MILLER'S

Antiques Shops, Fairs & Auctions

in the UK & Eire

2003

MILLER'S

Antiques Shops, Fairs & Auctions in the UK & Eire 2003

MILLER'S ANTIQUES SHOPS, FAIRS AND AUCTIONS IN THE UK & EIRE 2003

Compiled, edited and designed by Miller's Publications Ltd
The Cellars, High Street, Tenterden, Kent TN30 6BN
Tel: 01580 766411 Fax: 01580 766100

Project Director Valerie Lewis
Executive Art Editor Rhonda Fisher
Jacket Designer Victoria Bowen
Project Co-ordinator David Penfold, Edgerton Publishing Services
Assistant Project Co-ordinator Rosemary Cooke
Principal Researcher Carol Woodcock
Designers Simon Cook, Kari Reeves
Production Controller Angela Couchman
Advertising Co-ordinator & Administrator Melinda Williams
Advertising Assistants Emma Gillingham, Belinda Jones

First published in Great Britain in 2003 by Miller's,
a division of Mitchell Beazley, imprints of Octopus Publishing Group Ltd,
2–4 Heron Quays, London E14 4JP

ISBN 1 84000 681 1

Front cover illustrations:
A copper coal helmet, c1905, 15in (38cm) high. **£55–65/$80–95** ⊞
A walnut chair, French, c1680. **£3,200–3,500/$4,500–5,000** ⊞
A Lines Brothers rocking horse, 49¼in (125cm) high. **£1,100–1,300/$1,600–2,000** ⊞

Printed and bound by Mackays of Chatham Ltd

Exchange rate used in this edition: £1 = €1.57

BACA

BRITISH ANTIQUES AND COLLECTABLES AWARDS

presented by

MILLER'S

Celebrating the Winners of BACA 2002

The third annual Awards Ceremony took place on 26 June 2002 at The Dorchester, Park Lane, London. After a champagne reception, the 320 guests enjoyed a 3 course meal and, after eagerly awaiting the presentation ceremony, learned of the winners for the first time during the evening. Eric Knowles, Chairman of BACA, presented each winner with a certificate on stage.

The evening was a tremendous occasion continuing on into the early hours with guests and winners alike sharing in the celebrations.

How to Vote for 2003

The voting process for 2003 Awards begins now and the closing date is on 28th February 2003. For a voting form, please write to Melissa Boylen at BACA or log on to the website:

BACA/Miller's
2-4 Heron Quays
London E14 4JP
www.baca-awards.co.uk

2003 AWARDS CEREMONY: TUESDAY 24 JUNE 2003

PROUDLY SPONSORED BY

Scotland
Northern Ireland
Republic of Ireland
North East
North West
Yorks & Lincs
Midlands
East
Wales
Heart of England
South
South East
West Country
LONDON
Channel Islands

CONTENTS

HOW TO USE THIS BOOK

It is our aim to make *Miller's Antiques Shops, Fairs & Auctions in the UK & Eire 2003* simple to use. In order to make it easier to find entries, the book has been divided into three main sections: Dealers, Antiques Centres and Auction Houses; Associated Services; and Fairs.

Key to Symbols

- ⊞ Dealer
- Auction House
- Antiques Centre
- ✉ Address
- 🅿 Parking
- ☎ Telephone No.
- Ⓜ Mobile No.
- Ⓕ Fax No.
- Ⓔ E-mail address
- Ⓦ Web Address

SOUTH EAST

SOUTH EAST
KENT • APPLEDORE

KENT

APPLEDORE

Appledore Antiques Centre
Contact Roger Sinclair
✉ **The Old Forge, High Street, Appledore, Kent, TN26 2BX** 🅿
☎ 01233 758585
Est. 1985
No. of dealers 10
Stock General antiques
Open Mon–Sat 10am–5pm Sun 11am–5pm

⊞ **Back 2 Wood**
Contact Richard Moate
✉ **The Old Goods Shed, Station Road, Appledore, Kent, TN26 2DF**
☎ 01233 758109
Ⓔ pine@back2wood.com
Ⓦ www.back2wood.com
Est. 1987 *Stock size* Medium
Stock Antique pine furniture
Open Mon–Fri 9am–5pm Sat 9am–4pm
Services Pine stripping

⊞ **Victoria Lily**
Contact Victoria Grieveson-Moore
✉ **26 The Street, Appledore, Kent, TN26 2BX** 🅿
☎ 01233 758003
Est. 2002 *Stock size* Medium

ASHFORD

Hobbs Parker
Contact Marie Sessford
✉ **Monument Way, Orbital Park, Ashford, Kent, TN24 0HB** 🅿
☎ 01233 502222 Ⓕ 01233 502211
Ⓔ antiques@hobbsparker.co.uk
Ⓦ www.hobbsparker.co.uk
Est. 1850
Open Mon–Fri 9am–5.30pm
Sales Regular sales of antiques and collectables in the Amos Hall
Frequency Regular
Catalogues Yes

Parkinson Auctioneers
Contact Mrs L Parkinson
✉ **46 Beaver Road, Ashford, Kent, TN23 7RP** 🅿
☎ 01233 624426 Ⓕ 01233 624426
Ⓔ auctions@parkinson-uk.com
Ⓦ www.parkinson-uk.com
Est. 1979
Open Mon–Fri 9am–5pm
Sales General sale Mon 10am, viewing Sat 9am–1pm
Frequency Monthly
Catalogues Yes

ASHURST

⊞ **The Architectural Emporium**
Contact Michael Roberts
✉ **The Bald Faced Stag, Ashurst, Kent, TN3 9TE** 🅿
☎ 01892 740877

Dealers, Auction Houses and Antiques Centres

The United Kingdom has been divided into geographical regions, which are listed in the Contents on page 7. There is also a section for the Republic of Ireland. Each region is divided into counties and within each county, cities, towns and villages are listed alphabetically. Indexes to company name and place name can be found at the end of this Directory.

Each entry shows information such as address, phone number, opening hours, e-mail address and website, member organizations (eg LAPADA) and year established. Each **Dealer** entry contains details of stock and any services they provide. **Auction House** entries include information about their sales, frequency of sales and if catalogues are available. Entries for **Antiques Centres** include the number of dealers within the centre. **Associated Services** such as restorers, packers and valuers etc are listed alphabetically according to the service offered.

The **Fairs** section lists in date order, antiques fairs that will take place in the UK and Ireland throughout 2003. It is always advisable to contact the organisers in advance to check that information has not changed since going to press.

There are Indexes of **Specialists, Place Names** and a **General Index**, which are to be found beginning on page 566.

INTRODUCTION

It could surely not be considered too controversial or alarmist to suggest that the world of antiques is undergoing a period of change and revision at the moment. The prices for 'brown' furniture are not what they were; run-of-the-mill silver values are fairly static; the lower end of the picture market is more than a little sluggish; and the international political situation and economic projections continue to cast a pall over the future. What may surprise you, however, is that *Miller's Antiques Shops, Fairs & Auctions in the UK & Eire 2003* is in fact packed with even *more* entries than in previous editions, with listings of dealers, antiques fairs and auctioneers to tempt you wherever you are in the UK and Eire.

Of course, while many things change, some trends persist. When a new, young Labour MP was ushered into the presence of the diminutive but energetic post-war prime minister, Clement Atlee, he waited nervously for a word or two of guidance from the great man on how he might further his as yet embryonic career. 'Specialize and keep away from the bar,' Atlee snapped without looking up from his papers. This advice would seem to hold just as well for the field of antiques today as it did for politics in the brave new world of 1945 (and bear in mind, of course, that the bar to which Atlee referred had nothing to do with law).

A glance at the contents of this volume underlines just how specialized things have already become. Alongside the perennial standards 'Furniture', 'Ceramics' and 'Clocks', we have such esoteric delights as 'Breweriana', 'Celluloid & Bakelite' and 'Scripophily'. Devoted followers of the frenzied antics of the teams in popular TV programmes on garden and interior design can get their fix from 'Gardening Antiques' and 'Wallpaper' and, if that fails to do the trick, you can work out with 'Sporting Antiques'.

If you are simply cruising the countryside, the geographical listings will ensure that you pick off every treasure trove en route from St Peter Port to Pitlochry. When it comes to Fairs, you will find them all recorded in easy reference month-by-month date order and the invaluable 'Associated Services' listing will in turn help you take care of all your restoration and conservation needs.

In short, *Miller's Antiques Shops, Fairs & Auctions in the UK & Eire 2003* is the essential companion for anybody serious about collecting.

Leslie Gillham

2002 BACA *Winners...*

CATEGORY 1
General Antiques Dealer

LONDON (INSIDE M25)
sponsored by ebay.co.uk
Alistair Sampson Antiques Ltd
120 Mount Street

UK (OUTSIDE M25) *sponsored by*

Richard Gardner Antiques
Swan House, Market Square, Petworth, West Sussex

CATEGORY 2
Specialist Antiques Dealers

FURNITURE
sponsored by AON Artscope Incorporating Needham Johnson
Huntington Antiques Ltd
Church Street, Stow-on-the-Wold, Glos

MUSICAL INSTRUMENTS
Vintage and Rare Guitars
6 Denmark Street, London

ART NOUVEAU/ART DECO
The Fine Art Society plc
148 New Bond Street, London

COLLECTABLES
Manfred Schotten Antiques
The Crypt, 109 High Street, Burford, Oxon

SILVER & PLATE
Lowe & Sons
11 Bridge Street Row, Chester

SCULPTURE
Robert Bowman
8 Duke Street, St James's, London

PRINT
The O'Shea Gallery
120a Mount Street, London

WATERCOLOUR
Abbott & Holder
30 Museum Street, London

COSTUME & TEXTILES
Antique Textiles & Lighting
34 Belvedere, Lansdown Road, Bath, Somerset

POST WAR DESIGN
Target Gallery
7 Windmill St, London

CERAMICS
Andrew Dando
4 Wood Street, Bath, Somerset

CATEGORY 3
Auction Houses

LONDON (INSIDE M25)
sponsored by AON Artscope Incorporating Needham Johnson
Christie's South Kensington
85 Old Brompton Road, London

UK (OUTSIDE M25)
sponsored by AON Artscope Incorporating Needham Johnson
Gorringes incorporating Julian Dawson
15 North Street, Lewes, East Sussex

SPECIALIST DEPARTMENT WITHIN AN AUCTION HOUSE
Woolley & Wallis Ltd (Ceramics)
51-61 Castle Street, Wiltshire

CATEGORY 4
Associated Awards

FAIR OF THE YEAR
The Grosvenor House Art & Antiques Fair (June 2001)

Antiques Trade GAZETTE — The Antiques Trade Weekly
AWARD FOR: IN-HOUSE EXHIBITION
John Walker,
The English Joined Backstool 1660-1720

JOURNALIST OF THE YEAR
Brian Sewell, Evening Standard

AUCTIONEER OF THE YEAR
Rodney Tennant
Tennant Auctioneers, The Auction Centre, Leyburn, N Yorkshire

SERVICES AWARD: THIS YEAR FEATURING ANTIQUES ON THE INTERNET
www.christies.com

BBC HOMES & ANTIQUES MAGAZINE
AWARD FOR: FRIENDLY ANTIQUES SHOP
Megarry's
Jericho Cottage, The Duckpond Green, Blackmore, Essex

AWARD FOR: BEST ANTIQUES TOWN/VILLAGE
Saffron Walden

Antiques Shops, Centres & Auction Houses

If you wish your company to be entered in the next edition of the Directory, please complete the form at the end of the book or go to our website: http://www.mitchell-beazley.co.uk/mbeazley/miller/antiques_shops.htm

SOUTH EAST

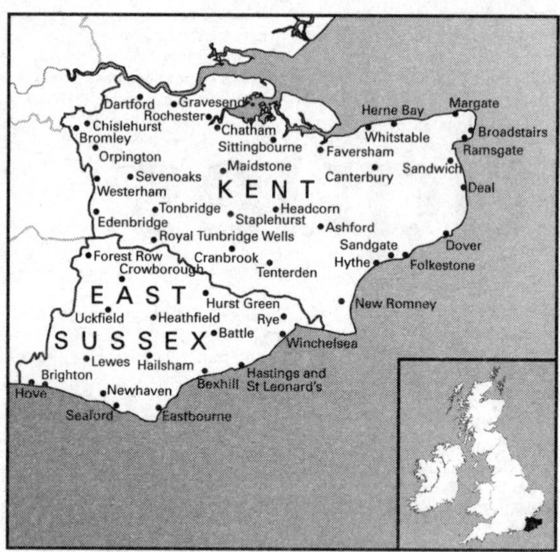

EAST SUSSEX

ALFRISTON

⊞ Alfriston Antiques
Contact John Tourell
✉ **The Square, Alfriston, East Sussex, BN26 5UD** 🅿
☎ 01323 870498 ⓕ 01323 870498
Est. 1967 *Stock size* Large
Stock Small collectables, porcelain, silver, jewellery, clocks
Open Wed–Sat 11am–5pm Sun 2.30–4.30pm
Services Valuations

⊞ The Old Apiary
Contact Tony Phillimore
✉ **High Street, Alfriston, East Sussex, BN26 5TB** 🅿
☎ 01323 870730
Est. 1995 *Stock size* Small
Stock Small furniture, decorative china
Open Mon–Sun 10am–5.30pm

BATTLE

⊞ Barnaby's of Battle
Contact Mr Barney Hance
✉ **50 High Street, Battle, East Sussex, TN33 0AN** 🅿
☎ 01424 772221
Est. 1997 *Stock size* Medium
Stock Old pine, oak, hardwood furniture
Open Mon–Sat 10am–6pm
Services Restorations

Burstow & Hewett
Contact Mr R Ellin
✉ **Abbey Auction Galleries & Granary Salerooms, Lower Lake, Battle, East Sussex, TN33 0AT** 🅿
☎ 01424 772374 ⓕ 01424 772302
ⓔ auctions@burstowandhewett.co.uk
ⓦ www.burstowandhewett.co.uk
Est. 1790
Open Mon–Fri 9am–5.30pm
Sales Sales of general antiques. Specialist sales of fine furniture, paintings and ceramics
Frequency Monthly
Catalogues Yes

⊞ Lavande
Contact Aryo Bakker or Sophie Hartley
✉ **53 High Street, Battle, East Sussex, TN33 0EN** 🅿
☎ 01424 774474 ⓕ 01424 774474
ⓜ 07710 098642
ⓔ info@lavande.co.uk
ⓦ www.lavande.co.uk
Est. 1998 *Stock size* Medium
Stock 18th–19thC French furniture, accessories
Open Mon–Sat 9.30am–5.30pm Sun by appointment
Fairs Decorative Antiques and Textiles Fair, Battersea
Services Upholstery, interior design

⊞ Spectrum Fine Jewellery Ltd (NAG, IPG)
Contact Mr Keith Ingram
✉ **46 High Street, Battle, East Sussex, TN33 0EE** 🅿
☎ 01424 774404
Est. 1975 *Stock size* Medium
Stock Jewellery, silver
Open Tues–Sat 9.30am–5.30pm
Fairs NEC
Services Repairs, enamelling, commissions

BEXHILL-ON-SEA

⊞ Acme Inc.
Contact Mrs Ruth Hardie
✉ **42 Sackville Road, Bexhill-on-Sea, East Sussex, TN39 3JE** 🅿
☎ 01424 211848 ⓜ 07973 402404
ⓔ ruth@acme-inc.com
ⓦ www.acme-inc.com
Est. 1993 *Stock size* Large
Stock 19th–20thC decorative arts, ceramics, glass, metalware, furniture
Open Mon Thurs Fri 11am–noon 2.30–4pm Sat 3–5pm Sun 3–4pm or by appointment

⊞ Annie's
Contact Priscilla Ann Rose
✉ **4 Bixlea Parade, Little Common Road, Little Common, Bexhill-on-Sea, East Sussex, TN39 4SD** 🅿
☎ 01424 846966
Est. 1992 *Stock size* Large
Stock Small furniture, collectables
Open Mon–Fri 10am–4pm Sat 10am–1pm closed Wed

⊞ Bexhill Antique Exporters
Contact Kim Abbott
✉ **56 Turkey Road, Bexhill-on-Sea, East Sussex, TN39 5HE** 🅿
☎ 01424 225103 ⓕ 01424 731430
ⓜ 07702 006982
Est. 1986 *Stock size* Large
Stock Furniture for the Spanish, Italian, French market
Open Mon–Fri 10am–5pm Sat Sun by appointment
Services Exporters

Gorringes Incorporating Julian Dawson (SOFAA, ISVA)
Contact Mr Ross Mercer
Terminus Road, Bexhill-on-Sea, East Sussex, TN39 3LR
01424 212994 F 01424 224035
bexhill@gorringes.co.uk
www.gorringes.co.uk
Est. 1926
Open Mon–Fri 8.30am–5.30pm Sat 9am–noon
Sales Fine art, antiques, collectables, Tues and Wed at 10am, viewing Fri 10am–5pm Sat 9.30am–4pm
Frequency 6 weeks
Catalogues Yes

Elizabeth Morgan Antiques
Contact Mr H Jenkins
50 Western Road, Bexhill-on-Sea, East Sussex, TN40 1DY
01424 218343
Stock size Medium
Stock General antiques
Open Mon–Sat 9am–5pm

Sivyer's
Contact Mrs V Sivyer
7 Sackville Road, Bexhill-on-Sea, East Sussex, TN39 3JB
01424 733821
Est. 1990 *Stock size* Medium
Stock General antiques, kitchenware
Open Mon–Sat 10am–5pm

Springfield Antiques
Contact Mr C Georgiou
127 Ninfield Road, Bexhill-on-Sea, East Sussex, TN39 5BD
01424 444498 M 07973 969244
Est. 1972 *Stock size* Large
Stock English pine furniture, kitchenware
Open Mon–Sun 10am–5.30pm

BRIGHTON

Alexandria Antiques
Contact Mr A H Ahmed
3 Hanover Place, Brighton, East Sussex, BN2 2SD
01273 688793 F 01273 688793
M 07880 625558
Est. 1978 *Stock size* Medium
Stock 18th–19thC furniture, porcelain, bronzes, paintings, decorative objects
Open Mon–Fri 9.30am–5.30pm Sat Sun by appointment
Fairs Newark, Ardingly
Services Valuations, restorations

Art Deco Etc
Contact Mr J Clark
73 Upper Gloucester Road, Brighton, East Sussex, BN1 3LQ
01273 329268 F 01273 329268
M 07971 268302
Est. 1979 *Stock size* Medium
Stock 1860–1980s pottery and glass, lighting, small furniture, metalwork
Open By appointment only
Fairs Newark, Alexandra Palace, Ardingly, Battersea
Services Valuations, insurance claims

Ashton's Antiques
Contact Pearl or Bob Ashton
1 & 3 Clyde Road, Brighton, East Sussex, BN1 4NN
01273 605253 F 01273 605253
M 07775 736041
Est. 1970 *Stock size* Medium
Stock Antiques, collectables
Open Thurs–Sat 10am–4pm

The Bookmark
Contact Sally May
91–93 Dyke Road, Brighton, East Sussex, BN1 3JE
01273 735577
Est. 1994 *Stock size* Medium
Stock General stock of antiquarian and modern books
Open Mon 1.30–6pm Tues–Fri 11.30am–6.30pm Sat 10.30am–6pm

Brighton Architectural Salvage
Contact Mr R L Legendre
33–34 Gloucester Road, Brighton, East Sussex, BN1 4AQ
01273 681656 F 01273 681656
M 07979 966245
Est. 1979 *Stock size* Large
Stock Restored architectural antiques, fireplaces, reclaimed flooring
Open Mon–Sat 10am–5pm
Services Fireplace installation

Brighton Flea Market
Contact Mr A R Wilkinson
31a Upper St James's Street, Brighton, East Sussex, BN2 1JN
01273 624006 F 01273 328665
arwilkinson@aol.com
Est. 1988 *Stock size* Large
Stock Antiques, bric-a-brac, collectables
Open Mon–Sun 9.30am–5.30pm

Brighton Postcard Shop (PTA)
Contact Mr K Davies
38 Beaconsfield Road, Brighton, East Sussex, BN1 4QH
01273 600035 F 01273 628660
keith.davies@pobox.com
www.postcard.co.uk/flair
Est. 1987 *Stock size* Large
Stock Postcards, ephemera, vintage glamour magazines
Open Tues–Sat 10.30am–4pm
Fairs Bloomsbury Fairs
Services Mail order

Brighton Retro
Contact Greg Wish
102a North Road, Brighton, East Sussex, BN1 1YE
01273 628444 M 07801 546709
Est. 1996 *Stock size* Medium
Stock Arts and Crafts, early 20thC furniture, retro furniture, clothes, fabrics
Open Mon–Sat 11am–6pm Sun noon–4pm
Services Valuations, restorations

Tony Broadfoot Antiques
Contact Mr Tony Broadfoot
39 Upper Gardner Street, Brighton, East Sussex, BN1 4AN
01273 695457 F 01273 620365
Est. 1982 *Stock size* Large
Stock Antique furniture
Open Mon–Fri 9am–5pm

C A R S (Classic Automobilia and Regalia Specialists)
Contact Mr G G Weiner
4–4a Chapel Terrace Mews, Kemp Town, Brighton, East Sussex, BN2 1HU
01273 622722/601960
F 01273 601960 M 07890 836734
cars@kemptown-brighton.freeserve.co.uk

SOUTH EAST

EAST SUSSEX • BRIGHTON

Ⓦ www.carsofbrighton.co.uk or www.brmmbrmm.com/pedalcars
Est. 1981 *Stock size* Medium
Stock Automobilia, collectors' car badges and mascots, hand-built collectors' and children's pedal cars
Open Mon–Sat 10am–6pm or by appointment
Fairs Classic car shows at NEC, Alexandra Palace
Services Valuations

Clock Tower Antiques
Contact Mr D Goss
128d Queens Road, Brighton, East Sussex, BN1 3WB Ⓟ
☎ 01273 747666 Ⓕ 01273 747666
Est. 1985 *Stock size* Large
Stock Antique pine furniture
Open Mon–Sun 9.30am–5.30pm
Services Kitchen specialists

Decorative Arts
Contact Anthony White
27 Gloucester Road, Brighton, East Sussex, BN1 4AQ Ⓟ
☎ 01273 676486 Ⓜ 07788 107101
Ⓦ www.decarts.net
Est. 1996 *Stock size* Medium
Stock Oak furniture 1880–1970, decorative arts, 1970s leather furniture
Open Mon–Sat 10am–5.30pm
Sun by appointment

Enhancements
Contact Lucille Robinson
11a Cavendish Street, Brighton, East Sussex, BN2 1RN Ⓟ
☎ 01273 677303 Ⓜ 07788 727878
Ⓔ lue80@hotmail.com
Est. 1992 *Stock size* Medium
Stock Kitchenware, tools, beds, pine furniture, shabby chic furniture
Open Mon–Sat 10am–5.30pm
Services Free delivery

Julie Griffin Antiques
Contact Julie Griffin
13a Prince Albert Street, Brighton, East Sussex, BN1 1HE Ⓟ
☎ 01273 773895
Est. 1996 *Stock size* Large
Stock Antique, reproduction and reclaimed pine furniture, mahogany, decorative pieces
Open Mon–Sat 10am–5pm

Hallmark Jewellers
Contact Mr J Hersheson
4 Union Street, The Lanes, Brighton, East Sussex, BN1 1HA Ⓟ
☎ 01273 725477 Ⓕ 01273 725477
Ⓜ 07885 298494
Est. 1959 *Stock size* Large
Stock Antique and modern silver, silver collectables, jewellery
Open Mon–Sat 9am–5pm
Sun 11am–4pm
Services Valuations

The House of Antiques (LAPADA)
Contact Mr A Margiotta
39 Upper North Street, Brighton, East Sussex, BN1 3FH Ⓟ
☎ 01273 327680 Ⓕ 01273 324961
Est. 1959 *Stock size* Medium
Stock General antiques, furniture, bronzes, porcelain, clocks
Open Mon–Fri 10am–5pm
closed 1–2.15pm
Services Pawnbrokers

Dudley Hume
Contact Mr D Hume
46 Upper North Street, Brighton, East Sussex, BN1 3FH
☎ 01273 323461 Ⓕ 01273 240422
Ⓜ 07977 598627
Ⓔ dudley@dudleyhume.freeserve.co.uk
Est. 1973 *Stock size* Medium
Stock 18th–19thC furniture, decorative items
Open Mon–Fri 10.30am–4.30pm
Sat 10am–noon
Fairs Olympia

Raymond P Inman
Contact Robert Inman
35 & 40 Temple Street, Brighton, East Sussex, BN1 3BH Ⓟ
☎ 01273 774777 Ⓕ 01273 735660
Ⓔ r.p.inman@talk21.com
Est. 1929
Open Mon–Fri 9am–5pm
Sales General antiques sales
Frequency 10 a year
Catalogues Yes

Jezebel
Contact Mrs A Davis
14 Prince Albert Street, Brighton, East Sussex, BN1 1HE Ⓟ
☎ 01273 206091 Ⓕ 01273 206091
Est. 1989 *Stock size* Medium
Stock Art Deco, Art Nouveau, costumes, vintage clothing, costume jewellery
Open Mon–Sat 11am–5.30pm
Fairs Newark

The Lanes Armoury
Contact Mark or David Hawkins
26 Meeting House Lane, Brighton, East Sussex, BN1 1HB Ⓟ
☎ 01273 321357 Ⓕ 01273 326453
Ⓔ hawkinsarms@hotmail.com
Ⓦ www.thelanesarmoury.co.uk
Est. 1992 *Stock size* Large
Stock Arms, armour, militaria and books from pre-Christian to WWII
Open Mon–Sat 10am–5.15pm

Leoframes
Contact Stephen Round
70 North Road, Brighton, East Sussex, BN1 1YD Ⓟ
☎ 01273 695862
Est. 1985 *Stock size* Medium
Stock Antique prints, maps
Open Mon–Sat 9am–5.30pm
Services Restorations, framing

Patrick Moorhead Antiques
Contact Mr P Moorhead
Spring Gardens, 76 Church Street, Brighton, East Sussex, BN1 1RL Ⓟ
☎ 01273 779696 Ⓕ 01273 220196
Ⓜ 07785 725202
Ⓔ patrick.moorhead@virgin.net
Est. 1984 *Stock size* Large
Stock 18th–19thC furniture, European and Oriental ceramics, paintings, clocks. Largest stock in south of England
Open Mon–Fri 9.30am–5.30pm
Services Valuations, restorations

Michael Norman Antiques (BADA)
Contact John Branch or Armando Fava
4 Fredrick Place, Brighton, East Sussex, BN1 4EA Ⓟ
☎ 01273 329253 Ⓕ 01273 206556
Ⓔ antiques@michaelnorman.com
Ⓦ www.michaelnorman.com
Est. 1965 *Stock size* Large
Stock Georgian and Regency period furniture
Open Mon–Sat 9am–1pm 2–5pm or by appointment
Services Restorations

North Laine Antiques & Flea Market
Contact Mr A Fitchett
5a Upper Gardner Street, Brighton, East Sussex, BN1 4AN P
01273 600894 F 01273 600894
M 07836 365411
E market@fitchett.freeserve.co.uk
Est. 2002 *Stock size* Large
No. of dealers 70
Stock Wide range of antiques and collectables
Open Mon–Fri 10am–5.30pm Sat 9am–5.30pm Sun 10am–4pm

Oasis
Contact Mr I Stevenson
39 Kensington Gardens, Brighton, East Sussex, BN1 4AL P
01273 683885
Est. 1979 *Stock size* Medium
Stock Period lighting, telephones, gramophones, furniture, Art Deco, Art Nouveau, watches, lighters, glass, textiles, clothes from 1920s and 1930s
Open Mon–Sat 10am–5.30pm

Odin Antiques
Contact Mr A Sjovold
43 Preston Street, Brighton, East Sussex, BN1 2HP P
01273 732738
W www.odinantiques.com
Est. 1979 *Stock size* Medium
Stock Antique furniture, maritime items, telescopes
Open Mon–Sat 10.30am–5.30pm

The Old Picture Shop
Contact Mr S Clark
2 Nile Street, Brighton, East Sussex, BN1 1HW P
01273 725609
Est. 1959 *Stock size* Medium
Stock Old paintings, watercolours, period furniture
Open Mon–Sat 10am–5pm
Services Valuations

Colin Page Antiquarian Books (ABA)
Contact Mr J Loska
36 Duke Street, Brighton, East Sussex, BN1 1AG P
01273 325954 F 01273 746246
E cpage@pavilion.co.uk
Est. 1969 *Stock size* Large
Stock Antiquarian and second-hand books, antiquarian literature, natural history, plate books, bindings
Open Mon–Sat 9.30am–5.30pm
Fairs ABA, Olympia, Chelsea
Services Valuations

Dermot & Jill Palmer Antiques
Contact Jill Palmer
7–8 Union Street, Brighton, East Sussex, BN1 1HA
01273 328669 F 01273 777641
M 07771 614331
Est. 1969 *Stock size* Large
Stock Mainly 19thC French and English furniture
Open Mon–Sat 9am–6pm or by appointment
Fairs Olympia

Sue Pearson Antique Dolls & Teddy Bears
Contact Sue Pearson
13½ Prince Albert Street, Brighton, East Sussex, BN1 1HE P
01273 329247 F 01273 494600
E enquire@sue-pearson.co.uk
W www.sue-pearson.co.uk
Est. 1981 *Stock size* Large
Stock Antique and modern bears, soft toys, dolls
Open Mon–Sat 10am–5pm
Fairs Kensington Town Hall
Services Repair of dolls and bears

Ben Ponting Antiques
Contact Michelle Ponting
53 Upper North Street, Brighton, East Sussex, BN1 3FH P
01273 329409 F 01273 558749
E pontingco@aol.com
Est. 1976 *Stock size* Large
Stock English Georgian–Edwardian antique furniture
Open Mon–Fri 9am–5pm
Services Valuations, restorations

Rin-Tin-Tin (ESoc)
Contact Mr Rick Irvine
34 North Road, Brighton, East Sussex, BN1 1YB P
01273 672424 F 01273 672424
E rick@rintintin.freeserve.co.uk
Est. 1982 *Stock size* Medium
Stock Old advertising, promotional matter, magazines, early glamour, games, toys, plastics, 20thC fixtures and fittings
Open Mon–Sat 11am–5.30pm
Fairs Alexandra Palace, Juke Box Fairs
Services Framing

Savery Antiques
Contact Ann Savery
257 Ditchling Road, Fireways, Brighton, East Sussex, BN1 6JH P
01273 564899
E hjamsavery@aol.com
Est. 1968 *Stock size* Medium
Stock Small furniture, porcelain, glass, metalwork
Open Mon 10.30am–5pm Thurs–Sat 9.30am–5pm
Fairs Ardingly, Sandown Park

Savery Books
Contact Mr James Savery
300 Ditchling Road, Brighton, East Sussex, BN1 6JG P
01273 503030
Est. 1990 *Stock size* Large
Stock Second-hand books, art, military, local studies
Open Wed–Sat 10am–4.30pm

Snooper's Paradise
Contact Mr N Drinkwater
7–8 Kensington Gardens, Brighton, East Sussex, BN1 4AL P
01273 602558 F 01273 686611
E snoopersparadisebrighton@btinternet.com
W www.snoopersparadise.co.uk
Est. 1994 *Stock size* Large
No. of dealers 70–80
Stock China, pictures, 1970s clothes and fabric, kitchenware, ephemera, jewellery, watches, records and CDs, phones and electrical, Art Deco, glass, treen, furniture, photographic, pens and lighters, militaria etc
Open Mon–Sat 9.30am–5.30pm Sun 11am–4pm

Studio Bookshop
Contact Mr P Brown
68 St James's Street, Brighton, East Sussex, BN2 1PJ P
01273 691253
E paul@studiobookshop.demon.co.uk
Est. 1995 *Stock size* Medium
Stock Reference books on glass, art and antiques
Open Mon–Sat 10am–6pm
Fairs Glass fairs
Services Catalogue, telephone orders

SOUTH EAST

EAST SUSSEX • BURWASH

Valelink Ltd
Contact Mr J Trory
26 Queen's Road, Brighton, East Sussex, BN1 3XA
01273 202906 Ⓕ 01273 202906
Est. 1970 *Stock size* Medium
Stock Collectables
Open Mon–Sat 10am–6pm
Fairs Brighton Centre

Wardrobe
Contact Mr Clive Parks or Philip Parfitt
51 Upper North Street, Brighton, East Sussex, BN1 3FH
01273 202201 Ⓕ 01273 202201
Ⓜ 07802 483056
Est. 1986 *Stock size* Medium
Stock Vintage clothing and accessories, textiles, jewellery, Art Deco, bakelite, collectable plastics
Open Wed–Sat 10am–5pm or by appointment
Fairs Alexandra Palace, Sandown Park, Horticultural Hall

E & B White
Contact Elizabeth or Ben White
43 & 47 Upper North Street, Brighton, East Sussex, BN1 3FH
01273 328706 Ⓕ 01273 207035
Est. 1965 *Stock size* Medium
Stock Antique and decorative furniture
Open Mon–Fri 9.30am–5pm
Sat 9.30am–1pm

Wilkinsons
Contact Mrs Wilkinson
23 New Road, Brighton, East Sussex, BN1 1WZ
01273 328665 Ⓕ 01273 328665
Ⓜ 07801 418495
Ⓔ arwilkinson@aol.com
Est. 1991 *Stock size* Small
Stock Furniture, decorative objects, lighting
Open Mon–Sat 10am–5.30pm
Sun noon–5pm
Services Free delivery, gift wrap, wedding lists

The Witch Ball
Contact Gina Daniels
48 Meeting House Lane, Brighton, East Sussex, BN1 1HB
01273 326618
Ⓜ 07889 420524
Ⓦ www.antiques-index.com
Est. 1967 *Stock size* Large
Stock 1550–1850 prints and maps
Open Mon–Sat 10.30am–6pm
Services Lists on request

Pamela Wright
Contact Mrs P Wright
45 Upper North Street, Brighton, East Sussex, BN1 3FH
01273 738838 Ⓕ 01273 724047
Est. 1987 *Stock size* Large
Stock Period furniture and metal, light fittings, paintings
Open Mon–Fri 10am–5pm

BURWASH

Chateaubriand Antiques Centre
Contact John Barker or Nick Morgan
High Street, Burwash, East Sussex, TN19 7ES
01435 882535
Ⓔ chateauframe@hotmail.com
Est. 1984 *Stock size* Large
Stock 4 showrooms. Furniture, pictures, prints, brass, copper, china, maps
Open Mon–Sat 10am–5pm
Sun noon–5pm
Services Valuations, tea room, picture framing

CROWBOROUGH

Ashdown Antiques
Contact Mrs J Lowther
The Wool Shop, Croft Road, Crowborough, East Sussex, TN6 1DL
01892 664180
Est. 1994 *Stock size* Large
Stock Furniture, jewellery, ceramics, silver, Art Deco, glass, Victoriana
Open Mon–Sat 10am–4pm
Fairs Ardingly
Services Valuations, jewellery repairs

EASTBOURNE

35 The Goffs
Contact Mrs Y Cole
35 The Goffs, Eastbourne, East Sussex, BN21 1HF
01323 737272
Est. 2000 *Stock size* Medium
Stock Decorative antiques, furniture, chandeliers
Open Tues–Sat 10.30am–4.30pm

W. Bruford
Contact John Burgess
11–13 Cornfield Road, Eastbourne, East Sussex, BN21 3NA
01323 725452 Ⓕ 01323 417873
Est. 1885 *Stock size* Small
Stock Jewellery, silver
Open Mon–Sat 9.30am–5pm
Services Valuations, restorations

Camilla's Bookshop
Contact Ms C Francombe or Mr S Broad
57 Grove Road, Eastbourne, East Sussex, BN21 4TX
01323 736001
Ⓔ c@millas.fsnet.co.uk
Est. 1975 *Stock size* Large
Stock Antiquarian and second-hand books, postcards, ephemera, children's books, needlework, military, aviation and nautical topics
Open Mon–Sat 10am–5.30pm
Services Valuations, book search

Francois Celada
Contact Francois Celada
26 South Street, Eastbourne, East Sussex, BN21 4XB
01323 644464 Ⓕ 01323 644464
Est. 1996 *Stock size* Large
Stock Postcards, stamps, cigarette cards, medals, coins, collectables
Open Mon–Sat 9.30am–5pm
Wed 2–5pm
Services Valuations

John Cowderoy Antiques (LAPADA)
Contact Mr Richard Cowderoy
42 South Street, Eastbourne, East Sussex, BN21 4XB
01323 720058 Ⓕ 01323 410163
Ⓔ john@cowderoyantiques.co.uk
Ⓦ www.cowderoyantiques.co.uk
Est. 1973 *Stock size* Large
Stock General antiques, collectables, clocks, musical boxes
Open Mon–Sat 8.30am–5pm
closed Wed pm
Services Restorations

Crest Collectables
Contact Mr C Powell
54 Grove Road, Eastbourne, East Sussex, BN21 4UD
01323 721185
Est. 1986 *Stock size* Medium

Stock Teddy bears, dolls, soft toys, collectables
Open Mon–Sat 10.30am–4pm closed Wed

Eastbourne Antiques Market
Contact Mr P C Barltrop
80 Seaside, Eastbourne, East Sussex, BN22 7QP
01323 642233
Est. 1969 ***Stock size*** Large
No. of dealers 25
Stock Antiques, collectables
Open Mon–Fri 10am–5.30pm Sat 10am–5pm

Eastbourne Auction Rooms
Contact Jeanette May
Auction House, Finmere Road, Eastbourne, East Sussex, BN22 8QL
01323 431444 01323 417638
enquiries@eastbourneauction.com
www.eastbourneauction.com
Est. 1994
Open Mon–Fri 9am–5pm
Sales General antiques fortnightly Sat 10am, viewing Fri 9am–7pm, antiques and collectables every six weeks Fri 10am, viewing Wed, Thurs 9am–7pm
Frequency Fortnightly
Catalogues Yes

The Enterprise Collectors Market
Contact Mr Lovegrove
Enterprise Centre, Station Parade, Eastbourne, East Sussex, BN21 1BD
01323 732690
Est. 1988 ***Stock size*** Large
No. of dealers 15
Stock Antiques, collectables, wrist watches
Open Mon–Sat 9.30am–5pm

Charles French
Contact Mr C McCleave
2 Kings Drive, Eastbourne, East Sussex, BN21 2NU
01323 720128
Est. 1969 ***Stock size*** Medium
Stock General antiques
Open Mon–Fri 10am–5.30pm
Services House clearance

A & T Gibbard (PBFA)
Contact Mrs M T Gibbard or Mr A Gibbard
30 South Street, Eastbourne, East Sussex, BN21 4XB
01323 734128 01323 734128
Est. 1910 ***Stock size*** Large
Stock Antiquarian and second-hand books, specializing in natural history, travel, topography, leather-bound books
Open Mon–Sat 9.30am–5.30pm
Fairs Russell Hotel

Edgar Horn's Fine Art Auctioneers
Contact David Holmes
46–50 South Street, Eastbourne, East Sussex, BN21 4XB
01323 410419 01323 416540
www.edgarhorns.com
Est. 1924
Open Mon–Fri 9am–5pm
Sales 6 Antiques sales per annum, Wed 11am, viewing Sat 9am–12.30pm Mon 9am–7pm Tues 9am–5pm
Frequency Bi-monthly
Catalogues Yes

More Than Music
Contact Mike Vandenbosch
PO Box 2809, Eastbourne, East Sussex, BN21 2EA
01959 565514 01959 565510
morethnmus@aol.com
www.mtmglobal.com
Est. 1995 ***Stock size*** Medium
Stock Vinyl, autographs, books, magazines, posters etc
Open Mon–Fri 10am–5.30pm Sat 10am–1pm
Services Worldwide mail order service

The Old Town Antiques Centre
Contact Mrs V Franklin
52 Ocklynge Road, Eastbourne, East Sussex, BN21 1PR
01323 416016
Est. 1989 ***Stock size*** Large
No. of dealers 16
Stock Mixed antiques, furniture, fine porcelain, glass, silver, Beswick, Copenhagen figures etc
Open Mon–Sat 10am–5pm
Services Valuations, restorations

Timothy Partridge Antiques
46 Ocklynge Road, Eastbourne, East Sussex, BN21 1PP
01323 638731
07860 864709
Stock size Medium
Stock General pre-war goods, furniture, smalls
Open Mon–Fri 10am–1pm 2–5pm

Pharoahs Antiques
Contact Mr W Pharoah
28 South Street, Eastbourne, East Sussex, BN21 4XB
01323 738655 0771 4398870
Est. 1988 ***Stock size*** Medium
Stock Lighting, linen, china, furniture, medical instruments, the bizarre, architectural ironmongery
Open Mon–Sat 10am–5pm
Fairs Ardingly, Brighton Racecourse

Seaquel Antiques & Collectors Market
Contact Mrs P Mornington-West
37 Seaside Road, Eastbourne, East Sussex, BN21 3PP
01323 645032
Est. 1998 ***Stock size*** Large
No. of dealers 18
Stock Furniture, collectables, bric-a-brac
Open Mon–Sat 10am–5pm Sun 10.30am–4.30pm

Shine's Antiques and Collectables
Contact Brian Shine
8 Crown Street, Eastbourne, East Sussex, BN21 1NX
01323 726261
Est. 1999 ***Stock size*** Large
Stock Antiques, collectables
Open Mon–Sat 10am–5pm

South Coast Collectables
Contact Sylvia Redford
85 Seaside Road, Eastbourne, East Sussex, BN21 3PL
01323 648811
Est. 1997 ***Stock size*** Large
No. of dealers 18
Stock Antiques, collectables, Georgian–Edwardian furniture
Open Tues–Sat 10am–5pm

SOUTH EAST

EAST SUSSEX • FOREST ROW

FOREST ROW

Cadari Ltd
Contact Marie Camp
6 Newlands Place, Hartfield Road, Forest Row, East Sussex, RH18 5DQ
01342 826644 F 01342 826655
Est. 1995 *Stock size* Medium
Stock English antiques, Georgian–Victorian furniture, French antiques, smalls
Open Tues–Sat 10am–5pm
Fairs Ardingly

The Dandelion Clock
Contact Mrs L Chapman
Lewes Road, Forest Row, East Sussex, RH18 5ES
01342 822335
W www.dandelion-clock.co.uk.
Est. 1994 *Stock size* Large
No. of dealers 12
Stock Pine and country furniture, antiques, Collectables
Open Mon–Sat 10am–5.30pm
Services Local delivery available

Jeroen Markies Antiques Ltd
Contact Mr J Markies
14–16 Hartfield Road, Forest Row, East Sussex, RH18 5HE
01342 824980 F 01342 823677
E sales@markies.co.uk
W www.markies.co.uk
Est. 1981 *Stock size* Large
Stock 18th–19thC fine antique furniture, decorative objects, silver
Open Mon–Sat 9.30am–5.30pm
Services Restorations

Trojan Antiques
Contact Mr Warren Hall
The Square, Forest Row, East Sussex, RH18 5HD
01342 826766 F 01342 826766
M 0788 788 1301
Est. 1998 *Stock size* Large
Stock Country furniture and associated items for home and garden
Open Mon–Sat 10am–5.30pm
Services Free delivery

GOLDEN CROSS

Golden Cross Antiques
Contact Mrs R R Buchan
A22, Golden Cross, Hailsham, East Sussex, BN27 4AN
01825 872144 F 01825 872144
M 07957 224165
E info@goldencrossantiques.co.uk
W www.goldencrossantiques.co.uk
Est. 1974 *Stock size* Medium
Stock Furniture, collectables, silver
Open Mon–Sat 9am–6pm
Sun 10am–6pm
Fairs Crowborough, Felbridge

GUESTLING

Hearth & Home
Contact Mr D Hance
Rye Road, Guestling Green, Hastings, East Sussex, TN35 4LS
01424 813220 F 01424 813220
Est. 1984 *Stock size* Medium
Stock Original Victorian and cast-iron fireplaces
Open Mon–Sat 9am–1pm
2–5.30pm
Services Advice, installation

HADLOW DOWN

Hadlow Down Antiques
Contact Mr Adrian Butler
Hastingford Farm, School Lane, Hadlow Down, Uckfield, East Sussex, TN22 4DY
01825 830707 F 01825 830172
M 07730 332331
Est. 1989 *Stock size* Large
Stock Antiques, decorative furniture, accessories
Open Mon–Sat 10am–5pm
Sun 2–5pm closed Wed
or by appointment
Services Valuations, restorations, custom-made oak furniture

HAILSHAM

Hawkswood Antiques
Contact Mr Barry Richardson
9–10 Carew Court, Hawkswood Road, Hailsham, East Sussex, BN27 1UL
01323 844454
Est. 1989 *Stock size* Medium
Stock General antiques, collectables
Open Mon–Fri 9.30am–5.30pm
Sat 9.30am–1pm closed Wed pm
Services Free local delivery

Horsebridge Antique Centre
Contact Roger Lane
1 North Street, Lower Horsebridge, Hailsham, East Sussex, BN27 4DJ
01323 844414 F 01323 844000
E lane_roger@hotmail.com
Est. 1978 *Stock size* Medium
Stock General antiques
Open By appointment

Stable Doors
Contact Mr K Skinner or Mr B Skinner
Market Street, Hailsham, East Sussex, BN27 2AE
01323 844033
Est. 1996 *Stock size* Large
Stock Antiques, collectables
Open Mon–Sat 9am–5pm
Sun 10am-4pm
Fairs Ardingly

Sunburst Antiques & Art Furniture
Contact Mr John Clements
1 Carriers Path, High Street, Hailsham, East Sussex, BN27 1AP
01323 441191
Est. 1998 *Stock size* Large
Stock Late 19thC furniture
Open Mon–Sat 10am–5.30pm
Services Restorations

Wealth of Weights (Cambridge Paperweight Circle)
Contact Mrs J Skinner or Mr K Skinner
Stable Doors, Market Street, Hailsham, East Sussex, BN27 2AE
01323 441150
E jaqui@weights.co.uk
W www.weights.co.uk
Est. 1997 *Stock size* Large
Stock Largest selection of paperweights in South England. registered PCA World Dealer
Open Mon–Sun 9am–5pm
Fairs Effingham Park, Copthorne, Woking Glass Fair
Services Valuations, collections bought

HASTINGS

Book Centre
Contact Mr R Naylor
18 West Street, Hastings, East Sussex, TN34 3AN
01424 729866
Est. 1996 *Stock size* Large

Stock Antiquarian and second-hand books
Open Mon–Sun 9am–5pm
Services Book search

Coach House Antiques
Contact Mr R J Luck
42 George Street, Hastings, East Sussex, TN34 3EA
01424 461849 01424 461849
07710 234803
Est. 1979 *Stock size* Large
Stock Longcase clocks, Victorian furniture, Dinky toys
Open Mon–Sun 10am–5pm
Services Valuations, restorations

John & Noel Connell
Contact Mr or Mrs J Connell
52–54 George Street, Hastings, East Sussex, TN34 3EE
01424 434373
Est. 1999 *Stock size* Medium
Stock Furniture, silver, glass
Open Thurs–Sun 11am–4pm or by appointment

George Street Antiques Centre
Contact Mrs F Stanley
47 George Street, Hastings, East Sussex, TN34 3EA
01424 429339
Est. 1984 *Stock size* Large
No. of dealers 8
Stock Collectables
Open Mon–Fri 9am–5pm
Sat 10am–5pm Sun 11am–5pm

Howes Bookshop Ltd (ABA, PBFA)
Contact Mr M Bartley
Trinity Hall, Braybrooke Terrace, Hastings, East Sussex, TN34 1HQ
01424 423437 01424 460620
rarebooks@howes.co.uk
www.howes.co.uk
Est. 1946 *Stock size* Large
Stock Antiquarian and second-hand books, arts and humanities a speciality
Open Tues–Sat 9.30am–5pm
Fairs Olympia, Chelsea, Russell Hotel
Services Valuations

Mollycoddles Collectables
Contact Gary Baker
24 George Street, Hastings, East Sussex, TN34 3EB
01424 433277
Est. 1995 *Stock size* Medium
Stock Collectables, pine furniture, textiles, jewellery
Open Mon–Sun 10am–5pm

Nakota Curios
Contact Mr R Kelly
12 Courthouse Street, Hastings, East Sussex, TN34 3AU
01424 438900
Est. 1969 *Stock size* Large
Stock Chandeliers, decorative china, silverware, rugs, pictures, mirrors
Open Mon–Sat 10.30am–1pm 2pm–4.30pm

Old Hastings Bookshop
Contact Mr Brian Richers
15 George Street, Hastings, East Sussex, TN34 3EG
01424 425989
Est. 1983 *Stock size* Small
Stock Antiquarian, rare and second-hand books
Open Mon–Sat 10am–4pm closed Wed

Reeves & Son
Contact Mr C Hawkins
4–6 Courthouse Street, Hastings, East Sussex, TN34 3AU
01424 437672
07778 311803
Est. 1818 *Stock size* Large
Stock Military collectables, china, smalls, books
Open Mon–Sat 9am–5pm
Services House clearance

HEATHFIELD

Colonial Times
Contact Tony Skinner
Lewes Road, Cross In Hand, Heathfield, East Sussex, TN21 0TA
01435 866442/862962
07860 441922
enquiries@colonial-times.com
www.colonial-times.com
Est. 1978 *Stock size* Large
Stock Furniture imported from India, China and the Far East
Open Mon–Sat 10am–5pm
Fairs Newark
Services Restorations

The Pig Sty
Contact Mrs Worton
49 High Street, Heathfield, East Sussex, TN21 8HU
01435 866671
Est. 1997 *Stock size* Medium
No. of dealers 10
Stock General antiques and collectables
Open Mon–Sat 9am–5pm
Services Coffee Shop

Toad Hall Antique Centre
Contact Patsy Quick
57 High Street, Heathfield, East Sussex, TN21 8HU
01435 863535 01435 863535
Est. 1996 *Stock size* Large
No. of dealers 16
Stock Furniture, general antiques, collectables
Open Mon–Sat 9am–5.30pm
Sun 11am–4pm

HORAM

John Botting
Contact Mr J Botting
Winston House, High Street, Horam, East Sussex, TN21 0ER
01435 813553
Est. 1981 *Stock size* Medium
Stock Georgian–Edwardian furniture and effects
Open By appointment only
Fairs Ardingly, Newark

HOVE

Antiques et Cetera
Contact Mr Ken Bomzer
190 Portland Road, Hove, East Sussex, BN3 5QN
01273 746159
antiques.etcetera@btinternet.com
Est. 1994 *Stock size* Large
Stock 200-year-old to modern porcelain, gold, silver, glassware, pictures, furniture, chandeliers, lighting, costume jewellery, 18th–20thC oriental objets d'art
Open Mon–Fri 10am–3pm
Sat 10am–1pm
Services Valuations of jewellery and porcelain, general valuations

Bonhams
19 Palmeira Square, Hove, East Sussex, BN3 2JN
01273 220000 01273 220335
hove@bonhams.com

SOUTH EAST

EAST SUSSEX • HURST GREEN

Ⓦ www.bonhams.com
Est. 1793
Open Mon–Fri 9am–1pm 2–5pm

J S Carter
Contact Mr J Carter
✉ **9 Boundary Road, Hove, East Sussex, BN3 4EH** 🅿
☎ 01273 439678 Ⓕ 01273 416053
Est. 1974 *Stock size* Large
Stock Georgian–Edwardian furniture
Open Mon–Fri 9.30am–6pm
Services Restorations

Simon Hunter Antique Maps
Contact Mr Simon Hunter
✉ **21 St Johns Road, Hove, East Sussex, BN3 2FB** 🅿
☎ 01273 746983 Ⓕ 01273 746983
Ⓔ simonhunter@fastnet.co.uk
Ⓦ www.antiquemaps.org.uk
Est. 1989 *Stock size* Large
Stock Antique maps
Open By appointment
Fairs AMPS Bonnington Hotel

Michael Norman Antiques Ltd (BADA)
Contact Michael Keehan
✉ **Palmeira House, 82 Western Road, Hove, East Sussex, BN3 1JB** 🅿
☎ 01273 329253/326712
Ⓕ 01273 206556
Ⓔ antiques@michaelnorman.com
Ⓦ www.michaelnorman.com
Est. 1964 *Stock size* Large
Stock 18th–19thC English furniture
Open Mon–Sat 9am–5.30pm closed 1–2pm

Scarborough Perry Fine Arts
Contact Mr S Perry
✉ **Hove Auction Rooms, Hove Street, Hove, East Sussex, BN3 2GL** 🅿
☎ 01273 735266 Ⓕ 01273 723813
Ⓔ gspfa@pavilion.co.uk
Ⓦ www.scarboroughperry.co.uk
Est. 1897
Open Mon–Fri 9am–5.30pm Sat 9am–noon
Sales General antique sales Thurs–Fri 10.30am, viewing Tues–Wed 10am–4.30pm Tues 6–8pm. Occasional special sales
Frequency 5–6 weeks
Catalogues Yes

Shirley-Ann's Antiques & Decorative Furniture
Contact Mrs S A Downes
✉ **69 Church Road, Hove, East Sussex, BN3 2BB** 🅿
☎ 01273 770045
Est. 1985 *Stock size* Large
Stock Georgian, Victorian, Edwardian furniture and antiques
Open Mon–Sat 10am–5.30pm
Services Free delivery

Sleeping Beauty Antique Beds
Contact Mrs Roberts
✉ **212 Church Road, Hove, East Sussex, BN3 2DJ** 🅿
☎ 01273 205115 or 020 7471 4711
Ⓔ info@antiquebeds.com
Ⓦ www.antiquebeds.com
Est. 1992 *Stock size* Large
Stock French, Victorian brass and iron bedsteads
Open Mon–Sat 10am–5pm

Yellow Lantern Antiques (LAPADA)
Contact B Higgins
✉ **34 Holland Road, Hove, East Sussex, BN3 1JL** 🅿
☎ 01273 771572 Ⓕ 01273 455476
Ⓜ 07860 342976
Est. 1950 *Stock size* Medium
Stock Period English town furniture pre-1840, ormolu and bronzes
Open Mon–Fri 10am–5.30pm Sat 10am–4pm
Fairs Olympia, Buxton
Services Valuations, restorations

HURST GREEN

Delmar Antiques
Contact Mr Harry Nicol
✉ **77 London Road, Hurst Green, East Sussex, TN19 7PN** 🅿
☎ 01580 860345 Ⓕ 01580 860099
Ⓜ 07712 543749
Est. 1951 *Stock size* Medium
Stock Period and Regency furniture, oils, watercolours, silver, clocks
Open Mon–Sat 9am–6pm or by appointment
Services Valuations, repairs

Hurst Green Antiques
Contact Mr S Atkinson
✉ **79 London Road, Hurst Green, East Sussex, TN19 7PN** 🅿
☎ 01580 860317
Ⓦ www.hurstgreenantiques.com
Est. 1988 *Stock size* Large
Stock English and French period furnishings for house and garden
Open Tues–Sat 9.30am–5.30pm

Libra Antiques
Contact Mrs Janice Hebert
✉ **81 London Road, Hurst Green, East Sussex, TN19 7PN** 🅿
☎ 01580 860569
Est. 1985 *Stock size* Medium
Stock Antique lamps, pine, collectables
Open Tues–Sat 9.30am–6pm Sun Mon by appointment

LEWES

Antique Interiors for Home & Garden
Contact Mr Kevin Hillman
✉ **7 Malling Street, Lewes, East Sussex, BN7 2RA** 🅿
☎ 01273 486822
Ⓜ 01273 486481
Est. 1990 *Stock size* Medium
Stock General antiques, decorative items, garden furniture, country pine
Open Mon–Sat 9.30am–5.30pm or by appointment
Fairs Ardingly, Newark

Bow Windows Bookshop (ABA, PBFA, ILAB)
Contact Alan or Jennifer Shelley
✉ **175 High Street, Lewes, East Sussex, BN7 1YE**
☎ 01273 480780 Ⓕ 01273 486686
Ⓔ rarebooks@bowwindows.com
Ⓦ www.bowwindows.com
Est. 1964 *Stock size* Medium
Stock General antiquarian books, all subjects
Open Mon–Sat 9.30am–5pm
Fairs Russell Hotel, International Book Fairs London
Services Valuations, 3 or 4 catalogues per year

David Cardoza Antiques
Contact David or Christina Cardoza
✉ **Milwards Farm, Lewes Road, Laughton, Lewes, East Sussex, BN8 6BN** 🅿
☎ 01323 811155
Ⓜ 07855 835991
Ⓔ dcardozaantiques@aol.com

Est. 1996 *Stock size* Large
Stock French furniture, armchairs, bedside tables, beds and bedroom suites
Open Every day by appointment only
Fairs Galloway
Services Restorations upholstery

Castle Antiques
Contact Mr Christopher Harris
163a High Street, Lewes, East Sussex, BN7 1XU
01273 475176
Est. 1984 *Stock size* Medium
Stock Pine furniture
Open Mon–Sat 10am–5pm Sun 11am–5pm

Church Hill Antique Centre
Contact Susan Miller or Simon Ramm
6 Station Street, Lewes, East Sussex, BN7 2DA
01273 474842 01273 846799
www.church-hill-antiques.co.uk
Est. 1995 *Stock size* Large
No. of dealers 60
Stock Art, collectables
Open Mon–Sat 9.30am–5pm or by appointment
Services Valuations

Cliffe Antiques Centre
Contact The Manager
47 Cliffe High Street, Lewes, East Sussex, BN7 2AN
01273 473266 01273 473266
Est. 1981 *Stock size* Medium
No. of dealers 15
Stock Wide range of antiques, collectables
Open Mon–Sat 9.30am–5pm

A & Y Cumming Ltd (ABA)
Contact Andrew Cumming
84 High Street, Lewes, East Sussex, BN7 1XN
01273 472319 01273 486364
a.y.cumming@ukgateway.net
Est. 1976 *Stock size* Large
Stock Antiquarian and second-hand books on travel, natural history, colour plate books, 1st editions, leather bound
Open Mon–Fri 10am–5pm Sat 10am–5.30pm
Fairs Olympia (June), Chelsea Book Fair
Services Valuations

The Emporium Antiques Centre
Contact Michelle Doyle or Steven Madigan
42 Cliffe High Street, Lewes, East Sussex, BN7 2AN
01273 486866
Est. 1993 *Stock size* Large
No. of dealers 60
Stock General antiques, collectables, studio ceramics, toys, textiles, silver, jewellery, books, clocks
Open Mon–Sat 9.30am–5.30pm Sun noon–4pm

The Emporium Antiques Centre Too
Contact Sean Lewis
24 High Street, Lewes, East Sussex, BN7 2LU
01273 477979
Est. 1989 *Stock size* Large
No. of dealers 100
Stock Antiques, collectables, furniture
Open Mon–Sat 9.30am–5pm Sun noon–5pm

The Fifteenth Century Bookshop (PBFA)
Contact Mrs Miraband
99–100 High Street, Lewes, East Sussex, BN7 1XH
01273 474160
07751 487642
www.15centurybookshop.co.uk
Est. 1930 *Stock size* Medium
Stock General stock, collectable children's books
Open Mon–Sat 10am–5.30pm Sun 10.30am–4.30pm
Services Book search for children's books, postal service

Gorringes Incorporating Julian Dawson (SOFAA, ISVA)
Contact Mr Julian Dawson
Garden Street, Lewes, East Sussex, BN7 1TJ
01273 478221 01273 487369
auctions@gorringes.co.uk
www.gorringes.co.uk
Est. 1920
Open Mon–Fri 9am–5.30pm Sat 9am–12.30pm
Sales Sales of general antiques and collectables Mon (not Bank Hols) 10am. Viewing Fri 10am–5pm Sat 9am–12.30pm
Frequency Weekly
Catalogues No

Gorringes Incorporating Julian Dawson (SOFAA, ISVA, BACA Award Winner 2002)
Contact Mr P Taylor
15 North Street, Lewes, East Sussex, BN7 2PD
01273 472503 01273 479559
auctions@gorringes.co.uk
www.gorringes.co.uk
Est. 1926
Open Mon–Fri 8.30am–5.15pm Sat 9am–11.45am
Sales Fine art and antiques 3-day sale Tues–Thurs at 10am, viewing Fri 10am–5pm, Sat 9.30am–4pm prior. Occasional house sales
Frequency 6 weeks
Catalogues Yes

Lewes Antique Centre
20 Cliffe High Street, Lewes, East Sussex, BN7 2AH
01273 476148/472173
01273 476148
Est. 1968 *Stock size* Large
No. of dealers 60
Stock Furniture, architectural salvage, bric-a-brac, china, clocks, metalware, glass
Open Mon–Sat 9.30am–5pm Sun Bank Hols 12.30–4.30pm
Services Storage, delivery, pine stripping, restorations, valuations

Lewes Book Centre
Contact Mr David Summerfield
38 Cliffe High Street, Lewes, East Sussex, BN7 2AN
01273 487053
Est. 1993 *Stock size* Medium
Stock Antiquarian and second-hand books to suit all tastes, military topics a speciality
Open Mon–Sat 10am–5pm
Fairs Lewes

The Lewes Clock Shop
Contact R I McColl
4 North Street, Lewes, East Sussex, BN7 2PA
01273 473123 01273 473123
rmccoll@lineone.net
Est. 1991 *Stock size* Medium
Stock Restored antique clocks
Open Mon–Sat 9am–4pm closed Wed
Services Valuations, restorations, shipping

SOUTH EAST

EAST SUSSEX • LITTLE HORSTEAD

Lewes Flea Market
Contact Mr A R Wilkinson
14a Market Street, Lewes, East Sussex, BN7 2NB
01273 480328 F 01273 328665
M 07801 4118496
E arwilkinson@aol.com
Est. 1993 *Stock size* Large
Stock Antiques, collectables, bric-a-brac
Open Mon–Fri 9.30am–5pm Sat Sun 10.30am–5pm

Pastorale Antiques
Contact Mr Soucek
15 Malling Street, Lewes, East Sussex, BN7 2RA
01273 473259 F 01273 473259
Est. 1980 *Stock size* Large
Stock English, French, East European and pine furniture, garden furniture and ornaments
Open Mon–Sat 10am–5pm
Services Restorations

School Hill Antiques
Contact Mrs Tina Allen
207 High Street, Lewes, East Sussex, BN7 2NS
01273 477782 F 01273 477782
Est. 1998 *Stock size* Medium
Stock Victorian–Edwardian furniture, decorative items
Open Mon–Sat 10am–5pm
Services Valuations, advice on decorations

Trade Antiques Centre
Contact Amanda Tollhurst
207 High Street, Lewes, East Sussex, BN7 2NS
01273 486688 M 08701 413783
Est. 2001 *Stock size* Large
Stock Pine, oak, mahogany furniture, enamel ware, pictures, jewellery, china and porcelain
Open Mon–Sat 10am–5.30pm Sun 12–5pm

The Treasury
Contact Pamela Marshall
89 High Street, Lewes, East Sussex, BN7 1XN
01273 480446 F 01273 838785
Est. 1986 *Stock size* Medium
Stock Collectables, small antiques, out-of-production figurines
Open Thurs–Sat 10am–5pm

Wallis & Wallis
Contact Mr Roy Butler (militaria) or Mr Glen Butler (toys)
West Street Auction Galleries, Lewes, East Sussex, BN7 2NJ
01273 480208 F 01273 476562
E auctions@wallisandwallis.co.uk (militaria) or grb@wallisandwallis.co.uk (toys)
W www.wallisandwallis.co.uk
Est. 1928
Open Mon–Fri 9am–5.30pm closed 1–2pm
Sales 9 militaria, medals, coins, arms and armour per annum. Tues 11am 2 connoisseur arms and armour per annum, Tues Wed 11am, 8 die-cast and tinplate toys per annum, Mon 10.30am, viewing prior Fri 9am–5pm Sat 9am–1pm, morning of sale 9am–10.30pm. Sales dates available on request
Frequency 6 weeks
Catalogues Yes (2 to 3 weeks before sales)

LITTLE HORSTEAD

Pianos Galore
Contact Jason Richards
Little Horstead, East Sussex, TN22 5TT
01825 750567 F 01825 750566
E info@pianosgalore.co.uk
Est. 1982 *Stock size* Large
Stock Pianos
Open Mon–Sat 9am–5pm Sat 10am–noon

NEWHAVEN

Newhaven Flea Market
Contact Mr R Mayne
28 Southway, Newhaven, East Sussex, BN9 9LA
01273 516065
M 0771 4660522
Est. 1979 *Stock size* Large
No. of dealers 40
Stock Furniture, collectables, bric-a-brac
Open Mon–Sun 10am–5.30pm

NINFIELD

Salehurst Auctioneers
Contact Jeremy Palmer
Bexhill Road, Ninfield, Battle, East Sussex, TN33 9EE
01424 893293 F 01424 893393
E sales@salehurstauctions.com
W www.salehurstauctions.com
Est. 2002
Open Mon–Fri 9am–5pm
Sales Fortnightly sale of Victorian and later furnishing and effects, Tues 10am, viewing Mon 9am–8pm and morning of sale
Catalogues Yes

NUTLEY

Nutley Antiques
Contact L Hall
Libra House, High Street, Nutley, East Sussex, TN22 3NF
01825 713220
Est. 1986 *Stock size* Large
Stock Rustic, country and decorative items
Open Mon–Sat 10am–5pm Sun 1.30–5pm
Fairs Ardingly
Services Caning, rushing

PEACEHAVEN

Hunters Antiques
Contact Colin Ancell
348 South Coast Road, Telscombe Cliffs, Peacehaven, East Sussex, BN10 7EP
01273 588841 F 01273 588841
M 07710 611311
Est. 1970 *Stock size* Large
Stock General antiques, furniture
Open Mon–Sun 10.30am–5pm
Fairs Ardingly, Newark
Services Valuations

PEVENSEY

The Old Mint House
Contact Mr Andrew Nicholson
High Street, Pevensey, East Sussex, BN24 5LF
01323 762337 F 01323 762337
E antiques@minthouse.co.uk
W www.minthouse.co.uk
Est. 1903 *Stock size* Large
Stock General antiques
Open Mon–Fri 9am–5pm Sat 10.30am–4pm
Services Shipping

POLEGATE

Graham Price Antiques Ltd
Contact Mr G Price
Applestore, Chaucer Industrial Estate, Dittons Road, Polegate, East Sussex, BN26 6JF
01323 487167 F 01323 483904
E mail@grahampriceantiques.co.uk
W www.grahampriceantiques.co.uk
Est. 1984 *Stock size* Large

Stock Decorative and antique country furniture, rural artefacts
Open Mon–Fri 8am–5pm
Fairs Newark
Services Packing, shipping

Summers Antiques
Contact Richard Millis
87 High Street, Polegate, East Sussex, BN26 6AE
01323 483834
Est. 2001 *Stock size* Small
Stock General antiques and collectables
Open Mon–Fri 9am–5pm Sat 9am–1pm
Fairs Ardingly

PORTSLADE

K Edwards Antiques
Contact Mr K Edwards
Unit 2, Bestwood Works, Drove Road, Portslade, Brighton, East Sussex, BN41 2PA
01273 420866
kedwa31024@aol.com
www.kedwardsantiques.co.uk
Est. 1988 *Stock size* Large
Stock Furniture, mainly chests-of-drawers
Open Mon–Fri 7.30am–6pm
Services Restorations

RINGMER

Bob Hoare Pine and Country Furniture
Contact Bob Hoare
Avery's Nursery, Lewes Road, Ringmer, East Sussex, BN8 5RU
01273 814181 01273 814714
bob@antiquebob.demon.co.uk
www.antiquebob.demon.co.uk
Est. 1980 *Stock size* Large
Stock Pine furniture, linen presses and pine dressers, decorative objects, etc
Open Mon–Fri 9am–6pm Sat 9am–5.30pm
Services Restorations

ROTHERFIELD

6a Antiques
Contact Mr B Samworth
6 High Street, Rotherfield, Crowborough, East Sussex, TN6 3LL
01892 852008
Est. 1979 *Stock size* Medium
Stock Georgian–Victorian furniture, antique pine
Open Mon–Sun 10am–5pm closed Wed

Country House Antiques
Contact Graham Blake
The Old Garage, The Square, Rotherfield, East Sussex, TN6 3LY
01892 853594 01892 853594
Est. 1992 *Stock size* Medium
Stock General antiques
Open Mon–Sat 10.30am–5pm

Forge Interiors
Contact Mr D Masham
South Street, Rotherfield, Crowborough, East Sussex, TN6 3LN
01892 853000 01892 853122
asiandecor@forgeinteriors.com
www.forgeinteriors.com
Est. 1999 *Stock size* Medium
Stock Asian and English furniture, decorative items
Open Tues–Sat 10am–1pm 2pm–5pm Sun 2pm–5pm
Services Chair caning

Olinda House Antiques
Contact David Hinton
Olinda House, South Street, Rotherfield, Crowborough, East Sussex, TN6 3LL
01892 852609/852412
07801 265764
David@olindahouse.freeserve.co.uk
Est. 1996 *Stock size* Large
No. of dealers 15
Stock Furniture, china, silver, glass
Open Mon–Sat 10am–5pm Sun 11am–4pm

ROTTINGDEAN

Georgina's Antiques
Contact Mrs Heldman
45 High Street, Rottingdean, Brighton, East Sussex, BN2 7HE
01273 308699
Est. 1995 *Stock size* Medium
Stock Antiques, collectables
Open Mon–Sat 9.30am–5pm Sun noon–5pm

Jordans of Rottingdean
Contact Mr Jordan Payne
98 High Street, Rottingdean, Brighton, East Sussex, BN2 7HF
01273 302003
Est. 2001 *Stock size* Medium
No. of dealers 40
Stock China, jewellery, books, ephemera
Open Mon–Sat 9.30–5pm Sun noon–5pm

RYE

Bears Galore
Contact Richard Tatham
c/o The Corner House, 27 High Street, Rye, East Sussex, TN31 7JF
01797 223187
bearsinrye@aol.com
www.bearsgalore.co.uk
Est. 1979 *Stock size* Large
Stock Handmade collectable teddy bears
Open Mon–Sat 10am–4.30pm Sun noon–4.30pm
Services Mail order, layaway service

Black Sheep Antiques
Contact Mrs S Wright
72 The Mint, Rye, East Sussex, TN31 7EW
01797 224508
Est. 1991 *Stock size* Medium
Stock Victorian china and glass
Open Mon–Sun 11am–5pm
Services China matching

Bragge & Sons
Contact Mr John Bragge
Landgate House, Landgate, Rye, East Sussex, TN31 7LH
01797 223358 01797 223358
Est. 1849
Stock 18thC English furniture and works of art
Open By appointment
Services Valuations, restorations

Chapter & Verse Booksellers
Contact Mr Spencer Rogers
105 High Street, Rye, East Sussex, TN31 7JE
01797 222692
07970 386905
chapterandverse@btconnect.com
Est. 1976 *Stock size* Medium

Stock Antiquarian and out-of-print books
Open Mon–Sat 9.30am–5pm closed Tues
Services Free book search

Cheyne House
Contact Keith Marshall
108 High Street, Rye, East Sussex, TN31 7JE
☎ 01797 222612
cheynehouse@ryeantiques.fsnet.co.uk
Est. 1999 *Stock size* Small
Stock Furniture, boxes
Open Mon–Sun 10am–5.30pm closed Tues

Collectors Corner
Contact Mr. Woolveridge
2 Market Road, Rye, East Sussex, TN31 7JA
☎ 01797 225796 Ⓕ 01797 229246
collectcor@hotmail.com
Est. 1994 *Stock size* Medium
Stock General antiques
Open Mon–Sun 10am–5pm

Herbert G Gasson
Contact Mr T J Booth
Lion Galleries, Lion Street, Rye, East Sussex, TN31 7LB
☎ 01797 222208 Ⓜ 07703 349431
hgassonantiques@hotmail.com
Est. 1909 *Stock size* Large
Stock Early oak, country, walnut, mahogany furniture
Open Mon–Sat 10am–5pm

Ann Lingard Ropewalk Antiques (LAPADA, BACA Award Winner 2001)
Contact Ann Lingard
18–22 Ropewalk, Rye, East Sussex, TN31 7NA
☎ 01797 223486 Ⓕ 01797 224700
ann-lingard@ropewalkantiques.freeserve.co.uk
Est. 1976 *Stock size* Large
Stock English antique pine furniture, glass, copper, wooden items, garden items, kitchen shop
Open Mon–Fri 9am–5pm Sat 10am–4.30pm

Masons Yard
Contact Mr A Frame
17 Wish Street, Rye, East Sussex, TN31 7DA
☎ 01797 224437
Est. 1996 *Stock size* Large
Stock Antique furniture, 1920s artefacts, lighting
Open Mon–Sun 10am–5pm

Mint Antiques
Contact Mr Charles Booth
54 The Mint, Rye, East Sussex, TN31 7EN
☎ 01797 224055
Est. 1984 *Stock size* Medium
Stock Antique furniture, decorative items
Open Phone call recommended

Mint Arcade
Contact John Bartholomew
71 The Mint, Rye, East Sussex, TN31 7EW
☎ 01797 225952 Ⓕ 01797 224834
johnbartholomew@freenet.co.uk
Est. 1982 *Stock size* Large
No. of dealers 5
Stock Jewellery, dolls' house furniture, hand-made military figures, chess sets, picture frames and mounts, cigarette and trade cards, framed sets of cards
Open Mon–Sun 10am–4.30pm

Needles Antique Centre
Contact Jenny King
15 Cinque Ports Street, Rye, East Sussex, TN31 7AD
☎ 01797 225064
needles.antiques@btinternet.com
Ⓦ www.btinternet.com/~needles_antiques_online/
Est. 1996 *Stock size* Large
No. of dealers 5
Stock Small antiques, collectables
Open Mon–Sun 10am–5pm

Quayside Antiques
Contact G T D Niall
The Corn Exchange, The Strand, Rye, East Sussex, TN31 7DB
☎ 01797 227088
Est. 1997 *Stock size* Large
Stock French antique furniture
Open Mon–Sun 11am–5pm

Rye Auction Galleries
Contact Mr A Paine
Rock Channel, Rye, East Sussex, TN31 7HL
☎ 01797 222124 Ⓕ 01797 222126
Ⓜ 07764 225457
sales@ryeauctions.fsnet.co.uk
Est. 1989
Open Mon–Fri 8.30am–5pm
Sales Antique and general sales 1st and 3rd Fri of each month 9.30am, viewing Thurs 9am–5pm, trade by appointment
Frequency Bi-monthly
Catalogues Yes

Rye Old Books
Contact Miss A Coleman
7 Lion Street, Rye, East Sussex, TN31 7LB
☎ 01797 225410 Ⓕ 01797 225410
Est. 1993 *Stock size* Medium
Stock Antiquarian and second-hand books, illustrated, fine bindings
Open Mon–Sat 10.30am–5.30pm Sun 2–5pm by appointment on Sundays during winter
Services Valuations

Strand Quay Antiques
Contact Ann Marie Sutherland
1–2 The Strand, Rye, East Sussex, TN31 7DB
☎ 01797 226790 Ⓜ 07775 602598
Est. 1994 *Stock size* Large
No. of dealers 12
Stock Victorian–Edwardian furniture, porcelain, glass, pictures, collectables
Open Mon–Sun 10am–5pm

Wish Barn Antiques
Contact Mr Robert Wheeler or Mr Joe Dearden
Wish Street, Rye, East Sussex, TN31 7DA
☎ 01797 226797
Est. 1993 *Stock size* Large
Stock 19thC pine and country furniture, 19thC mahogany furniture
Open Mon–Sun 10am–5pm

SEAFORD

The Barn Collectors Market & Bookshop
Contact Mr B J Wicks
Church Lane, Seaford, East Sussex, BN25 1HL
☎ 01323 890010
Est. 1969 *Stock size* Medium
No. of dealers 20
Stock Collectables, books, militaria, jewellery
Open Mon–Sat 9.30am–5pm

The Little Shop
Contact Mr C Keane
6 High Street, Seaford, East Sussex, BN25 1PG
☎ 01323 490742

Est. 1987 *Stock size* Large
Stock General curios, collectables, dolls' house furniture
Open Mon–Sat 9.30am–6pm

The Old House (Antiques China Glass) Ltd
Contact Mr S M Barrett
15–17 High Street, Seaford, East Sussex, BN25 1PD
01323 893795
Est. 1945 *Stock size* Large
Stock General antiques, furniture, china, glass, collectables
Open Mon–Sat 9am–5pm Wed 9am–1pm
Services Valuations

ST LEONARDS-ON-SEA

The Antique Shop
Contact A. Dwight
121 Bohemia Road, St Leonards-on-Sea, East Sussex, TN37 6RL
01424 423049
Est. 2001 *Stock size* Small
Stock Chinese and European ceramics, English and Continental glass
Open By appointment

The Book Jungle
Contact Mr M Gowen
24 North Street, St Leonards-on-Sea, East Sussex, TN38 0EX
01424 421187
Est. 1990 *Stock size* Medium
Stock Antiquarian and second-hand books
Open Mon–Sat 10am–5pm closed Wed

Bookman's Halt
Contact Mr C Linklater
127 Bohemia Road, St Leonards-on-Sea, East Sussex, TN37 6RL
01424 421413
Est. 1980 *Stock size* Medium
Stock Low-key general stock of antiquarian and second-hand books
Open Mon–Sat 10am–1pm 2.30pm–5pm closed Wed

Filsham Farmhouse Antiques
Contact John York
111 Harley Shute Road, St Leonards-on-Sea, East Sussex, TN38 8BY
01424 433109
Est. 1962 *Stock size* Large
Stock Oak and shipping furniture
Open Mon–Fri 9am–5pm

Hastings Antiques Centre
Contact Mr Robert Amstad
59–61 Norman Road, St Leonards-on-Sea, East Sussex, TN38 0EG
01424 428561 Ⓕ 01424 428561
Est. 1982 *Stock size* Large
No. of dealers 15
Stock Continental decorative furniture, sporting items, luggage, English furniture and general antiques
Services Valuations

Makins & Bailey
Contact Barbara Makins
42 Norman Road, St Leonards-on-Sea, East Sussex, TN38 0EG
01424 440777
Est. 2001 *Stock size* Small
Stock Antique and decorative furniture
Open Mon–Fri 10am–5pm Sat 10am–1pm closed Wed
Services Valuations

Monarch Antiques
Contact Mr Marcus King
6 & 19 Grand Parade, St Leonards-on-Sea, East Sussex, TN38 0DD
01424 445841 Ⓕ 01424 445841
Ⓜ 07802 217842 or 07809 027930
Ⓔ monarch.antiques@virgin.net
Ⓦ www.monarch-antiques.co.uk
Est. 1981 *Stock size* Large
Stock Victorian–Edwardian furniture, pine, bamboo, decorative items
Open Mon–Sat 8.30am–5.30pm or by appointment
Fairs Newark
Services Valuations, restorations

Woodstock Antiques
Contact Mr P Bebb
68 Norman Road, St Leonards-on-Sea, East Sussex, TN38 0EJ
Ⓜ 07720 086889
Est. 1994 *Stock size* Medium
Stock Architectural and garden antiques, contemporary garden ornaments
Open Mon–Sat 10am–5pm
Services Valuations, design, search

TICEHURST

Piccadilly Rare Books (ABA, PBFA)
Contact Mr P Minet
Church Street, Ticehurst, East Sussex, TN5 7AA
01580 201221 Ⓕ 01580 200957
Ⓔ minet.royalty@btinternet.com
Ⓦ www.abebooks.com/home/piccadilly
Est. 1968 *Stock size* Large
Stock Antiquarian and second-hand books
Open Mon–Sat 10am–5pm
Fairs Olympia, Chelsea
Services Valuations

WADHURST

Browsers Barn
Contact Brian Langridge
New Pond Farm, High Street, Wallcrouch, Wadhurst, East Sussex, TN5 7JN
01580 200938 Ⓕ 01580 200885
Ⓜ 07809 836662
Ⓔ brian.langridge@talk21.com
Ⓦ www.browsers-barn.co.uk
Est. 1973 *Stock size* Large
Stock General antiques and collectables
Open Mon–Sat 9am–5pm Sun 10.30am–4pm
Services Shipping

Park View Antiques
Contact Bunty Ross
High Street, Durgates, Wadhurst, East Sussex, TN5 6DE
01892 783630 Ⓕ 01892 740264
Ⓜ 07974 655120
Ⓔ info@parkviewantiques.co.uk
Ⓦ www.parkviewantiques.co.uk
Est. 1988 *Stock size* Medium
Stock Country furniture, stripped pine, artefacts, rural items, vintage tools, period oak
Open Wed–Sun 10am–4pm and by appointment
Services Restorations

SOUTH EAST

KENT • APPLEDORE

KENT

APPLEDORE

Appledore Antiques Centre
Contact Roger Sinclair
The Old Forge, High Street, Appledore, Kent, TN26 2BX P
☎ 01233 758585
Est. 1985
No. of dealers 10
Stock General antiques
Open Mon–Sat 10am–5pm Sun 11am–5pm

Back 2 Wood
Contact Richard Moate
The Old Goods Shed, Station Road, Appledore, Kent, TN26 2DF
☎ 01233 758109
pine@back2wood.com
www.back2wood.com
Est. 1987 *Stock size* Medium
Stock Antique pine furniture
Open Mon–Fri 9am–5pm Sat 9am–4pm
Services Pine stripping

Victoria Lily
Contact Victoria Grieveson-Moore
26 The Street, Appledore, Kent, TN26 2BX P
☎ 01233 758003
Est. 2002 *Stock size* Medium
Stock Antiques, clothes, soft furnishings
Open Tues–Sun 10am–5.30pm
Services Valuations, restorations

ASH

Henry's of Ash
Contact Mr P Robinson
51 The Street, Ash, Canterbury, Kent, CT3 2EN P
☎ 01304 812600
Est. 1988 *Stock size* Medium
Stock Victorian, Art Deco, pre-1950s items, general antiques, linens
Open Mon Thurs–Sat 10am–noon 2–5pm Tues 10am–noon
Fairs Copthorne, University of Kent, Ravenscourt School Bromley

ASHFORD

Hobbs Parker
Contact Marie Sessford
Monument Way, Orbital Park, Ashford, Kent, TN24 0HB P
☎ 01233 502222 F 01233 502211
antiques@hobbsparker.co.uk
www.hobbsparker.co.uk
Est. 1850
Open Mon–Fri 9am–5.30pm
Sales Regular sales of antiques and collectables in the Amos Hall
Frequency Regular
Catalogues Yes

Parkinson Auctioneers
Contact Mrs L Parkinson
46 Beaver Road, Ashford, Kent, TN23 7RP P
☎ 01233 624426 F 01233 624426
auctions@parkinson-uk.com
www.parkinson-uk.com
Est. 1979
Open Mon–Fri 9am–5pm
Sales General sale Mon 10am, viewing Sat 9am–1pm
Frequency Monthly
Catalogues Yes

ASHURST

The Architectural Emporium
Contact Michael Roberts
The Bald Faced Stag, Ashurst, Kent, TN3 9TE P
☎ 01892 740877
bfs@architecturalemporium.com
www.architecturalemporium.com
Est. 2000 *Stock size* Large
Stock Architectural antiques, garden statuary, sundials, fountains, fireplaces, lighting
Open Tues–Sat 9.30am–5.30pm

BARHAM

Stablegate Antiques
Contact Michael Giuntini,
Barham, Kent, CT4 6QD P
☎ 01227 831639 F 01227 831639
M 07802 439777
wwww.stablegateantiques.co.uk
Est. 1981 *Stock size* Large
Stock Period furniture, pictures, silver, silver plate, ceramics, mirrors
Open Mon–Sun 10am–5pm
Fairs Claridges, NEC, Harrogate

BECKENHAM

Antiques & Collectors Market
Contact Mrs Holley
Public Hall, Bromley Road, Beckenham, Kent, BR3 5JE
☎ 020 8660 1369
Est. 1975 *Stock size* Medium
No. of dealers 12
Stock Antiques, collectables
Open Wed 8am–2pm

Pepys Antiques
Contact Sonia Elton
9 Kelsey Park Road, Beckenham, Kent, BR3 6LH P
☎ 020 8650 0994
Est. 1968 *Stock size* Large
Stock Furniture, silver, porcelain, paintings
Open Mon–Sat 10am–2pm closed Wed
Services Valuations

Stabledoors and Co
Contact Mr R Pike
94–98 High Street, Beckenham, Kent, BR3 1ED
☎ 020 8650 9270 F 020 8650 9563
M 07899 892071
Est. 1967
Open Mon–Fri 9.30am–5.30pm
Sales General antiques sale Thurs 10am, viewing Wed 10am–4pm
Frequency Fortnightly
Catalogues Yes

BENENDEN

Mervyn Carey
Contact Mr M Carey
Twysden Cottage, Benenden, Cranbrook, Kent, TN17 4LD P
☎ 01580 240283 F 01580 240283
Est. 1991
Sales Antiques sales at Church Hall, Church Road, Tenterden, Kent. Further details by post
Frequency Five per year
Catalogues Yes

BETHERSDEN

Stevenson Brothers (British Toymakers Guild)
Contact Mark Stevenson or Sue Russell
The Workshop, Ashford Road, Bethersden, Ashford, Kent, TN26 3AP P

☎ 01233 820363 Ⓕ 01233 820580
Ⓔ sale@stevensonbros.com
Ⓦ www.stevensonbros.com
Est. 1982 *Stock size* Large
Stock Antique and new rocking horses
Open Mon–Fri 9am–6pm
Sat 10am–1pm
Services Restorations of children's classic cars

BEXLEY

Ellenor Hospice Projects
Contact Mrs June Lynch
✉ **18–20 High Street, Bexley, Kent, DA5 1AD** Ⓟ
☎ 01322 553996
Est. 1996 *Stock size* Large
Stock General antiques. All profits raised support hospice care in North West Kent and London Borough of Bexley
Open Mon–Sat 9.30am–4.30pm
Thurs 9.30am–1pm

BIDDENDEN

Period Piano Company
Contact David Winston
✉ **Park Farm Oast, Hareplain Road, Biddenden, Nr Ashford, Kent, TN27 8LJ** Ⓟ
☎ 01580 291393 Ⓕ 01580 291393
Ⓔ periodpiano@talk21.com
Ⓦ www.periodpiano.com
Est. 1980 *Stock size* Medium
Stock 1760–1930 pianos, piano stools, music stands, music cabinets
Open By appointment
Services Valuations, restorations, shipping

BILSINGTON

The Barn at Bilsington
Contact Gabrielle de Giles
✉ **Swanton Lane, Bilsington, Ashford, Kent, TN25 7JR** Ⓟ
☎ 01233 720917 Ⓕ 01233 720156
Ⓜ 07721 015263
Ⓔ gabrielle@gabrielledegiles.com
Ⓦ www.gabrielledegiles.com
Est. 1984 *Stock size* Large
Stock Antique and country furniture, architectural items
Open By appointment

BIRCHINGTON

Birchington Antiques
Contact Mr G Booker
✉ **63 Station Road, Birchington, Kent, CT7 9RE** Ⓟ
☎ 01843 842811
Est. 1997 *Stock size* Medium
Stock Reupholstered antique furniture, mostly Georgian–Edwardian mahogany and walnut, china, glass
Open Mon–Sat 10am–5pm
Services Re-upholstery

Galleria Pinocchio
Contact Frank or Olga Tramontin
✉ **28 Station Approach, Birchington, Kent, CT7 9RD** Ⓟ
☎ 01843 847592
Ⓔ olga@galpin.fsnet.co.uk
Est. 1997 *Stock size* Small
Stock General antiques and bric-a-brac, fishing tackle, militaria
Open Mon–Sat 10am–5pm
Services Valuations

Silvesters
Contact Mr S N Hartley
✉ **Albion Chambers, 1 Albion Road, Birchington, Kent, CT7 9DN** Ⓟ
☎ 01843 841524 Ⓕ 01843 845131
Est. 1954
Stock Decorative items, furniture, Georgian, Victorian, silver, porcelain, glass
Open By appointment only
Services Valuations

BLUEWATER

Bears 'n' Bunnies
Contact Mrs C Sales
✉ **Bluewater Shopping Centre, Upper Thames Walk, Greenhithe, Kent, DA9 9SR** Ⓟ
☎ 01322 624997
Ⓦ www.bearsnbunnies.com
Est. 1999 *Stock size* Large
Stock Collectable bears from leading manufacturers and artists
Open Mon–Fri 10am–9pm
Sat 9am–8pm Sun 11am–5pm

Famously Yours Ltd
Contact Lee Croxon
✉ **Upper Thames Walk, Unit U090B, Bluewater, Greenhithe, Kent, DA9 9SR** Ⓟ
☎ 01322 427072 Ⓕ 01322 427072
Ⓔ enquiries@famouslyyours.com
Ⓦ www.famouslyyours.com
Est. 1996 *Stock size* Large
Stock Autographed memorabilia
Open Mon–Fri 10am–9pm
Sat 9am–8pm Sun 11am–5pm

BRASTED

David Barrington
Contact Mr D Barrington
✉ **High Street, Brasted, Kent, TN16 1JL** Ⓟ
☎ 01959 562537
Est. 1947 *Stock size* Medium
Stock General antiques
Open Mon–Sun 9am–5pm
or by appointment

Bigwood Antiques
Contact Steven Bigwood
✉ **Roshleigh, High Street, Brasted, Kent, TN16 1JA** Ⓟ
☎ 01474 823866 Ⓕ 01474 823866
Ⓔ steve@sbigwood.force9.co.uk
Est. 1996 *Stock size* Medium
Stock Furniture
Open Mon–Sat 10.30am–5pm
Sun 1.30–5pm
Services Restorations, upholstery

Cooper Fine Arts
Contact Mr Jonathan Hill-Reid
✉ **Swan House, High Street, Brasted, Kent, TN16 1JJ** Ⓟ
☎ 01959 565818
Est. 1980 *Stock size* Medium
Stock Paintings and furniture
Open Mon–Sat 10am–6pm
Services Framing, restoration of oils and watercolours

Courtyard Antiques
Contact Gill Whyman
✉ **High Street, Brasted, Kent, TN16 1JA** Ⓟ
☎ 01959 564483 Ⓕ 01732 454726
Ⓦ www.courtyardantiques.co.uk
Est. 1982 *Stock size* Large
Stock Silver, jewellery, ceramics, 19thC furniture including extending dining tables, chairs, Tunbridge ware, glass, copper, brass, watercolours, oils, prints, objets d'art
Open Mon–Sat 10am–5pm Sun and Bank Holidays 12.30–4.30pm
Services Furniture restoration, French polishing, re-leathering, upholstery

SOUTH EAST

KENT • BROADSTAIRS

⊞ G A Hill Antiques
Contact Mrs G A Hill
✉ **5 High Street, Brasted, Kent, TN16 1JA** 🅿
☎ 01959 565500
Est. 1999 *Stock size* Medium
Stock Georgian furniture, decorative French mirrors and chandeliers
Open Tues–Fri 10 am–5pm Sat 10am–5.30pm

⊞ Celia Jennings
Contact Celia Jennings
✉ **High Street, Brasted, Kent, TN16 1JE** 🅿
☎ 01959 563616 Ⓕ 01689 853250
Ⓜ 07860 483292
Est. 1965 *Stock size* Medium
Stock Early European wood carvings, sculpture
Open Mon–Sat 9.30am–5.30pm
Fairs Summer Olympia

⊞ Keymer Son & Co Ltd
Contact P T Keymer
✉ **Swaylands Place, The Green, High Street, Brasted, Kent, TN16 1JY** 🅿
☎ 01959 564203 Ⓕ 01959 561138
Est. 1977 *Stock size* Small
Stock Small 19thC furniture
Open Mon–Fri 9.30am–5.30pm

⊞ Roy Massingham Antiques (LAPADA)
Contact Mr R Massingham
✉ **The Coach House, High Street, Brasted, Kent, TN16 1JJ** 🅿
☎ 01959 562408 Ⓕ 01959 562408
Est. 1967 *Stock size* Large
Stock 18th–19thC furniture, pictures and objects
Open By appointment any time
Services Buying 'pre-valued' antiques

⊞ Southdown House Antique Galleries
Contact Mr Graham Stead
✉ **High Street, Brasted, Kent, TN16 1JE** 🅿
☎ 01959 563522
Est. 1978 *Stock size* Medium
Stock 18th, 19thC and early 20thC furniture, porcelain, glass, metalware Chinese embroidery
Open Mon–Sat 10am–5pm
Services Restorations, shipping

⊞ Dinah Stoodley
Contact Mrs D Stoodley
✉ **High Street, Brasted, Kent, TN16 1JE** 🅿
☎ 01959 563616
Est. 1965 *Stock size* Medium
Stock Early oak, country furniture
Open Mon–Sat 9.30am–5.30pm

⊞ W W Warner Antiques (BADA)
Contact Mr Chris Jowitt
✉ **The Old Forge, The Green, Brasted, Kent, TN16 1JL** 🅿
☎ 01959 563698 Ⓕ 01959 563698
Est. 1957 *Stock size* Medium
Stock 18th–19thC porcelain, glass, pottery
Open Mon–Sat 10am–5pm

BROADSTAIRS

⊞ Bee Antiques
Contact Jane Burges
✉ **23b Albion Street, Broadstairs, Kent, CT10 1LU** 🅿
☎ 01843 864040
Ⓔ theteddymaster@aol.com
Est. 1997 *Stock size* Medium
Stock Dolls, toys, teddybears, postcards, jewellery, collectables, musical instruments
Open Mon–Sun 11am–5pm
Services Valuations, restorations, shipping, lectures

⊞ Broadstairs Antiques and Collectables
Contact Penny Edwards
✉ **49 Belvedere Road, Broadstairs, Kent, CT10 1PF** 🅿
☎ 01843 861965
Est. 1992 *Stock size* Large
Stock Small collectable items, medium-sized furniture
Open Mon–Sat 10am–5pm (winter 4.30pm) closed Wed

⊞ Gillycraft
Contact Mrs Gill Faulkner
✉ **15 Albion Street, Broadstairs, Kent, CT10 1LU** 🅿
☎ 01843 867983
Est. 1992 *Stock size* Large
Stock Dressed collector bears, accessories
Open Mon–Sat 9.30am–4.30pm or by appointment
Services Promotional bears, fund raising bears, personalised bears

⊞ Market Fayre
Contact Margaret Sage
✉ **69 High Street, Broadstairs, Kent, CT10 1NQ** 🅿
☎ 01843 862563
Est. 1989 *Stock size* Medium
Stock Antique bric-a-brac, china, glass, dolls' houses, dolls' house furniture, limited-edition bears
Open Mon–Sat 9.30am–4.30pm

⊞ Secondhand Department
Contact Mr Alan Kemp
✉ **44 Albion Street, Broadstairs, Kent, CT10 1NE** 🅿
☎ 01843 862876 Ⓕ 01843 860084
Est. 1956 *Stock size* Large
Stock Antiquarian and second-hand books
Open Mon–Sat 9am–5.30pm Sun 10.30am–4.30pm

BROMLEY

⊞ Bears 'n' Bunnies
Contact Mrs C Sales
✉ **18 The Mall, High Street, Bromley, Kent, BR1 1TS** 🅿
☎ 020 8466 9520 Ⓕ 020 8466 9570
Ⓔ bearsnbunnies@btinternet.com
Ⓦ www.bearsnbunnies.btinternet.com
Est. 1995 *Stock size* Large
Stock Collectable bears from leading manufacturers
Open Mon–Sat 10am–5pm

⊞ Patric Capon (BADA)
Contact Patric Capon
✉ **PO Box 581, Bromley, Kent, BR1 2WX** 🅿
☎ 020 8467 5722 Ⓕ 020 8295 1475
Ⓜ 07831 444924
Ⓔ patric.capon@netway.co.uk
Est. 1975 *Stock size* Medium
Stock Antique clocks, marine chronometers, barometers
Open Wed–Sat only
Fairs Olympia (Summer)
Services Valuations, restorations, shipping

⊞ Peter Morris (BNTA)
Contact Mr P Morris
✉ **1 Station Concourse, Bromley North Station, Bromley, Kent, BR1 4EQ** 🅿
☎ 020 8313 3410 Ⓕ 020 8466 8502
Ⓔ coins@petermorris.co.uk
Ⓦ www.petermorris.co.uk
Est. 1983 *Stock size* Large

Stock Coins, medals, bank notes, antiquities
Open Mon–Fri 10am–1pm 2–6pm Sat 9am–2pm closed Wed
Fairs BNTA Coinex
Services Mail order, 4 illustrated lists, valuations

⊞ The Studio
Contact Mr Ian Burt
✉ **2 Sundridge Parade, Plaistow Lane, Bromley, Kent, BR1 4DT** P
☎ 020 8466 9010
Est. 1998 *Stock size* Large
Stock Georgian–Edwardian furniture, Art Deco, ceramics
Open Tues–Sat 11am–4.30pm or by appointment closed Thurs

CANTERBURY

⊞ Antique & Design
Contact Mr S Couchman
✉ **The Old Oast, Hollow Lane, Canterbury, Kent, CT1 3SA** P
☎ 01227 762871 F 01227 780970
Est. 1987 *Stock size* Large
Stock English and Continental pine furniture
Open Mon–Sat 9am–6pm Sun 10am–4pm

⊞ Bygones Reclamation (Canterbury) Ltd
Contact Bob Thorpe
✉ **Nackington Road, Canterbury, Kent, CT4 7BA** P
☎ 01227 767453 F 01227 762153
M 07802 278424
E bob@bygones.net
W www.bygones.net
Est. 1991 *Stock size* Large
Stock Victorian fireplaces, cast-iron radiators, building materials, architectural salvage, 1000s of reclaimed items
Open Mon–Sun 9am–5.30pm
Services Paint stripping, spraying, sand blasting, welding repairs

The Canterbury Auction Galleries (SOFAA)
Contact Christine Wacker
✉ **40 Station Road West, Canterbury, Kent, CT2 8AN** P
☎ 01227 763337 F 01227 456770
E auctions@thecanterburyauctiongalleries.com
W www.thecanterburyauctiongalleries.com
Est. 1911
Open Mon–Fri 9am–1pm 2–5pm
Sales 6 specialist sales a year. Monthly sales of Victorian and later furniture
Frequency Monthly
Catalogues Yes

⊞ The Canterbury Book Shop (PBFA, ABA)
Contact David Miles
✉ **37 Northgate, Canterbury, Kent, CT1 1BL** P
☎ 01227 464773 F 01227 780073
Est. 1980 *Stock size* Medium
Stock Antiquarian and second-hand books
Open Mon–Sat 10am–5pm
Fairs PBFA fairs, ABA London
Services Valuations

⊞ Chaucer Bookshop (ABA)
Contact Robert Sherston-Baker
✉ **6–7 Beer Cart Lane, Canterbury, Kent, CT1 2NY** P
☎ 01227 453912 F 01227 451893
E chaucerbooks@canterbury.dialnet.com
W www.chaucer-bookshop.co.uk/main.html
Est. 1957 *Stock size* Large
Stock Antiquarian and out-of-print books
Open Mon–Sat 10am–5pm or by appointment
Services Valuations, Shipping

⊞ W J Christophers
Contact Mr W Christophers
✉ **9 The Borough, Canterbury, Kent, CT1 2DR** P
☎ 01227 451968
Est. 1970 *Stock size* Large
Stock General antiques, 1720s–1950s, pottery, porcelain, clocks, furniture, prints, books
Open Mon–Sat 9am–5pm

The Coach House Antique Centre
Contact Manager
✉ **2a Duck Lane, Northgate, Canterbury, Kent, CT1 2AE** P
☎ 01227 463117
Est. 1975 *Stock size* Large
No. of dealers 10
Stock General antiques, collectables, pressed glass
Open Mon–Sat 10am–4pm

⊞ Conquest House Antiques
Contact Mrs C Hill
✉ **17 Palace Street, Canterbury, Kent, CT1 2DZ** P
☎ 01227 464587 F 01227 451375
E empire@empire-antiques.co.uk
W www.empire-antiques.co.uk
Est. 1994 *Stock size* Large
Stock Georgian–Victorian furniture, small items, paintings, chandeliers, rugs
Open Mon–Sat 10am–5pm
Services Valuations, restorations

⊞ Stuart Heggie (Photographic Collectors Club)
Contact Mr Stuart Heggie
✉ **14 The Borough, Northgate, Canterbury, Kent, CT1 2DR** P
☎ 01227 470422 F 01227 470422
E heggie.cameras@virgin.net
Est. 1980 *Stock size* Medium
Stock Vintage cameras, optical toys, photographic images
Open Fri–Sat 10am–5pm
Fairs South London Photographic Fair, Photographica
Services Valuations, restorations

⊞ Housepoints
Contact Mr Robin Ross Hunt
✉ **13 The Borough, Canterbury, Kent, CT1 2DR** P
☎ 01227 451350
M 07808 784638
Est. 1984 *Stock size* Large
Stock French country pine furniture, Victorian–Edwardian pieces
Open Mon–Fri 10am–5pm Sat 9.30am–6pm
Services Restorations

⊞ Nan Leith's Brocanterbury
Contact Nan Leith
✉ **68 Stour Street, Canterbury, Kent, CT1 2NZ** P
☎ 01227 454519
Est. 1982 *Stock size* Medium
Stock Small collectables
Open Mon Wed Fri Sat 1–6pm or by appointment

⊞ The Neville Pundole Gallery
Contact Neville Pundole
✉ **8a and 9 The Friars, Canterbury, Kent, CT1 2AS** P
☎ 01227 453471 F 01227 453471
E neville@pundole.co.uk
W www.pundole.co.uk
Est. 1986 *Stock size* Large
Stock Moorcroft and

contemporary pottery, glass
Open Mon–Sat 10am–5pm or by appointment
Services Valuations

Pinetum
Contact Mr Alan Pattinson
25 Oaten Hill, Canterbury, Kent, CT1 3HZ
01227 780365 07710 243106
alan.pattinson@tiscali.co.uk
Est. 1972 *Stock size* Medium
Stock Antique, pine, country furniture
Open Mon–Sat 9.30am–5pm Sun 10am–3pm
Services Valuations, polishing

The Victorian Fireplace
Contact John Griffith
Thanet House, 92 Broad Street, Canterbury, Kent, CT1 2LU
01227 767723
info@victorianfireplace.co.uk
www.victorian fireplace.co.uk
Est. 1986 *Stock size* Large
Stock Fireplaces
Open Tue–Sat 9am–5.30pm closed Wed

Whatever Comics
Contact Mr M Armario
2 Burgate Lane, Canterbury, Kent, CT1 2HH
01227 453226
Est. 1988 *Stock size* Large
Stock Die-cast cars, Star Trek, Star Wars toys, movie-related items, sci-fi collectables, Beanie Babies, action figures
Open Mon–Sat 10am–5.30pm

World Coins
Contact David Mason
35–36 Broad Street, Canterbury, Kent, CT1 2LR
01227 768887
worldcoins@bigfoot.com
www.worldcoins.freeservers.com
Est. 1970 *Stock size* Large
Stock Coins, medals, militaria, bank notes, stamps, medallions, tokens
Open Mon–Sat 9.30am–5pm closed Thurs pm
Services Valuations, identification, quarterly catalogue

CHATHAM

The American Comic Shop
Contact Mr K Earl
1 Church Street, Chatham, Kent, ME4 4BS
01634 817410
Est. 1993 *Stock size* Large
Stock American imported comics, graphic novels, collectable toys, posters
Open Mon Wed–Fri 10am–5.30pm Tues 10am–5pm Sat 9am–5.30pm
Fairs Science Fiction Fair
Services Valuations, mail order, standing order

CHILHAM

Bagham Barn Antiques
Contact Peggy Boyd
Canterbury Road, Chilham, Kent, CT4 8DU
01227 732522
07780 675201
peggyboyd@baghambarn.com
www.baghambarn.com
Est. 2002 *Stock size* Large
Stock 17th–18thC furniture, ceramics, clocks, collectables, arms, coins, notes, marine
Open Tues–Sun Bank Holiday Mon 10am–5pm
Fairs Ardingly, Detling
Services Restorations

CHISLEHURST

Chislehurst Antiques (LAPADA)
Contact Margaret Crawley
7 Royal Parade, Chislehurst, Kent, BR7 6NR
020 8467 1530 020 8249 7705
07768 081577
Est. 1978 *Stock size* Large
Stock 1860–1910 lighting, mirrors, 1760–1900 furniture
Open Fri Sat Mon 10am–5pm Sun 11am–4pm or by appointment

Michael Sim
Contact Mr M Sim
1 Royal Parade, Chislehurst, Kent, BR7 6NR
020 8467 7040 020 8857 1313
Est. 1983 *Stock size* Large
Stock Clocks, barometers, Georgian furniture
Open Mon–Sat 9am–6pm
Services Restorations

Wrattan Antique & Craft Mews
Contact Mrs M Brown
51–53 High Street, Chislehurst, Kent, BR7 5AF
020 8295 5933
Est. 1996 *Stock size* Large
No. of dealers 45
Stock Antiques, collectables, crafts
Open Mon–Sat 9.30am–5pm
Services Café

CLIFTONVILLE

Cliftonville Antiques
Contact Mr F Al-Aldan
161 Northdown Road, Cliftonville, Margate, Kent, CT9 2PA
01843 223470 01843 223470
Est. 1994 *Stock size* Large
Stock Antique furniture, silver, china, clocks
Open Mon–Sat 10am–5pm

Cottage Antiques
Contact Mr P J Emsley
172 Northdown Road, Cliftonville, Margate, Kent, CT9 2RB
01843 298214/299166
07771 542872
Est. 1990 *Stock size* Large
Stock Georgian–1930s antiques, oak, china, silver, smalls
Open Mon–Sat 10am–5pm
Services Valuations

CRANBROOK

Antiques at Cranbrook
Contact Nick Everard
19 High Street, Cranbrook, Kent, TN17 3EE
01580 712173 07885 690913
nick@topdrawer.uk.com
Est. 1989 *Stock size* Large
No. of dealers 10
Stock 19thC country antiques, silver, small items of furniture, ceramics, prints
Open Mon–Sat 10am–5pm

Bentleys Fine Art Auctioneers (RADS)
Contact Mr Raj Bisram
The Old Granary, Waterloo Road, Cranbrook, Kent, TN17 3JQ
01580 715857 01580 715857
cranauct@aol.com
Est. 1995

Open Mon–Fri 10am–5pm
Sat 10am–1pm
Sales 1st Sat monthly antiques and fine art sale 11am, viewing 3 days prior 10am–6.30pm. Specialist sales throughout the year
Frequency Monthly
Catalogues Yes

⊞ Douglas Bryan Antiques (BADA, LAPADA)
Contact Douglas Bryan
✉ **The Old Bakery, St Davids Bridge, Cranbrook, Kent, TN17 3HN** Ⓟ
☎ 01580 713103 Ⓕ 01580 712407
Ⓜ 07774 737303
Est. 1980 *Stock size* Medium
Stock 17th–18thC oak furniture, associated items
Open By appointment only
Fairs Olympia, BADA

Desmond Judd Auctioneers
Contact Jude McArdle
✉ **Hazelden Farm Oast, Marden Road, Cranbrook, Kent, TN17 2LP** Ⓟ
☎ 01580 714522 Ⓕ 01580 715266
Ⓔ desjudd@dial.pipex.com
Est. 1988
Open Mon–Fri 9 am–5pm
Sat 9.30am–noon
Sales General antiques, collectables held at The Weald of Kent Golf Club, Headcorn, Kent, Sun 11am, viewing Sat 10am–5pm
Frequency Monthly
Catalogues Yes

⊞ The Old Tackle Box
Contact Richard Dowson
✉ **PO Box 55, Cranbrook, Kent, TN17 3ZY** Ⓟ
☎ 01580 713979 Ⓕ 01580 713979
Est. 1994 *Stock size* Large
Stock Antique fishing tackle
Open By appointment
Services Valuations and mail order

⊞ Past & Present
Contact D. Walters
✉ **Corner House, Stone Street, Cranbrook, Kent, TN17 3HF** Ⓟ
☎ 01580 720934
Ⓜ 07734 759590
Est. 1995 *Stock size* Medium
Stock General antiques
Open Mon–Sat 9.30am–5.30pm
Sun 11am–4pm

⊞ Swan & Foxhole Antiques
Contact Mr Robert White
✉ **Albert House, Stone Street, Cranbrook, Kent, TN17 3HG** Ⓟ
☎ 01580 712720
Ⓦ www.cranbrookpc.freeserve.co.uk
Est. 1979 *Stock size* Medium
Stock Folk art, country decorated furniture
Open Tues Thurs–Sat 10am–1pm 2pm–5pm closed Mon Wed
Fairs Olympia, Decorative Fair, Battersea
Services Restorations, chair caning, valuations

⊞ Vestry Antiques
Contact Mrs L Dawkins
✉ **3a Stone Street, Cranbrook, Kent, TN17 3HF** Ⓟ
☎ 01580 713563
Est. 1994 *Stock size* Large
Stock 18th–early 19thC oak, mahogany, pine furniture, decorative items
Open Mon–Sat 9.30am–5pm
Services Local delivery, full or part house clearance, single items purchased

DARTFORD

⊞ Watling Antiques
Contact John Leitch
✉ **139 Crayford Road, Dartford, Kent, DA1 4AS** Ⓟ
☎ 01322 523620
Est. 1970 *Stock size* Small
Stock Shipping goods, collectables
Open Mon–Sat 9.30am–5pm
Services Valuations

⊞ Wot-a-Racket (GCS [GB, USA], TCS)
Contact Mr B Casey
✉ **250 Shepherds Lane, Dartford, Kent, DA1 2PN** Ⓟ
☎ 01322 220619 Ⓕ 01322 220619
Ⓜ 07808 593467
Ⓔ wot-a-racket@talk21.com
Est. 1981 *Stock size* Large
Stock Sporting memorabilia
Open By appointment
Fairs Newark, Ardingly, Sandown Park, Alexandra Palace

DEAL

⊞ Decors
Contact Nicole Loftus-Potter
✉ **67a Beach Street, Deal, Kent, CT14 6HY** Ⓟ
☎ 01304 368030 Ⓕ 01304 368030
Est. 1990 *Stock size* Medium
Stock 17th–19thC antiques, modern St Louis, Baccarat, non-renewable pieces, textiles
Open Mon–Sun 10am–7pm or by appointment

⊞ Delpierre Antiques
Contact Margery Borley
✉ **132 High Street, Deal, Kent, CT14 6BE** Ⓟ
☎ 01304 371300 Ⓜ 07771 864231
Est. 1998 *Stock size* Medium
Stock Individual and specialist pieces, lighting, Art Deco, Art Nouveau, Oriental, French furniture
Open Tues–Sat 9.30am–5pm or by appointment
Services Valuations

⊞ Fordham's
Contact Mr A Fordham
✉ **3a Victoria Road, Deal, Kent, CT14 7AS** Ⓟ
☎ 01304 373599 Ⓕ 01304 389333
Est. 1974 *Stock size* Medium
Stock Silver, furniture, general antiques, antiquities, second-hand and antiquarian books
Open Mon–Sat 9.30am–4.30pm or by appointment
Services Valuations for probate and insurance

⊞ Mulbery Antiques
Contact Mrs Nina Spencer
✉ **7 St Georges Passage, Deal, Kent, CT14 6TA**
☎ 01304 381800 Ⓕ 01304 381800
Est. 1988 *Stock size* Medium
Stock General antiques, furniture, glass, china, textiles, lamps, lighting, jewellery
Open Tues Thurs–Sat 10am–4pm
Services Commissions undertaken

⊞ Pretty Bizarre
Contact Phillip Hartley
✉ **170 High Street, Deal, Kent, CT14 6BQ** Ⓟ
Ⓜ 07973 794537
Est. 1991 *Stock size* Medium

SOUTH EAST

KENT • EAST PECKHAM

Stock General antiques including Art Deco
Open Fri–Sat 10am–4pm

Quill Antiques
Contact Mr A J Young
12 Alfred Square, Deal, Kent, CT14 6LR
01304 375958
Est. 1969 *Stock size* Small
Stock General small antiques
Open Mon–Sat 9am–5pm

Ron's Emporium
Contact Mr Ron Blown
98 Church Lane, Sholden, Deal, Kent, CT14 9QL
01304 374784 F 01304 380294
Est. 1979 *Stock size* Large
Stock Unusual items, clocks, phone boxes, antique furniture, snooker tables, collectables
Open Mon–Sat 9.30am–5.30pm closed Thurs
Services House clearance

Serendipity
Contact Marion Short or Jayne Eschalier
125 High Street, Deal, Kent, CT14 6BB
01304 369165
E dipityantiques@aol.com
Est. 1979 *Stock size* Large
Stock Small furniture, ceramics, pictures
Open Mon–Wed Fri 10am–4.30pm closed 12.30–2pm Sat 9.30am–4.30pm or by appointment
Fairs Sandown Park
Services Restoration of pictures

Toby Jug Collectables
Contact Mrs S Pettit
South Toll House, Deal Pier, Beach Street, Deal, Kent, CT14 6HZ
01304 369917
Est. 1996 *Stock size* Large
Stock Royal Doulton, discontinued Toby and character jugs, other china collectables
Open Tues–Sun 11am–5.30pm closed 1.30–2.30pm
Fairs DMG Fair Detling, The Grand Hotel Folkestone

EAST PECKHAM

Desmond and Amanda North
Contact Desmond North
The Orchard, 186 Hale Street, East Peckham, Kent, TN12 5JB
01622 871353 F 01622 872998
Est. 1971 *Stock size* Medium
Stock Persian and other Oriental rugs, carpets, runners, and cushions 1800–1939
Open Mon–Sun appointment advisable
Services Valuations, restorations

EDENBRIDGE

Lennox Cato Antiques (BADA, LAPADA, WKADA, CINOA)
Contact Lennox or Susan Cato
1 The Square, Church Street, Edenbridge, Kent, TN8 5BD
01732 865988 F 01732 865988
M 07836 233473
E cato@lennoxcato.com
W www.lennoxcato.com
Est. 1979 *Stock size* Medium
Stock 18th–19thC furniture, works of art, accessories
Open Mon–Sat 9.30am–5.30pm
Fairs Olympia, BADA, Harrogate
Services Valuations, consultancy, restorations

Chevertons of Edenbridge Ltd (LAPADA)
Contact Angus or David Adam
67–73 High Street, Edenbridge, Kent, TN8 5AL
01732 863196 F 01732 864298
M 07711 234010
E chevertons@msn.com
W www.chevertons.com
Est. 1959 *Stock size* Large
Stock English and Continental antique and decorative furniture, accessories
Open Mon–Sat 9am–5.30pm
Fairs NEC, Olympia

Way Back When
Contact Mrs L Hayward
25 High Street, Edenbridge, Kent, TN8 5AB
01732 868280 F 01732 868280
Est. 1995 *Stock size* Large
Stock Worcester, Derby, Crown Derby, jewellery, clocks, furniture, general antiques, 18thC glass and silver
Open Tues–Sat 10am–5.30pm

Yew Tree Antiques
Contact Mr Bob Carter
Crossways, Four Elms Road, Edenbridge, Kent, TN8 6AF
01732 700215
Est. 1984 *Stock size* Large
Stock Small furniture, bric-a-brac, books, linen, pictures
Open Mon 1.30–5pm Tues–Sat 10am–5pm Sun 1.30–5pm
Services House clearance

ELHAM

Elham Antiques
Contact Mr Julian Chambers
High Street, Elham, Kent, CT17 9AH
01303 840085
Est. 1989 *Stock size* Large
Stock Architectural antiques, old metal toys
Open Tues–Sat 10.30am–5.30pm
Fairs Sandown Park, Newark
Services Valuations

Elham Valley Book Shop (PBFA)
Contact Mr Tim Parsons
St Mary's Road, Elham, Canterbury, Kent, CT4 6TH
01303 840359 F 01303 840359
E books@elham-valley.demon.co.uk or etchinghill@hotmail.com
W www.elham-valley.demon.co.uk
Est. 1992 *Stock size* Large
Stock Rare and second-hand books including those on art, travel, topography, modern 1st editions, illustrated, natural history, private press a speciality
Open Tues Thurs 2–4.30pm Fri 11.30am–4.30pm Sat 11am–5pm Sun noon–4pm closed Mon and Wed
Services Valuations

Old Bank Antiques
Contact Mrs J Swinbourne
Bank Buildings, High Street, Elham, Kent, CT4 6TD
01303 840140
Est. 2001 *Stock size* Medium
Stock General antiques, furniture, ceramics
Open Tues`–Sat 10 am–5.30 pm Sun 11am–4.30 pm

ERITH

Belmont Jewellers
Contact Mr S J Girt
5 Belmont Road, Northumberland Heath, Erith, Kent, DA8 1JY

☎ 01322 339646
Est. 1986 *Stock size* Small
Stock Jewellery, furniture, pictures, silver, silver plate
Open Mon–Sat 9am–5pm
Fairs Ardingly
Services Valuations, jewellery repairs

FARNINGHAM

Adams Arts & Antiques Ltd
Contact Mr M Adams
✉ **The Old Forge, 1 High Street, Farningham, Dartford, Kent, DA4 0DG** P
☎ 01322 866877 F 01322 866877
Est. 1998 *Stock size* Medium
Stock Mainly metalware, stoneware, garden statuary
Open Mon–Sun 9am–5pm

P T Beasley
Contact Mrs R Beasley
✉ **Forge Yard, High Street, Farningham, Dartford, Kent, DA4 0DB** P
☎ 01322 862453
Est. 1964 *Stock size* Large
Stock 17th–19thC furniture, small items, brass, pewter
Open Mon–Sun 9am–5pm or by appointment

Farningham Pine
Contact Mr P Dzierzek
✉ **The Old Bull Stores, Farningham, Kent, DA4 0DG** P
☎ 01322 863230 F 01322 863168
Est. 1987 *Stock size* Large
Stock Pine furniture
Open Mon–Sat 10am–5pm Sun 11am–3pm closed Wed

FAVERSHAM

Collectors' Corner
Contact Mrs Mavis Mileham
✉ **East Street, Crescent Road, Faversham, Kent, ME13 8AD** P
☎ 01795 539721
Est. 1988 *Stock size* Medium
Stock Second-hand tools, brassware, door knobs, furniture, coins, pictures, cigarette cards
Open Mon–Sat 10am–5pm closed Wed Thurs

Ecomerchant Ltd
Contact Paul Whitlock or Joe Hilton
✉ **The Old Filling Station, Head Hill Road, Goodnestone, Faversham, Kent, ME13 9BL** P
☎ 01795 530130 F 01795 530430
E sales@ecomerchant.co.uk
W www.ecomerchant.co.uk
Est. 1998 *Stock size* Medium
Stock Architectural antiques, floor boards, stone, bricks, wood/oak beams, conservation building materials
Open Mon–Fri 8am–5pm Sat 9am–5pm

Faversham Antiques and Collectables
Contact Mr Ralph Lane
✉ **7 Court Street, Faversham, Kent, ME13 7AN** P
☎ 01795 591471
Est. 1997 *Stock size* Large
Stock General furniture, collectables, blue and white china, Osborne plaques, jewellery
Open Mon–Sat 10am–5pm
Fairs Ardingly

Squires Antiques
Contact Ann Squires
✉ **3 Jacob Yard, Preston Street, Faversham, Kent, ME13 8NY** P
☎ 01795 531503 F 01795 591600
Est. 1984 *Stock size* Large
Stock General antiques
Open Mon Tues Fri Sat 10am–5pm

FOLKESTONE

Hogben Auctioneers & Valuers Ltd
Contact Mr M Hogben
✉ **Unit C, Highfields Industrial Estate, Warren Road, Folkestone, Kent, CT19 6DD** P
☎ 01303 246810 F 01303 246256
E hogbenauctions@btconnect.com
W www.hogbenauctioneers.com
Est. 1986
Open Mon–Fri 9am–5pm
Sales 3 weekly. Sat fine art and collectables, Sun Victorian and later, viewing Thurs 10am–6pm Fri 10am–8pm. Specialist jewellery, ephemera, books and Art Deco sales throughout the year
Catalogues Yes

Lawton's Antiques
Contact Ian Lawton
✉ **26 Canterbury Road, Folkestone, Kent, CT19 5NG** P
☎ 01303 246418
Est. 1987 *Stock size* Medium
Stock General antiques
Open Mon–Sat 9am–6pm
Services Valuations

Alan Lord Antiques
Contact Mr R Lord
✉ **71 Tontine Street, Folkestone, Kent, CT20 1JR** P
☎ 01303 253674 F 01303 240284
Est. 1953 *Stock size* Large
Stock General antiques, unrestored furniture
Open Mon–Fri 9am–5pm Sat 10am–1pm
Services House clearance of antiques to 1930

G & DI Marrin & Son (ABA, PBFA)
Contact John or Patrick Marrin
✉ **149 Sandgate Road, Folkestone, Kent, CT20 2DA** P
☎ 01303 253016 F 01303 850956
M 07765 663808, 07896 377201 or 07905 122182
E marrinbook@clara.co.uk
W www.marrinbook.clara.net, www.marrinbook.com or www.marrinbook.co.uk
Est. 1947 *Stock size* Medium
Stock Books on topography of Kent, history and literature of the Great War, prints, maps. Catalogues issued for each
Open Tues–Sat 9.30am–5.30pm
Fairs PBFA London Book Fair, Russell Hotel – monthly, major events in the UK and overseas
Services Valuations

FOUR ELMS

Treasures
Contact Christine Evans
✉ **Bough Beech Road, Four Elms, Kent, TN8 6NE** P
☎ 01732 700363
Est. 1974 *Stock size* Large
No. of dealers 6
Stock Antiques, collectable, bric-a-brac
Open Tue–Sat 10am–5.30pm (winter 5pm) Sun 2–5pm

SOUTH EAST
KENT • GOUDHURST

GOUDHURST

⊞ Mill House Antiques
Contact Brad Russell
✉ **Unit 3, Fountain House, High Street, Goudhurst, Kent, TN17 1AL** Ⓟ
☎ 01580 212476
Est. 1991 *Stock size* Medium
Stock Pine and country antiques, complementary items
Open Tues–Sat 10am–5pm
Services Valuations

GRAVESEND

⊞ Courtyard Antiques
Contact Mrs J Giles
✉ **7a Manor Road, Gravesend, Kent, DA12 1AA**
☎ 01474 369399
Est. 1987 *Stock size* Medium
Stock Victorian–1930s furniture, collectables
Open Mon–Sat 10am–4.30pm
Services Restorations

GREEN STREET GREEN

⊞ Antica Antiques
Contact Mrs Muccio
✉ **48 High Street, Green Street Green, Orpington, Kent, BR6 6BJ** Ⓟ
☎ 01689 851181
Est. 1980 *Stock size* Medium
Stock General antiques, bric-a-brac
Open Mon–Sat 10am–5pm closed Thurs

HADLOW

⊞ Lime Tree House Antiques
Contact Wendy Thomas
✉ **Lime Tree House, 2 High Street, Hadlow, Kent, TN11 0EE** Ⓟ
☎ 01732 852002 Ⓕ 01732 852002
Est. 1987 *Stock size* Large
Stock Oak, mahogany and decorative furniture
Open Tues–Sun 10am–4pm
Fairs Newark, Ardingly
Services Valuations, restorations

HAMSTREET

⊞ Woodville Antiques
Contact Andrew MacBean
✉ **The Street, Hamstreet, Ashford, Kent, TN26 2HG** Ⓟ
☎ 01233 732981 Ⓕ 01233 732981
Ⓜ 07762783354
Ⓔ woodvilleantique@netscapeonline.co.uk
Est. 1988 *Stock size* Medium
Stock Antique and collectable tools, glass, furniture
Open Tues–Sun 10am–5.30pm
Services Valuations

HARRIETSHAM

B J Norris
Contact Mrs Norris
✉ **The Quest, West Street, Harrietsham, Maidstone, Kent, ME17 1JD** Ⓟ
☎ 01622 859515/692515
Ⓕ 01622 859515
Ⓔ norris02@globalnet.co.uk
Ⓦ www.antiquesbulletin.com/bjnorris
Est. 1972
Open Mon–Fri 9am–5pm
Sales General antiques sale Thurs 10am, viewing Thurs 8am–1pm prior to sale
Frequency Fortnightly

HEADCORN

⊞ Headcorn Antiques
Contact Mr or Mrs Smith
✉ **61 High Street, Headcorn, Ashford, Kent, TN27 9QA** Ⓟ
☎ 01622 890050 Ⓕ 01622 890050
Est. 1994 *Stock size* Medium
Stock General antiques, Continental pine, mahogany, oak
Open Mon–Sat 10am–5pm Sun 11am–4pm

⊞ Penny Lampard
Contact Mrs Lampard
✉ **31–33 High Street, Headcorn, Ashford, Kent, TN27 9NE** Ⓟ
☎ 01622 890682
Est. 1985 *Stock size* Large
Stock Decorative pieces for the interior design trade
Open Mon–Sat 9.30am–5.30pm Sun 11am–5pm
Fairs Detling
Services Tea shop

HERNE BAY

⊞ Archaic Artifacts
Contact Miss E J Hooper
✉ **Wealden Forest Park, Herne Common, Herne Bay, Kent, CT6 7LQ** Ⓟ
☎ 01227 711840 Ⓕ 01227 711840
Est. 1996 *Stock size* Large
Stock Oak beams, bricks, slates, Kent peg tiles, floor tiles, architectural salvage, fireplaces, doors, floor boarding
Open Mon–Sat 9am–5pm Sun 10am–4pm
Services Demolition

⊞ Briggy's Antique Centre
Contact W. Briggs
✉ **75 High Street, Herne Bay, Kent, CT6 5LQ**
☎ 01227 370621
Est. 1998 *Stock size* Large
Stock General Antiques
Open Mon–Sat 9am–5pm
Fairs Newark, Swinderby

HIGH HALDEN

⊞ High Halden Antiques
Contact Mr Jennings
✉ **Ashford Road, High Halden, Ashford, Kent, TN26 3BY** Ⓟ
☎ 01233 850195
Est. 40 years *Stock size* Medium
Stock Victorian–Edwardian furniture, mahogany
Open Tues–Sat 10am–5pm
Services Valuations, restorations

⊞ Rother Reclamation (SALVO)
Contact Mrs Symonds
✉ **The Old Tile Centre, Ashford Road, High Halden, Tenterden, Kent, TN26 3BP** Ⓟ
☎ 01233 850075 Ⓕ 01233 850275
Ⓜ 07889 387136
Est. 1960 *Stock size* Medium
Stock Renovation materials, bricks, tiles, oak beams, flooring, doors, slate, stone, railway sleepers, garden statuary, pine furniture, sanitary ware etc
Open Mon–Sat 8am–5pm
Services Delivery (south east) & special requests

HYTHE

Malthouse Arcade
Contact Mr or Mrs Maxtone Graham
✉ **Malthouse Hill, Hythe, Kent, CT21 5BW** Ⓟ
☎ 01303 260103 Ⓕ 01304 615436
Ⓔ rmg@postmaster.co.uk
Est. 1974 *Stock size* Large
No. of dealers 37
Stock General antiques

Open Fri Sat Bank Holidays 9.30am–5.30pm
Services Café

Owlets
Contact Mrs A Maurice
99 High Street, Hythe, Kent, CT21 5JH P
☎ 01303 230333
www.owlets.co.uk
www.millenniumjewellers.co.uk
or www.kentjewellers.co.uk
Est. 1955 *Stock size* Large
Stock Antique and estate jewellery, silver
Open Mon–Sat 9.30am–5pm closed Wed
Services Valuations, restorations, jewellery repairs

Second Treasures
Contact Mr Alan Fairbairn
18 High Street, Hythe, Kent, CT14 5AT P
☎ 01303 267801 Ⓕ 0870 0554727
Ⓔ ha@applesys.demon.co.uk
Est. 1995 *Stock size* Large
Stock General antiques, clocks, collectables
Open Mon–Sat 10am–4.30pm
Services Clock repair and restoration

LAMBERHURST

Ascension Interiors
Contact Sonya Murton
Forstal Farm, Goudhurst Road, Lamberhurst, Kent, TN3 8AG P
☎ 01892 890102
Ⓔ sonya.murton@lineone.net
www.asint.co.uk
Est. 2001 *Stock size* Small
Stock Decorative French and English furnishings, exterior stonework design
Open By appointment
Fairs Ardingly
Services Interior design service

Forstal Farm Antique Workshops
Contact Mr D Johnstone
Forstal Farm, Goudhurst Road, Lamberhurst, Kent, TN3 8AG P
☎ 01892 891189 Ⓕ 01892 891189
www.forstalantiques.com
Est. 1997 *Stock size* Large
Stock Hand-painted beds and armoires, general bedroom furniture
Open Mon–Sun 10am–5pm or by appointment

Junk & Disorderly
Contact Rupert Chipchase
Forstal Farm, Goudhurst Road, Lamberhurst, Kent, TN3 8AG P
☎ 01892 890102
Ⓔ chipchase@compuserve.com
Est. 1998 *Stock size* Large
Stock Antiques, decorative items, French country furniture
Open Daily by appointment
Fairs Ardingly
Services House clearance

LITTLEBOURNE

Jimmy Warren
Contact Mr J Warren
Cedar Lodge, 28 The Hill, Littlebourne, Canterbury, Kent, CT3 1TA P
☎ 01227 721510 Ⓕ 01227 722431
Ⓔ enquiries@jimmywarren.co.uk
www.jimmywarren.co.uk
Est. 1973 *Stock size* Large
Stock Unusual antiques, garden ornaments
Open Mon–Sun 10am–5pm
Services Valuations

LOOSE

Loose Valley Antiques
Contact Mrs V Gibbons
Scriba House, Loose Road, Loose, Maidstone, Kent, ME15 0AA P
☎ 01622 743950
Est. 1998 *Stock size* Large
Stock Oak furniture, collectables, pine
Open Tues–Sat 10am–5pm Sun 10am–4pm
Services Free local delivery

LYMINGE

Valley Auctions
Contact Mr E T Hall
Claygate, Brady Road, Lyminge, Folkestone, Kent, CT18 8EU P
☎ 01303 862134 Ⓕ 01303 862134
Est. 1978
Open Mon–Fri 9am–5pm
Sales General antiques sale Sun 9.30am, viewing Sat 1–6pm
Frequency Monthly
Catalogues Yes

MAIDSTONE

Ad-Age Antique Advertising
Contact Mike Standen, **Maidstone, Kent, ME16 8JN** P
☎ 01622 670595
Est. 1972 *Stock size* Medium
Stock Advertising signs, enamel, tinplate, packaging, tobacco, confectionery collectables
Open By appointment

Cobnar Books (PBFA)
Contact Larry Icott
567 Red Hill, Wateringbury, Maidstone, Kent, ME18 5BE
☎ 01622 813230
Ⓔ books@cobnar.demon.co.uk
Est. 1994
Stock Antiquarian and English topography books
Open Mail order only
Fairs Royal National Hotel Book Fair
Services Valuations, books on the Internet

Crackpots
Contact Annie Smith
1b Hamilton House, Heath Road, Coxheath, Maidstone, Kent, ME17 4DF P
☎ 01622 741200
Est. 1984 *Stock size* Medium
Stock Furniture, bric-a-brac
Open Mon–Sat 10am–5pm closed Wed

Gem Antiques
Contact Mark Rackham
10 Gabriels Hill, Maidstone, Kent, ME15 6JG P
☎ 01622 763344
Ⓔ markrackham@ukonline.co.uk
Est. 1994 *Stock size* Medium
Stock Jewellery, pocket watches, objets d'art
Open Mon–Sat 10am–5pm
Services Valuations, repairs

Newnham Court Antiques
Contact Mrs S Draper
Newnham Court Shopping Village, Bearsted Road, Weavering, Maidstone, Kent, ME14 5LH P
☎ 01622 631526
Ⓔ newnhamcourt@antikes.co.uk
www.antikes.co.uk
Est. 1993 *Stock size* Large
No. of dealers 3

Stock Collectables, ceramics, dining furniture
Open Mon–Sat 9.30am–5.30pm Sun 10am–5pm

Sutton Valence Antiques (LAPADA)
Contact Nigel Mullarkey or Tony Foster
Unit 4, Haslemere Parkwood Estate, Sutton Road, Maidstone, Kent, ME15 9NL
01622 675332 F 01622 692593
E svantiques@aol.com
W www.svantiques.co.uk
Est. 1986 *Stock size* Large
Stock 18th–19thC furniture, clocks, china, glass
Open Mon–Sat 9am–5.30pm Sun 11am—4pm
Services Valuations, restorations, shipping

Whatever Comics
Contact Mr M Armario
5 Middle Row, High Street, Maidstone, Kent, ME14 1TF
01622 681041
Est. 1988 *Stock size* Medium
Stock Second-hand comics, Star Trek and Star Wars toys, movie-related items, sci-fi collectables, Beanie Babies, action figures
Open Mon–Sat 10am–5.30pm

NEW ROMNEY

The House Clearance Shop
Contact Mrs C S Bray
48 High Street, New Romney, Kent, TN28 8AT
01797 363000
Est. 1994 *Stock size* Medium
Stock Brass, copper, pictures, glass, mirrors, furniture
Open Mon–Sat Sun in Summer 9am–5pm
Services House clearance

NORTHFLEET

Northfleet Hill Antiques
Contact Martine Kilby
36 The Hill, Northfleet, Gravesend, Kent, DA11 9EX
01474 321521 F 01474 350921
M 07770 993906
Est. 1986 *Stock size* Medium
Stock Furniture, collectables, glass, china
Open Mon Tues Fri 10am–5pm
Fairs Mainwarings Chelsea Antiques Fair
Services Upholstery

ORPINGTON

Crescent Antiques
Contact Mrs B Harris
19 Crescent Way, Orpington, Kent, BR6 9LS
01689 857711
E ca@curioquest.com
W www.curioquest.com
Est. 1998 *Stock size* Large
Stock Victorian–modern collectables, china, glass, small items of furniture
Open Mon–Sat 10am–5.30pm closed Thurs
Services Valuations, auction sale agents

OTFORD

Ellenor Hospice Care Shop
Contact Mrs Gill Saunderson
11a High Street, Otford, Kent, TN14 5PG
01959 524322
Est. 1995 *Stock size* Medium
Stock General antiques
Open Mon–Sat 10am–5pm April–October, 10am–4pm November–March
Services Tea rooms

Mandarin Gallery
Contact Mr Joseph Liu
The Mill Pond, 16 High Street, Otford, Sevenoaks, Kent, TN14 5PQ
01959 522778 F 01732 457399
Est. 1984 *Stock size* Medium
Stock Mainly Chinese Oriental furniture, ivory, wood carvings, silk, paintings
Open Mon–Sat 10am–5pm closed Wed
Services Restorations

Otford Antique and Collectors Centre
Contact Mr David Lowrie
26–28 High Street, Otford, Sevenoaks, Kent, TN14 5PQ
01959 522025 F 01959 525858
E info@otfordantiques.co.uk
W www.otfordantiques.co.uk
Est. 1997 *Stock size* Large
No. of dealers 34
Stock General antiques, collectables
Open Mon–Sat 10am–5pm Sun 11am–4pm
Services Restorations, valuations, upholstery

PETTS WOOD

The Beehive
Contact Mr Johnson
22 Station Square, Petts Wood, Kent, BR5 1NA
01689 890675
Est. 1996 *Stock size* Medium
No. of dealers 50
Stock Collectables
Open Mon–Sat 9.30am–5pm

Memory Lane
Contact Mr R K Ludlam
105 Queensway, Petts Wood, Orpington, Kent, BR5 1DG
01689 826832
Est. 1972 *Stock size* Large
Stock General antiques
Open Mon–Sat 9.30am–5.30pm
Fairs Ardingly
Services House Clearance

PLUCKLEY

Catchpole and Rye (SALVO)
Contact Diana Rabjohns or Tony O'Donnel
Saracen's Dairy, Pluckley Road, Pluckley, Kent, TN27 0SA
01233 840457
E info@crye.co.uk
W www.crye.co.uk
Est. 1991 *Stock size* Large
Stock Baths, basins, cisterns, taps, sanitary ware
Open Mon–Fri 9am–5pm Sat by appointment
Services Design Service

RAINHAM

The Bookmark
Contact Mr G Harrison
Unit 15c, Rainham Shopping Centre, Rainham, Gillingham, Kent, ME8 7HW
01634 365987/401893
Est. 1992 *Stock size* Large
Stock Antiquarian, second-hand, general books, fiction, non-fiction
Open Mon–Sat 9.30am–5.30pm

RAMSGATE

B & D Collectors' Toys
Contact Mr R Smith
332 Margate Road, Ramsgate, Kent, CT12 6SQ
01843 589606 F 01843 589606
Est. 1991 *Stock size* Large
Stock Old and obsolete toys, Dinky, Corgi, new collectable toys, Star Wars
Open Mon–Thur 9.30am–5.30pm Wed 9.30am–1pm Fri Sat 9.30am–6pm
Services Valuations, mail order

Granny's Attic
Contact Miss Penny Warn
2 Addington Street, Ramsgate, Kent, CT11 9JL
01843 588955/596288
M 07773 155339
E GRANNYSATTIC@amserve.com
Est. 1986 *Stock size* Large
Stock Victorian, Edwardian, pre-1930s furniture, china, silver, glass, mirrors, pictures etc
Open Mon–Sat 10am–5pm closed 1–2pm Thurs 10am–1pm
Services Free local delivery, delivery in UK and abroad can be arranged

Thanet Antiques Trading Centre
Contact Mr Roy Fomison
45 Albert Street, Ramsgate, Kent, CT11 9EX
01843 597336
Est. 1983 *Stock size* Large
Stock General antiques, furniture, collectables
Open Mon–Sat 9am–5pm
Fairs Ardingly

Yesteryear Railwayana
Contact Patrick or Mary Mullen
Stablings Cottage, Goodwin Road, Ramsgate, Kent, CT11 0JJ
01843 587283 F 01843 587283
E mullen@yesrail.com
W www.yesrail.com
Est. 1980 *Stock size* Medium
Stock Out-of-print and scarce books, illustrations, documentation, printed ephemera, both important and trivial
Open Mail order only
Services Catalogue monthly

ROCHESTER

Amhuerst Auctions
Contact Ms S Duke
375 High Street, Rochester, Kent, ME1 1DA
01634 844759 F 01634 815713
W www.amhuerst.co.uk
Est. 1999
Open Mon–Sat 9am–5.30pm
Sales Antiques, collectables sale Sat 10.30am and general household sale Sat noon, viewing Fri 2–5pm Sat 9am–noon.
Frequency Weekly
Catalogues Yes

Baggins Book Bazaar
Contact Mr Godfrey George
19 High Street, Rochester, Kent, ME1 1PY
01634 811651 F 01634 840591
E godfreygeorge@btinternet.com
W www.bagginsbooks.co.uk
Est. 1986 *Stock size* Large
Stock Antiquarian, rare, second-hand books
Open Mon–Sun 10am–6pm
Services Book search, ordering service

Castlebridge Antiques
Contact Hazel Duckworth or Gemma Glover
30 High Street, Rochester, Kent, ME1 1LD
01634 880037
Est. 1996 *Stock size* Large
Stock Antiques, collectables
Open Mon–Fri 10am-4pm Sat 9.30am-5pm
Fairs Sandown Park, Ardingly
Services House clearance

Cathedral Antiques
Contact Jeanette Dickson
83 High Street, Rochester, Kent, ME1 1LX
01634 842735 F 01634 826480
M 07802 177800
Est. 1974 *Stock size* Large
Stock 17thC–1910 furniture
Open Mon–Sat 9.30am–5pm
Services Valuations for probate and insurance

City Antiques Ltd
Contact Mr Brian Ware
78 High Street, Rochester, Kent, ME1 1JY
01634 841278 M 07855 388620
E wareclockmad@aol.com
Est. 1997 *Stock size* Large
Stock Clocks, barometers, Georgian, Victorian, Edwardian furniture
Open Mon–Sat 10am–5pm closed some Wed
Services Clock and barometer repair, furniture restorations

Cottage Style Antiques
Contact Mr W Miskimmin
24 Bill Street Road, Frindsbury, Rochester, Kent, ME2 4RB
01634 717623
Est. 1982 *Stock size* Large
Stock Collectables, architectural salvage, fireplaces, interesting pieces
Open Mon–Sat 9.30am–5.30pm
Services Restorations, repairs

Dragonlee Collectables
Contact Janet Davies
Memories, 128 High Street, Rochester, Kent, ME1 1JT
01622 729502 M 07761 400128
Est. 1995 *Stock size* Medium
Stock Noritake, ceramic collectables, furniture
Open Tues Wed 9am–5pm
Fairs Detling

Field, Staff & Woods
Contact Jim Field
93 High Street, Rochester, Kent, ME1 1LX
01634 846144/840108
E john@woods-of-rochester.co.uk
Est. 1996 *Stock size* Large
Stock Furniture, small items, clocks, collectables, silver
Open Mon–Sat 10am–5pm call for seasonal Sun opening
Services Valuations, clock repairs and restorations

Kaizen International Ltd
Contact Jason Hunt or Jo Olivares
88 The High Street, Rochester, Kent, ME1 1JT
01634 814132
Est. 1997 *Stock size* Large
Stock Jewellery, silver, furniture, wine-related items
Open Mon–Sat 10am–5.30pm
Services Valuations

Medway Auctions
Contact Mr Bill Lucas
23 High Street, Rochester, Kent, ME1 1LN
01634 847444 F 01634 880555

SOUTH EAST

KENT • ROLVENDEN

Ⓔ medauc@dircon.co.uk
Ⓦ www.medwayauctions.co.uk
Est. 1997
Open Mon–Sat 10am–4pm
Sales Two sales a month of small furniture, collectables and general effects. Spring and Autumn Collectors' Auctions plus two or three postcard and ephemera auctions a year. Auction intake and valuation day Fri (except Good Friday) 10.30am–3pm. Contact auction office for details and viewing times
Catalogues Yes by subscription (email or post or from office Friday prior to sale)

Medway Auctions Retail
Contact Mr Bill Lucas
✉ **23 High Street, Rochester, Kent, ME1 1LN** Ⓟ
☎ 01634 847444 Ⓕ 01634 847444
Ⓜ 07976 565092
Ⓔ medauc@dircon.co.uk
Est. 1990 *Stock size* Large
Stock Collectables, curios including badges, glass, ceramics
Open Mon–Sat 10am–4pm closed Wed

Memories
Contact Mrs M Bond
✉ **128 High Street, Rochester, Kent, ME1 1JT** Ⓟ
☎ 01634 811044
Est. 1985 *Stock size* Large
No. of dealers 12
Stock Small furniture, china, general antiques
Open Mon–Fri 9.30am–5pm Sat 9am–5pm Sun 11am–4.30pm

ROLVENDEN

Falstaff Antiques
Contact C M Booth
✉ **63–67 High Street, Rolvenden, Kent, TN17 4LP** Ⓟ
☎ 01580 241234
Est. 1964 *Stock size* Medium
Stock General antiques and reproductions
Open Mon–Sat 10am–6pm

J D and R M Walters
Contact Mr John Walters
✉ **10 Regent Street, Rolvenden, Cranbrook, Kent, TN17 4PE** Ⓟ
☎ 01580 241563
Est. 1979 *Stock size* Medium
Stock 18th–19thC mahogany
Open Mon–Fri 8am–6pm Sat 11am–4.30pm or by appointment
Services Restorations

SANDGATE

Bespoke Furniture
Contact Mr M McEwan
✉ **55 Sandgate High Street, Sandgate, Kent, CT20 3AH** Ⓟ
☎ 01303 249515 Ⓕ 01303 249515
Est. 1994
Stock Chairs, tables, cabinets
Open Mon–Fri 10am–5pm Sat 10am–3pm Sun by appointment
Services Restorations

Christopher Buck Antiques (BADA)
Contact Christopher Buck
✉ **56–60 Sandgate High Street, Sandgate, Folkestone, Kent, CT20 3AP** Ⓟ
☎ 01303 221229 Ⓕ 01303 221229
Ⓜ 07836 551515
Ⓔ cb@christopherbuck.co.uk
Est. 1983
Stock 18thC and early 19thC English furniture and associated items
Open Mon–Sat 9.30am–5pm
Fairs Olympia, BADA
Services Valuations, restorations

Emporium Antiques
Contact Mr West
✉ **31–33 Sandgate High Street, Sandgate, Folkestone, Kent, CT20 3AH** Ⓟ
☎ 01303 244430 Ⓜ 07860 149387
Est. 1984 *Stock size* Medium
Stock Antique and decorative furniture
Open By appointment

Finch Antiques
Contact Mr Finch
✉ **40 Sandgate High Street, Sandgate, Folkestone, Kent, CT20 3AP** Ⓟ
☎ 01303 240725
Est. 1980 *Stock size* Medium
Stock Early 18thC–1930s furniture
Open Mon–Sat 9.30am–5.30pm Sun 10.30am–4pm
Services Restorations

Michael W Fitch Antiques (LAPADA)
Contact Mr Michael Fitch
✉ **95, 97 & 99 Sandgate High Street, Sandgate, Kent, CT20 3BY** Ⓟ
☎ 01303 249600 Ⓕ 01303 249600
Est. 1977 *Stock size* Large
Stock 18th–19thC furniture, furnishings, clocks
Open Mon–Sat 10am–5.30pm
Services Valuations

Freeman and Lloyd Antiques (BADA, LAPADA)
Contact Mr K Freeman or Mr R Lloyd
✉ **44 Sandgate High Street, Sandgate, Folkestone, Kent, CT20 3AP** Ⓟ
☎ 01303 248986 Ⓕ 01303 241353
Ⓜ 07860 100073
Ⓔ enquiries@freemanandlloyd.com
Ⓦ www.freemanandlloyd.com
Est. 1968 *Stock size* Large
Stock 18th–early 19thC furniture, accessories, pictures, clocks, bronzes
Open Tues Thurs–Sat 10am–5pm
Fairs Olympia (February, June, November), BADA (March)
Services Valuations

David Gilbert Antiques
Contact Mr D Gilbert
✉ **30 Sandgate High Street, Sandgate, Folkestone, Kent, CT20 3AP** Ⓟ
☎ 01303 850491
Est. 1984 *Stock size* Large
Stock Edwardian–Victorian Arts and Crafts
Open Mon–Sat 9.30am–4.30pm or by appointment
Services Delivery

Gabrielle de Giles
Contact Gabrielle de Giles
✉ **21 Sandgate High Street, Sandgate, Folkestone, Kent, CT20 3BD** Ⓟ
☎ 01233 720917 Ⓕ 01233 720156
Ⓜ 07721 015263
Ⓔ gabrielle@gabrielledegiles.com
Ⓦ www.gabrielledegiles.com
Est. 2002 *Stock size* Medium
Stock Antique and country furniture, architectural items
Open Tue–Sat 10.30am–5.30pm or by appointment
Fairs Battersea Decorative Antique & Textile Fair

⊞ Jonathan Greenwall Antiques (LAPADA)
Contact Mr J Greenwall
✉ **61–63 Sandgate High Street, Sandgate, Folkestone, Kent, CT20 3AH** 🅿
☎ 01303 248987 ⓕ 01303 248987
ⓜ 07799 133700
Est. 1969 *Stock size* Large
Stock Jewellery, clocks, watches, furniture, pictures, prints, glass
Open Mon–Sat 9.30am–5pm Sun Bank Holidays by appointment
Services Valuations, watch, clock and jewellery repair

⊞ David M Lancefield Antiques (LAPADA)
Contact David Lancefield
✉ **53 Sandgate High Street, Sandgate, Folkestone, Kent, CT20 3AH** 🅿
☎ 01303 850149 ⓕ 01303 850149
ⓔ david@antiquedirect.freeserve.co.uk
ⓦ www.davidmlancefield.co.uk
Est. 1976 *Stock size* Large
Stock General antiques
Open Mon–Sat 10am–6pm Sun & BH 11am–5pm
Services Valuations, restorations

⊞ John McMaster
Contact Mr J McMaster
✉ **56a Sandgate High Street, Sandgate, Folkestone, Kent, CT20 3AP** 🅿
☎ 01303 252725 ⓜ 07774 451179
Est. 1847 *Stock size* Large
Stock 18th–early 19thC English furniture, engravings
Open Mon–Sat 9.30am–5pm or by appointment
Fairs Goodwood, Guildford
Services Print and watercolour restorations

⊞ Sandgate Passage
Contact Mr John Rendle
✉ **82 Sandgate High Street, Sandgate, Folkestone, Kent, CT20 3BX** 🅿
☎ 01303 850973
Est. 1987 *Stock size* Medium
Stock Old postcards, prints
Open Mon–Sat 10.30am–4.30pm
Fairs DMG Detling, York, Twickenham, Guildford, Woking
Services Valuations

SANDWICH

⊞ All Our Yesterdays
Contact Sandy Baker
✉ **3 Cattle Market, Sandwich, Kent, CT13 9AE** 🅿
☎ 01304 614756
ⓔ chgramophones@aol.com
Est. 1994 *Stock size* Medium
Stock General antiques, collectables, unusual items
Open Mon–Sat 10.30am–2.30pm or by appointment closed Wed
Services Gramophone repairs

⊞ Chris Baker Gramophones (CLPGS)
Contact Mr Chris Baker
✉ **3 Cattle Market, Sandwich, Kent, CT13 9AE** 🅿
☎ 01304 614756/375767
ⓕ 01304 614696 ⓜ 07808 831462
ⓔ chgramophones@aol.com
Est. 1996 *Stock size* Large
Stock Mechanical music
Open Mon–Sat 10.30am–2.30pm closed Wed
Services Repairs, stock list available on request

⊞ Delf Stream Gallery
Contact Nick Rocke
✉ **14 New Street, Sandwich, Kent, CT13 9AB** 🅿
☎ 01304 617684 ⓕ 01304 615479
ⓔ oastman@aol.com
ⓦ www.delfstreamgallery.com
Est. 1984 *Stock size* Large
Stock 19th–20thC European and American art pottery
Open Mon Thurs–Sat 10am–5pm or by appointment
Fairs NEC
Services Valuations

⚒ Halifax Estate Agents
Contact Pat Kidman or Lyn Mills
✉ **15 Cattle Market, Sandwich, Kent, CT13 9AW** 🅿
☎ 01304 614369 ⓕ 01304 612023
ⓔ hpssandwich@halifax.co.uk
Est. 1900
Open Mon–Fri 9am–5.30pm
Sales 16 general antiques, household, collectables sales a year, held on Wed 9.45am, view Tues 10am–4pm at The Drill Hall, The Quay, Sandwich
Catalogues Yes

⊞ Sandwich Fine Books (ABA PBFA)
Contact Mr Nick McConnell
✉ **Cambridge House, 41 Strand Street, Sandwich, Kent, CT13 9DN** 🅿
☎ 01304 620300 ⓕ 01304 620300
ⓜ 07977 573766
ⓔ mcconnellbooks@aol.com
Est. 1976 *Stock size* Medium
Stock Antiquarian and second-hand books
Open By appointment
Fairs Russell Square, Olympia
Services Valuations

SEAL

⊞ Campbell and Archard (BADA)
Contact Paul Archard
✉ **Lychgate House, Church Street, Seal, Kent, TN15 0AR** 🅿
☎ 01732 761153
ⓔ campbellarchard@btclick.com
Est. 1970 *Stock size* Large
Stock Austro-Hungarian 1790–1850 clocks and regulators, English regulators and bracket clocks
Open By appointment only
Fairs Olympia, Duke of York's
Services Restorations

SEVENOAKS

⚒ Bonhams
✉ **49 London Road, Sevenoaks, Kent, TN13 1AR** 🅿
☎ 01732 740310 ⓕ 01732 741842
ⓔ sevenoaks@bonhams.com
ⓦ www.bonhams.com
Est. 1793
Open Mon–Fri 8.30am–5pm Sat 9am–noon
Catalogues Yes

⊞ Emma Antiques
Contact Mrs I Crow
✉ **28a Holly Bush Lane, Sevenoaks, Kent, TN13 3TH** 🅿
☎ 01732 459794
Est. 1979 *Stock size* Medium
Stock General antiques, furniture, china, silver, pictures, tapestry cushions
Open Mon Fri 2–5.15pm Tues Thurs 10am–5pm Sat 10am–1pm

⊞ Furniture and Effects
Contact Mr A Hardman
✉ **3 St Botolphs Road, Sevenoaks, Kent, TN13 3AJ** 🅿
☎ 01732 460400

SOUTH EAST
KENT • SIDCUP

Est. 1994 *Stock size* Large
Stock General antiques, furniture
Open Mon–Sat 10am–6pm
Services Valuations, restorations

Gem Antiques
Contact Mr M Rackham
28 London Road, Sevenoaks, Kent, TN13 1AP
☎ 01732 743540
Est. 1994 *Stock size* Medium
Stock Clocks, jewellery
Open Mon–Sat 10am–5pm
Services Clock repairs

Ibbett Mosely
Contact Mr Hodge
125 High Street, Sevenoaks, Kent, TN13 1UT
☎ 01732 456731 Ⓕ 01732 740910
Ⓔ auctions@ibbettmosely.co.uk
Ⓦ www.ibbettmosely.co.uk
Est. 1935
Open Office hours Mon–Fri 9am–5.30pm
Sales General antiques, 9 sales a year, call for viewing times
Frequency 9 a year
Catalogues Yes

John M Peyto & Co Ltd
Contact John Peyto
The Coach House, Row Dow Lane, Otford Hills, Sevenoaks, Kent, TN15 6XN
☎ 01959 524022 Ⓕ 01959 522100
Est. 1992
Open Mon–Fri 7.30am–6pm
Sales General antiques 1st and 3rd Sat 10am view Fri 8am–6pm
Frequency Monthly
Catalogues Yes

SIDCUP

Memory Lane Antiques and Collectables
Contact Lynn Brackley
143 Station Road, Sidcup, Kent, DA15 7AA
☎ 020 8300 0552 Ⓜ 0794 6649843
Est. 1998 *Stock size* Medium
Stock General antiques, collectables
Open Mon–Sat 10am–5.30pm closed Wed

SITTINGBOURNE

Newington Antiques (LAPADA)
Contact Georgina McKinnon
58–60 High Street, Newington, Sittingbourne, Kent, ME9 7JL
☎ 01795 844448 Ⓕ 01795 841448
Ⓜ 07802 844448
Ⓔ antiqueskent@btconnect.com
Ⓦ www.newingtonantiques.freeserve.co.uk
Est. 1994 *Stock size* Medium
Stock Decorative, antique furniture, small items, lighting, general antiques
Open Tues Thurs Fri 10am–5pm Sat 10am–4pm Sun 10am–2pm or by appointment
Fairs Ardingly, Kempton, Newark
Services Valuations, restorations, shipping

Past Sentence
Contact Mrs K Rowland
70 High Street, Sittingbourne, Kent, ME10 4PB
☎ 01795 428787
Ⓔ enquiries@pastsentence.com
Est. 1997 *Stock size* Medium
Stock Second-hand and antiquarian books
Open Mon–Thurs 9.30am–5.30pm Fri 10am–5pm Sat 9.30am–5pm

STAPLEHURST

Staplehurst Antiques
Contact Mrs Draper
Crampton House, High Street, Staplehurst, Kent, TN12 0AU
☎ 01580 890424
Ⓔ antiques@staplehurst-antiques.co.uk
Ⓦ www.staplehurst-antiques.co.uk
Est. 2001 *Stock size* Large
Stock Late Victorian and Edwardian oak, mahogany and walnut furniture, wide range of ceramics and glass
Open Mon–Sat 10am–4.30pm Sun by appointment
Services Restorations

STOCKBURY

Steppes Hill Farm Antiques (BADA)
Contact Mr William Buck
Steppes Hill Farm, Stockbury, Sittingbourne, Kent, ME9 7RB
☎ 01795 842205 Ⓜ 07931 594218
Ⓔ dwabuck@btinternet.com
Stock size Small
Stock General antiques, English porcelain, collectable silver
Open Mon–Fri 9am–5pm
Fairs Olympia, International Ceramics Fair, BADA Duke of York's
Services Valuations, restorations

SUTTON VALENCE

Sutton Valence Antiques (LAPADA, CINOA)
Contact Judith Mullarkey
North Street, Sutton Valence, Maidstone, Kent, ME17 3AP
☎ 01622 843333 Ⓕ 01622 843499
Ⓔ svantiques@aol.com
Ⓦ www.svantiques.co.uk
Est. 1978 *Stock size* Large
Stock 18th–19thC furniture, clocks, china, glass
Open Mon–Fri 9.30am–5pm Sat 10am–5pm Sun 11am–4pm
Services Valuations, restorations, shipping, container packing

TENTERDEN

Flower House Antiques
Contact Mr Q Johnson
90 High Street, Tenterden, Kent, TN30 6JB
☎ 01580 763764 Ⓕ 01580 291251 or 01797 270386
Est. 1995 *Stock size* Large
Stock 17th–early 19thC furniture, objets d'art, chandeliers, worldwide general antiques
Open Mon–Sat 9.30am–5.30pm Sun by appointment
Services Valuations, restorations, items purchased

Gaby's Clocks and Things
Contact Gaby Gunst
140 High Street, Tenterden, Kent, TN30 6HT
☎ 01580 765818 Ⓕ 01580 765818
Est. 1969 *Stock size* Medium
Stock Clocks, barometers
Open Mon–Sat 10.30am–5pm
Services Clock and barometer restoration

Heirloom Antiques
Contact Jan Byhurst
68 High Street, Tenterden, Kent, TN30 6AU
☎ 01580 765535
Est. 1994 *Stock size* Medium
No. of dealers 6
Stock Dolls, teddies, porcelain, prints, pictures, books,

Winstanley cats and dogs, jewellery, furniture, militaria
Open Mon–Sat 10am–5pm
Sun 11am–5pm

J & M Collectables (PTA)
Contact Maurice Coombs
64 High Street, Tenterden, Kent, TN30 6AU
01580 891657 07713 523573
jandmcollectables@tinyonline.co.uk
Est. 1993 *Stock size* Variable
Stock Postcards, crested china, Osborne plaques, other small collectables including Wade, Doulton etc
Open Mon–Sat 10am–5pm
Sun 11am–5pm
Services Major credit and debit cards accepted, mail order considered

Lambert and Foster
Contact Mrs G Brazier
102 High Street, Tenterden, Kent, TN30 6HT
01580 762083 01580 764317
saleroom@lambertandfoster.co.uk
www.lambertandfoster.co.uk
Est. 1830
Open Mon–Fri 9am–5.30pm
Sales General antiques sale Thurs 9.30am, viewing Sun 10.30am–4pm Tues 9.30am–4.30pm
Frequency Monthly
Catalogues Yes

Memories
Contact Mr Mark Lloyds
74 High Street, Tenterden, Kent, TN30 6AU
01580 763416
Est. 1995 *Stock size* Large
Stock Antiques, collectables, small furniture
Open Mon–Sat 10am–5pm
Sun 11am–4pm

Tenterden Antique & Silver Vaults
Contact T Smith
66 High Street, Tenterden, Kent, TN30 6AU
01580 765885
Est. 1991 *Stock size* Large
Stock Clocks, silver, china, furniture, glass, collectables, jewellery
Open Mon–Sat 10am–5pm
Sun 11am–10pm
Services House clearance

Tenterden Antiques Centre
Contact Mick Ellin
66a High Street, Tenterden, Kent, TN30 6AU
01580 765655
07776 203755
Est. 1990 *Stock size* Large
No. of dealers 8
Stock Furniture, Art Deco, china, clocks, silver, jewellery, militaria, postcards, porcelain, bric-a-brac
Open Mon–Sat 10am–5pm
Sun 11am–5pm

TEYNHAM

Jackson-Grant Antiques
Contact Mr David Jackson-Grant
133 London Road, Teynham, Sittingbourne, Kent, ME9 9QJ
01795 522027 01795 522027
07831 591881
david.jackson-grant@talk21.com
www.jackson-grantantiques.co.uk
Est. 1966 *Stock size* Large
Stock Antique furniture, small items
Open Mon–Sat 10am–5pm
Sun 1–5pm
Services Valuations

TONBRIDGE

Barden House Antiques
Contact Mrs Brenda Parsons
1 & 3 Priory Street, Tonbridge, Kent, TN2 2AP
01732 350142
Est. 1959 *Stock size* Large
No. of dealers 4
Stock General antiques, prints, watercolours, jewellery, china, small pieces of furniture
Open Tues–Sat 10am–5pm

Greta May Antiques
Contact Mrs G May
The New Curiosity Shop, Tollgate Buildings, Hadlow Road, Tonbridge, Kent, TN9 1NX
01732 366730
Est. 1988 *Stock size* Medium
Stock Furniture, silver, silver plate, china, glass
Open Tues Thurs–Sat 10am–4.30pm
Fairs Great Danes
Services Teddy bear repairs

Derek Roberts Antiques (BADA)
Contact Mr Derek Roberts
25 Shipbourne Road, Tonbridge, Kent, TN10 3DN
01732 358986 01732 771842
drclocks@clara.net
www.qualityantiqueclocks.com
Est. 1968 *Stock size* Large
Stock 17th–19thC clocks, books written by Derek Roberts
Open Mon–Sat 9.30am–5.30pm or by appointment
Services Valuations, annual catalogues

TUNBRIDGE WELLS

Aaron Antiques (RADS)
Contact Ron Goodman
77 St Johns Road, Tunbridge Wells, Kent, TN4 9TT
01892 517644
Est. 1967 *Stock size* Large
Stock Coins, medals, clocks, china, silver, paintings, prints, scientific and musical instruments, furniture, Chinese porcelain
Open Mon–Sat 10am–5pm or by appointment

Amadeus Antiques
Contact Pat Davies
32 Mount Ephraim, Tunbridge Wells, Kent, TN4 8AU
01892 544406
Est. 1982 *Stock size* Medium
Stock Antiques, collectables, lighting
Open Mon–Sat 10am–5pm

The Antiques Shop
Contact Joanne Chipchase
77a St John's Road, Tunbridge Wells, Kent, TN4 9TT
01892 676637
theantiquesshop@amserve.net
Est. 1998 *Stock size* Medium
Stock Decorative antiques and country furniture
Open Mon–Sat 10am–5pm
Fairs Ardingly

The Architectural Emporium
Contact Mick Bates
55 St Johns Road, Tunbridge Wells, Kent, TN4 9TP
01892 540368
www.architecturalemporium.com
Est. 1987 *Stock size* Medium

SOUTH EAST

KENT • TUNBRIDGE WELLS

Stock Antique fireplaces, period lighting, architectural
Open Tues–Sat 9.30am–5.30pm

⊞ Henry Baines (LAPADA, BADA)
Contact Mr H Baines
✉ **14 Church Road, Southborough, Tunbridge Wells, Kent, TN4 0RX** 🅿
☎ 01892 532099 ⓕ 01892 532099
ⓜ 07973 214406
Est. 1968 *Stock size* Large
Stock Oak, country furniture
Open Prior phone call advised
Fairs Olympia, West London

⊞ Baskerville Books
Contact D Smedley
✉ **13 Nevill Street, Tunbridge Wells, Kent, TN2 5RU** 🅿
☎ 01892 526776
Est. 1985 *Stock size* Small
Stock Antiques, collectables, antiquarian, second-hand books
Open Mon–Sat 9.30am–4.30pm
Services Valuations

⊞ Beau Nash Antiques
Contact Mr David Wrenn
✉ **29 Lower Walk, The Pantiles, Tunbridge Wells, Kent, TN2 5TD** 🅿
☎ 01892 537810
Est. 1990 *Stock size* Large
Stock Georgian–Edwardian period furniture, associated decorative items
Open Tues–Sat 11am–5pm

Bracketts Fine Arts
Contact Mr James Braxton ARICS
✉ **Auction Hall, Pantiles, Tunbridge Wells, Kent, TN1 1UU** 🅿
☎ 01892 544500 ⓕ 01892 515191
ⓦ www.bfaa.co.uk
Est. 1828
Open Mon–Fri 9am–5pm
Sales 2 monthly antiques sales Fri 10am, viewing Thurs 9am–7pm. Antiques and general sale Fri 10am, viewing Thurs 9am–7pm
Catalogues Yes

⊞ Calverley Antiques
Contact Mr P Nimmo
✉ **30 Crescent Road, Tunbridge Wells, Kent, TN1 2LZ** 🅿
☎ 01892 538254
Est. 1984 *Stock size* Large
Stock Pine, decorative and painted furniture
Open Mon–Sun 9.30am–5.30pm
Fairs Ardingly
Services House clearance

⊞ Chapel Place Antiques
Contact Mrs J A Clare
✉ **9 Chapel Place, Tunbridge Wells, Kent, TN1 1YQ**
☎ 01892 546561 ⓕ 01892 546561
Est. 1984 *Stock size* Large
Stock Antique and modern silver, hand-painted Limoges boxes, amber jewellery, silver photo frames, old silver plate, claret jugs
Open Mon–Sat 9am–6pm
Services Valuations

⊞ Claremont Antiques
Contact Mr A Broad
✉ **48 St Johns Road, Tunbridge Wells, Kent, TN4 9NY** 🅿
☎ 01892 511651 ⓕ 01892 517360
ⓜ 07786 262843
ⓔ ant@claremontantiques.com
ⓦ www.claremontantiques.com
Est. 1995 *Stock size* Large
Stock Pine, hardwood, painted country furniture
Open Mon–Sat 10am–5.30pm

⊞ Culverden Antiques
Contact Mr D Mason
✉ **49 St Johns Road, Tunbridge Wells, Kent, TN4 9TP** 🅿
☎ 01892 515264
Est. 1985 *Stock size* Medium
Stock 19thC furniture, decorative pieces
Open Tues–Sat 10am–5.30pm

⊞ Downlane Hall Antiques
Contact Mrs Hayes
✉ **Culverden Down, St Johns, Tunbridge Wells, Kent, TN4 9SA** 🅿
☎ 01892 522440
Est. 1980 *Stock size* Large
Stock Georgian–Victorian furniture
Open Mon–Sat 10am–4pm
Services Restorations

⊞ Glassdrumman
Contact Mr or Mrs G Dyson Rooke
✉ **7 Union Square, The Pantiles, Tunbridge Wells, Kent, TN4 8HE** 🅿
☎ 01892 538615
Est. 1989 *Stock size* Large
Stock Georgian, Victorian, second-hand jewellery, silver, pocket watches, decorative items, furniture
Open Tues–Sat 10am–5.30pm closed Sun, Mon
Services Repairs

⊞ Pamela Goodwin
Contact Pamela Goodwin
✉ **11 The Pantiles, Tunbridge Wells, Kent, TN2 5TD** 🅿
☎ 01892 618200 ⓕ 01892 618200
ⓜ 07751 816443
ⓔ mail@goodwinantiques.co.uk
ⓦ www.goodwinantiques.co.uk
Est. 1998 *Stock size* Large
Stock 18th–20thC furniture, clocks, silver, English porcelain, Moorcroft, Doulton, glass, sewing collectables
Open Mon–Fri 9.30am–5pm Sat 9.30am–5.30pm

Gorringes Incorporating Julian Dawson (SOFAA)
Contact Mr Leslie Gillham
✉ **15 The Pantiles, Tunbridge Wells, Kent, TN2 5TD** 🅿
☎ 01892 619670 ⓕ 01892 619671
ⓔ tunbridge.wells@gorringes.co.uk
ⓦ www.gorringes.co.uk
Est. 1926
Open Mon–Fri 8.30am–5.30pm Sat 9am–noon
Sales Fine art and antiques sales at The Spa Hotel, Tunbridge Wells, Tues 11.30am, viewing noon–8pm Mon prior and day of sale 8.30–11am
Frequency Quarterly
Catalogues Yes

⊞ Hall's Bookshop
Contact Sabrina Izzard
✉ **20 Chapel Place, Tunbridge Wells, Kent, TN1 1YQ**
☎ 01892 527842
Est. 1898 *Stock size* Large
Stock Antiquarian, second-hand books
Open Mon–Sat 9.30am–5pm

⊞ Peter Hoare Antiques
Contact Peter Hoare
✉ **35 London Road, Southborough, Tunbridge Wells, Kent, TN4 0PB** 🅿
☎ 01892 524623
Est. 1983 *Stock size* Medium
Stock Arts and Crafts furniture
Open Tues–Sat 10am–6pm
Services Valuations

⊞ Kent & Sussex Gold Refiners Ltd (NAG)
Contact A C & S B Padley
✉ **7 Vale Road, Tunbridge Wells, Kent, TN1 1BS** 🅿
☎ 01892 526084 Ⓕ 01892 543602
Est. 1937 *Stock size* Large
Stock Silver, jewellery, carriage clocks
Open Mon–Sat 9am–5.30pm closed Wed

⊞ Howard Neville
Contact Mr H Neville
✉ **21 The Pantiles, Tunbridge Wells, Kent, TN2 5TD** 🅿
☎ 01892 511461 Ⓕ 020 7491 7623
Ⓔ patrickboyd_carpenter@hotmail.com
Est. 1986 *Stock size* Large
Stock Antiques and works of art
Open Mon–Sat 10am–5pm or by appointment

⊞ Old Colonial
Contact Suzy Rees or Dee Martyn
✉ **56 St Johns Road, Tunbridge Wells, Kent, TN4 9NY** 🅿
☎ 01892 533993 Ⓕ 01892 513281
Est. 1994 *Stock size* Large
Stock Country antiques, decorative items, painted furniture
Open Mon–Sat 10am–5.30pm or by appointment

⊞ Pantiles Antiques
Contact Mrs E M Blackburn
✉ **31 The Pantiles, Tunbridge Wells, Kent, TN2 5TD** 🅿
☎ 01892 531291
Est. 1981 *Stock size* Medium
Stock Georgian and Edwardian furniture, porcelain, decorative pieces
Open Mon–Sat 9.30am–5pm
Fairs Copthorne
Services Restorations, upholstery

⊞ Pantiles Spa Antiques
Contact Mrs J A Cowpland
✉ **4/5/6 Union House, The Pantiles, Tunbridge Wells, Kent, TN4 8HE** 🅿
☎ 01892 541377 Ⓕ 01435 865660
Ⓜ 07711 283655
Ⓔ psa.wells@btinternet.com
Ⓦ www.antiques-tun-wells-kent.co.uk
Est. 1987 *Stock size* Large
Stock Specialist dining room tables and chairs, furniture, dolls, porcelain, glass, prints, watercolours, maps, clocks, silver
Open Mon–Fri 9.30am–5pm Sat 9.30am–5.30pm
Services Free delivery within 30 mile radius

⊞ Phoenix Antiques (WKADA)
Contact Robert Pilbeam, Jane Stott or Peter Janes
✉ **51–53 St Johns Road, Tunbridge Wells, Kent, TN4 9TP** 🅿
☎ 01892 549099 Ⓕ 01424 844365
Ⓔ robert.pilbeam@virgin.net
Est. 1989 *Stock size* Large
Stock 18th–19thC English and French country furniture, overmantel mirrors, associated decorative items
Open Mon–Sat 10am–5.30pm or by appointment

⊞ Sporting Antiques
Contact Mr L Franklin
✉ **10 Union Square, The Pantiles, Tunbridge Wells, Kent, TN4 8HE** 🅿
☎ 01892 522661 Ⓕ 01892 522661
Est. 1993 *Stock size* Large
Stock Sporting antiques, arms, armour, technical instruments, tools
Open Mon–Fri 9.30am–5pm Sat 9.30am–5.30pm closed Wed

⊞ John Thompson
Contact Mr J Thompson
✉ **27 The Pantiles, Tunbridge Wells, Kent, TN2 5TD** 🅿
☎ 01892 547215
Est. 1982 *Stock size* Medium
Stock 18th–early 19thC furniture, late 17th–20thC paintings, glass, porcelain
Open Mon–Sat 9.30am–1pm 2–5pm

⊞ Tunbridge Wells Antiques
Contact Mr Nick Harding
✉ **Union Square, The Pantiles, Tunbridge Wells, Kent, TN4 8HE** 🅿
☎ 01892 533708
Ⓔ nick@staffordshirefigures.com
Ⓦ www.staffordshirefigures.com
Est. 1986 *Stock size* Large
Stock Tunbridge ware, Staffordshire figures, watches, clocks, silver, porcelain, pottery, furniture
Open Mon–Sat 9.30am–5pm
Services Valuations, restorations

⊞ Up Country Ltd
Contact Mr C Springett
✉ **The Old Corn Stores, 68 St Johns Road, Tunbridge Wells, Kent, TN4 9PE** 🅿
☎ 01892 523341 Ⓕ 01892 530382
Ⓔ mail@upcountryantiques.co.uk
Ⓦ www.upcountryantiques.co.uk
Est. 1988 *Stock size* Large
Stock Antique and decorative country furniture, rural artefacts
Open Mon–Sat 9am–5.30pm

⊞ Variety Box
Contact Penny Cogan
✉ **16 Chapel Place, Tunbridge Wells, Kent, TN1 1YD** 🅿
☎ 01892 531868
Est. 1982 *Stock size* Large
Stock Tunbridge ware, hatpins, fans, sewing and collectors' items
Open Mon–Sat 9am–5pm closed Wed

⊞ World War Books (OMRS)
Contact Mr Tim Harper
✉ **Oaklands, Camden Park, Tunbridge Wells, Kent, TN2 5AE**
☎ 01892 538465 Ⓕ 01892 538465
Ⓔ wwarbooks@btinternet.com
Est. 1988 *Stock size* Large
Stock Military books including manuals, weapon books, regimental histories, maps, photographs, diaries
Open Mail order only
Fairs Arms and Armour Fair (Birmingham), World War Book Fair
Services Valuations, probate, book search, catalogue

SOUTH EAST

KENT • WALMER

WALMER

Grandma's Attic
Contact S J Marsh
60 The Strand, Walmer, Kent, CT14 7DP
01304 380121
Est. 1986 *Stock size* Medium
Stock Second-hand and antiques, mirrors
Open Mon–Sat 9.30am–5.30pm Sun by appointment
Services Restorations, gilding

WELLING

The Emporium Antiques, Collectables & Crafts Centre
Contact Miss J Marshall
138–140 Upper Wickham Lane, Welling, Kent, DA16 3DP
020 8855 8308 020 8855 8308
info@theemporiumwelling.co.uk
Est. 1999 *Stock size* Large
No. of dealers 30
Stock Antiques, collectables, craft ware
Open Tues–Sat 10am–5pm

WEST KINGSDOWN

East Meets West Antiques
Contact Philippa Dudley
Unit 7, West Kingsdown Industrial Estate, London Road, West Kingsdown, Kent, TN15 6EL
01474 854807 01474 852839
07973 756302
info@eastmeetswestantiques.co.uk
www.eastmeetswestantiques.co.uk
Est. 2001 *Stock size* Medium
Stock Furniture
Open Mon–Fri 10am–4pm Sat Sun 11am–3pm
Services Valuations, restorations

WEST MALLING

The Old Clock Shop
63 High Street, West Malling, Kent, ME19 6NA
01732 843246 01732 843246
theoldclockshop@tesco.net
www.theoldclockshop.co.uk
Est. 1975 *Stock size* Medium
Stock Clocks, barometers
Open Mon–Sat 9am–5pm
Services Restorations

Rose and Crown Antiques (GOMC)
Contact Mrs Candy Lovegrove
40 High Street, West Malling, Kent, ME19 6QR
01732 872707 01732 872810
jlantiques@hotmail.com
www.antiqueswestmalling.co.uk
Est. 1995 *Stock size* Medium
Stock 18th–early 20thC furniture, small items
Open Tues–Sat 9.30am–5.30pm
Fairs Antiques for Everyone at NEC, Penman and Wakefield Fairs
Services Restorations, upholstery

WEST WICKHAM

Nightingale Antiques and Craft Centre
Contact Maureen Haggerty
89–91 High Street, West Wickham, Kent, BR4 0LS
020 8777 0335 020 8776 2777
Est. 1998 *Stock size* Large
Stock Victorian–Edwardian furniture, 1930s oak, china
Open Mon–Sat 10am–5pm

West Wickham Bookshop (PBFA)
Contact Mr Ronald Davies
5 Bell Parade, Wickham Court Road, West Wickham, Kent, BR4 0RH
020 8777 3982 020 8777 3982
rondaviesbooks@aol.com
Est. 1995 *Stock size* Medium
Stock General stock including antiquarian, military topics a speciality
Open Mon–Sat 10am–5pm
Fairs Bloomsbury (H D Book Fairs), all Title Page Book Fairs
Services Book binding

WESTERHAM

20th Century Marks
Contact Mr M Marks
12 Market Square, Westerham, Kent, TN16 1AW
01959 562221 01959 569385
07831 778992
lambarda@btconnect.com
www.20thcenturymarks.co.uk
Est. 1960 *Stock size* Large
Stock Classic 20thC designs
Open Mon–Sat 10am–5.30pm
Services Valuations, restorations

Apollo Galleries (LAPADA)
Contact Mr S M Barr
19–21 Market Square, Westerham, Kent, TN16 1AN
01959 562200 01959 562986
aenq@ag.com
Est. 1974 *Stock size* Large
Stock Mainly Georgian–Edwardian furniture, bronzes, oil paintings, mirrors, objets d'art
Open Mon–Sat 9.30am–5.30pm
Fairs Olympia
Services Valuations for probate and insurance

Castle Antique Centre Ltd
Contact Stewart Ward Properties
1 London Road, Westerham, Kent, TN16 1BB
01959 562492
Est. 1986 *Stock size* Large
No. of dealers 8
Stock 4 showrooms. Linen, tools, silver, jewellery, china, glass, books, 19thC clothing, kitsch, retro clothing, small furniture
Open Mon–Sat 10am–5pm Sun 1–6pm
Services Valuations, advice, house clearance

Decorama
Contact Chrissie Painell or John Masters
5 The Green, Westerham, Kent, TN16 1AS
01959 561234
07974 322858 or 07785 503044
decorama@hotmail.com
Est. 2002 *Stock size* Medium
Stock Art Deco, Art Nouveau, Arts and Crafts, Gothic Revival and the Aesthetic Movement
Open Tues–Sat 9.30am–5pm
Services Restorations, shipping

Peter Dyke
Contact Mr Peter Dyke
3 The Green, Westerham, Kent, TN16 1AS
01959 565020
Est. 1993 *Stock size* Medium
Stock 18th–19thC furniture and works of art
Open Mon–Sat 10am–5pm

Anthony Hook Antiques
Contact Mr Anthony Hook
✉ **Westerham House Antiques, Fullers Hill, Westerham, Kent, TN16 1AA** P
☎ 01959 562161 F 01892 870041
M 07860 277099
Est. 1948 *Stock size* Small
Stock Period furniture, shipping goods, reproduction garden statuary
Open Mon–Fri 10am–5pm
Sat 10.30am–5pm
Services Valuations

London House Antiques
Contact Vivienne Graham
✉ **4 Market Square, Westerham, Kent, TN16 1AW** P
☎ 01959 564479 F 01959 565424
Est. 1995 *Stock size* Large
No. of dealers 4
Stock Furniture, clocks, bears, dolls, porcelain, glass
Open Mon–Sat 10am–5pm
or by appointment

Barbara Ann Newman
Contact Barbara Ann Newman
✉ **London House Antiques, 4 Market Square, Westerham, Kent, TN16 1AW** P
☎ 01959 564479 M 07850 016729
Est. 1991 *Stock size* Medium
Stock Antique dolls, teddy bears, children's antique furniture, rocking horses
Open Mon–Sat 10am–5pm
Fairs Kensington, Birmingham Doll Fair, Chelsea
Services Shipping

Regal Antiques (WKADA)
Contact Mrs T Lawrence
✉ **2 Market Square, Westerham, Kent, TN16 1AW** P
☎ 01959 561778 F 01959 561778
Est. 1991 *Stock size* Medium
Stock Antique jewellery, portrait miniatures, porcelain, watches, fine paintings
Open Wed–Sat 11am–5pm
Services Watch repairs

D H Sargeant
Contact Mr D H Sargeant
✉ **21 The Green, Westerham, Kent, TN16 1AX** P
☎ 01959 562130 F 01959 561989
Est. 1949 *Stock size* Large
Stock Chandeliers, table glass, glass wall lights
Open Mon–Sat 9am–5.30pm

Taylor-Smith Antiques (LAPADA)
Contact Ashton Taylor-Smith
✉ **4 The Grange, High Street, Westerham, Kent, TN16 1AH** P
☎ 01959 563100 F 01959 565300
E mountjoy@dircon.co.uk
Est. 1974 *Stock size* Medium
Stock Fine 18th and early 19thC furniture, objets d'art
Open Mon–Sat 10am–5pm
closed Wed

Westerham House Antiques
Contact Raymond Barr
✉ **The Old Sorting Office, Fullers Hill, London Road, Westerham, Kent, TN16 1AN** P
☎ 01959 561622 F 01959 562986
Est. 1997 *Stock size* Large
Stock General antiques
Open Mon–Sat 10am–5.30pm
Services Valuations, restorations

WESTGATE-ON-SEA

Berkeley House Antiques
Contact Barbara Croall
✉ **78 St Mildreds Road, Westgate-on-Sea, Kent, CT8 8RF** P
☎ 01843 833458
Est. 2001 *Stock size* Medium
Stock Decorative items, small furniture, paintings, mirrors, porcelain and reproduction jewellery
Open Thurs–Sat 10am–5pm

Westgate Auctions
Contact Mr Colin Langston
✉ **Rear of 70 St Mildred's Road, Westgate-on-Sea, Kent, CT8 8RF** P
☎ 01843 834891
Est. 1982
Open Mon–Sat 9am–5pm, auctions on Sun
Sales Antique and modern furniture and effects Sun, viewing Sat 9.30am–5pm
Frequency Monthly
Catalogues Yes

WHITSTABLE

Bonhams
✉ **95–97 Tankerton Road, Whitstable Road, Whitstable, Kent, CT5 2AJ** P
☎ 01227 275007 F 01227 266443
E whitstable@bonhams.com
W www.bonhams.com

Est. 1793
Open Mon–Fri 9am–5.30pm
Catalogues Yes

Boulevard Antiques
Contact Mrs J Baker
139 Tankerton Road, Whitstable, Kent, CT5 2AW
☎ 01227 273335
Est. 1997 *Stock size* Large
No. of dealers 5
Stock China, Art Deco, glass, furniture, postcards, books, records, Osborne plaques, dolls, toys, silver, silverplate
Open Mon–Sat 9.30am–5pm
Services Valuations

Inside Out
Contact John Perry
6 Oxford Street, Whitstable, Kent, CT5 1DD
☎ 01227 280111
Ⓜ 07850 365226
Est. 1985 *Stock size* Medium
Stock Country antiques, gardenalia, unusual decorative items
Open Mon–Sun 10.30am–5pm
Wed 10.30am–1pm
Fairs Ardingly, Kempton Park

Laurens Antiques
Contact Mr G Laurens
2 Harbour Street, Whitstable, Kent, CT5 1AG
☎ 01227 261940
Est. 1965 *Stock size* Medium
Stock General antiques
Open Mon–Sat 10am–5pm closed Wed
Services Valuations

Tankerton Antiques (BHI)
Contact Mr Paul Wrighton
136 Tankerton Road, Whitstable, Kent, CT5 2AN
☎ 01227 266490 Ⓜ 07702 244064
Est. 1985 *Stock size* Medium
Stock 18th–19thC clocks, watches, china, furniture, fabrics, ceramics
Open Tues Wed 10am–1pm
Thurs–Sat 10am–5pm
Fairs Brunel Clock and Watch Fair, Ardingly

WITTERSHAM

Old Corner House Antiques
Contact Gillian Shepherd
6 Poplar Road, Wittersham, Kent, TN30 7PG
☎ 01797 270236
Est. 1986 *Stock size* Medium
Stock Early English ceramics, needleworks, carvings, country furniture
Open Wed–Sat Sat 10am–5pm
Fairs Chiselhurst

WROTHAM

Barnaby's Antiques
Contact Cordelia McCartney
High Street, Wrotham, Kent, TN15 7AD
☎ 01732 886887 Ⓕ 01732 886887
Ⓔ cordelia@cordeliamc.free-online.co.uk
Est. 1996 *Stock size* Small
Stock Smalls, collectables, country furniture
Open Mon–Sat 9am–5pm or by appointment

LONDON

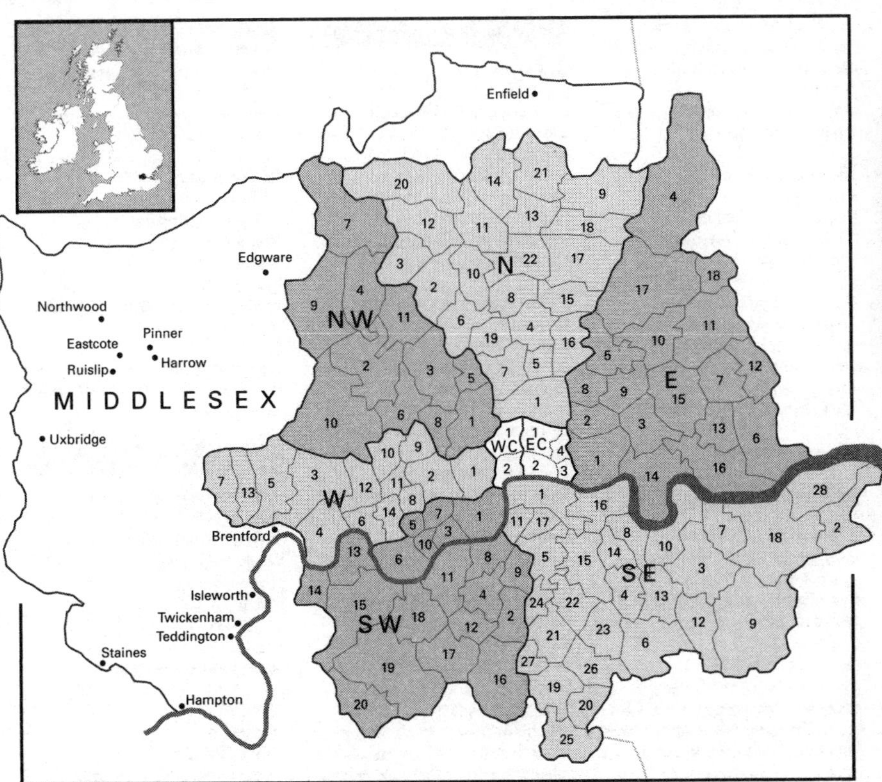

EAST

E1

⊞ AA Antiques
Contact Des King
✉ **145a Bacon Street, London, E1 6LF** 🅿
☎ 020 7739 4803 Ⓜ 07973 324814
Est. 1996 *Stock size* Medium
Stock Antique and shipping furniture
Open Mon–Sat 10am–5pm

⊞ Acme Planet
Contact Mr D Everington
✉ **Unit B1L/15, Metropolitan Wharf, Wapping Wall, London, E1W 3SS** 🅿
☎ 020 7480 5880
Ⓔ acmeplanet@hotmail.com
Est. 1996 *Stock size* Large
Stock Sci-fi, monster toys, bygones, kitsch
Open By appointment

⊞ Eat My Handbag Bitch
Contact George Enoch or Georgina Stead
✉ **6 Dray Walk, Off 91–95 Brick Lane, London, E1 6QL** 🅿
☎ 020 7375 3100 Ⓕ 020 7375 0959
Ⓜ 0780 350 2249
Ⓔ georges@eatmyhandbagbitch.co.uk
Ⓦ www.eatmyhandbagbitch.co.uk
Est. 1999 *Stock size* Large
Stock Post-war design, furniture, glass, small decorative items, clocks, ceramics, stereos, televisions, lighting
Open Mon noon–7pm
Wed Thurs 11am–7pm
Fri 11am–5pm
Sat Sun 11am–7pm closed Tues
Services Valuations

⊞ John Jackson (LAPADA)
Contact Fiona Atkins
✉ **5 Fournier Street, London, E1 6QE** 🅿
☎ 020 7247 4745 Ⓕ 020 7354 9591
Ⓜ 07711 319237
Est. 1984 *Stock size* Large
Stock Early and Georgian furniture, decorative items
Open Thurs–Sat 10am–5pm or by appointment

⊞ La Maison
Contact Mr Guillaume Bacou
✉ **107–108 Shoreditch High Street, London, E1 6JN** 🅿
☎ 020 7729 9646 Ⓕ 020 7729 6399
Ⓔ gui@lamaison.com
Ⓦ www.lamaison.co.uk
Est. 1991 *Stock size* Medium
Stock French and Italian beds
Open Mon–Sat 10am–6pm
Services Restorations, upholstery

E2

⊞ John Jackson (LAPADA)
Contact Fiona Atkins
✉ **116 Columbia Road, London, E2 7RG** 🅿
☎ 020 7613 2866 Ⓕ 020 7354 9591
Ⓜ 07711 319237

Est. 1984 *Stock size* Medium
Stock French and English decorative antiques and furniture
Open Sun 9am–2pm or by appointment

George Rankin Coin Co Ltd
Contact Mr G Rankin
325 Bethnal Green Road, London, E2 6AH
☎ 020 7729 1280 Ⓕ 020 7729 5023
Est. 1969 *Stock size* Large
Stock Jewellery, period, modern coins, medals, banknotes
Open Tues–Sat 10am–6pm closed Aug
Fairs Coinex, Cumberland and Europa
Services Valuations

E4

Record Detector
Contact Mr J Salter
3 & 4 Station Approach, Chingford, London, E4 6AL
☎ 020 8529 6361
Ⓔ nick@salter.co.uk
Ⓦ www.salter.co.uk
Est. 1991 *Stock size* Large
Stock Second-hand records, CDs, 1950–1990s, videos, magazines
Open Mon–Sat 9.30am–6pm

Nicholas Salter Antiques
Contact Mrs S Salter
8 Station Approach, Chingford, London, E4 6AL
☎ 020 8529 2938
Ⓔ nick@salter.co.uk
Ⓦ www.salter.co.uk
Est. 1969 *Stock size* Large
Stock General antiques
Open Mon–Wed 10am–5pm Fri Sat 10am–6pm

E9

Kelly Lordan
Contact Lesley Lordan or Christina Kelly
211a Victoria Park Road, London, E9 7JN
☎ 020 8985 7550
Est. 2002 *Stock size* Small
Stock Antiques, collectables, soft furnishings
Open Mon–Sat 10am–6pm Sun 11am–2pm

E11

I D Edrich
Contact Mr I Edrich
17 Selsdon Road, London, E11 2QF
☎ 020 8989 9541 Ⓕ 020 8989 9541
Est. 1965 *Stock size* Large
Stock First editions, antiquarian books, literary periodicals, literature a speciality
Open By appointment

Forrest Auctioneers and Valuers
Contact Mr J Wiggett
1–4 Hitchock Business Centre, High Road, Leytonstone, London, E11 4RP
☎ 020 8556 7009 Ⓕ 020 8532 8292
Est. 1965
Open Mon–Fri 9am–5pm
Sales Sale 11am Thurs, viewing Wed 10am–5pm
Frequency Fortnightly
Catalogues Yes

Wanstead Antiques Centre
Contact Mr Gill
21 High Street, Wanstead, London, E11 2AA
☎ 020 8532 9844
Est. 1992 *Stock size* Medium
Stock Georgian–Victorian furniture, ceramics, vintage radios, vintage pens, collectables
Open Mon–Sat 10am–5.30pm Sun 11am–4pm

E15

Robert Bush Antiques
Contact Mr Robert Bush
Bermondsey Antique Arches, 84 St James Road, Bermondsey, London, E15 1RN
Ⓜ 07836 236911
Ⓔ bush.antiques@virgin.net
Stock Antique and decorative furniture
Open Mon–Thurs 9.30am–5pm Fri 7.30am–4pm

E17

Peter Davis Antiques
Contact Mr P Davis
1 Georgian Village, 100 Wood Street, London, E17 3HX
☎ 020 8520 6638 Ⓕ 020 8520 6638
Est. 1972 *Stock size* Small
Stock Walking sticks, postcards, small silver, collectables
Open Mon–Wed 10.30am–4.30pm

Treasure World
Contact Ali Jewya
3 Central Parade, Hoe Street, Walthamstow, London, E17 4RT
☎ 020 8521 1255 Ⓕ 020 8521 1255
Ⓜ 07957 177283
Est. 2000 *Stock size* Medium
Stock Furniture, rugs
Open Mon–Sat 9.30am–6.30pm Sun 11am–5pm

E18

Thornwood Auction
Contact Mrs D Green
Thornwood Village Hall, Weald Hall Lane, Thornwood, Epping, London, E18
☎ 020 8553 1242 Ⓜ 07860 905667
Est. 1985
Open Mon–Fri 9am–5pm
Sales Antiques and general sale Mon 6.30pm
Frequency Fortnightly
Catalogues Yes

Victoria Antiques
Contact Mr M Holman
166a George Lane, London, E18 1AY
☎ 020 8989 1002
Est. 1998 *Stock size* Medium
Stock Silver, silver plate, brass, china, carved items, small furniture, coins, clocks
Open Mon–Sat 11am–5pm closed Tues Thurs
Services Valuations

Woodford Auctions
Contact Mrs D Green
209 High Road, South Woodford, London, E18 2PA
☎ 020 8553 1242 Ⓜ 07860 905667
Est. 1994
Open Mon–Fri 9am–5pm
Sales Antiques and general sale Mon 6.30pm, viewing Mon 4pm prior to sale
Frequency Fortnightly
Catalogues Yes

EC1

Bloomsbury Book Auctions
Contact Rupert Powell
3 & 4 Hardwick Street, London, EC1R 4RY
020 7833 2636/7
020 7833 3954
info@bloomsbury-book-auct.com
www.bloomsbury-book-auct.com
Est. 1983
Open Mon–Fri 9.30am–5.30pm
Sales 30–32 sales a year, Thurs 1pm, view Mon Tues 9.30am–5.30pm Wed 9.30am–8pm and morning of sale until 1pm. Occasional sales of prints, maps, atlases, photographs, posters
Catalogues Yes

City Clocks (BHI)
Contact Jeffrey Rosson
31 Amwell Street, Clerkenwell, London, EC1R 1UN
020 7278 1154 020 7476 7766
07074 767766
mail@cityclocks.co.uk
www.cityclocks.co.uk
Est. 1898 *Stock size* Medium
Stock Clocks
Open Mon–Fri 8.30am–5.30pm Sat 10am–3.30pm
Services Restorations, clock, watch repair

Eldridge London
Contact Mr B Eldridge
99–101 Farringdon Road, London, EC1R 3BN
020 7837 0379 020 7278 6167
Est. 1955 *Stock size* Large
Stock 18th–19thC English furniture, treen, items of social and historic interest
Open Mon–Fri noon–5pm 1st Sat of month 11am–5pm closed Wed

Frosts of Clerkenwell Ltd
Contact Mr G Redwood
60–62 Clerkenwell Road, London, EC1M 5PX
020 7253 0315
www.frostsofclerkenwell.co.uk
Est. 1938 *Stock size* Large
Stock Clocks, watches, cases, dials, movements
Open Mon–Fri 10am–5pm
Services Restorations

Hirsh Ltd
Contact Ben Stevenson
10 Hatton Garden, London, EC1N 8AH
020 7405 6080 020 7430 0107
www.hirsh.co.uk
Est. 1982 *Stock size* Large
Stock Fine antique jewellery, hand-made and designed diamond engagement rings
Open Mon–Fri 10.30am–5pm

Paragon Art
Contact Mr Hassbani
Office 7, 34–35 Hatton Garden, London, EC1 N8PJ
020 7404 3207 020 8551 4487
hassbanis@aol.com
Est. 1993 *Stock size* Large
Stock Ancient and Islamic art 2000BC–18thC
Open By appointment only

Andrew R Ullmann Ltd
Contact Mr J Ullmann
10 Hatton Garden, London, EC1N 8AH
020 7405 1877 020 7404 7071
Est. 1950 *Stock size* Large
Stock Antique gold and gem jewellery, clocks, silver, objets d'art, watches
Open Mon–Fri 9am–5pm Sat 9.30am–5pm
Services Restorations

EC2

LASSCO St Michael's (LAPADA, SALVO, BACA Award Winner 2001)
Contact Jack Nott-Bower or Anthony Reeve
St Michael's Church, Mark Street (Off Paul Street), London, EC2A 4ER
020 7749 9944 020 7749 9941
st.michaels@lassco.co.uk
www.lassco.co.uk
Est. 1978 *Stock size* Large
Stock Architectural antiques, chimney pieces, overmantels, carved stonework, panelled rooms, statuary, garden ornaments and furniture, stained glass, metalwork
Open Mon–Fri 9.30am–5.30pm Sat 10am–5pm
Services Shipping

Westland and Co (SALVO)
Contact Mr R Muirhead
St Michael's Church, Leonard Street, London, EC2A 4ER
020 7739 8094 020 7729 3620
07831 755566
westland@westland.co.uk
www.westland.co.uk
Est. 1969 *Stock size* Large
Stock Antique fireplaces, mantels, architectural elements, statuary, panelling
Open Mon–Fri 9am–6pm Sat Sun 10am–5pm
Services Valuations, restorations

EC3

Halcyon Days (BADA)
Contact Georgina Foster or Cheska Moon
4 Royal Exchange, London, EC3V 3LL
020 7626 1120 020 7283 1876
info@halcyondays.co.uk
www.halcyondays.co.uk
Est. 1950 *Stock size* Small
Stock Enamels, fans, snuff boxes, objects of virtue, tôle peinte, papier mâché, porcelain
Open Mon–Fri 10am–5.30pm
Fairs Grosvenor House

Nanwani & Co
Contact Shobna Pattani
2 Shopping Arcade, Bank Station Underground, Cornhill, London, EC3V 3LA
020 7623 8232 020 7283 2548
Est. 1962 *Stock size* Medium
Stock General antiques
Open Mon–Fri 9am–5pm

Searle & Co Ltd (NAG)
Contact Steve Carson
1 Royal Exchange, Cornhill, London, EC3V 3LL
020 7626 2456 020 7283 6384
mail@searleandcoltd.uk
www.searleandcoltd.uk
Est. 1893 *Stock size* Medium
Stock General antiques
Open Mon–Fri 9am–5pm
Services Valuations

NORTH

N1

After Noah
Contact Simon Tarr
121 Upper Street, London, N1 1QP
020 7359 4281 020 7359 4281
mailorder@afternoah.com
www.afternoah.com
Est. 1989 *Stock size* Medium
Stock Antique and contemporary furniture and houseware
Open Mon–Sat 10am–6pm Sun noon–5pm
Services Restorations

Annie's Vintage Costume and Textiles
Contact Mrs Annie Moss
12 Camden Passage, Islington, London, N1 8ED
020 7359 0796 020 7359 2116
Est. 1975 *Stock size* Small
Stock 1900–1940s costume, linen, textiles
Open Mon Tues Thurs Fri Sun 11am–6pm Wed Sat 9am–6pm

The Antique Trader at the Millinery Works
Contact Brian Thompson, Derek Rothera or Jeff Jackson
85–87 Southgate Road, London, N1 3JS
020 7359 2019 020 7359 5792
antiquetrader@millinery.demon.co.uk
www.millineryworks.co.uk
Est. 1970 *Stock size* Large
Stock Arts and Crafts movement, furniture, effects
Open Tues–Sat 11am–6pm Sun noon–5pm or by appointment
Services Valuations, bi-annual exhibitions held

R Arantes
Contact R Arantes
27 The Mall, Camden Passage, Islington, London, N1 0PD
020 7226 6367 020 7253 5303
07712 189160
rlaliqueglass@btinternet.com
Est. 1987 *Stock size* Large
Stock Lalique glass
Open Wed Sat 8am–5pm or by appointment
Services Valuations

Art Nouveau Originals C1900 (LAPADA)
Contact Mrs C Turner
4–5 Pierrepont Row Arcade, Camden Passage, London, N1 8EF
020 7359 4127 01733 244717
07774 718096
anoc1900@compuserve.com
Est. 1997 *Stock size* Medium
Stock Art Nouveau furniture, ceramics, bronzes, pictures, jewellery
Open Sat Wed 9am–4pm
Fairs NEC, LAPADA

Banana Dance Ltd
Contact Jonathan Daltrey
16 The Mall, 359 Upper Street, Camden Passage, Islington, London, N1 0PP
020 8699 7728/020 7354 3125
020 8699 7728
07976 296987
jonathan@bananadance.com
www.bananadance.com
Est. 1989 *Stock size* Large
Stock Clarice Cliff, 20thC ceramics
Open Wed Fri Sat 9am–5pm
Fairs NEC, Alexandra Palace
Services Valuations, shipping, mail order

Camden Passage Antiques Market
Contact Mrs S Lemkow
12 Camden Passage, London, N1 8ED
020 7359 0190 020 7704 2095
Est. 1960 *Stock size* Large
No. of dealers 300
Stock General antiques and specialist shops
Open Wed Sat 8am–3pm stalls 8am–5pm shops

Camel Art Deco
Contact Mrs E Durack
34 Islington Green, London, N1 8DU
020 7359 5242
Est. 1996 *Stock size* Small
Stock Art Deco ceramics, furniture, lighting
Open Wed Sat 9am–3.30pm
Fairs Specialist Art Deco fairs
Services French polishing, re-upholstering of Lloyd Loom furniture

Castle Gibson
Contact Joyce Gibson
106a Upper Street, London, N1 1QN
020 7704 0927 020 7704 0927
Stock size Large
Stock 19thC–1940s office furniture, polished metal items, 1930s leather chairs, sofas, early 20thC industrial furniture, 1920s–1940s shop fittings, garden furniture
Open Mon–Sat 10am–6pm Sun noon–5pm
Services Deliveries within London

Chancery Antiques Ltd
Contact Mr R Rote
2 The Mall, 359 Upper Street, London, N1 0PD
020 7359 9035 020 7359 9035
Est. 1951 *Stock size* Medium
Stock Japanese porcelain, pottery, ivory, 19thC Continental works of art, cloisonné
Open Tues–Sat 10.30am–5pm or by appointment closed Thurs

Peter Chapman Antiques and Restoration (LAPADA, CINOA)
Contact Peter Chapman or Zac Chapman
10 Theberton Street, Islington, London, N1 0QX
020 7226 5565 020 8348 4846
07831 093662
pchapmanantiques@easynet.co.uk
www.antiques-peterchapman.co.uk
Est. 1971 *Stock size* Medium
Stock English and Continental furniture 1700–1900, mirrors, Grand Tour souvenirs, bronzes, spelters and other smalls, paintings, lighting, hall lanterns, stained glass, architectural, garden and decorative items
Open Mon–Sat 9.30am–6pm or by appointment
Services Valuations, restorations, shipping

Charlton House Antiques
Contact Mr S Burrows or Mr R Sims
18/20 Camden Passage, Islington, London, N1 8ED
020 7226 3141 020 7226 1123
charlhse@aol.com

Est. 1979 *Stock size* Large
Stock Antique furniture
Open Mon–Sat 9.30am–5pm
Services Shipping

Chest of Drawers
Contact Vincent Glanvill
281 Upper Street, Islington, London, N1 2TZ
020 7359 5909 020 7704 6236
mail@chest of drawers.co.uk
www.chestofdrawers.co.uk
Est. 1987 *Stock size* Medium
Stock Antique pine, country and oak furniture
Open Mon–Sun 10am–6pm

Cloud Cuckoo Land
Contact Mrs C Harper
6 Charlton Place, London, N1 8AJ
020 7354 3141
cloudcuckoolandmail@yahoo.co.uk.
Est. 1981 *Stock size* Medium
Stock Vintage clothes, accessories, 1850s–1950s, some later
Open Mon–Sat 11am–5.30pm

Peter Collingridge
Contact Mr Peter Collingridge
Angel Arcade, 116 Islington High Street, London, N1 8EG
020 7354 9189
Est. 1987 *Stock size* Large
Stock 18th–19thC brassware
Open Wed Sat 7.30am–5pm
Fairs NEC

Rosemary Conquest
Contact Mrs R Conquest
4 Charlton Place, London, N1 8AJ
020 7359 0616
Est. 1996 *Stock size* Large
Stock Continental and Dutch lighting, decorative items
Open Tue Thurs Fri 11am–5.30pm
Wed Sat 9am–5.30pm

Criterion Auctioneers
Contact Daniel Webster
53 Essex Road, Islington, London, N1 2SF
020 7359 5707 020 7354 9843
info@criterion-auctioneers.co.uk
www.criterion-auctioneers.co.uk
Est. 1989
Open Mon–Fri 9.30am–6pm
Sales Mon 4pm sale of antiques and decorative furnishings, viewing Fri 4–8pm Sat Sun 10am–6pm and on the day of sale from 10am
Frequency Weekly
Catalogues Yes

Carlton Davidson Antiques
Contact Mr Carlton Davidson
33 Camden Passage, London, N1 8EA
020 7226 7491 020 7226 7491
Est. 1982 *Stock size* Medium
Stock Decorative French items, including lighting
Open Wed Sat 10am–4pm

Eclectica
Contact Liz Wilson
2 Charlton Place, London, N1 8AJ
020 7226 5625 020 7226 5625
Est. 1988 *Stock size* Large
Stock Vintage costume jewellery, 1920s–1960s
Open Wed Sat 9am–6pm
Tues Thurs Fri 11am–6pm
Services Theatre and film hire

Fandango
Contact Jonathan Ellis or Henrietta Palmer
50 Cross Street, Islington, London, N1 2BA
020 7226 1777 020 7226 1777
07979 650805
shop@fandango.uk.com
www.fandango.uk.com
Est. 1997 *Stock size* Medium
Stock Post-war design lighting and furniture
Open Wed–Sat 11am–6pm
Sun noon–5pm
Services Valuations, interior design

Feljoy Antiques
Contact Mrs Joy Humphreys
3 Angel Arcade, Camden Passage, London, N1 8EA
020 7354 5336 020 7831 3485
joy@feljoy-antiques.demon.co.uk
www.chintz.net/feljoy
Est. 1985 *Stock size* Large
Stock Chintzware, textiles, cushions, shawls, small decorative furniture, decorative items including beadwork cushions
Open Wed 8am–3.30pm Sat 10am–4pm
Services Mail order

Vincent Freeman Antiques
Contact Vincent Freeman
1 Camden Passage, Islington, London, N1 8EA
020 7226 6178 020 7226 7231
freemanvj@hotmail.com
Est. 1966 *Stock size* Medium
Stock 19thC music boxes
Open Wed Sat 10am–5pm or by appointment
Fairs Olympia

Furniture Vault
Contact Mr David Loveday
50 Camden Passage, London, N1 8AE
020 7354 1047 020 7354 1047
Est. 1984 *Stock size* Large
Stock 18th–19thC furniture
Open Tues–Sat 9.30am–4.30pm

Gateway Arcade Antiques Market
Contact Mike Spooner
357 Upper Street, Camden Passage, London, N1 0PD
020 7969 1500 020 7969 1639
Est. 2000 *Stock size* Large
No. of dealers 50
Stock Jewellery, silver, collectables, watches, militaria
Open Wed 6am–2pm Sat 8am–2pm

Get Stuffed
Contact Robert Sinclair
105 Essex Road, Islington, London, N1 2SL
020 7226 1364 020 7359 8353
07831 260062
taxidermy@thegetstuffed.co.uk
www.thegetstuffed.co.uk
Est. 1913 *Stock size* Large
Stock Victorian artefacts, birds, animals, insects, butterflies and glass domes
Open Mon–Fri 1am–5pm
Sat 1.30pm–3.30pm

Rosemary Hart
Contact Rosemary Hart
8 Angel Arcade, 116 Islington High Street, London, N1 8EG
020 7359 6839
rosemaryhart@cwcom.net
Est. 1980 *Stock size* Small
Stock Small plated tableware and silver pieces, decorative pieces and mother-of-pearl
Open Wed 9am–4pm
Fri Sat by appointment

House of Steel
Contact Judy Cole
400 Caledonian Road, London, N1 1DN
0207 6075889 0207 6075889
Est. 1977 *Stock size* Large
Stock Antique metalware, architectural ironwork
Open Mon–Fri 11am–5pm or by appointment
Services Valuations, restorations

Diana Huntley (LAPADA)
Contact Mrs Ross
8 Camden Passage, London, N1 8ED
020 7226 4605 020 7359 0240
diana@dianahuntleyantiques.co.uk
www.dianahuntleyantiques.co.uk
Est. 1970 *Stock size* Large
Stock Fine quality 19thC porcelain, Meissen, major English factories
Open Tues Fri Sat 10am–4pm Wed 7am–4pm

Intercol (ITA, Coin, Banknote and Map Collectors Societies)
Contact Mr Yasha Beresiner
114 Islington High Street, Camden Passage, The Angel, Islington, London, N1 8EG
020 8349 2207 020 8346 9539
07768 292066
yasha@compuserve.com
www.intercol.co.uk
Est. 1981 *Stock size* Medium
Stock Maps, charts, books, playing cards, currency
Open Tues–Sat 10am–5.30pm or by appointment
Fairs Playing cards fairs, Map Society fairs (phone for details)
Services Valuations

Jonathan James (LAPADA)
Contact Norman or James Petre
52–53 Camden Passage, London, N1 8EA
020 7704 8266
Est. 1994 *Stock size* Medium
Stock 18th–19thC English furniture
Open Tues–Sat 10am-5pm
Services Valuations

Japanese Gallery Ltd (Ukiyo-e Society)
Contact Mr C D Wertheim
23 Camden Passage, London, N1 8EA
020 7226 3347 020 7229 2934
07930 411991
princyw@hotmail.com or japanesegallerylondon@hotmail.com
Est. 1980 *Stock size* Large
Stock Japanese woodcut prints, Japanese ceramics, sword armour, Japanese dolls
Open Mon–Fri 9.30am–4.30pm Sat 10am–5pm
Services Restorations, free authentication

Judith Lassalle (PBFA)
Contact Mrs J Lassalle
7 Pierrepont Arcade, London, N1 8EF
020 7607 7121
Est. 1765 *Stock size* Small
Stock Toys, games, books, optical toys, ephemera, all pre-1914
Open Wed 7.30am–4pm Sat 9.30am–4pm or by appointment
Fairs English and American ephemera fairs, PBFA Bookfair at Russell Hotel

LASSCO Warehouse (SALVO)
Contact Jesse Carrington
101–108 Britannia Walk, London, N1 7LU
020 7490 1000 020 7490 0908
warehouse@lassco.co.uk
www.lassco.co.uk
Est. 1978 *Stock size* Large
Stock Architectural reclamation and salvage
Open Mon–Sat 10am–5pm
Services Shipping

John Laurie (LAPADA)
Contact Mr John Laurie
352 Upper Street, London, N1 0PD
020 7226 0913 020 7226 4599
rdgewirtz@aol.com
Est. 1963 *Stock size* Large
Stock Antique and modern silver, silver plate
Open Mon–Sat 9.30am–5pm
Services Restorations, re-plating

Leolinda
Contact Ms Leolinda Costa
3 The Mall, 359 Upper Street, Camden Passage, London, N1 0PD
020 7226 3450 020 7209 0143
leolinda@hotmail.com
www.islington.co.uk/leolinda
Est. 1989 *Stock size* Small
Stock Old and new silver jewellery, gemstone necklaces, ethnic art, jewellery
Open Tues–Sat 10am–4pm
Services After-sales service

Andrew Lineham Fine Glass (BADA, CINOA)
Contact Mr A Lineham
19 The Mall, Camden Passage, London, N1 8EA
020 7704 0195 01243 576241
07767 702722
andrewlineham@onetel.net.uk
www.andrewlineham.co.uk
Est. 1979 *Stock size* Large
Stock 19th–20thC colourful glass, porcelain
Open Wed 8am–3pm Sat 10.30am–4pm or by appointment
Fairs Olympia (June Nov)
Services Valuations, hire

The Mall Antiques Arcade
Contact Neil Jackson
359 Upper Street, Camden Passage, London, N1 0PD
020 7351 5353 020 7351 5350
antique@dial.pipex.com
www.visitlondon.com (search for antiques)
Est. 1979 *Stock size* Large
No. of dealers 35
Stock Furniture, decorative antiques
Open Tues Thurs Fri 10am–5pm Wed 7.30am–5.30pm Sat 8.30am–5.30pm

Metro Retro
Contact Mr Saxon Durrant
1 White Conduit Street, London, N1 9EL
020 7278 4884 020 7278 4884
07850 319116
saxon@metroretro.demon.co.uk
www.metroretro.co.uk
Est. 1994 *Stock size* Large
Stock Industrial style and stripped-steel furniture, lighting and design
Open Tues–Sat 11am–6pm
Fairs Syon Park, Jukebox Madness, Chiswick, Battersea
Services Props hire, consultancy

⊞ Michel André Morin (CPTA)
Contact Brian Trotman
✉ **7 Charlton Place, Islington, London, N1 8AQ** Ⓟ
☎ 020 7226 3803 Ⓕ 020 7704 0708
Ⓜ 07802 832496
Ⓔ michel.morin@aol.com
Est. 1989 *Stock size* Medium
Stock French decorative furniture, chandeliers, items for interior decorators
Open Wed–Sat 7.30am–4.30pm or by appointment
Fairs Olympia, Battersea Decorative Antiques and Textiles Fair
Services Valuations, restorations

⊞ Chris Newland Antiques
Contact Chris or George Newland
✉ **The Lower Level Georgian Village, 30–31 Islington Green, London, N1 8DU** Ⓟ
☎ 020 7359 9805 Ⓕ 020 7359 9805
Est. 1968 *Stock size* Large
Stock 18th–19thC period furniture, objets d'art
Open Tues Wed Fri Sat 9.30am–4.30pm
Services Restorations, polishing

⊞ Number 19
Contact Mr D Griffith
✉ **19 Camden Passage, London, N1 8EA** Ⓟ
☎ 020 7226 1999 Ⓕ 020 7226 1126
Est. 1982 *Stock size* Large
Stock Decorative antiques, campaign furniture, vintage shop fittings, leather seating, decorative accessories
Open Tues–Sat 10am–5pm closed Thurs

⊞ Origin 101
Contact Christopher Reen
✉ **Gateway Arcade, Islington High Street, London, N1 0PG**
☎ 020 7704 1326 Ⓜ 07769 686146
Ⓔ david@origin101.co.uk
Ⓦ www.origin101.co.uk
Est. 2001 *Stock size* Medium
Stock Modernist furniture, objects 1930–1950
Open Tues Thurs Fri noon–6pm Wed Sat 9am–6pm
Fairs 20thC Design Fair

⊞ Out of Time
Contact Mr E Farlow
✉ **110 Elmore Street, Islington, London, N1 3AH** Ⓟ
☎ 020 7354 5755 Ⓕ 020 7354 5755
Est. 1969 *Stock size* Large
Stock 1940s–1950s homestyle furniture, glass, fridges, tables, chairs
Open Mon–Sun 10am–6pm
Fairs Jukebox Madness, Ascot
Services Valuations, restorations

⊞ Kevin Page Oriental Art Ltd (LAPADA, CPADA)
Contact Mr K Page
✉ **2–6 Camden Passage, Islington, London, N1 8ED** Ⓟ
☎ 020 7226 8558 Ⓕ 020 7354 9145
Ⓔ kpageoriental@aol.com
Ⓦ www.kevinpage.co.uk
Est. 1969 *Stock size* Large
Stock Oriental art, bronze, lacquer, porcelain, ivory
Trade only Trade and export only
Open Tues–Sat 10.30am–4.30pm

⊞ John Pearman
Contact John Pearman
✉ **24 The Mall, Upper Street, London, N1 0PD** Ⓟ
☎ 020 7359 0591 Ⓕ 020 7359 0591
Ⓔ john.pearman@talk21.com
Est. 1983 *Stock size* Medium
Stock 19thC glass, ceramics
Open Wed 9am–5pm Sat 10am–5pm or by appointment

⊞ Phoenix Oriental Art (LAPADA)
Contact Elena Edwards
✉ **No 6 the Lower Mall, 359 Upper Street, Islington, London, N1 0PD** Ⓟ
☎ 020 7226 4474 Ⓕ 020 8521 8846
Ⓔ okinasan@aol.com
Ⓦ www.trocadero.com/okinasan
Est. 1981 *Stock size* Large
Stock Chinese and Japanese bronze from the last 1000 years
Open Wed Sat 10am–4pm or by appointment

⊞ Piers Rankin
Contact Mr P Rankin
✉ **14 Camden Passage, London, N1 8ED** Ⓟ
☎ 020 7354 3349 Ⓕ 020 7359 8138
Est. 1979 *Stock size* Large
Stock Silver, silver plate
Open Tues–Sat 9.30am–5.30pm
Services Packing for export

⊞ Regent Antiques
Contact Mr Tino Quaradeghini
✉ **King's Cross Freight Depot, Barpart House, York Way, London, N1 0UZ** Ⓟ
☎ 020 7833 5545 Ⓕ 020 7278 2236
Ⓜ 07836 294074
Ⓔ regentantiques@aol.com
Est. 1974 *Stock size* Large
Stock 18thC–Edwardian furniture
Open Mon–Fri 9am–5.30pm
Services Restoration of furniture

⊞ Relic Antiques
Contact Mr Gliksten
✉ **21 Camden Passage, London, N1 8EA**
☎ 020 7359 2597 Ⓕ 020 7388 2691
Ⓜ 07831 785059
Est. 1994 *Stock size* Large
Stock Decorative antiques, folk art, fairground art, country pieces, marine, architectural, trade signs, shop fittings
Open Wed Sat 10am–4pm or by appointment
Services Valuations

⊞ Marcus Ross Antiques
Contact Mr M Ross
✉ **16 Pierrepont Row, Camden Passage, Islington, London, N1 8EE** Ⓟ
☎ 020 7359 8494 Ⓕ 020 7359 0240
Est. 1973 *Stock size* Large
Stock Japanese and Chinese porcelain, 17thC onwards
Open Tues–Sat 10am–4pm closed Thurs

⊞ Rumours Decorative Arts (LAPADA)
Contact John Donovan
✉ **4 The Mall, 359 Upper Street, Camden Passage, Islington, London, N1 0PD** Ⓟ
☎ 020 7704 6549
Ⓜ 07836 277274 or 07831 103748
Ⓔ rumdec@aol.com
Est. 1988 *Stock size* Large
Stock Moorcroft pottery
Open Wed Sat 8am–4pm Sat 9am–5pm
Fairs NEC Antiques for Everyone
Services Valuations

⊞ At the Sign of the Chest of Drawers
Contact Daniel Harrison or Vincent Glanville
✉ **281 Upper Street, London, N1 2TZ**
☎ 020 7359 5909 Ⓕ 020 7704 6236

Est. 1986 Stock size Large
Stock Soft and hardwood old furniture, wooden and metal beds, sofas, armchairs, chests-of-drawers, wardrobes
Open Mon–Sun 10am–6pm

Sugar Antiques (CPTA)
Contact Mr T Sugarman
8–9 Pierrepont Arcade, Pierrepont Row, London, N1 8EF
☎ 020 7354 9896 Ⓕ 020 7931 5642
Ⓜ 07973 179980
Ⓔ tony@sugar-antiques.com
Ⓦ www.sugar-antiques.com
Est. 1990 Stock size Large
Stock Wristwatches, pocketwatches, pens, lighters, costume jewellery
Open Wed–Sat 8am–3.30pm

Tadema Gallery (BADA, LAPADA, CINOA)
Contact Sonya or David Newell-Smith
10 Charlton Place, Camden Passage, Islington, London, N1 8AJ
☎ 020 7359 1055 Ⓕ 020 7359 1055
Ⓜ 0771 0082395
Ⓔ info@tademagallery.com
Ⓦ www.tademagallery.com
Est. 1978 Stock size Large
Stock Art Nouveau, Arts and Crafts, Art Deco jewellery
Open Wed Sat 10am–5pm or by appointment
Fairs Grosvenor House

Chris Tapsell at Christopher House (CPADA)
Contact Mr C Tapsell
5 Camden Passage, Islington, London, N1 8EA
☎ 020 7354 3603
Est. 1993 Stock size Medium
Stock 18th–19thC English and Continental furniture, Oriental ceramics, Georgian–Victorian mirrors
Open Tues Wed 10am–5pm Fri Sat 10am–5pm or by appointment
Services Valuations, restorations

Turn On Lighting
Contact Janet Holdstock
116–118 Islington High Street, Camden Passage, Islington, London, N1 8EG
☎ 020 7359 7616 Ⓕ 020 7359 7616
Est. 1976 Stock size Large
Stock Antique lighting
Open Tues–Fri 10.30am–6pm Sat 9.30am–4.30pm
Services Museum work, interior design

Vane House Antiques
Contact Michael Till
15 Camden Passage, Islington, London, N1 8EA
☎ 020 7359 1343 Ⓕ 020 7359 1343
Est. 1962 Stock size Large
Stock 18th–early 19thC furniture
Open Tues Wed Fri and Sat 10am–5pm

Mike Weedon (LAPADA, CPADA)
7 Camden Passage, Islington, London, N1 8EA
☎ 020 7226 5319/020 7609 6826
Ⓕ 0207 700 6389
Ⓔ info@mikeweedonantiques.com
Ⓦ www.mikeweedonantiques.com
Est. 1979 Stock size Large
Stock Art Nouveau, Art Deco, general antiques, wholesale to Japanese trade
Open Wed 9am–5pm Sat 10am–5pm or by appointment

Agnes Wilton
Contact Agnes Wilton
3 Camden Passage, London, N1 8EA
☎ 020 7226 5679 Ⓕ 020 7226 0779
Est. 1972 Stock size Medium
Stock Furniture, silver, decorative objects
Open Tues–Sat 10am–2pm
Services Valuations

Woodage Antiques (LAPADA)
Contact Mr C Woodage
359 Upper Street, London, N1 0PD
☎ 020 7226 4173 Ⓕ 01753 529 047
Ⓔ woodage.antiques@btinternet.com
Est. 1995 Stock size Large
Stock 18th–20thC furniture
Open Wed 7.30am–5pm Sat 9am–5pm
Fairs TVADA

www.buymeissen.com (LAPADA)
Contact Laurence Mitchell
15 The Mall, Camden Passage, Islington, London, N1
☎ 0208 346 1444 Ⓕ 0209 346 1444
Ⓔ info@buymeissen.com
Ⓦ www.buymeissen.com
Est. 1974 Stock size Large
Stock 19thC Meissen, European, oriental works of art and ceramics
Open Tues–Fri 10am–5pm Sat 10am–5.30pm
Services Valuations, restorations

York Gallery Ltd (LAPADA)
Contact Mr G Beyer
51 Camden Passage, Islington, London, N1 8EA
☎ 020 7354 8012 Ⓕ 020 7354 8012
Ⓦ www.yorkgallery.co.uk
Est. 1989 Stock size Large
Stock 17th–19thC engravings
Open Wed–Sat 10am–5pm
Services Picture framing

Michael Young
Contact M Young
22 The Mall, 359 Upper Street, Camden Passage, London, N1 0PD
☎ 020 7226 2225
Est. 1985 Stock size Medium
Stock Marine models, pond yachts, general antiquities
Open Wed and Sat 9am–4pm
Services Valuations

N2

Martin Henham
Contact Mr M Henham
218 High Road, London, N2 9AY
☎ 020 8444 5274
Est. 1963 Stock size Medium
Stock 18th–20thC Victoriana, bronzes, ceramics, porcelain
Open Tues–Sat 10am–6pm closed Thurs or by appointment
Services Furniture restoration

N3

Martin Gladman Second-hand Books
Contact Mr M Gladman
235 Nether Street, London, N3 1NT
☎ 020 8343 3023
Est. 1991 Stock size Large
Stock Large range of rare and antiquarian books through the humanities, history, military history

Open Sat 10am–6pm
Tues–Fri 11am–8pm
Services Valuations

N4

The Antique Shop
Contact Michael Slade or Michael Kairis
42 Quernmore Road, London, N4 4QP
020 8341 3194 020 8348 7652
07973 800678
michael.kairis@btinternet.com
www.antiquesnorthlondon.co.uk
Est. 1982 *Stock size* Small
Stock Victorian–Edwardian furniture
Open Tues–Fri 10am–6pm
Sat by appointment
Fairs Alexandra Palace
Services Restorations

Kennedy Carpets
Contact Michael Kennedy or Vivien Eder
Oriental Carpet Centre, Building G, 105 Eade Road, London, N4 1TJ
020 8800 4455 020 8800 4466
kennedycarpets@ukonline.co.uk
www.cloudband.com/occ/kennedycarpets
Est. 1972 *Stock size* Large
Stock Antique Oriental large carpets and rugs
Open Mon–Fri 9.30am–6pm
Sat Sun by appointment
Services Valuations, restorations

Joseph Lavian
Contact Joseph Lavian
105 Eade Road, London, N4 1TJ
020 800 0707 020 800 0404
lavian@lavian.com
www.lavian.com
Est. 1962 *Stock size* Large
Stock Oriental carpets and textiles
Open Mon–Fri 9.30am–5.30pm
Services Valuations, restorations

Michael Slade
Contact M Slade
42 Quernmore Road, London, N4 4QP
020 8341 3194
mikeslade@ntl.com
Est. 1984
Stock Furniture
Open By appointment

N5

Gathering Moss
Contact Mrs S Murnane
193 Blackstock Road, London, N5 2LL
020 7354 3034
Est. 1999 *Stock size* Medium
Stock Furniture, gifts, reclaimed timber items
Open Sat 11am–6pm
Sun 11am–4pm

Nicholas Goodyer (PBFA, ABA)
Contact Mr N Goodyer
15 Calabria Road, London, N5 1JB
020 7226 5682 020 7354 4716
email@nicholasgoodyer.com
Est. 1950 *Stock size* Medium
Stock Antiquarian and rare books on architecture, travel, design, illustrated, natural history, colour-plate books
Open Mon–Fri 9am–5pm or by appointment, prior call advised
Fairs PBFA Russell Hotel, ABA
Services Valuations, restorations, shipping, book search

Sandby Fine Art
Contact B Ashley
72 Mountgrove Road, London, N5 2LT
020 7354 4759
Est. 1989 *Stock size* Medium
Stock General antiques, fireplaces, paintings
Open Mon–Sat 9am–6pm

Strike One Antique Clocks, Barometers & Music Boxes (BADA)
Contact Mr J G Mighell
48a Highbury Hill, London, N5 1AP
020 7354 2790 020 7354 2790
07860 335933
milo@strikeone.co.uk
www.strikeone.co.uk
Est. 1968 *Stock size* Medium
Stock Antique clocks, barometers, music boxes, 1700–1900 English tavern clocks a speciality
Open By appointment only
Services Valuations, repairs

N6

Fisher & Sperr (ABA)
46 Highgate High Street, London, N6 5JB
0208 3407244 0208 3484293
Est. 1945 *Stock size* Large
Stock General second-hand and antiquarian books
Open Mon–Sat 10am–5pm
Services Valuations

Ripping Yarns (PBFA)
Contact Mrs C Mitchell
355 Archway Road, London, N6 4EJ
020 8341 6111 020 7482 5056
yarns@rippingyarns.co.uk
www.rippingyarns.co.uk
Est. 1982 *Stock size* Large
Stock General stock, antiquarian and second-hand books including children's fiction, illustrated
Open Mon–Fri 10.30am–5.30pm
Sat 10am–5pm Sun 11am–4pm
Fairs PBFA
Services Book search, French and Spanish spoken, annual catalogue

At the Sign of the Chest of Drawers
Contact Mr Vincent Glanvill
164 Archway Road, London, N6 5BB
020 8340 7652 or 020 7359 5909
020 8340 7652
Est. 1999 *Stock size* Large
Stock Soft and hardwood old furniture, wooden and metal beds, chests-of-drawers, wardrobes
Open Tues–Sat 10am–6pm
Services Restorations

N7

Back in Time
Contact Mr Demetriou
93 Holloway Road, London, N7 8LT
020 7700 0744
mario000@btclick.com
www.backintime.com
Est. 1996 *Stock size* Large
Stock 1950s–1970s furniture, metal wardrobes, decorative items, metal kitchen furniture
Open Mon–Sat 10am–6pm
Services Valuations, restorations

Dome Antiques (LAPADA)
Contact Mr A Woolf
40 Queensland Road, London, N7 7AJ
020 7700 6266 020 7609 1692

LONDON

Ⓜ 07831 805888
Ⓔ info@domeantiques.co.uk
Ⓦ www.domeantiques.co.uk
Est. 1974 *Stock size* Large
Stock 19thC decorative furniture
Open Mon–Fri 9am–5pm
Fairs NEC, Olympia
Services Restorations

Ooh-la-La
Contact David or Andy
147 Holloway Road, London, N7 8LX
☎ 020 7609 6021
Ⓜ 07977 007590
Est. 1997 *Stock size* Medium
Stock Antiques, collectables, memorabilia
Open Mon–Sat 10am–6pm
Services Valuations

N8

Hornsey Auctions Ltd
Contact Miss C Connoly
54–56 High Street, Hornsey, London, N8 7NX
☎ 020 8340 5334 Ⓕ 020 8340 5334
Ⓔ hornseyauctions@ic24.net
Est. 1983
Open Thurs Fri 9.30am–5.30pm Sat 10am–4pm
Sales Antiques and general sale Wed 6.30pm, viewing Tues 5–7.30pm Wed 10am–6.30pm prior to sale
Frequency Weekly
Catalogues Yes

Of Special Interest
Contact Mr S Loftus
42–46 Park Road, London, N8 8TD
☎ 020 8340 0909 Ⓕ 020 8374 6990
Est. 1988 *Stock size* Large
Stock Antique pine furniture, porcelain, fabrics, Indian items, garden furniture
Open Mon–Fri noon–7pm Sat 10am–6pm Sun noon–4pm

Solomon
Contact Solomon
49 Park Road, London, N8 8SY
☎ 020 8341 1817 Ⓕ 020 8341 1817
Ⓔ solomon@solomonantiques.fsnet.co.uk
Est. 1981 *Stock size* Medium
Stock Arts & Crafts, Art Nouveau and Deco
Open Mon–Sat 9am–6pm
Services Valuations, restorations, upholstery

N9

Anything Goes
Contact C J Bednarz
83 Bounces Road, London, N9 8LD
☎ 020 8807 9399
Est. 1978 *Stock size* Small
Stock Antiques, collectables
Open Tues–Sat 10am–5pm
Services Valuations

N11

A Pine Romance
Contact Mr A Gray
111 Friern Barnet Road, New Southgate, London, N11 3EU
☎ 020 8361 5860 Ⓕ 020 83614697
Est. 1989 *Stock size* Medium
Stock British and Continental pine furniture, manufacturers of furniture from reclaimed timber
Open Mon–Sat 10am–5.30pm
Services Valuations, restorations

N12

Dean's Antiques Emporium
Contact Mr Dean Georgiou
218 Woodhouse Road, Friern Barnet, London, N12 0RS
☎ 020 8446 8409
Ⓜ 07770 445338
Est. 1996 *Stock size* Large
Stock English, Continental, Edwardian, Victorian furniture
Open Mon–Sat 10am–6pm closed Wed
Fairs Newark, Ardingly
Services Valuations, restorations

Nash & Company
Contact Mr S Nash
Lodge House, 9–17 Lodge Lane, London, N12 8JH
☎ 020 8445 9000 Ⓕ 020 8446 6068
Est. 1977
Open Mon–Fri 9am–5.30pm
Sales Antiques and general sale Mon 5pm, viewing Sun 9am–1pm Mon 9am–5pm
Frequency Weekly
Catalogues Yes

The New Curiosity Shop
Contact Mrs T Robins
211 Woodhouse Road, Friern Barnet, London, N12 9AY
☎ 020 8368 2117 Ⓕ 020 83682117
Est. 1994 *Stock size* Medium
Stock Coins, stamps, banknotes, sci-fi memorabilia, pop memorabilia, Star Wars toys, Corgi, Dinky, Matchbox collectables
Open Mon–Sat 10am–5.30pm
Services Valuations

N13

Palmers Green Antiques Centre
Contact Michael Webb
472 Green Lanes, Palmers Green, London, N13 5PA
☎ 020 8350 0878
Ⓜ 07855 067544
Est. 1996 *Stock size* Large
No. of dealers 40
Stock Furniture, clocks, pictures, jewellery, porcelain, china, glass, silver, lighting, general antiques
Open Mon Wed–Sat 10am–5.30pm Sun 11am–5pm
Services Valuations, house clearance

N14

C J Martin Coins Ltd (LAPADA)
Contact Chris Martin
85 The Vale, Southgate, London, N14 6AT
☎ 020 882 1509 Ⓕ 020 886 5253
Ⓔ ancientart@btinternet.com
Ⓦ www.ancientart.co.uk
Est. 1972 *Stock size* Large
Stock General antiquities and coins
Open By appointment
Services Valuations, restorations, shipping, mail order

Southgate Auction Rooms
Contact Mr J Nolan
55 High Street, Southgate, London, N14 6LD
☎ 020 8886 7888 Ⓕ 020 8882 4421
Ⓦ www.southgateauctionrooms.com
Est. 1986
Open Mon–Fri 9am–5.30pm
Sales General and antiques sales

Mon 5pm, viewing Sat 9am–1pm Mon 9am–5pm prior to sale
Frequency Weekly
Catalogues Yes

Southgate Bookshop
Contact Mr W Lobo
62 Chase Side, Southgate, London, N14 5PA
020 8886 4805 020 8363 8625
Est. 1985 *Stock size* Small
Stock Antiquarian, new and old books, furniture, silver, sport
Open Mon–Sat 11am–5.30pm
Services Valuations, book search

N15

Krypton Komics
Contact Mr G Ochiltree
252 High Road, Tottenham, London, N15 4AJ
020 8801 5378 020 8376 3174
krypton.komics@virgin.net
www.kryptonkomics.com
Est. 1980 *Stock size* Large
Stock 1950s–present day American comics
Open Mon–Fri 10.30am–6pm Sat 10am–6pm Sun 11am–6pm
Fairs Comic Convention at the Royal National Hotel
Services Valuations, mail order catalogue

M A Stroh Bookseller
Contact Mr M Stroh
1st Floor, 74–80 Markfield Road, Tottenham, London, N15 4QF
020 8885 2112 020 8885 2112
07974 413039
patents@stroh.demon.co.uk
www.webspawner.com/users/buttonbook
Est. 1957 *Stock size* Medium
Stock Books, patents 1617–1970, journals, scientific papers, ephemera, old bindings, dissertations
Open By appointment

N16

The Cobbled Yard
Contact Carole Lucas
1 Bouverie Road, Stoke Newington, London, N16 0AH
020 8809 5286
info@cobbled-yard.co.uk
www.cobbled-yard.co.uk
Est. 2002 *Stock size* Medium
Stock Furniture, pine ceramics, collectables, prints, pictures
Open Wed–Sun 11am–6pm
Services Restorations

I Ehrnfeld (NAWCC)
Contact Isaac Ehrnfeld
29 Leweston Place, London, N16 6RJ
020 8802 4584 020 8800 1364
07966 136495
Est. 1989 *Stock size* Medium
Stock Watches, wristwatches, ceramics, porcelain
Open By appointment
Fairs Major antiques fairs, clock/watch fairs
Services Shipping

N19

Chesney's Antique Fireplace Warehouse
Contact John Norman
734–736 Holloway Road, London, N19 3JF
020 7272 7462 020 7561 8288
sales@chesneys.co.uk
www.chesneys.co.uk
Est. 1985 *Stock size* Large
Stock Antique fireplaces
Open Mon–Fri 9am–5.30pm Sat 10am–5pm
Services Shipping

Old School
Contact Mr F Lascelles
130c Junction Road, Tufnell Park, London, N19 5LB
020 7272 5603 020 7272 5603
Est. 1996 *Stock size* Large
Stock Garden furniture, statuary, antique furniture, made-to-measure furniture
Open Mon–Sun 11am–6pm
Fairs Newark, Ardingly

N20

The Totteridge Gallery
Contact Mrs J Clarke
61 Totteridge Lane, London, N20 0HD
020 8446 7896 020 8446 7541
07836 777773
janet@totteridgegallery.com
www.totteridgegallery.com
Est. 1987 *Stock size* Large
Stock Fine art, 18th–20thC British and Continental oil paintings, watercolours, limited-edition Sir William Russell Flint prints
Open Mon–Sat 11am–6.30pm
Services Valuations, restorations

N21

Dollyland
864 Greenlanes, Winchmore Hill, London, N21 2RS
020 8360 1053 020 8364 1370
0780 821773
www.dollyland.com
Est. 1986 *Stock size* Large
Stock Dolls, Steiff bears, Scalextric, trains, die-cast toys
Open Tues Thurs Fri Sat 9.30am–4.30pm
Fairs Hugglets, Kensington Town Hall

Past Present Toys
Contact Mr Jim Parsons
862 Green Lanes, London, N21 2RS
020 8364 1370 020 8364 1370
Est. 1986 *Stock size* Large
Stock Dinkys, Hornby railways, tin-plate toys, Corgi, Matchbox
Open Tues Thurs–Sat 9.30am–4.30pm

Winchmore Antiques
Contact Mr D Hicks or Mr S Christian
14 The Green, London, N21 1AY
020 8882 4800
wa@keristal.freeuk.com
Est. 1980 *Stock size* Medium
Stock General antiques, furniture, porcelain, glass, china, silver, oil lamps and parts, architectural fittings, fireside accessories
Open Tues–Sat 9.30am–5.30pm
Services Valuations, restorations

NW1

Archive Books and Music
Contact Mr T Meaker
83 Bell Street, Marylebone, London, NW1 6TB
020 7402 8212
Est. 1975 *Stock size* Small
Stock Antiquarian and modern books, printed pop and classical music
Open Mon–Sat 10.30am–6pm

Art Furniture
Contact Liam Scanlon
158 Camden Street, London, NW1 9PA
020 7267 4324 020 7267 5199
arts-and-crafts@artfurniture.co.uk
www.artfurniture.co.uk
Est. 1989 *Stock size* Large
Stock Arts and Crafts furniture and objects including Liberty, Heals, Shapland and Petter
Open Mon–Sun noon–5pm
Services Shipping, restorations

Comic Book Postal Auctions Ltd (Eagle Society)
Contact Malcolm Phillips
40–42 Osnaburgh Street, London, NW1 3ND
020 7424 0007 020 7424 0008
comicbook@compuserve.com
www.compalcomics.com
Est. 1992
Open By appointment
Sales Quarterly, British and American comics, 1900–1970s, also annuals, artwork, TV-related merchandise. Sales in March, Jun, Sept, Dec
Frequency Quarterly
Catalogues Yes

Laurence Corner
Contact Sales Manager
62–64 Hampstead Road, London, NW1 2U
020 7813 1010 020 7813 1413
www.laurencecorner.com
Est. 1953 *Stock size* Small
Stock Militaria
Open Mon–Sat 10.30am–6pm

Madeline Crispin Antiques
Contact Mrs M Crispin or David Thomas
95 Lisson Grove, London, NW1 6UP
020 7402 6845
07956 289906
david@crispinantiques.fsnet.co.uk
Est. 1979 *Stock size* Medium
Stock Furniture, decorative items
Open Mon–Fri 10am–5.30pm
Sat 10am–4pm
Services Valuations

Elvisly Yours
Contact Mr Sid Shaw
233 Baker Street, London, NW1 6XE
020 7486 2005
elvisly@globalnet.co.uk
www.elvisly-yours.com
Est. 1978 *Stock size* Large
Stock Elvis memorabilia
Open Mon–Sat 11am–9pm
Sun 11am–8pm

Planet Bazaar
Contact Maureen Silverman
149 Drummond Street, London, NW1 2PB
020 7387 8326 020 7387 8326
maureen@planetbazaar.demon.co.uk
www.planetbazaar.co.uk
Est. 1997 *Stock size* Medium
Stock 1950–1980 designer furniture, art, glass, lighting, ceramics, books, eccentricities
Open Tues–Sat 11.30am–7pm or by appointment

The Relic Antiques Trade Warehouse
Contact Mr Gilksten
127 Pancras Road, London, NW1 1JN
020 7387 6039 020 7388 2691
Est. 1972 *Stock size* Large
Stock Decorative antiques, folk art, fairground art, Black Forest carvings, country pieces, architectural, marine, trade signs, shop fittings
Open Mon–Fri 10am–6pm
Sat by appointment
Services Valuations, framing, mirror restoration

Travers Antiques
Contact Mr S Kluth
71 Bell Street, London, NW1 6SX
020 7723 4376
Est. 1976 *Stock size* Large
Stock 1820–1920 furniture, decorative items
Open Mon–Sat 10.30am–5pm
Services Valuations, restorations

David J Wilkins
Contact Alex Wilkins
27 Princess Road, Regents Park, London, NW1 8JR
020 7722 7608 020 7483 0423
alexdwilkins@hotmail.com
www.orientalrugexperts.com
Est. 1990 *Stock size* Large
Stock Antique oriental rugs
Open Mon–Fri by appointment only

NW2

G and F Gillingham Ltd
Contact Mr Gillingham
62 Menelik Road, London, NW2 3RH
020 7435 5644 020 7435 5644
07958 484140
Est. 1960
Stock 1750–1950 furniture
Open By appointment
Services Valuations, exports, restorations

Gladstone's Furniture
Contact Mr Anthony Dwyer
1 Gladstone Parade, Off Edgware Road, London, NW2 1UJ
020 8208 1010 020 8450 9296
info@qfw.co.uk
www.qfw.co.uk
Est. 1998 *Stock size* Medium
Stock Reproduction Italian and French ormolu furniture, Victorian–Edwardian furniture
Open Mon–Sun 10.30am–6pm
Fairs Newark, Wembley
Services Repair, restoration

Quality Furniture Warehouse
Contact Mr Anthony Dwyer
Ionna House, Humber Road, London, NW2 6EN
020 8830 5888 020 8450 9296
info@qfw.co.uk
www.qfw.co.uk
Est. 1981 *Stock size* Large
Stock Victorian–Edwardian furniture and earlier, quality used furniture, English and Continental, reproduction French and Italian ormolu furniture
Open Sat Sun 10.30am–5.30pm or by appointment
Fairs Newark, Wembley
Services Restorations, repairs

Sabera Trading Oriental Carpets & Rugs
Contact Nawrozzadeh
Coles Green Road, London, NW2 7EU
020 8450 0012 020 8450 0012
Est. 1992 *Stock size* Medium
Stock Oriental carpets, rugs, Chinese porcelain, jewellery
Open Mon–Sat 10am–6pm

NW3

Keith Fawkes
Contact Keith Fawkes
1/3 Flask Walk, Hampstead, London, NW3 1HJ P
☎ 020 7435 0614 Ⓜ 07939 000921
Est. 1967 *Stock size* Large
Stock Antiquarian and second-hand books
Open Mon–Sat 10am–5.30pm Sun 1pm
Services Valuations

Brian Fielden (BADA)
Contact Brian Fielden
7 Chalcot Gardens, London, NW3 4YB P
☎ 020 7722 9192 Ⓕ 020 7722 9192
Est. 1965 *Stock size* Small
Stock English 18th–early 19thC furniture
Open By appointment

Gillian Gould Antiques
Contact Gill Gould
18a Belsize Park Gardens, Belsize Park, London, NW3 4LH P
☎ 020 7419 0500 Ⓕ 020 7419 0400
Ⓜ 07831 150060
Ⓔ gillgould@dealwith.com
Est. 1989 *Stock size* Small
Stock Scientific, marine, general gifts
Open By appointment only
Services Valuations, restorations

Hampstead Antique and Craft Emporium
Contact Mrs N Apple
12 Heath Street, London, NW3 6TE P
☎ 020 7794 3297 Ⓕ 020 7794 4620
Est. 1976 *Stock size* Large
No. of dealers 20
Stock Furniture, jewellery, first-edition teddy bears, trimmings, buttons, paintings, prints, gifts
Open Tues–Fri 10.30am–5.30pm Sat 10am–6pm courtyard open Sun 11.30am–5.30pm
Services Coffee shop

Sylvia Powell Decorative Arts (BADA, LAPADA)
Contact Mrs S Powell
400 Ceramic House, 573 Finchley Road, London, NW3 7BN P
Ⓜ 07802 714998
Ⓔ dpowell909@aol.com
Ⓦ www.sylvia-powell.com
Est. 1987 *Stock size* Large
Stock Art pottery, 20thC decorative arts
Open By appointment
Fairs Olympia, NEC, Harrogate, BADA
Services Valuations

Recollections Antiques Ltd
Contact Mrs June Gilbert
The Courtyard, Hampstead Antiques Emporium, 12 Heath Street, Hampstead, London, NW3 6TE P
☎ 020 7431 9907 Ⓕ 020 7794 9743
Ⓜ 07930 394014
Ⓔ junalantiques@aol.com
Est. 1991 *Stock size* Large
Stock Early 19thC blue-and-white transfer-printed pottery, early pine, miniature furniture, children's highchairs, kitchenware, collectors' teddy bears
Open Tues–Sat 10.30am–5pm

Malcolm Rushton Early Oriental Art
Contact Malcolm Rushton
Studio 3, 13 Belsize Grove, London, NW3 4UX P
☎ 020 7722 1989 Ⓕ 020 7722 1989
Ⓔ malcolmrushton@yahoo.co.uk
Est. 1988 *Stock size* Small
Stock Early Chinese pottery and bronze
Open By appointment

M & D Seligman (BADA)
Contact M or D Seligman
26 Belsize Park Gardens, London, NW3 4LH P
☎ 020 7722 4315 Ⓕ 020 7722 4315
Ⓜ 07946 634429
Est. 1947 *Stock size* Small
Stock Sophisticated 16th–early 19thC country furniture, associated works of art, antiquities
Open By appointment

Villa Grisebach Art Auctions
Contact Mrs Sabina Fliri
27 Kemplay Road, London, NW3 1TA
☎ 020 7431 9882 Ⓕ 020 7431 9756
Ⓦ www.villa-grisebach.de
Est. 1986
Open By appointment
Sales 19th–20thC art and photography, phone for details
Frequency Bi-annual in Berlin
Catalogues Yes

David Wainwright
Contact Mr D Wainwright
28 Rosslyn Hill, London, NW3 1NH
☎ 020 7431 5900
Stock Antique and old furniture, decorative items from India, Indonesia, China
Open Mon–Sat 10am–7pm Sun 11am–7pm
Services Delivery

NW4

Murray Cards (International) Ltd
Contact Mr I Murray
51 Watford Way, Hendon, London, NW4 3JH
☎ 020 8202 5688 Ⓕ 020 8203 7878
Ⓔ murraycards@ukbusiness.com
Ⓦ www.murraycards.com
Est. 1965 *Stock size* Large
Stock Cigarette and trading cards, albums, frames, books
Open Mon–Fri 9am–5pm
Services Annual Catalogue, auction catalogue

The Talking Machine
Contact Mr D Smith
30 Watford Way, London, NW4 3AL P
☎ 020 8202 3473
Ⓜ 07774 103139
Ⓔ davepaul50@hotmail.com
Ⓦ www.gramophones.endirect.co.uk
Est. 1975 *Stock size* Large
Stock Mechanical antiques, typewriters, radios, music boxes, photographs, sewing machines, juke boxes, calculators, televisions
Open Variable or by appointment
Services Valuations, restorations

NW6

Brondesbury Architectural Reclamation (SALVO)
Contact Tony Carroll
The Yard, 136 Willesden Lane, London, NW6 7TE P
☎ 020 7328 0820 Ⓕ 020 7328 0280
Est. 1993 *Stock size* Large

Stock Period fireplaces, cast-iron radiators, period doors, garden statuary, door furniture, sanitary ware, stained glass
Open Mon–Sat 10am–6pm

Frosts
Contact Mrs D Frost
205–207 West End Lane, London, NW6 1XF
☎ 020 7372 5788 Ⓕ 020 7372 5788
Est. 1989 *Stock size* Medium
Stock Pine, painted country furniture, textiles, porcelain, blue-and-white china, kitchenware
Open Mon–Sat 11am–5.30pm

Gallery Kaleidoscope incorporating Scope Antiques
Contact Mr K Barrie
64–66 Willesden Lane, London, NW6 7SX Ⓟ
☎ 020 7328 5833 Ⓕ 020 7624 2913
Est. 1970 *Stock size* Large
Stock Furniture, interior decorators' pieces, paintings, prints, sculptures, glass
Open Tues–Sat 10am–6pm
Thur 10am–9pm
Services Valuations, framing, silverwork

NW8

Alfie's Antique Market
Contact Rosalind Mena
13–25 Church Street, London, NW8 8DT Ⓟ
☎ 020 7723 6066 Ⓕ 020 7724 0999
Ⓔ post@ealfies.com
Ⓦ www.ealfies.com
No. of dealers 200
Stock General antiques, collectables, 20thC design
Open Tues–Sat 10am–6pm
Services Restoration, bureau de change, rooftop restaurant

Beverley
Contact Beverley
30 Church Street, Marylebone, London, NW8 8EP Ⓟ
☎ 020 7262 1576 Ⓕ 020 7262 1576
Ⓜ 07776 136003
Est. 1958 *Stock size* Large
Stock 1850–1950 English ceramics, glass, metal, wood, pottery, collectables, decorative items
Open Mon–Fri 10.30am–6pm
Sat 9.30am–6pm or by appointment
Fairs NEC, Peterborough Festival of Antiques
Services Mail order worldwide

D and A Binder
Contact Mr D Binder
34 Church Street, London, NW8 8EP Ⓟ
☎ 020 7723 0542 Ⓕ 020 7607 7800
Est. 1979 *Stock size* Large
Stock Period shop fittings, counters, cabinets
Open Tues–Sat 10am–5pm
Services Restorations

Bizarre
Contact Mr V Conti or Mr A Taramasco
24 Church Street, London, NW8 8EP Ⓟ
☎ 020 7724 1305 Ⓕ 020 7724 1316
Est. 1982 *Stock size* Large
Stock Art Deco, Continental furniture, wrought iron, glass, ceramics
Open Mon–Fri 10am–5pm
Sat 10am–4pm
Services Interior design

S Brunswick
Contact Ms S Brunswick
Alfie's, 13 Church Street, London, NW8 8DT Ⓟ
☎ 020 7724 9097 Ⓕ 020 8902 5656
Est. 1988 *Stock size* Large
Stock Functional and decorative furnishings for house, garden, conservatory
Open Tues–Sat 10am–6pm
Services Restorations, delivery

Camden Art Gallery
Contact Robert Gordon or Alan Silver
22 Church Street, London, NW8 8EP
☎ 020 7262 3613 Ⓕ 020 7723 1010
Stock size Large
Stock Paintings, 18th–early 20thC furniture
Open Tues–Sat 10am–6pm

Church Street Antiques
Contact Stuart Shuster
8 Church Street, London, NW8 8ED Ⓟ
☎ 020 7723 7415 Ⓕ 020 7723 7415
Est. 1980 *Stock size* Large
Stock 18th–20thC furniture, decorative items
Open Tues–Sat 10am–6pm

Davidson & Morgan
Contact Edward Davidson
5 Church Street, London, NW8 8EE Ⓟ
☎ 020 7724 9236 Ⓕ 020 7724 9387
Ⓔ enquiries@davidsonandmorgan.com
Ⓦ www.davidsonandmorgan.com
Est. 1958 *Stock size* Medium
Stock Furniture, decorative objects, clocks, chandeliers, lighting, architectural antiques
Open Mon–Sun 10am–6pm

Gallery of Antique Costume & Textiles
Contact L Segal
2 Church Street, London, NW8 8ED Ⓟ
☎ 020 7723 9981 Ⓕ 020 7723 9981
Ⓔ info@gact.co.uk
Ⓦ www.gact.co.uk
Est. 1980 *Stock size* Medium
Stock Antique textiles, curtains, cushions, antique costumes, mainly 1920s and 1930s, textiles by Lalya Moussa
Open Mon–Sat 10am–5.30pm
Fairs HALI Antique Textile Art Fair, Olympia

Gardiner & Gardiner
Contact Mrs H Gardiner
Stand FO13, Alfie's Antique Market, Church Street, London, NW8 8DT Ⓟ
☎ 020 7723 5595
Est. 1969 *Stock size* Medium
Stock Decorative items, interior accessories, Paisley and cashmere shawls
Open Tues–Sat 10am–6pm

Goldsmith & Perris (LAPADA)
Contact Mrs Goldsmith
13–25 Church Street, London, NW8 8DT Ⓟ
☎ 020 7724 7051 Ⓕ 020 7724 7051
Ⓜ 07831 447432
Ⓔ gandpalfies@aol.com
Est. 1975 *Stock size* Medium
Stock Antique silver, silver plate, lamps, collectables, cocktail shakers
Open Tues–Sat 10am–6pm
Fairs Portobello, Covent Garden
Services Valuations

Patricia Harvey Antiques (LAPADA)
Contact Mrs P Harvey
42 Church Street, London, NW8 8EP
020 7262 8989 020 7262 8989
info@patriciaharveyantiques.co.uk
www.patriciaharveyantiques.co.uk
Est. 1960 *Stock size* Large
Stock 18th–19thC English, French furniture, decorative, paintings, unusual objects,
Open Mon–Sat 10am–5.30pm
Fairs Decorative Antiques & Textiles Fair (Jan, April, Sept)
Services Valuations

Just Desks (LAPADA)
Contact Noelle Finch
20 Church Street, London, NW8 8EP
020 7723 7976 020 7402 6416
Est. 1972 *Stock size* Small
Stock Desks, tables, chairs, filing cabinets
Open Mon–Sat 9.30am–6pm

Marie Antiques
Stand G136–138, Alfie's Antique Market, 13–25 Church Street, London, NW8 8DT
020 7706 3727
marie136@globalnet.co.uk
www.marieantiques.co.uk
Est. 1987 *Stock size* Large
Stock Jewellery 1830–1930
Open Tues–Sat 10am–4.30pm
Services Valuations, restorations, shipping

Andrew Nebbett Antiques
Contact Andrew Nebbett
33–37 Church Street, Marylebone, London, NW8 8ES
020 7723 2303 07768 741595
anebbett@aol.com
Est. 1999 *Stock size* Large
Stock Simple, large, English and Swedish oak 17th–20thC
Open Tues–Sat 10am–5.30pm

Tara Antiques
Contact Mr G Robinson
6 Church Street, London, NW8 8ED
020 7724 2405
Est. 1984 *Stock size* Large
Stock Eclectic mix of decorative furniture and items, ivories, sculptures
Open Tues–Fri 10am–6pm Sat 1.30–6pm
Fairs Fine Art, Olympia, Decorative Textile Fairs, Battersea

Tin Tin Collectables
Contact Mr P Pinnington
Ground Units 38–42, Alfie's Antique Market, 13–25 Church Street, London, NW8 8DT
020 7258 1305
tin.tin@teleregion.co.uk
www.tintincollectables.com
Est. 1995 *Stock size* Large
Stock Handbags, Victorian–present day, decorative evening bags, luggage
Open Tues–Sat 10am–6pm
Fairs Sandown Park, Bath, Manchester
Services Valuations, film and TV hire

Wellington Gallery (LAPADA)
Contact Mrs M Barclay
1 St John's Wood High Street, London, NW8 7NG
020 7586 2620 020 7483 0716
Est. 1979
Stock Porcelain, silver, general antiques
Open Mon–Fri 10.30am–6pm Sat 10am–6pm

Young & Son (LAPADA)
Contact Mr Young
12 Church Street, London, NW8 8EP
020 7723 5910 07958 437043
www.youngandson.com
Est. 1990 *Stock size* Medium
Stock 18th–20thC antique decorative furniture, 19thC pictures, drawings, prints, fine frames, lighting, mirrors, oddities
Open Tues–Fri 10am–5.30pm Sat 11am–5.30pm
Services Valuations

NW10

Retrouvius Architectural Reclamation (SALVO)
Contact Adam Hills
2A Ravensworth Road, London, NW10 5NR
020 7724 3387 07778 210855
mail@retrouvius.com
www.retrouvius.com
Est. 1992 *Stock size* Medium
Stock Architectural antiques, reclamation
Open By appointment
Fairs Newark
Services Design service

Willesden Green Architectural Salvage
Contact Mr D Harkin
189 High Road, Willesden, London, NW10 2SD
020 8459 2947 020 8451 1515
Est. 1994 *Stock size* Large
Stock Radiators, stained glass windows, pine doors, lighting, architectural salvage, fireplaces
Open Mon–Sat 9am–6pm

SOUTH

SE1

The Antiques Exchange
Contact Ray Gibbs
170–172 Tower Bridge Road, London, SE1 3LS
020 7403 5568 020 7378 8828
info@AntiquesExchange.com
www.AntiquesExchange.com
Est. 1966 *Stock size* Large
Stock Furniture, glass, china, collectables, period style ighting
Open Mon–Fri 10am–6pm Sat10.30am–6pm Sun 11am–5pm

Antiques Trade Warehouse
Contact Mrs McCarthy
1 Bermondsey Square, London, SE1 3UN
020 7394 7856
Est. 1979 *Stock size* Medium
Stock Wide range of furniture, collectors' items
Open By appointment, trade welcome
Services Shipping

Sebastiano Barbagallo Antiques
Contact Mr S Barbagallo
Universal House, 294–304 St James's Road, London, SE1 5JX
020 7231 3680 020 7231 3680
Est. 1978 *Stock size* Large
Stock Chinese furniture, Indian and Tibetan antiques, crafts
Open By appointment only

Bermondsey Antiques Market
Contact Mike Spooner
✉ **Corner of Long Lane, Bermondsey Street, Bermondsey Square, London, SE1 3TQ** P
☎ 020 7969 1500 F 020 7969 1639
Est. 1950 *Stock size* Large
No. of dealers 400
Stock Wide range of general antiques and collectables, including specialists in jewellery and silver
Open Fri 5am–2pm and Bank Holidays

Victor Burness Antiques
✉ **241 Long Lane, Bermondsey, London, SE1 4PR** P
☎ 01732 454591
Est. 1975
Stock Scientific instruments
Open Fri 6am–12.30pm
Services Valuations, restorations

The Galleries Ltd
Contact Alan Bennett
✉ **157 Tower Bridge Road, London, SE1 3LW** P
☎ 020 7407 5371 F 020 7403 0359
Est. 1993 *Stock size* Large
No. of dealers 28
Stock Victorian, Edwardian, reproduction furniture, Arts and Crafts, Art Nouveau, reproduction leather Chesterfields
Open Mon–Thurs 9.30am–5.30pm Fri 8am–4pm Sat noon–6pm Sun noon–5pm

LASSCO Flooring (SALVO, Timber Trade Federation, TRADA)
Contact Bob Lovell
✉ **41 Maltby Street, London, SE1 3PA** P
☎ 020 7237 4488 F 020 7237 2564
E flooring@lassco.co.uk
W www.lassco.co.uk
Est. 1978 *Stock size* Large
Stock Reclaimed timber flooring in parquet strip and board
Open Mon–Sat 10am–5pm
Services Shipping

LASSCO RBK (SALVO)
Contact Bill Murphy or Douglas Kirk
✉ **41 Maltby Street, London, SE1 3PA** P
☎ 020 7336 8221 F 020 7336 8224
E rbk@lassco.co.uk
W www.lassco.co.uk
Est. 1978 *Stock size* Large
Stock Reclaimed radiators, bathrooms, kitchens
Open Mon–Sat 10am–5pm
Services Shipping

Mayfair Carpet Gallery Ltd
Contact Mr A H Khawaja
✉ **301–303 Borough High Street, London, SE1 1JH** P
☎ 020 7403 8228 F 020 7407 1649
Est. 1975 *Stock size* Large
Stock Fine antique Oriental carpets, rugs
Open Mon–Sat 10.30am–6.30pm
Services Valuations, restorations

Radio Days
Contact Mrs C Layzell
✉ **87 Lower Marsh, London, SE1 7AB** P
☎ 020 7928 0800 F 020 7928 0800
Est. 1993 *Stock size* Large
Stock 1930s–1970s lighting, telephones, radios, clothing, magazines, cocktail bars
Open Mon–Sat 11am–5pm or by appointment

Tower Bridge Antiques
Contact Joan Carter
✉ **71 Tanner Street, London, SE1 3PL** P
☎ 020 7403 3660 F 020 7403 6058
E towerbridgeant@aol.com
Est. 1967 *Stock size* Large
Stock A very large selection of English, French and American furniture
Open Mon–Fri 8am–5pm Sat 10am–6pm Sun 11am–5pm

G Viventi
Contact Giorgio
✉ **160 Tower Bridge Road, London, SE1 3LS** P
☎ 020 7403 0022 F 020 7394 1001
E viventi@btinternet.com
Est. 2000 *Stock size* Large
Stock Wide range of furniture, styles and periods
Open Mon–Sat 9.30am–6pm

SE3

The Bookshop Blackheath Ltd (ABA)
Contact Mr L Leff
✉ **74 Tranquil Vale, London, SE3 0BN** P
☎ 020 8852 4786
Est. 1947 *Stock size* Large
Stock Second-hand, new, antiquarian books, prints, maps
Open Mon–Sat 9am–4.30pm
Services Valuations, book search

Vale Stamps and Antiques (BNTA)
Contact Richard Varnham
✉ **21 Tranquil Vale, Blackheath, London, SE3 0BU** P
☎ 020 8852 9817
Est. 1952 *Stock size* Medium
Stock Georgian–Edwardian jewellery, ancient and medieval coins
Open Mon–Sat 10am–5.30pm closed Thur

SE4

Original Door Specialist (SALVO)
Contact Mr D Slattery
✉ **93 Endwell Road, Brockley Cross, London, SE4 2NF** P
☎ 020 7252 8109
Stock Doors, tables, flooring, handles, general architectural salvage
Open Mon–Sat 9am–6pm

SE5

Architectural Rescue
Contact Mr J Powell
✉ **1 Southampton Way, London, SE5 7JH** P
☎ 020 7277 0081 F 020 7277 0081
Est. 1993 *Stock size* Large
Stock Flooring, radiators, sanitary ware, doors, door furniture, fireplaces a speciality, York stone
Open Mon–Sat 10am–5pm Sun 10am–2pm
Fairs Newark, Swinderby

Camberwell Architectural Salvage & Antiques
Contact Mr M Tree
✉ **47 Southampton Way, London, SE5 7SW** P
☎ 020 7277 0315 M 07957 249722

Ⓔ matt.tree@btopenworld.com
Ⓦ www.camberwellsalvage.co.uk
Est. 1993 *Stock size* Medium
Stock Period doors, floor boards, stained-glass windows, fireplaces, cast-iron radiators, fixtures, fittings, sinks, basins, roll-top baths, taps, multi-fuel stoves
Open Tues–Sat 10am–5pm or by appointment
Services Fireplace fitting

SE6

The Old Mill
Contact Mr A Jackson
358 Bromley Road, Catford, London, SE6 2RT Ⓟ
☎ 020 8697 8006
Est. 1845 *Stock size* Medium
Stock Garden statuary, fireplaces
Open Mon–Sat 9.30am–5pm

Wilkinson PLC
Contact Jane Milnes
5 Catford Hill, London, SE6 4NU Ⓟ
☎ 020 8314 1080 Ⓕ 020 8690 1524
Ⓔ enquiries@wilkinson-plc.com
Ⓦ www.wilkinson-plc.com
Est. 1946 *Stock size* Large
Stock Lighting, chandeliers, candelabra
Open Mon–Fri 9am–5pm
Services Restorations

SE7

Ward's Antiques
Contact Terry or Michael Ward
267 Woolwich Road, London, SE7 7RB Ⓟ
☎ 020 8305 0963 Ⓕ 020 8305 2151
Ⓜ 07932 031936
Est. 1977 *Stock size* Large
Stock Victorian and Edwardian fireplaces, general antiques
Open Mon–Sat 9am–6pm Sun 11am–2pm

SE8

Antique Warehouse
Contact Mrs Tillet
9–14 Deptford Broadway, London, SE8 4PA Ⓟ
☎ 020 8691 3062 Ⓕ 020 8469 0295
Ⓔ martin@antiquewarehouse.co.uk
Ⓦ www.antiquewarehouse.co.uk
Est. 1983 *Stock size* Large
Stock General antiques
Open Mon–Sat 10am–6pm Sun 11am–4pm
Services Valuations via website

SE9

Chapman Antiques
Contact Mrs P Chapman
34 Well Hall Road, Eltham, London, SE9 6SF Ⓟ
☎ 020 8850 6464
Est. 1995 *Stock size* Large
Stock Pine furniture, china, collectables, mirrors, glass, garden ornaments
Open Mon–Fri 10am–6pm Sat 4–6pm Sun 2–4pm
Fairs Newark, Ardingly

Cobwebs
Contact Martin Baker
73 Avery Hill Road, New Eltham, London, SE9 2BJ Ⓟ
☎ 020 8850 5611 Ⓜ 0771 243 5842
Est. 1995 *Stock size* Medium
Stock Furniture, general antiques, collectables
Open Mon 2pm–5.30pm Tues Wed Fri Sat 10am–5.30pm
Services Valuations

Eltham Collectables
Contact Sue Almond
5 Arcade Chambers, Eltham High Street, London, SE9 1BG Ⓟ
☎ 020 8850 5001 Ⓜ 07899 758305
Est. 2000 *Stock size* Small
Stock Antiques, collectables, militaria, 1970s clothes section
Open Mon–Sat 10am–5pm

SE10

Beaumont Travel Books (ABA, PBFA, ILAB)
Contact Mr G Beaumont
Unit 6.2.9, Skillion Business Centre, 49 Greenwich High Road, London, SE10 8JL Ⓟ
☎ 020 8691 2023 Ⓕ 020 8691 2023
Ⓔ beaumont@dircon.co.uk
Ⓦ www.abebooks.com/home/beaumont
Est. 1996 *Stock size* Large
Stock Antiquarian, rare, second-hand books, anthropology, military, history, travel, exploration a speciality
Open Mon–Fri 9.30am–2pm or by appointment
Services Valuations, book search

Cassidy's Gallery
Contact Mr M Cassidy
20 College Approach, Greenwich, London, SE10 9HY Ⓟ
☎ 020 8858 7197 Ⓕ 020 8858 7197
Ⓜ 07710 012128
Ⓔ cassidysgallery@aol.com
Est. 1984 *Stock size* Small
Stock Antiquarian, plate books, atlases, illustrated books, maps, prints
Open By appointment
Fairs International Trade Antique Print and Plate Book Dealers Fair

Creek Antiques
Contact Dave
23 Greenwich South Street, London, SE10 8NW Ⓟ
☎ 020 8293 5721 Ⓜ 07778 427521
Est. 1986 *Stock size* Medium
Stock Jewellery, silver, enamel signs, amusement machines
Open By appointment
Fairs Sandown, Newark, Bermondsey

Decomania
Contact Mrs J Crompton
9 College Approach, London, SE10 9HY Ⓟ
☎ 020 8858 8180
Ⓦ www.decormania.co.uk
Est. 1998 *Stock size* Large
Stock Rare pieces of 1920s–1930s Art Deco, pictures, mirrors, furniture, decorative items, jewellery
Open Wed–Sun 10.30am–5.30pm or by appointment
Services Delivery, shipping

Finds
Contact Jeni Ferns
73 Trafalgar Road, London, SE10 9TS Ⓟ
☎ 020 8305 9665 Ⓜ 07778 013096
Est. 1997 *Stock size* Medium
Stock Collectables, furniture, books, pictures, mirrors
Open Mon–Sat 10am–5pm Sun 11am–5pm closed Wed
Fairs Detling, Ardingly
Services Book search

Flying Duck Enterprises
Contact Mr J Lowe or Ms C Shrosbree
320–322 Creek Road, Greenwich, London, SE10 9SW Ⓟ
☎ 020 8858 1964 Ⓕ 020 8852 3215
Ⓜ 07831 273303

ⓔ jimllkitschit@flying-duck.com
Est. 1985 *Stock size* Large
Stock 1950–1970s items, cocktail bars, furniture, lighting, fabrics, dinette sets, glassware, china, 1950s fridges
Open Tues–Fri noon–6pm
Sat Sun 10.30am–6pm
Services Mail order

Greenwich Collectables
Contact Lynn Lennon or Steve Mead
3–4 Nelson Road, London, SE10 9JB
☎ 020 8858 3311 ⓕ 020 8858 3311
ⓦ www.greenwichcollectables.com
Est. 1998 *Stock size* Large
Stock Ceramics, teddies
Open Mon–Sun 10am–5pm

Greenwich Gallery
Contact Richard Moy
9 Nevada Street, London, SE10 9JL
☎ 020 8305 1666 ext 24
ⓦ www.spreadeagle.org
Est. 1957 *Stock size* Medium
Stock 18th–19thC watercolours, modern British art, prints
Open Mon–Sun 10.30am–5.30pm

The Junk Box
Contact Mrs M Dodd
47 Old Woolwich Road, Greenwich, London, SE10 9PP
☎ 020 8293 5715
Est. 1988 *Stock size* Large
Stock Antiques, collectables, Victorian furniture, china, glass, copper, brass, kitchenware
Open Mon–Sun 10am–5pm
Services Bespoke framing, valuations

The Junk Shop
Contact Tobias Moy
9 Greenwich South Street, London, SE10 8NW
☎ 020 8305 1666 ext 25
ⓦ www.spreadeagle.org
Est. 1985
Stock Larger period furniture, architectural antiques, garden ornaments, decorative items
Open Mon–Sun 10.30am–5.30pm

Lamont Antiques Ltd (LAPADA)
Contact Mr F Llewellyn
Unit K, Tunnel Avenue Trading Estate, Greenwich, London, SE10 0QH
☎ 020 8305 2230 ⓕ 020 8305 1805
Est. 1974 *Stock size* Large
Stock Architectural items, stained glass, pub and restaurant fixtures, fittings
Open Mon–Fri 9.30am–5pm

Peter Laurie Maritime Antiques
Contact Mr P Laurie
28 Greenwich Church Street, Greenwich, London, SE10 9BJ
☎ 020 8853 5777 ⓕ 020 8853 5777
ⓜ 0771 8033150
ⓔ plaurie@maritimeantiques-uk.com
ⓦ www.maritimeantiques-uk.com
Est. 1978 *Stock size* Large
Stock Nautical, maritime items, navigational, scientific instruments, clocks, barometers, regalia, antique prints
Open Mon–Thurs Sat Sun 10.30am–5pm Fri 1–5pm

Marcet Books (PBFA)
Contact Mr M Kemp
4a Nelson Road, Greenwich, London, SE10 9JB
☎ 020 8853 5408
ⓔ marcet@dircon.co.uk
ⓦ www.marcetbooks.co.uk
Est. 1980 *Stock size* Medium
Stock Antiquarian, rare, second-hand books, maritime, foreign travel, British topography, art, natural history, poetry, specialities
Open Mon–Sun 10am–5.30pm
Fairs PBFA, Russell Hotel
Services Valuations

The Old Bottle Shop
Contact D Farrell
Unit 7, 17/18 Stockwell Street, Greenwich, London, SE10 9JN
ⓕ 020 8488 7048 ⓜ 07930 200584
ⓔ farrellinv@hotmail.com
Est. 1999 *Stock size* Large
Stock Antique bottles, breweriana
Open Mon & Wed 10.30am–4pm Fri 2–4pm Sat 10.30am–5.30pm Sun 8.30am–5.30pm
Fairs Ardingly
Services Valuations, shipping

Rogers Turner Books (ABA, PBFA)
Contact Mr P Rogers
23a Nelson Road, Greenwich, London, SE10 9JB
☎ 020 8853 5271 ⓕ 020 8853 5271
ⓔ rogersturner@compuserve.com
Est. 1976 *Stock size* Medium
Stock Rare, antiquarian and second-hand books on experimental science, scientific instruments, horology, dialling a speciality
Open Thurs Fri 10am–6pm or by appointment
Fairs ABA Fairs, Olympia, PBFA London (monthly)
Services Valuations, catalogues

Spread Eagle Antiques
Contact Richard Moy
1 Stockwell Street, London, SE10 9JN
☎ 020 8305 1666 ext 22
ⓦ www.spreadeagle.org
Est. 1957 *Stock size* Medium
Stock Antique furniture, silver, decorative antiques, curios, ethnic art
Open Mon–Sun 10.30am–5.30pm

Spread Eagle Books
Contact Richard Moy
8 Nevada Street, London, SE10 9JL
☎ 020 8305 1666 ext 23
ⓦ www.spreadeagle.org
Est. 1957 *Stock size* Medium
Stock Antiquarian books, collectables, ephemera
Open Mon–Sun 10.30am–5.30pm

The Warwick Leadlay Gallery (FATG)
Contact Mr Anthony Cross
5 Nelson Road, London, SE10 9JB
☎ 020 8858 0317 ⓕ 020 8853 1773
ⓔ wlg@ceasynet.co.uk
ⓦ www.wlgonline.com
Est. 1974 *Stock size* Large
Stock Antique maps, decorative maritime prints, fine arts, curios
Open Mon–Sat 9.30am–5.30pm Sun 11.30am–5.30pm
Services Valuations, restorations, conservation, framing

The Waterloo Trading Co
Contact Robert Boys
Unit D, Tunnel Avenue Trading Estate, Tunnel Avenue, Greenwich, London, SE10 0QH

☎ 020 8858 3355 Ⓕ 020 8858 3344
Ⓔ boysship@ftech.co.uk
Est. 1989 *Stock size* Large
Stock 10,000 sq ft of antique furniture
Open Mon–Fri 8am–6pm
Services Shipping

⊞ Robert Whitfield (LAPADA)
Contact Mr R Whitfield
✉ **Unit K, Tunnel Avenue Trading Estate, Greenwich, London, SE10 0QH** Ⓟ
☎ 020 8305 2230 Ⓕ 020 8305 1805
Ⓔ robertwhitfield@btinternet.com
Est. 1974 *Stock size* Large
Stock Oak, mahogany, walnut furniture
Trade only Yes
Open Mon–Fri 9am–5pm or by appointment

SE11

⊞ Kear of Kennington Antiques
Contact Mr S A Kear
✉ **4 Windmill Row, London, SE11 5DW** Ⓟ
☎ 020 7735 1304
Est. 1968 *Stock size* Small
Stock 18thC English drinking glasses, pottery, porcelain
Open By appointment

SE12

⊞ Book Aid Charitable Trust
Contact Mrs A Hiley
✉ **Christian Fellowship, Mayeswood Road, Grove Park, London, SE12** Ⓟ
☎ 020 8857 7794 Ⓕ 020 8857 9565
Est. 1987 *Stock size* Large
Stock Antiquarian, rare, second-hand religious books, bibles, general books
Open Thurs 9am–5pm or by appointment

SE13

⊞ The Old Station
Contact Mr R Jacob
✉ **72 Loampit Hill, Lewisham, London, SE13 7SX** Ⓟ
☎ 020 8694 6540/020 8692 8395
Ⓕ 020 8692 6824 Ⓜ 07710 489895
Ⓔ rob.jacob@btinternet.com
Ⓦ www.the-old-station.co.uk
Est. 1995 *Stock size* Large
Stock Large varied stock, architectural salvage, fireplaces, antique furniture, chimney pieces, sanitary ware
Open Mon–Sat 10am–5pm Sun by appointment only
Fairs Newark, Ardingly
Services Door stripping, fireplace restoration

SE17

⊞ Pub Paraphernalia UK Ltd
Contact Mr M Ellis
✉ **Unit 13, Newington Industrial Estate, Crampton Street, London, SE17 3AZ** Ⓟ
☎ 020 7701 8913 Ⓕ 020 7277 4100
Ⓔ sales@pub-paraphernalia.com
Ⓦ www.pub-paraphernalia.com
Est. 1980 *Stock size* Medium
Stock Water jugs, bar towels, beer mats, glassware, ashtrays, mirrors
Open Mon–Fri 9am–5pm by appointment
Fairs NEC (Spring)

SE19

⊞ The Book Palace
Contact Mr K Harman or Mr G West
✉ **Jubilee House, Bedwardine Road, London, SE19 3AP** Ⓟ
☎ 020 8768 0022 Ⓕ 020 8768 0563
Ⓔ david@totalise.co.uk
Ⓦ www.bookpalace.com
Est. 1996 *Stock size* Large
Stock Histories of comics and popular media, art books, science fiction, film and TV biographies, Disney, animation, old US and UK comics, pulps, paperbacks, graphic novels
Open Mon–Fri 10am–6pm or by appointment
Fairs CIAMA, London Memorabilia Fair, NEC
Services Valuations, wanted titles list

SE20

⊞ Bearly Trading of London
Contact Cindy Hamilton-Aust
✉ **202 High Street, London, SE20 7QB** Ⓟ
☎ 020 8659 0500/8466 6696
Ⓕ 020 8460 3166
Est. 1998 *Stock size* Large
Stock Old and new artists' teddy bears, rocking horses, antique furniture
Open Sat 10am–6pm or by appointment
Fairs Kensington Bear Fair (Nov)
Services Lay-a-way, mail order

SE21

⊞ Francis Jevons
Contact Mr F Jevons
✉ **80 Dulwich Village, London, SE21 7AJ** Ⓟ
☎ 020 8693 1991
Est. 1983 *Stock size* Small
Stock Antique furniture, china, glass, interior design items
Open Mon–Fri 9.30am–1pm 2.30–5.30pm Sat close 5pm closed Wed
Services Valuations, restorations

SE22

⊞ Melbourne Antiques & Interiors
Contact Ian Peters
✉ **67 Lordship Lane, London, SE22 8EP** Ⓟ
☎ 020 8299 6565 Ⓕ 020 8299 4257
Ⓔ ian@melbourneantiques.co.uk
Ⓦ www.melbourneantiques.co.uk
Est. 1998 *Stock size* Large
Stock French furniture, mirrors, chandeliers, armoires, beds, commodes, linens, fire surrounds
Open Mon–Sat 10am–6pm

⊞ Melbourne Antiques & Interiors
Contact Ian Peters
✉ **8 Melbourne Grove, London, SE22 8QZ** Ⓟ
☎ 020 8299 6565 Ⓕ 020 8299 4257
Ⓔ melbourneantiques@lineone.net
Est. 1998 *Stock size* Large
Stock French furniture, mirrors, chandeliers, armoires, linens, beds, commodes, fire surrounds
Open Mon–Sat 10am–6pm or by appointment

⊞ Still Useful
Contact Mr R H Honour
✉ **52 Grove Vale, London, SE22 8DY** Ⓟ

LONDON

☎ 020 8299 2515
Est. 1979 *Stock size* Large
Stock Oak and mahogany furniture, decorative items, lighting
Open Mon–Sat 10am–5pm

SE24

Under Milkwood Fireplaces
Contact Nick or Sue Williams
379 Milkwood Road, London, SE24 1HB
☎ 020 7733 3921
Ⓜ 07801 219156/7
Est. 1987 *Stock size* Medium
Stock Mantel pieces, chimney pieces
Open Mon–Sat 9.30am–4pm

SE26

Grenadiers
Contact Mr C Chin-See
102 Sydenham Road, London, SE26 5JX
☎ 020 8659 1588 Ⓕ 020 8659 1588
Ⓔ grenadiers@btinternet.com
Ⓦ www.grenadiers.co.uk
Est. 1998 *Stock size* Medium
Stock Wide range of militaria
Open Mon–Fri 9.30am–6pm
Sat 9.30am–5.30pm

Oola Boola Antiques London
Contact Mrs S Bramley
139–147 Kirkdale, London, SE26 4QJ
☎ 020 8291 9999 Ⓕ 020 8291 5759
Ⓜ 07956 261252
Ⓔ oola.boola@telco4u.net
Est. 1970 *Stock size* Large
Stock Victorian, Edwardian, Art Nouveau, Art Deco, Arts and Crafts furniture
Open Mon–Sat 10am–6pm, Sun 11am–5pm
Services Restorations, shipping

Sydenham Antiques Centre
Contact Mr P Cockton
48 Sydenham Road, London, SE26 5QF
☎ 020 8778 1706
Est. 1996 *Stock size* Large
No. of dealers 10
Stock Antiques, china, glass, furniture, jewellery, pictures, silver
Open Mon–Sat 10am–5pm

Vintage Cameras Ltd
Contact John or Mark Jenkins
256 Kirkdale, London, SE26 4NL
☎ 020 8778 5416 Ⓕ 020 8778 5841
Ⓔ info@vintagecameras.co.uk
Ⓦ www.vintagecameras.co.uk
Est. 1970 *Stock size* Large
Stock Antique and modern cameras, photographica, classic cameras
Open Mon–Sat 9am–5pm
Services Repairs

SE27

Rosebery Fine Art Ltd (ISVA)
Contact Miss L Lloyd
74–76 Knights Hill, London, SE27 0JD
☎ 020 8761 2522 Ⓕ 020 8761 2524
Ⓔ auctions@roseberys.co.uk
Ⓦ www.roseberys.co.uk
Est. 1987
Open Mon–Fri 9.30am–5.30pm
Sales Antiques and collectors' sale Tues Wed 11am. General sale Mon 1pm, viewing
Sun 10am–2pm
Mon 10am–7.30pm
Tues Wed 9.30–10.45am.
Quarterly select antiques, Decorative Arts & Modern Design, musical instruments, toys and collectors, books
Frequency Fortnightly
Catalogues Yes

SW1

ADC Heritage Ltd (BADA)
Contact Francis Raeymaekers or Elisabeth Bellord
95a Charlwood Street, London, SW1V 4PB
☎ 020 7976 5271 Ⓕ 020 7828 7432
Ⓜ 07747 692554
Ⓔ elbellord@btinternet.com
Est. 1980 *Stock size* Small
Stock Antique English silver and old Sheffield plate
Open By appointment only
Services Valuations, restorations

Adec Antiques & Interior Design
Contact Mr André de Cacqueray
227 Ebury Street, London, SW1W 8UT
☎ 020 7730 0005 Ⓕ 020 7730 8681
Est. 1992 *Stock size* Medium
Stock 18th–19thC Continental furniture
Open Mon–Fri 10am–6pm
Sat by appointment
Services Interior design

Albert Amor (RWHA)
Contact Mark Law or Nicholas Lyne
37 Bury Street, London, SW1Y 6AU
☎ 020 7930 2444 Ⓕ 020 7930 9067
Ⓔ info@albertamor.co.uk
Ⓦ www.albertamor.co.uk
Est. 1899 *Stock size* Small
Stock 18thC English porcelain
Open Mon–Fri 9.30am–5pm
Fairs Park Lane International Ceramics Fair

Anno Domini Antiques (BADA)
Contact Mr D Cohen
66 Pimlico Road, London, SW1W 8LS
☎ 020 7730 5496
Est. 1969 *Stock size* Large
Stock 18th–19thC furniture, mirrors, pictures, glass, porcelain
Open Mon–Fri 10am–1pm 2.15–5.30pm Sat 10am–3pm or by appointment
Services Valuations, restorations

Antiquus
Contact Elizabeth Amati
90–92 Pimlico Road, London, SW1W 8PL
☎ 020 7730 8681 Ⓕ 020 7823 6409
Ⓔ antiquus@antiquus-london.co.uk
Ⓦ www.antiquus-london.co.uk
Est. 1971 *Stock size* Large
Stock Gothic, Renaissance works of art, sculpture, textiles
Open Mon–Sat 9.30am–5.30pm

The Armoury of St James (OMRS)
Contact Mr Rawlins or Mr Davis
17 Piccadilly Arcade, London, SW1Y 6NH
☎ 020 7493 5082 Ⓕ 020 7499 4422
Ⓔ welcome@armoury.co.uk
Ⓦ www.armoury.co.uk
Est. 1969 *Stock size* Large
Stock Royal memorablilia, model soldiers

Open Mon–Fri 10am–6pm
Sat noon–6pm
Services Valuations, world orders, decorations

⊞ Belgrave Carpet Gallery Ltd
Contact Mr Khawaja
✉ **91 Knightsbridge, London, SW1X 7RV** 🅿
☎ 020 7235 2541 Ⓕ 020 7407 1649
Est. 1975 *Stock size* Large
Stock Antique Oriental carpets
Open Mon–Sat 10.30am–6.30pm

⊞ Blanchard Ltd (LAPADA)
Contact Mr Piers Ingall
✉ **86–88 Pimlico Road, London, SW1W 8PL**
☎ 020 7823 6310 Ⓕ 020 7823 6303
Ⓔ piers@jwblanchard.com
Est. 1989 *Stock size* Medium
Stock English and Continental furniture, decorative items, works of art
Open Mon–Fri 10am–6pm
Sat 10am–3pm
Fairs Olympia (June)
Services Valuations, restorations, shipping

⊞ John Bly (BADA, CINOA)
Contact Mr John Bly or Mr James Bly
✉ **27 Bury Street, London, SW1Y 6AL** 🅿
☎ 020 7930 1292 Ⓕ 020 7839 4775
Ⓔ james@johnbly.com
Ⓦ www.johnbly.com
Est. 1891 *Stock size* Large
Stock 18th–19thC English furniture, works of art, objets d'art, paintings, silver, glass, porcelain, tapestries
Open Mon–Fri 9.30am–5.30pm
Sat by appointment
Fairs Grosvenor House (June), BADA (March), Palm Beach, Florida (Feb)
Services Valuations, restorations

⊞ J H Bourdon-Smith Ltd (BADA, CINOA)
Contact Mr J Bourdon-Smith
✉ **24 Masons Yard, Duke Street, St James's, London, SW1Y 6BU** 🅿
☎ 020 7839 4714 Ⓕ 020 7839 3951
Est. 1953 *Stock size* Large
Stock Georgian–Victorian silver, modern reproduction silver
Open Mon–Fri 9.30am–6pm
Fairs Grosvenor House, BADA, Olympia (Nov)

⊞ John Carlton-Smith (BADA)
Contact Mr J Carlton-Smith
✉ **17 Ryder Street, London, SW1Y 6PY** 🅿
☎ 020 7930 6622 Ⓕ 020 7930 6622
Ⓔ jcarltonsm@aol.com
Ⓦ www.fineartantiqueclocks.com
Est. 1968 *Stock size* Large
Stock Fine antique clocks and barometers
Open Mon–Fri 9am–5.30pm
Fairs March BADA, Grosvenor House, Winter Olympia
Services Valuations

⊞ Chelsea Antique Mirrors
Contact Mr A Koll
✉ **72 Pimlico Road, London, SW1W 8LS** 🅿
☎ 020 7824 8024 Ⓕ 020 7824 8233
Est. 1980 *Stock size* Medium
Stock 18th–19thC mirrors, furniture
Open Mon–Fri 10am–6pm
Sat 10am–2pm
Services Restorations

Christie's
✉ **8 King Street, London, SW1Y 6QT** 🅿
☎ 020 7839 9060 Ⓕ 020 7839 1611
Ⓦ www.christies.com
Est. 1766
Open Mon–Fri 9am–5pm
Sales Sales throughout the year, except Aug and Jan, viewing 4 days prior to sales and weekends, evenings. Free verbal auction estimates
Catalogues Yes

⊞ Ciancimino Ltd
Contact Mr J Ciancimino
✉ **99 Pimlico Road, London, SW1W 8PH** 🅿
☎ 020 7730 9950 Ⓕ 020 7730 5365
Ⓔ info@ciancimino.com
Ⓦ www.ciancimino.com
Est. 1965 *Stock size* Medium
Stock Art Deco furniture, Oriental furniture, ethnography
Open Mon–Fri 10am–6pm
Sat 10am–5pm
Fairs International Fine Art & Antique Dealers Show, New York

⊞ Classic Bindings
Contact Mr S Poklewski-Koziell
✉ **61 Cambridge Street, London, SW1V 4PS** 🅿
☎ 020 7834 5554 Ⓕ 020 7630 6632
Ⓔ info@classicbindings.net
Ⓦ www.classicbindings.net
Est. 1990 *Stock size* Large
Stock General antiquarian books, classic bindings
Open Mon–Fri 9.30am–5.30pm or by appointment
Services Valuations

⊞ Cobra & Bellamy
Contact Tanya Hunter
✉ **149 Sloane Street, London, SW1X 9BZ** 🅿
☎ 020 7730 9993 Ⓕ 020 7824 8996
Ⓔ cobrabellamy@hotmail.com
Est. 1980 *Stock size* Medium
Stock Jewellery, amber, glass, ivory, coral
Open 10.30am–6pm Mon–Sat
Services Valuations

⊞ Peter Dale Ltd (LAPADA)
Contact Mr Robin Dale
✉ **12 Royal Opera Arcade, London, SW1Y 4UY** 🅿
☎ 020 7930 3695 Ⓕ 020 7930 2223
Ⓜ 07785 580396
Ⓔ robin@peterdaleltd.com
Est. 1960 *Stock size* Medium
Stock European antique arms, armour
Open Mon–Fri 9.15am–5pm
Services Valuations

⊞ Kenneth Davis (Works of Art) Ltd
Contact Danielle Fluer
✉ **15 King Street, London, SW1Y 6QU** 🅿
☎ 020 7930 0313 Ⓕ 020 7976 1306
Est. 1965 *Stock size* Medium
Stock Antique English and Continental silver, works of art
Open Mon–Fri 9.30am–5pm
Services Valuations, restorations

⊞ Alastair Dickenson Fine Silver Ltd (BADA)
Contact Mr A Dickenson or Mrs M Cuchet
✉ **90 Jermyn Street, London, SW1Y 6JD** 🅿
☎ 020 7839 2808 Ⓕ 020 7839 2809
Ⓜ 07976 283530
Est. 1996 *Stock size* Small

LONDON

Stock 16th–19thC fine, rare English silver
Open Mon–Fri 9.30am–5.30pm
Services Valuations, restorations

⊞ Didier Aaron (London) Ltd (BADA)
Contact Didier Leblanc
✉ **21 Ryder Street, London, SW1Y 6PX** Ⓟ
☎ 020 7839 4716 Ⓕ 020 7930 6699
Ⓔ contact@didieraaronltd.com
Est. 2985 *Stock size* Medium
Stock 18thC–early 19thC Continental furniture, old master drawings, paintings
Open Mon–Fri 11am–1pm 2–5pm and by appointment
Fairs Maastricht, Paris Bienniale

⊞ Filippa & Co
Contact Filippa Naess
✉ **51 Kinnerton Street, London, SW1X 8ED** Ⓟ
☎ 020 7235 1722 Ⓕ 020 7245 9160
Ⓔ filippa@dircon.co.uk
Ⓦ www.filippaandco.com
Est. 1998 *Stock size* Medium
Stock Swedish furniture, chandeliers, mirrors, decorative accessories
Open Tues–Fri 11am–5.30pm Sat noon–4.30pm Sun by appointment
Services Shipping

⊞ N & I Franklin (BADA)
Contact Mr N Franklin or Mr I Franklin
✉ **11 Bury Street, London, SW1Y 6AB**
☎ 020 7839 3131 Ⓕ 020 7839 3132
Ⓔ neil@franklinsilver.com
Est. 1980 *Stock size* Large
Stock 17th–18thC English domestic silver
Open Mon–Fri 10am–5pm or by appointment
Fairs Grosvenor House
Services Valuations

⊞ J A L Franks and Co
Contact Mr G Franks
✉ **7 Allington Street, London, SW1E 5EB** Ⓟ
☎ 020 7233 8433 Ⓕ 020 7233 8655
Ⓔ jalfranks@btinternet.com
Ⓦ www.jalfranks.btinternet.co.uk
Est. 1947 *Stock size* Medium
Stock 16th–19thC antique maps
Open Mon–Fri 10am–5pm
Fairs Bonnington, IMCOS

⊞ Victor Franses Gallery (BADA)
Contact Graham Franses
✉ **57 Jermyn Street, St James's, London, SW1Y 6LX**
☎ 020 7493 6284/7629 1144
Ⓕ 020 7495 3668
Ⓔ bronzes@vfranses.com
Ⓦ www.vfranses.com
Est. 1972 *Stock size* Large
Stock 19thC animalier sculpture, paintings, drawings, watercolours
Open Mon–Fri 10am–5pm or by appointment
Fairs Grosvenor House
Services Valuations, restorations

⊞ Nicholas Gifford-Mead (BADA, LAPADA)
Contact Mr N Gifford-Mead
✉ **68 Pimlico Road, London, SW1W 8LS** Ⓟ
☎ 020 7730 6233 Ⓕ 020 7730 6239
Est. 1969 *Stock size* Medium
Stock Pre-1840 English and European chimney pieces, sculpture
Open Mon–Fri 9.30am–5.30pm
Services Valuations

⊞ Joss Graham Orientals
Contact Joss Graham
✉ **10 Eccleston Street, London, SW1W 9LT** Ⓟ
☎ 020 7730 8200 Ⓕ 020 7730 4370
Ⓔ jossgraham@btinternet.com
Est. 1982 *Stock size* Large
Stock Oriental antiques
Open Mon–Fri 10am–6pm
Services Valuations, restorations

⊞ Nicolas Guedroitz Ltd
Contact Simon Pugh
✉ **24 Pimlico Road, London, SW1W 8JA** Ⓟ
☎ 020 7730 3111
Ⓕ 020 7730 1441
Ⓔ guedroitz@russianfurniture.co.uk
Ⓦ www.russianfurniture.co.uk
Est. 1996 *Stock size* Medium
Stock 18th–19thC Russian furniture
Open Mon–Fri 10am–5.30pm Sat 10am–1pm

⊞ Ross Hamilton (Antiques) Ltd (LAPADA, CINOA)
Contact Mr C M Boyce
✉ **95 Pimlico Road, London, SW1W 8PH** Ⓟ
☎ 020 7730 3015 Ⓕ 020 7730 3015
Ⓦ www.lapada.co.uk/rosshamilton/
Est. 1973 *Stock size* Large
Stock 17th–19thC fine English/ Continental furniture, 16th–20thC paintings, Oriental porcelain, objets d'art, bronzes
Open Mon–Fri 9am–6pm Sat 10.30am–5pm
Services Shipping worldwide

⊞ Brian Harkins
Contact Ms Erica Quan or Brian Harkins
✉ **3 Bury Street, St James's, London, SW1Y 6AB** Ⓟ
☎ 020 7839 3338 Ⓕ 020 7839 9339
Ⓔ info@brianharkins.co.uk
Ⓦ www.brianharkins.co.uk
Est. 1978
Stock Chinese and Japanese antiques, scholars' items, furniture, decorative items, ceramics, bronzes, rocks, baskets
Open Mon–Fri 10am–6pm

⊞ Harris Lindsay (BADA, CINOA)
Contact Jonathan Harris or Bruce Lindsay
✉ **67 Jermyn Street, London, SW1Y 6NY** Ⓟ
☎ 020 7839 5767 Ⓕ 020 7839 5768
Est. 1967 *Stock size* Medium
Stock English, Continental and Oriental works of art
Open Mon–Fri 9.30am–6pm and by appointment
Fairs Grosvenor House

⊞ Harvey & Gore (BADA)
Contact Barry Norman
✉ **41 Duke Street, St James's, London, SW1Y 6DF** Ⓟ
☎ 020 7839 4033 Ⓕ 020 7839 3313
Ⓔ norman@harveyandgore.co.uk
Est. 1723 *Stock size* Large
Stock Jewellery, bijouterie, snuff boxes, old Sheffield plate, miniatures
Open Mon–Fri 9.30am–5pm
Fairs BADA
Services Valuations, restorations, VAT margin and standard

⊞ Thomas Heneage Art Books (ABA, LAPADA)
Contact Antonia Howard-Sneyd
✉ **42 Duke Street, St James's, London, SW1Y 6DJ** Ⓟ
☎ 020 7930 9223 Ⓕ 020 7839 9223

artbooks@heneage.com
www.heneage.com
Stock size Large
Stock Art reference books
Open Mon–Fri 9.30am–6pm or by appointment
Services Valuations

Hermitage Antiques Plc
Contact Mr Vieux-Pernon
97 Pimlico Road, London, SW1W 8PH
020 7730 1973 020 7730 6586
info@hermitage-antiques.co.uk
www.hermitage-antiques.co.uk
Est. 1970 *Stock size* Large
Stock Biedermeier and Russian furniture, chandeliers, oil paintings, decorative arts, bronzes
Open Mon–Fri 10am–6pm Sat 10am–5pm
Fairs Olympia (June)
Services Consultancy

Appley Hoare Antiques
Contact Appley or Zoe Hoare
30 Pimlico Road, London, SW1W 8LJ
020 7730 7070 020 7730 8188
appley@appleyhoare.com
www.appleyhoare.com
Est. 1980 *Stock size* Large
Stock 18th–19thC French country furniture, accessories
Open Mon–Fri 10.30am–6pm Sat 11am–5pm
Services Shipping

John Hobbs Ltd (BADA)
Contact Mr C Mortimer or Mr R Hobbs
107a Pimlico Road, London, SW1W 8PH
020 7730 8369 020 7730 0437
info@johnhobbs.demon.co.uk
www.johnhobbs.co.uk
Est. 1994 *Stock size* Large
Stock 18th–19thC Continental and English furniture, objets d'art, statuary
Open Mon–Fri 9am–6pm Sat 11am–4pm

Christopher Hodsoll Ltd (BADA)
Contact Mr C Hodsoll
89–91 Pimlico Road, London, SW1W 8PH
020 7730 3370 020 7730 1516
c.hodsoll@btinternet.com
www.hodsoll.com
Est. 1991 *Stock size* Large
Stock 18th–19thC furniture, works of art
Open Mon–Fri 9am–6pm Sat 10am–5pm
Fairs Olympia
Services Finders service, interior design

Hotspur Ltd (BADA)
Contact Mr R Kern
14 Lowndes Street, London, SW1X 9EX
020 7235 1918 020 7235 4371
hotspurltd@msn.com
Est. 1924 *Stock size* Medium
Stock 18thC quality furniture, works of art
Open Mon–Fri 9am–6pm Sat 9am–1pm
Fairs Grosvenor House

Christopher Howe Antiques
Contact Christopher Howe or Olivia Bishop
93 Pimlico Road, London, SW1W 8PH
020 7730 7987 020 7730 0157
christopherhowe@easynet.co.uk
Est. 1987 *Stock size* Large
Stock General antiques
Open Mon-Fri 9am–6pm Sat 10.30am–4.30pm

Humphrey-Carrasco
Contact Mr David Humphrey or Miss Marylise Carrasco
43 Pimlico Road, London, SW1W 8NE
020 7730 9911 020 7730 9944
hc@humphreycarrasco.demon.co.uk
Est. 1990 *Stock size* Medium
Stock English furniture, 18th–19thC lighting
Open Mon–Fri 10am–6pm Sat by appointment
Fairs Olympia (Nov)

Iconastas Russian Works of Art
Contact Chris Martin
5 Piccadilly Arcade, London, SW1Y 6NH
020 7629 1433 020 7408 2015
info@iconastas.com
www.iconastas.com
Est. 1972 *Stock size* Large
Stock 10thC–1974 Russian works of art
Open Mon–Fri 10am–6pm Sat 2–5pm
Services Valuations

Jeremy Ltd (BADA)
Contact Mr M Hill
29 Lowndes Street, London, SW1X 9HX
020 7823 2923 020 7245 6197
jeremy@jeremique.co.uk
www.jeremy.ltd.co.uk
Est. 1946 *Stock size* Large
Stock 18th–early 19thC English and Continental furniture, works of art, clocks, antiques
Open Mon–Fri 8.30am–6pm Sat by appointment
Fairs Grosvenor House, New York

Keshishian (BADA)
Contact Mr Arto or Eddy Keshishian
73 Pimlico Road, London, SW1W 8NE
020 7730 8810
rujbics@yahoo.com or amale88@hotmail.com
Est. 1989 *Stock size* Large
Stock Aubussons, British Arts and Crafts, Art Deco, antique and modernist carpets and tapestries
Open Mon–Fri 9.30am–6pm Sat 10am–5pm

John King (BADA)
Contact Mr J King
74 Pimlico Road, London, SW1W 8LS
020 7730 0427 020 7730 2515
Est. 1967 *Stock size* Large
Stock Period furniture, associated items, 20thC items
Open Mon–Fri 10am–6pm or by appointment
Fairs Olympia (June)

Knightsbridge Coins (BNTA)
Contact Mr J Brown
43 Duke Street, London, SW1Y 6DD
020 7930 8215 020 7930 8214
Est. 1975
Stock English and foreign medieval–present day coins
Open Mon–Fri 10.15am–6pm
Fairs Coinex, Cumberland
Services Valuations

M & D Lewis
Contact Mr D Vaughan
84 Pimlico Road, London, SW1W 8PL
020 7730 1015
Est. 1959 *Stock size* Large

Stock English and Continental furniture, Oriental porcelain
Open Mon–Fri 10am–5pm Sat 10am–noon

⊞ Jeremy Mason
Contact Mr J Mason
✉ **145 Ebury Street, London, SW1W 9QN** Ⓟ
☎ 020 7730 8331 Ⓕ 020 7730 8334
Est. 1974 ***Stock size*** Small
Stock Oriental works of art from all periods
Open By appointment only

⊞ Alexander von Moltke
Contact Alexander von Moltke
✉ **46 Bourne Street, London, SW1W 8JD** Ⓟ
☎ 020 7730 9020 Ⓕ 020 7730 2945
Ⓔ alexandervonmoltke@btinternet.com
Ⓦ www.alexandervonmoltke.com
Est. 1992 ***Stock size*** Large
Stock French furniture 1920–1950, Italian lighting
Open Mon–Fri 10am–6pm Sat 10am–5pm
Fairs Olympia, Decorative Antiques & Textile Fair, Battersea

⊞ Peter Nahum at the Leicester Galleries (BADA)
Contact Peter Nahum
✉ **5 Ryder Street, London, SW1Y 6PY** Ⓟ
☎ 020 7930 6059 Ⓕ 020 7930 4678
Ⓜ 07770 220851
Ⓔ peternahum@leicestergalleries.com
Ⓦ www.leicestergalleries.com
Est. 1984 ***Stock size*** Large
Stock 19th–20thC paintings, drawings, sculpture
Open Mon–Fri 9.30am–6pm
Fairs Grosvenor House Art and Antiques Fair and International Fine Art Fair, New York
Services Valuations, restorations, shipping, book search

⊞ Odyssey Fine Arts Ltd (LAPADA)
Contact Martin MacRodain
✉ **24 Holbein Place, London, SW1W 8NL**
☎ 020 7730 9942 Ⓕ 020 7259 9941
Ⓔ martin@odysseyart.co.uk
Ⓦ www.odysseyart.co.uk
Est. 1993 ***Stock size*** Large
Stock Decorative antiques
Open Mon–Fri 10.30am–5.30pm Sat 10.30am–3.30pm
Fairs Olympia, Decorative Antiques and Textiles

⊞ The O'Shea Gallery (BADA, BACA Award Winner 2002)
Contact Mr D Isaac
✉ **No 4 St James's Street, London, SW1A 1EF** Ⓟ
☎ 020 7930 5880 Ⓕ 020 7930 9500
Ⓔ prints@osheagallery.com
Ⓦ www.osheagallery.com
Est. 1969 ***Stock size*** Large
Stock 15th–19thC maps, decorative, natural history, sporting, marine prints, publisher of Annie Tempest, Tottering-by-Gently cartoons
Open Mon–Fri 9.30am–6pm
Fairs Olympia, International New York, Fall Antiques Show San Francisco
Services Restorations, framing

⊞ Ossowski (BADA)
Contact Mr M Ossowski
✉ **83 Pimlico Road, London, SW1W 8PH**
☎ 020 7730 3256 Ⓕ 020 7823 4500
Ⓔ markossowski@hotmail.com
Est. 1960 ***Stock size*** Large
Stock 18thC English giltwood mirrors, tables, decorative wood carving
Open Mon–Fri 10am–6pm Sat 10am–1pm
Fairs Olympia (June), Palm Beach (Feb), New York International (Oct)
Services Restorations

⊞ Trevor Philip & Son Ltd (BADA)
Contact Mr T Waterman
✉ **75a Jermyn Street, St James's, London, SW1Y 6NP** Ⓟ
☎ 020 7930 2954 Ⓕ 020 7321 0212
Ⓔ globe@trevorphilip.com
Ⓦ www.trevorphilip.com
Est. 1972 ***Stock size*** Large
Stock Globes, ships' models, marine and navigation instruments
Open Mon–Fri 9.30am–6pm Sat by appointment only
Fairs Grosvenor House
Services Valuations, restorations

⊞ Pullman Gallery Ltd
Contact Mr S Khachadourian
✉ **14 King Street, St James's, London, SW1Y 6QU** Ⓟ
☎ 020 7930 9595 Ⓕ 020 7930 9494
Ⓔ pullman.gallery@dial.pipex.com
Ⓦ www.pullmangallery.com
Est. 1998 ***Stock size*** Large
Stock Cocktail shakers, bar accessories, smoking accessories, automobilia, vintage Louis Vuitton and Hermes luggage, motor racing posters, René Lalique glass, 1900–1940
Open Mon–Fri 10am–6pm or by appointment
Services Usual gallery services

⊞ Mark Ransom Ltd
Contact Mr C Walker or Mr M James
✉ **62/64 Pimlico Road, London, SW1W 8LS** Ⓟ
☎ 020 7259 0220 Ⓕ 020 7259 0323
Ⓔ contact@markransom.co.uk
Ⓦ www.markransom.co.uk
Est. 1992 ***Stock size*** Medium
Stock Russian and French Empire, Continental furniture, decorative items, objets d'art, prints, pictures
Open Mon–Sat 10am–6pm

⊞ Mark Ransom Ltd
Contact Mr C Walker or Mr M James
✉ **130 Pimlico Road, London, SW1W 8LS** Ⓟ
☎ 020 7259 0220 Ⓕ 020 7259 0323
Ⓔ contact@markransom.co.uk
Ⓦ www.markransom.co.uk
Est. 1992 ***Stock size*** Medium
Stock Russian and French Empire, Continental furniture, decorative items, objets d'art, prints, pictures
Open Mon–Sat 10am–6pm

⊞ Rogier Antiques
Contact Mr Elene Rogier
✉ **20a Pimlico Road, London, SW1W 8LJ** Ⓟ
☎ 020 7823 4780 Ⓕ 020 7823 4780
Est. 1988 ***Stock size*** Medium
Stock French and Continental 18–19thC decorative furniture, unusual lamps, reproductions, lighting
Open Mon–Fri 10am–6pm Sat 11am–4pm
Services Restorations

⊞ Rossi & Rossi Ltd
Contact Mr Fabio Rossi
✉ **Barrington Court, 91c Jermyn Street, London, SW1Y 6JB** Ⓟ
☎ 020 7321 0208 Ⓕ 020 7321 0546

ⓔ rossirossi@compuserve.com
ⓦ www.asianart.com/rossi
Est. 1986 *Stock size* Medium
Stock Asian art, sculpture, paintings from India, the Himalayas, Chinese textiles
Open Mon–Fri 10.30am–5.30pm

The Silver Fund Ltd (LAPADA)
Contact A Crawford
40 Bury Street, London, SW1Y 6AU
☎ 020 7839 7664 ⓕ 020 7839 8935
ⓔ dealers@thesilverfund.com
ⓦ www.thesilverfund.com
Est. 1996 *Stock size* Large
Stock Georg Jensen, Tiffany, Martele and Puiforcat silver
Open Mon–Fri 9am–6pm
Fairs NEC, LAPADA, Claridges
Services Valuations

Sims Reed Ltd (ABA)
Contact Mr J Sims
43a Duke Street, St James's, London, SW1Y 6DD
☎ 020 7493 5660 ⓕ 020 7493 8468
ⓔ info@simsreed.com
ⓦ www.simsreed.com
Est. 1977 *Stock size* Large
Stock Antiquarian, rare, second-hand books, including books illustrated by artists, books on fine and applied arts
Open Mon–Fri 10am–6pm or by appointment
Fairs ABA, Olympia

Peta Smyth Antique Textiles (LAPADA, CINOA)
Contact Mrs P Smyth
42 Moreton Street, London, SW1V 2PB
☎ 020 7630 9898 ⓕ 020 7630 5398
Est. 1975 *Stock size* Large
Stock Early European textiles, needlework, silks, tapestries, hangings
Open Mon–Fri 9.30am–5.30pm
Fairs Olympia (June, Nov)
Services Valuations

Somlo Antiques Ltd (BADA)
Contact Mr Paul Symons
7 Piccadilly Arcade, London, SW1Y 6NH
☎ 020 7499 6526 ⓕ 020 7499 0603
ⓔ mail@somlo.com
ⓦ www.somloantiques.com
Est. 1970 *Stock size* Large
Stock Vintage wristwatches, antique pocket watches
Open Mon–Fri 10am–5.30pm Sat 10.30am–5.30pm
Fairs Olympia (Feb, June)
Services Valuations, repairs

Alexe Stanion Antiques
Contact Alexe Stanion
73 Elizabeth Street, London, SW1W 8PH
☎ 020 7824 8808 ⓕ 020 7824 8828
ⓔ alexestanion@aol.com
ⓦ www.alexestanion.com
Est. 1999 *Stock size* Medium
Stock Mid 20thC, post-war design and modernism
Open Mon–Sat 10am–6pm
Fairs Alexandra Palace

Un Français à Londres
Contact Mr P Sumner
202 Ebury Street, London, SW1W 8UN
☎ 020 7730 1771 ⓕ 020 7730 1661
ⓔ eburystreet@aol.com
ⓦ www.unfrancaisalondres.com
Est. 1998 *Stock size* Large
Stock French and Continental furniture, works of art, 17th–19thC
Open Mon–Fri 10am–6pm Sat 10am–4pm or by appointment
Services Valuations, restorations, upholstery

Westenholz Antiques Ltd
Contact Andrew Damonte
76–78 Pimlico Road, London, SW1W 8PL
☎ 020 7824 8090 ⓕ 020 7823 5913
ⓔ shop@westenholz.co.uk
ⓦ www.westenholz.co.uk
Stock 18th–19thC English furniture, decorative items
Open Mon–Fri 8.30am–6pm
Fairs Olympia (June, Nov)
Services Interior design

SW3

Jaki Abbott
Contact Jaki Abbott
Antiquarius, 135 Kings Road, London, SW3 4PW
☎ 0777 486 4442
Stock size Small
Stock Antique and period jewellery
Open Mon–Sat 10am–5pm

Norman Adams Ltd (BADA, BACA Award Winner 2001)
Contact R S G Whittington or C Claxton-Stevens
8–10 Hans Road, London, SW3 1RX
☎ 020 7589 5266 ⓕ 020 7589 1968
ⓔ antiques@normanadams.com
ⓦ www.normanadams.com
Est. 1923 *Stock size* Large
Stock Fine 18thC English furniture, works of art, mirrors, paintings, chandeliers
Open Mon–Fri 9am–5.30pm or Sat Sun by appointment
Fairs BADA (March), Grosvenor House (June)
Services Annual catalogue

Aesthetics (BADA, LAPADA)
Contact Peter A Jeffs
Stand V2, Antiquarius, 131–141 Kings Road, London, SW3 4PW
☎ 020 7352 0395 ⓕ 020 7376 4057
Est. 1983 *Stock size* Large
Stock Ceramics and silver
Open Mon–Sat 10am–6pm
Fairs Olympia (June)
Services Shipping

After Noah
Contact Simon Tarr
261 King's Road, London, SW3 5EL
☎ 020 7351 2610
ⓔ mailorder@afternoah.com
ⓦ www.afternoah.com
Est. 1995 *Stock size* Medium
Stock Antique and contemporary furniture and houseware
Open Mon–Sat 10am–6pm Sun noon–5pm
Services Restorations

Alexia Amato Antiques
Contact Alexia Amato
Stand V8, Antiquarius, 135 Kings Road, London, SW3 4PW
☎ 020 7352 3666 ⓕ 020 7352 3666
ⓜ 07770 826254
ⓔ alexia@amato.freeserve.co.uk
ⓦ www.amato.freeserve.co.uk
Est. 1993 *Stock size* Medium
Stock Continental 19thC glass especially French and Bohemian
Open Mon–Sat 10am–6pm
Services Shipping

Antiquarius Antique Centre
Contact Mike Spooner
✉ **131–141 Kings Road, London, SW3 4PW** P
☎ 020 7351 5353 F 020 7351 5350
E antique@dial.pipex.com
Est. 1969 *Stock size* Large
No. of dealers 100
Stock General and specialist antiques of all periods
Open Mon–Sat 10am–6pm

Apter-Fredericks Ltd (BADA)
Contact Harry or Guy Apter
✉ **265–267 Fulham Road, London, SW3 6HY**
☎ 020 7352 2188 F 020 7376 5619
E antiques@apter-fredericks.com
W www.apter-fredericks.com
Est. 1946 *Stock size* Large
Stock 18thC English furniture
Open Mon–Fri 9.30am–5.30pm
Fairs Grosvenor House

Joanna Booth (BADA, CINOA)
Contact Joanna Booth
✉ **247 King's Road, London, SW3 5EL** P
☎ 020 7352 8998 F 020 7376 7350
E joanna@joannabooth.co.uk
W www.joannabooth.co.uk
Est. 1966 *Stock size* Large
Stock Old master drawings, early sculptures, tapestries, oak furniture, textiles
Open Mon–Sat 10am–6pm
Fairs Olympia
Services Valuations, restorations

Bourbon Hanby Antique Centre
Contact Mr I Towning
✉ **151 Sydney Street, London, SW3 6NT** P
☎ 020 7352 2106 F 020 7565 0003
W www.antiques-uk.co.uk/bourbon-hanby
Est. 1974 *Stock size* Large
No. of dealers 30
Stock China, glass, silver, porcelain, jewellery, textiles, furniture, carpets, rugs, paintings
Open Mon–Sat 10am–6pm
Sun 11am–5pm
Services Restorations, jewellery manufacturing

Brown & Kingston
Contact Alan Brown or Dennis Kingston
✉ **Antiquarius, 131–141 Kings Road, London, SW3 4PW** P
☎ 020 7376 8881 F 020 7376 8881
Est. 1978 *Stock size* Large
Stock Japanese Imari, oil paintings, George III furniture
Open Mon–Sat 10am–5pm
Services Shipping

Jasmin Cameron (Glass Circle)
Contact Jasmin Cameron
✉ **Stand M16, Antiquarius, 131–141 Kings Road, London, SW3 4PW** P
☎ 020 7351 4154 F 020 7351 4154
M 07774 871257
E jasmin.cameron@mail.com
Est. 1980 *Stock size* Large
Stock 18th–19thC English and Irish drinking glasses, decanters, fountain pens, writing materials
Open Mon–Fri 10am–5.30pm
Sat 10am–5.45pm
Services Valuations, restorations

Chelsea Military Antiques
Contact Richard Black
✉ **Stands N13–14, Antiquarius, 131–141 Kings Road, London, SW3 4PW** P
☎ 020 7352 0308 F 020 7352 0308
E richard@chelseamilitaria.com
W www.chelseamilitaria.com
Est. 1996 *Stock size* Large
Stock British campaign medals, 19th and 20thC Allied and Axis militaria
Open Mon–Sat 10.30am–5.30pm
Fairs Britannia and South England Militaria Fairs
Services Valuations, medal mounting

Classic Prints
Contact Mr Paul Dowling
✉ **265 King's Road, London, SW3 5EL**
☎ 020 7376 5056 F 020 7460 5356
M 07770 431855
E art@classicprints.com
W www.classicprints.com
Est. 1983 *Stock size* Large
Stock Antique prints of all ages, maps
Open Mon–Sat 10am–6pm
Sun noon–5pm
Services Valuations

L and D Collins
Contact Louise Collins or David Collins
☎ 020 7584 0712 F 020 7584 0712
Est. 1994 *Stock size* Medium
Stock Paintings, fans, decorative objects
Open By appointment
Fairs Decorative Antiques and Textiles Fair, Penman Fairs

Richard Courtney Ltd (BADA)
Contact Mr R Courtney
✉ **114 Fulham Road, London, SW3 6HU** P
☎ 020 7370 4020 F 020 7370 4020
Est. 1965 *Stock size* Large
Stock Finest early 18thC English walnut furniture
Open Mon–Fri 9.30am–5.30pm
Fairs Grosvenor House, BADA Duke of York's

The Cufflink Shop
Contact Mr John Szwarl
✉ **Stand G2, Antiquarius, 137 Kings Road, London, SW3 4PW** P
☎ 020 7352 8201
M 07715 381175
Est. 1990 *Stock size* Large
Stock Antique, vintage and modern cufflinks
Open Mon–Sat 10.30am–5.30pm

Jesse Davis Antiques (LAPADA)
Contact Mr J Davis
✉ **Stands A9–11, Antiquarius, 131–141 Kings Road, London, SW3 4PW** P
☎ 020 7352 4314
Est. 1984 *Stock size* Large
Stock 19thC pottery, majolica, Staffordshire and other collectable factories, decorative objects
Open Mon–Sat 10.30am–6pm
Fairs Olympia (June), LAPADA Fair, Decorative Antiques and Textiles Fair

Dernier and Hamlyn Ltd
✉ **3 Egerton Terrace, London, SW3 2EJ** P
☎ 020 7225 5030 F 020 7838 1030
W www.dernier-hamlyn.com
Stock size Large
Stock Fine lighting, high-quality period lighting

Open Mon–Sat 10am–7pm
Services Restorations

Robert Dickson and Lesley Rendall Antiques (BADA)
Contact Robert Dickson or Lesley Rendall
263 Fulham Road, London, SW3 6HY P
☎ 020 7351 0330
W www.dicksonrendallantiques.co.uk
Est. 1969 *Stock size* Large
Stock Antique furniture, English and French works of art, English Regency
Open Mon–Fri 10am–6pm
Sat 10am–4.30pm
Services Valuations, restorations

Eclectic Antiques and Interiors
Contact Graham Tomlinson
Stands T3–4, Antiquarius, 131–141 Kings Road, London, SW3 4PW P
☎ 020 7286 7608 F 020 7286 7608
M 07778 470983
Stock size Medium
Stock English and French decorative antiques and furniture
Open Mon–Sat 10am–6pm
Services Shipping, valuations

Michael Foster (BADA)
Contact Margaret Susands
118 Fulham Road, Chelsea, London, SW3 6HU
☎ 020 7373 3636 F 020 7373 4042
Est. 1967 *Stock size* Medium
Stock Fine 18th–early 19thC furniture, works of art
Open Mon–Fri 9.30am–5.30pm
Fairs Grosvenor House, Olympia
Services Valuations

Angelo Gibson
Contact Angelo Gibson
Antiquarius, 131–141 Kings Road, London, SW3 4PW P
☎ 020 8352 4690 M 07951 929015
Est. 1972 *Stock size* Small
Stock Antique silver and silver plate
Open Mon–Sat 10am–6pm
Services Silver plating

James Hardy & Co
Contact Mr H P Ross
235 Brompton Road, London, SW3 2EP P
☎ 020 7589 5050 F 020 7589 9009
Est. 1853 *Stock size* Medium
Stock Silver, jewellery
Open Mon–Sat 10am–5.30pm
Services Valuations, restorations

Robin Haydock Rare Textiles (LAPADA)
Contact Robin Haydock
Stands L1–10, Antiquarius, 131–141 Kings Road, London, SW3 4PW
☎ 020 7349 9110 F 020 7349 9110
M 07770 931240
E robinhaydock@talk21.com
W www.robinhaydock.com
Est. 1996 *Stock size* Medium
Stock Antique textiles, mostly 18thC European and earlier, decorative furnishings
Open Tues–Sat 10.30am–5.30pm
Fairs Olympia (June) Decorative Antiques & Textile Fairs
Services Valuations, restorations

Hayman & Hayman
Contact Georgina Hayman
Antiquarius, 131–141 Kings Road, London, SW3 4PW P
☎ 020 7351 6568
E hayman@wahlgren.demon.co.uk
Est. 1976 *Stock size* Large
Stock Photograph frames, Limoges boxes, scent bottles
Open Mon–Sat 10am–5.30pm
Services Valuations, restorations, shipping

Peter Herington Antiquarian Bookseller (ABA, PBFA)
Contact Kevin Finch
100 Fulham Road, Chelsea, London, SW3 6HS P
☎ 020 7591 0220 F 020 7225 7054
E mail@peter-herington-books.com
W www.peter-herington-books.com
Est. 1969 *Stock size* Large
Stock Antiquarian books, illustrated, fine bindings, English literature, travel, children's etc, modern first editions
Open Mon–Sat 10am–6pm
Fairs Olympia ABA, Chelsea ABA

Hill House Antiques & Decorative Arts
Contact S Benhalim
PO Box 17320, London, SW3 3WE
☎ 07973 842777
E info@hillhouse-antiques.co.uk
W www.hillhouse-antiques.co.uk
Est. 1999 *Stock size* Small
Stock Small furniture, metalware, ceramics, decorative arts
Open By appointment
Fairs P & A fairs, Take Five Fairs
Services Sourcing, design consultancy

Paul Howard
Contact Mr P Howard
Within Bourbon Hanby Antique Centre, Shop 2, 151 Sydney Street, Chelsea, London, SW3 6NT
☎ 020 7352 4113 F 020 7351 0003
M 07881 862375
Est. 1972 *Stock size* Medium
Stock Antique sextants, octants, theodolites, microscopes, telescopes, scientific instruments, other related items
Open Mon–Sat 10am–6pm

Michael Hughes (BADA)
Contact Michael Hughes
88 Fulham Road, London, SW3 6HR P
☎ 020 7589 0660 F 020 7823 7618
E antiques@michaelhughes.freeserve.com
Est. 1995 *Stock size* Large
Stock 18th–early 19thC English furniture and works of art
Open Mon–Fri 9.30am–5.30pm
Fairs Olympia

Anthony James & Son Ltd (BADA, CINOA)
Contact James Millard
88 Fulham Road, London, SW3 6HR P
☎ 020 7584 1120 F 020 7823 7618
E anthony.james10@virgin.net
W www.anthony-james.com
Est. 1949 *Stock size* Large
Stock Fine 18th–19thC English and Continental furniture, decorative items
Open Mon–Fri 9.30am–5.45pm
Fairs Olympia (June, Nov)
Services Valuations, restorations

Peter Jones/PJ2
Contact Annie Mihell
Draycott Avenue, London, SW3 2NA P
☎ 020 7730 3434 F 020 7808 4006
W www.peterjones.co.uk
Est. 1915 *Stock size* Large

Stock 18th–19thC furniture, gilt mirrors, accessories
Open Mon–Sat 9.30am–7pm
Services Shipping

John Keil Ltd (BADA)
Contact Diana Yates-Watson
First Floor, 154 Brompton Road, London, SW3 1HX
020 7589 6454 F 020 7823 8235
antiques@johnkeil.com
www.johnkeil.com
Est. 1959 *Stock size* Medium
Stock 18thC English furniture
Open Mon–Fri 9.30am–5.30pm

M Lexton
Contact Michael Lexton
Antiquarius, 131–141 Kings Road, London, SW3 4PW
020 7351 5980 F 020 7351 5980
mlextonltd@hotmail.com
Stock size Medium
Stock Silver
Open Mon–Sat 10.30am–6pm
Services Valuations, restorations

Michael Lipitch (BADA)
Contact Mr M Lipitch
98 Fulham Road, London, SW3 6HS
020 8441 4340
Est. 1969 *Stock size* Large
Stock 18th–19thC fine furniture, mirrors, objets d'art
Open By appointment
Fairs Grosvenor House
Services Specialist advice on forming collections

Peter Lipitch Ltd (BADA)
Contact Melvyn Lipitch
120–124 Fulham Road, London, SW3 6HU
020 7373 3328 F 020 7373 8888
lipitch.al@aol.com
Est. 1950 *Stock size* Medium
Stock 18thC English furniture
Open Mon–Fri 9.30am–5.30pm Sat 10am–2pm

Little River Oriental Antiques
Contact Mr D Dykes
Antiquarius, 131–141 Kings Road, London, SW3 4PW
020 7349 9080 F 01342 300131
Est. 1997 *Stock size* Large
Stock Chinese antiquities, domestic ceramics
Open Mon–Sat 10am–6pm
Services Restorations

The Map House (BADA, ABA)
Contact Mr P Stuchlik
54 Beauchamp Place, London, SW3 1NY
020 7584 8559 F 020 7589 1041
maps@themaphouse.com
www.themaphouse.com
Est. 1973 *Stock size* Large
Stock Antique maps, 15th–19thC, decorative engravings, 16th–19thC, globes, atlases
Open Mon–Fri 9.45am–5.45pm Sat 10.30am–5pm
Services Valuations

Mariad Antiques
Contact Mrs H McClean
Antiquarius, 131–141 King's Road, London, SW3 6NT
020 7351 9526
Est. 1971 *Stock size* Large
Stock Georgian, Victorian, Edwardian jewellery, cold-painted Vienna bronzes, animal subjects
Open Mon–Sun 10am–6pm
Fairs NEC
Services Valuations, restorations

Gerald Mathias
Contact Gerald Mathias
Stands R5–6, Antiquarius, 135 Kings Road, London, SW3 4PW
020 7351 0484
fineantiqueboxes@geraldmathias.com
www.geraldmathias.com
Est. 1979 *Stock size* Large
Stock Antique boxes
Open Mon–Sat 10am–5.30pm

Sue Mautner Costume Jewellery
Contact Mrs S Mautner
Stand N16, Antiquarius, 131-141 Kings Road, London, SW3 4PW
020 7376 4419
Est. 1990 *Stock size* Large
Stock 1940s–1950s costume jewellery, Christian Dior, Miriam Haskell, Schiaparelli, Coppolo Toppo, Har, Schreiner
Open Mon–Sat 10.30am–5pm

McKenna & Co (LAPADA, NAG)
Contact Catherine McKenna
28 Beauchamp Place, London, SW3 1NJ
020 7584 1966 F 020 7225 2893
info@mckennajewels.com
Est. 1983 *Stock size* Large
Stock Antique, period and contemporary jewellery
Open Mon–Sat 10.15am–5.45pm
Services Valuations, restorations

C Negrillo Antiques and Jewellery
Contact C Negrillo
Stand P1–P3, Antiquarius, 135 Kings Road, London, SW3 4PW
020 7349 0038 M 07778 336781
negrilloc@aol.com
Est. 1994 *Stock size* Large
Stock Jewellery
Open Mon–Sat 10am–6pm

No. 12
Contact Mrs Isabel Haines
12 Cale Street, London, SW3 3QU
020 7581 5022 F 020 7581 3966
Est. 1990 *Stock size* Large
Stock French country antiques
Open Mon–Sat 10am–6pm
Services Interior design

Sue Norman
Contact Sue Norman
Antiquarius, 135 Kings Road, London, SW3 4PW
020 7352 7217 F 020 8870 4677
M 07720 751162
sue@sue-norman.demon.co.uk
www.sue-norman.demon.co.uk
Est. Olympia *Stock size* Large
Stock Blue-and-white transfer ware
Open Mon–Sat 10.30am–5.30pm

Jacqueline Oosthuizen Antiques (LAPADA)
Contact Mrs J Oosthuizen
23 Cale Street, Chelsea, London, SW3 3QR
020 7352 6071 F 020 7376 3852
M 07785 258806
Est. 1979 *Stock size* Large
Stock Staffordshire animals, cottages, figures, jewellery
Open Mon–Sat 10am–5pm Sun by appointment only

Rogers de Rin (BADA)
Contact Mrs V de Rin
76 Royal Hospital Road, London, SW3 4HN
020 7352 9007 020 7351 9407
rogersderin@rogersderin.co.uk
Est. 1965 *Stock size* Medium
Stock Collectors' items, snuff boxes, enamels, Vienna bronzes, Staffordshire, Scottish Wemyss ware
Open Mon–Fri 10am–5.30pm Sat 10am–1pm
Fairs Olympia (June, Nov), BADA (March)
Services Shipping arranged

Russell Rare Books (ABA, PBFA)
Contact Charles Russell
239a Fulham Road, Chelsea (at junction of Old Church Street), London, SW3 6HY
020 7351 5119 020 7376 7227
crussell@russellrarebooks.com
www.russellrarebooks.com
Est. 1978 *Stock size* Medium
Stock Rare books, leather bound books, library sets, illustrated books, prints, maps
Open Mon–Fri 11am–6pm
Fairs Olympia, Russell Hotel
Services Valuations

Salamanca
Contact Mrs Martin
Stands 14–15, Antiquarius, 131–141 Kings Road, London, SW3 4PW
020 7351 5829 020 7351 5829
Est. 1976 *Stock size* Large
Stock Moorcroft pottery, Sabino glass, porcelain, silver
Open Mon–Sat 10.30am–5.30pm
Services Valuations, restorations

Charles Saunders Antiques
Contact Mr Charles Saunders
255 Fulham Road, London, SW3 6HY
020 7351 5242 020 7352 8142
Est. 1987 *Stock size* Medium
Stock Antique lighting, English and Continental 18th–early 19thC furniture, objects, decorations, some 20thC furniture, lighting, decorative objects
Open Mon–Fri 9.30am–5.30pm

Christine Schell (LAPADA)
Contact Ms Christine King
15 Cale Street, London, SW3 3QS
020 7352 5563
020 7589 7161
c.schell@eidosnet.co.uk
Est. 1973 *Stock size* Medium
Stock Tortoiseshell, ivory, silver, Arts and Crafts, decorative items, mirrors
Open Mon–Sat 10am–5.30pm
Services Valuations, restorations

Snap Dragon
Contact Leonie Whittle
247 Fulham Road, London, SW3 6HY
020 7376 8889
leonie@snapdragon.sonnet.co.uk
Stock size Large
Stock 18th–19thC Chinese furniture, chairs
Open Mon–Sat 10am–6pm

Miwa Thorpe
Contact Ms Miwa Thorpe
Stands M8–9, Antiquarius, 131–141 Kings Road, London, SW3 4PW
020 7351 2911 020 7351 6690
07768 455679
Est. 1987 *Stock size* Medium
Stock Jewellery and decorative silver
Open Mon–Sat 10am–6pm

Geoffrey Waters Ltd (LAPADA)
Contact Geoffrey Waters
Stands F1–6, Antiquarius, 135 Kings Road, London, SW3 4PW
020 7376 5467 020 7376 5467
Est. 1992 *Stock size* Medium
Stock 16th–18thC Chinese porcelain
Open Mon–Sat 10am–5.30pm

Gordon Watson Ltd (LAPADA)
Contact Mr S Berg
50 Fulham Road, London, SW3 6HH
020 7589 3108 020 7584 6328
Stock size Medium
Stock Art Deco furniture, lighting
Open Mon–Sat 11am–6pm
Fairs Olympia

O F Wilson Ltd (BADA, LAPADA)
Contact Mr P Jackson
Queens Elm Parade, Old Church Street, Chelsea, London, SW3 6EJ
020 7352 9554 020 7351 0765
ofw@email.msn.com
Est. 1949 *Stock size* Medium
Stock Continental furniture, French chimney pieces, English painted decorative furniture, mirrors
Open Mon–Fri 9.30am–5.30pm Sat 10.30am–1pm
Services Valuations

World's End Bookshop
Contact Mr S Dickson
357 King's Road, London, SW3 5ES
020 7352 9376
07961 316 918
stephen.dickson@virgin.net
Est. 1999 *Stock size* Medium
Stock Antiquarian, rare, second-hand books, non-fiction, art, literature etc
Open Mon–Sun 10am–6.30pm
Fairs Royal National Hotel, Bloomsbury (H D)
Services Valuations

Clifford Wright Antiques Ltd (BADA)
Contact Clifford Wright
104–106 Fulham Road, London, SW3 6HS
020 7589 0986 020 7589 3565
Est. 1960 *Stock size* Large
Stock English furniture early 18thC–Regency, English giltwood furniture, period giltwood mirrors
Open Mon–Fri 9am–6pm

SW4

Antiques and Things
Contact Mrs V Crowther
020 7498 1303 020 7498 1303
07767 262096
info@antiquesandthings.co.uk
www.antiquesandthings.co.uk
Est. 1985 *Stock size* Medium
Stock Lighting, chandeliers, curtain furniture, accessories, French decorative furniture, textiles
Open By appointment
Fairs Decorative Antiques and Textiles Fair

Places and Spaces
Contact Paul Carroll or Nick Hannam
30 Old Town, Clapham, London, SW4 0LB
020 7498 0998 020 7627 2625
contact@placesandspaces.com
www.placesandspaces.com
Est. 1997 *Stock size* Large
Stock 20thC classic designs, 1950s Scandinavian furniture, Italian lighting, Eames, Panton
Open Tues–Sat 10.30am–6pm Sun noon–4pm
Fairs 100% Design
Services Valuations, design consultancy

SW6

275 Antiques
Contact Mr D Fisher
275 Lillie Road, London, SW6 7LL
020 7386 7382 020 7381 8320
Est. 1991 *Stock size* Large
Stock 1880s–1930s furniture, decorative items, American Lucite furniture, lighting, 1930s–1970s
Open Mon–Sat 10am–5.30pm

Sebastiano Barbagallo Antiques
Contact Mr S Barbagallo
61 Fulham Road, London, SW6 5PZ
020 7751 0691 020 7751 0691
Est. 1978 *Stock size* Large
Stock Chinese furniture, Indian and Tibetan antiques, crafts
Open Mon–Sun 10am–6pm

Sebastiano Barbagallo Antiques
Contact Mr S Barbagallo
310 Wandsworth Bridge Road, London, SW6 2UA
020 7751 0586 020 7751 0586
Est. 1978 *Stock size* Medium
Stock Chinese furniture, objects
Open Mon–Sun 10am–6pm

Big Ben Clocks and Antiques
Contact Mr R Lascelles
5 Broxholme House, New King's Road, London, SW6 4AA
020 7736 1770 020 7384 1957
info@lasc.demon.co.uk
Est. 1974 *Stock size* Large
Stock Longcase, mantel, Grandfather and traditional reproduction clocks
Open Tues Wed Sat 10am–5pm or by appointment

Alasdair Brown
Contact Mr A Brown
3 & 4 The Cranewell, The Gas Works, 2 Michael Road, London, SW6 2AD
020 7736 6661 020 7384 3334
07836 672857
ab@ajcb.demon.co.uk
Est. 1984 *Stock size* Medium
Stock 19th–20thC furniture, lighting, upholstery, unusual items
Open Wed Thurs 10am–6pm
Fairs Olympia
Services Valuations

I and J L Brown Ltd
Contact Mr S Hilton
632–636 King's Road, London, SW6 2DU
020 7736 4141 020 7736 9164
enquiries@brownantiques.com
www.brownantiques.com
Est. 1978 *Stock size* Large
Stock The largest antique showroom on the Kings Road with over 8,000 square feet of English country, French provincial antique and reproduction furniture, extensive range of decorative items including lighting
Open Mon–Sat 9am–5.30pm or by appointment
Services Restorations, re-rushing

Rupert Cavendish Antiques
Contact Mr Francois Valcke
610 King's Road, London, SW6 2DX
020 7731 7041 020 7731 8302
rcavendish@aol.com
www.rupertcavendish.co.uk
Est. 1984 *Stock size* Large
Stock European 20thC paintings
Open Mon–Sat 10am–6pm

Cheyne Antiques
Contact G. Watson
314 Munster Road, London, SW6 6BH
020 7727 1304
Est. 1996 *Stock size* Small
Stock General antiques
Open Mon–Sat 9am–6pm
Services Valuations, restorations

Fergus Cochrane Leigh Warren
Contact Mr F Cochrane
570 King's Road, London, SW6 2DY
020 7736 9166 020 7736 6687
Est. 1979 *Stock size* Large
Stock 19th–20thC lighting
Open Mon–Fri 10am–5pm Sat 10am–4pm

Marc Costantini Antiques
Contact Mr M Costantini
313 Lillie Road, London, SW6 7LL
020 7610 2380 020 7610 2380
07941 075289
Est. 1999 *Stock size* Large
Stock English and Continental antique furniture
Open Mon–Sat 10.30am–5.30pm

Deans Antiques
Contact Mr D Gipson
Core One, The Gas Works, 2 Michael Road, London, SW6 2AN
020 7610 6997
07770 231687
dean.antiques@virgin.net
Est. 1988 *Stock size* Large
Stock 18th–19thC French and Italian decorative antiques
Open Wed–Fri 10am–6pm Sat 11am–4pm or by appointment
Fairs Battersea Decorative Antiques and Textiles Fair

Decorative Antiques (LAPADA)
Contact Mr T Harley
284 Lillie Road, Fulham, London, SW6 7PX
020 7610 2694 020 7386 0103
Est. 1992 *Stock size* Large
Stock 18th–19thC French provincial furniture, Irish furniture
Open Mon–Sat 10am–5.30pm

Charles Edwards (BADA, CINOA)
Contact Annabel or Louise
19a Rumbold Road, London, SW6 2HX
020 7736 7172 020 7731 7388
charles@charlesedwards.demon.co.uk
Est. 1969 *Stock size* Medium
Stock Antique lighting,

18th–19thC furniture, bookcases, general antiques
Open Mon–Fri 9.30am–6pm
Sat 10am–5pm

Nicole Fabre French Antiques (LAPADA)
Contact Mrs N Fabre
592 King's Road, London, SW6 2DX
020 7384 3112 020 7610 6410
antiques@nicolefabre.com
Stock size Medium
Stock French Provencale furniture and beds, Provencale quilts, linens, textiles, 18th–19thC toiles, decorative items, antique fabrics
Open Mon–Fri 10am–6pm
Sat 11am–5pm
Fairs Decorative Antiques and Textiles Fair

Hector Finch Lighting
Contact Mr H Finch
88–90 Wandsworth Bridge Road, London, SW6 2TF
020 7731 8886 020 7731 7408
hector@hectorfinch.com
www.hectorfinch.com
Est. 1987 *Stock size* Large
Stock Specialist period lighting shop, large range of antique and contemporary decorative lighting
Open Mon–Sat 10am–5.30pm

Birdie Fortescue Antiques (LAPADA)
Contact Birdie Fortescue
Unit GJ, Cooper House, 2 Michael Road, London, SW6 2AD
01206 337567 01206 337557
07778 263467
Est. 1991 *Stock size* Large
Stock 18th–early 19thC Continental furniture
Open By appointment
Fairs Olympia (Feb, June), Decorative Antiques Fair, Battersea Park (Jan, April, Sept)

Fulham Antiques
Contact Mr A Eves
320 Munster Road, London, SW6 6BH
020 7610 3644
Est. 1993 *Stock size* Large
Stock Antique and decorative furniture, lighting, mirrors
Open Mon–Sat 10am–5.30pm
Services Delivery

Ena Green
Contact Ms Ena Green
566 King's Road, London, SW6 2DY
020 7736 2485 020 7610 9028
07831 106002
Est. 1979 *Stock size* Medium
Stock 18th–20thC painted furniture, lighting, mirrors, decorative items
Open Mon–Sat 10.30am–5.30pm

Judy Greenwood Antiques
Contact Ms J Greenwood
657–659 Fulham Road, London, SW6 5PY
020 7736 6037 020 7736 1941
07768 347669
judyg@dial.pipex.com
Est. 1978 *Stock size* Large
Stock 19th–20thC French decorative items, beds, textiles, lighting, furniture, mirrors, quilts
Open Mon–Fri 10am–5.30pm
Sat 10am–5pm
Services Restorations, painting

Gutlin Clocks & Antiques
Contact Mr. Coxhead
606 Kings Road, London, SW6 2DX
020 7384 2439/2804
020 7384 2439 07973 123921
mark@gutlin.com
www.gutlin.com
Est. 1992 *Stock size* Medium
Stock Furniture, clocks, chandeliers
Open Mon–Sat 10am–6.30pm
Services Restorations

H R W Antiques Ltd (LAPADA)
Contact Mr I Henderson-Russell
26 Sulivan Road, London, SW6 3DT
020 7371 7995 020 7371 9522
ian@hrw-antiques.freeserve.co.uk
www.hrw-antiques.com
Est. 1988 *Stock size* Large
Stock Decorative items
Open Mon–Fri 9am–5pm

Nigel Hindley
Contact Mr N Hindley
281 Lillie Road, London, SW6 7LL
020 7385 0706
Est. 1979 *Stock size* Large
Stock English period antiques, French furniture, eccentricities, lighting, mirrors
Open Mon–Sat 10.30am–5pm
Services Valuations

House of Mirrors
Contact Miss Witek
597 Kings Road, London, SW6 2EL
020 7736 5885 020 7610 9188
grazyna@houseofmirrors.co.uk
www.houseofmirrors.co.uk
Est. 1972 *Stock size* Large
Stock 19thC English mirrors
Open Mon–Fri 9am–6pm
Sat 10am–6pm

Indigo
Contact Marion Bender
275 New King's Road, London, SW6 4RD
020 7384 3101 020 7384 3102
indigo_uk@compuserve.com
www.indigo-uk.com
Est. 1982 *Stock size* Large
Stock Indian, Chinese and Japanese furniture, decorative items, handicrafts, Indonesian furniture from recycled teakwood
Open Mon–Sat 10am–6pm
Fairs House and Garden Fair

Jackdawes (LAPADA)
Contact Princess Sevilla Hercolani
297 Lillie Road, London, SW6 7LL
020 7386 0880 020 7602 4800
Est. 1989 *Stock size* Large
Stock Decorative French, Italian, English painted furniture, lighting, gilded mirrors
Open Mon–Sat 10.30am–5.30pm
Fairs Decorative Fair, Battersea, Kensington Penman Fair
Services Restorations

Christopher Jones Antiques
Contact Rene Sanderson
618–620 King's Road, London, SW6 2DU
020 7731 4655 020 7371 8682
florehouse@msn.com
www.christopherjonesantiques.co.uk
Est. 1984 *Stock size* Large
Stock French furniture, mirrors, screens, 1860–1890 Chinese porcelain
Open Mon–Sat 10am–5.30pm

King's Court Galleries
Contact Mrs J Joel

✉ 949–953 Fulham Road, London, SW6 5HY 🅿
☎ 020 7610 6939 Ⓕ 020 7731 4737
Ⓔ sales@kingscourtgalleries.co.uk
Ⓦ www.kingscourtgalleries.co.uk
Est. 1984 *Stock size* Large
Stock Antique maps, engravings, sporting, decorative prints
Open Mon–Sat 10am–5.30pm
Services Framing

⊞ L & E Kreckovic
Contact Joanna Christopher
✉ **559 King's Road, London, SW6 2EB** 🅿
☎ 020 7736 0753 Ⓕ 020 7731 5904
Est. 1969 *Stock size* Large
Stock Early 18th–19thC furniture
Open Mon–Sat 10am–6pm
Services Valuations, restorations

⊞ L'Accademia Antiques
Contact Mrs P Villanueva
✉ **643c Fulham Road, London, SW6 5PU** 🅿
☎ 020 7736 7088
Est. 1996 *Stock size* Large
Stock Antiques, decorative items, chandeliers, bedroom furniture, mirrors, French and Italian furniture
Open Mon–Sat 10am–6pm

⊞ Roger Lascelles Clocks Ltd
Contact Mr R Lascelles
✉ **29 Carnwath Road, London, SW6 3HR** 🅿
☎ 020 7731 0072 Ⓕ 020 7384 1957
Ⓔ info@lasc.demon.co.uk
Ⓦ www.rogerlascelles.com
Est. 1984 *Stock size* Large
Stock Antique and reproduction clocks
Open Mon–Fri 10am–5pm
Fairs Birmingham, Frankfurt, New York Gift Fair
Services Annual catalogue

⊞ Lewin
Contact Harriet Lewin
✉ **638 Fulham Road, London, SW6 5RT**
☎ 020 7731 3738
Est. 1992 *Stock size* Medium
Stock Original 1829–40 Dutch colonial furniture
Open Mon–Sat 10.30am–6pm
Services Restorations

⊞ M Luther Antiques
Contact Mr M Luther
✉ **590 King's Road, Chelsea, London, SW6 2DX** 🅿
☎ 020 7371 8492 Ⓕ 020 7371 8492
Est. 1992 *Stock size* Medium
Stock 18th–19thC English and Continental furniture, tables, chairs, mirrors, lighting etc
Open Mon–Sat 9.30am–6pm

⊞ Michael Marriott
Contact Mr M Marriott
✉ **Unit 7, 72 Farm Lane, London, SW6 1QA** 🅿
☎ 020 7610 3922
Ⓜ 07740 633012
Est. 1979 *Stock size* Medium
Stock English 18th–19thC furniture
Open Mon–Fri 9am–5pm Sat 9am–1pm
Services Valuations, restorations

⊞ David Martin-Taylor Antiques (LAPADA)
Contact Mr Cavet
✉ **558 King's Road, London, SW6 2DZ** 🅿
☎ 020 7731 4135 Ⓕ 020 7371 0029
Ⓜ 07889 437306
Ⓔ dmt@davidmartintaylor.com
Ⓦ www.davidmartintaylor.com
Est. 1965 *Stock size* Large
Stock 18th–19thC Continental and English furniture, objets d'art, decorative art, from the eccentric to the unusual
Open Mon–Fri 10am–6pm Sat 11am–4.30pm or by appointment
Fairs Olympia (June), London Decorative Arts

⊞ Ann May
Contact Mrs A May
✉ **80 Wandsworth Bridge Road, London, SW6 2TF** 🅿
☎ 020 7731 0862
Est. 1969 *Stock size* Medium
Stock Painted French furniture, decorative items
Open Mon–Sat 10am–6pm

⊞ Mark Maynard
Contact Mr M Maynard
✉ **651 Fulham Road, London, SW6 5PU** 🅿
☎ 020 7731 3533
Est. 1985 *Stock size* Medium
Stock Painted French furniture, decorative items
Open Mon–Sat 10am–6pm

⊞ Mora & Upham Antiques
Contact Mr M Upham
✉ **584 King's Road, London, SW6 2DX** 🅿
☎ 020 7731 4444 Ⓕ 020 7736 0440
Ⓔ mora.upham@talk21.com
Est. 1980 *Stock size* Large
Stock Gilded French chairs, antique chandeliers, 18th–19thC English and Continental furniture, mirrors
Open Mon–Sat 10am–6pm

⊞ Sylvia Napier Ltd
Contact Mrs S Napier
✉ **554 King's Road, London, SW6 2DZ** 🅿
☎ 020 7371 5881
Ⓜ 07802 309081
Est. 1981 *Stock size* Large
Stock Painted Continental furniture, ironwork, chandeliers, urns
Open Mon–Sat 10am–6pm

⊞ Nimmo & Spooner
Contact Myra Spooner or Catherine Nimmo
✉ **277 Lillie Road, London, SW6 7LL** 🅿
☎ 020 7385 2724 Ⓕ 020 7385 2724
Est. 1990 *Stock size* Medium
Stock Decorative antiques, unusual objects, 18thC French furniture
Open Mon–Sat 10am–5.30pm
Fairs Decorative Antiques and Textiles Fair

⊞ Old World Trading Co
Contact Mr R Campion
✉ **565 King's Road, London, SW6 2EB** 🅿
☎ 020 7731 4708
Ⓕ 020 7731 1291
Ⓔ oldworld@btinternet.com
Est. 1970 *Stock size* Large
Stock 18th–19thC English and French chimney places, fire dogs, grates
Open Mon–Fri 9.30am–6pm Sat 10am–3pm
Services Valuations, restorations

⊞ Orient Expressions Ltd (BABAADA)
Contact Amanda Leader
✉ **Studio 3B2, 3rd Floor, Cooper House, 2 Michael Road, London, SW6 2ER** 🅿

☎ 020 7610 9311 Ⓕ 020 7610 6872
Ⓜ 07887 770406
Ⓔ amanda@orientexpressions.com
Ⓦ www.orientexpressions.com
Est. 1996 *Stock size* Medium
Stock Mostly early 19thC provincial Chinese furniture, accessories
Open By appointment

⊞ Anthony Outred Antiques Ltd (BADA)
Contact Anthony Outred
✉ **69 Finlay Street, London, SW6 6HS** Ⓟ
☎ 020 7371 9863 Ⓕ 020 7371 9869
Ⓜ 07767 848132
Ⓔ antiques@outred.co.uk
Ⓦ www.outred.co.uk
Est. 1977 *Stock size* Medium
Stock 18th–19thC English, Irish and Continental furniture, sculptures, lighting, oil paintings
Open By appointment
Fairs Olympia (June)

⊞ Rainbow Antiques
Contact Mr Fabio Bergomi
✉ **329 Lillie Road, London, SW6 7NR** Ⓟ
☎ 020 7385 1323 Ⓕ 020 7385 4190
Ⓔ rainbowlondon@aol.com
Ⓦ www.rainbowlondon.com
Est. 1998 *Stock size* Large
Stock Italian, French 1880–1940 period lighting, chandeliers, lamps, lanterns
Open Mon–Sat 10.30am–5.30pm or by appointment
Fairs Battersea Decorative Antiques Fair, House and Garden
Services Restorations, re-wiring

⊞ Daphne Rankin & Ian Conn Oriental Antiques (LAPADA)
Contact Ms Sara Reynolds
✉ **608 King's Road, London, SW6 2DX** Ⓟ
☎ 020 7384 1847 Ⓕ 020 7384 1847
Ⓜ 07774 487713
Ⓔ daphnerankin@aol.com
Ⓦ www.china-trade.com
Est. 1979 *Stock size* Large
Stock 17th–19thC Japanese Imari, Chinese Export porcelain, Rose Mandarin, Blue Canton, tortoiseshell tea caddies, Dutch Delft
Open Mon–Sat 10.30am–6pm or by appointment
Fairs Olympia (June, Nov)

⊞ Red Room
Contact Ms Lei Jia
✉ **72 Farm Lane, Fulham, London, SW6 1QA** Ⓟ
☎ 020 7386 8777 Ⓕ 020 7385 3747
Ⓜ 07798 801707
Ⓔ compact@red-room.com
Ⓦ www.red-room.com
Est. 1997 *Stock size* Medium
Stock 18th–19thC Chinese decorative antique furniture
Open Wed–Fri 11am–5pm Sat 11am–3pm
Fairs Battersea

⊞ Rogers & Co (LAPADA)
Contact Christine or Michael Rogers
✉ **604 Fulham Road, London, SW6 5RP** Ⓟ
☎ 020 7731 8504 Ⓕ 020 7610 6040
Est. 1971 *Stock size* Medium
Stock 19thC English antiques
Open Mon–Fri 10am–6pm Sat 10am–5pm

⊞ Soosan
Contact Suzanne or Murray
✉ **598a Kings Road, London, SW6 2DX**
☎ 020 7373 4489 Ⓕ 020 7311 1566
Ⓔ suze@soosan.co.uk
Ⓦ www.soosan.co.uk
Est. 1995 *Stock size* Large
Stock Oriental antiques and interiors
Open Mon–Sat 10am–6pm

⊞ Stephen Sprake Antiques
Contact Mr S Sprake
✉ **283 Lillie Road, London, SW6 7LL** Ⓟ
☎ 020 7381 3209 Ⓕ 020 7381 9502
Ⓜ 07710 922225
Est. 1998 *Stock size* Medium
Stock 18th–20thC English and French furniture, lighting, unusual architectural pieces
Open Mon–Sat 10.30am–5.30pm

⊞ Through The Looking Glass
Contact John Pulton
✉ **563 King's Road, London, SW6 2EB**
☎ 020 7736 7799 Ⓕ 020 7602 3678
Stock size Large
Stock 19thC mirrors
Open Mon–Sat 10am–5.30pm closed Sun

⊞ Whiteway & Waldron Ltd
Contact Mr G Kirkland
✉ **305 Munster Road, London, SW6 6BJ** Ⓟ
☎ 020 7381 3195 Ⓕ 020 7381 3195
Ⓔ sales@whiteway-waldron.co.uk
Ⓦ www.whiteway-waldron.co.uk
Est. 1978 *Stock size* Large
Stock Religious Victoriana, statues, chalices, sanctuary lamps, crucifixes, candlesticks
Open Mon–Fri 10am–5.30pm Sat 11am–4pm

⊞ York Gallery Ltd
Contact Mr G Beyer
✉ **569 King's Road, London, SW6 2EB** Ⓟ
☎ 020 7736 2260 Ⓕ 020 7736 2260
Ⓔ prints@yorkgallery.co.uk
Ⓦ www.yorkgallery.co.uk
Est. 1989 *Stock size* Large
Stock Antique prints
Open Mon–Sat 10.30am–6pm
Services Picture framing

SW7

⊞ Atlantic Bay Gallery (BADA)
Contact Mr Wojtek Grodzinski
✉ **14 Gloucester Road, London, SW7 4RB** Ⓟ
☎ 020 7589 8489 Ⓕ 020 7589 8189
Ⓜ 07831 455492
Ⓔ atlanticbaygallery@btinternet.com
Ⓦ www.atlanticbaycarpet.com
Est. 1945 *Stock size* Large
Stock Oriental and European carpets and textiles, Islamic and Indian art
Open Mon–Fri 9am–5.30pm
Services Valuations, restorations

Bonhams
✉ **Montpelier Street, London, SW7 1HH** Ⓟ
☎ 020 7393 3900 Ⓕ 020 7393 3905
Ⓔ info@bonhams.com
Ⓦ www.bonhams.com
Est. 1793
Open Mon–Fri 9am–4.30pm Sun 11am–3pm
Sales Regular sales of antique and modern guns and militaria, antiquities, books, maps and manuscripts, clocks and watches, coins, collectables, including toys, scientific instruments and entertainment memorabilia, carpets and rugs, contemporary ceramics, ceramics and glass,

decorative arts, design, furniture, Islamic works of art, jewellery, musical instruments, pictures, frames, Oriental works of art, portrait miniatures, silver, textiles, tribal art and vintage pens. In addition to general sales, regional salerooms offer more specialized areas of interest including sporting memorabilia and wines and spirits. Regular house and attic sales across the country; contact London offices for further details
Catalogues Yes

Christie's South Kensington (BACA Award Winner 2002)
85 Old Brompton Road, London, SW7 3LD
020 7581 7611 Ⓕ 020 7321 3311
Ⓦ www.christies.com
Est. 1766
Open Tues–Fri 9am–5pm
Mon 9am–7.30pm
Sales Weekly furniture sale Wed 10.30am. Fortnightly sale of silver Tues 2pm and ceramics Tues 10.30am and 2pm. Fortnightly jewellery sale Tues 2pm and pictures Thurs 10.30am, viewing Sun 1–4pm Mon 9am–7.30pm Tues–Fri 9am–5pm
Catalogues Yes

Gloucester Road Bookshop
Contact Vivi Gregory
123 Gloucester Road, London, SW7 4TE Ⓟ
020 7370 3503 Ⓕ 020 7373 0610
Ⓔ manager@gloucesterbooks.co.uk
Ⓦ www.gloucesterbooks.co.uk
Est. 1983 *Stock size* Large
Stock Antiquarian, rare, second-hand books, modern literature, academic, art, first editions
Open Mon–Fri 9.30am–10.30pm
Sat Sun 10.30am–6.30pm
Services Catalogues, shipping, booksearch

M P Levene Ltd (BADA)
Contact Mr Martin Levene
5 Thurloe Place, London, SW7 2RR Ⓟ
020 7589 3755 Ⓕ 020 7589 9908
Ⓔ silver@mplevene.co.uk
Ⓦ mplevene.co.uk
Est. 1989 *Stock size* Medium
Stock Antique and modern English silver, silver cufflinks, cutlery sets, handmade silver scale models
Open Mon–Fri 9am–6pm
Sat 9am–1.30pm
Services Valuations

Robert Miller
Contact Robert Miller
15 Glendower Place, South Kensington, London, SW7 3DR Ⓟ
020 7584 4733
Est. 1968 *Stock size* Medium
Stock Furniture, pictures and works of art
Open Mon–Fri 9am–5pm
Sat 2–6pm or by appointment
Fairs Olympia

SW8

French House Antiques
Contact Marcus Hazell
125 Queenstown Road, Battersea, London, SW8 3RH Ⓟ
020 7978 2228 Ⓕ 020 7978 2340
Ⓔ info@thefrenchhouse.co.uk
Ⓦ www.thefrenchhouse.co.uk
Est. 1998 *Stock size* Medium
Stock French furniture, beds, mirrors
Open Mon–Sat 10am–6pm

Paul Orssich (PBFA)
Contact Paul Orssich
2 St Stephens Terrace, South Lambeth, London, SW8 1DH Ⓟ
020 7787 0030 Ⓕ 020 7735 9612
Ⓔ paulo@orssich.com
Ⓦ www.orssich.com
Est. 1980 *Stock size* Large
Stock Antiquarian, rare and out-of-print books on Hispanic topics
Open By appointment
Fairs Bonnington North Map Fair
Services Valuations, book search

SW10

Adam & Eve Books
Contact Mr S Dickson
18a Basement, Redcliffe Square, London, SW10 9JZ Ⓟ
020 7370 4535 Ⓜ 07961 316 918
Ⓔ stephen.dickson@virgin.net
Est. 1999 *Stock size* Small
Stock Antiquarian books, Middle East, travel, first editions, modern first editions a speciality
Open By appointment
Fairs Royal National Hotel Book Fair

Paul Andrews Antiques
Contact Lizzie Bluff
The Furniture Cave, 533 King's Road, London, SW10 0TZ Ⓟ
020 7352 4584 Ⓕ 020 7351 7815
Ⓔ mail@paulandrews.co.uk
Ⓦ www.paulandrewsantiques.co.uk
Est. 1969 *Stock size* Large
Stock Eclectic furniture, sculpture, tapestries, paintings, works of art
Open Mon–Sat 10am–6pm
Sun noon–5pm

Bonhams
65–69 Lots Road, London, SW10 0RN
020 7393 3900 Ⓕ 020 7393 3906
Ⓔ info@bonhams.com
Ⓦ www.bonhams.com
Est. 1793
Open 9am–4.30pm Mon–Fri
11am–3pm Sun viewing only
Sales Regular sales of furniture, carpets, ceramics, glass, Oriental works of art, 19thC oils, watercolours, modern pictures, prints, frames, toys, dolls, textiles, rock and pop, tribal art, decorative arts
Catalogues Yes

Brown's
Contact Mr N McAuliffe
First Floor, The Furniture Cave, 533 King's Road, London, SW10 0TZ Ⓟ
020 7352 2046
Ⓦ www.thecave.co.uk
Est. 1972 *Stock size* Medium
Stock 18th–20thC furniture, chandeliers, lighting, tapestries, furniture, accessories
Open Mon–Sat 10am–6pm
Sun noon–4pm

Chelsea Gallery (LAPADA)
Contact Mr S Toscani
The Plaza, 535 King's Road, Chelsea, London, SW10 0SZ Ⓟ
020 7823 3248 Ⓕ 020 7352 1579

e info@chelseagallery.co.uk
w www.chelseagallery.co.uk
Est. 1978 *Stock size* Medium
Stock Antique illustrated books, literature, prints, maps, specializing in natural history, travel, architecture, history
Open Mon–Sat 10.30am–7pm
Services Framing

The Classic Library
Contact Gerry Freeman
1st floor, 533 King's Road, London, SW10 0TZ
☎ 020 7376 7653 f 020 7376 7653
Stock size Large
Stock Antiquarian books, bookcases, library furniture, prints
Open Mon–Sat 10am–6pm
Sun noon–5pm

Kenneth Harvey Antiques (LAPADA)
Contact Mr K Harvey
The Furniture Cave, 533 King's Road, London, SW10 0TZ P
☎ 020 7352 3775 f 020 7352 3759
e mail@kennethharvey.com
Est. 1982 *Stock size* Large
Stock English and French furniture, chandeliers, mirrors, late 17thC–20thC, leather armchairs
Open Mon–Sat 10am–6pm
Sun 11am–5pm

Simon Hatchwell Antiques
Contact Mr A Hatchwell
533 King's Road, London, SW10 0TZ P
☎ 020 7351 2344 f 020 7351 3520
e hatchwell@callnetuk.com
Est. 1961 *Stock size* Large
Stock English and Continental furniture, early 19th–20thC chandeliers, lighting, bronzes, barometers, clocks including grandfather clocks
Open Mon–Sat 10am–6pm
Sun 11.30am–5pm
Fairs Olympia (June)
Services Valuations, restorations

John Nicholas Antiques
Contact Mr Nicholas McAuliffe
First Floor, 533 King's Road, London, SW10 0TZ P
☎ 020 7352 2046
w www.thecave.co.uk
Est. 1999 *Stock size* Medium
Stock 18th–20thC furniture, accessories, chandeliers, lighting, tapestries
Open Mon–Sat 10am–6pm
Sun noon–4pm

Langfords Marine Antiques (BADA, LAPADA)
Contact Mrs J Langford
The Plaza, 535 King's Road, London, SW10 0SZ P
☎ 020 7351 4881 f 020 7352 0763
e langford@dircon.co.uk
w www.langfords.co.uk
Est. 1950 *Stock size* Large
Stock Nautical artefacts
Open Mon–Sat 10am–5.30pm

L'Encoignure
Contact Thomas Kerr
517 King's Road, London, SW10 0TX P
☎ 020 7351 6465 f 020 7351 4744
e kerrant@globalnet.co.uk
w www.thomaskerrantiques.com
Est. 1994 *Stock size* Large
Stock 18th–19thC French furniture, decorative items, Continental furniture
Open Mon–Sat 10am–6pm
Services Interior design

Stephen Long
Contact Mr S Long
348 Fulham Road, London, SW10 9UH P
☎ 020 7352 8226
Est. 1966 *Stock size* Medium
Stock Painted furniture, small decorative items, English pottery, 1780–1850
Open Mon–Fri 9.30am–1pm
2.15–5pm Sat 10am–12.30pm

Lots Road Galleries
Contact Patricia Roos or Melina Papadopolous
71–73 Lots Road, Chelsea, London, SW10 0RM P
☎ 020 7351 7771 f 020 7376 6899
e info@lotsroad.com
w www.lotsroad.com
Est. 1979
Open Mon–Wed 9am–6pm
Thurs 9am–7pm Fri 9am–4pm
Sat 10am–4pm Sun 10am–7pm
Sales 2 sales each Monday, 1pm modern and reproduction furnishings, 6pm antiques sale, viewing Thurs 5–7pm
Fri–Sun 10am–4pm
Mon 9am–6pm
Catalogues Yes

James McWhirter
Contact James McWhirter
22 Park Walk, London, SW10 0AQ P
☎ 020 7351 5399 f 020 7352 9821
e mail@jamesmcwhirter.com
w www.jamesmcwhirter.com
Est. 1988 *Stock size* Medium
Stock 17th–20thC unusual objects and furniture
Open Mon–Fri 9am–6pm

Phoenix Trading Co
Contact Mr T Shalloe
The Furniture Cave, 533 King's Road, London, SW10 0TZ P
☎ 020 7351 6543 f 020 7352 9803
w www.phoenixtrading.co.uk.
Est. 1979 *Stock size* Large
Stock Antique and reproduction decorative accessories, furniture, porcelain, bronze, marble
Open Mon–Sat 10am–6pm
Sun 11am–5pm

H W Poulter & Son
Contact Mr D Poulter
279 Fulham Road, London, SW10 9PZ P
☎ 020 7352 7268 f 020 7351 0984
Est. 1946 *Stock size* Large
Stock 18th–19thC marble, wooden, stone fireplaces, accessories
Open Mon–Fri 9am–5pm
Sat 9am–noon
Services Restoration of marble

Francis Smith Ltd
Contact Mr Norman Ashford
107 Lots Road, Chelsea, London, SW10 0RN P
☎ 020 7349 0011 f 020 7349 0770
Est. 1835
Open Mon–Fri 9am–6pm
Sales Antiques and general sale Tues 6pm, viewing Sun 11am–4pm Mon 9am–7pm Tues 9am–6pm prior to sale
Frequency Fortnightly
Catalogues Yes

John Thornton
Contact John or Caroline Thornton
455 Fulham Road, London, SW10 9UZ P
☎ 020 7352 8810
Est. 1964 *Stock size* Medium
Stock Antiquarian and

LONDON

second-hand books, Catholic and Anglo-Catholic theology
Open Mon–Sat 10am–5.30pm

SW11

⊞ Banana Dance Ltd (LAPADA)
Contact Mr J Daltrey
✉ **Unit 20, The Northcote Road, Antiques Market, 155a Northcote Road, Battersea, London, SW11 2QT** 🅿
☎ 020 8699 7728/7354 3125
Ⓕ 020 8699 7728
Ⓜ 07976 296987
Ⓔ jonathan@bananadance.com
Ⓦ www.bananadance.com
Est. 1988 *Stock size* Large
Stock Clarice Cliff, Art Deco, ceramics, silver, silver plate
Open Mon–Sat 10am–6pm
Sun noon–5pm
Fairs NEC April, Alexandra Palace
Services Valuations, mail order

⊞ Battersea Collectables
Contact Mr David Nurse
✉ **495 Battersea Park Road, London, SW11 4LW** 🅿
☎ 020 7228 8820 Ⓕ 020 7978 6188
Ⓜ 07939 087757
Ⓔ revdavidnurse@onetel.net.uk
Est. 1998 *Stock size* Medium
Stock China, clocks, furniture, pictures, mirrors, collectables, Asian, Far East furniture
Open Mon–Sat 10am–6pm
Services Valuations, shipping

⊞ Braemar Antiques
Contact Mrs Marlis Ramos de Deus
✉ **Braemar Villas, 113 Northcote Road, London, SW11 6PW** 🅿
☎ 020 7924 5628
Est. 1994 *Stock size* Medium
Stock Decorative antiques, furniture, chandeliers, mirrors, fabrics
Open Mon–Sat 10am–5.30pm
Fairs Horticultural Hall, Kensington Brocante

⊞ Chesney's Antique Fireplaces
Contact Henry Masterton
✉ **194–202 Battersea Park Road, London, SW11 4ND** 🅿
☎ 020 7627 1410 Ⓕ 020 7622 1078
Ⓔ sales@chesneys.co.uk
Ⓦ www.chesneys.co.uk
Est. 1985 *Stock size* Large
Stock Antique fireplaces
Open Mon–Fri 9am–5.30pm
Sat 10am–5pm

⊞ Eccles Road Antiques
Contact Mrs H Rix
✉ **60 Eccles Road, London, SW11 1LX** 🅿
☎ 020 7228 1638 Ⓕ 020 8767 5313
Ⓜ 07885 172087
Est. 1985 *Stock size* Large
Stock Victoriana, pine and mahogany furniture, collectables, kitchenware
Open Tues–Sat 10am–5pm
Sun noon–5pm
Fairs Ardingly

⊞ Garland Antiques
Contact Mrs Garland Beech
✉ **74 Chatham Road, London, SW11 6HG** 🅿
☎ 020 7924 4284 Ⓕ 020 7924 4284
Est. 1998 *Stock size* Medium
Stock English and Continental furniture, decorative items
Open Tues–Sat 10am–6pm
Sun noon–5pm
Services Pine stripping

⊞ Gideon Hatch Rugs & Carpets
Contact Gideon Hatch
✉ **1 Port House, Plantation Wharf, London, SW11 3GY** 🅿
☎ 020 7223 3996 Ⓜ 07801 748962
Ⓦ www.gideonhatch.co.uk
Est. 1998 *Stock size* Medium
Stock Rugs and carpets
Open By appointment
Fairs Olympia
Services Restorations, cleaning

⌂ Northcote Road Antiques Market
Contact Mrs Gill Wilkins
✉ **155a Northcote Road, London, SW11 6QB** 🅿
☎ 020 7228 6850
Est. 1986 *Stock size* Large
No. of dealers 30
Stock Jewellery, prints, pictures, glass, Victoriana, Art Deco, furniture, lighting, silver, plate, textiles, old advertising
Open Mon–Sat 10am–6pm
Sun noon–5pm
Services Café

⊞ Overmantels
Contact Seth Taylor
✉ **66 Battersea Bridge Road, London, SW11 3AG** 🅿
☎ 020 7223 8151 Ⓕ 020 7924 2283
Ⓦ www.overmantels.co.uk
Est. 1982 *Stock size* Small
Stock Mirrors, console tables
Open Mon–Sat 9.30am–5.30pm

⊞ Pairs Antiques
Contact Iain Brunt
✉ **Unit 6, Parkfields Industrial Estate, Culvert Road, Battersea, London, SW11 5BA** 🅿
☎ 020 7622 6446 Ⓕ 0870 1273570
Ⓜ 07798 684694
Ⓔ iain@pairsantiques.co.uk
Ⓦ www.pairsantiques.co.uk
Est. 1995 *Stock size* Large
Stock 18th–19thC English and Continental pairs of furniture
Open By appointment
Services Valuations, restorations, shipping, upholstery

⊞ Wood Pigeon
Contact Mr J Taylor or Mrs B Cunnell
✉ **71 Webb's Road, London, SW11 6SD** 🅿
☎ 020 7223 8668 Ⓕ 020 8647 8790
Ⓜ 07958 787676 or 07932 780707
Est. 1996 *Stock size* Medium
Stock French, country, painted, upholstered furniture, decorative items
Open Tues–Sat 10.30am–5.30pm
Sun noon–4pm
Services Decorative furniture painting, upholstery

⊞ Robert Young Antiques (BADA)
Contact Sharon Fraser
✉ **68 Battersea Bridge Road, London, SW11 3AG** 🅿
☎ 020 7228 7847 Ⓕ 020 7585 0489
Ⓔ office@robertyoungantiques.com
Ⓦ robertyoungantiques.com
Est. 1975 *Stock size* Medium
Stock Country furniture, folk art, treen
Open Tues–Fri 9.30am–6pm
Sat 10am–5pm
Fairs Olympia (June), Chelsea

SW13

⊞ Christine Bridge Antiques (BADA, LAPADA, CINOA)
Contact Christine Bridge or Darryl Bowles

⊠ 78 Castelnau, London, SW13 9EX P
☎ 07000 4 GLASS or 020 8741 5501
F 07000 FAX GLASS or 020 8255 0172 M 07831 126668
E christine@bridge-antiques.com
W www.bridge-antiques.com or www.antiqueglass.co.uk
Est. 1970 *Stock size* Medium
Stock 18thC collectors' glass, 19thC coloured and decorative glass
Open By appointment
Fairs BADA, Olympia, fairs in USA and Far East

Simon Coleman Antiques
Contact Simon Coleman
⊠ 40 White Hart Lane, Barnes, London, SW13 0PZ P
☎ 020 8878 5037
Est. 1977 *Stock size* Large
Stock Fully restored farmhouse tables, narrow serving tables
Open Mon–Fri 9.30am–6pm Sat 9.30am–5pm

The Dining Room Shop
Contact David Hur
⊠ 62–64 White Hart Lane, Barnes, London, SW13 0PZ P
☎ 020 8878 1020 F 020 8876 2367
E enquiries@thediningroomshop.co.uk
W www.thediningroomshop.co.uk
Est. 1985 *Stock size* Medium
Stock Everything for formal and country dining rooms, furniture, china, glass, silver, linens, lighting, prints
Open Mon–Sat 10am–5.30pm
Fairs Olympia June
Services Valuations, restorations

Joy McDonald Antiques
Contact Ms Angela McDonald
⊠ 50 Station Road, Barnes, London, SW13 0LP P
☎ 020 8876 6184 F 020 8876 6184
Est. 1966 *Stock size* Medium
Stock 18th–20thC mirrors, chandeliers, lighting, upholstered chairs, decorative items
Open Tues–Sat 10.30am–5.30pm

Tobias & The Angel
Contact Angel Hughes
⊠ 68 White Hart Lane, London, SW13 0PZ P
☎ 020 8878 8902 F 020 8296 0058
Est. 1985 *Stock size* Large
Stock Country antiques, furniture, lampshades, pictures, mirrors, linen, pretty, useful objects for the home
Open Mon–Sat 10am–6pm
Services Mail order, bespoke furniture

SW14

The Arts and Crafts Furniture Co Ltd
Contact Mr P Rogers
⊠ 49 Sheen Lane, East Sheen, London, SW14 8AB P
☎ 020 8876 6544 F 020 8876 6544
E acfc@49sheen.fsnetco.uk
W www.acsc.co.uk
Est. 1989 *Stock size* Large
Stock Arts and Crafts furniture, copperware, ceramics, fabrics, artworks
Open Mon–Fri 10am–6pm Sat 10am–5pm
Services Restorations

Paul Foster Books (ABA, PBFA)
Contact Paul Foster
⊠ 119 Sheen Lane, East Sheen, London, SW14 8AE P
☎ 020 8876 7424 F 020 8876 7424
E paulfosterbooks@btinternet.com
Est. 1990 *Stock size* Medium
Stock Antiquarian, rare, second-hand, out-of-print books
Open Mon–Sat 10.30am–6pm
Fairs Olympia, Chelsea

SW15

30th Century Comics
Contact Mr H Stangroom
⊠ 18 Lower Richmond Road, London, SW15 1JP P
☎ 020 8788 2052
E rob@thirtiethcentury.free-online.co.uk
W www.thirtiethcentury.free-online.do.uk
Est. 1994 *Stock size* Large
Stock British and American vintage and new collectors' comics, annuals, 1930s–1970s
Open Mon–Wed Sat 10.30am–6pm Thurs Fri 10.30am–7pm Sun 11am–5pm
Fairs Royal National Comic Marts, Camden Centre Comic Marts
Services Quarterly catalogue

The Clock Clinic Ltd (LAPADA)
Contact Mr R Pedler FBHI
⊠ 85 Lower Richmond Road, Putney, London, SW15 1EU P
☎ 020 8788 1407 F 020 8780 2838
E clockclinic@btconnect.com
W www.clockclinic.co.uk
Est. 1971 *Stock size* Medium
Stock Antique clocks, barometers, all overhauled and guaranteed
Open Tues–Fri 9am–6pm Sat 9am–1pm
Fairs Olympia (Feb, June, Nov)
Services Valuations, restorations, repairs

Hanshan Tang Books (ABA)
Contact Mr J Cayley
⊠ Unit 3, Ashburton Centre, 276 Cortis Road, London, SW15 3AY P
☎ 020 8788 4464 F 020 8780 1565
E hst@hanshan.com
W www.hanshan.com
Est. 1974 *Stock size* Medium
Stock East Asian art, archaeology
Open By appointment
Services Book search, library purchases

SW16

H C Baxter & Sons (BADA, LAPADA)
Contact Mr G Baxter
⊠ 40 Drewstead Road, London, SW16 1AB P
☎ 020 8769 5969 F 020 8769 0898
E partners@hcbaxter.co.uk
W www.hcbaxter.co.uk
Est. 1928 *Stock size* Medium
Stock 18th–19thC English furniture, decorative items
Trade only Public by appointment only
Open Wed Thurs 9am–5pm
Fairs Olympia (Nov) BADA, Duke of York, Grosvenor House
Services Valuations

A and J Fowle
Contact Mr A Fowle
⊠ 542 Streatham High Road, London, SW16 3QF P
☎ 020 8764 2896 M 07968 058790
Est. 1950 *Stock size* Medium
Stock General antiques, furniture, silver, china, paintings

Open Mon–Sun 9am–6pm or by appointment
Fairs Ardingly

Kantuta
Contact Mrs N Wright
1d Gleneagle Road, London, SW16 6AX
020 8677 6701
Est. 1986 *Stock size* Medium
Stock Antique furniture
Open Mon–Sat 10am–6pm
Services Restorations

SW17

Kerry Ward Antiques
Contact Mrs K Sparkes
30 Bellevue Road, London, SW17 7EF
020 8682 2682
Est. 1993 *Stock size* Large
Stock 19thC painted French furniture, country-look items, French shutters
Open Tues–Sat 10.30am–5.30pm Sun noon–4pm

SW18

Bertie's
Contact Mrs B Ferguson
1st Floor, 284 Merton Road, London, SW18 5JN
020 8874 2520
Est. 1985 *Stock size* Small
Stock Antique and reproduction pine furniture, china, collectables
Open Tues–Sat 9.30am–5.30pm
Services Bespoke pine furniture

The Earlsfield Bookshop
Contact Mr C Dixon
513 Garratt Lane, Wandsworth, London, SW18 4SW
020 8946 3744
Est. 1994 *Stock size* Medium
Stock General books
Open Mon–Thurs 4am–6pm Fri 11am–6pm Sat 10am–5pm
Fairs Kempton Park, Bloomsbury
Services Valuations

Eastern Books of London
Contact Mr P Eastman
81 Replingham Road, London, SW18 5LU
020 8871 0880 020 8877 9757
info@easternbooks.com
www.easternbooks.com
Est. 1989 *Stock size* Large
Stock Antiquarian, rare, second-hand books, Oriental, Middle Eastern, African, maps, prints
Open Mon–Sun noon–7pm
Services Valuations, book search, library building

The House Hospital
Contact Mr J Brunton
9 Ferrier Street, London, SW18 1SW
020 8870 8202
Est. 1983 *Stock size* Medium
Stock Fireplaces, cast-iron radiators, doors, handles, general architectural salvage
Open Mon–Sat 10am–5pm
Services Sandblasting, paint stripping

Just a Second
Contact Mr J Ferguson
284 Merton Road, London, SW18 5JN
020 8874 2520
Est. 1980 *Stock size* Medium
Stock General antiques, good quality furniture
Open Tues–Sat 9.30am–5.30pm
Services Valuations, restorations

Lini Designs
Contact Rupali Varma
Unit F, 260–261 Riverside Business Centre, Haldane Place, London, SW18 4UH
020 8870 6895 020 8546 8394
linidesign@aol.com
Stock size Medium
Stock Antique Indian furniture, cushions, artefacts, Christmas decorations
Open Mon–Sat 11am–6pm Sun noon–6pm
Fairs Top Drawer, NEC

Lloyds International Auction Galleries Ltd
Contact Mr Mick Bown
9 Lydden Road, Earlsfield, London, SW18 4LT
020 8788 7777 020 8874 5390
lloyds_international@compuserve.com
www.lloyds-auction.co.uk
Est. 1944
Open Mon–Fri 9.30am–5.30pm
Sales Furniture, paintings and collectables sale Sat 11am, viewing Fri 10.30am–7.30pm Sat 9am prior to sale. Jewellery sale Tues 11am, viewing Mon 9.30am–4pm. General Met Police 'Lost Property' sale Wed 5pm, viewing Wed 10.30am–4.45pm prior to sale
Frequency Fortnightly all sales
Catalogues Yes

SW19

Corfield Potashnick (LAPADA)
Contact Jonathan Fry
39 Church Road, Wimbledon Village, London, SW19 5DG
020 8944 9022 07974 565659
jonfry@btopenworld.com
Est. 1997 *Stock size* Medium
Stock 18–19thC furniture
Open Mon–Sat 10am–6pm
Fairs Lapada, Commonwealth Institute, London
Services Valuations, restorations

Priestley and Ferraro
Contact David Priestley
17 King Street, London, SW19 6QU
020 7930 6228 020 7930 6226
info@priestleyandferraro.com
www.priestleyandferraro.com
Est. 1994 *Stock size* Medium
Stock Early Chinese art
Open Mon–Fri 9.30am–5.30pm
Fairs International Ceramics Fair, Asian Art

Mark J West (BADA)
Contact Mr M West
39b High Street, London, SW19 5BY
020 8946 2811
Est. 1977 *Stock size* Large
Stock 18th–19thC English and Continental glassware
Open Mon–Sat 10am–5.30pm

SW20

W F Turk Fine Antique Clocks (LAPADA, CINOA)
Contact Mr W Turk
355 Kingston Road, London, SW20 8JX
020 8543 3231 020 8543 3231
sales@wfturk.com
www.wfturk.com
Est. 1979 *Stock size* Large

Stock Antique clocks, 17th–19thC longcase and bracket clocks, French decorative mantel and carriage clocks
Open Tues–Fri 9am–5.30pm
Sat 9am–4pm
Fairs Olympia, LAPADA, NEC
Services Valuations, restorations, repairs, sales

WEST

W1

David Aaron
Contact Mr David Aaron
22 Berkeley Square, London, W1J 6EH
020 7491 9588 Ⓕ 020 7491 9522
Ⓔ david_aaron@hotmail.com
Est. 1910 *Stock size* Large
Stock Worldwide ancient art, rare carpets
Open Mon–Fri 9am–6pm
Sat by appointment only
Services Valuations, restorations

Aaron Gallery (ADA)
Contact Simon Aaron
125 Mount Street, London, W1K 3NS
020 7499 9434 Ⓕ 020 7499 0072
Ⓔ simon@aarongallery.com
Ⓦ www.aarongallery.com
Est. 1910 *Stock size* Large
Stock Islamic, near Eastern, Greek, Roman, Egyptian ancient art
Open Mon–Fri 10am–5.30pm
Services Valuations, restorations

Adrian Alan Ltd (BADA, LAPADA)
Contact Miss H Alan
66/67 South Audley Street, London, W1YK 2QX
020 7495 2324 Ⓕ 020 7495 0204
Ⓔ enquiries@adrianalan.com
Ⓦ www.adrianalan.com
Est. 1964 *Stock size* Large
Stock Furniture, light fittings, mirrors, objets d'art, paintings, statues, garden furniture, pianos, 19thC Continental furniture a speciality
Open Mon–Fri 9.30am–6pm
Fairs Olympia (June)
Services Restorations, shipping, storage

Altea Maps and Books (PBFA, ABA)
Contact Mr M Demartini
3rd Floor, 91 Regent Street, London, W1RB 4EL
020 7494 9060 Ⓕ 020 7287 7938
Ⓔ info@alteamaps.com
Ⓦ www.alteamaps.com
Est. 1993 *Stock size* Medium
Stock 15th–19thC maps, atlases, travel books
Open By appointment
Fairs PBFA, Russell Hotel, Chelsea Book Fair
Services Valuations, sale on commission

Argyll Etkin Ltd (PTS)
Contact Jim Hanson or Ian Shapiro
1–9 Hills Place, Oxford Circus, London, W1F 7SA
020 7437 7800
Ⓔ royalty@argyll-etkin.com
Ⓦ www.argyll-etkin.com
Est. 1950 *Stock size* Large
Stock Royal memorabilia, manuscripts, autographs, history of the posts
Open Mon–Fri 8.30am–5pm
Fairs Olympia, Stampex

ATLAS
Contact Mr B Burdett
49 Dorset Street, London, W1U 7NF
020 7224 4192 Ⓕ 020 7224 3351
Ⓔ info@atlasgallery.com
Ⓦ www.atlasgallery.com
Est. 1993 *Stock size* Medium
Stock Antiquarian, rare, second-hand books, travel a speciality. Fine art photographs from vintage prints to limited edition modern prints
Open Mon–Fri 9am–5.30pm
Fairs Bloomsbury, Phillips
Services Valuations, book search

Automatomania
Contact Michael Start
Stand 124, Grays Antique Markets, 58 Davies Street, London, W1K 5LP
020 7495 5259 Ⓕ 020 8343 7809
Ⓜ 07790 719097
Ⓔ magic@automatomania.com
Ⓦ www.automatomania.com
Est. 1990 *Stock size* Large
Stock Automata, mechanical antiques, small music boxes, some magic items
Open Mon–Fri 11am–5pm
Fairs Olympia June
Services Valuations, restorations

Aytac Antiques (NAWCC)
Contact Mr O Aytac
Grays Antique Markets, Unit 331–332, 58 Davies Street, London, W1Y 1LB
020 7629 7380 Ⓕ 020 7629 7380
Ⓔ ossiemania@aol.com
Est. 1982 *Stock size* Large
Stock Vintage wristwatches, clocks, 19thC French bronzes
Open Mon–Fri 10.30am–5pm
Services Wristwatch restoration, repair

J and A Beare Ltd (BADA)
Contact Simon Morris or Frances Gilham
30 Queen Anne Street, London, W1G 8HX
020 7307 9666 Ⓕ 020 7307 9651
Ⓔ violins@beares.com
Ⓦ www.beares.com
Stock size Large
Stock Musical instruments of the violin family
Open Mon–Fri 10am–12.30pm 1.30pm–5pm
Services Valuations

Linda Bee
Contact Linda Bee
1–7 Davies Mews, London, W1Y 1AR
020 7629 5921 Ⓕ 020 7629 5921
Ⓜ 07956 276384
Ⓦ www.emews.com
Est. 1992 *Stock size* Large
Stock Vintage fashion accessories, handbags, perfume bottles, powder compacts, costume jewellery
Open Mon–Fri 1–6pm or by appointment
Fairs Alexandra Palace
Services Valuations

Paul Bennett (LAPADA)
Contact Mr Dubiner
48A George Street, London, W1H 5RF
020 7935 1555
Ⓔ paulbennet@ukgateway.net
Ⓦ www.paulbennet.ukgateway.net
Est. 1967
Stock Antique and modern silver, Sheffield plate
Open Mon–Fri 10am–6pm
Fairs Olympia, Claridges
Services Valuations

⊞ Daniel Bexfield Antiques (LAPADA, BADA, CINOA)
Contact Mr D Bexfield
✉ **26 Burlington Arcade, Mayfair, London, W1J 0PU** 🅿
☎ 020 7491 1720 ⓕ 020 7491 1730
ⓔ antiques@bexfield.co.uk
ⓦ www.bexfield.co.uk
Est. 1981 *Stock size* Large
Stock Fine quality silver, objects of virtue, 17th–20thC
Open Mon–Sat 9am–6pm
Services Valuations, restorations

Biblion
Contact Leo Harrison or Stephen Poole
✉ **Grays in the Mews, 1–7 Davies Mews, London, W1Y 2LP** 🅿
☎ 020 7629 1374 ⓕ 020 7493 7158
ⓔ info@biblion.co.uk
ⓦ www.biblion.com
Est. 1999 *Stock size* Large
No. of dealers 100
Stock Antiquarian, rare books, prints, manuscripts, modern first editions
Open Mon–Sat 10am–6pm
Services Book binding, book search, shipping

⊞ H Blairman & Sons Ltd (BADA)
Contact Martin Levy, Patricia Levy or Sara Sowerby
✉ **119 Mount Street, London, W1K 3NL** 🅿
☎ 020 7493 0444 ⓕ 020 7495 0766
ⓔ blairman@atlas.co.uk
ⓦ www.blairman.co.uk
Est. 1884 *Stock size* Large
Stock 18th–19thC furniture, works of art
Open Mon–Fri 9am–6pm or by appointment
Fairs Grosvenor House Fair, International Fine Art & Antique Dealers Show, New York
Services Catalogues

⊞ N Bloom and Son (1912) Ltd (LAPADA, CINOA, BACA Award Winner 2001)
Contact Ian Harris
✉ **Bond Street Antiques Centre, 124 New Bond Street, London, W1S 1DX**
☎ 020 7629 5060 ⓕ 020 7493 2528
ⓔ nbloom@nbloom.com
ⓦ www.nbloom.com
Est. 1912 *Stock size* Large
Stock 1860–1960 jewellery, silver
Open Mon–Fri 10.30am–5.30pm Sat 11am–5.30pm
Fairs Olympia (June), LAPADA, Claridges (April), Miami (Jan)
Services Valuations, restorations, catalogue

⊞ Blunderbuss Antiques
Contact Mr C Greenaway
✉ **29 Thayer Street, London, W1U 2QW** 🅿
☎ 020 7486 2444 ⓕ 020 7935 1645
ⓔ mail@blunderbuss-antiques.co.uk
ⓦ www.blunderbuss-antiques.co.uk
Est. 1968 *Stock size* Large
Stock 16thC–WWII weapons, militaria
Open Tues–Fri 9.30am–4.30pm

The Bond Street Antiques Centre
Contact Neil Jackson
✉ **124 New Bond Street, London, W1Y 9AE** 🅿
☎ 020 7493 1854 ⓕ 020 7351 5350
ⓔ antique@dial.pipex.com
Est. 1968 *Stock size* Large
No. of dealers 35
Stock Jewellery, silver, fine vintage watches
Open Mon–Fri 10am–6.45pm Sat 11am–5.30pm

Bonhams
✉ **101 New Bond Street, London, W1S 1SR** 🅿
☎ 020 7629 6602 ⓕ 020 7629 8876
ⓔ info@bonhams.com
ⓦ www.bonhams.com
Est. 1793
Open Mon–Fri 9am–4.30pm Sun 11am–3pm
Catalogues Yes

⊞ David Bowden Chinese and Japanese Art
Contact David Bowden
✉ **58 Davies Street, London, W1K 5LP** 🅿
☎ 020 7495 1773
Est. 1980 *Stock size* Large
Stock Japanese Netsuke, works of art, Chinese works of art
Open Mon–Fri 10am–6pm
Fairs NEC

⊞ Patrick Boyd-Carpenter and Howard Neville
Contact Mr P Boyd-Carpenter or Mr H Neville
✉ **Grays Antique Markets, 58 Davies Street, London, W1Y 2LP** 🅿
☎ 020 7491 7623 ⓕ 020 7491 7623
ⓔ patrickboyd_carpenter@hotmail.com
Est. 1986 *Stock size* Large
Stock Wide range of antiques, 16th–18thC sculpture, paintings, prints
Open Mon–Fri 10.30am–5.30pm or by appointment
Services Valuations, restorations

⊞ Brandt Oriental Antiques (BADA)
Contact Robert Brandt
✉ **1st Floor, 29 New Bond Street, London, W1S 2RL** 🅿
☎ 020 7499 8835 ⓕ 020 7409 1882
Ⓜ 07774 989661
ⓔ brandt@nildram.co.uk
Est. 1980 *Stock size* Medium
Stock Japanese metalwork and screens, the China trade
Open By appointment
Fairs June Olympia, New York

⊞ John Bull (Antiques) Ltd (LAPADA)
Contact Elliot or Ken Bull
✉ **139a New Bond Street, London, W1S 2TN** 🅿
☎ 020 7629 1251 ⓕ 020 7495 3001
ⓔ sales@jbsilverware.co.uk
ⓦ www.antique-silver.co.uk
Est. 1952 *Stock size* Medium
Stock Antique silver giftware
Open Mon–Fri 9am–5pm
Fairs Antiques for Everyone

⊞ The Button Queen Ltd
Contact Martin Frith
✉ **19 Marylebone Lane, London, W1U 2NF**
☎ 020 7935 1505 ⓕ 020 7935 1505
ⓦ www.thebuttonqueen.co.uk
Est. 1950 *Stock size* Large
Stock Buttons
Open Mon–Wed 10am–5pm Thur–Fri 10am–6pm Sat 10am–4pm

⊞ Paul Champkins Oriental Art (BADA)
Contact Mr P Champkins
✉ **41 Dover Street, London, W1S 4NS** 🅿
☎ 020 7495 4600 ⓕ 01235 751658
ⓔ pc@paulchampkins.demon.co.uk
Est. 1995 *Stock size* Medium
Stock Chinese, Korean, Japanese porcelain, works of art

Open By appointment
Fairs Grosvenor House, New York Ceramics Fair, Olympia (Winter)
Services Valuations, restorations, auction purchasing advice

⊞ Antoine Chenevière Fine Arts Ltd (BADA)
Contact Mr Chenevière
✉ **27 Bruton Street, London, W1X 7DB** 🅿
☎ 020 7491 1007 ⓕ 020 7495 6173
ⓔ finearts@antoinecheneviere.com
Stock size Medium
Stock 18th–19thC Russian, Austrian, German and Italian furniture, objets d'art
Open Mon–Sat 9.30am–6pm
Fairs Grosvenor House, The Armoury Fair

⊞ Classical Numismatic Group Inc. (BNTA)
Contact Irene Tilmont
✉ **14 Old Bond Street, London, W1S 4PP** 🅿
☎ 020 7495 1888 ⓕ 020 7499 5916
ⓔ cng@cngcoins.com
ⓦ www.cngcoins.com
Est. 1990 *Stock size* Large
Stock Coins, Greek, Roman, Medieval, European to end of 18thC
Open Mon–Fri 9.30am–5.30pm
Fairs Coinex
Services Valuations, auctions, phone for details

⊞ Sibyl Colefax & John Fowler
Contact Roger Jones
✉ **39 Brooks Street, London, W1K 4JE** 🅿
☎ 020 7493 2231 ⓕ 020 7355 4037
ⓔ antiques@sibylcolefax.com
ⓦ www.colefaxantiques.com
Stock size Large
Stock 18th–19thC Continental and English furniture, objects, pictures
Open Mon–Fri 9.30am–5.30pm
Fairs Olympia

⊞ Sandra Cronan Ltd (BADA)
Contact Sandra Cronan or Blane Thompson
✉ **18 Burlington Arcade, London, W1J 0PN** 🅿
☎ 020 7491 4851 ⓕ 020 7493 2758
ⓔ sandracronanltd@btinternet.com
Est. 1978 *Stock size* Medium
Stock 18th–early 20thC jewellery
Open Mon–Fri 10am–5pm
Fairs Grosvenor House, March BADA, The Armoury
Services Valuations, restorations, repairs, design commission

⊞ Cyjer Jewellery Ltd
Contact Mrs E M Plampton
✉ **Stands 143–144, Grays Antique Markets, 58 Davies Street, London, W1Y 2LP** 🅿
☎ 020 7629 3206
Est. 1989 *Stock size* Large
Stock Georgian–Edwardian, Art Deco, modern jewellery
Open Mon–Fri 10.30am–5.30pm closed Tues
Fairs Copthorne Hotel, Runnymede Hotel
Services Restorations

⊞ Barry Davies Oriental Art (BADA)
Contact Barry Davies
✉ **1 Davies Street, London, W1K 3DB** 🅿
☎ 020 7408 0207 ⓕ 020 7493 3422
ⓔ bdoa@btinternet.com
ⓦ www.barrydavies.com
Est. 1976 *Stock size* Large
Stock Japanese works of art
Open Mon–Fri 9am–6pm

⊞ Adèle De Havilland
Contact Adèle De Havilland
✉ **The Bond Street Antique Centre, 124 New Bond Street, London, W1S 1DX**
☎ 020 7499 7127
Est. 1971 *Stock size* Medium
Stock Oriental porcelain, netsuke, jade, ivory carvings, bronze figures, objects of virtue
Open Mon–Sat 10am–4pm

🔨 Dix Noonan Webb (BNTA, OMRS, OMSA)
Contact Mr C Webb
✉ **1 Old Bond Street, London, W1S 4PB** 🅿
☎ 020 7499 5022 ⓕ 020 7499 5023
ⓔ auction@dnw.co.uk
ⓦ www.dnw.co.uk
Est. 1991
Open Mon–Fri 8.30am–5.30pm
Sales Coins and military medals sale Wed, viewing Tues noon–1pm prior to sale
Frequency 10 per annum
Catalogues Yes

⊞ Charles Ede Ltd (BADA, ADA, IADA)
Contact Mr J Ede
✉ **20 Brook Street, London, W1K 5DE** 🅿
☎ 020 7493 4944 ⓕ 020 7491 2548
ⓔ charlesede@attglobal.net
ⓦ www.charlesede.com
Est. 1976 *Stock size* Medium
Stock Egyptian, Greek, Roman classical and pre-classical antiquities
Open Tues–Fri 12.30–4.30pm or by appointment
Fairs Grosvenor House
Services Valuations, bidding at auction, mail order

⊞ Peter Edwards
Contact Mr P Edwards
✉ **31 Burlington Arcade, London, W1J 0PY** 🅿
☎ 020 7491 1589 ⓕ 020 7408 2405
ⓔ peter@edwards-jewels.co.uk
ⓦ www.edwards-jewels.co.uk
Est. 1966 *Stock size* Medium
Stock 20thC jewellery, signed pieces
Open Mon–Sat 10am–6pm
Fairs Olympia, Harrogate
Services Valuations, restorations

⊞ Emanouel Corporation (UK) Ltd (LAPADA)
Contact Emanouel Naghi
64–64a South Audley Street, London, W1K 2QT 🅿
☎ 020 7493 4350 ⓕ 0207 629 3125
Est. 1975 *Stock size* Large
Stock General antiques
Open Mon–Fri 8am–6pm
Services Valuations

⊞ Eskenazi Ltd (BADA)
Contact Mr J Eskenazi
✉ **10 Clifford Street, London, W1S 2LJ** 🅿
☎ 020 7493 5464 ⓕ 020 7499 3136
ⓔ eskArt@ad.com
Est. 1960 *Stock size* Medium
Stock Early Chinese works of art
Open Mon–Fri 9am–5.30pm

⊞ John Eskenazi Ltd (BADA)
Contact Kate Cook
✉ **15 Old Bond Street, London, W1S 4AX** 🅿
☎ 020 7409 3001 ⓕ 020 7629 2146
ⓔ john.eskenazi@john-eskenazi.com
ⓦ www.john-eskenazi.com
Est. 1994 *Stock size* Medium
Stock South East Asian,

Himalayan and Indian works of art, Oriental textiles and carpets
Open Mon–Fri 9am–6pm or by appointment
Fairs International Asian Art Fair

Essie Carpets
Contact Mr Essie
62 Piccadilly, London, W1J 0DZ
020 7493 7766 020 7495 3456
Est. 1766 *Stock size* Large
Stock Persian, Oriental rugs, tapestries
Open Sun Bank Holidays 10.30am–5.30pm Mon–Fri 9.30am–6pm

Simon Finch Rare Books (ABA, PBFA)
Contact Mr S Finch
53 Maddox Street, London, W1S 2PN
020 7499 0974 020 7499 0799
rarebooks@simonfinch.com
www.simonfinch.com
Est. 1982 *Stock size* Medium
Stock 15th–20thC books on art, architecture, literature, science, medicine
Open Mon–Fri 10am–6pm
Fairs Olympia, Chelsea, Grosvenor House
Services Valuations, library advice

J First Antiques
Contact Mr J First
Stand 310, Grays Antique Markets, 58 Davies Street, London, W1Y 1LB
020 7409 2722 020 7409 2722
www.firstsilver18@hotmail.com
Est. 1967 *Stock size* Large
Stock Antique English silver collectables
Open Mon–Fri 10am–6pm
Fairs NEC

Matthew Foster
Contact Mr M Foster or Mr J Silver
Units 4, 5 & 6, Bond Street Antiques Centre, 124 New Bond Street, London, W1S 1DX
020 7629 4977 020 7629 4977
Est. 1987 *Stock size* Large
Stock Large stock of Victorian gold jewellery
Open Mon–Fri 10am–5.30pm Sat 11am–5.30pm
Fairs Olympia (June)

O Frydman
Contact Mr G Barnett
The Bond Street Silver Galleries, 111–112 New Bond Street, London, W1S 1DP
020 7493 4895 020 7493 4895
Est. 1929 *Stock size* Medium
Stock Second-hand and antique silver, Victorian silver, old Sheffield plate
Open Mon–Fri 9.30am–5.30pm
Fairs Park Lane, The Marriot
Services Valuations, renovations

Peter Gaunt
Contact Mr P Gaunt
Stand 120, Grays Antique Markets, 58 Davies Street, London, W1K 5JF
020 7629 1072 020 7629 5253
ptg@peter-gaunt.fsnet.co.uk
Est. 1978 *Stock size* Large
Stock Antique silver including Georgian teaspoons, 17thC candlesticks
Open Mon–Fri 10am–5pm
Services Valuations

Gentry Antiques
Contact Marilyn Gentry
Grays Antiques Market Mews, Davies Street, London, W1Y 2LP
01503 272361
info@cornishwarecollector.co.uk
www.cornishwarecollector.co.uk
Est. 1998 *Stock size* Medium
Stock Cornish ware by T G Green and other kitchenware
Open Mon–Fri 11am–5pm

The Gilded Lily Jewellery Ltd (LAPADA, CINOA)
Contact Ms Korin Harvey
Stand 145–146, Grays Antique Markets, 58 Davies Street, London, W1K 5LP
020 7499 6260 020 7499 6260
jewellery@gilded-lily.co.uk
www.graysantiques.com
Est. 1970 *Stock size* Large
Stock Glamorous jewellery, signed pieces
Open Mon–Fri 10am–6pm
Fairs Olympia, LAPADA, Miami Beach, Hong Kong

Glendining's (BNTA, SOFAA)
Contact Mr A Litherland
101 New Bond Street, London, W1S 1SR
020 7493 2445
Est. 1900
Open Mon–Fri 8.30am–5pm
Sales 4 coin sales, 3 medal sales, also arms, armour, militaria
Frequency 7 per annum
Catalogues Yes

Gordon's Medals (OMRS)
Contact Mr M Gordon
Stand G14–16, Grays Mews Antiques Market, Davies Mews, London, W1K 5AB
020 7495 0900 020 7495 0115
07976 266293
malcolm@gordonsmedals.co.uk
www.gordonsmedals.co.uk
Est. 1979 *Stock size* Large
Stock Militaria, uniforms, headgear, badges, medals, documents
Open Mon–Fri 10.30am–6pm
Fairs Brittania Fair, OMRS
Services Valuations

The Graham Gallery (LAPADA)
Contact Mr G Whittall
60 South Audley Street, Mayfair, London, W1K 2QW
020 7495 3151 020 7495 3171
07710 407 885
Est. 1979 *Stock size* Large
Stock 18–19thC furniture, 19thC oil paintings, objets d'art
Open Mon–Fri 10.30am–6pm or by appointment
Fairs Olympia (June), LAPADA

Graus Antiques
Contact Jackie Stern
Bond Street Silver Galleries, 111–112 New Bond Street, London, W1S 1DP
020 7629 6680 020 7629 6651
eric@graus-antiques.demon.co.uk
Est. 1945 *Stock size* Large
Stock Antique pocket watches, jewellery
Open Mon–Fri 9am–5pm

Anita Gray (LAPADA)
Contact Mrs A Gray
Grays Antique Markets, 58 Davies Street, London, W1K 5LP
020 7408 1638 020 7495 0707
info@chinese-porcelain.com
www.chinese-porcelain.com

Est. 1975 *Stock size* Medium
Stock Asian and European porcelain, works of art, 16th–18thC
Open Mon–Fri 10am–6pm
Fairs Olympia (June)

Grays Antique Markets
Contact William Griffith or Kirstine Wallace
58 Davies Street, London, W1K 5AB
020 7629 7034 020 7629 3279
grays@clara.net
www.egrays.uk
Est. 1977 *Stock size* Large
No. of dealers 300
Stock Automata, British and Oriental ceramics, gems, precious stones, glass, Islamic jewellery, objects, prints, paintings, silver, textiles, lace, linen, watches
Open Mon–Fri 10am–6pm special hours at Christmas
Services Café, bureau de change, jewellery repair, glass and metal engraving, pearl stringing

Anthony Green Antiques
Contact Anthony Green
Unit 39, The Bond Street Antiques Centre, 124 New Bond Street, London, W1S 1DX
0207 409 2854 0207 409 7032
07900 681469
vintagewatches@hotmail.com
www.anthonygreen.com
Est. 1985 *Stock size* Large
Stock Vintage wristwatches and antique pocket watches
Open Mon–Fri 10am–5pm Sat 11am–5pm

Simon Griffin Antiques Ltd
Contact Mr S Griffin
3 Royal Arcade, 28 Old Bond Street, London, W1S 4SB
020 7491 7367
Est. 1979 *Stock size* Medium
Stock Antique, modern silverware, old Sheffield plate
Open Mon–Sat 10am–5.30pm

Nicholas Grindley (BADA)
Contact Ms Rebecca Gardner
13 Old Burlington Street, London, W1S 3AJ
020 7437 5449 020 7494 2446
nick@nicholasgrindley.co.uk
Est. 1993 *Stock size* Small
Stock Chinese works of art, sculptures, wall paintings, furniture etc
Open Mon–Fri 2–5pm or by appointment
Fairs Asian Art, London (Nov)
Services Valuations by mail

Sarah Groombridge (LAPADA)
Contact Sarah Groombridge
Stand 335, 58 Davies Street, London, W1Y 1LB
020 7629 0225 01252 616201
07770 920277
Est. 1974 *Stock size* Medium
Stock Fine antique jewellery, Georgian–1920s including natural pearls, cameos
Open Mon–Fri 10am–6pm
Fairs Olympia (Nov, June) Miami Jan

Guest and Gray
Contact Anthony Gray
1–7 Davies Mews, London, W1Y 2LP
020 7408 1252 020 7499 1445
07968 719496
info@chinese-porcelain-art.com
www.guest-gray.demon.co.uk
Est. 1970 *Stock size* Large
Stock Asian and European ceramics, works of art and art reference books
Open 10am–6pm Mon–Fri
Fairs International Ceramics Fair, Olympia
Services Valuations

Claire Guest at Thomas Goode & Co. Ltd
Contact Claire Guest
19 South Audley Street, London, W1Y 6BH
020 7499 2823/7243 1423
020 7629 4230/7792 5450
Est. 1969 *Stock size* Medium
Stock Antique furniture, silver, silver plate, glass, china
Open Mon–Sat 10am–6pm

Hadji Baba Ancient Art Ltd (IADA)
Contact R Soleimani
34a Davies Street, London, W1K 4NE
020 7499 9363 020 7493 5504
info@hadjibaba.co.uk
www.hadjibaba.co.uk
Est. 1979 *Stock size* Medium
Stock Near and Middle East antiquities
Open Mon–Fri 10am–6pm
Services Valuations

Halcyon Days (BADA)
Contact Cheska Moon or Susan Benjamin
14 Brook Street, London, W1S 1BD
020 7629 8811 020 7514 5472
info@halcyondays.co.uk
www.halcyondays.co.uk
Est. 1950 *Stock size* Small
Stock 18thC English enamels, fans, objects of virtue, tortoiseshell, pique, scent bottles
Open Mon–Fri 9.30am–6pm Sat 10am–6pm
Fairs Grosvenor House

Robert Hall (BADA)
Contact Mr R Hall
15c Clifford Street, London, W1X 1RF
020 7734 4008 020 7734 4408
roberthall@snuffbottle.com
www.snuffbottle.com.
Est. 1976 *Stock size* Large
Stock 18th–19thC Chinese snuff bottles
Open Mon–Fri 10am–5.30pm or by appointment
Fairs Grosvenor House
Services Valuations, bi-annual catalogues

Hallmark Antiques
Contact Mr Ralph
Stands 319 & 356, Grays Antique Markets, Davies Street, London, W1K 5LP
020 7354 1616
Est. 1979 *Stock size* Medium
Stock Victorian–Edwardian jewellery, amber, silver, silver photo frames
Open Mon–Fri 10am–6pm

Hancocks and Co (Jewellers) Ltd (BADA)
Contact Mr Steven Burton
52–53 Burlington Arcade, London, W1J 0HH
020 7493 8904 020 7493 8905

ⓔ info@hancockslondon.com
ⓦ www.hancockslondon.com
Est. 1849 ***Stock size*** Large
Stock Jewellery, silver
Open Mon–Fri 9.30am–5pm
Sat 10am–4pm
Fairs Grosvenor House, Maastricht, The Armoury, Palm Beach
Services Valuations, restorations, purchase of second-hand items

⊞ Brian Haughton Antiques
Contact Brian Haughton
✉ **3b Burlington Gardens, London, W1S 3EP** 🅿
☎ 020 7734 5491 ⓕ 020 7494 4604
ⓔ info@haughton.com
ⓦ www.haughton.com
Est. 1965 ***Stock size*** Large
Stock 18th–19thC English and Continental ceramics
Open Mon–Fri 10am–5pm
Fairs International Ceramics Fair and Seminar (June), The International Fine Art & Antique Dealers Show, New York (Oct)

⊞ Gerard Hawthorn Ltd (BADA)
Contact Mr G Hawthorn
✉ **104 Mount Street, London, W1K 2TL** 🅿
☎ 020 7409 2888 ⓕ 020 7409 2777
ⓜ 07775 917487
ⓔ mail@gerardhawthorn.com
Est. 1996 ***Stock size*** Medium
Stock Chinese, Japanese, Korean ceramics, works of art
Open Mon–Fri 10am–late
Fairs 2 exhibitions at gallery (June, Nov), International Asian Art Fair, New York (March)
Services Valuations, restorations, photography

⊞ G Heywood Hill Ltd (ABA)
Contact Mr John Saumarez Smith
✉ **10 Curzon Street, London, W1J 5HH** 🅿
☎ 020 7629 0647 ⓕ 020 7408 0286
ⓔ books@gheywoodhill.com
ⓦ www.gheywoodhill.com
Est. 1936 ***Stock size*** Medium
Stock Fiction, history, travel, memoirs, children's antiquarian, second-hand, new books
Open Mon–Fri 9am–5.30pm
Sat 9am–12.30pm
Services Book search

⊞ Hirsh Ltd
Contact Ben Stevenson
56–57 Burlington Arcade, London, W1J 0QN 🅿
☎ 020 7499 6814 ⓕ 020 7629 9946
ⓦ www.hirsh.co.uk
Est. 1982 ***Stock size*** Large
Stock Fine antique jewellery, hand-made and designed diamond engagement rings
Open Mon–Fri 10.30am–5pm

⊞ Brian and Lynn Holmes (LAPADA)
Contact Brian or Lynn Holmes
✉ **Stand 304–306, Grays Antique Markets, 58 Davies Street, London, W1Y 2LP** 🅿
☎ 020 7629 7327 ⓕ 020 7629 7327
ⓦ www.graysantiques.com
Est. 1971 ***Stock size*** Large
Stock Antique Georgian, Victorian silver, gold, jewellery, Scottish antique jewellery
Open Mon–Fri 10am–6pm
Services Valuations, restorations

⊞ Holmes Ltd
Contact Mr Eldred
✉ **24 Burlington Arcade, London, W1J 0PS**
☎ 020 7629 8380
Est. 1923 ***Stock size*** Small
Stock Antique, modern jewellery and silver
Open Mon–Sat 9.45am–5pm

⊞ C John Ltd (BADA)
Contact Mr L Sassoon
✉ **70 South Audley Street, London, W1K 2RA** 🅿
☎ 020 7493 5288 ⓕ 020 7409 7030
ⓔ cjohn@dircom.co.uk
Est. 1948 ***Stock size*** Large
Stock Persian, French, Russian, Caucasian tapestries, Indian, Turkish, Chinese carpets, rugs, textiles
Open Mon–Fri 9.30am–5pm
Fairs Grosvenor House
Services Valuations, restorations

⊞ Johnson Walker Ltd (BADA)
Contact Miss R Gill
✉ **64 Burlington Arcade, London, W1J 0QT** 🅿
☎ 020 7629 2615/6
ⓕ 020 7409 0709
Est. 1849 ***Stock size*** Medium
Stock Jewellery, bijouterie
Open Mon–Sat 9.30am–5.30pm
Services Valuations, repairs

⊞ John Joseph (LAPADA, LJAJDA)
Contact Mr J Joseph
✉ **Stand 34b, Grays Antique Markets, 58 Davies Street, London, W1Y 2LP** 🅿
☎ 020 7629 1140 ⓕ 020 7629 1140
ⓔ jewellery@john-joseph.co.uk
ⓦ www.john-joseph.co.uk
Est. 1995 ***Stock size*** Large
Stock Victorian, Edwardian, Art Deco jewellery, gem set, gold, platinum
Open Mon–Fri 10am–6pm
Fairs Olympia (June)

⊞ Daniel Katz Ltd (SLAD)
Contact Daniel Katz or Stuart Lochhead
✉ **13 Old Bond Street, London, W1S 4SX**
☎ 020 7493 0688 ⓕ 020 7499 7493
ⓔ info@katz.co.uk
ⓦ www.katz.co.uk
Est. 1969 ***Stock size*** Large
Stock European sculpture
Open Mon–Fri 9am–6pm

⊞ Roger Keverne Ltd (BADA)
Contact Mr R Keverne
✉ **2nd Floor, 16 Clifford Street, London, W1S 3RQ** 🅿
☎ 020 7434 9100 ⓕ 020 7434 9101
ⓔ rogerkeverne@keverne.co.uk
ⓦ www.keverne.co.uk
Est. 1996 ***Stock size*** Large
Stock Chinese ceramics, jade, lacquer, bronzes, enamels, hard stones, ivory, bamboo
Open Mon–Fri 9.30am–5.30pm
Sat for exhibitions
Fairs Exhibition at 16 Clifford Street (Jun, Nov), International Asian Art Fair, New York (March)
Services Valuations, restorations

⊞ D S Lavender Antiques Ltd (BADA)
Contact Mr D Lavender
✉ **26 Conduit Street, London, W1S 2XX** 🅿
☎ 020 7409 2305 ⓕ 020 7629 3106
ⓔ dslavender@clara.net
Est. 1946 ***Stock size*** Large
Stock Gold, silver, enamel, fine snuff boxes, fine jewels, 16th–early 19thC portrait miniatures
Open Mon–Fri 9.30am–5pm
Fairs Grosvenor House
Services Valuations, restorations

⊞ Leuchers & Jefferson
Contact Mr H Leuchers
✉ **94 Mount Street, London, W1Y 5HG** P
☎ 020 7491 4931 Ⓕ 020 7491 5027
Est. 1829 *Stock size* Medium
Stock 18thC English furniture, decorative items
Open Mon–Sat 9.30am–5.30pm
Services Valuations, restorations

⊞ Sanda Lipton (BADA, CINOA)
Contact Sanda Lipton
✉ **3rd Floor, Elliot House, 28A Devonshire Street, London, W1G 6PS** P
☎ 020 7431 2688 Ⓕ 020 7431 3224
Ⓜ 07836 660008
Ⓔ sanda@antique-silver.com
Ⓦ www.antique-silver.com
Est. 1979 *Stock size* Medium
Stock 16th–mid 19thC silver, collectors items, early English spoons, historical medals
Open By appointment
Fairs Olympia, March BADA
Services Valuations, restorations, consultancy, bidding at auction

⊞ Monty Lo Antiques
Contact Mr M Lo
✉ **Grays Antique Markets, 58 Davies Street, London, W1Y 1LB** P
☎ 020 7493 9457
Est. 1980 *Stock size* Medium
Stock European and English ceramics, glass
Open Mon–Fri 10am–6pm
Services Valuations, repair

⊞ Michael Longmore and Trianon Antiques Ltd (LAPADA)
Contact Mr Bruce Rowley
✉ **Stand 378, Grays Antiques Markets, 58 Davies Street, London, W1K 5LP** P
☎ 020 7491 2764 Ⓕ 020 7409 1587
Ⓔ michaellongmore@aol.com
Est. 1974 *Stock size* Large
Stock Fine jewellery, objets d'art
Open Mon–Fri 10am–5.30pm
Fairs Olympia (June)

⊞ Maggs Bros Ltd (ABA, BADA)
Contact Mr Edward F Maggs
✉ **50 Berkeley Square, London, W1J 5BA** P
☎ 020 7493 7160 Ⓕ 020 7499 2007
Ⓔ ed@maggs.com
Ⓦ www.maggs.com
Est. 1853 *Stock size* Large
Stock Military history, travel, natural history, science, modern literature, early English and Continental books, illustrated manuscripts, autographed letters
Open Mon–Fri 9.30am–5pm
Fairs Olympia
Services Catalogues issued by all departments

⊞ Mallett (BADA)
✉ **Bourden House, 2 Davies Street, London, W1K 3DJ**
☎ 020 7629 2444 Ⓕ 020 7499 2670
Ⓔ antiques@mallett.co.uk
Ⓦ www.mallettantiques.com
Est. 1865 *Stock size* Large
Stock Fine antique furniture, works of art, glass, paintings, watercolours, needlework
Open Mon–Fri 9am–6pm
Sat 10am–4pm
Fairs Grosvenor House, International Ceramics Fair

⊞ Mallett (BADA)
✉ **141 New Bond Street, London, W1S 2BS**
☎ 020 7499 7411 Ⓕ 020 7495 3179
Ⓔ antiques@mallett.co.uk
Ⓦ www.mallettantiques.com
Est. 1865 *Stock size* Large
Stock Fine antique furniture, works of art, glass, paintings, watercolours, needlework
Open Mon–Fri 9am–6pm
Sat 10am–4pm
Fairs Grosvenor House, International Ceramics Fair

⊞ Carol Manheim at Biblion (ABA, PBFA)
Contact Carol Manheim
✉ **Grays, 1–7 Davies Mews, London, W1Y 2LP**
☎ 020 8994 9740
Ⓔ art.photo@lineone.net
Ⓦ www.carolmanheimartbooks.co.uk
Est. 1984
Stock 20thC fine art monographs and illustrated books, exhibition catalogues
Open Mon–Sat 10am–6pm
Fairs ABA

⊞ Map World (LAPADA)
Contact Jeffrey Sharpe
✉ **25 Burlington Arcade, Piccadilly, London, W1V 9AD**
☎ 020 7495 5377 Ⓕ 020 7495 5377
Ⓔ info@map-world.com
Ⓦ www.map-world.com
Est. 1982 *Stock size* Large
Stock 15th–19thC antique maps
Open Mon–Sat 10am–5.30pm
Services Valuations

⊞ Marks Antiques (BADA, LAPADA)
Contact Anthony Marks
✉ **49 Curzon Street, London, W1J 7UN**
☎ 020 7499 1788 Ⓕ 020 7409 3183
Ⓔ marks@marksantiques.com
Ⓦ www.marksantiques.com
Est. 1921 *Stock size* Large
Stock Antique silver, Russian works of art
Open Mon–Fri 9.30am–6pm
Sat 9.30am–5pm
Fairs Olympia, Grosvenor House
Services Valuations, Shipping

⊞ Marlborough Rare Books Ltd (ABA)
Contact Jonathan Gestetner
✉ **4th Floor, 144–146 New Bond Street, London, W1S 2TR**
☎ 020 7493 6993 Ⓕ 020 7499 2479
Ⓔ sales@mrb-books.co.uk
Est. 1948 *Stock size* Medium
Stock Antiquarian and rare art, architecture, illustrated, colour plate, fine bindings, English literature, topography
Open Mon–Fri 9.30am–5.30pm
Fairs Olympia, Chelsea
Services Valuations

⊞ Massada Antiques (LAPADA, LJAJDA)
Contact Mr B Yacobi
✉ **Bond Street Antiques Centre, 124 New Bond Street, London, W1S 1DX** P
☎ 020 7493 5610 Ⓕ 020 7491 9852
Est. 1970 *Stock size* Large
Stock Georgian–Edwardian wearable, decorative jewellery
Open Mon–Fri 10am–5.30pm
Fairs Olympia (June, Nov)
Services Valuations, repairs

⊞ Mayfair Carpet Gallery Ltd
Contact Mr A H Khawaja
✉ **10A Berkeley Street, London, W1J 8DR** P
☎ 020 7493 0126 Ⓕ 020 7407 1649
Est. 1975 *Stock size* Large
Stock Fine antique Oriental carpets, rugs

Open Mon–Sat 10.30am–6.30pm
Services Valuations, restorations

Mayfair Gallery Ltd
Contact Mrs C Giese
39 South Audley Street, London, W1K 2PP
020 7491 3435/3436
020 7491 3437
mayfairgallery@mayfairgallery.net
www.artnet.com/mayfairgallery.html
Est. 1974 *Stock size* Large
Stock 19thC antiques, decorative arts, bronzes, marbles, Continental porcelain, furniture
Open Mon–Fri 9.30am–6pm
Sat by appointment
Fairs Olympia, Miami Beach
Services Valuations, restorations

Melton's
Contact Cecilia Neale
27 Bruton Place, London, W1J 6NQ
020 7409 2938 020 7495 3196
meltons.uk@virgin.net
www.meltons.co.uk
Est. 1980 *Stock size* Medium
Stock Antiques and collectables
Open Mon–Fri 9.30am–5.30pm

The Mews Antique Market
Contact William Griffith or Kirstine Wallace
1–7 Davies Mews, London, W1K 5AB
020 7629 7034 020 7493 9344
grays@clara.net
www.ethemews.co.uk
Est. 1978 *Stock size* Large
No. of dealers 100
Stock Asian, Islamic antiquities, books, perfume bottles, Bohemian glass, ceramics, handbags, carpets, jewellery, militaria, pewter, teddy bears, dolls, toys, clocks, timepieces
Open Mon–Fri 10am–6pm
Services Restorations, repairs, restaurant

Michael's Boxes (PADA)
Contact Michael Cassidy
Unit L15, Grays Mews, Grays Antique Markets, 58 Davies Street, London, W1K 5AB
020 7629 5716 020 8930 8318
info@michaelsboxes.com
www.michaelsboxes.com
Est. 1997 *Stock size* Large
Stock Limoges, enamel and porcelain antique boxes
Open Mon–Fri 10am–5pm
Fairs Portobello
Services Personalized boxes

Moira
Contact Mrs S Lauder
11 New Bond Street, London, W1S 3SR
020 7629 0160 020 7495 3343
info@moira-jewels.com
Est. 1970 *Stock size* Large
Stock Antique, modern and own design jewellery
Open Mon–Sat 10am–5pm

Sydney L Moss Ltd (BADA)
Contact Paul G Moss or Mr M Rutherston
51 Brook Street, London, W1Y 1AU
020 7629 4670 020 7491 9278
mail@slmoss.com
www.slmoss.com
Est. 1904 *Stock size* Large
Stock Chinese and Japanese antiques, works of art, paintings
Open Mon–Fri 10am–5.30pm
Fairs International Asian Art Fair New York
Services Valuations

Morris Namdar
Contact Mr Morris Namdar
Stand B18, Grays Mews Antiques Market, 1–7 Davies Mews, London, W1K 5AB
020 7629 1183 020 7493 9344
Est. 1979 *Stock size* Medium
Stock Chinese, Japanese, European ceramics, glass, textiles
Open Mon–Fri 10am–6pm

Pelham Galleries Ltd (BADA, CINOA)
Contact Mr Alan Rubin
24 & 25 Mount Street, London, W1K 2RR
020 7629 0905 020 7495 4511
antiques@pelhamgalleries.com
www.pelhamgalleries.com
Est. 1928 *Stock size* Large
Stock English and European furniture, works of art 16th–19thC, early keyboard instruments
Open Mon–Fri 9am–5.30pm
Sat by appointment
Fairs Grosvenor House
Services Valuations, shipping

Pendulum of Mayfair
Contact Mr J Clements
King House, 51 Maddox Street, London, W1R 9LA
020 7629 6606
www.pendulumofmayfair.com
Est. 1995 *Stock size* Large
Stock Clocks, including longcase, bracket, wall, Georgian period furniture
Open Mon–Fri 10am–6pm
Sat 10am–5pm or by appointment

Ronald Phillips Ltd (BADA)
Contact Mr S Phillips
26 Bruton Street, London, W1J 6QL
020 7493 2341 020 7495 0843
ronphill@aol.com.
www.rp-antique-furniture.com
Est. 1952 *Stock size* Large
Stock 18thC English furniture, glass, clocks, barometers, mirrors
Open Mon–Fri 9am–5.30pm
Sat by appointment
Fairs Grosvenor House

S J Phillips Ltd (BADA)
Contact Mr F Norton
139 New Bond Street, London, W1A 3DL
020 7629 6261 020 7495 6180
enquiries@sjphillips.com
www.sjphillips.com
Est. 1869 *Stock size* Large
Stock Silver jewellery, snuff boxes
Open Mon–Fri 10am–5pm
Fairs Grosvenor House, TEFAF, Maastricht
Services Restorations

Pickering and Chatto (ABA, PBFA)
Contact Mr J Hudson
36 St George Street, London, W1R 9FA
020 7491 2656 020 7491 9161
rarebook@pickering-chatto.com
www.pickering-chatto.com
Est. 1820 *Stock size* Medium
Stock Antiquarian, rare, second-hand books on economics, philosophy, medicine, general literature
Open Mon–Fri 9.30am–5.30pm
or by appointment

Fairs Olympia
Services Book search valuations

⊞ Pieces of Time (BADA)
Contact Mr J Wachsmann
✉ **1–7 Davies Mews, London, W1Y 2LP** Ⓟ
☎ 020 7629 2422 Ⓕ 020 7409 1625
Ⓔ info@antique-watch.com
Ⓦ www.antique-watch.com
Est. 1973 *Stock size* Large
Stock Antique pocket watches, Judaica
Open Mon–Fri 10.30am–5pm
Services Valuations

⊞ Nicholas S Pitcher Oriental Art
Contact Mr N S Pitcher
✉ **1st Floor, 29 New Bond Street, London, W1S 2RL** Ⓟ
☎ 020 7499 6621 Ⓕ 020 7499 6621
Ⓜ 07831 391574
Ⓔ nickpitcher@cs.com
Est. 1990 *Stock size* Medium
Stock Early Chinese ceramics, works of art
Open By appointment
Fairs Arts of Pacific Asia Show, New York
Services Valuations

⊞ Jonathan Potter Ltd (ABA, BADA, LAPADA, PBFA)
Contact Mr J Potter
✉ **125 New Bond Street, London, W1S 1DY** Ⓟ
☎ 020 7491 3520 Ⓕ 020 7491 9754
Ⓔ jpmaps@attglobal.net
Ⓦ www.jpmaps.co.uk
Est. 1974 *Stock size* Large
Stock History of cartography books, atlases, maps, reproduction globes
Open Mon–Fri 10am–6pm
Fairs ABA, Olympia, IMCoS, International Map Fair
Services Valuations, restorations, framing

⊞ Bernard Quaritch Ltd (PBFA, ABA, BADA)
Contact Mr I Smith
✉ **5–8 Lower John Street, London, W1R 4AU**
☎ 020 7734 2983 Ⓕ 020 7734 0967
Ⓔ rarebooks@quaritch.com
Ⓦ www.quaritch.com
Est. 1847 *Stock size* Large
Stock Antiquarian books
Open Mon–Fri 9am–5.30pm
Fairs Olympia
Services Valuations

⊞ Retrouvius Architectural Reclamation (SALVO)
Contact Adam Hills or Maria Speake
✉ **32 York House, Upper Montague Street, London, W1H 1FR** Ⓟ
☎ warehouse: 020 8960 6060 office: 020 7724 3387
Ⓜ 07778 210855
Ⓔ mail@retrouvius.com
Est. 1992 *Stock size* Medium
Stock Architectural antiques, reclamation
Open By appointment
Fairs Newark
Services Design service

⊞ David Richards & Sons (LAPADA)
Contact Mr Richards
✉ **10 New Cavendish Street, London, W1G 8UL** Ⓟ
☎ 020 7935 3206/0322
Ⓕ 020 7224 4423
Est. 1970 *Stock size* Large
Stock Modern and antique silver plate, decorative items, flatware
Open Mon–Fri 9.30am–5.30pm
Services Valuations, restorations

⊞ Samiramis (LAPADA)
Contact Mr H Ismael
✉ **M14–16 Grays Mews, Davies Mews, London, W1Y 1FH** Ⓟ
☎ 020 7629 1161 Ⓕ 020 7493 5106
Est. 1978 *Stock size* Medium
Stock Islamic pottery, silver, Eastern items, calligraphy
Open Mon–Fri 10am–6pm

⊞ Alistair Sampson Antiques Ltd (BADA, BACA Award Winner 2002)
Contact Mr A Sampson or Mr C Banks
✉ **120 Mount Street, London, W1K 3NN** Ⓟ
☎ 020 7409 1799 Ⓕ 020 7409 7717
Ⓔ info@alistairsampson.com
Ⓦ www.alistairsampson.com
Est. 1969 *Stock size* Large
Stock English pottery, oak, country furniture, metalwork, needlework, pictures, 17th–18thC decorative items
Open Mon–Fri 9.30am–5.30pm or Sat by appointment
Fairs Olympia, Grosvenor House,

⊞ Seaby Antiquities (ADA)
Contact Peter Clayton
✉ **14 Old Bond Street, London, W1S 4PP** Ⓟ
☎ 020 7495 2590 Ⓕ 020 7491 1595
Ⓔ minerva.mag@virgin.net
Ⓦ www.royalathena.com
Est. 1942 *Stock size* Small
Stock Museum-quality antiquities
Open Mon–Fri 10am–5pm
Services Valuations

⊞ Bernard J Shapero Rare Books (ABA, PBFA, BADA)
Contact Lucinda Boyle
✉ **32 St George Street, London, W1S 2EA** Ⓟ
☎ 020 7493 0876 Ⓕ 020 7229 7860
Ⓔ rarebooks@shapero.com
Ⓦ www.shapero.com
Est. 1979 *Stock size* Large
Stock 16th–20thC guide books, antiquarian and rare books, English and Continental literature, specializing in travel, natural history, colour plate
Open Mon–Fri 9.30am–6.30pm Sat 11am–5pm August Mon–Fri 10am–5pm
Fairs Olympia
Services Valuations, restorations

⊞ Shapiro & Co (LAPADA)
Contact Sheldon Shapiro
✉ **Stand 380, Grays Antique Markets, 58 Davies Street, London, W1K 5LP**
☎ 020 7491 2710 Ⓕ 020 7491 2710
Ⓜ 07768 840930
Est. 1982
Stock Jewellery, silver, objets d'art, Imperial Russian works of art
Open Mon–Fri 10am–6pm
Fairs Olympia, NEC

⊞ Shiraz Antiques (BADA)
Contact Mr Reza Kiadeh
✉ **1 Davies Mews, London, W1K 5AB** Ⓟ

☎ 020 7495 0635 Ⓕ 020 7495 0635
Est. 1990 *Stock size* Medium
Stock Asian art, antiquities, glass, marble, pottery
Open Mon–Fri 10am–6pm
Fairs BADA

W Sitch (Antique) Co Ltd
Contact Mr Sitch
✉ **48 Berwick Street, London, W1V 4JD** Ⓟ
☎ 020 7437 3776 Ⓕ 020 7437 5707
Ⓔ wsitch-co@hotmail.com
Ⓦ www.w.sitch.co.uk
Est. 1776 *Stock size* Large
Stock Lighting
Open By appointment
Services Restorations

R Solaimany
Contact Mr R Solaimany
✉ **Unit H, Davies Mews, London, W1K 5AB** Ⓟ
☎ 020 7491 2562 Ⓕ 020 7493 9344
Est. 1981 *Stock size* Medium
Stock Oriental ceramics, bronzes, Roman glass
Open Mon–Fri 10am–6pm

Sotheby's
✉ **34–35 New Bond Street, London, W1A 2AA** Ⓟ
☎ 020 7293 5000
Ⓦ www.sothebys.com
Est. 1744
Open Mon–Fri 9am–5.30pm
Sales International auctioneer of fine art, furniture, jewellery, decorative arts, collectables and more. Services include restoration, valuation, financial service, picture library, on-line auctions, Sotheby's International Realty and Sotheby's Bookshop
Frequency Varies by month
Catalogues Yes

Henry Sotheran Ltd (ABA, PBFA, ILAB)
Contact Mr A McGeachin
✉ **2 Sackville Street, Piccadilly, London, W1S 3DP** Ⓟ
☎ 020 7439 6151 Ⓕ 020 7434 709
Ⓔ sotherans@sotherans.co.uk
Ⓦ www.sotherans.co.uk
Est. 1761 *Stock size* Large
Stock Antiquarian books on English literature, natural history, travel, children's illustrated, modern first editions, prints, art, architecture

Open Mon–Fri 9.30am–6pm
Sat 10am–4pm

Spectrum
Contact Mrs S Spectrum
✉ **Stand 372, Grays Antique Markets, 58 Davies Street, London, W1K 5LP0** Ⓟ
☎ 020 7629 3501 Ⓕ 020 8883 5030
Ⓜ 07770 753302
Est. 1979 *Stock size* Large
Stock Georgian seedpearl necklaces, brooches, Georgian–Victorian jewellery, Georg Jensen jewellery
Open Mon–Fri 10am–6pm
Services Valuations, repairs, stringing, designing

A and J Speelman Ltd (BADA)
Contact Mr J Speelman or J Mann
✉ **129 Mount Street, London, W1K 3NX** Ⓟ
☎ 020 7499 5126 Ⓕ 020 7355 3391
Ⓔ speelman@enterprise.net
Est. 1976 *Stock size* Large
Stock Oriental furniture, porcelain, works of art
Open Mon–Fri 10am–6pm
Fairs New York, Asian Art Fair
Services Valuations, restorations

St. Petersburg Collection Ltd
Contact Mr B Lynch
✉ **42 Burlington Arcade, London, W1J 0QG** Ⓟ
☎ 020 7495 2883 Ⓕ 01895 810566
Ⓔ creations@stpetersburgcollection.com
Ⓦ www.stpetersburgcollection.com
Est. 1989 *Stock size* Medium
Stock English and French objets d'art, boxes, 19th–20thC silver, glass, ormolu
Open Mon–Sat 10am–5pm

Stair & Company Ltd (BADA, CINOA)
Contact Mr R Luck
✉ **14 Mount Street, London, W1K 2RF** Ⓟ
☎ 020 7499 1784 Ⓕ 020 7269 1050
Ⓔ stairandcompany@talk21.com
Ⓦ www.stairandcompany.com
Est. 1911 *Stock size* Large
Stock 18thC fine English furniture, works of art
Open Mon–Fri 9.30am–5.30pm or by appointment

Fairs Grosvenor House, BADA
Services Valuations, restorations

Jacob Stodel (BADA)
Contact Jacob Stodel
✉ **Flat 53, Macready House, 75 Crawford Street, London, W1H 5LP** Ⓟ
☎ 020 7723 3732
Ⓔ jacobstodel@aol.com
Stock 18thC English and Continental furniture, 17th–early 19thC Oriental and European ceramics and works of art
Open By appointment
Fairs Maastricht
Services Valuations

E Swonnell Ltd
Contact Miss S Swonnell
✉ **111–112 New Bond Street, London, W1Y 0BQ** Ⓟ
☎ 020 7629 9649 Ⓕ 020 7629 9649
Est. 1957 *Stock size* Large
Stock 17th–19thC silver and plate, large decorative items
Open Mon–Fri 10am–5pm
Services Valuations, restorations

Tagore Ltd
Contact Mr R Falloon
✉ **Stand 302, Grays Antique Markets, 58 Davies Street, London, W1Y 2LP** Ⓟ
☎ 020 7499 0158 Ⓕ 020 7499 0158
Ⓔ grays@clara.net
Est. 1977 *Stock size* Large
Stock 20thC drinking, smoking, gambling collectors' items, silver, glass, gentlemen's gifts
Open Mon–Fri 10am–6pm
Services Valuations

Textile-Art: The Textile Gallery (BADA)
Contact Michael Franses or Nicholas Waterhouse
✉ **12 Queen Street, Mayfair, London, W1J 5PG** Ⓟ
☎ 020 7499 7979 Ⓕ 020 7409 2596
Ⓜ 07836 321461
Ⓔ post@textile-art.com
Ⓦ www.textile-art.com
Est. 1972
Stock Textile art from China, Central Asia, India and Ottoman Empire, 300BC–1800AD, classical carpets 1400–1700
Open Mon–Fri by appointment 10.30am–6pm

Fairs The European Fine Art Fair, Maastricht, Asian Art in London
Services Conservation of important textiles to museum standards

⊞ Tosi Gold Ltd
Contact Sergio Tencati
✉ **Unit 16, Bond Street Antiques Centre, 124 New Bond Street, London, W1Y 9AE** P
☎ 020 7493 6272 F 020 7493 6272
M 07929 875822
Est. 1897 *Stock size* Medium
Stock Antique and contemporary 18ct gold jewellery
Open Mon–Sat 10.30am–5.30pm
Services Valuations, repair, shipping

⊞ Toynbee-Clarke Interiors Ltd
Contact Mrs Daphne Toynbee-Clarke
✉ **95 Mount Street, London, W1Y 5HG** P
☎ 020 7499 4472 F 020 7495 1204
Est. 1959 *Stock size* Medium
Stock Continental furniture, works of art, 18th–19thC Chinese hand-painted export wallpapers, early 19thC French panoramic papers
Open Mon–Fri 11am–5.30pm or by appointment
Services Restorations

⊞ Trianon Antiques Ltd and Michael Longmore (LAPADA, LJAJDA)
Contact Miss L Horton
✉ **Bond Street Antiques Centre, 124 New Bond Street, London, W1Y 9AE** P
☎ 020 7629 6678 F 020 7355 2055
Est. 1974 *Stock size* Large
Stock Fine jewellery, objets d'art
Open Mon–Fri 10am–5.30pm
Fairs Olympia (June)

⊞ Jan Van Beers Oriental Art (BADA)
Contact Mr J Van Beers
✉ **34 Davies Street, London, W1Y 1LG** P
☎ 020 7408 0434 F 020 7355 1397
E jan@vanbeers.demon.co.uk
Est. 1978 *Stock size* Large
Stock Chinese and Japanese antiques, ceramics, works of art
Open Mon–Fri 10am–6pm
Services Valuations

⊞ Vinci Antiques
Contact Mr A Vinci
✉ **27 Avery Row, London, W1X 9HD** P
☎ 020 7499 1041
Est. 1974 *Stock size* Large
Stock Objets d'art, objects of virtue, silver, porcelain, glass, paintings, Russian icons, jewellery
Open Mon–Sat 9am–7pm
Services Valuations, restorations

⊞ Rupert Wace Ancient Art Ltd (ADA, IADAA, BADA)
Contact Mr R Wace
✉ **14 Old Bond Street, London, W1X 3DB** P
☎ 020 7495 1623 F 020 7495 8495
E rupert.wace@btinternet.com
Est. 1987 *Stock size* Large
Stock Antiquities, Greek, Roman, ancient Egyptian, Near Eastern, Celtic, Dark Ages
Open Mon–Fri 10am–5pm or by appointment
Fairs Olympia (June, Feb)
Services Valuations

⊞ Wartski Ltd (BADA)
Contact Geoffrey Munn or Katherine Purcell
✉ **14 Grafton Street, London, W1S 4DE** P
☎ 020 7493 1141 F 020 7409 7448
E wartski@wartski.com
W www.wartski.com
Est. 1865 *Stock size* Medium
Stock Jewellery, works by Fabergé, 18thC gold snuff boxes
Open Mon–Fri 9.30am–5pm
Services Repairs

⊞ Westminster Group Antique Jewellery (LAPADA)
Contact Mr R Harrison
✉ **Stand 150, Grays Antique Markets, 58 Davies Street, London, W1K 2LP** P
☎ 020 7493 8672 F 020 7493 8672
Est. 1976 *Stock size* Large
Stock Victorian–Edwardian second-hand jewellery, watches
Open Mon–Fri 10am–6pm

⊞ Wheels of Steel
Contact Jeff Williams
✉ **Stand A12–13 Unit B10, Basement, 1–7 Davies Mews, London, W1Y 2LP**
☎ 020 7629 2813
Est. 1976 *Stock size* Large
Stock Model trains
Open Mon–Fri 10am–6pm

⊞ Wilkinson PLC
Contact Mark Savin
✉ **1 Grafton Street, London, W1S 4EA** P
☎ 020 7495 2477 F 020 7491 1737
E enquiries@wilkinson-plc.com
W www.wilkinson-plc.com
Est. 1946 *Stock size* Large
Stock Lighting, chandeliers, candelabra
Open Mon–Fri 9.30am–5pm
Services Restorations

⊞ Wimpole Antiques (LAPADA)
Contact Lyn Lindsay
✉ **Stand 349, Grays Antiques Markets, Davies Street, London, W1Y 1LB** P
☎ 020 7499 2889 F 020 7372 2405
E 100046.1430@compuserve.com
Est. 1977 *Stock size* Large
Stock Affordable, wearable jewellery, 1780–1960, Victorian jewellery
Open Mon–Fri 10am–6pm
Fairs Olympia, NEC, LAPADA
Services Valuations, repairs

⊞ Linda Wrigglesworth Ltd
Contact Gary Dickinson
✉ **34 Brook Street, London, W1K 5DN** P
☎ 020 7408 0177 F 020 7491 9812
E info@lindawrigglesworth.com
W www.cloudband.com/arcade/lindawrigglesworth
Est. 1977
Stock Chinese court costumes, Tibetan and Korean textiles
Open Mon–Fri 11am–7pm
Fairs Grosvenor House

⊞ Yamamoto Antiques
Contact Mrs M Yamamoto
✉ **Units 14 & 15, Bond Street Antique Centre, 124 New Bond Street, London, W1Y 9AE**
☎ 020 7491 0983 F 020 7491 0983
E m@bondst.plus.com
Est. 1995 *Stock size* Medium
Stock Jewellery, porcelain
Open Mon–Sat 11am–5.30pm
Services Shipping

LONDON

W2

Sean Arnold Sporting Antiques (PADA)
Contact Sean Arnold
21–22 Chepstow Corner, off Westbourne Grove, London, W2 4XE
☎ 020 7221 2267 Ⓕ 020 7221 5464
Est. 1977 *Stock size* Large
Stock Sporting antiques, luggage, globes
Open Mon–Sat 10am–6pm or by appointment
Services Valuations, restorations

Bonhams
✉ **10 Salem Road, London, W2 4DL**
☎ 020 7313 2700 Ⓕ 020 7313 2701
Ⓔ info@bonhams.com
Ⓦ www.bonhams.com
Est. 1793
Open Mon–Fri 9am–4.30pm Sun 11am–3pm
Catalogues Yes

Mark Gallery (BADA, CINOA)
Contact Helen Mark
✉ **9 Porchester Place, Marble Arch, London, W2 2BS**
☎ 020 7262 4906 Ⓕ 020 7224 9416
Est. 1970
Stock 16th–19thC Russian and Greek icons, contemporary and modern French lithographs and etchings
Open Mon–Fri 10am–1pm 2pm–6pm Sat by appointment 11am–1pm
Fairs Olympia, Cologne
Services Valuations, restorations

Quest
Contact Fay Lambert
✉ **1 Garway Road, Bayswater, London, W2 4PH**
☎ 020 7221 1863 Ⓕ 020 7221 1863
Ⓜ 07850 878994
Ⓔ fay.lambert@btinternet.com
Est. 1995
Stock Fine art, decorative antiques
Open By appointment
Services Acquisition and disposal of fine art and antiques

Reel Poster Gallery
Contact Mr Tony Nourmand
✉ **72 Westbourne Grove, London, W2 5SH**
☎ 020 7727 4488 Ⓕ 020 7727 4499
Ⓔ info@reelposter.com
Ⓦ www.reelposter.com
Est. 1989
Stock Original vintage film posters
Open Mon–Fri 11am–7pm Sat noon–6pm
Services Valuations, annual catalogue

W3

Chiswick and West Middlesex Auctions
Contact Mr D Wells or Mr T Stead
✉ **1 Colville Road, London, W3 8BL**
☎ 020 8992 4442 Ⓕ 020 8896 0541
Est. 1992
Open Mon–Fri 10am–6pm
Sales Antiques and general effects Tues 5pm, viewing Sun noon–6pm Mon 10am–6pm Tues 10am–5pm
Frequency Weekly
Catalogues Yes

W4

The Chiswick Fireplace Co
Contact Rosemary O'Grady
✉ **68 Southfield Road, London, W4 1BD**
☎ 020 8995 4011 Ⓕ 020 8995 4012
Est. 1990 *Stock size* Medium
Stock Original Art Nouveau, Edwardian, Victorian fireplaces, marble, limestone and wood surrounds
Open Mon–Sat 9.30am–5pm
Services Restorations

Chiswick Park Antiques
Contact Mr Azzariti
✉ **2 Chiswick Park Station, London, W4 5EB**
☎ 020 8995 8930
Est. 1965 *Stock size* Medium
Stock Mirrors, furniture, clocks
Open Mon–Sat 11am–6pm
Services Valuations, restorations

David Edmonds Indian Furniture
✉ **1–4 Prince of Wales Terrace, London, W4 2EY**
☎ 020 8742 1920 Ⓕ 020 8742 3030
Ⓜ 07831 666436
Ⓔ dareindia@aol.com
Est. 1987 *Stock size* Large
Stock Fine quality Indian furniture, antiques, architectural items
Open Mon–Sat 11am–6pm Sun noon–4pm
Services Valuations, repairs

W A Foster (PBFA)
Contact Mr Foster
✉ **183 Chiswick High Road, London, W4 2DR**
☎ 020 8995 2768
Est. 1968 *Stock size* Medium
Stock Antiquarian, rare and second-hand books, fine bindings, illustrated children's books
Open Thurs–Sat 10.30am–5.30pm
Fairs PBFA Hotel Russell

Harmers of London Stamp Auctioneer Ltd (Philatelic Traders Society)
Contact Mr G Childs
✉ **111 Power Road, Chiswick, London, W4 5PY**
☎ 020 8747 6100 Ⓕ 020 8996 0649
Ⓔ auctions@harmers.demon.co.uk
Ⓦ www.harmers.com
Est. 1918
Open Mon–Fri 9am–5pm
Sales Philatelic auctions every 6 weeks, ring for details
Frequency Every 6 weeks
Catalogues Yes

The Old Cinema (LAPADA)
Contact Mr K Norris
✉ **160 Chiswick High Road, London, W4 1PR**
☎ 020 8995 4166 Ⓕ 020 8995 4167
Ⓔ theoldcinema@antiques-uk.co.uk
Ⓦ www.antiques-uk.co.uk/theoldcinema
Est. 1980 *Stock size* Large
Stock Georgian–Art Deco furniture, large items of furniture, clocks, silver
Open Mon–Sat 9.30am–6pm Sun noon–5pm

Strand Antiques
Contact Mrs A Brown
✉ **46 Devonshire Road, London, W4 2HD**
☎ 020 8994 1912
Est. 1977 *Stock size* Large
Stock English and French furniture, glass, lighting, jewellery, silver, garden items, kitchenware, books, prints, textiles, collectables
Open Mon–Sat 10.30am–5.30pm
Services Furniture restoration

W5

Aberdeen House Antiques (LAPADA, CINOA)
Contact Mr N Schwartz
75 St Mary's Road, London, W5 5RH
020 8567 1223
Est. 1972 *Stock size* Medium
Stock 18th–19thC antiques, decorative items, lighting, furniture, mirrors
Open Mon–Sat 10am–5.30pm or by appointment
Services Valuations

Harold's Place
Contact Mr H Bowman
148 South Ealing Road, Ealing, London, W5 4QJ
020 8579 4825
Est. 1976 *Stock size* Medium
Stock Antique china, glass, decorative items
Open Mon–Sat 9.30am–5.30pm closed Wed

Terrace Antiques
Contact Mr N Schwartz
10–12 South Ealing Road, London, W5 4QA
020 8567 5194
Est. 1972 *Stock size* Medium
Stock Furniture, collectables, china, silver plate, glass
Open Mon–Sat 10am–5.30pm or by appointment
Services Valuations

W8

Abstract/Noonstar (LAPADA)
Contact Galya Aytac or Juliette Boagers
58–60 Kensington Church Street, London, W8 4DB
020 7376 2652 020 7376 2652
07770 281301
galya53@aol.com
www.abstract-antiques.com
Est. 1980 *Stock size* Medium
Stock 20thC Decorative Arts, Art Nouveau, Art Deco
Open Mon–Sat 11am–5pm
Services Valuations, shipping

Antiquewest Ltd at Patrick Sandberg Antiques (CINOA)
Contact Mr J Robinson
150/152 Kensington Church Street, London, W8 4BH
020 7229 4115 020 7792 3467
china@antikwest.com
www.antikwest.com
Est. 1980 *Stock size* Large
Stock Oriental porcelain, pottery, Chinese carpets, furniture
Open Mon–Fri 10am–6pm Sat 10am–4pm
Fairs Olympia (June), Gothenburg, Sweden (Oct), Asian Art in London (Nov)
Services Valuations, restorations

Artemis Decorative Arts Ltd (LAPADA)
Contact Mr M Jones
36 Kensington Church Street, London, W8 4BX
020 7376 0377 020 7376 0377
artemis.w8@btinternet.com
Est. 1994 *Stock size* Medium
Stock Art Nouveau, Art Deco, glass, bronze, ivory, furniture
Open Mon–Sat 10am–6pm

Garry Atkins
Contact Mr G Atkins
107 Kensington Church Street, London, W8 7LN
020 7727 8737 020 7792 9010
garry.atkins@englishpottery.com
www.englishpottery.com
Est. 1983 *Stock size* Large
Stock English and Continental pottery, 18thC and earlier
Open Mon–Fri 10am–5.30pm
Fairs New York Ceramics Fair

Gregg Baker Asian Art (BADA, LAPADA, CINOA)
Contact Mr G Baker
132 Kensington Church Street, London, W8 4BH
020 7221 3533 020 7221 4410
gbakerart@aol.com
www.greggbaker.com
Est. 1984 *Stock size* Medium
Stock Japanese and Chinese works of art
Open Mon–Fri 10am–6pm or by appointment
Fairs Olympia

Eddy Bardawil (BADA)
Contact Mr E Bardawil
106 Kensington Church Street, London, W8 4BH
020 7221 3967 020 7221 5124
Est. 1982 *Stock size* Medium
Stock 18th–19thC English furniture, works of art
Open Mon–Fri 10am–6pm Sat 10am–1pm
Services Restorations

Nigel Benson 20th Century Glass (KCSADA)
Contact Mr N Benson
Unit 7, The Antique Centre, 58–60 Kensington Church Street, London, W8 4DB
020 7938 1137 020 7729 9875
07971 859848
Est. 1986 *Stock size* Large
Stock 1870–1980 British glass, post-war Scandinavian, Continental glass
Open Thurs–Sat noon–6pm or by appointment
Fairs NEC (April, Aug, Nov), Glass Fair, Birmingham

Berwald Oriental Art (BADA, CINOA)
Contact Isabella Corble
101 Kensington Church Street, London, W8 7LN
020 7229 0800 020 7229 1101
berwald@aapi.co.uk
www.berwald-oriental.com
Est. 1986 *Stock size* Medium
Stock Fine Chinese pottery and porcelain, Han to Qing and Chinese works of art
Open Mon–Fri 10am–6pm or by appointment

Nicolaus Boston Antiques
Contact Mr N Boston
58–60 Kensington Church Street, London, W8 4DB
020 7937 2237 020 8944 1280
sales@majolica.co.uk
www.majolica.co.uk
Est. 1983 *Stock size* Large
Stock Majolica, Christopher Dresser, aesthetic pottery
Open Fri Sat 10am–6pm
Fairs Olympia, Ceramic Fair, New York

David Brower (KCSADA)
Contact Mr D Brower
113 Kensington Church Street, London, W8 7LN
020 7221 4155 020 7221 6211
07831 234343
David@davidbrower-antiques.com
www.davidbrower-antiques.com
Est. 1969 *Stock size* Large
Stock Meissen, KPM, European and Asian porcelain, French

bronzes, Japanese works of art
Open Mon–Fri 10am–6pm
Sat by appointment
Fairs Olympia (June)

Butchoff Antiques (LAPADA)
Contact Mr A Kaye
154 Kensington Church Street, London, W8 4BN
020 7221 8174 020 7792 8923
enquiries@butchoff.com
www.butchoff.com
Est. 1964 *Stock size* Large
Stock English and Continental furniture, decorative items, porcelain, mirrors
Open Mon–Fri 9.30am–6pm
Sat 9.30am–5pm
Fairs Olympia
Services Valuations

Cohen & Cohen (BADA, KCSADA)
Contact Mr M Cohen
101b Kensington Church Street, London, W8 7LN
020 7727 7677 020 7229 9653
cohenandcohen@aol.com
Est. 1973 *Stock size* Large
Stock Chinese export porcelain, works of art
Open Mon–Fri 10am–6pm
Sat 11am–3pm
Fairs New York Ceramics Fair, Palm Beach, Grosvenor House

Davies Antiques (LAPADA)
Contact Mr H Davies
40 Kensington Church Street, London, W8 4BX
020 7937 9216 020 7938 2032
hugh.davies@btconnect.com
Est. 1975 *Stock size* Large
Stock 1710–Art Deco Continental porcelain, Meissen porcelain
Open Mon–Fri 10am–5.30pm
Sat 10am–3pm

Denton Antiques
Contact Mr N Denton
156 Kensington Church Street, London, W8 4BN
020 7229 5866 020 7792 1073
Est. 1897 *Stock size* Large
Stock French and English chandeliers, lighting, table lamps, 1750–1920
Open Mon–Fri 9.30am–5.30pm

Didier Antiques (LAPADA)
Contact Didier Haspeslagh
58–60 Kensington Church Street, Kensington, London, W8 4DB
020 7938 2537 020 7938 2537
didier.antiques@virgin.net.
www.didierantiques.com
Est. 1989 *Stock size* Large
Stock Late 19th–early 20thC Arts and Crafts, Art Nouveau, jewellery, silver, 1960s–1970s designer jewellery
Open By appointment
Fairs Olympia (June, Nov)

C. Fredericks and Son (BADA, KCSADA)
Contact Richard Fredericks
142 Kensington Church Street, London, W8 4BN
020 7727 2240 020 7727 2240
antiques@cfredericksandson.freeserve.co.uk
Est. 1947 *Stock size* Medium
Stock 18thC English furniture
Open Mon–Fri 9.30am–5.30pm
Fairs BADA Olympia (Nov)
Services Restorations

Michael German Antiques Ltd (BADA, LAPADA)
Contact Mr M German or Mr D Strickland
38b Kensington Church Street, London, W8 4BX
020 7937 2771 020 7937 8566
info@antiquecanes.com or info@antiqueweapons.com
www.antiquecanes.com or www.antiqueweapons.com
Est. 1973 *Stock size* Large
Stock Antique walking canes, antique arms, armour
Open Mon–Fri 10am–5pm
Sat 10am–1pm

Green's Antique Galleries
Contact Sidney Green
117 Kensington Church Street, London, W8 7LN
020 7229 9618
Est. 1952 *Stock size* Medium
Stock General antiques
Open Mon–Sat 9.30am–5.30pm

Robert Hales Antiques
Contact Mr R Hales
131 Kensington Church Street, London, W8 7LP
020 7229 3887 020 7229 3887
RHAntique@aol.com
Est. 1967 *Stock size* Medium
Stock Oriental and Islamic arms, armour, Medieval–19thC
Open Tues–Fri 9.30am–5.30pm
Fairs Park Lane Arms Fair
Services Valuations

Adrian Harrington (ABA, PBFA, ILAB)
Contact Adrian Harrington, Jon Gilbert or Pierre Lambardini
64a Kensington Church Street, London, W8 4DB
020 7937 1465 020 7368 0912
rare@harringtonbooks.co.uk
www.harringtonbooks.co.uk
Est. 1964 *Stock size* Large
Stock Antiquarian and rare books specializing in literature, modern first editions, children's books, library sets, travel
Open Mon–Sat 10am–6pm
Fairs Olympia, Chelsea Town Hall
Services Valuations

Haslam & Whiteway
Contact Helen Duntan
105 Kensington Church Street, London, W8 7LN
020 7229 1145
Est. 1972 *Stock size* Medium
Stock 19thC British design
Open Mon–Fri 10am–6pm
Sat 10am–4pm

Jeanette Hayhurst (BADA)
Contact Mrs J Hayhurst
32a Kensington Church Street, London, W8 4HA
020 7938 1539
Est. 1979 *Stock size* Medium
Stock 18thC glass, specializing in English drinking glasses
Open Mon–Fri 10am–5pm
Sat noon–5pm or by appointment
Fairs BADA, Harrogate, NEC

D Holmes
Contact Mr D Holmes
47c Earls Court Road, in Abingdon Villas, London, W8 6EE
020 7937 6961 020 8880 254
07710 249471
Est. 1965 *Stock size* Small
Stock 18th–19thC English mahogany furniture
Open Fri 9am–7pm Sat 9am–3pm

Fairs Olympia (June)
Services Also showrooms at Oudenaarde, Belgium

Hope & Glory
Contact Mr J Pym
131a Kensington Church Street (Entrance in Peel Street), London, W8 7LP
020 7727 8424
Est. 1982 *Stock size* Large
Stock Commemorative ceramics, Royal, political etc
Open Mon–Sat 10am–5pm

Jonathan Horne (BADA, CINOA)
Contact Mr S Westman or Jonathan Horne
66c Kensington Church Street, London, W8 4BY
020 7221 5658 F 020 7792 3090
E jh@jonathanhorne.co.uk
W www.jonathanhorne.co.uk
Est. 1968 *Stock size* Large
Stock Early English pottery, medieval–1820
Open Mon–Fri 9.30am–5.30pm
Fairs BADA, Olympia (June, Nov)
Services Valuations

Valerie Howard (LAPADA)
Contact Mrs Valerie Howard
4 Campden Street, London, W8 7EP
020 7792 9702 F 020 7221 7008
E valeriehoward@quimperpottery.co.uk
W www.masonsironstonechina.co.uk or www.quimperpottery.co.uk
Est. 1988 *Stock size* Medium
Stock Mason's ironstone, other English ironstone, Miles Mason porcelain 1796–1840, Quimper pottery 19thC–1920
Open Mon–Fri 10am–5.30pm Sat 10am–4.30pm
Fairs International Ceramics Fair and Seminar
Services Valuations, shipping, restoration

Iona Antiques
Contact Stephen Joseph
P O Box 285, London, W8 6HZ
020 7602 1193
F 020 7371 2843
E iona@ionaantiques.com
W www.ionaantiques.com
Est. BADA *Stock size* Large
Stock 19thC animal paintings
Open By appointment
Fairs Grosvenor House, Olympia (June)

Isaac Carpets
Contact Mr Javid
347 Kensington High Street, London, W8 6NW
020 8838 3399 F 020 8388 3102
Est. 1978 *Stock size* Large
Stock Antique Oriental carpets, European carpets, tapestries
Open Mon–Sat 10am–6pm
Services Valuations, repair, cleaning

Jag Applied and Decorative Arts (Decorative Arts Society)
Contact C A Warner, G J Morgan or G S Strickland
58–60 Kensington Church Street, London, W8 4DB
020 7938 4404 F 020 7938 4404
M 07974 567507
E jag@jagdecorativearts.com
W www.jagdecorativearts.com
Est. 1990 *Stock size* Medium
Stock Liberty pewter and silver, Art Nouveau metal, glass decorative items
Open Mon–Sat 10.30am–5.30pm

J A N Fine Art (KCSADA)
Contact F K Shimizu
134 Kensington Church Street, Kensington, London, W8 4BH
020 7792 0736 F 020 7221 1380
E shimizu@jan-fineart-london.com
W www.jan-fineart-london.com
Est. 1979 *Stock size* Medium
Stock Japanese, Chinese, Korean ceramics, bronzes, works of art
Open Mon–Fri 10am–6pm Sat by appointment

Japanese Gallery Ltd (Ukiyo-e Society)
Contact Mr C D Wertheim
66d Kensington Church Street, London, W8 4BY
020 7229 2934 F 020 7229 2934
M 07930 411991
E princyw@hotmail.com
Est. 1978 *Stock size* Large
Stock Japanese woodcut prints, Japanese ceramics, sword armour, Japanese dolls
Open Mon–Sat 10am–6pm
Services Exhibitions every 3 months of Japanese prints, Japanese-speaking staff

Roderick Jellicoe (BADA, KCSADA, BACA Award Winner 2001)
3a Camden Street, off Kensington Church Street, London, W8 7EP
020 7727 1571 F 020 7727 1805
E jellicoe@englishporcelain.com
W www.englishporcelain.com
Est. 1975
Stock 18thC English porcelain
Open Mon–Fri 10am–5.30pm Sat by appointment
Fairs NY Ceramics fair

John Jesse
Contact John Jesse
160 Kensington Church Street, London, W8 4BN
020 7229 0312 F 020 7229 4732
M 07767 497880
E jj@johnjesse.com
Est. 1963 *Stock size* Medium
Stock 20thC decorative arts, sculpture, glass, ceramics, silver, jewellery
Open Mon–Fri 10am–5.30pm Sat 11am–4pm

Howard Jones Antiques (LAPADA)
Contact Mr Tristan Wright
43 Kensington Church Street, London, W8 4BA
020 7937 4359 F 020 7937 4359
Est. 1979 *Stock size* Small
Stock Antique and modern silver, trinket boxes, picture frames, cufflinks
Open Mon–Sat 9.30am–5.30pm

Peter Kemp
Contact Mr P Kemp
170 Kensington Church Street, London, W8 4BN
020 7229 2988 F 020 7229 2988
E peterkemp@btinternet.com
Est. 1971 *Stock size* Large
Stock 18thC Oriental, European porcelain, works of art
Open Mon–Fri 10.30am–5.30pm or by appointment

Kensington Church Street Antique Centre
Contact Jody Barry
58–60 Kensington Church Street, London, W8 4DB

LONDON

☎ 020 7937 4600 Ⓕ 020 7937 3400
Ⓔ themanager@vh-businesscentres.com
Ⓦ www.vh-businesscentres.com
Est. 1989 *Stock size* Large
No. of dealers 9
Stock 19th–20thC Decorative arts, Oriental and English ceramics
Open Mon–Sat 10am–6pm
Services Valuations, restorations, shipping

The Lacquer Chest
Contact Mrs G Andersen
✉ **75 Kensington Church Street, London, W8 4BG** Ⓟ
☎ 020 7937 1306 Ⓕ 020 7376 0223
Est. 1959 *Stock size* Large
Stock Military chests, china, clocks, samplers, lamps
Open Mon–Fri 9.30am–5.30pm Sat 11am–3pm
Services Prop hire of antiques

Lev Antiques Ltd
Contact Alyson Lawrence
✉ **97a Kensington Church Street, London, W8 7LN** Ⓟ
☎ 020 7727 9248 Ⓕ 020 7727 9248
Ⓔ alyson@richardlawrence.co.uk
Est. 1882 *Stock size* Medium
Stock Jewellery, silver, paintings, objets d'art, antiquities
Open Tues–Sat 10.30am–5.45pm Mon noon–5.30pm
Services Oil painting restoration

Lewis & Lloyd (BADA)
Contact Mr Paul C Lewis
✉ **65 Kensington Church Street, London, W8 4BA** Ⓟ
☎ 020 7938 3323 Ⓕ 020 7361 0086
Ⓔ paulclewis@aol.com
Ⓦ www.lewisandlloyd.co.uk
Est. 1977 *Stock size* Medium
Stock 18th–early 19thC English and Continental furniture
Open Mon–Fri 10.15am–5.15pm
Fairs Olympia (June, Nov)

Libra Antiques
Contact Mrs A Wolsey
✉ **131d Kensington Church Street, London, W8 7PT** Ⓟ
☎ 020 7727 2990
Est. 1979 *Stock size* Large
Stock English blue-and-white pottery 1790–1820, creamware
Open Mon–Fri 10am–5pm Sat 10am–4pm

London Antique Gallery
Contact Mr C D Wertheim
✉ **66e Kensington Church Street, London, W8 4BY** Ⓟ
☎ 020 7229 2934 Ⓕ 020 7229 2934
Ⓜ 07930 411991
Ⓔ centrallondon@hotmail.com
Est. 1996 *Stock size* Medium
Stock Meissen, Dresden, Worcester, Minton, Shelley, Sèvre, Lalique, bisque dolls
Open Mon–Sat 10am–6pm
Services Restorations, framing

Mah's Antiques
Contact Mr Mah
✉ **141 Kensington Church Street, London, W8 7LP** Ⓟ
☎ 020 7229 9047 Ⓕ 020 7354 1860
Est. 1994 *Stock size* Large
Stock Oriental and European porcelain, works of art
Open Mon–Fri 10.30am–5.30pm
Services Valuations, restorations

C H Major
Contact Sally Major
✉ **154 Kensington Church Street, London, W8 4BN** Ⓟ
☎ 01296 624402
Est. 1919 *Stock size* Large
Stock 18th–19thC English furniture
Open Mon–Fri 10am–5.30pm Sat 10am–2pm
Services Valuations, restorations

E and H Manners (BADA)
Contact Errol Manners
✉ **66a Kensington Church Street, London, W8 4BY** Ⓟ
☎ 020 7229 5516 Ⓕ 020 7229 5516
Ⓔ manners@europeanporcelain.com
Ⓦ www.europeanporcelain.com
Est. 1986 *Stock size* Medium
Stock 18thC European porcelain, pottery
Open Mon–Fri 10am–5.30pm
Fairs International Ceramics Fair

S Marchant & Son (BADA, KCSADA)
Contact Mr S Marchant or Mr R Marchant
✉ **120 Kensington Church Street, London, W8 4BH** Ⓟ
☎ 020 7229 5319 Ⓕ 020 7792 8979
Ⓔ marchant@dircon.co.uk
Ⓦ www.marchantasianart.com
Est. 1925 *Stock size* Large
Stock Chinese porcelain, works of art, snuff bottles, jade
Open Mon–Fri 9.30am–5.30pm
Fairs Grosvenor House, International Asian Art
Services Valuations

R & G McPherson Antiques at Stockspring (PADA)
Contact Robert McPherson
✉ **114 Kensington Church Street, London, W8 4BH** Ⓟ
☎ 020 7727 7995 Ⓕ 020 7727 7995
Ⓜ 07768 432630
Ⓔ robertmcpherson@orientalceramics.com
Ⓦ www.orientalceramics.com
Est. 1987 *Stock size* Medium
Stock Oriental ceramics
Open Mon–Fri 10.30am–5.30pm Sat 10am–1pm

Michael Coins
Contact Mr M Gouby
✉ **6 Hillgate Street, London, W8 7SR** Ⓟ
☎ 020 7727 1518 Ⓕ 020 7727 1518
Est. 1966 *Stock size* Medium
Stock English and foreign, medieval–present day coins, banknotes
Open Mon–Fri 10am–5pm

Colin D Monk
Contact Mr C Monk
✉ **58–60 Kensington Church Street, London, W8 4DB** Ⓟ
☎ 020 7229 3727 Ⓕ 020 7376 1501
Stock size Medium
Stock Oriental porcelain
Open Mon–Sat 11am–5pm

Nassirzadeh Antiques
Contact Mr Houshang
✉ **178 Kensington Church Street, London, W8 4DP** Ⓟ
☎ 020 7243 8262 Ⓕ 020 7243 8262
Ⓜ 07958 626777
Est. 1984 *Stock size* Large
Stock Porcelain, glass, textiles
Open Mon–Sat 11am–6pm

New Century
Contact Mr H Lyons
✉ **69 Kensington Church Street, London, W8 4BG** Ⓟ
☎ 020 7937 2410 Ⓕ 020 7937 2410
Ⓜ 07711 098941
Est. 1989 *Stock size* Medium
Stock Design, 1860–1910
Open Mon–Sat 10am–6pm

Pruskin Galleries
Contact Michael Pruskin
50 & 73 Kensington Church High Street, London, W8 4BG
020 7937 1994 020 7376 1285
pruskin@pruskingallery.demon.co.uk
Est. 1977 *Stock size* Large
Stock Decorative art, paintings, furniture, ceramics, jewellery, glass
Open Mon–Fri 10am–6pm
Sat 11am–5pm

Mrs Quick Chandeliers
Contact Mr N Denton
166 Kensington Church Street, London, W8 4BN
020 7229 1338 020 7792 1073
Est. 1897 *Stock size* Large
Stock French and English chandeliers, lighting, table lamps, 1750–1920
Open Mon–Fri 9.30am–5.30pm

Raffety & Walwyn (BADA)
Contact Nigel Raffety or Howard Walwyn
79 Kensington Church Street, London, W8 4BG
020 7938 1100 020 7938 2519
raffety@globalnet.co.uk
www.raffetyantiqueclocks.com
Est. 1982 *Stock size* Medium
Stock Late 17th–18thC clocks, furniture
Open Mon–Fri 1–6pm
Sat by appointment

Paul Reeves
Contact Mr P Reeves or S Barrett
32b Kensington Church Street, London, W8 4HA
020 7937 1594 020 7938 2163
Est. 1976 *Stock size* Large
Stock Victorian–Edwardian furniture, artefacts, textiles, glass, ceramics, metalwork, Arts and Crafts, aesthetic movement, Gothic Revival
Open Mon–Fri 10am–6pm
Sat 11am–4pm

Reindeer Antiques Ltd (BADA, LAPADA)
Contact Adrian Butterworth
81 Kensington Church Street, London, W8 4BG
020 7937 3754 020 7937 7199
adrianbutterworth@btinternet.com
www.reindeerantiques.co.uk
Est. 1969 *Stock size* Large
Stock Fine period English furniture, 17th–19thC mahogany, walnut, oak mirrors, paintings, objets d'art
Open Mon–Fri 9.30am–6pm
Sat 10am–5pm
Fairs BADA (March), LAPADA (Oct), NEC
Services Valuations, restorations

Roderick Antiques (LAPADA, KCSADA)
Contact Mr R Mee
23 Vicarage Gate, (Junction Kensington Church Street), London, W8 4AA
020 7937 8517 020 7937 8517
Est. 1975 *Stock size* Large
Stock Antique clocks, 1700–1900, including bracket, Vienna, longcase, carriage, English, French, German
Open Mon–Fri 10am–5.30pm
Sat 10am–4pm
Services Valuations, repairs

Brian Rolleston Antiques Ltd (BADA)
Contact Mr B Rolleston
104a Kensington Church Street, London, W8 4BU
020 7229 5892 020 7229 5892
Est. 1955 *Stock size* Medium
Stock 18thC English furniture
Open Mon–Fri 10am–1pm
2–5.30pm
Fairs Grosvenor House

Dyala Salam Antiques (KCSADA)
Contact Miss Dyala Salam
174a Kensington Church Street, London, W8 4DP
020 7229 4045 020 7229 2433
Est. 1991 *Stock size* Large
Stock 18th–19thC Ottoman antiques, textiles, Bohemian glass, Islamic furniture
Open Mon–Fri 11am–6pm
Sat 11.30am–3.30pm

Patrick Sandberg Antiques (BADA, CINOA)
Contact Mr C Radford
150–152 Kensington Church Street, London, W8 4BH
020 7229 0373 020 7792 3467
psand@antiquefurniture.net
www.antiquefurniture.net
Est. 1983 *Stock size* Large
Stock 18th–19thC English furniture, mirrors, accessories
Open Mon–Fri 10am–6pm
Sat 10am–4pm
Fairs Olympia

Santos (BADA)
Contact Mr A Santos
21 Old Court House, London, W8 4PD
020 7937 6000 020 7937 3351
www.santoslondon.com
Est. 1979 *Stock size* Small
Stock 17th–18thC Chinese export porcelain
Open By appointment only
Fairs International Ceramics Fair & Seminar London, The International Asian Art Fair, The New York Ceramics Fair, Lisbon International Fair

Simon Spero
Contact Mr S Spero
109 Kensington Church Street, London, W8 7LN
020 7727 7413 020 7727 7414
Est. 1964 *Stock size* Large
Stock 18thC English porcelain, enamels
Open Mon–Fri 10am–5pm
closed 1–2pm
Services Valuations, author of 5 reference books, lecturer

Stockspring Antiques (BADA, LAPADA, KCSADA)
Contact Mrs F Marno
114 Kensington Church Street, London, W8 4BH
020 7727 7995 020 7727 7995
stockspring@antique-porcelain.co.uk
www.antique-porcelain.co.uk
Est. 1979 *Stock size* Large
Stock 18th–early 19thC English porcelain
Open Mon–Fri 10am–5.30pm
Sat 10am–1pm
Fairs Olympia (Nov, June), Harrogate (Sept)
Services Packing, shipping

Pamela Teignmouth & Son
Contact Pamela Teignmouth
108 Kensington Church Street, London, W8 4BH
020 7229 1602 020 7792 5042
Est. 1981 *Stock size* Medium
Stock Decorative antiques
Open Mon–Fri 10am–6pm
Sat 10am–1pm
Services Valuations, restorations

Through The Looking Glass
Contact Mr J Pulton
137 Kensington Church Street, London, W8 7LP
020 7221 4026 020 7602 3678
Est. 1988 *Stock size* Large
Stock 19thC mirrors
Open Mon–Sat 10am–5.30pm

Jorge Welsh (BADA)
Contact Mr J Welsh
116 Kensington Church Street, London, W8 4BH
020 7229 2140 020 7792 3535
uk@jorgewelsh.com
www.jorgewelsh.com
Est. 1997 *Stock size* Large
Stock Chinese porcelain
Open Mon–Fri 10am–5.30pm
Sat 10am–2pm
Fairs International Ceramics Fair, Olympia (June)

Mary Wise & Grosvenor Antiques (BADA)
Contact Mrs M Wise
27 Holland Street, London, W8 4NA
020 7937 8649 020 7937 7179
07850 863050
info@wiseantiques.com
www.wiseantiques.com
Est. 1970 *Stock size* Small
Stock Porcelain, small bronzes, works of art, Chinese watercolours on pith paper
Open Mon–Fri 10am–5pm
Fairs New York Ceramics Fair, San Francisco Fall Antiques Show
Services Bid at auction

Zeitgeist Antiques
Contact Mr A Self
58 Kensington Church Street, London, W8 4DB
020 7938 4817 020 7938 4817
zeitgeistantiques@virgin.net
www.zeitgeistantiques.com
Est. 1988 *Stock size* Small
Stock Art Nouveau, Art Deco, glass, ceramics, metalware
Open Mon–Sat 10am–6pm
Fairs 20thC Olympia, Great Antiques Fair

W9

Vale Antiques
Contact Mr P Gooley
245 Elgin Avenue, Maida Vale, London, W9 1NJ
020 7328 4796
Est. 1973 *Stock size* Large
Stock Eclectic mix of antiques, Victorian–1950s, pictures, mirrors, silver, silver plate, china etc
Open Mon–Sat 10am–6pm
Services Restorations, pearl stringing, clock and watch repairs, framing

W10

88 Antiques
Contact Mr D Lucas
88 Golborne Road, London, W10 5PS
020 8960 0827
Est. 1977 *Stock size* Large
Stock Antique pine, country furniture
Open Tues–Sat 10am–6pm
Services Makers of tables from reclaimed 100-year-old wood

Bazar
Contact Ms M Davis or Ms C Rogers
82 Golborne Road, London, W10 5PS
020 8969 6262
Est. 1992 *Stock size* Medium
Stock French decorative country furniture, beds, tables, armchairs, kitchenware, garden furniture etc
Open Tues–Thurs 10am–5pm
Fri Sat 9.30am–5.30pm

David Wainwright
Contact Mr Jeremy Schroder
16–18 Malton Road, London, W10 5UP
020 8960 8181
Stock size Large
Stock Antique and old furniture, decorative items from India, Indonesia, China
Open By appointment
Services Delivery

W11

51 Antiques
Contact Mr Justin Raccanello
51 Ledbury Road, London, W11 2AA
020 7229 6153 020 7229 6153
Est. 1975 *Stock size* Medium
Stock Italian ceramics, 1500–1900, Venetian glass
Open Mon–Fri 9.30am–5.30pm
Sat 9.30am–1pm

Alice's
Contact Mrs D Carter
86 Portobello Road, London, W11 2QD
020 7229 8187 020 7792 2456
Est. 1887 *Stock size* Large
Stock Painted furniture, decorative items, general antiques
Open Tues–Fri 9am–5pm
Sat 7am–4pm

Anthea's Antiques
Contact A Mcilroy
Burton's Arcade, 296 Westbourne Grove, Portobello Market, London, W11 2PS
020 8690 7207
07961 838780
Est. 1985 *Stock size* Medium
Stock 19thC English and continental glass and ceramics
Trade only Yes
Open Sat 7am–4pm
Fairs Newark, Ardingly
Services Will arrange shipping if required

Appleby Antiques (PADA)
Contact Mike or Sue Witts
Geoffrey Van Gallery, 105–107 Portobello Road, London, W11 2QB
01453 753126 07778 282532
applebyantiques@aol.com
www.applebyantiques.co.uk
Est. 1986 *Stock size* Medium
Stock English pottery 1750–1930, specializing in Wedgwood Lustreware, culinary moulds in pewter, copper, ceramic
Open Sat 6.45am–3pm
Fairs NEC
Services Shipping

Arbras
Contact Sandy
Arbras Gallery, 292 Westbourne Grove, London, W11 2PS
020 7229 6772 020 7229 6772
info@arbras.freeserve.co.uk
www.arbras.freeserve.co.uk
Est. 1973 *Stock size* Large
Stock Silver picture frames, giftware
Open Mon–Fri 10am–4.30pm
Sat 7am–4.30pm
Services Mail order

Arenski Fine Art (BADA, LAPADA)
Contact Katie Kirkland
The Coach House, Ledbury Mews North, London, W11 2AF
020 7727 8599 F 020 7727 7584
arenski@netcomuk.co.uk
www.arenski.com
Stock size Large
Stock Exotic, unusual and colonial furniture, sculpture, animals in art
Open By appointment only
Fairs Olympia (summer and winter), Dallas, Palm Beach

Atlam Sales and Service (PADA)
Contact B Skogland-Kirk
111 Portobello Road, London, W11 2QB
020 7602 7573 F 020 7602 2997
info@atlam-watches.co.uk
www.atlam-watches.co.uk or www.atlamsilver.com
Est. 1979 *Stock size* Large
Stock Silver and antique pocket watches, decorative silver
Open Mon–Fri 9am–5pm Sat 8am–5pm

B and T Antiques Ltd (LAPADA, PADA)
Contact Bernadette Lewis or Vigi Sawdon
79–81 Ledbury Road, London, W11 2AG
020 7229 7001 F 020 7229 2033
bt.antiques@virgin.net
Est. 1994 *Stock size* Large
Stock Decorative antiques, Art Deco furniture and objects
Open Mon–Sat 10am–6pm
Services Restorations, gilding

Sebastiano Barbagallo Antiques
Contact Mr S Barbagallo
15 Pembridge Road, London, W11 3HG
020 7792 3320 F 020 7792 3320
Est. 1978 *Stock size* Large
Stock Chinese furniture, Indian and Tibetan antiques, crafts
Open Mon–Fri 10.30am–6.30pm Sat 9am–7pm Sun 10.30am–5pm

Barham Antiques (PADA)
Contact Mr M Barham
83 Portobello Road, London, W11 2QB
020 7727 3845 F 020 7727 3845
mchlbarham@aol.com
Est. 1970 *Stock size* Large
Stock Boxes, caddies, inkwells, clocks, glassware, inkstands, small furniture, silver plate
Open Mon–Fri 10am–4.30pm Sat 7am–5pm
Services Valuations, restorations

Beagle Gallery and Asian Antiques
Contact Mr Beagle
303 Westbourne Grove, London, W11 2QA
020 7229 9524 F 020 7792 0333
Est. 1984 *Stock size* Medium
Stock Oriental furniture, sculpture
Open By appointment

Book and Comic Exchange
Contact Mrs S Dawson
14 Pembridge Road, London, W11 3HL
020 7229 8420
www.buy-sell-trade.co.uk
Est. 1967 *Stock size* Medium
Stock Modern first editions, cult books, comics
Open Mon–Sun 10am–8pm

Tony Booth Antiques (PADA)
Contact Mr Tony Booth
135 Portobello Road, London, W11 2DY
020 8810 6339 F 020 8810 6339
M 07770 390749
tonybooth44@hotmail.com
Est. 1990 *Stock size* Medium
Stock Silver
Open Sat 7am–5pm
Fairs Ardingly, NEC

F E A Briggs Ltd
Contact Joan Wilson
77 Ledbury Road, London, W11 2AG
020 7727 0909 F 023 8081 2595
feabriggs@aol.com
Est. 1966 *Stock size* Small
Stock Victorian furniture
Open Mon–Fri 9am–5.30pm
Fairs Newark
Services Restorations

Butchoff Interiors (LAPADA)
Contact Mr A Kaye
220 Westbourne Grove, London, W11 2RH
020 7221 8174 F 020 7792 8923
ian@butchoff.com
www.butchoff.com
Est. 1999 *Stock size* Medium
Stock One-off items, textiles, collectables, dining tables, chairs, consoles, accessories
Open Mon–Fri 9.30am–6pm Sat 9.30am–5pm

Canonbury Antiques Ltd
Contact Miss A Worster
174 Westbourne Grove, London, W11 2RW
020 7229 2786 F 020 7229 5840
martin@canonbury-antiques.co.uk
Est. 1964 *Stock size* Large
Stock 18th–19thC furniture, reproduction furniture, accessories
Open Mon–Sat 10am–5.30pm
Fairs Newark
Services Restorations

Aurea Carter (LAPADA)
Contact Aurea Carter
Burton's Antique Arcade, 296 Westbourne Grove, London, W11 2PS
020 7731 3486 F 020 7731 3486
M 07815 912477
aureacarter@englishceramics.com
www.englishceramics.com
Est. 1980 *Stock size* Large
Stock 18th–early 19thC English pottery and porcelain
Open Sat 7.30am–2.30pm Fri afternoon by appointment
Fairs Olympia, New York Ceramic Fair
Services Valuations, shipping

Jack Casimir Ltd (BADA, LAPADA)
23 Pembridge Road, London, W11 3HG
020 7727 8643
Est. 1931 *Stock size* Large
Stock 16th–19thC British and European domestic brass, copper, pewter, paktong
Open Mon–Sat 9.30am–5.30pm
Services Shipping

Chamade Antiques
Contact George Walters
65 Portobello Road, London, W11 2QB
020 8446 0130
Stock size Medium
Stock Antique Rolex watches
Open Sat 7am–3pm

田 Nicholas Chandor Antiques
Contact Mr N Chandor
✉ **4a Ladbroke Grove, London, W11 3BG** 🅿
☎ 020 7229 4044 Ⓕ 020 7229 4044
Ⓔ nicholaschandor@aol.com
Est. 1990 *Stock size* Medium
Stock Eclectic Continental furniture
Open Tues–Sat 10am–6pm

田 Chelsea Clocks and Antiques
Contact Mr Donald Lynch
✉ **73 Portobello Road, Notting Hill, London, W11 2QB** 🅿
☎ 020 7229 7762 Ⓕ 020 7274 5198
Ⓔ info@chelseaclocks.co.uk
Ⓦ www.chelseaclocks.co.uk
Est. 1979 *Stock size* Medium
Stock Clocks, scales, boxes, collectables, ink stands and wells
Open Mon–Sat 10am–5pm

田 Sheila Cook Textiles
Contact Mrs S Cook
✉ **283 Westbourne Grove, London, W11 2QA** 🅿
☎ 020 7792 8001 Ⓕ 020 7229 3855
Ⓔ sheilacook@sheilacook.co.uk
Ⓦ www.sheilacook.co.uk
Est. 1970 *Stock size* Small
Stock Mid-18thC–1970s European costume, textiles, accessories
Open Fri & Sat 10am–6pm other times by appointment
Services Valuations

田 Stuart Craig (PADA)
Contact Stuart Craig
✉ **Unit 72, Ground Floor, Admiral Vernon Antiques Market, 141–149 Portobello Road, London, W11 2DY** 🅿
☎ 020 7221 8662 Ⓜ 07947 889012
Est. 1991 *Stock size* Medium
Stock Early 19thC–1950s antique ladies' clothing, accessories
Open Sat 8.30am–4pm or by appointment

田 Cura Antiques
Contact Mr Cura
✉ **34 Ledbury Road, London, W11 2AB** 🅿
☎ 020 7229 6880 Ⓕ 020 7792 3731
Ⓔ mail@cura-antiques.com
Ⓦ www.cura-antiques.com
Est. 1969 *Stock size* Medium
Stock Continental works of art, furniture, old master paintings
Open Mon–Fri 10.30am–5.30pm Sat 10.30am–1pm
Fairs Olympia (June)
Services Restorations

🏠 John Dale Antiques (PADA)
Contact Mrs Jo Cairns
✉ **87 Portobello Road, London, W11 2QB** 🅿
☎ 020 7727 1304
Est. 1960 *Stock size* Medium
No. of dealers 6
Stock Stained glass, books, prints, antiquities, collectables, cameras, decorative antiques
Open Sat 7am–5pm Mon–Fri 11am–4pm or by appointment

田 Gavin Douglas (LAPADA, PADA)
Contact Gavin Douglas
✉ **75 Portobello Road, London, W11 2QB** 🅿
☎ 01825 723441 Ⓕ 01825 724418
Ⓔ gavin@antique-clocks.co.uk
Ⓦ www.antique-clocks.co.uk
Est. 1992 *Stock size* Large
Stock Antique clocks, ormolu, bronzes and porcelain
Open Mon–Sat 10.30am–4.30pm
Fairs Olympia, LAPADA
Services Valuations, restorations

田 Simon Finch (ABA, PBFA)
Contact Simon Finch
✉ **61a Ledbury Road, London, W11 2AL** 🅿
☎ 020 7792 3303
Ⓔ rarebooks@simonfinch.com
Ⓦ www.simonfinch.com
Est. 1982 *Stock size* Medium
Stock Modern first editions, art and photography
Open Mon–Sat 10am-6pm
Fairs Olympia, Chelsea, Grosvenor House

田 Henry Gregory (PADA)
Contact Camy Gregory
✉ **82E Portobello Road, London, W11 2QD** 🅿
☎ 020 7792 9221
Est. 1970 *Stock size* Medium
Stock Silver plate, silver, sporting goods, decorative antiques
Open Mon–Fri 10am–4.30pm Sat 8am–4.30pm
Services Shipping

田 Hart & Rosenberg
Contact Mrs E Hart
✉ **Units L52/L53, Lower Trading Hall, Admiral Vernon Antiques Market, 141–149 Portobello Road, London, W11 2DY** 🅿
☎ 020 7359 6839 Ⓕ 020 7359 6839
Est. 1968 *Stock size* Large
Stock Oriental and Continental ceramics, decorative items
Open Wed–Sat 10am–5pm Tues–Fri 10.30am–5pm or by appointment
Services Valuations, restorations

田 Helios Gallery (ADA, PADA, BABAADA)
Contact Rolf Kiaer
✉ **292 Westbourne Grove, London, W11 2PS** 🅿
Ⓕ 01225 336097 Ⓜ 07711 955997
Ⓔ heliosgallery@btinternet.com
Ⓦ www.heliosgallery.com
Est. 1995 *Stock size* Medium
Stock Roman, Greek, Egyptian, Chinese, ancient art
Open Sat 8am–4pm or by appointment
Fairs ADA Fair
Services Valuations, restorations, shipping

田 Hirst Antiques
Contact Mrs S Hirst
✉ **59 Pembridge Road, London, W11 3HN** 🅿
☎ 020 7727 9364 Ⓕ 020 7460 6480
Est. 1969 *Stock size* Large
Stock General antique furniture, antique beds, bronzes, sculpture, pictures
Open Mon–Sat 10am–6pm

田 Erna Hiscock (PADA)
Contact Erna Hiscock
✉ **Chelsea Galleries, 69 Portobello Road, London, W11 2PS**
☎ 01233 661407 Ⓕ 01233 661407
Ⓔ erna@ernahiscockantiques.com
Ⓦ www.ernahiscockantiques.com
Est. 1975 *Stock size* Large
Stock 17th–19thC samplers, needlework
Open Sat 7am–3pm
Fairs NEC
Services Valuations

Humbleyard Fine Art (PADA)
Contact James Layte
Unit 32, Admiral Vernon Arcade, Portobello Road, London, W11 2DY
☎ 01362 637793 Ⓕ 01362 637793
Ⓜ 07836 349416
Est. 1974 *Stock size* Medium
Stock Scientific, medical, decorative and collectors' items
Open Sat 6am–1.30pm
Fairs Olympia
Services Valuations

Kleanthous Antiques Ltd (LAPADA)
Contact Mr C Kleanthous
144 Portobello Road, London, W11 2DZ
☎ 020 7727 3649 Ⓕ 020 7243 2488
Ⓜ 07850 375501
Ⓔ antiques@kleanthous.com
Ⓦ www.kleanthous.com
Est. 1969 *Stock size* Medium
Stock Jewellery, wrist watches, furniture, clocks, pocket watches, porcelain, china, silver, works of art, 20thC decorative items
Open Sat 8am–4pm or by appointment
Fairs Olympia

M & D Lewis
Contact Mr M Lewis
83–85 Ledbury Road, London, W11 2AG
☎ 020 7727 3908 Ⓕ 020 7727 3908
Est. 1959 *Stock size* Large
Stock English and Continental furniture, Oriental porcelain
Open Mon–Fri 10am–5pm
Sat 10am–4pm

M & D Lewis (PADA)
Contact Mr M Lewis
1 Lonsdale Road, London, W11 2BY
☎ 020 7727 3908 Ⓕ 020 7727 3908
Est. 1959 *Stock size* Large
Stock English and Continental furniture, Oriental porcelain
Open Mon–Fri 10am–5pm
Sat 10am–4pm

M & D Lewis
Contact Mr M Lewis
172 Westbourne Grove, London, W11 2RW
☎ 020 7727 3908 Ⓕ 020 7727 3908
Est. 1959 *Stock size* Large
Stock English and Continental furniture, Oriental porcelain
Open Mon–Fri 10am–5pm
Sat 10am–3pm

Caira Mandaglio
Contact Anne or Sharon
31 Pembridge Road, London, W11 3HG
☎ 020 7727 5496 Ⓕ 020 7229 4889
Est. 1998 *Stock size* Large
Stock 14th–20thC furniture, lighting, glassware, objets d'art, chandeliers
Open Tues–Fri 11am–5pm Sat 10.30am–5.30pm

Mario's Antiques (LAPADA, PADA)
Contact M Barazi
115 Portobello Road, London, W11 2DY
☎ 020 8902 1600 Ⓕ 020 8900 0810
Ⓜ 07956 580772
Ⓔ marwan@barazi.screaming.net
Ⓦ www.marios-antiques.com
Est. 1986 *Stock size* Medium
Stock Porcelain, Meissen, Sèvres, Vienna
Open Wed Fri 10am–4pm
Sat 7am–5pm
Fairs Olympia, LAPADA, NEC

Robin Martin Antiques
Contact Mr P Martin
44 Ledbury Road, London, W11 2AB
☎ 020 7727 1301 Ⓕ 020 7727 1301
Ⓔ paul.martin11@virgin.net
Est. 1971 *Stock size* Medium
Stock Mirrors, Regency furniture, Continental furniture, works of art, lighting
Open Mon–Fri 10am–6pm
Sat 10am–1pm
Fairs Olympia (June, Nov)

Mayflower Antiques (PADA)
Contact Mr John Odgers
117 Portobello Road, London, W11 2DY
☎ 020 7727 0381 Ⓜ 07860 843569
Ⓔ antiques@johnodgers.com
Est. 1970 *Stock size* Medium
Stock Music boxes, clocks, dolls, scientific instruments, pistols, collectable items
Open Sat 7am–4pm
Fairs Newark, Ardingly

MCN Antiques
Contact Makoto Umezawa
183 Westbourne Grove, London, W11 2SB
☎ 020 7727 3796 Ⓕ 020 7229 8839
Est. 1980 *Stock size* Large
Stock Japanese porcelain, works of art
Open Mon–Fri 10am–6pm
Sat 11am–3pm

Mimi Fifi
Contact Rita Delaforge
27 Pembridge Road, Notting Hill Gate, London, W11 3HG
☎ 020 7243 3154 Ⓕ 020 7938 4222
Ⓜ 07956 222238
Ⓔ info@mimififi.com
Ⓦ www.mimififi.com
Est. 1992 *Stock size* Large
Stock Collectors' and vintage toys, Coca-Cola memorabilia, Pokemon, perfume-related items, vintage badges, tobacco memorabilia, Michelin memorabilia, Kewpie dolls, Japanese collectables
Open Tues–Sat 11am–6pm
Services Overseas postal service

Myriad Antiques
Contact Mrs S Nickerson
131 Portland Road, London, W11 4LW
☎ 020 7229 1709 Ⓕ 020 7221 3882
Est. 1975 *Stock size* Large
Stock French painted furniture, garden furniture, bamboo, Victorian–Edwardian upholstered chairs, mirrors, objets d'art
Open Tues–Sat 11am–6pm

Ormonde Gallery (LAPADA)
Contact Mr F Ormonde
156 Portobello Road, London, W11 2EB
☎ 020 7229 9800 Ⓕ 020 7792 2418
Stock size Large
Stock 19thC Chinese and Indonesian furniture, ceramics 2000BC–Ching Dynasty, Oriental art, jade, snuff bottles
Open Mon–Fri 10am–6pm
Sat 9am–6pm

Polly Pallister (PADA)
Contact Polly Pallister
Geoffrey Van Gallery, 105–107 Portobello Road, London, W11 2QB

☎ 020 7267 7864
Ⓦ www.polly-pallister-antiques.com
Est. 1996 *Stock size* Medium
Stock 18th–19thC decorative antiques, 18thC engravings, creamware, silk patchworks, textiles
Open Sat 7am–2.30pm
or by appointment

Peter Petrou (BADA, LAPADA)
Contact Katie Kirkland
✉ **The Coach House, Ledbury Mews North, London, W11 2AF** Ⓟ
☎ 020 7229 9575 Ⓕ 020 7727 7584
Ⓔ peterpetrou@btinternet.com
Ⓦ www.peterpetrou.com
Est. 1974 *Stock size* Large
Stock Exotic, unusual and colonial furniture, sculpture, animals in art
Open By appointment only
Fairs Olympia (summer and winter), Dallas, Palm Beach

Portobello Antique Store
Contact Mr J Ewing
✉ **79 Portobello Road, London, W11 2QB** Ⓟ
☎ 020 7221 1994 Ⓕ 020 7221 1994
Est. 1984 *Stock size* Large
Stock Silver, silver plate, decorative items, flatware
Open Tues–Fri 10am–4pm
Sat 8.15am–4pm

Principia Fine Art
Contact Mr M Forrer
✉ **Stand 9–10, Lipka Arcade, 282 Westbourne Grove, London, W11 2DX** Ⓟ
☎ 01488 682873 Ⓕ 01672 511551
Ⓜ 07899 926020
Est. 1970 *Stock size* Large
Stock Scientific instruments, small furniture, Oriental art, books, paintings, works of art
Open Mon–Fri 10.30am–5pm
Sat 7am–12.30pm
Services Valuations, restorations, shipping, book search

Rogers Antiques Gallery
Contact Mike Spooner
✉ **65 Portobello Road, London, W11 2QB** Ⓟ
☎ 020 7969 1500 Ⓕ 020 7969 1639
Est. 1969 *Stock size* Large
No. of dealers 65
Stock Wide range of antiques and collectables, specialist dealers in most fields
Open Sat 7am–4.30pm
Services Valuations

Schredds of Portobello (LAPADA, CINOA, PADA)
Contact George R Schrager
✉ **107 Portobello Road, London, W11 2QB** Ⓟ
☎ 020 8348 3314 Ⓕ 020 8341 5971
Ⓔ silver@schredds.demon.co.uk
Ⓦ www.schredds.com
Est. 1972 *Stock size* Large
Stock Small pieces of pre-1880 silver
Open Sat 7am–2.30pm
Fairs Penman fairs
Services Valuations, shipping

Justin F Skrebowski Prints (PBFA, PADA)
Contact Mr J Skrebowski
✉ **Ground Floor, 177 Portobello Road, London, W11 2DY** Ⓟ
☎ 020 7792 9742 Ⓕ 020 7792 9742
Ⓜ 07774 612474
Ⓔ justin@skreb.co.uk
Ⓦ www.skreb.co.uk
Est. 1979 *Stock size* Large
Stock 18–19thC decorative prints, 18th–20thC frames for prints and watercolours, oils, watercolours
Open Sat 9am–4pm
or by appointment
Fairs PBFA, Russell Hotel
Services Folio stands, easels, display equipment

Solaris Antiques
Contact Hassan Abdullah
✉ **170 Westbourne Grove, London, W11 2RW** Ⓟ
☎ 020 7229 8100 Ⓕ 020 7229 8300
Est. 1994 *Stock size* Medium
Stock Decorative antiques from France and Sweden, all periods up to 1970s
Open Mon–Sat 10.30–6pm

Staffordshire Pride
Contact Sharon Racklyeft
✉ **Stand 30 & 31, 290 Westbourne Grove, London, W11 2PS**
☎ 020 8883 6180 Ⓜ 07958 453295
Est. 1975 *Stock size* Large
Stock 1790–1900 Staffordshire figures
Open Sat 8am–2.30pm

June and Tony Stone Fine Antique Boxes (PADA LAPADA)
Contact Tony Stone
✉ **75 Portobello Road, London, W11 2QB** Ⓟ
☎ 07092 106600 Ⓕ 07092 106611
Ⓔ jts@boxes.co.uk
Ⓦ www.boxes.co.uk
Est. 1990 *Stock size* Large
Stock 18th–19thC boxes, rare and unusual tea caddies
Open Mon–Fri 10.30am–4.30pm
Sat 8am–5pm
Fairs All Olympias, LAPADA
Services Shipping included in prices

Pam Taylor Antiques (PADA)
Contact Mrs P Taylor
✉ **Portobello Studios, The Red Teapot, 101 Portobello Road, London, W11 2QB** Ⓟ
Ⓜ 07850 416717
Ⓔ pamlet@globalnet.co.uk
Est. 1982 *Stock size* Medium
Stock Late 19th–early 20thC ceramics, glass, oil lamps
Open Sat 6.30am–3.30pm
Fairs Antiques for Everyone

Themes and Variations
Contact Liliane Fawcett
✉ **231 Westbourne Grove, London, W11 2SE** Ⓟ
☎ 020 7727 5531 Ⓕ 020 7727 6378
Ⓔ go@themesandvariations.co.uk
Ⓦ www.themesandvariations.co.uk
Est. 1984 *Stock size* Large
Stock Post-war Scandinavian, Italian furniture, decorative arts
Open Mon–Fri 10am–1pm
2pm–6pm

Christina Truscott (PADA)
Contact Christina Truscott
✉ **Geoffrey Van Gallery, 105–107 Portobello Road, London, W11 2QB**
☎ 01403 730554 Ⓜ 07968 371036
Est. 1977 *Stock size* Medium
Stock Chinese export lacquer, papier mâché, decorative items
Open Sat 7am–3pm

Virginia
Contact Mrs V Bates
98 Portland Road, London, W11 4LQ
020 7727 9908 020 7229 2198
Est. 1971 *Stock size* Medium
Stock Vintage clothes, late 19thC–late 1930s
Open 11am–6pm by appointment only

Visto
Contact Mrs H Little
41 Pembridge Road, Notting Hill, London, W11 3HG
020 7243 4392 020 7243 1374
07788 136906
Est. 1997 *Stock size* Medium
Stock 1950s–1960s collectables, lighting, textiles, furniture, ceramics, glass
Open Wed–Fri 11am–6pm Sat 10am–6pm

David Wainwright
Contact Mr D Wainwright
63 Portobello Road, London, W11 3DB
020 7727 0707 *Stock size* Small
Stock Antique and old furniture, decorative items from India, Indonesia, China
Open Mon–Sat 9am–6pm
Services Delivery

David Wainwright
Contact Mr D Wainwright
251 Portobello Road, London, W11 1LT
020 7792 1988
Stock size Medium
Stock Antique and old furniture, decorative items from India, Indonesia, China
Open Mon–Sat 9.30am–6.30pm Sun 11am–6pm
Services Delivery

Trude Weaver (LAPADA)
Contact Mr B Weaver
71 Portobello Road, London, W11 2QB
020 7229 8738 020 7229 8738
07768 551269
Est. 1968 *Stock size* Large
Stock 18th–19thC English and Continental furniture, complementary accessories
Open Wed–Sat 9.30am–5.30pm
Fairs Olympia (June, Nov)

W12

Neil Freeman Angling Auctions
Contact Mr N Freeman
PO Box 2095, London, W12 8RU
020 8749 4175 020 8743 4855
07785 281349
neil@anglingauctions.demon.co.uk.
www.thesaurus.co.uk/angling-auctions/
Est. 1990
Sales Angling auctions twice yearly, first Sat April noon, first Sat October noon, viewing The Grand Hall, Chiswick Town Hall, Heathfield Terrace, London W4 Fri 1.30–7pm Sat 8.30am to sale
Frequency Twice yearly
Catalogues yes

W13

C and L Burman (BADA)
Contact Charles Truman or Lucy Burniston
5 Vigo Street, London, W13 3HF
020 7439 6604 020 7439 6605
charles-truman@lineone.net
Est. 2001 *Stock size* Medium
Stock Antiques and works of art including silver, glass, ceramics, furniture, sculpture
Open By appointment
Fairs March BADA, Grosvenor House, Winter Olympia
Services Valuations, restorations

W14

Asenbaum Fine Arts Ltd
Contact Mrs C Fells
10 Carlton Mansions, Holland Park Gardens, London, W14 8DW
020 7602 5373 020 7602 5373
Est. 1998 *Stock size* Medium
Stock English and Viennese silver, Viennese furniture, Victorian jewellery
Trade only Yes
Open By appointment only

Kate Thurlow, David Alexander Antiques and Lucy Johnson (LAPADA, CINOA)
Contact Kate Thurlow, Rodney Robertson or Lucy Johnson
The Warehouse, 7A North End Road, London, W14 8ST
020 7602 8388 020 7602 8388
katethurlow@onetel.net.uk
Est. 1978 *Stock size* Medium
Stock 16th–17thC European furniture, associated works of art
Open By appointment
Fairs Olympia
Services Restorations

WC1

Amherst Antiques (LAPADA)
Contact Mrs Dianne Brick
Monomark House, 27 Old Gloucester Street, London, WC1 N3XX
01892 725552 01892 725552
07850 350212
Est. 1987 *Stock size* Medium
Stock Tunbridge ware, 19thC English ceramics, coloured glass, silver
Open By appointment
Fairs Olympia, NEC, Chester, Buxton, Petersfield
Services Valuations of Tunbridge ware

The Bloomsbury Bookshop
Contact Mr M Thompson
12 Bury Place, London, WC1A 2JL
020 7404 7433
dullbooks@aol.com
Est. 1989 *Stock size* Large
Stock Non-fiction, history, humanities, social sciences
Open Mon–Sat 11am–6pm Sun 11am–5pm
Services Valuations, book search

Book Art and Architecture Ltd
Contact Mr D C Sharp
12 Woburn Walk, London, WC1H 0JL
020 7387 5006 01707 875286
07710 207404
sharpd@globalnet.co.uk
www.sharparchitects.co.uk
Est. 1998 *Stock size* Large
Stock Antiquarian, rare, out-of-print, second-hand books, also the volume gallery, modern architecture, art, design a speciality
Open Mon–Fri 11am–6pm

Fairs Russell Hotel, Hatfield
Services Book searches, valuations, library lists

George & Peter Cohn
Contact Peter Cohn
Unit 21, 21 Wren Street, London, WC1X 0HF
020 7278 3749
Est. 1947 *Stock size* Medium
Stock Chandeliers, wall lights, lanterns, chandelier parts
Open Mon–Fri 9.30am–4pm
Services Restorations

Coincraft (ADA, IBNS, PNG, ANA)
Contact Mr B Clayden
44–45 Great Russell Street, London, WC1B 3LU
020 7636 1188 F 020 7323 2860
info@coincraft.com
ww.coincraft.com
Est. 1955
Stock Greek, Roman, English, Medieval–present day coins, British and foreign banknotes, ancient artefacts
Open Mon–Fri 9.30am–5pm
Sat 10am–2.30pm or by appointment
Fairs Marriott, Cumberland
Services Catalogue of British coins

Collinge & Clark (PBFA)
Contact Mr O Clark
13 Leigh Street, London, WC1H 9EW
020 7387 7105 F 020 7388 1315
Est. 1989 *Stock size* Medium
Stock Antiquarian, rare, second-hand books, private press books, limited editions, 18th–19thC political and social history, typography
Open Mon–Fri 11am–6.30pm
Sat 11am–3.30pm

Fine Books Oriental Ltd (PBFA)
Contact Mr J Somers
38 Museum Street, London, WC1A 1LP
020 7242 5288 F 020 7242 5344
oriental@finebooks.demon.co.uk
www.finebooks.demon.co.uk
Est. 1977 *Stock size* Medium
Stock South Asian and Indian, out-of-print, rare books
Open Mon–Fri 9.30am–6pm
Sat 11am–6pm
Fairs PBFA, Russell Hotel
Services Valuations

Robert Frew Ltd (PBFA, ABA)
Contact Mr R Frew
106 Great Russell Street, London, WC1B 3NB
020 7580 2311 F 020 7580 2313
shop@robertfrew.com
www.robertfrew.com
Est. 1976 *Stock size* Medium
Stock Antiquarian and rare books, travel, literature, classics, maps, prints
Open Mon–Fri 10am–6pm
Sat 10am–2pm
Fairs PBFA Bookfairs, Russell Hotel, ABA Olympia Chelsea

R A Gekoski Booksellers (ABA, ILAD)
Contact Rick Gekoski or Peter Grogan
Pied Bull Yard, 15a Bloomsbury Square, London, WC1A 2LP
020 7404 6676 F 020 7404 6595
gekoski@dircon.co.uk
Est. 1984 *Stock size* Small
Stock First editions, letters, paintings, manuscripts
Open Mon–Fri 10am–5.30pm
Fairs ABA
Services Valuations

Griffith & Partners Ltd
Contact David Griffith
31–35 Great Ormond Street, London, WC1N 3HZ
020 7430 1394
Est. 1992 *Stock size* Medium
Stock Antiquarian, rare, second-hand books, London topography, Middle East, poetry, Anglo and Welsh topics a speciality
Open Mon–Fri noon–6pm
or by appointment
Services Valuations, book search, catalogues, mail order

Jarndyce Antiquarian Booksellers (ABA, PBFA)
Contact Mr B Lake or Ms Janet Nassau
46 Great Russell Street, London, WC1B 3PA
020 7631 4220 F 020 7631 1882
books@jarndyce.com
www.jarndyce.com
Est. 1969 *Stock size* Large
Stock Antiquarian, rare, second-hand books on English language, English literature, Dickens, 18th–20thC economic and social history
Open Mon–Fri 10.30am–5.30pm
Fairs Olympia, Chelsea ABA, York PBFA
Services Valuations, catalogues

Jessop Classic Photographic
Contact Martin Frost or Steve Johnson
67 Great Russell Street, London, WC1B 3BN
020 7831 3640 F 020 7831 3956
www.jessops.com/classic
Est. 1989 *Stock size* Large
Stock 1900–1970 classic cameras
Open Mon–Sat 9am–5.30pm
Services Repairs

Robert Johnson Coin Co
Contact Mr R Johnson
15 Bury Place, London, WC1A 2JB
020 7831 0305 F 01494 681084
Est. 1971
Stock Greek, Roman, English, hammered and milled coins
Open Mon–Fri 10am–6pm
Sat 11am–4pm
Services Valuations

Marchmont Bookshop
Contact Mr D Holder
39 Burton Street, London, WC1H 9AL
020 7387 7989 F 020 7387 7989
Est. 1977 *Stock size* Medium
Stock Rare, antiquarian, second-hand books, literature, poetry a speciality
Open Mon–Fri 11am–6.30pm

Rennies (ESoc)
Contact Mr P Rennie
13 Rugby Street, London, WC1N 3QT
020 7405 0220
info@rennart.co.uk
www.rennart.co.uk
Est. 1990 *Stock size* Small
Stock 20thC art and design, inter-war period posters, graphics
Open Tues–Fri noon–6.30pm
Sat noon–6pm
Services Valuations

Roe and Moore
Contact Mr T Roe
29 Museum Street, London, WC1A 1LH
020 7636 4787 Fax 020 7636 6110
roeandmoore@fsbdial.co.uk
www.abebooks.com
Est. 1992 *Stock size* Medium
Stock Prints, posters, 19th–20thC rare books, children's books, photography, European language books
Open Mon–Sat 10.30am–6pm

Simmons Gallery (BNTA)
Contact Mr H Simmons
53 Lambs Conduit Street, London, WC1N 3NB
020 7831 2080 Fax 020 7831 2090
info@simmonsgallery.co.uk
www.simmonsgallery.co.uk
Est. 1982 *Stock size* Large
Stock Worldwide coins, contemporary, prize, commemorative medals, art, sculpture, jewellery
Open Mon–Fri 10.30am–5.30pm or by appointment
Fairs London Coin Fair, Coinex
Services Valuations, bi-annual metrology mail auction

Skoob Books Ltd
Contact Mr I Ong or Mark Lovell
15 Sicilian Avenue, off Bernard Street, London, WC1A 2QH
020 7404 3063 Fax 020 7404 4398
books@skoob.com
www.skoob.com
Est. 1980 *Stock size* Large
Stock Second-hand and antiquarian books, philosophy a speciality
Open Mon–Sat 11am–7pm Sun noon–5pm

Skoob Russell Square
Contact Mr I Ong or Mark Lovell
10 Brunswick Centre, off Bernard Street, London, WC1N 1AE
020 7278 8760 Fax 020 7278 3137
books@skoob.com
www.skoob.com
Est. 2001 *Stock size* Large
Stock Second-hand and antiquarian books, philosophy a speciality
Open Mon–Sat 11am–7pm Sun noon–5pm

Unsworths Booksellers Ltd (ABA, PBFA)
Contact Mr Charlie Unsworth
12 Bloomsbury Street, London, WC1B 3QA
020 7436 9836 Fax 020 7637 7334
books@unsworths.com
www.unsworths.com
Est. 1986 *Stock size* Large
Stock Antiquarian, second-hand and remainder books on the humanities
Open Mon–Sat 10am–8pm Sun 11am–7pm
Fairs See website for details

Woburn Book Shop (PBFA)
Contact Mr B Buitekant
10 Woburn Walk, London, WC1H 0JL
020 7388 7278 Fax 020 7263 5196
bb@ukgateway.net
Est. 1994 *Stock size* Medium
Stock Second-hand and antiquarian books on social history, psychoanalysis, philosophy
Open Mon–Fri 11am–6pm Sat 11am–5pm

WC2

Anchor Antiques Ltd
Contact Mrs Samne
26 Charing Cross Road, London, WC2H 0DG
020 7836 5686
Est. 1964 *Stock size* Medium
Stock European and Oriental ceramics
Trade only Yes
Open By appointment

Any Amount of Books (PBFA, ABA, ILAB)
Contact N Burwood
56 Charing Cross Road, London, WC2H 0QA
020 7836 3597 Fax 020 7240 1769
charingx@anyamountofbooks.com
www.anyamountofbooks.com
Est. 1975 *Stock size* Large
Stock Antiquarian, rare and second-hand books
Open Mon–Sat 10.30am–9.30pm Sun 11.30am–8.30pm
Fairs PBFA Russell Hotel, Olympia
Services Shipping, appraisals

The Apple Market
Contact Anne Surs
Covent Garden Market, London, WC2E 8RF
020 7836 9136
www.coventgardenmarket.co.uk
Est. 1980 *Stock size* Small
No. of dealers 40
Stock 40 traders use the traditional wrought iron stalls of the original Covent Garden, jewellery, china, small collectable items
Open Mon 10am–6pm

Argenteus Ltd (LAPADA)
Contact Mr M Feldman
Vault 2, The London Silver Vaults, 53 Chancery Lane, London, WC2A 1QS
020 7831 3637 Fax 020 7430 0126
Est. 1991 *Stock size* Medium
Stock Antique silver, Sheffield plate, flatware
Open Mon–Fri 9am–5.30pm Sat 9am–1pm

A H Baldwin and Son (BADA)
Contact Tim Wilkes
11 Adelphi Terrace, London, WC2N 6BJ
020 7930 6879 Fax 020 7930 9450
coins@baldwin.sh
www.baldwin.sh
Est. 1872
Stock Coins, commemorative medals
Open Mon–Fri 9am–5pm
Services Valuations

Bell, Book and Radnell (ABA)
Contact Mr John Bell or Mr James Tindley
4 Cecil Court, London, WC2N 4HE
020 7240 2161 Fax 020 7379 1062
bellbr@dial.pipex.com
Est. 1972 *Stock size* Medium
Stock 20thC first editions, literature, novels, poetry
Open Mon–Fri 10am–5.30pm Sat 11am–4pm
Services Valuations

Malcolm Bord
Contact Mr M Bord
16 Charing Cross Road, London, WC2H 0HR
020 7836 0631 Fax 020 7240 1920
Est. 1970 *Stock size* Large
Stock Worldwide old silver and bronze coins
Open Mon–Sat 10.30am–5.30pm
Services Valuations

Charing Cross Markets
Contact Rodney Bolwell
1 Embankment Place, London, WC2N 6NN
01483 281771 01483 281771
rodney@chicane.fsbusiness.co.uk
Est. 1974 *Stock size* Large
No. of dealers 35
Stock Stamps, postcards, coins
Open Sat 7.30am–3pm

Coins and Bullion (BNTA, ANA)
Contact Mr P Cohen
20 Cecil Court, London, WC2N 4HE
020 7379 0615
Est. 1977
Stock British coins from 1500, world coins
Open Mon–Fri 10.30am–5.30pm
Sat noon–5pm
Services Valuations

Paul Daniel (LSVA)
Contact Paul Daniel
51 The London Silver Vaults, Chancery Lane, London, WC2A 1QS
020 7430 1327 020 7430 1327
07831 338461
paveldaniel@aol.com
Est. 1979 *Stock size* Medium
Stock Commercial English and Continental silver
Open Mon–Fri 10am–4pm
Services Valuations, restorations

Bryan Douglas (LAPADA)
Contact Mr B Douglas
12 & 14 The London Silver Vaults, Chancery Lane, London, WC2A 1QS
020 7242 7073 020 7242 7073
sales@bryandouglas.co.uk
www.bryandouglas.co.uk
Est. 1971 *Stock size* Large
Stock Antique, vintage, modern silver, silver plate, old Sheffield plate
Open Mon–Fri 9.30am–5pm
Sat 9.30am–1pm
Services Valuations

R Feldman Ltd Antique Silver (LAPADA)
Contact Mr R Feldman
4 & 6 The London Silver Vaults, 53 Chancery Lane, London, WC2A 1QB
020 7405 6111 020 7430 0126
rfeldman@rfeldman.co.uk
www.rfeldman.co.uk
Est. 1954 *Stock size* Large
Stock Antique Victorian silver, old Sheffield plate
Open Mon–Fri 9am–5.30pm
Sat 9am–1pm
Services Valuations, repairs

Frasers Autographs (IADA, UACC)
Contact Poppy Collinson
399 The Strand, London, WC2R 0LX
020 7557 4404 020 7836 7342
sales@frasersautographs.co.uk
www.frasersautographs.com
Est. 1978 *Stock size* Large
Stock Signed photos, letters, documents, stage and film costumes and props, signed guitars, sports equipment
Open Mon–Sat 9.30am–5.30pm
Fairs Stanley Gibbons Fairs
Services Valuations, want list, bi-monthly postal Internet autograph auction, lifetime authenticity guarantee

Stanley Gibbons Auctions Ltd (PTS, ASDA)
Contact Mr Colin Avery
399 Strand, London, WC2R 0LX
020 7836 8444 020 7836 7342
auctions@stanleygibbons.co.uk
www.stanleygibbons.com/auction
Est. 1856
Open Mon–Fri 9am–5pm
Sales 6 Postbid sales per year, 6 Collections & Ranges sales, occasional Web-only sales, viewing for all sales by appointment
Frequency Every 4–6 weeks
Catalogues Yes

Gillian Gould Antiques
Contact Gill Gould
Ocean Leisure, 11–14 Northumberland Avenue, London, WC2N 5AQ
020 7419 0500 020 7419 0400
07831 150060
gillgould@dealwith.com
Est. 1989 *Stock size* Small
Stock Scientific, marine, general gifts
Open Mon Tues Wed Fri 9.30am–6.30pm
Thur 9.30am–7pm
Sat 9.30am–5.30pm
Services Valuations, restorations

Grosvenor Prints
Contact Ms McDiarmid
28 Shelton Street, London, WC2H 9JE
020 7836 1979 020 7379 6695
grosvenorprints@btinternet.com
www.grosvenorprints.com
Est. 1976 *Stock size* Large
Stock Topographical, sporting, dogs, portraits, decorative prints
Open Mon–Fri 10am–6pm
Sat 11am–4pm

M & J Hamilton
Contact Mr M Hamilton
25 The London Silver Vaults, Chancery Lane, London, WC2A 1QS
020 7831 7030 020 7831 5483
Stock size Large
Stock Antique silver, flatware services a speciality
Open Mon–Fri 9.30am–5.30pm
Sat 9.30am–1pm

P J Hilton Books
Contact Mr P Hilton
12 Cecil Court, London, WC2N 4HE
020 7379 9825
paul.hilton@rarebook.globalnet.co.uk
www.rarebookweb.com
Est. 1986 *Stock size* Medium
Stock Antiquarian, second-hand, rare books, pre-1700 a speciality
Open Mon–Fri 10.30am–6pm
Sat 10.30am–5pm
Services Book search

Raymond D Holdich (OMRS)
Contact Mr R Holdich
7 Whitcomb Street, London, WC2H 7HA
020 7930 1979 020 7930 1152
07774 133493
rdhmedals@aol.com
www.rdhmedals.com
Est. 1969 *Stock size* Large
Stock Cap badges, militaria including medals, orders, decorations
Open Mon–Fri 10am–4.30pm
Services Valuations, restorations

S & H Jewell Ltd
Contact Mr R Jewell or Mr G Korkis
26 Parker Street, London, WC2B 5PH
020 7405 8520 020 7405 8521
07973 406 255

Est. 1830 *Stock size* Large
Stock Quality English antique and period style 19th–20thC furniture
Open Mon–Fri 9am–5.30pm other times by appointment
Fairs Newark
Services Valuations, restorations

Stephen Kalms Antiques (LAPADA)
Contact Mr S Kalms
The London Silver Vaults, Chancery Lane, London, WC2A 1QS
020 7430 1254 020 7405 6206
stephen@kalms.freeserve.co.uk
Est. 1990 *Stock size* Large
Stock Victorian–Edwardian silver, silver plate, decorative items
Open Mon–Fri 9am–5.30pm Sat 9am–1pm
Fairs Olympia (June)
Services Valuations, restorations, repairs

Nat Leslie Ltd
Contact Mr M Hyams
21 The London Silver Vaults, 53 Chancery Lane, London, WC2A 1QS
020 7242 4787
Est. 1947 *Stock size* Large
Stock Modern, antique, contemporary silverware, silver plate, flatware a speciality
Open Mon–Fri 9.30am–5pm

C and T Mammon (LSVA)
Contact Mr C Mammon
55 and 64 The London Silver Vaults, Chancery Lane, London, WC2A 1QT
020 7405 2397 020 7405 4900
07785 325642
Est. 1969 *Stock size* Large
Stock Decorative silver, silver-plate items
Open Mon–Fri 9am–5.30pm or by appointment
Services Valuations

E W Marchpane Ltd (ABA, PBFA)
Contact K Fuller
16 Cecil Court, Charing Cross Road, London, WC2N 4HE
020 7836 8661 020 7497 0567
kenneth@marchpane.com
www.marchpane.com
Est. 1989 *Stock size* Medium
Stock Antiquarian, rare, second-hand books, children's and illustrated books a speciality
Open Mon–Sat 10.30am–6.30pm

Arthur Middleton Ltd (SIS)
Contact Mr A Middleton or Miss Morgan
12 New Row, London, WC2N 4LF
020 7836 7042 020 7497 2486
arthur@antique-globes.com
www.antique-globes.com
Est. 1978 *Stock size* Large
Stock Marine and scientific instruments, globes
Open Mon–Fri 10am–6pm
Fairs Scientific Instruments Fair, Portman Hotel (April, Oct)
Services Valuations

E C Molan
Contact Mr E Molan
1 Cecil Court, London, WC2N 4EZ
020 7497 9228 020 7497 2328
Est. 1971 *Stock size* Small
Stock Prints, maps, antiquarian books
Open Mon–Sat 10.30am–6.30pm

Murray Cards (International) Ltd
Contact Mr I Murray
20 Cecil Court, London, WC2N 4HE
020 8202 5688 020 8203 7878
murraycards@ukbusiness.com
www.murraycards.com
Est. 1965 *Stock size* Medium
Stock Cigarette and trading cards, albums, frames, books
Open Mon–Sat 10.30am–5.30pm
Services Annual Catalogue, auction catalogue

Colin Narbeth and Son (IBNS)
Contact Mr Simon Narbeth
20 Cecil Court, London, WC2N 4HE
020 7379 6975 0172 811244
colin.narbeth@btinternet.com
www.colin-narbeth.com
Est. 1982 *Stock size* Large
Stock Banknotes, bonds, shares of all countries and periods
Open Mon Sat 10.30am–4pm Tues–Fri 10am–5pm
Fairs Bonnington Paper Money Fair, IBNS (Oct)

Percy's Ltd (LAPADA)
Contact Mr D Simmons
16 The London Silver Vaults, Chancery Lane, London, WC2A 1QS
020 7242 3618 020 7831 6541
sales@percys-silver.com
www.percys-silver.com
Est. 1935 *Stock size* Large
Stock 18th–19thC decorative silver and plate
Open Mon–Fri 9.30am–5pm Sat 10am–1pm
Fairs Olympia (June, Nov)
Services Valuations, repairs

Henry Pordes Books Ltd
Contact Mr G Della-Ragione
58–60 Charing Cross Road, London, WC2H 0BB
020 7836 9031 020 7240 4232
henrypordes@clara.net
www.home.clara.net/henrypordes
Est. 1983 *Stock size* Medium
Stock Remainders, second-hand, antiquarian books, art, literature, Judaica a speciality
Open Mon–Sat 10am–7pm

Quinto Bookshop
Contact Mr I Marchant
48a Charing Cross Road, London, WC2H 0BB
020 7379 7669
Est. 1979 *Stock size* Medium
Stock General second-hand, antiquarian books
Open Mon–Sat 9am–9pm Sun noon–7pm

Rare Art Ltd (BADA)
Contact Mr L Smith
London Silver Vaults, Chancery Lane, London, WC2A 1QS
020 7242 7624 020 7831 0221
rareart@compuserve.com
www.rareartlondon.com
Est. 1984 *Stock size* Large
Stock Antique silver
Open Mon–Fri 9am–5.30pm Sat 10am–1pm
Fairs Olympia (June), IFAADS, New York

Reg & Philip Remington (ABA)
Contact Mr R Remington
18 Cecil Court, London, WC2N 4HE

☎ 020 7836 9771 Ⓕ 020 7497 2526
Ⓔ philip@remingtonbooks.com
Ⓦ remingtonbooks.com
Est. 1979 *Stock size* Medium
Stock Antiquarian, rare, second-hand books, voyages, travel books a speciality
Open Mon–Fri 9am–5pm
Fairs Olympia

Bertram Rota Ltd (ABA, ILAB)
Contact Mr J Rota
✉ 1st Floor, 31 Long Acre, London, WC2E 9LT Ⓟ
☎ 020 7836 0723 Ⓕ 020 7497 9058
Ⓔ bertramrota@compuserve.com
Ⓦ www.bertramrota.co.uk
Est. 1923 *Stock size* Small
Stock Antiquarian, rare, second-hand books, 1890–present day first editions of English and American literature
Open Mon–Fri 9.30am–5.30pm
Services Valuations, book search, catalogues (4–6 a year)

Silstar Antiques Ltd
Contact Mr J Langer
✉ 29 The London Silver Vaults, Chancery Lane, London, WC2A 1QS Ⓟ
☎ 020 7242 6740 Ⓕ 020 7430 1745
Est. 1955 *Stock size* Large
Stock Antique and modern silver of all descriptions
Open Mon–Fri 10am–5pm

B Silverman (BADA)
Contact Robin Silverman or Bill Brackenbury
✉ 26 London Silver Vaults, Chancery Lane, London, WC2A 1QS
☎ 020 7242 3269 Ⓕ 020 7430 1949
Ⓔ silver@silverman-london.com
Ⓦ www.silverman-london.com
Stock size Large
Stock 17th–19thC fine English silverware, silver flatware
Open Mon–Fri 9am–5pm
Sat 9am–1pm
Fairs Olympia, BADA
Services Valuations

Jack Simons Antiques Ltd (LAPADA)
Contact Mr J Simons
✉ 37 The London Silver Vaults, Chancery Lane, London, WC2A 1QS Ⓟ
☎ 020 7242 3221 Ⓕ 020 7831 6541
Est. 1955 *Stock size* Large
Stock Fine antique English and Continental silver, objets d'art
Open Mon–Fri 9.30am–5pm
Services Valuations, restorations

Stage Door Prints (UACC)
Contact Mr A L Reynold
✉ 9 Cecil Court, St Martins Lane, London, WC2N 4EZ Ⓟ
☎ 020 7240 1683 Ⓕ 020 7379 5598
Est. 1979 *Stock size* Large
Stock Antique prints, maps, autographs, movie posters, out-of-print books, film memorabilia, Victorian cards, Valentines
Open Mon–Fri 11am–6pm
Sat 11.30am–6pm

S & J Stodel (BADA)
Contact Mr S Stodel
✉ 24 The London Silver Vaults, Chancery Lane, London, WC2A 1QS Ⓟ
☎ 020 7405 7009 Ⓕ 020 7242 6366
Ⓦ www.chinesesilver.co.uk
Est. 1973
Stock Chinese export silver, Art Deco silver, antique silver flatware
Open Mon–Fri 9.30am–5.30pm
Sat 9am–1pm
Fairs Olympia (June)

Tom Tom
Contact Gary Mitchell
✉ 42 New Compton Street, London, WC2H 8DA Ⓟ
☎ 020 7240 7909 Ⓕ 020 7240 7909
Ⓔ sales@tomtomshop.co.uk
Ⓦ www.tomtomshop.co.uk
Est. 1993 *Stock size* Large
Stock Post-war designer furniture and technology, classics by Eames, Jacobsen, Saarinen
Open Tues–Fri noon–7pm
Sat 11am–6pm or by appointment
Services Valuations

Travis & Emery Books on Music (ABA)
Contact Mr Coleman
✉ 17 Cecil Court, London, WC2N 4EZ
☎ 020 7240 2129 Ⓕ 020 7497 0790
Ⓔ enquiries@travis-and-emery.com
Est. 1960 *Stock size* Medium
Stock Antiquarian sheet music, prints, ephemera, books on music
Open Mon–Sat 11am–6pm
Sun noon–4pm or by appointment
Services Valuations

William Walter Antiques Ltd (BADA, LAPADA)
Contact Miss E Simpson
✉ 3 The London Silver Vaults, Chancery Lane, London, WC2A 1QS Ⓟ
☎ 020 7242 3248 Ⓕ 020 7404 1280
Ⓔ enq@wwantiques.prestel.co.uk
Ⓦ www.williamwalter.co.uk
Est. 1949 *Stock size* Large
Stock Georgian silver, decorative silver, flatware etc
Open Mon–Fri 9.30am–5.30pm
Sat 9.30am–1pm
Services Valuations, repairs

Watkins Books Ltd
Contact Jeremy Cranswick or Ricky James
✉ 19 Cecil Court, London, WC2N 4EZ Ⓟ
☎ 020 7836 2182
Ⓔ service@watkinsbooks.com
Ⓦ www.watkinsbooks.com
Est. 1894 *Stock size* Large
Stock Antiquarian books specializing in mystical, occult, Eastern religions
Open Mon–Fri 10am–8pm
Sat 10.30am–6pm
Services Shipping

Peter K Weiss
Contact Mr P Weiss
✉ 18 The London Silver Vaults, Chancery Lane, London, WC2A 8QS Ⓟ
☎ 020 7242 8100
Ⓔ peterweiss@mymailstation.com
Est. 1958 *Stock size* Large
Stock Antique clocks, watches, objets d'art
Open Mon–Fri 10am–4pm
Sat 10am–1pm
Services Valuations, restorations

Nigel Williams Rare Books (PBFA, ABA)
Contact Mr Nigel Williams
✉ 22 & 25 Cecil Court, Charing Cross Road, London, WC2N 4HE Ⓟ
☎ 020 7836 7757 Ⓕ 020 7379 5918
Ⓔ nwrarebook@tcp.co.uk
Ⓦ www.nigelwilliams.com
Est. 1989 *Stock size* Medium
Stock Antiquarian, rare, second-

hand books, collectable children's, illustrated, 19th–20thC first editions
Open Mon–Sat 10am–6pm
Fairs Olympia, Russell Hotel
Services Monthly catalogue

The Witch Ball
Contact Rosslyn Glassman
2 Cecil Court, London, WC2N 4HE
020 7836 2922 020 7836 2922
thewitchball@btinternet.com
www.thewitchball.co.uk
Est. 1967 *Stock size* Medium
Stock Antique prints, posters of the performing arts
Open Mon–Sat 10.30am–7pm

MIDDLESEX

ASHFORD

Magnet Antiques
Contact Mr Ted Pullen
23 Woodthorpe Road, Ashford, Middlesex, TW15 2RP
01784 253107
Est. 1989 *Stock size* Medium
Stock Edwardian, Victorian, reproduction furniture, Doulton, Beswick, Kevin Francis ceramics
Open Mon–Sat 10am–5pm

EASTCOTE

Eastcote Bookshop (PBFA)
Contact Mrs E May
156–160 Field End Road, Eastcote, Middlesex, HA5 1RH
020 8866 9888 020 8985 9383
Est. 1994 *Stock size* Large
Stock Antiquarian, rare, second-hand books
Open Tues–Sat 10am–5pm
Fairs Russell Hotel

ENFIELD

Designer Classics
Contact Mr L Wilkin
70 Goat Lane, Enfield, Middlesex, EN1 4UB
020 8342 1221 020 8366 8786
mail@designclassic.com
www.designclassic.com
Est. 1998 *Stock size* Large
Stock 1950s–present day classics by famous designers, Bellini, Herman Miller, Verna Panton, computers, hi-fi, radios etc
Open Mail order via Internet

Enfield Collectors Centre
Contact Mr R E Kent
St Onge Parade, 6 Genotin Road, Enfield, Middlesex, EN1 1YU
020 8363 9375
Est. 1970 *Stock size* Large
Stock Militaria, old toys, Dinky, Corgi, Meccano, pocket watches, wind-up gramophones, cigarette cards, postcards, coins
Open Mon–Sat 10am–5pm
Fairs Lea Valley Leisure Centre
Services Medal mounting

Gallerie Veronique
Contact Ms V Aslangul
66 Chase Side, Enfield, Middlesex, EN2 6NJ
020 8342 1005 020 8342 1005
07770 410041
antiques@gallerieveronique.co.uk
Est. 1993 *Stock size* Large
Stock Victorian, Edwardian, 1970s furniture
Open Mon–Fri 10am–3pm Sat 10am–5pm closed Wed
Services Restorations, reupholstery

Griffin Antiques
Contact Mr J Gardner
6 Chase Side, Enfield, Middlesex, EN2 6NF
020 8366 5959
Est. 1970 *Stock size* Medium
Stock Wide range of antiques, porcelain, silver, metalware, scales, weights, measures, candlesticks
Open Mon–Fri 10.30am–6pm Sat 4.30am–6pm
Fairs Newark
Services Valuations

Period Style Lighting (Lighting Association)
Contact Gillian Day
8–9 East Lodge Lane, Botany Bay, Enfield, Middlesex, EN2 8AS
020 8363 9789
Est. 1991 *Stock size* Large
Stock Antique, period lighting, chandeliers
Open Tues–Sun 10am–5pm
Services Valuations, restorations

HAMPTON

Hunters of Hampton
Contact Mr R Hunter
76 Station Road, Hampton, Middlesex, TW12 2AX
020 8979 5624 020 8979 5624
Est. 1991 *Stock size* Large
Stock Victorian, Edwardian furniture, clocks
Open Mon 10am–5.30pm Fri Sat 10am–6pm or by appointment

HAREFIELD

David Ansell (BHI, BAFRA)
Contact David Ansell
48 Dellside, Harefield, Middlesex, UB9 6AX
01895 824648 07976 222610
dansell@globalnet.co.uk
Est. 1990 *Stock size* Medium
Stock Clocks, photographica
Open Mon–Sun 8.30am–5.30pm or by appointment
Fairs NEC, Newark
Services Restorations

Harefield Antiques
Contact Mrs J Davie
42 High Street, Harefield, Uxbridge, Middlesex, UB9 6BX
01895 825224
antiques@nildram.co.uk
www.homepages.nildram.co.uk/~antiques
Est. 1998 *Stock size* Medium
No. of dealers 10
Stock Furniture, china, glass, stamps, radios, militaria, civil war books, sporting memorabilia, jewellery, collectables
Open Mon–Sat 10am–5.30pm Sun 11am–5pm
Services Finding service

HARROW

The Collectors Shop (PTA, ESoc)
Contact Mr I Crawford
16 Village Way East, Rayners Lane, Harrow, Middlesex, HA2 7LU
020 8866 1053
Est. 1992 *Stock size* Large
Stock Postcards, cigarette cards,

illustrated sheet music, toys, sporting items, records, illustrated song sheets, film memorabilia, militaria, china, collectables
Open Mon–Sat 9.30am–4.30pm closed Wed
Services Valuations

HATCH END

Calvers Collectables
Contact Mrs I Calver
266–268 Uxbridge Road, Hatch End, Middlesex, HA5 4HS
020 8421 1653
Est. 1994 *Stock size* Large
No. of dealers 26
Stock Doulton, Art Deco, ceramics, small furniture, collectables
Open Mon–Sat 10am–5.30pm Sun 11.30am–4pm
Services Ceramic repairs

ISLEWORTH

Antique Traders
Contact Mr T Keane
156 London Road, Isleworth, Middlesex, TW7 5BG
020 8847 1020 020 8847 1020
Est. 1997 *Stock size* Large
Stock Wide range of antiques, furniture, porcelain, glass, pictures, mirrors
Open Mon–Sun 10.30am–6pm
Services Valuations

LALEHAM

Laleham Antiques
Contact Mrs H Potter
23 Shepperton Road, Laleham, Middlesex, TW18 1SE
01784 450353
Est. 1973 *Stock size* Medium
Stock Antique and reproduction furniture, old pine, silver, plated items, pictures, brass, copper, jewellery, collectables
Open Mon–Sat 10.30am–5.30pm closed Wed

NORTHWOOD HILLS

Golden Days
Contact Mrs J Bryne
37 The Broadway, Joel Street, Northwood Hills, Middlesex, HA6 1NZ
01923 841255
Est. 1996 *Stock size* Large
Stock Antique furniture, ceramics, brass, mirrors, lighting, collectables
Open Mon–Sat 10am–4.30pm closed Wed or by appointment
Services Valuations, glass and china repairs, re-planing, house clearance

PINNER

The Curiosity Shop
Contact Mr P August
7 High Street, Pinner, Middlesex, HA5 5PJ
020 8868 9953 020 8429 1585
www.the-curiosity-shop.co.uk
Est. 1987 *Stock size* Medium
Stock Antique maps, engravings, Regency, Georgian, Victorian silver, decorative items
Open Mon–Sat 10am–5pm
Services Valuations, restorations

RUISLIP

Alberts of Kensington
Contact Mr J A Wooster
PO Box 147, Ruislip, Middlesex, HA4 9WD
020 8869 9292 020 8869 9393
Est. 1964
Open Tues–Fri 10am–6pm Sat 10am–4pm postal only
Sales 10–12 postal auctions of cigarette cards and ephemera per year
Catalogues Yes

Hobday Toys (Dolls Club of Great Britain)
Contact Wendy Hobday
01895 636737 01895 621042
wendyhobday@freenet.co.uk
Est. 1985 *Stock size* Large
Stock Dolls houses and furniture, tin-plate toys
Open By appointment
Fairs Sandown, Lyndhurst, Pudsey, Stafford
Services Valuations

The Old Trinket Box
Contact Eilleen Cameron
1B High Street, Ruislip, Middlesex, HA4 7AU
01895 675658
Est. 1995 *Stock size* Medium
No. of dealers 10
Stock Wide range of collectables, antiques
Open Mon–Sat 10am–5pm Sun 11am–4pm

STAINES

K W Dunster Antiques
Contact Mr K W Dunster
23 Church Street, Staines, Middlesex, TW18 4EN
01784 453297 01784 483146
07831 649626
Est. 1973 *Stock size* Medium
Stock Brass, furniture, jewellery, marine items
Open Mon–Sat 9am–4pm
Services Valuations, house clearance

Staines Antiques
Contact Mr D Smith
145–147 Kingston Road, Staines, Middlesex, TW18 1PD
01784 461306 01784 461306
Est. 1978 *Stock size* Large
Stock Furniture, ceramics
Open Mon–Sat 9am–5.30pm
Services Valuations, restorations

TEDDINGTON

Chris Hollingshead
Contact Chris Hollingshead
10 Linden Grove, Teddington, Middlesex, TW11 8LT
020 8255 4774
c.hollingshead@btinternet.com
Est. 1993 *Stock size* Medium
Stock Scarce, out-of-print, antiquarian books on landscape, architecture, garden design, botany, horticulture, funeral customs, cemeteries
Open 9.30am–6pm
Services Mail order, annual catalogue

Waldegrave Antiques
Contact Mrs J Murray
197 Waldegrave Road, Teddington, Middlesex, TW11 8LX
020 8404 0162
07946 506145
Est. 1997 *Stock size* Large
Stock Wide selection of antiques, furniture, silver, porcelain, glass etc
Open Mon–Sat 10.30am–5.30pm
Fairs Kempton Park

TWICKENHAM

Antique Interiors
Contact Mr A Mundy
93 Crown Road, Twickenham, Middlesex, TW1 3EX
020 8607 9853
Est. 1995 *Stock size* Medium
Stock English, French and 19thC mahogany and old pine furniture, other quality English items, garden items
Open Tues–Sat 10am–5.30pm
Services Restorations, upholstery

Cheyne Galleries
Contact Mrs C Cox
8 Crown Road, Twickenham, Middlesex, TW1 3EE
020 8892 6932
Est. 1977 *Stock size* Medium
Stock Wide range of antique and second-hand items, collectables
Open Mon–Sat 10am–6pm closed Wed
Services Valuations, house clearance

Anthony C Hall (ABA, PBFA)
Contact Mr A C Hall
30 Staines Road, Twickenham, Middlesex, TW2 5AH
020 8898 2638 020 8893 8855
achallbooks@btinternet.co.uk
www.hallbooks.co.uk
Est. 1966 *Stock size* Large
Stock Out-of-print and rare books, Russian and eastern European topics a speciality
Open Mon–Sat 9am–5.30pm closed Wed
Fairs Richmond Book Fair

John Ives (PBFA)
Contact Mr J Ives
5 Normanhurst Drive, Twickenham, Middlesex, TW1 1NA
020 8892 6265 020 8744 3944
jives@btconnect.com
www.ukbookworld.com/members/johnives
Est. 1979
Stock Reference books on antiques and collecting, 1,000s of titles in stock including scarce items
Open By appointment
Services Mail order only, catalogue

David Morley Antiques
Contact Mr D Morley
371 Richmond Road, Twickenham, Middlesex, TW1 2EF
020 8892 2986
Est. 1968 *Stock size* Large
Stock Wide range of antiques including small furniture, silver, porcelain, silver plate, telephones, old toys
Open Mon Tues Thurs–Sat 10am–5pm closed 1–2pm
Services Valuations

Phelps Ltd (LAPADA)
Contact Robert Phelps
133–135 St Margarets Road, East Twickenham, Middlesex, TW1 1RG
020 8892 1778/7129
020 8892 3661
antiques@phelps.co.uk
www.phelps.co.uk
Est. 1870 *Stock size* Large
No. of dealers 16
Stock Antique furniture
Open Mon–Fri 9am–5.30pm Sat 9.30am–5.30pm Sun noon–4pm
Services Restorations, gilding, caning, French polishing, reupholstery, cabinet making

The Twickenham Antiques Warehouse
Contact Mr A Clubb
80 Colne Road, Twickenham, Middlesex, TW2 6QE
020 8894 5555 07973 132847
andclubb@aol.com
Est. 1984 *Stock size* Large
Stock 1700–1930s English and Continental furniture, decorative items
Open Mon–Sat 9.30am–5pm
Services Valuations, restorations

UXBRIDGE

Antiques Warehouse & Restoration
Contact Mr M Allenby
34 Rockingham Road, Uxbridge, Middlesex, UB8 2TZ
01895 256963
Est. 1979 *Stock size* Large
Stock 1800–1950 furniture, collectables
Open Mon–Sat 10am–6pm
Services Restorations

Anthony Smith
Contact Mr Anthony Smith
45 Windsor Street, Uxbridge, Middlesex, UB8 1AB
01895 814442 01895 253756
Est. 1997 *Stock size* Large
Stock Georgian, Victorian, Edwardian furniture
Open Mon–Sat 10am–6pm Sun 11am–4pm
Services Restorations, upholstery

WEST RUISLIP

A Bainbridge & Co
Contact Mr P Bainbridge
The Auction House, Ickenham Road, West Ruislip, Middlesex, HA4 7DL
01895 621991 01895 623621
Est. 1979
Open Mon–Fri 9am–5pm
Sales Antiques and general effects Thurs 11am, viewing Wed 1–7pm Thurs from 9.30am
Frequency Every 4 weeks
Catalogues Yes

WRAYSBURY

Wyrardisbury Antiques
Contact Mr C Tuffs
23 High Street, Wraysbury, Staines, Middlesex, TW19 5DA
01784 483225 01784 483225
Est. 1978 *Stock size* Medium
Stock All types, ages of clocks up to Edwardian, small furniture, barometers
Open Tues–Sat 10am–5pm
Services Valuations, repairs

BERKSHIRE

ALDERMASTON

⊞ Village Antiques Aldermaston
Contact Mrs Vivian Green
✉ **The Old Dispensary, The Street, Aldermaston, Reading, Berkshire, RG7 4LW** Ⓟ
☎ 0118 971 2370
Est. 1997 *Stock size* Large
Stock Clocks, architectural antiques, furniture, china, glass, silver, garden items
Open Tues–Sun 10am–5.30pm

ASCOT

⊞ The Coworth Gallery
Contact Mr S Paddon
✉ **9 Coworth Road, Ascot, Berkshire, SL5 0NX** Ⓟ
☎ 01344 626532 Ⓕ 01344 626532
Ⓜ 07831 182076
Est. 1990 *Stock size* Small
Stock Architectural antiques, garden ornaments
Open By appointment
Services Garden design

Edwards and Elliott
Contact Mr Francis Ogley
✉ **32 High Street, Ascot, Berkshire, SL5 7HG** Ⓟ
☎ 01344 872588 Ⓕ 01344 624700
Ⓜ 07885 333627
Ⓔ edwards2@netcomuk.co.uk
Ⓦ www.edwardsandelliott.co.uk
Est. 1994
Open Mon–Fri 9am–5.30pm
Sat 10am–4pm Sun 10am–2pm
Sales Wed Thurs every 5–6 weeks antiques and modern, viewing day of sale 9am–noon. Held at Silver Ring Grandstand, Ascot Racecourse
Frequency Every 5–6 weeks
Catalogues Yes

⊞ Melnick House Antiques (ESoc)
Contact Mrs J Collins
✉ **16 Brockenhurst Road, Ascot, Berkshire, SL5 9DL** Ⓟ
☎ 01344 628383 Ⓕ 01344 291800
Ⓔ antiquarian@melnick-house.demon.co.uk
Est. 1972 *Stock size* Large
Stock Antique maps, prints, furniture, decorative antiques
Open Tues–Sat 10am–5pm
Services Restorations, free postage worldwide

BRIMPTON

Law Fine Art Ltd
Contact Mr Mark Law
✉ **Firs Cottage, Brimpton, Berkshire, RG7 4TJ** Ⓟ
☎ 01189 710353 Ⓕ 01189 713741
Ⓔ info@lawfineart.co.uk
Ⓦ www.lawfineart.co.uk
Est. 2000
Open Mon–Fri 9am–5.30pm
Sales Eight sales a year including five specialist ceramics and glass sales
Frequency Monthly
Catalogues Yes

CAVERSHAM

⊞ Amber Antiques
Contact Clair Hughes
✉ **12 Bridge Street, Caversham, Berkshire, RG4 8AA**
☎ 01189 541394 Ⓕ 01189 541394
Ⓜ 07977 499234
Ⓔ amberantiques@btinernet.com
Ⓦ www.amberantiques.co.uk
Est. 1995 *Stock size* Medium
Stock French antiques, decorative items
Open Mon–Sat 10.30am–5.30pm
Fairs TVADA
Services Restorations, in-house traditional upholstery

⊞ D Card (BHI)
Contact D Card
✉ **1a Chester Street, Caversham, Reading, Berkshire, RG4 8JH** Ⓟ
☎ 0118 947 0777 Ⓕ 0118 947 0777
Ⓔ d.card@ntlworld.com
Est. 1971 *Stock size* Small
Stock Longcase, carriage, table clocks and music boxes
Open Mon–Fri 9am–5pm appointment preferred
Services Valuations, restorations

⊞ The Clock Workshop (LAPADA, TVADA, BHI)
Contact Mr J Yealland

✉ **17 Prospect Street, Caversham, Reading, Berkshire, RG4 8JB** 🅿
☎ 0118 947 0741
Ⓦ www.lapada.co.uk
Est. 1981 *Stock size* Medium
Stock English clocks, French carriage clocks
Open Mon–Fri 9.30am–5.30pm Sat 10am–1pm
Fairs Olympia, LAPADA, TVADA
Services Valuations, restorations

COOKHAM

Cookham Antiques
Contact Mr G Wallis
✉ **35 Station Parade, Cookham, Maidenhead, Berkshire, SL6 9BR** 🅿
☎ 01628 523224 Ⓜ 07778 020536
Est. 1989 *Stock size* Large
Stock Furniture, decorative items, architectural
Open Mon–Sat 10am–5pm Sun 11am–5pm
Services Valuations

DONNINGTON

Dreweatt Neate (SOFAA, ARVA)
Contact Clive Stewart-Lockhart
✉ **Donnington Priory, Donnington, Newbury, Berkshire, RG14 2JE** 🅿
☎ 01635 553553 Ⓕ 01635 553599
Ⓔ auctions@dreweatt-neate.co.uk or fineart@dreweatt-neate.co.uk
Est. 1759
Open Mon–Fri 9am–5.30pm Sat 9am–12.30pm
Sales General sales fortnightly Tues at 10am, antiques sales every six weeks Wed 10am, viewing prior Sat 9am–12.30pm Mon 9.30am–7pm and 9.30am–4pm for Wed sales
Frequency Six weeks
Catalogues Yes

ETON

Art and Antiques (Eton Traders)
Contact Mrs V Rand
✉ **69 High Street, Eton, Windsor, Berkshire, SL4 6AA** 🅿
☎ 01753 855727 Ⓜ 07903 921168
Est. 1982 *Stock size* Large
Stock Furniture, china, brass, silver plate, jewellery, collectors' items
Open Mon–Fri 10.30am–5.30pm Sat 10.30am–6pm Sun 2.30–6pm

Roger Barnett
Contact Roger Barnett
✉ **91 High Street, Eton, Windsor, Berkshire, SL4 6AF** 🅿
☎ 01753 867785
Est. 1976 *Stock size* Medium
Stock Brown furniture, brass, longcase clocks
Open Variable

Eton Antiques
Contact Mr M Procter
✉ **80 High Street, Eton, Windsor, Berkshire, SL4 6AF** 🅿
☎ 01753 860752 Ⓕ 01753 818222
Ⓦ www.etonantiques.com
Est. 1969 *Stock size* Large
Stock 18th–19thC English furniture
Open Mon–Sat 10am–5pm Sun 2.30–5pm
Services Valuations, restorations, shipping

Marcelline Herald Antiques (LAPADA, TVADA)
Contact Marcelline Herald
✉ **41 High Street, Eton, Windsor, Berkshire, SL4 6BD** 🅿
☎ 01753 833924 Ⓕ 0118 9714683
Ⓦ www.tvada.co.uk
Est. 1998 *Stock size* Medium
Stock 17thC shop in historic Eton High Street selling18th–19thC furniture, mirrors and decorative items
Open Tues–Sat 10am–5pm
Fairs Decorative Fair Battersea, TVADA
Services Valuations

Peter J Martin and Son (TVADA, LAPADA)
Contact Mr P Martin
✉ **40 High Street, Eton, Windsor, Berkshire, SL4 6BD** 🅿
☎ 01753 864901
Ⓜ 07850 975889
Ⓔ pjmartin.antiques@btopenworld.com
Ⓦ www.pjmartin-antiques.co.uk
Est. 1967 *Stock size* Large
Stock 18th–20thC furniture, copper, brass, mirrors
Open Mon–Fri 9am–5pm closed 1–2pm Sat 10am–1pm or by appointment
Services Restorations

Mostly Boxes
Contact Mr G Munday
✉ **93 High Street, Eton, Windsor, Berkshire, SL4 6AF** 🅿
☎ 01753 858470 Ⓕ 01753 857212
Est. 1982 *Stock size* Large
Stock Ivory, tortoiseshell, decorative antique boxes
Open Mon–Sat 10am–6.30pm
Fairs K & M London

Sebastian of Eton
Contact Hannah West
✉ **4 High Street, Eton, Berkshire, SL4 6AS**
☎ 01753 851897 Ⓕ 01753 851897
Ⓔ sebastians@wingchairs.co.uk
Est. 2000 *Stock size* Small
Stock Antiques and decorative items
Open Mon–Sat 10am–6pm

Studio 101
Contact Anthony Cove
✉ **101 High Street, Eton, Berkshire, SL4 6AF** 🅿
☎ 01753 863333
Est. 1959 *Stock size* Small
Stock General antiques
Open By appointment

Times Past Antiques (BHI)
Contact Mr P Jackson
✉ **59 High Street, Eton, Windsor, Berkshire, SL4 6BL** 🅿
☎ 01753 856392 Ⓕ 01753 856392
Ⓜ 07768 454444
Ⓔ phillipstimespast@aol.com
Est. 1974 *Stock size* Medium
Stock Clocks, barometers, small furniture
Open By appointment
Services Valuations, restorations

Turks Head Antiques
Contact Mrs A Baillie or Mr A Reeve
✉ **98 High Street, Eton, Windsor, Berkshire, SL4 6AF** 🅿
☎ 01753 863939
Est. 1975 *Stock size* Medium
Stock Porcelain, silver, glass, pictures
Open Mon–Sat 10am–5pm
Services Restorations of porcelain, silver-plating

Windsor & Eton Antiques Centre
Contact Mrs Thomas
✉ **17 High Street, Eton, Berkshire, SL4 6AX** 🅿

☎ 01753 840412 Ⓕ 01628 630041
Est. 2000 *Stock size* Medium
No. of dealers 22
Stock General antiques and collectables
Open Mon–Fri 10.30am–5pm Sun 1–4pm
Services Valuations

FIFIELD

Jan Hicks Antiques (TVADA, LAPADA)
Contact Jan Hicks
✉ **Fifield, Near Windsor, Berkshire**
☎ 01488 683986 Ⓕ 01488 683986
Ⓜ 07770 230686
Ⓔ antiques@janhicks.com
Est. 1987 *Stock size* Large
Stock French provincial furniture, particularly armoires, beds, farm tables, buffets, mirrors, chandeliers, decorative items
Open By appointment
Fairs Decorative Antiques and Textiles Fair

GORING ON THAMES

Barbara's Antiques and Bric-a-Brac
Contact Mrs M Bateman
✉ **Wheel Orchard, Station Road, Goring on Thames, Reading, Berkshire, RG8 9HB** Ⓟ
☎ 01491 873032
Est. 1981 *Stock size* Large
Stock Furniture, linen, lace, jewellery, china, brass, silver, plate, railwayana
Open Mon–Sat 10am–1pm 2.15–5pm

HUNGERFORD

Beedham Antiques Ltd (BADA)
Contact Herbert or Paul Beedham
✉ **26 Charnham Street, Hungerford, Berkshire, RG17 0EJ** Ⓟ
☎ 01488 684141 Ⓕ 01488 684050
Est. 1971 *Stock size* Medium
Stock 16th–17thC English and Continental oak furniture
Open Mon–Sat 11am–5pm or by appointment
Fairs Olympia June, Nov

Below Stairs of Hungerford
Contact Stewart Hofgartner
✉ **103 High Street, Hungerford, Berkshire, RG17 0NB** Ⓟ
☎ 01488 682317 Ⓕ 01488 684294
Ⓔ hofgartner@belowstairs.co.uk
Ⓦ www.belowstairs.co.uk
Est. 1972 *Stock size* Large
Stock Collectables, furniture, taxidermy, garden items, kitchenware, lighting, interior fittings
Open Mon–Sun 10am–6pm
Services Valuations

Sir William Bentley Billiards
Contact Charles Saunders
✉ **Standen Manor Farm, Hungerford, Berkshire, RG17 0RB** Ⓟ
☎ 01488 681711 Ⓕ 01488 685197
Ⓦ www.billiards.co.uk
Stock size Large
Stock Billiard tables, accessories, build contemporary and traditional billiard tables including convertible dining and billiard tables
Open Mon–Sun or by appointment
Fairs Daily Telegraph House and Garden, Ideal Homes
Services Valuations, restorations

Paula Biggs
Contact Paula Biggs
✉ **Great Grooms Antique Centre, Riverside House, Hungerford, Berkshire, RG17 0EP** Ⓟ
☎ 01993 869245 Ⓕ 01993 869247
Ⓔ john@thebiggs.co.uk
Est. 1978 *Stock size* Large
Stock Antiques, collectable silver items, objects of virtue
Open Tues–Sat 10am–5.30pm
Fairs NEC 3 times

Bowhouse Antiques
Contact Jo Preston
✉ **3–4 Faulkener Square, Charnham Street, Hungerford, Berkshire, RG17 0EP** Ⓟ
☎ 01488 680826 Ⓕ 01488 608593
Ⓜ 07710 921331
Est. 2000 *Stock size* Large
Stock 19thC decorative interiors
Open Mon–Sat 9.30am–5.30pm Sun 11am–4pm
Services Upholstery

Bridge House Antiques & Interiors
Contact Kate Pols
✉ **7 Bridge Street, Hungerford, Berkshire, RG17 0EH** Ⓟ
☎ 01488 681999 Ⓕ 01488 681999
Ⓔ bridgehouse@kpols.fsnet.co.uk
Est. 1992 *Stock size* Medium
Stock Antiques, decorative items for interiors
Open Tues–Sat 10am–5.30pm
Services Shipping

Countryside Books (PBFA)
Contact Mr Martin Smith
✉ **The Hungerford Antiques Centre, High Street, Hungerford, Berkshire, RG17 0NB**
☎ 01264 773943
Est. 1980 *Stock size* Medium
Stock Antiquarian, rare, second-hand books
Open Mon–Fri 9.15am–5.30pm Sat 9.15am–6pm Sun 11am–5pm
Fairs PBFA fair, Russell Hotel

Franklin Antiques
Contact Mrs L Franklin
✉ **25 Charnham Street, Hungerford, Berkshire, RG17 0EJ** Ⓟ
☎ 01488 682404 Ⓕ 01488 686069
Ⓔ antiques@lyndafranklin.com
Est. 1974 *Stock size* Large
Stock 18th–19thC English and French furniture
Open Mon–Sat 10am–5.30pm
Services Interior decoration

Garden Art
Contact Mr Arnie Knowles
✉ **Barrs Yard, 1 Bath Road, Hungerford, Berkshire, RG17 0HE** Ⓟ
☎ 01488 681881 Ⓕ 01488 681882
Ⓔ garden.art@dial.pipex.com
Est. 1976 *Stock size* Large
Stock Architectural antiques for the garden including gates, neo-classical statuary, bronze
Open Mon–Sat 10am–6pm Sun 11am–4pm or by appointment
Services Valuations, restorations, garden design

Great Grooms of Hungerford
Contact Mr J Podger
✉ **Riverside House, Charnham Street, Hungerford, Berkshire, RG17 0EP** Ⓟ

☎ 01488 682314 ℱ 01488 686677
ⓔ antiques@great-grooms.co.uk
ⓦ www.great-grooms.co.uk
Est. 1998 ***Stock size*** Large
No. of dealers 65
Stock General antiques, furnishings, country furniture, porcelain, clocks, silver, rugs, glass, bronzes, lighting, pictures
Open Mon–Sat 9.30am–5.30pm Sun 10am–6pm
Services Valuations, restorations

Hungerford Arcade
Contact Trevor Butcher
✉ **26 High Street, Hungerford, Berkshire, RG17 0ER** Ⓟ
☎ 01488 683701
Est. 1978 ***Stock size*** Large
No. of dealers 80
Stock General antiques and collectables
Open Mon–Sun 9.15am–5.30pm

Roger King Antiques
Contact Mrs A King
✉ **111 High Street, Hungerford, Berkshire, RG17 0NB** Ⓟ
☎ 01488 682256
Est. 1974 ***Stock size*** Large
Stock Furniture, George III–Edwardian
Open Mon–Sat 9.30am–5pm Sun 11am–5pm

M J M Antiques
Contact Michael Mancey
✉ **13 Bridge Street, Hungerford, Berkshire, RG17 0EH** Ⓟ
☎ 01488 684905 ℱ 01488 684090
Ⓜ 07774 479997
ⓔ mike@oldguns.co.uk
ⓦ www.oldguns.co.uk
Est. 1999 ***Stock size*** Medium
Stock Fine antique arms
Open Mon–Sat 10am–5pm or by appointment
Fairs Arms & Armour Fairs
Services Valuations

Medalcrest Ltd
Contact Mrs M Farrow
✉ **Charnham House, 29–30 Charnham Street, Hungerford, Berkshire, RG17 0EJ** Ⓟ
☎ 01488 684157 ℱ 01488 684157
Ⓜ 07901 898585
Est. 1974 ***Stock size*** Large
Stock 18th–19thC walnut, mahogany, oak, country furniture, barometers
Open Mon–Sat 10am–5.30pm Sun by appointment

The Old Malthouse (BADA, CINOA)
Contact Mr or Mrs P Hunwick
✉ **15 Bridge Street, Hungerford, Berkshire, RG17 0EG** Ⓟ
☎ 01488 682209 ℱ 01488 682209
Ⓜ 07771 862257
ⓔ hunwick@oldmalthouse30.freeserve.co.uk
Est. 1959 ***Stock size*** Large
Stock 18th–19thC furniture, brass, mirrors, paintings, clocks, barometers, decorative items
Open Mon–Sat 10am–5.30pm
Fairs Chelsea
Services Valuations

Principia Fine Art
Contact Mr M Forrer
✉ **35a High Street, Hungerford, Berkshire, RG17 0NF** Ⓟ
☎ 01488 682873 Ⓜ 07899 926020
ⓦ www.antiquesportfolio.com
Est. 1970 ***Stock size*** Large
Stock Scientific instruments, small furniture, Oriental art, books, paintings, works of art
Open Mon–Fri 10.30am–5pm Sat 10am–5pm
Services Valuations, restorations, shipping, book search

Styles Silver (LAPADA)
Contact Mr or Mrs Styles
✉ **12 Bridge Street, Hungerford, Berkshire, RG17 0EH**
☎ 01488 683922 ℱ 01488 683488
Ⓜ 07778 769559
ⓔ pdstyles@hotmail.com
ⓦ www.styles-silver.co.uk
Stock size Large
Stock Silver of all periods, flatware services a speciality, collectables, christening, wedding presents
Open Mon–Sat 9am–5.30pm or by appointment
Services Restorations

Turpins Antiques (BADA, LAPADA, CINOA)
Contact Mrs J Summer
✉ **17 Bridge Street, Hungerford, Berkshire, RG17 0EG** Ⓟ
☎ 01488 681886
Est. 1959 ***Stock size*** Medium
Stock 18thC English and Regency walnut furniture
Open Wed Fri Sat 10am–5pm or by appointment
Fairs Olympia

Youll's Antiques
Contact Mr B Youll
✉ **27–28 Charnham Street, Hungerford, Berkshire, RG17 0EJ** Ⓟ
☎ 01488 682046 ℱ 01488 684335
ⓔ bruce.youll@virgin.net
ⓦ www.youll.com
Est. 1935 ***Stock size*** Large
Stock 17th–20thC English and French furniture, porcelain, silver, decorative items
Open Mon–Sun 10.30am–5.30pm
Fairs Newark
Services Valuations, restorations

KINGSCLERE

Wyseby House Books (PBFA)
Contact Dr Tim Oldham
✉ **Kingsclere Old Bookshop, 2a George Street, Kingsclere, Newbury, Berkshire, RG20 5NQ** Ⓟ
☎ 01635 297995 ℱ 01635 297677
ⓔ info@wyseby.co.uk
ⓦ www.wyseby.co.uk
Est. 1977 ***Stock size*** Large
Stock General antiquarian, rare, second-hand books, fine art, decorative arts, architectural a speciality
Open Mon–Sat 9am–5pm
Services Catalogue 10 times a year

LECKHAMPSTEAD

Hill Farm Antiques
Contact Mr M Beesley
✉ **Hill Farm, Shop Lane, Leckhampstead, Newbury, Berkshire, RG20 8QG** Ⓟ
☎ 01488 638541/638361
ℱ 01488 638541
ⓔ beesley@hillfarmantiques.demon.co.uk
Est. 1987 ***Stock size*** Large
Stock 19thC extending dining tables in mahogany, oak, walnut
Open By appointment

MIDGHAM

Berkshire Antiques Centre
Contact Mrs J Bradley

✉ Unit 1, Kennet Holme Farm Buildings, Bath Road, Midgham, Berkshire, RG7 5UX P
☎ 01189 710477 F 01189 710477
E enquiries@berkshire-antiques.fsnet.co.uk
Est. 2000 *Stock size* Large
No. of dealers 10
Stock Furniture, general antiques and collectables
Open Mon–Sun 10.30am–4.30pm closed Wed

Special Auction Services
Contact Andrew Hilton
✉ **The Coach House, Midgham Park, Reading, Berkshire, RG7 5UG** P
☎ 0118 971 2949 F 0118 971 2420
E commemorative@aol.com
Est. 1991
Open 8.30am–6pm by appointment
Sales Special auctions of commemoratives, pot lids, Prattware, fairings, Goss & Crested, Baxter and Le Blond prints, toys for the collector. Held at The Courtyard Hotel, Padworth, Nr Reading. Please phone for details
Frequency 8 per annum
Catalogues Yes

MORTIMER

Frank Milward (BNTA, ANA)
Contact Mr F Milward
✉ **2 Ravensworth Road, Mortimer, Reading, Berkshire, RG7 3UU** P
☎ 0118 933 2843 F 0118 933 2843
Est. 1975 *Stock size* Medium
Stock English and foreign coins, banknotes
Open By appointment
Fairs International Coin Fair, Coinex, London
Services Valuations

NEWBURY

Invicta Bookshop (PBFA)
Contact Mr S Hall
✉ **8 Cromwell Place, Newbury, Berkshire, RG14 1AF** P
☎ 01635 31176
Est. 1969 *Stock size* Medium
Stock Antiquarian, rare and second-hand books, cookery, cricket, military topics a speciality
Open Mon–Sat 10.30am–5.30pm closed Wed
Fairs Oxford, Bath PBFA
Services Book search

Newbury Salvage Ltd
Contact Mrs H Bromhead
✉ **Kelvin Road, Newbury, Berkshire, RG14 2DB** P
☎ 01635 528120 F 01635 551007
M 07776 174875
Est. 1988 *Stock size* Large
Stock Bricks, tiles, slates, chimney pots, fireplaces, doors, windows, statuary, sanitary ware, oak beams
Open Mon–Fri 8am–5pm Sat 9am–1pm

Alan Walker (BADA, TVADA)
Contact Mr A Walker
✉ **Halfway Manor, Halfway, Newbury, Berkshire, RG20 8NR** P
☎ 01488 657670 F 01488 657670
W www.alanwalker-barometers.com
Est. 1987 *Stock size* Large
Stock 18th–19thC barometers, barographs, related instruments
Open By appointment
Fairs Olympia, BADA, Duke of York's
Services Valuations, restorations, barometers purchased

PANGBOURNE

R Butler
Contact Rita Butler
✉ **4 Station Road, Pangbourne, Reading, Berkshire, RG8 7AN** P
☎ 0118 984 5522 F 0118 984 4520
Est. 1999 *Stock size* Medium
No. of dealers 5
Stock Small to medium-sized furniture 17th–20thC, Art Deco, decorative interiors, Georgian and other glass
Open Wed–Mon 10am–5pm closed Sun
Services Valuations

READING

Addington Antiques
Contact Paul Schneiderman
✉ **41 Addington Road, Reading, Berkshire, RG1 5PZ** P
☎ 0118 935 3435
Est. 1996 *Stock size* Small
Stock General antiques 18thC–1960s design
Open Thurs–Sat 10am–6pm
Fairs Newark, Ardingly

Fanny's Antiques
Contact Mrs Lyons
✉ **1 Lynmouth Road, Reading, Berkshire, RG1 8DE** P
☎ 0118 950 8261
Est. 1995 *Stock size* Large
No. of dealers 20
Stock General antiques, furniture, smalls, gardenalia
Open Mon–Sat 10.30am–4pm Sun noon–4pm

Graham Gallery
Contact John Steeds
✉ **Highwoods, Burghfield Common, Reading, Berkshire, RG7 3BG** P
☎ 01189 831070 F 01189 831070
E jfsteeds@aol.com
Est. 1975 *Stock size* Medium
Stock 19th–20thC oils, watercolours, prints
Open By appointment

P D Leatherland Antiques (TVADA)
Contact Mr P D Leatherland
✉ **68 London Street, Reading, Berkshire, RG1 4SQ** P
☎ 0118 958 1960
Est. 1965 *Stock size* Large
Stock 18th–19thC furniture, porcelain, clocks, paintings, decorative items
Open Mon–Sat 9am–5.15pm Sun 10am–4pm

SLOUGH

Randtiques
Contact Mr Tony Lowe
✉ **23 Stoke Road, Slough, Berkshire, SL2 5AH** P
☎ 01753 572512
Est. 1984 *Stock size* Medium
Stock Furniture, china, glass, pine, prints, watercolours
Open Mon–Sat 10am–5pm closed Wed
Services Framing, paint stripping

SONNING-ON-THAMES

Cavendish Fine Art (BADA)
Contact Janet Middlemiss

✉ Dower House, Pearson Road, Sonning-on-Thames, Berkshire, RG4 6UL Ⓟ
☎ 0118 969 1904 Ⓜ 07831 295575
Ⓔ info@cavendishfineart.com
Ⓦ www.cavendishfineart.com
Est. 1973 *Stock size* Large
Stock Georgian furniture
Open By appointment
Fairs Olympia, BADA

TWYFORD

Bell Antiques
Contact Mr N Timms
✉ 2b High Street, Twyford, Reading, Berkshire, RG10 9AE Ⓟ
☎ 0118 934 2501
Est. 1989 *Stock size* Large
Stock General antiques, collectables
Open Mon–Sat 9.30am–5.30pm Sun 10am–5.30pm

Brocante Antiques & Interiors
Contact Tony Wilkinson
✉ 19–21 Church Street, Twyford, Reading, Berkshire, RG10 9DN Ⓟ
☎ 0118 932 0850 Ⓜ 07932 153009
Ⓔ brocante.wilkinson@virgin.net
Est. 2000 *Stock size* Medium
Stock Late 18thC–early 19thC French and Oriental furniture, decorative items
Open Tues–Sun 10.30am–5.30pm
Fairs East Berkshire Antique Fair, Newark, Ardingly
Services Valuations, restorations

Jem's Collectables
Contact Mr Belli
✉ 7 The High Street, Twyford, Reading, Berkshire, RG10 9AB Ⓟ
☎ 0118 932 1414
Est. 1993 *Stock size* Medium
Stock Bunnykins, Royal Doulton, collectables
Open Mon–Sat 10am–5.30pm Sun 11am–4.30pm
Services Valuations

WARFIELD

Moss End Antiques Centre (TVADA)
Contact Maureen Staite or Maura Dorrington
✉ Moss End, Warfield, Berkshire, RG42 6EJ Ⓟ
☎ 01344 861942
Est. 1988 *Stock size* Large
No. of dealers 20
Stock Antique furniture, clocks, silver, glass, porcelain, linen, collectables
Open Tues–Sun 10.30am–5pm
Services Restorations, coffee shop

WARGRAVE

Ferry Antiques
Contact Peter or Kate Turner
✉ 70 High Street, Wargrave, Berkshire, RG10 8BY Ⓟ
☎ 0118 940 4415 Ⓜ 07778 615975
Est. 1993 *Stock size* Medium
Stock 18th–19thC furniture, general antiques, glass, porcelain, silver, decorative objects
Open Wed–Sun 10am–5.30pm
Fairs The East Berkshire Antiques Fair
Services Valuations, restorations

Wargrave Antiques
Contact Mr J Connell
✉ 66 High Street, Wargrave, Berkshire, RG10 8BY Ⓟ
☎ 0118 940 2914
Est. 1979 *Stock size* Large
Stock Furniture, porcelain, glass, silver, copper, brass, 19thC furniture a speciality
Open Wed–Sun 10am–5pm
Services Valuations, restorations

WINDSOR

Berkshire Antiques Co Ltd
Contact Mr Sutton
✉ 42 Thames Street, Windsor, Berkshire, SL4 1YY Ⓟ
☎ 01753 830100 Ⓕ 01753 832278
Ⓔ sales@jewels2go.co.uk
Est. 1981 *Stock size* Large
Stock Silver, dolls, jewellery, furniture, pictures, porcelain, Art Deco, Art Nouveau, commemorative memorabilia, royal commemoratives
Open Mon–Sat 10.30am–5.30pm Sun by appointment
Services Valuations, restorations

Dee's Antique Pine
Contact Mrs Dee Waghorn
✉ 89 Grove Road, Windsor, Berkshire, SL4 1HT Ⓟ
☎ 01753 865627 Ⓕ 01753 850926
Ⓔ deesantiquepine@aol.com
Stock size Large
Stock Decorative items, furniture
Open Tues–Sat 10.30am–6pm or by appointment

Old Barn Antiques
Contact Mrs Sue Lakey
✉ Wyedale Garden Centre, Dedworth Road, Windsor, Berkshire, SL4 4LH Ⓟ
☎ 01753 833099
Est. 1991 *Stock size* Large
Stock Furniture, porcelain, jewellery, garden antiquities, militaria, silver, dolls, glassware
Open Mon–Sat 10am–5pm Sun 10.30am–4.30pm

Rule's Antiques (TVADA)
Contact Miss Sue Rule
✉ 62 St Leonards Road, Windsor, Berkshire, SL4 3BY Ⓟ
☎ 01753 833210
Est. 1995 *Stock size* Medium
Stock Decorative pieces, brass, lighting, door furniture and fittings
Open Mon–Sat 11am–5pm
Fairs TVADA

WOKINGHAM

Barkham Antiques Centre
Contact Len or Mary Collins
✉ Barkham Street, Wokingham, Berkshire, RG40 4PJ Ⓟ
☎ 01189 761355
Ⓦ www.neatsite.com
Est. 1984 *Stock size* Large
Stock Collectables, toy specialists, Doulton, general antiques, architectural salvage
Open Mon–Sun 10.30am–5pm
Services Restorations

Martin & Pole
Contact Mr G J R Lewis
✉ The Auction House, Milton Road, Wokingham, Berkshire, RG40 1DB Ⓟ
☎ 0118 979 0460 Ⓕ 0118 977 6166
Ⓔ a@martinpole.co.uk
Ⓦ www.martinpole.co.uk
Est. 1846
Open Mon–Fri 9am–5pm
Sales Monthly antiques and collectables, also modern and household. No sales in August. Phone for details
Frequency 2 per month
Catalogues Yes

Wokingham Antiques
Contact Liz Ballard
152 London Road, Wokingham, Berkshire, RG40 1SU
01189 790202
Est. 1998 *Stock size* Small
Stock General antiques and collectables
Open Mon–Sat 10.30am–5.30pm 1st Sun of each month 9am–5.30pm closed Wed

WOOLHAMPTON

The Old Bakery Antiques
Contact Susan Everard
Bath Road, Woolhampton, Reading, Berkshire, RG10 8BY
0118 971 2116
Est. 1974 *Stock size* Medium
Stock Antiques and collectables
Open Thurs–Sat 10am–5pm
Fairs Newark, Ardingly

HAMPSHIRE

ALDERSHOT

Aldershot Antiques
Contact Mr N Powell-Pelly
2a Elms Road, Aldershot, Hampshire, GU11 1LJ
01252 408408 01252 408408
07768 722152
Est. 1979 *Stock size* Small
Stock Furniture including pine
Open By appointment
Services Valuations

Traders Antiques and Country Pine Centre
Contact Mrs J Burns
Norfolk House, 131 Grosvenor Road, Aldershot, Hampshire, GU11 3ER
01252 322055
Est. 1969 *Stock size* Large
Stock Furniture, fireplaces, doors, pine, mahogany, oak
Open Mon–Sat 10am–5.30pm
Services Restorations, French polishing

ALRESFORD

Artemesia
Contact Mr Tim Wright
16 West Street, Alresford, Hampshire, SO24 9AT
01962 732277
Est. 1969 *Stock size* Large
Stock English and Continental furniture, ceramics, works of art
Open Mon–Sat 10am–1pm 2–5pm
Services Valuations

Laurence Oxley (ABA, FATG)
Contact Anthony Oxley
17 Broad Street, Alresford, Hampshire, SO24 9AW
01962 732188 01962 732998
07769 715510
aoxley@freenet.co.uk
Est. 1950
Stock Victorian watercolours, old maps, antiquarian books
Open Mon–Sat 9am–5pm
Fairs Chelsea Book Fair
Services Restorations, picture framing

Pineapple House
Contact Peter Radford
49 Broad Street, Alresford, Hampshire, SO24 9AS
01962 736575
07973 254749
Est. 1979 *Stock size* Small
Stock 19th–20thC general antiques especially walnut and mahogany furniture
Open Thur 11am–3pm Fri Sat 11am–5pm Sun 11am–4pm or by appointment

Tudor Antiques and Fine Arts Ltd (AAFAA)
Contact Eric or Penelope Tudor
The Old Exchange, Station Road, Alresford, Hampshire, SO24 9JG
01962 735345 01962 736345
07774 908888
eandptudor@tudor-antiques.co.uk
www.tudor-antiques.co.uk
Est. 1980 *Stock size* Large
Stock 17th–19thC English, Continental Oriental furniture, works of art
Open Mon–Sat 10am–4pm Sun by appointment closed Wed
Services Valuations, shipping arranged

ALTON

Artisan Restoration
Contact Mr W Dalton
86 Victoria Road, Alton, Hampshire, GU34 2DD
01420 549554
artisan@britannia.uk.com
Est. 1984 *Stock size* Medium
Stock Antique writing furniture, display cabinets, rocking horses
Open Mon–Sat 9am–1pm or by appointment
Services Restorations

Jardinique (SALVO)
Contact Mr Edward Neish
Old Park Farm, Kings Hill, Beech, Alton, Hampshire, GU34 4AW
01420 560055 01420 560050
jardinique@aol.com
www.jardinique.co.uk
Est. 1994 *Stock size* Large
Stock Statuary, sundials, urns, garden items, seats, fountains, stone troughs, staddle stones
Open Tues–Sat 10am–5pm or by appointment
Services Valuations

ANDOVER

Andover Saleroom (Pearsons)
Contact Dominic Foster
41a London Street, Andover, Hampshire, SP10 2NU
01264 364820 01264 323402
www.pearsons.com
Est. 1979
Open Mon–Fri 8.30am–6pm
Sales Pictures and jewellery Sat, antique and general Mon, viewing Fri 9am–9pm Sat 9am–6pm. Advisable to telephone for details
Frequency Fortnightly
Catalogues Yes

Ludgershall Antiques Centre
Contact Mrs I Haylen
4–6 Andover Road, Ludgershall, Andover, Hampshire, SP11 9LZ
01264 791372 01264 710704
lac@hayland.demon.co.uk
Est. 1996 *Stock size* Medium
Stock Furniture, jewellery, silver, bronzes, paintings, porcelain, objets d'art
Open Tues–Sat 10am–5pm Sun 11am–4pm
Services Valuations, free local delivery

May and Son
Contact Mr J May
9a The Old Stables, Winchester Road, Andover, Hampshire, SP10 2EG
01264 323417 01264 338841
07710 001660
office@mayandson.com
www.mayandson.com
Est. 1925
Open Mon–Fri 9am–3pm Sat 9am–noon
Sales Antique furniture and effects 3rd Wed of the month at 10.30am, viewing Tues 8.30am–6pm and morning of sale from 8.30am. Sales take place in Village Hall, Penton Mewsey, Andover. Periodic specialist auctions
Frequency Monthly
Catalogues Yes

ASH VALE

The House of Christian
Contact Mrs Bail
5 Vale Road, Ash Vale, Aldershot, Hampshire, GU12 5HH
01252 314478
Est. 1975 *Stock size* Medium
Stock Pine furniture
Open Mon–Fri 10am–5pm Sat 12.30–3.30pm
Services Valuations, restorations

ASHURST

Nova Foresta Books (PBFA)
Contact Mr Peter Roberts
185 Lyndhurst Road, Ashurst, Southampton, Hampshire, SO40 7AR
023 8029 3389
Est. 1994 *Stock size* Medium
Stock Antiquarian, rare, second-hand books, New Forest, 20thC literature and art a speciality
Open Tues–Sat 10am–5.30pm
Fairs PBFA fairs
Services Valuations, book search

BASINGSTOKE

Anticks
Contact Jean Stone
5 Church Street, Basingstoke, Hampshire, RG21 7QH
01256 471000
Est. 1995 *Stock size* Medium
Stock Jewellery, antiques and collectable china
Open Mon–Sat 10am–5pm closed Tues
Fairs Magnum
Services Jewellery repairs

Hickley's Cards
Contact Mr R Hickley
PO Box 6090, Basingstoke, Hampshire, RG23 8YR
01256 411893 01256 411894
sales@hickleysautographs.com
www.hickleysautographs.com
Est. 1993 *Stock size* Large
Stock Japanese and American music memorabilia
Open By appointment only
Services Valuations, search service

The Squirrel Antique & Collectors Centre
Joyce's Yard, 9a New Street, Basingstoke, Hampshire, RG21 7DE
01256 464885
Est. 1981 *Stock size* Large
Stock Antique jewellery, silver, dolls, teddy bears, Art Deco ceramics, china, furniture
Open Mon–Sat 10am–5.30pm
Services Valuations

BOTLEY

The Furniture Trading Co
Contact Mr Davies
The Old Flour Mills, Mill Hill, Botley, Hampshire, SO30 2GB
01489 788194 01489 797337
Est. 1984 *Stock size* Large
Stock General antiques, furniture, accessories, porcelain, lighting, mirrors
Open Mon–Sat 10am–5pm Sun 11am–4pm
Services Restorations

BROCKENHURST

Antiquiteas
Contact Mr R Wolstenholme
37 Brockley Road, Brockenhurst, Hampshire, SO42 7RB
01590 622120
antiquiteas@aol.com
www.antiquiteas.co.uk
Est. 1999 *Stock size* Medium
Stock Pine furniture, copper, brass, porcelain, watercolour originals, prints
Open Mon–Sat 10am–5pm Sun 10am–4pm

Squirrels
Contact Sue Crocket
Lyndhurst Road, Brockenhurst, Hampshire, SO42 7RL
01590 622433
Est. 1989 *Stock size* Medium
Stock Antiques, collectables, stripped pine, furniture, Victoriana, Art Deco, Art Nouveau, kitchenware, garden items, pictures, mirrors
Open Wed–Sun 10am–5pm winter10am–4pm

BROOK

F E A Briggs Ltd
Contact Frank Briggs
Birchenwood Farm, Brook, Hampshire, SO43 7JA
023 8081 2595 023 8081 2595
07831 315838
feabriggs@aol.com
Est. 1966 *Stock size* Large
Stock Victorian furniture
Open Mon–Fri 9am–5.30pm
Fairs Newark
Services Restorations

CHANDLERS FORD

Boris Books (PBFA)
Contact Mrs P Stevenson
2 Holland Close, Chandlers Ford, Eastleigh, Hampshire, SO53 3NA
023 8027 5496 023 8027 5496
07801 111886
borisbooks@aol.com
Est. 1995 *Stock size* Small
Stock Antiquarian, rare, collectable, second-hand books, specializing in literature, music, children's, illustrated
Open By appointment
Fairs Romsey Antique and Collectors Fair, Forest Fairs
Services Book search

CRAWLEY

The Pine Barn
Contact Mr P Chant
Folly Farm, Crawley, Winchester, Hampshire, SO21 2PH
01962 776687 01962 776687
Est. 1987 *Stock size* Large

Stock Furniture made from reclaimed pine, antique and reproduction pine furniture
Open Mon–Sat 9am–5pm Sun 10am–4pm
Services Valuations, restorations, shipping

EMSWORTH

Antique Bed Company
Contact Mr I Trewick
32 North Street, Emsworth, Hampshire, PO10 7DG
01243 376074 Ⓕ 01243 376074
Ⓔ antiquebeds@aol.com
Ⓦ www.antiquebedsemsworth.co.uk
Est. 1992 *Stock size* Large
Stock Victorian–Edwardian brass, iron and wooden beds
Open Mon–Sat 9am–5.30pm
Services Valuations, restorations

Bookends
Contact Mrs C Waldron
7 High Street, Emsworth, Hampshire, PO10 7AQ
01243 372154 Ⓜ 07796 263508
Ⓔ cawaldron@tinyworld.co.uk
Est. 1982 *Stock size* Medium
Stock Antiquarian, rare, second-hand books, sheet music
Open Mon–Sat 9.30am–5pm Sun 10.30am–3pm
Services Valuations, book search

Dolphin Quay Antique Centre
Contact Mrs M Farmer or Mr M Farmer
Queen Street, Emsworth, Hampshire, PO10 7BU
01243 379994 Ⓕ 01243 379251
Ⓔ enquiriesnancy@dqantiques.co.uk
Ⓦ www.dqantiques.co.uk
Est. 1969 *Stock size* Large
No. of dealers 30
Stock Fine antique furniture, porcelain, clocks, watches, jewellery, silver
Open Mon–Sat 10am–5pm Sun 10am–4pm
Services Restorations, furniture upholstery

Tiffins Antiques
Contact Phyl Hudson
12 Queen Street, Emsworth, Hampshire, PO10 7BL
01243 372497
Est. 1989 *Stock size* Small
Stock General antiques, silver, oil lamps
Open Wed–Sat 9.30am–5pm

EVERSLEY

Eversley Antiques
Contact Hilary Craven
Church Lane, Eversley, Hampshire, RG27 0PX
0118 932 8518
Est. 1998 *Stock size* Large
No. of dealers 11
Stock General antiques, collectables
Open Mon Thurs–Sun 10.30am–5.30pm
Services Delivery

FARNBOROUGH

Clarice Cliff Ltd (ADDA)
Contact Mr J Motley
The Clarice Cliff Nostalgia Store, Kingsmead, Farnborough, Hampshire, GU14 7SL
01252 372188 Ⓕ 01252 513671
Ⓔ admin@claricecliff.net
Ⓦ www.claricecliff.co.uk
Est. 1973 *Stock size* Large
Stock Clarice Cliff, English 20thC ceramics
Open Mon–Sat 10.30am–5pm
Services Valuations, archive information

FLEET

Yesterdays
258 Fleet Street, Fleet, Hampshire, GU13 8BX
01252 669971 Ⓕ 01252 669971
Ⓔ enquiries@yesterdays.co.uk
Ⓦ www.yesterdays.co.uk
Est. 1998 *Stock size* Large
Stock Georgian–1940s furniture, glass, china, collectables
Open Mon–Wed Fri 10.30am–5.30pm Thurs 10.30am–5pm Sun 11am–4.30pm

FORDINGBRIDGE

Bristow and Garland
Contact Mr David Bristow
45–47 Salisbury Street, Fordingbridge, Hampshire, SP6 1AB
01425 657337 Ⓕ 01425 657337
Ⓔ davidbristow@bristowandgarland.fonet.co.uk
Est. 1960 *Stock size* Small
Stock Antiquarian, rare, second-hand books, manuscripts, ephemera
Open Mon–Sat 9.30am–5pm closed Wed

Mark Collier
Contact Mark Collier
24 High Street, Fordingbridge, Hampshire, SP6 1AX
01425 652555
Est. 1966 *Stock size* Medium
Stock Antique and contemporary works of art
Open By appointment
Services Gallery open daily

Quatrefoil
Contact C D Aston
Burgate, Fordingbridge, Hampshire, SP6 1LX
01425 653309 Ⓕ 01425 653309
Ⓜ 07802 361804
Est. 1972 *Stock size* Medium
Stock 17th–18thC oak furniture, 15th–17thC oak carvings and sculpture
Open Mon–Sun 9am–8pm

West Essex Coin Investments (BNTA, IBNS)
Contact Mr R Norbury
Croft Cottage, Station Road, Alderholt, Fordingbridge, Hampshire, SP6 3AZ
01425 656459 Ⓕ 01425 656459
Est. 1977 *Stock size* Medium
Stock English coinage medieval–present day including English milled, British colonial, coins of the USA
Open By appointment only
Fairs York Racecourse, BNTA Fairs
Services Valuations

GOSPORT

Easter Antiques
Contact Mr R Easter
333 Forton Road, Gosport, Hampshire, PO12 3HF
023 9250 3621
Est. 1984 *Stock size* Small
Stock Small decorative items
Open Mon–Sat 10am–5pm closed Wed
Services Valuations, restorations

Former Glory
Contact Mr L Brannon
49 Whitworth Road, Gosport, Hampshire, PO12 3NJ
023 9250 4869

Est. 1986 *Stock size* Medium
Stock Victorian–Edwardian furniture, china
Open Mon–Sat 9am–5pm closed Wed
Services Restorations, traditional upholstery

HARTLEY WINTNEY

Nicholas Abbott (LAPADA)
Contact Mr C N Abbott
High Street, Hartley Wintney, Hook, Hampshire, RG27 8NY
☎ 01252 842365 Ⓕ 01252 842365
Ⓔ nicholasabbott@web-hq.com
Ⓦ nicholas-abbott.com
Est. 1964 *Stock size* Medium
Stock 18thC furniture
Open Mon–Sat 9.30am–5.30pm

Andwells Antiques (LAPADA)
Contact Alastair Mackenzie
The Row, High Street, Hartley Wintney, Hampshire, RG27 8NY
☎ 01252 842305 Ⓕ 01252 845149
Est. 1967 *Stock size* Large
Stock 18thC English furniture
Open Mon–Fri 9am–5.30pm Sat 9.30am–5.30pm

Antique House
Contact P Weaver
22 High Street, Hartley Wintney, Hook, Hampshire, RG27 8NY
☎ 01252 844499 Ⓕ 01252 845270
Ⓜ 07467 603443
Ⓔ clancampbell1@aol.com
Est. 1977 *Stock size* Large
Stock Georgian–Victorian mahogany and walnut furniture
Open Mon–Sat 9.30am–5.30pm
Services Valuations, restorations

The Antiques Centre
Contact Mrs S Lister
Primrose House, London Road, Hartley Wintney, Hampshire, RG27 8RJ
☎ 01252 843393 Ⓕ 0118 934 9311
Ⓜ 07836 734838
Ⓔ invogueantiques@aol.com
Ⓦ www.invogueantiques.co.uk
Est. 1996 *Stock size* Large
No. of dealers 9
Stock Georgian–Victorian, fine and country furniture, clocks, paintings, china (including Art Deco)
Open Mon–Sat 10am–5pm Sun noon–4pm
Services Shipping

Cedar Antiques Centre Ltd
Contact Derek Green
High Street, Hartley Wintney, Hampshire, RG27 8NY
☎ 01252 843222 Ⓕ 01252 842111
Ⓔ cac@cedar-ltd.demon.co.uk
Ⓦ www.cedar-antiques.com
Est. 1998 *Stock size* Large
No. of dealers 50
Stock Early English furniture, silver, glass, water colours, carpets
Open Mon–Sat 10am–5.30pm Sun 11am–5pm
Services Café, Museum of T G Green pottery

Cedar Antiques Ltd
Contact Sally Green
High Street, Hartley Wintney, Hampshire, RG27 8NT
☎ 01252 843252
Est. 1964 *Stock size* Large
Stock 17th–20thC English and continental country furniture with colour
Open Mon–Sat 10am–5pm
Services Valuations, restorations

Bryan Clisby (LAPADA)
Contact Mr B Clisby
High Street, Hartley Wintney, Hampshire, RG27 8NY
☎ 01252 716436 Ⓕ 01252 716436
Ⓔ bryanclisby@cwcom.net
Est. 1978 *Stock size* Large
Stock Longcase, bracket, wall clocks, mantel clocks, barometers
Open Mon–Sat 9.30am–5.30pm
Services Restorations

Deva Antiques
Contact Mr A Gratwick
High Street, Hartley Wintney, Hook, Hampshire, RG27 8NY
☎ 01252 843538 Ⓕ 01252 842946
Ⓔ devaants@aol.com
Ⓦ www.deva-antiques.com
Est. 1986 *Stock size* Medium
Stock 18th–19thC mahogany, walnut, country furniture, decorative accessories
Open Mon–Sat 9am–5.30pm
Services Collection from BR station by arrangement

Sally Green Designs
Contact Sally Green
63 High Street, Hartley Wintney, Hampshire, RG27 8NT
☎ 01252 843252 Ⓕ 01252 842111
Ⓔ sg@cedar-ltd.deom.co.uk
Ⓦ www.cedar-antiques.com
Est. 1965 *Stock size* Medium
Stock 18th–19thC English and Continental country furniture
Open Mon–Sat 10am–5pm

David Lazarus Antiques (BADA)
Contact Mr D Lazarus
High Street, Hartley Wintney, Hook, Hampshire, RG27 8NS
☎ 01252 842272 Ⓕ 01252 842272
Est. 1973 *Stock size* Medium
Stock Furniture, sculpture, objets d'art
Open Mon–Sat 9.30am–5.30pm
Services Valuations

HEADLEY

Victorian Dreams
Contact Mrs S Kay
The Old School, Crabtree Lane, Headley, Bordon, Hampshire, GU35 8QH
☎ 01428 717000 Ⓕ 01428 717111
Ⓔ sales@victorian-dreams.co.uk
Ⓦ www.victorian-dreams.co.uk
Est. 1985 *Stock size* Large
Stock Brass, iron, wooden, upholstered and caned bedsteads
Open Mon–Sat 9am–5.30pm Sun 10am–4pm
Fairs Newark, Ardingly
Services Valuations, restorations, world and nationwide delivery

HIGHBRIDGE

Brambridge Antiques
Contact Mr D May
Bugle Farm, Highbridge Road, Highbridge, Eastleigh, Hampshire, SO50 6HS
☎ 01962 714386
Est. 1973 *Stock size* Medium
Stock Mahogany, walnut furniture
Open Mon–Sat 9am–5pm
Services Restorations

HORNDEAN

The Goss & Crested China Club
Contact Lynda Pine
62 Murray Road, Horndean, Hampshire, PO8 9JL
023 9259 7440 F 023 9259 1975
E info@gosschinaclub.demon.co.uk
W www.gosscrestedchina.co.uk
Est. 1969 *Stock size* Large
Stock Over 5,000 pieces of Goss & Crested china
Open Mon–Sat 9am–5pm
Services Monthly mail order catalogue, museum on site, search service for wants lists

LISS

Mother Hubbard Antiques
Contact Mr J Worboys
20 Station Road, Liss, Hampshire, GU33 7DT
01730 894989 F 01252 812311
Est. 1975 *Stock size* Medium
Stock Pine furniture
Open Mon–Sat 9am–6pm
Sun 11am–3pm
Services Restorations, paint stripping

Plestor Barn Antiques
Contact Mr McCarthy
Farnham Road, Liss, Hampshire, GU33 6JQ
01730 893922
M 07850 539998
E craigmccarthy@btopenworld.com
Est. 1984 *Stock size* Medium
Stock Victorian–Edwardian, stripped pine, 1920s furniture, used and reproduction soft furnishings
Open Mon–Fri 10am–5pm
Sat 10am–2pm
Services Light removals service

LYMINGTON

Carlsen's Antiques and Fine Arts
Contact Mr D Carlsen
8 St Thomas Street, Lymington, Hampshire, SO41 9NA
01590 676370
Est. 1987 *Stock size* Large
Stock Watercolours, pencils, etchings, mirrors, small Georgian–Victorian furniture
Open Mon–Sat 9.30am–5.30pm
Fairs Winchester, Lymington
Services Valuations

Corfield Ltd
Contact Mr A Roberts
120 High Street, Lymington, Hampshire, SO41 9AQ
01590 673532 F 01590 678855
Est. 1995 *Stock size* Medium
Stock Porcelain, paintings, Regency, Georgian, Victorian furniture
Open Mon–Sat 9.30am–5.30pm
Services Restorations

George Kidner
Contact Mrs K Chamberlain
The Old School, The Square, Pennington, Lymington, Hampshire, SO41 8GN
01590 670070 F 01590 675167
E info@georgekidner.co.uk
W www.georgekidner.co.uk
Est. 1991
Open Mon–Fri 9am–5pm
Sales Furniture and decorative items, silver, jewellery, paintings, collectors items. Sales on Wed, viewing Sat 9.30am–1pm
Mon 9.30am–4.30pm
Tues 9.30am–7pm
Frequency Monthly
Catalogues Yes

Landfall
Contact Mrs E P Moody
96 High Street, Milford on Sea, Lymington, Hampshire, SO41 0QE
01590 643951
Est. 1973 *Stock size* Small
Stock General, small furniture, pictures, clothes, books, jewellery, linen
Open Mon–Sat 9am–5.30pm
Sun 2–5pm

Lymington Antique Centre
Contact Lisa Reeves
76 High Street, Lymington, Hampshire, SO41 9AL
01590 670934
Est. 1990 *Stock size* Large
No. of dealers 30
Stock Furniture, porcelain, books, jewellery, silver, pictures
Open Mon–Fri 10am–5pm
at 9am–5pm
Services Restorations

Barry Papworth
Contact Steve Park
28 St Thomas Street, Lymington, Hampshire, SO41 9NE
01590 676422
Est. 1978 *Stock size* Medium
Stock Jewellery and silver
Open Mon–Sat 9.15am–5.15pm
Services Valuations

Pennyfarthing Antiques
Contact Roberta Payne
Lymington Antiques Centre, 76 High Street, Lymington, Hampshire, SO41 9AL
023 8086 0846
M 07970 847690
Est. 1996 *Stock size* Large
Stock Georgian–Edwardian furniture, clocks, Oriental items, watches
Open Mon–Sat 10am–5pm
Services Valuations, restorations

Platt's of Lymington
Contact Mrs Kay Boyd-Platt
15 St Thomas Street, Lymington, Hampshire, SO41 9NB
01590 688769
Est. 1997 *Stock size* Large
Stock Superb selection of good quality porcelain, furniture, especially small pieces, all stock dated, priced, guaranteed
Open Wed–Sat 10am–5pm
or by appointment
Services Valuations

Treasure Trove
Contact Mrs M Wall
1a Captains Row, Lymington, Hampshire, SO41 9RP
01590 673974
Est. 1993 *Stock size* Medium
Stock Collectables, glass, clocks
Open Tues–Sat 10am–4pm

Wick Antiques (LAPADA, CINOA)
Contact Mr Charlie Wallrock
Fairlea House, 110–112 Marsh Lane, Lymington, Hampshire, SO4 19EE
01590 677558 F 01590 677558
E charles@wickantiques.co.uk
W www.wickantiques.co.uk
Est. 1984 *Stock size* Large
Stock 18th–19thC English and French furniture
Open Mon–Fri 9am–5pm
Sat by appointment

SOUTH

Fairs Olympia Fine Arts Fair, Fall Fair New York
Services Restorations

LYNDHURST

Lita Kaye Antiques
Contact Mr S Ferder
13 High Street, Lyndhurst, Hampshire, SO43 7BB
023 8028 2337
Est. 1950 *Stock size* Large
Stock English period, 18thC Regency furniture, porcelain, decorative items
Open Mon–Sat 9.30am–5.30pm

Lyndhurst Antique Centre
Contact Mrs G Ashley
19–21 High Street, Lyndhurst, Hampshire, SO43 7BB
023 8028 4000
Est. 1998 *Stock size* Large
No. of dealers 50
Stock Collectables, furniture, militaria
Open Mon–Sun 10am–5pm

MATTINGLEY

Odiham Auction Sales
Contact Mr S R Thomas
Unit 4, Priors Farm, West Green Road, Mattingley, Hampshire, RG29 8JU
01189 326824 F 01189 326797
M 07836 201764
Est. 1989
Open Mon–Fri 9.30am–4pm
Sales General antiques sales Wed. Smalls sales at 2pm, furniture sales at 6.30pm, viewing Tues 6–9pm Wed 9am–2pm
Frequency Fortnightly
Catalogues Yes

NEW MILTON

Forest House Antiques
Contact Mr K Plater
4 Winston Parade, Lymington Road, New Milton, Hampshire, BH25 6PT
01425 614441
Est. 1984 *Stock size* Large
Stock 18th–19thC English furniture, ceramics, collectables
Open Mon–Sat 10am–5pm closed Wed

Fairs Antiques for Everyone, Newark
Services Valuations, restorations

NORTH WARNBOROUGH

Second Chance Antique Centre
Contact Mrs Paula Vaisey
The Albion Centre, Dunleys Hill, North Warnborough, Near Odiham, Hampshire, RG25 1DX
01256 704273 M 07932 664086
Stock size Large
No. of dealers 18
Stock General antiques
Open Mon–Sat 10am–5.30pm Sun 11am–5.30pm

OLD BEDHAMPTON

J F F Militaria & Fire Brigade Collectables
Contact Mr J Franklin
Ye Olde Coach House, Mill Lane, Old Bedhampton, Hampshire, PO9 3JH
023 9248 6485 M 07786 012316
Est. 1995 *Stock size* Medium
Stock Militaria, brass fire helmets, medals, badges, cloth insignia, equipment, buttons
Open By appointment only
Fairs Stoneleigh, Beltring
Services Valuations

PETERSFIELD

Wayne Buckner Antiques
Contact Audrey Buckner
62 Station Road, Petersfield, Hampshire, GU32 3ES
01730 268822 F 023 923 27584
M 07801 254494
Est. 1996 *Stock size* Medium
Stock Collectables, clocks, small items of furniture, music boxes, barometers, china toys, Meccano, steam engines
Open Wed–Sat 9.30am–4pm or by appointment
Fairs Kempton, Goodwood
Services Valuations, restorations, house clearance

Dragon Treasures
Contact Elizabeth or Rose
10–12 College Street, Petersfield, Hampshire, GU31 4AD
01730 269888
Est. 1998 *Stock size* Medium
Stock Small items of furniture, china, glass, gold and silver jewellery, pictures, prints
Open Mon–Sat 9.30am–5pm

Folly Four Antiques & Collectables
Contact Diane
10–12 College Street, Petersfield, Hampshire, GU31 4AD
01730 266650
Est. 1999 *Stock size* Small
Stock Antiques and collectables
Open Mon–Sat 9.30am–5pm

Jacobs and Hunt Fine Art Auctioneers
Contact Kevin Baker or Alicia Boorne
26 Lavant Street, Petersfield, Hampshire, GU32 3EF
01730 233933 F 01730 262323
W www.jacobsandhunt.co.uk
Est. 1895
Open Mon–Fri 9am–5pm Sat 9am–noon
Sales General antiques sales Fri, viewing Wed 10am–4.30pm Thurs 10am–6.30pm and morning of sale from 9am
Frequency Monthly
Catalogues Yes

The Petersfield Bookshop (ABA, PBFA)
Contact Frank Westwood
16a Chapel Street, Petersfield, Hampshire, GU32 3DS
01730 263438 F 01730 269426
E sales@petersfieldbookshop.com
W www.petersfieldbookshop.com
Est. 1918 *Stock size* Large
Stock Antiquarian and modern books
Open Mon–Sat 9am–5.30pm
Fairs ABA, Olympia, Chelsea
Services Valuations, quarterly catalogues

Underwood Oak
Contact Ms Ann Egerton
Langrish, Petersfield, Hampshire, GU32 1QY
01730 263972
E antiques@underwoodoak.co.uk
W www.underwood.co.uk
Est. 1999 *Stock size* Medium
Stock 17th–19thC oak, country furniture

Open By appointment
Fairs Avington
Services Valuations, restorations

PORTSMOUTH

The Architectural Warehouse
Contact Mr Byng
17 Beck Street, Portsmouth, Hampshire, PO1 3AN
023 9287 7070 Ⓕ 023 922 94777
Ⓔ des_res@hotmail.com
Est. 2000 *Stock size* Large
Stock Architectural antiques, doors, baths, sinks, stained glass, pine flooring, fireplaces
Open Mon–Sat 9am–5pm

Good Day Antiques and Decor
Contact Mrs G Day
22 The Green, Rowlands Castle, Portsmouth, Hampshire, PO9 6AB
023 9241 2924 Ⓜ 0795 8619413
Ⓔ Gillday@aol.com
Est. 1979 *Stock size* Medium
Stock Victorian furniture, small cabinets, jewellery, silver, porcelain, pottery, pictures
Open Thurs–Mon 11am–5pm Sun noon–4pm
Services Silver-plating, gilding, engraving

Alexandra Gray Antiques & Decorative Ideas
Contact Alexandra Gray
129–131 Havant Road, Drayton, Portsmouth, Hampshire, PO6 2AA
023 9237 6379 Ⓜ 07752 781835
Est. 1997 *Stock size* Large
No. of dealers 15
Stock General antiques, chandeliers, French beds, china, clocks, oil lamps
Open Mon–Sat 10am–5pm Sun noon–4pm closed Wed
Services Upholstery

RINGWOOD

Bonhams
54 Southampton Road, Ringwood, Hampshire, BH24 1JD
01425 6473333 Ⓕ 01425 470989
Ⓔ ringwood@bonhams.com
Ⓦ www.bonhams.com
Open Mon–Fri 9am–5pm
Sales Regional Representative for Hampshire and Dorset

E Chalmers Hallam (PBFA)
Contact Mrs L Hiscock
9 Post Office Lane, St Ives, Ringwood, Hampshire, BH24 2PG
01425 470060 Ⓕ 01425 470060
Ⓔ laura@chalmershallam.freeserve.co.uk
Est. 1946 *Stock size* Large
Stock Antiquarian, rare, second-hand books, angling, field sports, travel, Africana
Open By appointment
Services Valuations

Hugh and Favia Lister
Contact Mrs Favia Lister
Ringwood Road, Burley, Ringwood, Hampshire, BH24 4BU
01425 402404
Est. 1974 *Stock size* Small
Stock Porcelain, small collectables
Open Mon–Sun 10am–5pm
Services Repairs to jewellery including re-threading, plating, silver, small furniture

Millers Antiques Ltd (LAPADA)
Contact Mr A J Miller
Netherbrook House, Christchurch Road, Ringwood, Hampshire, BH24 1DR
01425 472062 Ⓕ 01425 472727
Ⓜ 07806 711280
Ⓔ mail@millers-antiques.co.uk
Ⓦ www.millers-antiques.co.uk
Est. 1897 *Stock size* Large
Stock English and Continental country furniture, 19thC majolica, Quimper, treen, decorative items
Open Mon 9.30am–1.30pm Tue–Fri 9.30am–5pm Sat 10am–3pm
Fairs Decorative Antiques and Textiles Fair, Great Antiques Fair
Services Restorations, packing, shipping

Robert Morgan Antiques
Contact Mr C King
90 Christchurch Road, Ringwood, Hampshire, BH24 1DR
01425 479400 Ⓕ 01425 479400
Est. 1985 *Stock size* Medium
Stock Postcards, ephemera
Open Tues–Sat 10am–5pm
Fairs Twickenham, Yeovil, Woking postcard fairs
Services Valuations

Sci-Fi World
Contact Mr J Wilson
42a High Street, Ringwood, Hampshire, BH24 1AG
01425 474506
Ⓔ james.wilson5@virgin.net
Est. 1996 *Stock size* Medium
Stock Cards, badges, mugs, videos, books, toys
Open Mon–Sat 10am–5pm
Services Valuations

Lorraine Tarrant Antiques
Contact Mrs L Tarrant
23 Market Place, Ringwood, Hampshire, BH24 1AN
01425 461123
Est. 1991 *Stock size* Medium
Stock Furniture, carved oak, old pine, bears, collectors' items, tapestry cushions
Open Tues–Sat 10am–5pm

ROMSEY

Antique Enterprises
Contact Mr M Presterfield
19 Cavendish Close, Romsey, Hampshire, SO51 7HT
01794 515589
Est. 1976 *Stock size* Medium
Stock Furniture, china, glass, collectables
Open By appointment

Bell Antiques (Gemmological Association)
Contact Mr M Gay
8 Bell Street, Romsey, Hampshire, SO51 8GA
01794 514719
Est. 1979 *Stock size* Large
Stock Jewellery, silver, glass, china, small furniture, maps, topographical prints
Open Mon–Sat 9.30am–5.30pm closed Wed in Winter

Rick Hubbard Art Deco
Contact Rick Hubbard
3 Tee Court, Bell Street, Romsey, Hampshire, SO51 8GY
01794 513133 Ⓜ 07767 267607
Ⓦ www.rickhubbard-artdeco.co.uk

Est. 1995 *Stock size* Large
Stock 20thC ceramics
Open Mon–Fri 10am–3pm
Sat 9am–4pm
Fairs Alexander Palace, Shelley Collectors Fair

Romsey Auction Rooms
Contact Mrs Vanessa Blair
86 The Hundred, Romsey, Hampshire, SO51 8BX
01794 513331 01794 511770
gavelman@waitrose.com
Est. 1966
Open Mon–Thurs 9am–5.30pm
Fri 9am–5pm
Sales General antiques sales monthly, first or second Tues. 5 silver sales and 3 toy sales a year, viewing day before sale noon–7.30pm. Advisable to phone for sale details
Frequency Monthly
Catalogues Yes

SOUTHAMPTON

Amber Antiques
Contact Mr R Boyle
115 Portswood Road, Portswood, Southampton, Hampshire, SO17 2FX
023 8058 3645 023 8058 3645
Est. 1970 *Stock size* Large
Stock Furniture
Open Mon–Sun 9am–5pm
Services Restorations

The Antique Centre
Contact Mrs S O'Shea
Britannia Road, Southampton, Hampshire, SO14 0QL
023 8022 1022
Est. 1999 *Stock size* Large
No. of dealers 40
Stock Furniture, porcelain, jewellery, pictures, glass, medals, ocean memorabilia, Clarice Cliff
Open Mon–Sat 10.30am–5.30pm
Sun 11am–4pm
Services Restorations, upholstery

Clocktower Antiques Centre
Contact Mr Chris White
1 Manor Farm Road, Bitterne Park Triangle, Southampton, Hampshire, SO18 1DE
023 8055 4303
Est. 1999 *Stock size* Large
No. of dealers 20
Stock Furniture, porcelain, brass, silver, clocks
Open Mon–Sat 10am–5.30pm
closed Wed
Services Valuations

Cobwebs
Contact Mr P Boyd-Smith
78 Northam Road, Southampton, Hampshire, SO14 0PB
023 8022 7458 023 8022 7458
www.cobwebs.uk.com
Est. 1974 *Stock size* Large
Stock Ocean liner memorabilia, Titanic and White Star Line, Aviation items, Royal and Merchant Navy items
Open Mon–Sat 10am–4pm
closed Wed
Fairs Transportation 2000, British Titanic Convention
Services Valuations

Highfield Antiques
Contact Clive Madge
33 Highfield Lane, Southampton, Hampshire, SO17 1QD
023 8032 2025
cmadge@aol.com
Est. 1983 *Stock size* Medium
Stock Georgian–1930s furniture, pictures, prints, garden furniture, ceramics, glass, toys
Open Mon–Sat 9am–5.30pm
Fairs Swinderby, Kempton
Services Free delivery

Memory Lane
Contact Mr A Dittrich
26 Manor Farm Road, Southampton, Hampshire, SO18 1HP
023 8055 1166
Est. 1997 *Stock size* Medium
Stock Furniture, pictures, collectables
Open Mon–Sat 10am–5pm
closed Wed
Services House clearance

Peter Rhodes Books
Contact Peter Rhodes
21 Portswood Road, Southampton, Hampshire, SO17 2ES
023 8039 9003
peterrhodes21@hotmail.com
Est. 1997 *Stock size* Large
Stock Antiquarian, rare, second-hand books, architecture, art, design, illustrators a speciality
Open Mon–Sat 11am–5pm
Fairs HD Fairs
Services Valuations, book search

Kenneth Standrin
Contact Mr K Standrin
307a Burlesdon Road, Southampton, Hampshire, SO19 8NE
023 8044 4200
Est. 1998 *Stock size* Small
Stock Antique furniture, mirrors, decorative items
Open Mon–Sat 9am–5pm
Services Restorations

SOUTHSEA

Book Academy (ABA)
Contact Mr Robinson
13 Marmion Road, Southsea, Hampshire, PO5 2AT
023 9281 6632 023 9281 6632
www.book-academy.com
Est. 1970 *Stock size* Large
Stock Antiquarian and new, reformed theology books including bibles, prayer, hymn books, Dickens, Hampshire a speciality
Open Mon–Sat 9.30am–4.30pm
Services Valuations, book repair, rebinding

The Clock Shop
Contact Mr G Carrington
155 Highland Road, Southsea, Hampshire, PO4 9EY
023 9285 1649
Est. 1999 *Stock size* Large
Stock Clocks, watches, general antiques
Open Wed–Sat 9am–5pm
Fairs Kempton Park, DMG
Services Valuations, clock restorations

Design Explosion
Contact Susan Mosely
2 Exmouth Road, Southsea, Hampshire, PO5 2QL
023 9229 3040 07850 131414
susan.moseley@btclick.com
www.ianparmiter.co.uk
Est. 1998 *Stock size* Medium
Stock 1950s–1970s china, glass, lighting, furniture
Open Fri Sat 9am–5pm
Fairs Ardingly

A Fleming (Southsea) Ltd
Contact Mr Alfred Fleming

✉ **The Clock Tower, Castle Road, Southsea, Hampshire, PO5 3DE** Ⓟ
☎ 023 9282 2934 Ⓕ 023 9229 3501
Ⓜ 07885 334545
Ⓔ mail@flemingsantiques.fsnet.co.uk
Ⓦ www.flemingsantiques.com
Est. 1908 ***Stock size*** Medium
Stock 18th–19thC English and Continental furniture, silver, boxes, barometers
Open Mon–Fri 9.30am–5.30pm Sat 9.30am–1pm or by appointment
Fairs Goodwood, Surrey Antiques Fair Guildford, Petersfield
Services Valuations, furniture and silver restorations

⊞ Langford Antiques
Contact Mr I Langford
✉ **70 Albert Road, Southsea, Hampshire, PO5 2SL** Ⓟ
☎ 023 9283 0517
Est. 1982 ***Stock size*** Medium
Stock Victorian–20thC furniture, collectables, silver, costume jewellery
Open Mon–Fri 11am–5pm Sat 10am–6pm closed Wed

D M Nesbit & Co
Contact Mr M Jarrett
✉ **7 Clarendon Road, Southsea, Hampshire, PO5 2ED** Ⓟ
☎ 023 9286 4321 Ⓕ 023 9229 5522
Ⓔ auctions@nesbits.co.uk
Ⓦ www.invaluable.com/dmnesbitandco
Est. 1921
Open Mon–Fri 9.30am–5pm
Sales General antiques sale monthly. Phone for details
Catalogues Yes

⊞ Oldfield Gallery
Contact Ann Downs
✉ **76 Elm Grove, Southsea, Hampshire, PO5 1LN** Ⓟ
☎ 023 9283 8042
Est. 1972 ***Stock size*** Large
Stock Antique maps and prints
Open Tues–Sat 10am–5pm
Fairs London Map Fairs
Services Valuations, framing

⊞ Ian Parmiter
Contact Mr I Parmiter
✉ **18a Albert Road, Southsea, Hampshire, PO5 2SH** Ⓟ
☎ 023 9229 3040
Ⓦ www.ianparmiter.co.uk
Est. 1987 ***Stock size*** Medium
Stock Architectural antiques, unusual items
Open Mon 11am–2.30pm Fri Sat 11am–5pm or by appointment

STOCKBRIDGE

Evans and Partridge
Contact John Partridge
✉ **Agriculture House, Stockbridge, Hampshire, SO20 6HF** Ⓟ
☎ 01264 810702 Ⓕ 01264 810944
Ⓔ auctions@evansandpartridge.co.uk
Est. 1973
Open Mon–Fri 9am–5.30pm Sat 9am–4pm
Sales Sales of early and modern fishing tackle, sporting guns, antique weapons, steam, tractors and farming bygones
Frequency Annual
Catalogues Yes

⊞ Lane Antiques
Contact Mrs E Lane
✉ **High Street, Stockbridge, Hampshire, SO20 6EU** Ⓟ
☎ 01264 810435
Est. 1982 ***Stock size*** Medium
Stock 18th–19thC porcelain, silver, glass, small furniture, objets d'art, fine art
Open By appointment

⊞ Stockbridge Antiques Centre
Contact Tim Baker
✉ **Old London Road, Stockbridge, Hampshire, SO20 6EJ** Ⓟ
☎ 01264 811008 Ⓜ 07966 539993
Ⓔ rona@oakchairs.com
Ⓦ www.oakchairs.com
Est. 1978 ***Stock size*** Medium
Stock Pine and oak country furniture
Open Mon–Sat 10am–5pm Sun 11am–2pm closed Wed

⊞ Elizabeth Viney (BADA)
Contact Miss E A Viney MBE
✉ **Jacobs House, High Street, Stockbridge, Hampshire, SO20 6HF** Ⓟ
☎ 01264 810761
Est. 1967 ***Stock size*** Small
Stock 18th–19thC furniture, treen, domestic metalware, brass, candlesticks, police truncheons
Open By appointment only

WARSASH

⊞ Athena Antiques
Contact Mr Alan Tonks
✉ **31 Newtown Road, Warsash, Southampton, Hampshire, SO31 9FY** Ⓟ
☎ 01489 578093
Ⓔ athenaantq@aol.com
Est. 1980 ***Stock size*** Large
Stock China, glass, figurines, chandeliers, railwayana
Open Telephone for opening hours
Fairs Athena Fayres, Antiques and Collectables Fairs at Wickham, Locks Heath, Minstead

WICKHAM

Solent Railwayana Auctions
Contact Mr Alan Tonks
✉ **Community Centre, Mill Lane, Wickham, Hampshire, PO17 5AL** Ⓟ
☎ 01489 574029
Ⓔ solentry@aol.com
Est. 1992
Open Sale 11am–5pm
Sales Railwayana auctions. Dates for 2003 15 March, 21 June, 18 October
Frequency 3 per annum
Catalogues Yes

WINCHESTER

Bonhams
✉ **The Red House, Hyde Street, Winchester, Hampshire, SO23 7DX** Ⓟ
☎ 01962 862515 Ⓕ 01962 865166
Ⓔ winchester@bonhams.com
Ⓦ www.bonhams.com
Est. 1793
Open Mon–Fri 8.30am–5pm

⊞ Burgess Farm Antiques
Contact Mr Brown
✉ **39 Jewry Street, Winchester, Hampshire, SO23 8RY** Ⓟ
☎ 01962 777546
Est. 1982 ***Stock size*** Large
Stock Antique pine and country furniture, general antiques
Open Mon–Sat 9.30am–5pm
Services Valuations, restorations

The Clock-Work-Shop (Winchester) (BHI, AHS)
Contact Mr P Ponsford-Jones
6a Parchment Street, Winchester, Hampshire, SO23 8AT
01962 842331 07973 736155
Est. 1994 *Stock size* Large
Stock Furniture, clocks, barometers
Open Mon–Sat 9am–5pm
Services Restorations of clocks and barometers

G E Marsh (Antique Clocks) Ltd (BADA, CINOA, CC, BHI, NAWCC)
Contact Mr D Dipper
32a The Square, Winchester, Hampshire, SO23 9EX
01962 844443 01962 844443
gem@marshclocks.co.uk
www.marshclocks.co.uk
Est. 1947 *Stock size* Medium
Stock Carriage clocks, English longcase clocks, Continental clocks
Open Mon–Fri 9.30am–5pm Sat 9.30am–1pm 2–5pm
Services Valuations, restorations, home visits

The Pine Cellars
Contact Mr N Brain
39 Jewry Street, Winchester, Hampshire, SO23 8RY
01962 777546
Est. 1971 *Stock size* Large
Stock Antique pine, country furniture
Open Mon–Sat 9.30am–5.30pm
Services Restorations

The Silver Shop
Contact Christopher Barbour
Unit 3, Antique Market, Kings Walk, Winchester, Hampshire, SO23 8AF
01962 855575
acbsilwin@aol.com
Est. 1992 *Stock size* Small
Stock Antique silver, jewellery and plate
Open Mon–Sat 10.30am–4.30pm
Services Valuations, restorations

Studio Coins (BNTA)
Contact Mr S Mitchell
16 Kilham Lane, Winchester, Hampshire, SO22 5PT
01962 853156 01962 624246
Est. 1987
Stock Old English coins
Open By appointment only
Fairs Coinex, Cumberland, York
Services Free bi-monthly list

Todd & Austin Antiques & Fine Art
Contact Gerald Austin
2 Andover Road, Winchester, Hampshire, SO23 7BS
01962 869824
Est. 1974 *Stock size* Medium
Stock 18th–early 20thC pottery, porcelain, glass paperweights 1845–60, decorative silver, boxes, silver plate, Oriental arts, 18th–19thC glass, objets d'art
Open Tues–Fri 9.30am–5pm Nov Dec Sat 9am–noon
Services Valuations

Irene S Trudgett Collectables
Contact Irene S Trudgett
3 Andover Road, Winchester, Hampshire, SO23 7BS
01962 854132/862070
Est. 1966 *Stock size* Medium
Stock Pottery, porcelain, cigarette cards, Goss & Crested china, glass, collectables
Open Mon–Fri 9.15am–4pm Thurs Sat 9.15am–noon
Services Valuations, restorations, book search

Webb Fine Arts
Contact Mr Webb
38 Jewry Street, Winchester, Hampshire, SO23 8RY
01962 842273 01962 863516
davieswebb@hotmail.com
www.webbfinearts.co.uk
Est. 1972 *Stock size* Medium
Stock Small furniture, Victorian paintings
Open Mon–Fri 9.30am–5pm Sat 9.30am–2pm
Services Valuations, restorations

The Winchester Bookshop (PBFA)
Contact Mr M Green
10a St Georges Street, Winchester, Hampshire, SO23 8BG
01962 855630
Est. 1991 *Stock size* Medium
Stock Antiquarian, rare, second-hand books, topography, archaeology, travel, literature a speciality
Open Mon–Sat 10am–5.30pm
Fairs PBFA fairs
Services Valuations, book search

ISLE OF WIGHT

BEMBRIDGE

Cobwebs Antiques and Collectables (GADAR)
Contact Mrs Sue Williams
Foreland Road, Bembridge, Isle of Wight, PO35 5XN
01983 874487
Est. 1997 *Stock size* Medium
Stock Bunnykins, Beatrix Potter, Doulton
Open Tues–Sat 10am–5pm

COWES

Copperwheat Restoration (RICS)
Contact Carole Copperwheat
Rear of Pascall Atkey, 29–30 High Street, Cowes, Isle of Wight, PO31 7RX
01983 281011 07720 399670
Est. 1985 *Stock size* Small
Stock 17th–18thC furniture, metalware, ceramics
Open Any time by prior phone call
Services Valuations, restorations

Flagstaff Antiques
Contact Mr T A M Cockram
Tudor House, Bath Road, Cowes, Isle of Wight, PO31 7RH
01983 200138
Est. 1995 *Stock size* Medium
Stock Jewellery, porcelain, silver
Open Mon–Sat 10.30am–4pm closed Wed
Fairs Miami, Florida
Services Valuations

Gaby Goldscheider (ABA)
Contact Miss G Goldscheider
Charles Dickens Bookshop, 65 High Street, Cowes, Isle of Wight, PO31 7RL
01983 280586
Est. 1987 *Stock size* Medium
Stock Second-hand, antiquarian,

rare books, prints, children's books, literature, fiction, topography, travel, nautical a speciality
Open By appointment
Fairs ABA fairs at Chelsea, Bath
Services Catalogues

Royal Standard Antiques
Contact Mrs C Bradbury
70–72 Park Road, Cowes, Isle of Wight, PO31 7LY
01983 281672 Ⓜ 07890 962262
caroline@royalstandardantiques.fsbusiness.co.uk
www.royalstandardantiques.fsbusiness.co.uk
Est. 1994 *Stock size* Medium
Stock Georgian–Edwardian English and French furniture, pictures, engravings, commemoratives, architectural antiques
Open Mon–Sat 10.30am–5.30pm Wed 10.30am–1pm or by appointment
Services Furniture restoration, stained glass restoration, upholstery, chair caning

FRESHWATER

Aladdin's Cave
Contact Mrs Dunn
147–149 School Green Road, Freshwater, Isle of Wight, PO40 9BB
01983 752934/753846
Ⓜ 07867 558424
Est. 1984 *Stock size* Large
Stock Old pine furniture, glass, china, collectables
Open Mon–Sat 9.30am–4.30pm closed Tues
Services House clearance

The Old Village Clock Shop
Contact Mr R Taylor
3 Moa Place, Freshwater, Isle of Wight, PO40 9DS
01983 754193
Est. 1970 *Stock size* Medium
Stock 17th–19thC English longcase and dial clocks, Vienna regulators, early German, English bracket, French ormolu, carriage clocks
Open Wed Fri Sat 9.30am–1pm or by appointment
Services Valuations

GODSHILL

Style
Contact Mrs R Brooks
High Street, Godshill, Isle of Wight, PO38 3HH
01983 840194 Ⓕ 01983 840438
Est. 1992 *Stock size* Large
Stock China, glass, collectables, items of interest, furniture
Open Mon–Sun 10am–5pm

NEWPORT

Mike Heath Antiques
Contact Mr M Heath
3–4 Holyrood Street, Newport, Isle of Wight, PO30 5AU
01983 525748
Est. 1979 *Stock size* Medium
Stock Furniture, oil lamps, porcelain, glass, collectables
Open Mon–Sat 9.30am–5pm closed Thurs
Services Metal restoration, polishing

Lugley Street Antiques
Contact Mr D Newman
13 Lugley Street, Newport, Isle of Wight, PO30 5HD
01983 523348
Est. 1986 *Stock size* Large
Stock Furniture, clocks, china, collectables, 19thC furniture a speciality
Open Mon–Sat 9.30am–5pm closed Thurs

Online Antiques
Contact Kim or Steve Snow
5 Watchbell Lane, Newport, Isle of Wight, PO30 5XU
01983 526282
vintage.uk@virgin.net
www.vintage-uk.com
Est. 2001 *Stock size* Small
Stock Anything old and interesting
Open Mon–Sat 10am–4pm
Services Online auction service

RYDE

Antiques Etc
Contact Mr B Walker
27 Cross Street, Ryde, Isle of Wight, PO33 2AA
Ⓜ 07790 874181
Est. 1969 *Stock size* Large
Stock China, collectables, glass, furniture
Open Mon–Sat 10am–4pm

Heritage Books
Contact Rev D H Nearn
7 Cross Street, Ryde, Isle of Wight, PO33 2AD
01983 562933 Ⓕ 01983 812634
dhnearn.heritagebooksryde@virgin.net
Est. 1977 *Stock size* Medium
Stock General, Isle of Wight antiquarian prints, books on modern theology, history, culture of Africa a speciality
Open Mon–Sat 10am–5pm closed Thurs
Fairs Guildford Book Fair
Services Book search

Nooks and Crannies
Contact Mr D Burnett
60 High Street, Ryde, Isle of Wight, PO33 2RJ
01983 568984
Est. 1986 *Stock size* Medium
Stock Collectables, lamps, 78 rpm records, telephones, radio, glass, china, furniture
Open Mon–Sat 9.30am–1.30pm 2.30–5pm closed Thurs pm
Fairs Ardingly

Ryde Antiques
Contact Roger Rowan
61 High Street, Ryde, Isle of Wight, PO33 2RJ
01983 615703
rowantobyb@aol.com
Est. 1968 *Stock size* Medium
Stock Jewellery and militaria, small antiques
Open Mon–Sat 10am–4.30pm

Ways
Contact Mr T L Smith
The Auction House, Garfield Road, Ryde, Isle of Wight, PO33 2PT
01983 562255 Ⓕ 01983 565108
www.waysauctionrooms.fsbusiness.co.uk
Est. 1815
Open Mon–Fri 9am–5pm
Sales Antique and modern furnishings sale on Thurs, viewing day prior 10am–6pm. No buyer's premium
Frequency Every 5 weeks
Catalogues Yes

SANDOWN

Lake Antiques
Contact Mrs J Marchant
18 Sandown Road, Sandown, Isle of Wight, PO36 9JP
01983 406888 07710 067678
Est. 1982 *Stock size* Medium
Stock Antique furniture, clocks, pictures, decorative items
Open Mon–Sat 10am–4pm closed Wed or by appointment
Services Valuations, mainland deliveries arranged

SHANKLIN

Regency Antiques
Contact Mr D Cooper
64 Regent Street, Shanklin, Isle of Wight, PO37 7AE
01983 868444
Est. 1955 *Stock size* Medium
Stock Oriental and English antiques
Open Mon–Sat 11am–2pm or by appointment
Services Valuations

Shanklin Auction Rooms (NAVA)
Contact Mr H Riches
79 Regent Street, Shanklin, Isle of Wight, PO37 7AP
01983 863441 01983 863890
shanklin.auction@tesco.net
Est. 1850
Open Mon–Fri 9am–5pm
Sales Collective antiques monthly. Antiques quarterly. Phone for details
Frequency Monthly
Catalogues Yes

VENTNOR

Curios
Contact Mr M Gregory
3 Church Place, Chale, Ventnor, Isle of Wight, PO38 2HA
01983 730230
Est. 1995 *Stock size* Large
Stock Taxidermy, architectural antiques, fireplaces, staddle stones, unusual curiosities
Open Mon–Sun noon–5.30pm
Services Valuations

Plumridge Antiques
Contact Mr R Plumridge
Unit 2, Caxton House, Ventnor Industrial Estate, Ventnor, Isle of Wight, PO38 1DX
01983 856666 01983 855325
07855 649297
plumridge@lineone.net
Est. 1999 *Stock size* Large
Stock Pianos, furniture
Open Mon–Fri 8.30am–5pm Sat 8.30am–1pm
Services Packers, shippers

Ultramarine
Contact Mrs M Stevens
40b High Street, Ventnor, Isle of Wight, PO38 1RZ
01983 854062
Est. 1999 *Stock size* Large
Stock Collectables, costume jewellery, china, stoneware, glass
Open Mon Tues 10am–1pm Thurs Fri Sat 10am–2pm closed Wed

Ventnor Antiques Centre
Contact Mrs P Huntley
66 High Street, Ventnor, Isle of Wight, PO38 1LU
01983 855302 01983 855325
Est. 1994 *Stock size* Medium
No. of dealers 4
Stock General antiques, collectables, furniture
Open Mon–Sat 10am–5pm
Services Valuations, delivery

Ventnor Junction
Contact Mr or Mrs P Dolby
48 High Street, Ventnor, Isle of Wight, PO38 1LT
01983 853996
shop@ventjunc.freeserve.co.uk
www.ventjunc.freeserve.co.uk
Est. 1987 *Stock size* Large
Stock Old toys, collectables, tin trains
Open Most mornings or by appointment
Fairs Sandown Park Toy Fair, Esher
Services Mail order

YARMOUTH

Yarmouth Antiques and Books
Contact Mrs V Blakeley & Mr M Coyle
The House, The Square, Yarmouth, Isle of Wight, PO41 0NP
01983 760046
yarmouth-antiquesiow@btinternet.com
Est. 1996 *Stock size* Medium
Stock Antiquarian, second-hand books, china, collectables
Open Mon–Sun 10am–5pm
Fairs Kempton Park, February

SURREY

ABINGER HAMMER

Abinger Bazaar
Contact Mike Gammon
Guildford Road, Abinger Hammer, Dorking, Surrey, RH5 6QA
01306 730756
g.tovey@virgin.net
Est. 1979 *Stock size* Medium
Stock French Art Deco stoves, porcelain, books, Victorian fireplaces, dolls' houses
Open Tues–Sun 10am–6pm

Stirling Antiques
Contact Mr U Burrell
Aberdeen House, Guildford Road, Abinger Hammer, Dorking, Surrey, RH5 6RY
01306 730706 01306 731575
07748 005619
Est. 1968 *Stock size* Medium
Stock Architectural stained glass, metalware, furniture, jewellery, silver, curios
Open Mon–Sat 9.30am–6pm closed Thurs

ADDLESTONEMOOR

Small Wood Ltd
Contact Julian Faulkner
The Elephant House, Addlestonemoor, Surrey, KT15 2QF
01932 848122 01932 831690
enquiries@small-wood.com
Est. 1998 *Stock size* Medium
Stock Architectural salvage, contemporary furniture, art and antiques
Open Mon–Sat 10am–5pm

ASHTEAD

Bumbles
Contact Mrs B Kay
90 The Street, Ashtead, Surrey, KT21 1AW
01372 276219 01798 875545
Est. 1978 *Stock size* Medium
Stock General furniture, clocks, porcelain, silver, coins, cigarette cards, lighting, oil-lamp parts

Open Mon–Sat 10am–5.30pm
Services Furniture restorations, re-upholstery

BETCHWORTH

Stoneycroft Farm (LAPADA)
Contact Michael Head
Reigate Road, Betchworth, Surrey, RH3 7EY
01737 845215
www.desk.uk.com
Est. 1987 ***Stock size*** Large
Stock Country furniture, bookcases, linen presses, dining room tables
Open Mon–Fri 8am–5.30pm
Sat 10am–3pm

BLETCHINGLEY

John Anthony
Contact Mrs N Hart
71 High Street, Bletchingley, Redhill, Surrey, RH1 4LJ
01883 743197 F 01883 742108
M 07836 221689
johnanthonyantiques@hotmail.com
Est. 1974 ***Stock size*** Medium
Stock 18th–19thC furniture
Open By appointment only

Lawrences Auctioneers Ltd
Contact Miss S Debnam
Norfolk House, High Street, Bletchingley, Redhill, Surrey, RH1 4PA
01883 743323 F 01883 744578
www.lawrencesbletchingley.co.uk
Est. 1960
Open Mon–Fri 9am–5pm
Sales General antiques sales on Tues Wed Thurs, viewing Fri Sat 10am–5pm
Frequency Every 6 weeks
Catalogues Yes

Post House Antiques
Contact Mr P Bradley
High Street, Bletchingley, Surrey, RH1 4PA
01883 743317 F 01883 743317
Est. 1975 ***Stock size*** Large
Stock Antique lighting
Open Mon–Sat 10am–5pm
Services Restorations

Quill Antiques
Contact Mrs J Davis
86 High Street, Bletchingley, Surrey, RH1 4PA
01883 743755
Est. 1973 ***Stock size*** Large
Stock Agricultural, rural bygones, copper, brass, glass, porcelain
Open Tues–Sat 10am–5.30pm
Fairs Dorking

BRAMLEY

Memories Antiques
Contact Mrs P S Kelsey
High Street, Bramley, Guildford, Surrey, GU5 0HB
01483 892205 M 07774 885014
Est. 1985 ***Stock size*** Medium
No. of dealers 8
Stock Georgian–Victorian French, pine furniture, silver, jewellery, porcelain, collectables, garden items, kitchenware, French antiques
Open Mon–Sat 10am–5pm
Services 'Wanted' service

The Old Works Antiques
Contact Mr A Sutherland
24 High Street, Bramley, Guildford, Surrey, GU5 0HB
01483 894648 M 07968 971444
Est. 1994 ***Stock size*** Medium
Stock English, Continental, Victorian, pre-Victorian furniture
Open Mon–Fri 9am–5.30pm
Sat 9.30am–5pm
Sun 10.30am–4pm
Services Restorations

BROCKHAM

Cartels Auctioneers and Valuers
Contact Mr Carter
2 Tanners Court, Middle Street, Brockham, Dorking (on A25), Surrey, RH3 7NH
01737 844646 F 01737 844646
M 07768 004293
Est. 1978
Open Mon–Fri 9.30am–5pm
Sales General antiques, fine art, pre-1930s, viewing all day Fri 10am–7pm and morning of sale 8.30–10am
Frequency Monthly excluding August
Catalogues Yes

CARSHALTON

Cherub Antiques
Contact Mr M Wisdom
312–314 Carshalton Road, Carshalton, Surrey, SM5 3QB
020 8643 0028 M 07740 178093
Est. 1985 ***Stock size*** Large
Stock Continental and English antique pine, mahogany
Open Mon–Sat 10am–5.30pm
Services Pine stripping, French polishing

The Clock House (BWCG)
Contact Mark Cocklin
75 Pound Street, Carshalton, Surrey, SM5 3PG
020 8773 4844 M 07850 363317
mark@theclockhouse.co.uk
www.theclockhouse.co.uk
Est. 1989 ***Stock size*** Medium
Stock Antiquarian horology, longcase clocks
Open Tues–Fri 9.30am–4.30pm
Sat 9am–6pm or by appointment
Fairs Brunel University
Services Valuations, restorations, spares

CATERHAM

Chaldon Books and Records
Contact Mr K Chesson
1 High Street, Caterham, Surrey, CR3 5UE
01883 348583
Est. 1994 ***Stock size*** Medium
Stock Rare and second-hand books
Open Mon–Sat 9.30am–5.30pm closed Wed
Services Book search

CHEAM

Parkins
Contact Mrs Mary Zenthon
18 Malden Road, Cheam, Surrey, SM3 8QF
020 8644 6633
www.urus.globalnet.co.uk/~parkins
Est. 1945
Open Mon–Fri 9am–1pm 2–5pm
Sales Antique furniture and effects 1st Mon of month 10am, general furniture and effects 2nd and 4th Mon of month 10am, viewing Fri 2–4pm Sat 10am–4pm. Smaller antiques and collectables monthly evening sale, viewing 2–7pm
Catalogues Yes

Village Antiques
Contact Miss S Jenner
16 Malden Road, Cheam, Sutton, Surrey, SM3 8QF
020 8644 8567
Est. 1986 *Stock size* Large
Stock Furniture, lighting, porcelain, glass, silver, jewellery, collectors' items
Open Mon–Sat 11am–5pm closed Tues Thurs
Services House clearance

CHERTSEY

Chertsey Antiques
Contact Judy Carroway
10 Windsor Street, Chertsey, Surrey, KT16 8AS
0118 976 1355
Est. 1996 *Stock size* Medium
No. of dealers 6
Stock Collectables, furniture, clocks, silver, jewellery, memorabilia
Open Mon–Fri 10am–5pm Sat 10am–5.30pm

D'Eyncourt Antiques
Contact Mr G D H Davies
21 Windsor Street, Chertsey, Surrey, KT16 8AY
01932 563411
Est. 1970 *Stock size* Large
Stock Furniture, jewellery, china, collectables, fireplaces
Open Mon–Fri 10am–5.15pm Sat 7am–5.30pm Sun 11am–4pm
Fairs London Photographic Fair
Services Valuations

Wellers Auctioneers (ISVA)
Contact Mr Glen Snelgar or Mr Mark Longson
70 Guildford Street, Chertsey, Surrey, KT16 9BB
01932 568678 01932 568626
Est. 1980
Open Mon–Fri 9am–5.30pm
Sales Antique sales 2nd Sat monthly at 9.30am, Bygones auction March and September
Frequency Monthly
Catalogues Yes

CHOBHAM

Chobham Antique Clocks (BHI)
Contact Mike Morris
73–75 High Street, Chobham, Woking, Surrey, GU24 8AF
01276 682560
Est. 1989 *Stock size* Medium
Stock Antique clocks, barometers
Open Tues–Sat 10am–5pm
Services Valuations, restorations

Mimbridge Antiques and Collectables
Contact Mrs J Monteath Scott
Mimbridge Garden Centre, Station Road, Chobham, Woking, Surrey, GU24 8AS
01276 855736 0771 862284
Est. 1987 *Stock size* Medium
Stock Small antiques, pictures, prints, maps, garden items, period furniture, decorative items, porcelain, glass, dolls
Open Mon–Sun 10am–5pm
Fairs Kempton
Services Picture framing

CHURT

Churt Curiosity Shop
Contact Mrs G Gregory
Crossways, Churt, Farnham, Surrey, GU10 2JE
01428 714096
Est. 1995 *Stock size* Medium
Stock Victorian–Edwardian small furniture, Victorian china, glass, collectables
Open Tues–Sat 10.15am–5pm closed Wed

COBHAM

Village Antiques
Contact Mr N Tsangari
38 Portsmouth Road, Cobham, Surrey, KT11 1HZ
01932 589841 07973 549221
Est. 1998 *Stock size* Medium
Stock General antiques, small furniture, pictures, porcelain, glass
Open Mon–Fri 10am–6pm or by appointment
Services Picture restoration

COMPTON

Country Rustics
Contact Veronica Dewey
45 The Street, Compton, Guildford, Surrey, GU3 1EG
01483 810505
Est. 2001 *Stock size* Small
Stock Rustic furniture and collectables
Open Tues–Sun 10am–6pm

Old Barn Antiques
Contact Mrs Chris Thurner
Old Barn, The Street, Compton, Guildford, Surrey, GU3 1EB
01483 810819
Est. 1993 *Stock size* Small
No. of dealers 6
Stock Country items, blue-and-white pottery, Victoriana, china, glass, collectables
Open Mon–Sat 10am–4pm

COULSDON

Decodream
Contact David Mobbs
233 Chipstead Valley Road, Coulsdon, Surrey, CR5 3BY
020 8668 5534 01737 556079
Est. 1987 *Stock size* Large
Stock Art Deco pottery
Open Mon–Sat by appointment
Services Valuations

CROYDON

Croydon Coin Auctions
Contact Mr G J Monk
PO Box 201, Croydon, Surrey, CR9 7AQ
020 8656 4583 020 8656 4583
cca@eigo.co.uk
www.eigo.co.uk/cca
Est. 1983
Open Mon–Fri 9am–5pm
Sales 6 sales a year of English, foreign and ancient coins, medallions, tokens and bank notes. Held at the United Reformed Church Hall, East Croydon Tues noon
Frequency Bi-monthly

McNally Antiques
Contact I McNally
322 Brighton Road, South Croydon, Surrey, CR2 6AJ
020 8686 8387 020 8686 8387
Est. 1972 *Stock size* Large
Stock Oak, walnut, mahogany furniture
Open Mon–Fri 9.30am–5.30pm Sat 9.30am–1pm or by appointment
Services Shipping

Miss Ellany
Contact Mr or Mrs J A Cusden
✉ **28 Croham Road, South Croydon, Surrey, CR2 7BA** P
☎ 020 8688 338
Est. 1984 *Stock size* Small
Stock Antiquarian, rare and second-hand books, transport a speciality
Open Mon–Sat 11am–4pm closed Thurs

DORKING

Antique Clocks by Patrick Thomas
Contact Mr P Thomas
✉ **62a West Street, Dorking, Surrey, RH4 1BS** P
☎ 01306 743661 F 01306 743661
M 07779 640319
Est. 1992 *Stock size* Large
Stock Clocks, scientific instruments, sporting antiques
Open Mon–Sat 9.30am–5.30pm Sun 11am–4pm
Services Valuations, restorations

G D Blay Antiques (BADA)
Contact Geoffrey Blay
✉ **56 West Street, Dorking, Surrey, RH4 1BS** P
☎ 01306 743398 M 07785 767718
E gblayantiques@gblay.freeserve.co.uk
W www.gdblayantiques.com
Stock size Medium
Stock Pre-1830s furniture
Open Tues–Sat 10am–5pm or by appointment
Fairs Summer and Winter Olympia, BADA Chelsea

J and M Coombes (DADA)
Contact Mr M Coombes
✉ **44 West Street, Dorking, Surrey, RH4 1BU** P
☎ 01306 885479 F 01306 885479
Est. 1967 *Stock size* Large
Stock Victorian–Edwardian furniture
Open Mon–Fri 9am–5pm Sat 10am–5pm Sun 1–4pm

Crows Auction Gallery
Contact Mrs H Farquhar
✉ **Rear of Dorking Halls, Reigate Road, Dorking, Surrey, RH4 1SG** P
☎ 01306 740382 F 01306 881672
Est. 1988
Open Mon–Fri 9am–4pm Sat 9.30am–noon
Sales Antiques and collectables sale last Wed in month 10am, viewing Sat 9am–1pm Mon–Tues 9am–4pm and morning of sale
Frequency Monthly
Catalogues Yes

Dolphin Square Antiques
Contact Diana Jones
✉ **42 West Street, Dorking, Surrey, RH4 1BU** P
☎ 01306 887901
Est. 1995 *Stock size* Medium
Stock Georgian–Edwardian furniture, clocks, mirrors, Staffordshire, porcelain, glass, copper, brass ware, bronzes
Open Mon–Sat 10am–5.30pm

Dorking Desk Shop (LAPADA, DADA)
Contact J G Elias
✉ **41 West Street, Dorking, Surrey, RH4 1BU**
☎ 01306 883327 F 01306 875363
W www.desk.uk.com
Est. 1973 *Stock size* Large
Stock Library and writing furniture, pedestal and partner desks
Open Mon–Fri 8am–5.30pm Sat 10.30am–5.30pm
Services Desk finding service

Dorking House Antiques
Contact Mrs G Emburey
✉ **17–18 West Street, Dorking, Surrey, RH4 1BS** P
☎ 01306 740915
Est. 1988 *Stock size* Large
No. of dealers 25
Stock Period furniture, silver, porcelain, paintings, collectables, treen, clocks
Open Mon–Sat 10am–5pm

Gallery Eleven (LAPADA)
✉ **11 West Street, Dorking, Surrey, RH4 1BL** P
☎ 01306 887771 F 01306 887771
Est. 1990 *Stock size* Large
Stock Fine 18th–19thC furniture, quality ceramics, decorative items
Open Mon–Sat 10am–5pm
Services Valuations

Hampshires of Dorking (LAPADA)
Contact Mr Michael Pay
✉ **50–52 West Street, Dorking, Surrey, RH4 1BU** P
☎ 01306 887076 F 01306 881029
M 07973 819783
E sales@hampshires.co.uk
W www.hampshires.co.uk
Est. 1970 *Stock size* Large
Stock 18thC, Edwardian and Georgian furniture, satinwood
Open Mon–Sat 9.30am–5.30pm Sun Bank Holidays 10am–4pm

Harmans Antiques (LAPADA)
Contact Mr P Harman
✉ **19 West Street, Dorking, Surrey, RH4 1QH** P
☎ 01306 743330 F 01306 742593
E enquiries@harmans-antiques.co.uk
W www.harmans-antiques.co.uk
Est. 1956 *Stock size* Large
Stock Georgian–Edwardian furniture
Open Mon–Sat 10am–5pm Sun 11am–4pm
Fairs Guildford
Services Restorations

The Howard Gallery (LAPADA)
Contact Mrs F Howard
✉ **5 West Street, Dorking, Surrey, RH4 1BL** P
☎ 01306 880022
W www.thehowardgallery.co.uk
Est. 1989 *Stock size* Medium
Stock 17th–18thC early Georgian, Queen Anne, Regency, oak, country furniture, longcase, bracket clocks
Open Wed–Fri 1–5pm Sat noon–11am or by appointment
Services Restorations, shipping

King's Court Galleries (FATG)
Contact Mrs J Joel
✉ **54 West Street, Dorking, Surrey, RH4 1BS** P
☎ 01306 881757 F 01306 875305
E sales@kingscourtgalleries.co.uk
W www.kingscourtgalleries.co.uk
Est. 1984 *Stock size* Large
Stock Antique maps, engravings, sporting and decorative prints
Open Mon–Sat 9.30am–5.30pm
Services Bespoke framing, mounting

Malthouse Antiques
Contact Mr R Dodsworth or Mr C Waters
49 West Street, Dorking, Surrey, RH4 1BU
01306 886169
Est. 1993 ***Stock size*** Large
No. of dealers 5
Stock 17th–19thC antiques
Open Mon–Sat 10am–5pm
Services Valuations, restorations, shipping

Mayfair Antiques
43 West Street, Dorking, Surrey, RH4 1BU
01306 885007 01306 742636
Est. 1968
Stock General antiques, furniture
Open Mon–Sat 10am–5.30pm
Services Restorations

Norfolk House Galleries Ltd
Contact Mr M Share
48 West Street, Dorking, Surrey, RH4 1BU
01306 881028
Est. 1975 ***Stock size*** Large
Stock 18th–19thC furniture
Open Mon–Sat 10am–5pm
Services Valuations, shipping

The Olde Bakehouse Antiques
Contact Mr D Kenney
1a West Street, Dorking, Surrey, RH4 1BL
01306 876646
Est. 1987 ***Stock size*** Large
Stock George III–Edwardian mahogany furniture, decorative items, china, pictures, silver, books
Open Tues–Sat 10.30am–5pm

Pilgrims Antique Centre
Contact Mrs M Pritchard
7 West Street, Dorking, Surrey, RH4 1BL
01306 875028
Est. 1990 ***Stock size*** Medium
No. of dealers 10
Stock Glass, furniture, paintings, books, Art Deco, barometers, Jobling glass, collectables
Open Mon–Fri 10am–5pm
Sat 10am–5.30pm
Services Restaurant

The Refectory
Contact Mr Chris Marks
38 West Street, Dorking, Surrey, RH4 1BU
01306 742111 01306 742111
Est. 1995
Stock 16th–19thC English country furniture, refectory tables, coffers, Windsor chairs, country items
Open Mon–Sat 10.30am–5.30pm
Sun by appointment

Eric Tombs
Contact Mr Eric Tombs
62a West Street, Dorking, Surrey, RH4 1BS
01306 743661 07720 561680
ertombs@aol.com
Est. 1992 ***Stock size*** Medium
Stock Scientific instruments
Open Mon–Sat 9.30am–5.30pm
Sun 11am–4pm
Fairs Scientific Instruments Fair
Services Valuations, restorations

Victoria and Edward Antique Centre (WSADA)
Contact Mr Tony Crowe
61 West Street, Dorking, Surrey, RH4 1BS
01306 889645
Est. 1983 ***Stock size*** Large
No. of dealers 26
Stock General antiques, furniture, metalware, porcelain, jewellery, silver
Open Mon–Sat 9.30am–5.30pm

The Vinery Antiques
Contact Cindy King or Pauline Schwarz
55 West Street, Dorking, Surrey, RH4 1BS
01306 743440 01306 743440
Stock size Medium
Stock 18th–19thC mahogany, walnut furniture, upholstery, early porcelain, decorative items
Open Tues–Sat 10.30am–5pm or by appointment
Services Valuations, restorations, furniture search

West Street Antiques
Contact Mr J G Spooner
63 West Street, Dorking, Surrey, RH4 1BS
01306 883487 01306 883487
weststant@aol.com
antiquearmsandarmour.com
Est. 1986 ***Stock size*** Medium
Stock English furniture, arms, armour. Comprehensive on-line catalogue
Open Mon–Sat 9.30am–1pm 2.15–5.30pm or by appointment
Fairs London Arms Fair, Park Lane Arms Fair
Services Valuations

P F Windibank
Contact Mr S Windibank
Dorking Halls, Reigate Road, Dorking, Surrey, RH4 1SG
01306 884556 01306 884669
sjw@windibank.co.uk
www.windibank.co.uk
Est. 1945
Open Mon–Fri 9am–5pm
Sat 10am–1pm
Sales Antique and quality sales on Sat, viewing Thurs 5–9pm Fri 9am–5pm
Frequency 4–6 weeks
Catalogues Yes

EAST MOLESEY

Antique Centre
Contact Mr Stuart James
77 Bridge Road, East Molesey, Surrey, KT8 9HH
020 8979 7954
Est. 1972 ***Stock size*** Large
No. of dealers 8
Stock Furniture, silver, glass, ceramics, jewellery, collectors' items
Open Mon–Sat 10am–5pm
Sun noon–5pm

Books Bought and Sold
Contact Mr P Sheridan
68 Walton Road, East Molesey, Surrey, KT8 0DL
020 8224 3232 020 8224 3576
booksbought@yahoo.co.uk
Est. 1973 ***Stock size*** Medium
Stock Antiquarian, rare, second-hand books, transport, collectable children's books a speciality
Open Tues–Sat 10am–5pm
Fairs H D Book Fairs

Elizabeth R Antiques
Contact E L Mallah
39 Bridge Road, Hampton Court, East Molesey, Surrey, KT8 9ER

☎ 020 8979 4004 Ⓕ 020 8979 4004
Ⓔ lizaantiques@hotmail.com
Est. 1994 *Stock size* Large
Stock 18th–19thC furniture, porcelain, glass, jewellery, 20thC dolls and toys
Open Tues–Sat 10am–4.30pm Sun 11am–3pm
Fairs Alexandra Palace, Sandown
Services Valuations, restorations

The Hampton Court Emporium
Contact Mr A Smith
52–54 Bridge Road, East Molesey, Surrey, KT8 9HA Ⓟ
☎ 020 8941 8876
Est. 1992 *Stock size* Large
No. of dealers 42
Stock Cameras, books, jewellery, lace, silver, brass, copper, toys, war ephemera, French arts, bronzes, furniture
Open Mon–Sat 10am–5.30pm Sun 11am–5.30pm

Nostradamus
Contact Heather Ferri
30 & 32 Bridge Road, East Molesey, Surrey, KT8 9HA Ⓟ
☎ 020 8979 6766 Ⓜ 07979 591022
Est. 1998 *Stock size* Large
No. of dealers 20
Stock General antiques, old cameras, brass, porcelain, Art Deco, jewellery, furniture
Open Tues–Sun 10am–5.30pm

Nostradamus II
Contact Kristina Carson
53 Bridge Road, East Molesey, Surrey, KT8 9HA Ⓟ
☎ 020 8783 0595
Est. 1980 *Stock size* Medium
No. of dealers 20
Stock Furniture, crystal, silver, old toys, Art Deco
Open Tues–Sun 10am–5.30pm

Palace Antiques
Contact John Prince
29 Bridge Road, East Molesey, Surrey, KT8 9ER Ⓟ
☎ 020 8979 2182
Est. 2000 *Stock size* Large
No. of dealers 10
Stock General antiques
Open Mon–Sun 10am–6pm

Rhombus
Contact Jackie Griffin
28 Bridge Road, East Molesey, Surrey, KT8 9HA Ⓟ
☎ 020 8224 5035
Ⓜ 07941 292049
Est. 2000 *Stock size* Medium
No. of dealers 4
Stock Art Deco centre
Open Tues–Sun 11am–5.30pm closed Fri

Alexis F J Turner Antiques
Contact Mr Turner
Antiques at 144a Bridge Road, East Molesey, Surrey, KT8 9HW Ⓟ
☎ 020 8542 5926 Ⓜ 07770 880960
Est. 1992 *Stock size* Medium
Stock Natural history, taxidermy, gentlemen's effects, curiosities
Open Sat 10am–4pm or by appointment

EWELL

Julian Eade
Ewell, Surrey
☎ 01491 575059 Ⓜ 07973 542971
Ⓔ julian.eade@insignia-re.com
Est. 1983 *Stock size* Medium
Stock Worcester, Minton, Derby, Artist ceramics, Doulton stoneware
Open By appointment
Fairs NEC
Services Valuations

J W McKenzie
Contact Mr J W McKenzie
12 Stoneleigh Park Road, Ewell, Epsom, Surrey, KT19 0QT Ⓟ
☎ 020 8393 7700 Ⓕ 020 8393 1694
Ⓔ jwmck@netcomuk.co.uk
Ⓦ www.mckenzie-cricket.co.uk
Est. 1972 *Stock size* Medium
Stock Antiquarian, rare and second-hand cricket books
Open Mon–Fri 9.30am–5.30pm Sat 10am–noon or by appointment

FARNHAM

Annie's Antiques
1 Ridgway Parade, Frensham Road, Farnham, Surrey, GU9 8UZ Ⓟ
☎ 01252 713447
Est. 1982 *Stock size* Medium
Stock General antiques
Open Mon–Fri 10am–5.30pm

Bourne Mill Antiques
Contact Mrs Vicky Bowers
39–43 Guildford Road, Farnham, Surrey, GU9 9PY Ⓟ
☎ 01252 716663
Est. 1960 *Stock size* Large
No. of dealers 65–85
Stock Antiques, collectables in 38 rooms
Open Mon–Sat 9.30am–5pm Sun 10am–5pm

Casque and Gauntlet Militaria
Contact R L Colt or A Colt
57 Badshot Lea Road, Badshot Lea, Farnham, Surrey, GU9 9LP Ⓟ
☎ 01252 320745 Ⓕ 01252 320745
Ⓦ www.armsandarmour.co.uk/dealers/casque/casque.htm
Est. 1972 *Stock size* Large
Stock Militaria, 15thC–modern times including swords, bayonets, armour
Open Mon–Sat 11am–5pm
Services Restoration of antique weapons

Christopher's Antiques
Contact Mr C Booth
39a West Street, Farnham, Surrey, GU9 7DX Ⓟ
☎ 01252 713794 Ⓕ 01252 713266
Ⓔ cbooth7956@aol.com
Est. 1972 *Stock size* Large
Stock French provincial country furniture
Open Mon–Fri 8am–5.30pm Sat 8am–noon
Services Valuations, restorations

FERNHURST

John Nicholson Fine Art Auctioneers
Contact Mr G Nugent
The Auction Rooms, Longfield, Midhurst Road, Fernhurst, Surrey, GU27 3HA Ⓟ
☎ 01428 653727 Ⓕ 01428 641509
Ⓔ nicholfineart@aol.com
Ⓦ www.antiquestradegazetter.co.uk
Est. 1992
Open Mon–Fri 9am–5.30pm
Sales Fine art auctions 6 weekly Wed Thurs. Paintings, prints, antiquarian books 3–4 times a year
Catalogues Yes

GODALMING

Michael Andrews Antiques
Contact Mr M Andrews

✉ **Portsmouth Road, Milford, Godalming, Surrey, GU8 5AU** 🅿
☎ 01483 420765
Est. 1982 *Stock size* Medium
Stock 18th–early 19thC furniture, mainly mahogany
Open Mon–Sat 9.30am–5.30pm closed Thurs or by appointment

E Bailey
Contact E Bailey
✉ **Portsmouth Road, Milford, Godalming, Surrey, GU8 5DR** 🅿
☎ 01483 422943
Est. 1978 *Stock size* Medium
Stock General antiques, collectables, curios, golf clubs, woodworking, engineering tools
Open Mon–Sat 8.30am–5pm closed Thurs

Church Street Antiques
Contact Mr L Bambridge
✉ **10 Church Street, Godalming, Surrey, GU7 1EH**
☎ 01483 860894
ⓔ churchst.antiques@virgin.net
ⓦ www.freespace.virgin.net/churchstreetantiques
Est. 1984 *Stock size* Large
Stock Early 19th–20thC ceramics
Open Mon–Sat 10am–5pm Wed 10am–1pm
Services Valuations

Godalming Antiques
Contact Gillian Noble-Jones
✉ **72a Ockford Road, Godalming, Surrey, GU7 1RF**
☎ 01483 414428
Est. 1993 *Stock size* Medium
No. of dealers 7
Stock Antiques, furniture, collectables, uniforms, books, trivia, memorabilia
Open Mon–Sat 10am–4.30pm

Hamptons International Auctioneers and Valuers
Contact Liz Bryder
✉ **Queen Street Salerooms, Queen Street, Godalming, Surrey, GU7 1BA**
☎ 01483 423497 ⓕ 01483 415699
ⓔ queenstreetauctions@hamptons-int.com
ⓦ www.hamptons.co.uk
Open Mon–Fri 9am–5.30pm Sat 8.30am–12.30pm (sale days only)
Sales Victorian, Edwardian and later furniture and effects sales on Sat at 9.30am, viewing Fri 10am–7pm Sat 8.30–9.30am
Frequency Fortnightly
Catalogues Yes

Hamptons International Auctioneers and Valuers
Contact Liz Bryder
✉ **Baverstock House, 93 High Street, Godalming, Surrey, GU7 1AL** 🅿
☎ 01483 423567 ⓕ 01483 426392
ⓔ fineartauctions@hamptons-int.com
ⓦ www.hamptons.co.uk
Est. 1996
Open Mon–Fri 9am–5.30pm
Sales Sales of antiques, furniture, carpets, pictures, clocks, china, glass, jewellery, silver, objects of virtue Wed and Thurs at 11am, viewing Sat 9.30am–12.30pm Mon 9.30am–7pm Tues 9.30am–3pm and up to 10.30am on day of sale
Frequency 4 sales every 6–8 weeks
Catalogues Yes

Heath-Bullocks (BADA)
Contact Mrs Mary Heath-Bullock
✉ **8 Meadrow, Godalming, Surrey, GU7 3HN** 🅿
☎ 01483 422562 ⓕ 01483 426077
ⓔ rogrheathbullock@aol.com
ⓦ www.heath-bullocks.com
Est. 1925 *Stock size* Large
Stock 17th–19thC furniture
Open Fri Sat 10am–5pm and by appointment
Fairs BADA, The Surrey Antiques Fair, The Buxton Antiques Fair
Services Valuations, restorations, upholstery

Honeypot Antiques
Contact Bob Holroyd
✉ **Milford Road, Elstead, Godalming, Surrey, GU8 6HR** 🅿
☎ 01252 703614 ⓕ 01252 733909
Est. 1996 *Stock size* Large
No. of dealers 25
Stock General antiques and collectables
Open Mon–Sat 10am–5.30pm Sun 11am–5.30pm

GOMSHALL

Reeves Restoration at the Coach House Antiques
Contact Mr P W Reeves
✉ **The Coach House, 60 Station Road, Gomshall, Guildford, Surrey, GU5 9NP** 🅿
☎ 01483 203838 ⓕ 01483 202999
ⓜ 07774 729325
ⓔ coach_house.antiques@virgin.net
ⓦ www.coachhouseantiques.com
Est. 1984 *Stock size* Large
Stock Regency, William IV furniture
Open Mon–Sun 10am–5pm closed Thurs
Fairs Guildford, Olympia
Services Restorations

The Studio
Contact Mrs M Ellenger
✉ **Station Road, Gomshall, Guildford, Surrey, GU5 9LQ** 🅿
☎ 01483 202449
Est. 1984 *Stock size* Large
Stock Furniture, china, silver, pictures
Open Mon–Sun noon–5pm

GREAT BOOKHAM

Roger A Davis Antiquarian Horologist
Contact Roger Davis
✉ **19 Dorking Road, Great Bookham, Surrey, KT23 4PU** 🅿
☎ 01372 457655
Est. 1972 *Stock size* Medium
Stock Antique clocks
Open Tues Thurs Sat 9.30am–12.30pm 2–5pm
Services Valuations, restorations

Memory Lane Antiques
Contact Mrs J Westwood
✉ **30 Church Road, Great Bookham, Leatherhead, Surrey, KT23 3PW** 🅿
☎ 01372 459908
Est. 1984 *Stock size* Medium
Stock Antiques, toys
Open Mon–Fri 10am–5pm Sat 10am–2pm closed Wed

GUILDFORD

Bonhams
✉ **Millmead, Guildford, Surrey, GU2 4BE** 🅿
☎ 01483 504030 ⓕ 01483 450205
ⓔ guildford@bonhams.com
ⓦ www.bonhams.com
Est. 1793
Open Mon–Fri 9am–1pm 2–5pm

Clarke Gammon Auctioneers and Valuers (RICS)
Bedford Road, Guildford, Surrey, GU1 4SJ
01483 880915 F 01483 880918
www.invaluable.com/clarkegammon
Est. 1919
Open Mon–Fri 9am–5.30pm
Sales Fine art, antiques and collectors' sales, viewing Sat 9am–noon Mon 9am–7pm prior to sale
Frequency 6 weeks
Catalogues Yes

Denning Antiques
Contact Mrs C Denning
1 Chapel Street, Guildford, Surrey, GU1 3UH
01483 539595
Est. 1984 *Stock size* Large
Stock Silver, textiles, jewellery
Open Mon–Sat 10am–5pm

Horological Workshops (BADA, BHI)
Contact Mr M D Tooke
204 Worplesdon Road, Guildford, Surrey, GU2 9UY
01483 576496 F 01483 452212
enquiries@horologicalworkshops.com
Est. 1968 *Stock size* Large
Stock Clocks, watches, barometers
Open Tues–Fri 8.30am–5.30pm Sat 9am–12.30pm
Services Valuations, restorations, shipping

Pew Corner Ltd (SALVO)
Contact David Bouldin
Artington Manor Farm, Old Portsmouth Road, Guildford, Surrey, GU3 1LP
01483 533337 F 01483 535554
pewcorner@pewcorner.co.uk
www.pewcorner.co.uk
Est. 1988 *Stock size* Large
Stock Period ecclesiastical interiors, furniture, hand-made furniture
Open Mon–Sat 10am–5pm Sun 11am–5pm

Thomas Thorp
Contact Mr J Thorp
170 High Street, Guildford, Surrey, GU1 3HP
01483 562770 F 01438 562770
www.thorpsbooks.co.uk
Est. 1883 *Stock size* Medium
Stock Antiquarian, rare and second-hand books
Open Mon–Sat 9am–5.30pm

Charles W Traylen (ABA)
Contact Mr C W Traylen
Castle House, 49–50 Quarry Street, Guildford, Surrey, GU1 3UA
01483 572424 F 01483 450048
Est. 1945 *Stock size* Large
Stock Antiquarian, rare and second-hand books
Open Tues–Sat 9am–5pm
Fairs Olympia Book Fair, Chelsea
Services Book search

HAM COMMON

Glencorse Antiques (LAPADA)
Contact Mr Prydal
321 Richmond Road, Ham Common, Surrey, KT2 5QU
020 8541 0871
M 07740 779917
Est. 1983 *Stock size* Medium
Stock 19thC furniture, Victorian, modern British paintings
Open Mon–Sat 10am–5.30pm
Fairs Olympia (Spring), Claridges (April), Harrogate (May)

HAMPTON WICK

Gill Parkin Furniture
Contact Mr D Beard
7 High Street, Hampton Wick, Kingston upon Thames, Surrey, KT1 4DA
020 8977 5402 F 020 8977 5403
Est. 1980 *Stock size* Medium
Stock Handcrafted 17th–18thC style oak and country furniture
Open Mon–Sat 9am–5.30pm or by appointment

HASLEMERE

Serendipity
Contact Mrs E Moore
7 Petworth Road, Haslemere, Surrey, GU27 2BJ
01428 642682
Est. 1997 *Stock size* Medium
No. of dealers 14
Stock Period, pine furniture, china, glass, books, maps, pictures, collectables
Open Mon–Sat 10am–5pm

West Street Antiques (LAPADA)
Contact Mr M Holden
8–10 West Street, Haslemere, Surrey, GU27 2AB
01428 644911 F 01428 645201
info@weststreetantiques.co.uk
www.weststreetantiques.co.uk
Est. 1998 *Stock size* Medium
Stock 17thC–early 20thC furniture, dinner services, maps, prints, Georgian and Victorian silver
Open Mon–Sat 9.30am–5pm
Services Valuations, restorations

Woods Wharf Antiques Market
Contact Mrs C Lunnon
56 High Street, Haslemere, Surrey, GU27 2LA
01428 642125 F 01428 642125
Est. 1975 *Stock size* Medium
No. of dealers 8
Stock Antiques, collectables
Open Mon–Sat 9.30am–5pm

HINDHEAD

Albany Antiques
Contact Mr T Winstanley
8–10 London Road, Hindhead, Surrey, GU26 6AF
01428 605528 F 01428 605528
M 07931 672345
Est. 1949 *Stock size* Large
Stock Georgian furniture, 18thC brass, Victorian antiques, porcelain, statuary
Open Mon–Sat 9.30am–5pm or by appointment

M J Bowdery (BADA)
Contact Mr Malcolm John Bowdery
12 London Road, Hindhead, Surrey, GU26 6AF
01428 606376
M 07774 821444
Est. 1970 *Stock size* Small
Stock 18th–19thC furniture
Open Mon–Sat 9am–1pm or by appointment
Fairs The Buxton Antiques Fair, Surrey Antiques Fair
Services Valuations

Drummonds Architectural Antiques Ltd (SALVO)
Contact Mr Drummond Shaw
The Kirkpatrick Buildings, 25 London Road, Hindhead, Surrey, GU26 6AB
☎ 01428 609444 Ⓕ 01428 609445
Ⓔ info@drummonds-arch.co.uk
Ⓦ www.drummonds-arch.co.uk
Est. 1989 *Stock size* Large
Stock Period bathrooms, oak and pine flooring, fireplaces, statues, garden furniture and lighting, brass door furniture and fittings, radiators, furniture, windows, doors, gates, railings, conservatories
Open Mon–Fri 9am–6pm Sat Sun 10am–5pm

Grayshott Pine
Contact Julia Dickens
5 Victoria Terrace, Crossways Road, Grayshott, Hindhead, Surrey, GU26 6HF
☎ 01428 607478
Est. 1960 *Stock size* Large
Stock Pine, painted furniture, kitchenware
Open Mon–Sat 10am–1pm 2–5pm closed Wed
Services Restorations

HORLEY

Surrey Antiques
Contact Mr M Bradnum
3 Central Parade, Massetts Road, Horley, Surrey, RH6 7PP
☎ 01293 775522
Est. 1989 *Stock size* Large
Stock Antiques, collectables, furniture, silver, china, glass, brass, linen, pictures, books
Open Mon–Sat 10am–5pm
Services House clearance

KINGSTON-UPON-THAMES

Glydon and Guess (NAG, NPA, GMC)
Contact Mr A Fleckney
14 Applemarket, Kingston-upon-Thames, Surrey, KT1 1JE
☎ 020 8546 3758 Ⓕ 020 8541 5743
Ⓔ glydonandguess@finegem.co.uk
Ⓦ www.finegem.co.uk
Est. 1940 *Stock size* Medium
Stock Jewellery, antique and modern furniture, clocks, barometers
Open Mon–Sat 9.30am–5pm
Services Valuations, restorations, pawnbrokers

The Kingston Antiques Centre
Contact Miss R Bean
29–31 London Road, Kingston-upon-Thames, Surrey, KT2 6ND
☎ 020 8549 2004 Ⓕ 020 8549 3839
Ⓔ enquiries@antiquesmarket.co.uk
Ⓦ www.kingstonantiquescentre.co.uk
Est. 1996 *Stock size* Large
No. of dealers 80
Stock Furniture, jewellery, porcelain, silver, pictures, 20thC design, lighting, Oriental
Open Mon–Sat 9.30am–6pm Sun 10am–6pm

LEATHERHEAD

Alan's Antiques
Contact Mr M Laikin
1–3 Church Street, Leatherhead, Surrey, KT22 8DN
☎ 01372 360646
Ⓔ michael.laikin@virgin.net
Est. 1989 *Stock size* Medium
Stock Period furniture, silver, porcelain, lighting, glass
Open Mon–Sat 9am–5.30pm closed Wed Sun
Fairs Sandown Park, Epsom Racecourse
Services Valuations, restorations

MERSTHAM

Elm House Antiques
3 High Street, Merstham, Redhill, Surrey, RH1 3BA
☎ 01737 643983
Est. 1995 *Stock size* Medium
Stock General antiques, decorative items, mahogany, oak, pine furniture
Open Mon–Sat 11am–6pm
Services Furniture and textile valuations, restorations

Geoffrey Van-Hay Antiques
Contact Geoffrey Van-Hay
The Old Smithy, 7 High Street, Merstham, Surrey, RH1 3BA
☎ 01737 645131 Ⓕ 01737 645131
Ⓔ olliev@hotmail.com
Est. 1992 *Stock size* Medium
Stock General antiques
Open Mon–Sat 9.30am–5.30pm
Services Valuations, restorations

OXTED

Books in the Basement
Contact Mr David Neal
Wagstaffs, 80–84 Station Road East, Oxted, Surrey, RH8 OPG
☎ 01883 723131
Est. 1999 *Stock size* Medium
Stock General second-hand books
Open Mon–Sat 9.30am–5.30pm
Fairs H & D, Titlepage

The Second-Hand Bookshop
Contact Mr David Neal
56 Station Road West, Oxted, Surrey, RH8 9EU
☎ 01883 715755
Est. 1994 *Stock size* Medium
Stock Rare and second-hand books, mainly non-fiction
Open Mon–Sat 10am–5pm
Fairs H & D, Titlepage
Services Valuations

PURLEY

Aladdin's Antiques
Contact Mrs I Ford
947 Brighton Road, Purley, Surrey, CR8 2BP
☎ 020 8668 5600
Est. 1997 *Stock size* Medium
Stock Porcelain, furniture, mirrors, pictures, collectables
Open Mon–Sat 10am–5.30pm closed Wed
Services Valuations

REDHILL

F G Lawrence and Son
Contact Mr C Lawrence
Rear of 89 Brighton Road, Redhill, Surrey, RH1 6PS
☎ 01737 764196 Ⓕ 01737 764196
Ⓜ 07850 787873
Ⓔ catherine.lawrence@btinternet.com
Est. 1890 *Stock size* Large
Stock Georgian, Edwardian and 1920s furniture
Open Mon–Fri 9am–5pm Sat 9am–1pm
Fairs Newark
Services Valuations, restorations

REIGATE

Knoller, Bertram
Contact Bertram Knoller
14a London Road, Reigate, Surrey, RH2 9HY
01737 242548
Est. 1970 *Stock size* Small
Stock Copper, brass, silver, fireplace accessories, lighting
Open Tues Thurs Sat 10am–5pm
Services Clock repairs, metal repairs and polishing

Reigate Galleries (PBFA)
Contact J S Morrish
45a Bell Street, Reigate, Surrey, RH2 7AQ
01737 246055
Est. 1958 *Stock size* Large
Stock Antiquarian, rare, second-hand books, antique engravings
Open Mon–Sat 9am–5.30pm Wed 9am–1pm
Fairs PBFA fairs in London

M & M White Antiques and Reproduction Centre
Contact Mr M White
57 High Street, Reigate, Surrey, RH2 9AE
01737 222331
Est. 1994 *Stock size* Medium
Stock Regency, Victorian, reproduction furniture
Open Mon–Sat 10am–5.30pm
Fairs Newark, Ardingly

RICHMOND

Antigone
Contact Mr S Bolster
3 Brewers Lane, Richmond, Surrey, TW9 1HH
020 8940 6894
07785 222082
Est. 1982 *Stock size* Large
Stock Antique jewellery, objects of virtue
Open Mon–Sat 10am–5pm
Services Valuations, probate

Antique Mart
Contact Mr G Katz
72–74 Hill Rise, Richmond, Surrey, TW10 6UB
020 8940 6942 020 8715 4668
07775 626423
Est. 1963 *Stock size* Medium
Stock 18th–19thC furniture
Open Thurs–Sun 2–5.15pm or by appointment

Andrew Davis Antiques
Contact Mr A Davis
6 Mortlake Terrace, Kew Green, Richmond, Surrey, TW9 3DT
020 8948 4911
07768 904041
Est. 1969 *Stock size* Medium
Stock General antiques, furniture, clocks, pictures, prints, ceramics, glass
Open Open most days and by appointment
Services Valuations, house clearance

The Gooday Gallery
Contact Mrs D Gooday
14 Richmond Hill, Richmond, Surrey, TW10 6QX
020 8940 8652 07710 124540
goodaygallery@aol.com
Est. 1971 *Stock size* Medium
Stock Arts and Crafts, Art Nouveau, Art Deco, postmodernism, tribal art, African and Oceanic masks
Open Thurs–Sat 11am–5pm or by appointment
Services Valuations

Hill Rise Antiques (LAPADA)
Contact Patrick Hinde
26 Hill Rise, Richmond, Surrey, TW10 6UA
020 8332 2941
antiques@hillrisehouse.com
www.hillrisehouse.com/antiques
Est. 1978 *Stock size* Medium
Stock 18th–19thC mahogany, walnut, rosewood furniture and accessories
Open Mon Tues Thurs Fri Sat 10.30am–5.30 Wed by appointment Sun 2.30–5.30pm

Lionel Jacobs (NAG)
Contact Tom French
12–14 Brewers Lane, Richmond, Surrey, TW9 1HH
020 8940 8069 020 8332 1841
lioneljames@lioneljames.com
www. lioneljames.com
Est. 1977 *Stock size* Medium
Stock Antique fine jewellery, silver, watches
Open Tues–Sat 10am–5pm
Services Valuations, jewllery and watch repair

F and T Lawson Antiques
Contact Mr Lawson
13 Hill Rise, Richmond, Surrey, TW10 6UQ
020 8940 0461
Est. 1965 *Stock size* Medium
Stock Furniture, collectables, brass, copper, costume jewellery, china
Open Mon–Sat 11am–5.30pm closed Wed
Services Valuations

Linden Antique Prints
Contact Mr M Synan
1a Church Court, Richmond, Surrey, TW9 1JL
020 8332 7019
020 8223 26516
martin@lindenprints.com
www.lindenprints.com
Est. 1997 *Stock size* Medium
Stock Antique prints, maps, watercolours
Open Mon–Fri 10.30am–5.30pm or by appointment
Fairs Royal National

Marryat Antiques Ltd (LAPADA)
Contact Mrs M Samuels
88 Sheen Road, Richmond, Surrey, TW9 1UF
020 8332 0262
Est. 1990 *Stock size* Large
Stock Furniture, pictures, silver, porcelain, Oriental antiques
Open Mon–Fri 10am–5.30pm Sat 9.30am–5.30pm Sun by appointment
Services Restorations

Richmond Hill Antiques
Contact Mrs M Hobson
82 Hill Rise, Richmond, Surrey, TW10 6UB
020 8940 5755 020 8940 5755
07909 912382
richmondhillant@hotmail.com
Est. 1970 *Stock size* Medium
Stock Georgian and Victorian furniture
Open Mon Thurs Fri noon–4pm Sat 10.30am–5.30pm Sun 1.30–5.30pm Tues Wed by appointment
Services Valuations, restorations, shipping

Succession
Contact Michael John
✉ **18 Richmond Hill, Richmond, Surrey, TW10 6QX**
☎ 020 8940 6774
Ⓜ 07885 275694
Est. 1969 *Stock size* Medium
Stock Art Nouveau, Art Deco, furniture, bronzes, glass, pictures
Open Fri Sat 11am–6pm
Sun 1–6pm or by appointment
Fairs Olympia Spring, 20thC Specialist Fair

Town & Country Decorative
Contact Benson Charlton
✉ **24 Hill Rise, Richmond, Surrey, PW10 6BA**
☎ 020 8948 4638
Est. 1999 *Stock size* Medium
No. of dealers 6
Stock French decorative, gardenalia, 1950–1970s collectables
Open Mon–Sun 10.30am–5.30pm

Vellantiques
Contact S Vella
✉ **127 Kew Road, Richmond, Surrey, TW9 2PN** Ⓟ
☎ 020 8940 5392
Est. 1983 *Stock size* Large
Stock Furniture, pictures, jewellery
Open Mon–Sat 10am–6pm
Fairs Ardingly, Kempton
Services Valuations

RIPLEY

J Hartley Antiques Ltd (LAPADA)
Contact Mr J Hartley
✉ **186 High Street, Ripley, Woking, Surrey, GU23 6BB** Ⓟ
☎ 01483 224318
Est. 1973 *Stock size* Medium
Stock Antique furniture
Open Mon–Fri 9am–6pm
Sat 9.30am–5pm
Services Free local delivery

The Lamp Gallery
Contact Graham Jones
✉ **Talbot Walk Antique Centre, Talbot Hotel, High Street, Ripley, Surrey, GU23 6BB** Ⓟ
☎ 01483 211724 Ⓕ 01483 211724
Est. 1986 *Stock size* Medium
Stock Interior lighting, including Art Nouveau and Art Deco lamps
Open Mon–Sat 10am–5pm
Sun 11am–4pm or by appointment
Services Valuations, shipping

Ripley Antiques (LAPADA)
Contact Mrs H Denham
✉ **67 High Street, Ripley, Surrey, GU23 6AX** Ⓟ
☎ 01483 224981 Ⓕ 01483 224333
Est. 1959 *Stock size* Large
Stock Large showrooms specializing in English and French 18th–19thC furniture, decorative items for trade and export
Open Mon–Sat 9.30am–5.30pm
Services Shipping

Talbot Walk Antique Centre
Contact Graham Jones
✉ **Talbot Hotel, High Street, Ripley, Surrey, GU23 6BB** Ⓟ
☎ 01483 211724 Ⓕ 01483 211724
Est. 1999 *Stock size* Medium
No. of dealers 40
Stock Interior lighting, including Art Nouveau and Art Deco lamps, general antiques, furniture
Open Mon–Sat 10am–5pm
Sun 11am–4pm
Services Valuations, restorations, shipping

Anthony Welling (BADA)
Contact Mr A Welling
✉ **Broadway Barn, High Street, Ripley, Woking, Surrey, GU23 6AQ** Ⓟ
☎ 01483 225384 Ⓕ 01483 225384
Est. 1970 *Stock size* Medium
Stock Large 17th–18thC oak, country furniture
Open Mon–Sat 9.30am–5pm
Services Valuations, restorations

RUNFOLD

The Antiques Warehouse
Contact Mrs H Burroughs
✉ **Badshot Farm, St Georges Road, Runfold, Farnham, Surrey, GU9 9HY** Ⓟ
☎ 01252 317590 Ⓕ 01252 879751
Ⓔ prjb01@globalnet.co.uk
Est. 1995 *Stock size* Large
No. of dealers 40
Stock Wide variety of antiques including militaria, glass, silver, china, furniture, paintings, prints, garden artefacts
Open Mon–Sun 10am–5.30pm including Bank Holidays
Services Restorations, caning

The Packhouse Antiques Centre
Contact Lynn or Geoff Lackford
✉ **Hewetts Kilns, Tongham Road, Runfold, Farnham, Surrey, GU10 1PQ** Ⓟ
☎ 01252 781010 Ⓕ 01252 783876
Ⓦ www.packhouse.com
Est. 1990 *Stock size* Large
No. of dealers 109
Stock Furniture, collectables, garden artefacts, clocks, paintings, mirrors
Open Mon–Fri 10.30am–5.30pm
Sat–Sun 10am–5.30pm
Services Delivery service, finders file

SHERE

Helena's Collectables
Contact Mrs H Lee
✉ **Middle Street, Shere, Guildford, Surrey, GU5 9HF** Ⓟ
☎ 01483 203039 Ⓕ 01483 203039
Ⓔ helena@collectables.demon.co.uk
Ⓦ www.collectables.demon.co.uk
Est. 1996 *Stock size* Large
Stock Royal Worcester, Wedgwood, Coalport, Doulton, Beswick, classic Disney, porcelain, collectable ceramics
Open Mon–Sat 9.30am–5.30pm
Sun 10.30am–4.30pm
Services Mail order service

Shere Antiques Centre
Contact Mrs Jean Watson
✉ **Middle Street, Shere, Guildford, Surrey, GU5 9HF** Ⓟ
☎ 01483 202846 Ⓕ 01483 830762
Est. 1987 *Stock size* Large
Stock Majolica, flow blue, Continental ceramics, chintz, silver, antique furniture, maps, prints
Open Mon–Fri 10am–5pm Sat Sun 11am–5pm or by appointment
Services Restorations, shipping, house clearance

SOUTH HOLMWOOD

Holmwood Antiques
Contact R Dewdney
Charlwyns, Norfolk Road, South Holmwood, Dorking, Surrey, RH5 4LA
01306 888468 F 01306 742636
Est. 1968
Stock General antiques
Open Mon–Fri 9am–6pm or by appointment
Services Restorations

SURBITON

Cockrell Antiques
Contact Peter or Sheila Cockrell
278 Ewell Road, Surbiton, Surrey, KT6 7AG
020 8390 8290
W www.cockrellantiques.co.uk
Est. 1984 *Stock size* Large
Stock General antiques, mainly furniture
Open Mon–Sat 9am–6pm
Services Valuations

Maple Antiques
Contact Lynda or Geof Morris
4 Maple Road, Surbiton, Surrey, KT6 4AB
020 8399 6718
Est. 1981 *Stock size* Medium
Stock Mahogany, pine, oak, walnut furniture, mirrors, rugs, garden art
Open Mon–Sat 10am–5.30pm
Fairs Ardingly, Kempton Park
Services Valuations

Laurence Tauber Antiques
Contact Laurence Tauber
131 Ewell Road, Surbiton, Surrey, KT6 6AL
020 8390 0020
M 07710 443293
Est. 1973 *Stock size* Large
Stock 19thC–1930s Continental and decorative items
Trade only Yes
Open By appointment

TADWORTH

Ian Caldwell (LAPADA)
Contact Mr I Caldwell
9a The Green, Dorking Road, Tadworth, Surrey, KT20 5SQ
01737 813969
E caldwell.antiques@virgin.net
W www.lapada.co.uk/homepages/2486.htm
Est. 1978 *Stock size* Medium
Stock Town furniture, from William and Mary to Edwardian
Open Mon–Sat 10am–5pm closed Wed
Services Valuations, restorations

F and R Restorations
Contact Mr G R Fisher
39b Walton Street, Tadworth, Surrey, KT20 7RR
01737 819918 F 01737 819518
E fandr.restoration@virgin.net
W www.fandrrestorations.co.uk
Est. 1999 *Stock size* Medium
Stock Antique and contemporary design furniture
Open Mon–Sat 8.30am–6pm

THAMES DITTON

Clifford and Roger Dade
Contact Mr R Dade
Boldre House, Weston Green, Hampton Court Way, Thames Ditton, Surrey, KT7 0JP
020 8398 6293 F 020 8398 6293
M 07932 158949
Est. 1937 *Stock size* Medium
Stock Georgian furniture, particularly mahogany
Open Sat 9.30am–5pm or by appointment

WALLINGTON

An-Toy-Ques
Contact Mrs Britt Grace
85 Stafford Road, Wallington, Surrey, SM6 9AP
020 8288 8124 M 077 478 31043
E antoyques@tinyworld.co.uk
Est. 1994 *Stock size* Large
Stock Old toys including dolls, dolls' houses, bears, trains, lead figures
Open Tues–Sat 10.30am–5pm closed Wed
Fairs Sandown Park, Train fairs, Reading Vintage
Services Valuations, restorations

WALTON-ON-THAMES

Antique Church Furnishings (SALVO)
Contact Mr L Skilling
Rivernook Farm, Sunnyside, Walton-on-Thames, Surrey, KT12 2ET
01932 252736 F 01932 252736
E antchurch@aol.com
W www.churchantiques.com
Est. 1989 *Stock size* Large
Stock Church furniture, fixtures and fittings
Open Mon–Fri 10am–6pm

Chancellors Church Furnishings (SALVO)
Contact Mr S Williams
Rivernook Farm, Sunnyside, Walton-on-Thames, Surrey, KT12 2ET
01932 230284 F 01932 230284
M 07973 139308
E antchurch@aol.com
W www.churchantiques.com
Est. 1992 *Stock size* Large
Stock All pre-war church furnishings, fixtures and fittings
Open Mon–Fri 10am–6pm

WARLINGHAM

Trengove Antiques
Contact Mr B Trengove
397 Limpsfield Road, Warlingham, Surrey, CR6 9LA
01883 624422
Est. 1900 *Stock size* Large
Stock Small pieces of furniture, china, glass, silver, objets d'art
Open Thurs Fri 10am–12.30pm

WEST BYFLEET

Academy Billiard Company
Contact Robert Donachie
5 Camp Hill Industrial Estate, Camp Hill Road, West Byfleet, Surrey, KT14 6EW
01932 352067 F 01932 353904
Est. 1983 *Stock size* Large
Stock Antique and modern games room equipment
Open By appointment
Services Valuations, restorations, shipping

WEYBRIDGE

Ariel Antiques
Contact Mrs Pat Harvey or Gail Rees
89 Queens Road, Weybridge, Surrey, KT13 9UQ
01932 850135
E gailrees@compuserve.com

Est. 1994 *Stock size* Medium
Stock Furniture, porcelain, mirrors, silver, jewellery, clocks
Open Mon–Sat 10am–5pm closed Wed
Services Porcelain, furniture restorations, clock repairs

Church House Antiques (LAPADA)
Contact Mary Foster
42 Church Street, Weybridge, Surrey, KT13 8DP
01932 842190
Est. 1886 *Stock size* Medium
Stock Antique jewellery, furniture, silver, decorative accessories
Open Thurs–Sat 10am–5.30pm

The Clockshop
Contact Mr A Forster
64 Church Street, Weybridge, Surrey, KT13 8DL
01932 855503 F 01932 840407
Est. 1969 *Stock size* Large
Stock Antique clocks, barometers
Open Mon–Sat 10am–6pm closed Wed
Services Restorations

Not Just Silver (NAG)
Contact Susan Hughes
16 York Road, Weybridge, Surrey, KT13 9DT
01932 842468 F 01932 830054
M 07774 298151
E sales@not-just-silver.com
W www.not-just-silver.com
Est. 1969 *Stock size* Medium
Stock Silver
Open Mon–Sat 9.30am–5.30pm
Services Valuations, restorations

Village Antiques
Contact Barry Mulvany
39 St Marys Road, Weybridge, Surrey, KT13 9PT
01932 846554
M 07803 372399
W www.villantiques.co.uk
Est. 1980 *Stock size* Medium
Stock Mahogany, pine furniture, silver
Open Mon–Sat 10am–3pm

WHYTELEAFE

Modellers Loft
Contact Mr A Hall
4 Wellesley Parade, Godstone Road, Whyteleafe, Surrey, CR3 0BL
01883 625417 F 01883 625417
E info@modellersloft.co.uk
W www.modellersloft.co.uk
Est. 1980 *Stock size* Large
Stock Action Man, both old and new, soldiers, Dinky, Corgi, Scalextric, railways, all scale, Star Wars, sci-fi collectables
Open Mon–Sat 9am–5.15pm
Fairs Lee Valley Park, Sandown Park

WOKING

Barbers Fine Art Auctioneers (West Sussex Estate Agents, Surveyors and Auctioneers)
Contact Mr K Mansfield
Mayford Centre, Mayford Green, Woking, Surrey, GU22 0PP
01483 728939 F 01483 762552
Est. 1971
Open Mon–Sat 9am–1pm
Sales General and fine art sales. Please telephone for further details
Frequency Every 5–6 weeks
Catalogues Yes

Ewbank Fine Art Auctioneers (SOFAA)
Contact Mr C T J Ewbank
Burnt Common Auction Rooms, London Road, Send, Woking, Surrey, GU23 7LN
01483 223101 F 01483 222171
E antiques@ewbankauctions.co.uk
W www.ewbankauctions.co.uk
Est. 1994
Open Mon–Fri 9.30am–5pm
Sales 4 antiques sales and 14 sales of Victorian and later furnishings annually, viewing Tues week of sale 2–5pm and Wed 10am–8pm. Phone for sale details
Frequency Monthly
Catalogues Yes

Philip Gilbert
Contact Mr P Gilbert
77 High Street, Horsell, Woking, Surrey, GU21 4UA
01483 756807
E philip@pgilbert.fsnet.co.uk
Est. 1975 *Stock size* Small
Stock Georgian–Edwardian furniture
Open Mon–Fri 10.30am–5.30pm Sat 10am–1pm
Services Restorations

Goldsworth Books and Prints (PBFA)
Contact Mr Brian Hartles
47 Goldsworth Road, Woking, Surrey, GU21 1JY
01483 767670 F 01483 767670
E goldsworth@cwcom.net
Est. 1986 *Stock size* Medium
Stock Antiquarian, rare and second-hand books, antiquarian maps, books illustrated by Arthur Rackham a speciality
Open Tues–Sat 10am–5pm Sat 9am–4.30pm
Fairs Russell Hotel, London, York National
Services Worldwide book search

WEST SUSSEX

ARDINGLY

Ardingly Antiques
Contact Mary Burke
64 High Street, Ardingly, West Sussex, RH 17 6TD
01444 892680
Est. 1990 *Stock size* Medium
Stock General antiques and collectables
Open Mon–Sun 2–5.30pm closed Tues
Fairs Ardingly, Sandown Park

Rocking Horse Antique Market
Contact Mrs J Livett or Mr P Livett
16 High Street, Ardingly, West Sussex, RH17 7TD
01444 892205
Est. 1993 *Stock size* Large
No. of dealers 20
Stock Antiques, collectables, books, ephemera
Open Mon–Sat 9.30am–5.30pm Sun 10am–5.30pm 5pm during Winter

ARUNDEL

Antiquities
Contact Mr Ian Fenwick or Mrs Christina Fenwick
5–7 Tarrant Street, Arundel, West Sussex, BN18 9DG
01903 884355 F 01903 884355
E antiquities@btconnect.com
Est. 1991 *Stock size* Large
Stock 19thC English and French furniture, decorative items, majolica, blue-and-white pottery, pond boats, French mirrors

Trade only Trade and export, public by appointment
Open Mon–Sat 10am–5pm or by appointment
Services Shipping, major credit cards accepted

Arundel Antique Galleries
Contact Herbert Smith
Castle Mews, Tarrant Street, Arundel, West Sussex, BN18 9DG
01903 883066
Est. 1980 *Stock size* Medium
Stock Georgian–Edwardian furniture
Open Mon–Sat 10.30am–4.30pm Sun 2.30–4.30pm

Arundel Antiques Centre
51 High Street, Arundel, West Sussex, BN18 9AJ
01903 882749
Est. 1975
No. of dealers 30
Stock Furniture, china, silver, porcelain, general antiques
Open Mon–Sun 10am–5pm
Services Valuations

The Arundel Bookshop
Contact G or A Shepherd
10 High Street, Arundel, West Sussex, BN18 9AB
01903 882680
Est. 1977 *Stock size* Medium
Stock Rare, antiquarian, second-hand books
Open Mon–Sat 9.30am–1pm 2.15–5.30pm

Arundel Clocks
Contact Mr Henderson
Lasseters Corner, 8A High Street, Arundel, West Sussex, BN18 9AE
01903 884525
arundelclockman@btinternet.com
Est. 1979 *Stock size* Medium
Stock Clocks, watches, barometers, barographs
Open Mon–Sat 10am–1pm 2.15–5pm
Services Restorations

Baynton-Williams
Contact Sarah or Roger Baynton-Williams
37A High Street, Arundel, West Sussex, BN18 9AG
01903 883588 F 01903 883588
gallery@baynton-williams.freeserve.co.uk
www.baynton-williams.com
Est. 1946 *Stock size* Medium
Stock Antiquarian maps, prints, decorative and botanical
Open Mon–Sat 10am–6pm or by appointment
Services Valuations

Castle Antiques
Contact Mr J Hughes
34 High Street, Arundel, West Sussex, BN18 9AB
01903 882208
Est. 1990 *Stock size* Medium
Stock Georgian–Edwardian furniture
Open Mon–Sat 10am–5pm

Decorum
Contact Caroline Baker
9 Tarrant Street, Arundel, West Sussex, BN18 9DG
01903 884436 F 01903 889527
caroline@decorum-arundel.co.uk
Est. 1989 *Stock size* Medium
Stock French furniture and antiques
Open Mon–Sun 10am–5pm

The Jolly Pedlars
Contact Mr Travers
43 High Street, Arundel, West Sussex, BN18 9AG
01903 884401 F 01903 723381
Est. 1982 *Stock size* Medium
Stock General antiques, collectables, toys, dolls
Open Mon–Sun 10.30am–4.30pm

The Old Cornstore Antiques Centre
Contact Peter Francis
31 High Street, Arundel, West Sussex, BN18 9AG
01903 885456 F 01903 892481
Est. 2001 *Stock size* Large
No. of dealers 30
Stock Georgian–Edwardian furniture, jewellery, ceramics, silver, paintings, clocks
Open Mon–Sat 10am–5pm Sun 11am–5pm closed Wed
Services Valuations, shipping

Old Maps
Contact Mr K R Goddard
59 High Street, Arundel, West Sussex, BN18 9AJ
01903 882522
Est. 1975 *Stock size* Medium
Stock Maps, prints
Open Mon–Sun 10am–5pm
Services Valuations

Passageway Antiques
Contact J Saxon
18 High Street, Arundel, West Sussex, BN18 9AB
01903 884602
Est. 1994 *Stock size* Large
Stock Antiques, collectables
Open Mon–Sat 10am–5pm Sun 11am–5pm
Services Valuations

Spencer Swaffer (LAPADA)
Contact Spencer Swaffer
30 High Street, Arundel, West Sussex, BN18 9AB
01903 882132 F 01903 884564
spencerswaffer@btconnect.com
Est. 1974 *Stock size* Large
Stock Eclectic mix of decorative items
Open Mon–Sat 9am–6pm Sun 10am–6pm

Tarrant Street Antique Centre
Contact Louis de Marigny
Nineveh House, Tarrant Street, Arundel, West Sussex, BN18 9DJ
01903 884307
Est. 1989 *Stock size* Large
No. of dealers 14
Stock Furniture, clocks, jewellery, brass, silver, porcelain, French antique furniture
Open Mon–Fri 10am–5pm Sat 9.30am–5pm Sun 11am–5pm

The Walking Stick Shop
Contact Stuart Thompson
8 & 9 The Old Printing Works, Tarrant Street, Arundel, West Sussex, BN18 9JH
01903 883796
www.walkingsticks.uk.com
Est. 1978 *Stock size* Large
Stock Walking sticks
Open Mon–Sat 9am–5.30pm

BALCOMBE

Woodall & Emery Ltd
Contact Mrs Chinn
Haywards Heath Road, Balcombe, Haywards Heath, West Sussex, RH17 6PG
01444 811608 F 01444 811608
Est. 1860 *Stock size* Large

Stock Antique lighting, chandeliers, table lights, lanterns
Open Mon–Sat 10am–5pm closed Wed

BARNHAM

Howard's Reclamation
Contact Craig Howard
The Yard, Lake Lane, Barnham, West Sussex, PO22 0AE
01243 552095
howardsreclaim@callnetuk.com
Est. 1971 *Stock size* Large
Stock Old and new planked timber floors, oak beams, oak sleepers, telegraph poles, bricks, doors, stone, fireplaces and architectural antiquities
Open Mon–Fri 9am–1pm 2–5pm Sat 8am–1pm closed Wed

BILLINGSHURST

Great Grooms Antique Centre
Contact Mr J Podger
Great Grooms, Parbrook, Billingshurst, West Sussex, RH14 9EU
01403 786202 01403 786224
antiques@great-grooms.co.uk
www.great-grooms.co.uk
Est. 1993 *Stock size* Large
Stock Furniture, porcelain, jewellery, silver, glass, pictures
Open Mon–Sat 9.30am–5.30pm Sun 10am–6pm
Services Valuations, restorations, interior design

Old House Antiques Centre
Contact Mr D Jull
Adversane, Billingshurst, West Sussex, RH14 9JJ
01403 782186
Est. 1976 *Stock size* Medium
Stock Antiques, collectables
Open Mon–Sun 10am–5pm

The Old Orchard Antique Market
Contact Jean or Sheila
Old House, Adversane, Billingshurst, West Sussex, RH14 9JF
01403 783594
Est. 1985 *Stock size* Medium
Stock China, glass, collectables
Open Mon–Sun 10am–5pm

Sotheby's South
Summers Place, Billingshurst, West Sussex, RH14 9AD
01403 833500 01403 833696
www.sothebys.com
Est. 1744
Open Mon–Fri 9.30am–1pm 2.15–4.30pm
Sales Garden statuary sales in May and September. Valuations given for items to be sold in London saleroom
Frequency Twice a year
Catalogues Yes

BIRDHAM

Whitestone Farm Antiques
Contact Carey Mordue
Whitestone Farm, Main Road, Birdham, Chichester, West Sussex, PO20 7HU
01243 513706
antiques@whitestonefarm.force9.co.uk
Est. 1970 *Stock size* Large
Stock 18th–20thC furniture and objets d'art
Open Mon–Sat 10am–5.30pm

BOSHAM

Mr Pickett's
Contact Mr M Pickett
Top Barn, Old Park Lane, Bosham, Nr Chichester, West Sussex, PO18 8EX
01243 574573 01243 572255
07779 997012
info@mrpicketts.com
www.mrpicketts.com
Est. 1991 *Stock size* Large
Stock Victorian pine furniture
Open Mon–Fri 8am–5pm Sat 8am–4pm Sun by appointment
Services Stripping, restoration, bespoke pine furniture

BUCKS GREEN

Music Room Antiques (BADA)
Contact Andrew Lancaster
School House, Bucks Green, Horsham, West Sussex, RH12 3JP
01403 822189 01403 823089
07744 986926
andrew@musicroomantiques.co.uk
www.musicroomantiques.co.uk
Est. 1986 *Stock size* Medium
Stock Square pianos and associated music-related antiques
Open By appointment
Fairs BADA, Harrogate Antique Fair
Services Restorations

BURGESS HILL

British Antique Replicas
22 School Close, Queen Elizabeth Avenue, Burgess Hill, West Sussex, RH15 9RX
01444 245577 01444 232014
www.1760.com
Est. 1963 *Stock size* Large
Stock English antique replica furniture
Open Mon–Sat 9am–5.30pm
Services Restoration of antique furniture

Recollect The Dolls Hospital
Contact Paul Jago
17 Junction Road, Burgess Hill, West Sussex, RH15 0HR
01444 871052 01444 871052
dollshopuk@aol.com
Est. 1973 *Stock size* Medium
Stock Antique dolls
Open Tues–Fri 10am–4pm Sat 10am–1pm or by appointment
Services Restoration of dolls

CHICHESTER

Henry Adams Fine Art Auctioneers (ARVA, SOFA)
Contact Kate Lawson-Paul
Baffins Hall, Baffins Lane, Chichester, West Sussex, PO19 1UA
01243 532223 01243 532299
enquiries@henryadamsfineart.co.uk
www.henryadamsfineart.co.uk
Est. 2000
Open Mon–Fri 9am–5.30pm
Sales Antiques and fine art
Frequency Six weekly
Catalogues Yes

Almshouse Arcade
Contact Mrs V Barnet
19 The Hornet, Chichester, West Sussex, PO19 7JL
01243 528089 01423 778126
www.almshousearcade.co.uk
Est. 1977 *Stock size* Medium
Stock Toys, china, furniture, automobilia
Open Mon–Sat 10am–4.30pm

Antics
Contact Peter German
19 The Hornet, Chichester, West Sussex, PO19 4JL
01243 786327
Est. 1981 *Stock size* Small
Stock General antiques
Open Mon–Sat 9am–4pm

Antiques and Bygones
Contact Mrs M Haydon
24 The Buttermarket, North Street, Chichester, West Sussex, PO19 1LQ
01243 788071
Est. 1975 *Stock size* Medium
Stock China, glass, collectors' items
Open Tues–Sat 10am–4pm

Barnett Antiques
Contact Mrs U Barnett
Unit 1, Almshouse Arcade, 19 The Hornet, Chichester, West Sussex, PO19 4JL
01243 528089
Est. 1970 *Stock size* Medium
Stock Furniture, china, toys
Open Mon–Sat 10am–4.30pm

Canon Gate Bookshop (PBFA)
Contact W or P Pegler
28 South Street, Chichester, West Sussex, PO19 1EL
01243 778477
Est. 1980 *Stock size* Medium
Stock Rare, antiquarian, second-hand books
Open Mon–Sat 10.30am–5pm

Canute Antiques
Contact Wendy Rowden
Bosham Walk, Bosham Lane, Chichester, West Sussex, PO18 8HX
01243 576111
Est. 1977 *Stock size* Small
Stock Silver, jewellery, porcelain and collectors' items
Open Mon–Sun 10am–5.30pm

Chichester Antiques Centre
Contact Michael Carter
46–48 The Hornet, Chichester, West Sussex, PO19 4JG
01243 530100
www.antiqueschichester.com
Est. 1994 *Stock size* Large
No. of dealers 40
Stock General antiques, collectables, 18th–20thC furniture
Open Mon–Sat 10am–5pm
Sun 11am–5pm
Services Valuations

The Chichester Bookshop
Contact Mr N Howell
39 Southgate, Chichester, West Sussex, PO19 1DP
01243 785473
chibooks@supanet.com
Est. 1965 *Stock size* Large
Stock Rare, second-hand books, specialists in railway books, Sussex books, maps, prints
Open Mon–Sat 9.30am–5pm
Services Book search

Gems
Contact Maureen Hancock
39 West Street, Chichester, West Sussex, PO19 1RP
01243 786173 01243 778865
Est. 1985 *Stock size* Large
Stock Edwardian furniture, dolls, Staffordshire, Dresden
Open Tues–Sat 10am–1pm 2.30–5pm or by other appointment
Services Restorations

Peter Hancock
Contact Peter Hancock
40 West Street, Chichester, West Sussex, PO19 1RP
01243 786173 01243 778865
Est. 1965 *Stock size* Large
Stock A comprehensive range of antiques and collectables
Open Tues–Sat 10am–1pm 2.15–5.30pm or by appointment
Services Restorations

Heirloom Antiques
Contact Alan Hayes
57 Pound Farm Road, Chichester, West Sussex, PO19 2LU
01243 530489
Est. 1986 *Stock size* Large
Stock Furniture, collectables, curios
Open Mon–Sat 9.30am–5pm
Sun 11am–4pm
Fairs Goodwood, Kempton

Heritage Antiques
Contact Mr D Grover
77d, 83 & 84 St Pancras, Chichester, West Sussex, PO19 4LS
01243 783796
Est. 1987 *Stock size* Medium
Stock Georgian–Edwardian, 1920s furniture
Open Mon–Sat 9am–5.30pm

W D Priddy Antiques, Chichester Furniture Warehouse
Contact Mr W D Priddy
Unit 6, Terminus Mill, Terminus Road, Chichester, West Sussex, PO19 2UN
01243 783960 01243 783960
07712 002371
bill@priddyantiques.fsnet.co.uk
www.priddyantiques.co.uk
Est. 1983 *Stock size* Medium
Stock Georgian–Edwardian furniture
Open Mon–Fri 10am–4pm
Sat 10am–5pm variable Sundays 11am–4pm or by appointment

St Pancras Antiques
Contact Mr R Willatt
150 St Pancras, Chichester, West Sussex, PO19 5SH
01243 787645
Est. 1980 *Stock size* Medium
Stock Arms, armour, pre-1800 furniture, ceramics, numismatics, militaria
Open Mon–Sat 9.30am–5pm
Thurs 9.30am–1pm
Services Valuations

Stride & Son
Contact Mr M Hewitt or Mr K Warne
Southdown House, St Johns Street, Chichester, West Sussex, PO19 1XQ
01243 780207 01243 786713
stride-auctions@cyberquest.co.uk
www.strideandson.co.uk
Est. 1890
Open Mon–Fri 9am–5.30pm closed 1–2pm
Sales Monthly sale of general antiques, periodic book auctions
Frequency Monthly
Catalogues Yes

COCKING

The Victorian Brass Bedstead Co
Contact David Woolley
Hoe Copse, Cocking, Midhurst, West Sussex, GU29 0HL
01730 812287
toria@netcomuk.co.uk

Est. 1982 *Stock size* Large
Stock Brass and iron bedsteads, mattresses, bases, quilts
Open Mon–Sun By appointment
Services Valuations, restorations

CUCKFIELD

David Foord-Brown Antiques (LAPADA, BADA)
Contact David Foord-Brown
3 Bank Buildings, High Street, Cuckfield, West Sussex, RH17 5JU
☎ 01444 414418 Ⓜ 07850 188250
Est. 1988 *Stock size* Large
Stock 18th–19thC furniture, porcelain, silver, glass
Open Mon–Sat 10am–5.30pm and by appointment
Fairs BADA Fair

Richard Usher Antiques
Contact Richard Usher
23 South Street, Cuckfield, West Sussex, RH17 5LB
☎ 01444 451699
Est. 1978 *Stock size* Small
Stock Furniture and decorative items
Open Mon–Sat 10am–5pm closed Wed Sat pm

DIAL POST

de Montfort Antiques (LAPADA)
Contact Mr Alexander Stone
Dial Post House, Dial Post, Nr Horsham, West Sussex, RH13 8NQ
☎ 01403 713388 Ⓕ 01493 713388
Ⓜ 07860 632822
Ⓔ alexander@demontfortantiques.fsnet.co.uk
Est. 1965 *Stock size* Large
Stock Oak furniture, Italian furniture, Delft, English and Dutch majolica, treen
Open By appointment only
Fairs Olympia, LAPADA, Guildford, Goodwood

DITCHLING

Dycheling Antiques
Contact Mrs E A Hudson
34 High Street, Ditchling, West Sussex, BN6 8TA
☎ 01273 842929
Ⓜ 07785 456341
Ⓔ hudson@icsgroup.demon.co.uk
Est. 1979 *Stock size* Large
Stock Sets of Georgian–Victorian dining furniture, upholstered furniture, chiffoniers, dining tables
Open Tues Thurs–Sat 10.30am–5.30pm or by appointment
Services Chair search service

HAYWARDS HEATH

Roundabout Antiques
Contact Angie Craik
7 Commercial Square, Haywards Heath, West Sussex, RH16 1DW
☎ 01273 835926 Ⓕ 01273 835659
Ⓔ roundabout@mistral.co.uk
Est. 1993 *Stock size* Medium
Stock Collectables, silver, jewellery, furniture, musical instruments
Open Mon–Sat 9.30am–5.30pm

HENFIELD

Ashcombe Coach House Antiques (BADA, CINOA)
Contact Mr Roy Green
PO Box No 2527, Brighton Road, Henfield, West Sussex, BN5 9SU
☎ 01273 491630 Ⓕ 01273 491630
Ⓜ 07803 180098
Ⓔ sharon@anglocontinental.fsnet.co.uk
Est. 1953 *Stock size* Large
Stock 18th–early 19thC furniture, decorative objects
Open By appointment only
Fairs Olympia, BADA

Henfield Antiques and Collectables
Contact Mrs D Evans
2 Commercial Buildings, High Street, Henfield, West Sussex, BN5 9DE
☎ 01273 495300
Est. 1999 *Stock size* Large
Stock Kitchenware, pine furniture, Beswick, Wade
Open Mon–Sun 10.30am–5pm
Services Verbal valuations

HORSHAM

Denham's
Contact Kate Tyekiff or Louise Shelley
The Auction Galleries, Warnham, Horsham, West Sussex, RH12 3RZ
☎ 01403 255699 Ⓕ 01403 253837
Ⓔ denhams@lineone.net
Ⓦ www.invaluable.com/denhams
Est. 1884
Open Mon–Thurs 9am–5.30pm Fri 9am–5pm Sat 9am–noon
Sales Sales of antiques and collectors' items every four weeks
Frequency Every 4 weeks
Catalogues Yes

The Horsham Antiques Centre
Contact Mr T Costin
7–9 Park Place, Horsham, West Sussex, RH12 1DF
☎ 01403 259181 Ⓕ 01403 259181
Est. 1997 *Stock size* Large
No. of dealers 25
Stock Furniture, pictures, pottery, toys, porcelain, glass, silver, jewellery, other collectables
Open Tues–Sat 10am–5.30pm Sun 10.30am–4pm

The Horsham Bookshop
Contact Mr T Costin
4 Park Place, Horsham, West Sussex, RH12 1DG
☎ 01403 252187
Ⓔ horshambs@btinternet.com
Ⓦ www.horshambookshop.com
Est. 1986 *Stock size* Medium
Stock Rare, antiquarian and second-hand books, cricket, aviation a speciality
Open Tues–Sat 9.30am–5.15pm
Services Book search

Murray and Kemmett
Contact J Murray
102 Bishopric, Horsham, West Sussex, RH12 1QN
☎ 01403 254847
Est. 1980 *Stock size* Medium
Stock Rare, second-hand books, crime fiction, religious books a speciality
Open Mon–Sat 9.15am–1pm 2–5pm
Services Book search

HOUGHTON

Stable Antiques at Houghton
Contact Ian Wadey
Main Road (B2139), Houghton, West Sussex, BN18 9LW
☎ 01798 839555/01903 740555
Ⓕ 01903 740441

www.stableantiques.co.uk
Est. 2000 *Stock size* Medium
No. of dealers 12
Stock Antiques, furniture and design
Open Tues–Sun 11am–4pm

HUNSTON

J and M Riley
Contact Mr J Riley
Frensham House, Hunston, Chichester, West Sussex, PO20 6NX
01243 782660
Est. 1966 *Stock size* Medium
Stock 18thC English furniture
Open Mon–Sat 9am–6pm and by appointment

HURSTPIERPOINT

Heather Boardman Antiques
Contact Heather Boardman
40 High Street, Hurstpierpoint, West Sussex, BN16 9RG
01273 832101
Est. 1987 *Stock size* Small
Stock Decorative items, collectables
Open Mon–Sat 9.30am–5pm closed Wed
Fairs Ardingly

Graham Foster Antiques
Contact Graham Foster
The Old Telephone Exchange, 41 Cuckfield Road, Hurstpierpoint, West Sussex, BN6 9RW
01273 833099 01273 833099
07850 576434
graham.foster-antiques@ukonline.co.uk
Est. 1982 *Stock size* Large
Stock Iron gates, furniture
Open Mon–Sat 8.30am–6pm
Fairs Ardingly, Newark
Services Valuations, restorations

Julian Antiques
Contact Mrs C Ingram or Mr J Ingram
124 High Street, Hurstpierpoint, West Sussex, BN6 9PX
01273 832145
Est. 1969 *Stock size* Medium
Stock 19thC French mirrors, clocks, candelabra, fireplaces, bronzes, sculptures, fenders, furniture
Open By appointment
Fairs Olympia
Services Shipping

Samuel Orr (LAPADA)
Contact Mr S Orr
34–36 High Street, Hurstpierpoint, West Sussex, BN6 9RG
01273 832081 01273 832081
07860 230888
clocks@samorr.co.uk
www.samorr.co.uk
Est. 1977 *Stock size* Large
Stock Antique clocks, barometers
Open Mon–Sat 10am–6pm or by appointment
Services Clock restoration

LINDFIELD

Lindfield Galleries (BADA)
Contact David Adam
62 High Street, Lindfield, West Sussex, RH16 2HL
01444 483817 01444 484682
david@orientalandantiquerugs.com
www.orientalandantiquerugs.com
Est. 1973 *Stock size* Large
Stock Oriental carpets and tapestries
Open Tues–Fri 9.30am–5pm Sat 10am–4pm
Services Valuations, restorations

Spongs Antique Centre
Contact Ashley or Karen Richardson
102 High Street, Lindfield, West Sussex, RH16 2HS
01444 487566
Est. 2000 *Stock size* Medium
No. of dealers 34
Stock Furniture, china, silver, ceramics, Carlton ware
Open Mon–Fri 10am–5pm Sun 2–5pm
Services Restorations

Stable Antiques
Contact Adrian Hoyle
98a High Street, Lindfield, West Sussex, RH16 2HP
01444 483662 01444 483662
Est. 1989 *Stock size* Large
Stock George III, Regency, Victorian, Edwardian furniture, antique country pine 1850–1920, some porcelain
Open Mon–Sun 10am–5.30pm
Services Free local delivery

LITTLEHAMPTON

Peter Cheney Auctioneers and Valuers (SSA)
Contact Mr P Cheney
Western Road Auction Rooms, Western Road, Littlehampton, West Sussex, BH17 5NP
01903 722264/713418
01903 713418
Est. 1940
Open Mon–Fri 9am–1pm 2–5pm
Sales Monthly auction sales of antiques, furniture, pictures, silver, porcelain and collectors items. Valuations for insurance and probate. No buyer's premium
Frequency Monthly
Catalogues Yes

Joan's Antiques
Contact Mrs J Walkden
1 New Road, Littlehampton, West Sussex, BN17 5AX
01903 722422
Est. 1977 *Stock size* Large
Stock China, glass, 1930s items, Victoriana, collectables
Open Thurs–Sat 10.30am–4.30pm
Fairs Goodwood

MIDHURST

Churchill Clocks (BHI)
Contact Mr W P Tyrell
Rumbolds Hill, Midhurst, West Sussex, GU29 9BZ
01730 813891
info@churchillclocks.co.uk
www.churchillclocks.co.uk
Est. 1970 *Stock size* Medium
Stock Clocks, longcase, mantel, French bracket etc
Open Mon–Sat 9am–5pm closed Wed pm
Services Valuations, restorations, shipping

The Old Town Hall Antiques Centre
Contact Mr P Baker
The Old Town Hall, Market Square, Midhurst, West Sussex, GU29 9HJ

☎ 01730 817166
Est. 1974 *Stock size* Medium
Stock Furniture, glass, porcelain
Open Mon–Sat 10am–5pm

PETWORTH

Angel Antiques
Contact Nick or Barbara Swanson
✉ **Church Street, Petworth, West Sussex, GU28 0AD** P
☎ 01798 343306 F 01798 342665
E swan189@aol.com
W www.angel-antiques.com
Est. 1991 *Stock size* Medium
Stock Oak and country furniture, decorative items
Open Mon–Sat 10am–5.30pm or by appointment

Antiquated (LAPADA)
Contact Vicki Emery
✉ **10 New Street, Petworth, West Sussex, GU28 0AS** P
☎ 01798 344011 F 01798 344011
Est. 1989 *Stock size* Medium
Stock 18th–19thC painted furniture, 19thC rocking horses
Open Mon–Sat 10am–5.30pm

Bacchus Gallery
Contact Mr R Gillett
✉ **Lombard Street, Petworth, West Sussex, GU28 0AG** P
☎ 01798 342844 F 01798 342634
E bacchus@cavovin.com
Est. 1988 *Stock size* Medium
Stock Decanters, glasses, corkscrews, anniversary wines
Open Mon–Sat 10am–5pm

Baskerville Antiques (BADA)
Contact Mr B Baskerville
✉ **Saddlers House, Saddlers Row, Petworth, West Sussex, GU28 0AH** P
☎ 01798 342067 F 01798 343956
E brianbaskerville@aol.com
Est. 1971 *Stock size* Medium
Stock Antiquarian horologist, clocks, barometers
Open Tues–Sat 10am–6pm

John Bird Antiques
Contact John Bird
✉ **High Street, Petworth, West Sussex, GU28** P
☎ 01798 343933 F 01273 483366
M 07973 421070 or 07970 683949
E bird.puttnam@virgin.net
Est. 1976 *Stock size* Medium
Stock Decorative objects and furniture, upholstery, Arts and Crafts
Open Mon–Sat 10.15am–5.15 pm
Fairs Olympia

Bradley's Past and Present Shop
Contact Mr & Mrs M Bradley
✉ **21 High Street, Petworth, West Sussex, GU28 0AU** P
☎ 01798 343533
Est. 1979 *Stock size* Medium
Stock Furniture and bygones
Open Tues–Sat 10am–1pm 2–5pm
Services Restoration of gramophones

Callingham Antiques Ltd
Contact Nigel Callingham
✉ **Northchapel, Petworth, West Sussex, GU28 9HL** P
☎ 01428 707379
Est. 1979 *Stock size* Medium
Stock 17th–18thC English furniture
Open Mon–Sat 9am–5.30pm closed Wed
Services Restorations

Ronald G Chambers – Fine Antiques (LAPADA, CINOA, PAADA)
Contact Mr R G Chambers or Mrs J F Tudor
✉ **Market Square, Petworth, West Sussex, GU28 0AH** P
☎ 01798 342305 F 01798 342724
M 07932 161968
E jackie@ronaldchambers.com
W www.ronaldchambers.com
Est. 1985 *Stock size* Large
Stock Fine-quality antique furniture and objets d'art 1700–1910 Queen Anne–Edwardian period, paintings, longcase clocks, gilded mirrors, bronze statuary and decorative items, jewellery
Open Mon–Sat 10am–5.30pm Sun 10am–4.30pm
Services Valuations, restorations, exchange and finder service, shipping

Oliver Charles Antiques Ltd (PAADA)
Contact Mr T G Wilkinson
✉ **Lombard Street, Petworth, West Sussex, GU28 0AG** P
☎ 01798 344443
E olivercharles@aol.com
W www.olivercharles.com
Est. 1987 *Stock size* Medium
Stock 18th–19thC English furniture, related items, 19thC paintings
Open Mon–Sat 10am–5.30pm Sun by appointment

Du Cros Antiques
Contact Mr J Du Cros
✉ **1 Pound Street, Petworth, West Sussex, GU28 0DX** P
☎ 01798 342071
Est. 1982 *Stock size* Medium
Stock 17th–19thC English furniture, metalware
Open Mon–Sat 10am–5.30pm
Services Verbal valuations

Elliott's (PAADA)
Contact Mrs P Elliott
✉ **19 East Street, Petworth, West Sussex, GU28 0AB** P
☎ 01798 343408
Est. 1993 *Stock size* Large
Stock Georgian–Edwardian furniture
Open Wed Fri Sat 10am–5pm

Richard Gardner Antiques (LAPADA, CINOA, PAADA, BACA Award Winner 2002)
Contact Richard Gardner
✉ **Market Square, Petworth, West Sussex, GU28 0AN** P
☎ 01798 343411
E rg@richardgardnerantiques.co.uk
W www.richardgardnerantiques.co.uk
Est. 1990 *Stock size* Large
Stock Period furniture, works of art, bronzes, Staffordshire figures, paintings, silver, mirrors, 18th–19thC porcelain, etchings
Open Mon–Sat 10am–5.30pm Sun 10am–5pm

Granville Antiques (BADA)
Contact Mr Ian Miller
✉ **6 High Street, Petworth, West Sussex, GU28 0AU** P
☎ 01798 343250 F 01798 343250
M 07966 279761
Est. 1985 *Stock size* Large
Stock Furniture, fine art, decorative antiques
Open Mon–Sat 9.30am–5.30pm
Services Valuations

SOUTH

John Harris Antiques and Restorations
Contact Mr J Harris
Stables, London Road, Northchapel, Petworth, West Sussex, GU28 9EQ
01428 707667
Est. 1976 *Stock size* Medium
Stock 18th–19thC furniture, decorative items
Open Mon–Sat 8am–5pm
Services Restorations

William Hockley Antiques
Contact Val Thrower
East Street, Petworth, West Sussex, GU28 0AB
01403 701917
Est. 1982 *Stock size* Medium
Stock Early English oak, country furniture and interiors
Open Mon–Sun 10am–5.30pm
Services Restorations, shipping, interior design

John's Corner Allsorts
Contact Mr J H Mason
Market Square, Petworth, West Sussex, GU28 0AH
01798 343270
johns@corner99.freeserve.co.uk
Est. 1991 *Stock size* Medium
Stock Netsuke, okimonos, ivory, small bronzes, silver
Open Mon–Sat 10am–5pm
Fairs Ardingly

Madison Gallery (PAADA)
Swan House, Market Square, Petworth, West Sussex, GU28 0AH
01798 343638
Est. 1987 *Stock size* Large
Stock Oak, walnut, mahogany furniture, country furniture, silver, porcelain, decorative items, paintings
Open Mon–Sun 10am–5pm
Services Valuations, restorations

Octavia Antiques (PAADA)
Contact Aline Bell
East Street, Petworth, West Sussex, GU28 0AB
01798 342771
Est. 1972 *Stock size* Small
Stock Decorative antiques, small furniture, mirrors, lamps, chairs, china
Open Mon–Sat 10.30am–5.30pm closed Fri

Petworth Antique Market
Contact Mrs D M Rayment
East Street, Petworth, West Sussex, GU28 0AB
01798 342073 01798 344566
Est. 1974 *Stock size* Large
Stock English oak furniture, silver, linen, books, soft furnishings, porcelain, glass, fans, general antiques
Open Mon–Sat 10am–5.30pm

Petworth Collectables and Bookshop
Contact Mr Hanson
Middle Street, Petworth, West Sussex, GU28 0BE
01798 342154
Est. 1987 *Stock size* Large
Stock Rare, second-hand, out-of-print books and collectables
Open Mon–Sat 10am–6pm

Annette Puttnam Antiques
Contact Annette Puttnam
2 Leppards, High Street, Petworth, West Sussex, GU28 0AU
01798 343933 01798 343933
07973 421070/07970 683940
bird.puttnam@virgin.net
Est. 1986 *Stock size* Medium
Stock Decorative objects and furniture, upholstery
Open Mon–Sat 10.15am–5.15 pm
Fairs Olympia

Red Lion Antiques (LAPADA)
Contact Mr R Wilson
New Street, Petworth, West Sussex, GU28 0AS
01798 344485 01798 342367
rod@redlion-antiques.com
www.redlion-antiques.com
Est. 1980 *Stock size* Large
Stock 17th–19thC furniture
Open Mon–Sat 10am–5.30pm or by appointment
Fairs LAPADA

Riverbank Gallery Ltd (PAADA)
Contact Linda Burke White
High Street, Petworth, West Sussex, GU28 0AU
01798 344401 01798 343135
riverbank@riverbank-antiques.com
Est. 1997 *Stock size* Large
Stock Large English 18th–19thC furniture, decorative items, garden furniture, decorative paintings
Open Mon–Sat 10am–5.30pm

Roughshed
Contact Kirstine St John Best
Pound Street, Petworth, West Sussex, GU28 0DX
01798 344446 07970 599464
sk.best.roughshed@cwcom.net
www.roughshed.co.uk
Est. 2000 *Stock size* Medium
Stock French and English decorative antiques
Open Fri Sat 10am–5pm or by appointment
Services Design service

Ruddy Antiques
Contact Robin Ruddy
10a New Street, Petworth, West Sussex, GU28 0AS
01798 344622 07710 346222
ruddy.antiques@virgin.net
Est. 1981 *Stock size* Medium
Stock Decorative, painted furniture, garden furniture
Open Mon–Sat 10am–5pm

H G Saunders Fine Antiques (LAPADA)
Contact H G Saunders
Market Square, Petworth, West Sussex, GU28 0AH
01798 344333 01798 342724
jackie@ronaldchambers.com
www.ronaldchambers.com
Est. 1986 *Stock size* Medium
Stock 18th–19thC furniture, paintings, objets d'art, jewellery
Open Mon–Sun 10am–5.30pm
Services Valuations, restorations

Nicholas Shaw Antiques (BADA, LAPADA, CINOA)
Contact Nicholas Shaw
Virginia Cottage, Petworth, West Sussex, GU28 0AG
01798 345146 01798 345146
07817 572746 or 07885 643000
silver@nicholas-shaw.com
www.nicholas-shaw.com
Est. 1992 *Stock size* Large
Stock Scottish and Irish fine silver, small silver collectors' items
Open Mon–Sat 10am–5.30pm Sun noon–4pm

SOUTH

Fairs BADA Fair, Olympia, Antiques for Everyone, LAPADA
Services Valuations, restorations

Stewart Antiques
Contact J Moore
High Street, Petworth, West Sussex, GU28 0AU
☎ 01798 342136
Est. 1980 *Stock size* Large
Stock Victorian, Edwardian stripped pine and fruitwood furniture, kitchenware, Continental decorative items
Open Mon–Sat 10am–5.30pm

T and S Blues Antiques
Contact Susan Boyles and Albert Thomas
The Hut, Lombard Street, Petworth, West Sussex, GU28 0AG
☎ 01798 344155 Ⓕ 01798 344155
Est. 2001 *Stock size* Medium
Stock French furniture, 20thC British pictures
Open Mon–Sat 10am–5.30pm
Services Small restorations

Tudor Rose Antique Centre
Contact Elizabeth Lee
East Street, Petworth, West Sussex, GU28 0AB
☎ 01798 343621 Ⓕ 01798 344951
Ⓜ 07980 927331
Est. 2001 *Stock size* Large
No. of dealers 12
Stock General antiques, brown and decorative furniture, silver, porcelain, blue-and-white pottery, books, reclamation, including William Hockley, early country furniture and interiors
Open Mon–Sat 10am–5.15pm Sun 11am–4.15pm

J C Tutt Antiques
Contact J C Tutt
Angel Street, Petworth, West Sussex, GU28 0BQ
☎ 01798 343221 Ⓕ 01798 343221
Est. 1984 *Stock size* Large
Stock Mahogany, country furniture, accessories
Open Mon–Sat 10am–5pm

PULBOROUGH

Brand Inglis (BADA)
Contact Brand Inglis or Jackie Kyte
Besley Farmhouse, Pulborough, West Sussex, RH20 1NG
☎ 01798 839180 Ⓕ 01798 839180
Ⓜ 07950 931911
Est. 1975 *Stock size* Medium
Stock Antique silver
Open By appointment only
Fairs BADA (Mar), Olympia (Nov)
Services Valuations for insurance, probate or family division

Thakeham Furniture
Contact Mr T Chavasse
Mare Hill Road, Pulborough, West Sussex, RH20 2DY
☎ 01798 872006 Ⓕ 01798 872006
Ⓜ 07803 086828
Est. 1979 *Stock size* Medium
Stock 18th–19thC English furniture
Open Mon–Fri 9am–5pm
Fairs Malthouse Dorking
Services Restorations

SHOREHAM BY SEA

Bookworms of Shoreham
Contact Mrs P A Liddell
4 High Street, Shoreham by Sea, West Sussex, BN43 5DA
☎ 01273 453856
Est. 1992 *Stock size* Medium
Stock Rare, second-hand books, military, modern art
Open Tues–Sat 10am–5pm

SMALL DOLE

Alexander Antiques
Contact Judith Goodinge
Small Dole, Henfield, West Sussex, BN5 9XE
☎ 01273 493121
Est. 1972 *Stock size* Medium
Stock Country furniture, treen, boxes, brass, copper
Open Telephone call advisable
Fairs Chester, Petersfield

STORRINGTON

Stable Antiques
Contact Ian Wadey
46 West Street, Storrington, West Sussex, RH20 4EE
☎ 01903 740555 or 01798 839555
Ⓕ 01903 740441
Ⓦ www.stableantiques.co.uk
Est. 1993 *Stock size* Large
No. of dealers 35
Stock Antiques, furniture and bric-a-brac
Open Mon–Sun 10am–6pm

STREAT

Fisher Nautical (PBFA)
Contact S D Fisher
Huntswood House, St Helena Lane, Streat, Hassocks, West Sussex, BN16 8SD
☎ 01273 890273 Ⓕ 01273 891439
Ⓔ fishernautical@seabooks.fsnet.co.uk
Ⓦ www.fishernautical.co.uk
Est. 1963 *Stock size* Large
Stock Rare, antiquarian, second-hand nautical books
Open Mail order Mon–Fri 9am–5pm
Services Mail order

TURNERS HILL

Albion House Antiques
Contact Janet Avery
Albion House, North Street, Turners Hill, Worth, West Sussex, RH10 4NS
☎ 01342 715670
Est. 1971 *Stock size* Large
Stock 18th–19thC brass, copper, furniture, collectables
Open Mon–Sun 9am–6pm during Summer 9am–7pm

WASHINGTON

Rupert Toovey & Co (RICS)
Contact Alan Toovey
Spring Gardens, Washington, Ashington, West Sussex, RH20 3BS
☎ 01403 711744
Ⓔ auctions@rupert-toovey.com
Ⓦ www.rupert-toovey.com
Est. 1995
Open Mon–Fri 9am–5pm
Sales Monthly sales of antiques, fine art, collectables, silver, jewellery, clocks and furniture. Sales of books and postcards 2–3 times a year
Frequency Monthly
Catalogues Yes

WISBOROUGH GREEN

John Bellman Ltd
Contact John Ireland
New Pound, Wisborough Green, West Sussex, RH14 0AZ

☎ 01403 700858 Ⓕ 01403 700059
Ⓔ enquiries@bellmans.co.uk
Ⓦ www.bellmans.co.uk
Est. 1989
Open Mon–Fri 9am–5pm
Sales Monthly sales of antiques and collectables Thurs Fri 10am and 2pm, viewing Sat prior 9am–noon, Mon 9am–4pm, Tues 9am–7pm, Wed 9am–1pm
Frequency Monthly
Catalogues Yes

WORTHING

Acorn Antiques
Contact Henry Nicholls
91 Rowlands Road, Worthing, West Sussex, BN11 3JX
☎ 01903 216926
Ⓔ hnick@pavilion.co.uk
Est. 1992 *Stock size* Large
Stock Georgian–Edwardian furniture, china, silver, jewellery
Open Mon–Sat 9am–5.30pm
Services Valuations, restorations

Badgers Books
Contact Ray Potter
8–10 Gratwicke Road, Worthing, West Sussex, BN11 4BH
☎ 01903 211816
Est. 1982 *Stock size* Large
Stock Rare, antiquarian, second-hand books
Open Mon–Sat 9am–5.30pm

Chloe Antiques
Contact Mrs Dorothy Peters
61 Brighton Road, Worthing, West Sussex, BN11 3EE
☎ 01903 202697
Est. 1967 *Stock size* Large
Stock Small collectables, jewellery, china, glass
Open Mon–Sat 10am–4.30pm closed Wed

Corner Antiques
Contact Richard Mihok
9–10 Havercroft Building, North Street, Worthing, West Sussex, BN11 1DY
☎ 01903 537669 Ⓕ 01903 206881
Est. 1997 *Stock size* Small
Stock General antiques, textiles, collectables
Open Mon–Sat 10am–5pm
Fairs Charmandan Centre Worthing

R H Ellis and Son Auctioneers and Valuers
Contact Mr K Ellis
44–46 High Street, Worthing, West Sussex, BN11 1LL
☎ 01903 238999 Ⓕ 01903 215959
Ⓦ www.rhellisestateagents.co.uk
Est. 1928
Open Mon–Fri 9am–1pm 2–5pm
Sales Monthly sales of Edwardian–Victorian furniture and collectables. Quarterly sales of silver, paintings, Oriental and rugs, Mon 10am and 2pm, viewing Sat 9am–1pm 2–4pm Mon 9–10am prior to sale
Frequency Monthly and quarterly
Catalogues Yes

Interiors and Antiques
Contact Pat or Janet Cassie
162 Findon Road, Worthing, West Sussex, BN14 0EL
☎ 01903 261134
Est. 1998 *Stock size* Medium
Stock Furniture, china, glass, garden statues, bird baths
Open Mon–Sun 10am–6pm closed Tues

Postcard Cabin
Contact Colin Clissold
1 West Buildings, Worthing, West Sussex, BN11 3BS
☎ 01903 823126 Ⓕ 01903 236254
Est. 1988 *Stock size* Medium
Stock Postcards, coins, medals, bank notes
Open Mon–Fri 10am–5pm Sat 10am–2pm closed Wed

Wilson's Antiques (LAPADA)
Contact Mr F Wilson
45–47 New Broadway, Tarring Road, Worthing, West Sussex, BN11 4HS
☎ 01903 202059 Ⓜ 0778 813395
Ⓔ frank@wilsons-antiques.com
Ⓦ www.wilsons-antiques.com
Est. 1936 *Stock size* Large
Stock Georgian–Edwardian formal English furniture
Open Mon–Fri 10am–5pm other times by appointment
Fairs Olympia, NEC Antiques for Everyone

Worthing Auction Galleries Ltd
Contact Mr R Rood
Fleet House, Teville Gate, Worthing, West Sussex, BN11 1UA
☎ 01903 205565 Ⓕ 01903 214365
Ⓔ info@worthing-auctions.co.uk
Ⓦ www.worthing-auctions.co.uk
Est. 1964
Open Mon–Fri 8.30am–5pm closed 1–2pm
Sales Monthly sales of general antiques
Frequency Monthly
Catalogues Yes

WEST COUNTRY

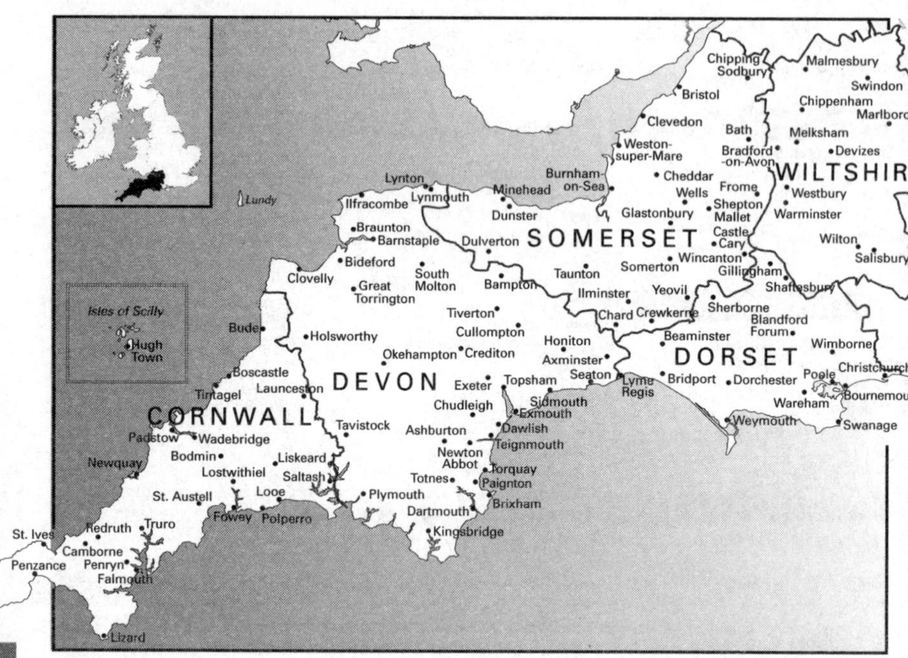

CORNWALL

BODMIN

Bodmin Antiques Centre
Contact Ralph Solomons
✉ **Townend, Bodmin, Cornwall, PL31 2LN** P
☎ 01208 78661 Ⓜ 0771 2431837
Ⓔ bodminantiques@hotmail.com
Ⓦ www.bodminantiquescentre.co.uk
Est. 1996 ***Stock size*** Large
No. of dealers 10
Stock General antiques, small items, porcelain, pottery, commemoratives, jewellery, collectables, furniture, glass
Open Mon–Sat 10am–4pm
Services Valuations

CALLINGTON

Country Living Antiques
Contact Ian Baxter CBE
✉ **Weston House, Haye Road, Callington, Cornwall, PL17 7JJ** P
☎ 01579 382245
Est. 1988 ***Stock size*** Medium
Stock Country furniture and effects
Open Mon–Sat 9.30am–5.30pm
Services Free valuations

CAMBORNE

The Victoria Gallery and Bookshop
Contact Jennifer Maker
✉ **28 Cross Street, Camborne, Cornwall, TR14 8EX** P
☎ 01209 719268
Est. 1983 ***Stock size*** Medium
Stock Antiquarian and second-hand books, general antiques, silver, jewellery
Open Mon–Fri 10.30am–5.15pm
Services Valuations for insurance, probate, china and furniture restoration, jewellery repairs

CAMELFORD

Corner Shop Antiques and Gallery
Contact Mr P J Tillett
✉ **68 Fore Street, Camelford, Cornwall, PL32 9PG** P
☎ 01840 212573
Ⓜ 07884 456247
Ⓔ tillett18@aol.com
Est. 1989 ***Stock size*** Medium
Stock General antiques, collectables, Victorian watercolours
Open Mon–Sat 9.30am–5.30pm

CHACEWATER

Chacewater Antiques
Contact Ray McCall
✉ **5 Fore Street, Chacewater, Truro, Cornwall, TR4 8PS** P
☎ 01872 561411
Est. 1992 ***Stock size*** Medium
Stock Georgian–Edwardian furniture, paintings, 19thC brassware
Open Mon–Fri 10.30am–4pm Sat 10am–1pm closed Wed

CHARLESTOWN

Charlestown Trading
Contact Pippa Kennedy
✉ **The Old Gun Store, Charlestown, Cornwall, PL25 3NJ** P
☎ 01726 76018
Est. 1997 ***Stock size*** Medium

Stock General antiques, garden statuary, original fireplaces, Cornish ranges
Open Mon–Sun 10am–4.30pm

FALMOUTH

Arcade Antiques
Contact G Springfield
16 St George's Arcade, Church Street, Falmouth, Cornwall, TR11 3DH
01326 212472
Est. 1995 *Stock size* Medium
Stock General antiques, clocks
Open Mon–Sat 10.30am–5pm

Browsers Bookshop
Contact Mr Floyd
13–15 St George's Arcade, Church Street, Falmouth, Cornwall, TR11 3DH
01326 313464
Est. 1981 *Stock size* Medium
Stock Antiquarian, second-hand books, printed music
Open Mon–Sat 9.30am–5pm
Services Valuations

Isabelline Books
Contact Mr M Whetman
2 Highbury House, 8 Woodlane Crescent, Falmouth, Cornwall, TR11 4QS
01326 210412 F 0870 051 6387
E mikann@beakbook.demon.co.uk
W www.beakbook.demon.co.uk
Est. 1997 *Stock size* Small
Stock Antiquarian books on ornithology
Open By appointment
Services Valuations, 3 catalogues a year

Marine Instruments
Contact Alistair Heane
The Wheelhouse, Upton Slip, Falmouth, Cornwall, TR11 3DQ
01326 312414 F 01326 211414
E info@marineinstruments.co.uk
W www.marineinstruments.co.uk
Est. 1960 *Stock size* Large
Stock Marine-related charts, publications, sextants, compasses
Open Mon–Fri 9am–5pm
Sat 9am–4pm
Services Worldwide mail order, valuations, repair of sextants and compasses

Old Town Hall Antiques
Contact Terry Brandreth or Mary Sheppard
Old Town Hall, 3 High Street, Falmouth, Cornwall, TR11 2AB
01326 319437
Est. 1986 *Stock size* Large
Stock 17th–early 20thC furniture, general antiques and collectables
Open Mon–Sat 10am–5.30pm
Services Deliveries abroad

P S I Collectables
Contact Phil Hart
2a Berkeley Court, Falmouth, Cornwall, TR11 3XE
01326 212540 F 01326 212540
M 07929 880230
E psicomadasafish.com
Est. 1998 *Stock size* Medium
Stock Wade, American comics, collectable bears, annuals
Open Mon–Sat 10am–5pm

Waterfront Antiques Market
Contact Mr Rickard
4 Quay Street, Falmouth, Cornwall, TR11 3HH
01326 311491
Est. 1984 *Stock size* Medium
No. of dealers 20
Stock Furniture, brass, copper, silver, glass, porcelain, pictures, prints, linen, collectables
Open Mon–Sat 10am–4.30pm

FOWEY

Bookends of Fowey (IPG)
Contact Mrs C Alexander
4 South Street, Fowey, Cornwall, PL23 1AR
01726 833361 F 01726 833900
E alex@nder.com
W www.nder.com
Est. 1987 *Stock size* Large
Stock Antiquarian, second-hand and publishers of Cornish literature books
Open Mon–Sat 9.30am–1pm 2–6pm
Services Valuations, book search

GRAMPOUND

Pine & Period Furniture
Contact Simon Payne
Fore Street, Grampound, Cornwall, TR2 4QT
01726 883117
M 07850 318298
Est. 1971 *Stock size* Medium
Stock Pine and period furniture
Open Mon–Sat 10.30am–5pm
Services Restorations

Radnor House Antiques
Contact Geoff or Penny Hodgson
Fore Street, Grampound, Truro, Cornwall, TR2 4QT
01726 882921
Est. 1975 *Stock size* Medium
Stock Victorian, Edwardian and Georgian oak, pine and mahogany furniture
Open Mon–Sat 10am–6pm

HAYLE

Copperhouse Gallery
Contact Paul Dyer
14 Fore Street, Copperhouse, Hayle, Cornwall, TR27 4DY
01736 752787
Est. 1900 *Stock size* Large
Stock Victorian and early 20thC watercolours, art pottery
Open Tues–Sat 9am–5pm

HELSTON

Butchers Antiques
Contact Howard Jones
12 Wendron Street, Helston, Cornwall, TR13 8PS
01326 565117
Est. 1991 *Stock size* Medium
Stock Country and pine furniture, cottageware and very unusual items
Open Mon–Sat 8am–5pm

The Helston Bookworm (PBFA)
Contact Mr and Mrs Summers
9 Church Street, Helston, Cornwall, TR13 8TA
01326 565079
Est. 1994 *Stock size* Medium
Stock Antiquarian and second-hand books
Open Mon–Fri 10am–5.30pm
Sat 10am–2pm
Fairs Local fairs (phone for details)
Services Restorations, book search

LAUNCESTON

Antique Chairs and Museum
Contact Alice or Tom Brown
Colhay Farm, Polson, Launceston, Cornwall, PL15 9QS

☎ 01566 777485 ⓕ 01566 777485
Est. 1987 *Stock size* Large
Stock Period chairs
Open Mon–Sun 9am–5.30pm
Services Restorations, upholstery

The Junk Shop
Contact Mrs L Deeble
✉ **31 St Thomas Road, Launceston, Cornwall, PL15 8DA** Ⓟ
☎ 01566 773333
Est. 2001 *Stock size* Medium
Stock French furniture, general antiques, second-hand furniture, bric-a-brac
Open Tue–Sat 9am–5pm

Todd's Antiques
Contact Mr T Mead
✉ **2 High Street, Launceston, Cornwall, PL15 8ER** Ⓟ
☎ 01566 775007 ⓕ 01566 775007
Est. 1997 *Stock size* Large
Stock Small furniture, collectables, ceramics
Open Mon–Fri 9am–5pm Thurs–Sat 9am–4pm

LISKEARD

Collage
Contact Mrs Dempsey
✉ **Station Road, Liskeard, Cornwall, PL14 4BX**
☎ 01579 348471
Est. 1995 *Stock size* Medium
Stock Antique furniture, new pine, crafts, juggling equipment
Open Mon–Sat 10am–5pm

Olden Days
Contact Mrs F Nancarrow
✉ **Five Lanes, Dobwalls, Liskeard, Cornwall, PL14 6JD** Ⓟ
☎ 01579 321577 ⓕ 01579 321804
Ⓜ 07780 687944
Est. 1989 *Stock size* Medium
Stock General antiques, old furniture, new pine
Open Mon–Sun 10am–5pm
Services Bespoke fitted kitchens, bedrooms etc

LOOE

Tony Martin
Contact Mr Tony Martin
✉ **Fore Street, East Looe, Looe, Cornwall, PL13 1AE** Ⓟ
☎ 01503 262734
Est. 1965 *Stock size* Medium
Stock General small furniture, china, ceramics, pictures
Open Appointment advisable

LOSTWITHIEL

John Bragg Antiques
Contact Ann Bragg
✉ **35 Fore Street, Lostwithiel, Cornwall, PL22 0BN** Ⓟ
☎ 01208 872827
Est. 1973 *Stock size* Large
Stock Period furniture
Open Mon–Sat 10am–5pm closed Wed pm
Services Valuations

Déja-Vu Antiques & Collectables
Contact Adrian or Marianne Barratt
✉ **31 Fore Street, Lostwithiel, Cornwall, PL22 0BN** Ⓟ
☎ 01208 873912
ⓔ antiquedejavu@hotmail.com
Est. 1998 *Stock size* Medium
Stock Furniture, pictures, collectables, curios, silver, large selection of books
Open Mon–Sat 10am–5pm closed Wed pm
Fairs Charlestown, Trenython Manor
Services Book search

The Furniture Store
Contact Mike Edwards
✉ **2 Queen Street, Lostwithiel, Cornwall, PL22 0AB**
☎ 01208 873408 ⓕ 01208 873408
Ⓜ 07790 759540
Est. 1986 *Stock size* Large
Stock Pine furniture, turn-of-the-century oak, Bakelite radios
Open Mon–Sat 10am–5.30pm Wed close 1pm

The Higgins Press
Contact Doris Roberts
✉ **South Street, Lostwithiel, Cornwall, PL22 0BZ** Ⓟ
☎ 01208 872755
Est. 1980 *Stock size* Medium
Stock Antiques and collectables
Open Mon–Sat 10am–4pm closed Wed pm

Jefferys
Contact Ian Morris
✉ **5 Fore Street, Lostwithiel, Cornwall, PL22 0BP** Ⓟ
☎ 01208 872245 ⓕ 01208 873260
ⓔ jefferys.lostwithiel@btinternet.com
Ⓦ www.jefferys.uk.com
Est. 1865
Open Mon–Fri 9am–5.30pm
Sales Antique and fine art sales every two months Wed 10am. Viewing prior Mon 2–7pm Tues 10am–1pm 2–5pm. General household sales fortnightly Wed 10am, viewing prior Tues 10am–1pm 2–5pm
Frequency 8 weekly
Catalogues Yes

The Old Palace Antiques
Contact Mrs D Bryant
✉ **Quay Street, Lostwithiel, Cornwall, PL22 0BS** Ⓟ
☎ 01208 872909
Est. 1979 *Stock size* Medium
Stock Pine furniture, china, brass, prints, postcards
Open Mon–Sat 10am–5pm closed 1–2pm and Wed pm

Yesterdays
Contact John Fairclough
✉ **9 Fore Street, Lostwithiel, Cornwall, PL22 0BP** Ⓟ
☎ 01208 872344 ⓕ 01208 872344
Est. 1997 *Stock size* Medium
Stock Antique pine furniture, prints, watercolours, brass, ceramics
Open Tues–Sat 10am–5pm
Services Picture framing

MARAZION

Antiques
Contact Andrew S Wood
✉ **The Shambles, Market Place, Marazion, Cornwall, TR17 0AR** Ⓟ
☎ 01736 711381
Est. 1988 *Stock size* Medium
Stock General antiques and collectors' items particularly 19th–20thC pottery, porcelain and glass
Open 1 Apr–31 Oct Mon–Fri 10.15am–5.30pm 1 Nov–31 Mar Mon–Sat 10.15am–5pm

MEVAGISSEY

Cloud Cuckoo Land (UACC)
Contact Paul Mulvey
✉ **12 Fore Street, Mevagissey, St Austell, Cornwall, PL26 6UQ** Ⓟ

☎ 01726 842364 Ⓜ 07973 135906
ⓔ oy91@dial.pipex.com
Est. 1993 *Stock size* Medium
Stock Autographs
Open Mon–Sun 10am–5pm

MILLENDREATH

County Auctions
Contact Mrs Joy Walker
✉ **Millendreath, Looe, Cornwall, PL13 1NY** P
☎ 01503 265553 Ⓕ 01503 264467
Est. 1995
Open Tues–Thurs 10am–5pm
Sales Quarterly antiques sale Thurs 10am
Frequency Quarterly

PADSTOW

Jacob & His Fiery Angel
Contact Mrs Sonya Fancett
✉ **7 Middle Street, Padstow, Cornwall, PL28 8AP** P
☎ 01841 532130/01209 831616
Ⓕ 01841 532130
ⓔ debbiemorriskirby@tesco.net
Ⓦ www.jacobandhisfieryangel.com
Est. 1992 *Stock size* Large
Stock Antiques, eccentricities, eg angels, chandeliers, cats, curiosities. Taxidermy (birds)
Open Mon–Sat 11am–5pm winter Mon Thurs Sat noon–4pm or by appointment

Taclow Coth
Contact Patricia or Malcolm McCarthy
✉ **The Drang, South Quay, Padstow, Cornwall, PL28 8BL** P
☎ 01841 532326
Est. 1998 *Stock size* Medium
Stock Cutlery, antiques and collectables
Open Mon–Sat 10am–6pm

PAR

Bonhams
✉ **Cornubia Hall, Eastcliffe Road, Par, Cornwall, PL24 2AQ**
☎ 012726 814047
Ⓕ 012726 817979
ⓔ par@bonhams.com
Ⓦ www.bonhams.com
Open Mon–Fri 9am–5.30pm
Sales Par Saleroom

PENRYN

The Old School Antiques
Contact Mr J Gavin
✉ **The Old School, Church Road, Penryn, Cornwall, TR10 8DA** P
☎ 01326 375092
Est. 1985 *Stock size* Large
Stock Antique furniture, glass, china, clocks
Open Mon–Sun 9am–5.30pm
Services Clock repairs and furniture restoration

Leon Robertson Antiques
Contact Mr L Robertson
✉ **Unit 2, The Old School, Church Road, Penryn, Cornwall, TR10 8DA** P
☎ 01326 372767 Ⓜ 07971 171909
Est. 1973 *Stock size* Medium
Stock Furniture, paintings, general antiques
Open Mon–Sun 9am–5.30pm
Services Valuations

Ruby Antiques
Contact M or T Platt
✉ **Grays Wharf, Commercial Road, Penryn, Cornwall, TR10 8AE** P
☎ 01326 379322 Ⓜ 07989 537892
ⓔ mandtplatt@ntlworld.com
Est. 2001 *Stock size* Large
Stock Chairs, sofas, chaises longues, mirrors, brass fire fenders, vintage feather eiderdowns, furniture
Open Tues–Sat 10am–5pm Sun 11am–4pm

PENZANCE

Antiques and Fine Art
Contact Elinor Davies or Geoffrey Mills
✉ **1–3 Queens Buildings, The Promenade, Penzance, Cornwall, TR18 4HH** P
☎ 01736 350509
Est. 1994 *Stock size* Medium
Stock Georgian–Edwardian furniture
Open Mon–Sat 10am–4pm
Services Valuations, restorations and upholstery

Chapel Street Arcades
Contact Mr Bentley
✉ **61–62 Chapel Street, Penzance, Cornwall, TR18 4AE** P
☎ 01736 363267
Est. 1984 *Stock size* Medium
No. of dealers 20–25
Stock Furniture, brass, copper, silver, glass, porcelain, pictures, prints, linen, collectors' items
Open Mon–Sat 10am–5pm

R W Jeffery
Contact Mr R W Jeffery
✉ **Trebehor, St Levan, Penzance, Cornwall, TR19 6LX** P
☎ 01736 871263
Est. 1968 *Stock size* Large
Stock Coins, banknotes
Open By appointment

Peter Johnson
Contact Mr P Johnson
✉ **62 Chapel Street, Penzance, Cornwall, TR18 4AE** P
☎ 01736 363267
Est. 1992 *Stock size* Medium
Stock Period lighting, Oriental ceramics, furniture, handmade silk lampshades
Open Tue–Sat 9.30am–5pm
Services Valuations

W H Lane & Son, Fine Art Auctioneer and Valuers
Contact Graham J Bazley
✉ **Jubilee House, Queen Street, Penzance, Cornwall, TR18 4DF** P
☎ 01736 361447 Ⓕ 01736 350097
ⓔ info@whlane.co.uk
Est. 1934
Open Mon–Fri 9am–1pm 2–5pm
Sales 6 major picture sales per annum, occasional country house sales
Frequency 6+ per annum
Catalogues Yes

David Lay
Contact Mr D Lay FRICS
✉ **The Penzance Auction House, Alverton, Penzance, Cornwall, TR18 4RE** P
☎ 01736 361414 Ⓕ 01736 360035
ⓔ david.lay@byoprneotld.com
Ⓦ www.invaluable.com
Est. 1985
Open Mon–Fri 9am–5pm
Sales Auctioneers and valuers General sales every 3 weeks Tues 10am, viewing Sat 9am–1pm, Mon 9am–5pm. Bi-monthly 2-day antiques auctions Thurs Fri 10am, viewing

Sat, day prior and day of sale 8.30–10am. Traditional contemporary art auctions 3 per annum Feb June Oct Thurs 11am, viewing Sat 9am–1pm day prior 9am–5pm day of sale 8.30–11am. Book and collectors' sales 2 per annum Aug and Dec Tues 10am, viewing Sat 9am–1pm day prior 9am–5pm morning of sale 8.30–10am
Catalogues Yes

New Street Books
Contact Mr K Hearn
4 New Street, Penzance, Cornwall, TR18 2LZ
☎ 01736 362758
eankelvin@yahoo.com
Est. 1991 *Stock size* Medium
Stock Antiquarian and second-hand books, Cornish topics a speciality
Open Mon–Sat 10am–5pm
Services Book search

The Old Custom House
Contact Mr M Bauer
53 Chapel Street, Penzance, Cornwall, TR18 4AF P
☎ 01736 331030 F 01736 331030
Est. 1997 *Stock size* Medium
Stock Glass, china
Open Mon–Sat 9am–5.30pm Sun by appointment

Penzance Rare Books
Contact Pat Johnstone
43 Causewayhead, Penzance, Cornwall, TR18 2SS P
☎ 01736 362140
pat@boscathnoe.free-online.co.uk
Est. 1991 *Stock size* Large
Stock Antiquarian and second-hand books
Open Mon–Sat 10am–5pm
Services Valuations

Tony Sanders Gallery
Contact Mr Tony Sanders
14 Chapel Street, Penzance, Cornwall, TR18 4AW P
☎ 01736 366620
Est. 1969 *Stock size* Large
Stock Antique furniture, paintings, silver, glass, Newlyn copper
Open Mon–Sat 9am–5.30pm

Shiver Me Timbers
Contact Mr T R E Gray
Station Road, Long Rock, Penzance, Cornwall, TR20 9TT P
☎ 01736 711338
Est. 1983 *Stock size* Medium
Stock Reclaimed materials
Open Mon–Sat 9am–6pm
Services Hire of materials to film companies, makes reproduction furniture

Ursus
Contact Judith Piper
1 Arcade Steps, Market Jew Street, Penzance, Cornwall, TR18 2HW
☎ 01736 364605/871537
M 07790 442827
piper@tredavoe.freeserve.co.uk
www.ursus.co.uk
Est. 1999 *Stock size* Medium
Stock Old teddy bears and their toy-box companions
Open Ring for opening hours
Services Repairs to bears, identifications, valuations, mail order

POLPERRO

Expectations
Contact John Walker
The Old Bank, Fore Street, Polperro, Cornwall, PL13 2QR
☎ 01503 272552
Est. 2001 *Stock size* Medium
Stock Furniture, lamps, brass, copper
Open Summer Mon–Sun 10.30am–5.30pm winter by appointment
Services Search service for oil lamp parts

Gentry Antiques
Contact Pauline Black
Little Green, Polperro, Cornwall, PL13 2RF
☎ 01503 272361
info@gentryantiques.co.uk
www.gentryantiques.co.uk
Est. 1998 *Stock size* Medium
Stock Country pine, oak, pottery, porcelains and decorative items
Open Mon–Sun 10am–5pm
Fairs Battersea Antiques and Decorators Fair

Past & Presents
Contact Joe Askew
1 Lansalos, Polperro, Cornwall, PL13 2QU P
☎ 01503 272737
info@polperro-antiques.com
Est. 2000 *Stock size* Medium
Stock Stripped pine and dark wood furniture, collectables, Beswick, Royal Doulton, Crested china, other antiques
Open Mon–Sun 10am–5pm

REDRUTH

Evergreen Antiques & Interiors
Contact Michele Jelf
38 Fore Street, Redruth, Cornwall, TR15 2AE P
☎ 01209 215634
mickee@oxbury.freeserve.co.uk
Est. 2000 *Stock size* Medium
Stock General antiques
Open Mon–Sat 10am–4.30pm

La Belle
Contact Danny Everard
47 Fore Street, Redruth, Cornwall, TR15 2AE P
☎ 01209 216228
Est. 1991 *Stock size* Medium
Stock General antiques
Open Mon–Sat 9am–5pm
Services Valuations

The Old Steam Bakery
Contact Mr Stephen Phillips
60a Fore Street, Redruth, Cornwall, TR15 2AF P
☎ 01209 315099
Est. 1994 *Stock size* Large
Stock Late Victorian and Edwardian oak and pine furniture
Open Mon–Sat 10.30am–5pm
Services Restorations, furniture designed and made to order

Pool Auctions
Contact Mr or Mrs Duncan
Unit 1, Trevenson Road, Pool, Redruth, Cornwall, TR15 3PH P
☎ 01209 717111
Est. 1995
Open Mon–Fri 9am–3pm
Sales Antiques and general household sale Tues 6pm, viewing Tues 9am–6pm prior to sale

Frequency Weekly
Catalogues No

Portreath Furniture & Curios
Contact P A Chivers
Unit 4, New Portreath Road, Guilberts Coombe, Redruth, Cornwall, TR16 4HN
01209 219641
Est. 2002 *Stock size* Medium
Stock Furniture
Open Mon–Sat 10am–5pm
Services Restorations

Richards Son & Murdoch
Contact Mr Eddy
Alma Place, Redruth, Cornwall, TR15 2AT
01209 216367 01209 314959
Est. 1876
Open Mon–Fri 9am–1pm 2–5pm Sat 9am–noon
Sales Tuesday, general antiques, household furniture, 11am
Frequency 5–6 weekly
Catalogues Yes

Romantiques
Contact Patrick Ludford
Old Rectory, Churchtown, Redruth, Cornwall, TR15 3BT
07980 500490
Est. 1999 *Stock size* Medium
Stock Period antiques and ornamental garden antiques, staddle stones, troughs
Open Mon–Sat 10am–5pm or by appointment

Thornleigh Trading Antique Lighting
Contact Mr Duncan
46 Fore Street, Redruth, Cornwall, TR15 2AE
01209 315454
Est. 1992 *Stock size* Large
Stock Antique lighting, Victorian oil lamps
Open Mon–Sat 9am–5pm
Services Restorations

Upstairs Downstairs
Contact Michelle or Danny Everard
3a Higher Fore Street, Redruth, Cornwall, TR15 2AE
01326 216186
Est. 1991 *Stock size* Large
Stock General antiques
Open Mon–Sat 9am–5pm
Services Valuations

SALTASH

Eric Distin Auctioneers and Chartered Surveyors
Contact Mr E Distin
46 Fore Street, Saltash, Cornwall, PL12 6JL
01752 842355 01752 843768
Est. 1973
Open Mon–Fri 9am–5pm
Sales Antiques and collectables sale Sat 10.30am at New Road, Callington, viewing morning of sale
Frequency Fortnightly
Catalogues Yes

ST AUSTELL

Once Upon a Time
Contact Pippa and Graham Kennedy
The Old Workshop, Charles Town, St Austell, Cornwall, PL25 3NJ
01726 76018 01872 262520
Est. 1992 *Stock size* Large
Stock China, furniture, garden statuary, coins, general antiques
Open Mon–Sat 10am–4.30pm
Services Valuations, house clearances

ST COLUMB

M R Dingle
Contact Mr Dingle
Station Yard, Station Approach, St Columb Road, St Columb, Cornwall, TR9 6QR
01726 861119
Est. 1989 *Stock size* Large
Stock Architectural antiques including reclaimed timber
Open Mon–Fri 8am–5pm Sat 8am–noon

ST IVES

The Book Gallery
Contact David and Tina Wilkinson
2 Bedford Road, St Ives, Cornwall, TR26 1SP
01736 793545
Est. 1991 *Stock size* Medium
Stock Antiquarian and second-hand books. Art on St Ives a speciality
Open Mon–Fri 10am–5pm Sat 10am–2pm winter closed Mon
Services Book search and catalogue of St Ives books

Collectors Corner (PTA)
Contact Steve Prescott
Market Place, St Ives, Cornwall, TR26 1RZ
01736 798484 01736 798417
cprescott@btclick.com
Est. 1985 *Stock size* Small
Stock Stamps, postcards, cigarette cards, coins
Open Mon–Sat 10am–5pm
Fairs Shepton Mallet

Courtyard Collectables
Contact Janice Mosedale
Cyril Noall Square, Fore Street, St Ives, Cornwall, TR26 1HE
01736 798809
Est. 1994 *Stock size* Large
Stock General collectables
Open May–October Mon–Sun 10am–10pm Nov–April Mon–Sat 10am–5pm Sun noon–5pm

Dragons Hoard
Contact Chris Prescott
2 Tre-Pol-Pen, Street-an-Pol, St Ives, Cornwall, TR26 2DS
01736 798484 01736 798417
dragonshoard@dragonshoard.ws
www.dragonshoard.ws
Est. 1985 *Stock size* Small
Stock Collectables, bottles, cigarette cards, sugarlump labels
Open Mon–Fri 1.30pm–5pm
Fairs Newark

Mike Read Antique Sciences (SIS)
Contact Mr M Read
1 Abbey Meadow, Lelant, St Ives, Cornwall, TR26 3LL
01736 757237 01736 757237
mikeread@appleonline.net
Est. 1978 *Stock size* Medium
Stock Scientific instruments, maritime works of art and nautical artefacts
Open By appointment
Fairs International Antique Scientific and Medical Instruments Fair, Portman Square
Services Valuations

Tremayne Applied Arts
Contact Roger or Anne Tonkinson
Street-an-Pol, St Ives, Cornwall, TR26 2DS

☎ 01736 797779 Ⓕ 01736 793222
Ⓔ tomkinson@btinternet.com
Est. 1997 ***Stock size*** Large
Stock 20thC antiques, 1960s, Arts and Crafts, Art Deco, Art Nouveau
Open Summer Mon–Fri 10.30am–4.30pm Sat 10am–1.30pm closed Wed winter by appointment

ST JUST

St Just Bygones
Contact S A Wallis
✉ **42 Fore Street, St Just, Penzance, Cornwall, TR19 7LJ** Ⓟ
☎ 01736 787860
Est. 1990 ***Stock size*** Large
Stock Furniture, general antiques, bric-a-brac
Open Mon–Sat 9.30am–5pm

ST MAWGAN

The Forge
Contact M Jenner
✉ **Penpont, St Mawgan, Cornwall, TR8 4DT**
☎ 01636 860999
Est. 2001 ***Stock size*** Small
Stock General antiques
Open Mon–Fri 10am–4pm

TIDEFORD

Cutcrew Antiques
Contact Robert Stewart
✉ **Cutcrew Sawmills, Tideford, Cornwall, PL12 5JS** Ⓟ
☎ 01752 851402
Est. 1984 ***Stock size*** Large
Stock Georgian–Edwardian furniture situated in an 18thC water mill
Open Mon–Sun 9am–5.30pm

TRURO

Alan Bennett
Contact Mr Alan Bennett or Justin Bennett
✉ **24 New Bridge Street, Truro, Cornwall, TR1 2AA** Ⓟ
☎ 01872 273296
Est. 1954 ***Stock size*** Large
Stock Furniture pre-1910, general antiques
Open Mon–Sat 9am–5.30pm
Services Valuations

Blackwater Pine Antiques
Contact Linda Cropper
✉ **Blackwater, Truro, Cornwall, TR4 8ET** Ⓟ
☎ 01872 560919
Est. 1989 ***Stock size*** Large
Stock Antique pine and oak furniture
Open Mon–Sat 10am–5.30pm Wed 10am–1pm
Services Valuations, restorations, pine stripping

Bonython Bookshop
Contact Mrs R Carpenter
✉ **16 Kenwyn Street, Truro, Cornwall, TR1 3BU**
☎ 01872 262886
Est. 1996 ***Stock size*** Small
Stock Antiquarian, second-hand and art books. Cornish interest a speciality
Open Mon–Sat 10.30am–4.30pm
Services Valuations, book search

Bric-a-Brac
Contact Richard Bonehill
✉ **16a Walsingham Place, Truro, Cornwall, TR1 2RP** Ⓟ
☎ 01872 225200
Ⓔ richard@bonehill3.freeserve.co.uk
Ⓦ www.bonehill3.freeserve.co.uk
Est. 1974 ***Stock size*** Large
Stock Militaria, small collectables, Royal commemorative china
Open Mon–Sat 9.30am–5pm
Fairs Lostwithiel
Services Research into WWI and WWII war deaths

Philip Buddell
Contact Linda Buddell
✉ **The Elms, Tresillian, Truro, Cornwall, TR2 4BA**
☎ 01872 2520173 Ⓜ 07974 022893
Ⓔ lulubudd@aol.com
Est. 1989
Open Mon–Fri 10am–5pm Sat by appointment
Sales Auctions and viewing at a hall in Ladock. Antiques and general household sale 3-weekly on Sat 10am viewing Fri 2–8pm. Specialist wine sale, toy sale and book sale quarterly. Phone for details
Catalogues Yes

Philip Buddell Antiques
Contact Philip or Linda Buddell
✉ **The Elms, Tresillian, Truro, Cornwall, TR2 4BA** Ⓟ
☎ 01872 520173
Ⓜ 07974 022893
Ⓔ lulubudd@aol.com
Est. 2000 ***Stock size*** Medium
Stock Fine furniture, paintings
Open Mon–Fri 10am–5pm Sat by appointment
Services Valuations

Coinage Hall Antique Centre
Contact Tony Martin
✉ **1 Boscawen Street, Truro, Cornwall, TR1 2QV** Ⓟ
☎ 01872 262520 Ⓕ 01872 261133
Est. 1996 ***Stock size*** Medium
No. of dealers 6
Stock Fine furniture, collectables, general antiques, fabrics, fine art
Open Mon–Sat 10am–4.30pm
Services Valuations

Collectors Corner
Contact Alan McLoughlin
✉ **Unit 45–46, Pannier Market, Back Quay, Truro, Cornwall, TR1 2LL** Ⓟ
☎ 01872 272729
Ⓔ almacmedal@aol.com
Ⓦ www.militarycollectables.co.uk
Est. 1997 ***Stock size*** Medium
Stock Coins, banknotes, medals, militaria, stamps, postcards, cigarette cards
Open Mon–Sat 9.30am–4.30pm
Services Valuations, medal mounting

Count House Antiques
Contact Mrs M Such
✉ **Coinage Hall, 1 Princess Street, Truro, Cornwall, TR1 2ES** Ⓟ
☎ 01872 264269
Est. 1998 ***Stock size*** Medium
Stock General antiques
Open Mon–Sat 10am–4.30pm
Fairs Exeter

Just Books
Contact Jenny Wicks
✉ **9 Pydar Mews, Truro, Cornwall, TR1 2UX** Ⓟ
☎ 01872 242532
Est. 1986 ***Stock size*** Medium
Stock Antiquarian, collectable, second-hand and out-of-print books, Cornish topography
Open Mon–Sat 9.30am–5pm
Services Valuations, book search, repairs referral

Lodge and Thomas
Contact Mr Lodge
58 Lemon Street, Truro, Cornwall, TR1 2PY
☎ 01872 272722 Ⓕ 01872 223665
Ⓔ landt@cwcom.net
Ⓦ www.lodgeandthomas.co.uk
Est. 1892
Open Mon–Fri 9am–5.30pm Sat 9am–noon
Sales General antiques and collectables sale, viewing 9–11am prior to sale. Phone for details. Sales held at Ludgvan Community Hall, Ludgvan, Penzance, Cornwall
Frequency 8 per year
Catalogues Yes

Once Upon A Time
Contact Graham Kennedy
The Coinage Hall, Truro, Cornwall, TR1 2QU Ⓟ
☎ 01872 262520 Ⓕ 01872 262520
Est. 1996 *Stock size* Medium
No. of dealers 6
Stock General antiques, English, French and Continental furniture, paintings, sculpture
Open Mon–Sat 10am–5pm
Services Restorations, upholstery

Taylors Collectables
Contact Mr D Taylor
The Antique Centre (Upstairs), 1 Princes Street, Truro, Cornwall, TR1 2ER
☎ 01872 262336 Ⓜ 07775 811686
Est. 1996 *Stock size* Large
Stock Collectables, postcards, coins, medals, stamps, ceramics, books, toys, cigarette cards, militaria
Open Mon–Sat 10am–4pm
Fairs Ardingly, Newark, West Point, Brentwood
Services Valuations

The Truro Auction Centre
Contact Martyn Rowe
City Wharf, Malpas Road, Truro, Cornwall, TR1 1QH Ⓟ
☎ 01872 260020 Ⓕ 01872 261794
Est. 1990
Open Mon–Fri 9am–5.30pm except Wed 9am–6pm Sat 9am–1pm
Sales Victorian and general sale every Thurs 10am, viewing Wed 2–6pm. Antiques and picture sale, also collectors' and sporting sale every 6 to 8 weeks Fri 10.30am, viewing Wed 2–6pm Thurs 2–4pm. 3 vintage and classic automobile sales every year, telephone for details
Frequency Weekly
Catalogues Yes

WADEBRIDGE

Acorn Antique Interiors
Contact Brian or Margaret
Eddystone Road, Wadebridge, Cornwall, PL27 7AL Ⓟ
☎ 01208 812815
Est. 1982 *Stock size* Medium
Stock Antique pine furniture
Open Mon–Sat 9am–5pm
Services Restorations

Lambrays
Contact Richard J Hamm
Polmorla Walk, The Platt, Wadebridge, Cornwall, PL27 7AE Ⓟ
☎ 01208 813593 Ⓕ 01208 814986
Est. 1981
Open Mon–Fri 9am–5.30pm Sat 9am–noon (prior to sale)
Sales Quarterly specialist antique sales. Victoriana sales fortnightly Mon at 11am
Catalogues Yes

Polmorla Bookshop
Contact Joan Buck
1 Polmorla Road, Wadebridge, Cornwall, PL27 7NB Ⓟ
☎ 01208 814399
Est. 1991 *Stock size* Large
Stock Antiquarian, rare, second-hand and out-of-print books
Open Mon–Sat 10.30am–5pm
Services Valuations, house clearance, book search

Relics
Contact Mr K Brenton
4 Polmorla Road, Wadebridge, Cornwall, PL27 7NB Ⓟ
☎ 01208 815383
Est. 1991 *Stock size* Large
Stock Furniture, china, brass, kitchenware, pictures
Open Mon–Sat 10am–5pm

Victoria Antiques
Contact Mr Daly
21 Molesworth Street, Wadebridge, Cornwall, PL27 7DD Ⓟ
☎ 01208 814160 Ⓕ 01208 814160
Est. 1974 *Stock size* Large
Stock General antiques, clocks, barometers, period furniture
Open Mon–Sat 9am–5pm

DEVON

ASHBURTON

Adrian Ager
Contact Adrian Ager
Ashburton Marbles, Great Hall, North Street, Ashburton, Devon, TQ13 7QD Ⓟ
☎ 01364 653189 Ⓕ 01364 653189
Ⓔ afager@tinyworld.co.uk
Ⓦ www.adrianager.co.uk
Est. 1975 *Stock size* Large
Stock Victorian furnishings, interior fittings, fireplaces, dining room tables, garden statuary, garden ornaments
Open Mon–Fri 8am–5pm Sat 10am–4pm
Services Valuations, restorations

The Dartmoor Bookshop (PBFA)
Contact Mr Paul Heatley
2 Kingsbridge Lane, Ashburton, Newton Abbot, Devon, TQ13 7DK Ⓟ
☎ 01364 653356
Ⓔ Dartmoorbks@aol.com
Ⓦ www.dartmoorbks.dabsol.co.uk
Est. 1974 *Stock size* Large
Stock Antiquarian, second-hand, rare and out-of-print books
Open Mon–Sat 9.30am–5.30pm

Kessler Ford Antiques
Contact Matthew Ford or Elizabeth Kessler
9 North Street, Ashburton, Devon, TQ13 7QJ Ⓟ
☎ 01364 654310 Ⓕ 01364 654141
Ⓜ 07770 782402
Ⓔ kessler.ford@netmatters.co.uk
Est. 1998 *Stock size* Medium
Stock 17th–18thC English oak and mahogany furniture
Open Tues–Sat 10am–5pm closed Wed or by appointment

Memories
Contact Julia Walters
Globe Buildings, 15 North Street, Ashburton, Devon, TQ13 7QH Ⓟ
☎ 01364 654681 Ⓜ 07773 795777
Est. 1996 *Stock size* Medium
Stock A varied range of period furniture Georgian–Edwardian, collectables

Open Mon–Sat 10am–4pm closed Wed pm
Fairs Shepton Mallet, Westpoint, Exeter
Services Restorations

Moor Antiques
Contact Mr or Mrs Gatland
19a North Street, Ashburton, Newton Abbot, Devon, TQ13 7QH
01364 653767 07720 183414
moorantiques@aol.com
Est. 1984 *Stock size* Medium
Stock 18th–19thC furniture, silver, glass, porcelain, clocks, jewellery
Open Mon–Sat 10am–4.30pm Wed 10am–1pm
Services Valuations

Rendells
Contact Mr Clive Morgan
Stonepark, Ashburton, Newton Abbot, Devon, TQ13 7RH
01364 653017 01364 654251
stonepark@rendells.co.uk
www.rendells.co.uk
Est. 1816
Open Mon–Fri 9am–5.30pm
Sales Antiques and selected items monthly Thurs Fri 10am, viewing Tues 10am–7pm Wed 10am–5pm
Frequency Monthly
Catalogues Yes

The Shambles
Contact Mrs Pam Paice
22 North Street, Ashburton, Devon, TQ13 7QD
01364 653848
Est. 1986 *Stock size* Large
Stock Furniture, collectables, marine antiques, textiles, pictures, rugs, silver, Staffordshire figures
Open Mon–Sat 10am–5pm

The Snug
Contact Jill Stubbs or Ros Gregg
15 North Street, Ashburton, Devon, TQ13 7QH
01364 653096
Est. 1991 *Stock size* Medium
Stock Antiques, decorative items and textiles
Open Mon–Sat 10am–4.30pm
Fairs Hyson Fairs

Taylors
Contact Wendy Taylor
5 North Street, Ashburton, Devon, TQ13 7QJ
01364 652631
Est. 1985 *Stock size* Medium
Stock 18thC–Edwardian oak furniture, 18thC blue-and-white Chinese porcelain
Open Mon–Sat 10am–5pm Wed closed pm

AXMINSTER

Axminster Salerooms
Contact John Bloxham
Coombe Lane, Axminster, Devon, EX13 5AY
01297 35693 01297 35693
Est. 1858
Open Mon–Fri 9am–5pm
Sales General antiques sale second and last Wed of the month 10am, viewing Tues 2–8pm
Frequency Monthly

South Street Antiques
Contact Philip Atkins
South Street, Axminster, Devon, EX13 5AD
01297 33701
Est. 1987 *Stock size* Medium
Stock General antiques
Open Mon–Sat 9.30am–5pm
Fairs Shepton Mallet
Services Valuations

BAMPTON

Bampton Gallery
Contact Gerald Chidwick
2–4 Brook Street, Bampton, Devon, EX16 9LY
01398 331119/331354
01398 331119
bampgall@aol.com
Est. 1997 *Stock size* Medium
Stock Antique porcelain, glass, small furniture, pictures
Open Mon–Sun 10am–5pm
Services Restorations

BARNSTAPLE

The Barn Antiques
Contact Mr T Cusack
73 Newport Road, Barnstaple, Devon, EX32 9BG
01271 323131
Est. 1987 *Stock size* Large
Stock General antiques
Open Mon–Sat 9.30am–5pm closed Wed pm
Services Valuations, restorations

Barnstaple Auctions
Contact Mr Mugleston
Pilton Quay, Barnstaple, Devon, EX31 1PB
01271 327087 01271 327087
Est. 1993
Open Mon–Fri 9am–5pm Sat 10am–2pm
Sales General antiques sale last Thurs 6.30pm every month viewing Wed 4–7pm
Frequency Monthly
Catalogues Yes

Medina Gallery
Contact Richard Jennings
80 Boutport Street, Barnstaple, Devon, EX31 1SR
01271 371025
Est. 1973 *Stock size* Medium
Stock Antique prints, maps, oils, watercolours
Open Mon–Sat 9.30am–5pm

North Devon Antiques Centre
Contact Patrick Broome
The Old Church, Cross Street, Barnstaple, Devon, EX31 1BD
01271 375788 01271 375788
07967 930917
patrick-broome@top-finish-designs.freeserve.co.uk
Est. 1998 *Stock size* Large
No. of dealers 27
Stock Georgian to contemporary furniture, Royal Worcester, Clarice Cliff, Crested china ware, Barum and Brannam, militaria, clocks, architectural salvage, pictures and prints, Art Deco
Open Mon–Sat 10am–4.30pm
Services Restorations, café also open 6 days

Tarka Books (BA)
Contact Fiona Broster
5 Bear Street, Barnstaple, Devon, EX32 7BU
01271 374997
info@tarkabooks.co.uk
www.tarkabooks.co.uk
Est. 1987 *Stock size* Large
Stock Second-hand books. Henry Williamson titles a speciality
Open Mon–Sat 9.45am–5pm
Services Book search

BEAWORTHY

Alan Jones Antiques
Contact Mr A Jones
Beara Court, Highampton, Beaworthy, Devon, EX21 5JJ
01409 231428 F 01409 231528
M 07836 530819
Est. 1974 *Stock size* Small
Stock Antiques and furniture
Trade only Yes
Open By appointment
Services Delivery can be arranged to most parts of the world

BEER

Beer Collectables
Contact Mr Forkes
Dolphin Hotel, Fore Street, Beer, Seaton, Devon, EX12 3EQ P
01297 24362
Est. 1993 *Stock size* Medium
Stock Collectables, china, glass, fishing tackle, jewellery
Open Mon–Sun 10am–5pm
Fairs Exeter Livestock, Salisbury, T&T Fairs

BIDEFORD

J Collins & Son (BADA, LAPADA, CINOA)
Contact Mr John Biggs
28 High Street, Bideford, Devon, EX39 2AN P
01237 473103 F 01237 475658
E biggs@collinsantiques.co.uk
W www.collinsantiques.co.uk
Est. 1953 *Stock size* Large
Stock Georgian and Regency furniture, Victorian oil paintings, watercolours
Open By appointment
Fairs BADA, Olympia (Nov)
Services Restorations of English furniture, watercolours and oil paintings

Peter Hames (PBFA)
Contact Mr P Hames
Old Bridge Antiques Centre, Market Place, Bideford, Devon, EX39 2DR
01237 421065 F 01237 421065
E peterhames@hotmail.com
W www.members.aol.com/tarkabooks
Est. 1979 *Stock size* Medium
Stock Small selection of general books. Jazz and North Devon books a speciality
Open Mon–Sat 9am–5.30pm
Fairs PBFA

Medina Gallery
Contact Caroline Jennings
55 Mill Street, Bideford, Devon, EX39 2JR P
01237 476483
Est. 1973 *Stock size* Medium
Stock Antique prints, maps, oils, watercolours
Open Mon–Sat 9.30am–5pm

Stuff
Contact David Marochan
27 Market Place, Bideford, Devon, EX39 2DR P
01237 423535
M 0778 8467 727
Est. 1988 *Stock size* Medium
Stock General antiques, collectables, furniture, smalls
Open Mon–Sat 10am–4pm
Fairs Westpoint, Exeter Livestock

BRAUNTON

Book Cellar
Contact Mr Dennis Stow
5a The Square, East Street, Braunton, Devon, EX33 2JD P
01271 815655 F 01271 815655
Est. 1988 *Stock size* Large
Stock Antiquarian and second-hand books
Open Summer Mon–Sat 10am–5pm closed Wed winter Tues Thurs Sat 10am–4pm

BRIXHAM

Devon Clocks
Contact Dr Paul Strickland
Ye Olde Coffin House, King Street, Brixham, Devon, TQ5 9TF P
01803 856307
E clocks@forall.fsnet.co.uk
W www.forall.fsnet.co.uk
Est. 1997 *Stock size* Large
Stock Clocks, related tools, books
Open Mon–Sun 9am–5pm
Services Restorations

John Luce Antiques
Contact Mr J Luce
King Street Rooms, King Street, Brixham, Devon, TQ5 9TF P
01803 858303
Est. 1971 *Stock size* Medium
Stock Early motoring, clocks, general antiques
Open Mon–Sat 10am–5pm
Services Restoration of woodwork and clocks

John Prestige Antiques
Contact Mr Prestige
Greenswood Court, Greenswood Road, Brixham, Devon, TQ5 9HN P
01803 856141 F 01803 851649
E sales@john-prestige.co.uk
W www.john-prestige.co.uk
Est. 1971 *Stock size* Large
Stock Furniture, pictures, mirrors, ceramics
Trade only Yes
Open Mon–Fri 8.45am–6pm or by appointment
Services Valuations, restorations

BUDLEIGH SALTERTON

Alison Gosling Antiques
Contact Mrs Gosling
46a High Street, Budleigh Salterton, Devon, EX9 6LJ P
01395 443737/271451
M 07798 782444
Est. 1983 *Stock size* Medium
Stock Late Georgian–1930s decorative items, early 1700–1830s period furniture, mostly Georgian and Regency
Open Mon 11am–5pm Tues Wed 3–5pm Fri 11.30am–5pm or by appointment
Services Valuations

B & T Thorn and Son
Contact Mr Thorn
2 High Street, Budleigh Salterton, Devon, EX9 6LQ P
01395 442448
Est. 1950 *Stock size* Medium
Stock Ceramics, English pottery and porcelain
Open Tues Fri Sat 10am–1pm
Services Valuations

CATTEDOWN

Plymouth Auction Rooms
Contact Mr P Keen
Edwin House, St John's Road, Cattedown, Plymouth, Devon, PL4 0NZ P
01752 254740 F 01752 254740
E info@plymouthauctions.co.uk
W www.plymouthauctions.co.uk
Est. 1992

Open Mon–Fri 9am–5pm
Sales Antiques and collectables fortnightly Wed 10.30am, viewing Tues 10am–7pm Wed 9–10.30am.
Frequency Fortnightly
Catalogues Yes

CHAGFORD

Whiddons Antiques & Tearooms
Contact Pippa or Mark Phillips
4 High Street, Chagford, Devon, TQ13 8AJ P
☎ 01647 433406
Est. 1979 *Stock size* Medium
Stock Royal Doulton, Beswick figures, small furniture
Open Mon–Sat 10am–6pm Sun noon–6pm

CLYST HONITON

Pennies Antiques
Contact Mrs Clark
Home Farm, Clyst Honiton, Devon, EX25 2LX P
☎ 01392 276532
W www.penniesantiques.co.uk
Est. 1979 *Stock size* Medium
Stock General antiques
Open By appointment

COLYTON

D Barney
Contact Mr D Barney
Greenfield, Colyton Hill, Colyton, Devon, EX24 6HY P
☎ 01297 552702 F 01297 552702
E doug.barney@talk21.com
Est. 1969 *Stock size* Medium
Stock English and foreign coins
Open By appointment and mail order
Services Valuations

Colyton Antique Centre
Contact R C Hunt
Dolphin Street, Colyton, Devon, EX24 6LU P
☎ 01297 552339 F 01297 552339
M 07973 678989
E colytonantiques@modelgarage.co.uk
W www.modelgarage.co.uk
Est. 1988 *Stock size* Medium
No. of dealers 30
Stock Antiques and collectables
Open Summer Mon–Sun 10am–5pm winter/Bank Holidays 11am–4pm

COMBE MARTIN

Combe Martin Clock Shop
Contact Robin Westcott
1 High Street, Combe Martin, Ilfracombe, Devon, EX34 0EP P
☎ 01271 882607
E robin@robinw.force9.co.uk
W www.robinw.force9.co.uk
Est. 1980 *Stock size* Medium
Stock Clocks from longcase to mantel and barometers
Open Mon–Sat 9am–6pm
Services Restorations of clocks

CREDITON

Mid Devon Antiques
Contact Colin Knowles
The Corn Store, Morchard Road, Copplestone, Crediton, Devon, EX17 5LP P
☎ 01363 84066 M 07718 583086
Est. 1965 *Stock size* Medium
Stock Country furniture, tables, beds
Open By appointment
Services Restorations, repairs

Musgrave Bickford Antiques (BHI)
Contact Dennis Bickford
15 East Street, Crediton, Devon, EX17 3AT P
☎ 01363 775042
Est. 1987 *Stock size* Medium
Stock Clocks, barometers and small furniture
Open By appointment
Fairs Westpoint, Shepton Mallet
Services Valuations, restorations

Woods Emporium
Contact Martin Wood
1 Exeter Road, Crediton, Devon, EX17 3BH
☎ 01363 774702/772503
F 01363 776082
E woodsgroup@eclipse.co.uk
Est. 1972 *Stock size* Large
Stock Marine antiques
Open Mon–Fri 9am–5.30pm Sat 9am–3.30pm

Woods Emporium
Contact Martin Wood
32 Exeter Road, Crediton, Devon, EX17 3BP P
☎ 01363 772503 F 01363 776082
E woodsgroup@eclipse.co.uk
Est. 1972 *Stock size* Large
Stock Government surplus Navy equipment
Open Mon–Fri 9am–5.30pm Sat 9am–3.30pm

CULLOMPTON

Cobweb Antiques
Contact Richard Holmes
The Old Tannery, Exeter Road, Cullompton, Devon, EX15 1DT P
☎ 01884 855748 F 01884 38476
E tannery@cullompton-antiques.co.uk
W www.cullompton-antiques.ltd.uk
Est. 1986 *Stock size* Large
Stock General antiques, country furniture
Open Mon–Sat 10am–5pm

Country Antiques & Interiors
Contact Mr M C Mead
The Old Brewery, High Street, Uffculme, Cullompton, Devon, EX15 3AB P
☎ 01884 841110 F 01803 845480
M 07768 328433
E mike@englishcountryantiques.co.uk
W www.englishcountryantiques.co.uk
Est. 1994 *Stock size* Medium
Stock Country furniture, decorative items
Open Mon–Fri 9am–6pm by appointment
Services Shipping arranged

Cullompton Old Tannery Antiques
Contact George Mills
The Old Tannery, Exeter Road, Cullompton, Devon, EX15 1DT P
☎ 01884 38476 F 01884 38476
E mail@cullompton-antiques.ltd.uk
W www.cullompton-antiques.ltd.uk
Est. 1987 *Stock size* Large
Stock Antique country furniture, English, French and European clocks, mirrors, decorative items
Open Mon–Sat 10am–5pm
Services Shipping, courier

English Country Antiques
Contact Mr M C Mead
The Old Brewery, High Street, Uffculme, Cullompton, Devon, EX15 3AB P
☎ 01803 845480 F 01803 845480
M 07768 328 433
E mike@englishcountryantiques.co.uk

Ⓦ www.englishcountryantiques.co.uk
Est. 1984 *Stock size* Medium
Stock Country antiques, decorative items of all types
Open By appointment

Oaks & Partners
Contact Katy Rombold
The Old Tannery, Exeter Road, Cullompton, Devon, EX15 1DT Ⓟ
☎ 01884 35848 Ⓕ 01884 38000
Ⓔ roger.shenton@btclick.com
Ⓦ www.invaluable.com/oaksandpartners
Est. 1979
Open Mon–Fri 9am–4pm
Sales Antiques and general sale Sat 10.30am, viewing Thurs 9am–5pm Fri 9am–8pm
Frequency 3-weekly
Catalogues Yes

DARTMOUTH

Looking Back
Contact Paddy Distin
32 Lower Street, Dartmouth, Devon, TQ6 9AN Ⓟ
☎ 01803 832615
Est. 1990 *Stock size* Medium
Stock General antiques
Open Summer Mon–Sat 9.30am–10.30pm Sun 10am–5pm winter Mon–Sun 10am-5pm
Services House clearance

DAWLISH

Emporium
Contact Michael Peters
40b The Strand, Dawlish, Devon, EX7 9PT Ⓟ
☎ 01626 862222 Ⓕ 01626 774689
Ⓜ 07768 076360
Est. 1983 *Stock size* Medium
Stock General antiques
Open Tues–Sat 10am–5pm
Fairs West Point, Shepton Mallet
Services Valuations

EAST BUDLEIGH

Antiques at Budleigh House
Contact Wendy Cook
Budleigh House, East Budleigh, Devon, EX9 7ED Ⓟ
☎ 01395 445368
Est. 1981 *Stock size* Small
Stock 17th–18thC country furniture
Open Tues Thur Fri Sat 10am–5pm

EXETER

Bearnes (SOFAA)
Contact Mr R Barlow
St Edmund's Court, Okehampton Street, Exeter, Devon, EX4 1DU Ⓟ
☎ 01392 422800 Ⓕ 01392 207007
Ⓔ enquiries@bearnes.co.uk
Ⓦ www.bearnes.co.uk
Est. 1945
Open Mon–Fri 9.30am–5pm
Sales General sale Tues am, viewing Sat am Mon 9.30am–7.30pm. Specialist sale 3 times a year Tues Wed. Phone for details
Frequency Fortnightly
Catalogues Yes

Bonhams
38/39 Southernhay East, Exeter, Devon, EX14 1PE Ⓟ
☎ 01392 455955 Ⓕ 01392 455962
Ⓔ exeter@bonhams.com
Ⓦ www.bonhams.com
Open Mon–Fri 9am–1pm 2–5pm
Catalogues Yes

Lisa Cox Music (ABA)
Contact Lisa Cox
Heath House, Heath Lane, Whitestone, Exeter, Devon, EX4 2HJ Ⓟ
☎ 01647 61140 Ⓕ 01647 61138
Ⓔ music@lisacoxmusic.co.uk
Ⓦ www.lisacoxmusic.co.uk
Est. 1984 *Stock size* Large
Stock Antiquarian music, pictures, ephemera, autographs
Open By appointment
Services Valuations

Eclectique
Contact Sue Bellamy
26–27 Commercial Road, The Quay, Exeter, Devon, EX2 4AE Ⓟ
☎ 01392 250799
Est. 1994 *Stock size* Medium
Stock Antique and painted furniture, ceramics, lamps, objets d'art, collectables
Open Mon–Sun 11am–5.30pm
Services Interior design

Exeter Antique Lighting
Contact Julian Wood
Cellar 15, The Quay, Exeter, Devon, EX2 4AP Ⓟ
☎ 01392 490848 Ⓜ 07702 969438
Est. 1990 *Stock size* Large
Stock Antique lighting, fireplaces, iron beds
Open Mon–Sun 11am–5pm or by appointment
Fairs Newark, Ardingly
Services Valuations, restorations

Exeter Rare Books (ABA, PBFA)
Contact Mr R C Parry
12a Guildhall Shopping Centre, Exeter, Devon, EX4 3HG Ⓟ
☎ 01392 436021
Est. 1974 *Stock size* Medium
Stock Antiquarian, rare and second-hand books
Open Mon–Sat 10am–1pm 2–5pm
Fairs Chelsea ABA, Olympia Hilton

Exeter's Antiques Centre on the Quay
Contact Patsy Bliss
The Quay, Exeter, Devon, EX2 4AN Ⓟ
☎ 01392 493501
Ⓦ www.exeterquayantiques.co.uk
Est. 1984 *Stock size* Large
No. of dealers 21
Stock Antiques, collectables, books, postcards, jewellery, tools, cameras etc
Open Mon–Sun summer 10am–6pm winter 10am–5pm
Services Restaurant

McBains Antiques (LAPADA)
Contact Mr Gordon McBain
Exeter Airport Industrial Estate, Exeter, Devon, EX5 2BA Ⓟ
☎ 01392 366261 Ⓕ 01392 365572
Ⓔ mcbains@netcom.co.uk
Est. 1980 *Stock size* Large
Stock Georgian, Victorian, Edwardian furniture, also selection of French and Continental furniture
Open Mon–Fri 9am–6pm Sat 10am–1pm closed Bank Holiday weekends
Fairs Newark
Services Full container and export facility

Mortimers
Contact Ian Watson
87 Queen Street, Exeter, Devon, EX4 3RP Ⓟ
☎ 01392 279994 Ⓜ 07767 492815
Est. 1970 *Stock size* Large

Stock Antique jewellery, watches, clocks and silver
Open Mon–Sat 9.30am–5pm
Services Valuations, restorations

Pennies Antiques
Contact Mrs Clark
6 Marsh Green Road, Marsh Barton, Exeter, Devon, EX2 8NY
01392 276532
www.penniesantiques.co.uk
Est. 1979 *Stock size* Medium
Stock General antiques
Open Mon–Sun 10am–5pm

Phantique
Contact Mrs Bliss
Unit 5–7, 47 The Quay, Exeter, Devon, EX2 4AN
01392 498995
www.phantique.co.uk
Est. 1996 *Stock size* Large
No. of dealers 9
Stock General antiques and collectables, prints, books, Torquay pottery
Open Summer Mon–Fri 10.30am–5.30pm
Sat Sun 10.30am–6pm
winter 10.30am–5pm

The Quay Gallery Antiques Emporium
Contact Mark Davis
43 The Quay, Exeter, Devon, EX2 4AN
01392 213283
Est. 1984 *Stock size* Large
Stock Fine mahogany and oak furniture, porcelain, silver, glass, paintings, prints, general antiques, antiquities, clocks, Art Deco, 20thC furniture
Open Mon–Sun 10am–5pm
Fairs West Point, Shepton Mallet, Cooper Fairs
Services Valuations

St David's Auctions
Contact Nick Magnum
1 & 2 Wessex Estate, Station Road, Exeter, Devon, EX4 4NZ
01392 217412/3 01392 217414
07788 428931
info@stdavidsauctions.co.uk
www.stdavidsauctions.co.uk
Est. 2001
Open Mon–Sat 9am–5pm
Sales General antiques sale Sat, viewing Fri 9am–7pm
Frequency Weekly
Catalogues Yes

Tobys (SALVO)
Contact Mr P Norrish
Station House, Station Road, Exminster, Exeter, Devon, EX6 8DZ
01392 833499 01392 833429
www.tobysreclamation.co.uk
Est. 1983 *Stock size* Large
Stock Architectural antiques, sanitary ware, fireplaces, reclaimed building materials
Open Mon–Fri 9am–5pm Sat 9.30am–4.30pm Sun Bank Holidays 10.30am–4.30pm
Services House clearance, nationwide delivery

Tredantiques
Contact Jon Tredant
Adjacent to Exeter Airport, Exeter, Devon, EX5 2BA
01392 447082 07967 447082
www.tredantiques.com
Est. 1982 *Stock size* Large
Stock Good quality furniture and decorative items
Open Mon–Fri 9am–6pm or Sat by appointment
Fairs Newark, Decorative Antiques and Textiles Fair (Battersea)

Victoriana Antiques and Kents Jewellers
Contact Mr Kent
68 Sidwell Street, Exeter, Devon, EX4 6PH
01392 275204/275291
Est. 1945 *Stock size* Medium
Stock General antiques, porcelain, jewellery, silver
Open Mon Tues Thurs–Sat 9.30am–5pm
Services Jewellery, silver and porcelain restorations and repair

EXMOUTH

Antiques and Collectables
Contact Antonio Newton
Unit 3, The Indoor Market, The Strand, Exmouth, Devon, EX8 1AB
07831 095951
Est. 1990 *Stock size* Medium
Stock Jewellery, clocks, Art Deco, glass, Beswick, Wade, commemorative ware, Poole, Royal Doulton
Open Mon–Sat 9am–5.30pm
Services Valuations, restorations

Browsers
Contact Mr or Mrs Spiller
1–2 The Strand, Exmouth, Devon, EX8 1HL
01395 265010
Est. 1988 *Stock size* Large
Stock Collectables, toys, advertising, books, china
Open Mon–Sat 10.30am–6pm

Martin Spencer-Thomas (NAVA)
Contact Mr M Spencer-Thomas
Bicton Street Auction Rooms, Bicton Street, Exmouth, Devon, EX8 2RT
01395 267403 01395 222598
martin@martinspencerthomas.co.uk
www.martinspencerthomas.co.uk
Est. 1984
Open Mon–Fri 9am–5pm
Sales Antiques sale Mon 1.30pm, modern furniture sale Mon 10.30am, viewing Thurs 9am–6pm Fri 9am–5pm Sat 10am–4pm
Frequency 5 weeks
Catalogues Yes

HATHERLEIGH

Hatherleigh Antiques (BADA)
Contact Michael Dann
15 Bridge Street, Hatherleigh, Devon, EX20 3HU
01837 810159
Stock size Large
Stock Gothic and Renaissance furniture
Open Mon–Sat please telephone to confirm opening times
Services Valuations, restorations

HELE

Fagins Antiques
Contact Jean Pearson
Old Whiteways Cider Factory, Hele, Exeter, Devon, EX5 4PW
01392 882062 01392 882194
cstrong@fagins-antiques.co.uk
www.fagins-antiques.co.uk
Est. 1978 *Stock size* Large
Stock Stripped pine, dark wood, general antiques, china, architectural antiques
Open Mon–Fri 9.15am–5pm
Sat 11am–5pm
Services Pine stripping

HOLSWORTHY

The Mill Emporium
Contact Tim Coleman
Bude Road, Holsworthy, Devon, EX22 6HZ
01409 254800
Est. 1996 *Stock size* Large
Stock Pine, mahogany and oak furniture, china and general antiques
Open Tues–Sat 9am–5pm
Fairs West Point
Services Restorations, pine stripping, re-upholstery

HONITON

Abingdon House Antique Centre
Contact Nick Thompson
136 High Street, Honiton, Devon, EX14 1JP
01404 42108
Est. 1985 *Stock size* Large
Stock General antiques, 17th-20thC furniture, country, tools, prints, equestrian
Open Mon–Sat 9.30 am–5.30pm April–Dec Sun 11am-5pm

Antique Toys
38 High Street, Honiton, Devon, EX14 1PJ
01404 41194
honitonantiquetoys38@hotmail.com
Est. 1976 *Stock size* Large
Stock Toys, teddies, dolls
Open Tues–Sat 10.30am–5pm closed Mon Thurs
Services Dolls' hospital

Jane Barnes Antiques and Interiors
Contact Mrs Barnes
59 High Street, Honiton, Devon, EX14 1PW
01404 41712/861300
01404 861300 07971 328618
Est. 1985 *Stock size* Large
Stock General antiques, Victorian and Edwardian
Open Mon–Sat 10am–4pm closed Wed or by appointment
Services Chairs copied to order

Bonhams
Dowell Street, Honiton, Devon, EX14 1LX
01404 41872 01404 43137
honiton@bonhams.com
www.bonhams.com
Open Mon–Fri 9am–5.30pm
Sales Honiton Saleroom

Roderick Butler (BADA)
Contact Mr R Butler or Mrs V Butler
Marwood House, Honiton, Devon, EX14 1PY
01404 42169
Est. 1948 *Stock size* Large
Stock 17th–18thC Regency furniture, works of art and metalwork
Open Mon–Sat 9.30am–5pm in August by appointment only
Services Restorations

Collectables
Contact Mr Chris Guthrie
134B High Street, Honiton, Devon, EX14 1JP
01404 47024
chris@collectableshoniton.co.uk
www.collectableshoniton.co.uk
Est. 1995 *Stock size* Large
Stock Ceramics, Wade, cameras, railwayana, toys, militaria, annuals, phone cards, cigarette cards, breweriana, commemorative, games, postcards, Crested china
Open Mon–Sat 10am–5pm

Colystock Antiques
Contact Dave McCollum
Rising Sun Farm, Stockland, Honiton, Devon, EX14 9NH
01404 861271 01404 861271
Est. 1985 *Stock size* Large
Stock 18th–19thC pine and reproduction furniture, reclaimed pine kitchens
Open Mon–Sat 8.30am–6pm Sun 1–4pm

Fountain Antiques
Contact J Palmer or G York
132 High Street, Honiton, Devon, EX14 1JP
01404 42074 01404 44993
07831 138011
antiques@gyork.co.uk
Est. 1988 *Stock size* Large
No. of dealers 15
Stock Linen, books, cutlery, telephones, china, furniture, lighting
Open Mon–Sat 9.30am–5.30pm

The Globe Antiques & Art Centre
Contact A J Littler
165 High Street, Honiton, Devon, EX14 1LQ
01404 549372 01404 41465
theglobe@honitonantiques.com
www.honitonantiques.com
Est. 2000 *Stock size* Large
No. of dealers 25
Stock Period furniture, Art Deco, silver, porcelain, glass, corkscrews, lamps, ephemera, collectables, bespoke furniture, Oriental rugs, clocks, barometers, jewellery, permanent art exhibition, pictures
Open Mon–Sat 10am–5pm
Services Restorations

The Grove Antique Centre
Contact Lesley Phillips
55 High Street, Honiton, Devon, EX14 1PW
01404 43377 01404 43390
07980 202976
info@groveantiquescentre.com
www.groveantiquescentre.com
Est. 1998 *Stock size* Medium
Stock Bears, silver, porcelain, 18th–20thC furniture, collectables, paintings, clocks, barometers, rugs, decorative items, china, glassware, beds
Open Mon–Sat 10am–5pm
Services Shipping deliveries

Hermitage Antiques
Contact Christian Giltsoff
37 High Street, Honiton, Devon, EX14 8PW
01404 44406 01404 42471
07768 960144
antiquesmerchant@ndirect.co
Est. 1980 *Stock size* Large
Stock General antiques, furniture
Open Mon–Sat 10am–5pm
Services Valuations, buying and selling

High Street Books (PBFA)
Contact Geoff Tyson
150 High Street, Honiton, Devon, EX14 8JX
01404 45570 01404 45570
07930 171380
shegeoff@ukonline.co.uk
Est. 1982 *Stock size* Medium
Stock Antiquarian, books, maps and prints
Open Mon–Sat 10am–5pm
Fairs PBFA
Services Valuations

Honiton Antique Centre
Contact Nick Thompson
Abingdon House, 136 High Street, Honiton, Devon, EX14 8JP
01404 42108
Est. 1982 *Stock size* Large
No. of dealers 20
Stock Early 17th–20thC furniture, metalware, sporting, ceramics, china, glass, paintings
Open Mon–Sat 9.30am–5.30pm Sun 11am–5pm
Services Valuations, restorations, delivery

Honiton Galleries
Contact Mr Richard Connor
205 High Street, Honiton, Devon, EX14 1LQ
01404 42404 01404 46510
sales@honitongalleries.com
www.honitongalleries.com
Est. 1949
Open Mon–Fri 9am–5pm
Sales Antiques and collectors' items bi-monthly Fri 10.30am, viewing Wed 9am–5pm Thurs 9am–7pm Fri 9–10.30am. 6 Fine arts and collectables sales per annum
Frequency Bi-monthly
Catalogues Yes

The Honiton Lace Shop
Contact Jonathan Page
44 High Street, Honiton, Devon, EX14 1PJ
01404 42416 01404 47797
shop@honitonlace.com
www.honitonlace.com
Est. 1984 *Stock size* Large
Stock Antique lace, textiles, bobbins and lace-making equipment
Open Mon–Sat 9.30am–1pm 2–5pm
Services Restoration and cleaning of antique lace

Honiton Old Book Shop (PBFA, ABA)
Contact Roger Collicott or Adele
Felix House, 51 High Street, Honiton, Devon, EX14 1PW
01404 47180 01404 47180
Est. 1978 *Stock size* Medium
Stock Antiquarian, rare and second-hand books, leather bindings, antiquarian maps and prints
Open Mon–Sat 10am–5.30pm
Fairs PBFA, Russell, ABA, Chelsea Town Hall, Olympia (June)
Services Valuations

Kings Arms Antiques Centre
Contact Mrs Heather Grabham
56 High Street, Honiton, Devon, EX14 1PQ
01404 46269
Est. 1989 *Stock size* Large
Stock General antiques, early oak to reproduction furniture
Open Mon–Sat 10am–4.30pm closed Thurs pm or by appointment

Kingsway House Antiques
Contact Mrs M Peache
3 High Street, Honiton, Devon, EX14 8PR
01404 46213
Est. 1981 *Stock size* Medium
Stock Georgian furniture, china, clocks
Open Mon–Sat 10am–5.30pm or by appointment

Maya Antiques
Contact Pauline Brown
46 High Street, Honiton, Devon, EX14 1PJ
01404 46009
Est. 1997 *Stock size* Large
Stock Large Georgian, Victorian, and Edwardian furniture
Open Mon–Sat 10am–5pm
Services Restorations

Merchant House Antiques
Contact Christian Giltsoff
19 High Street, Honiton, Devon, EX14 1PR
01404 42694 01404 42471
antiquesmerchant@ndirect.co
Est. 1980 *Stock size* Large
Stock Fine furniture, general antiques and collectables
Open Mon–Sat 10am–5pm
Services Valuations and interior design

Otter Antiques
Contact Kate Skailes
69 High Street, Honiton, Devon, EX14 1PW
01404 42627 01404 43337
otterantiques@jspencer.co.
www.jspencer.co.uk
Est. 1979 *Stock size* Large
Stock Fine and antique silver, silver plate
Open Mon–Sat 9.30am–5pm Thurs 9.30am–1.30pm
Services Valuations, restorations, silver plating, engraving

Alexander Paul Restorations
Contact Dave Steele
Fenny Bridges, Honiton, Devon, EX14 1PJ
01404 850881 01404 850881
alexanderpaulre@aol.com
Est. 2000 *Stock size* Medium
Stock French and English country furniture
Open Mon–Fri 9am–5.30pm Sat 10am–4pm
Services Restorations

Pilgrim Antiques (LAPADA)
Contact Mrs Mills
145 High Street, Honiton, Devon, EX14 1LJ
01404 41219 01404 45317
Est. 1971 *Stock size* Large
Stock 17th–18thC English and French oak and country furniture, longcase clocks
Open Mon–Sat 9am–5.30pm
Services Valuations, shipping

Plympton Antiques
Contact Mr Button-Stephens
59 High Street, Honiton, Devon, EX14 8PW
01404 42640
Est. 1966 *Stock size* Medium
Stock Mostly mahogany furniture, copper, brass, porcelain
Open Mon–Sat 10am–4.30pm

Jane Strickland & Daughters (LAPADA)
Contact Jane Strickland
71 High Street, Honiton, Devon, EX14 1PW
01404 44221
JSandDaughtersUK@aol.com
Est. 1980 *Stock size* Medium
Stock 18th–19thC English and Continental furniture, upholstery, mirrors, lights, Aubussons, needlepoints
Open Mon–Sat 10am–5pm

⊞ Geoffrey M Woodhead
Contact Mr G Woodhead
✉ **Monkton House, 53 High Street, Honiton, Devon, EX14 1PW** P
☎ 01404 42969
Est. 1950 *Stock size* Large
Stock General antiques and books
Open Mon–Sat 9.30am–1pm 2.15–5pm
Fairs West Point, Shepton Mallet, Livestock Centre Matford Exeter

ILFRACOMBE

⊞ Relics
Contact Nicola Bradshaw
✉ **113 High Street, Ilfracombe, Devon, EX34 9ET**
☎ 01271 865486 Ⓜ 07967 892998
Est. 1980 *Stock size* Medium
Stock General antiques and collectables
Open Mon–Sat 10am–5pm

⊞ Sherbrook Antiques & Collectables
Contact Mr T Pickard
✉ **1 Borough Road, Combe Martin, Ilfracombe, Devon, EX34 0AN** P
☎ 01271 889060 Ⓜ 07887 806493
Est. 2000 *Stock size* Medium
Stock General antiques, glass, ceramics, small furniture
Open Mon–Sun 10am–5.30pm closed Wed
Fairs Westpoint, Exeter
Services Valuations

KINGSBRIDGE

⊞ Avon House Antiques
Contact Mrs Hayward
✉ **13 Church Street, Kingsbridge, Devon, TQ7 1BT** P
☎ 01548 853718
Ⓜ 07977 451223
Est. 1969 *Stock size* Medium
Stock General antiques and collectables
Open Mon–Sat 10am–5pm Thurs closed Sat pm
Fairs Devon County Antiques Fairs
Services Valuations, restorations

⊞ Curiosity Shop
Contact Miss Williams
✉ **9 Church Street, Kingsbridge, Devon, TQ7 1BT** P
☎ 01548 857117/853824
Est. 1997 *Stock size* Small
Stock Antiques, bric-a-brac
Open Mon–Fri 10am–5pm Sat 10am–1pm

⊞ Haywards Antiques & Avon House Antiques
Contact Mr D Hayward
✉ **13 Church Street, Kingsbridge, Devon, TQ7 1BT** P
☎ 01548 853718 Ⓜ 07977 451223
Ⓦ www.haywardsantiques.fsbusiness.co.uk
Est. 1985 *Stock size* Large
Stock General antiques and collectables
Open Mon–Wed 10am–5pm Thurs Fri Sat 10am–1pm
Fairs West Point, Exeter
Services Valuations

⊞ Salters Bookshelf 'The Bookshelf at the Top'
Contact Steve Salter
✉ **89 Fore Street, Kingsbridge, Devon, TQ7 1AB** P
☎ 01548 8856176/857503
Ⓕ 01548 857503
Est. 1997 *Stock size* Medium
Stock Old picture postcards, postal history, postal stationery, accessories
Open Mon–Sat 9am–5.30pm summer Sun10am–2.30pm
Services Picture framing, booksearch agents

LYNTON

⊞ Farthings
Contact Jane or Lucy Farthing
✉ **Church Hill House, Church Hill, Lynton, Devon, EX35 6HY** P
☎ 01598 753744 Ⓕ 01598 753744
Ⓔ jane@farthings1.freeserve.co.uk
Ⓦ farthings.antiques.com
Est. 1984 *Stock size* Large
Stock Antiques, bronzes 18th–20thC, contemporary art, collectables, crafts
Open Mon–Sun 10am–4.30pm
Fairs Westpoint
Services Search service, delivery

⊞ Wood's Antiques
Contact Mr or Mrs Wood
✉ **29a Lee Road, Lynton, Devon, EX35 6BS** P
☎ 01598 752722
Est. 1995 *Stock size* Medium
Stock Antiques, collectables, furniture, clocks
Open Mon–Sun 9am–6pm closed Thurs

MODBURY

⊞ Collectors Choice
Contact Allan Jenkins
✉ **27 Church Street, Modbury, Ivybridge, Devon, PL21 0QR** P
☎ 01548 831111 Ⓜ 07884 365361
Est. 1994 *Stock size* Medium
Stock Small furniture, ceramics, Bakelite, radios, general antiques
Open Mon–Sat 10am–5.30pm
Services Valuations, restoration of valve radios and clocks

⊞ Wild Goose Antiques
Contact Kay or Ty Freeman
✉ **34 Church Street, Modbury, Devon, PL21 0QU** P
☎ 01548 830715
Ⓔ wildgoose@kfreeman0.fsnet.co.uk
Est. 2000 *Stock size* Medium
Stock Antique pine, country furniture, decorative items, brass, iron beds
Open Mon–Sat 10am–5.30pm

MONKTON

⊞ Pughs Antiques
Contact Mr Guy Garner
✉ **Pughs Farm, Monkton, Honiton, Devon, EX14 9QH** P
☎ 01404 42860 Ⓕ 01404 47792
Ⓔ sales@pughsantiques.com
Ⓦ www.pughsantiques.com
Est. 1986 *Stock size* Large
Stock Victorian–Edwardian furniture in mahogany, oak, walnut and pine, French furniture, antique beds
Open Mon–Sat 9am–5.30pm
Services Export

NEWTON ABBOT

⊞ The Attic
Contact Mr Gillman
✉ **9 Union Street, Newton Abbot, Devon, TQ12 2JX** P
☎ 01626 355124
Est. 1976 *Stock size* Large
Stock General antiques and small furniture
Open Tues–Sat 9am–5.30pm closed Thurs

Michael J Bowman (ICA, BACA Award Winner 2002)
Contact Mr M Bowman ARICS
6 Haccombe House, Netherton, Newton Abbot, Devon, TQ12 4SJ
01626 872890 F 01626 872890
Est. 1986
Open By appointment
Sales 7 antiques and effects sales per annum Sat 2pm, viewing Fri 4.30–8.30pm. Held at Chudleigh Town Hall, also free valuations Mon 2–5pm at same venue
Catalogues Yes

The Jolly Roger
Contact Mr Chris Sims
4 Western Units, Pottery Road, Newton Abbot, Devon, TQ13 9JJ
01626 835105 F 01626 835105
M 07860 680181
E jollyrog@eclipse.co.uk
W www.jollyroger.eclipse.co.uk
Est. 1994 *Stock size* Large
Stock General antiques and nautical antiques
Open Mon–Fri 9am–4pm Sat 9am–noon (phone first)
Fairs Newark
Services Valuations and restoration of nautical antiques

St Leonard's Antiques and Craft Centre
Contact Mr Derick Wilson
St Leonard's, Wolborough Street, Newton Abbot, Devon, TQ12 1JQ
01626 335666 F 01626 335666
M 07860 178969
Est. 1999 *Stock size* Large
Stock General antiques, furniture, jewellery
Open Mon–Sun 10am–4.30pm

Tobys (SALVO)
Contact Mr P Norrish
Brunel Road, Newton Abbot, Devon, TQ12 4PB
01626 351767 F 01626 336788
W www.tobysreclamation.co.uk
Est. 1985 *Stock size* Large
Stock General antiques, reclaimed material
Open Mon–Fri 9am–5pm Sat 9.30am–4.30pm
Fairs Exeter Ideal Home, Devon County Show
Services House clearance

NEWTON FERRERS

Toad Hall Medals (OMRS)
Contact Mr Hitchings
Toad Hall, Court Road, Newton Ferrers, Plymouth, Devon, PL8 1DH
01752 872672 F 01752 872723
E chrissie@toadhallmedals.com
W www.toadhallmedals.com
Est. 1974 *Stock size* Large
Stock Collectors' replacement and veterans' medals
Open Mail order only
Fairs Britannia (London)
Services Valuations

OAKHAMPTON

Barometer World
Contact Phiip Collins
Quicksilver Barn, Merton, Oakhampton, Devon, EX20 3DS
01805 603443 F 01805 603344
E enquiries@barometerworld.co.uk
W www.antiquebarometers.org.uk
Est. 1979 *Stock size* Large
Stock 1780–1930s barometers
Open Tues–Sat 9am–5pm
Services Valuations, restorations

Tarka Antiques
Contact Henrietta Robertshaw
52 Red Lion Yard, Okehampton, Devon, EX20 1AW
01837 54222
Est. 1998 *Stock size* Large
Stock Traditional upholstery, porcelain, glass, lighting, furniture, Lloyd Loom, decorative items
Open Mon–Sat 10am–5pm closed Wed or by appointment
Fairs West Point
Services Upholstery

PAIGNTON

Hyde Road Antiques
Contact David Pentecost
23 Hyde Road, Paignton, Devon, TQ4 5BW
01803 554000
Est. 1992 *Stock size* Large
Stock General antiques and collectables
Open Mon–Sat 10am–5pm
Fairs West Point, Exeter Livestock
Services Valuations and ceramic repairs

The Pocket Bookshop
Contact Mr L Corrall
159 Winner Street, Paignton, Devon, TQ3 3BP
01803 529804
Est. 1985 *Stock size* Large
Stock Antiquarian, second-hand and out-of-print books
Open Summer Mon–Sat 10.30am–5.30pm winter Tues–Sat 10.30am–5.30pm

PLYMOUTH

Anita's Antiques
Contact Anita Walker
27 New Street, Plymouth, Devon, PL1 2NB
01752 269622
Est. 1984 *Stock size* Large
Stock Furniture, silver, china, jewellery, lighting, glass, clocks, barometers, general antiques
Open Mon–Sat 9am–5pm Sun 11am–4pm May to September

Annterior Antiques
Contact Anne Tregenza
22 Molesworth Road, Stoke, Plymouth, Devon, PL1 5LZ
01752 558277 F 01752 564471
M 07815 618659
E sales@annterior.co.uk
Est. 1984 *Stock size* Medium
Stock 19th–early 20thC country furniture, stripped pine, small accessories
Open Mon–Fri 9.30am–5.30pm Sat 10am–5pm closed Tues
Services Restorations and finding service

Barbican Antique Centre
Contact Tony Cremer-Price
82–84 Vauxhall Street, Plymouth, Devon, PL4 0EX
01752 201752 F 020 8546 1618
M 07836 291791
Est. 1971 *Stock size* Large
No. of dealers 60
Stock Silver, jewellery, porcelain, glass, pictures, furniture, collectables
Open Mon–Sat 9.30am–5pm

Eric Distin Auctioneers & Chartered Surveyors (RICS)
Contact Mr E Distin
72 Mutley Plain, Plymouth, Devon, PL4 6LF
01752 663046 F 01752 255371

Est. 1973
Sales Antiques and collectables Sat 10.30am, viewing morning of sale or afternoon prior. Coins and stamps 2nd Mon monthly, viewing from 4pm
Frequency Fortnightly
Catalogues Yes

Grosvenor Chambers Restoration
Contact Robert Miller
180 Rendle Street, Plymouth, Devon, PL1 1UQ
☎ 01752 257544
robbie@grosvenor-restoration.co.uk
Est. 1989 *Stock size* Large
Stock General architectural antiques, pine furniture, lighting, etc
Open Mon–Sat 9am–5.30pm
Services Valuations, restorations, wood and metal stripping

Frederick Harrison
Contact Mr Harrison
43 Bridwell Road, Weston Mill, Plymouth, Devon, PL5 1AB
☎ 01752 365595
Est. 1974 *Stock size* Large
Stock Antiquarian, rare and second-hand books, particularly on diving, Dartmoor and local topography
Open By appointment
Services Valuations

New Street Antique and Craft Centre
Contact Mrs Cuthill
27 New Street, Barbican, Plymouth, Devon, PL1 2NB
☎ 01752 256265 F 01752 256265
Est. 1980 *Stock size* Large
No. of dealers 11
Stock General collectables, books, stamps, postcards, craft materials, locally made crafts
Open Mon–Sat Sun during holiday season 10am–5pm
Services Café

Parade Antiques
Contact Mr Cabello
17 The Parade, The Barbican, Plymouth, Devon, PL1 2JW
☎ 01752 221443
Est. 1992 *Stock size* Large
Stock General antiques, militaria
Open Mon–Sun 10am–5pm
Services Tea room

G S Shobrook and Co incorporating Fieldens (RICS)
Contact Roger Shobrook
20 Western Approach, Plymouth, Devon, PL1 1TG
☎ 01752 663341 F 01752 255157
info@shobrook.co.uk
www.shobrook.co.uk
Est. 1920
Open Mon–Fri 9am–5pm Sat 9am–11am
Sales Antiques and collectables sale Wed 1.30pm, viewing Tues 9am–5pm or by appointment. Weekly general household sale Wed 10am, viewing Tues 9am–5pm
Frequency Monthly
Catalogues Yes

Michael Wood Fine Art
Contact Alvin Tull
The Gallery, 1 Southside Ope, The Barbican, Plymouth, Devon, PL1 2LL
☎ 01752 225533 F 01752 225533
Est. 1967 *Stock size* Medium
Stock 1850–present day paintings, watercolours, original prints, sculptures, art pottery, studio glass
Open Mon–Sat 10am–6pm
Fairs NEC, Battersea Contemporary Art Fair

Woodford Antiques & Collectables
Contact Mr Bill Humphries
17–18 New Street, The Barbican, Plymouth, Devon, PL1 2NA
☎ 01752 344562 F 01752 344562
M 07711 723006
Est. 1996 *Stock size* Medium
Stock Ceramics, kitchenware, general antiques and Torquay pottery
Open Mon–Sat 10am–4.30pm Sun noon–4.30pm
Fairs Westpoint, Devon Ceramic Fairs
Services Shipping

PLYMPTON

Eldreds Auctioneers and Valuers
Contact Anthony Eldred
13–15 Ridge Park Road, Plympton, Plymouth, Devon, PL7 2BS
☎ 01752 340066 F 01752 341760
enquiries@eldreds.net
www.eldreds.net
Est. 1992
Open Mon–Fri 8.30am–5pm
Sales Fortnightly 19th–20thC sales, 6–8 weekly antiques and specialist sales, phone for details
Frequency Fortnightly
Catalogues Yes

SEATON

Carol's Curiosity Shop
Contact Mrs Spurgeon
4 Marine Crescent, Seaton, Devon, EX12 2QN
☎ 01297 22039
Est. 1996 *Stock size* Large
No. of dealers 5
Stock General antiques, English ceramics, Oriental, lace, books
Open Mon–Sun 10am–6pm

Etcetera Antiques
Contact Mrs Rymer
12 Beer Road, Seaton, Devon, EX12 2PA
☎ 01297 21965
M 07780 840507
Est. 1965 *Stock size* Large
Stock Furniture and small items
Open Mon–Fri 10am–1pm 2–5pm Thurs by appointment
Services Restorations, house clearances, shipping

SIDMOUTH

The Lantern Shop Gallery
Contact Julia Creeke
5 New Street, Sidmouth, Devon, EX10 8AP
☎ 01395 578462 F 01395 578462
Est. 1977 *Stock size* Medium
Stock Porcelain, watercolours, oils
Open Mon–Sat 9.45am–4.45pm

The Old Curiosity Shop
Contact Mr or Mrs T Koch
Old Fore Street, Sidmouth, Devon, EX10 8LP
☎ 01395 515299
Est. 1995 *Stock size* Large
Stock General collectables
Open Mon–Sat 9am–5.30pm Sun 11am–5pm

Sidmouth Antiques Centre
Contact Mr R Hair

✉ **Devonshire House, All Saints Road, Sidmouth, Devon, EX10 8ES** 🅿
☎ 01395 512588 Ⓜ 07714 376918
Ⓦ www.sidmouthantiques.com
Est. 1994 *Stock size* Medium
No. of dealers 10
Stock General antiques, antiquarian books
Open Mon–Sat 10am–5pm summer Sun 2–5pm

The Vintage Toy & Train Shop
Contact David Salisbury
✉ **Devonshire House, All Saints Road, Sidmouth, Devon, EX10 8ES** 🅿
☎ 01395 512588 Ⓕ 01395 513399
Est. 1982 *Stock size* Medium
Stock Hornby Gauge O and Dublo trains, original Meccano, Dinky toys
Open Mon–Sat 10am–5pm

SOUTH BRENT

Patrick Pollak Rare Books (ABA)
Contact Patrick Pollak
✉ **Moorview, Plymouth Road, South Brent, Devon, TQ10 9HT** 🅿
☎ 01364 73457 Ⓕ 01364 649126
Ⓔ patrick@rarevols.co.uk
Ⓦ www.rarevols.co.uk
Est. 1973 *Stock size* Large
Stock Rare, antiquarian scholarly books
Open By appointment
Services Mail order

SOUTH MOLTON

Antique Centre
Contact Bob Golding
✉ **14a Barnstaple Street, South Molton, Devon, EX36 3BQ** 🅿
☎ 01769 573401
Est. 1990 *Stock size* Large
No. of dealers 10
Stock General antiques, furniture, clocks, bric-a-brac
Open Tues–Sat 10am–5pm

C R Boumphrey
Contact Mr Boumphrey
✉ **Finehay, Mariansleigh, South Molton, Devon, EX36 4LL** 🅿
☎ 01769 550419
Est. 1969
Stock 17th–18thC furniture
Open By appointment
Services Finds and orders stock

The Dragon
Contact Jenny Aker
✉ **80 South Street, South Molton, Devon, EX36 4AG** 🅿
☎ 01769 572374
Ⓜ 07712 079818
Ⓔ snapdragonantiques@hotmail.com
Ⓦ www.snapdragoncollectables-northdevon.co.uk
Est. 1998 *Stock size* Medium
Stock General antiques, furniture, books, collectables
Open Mon–Sat 9.30am–4.30pm

Snapdragon
Contact Jenny Aker
✉ **77 South Street, South Molton, Devon, EX36 3AG** 🅿
☎ 01769 572374 Ⓜ 07712 079818
Ⓔ snapdragonantiques@hotmail.com
Ⓦ www.snapdragoncollectables-northdevon.co.uk.
Est. 1998 *Stock size* Medium
Stock General antiques, pine furniture, books, farming bygones, kitchenware
Open Mon–Sat 9.30am–4.30pm

R M Young Bookseller
Contact Mr M Young
✉ **17 Broad Street, South Molton, Devon, EX36 3AQ** 🅿
☎ 01769 573350
Est. 1985 *Stock size* Large
Stock Antiquarian, second-hand, rare and out-of-print books. Countryside topics a speciality
Open Mon–Sat 10am–5pm
Services Book search, book binding

TAVISTOCK

Archways
Contact Mrs Diana Hunter
✉ **Court Gate, Bedford Square, Tavistock, Devon, PL19 0AE**
☎ 01822 612773
Est. 1989 *Stock size* Medium
Stock General antiques, small items, clocks
Open Tues–Sat 10am–4pm closed Thurs

Bassett Books
Contact Mr J J Bassett
✉ **Baggator Farm, Wapsworthy, Tavistock, Devon, PL19 9NA** 🅿
☎ 01822 617599
Ⓔ b@ssett-books.com
Ⓦ www.bassett-books.co.uk
Est. 1990 *Stock size* Medium
Stock Antiquarian books and smalls
Open Mon–Sat 10am–6pm Wed 10am–1pm
Services Valuations, china and book restorations

Den of Antiquity
Contact Shelly Barlow
✉ **7 Pixon Lane, Crelake Industrial Estate, Tavistock, Devon, PL19 8DH** 🅿
☎ 01822 610274 Ⓜ 07971 182381
Est. 1999 *Stock size* Large
Stock Georgian–Edwardian and French furniture
Open Mon–Sat 10am–5.30pm Sun 2–5pm

Robin A Fenner and Co
Contact Mr Fenner
✉ **Stannary Gallery, Drake Road, Tavistock, Devon, PL19 0AX** 🅿
☎ 01822 617799 Ⓕ 01822 617595
Ⓜ 07712 874689
Ⓔ raf2536500@aol.com
Ⓦ www.invaluable.com/rafenner
Est. 1968
Open Mon–Fri 9am–5pm
Sales 6 antiques, 2 vintage toys and models, 2 collectors', 1 antiquarian books and ephemera and 1 postcards and cigarette cards sale every year. All sales Mon 11am, viewing Fri–Sun noon–5pm. Phone for dates
Frequency Irregular
Catalogues Yes

Tavistock Furniture Store
Contact Shelley Barlow
✉ **7 Pixon Lane, Tavistock, Devon, PL19 9AZ** 🅿
☎ 01822 610274
Ⓔ doa@pixonlane.fsnet.co.uk
Est. 1999 *Stock size* Large
Stock English and French country furniture and decorative items
Open Mon–Sat 10am–5pm

Ward and Chowen Auction Rooms
Contact Mrs Pat Smith

Market Road, Tavistock, Devon, PL19 0BW
01822 612603 01822 617311
tavistockauctionrooms@wardchowen.co.uk
Est. 1830
Open Mon–Fri 8.30am–4.30pm
Sales Quarterly antiques sale Tues, viewing Mon 10am–6pm. Fortnightly general household sale Thurs 10am (no catalogue), viewing Wed 1–6pm
Catalogues Yes

TEDBURN ST MARY

A E Wakeman and Sons Ltd
Contact Mr Wakeman
Newhouse Farm, Tedburn St Mary, Exeter, Devon, EX6 6AL
01647 61254 01647 61254
07836 284765/636525
Est. 1971 *Stock size* Medium
Stock 19thC furniture
Trade only Yes
Open Mon–Fri 8.30am–5.30pm or by appointment
Fairs Newark

TEIGNMOUTH

Leigh Extence Antique Clocks (BHI)
Contact Mr Leigh Extence
49 Fore Street, Shaldon, Teignmouth, Devon, TQ14 0EA
01626 872636 01626 873457
07967 802160
clocks@extence.co.uk
www.extence.co.uk
Est. 1981 *Stock size* Medium
Stock Antique clocks and barometers
Open By appointment or telephone call
Services Valuations, restorations, clock research

Extence Antiques
Contact Mr T E or L E Extence
2 Wellington Street, Teignmouth, Devon, TQ14 8HH
01626 773353
Est. 1928 *Stock size* Large
Stock Jewellery, silver and objets d'art
Open Mon–Sat 10am–5pm
Services Valuations, repair and restoration of jewellery and silver

The Old Salty
Contact Kate Worden
42 Northumberland Place, Teignmouth, Devon, TQ14 8DE
01626 775754
Est. 1978 *Stock size* Medium
Stock Old and new nautical items, bygones, kitchenware, decorative items, collectable teddy bears
Open Tues–Sat 10am–4pm closed Thurs

Queens House Antiques
Contact Teresa Nicholls
27 Fore Street, Teignmouth, Devon, TQ14 8DZ
01626 776675 01626 774689
Est. 1976 *Stock size* Medium
Stock General antiques and furniture
Open Tues–Sat 10am–5pm
Fairs West Point, Livestock – Exeter
Services Valuations

Timepiece Antiques
Contact Clive or Willow Pople
125 Bitton Park Road, Teignmouth, Devon, TQ14 9BZ
01626 770275
Est. 1988 *Stock size* Medium
Stock Country, mahogany and oak furniture, longcase clocks, brass, copper, metalware, gramophones, general antiques
Open Tues–Sat 9.30am–5.30pm

TIVERTON

Judith Christie
Contact Judith Christie
42 Gold Street, Tiverton, Devon, EX16 6PX
01884 258795 07770 741885
Est. 1974 *Stock size* Medium
Stock General antiques, interiors and decorative arts
Open Tues Fri Sat 10.30am–5pm

TOPSHAM

Bizarre!
Contact Alexandra Fairweather
The Quay Antiques Centre, The Quay, Topsham, Exeter, Devon, EX3 OJA
01392 874006
office@antiquesattopshamquay.co.uk
www.antiquesattopshamquay.co.uk
Est. 1991 *Stock size* Large
Stock Vintage clothes, textiles and accessories
Open Mon–Sun 10am–5pm
Fairs Hammersmith Textile and Costume, Hyson Textile Fair

Bounty Antiques
Contact J Harding or J Purves
76 Fore Street, Topsham, Devon, EX3 0HQ
01395 266007 07939 526504
Est. 1997 *Stock size* Large
No. of dealers 18
Stock General antiques, collectables, scientific instruments, maritime items
Open Mon–Sat 9.30am–5pm
Services Valuations

Charis
Contact Chris Evans
The Quay Antiques Centre, The Quay, Topsham, Exeter, Devon, EX3 OJA
01392 874006
office@antiquesattopshamquay.co.uk
www.antiquesattopshamquay.co.uk
Est. 1993 *Stock size* Medium
Stock Old glass, crystal, china, jewellery
Open Mon–Sun 10am–5pm

Curzon Pictures
The Quay Antiques Centre, The Quay, Topsham, Exeter, Devon, EX3 OJA
01392 874006
office@antiquesattopshamquay.co.uk
www.antiquesattopshamquay.co.uk
Est. 1993 *Stock size* Medium
Stock Prints, Louis Wain, Russell Flint
Open Mon–Sun 10am–5pm

Gudrun Doel
Contact Gudrun (Goody) Doel
The Quay Antiques Centre, The Quay, Topsham, Exeter, Devon, EX3 OJA
01392 874006
office@antiquesattopshamquay.co.uk
www.antiquesattopshamquay.co.uk
Est. 1993 *Stock size* Medium
Stock Decorative items, porcelain, glass, pictures, silver, textiles
Open Mon–Sun 10am–5pm
Fairs Livestock Centre, Exeter

Farthings
The Quay Antiques Centre, The Quay, Topsham, Exeter, Devon, EX3 OJA
01392 874006
office@antiquesattopshamquay.co.uk

Ⓦ www.antiquesattopshamquay.co.uk
Est. 1993 *Stock size* Medium
Stock Ceramics, commemorative china
Open Mon–Sun 10am–5pm

Rob Gee
Contact Rob Gee
✉ **The Quay Antiques Centre, The Quay, Topsham, Exeter, Devon, EX3 OJA** Ⓟ
☎ 01392 874006
Ⓔ office@antiquesattopshamquay.co.uk
Ⓦ www.antiquesattopshamquay.co.uk
Est. 1993
Stock Pot lids, Pratt ware, chemist items, steam and toy locomotives
Open Mon–Sun 10am–5pm

Nicky Gowing
Contact Nicky Gowing
✉ **The Quay Antiques Centre, The Quay, Topsham, Exeter, Devon, EX3 OJA** Ⓟ
☎ 01392 874006
Ⓔ office@antiquesattopshamquay.co.uk
Ⓦ www.antiquesattopshamquay.co.uk
Est. 1993 *Stock size* Medium
Stock Decorative china, character jugs, Toby jugs
Open Mon–Sun 10am–5pm

Sheila Hyson
Contact Sheila Hyson
✉ **The Quay Antiques Centre, The Quay, Topsham, Exeter, Devon, EX3 OJA** Ⓟ
☎ 01392 874006 Ⓜ 07798 808701
Ⓔ shyson@freenetname.co.uk
Ⓦ www.antiquesattopshamquay.co.uk
Est. 1993 *Stock size* Large
Stock Kitchenware
Open Mon–Sun 10am–5pm
Fairs Hyson Fairs, Deco '50s and '60s Fair, Exmouth Fair

Robin Jeffreys
Contact Robin Jeffreys
✉ **The Quay Antiques Centre, The Quay, Topsham, Exeter, Devon, EX3 OJA** Ⓟ
☎ 01392 874006
Ⓔ office@antiquesattopshamquay.co.uk
Ⓦ www.antiquesattopshamquay.co.uk
Est. 1966 *Stock size* Large
Stock Ceramics and Oriental ware
Open Mon–Sun 10am–4pm
Fairs Hyson Pottery and Glass Fair, Chafford Antiques and Collectors' Fair

Bart and Julie Lemmy
Contact Bart and Julie Lemmy
✉ **The Quay Antiques Centre, The Quay, Topsham, Exeter, Devon, EX3 OJA** Ⓟ
☎ 01392 874006 Ⓜ 07809 172468
Ⓔ rosettibrides@btinternet.com
Ⓦ www.antiquesattopshamquay.co.uk
Est. 1993
Stock Royal Doulton figurines
Open Mon–Sun 10am–5pm
Services Shipping furniture

Betty Lovell
Contact Betty Lovell
✉ **The Quay Antiques Centre, The Quay, Topsham, Exeter, Devon, EX3 OJA** Ⓟ
☎ 01392 874006
Ⓔ office@antiquesattopshamquay.co.uk
Ⓦ www.antiquesattopshamquay.co.uk
Est. 1993 *Stock size* Medium
Stock Linen and lace
Open Mon–Sun 10am–5pm
Fairs Hysons Textile Fair

D Lovell
Contact D Lovell
✉ **The Quay Antiques Centre, The Quay, Topsham, Exeter, Devon, EX3 OJA** Ⓟ
☎ 01392 874006
Ⓔ office@antiquesattopshamquay.co.uk
Ⓦ www.antiquesattopshamquay.co.uk
Est. 1986 *Stock size* Medium
Stock Silver and silver plate
Open Mon–Sun 10am–5pm

Mere Antiques (LAPADA)
Contact Mrs M Hawkins or Mrs M Reed
✉ **13 Fore Street, Topsham, Exeter, Devon, EX3 0HF** Ⓟ
☎ 01392 874224 Ⓜ 07957 867751
Ⓔ bob@ntlbusiness.com
Ⓦ www.mereantiques.co.uk
Est. 1986 *Stock size* Medium
Stock 18th–19thC porcelain, Japanese Satsuma ware, period furniture, paintings
Open Mon–Sat 9.30am–5.30pm
Fairs NEC (LAPADA and Antiques for Everyone)
Services Appraisals, deliveries

Number 38
Contact Stuart Westaway
✉ **The Quay Antiques Centre, The Quay, Topsham, Exeter, Devon, EX3 OJA** Ⓟ
☎ 01392 874006
Ⓔ office@antiquesattopshamquay.co.uk
Ⓦ www.antiquesattopshamquay.co.uk
Est. 1993 *Stock size* Medium
Stock Restored period lighting
Open Mon–Sun 10am–5pm
Services Restorations

Old Tools Feel Better!
Contact Barry Cook
✉ **The Quay Antiques Centre, The Quay, Topsham, Exeter, Devon, EX3 OJA** Ⓟ
☎ 01392 874006 Ⓕ 01392 874006
Ⓜ 07799 054565
Ⓔ office@antiquesattopshamquay.co.uk
Ⓦ www.antiquesattopshamquay.co.uk
Est. 1993 *Stock size* Large
Stock Antique and collectable quality used tools
Open Mon–Sun 10am–5pm

Pennies Antiques
Contact Mrs Clark
✉ **40 Fore Street, Topsham, Exeter, Devon, EX3 0HU** Ⓟ
☎ 01392 877020
Ⓦ www.penniesantiques.co.uk
Est. 1979 *Stock size* Medium
Stock General antiques
Open Mon–Sat 10am–5pm Sun 11am–4pm

The Quay Centre
Contact Beverley Cook
✉ **The Quay, Topsham, Exeter, Devon, EX3 OJA** Ⓟ
☎ 01392 874006
Ⓔ office@antiquesattopshamquay.co.uk
Ⓦ www.antiquesattopshamquay.co.uk
Est. 1993 *Stock size* Large
No. of dealers 80
Stock Furniture, collectables, ephemera, Exeter silver, Torquay ware, studio pottery, jewellery, tools, period lighting, textiles
Open Mon–Sun 10am–5pm
Services Cards accepted, online buying, shipping advice

Joel Segal Books
Contact Mrs Neal
✉ **27 Fore Street, Topsham, Exeter, Devon, EX3 0HD**
☎ 01392 877895
Est. 1993 *Stock size* Large
Stock Antique, rare and second-hand books
Open Mon–Sat 10.30am–5pm

Traditional Telephones
Contact Gary Richardson
✉ **The Quay Antiques Centre, The Quay, Topsham, Exeter, Devon, EX3 OJA** Ⓟ

☎ 01752 845188
Ⓦ www.traditionaltelephones.co.uk
Est. 1993 ***Stock size*** Medium
Stock Restored and vintage telephones, converted and working
Open Mon–Sun 10am–5pm

The Venerable Bead
Contact Daphne King
✉ **The Quay Antiques Centre, The Quay, Topsham, Exeter, Devon, EX3 OJA** Ⓟ
☎ 01392 874006 Ⓜ 07787 561681
Ⓔ office@antiquesattopshamquay.co.uk
Ⓦ www.antiquesattopshamquay.co.uk
Est. 1993 ***Stock size*** Large
Stock Costume jewellery
Open Mon–Sun 10am–4pm
Fairs Westpoint, Shepton Mallet

S Vye
Contact S Vye
✉ **The Quay Antiques Centre, The Quay, Topsham, Exeter, Devon, EX3 OJA** Ⓟ
☎ 01392 874006
Ⓔ s.vye@virgin.net
Ⓦ www.antiquesattopshamquay.co.uk
Est. 1993 ***Stock size*** Medium
Stock Furniture, ceramics, paintings, samplers
Open Mon–Sun 10am–5pm

Yesteryears
Contact Paul Gowing
✉ **The Quay Antiques Centre, The Quay, Topsham, Exeter, Devon, EX3 OJA** Ⓟ
☎ 01392 874006 Ⓜ 07813 569391
Ⓦ www.antiquesattopshamquay.co.uk
Est. 1993 ***Stock size*** Medium
Stock Furniture, including compactums, wardrobes, dressing tables
Open Mon–Sun 10am–5pm

TORQUAY

The Old Cop Shop
Contact Mr L Rolfe or Brian Harper
✉ **Castle Lane, Torquay, Devon, TQ1 3AN** Ⓟ
☎ 01803 294484 Ⓕ 01803 316620
Est. 1974 ***Stock size*** Large
Stock General antiques
Open Mon–Sat 9am–5pm
Services Valuations

Tobys (SALVO)
Contact Mr P Norrish
✉ **Torre Station, Newton Road, Torquay, Devon, TQ2 2DD** Ⓟ
☎ 01803 212222 Ⓕ 01803 200523
Ⓦ www.tobysreclamation.co.uk
Est. 1985 ***Stock size*** Large
Stock General antiques, furniture, architectural antiques, gifts
Open Mon–Fri 9am–5pm Sat 9.30am–4.30pm Sun Bank Holidays 10.30am–4.30pm
Fairs Exeter Ideal Home, Devon County Show
Services House clearance, nationwide delivery

Upstairs Downstairs
Contact Ms Linda Nicholls
✉ **53 Fore Street, St Marychurch, Torquay, Devon, TQ1 4PR** Ⓟ
☎ 01803 313010
Est. 1997 ***Stock size*** Large
Stock Antique and modern jewellery, glass, rocking horses, paintings, china, furniture
Open Mon–Sat 9am–5pm
Services Valuations

West Country Old Books (PBFA)
Contact Mr D Neil
✉ **22 Perinville Road, Torquay, Devon, TQ1 3NZ** Ⓟ
☎ 01803 322712
Est. 1989 ***Stock size*** Small
Stock Antiquarian and good quality second-hand books. Specializing in topography, and literature
Open By appointment only
Fairs PBFA
Services Valuations and books bought

West of England Auctions
Contact Mr Warren Hunt
✉ **3 Warren Road, Torquay, Devon, TQ2 5TQ** Ⓟ
☎ 01803 211266 Ⓕ 01803 212286
Est. 1949
Open Mon–Fri 9am–1pm 2pm–5pm
Sales Sales of antiques, silver, jewellery Mon 11am, viewing Sat 9am–noon Sun 1–5pm Mon 9–11am prior to sale
Frequency Fortnightly
Catalogues yes

TORRINGTON

C Short
Contact Mr C Short
✉ **12 Potacne, Torrington, Devon, EX38 8BH**
☎ 01805 624796
Est. 1984 ***Stock size*** Large
Stock Furniture
Open Mon Tues Thurs Fri 10am–4pm Wed Sat 10am–1pm

TOTNES

Bogan House Antiques
Contact Mr M Mitchell
✉ **43 High Street, Totnes, Devon, TQ9 5NP** Ⓟ
☎ 01803 862075
Ⓜ 07974 808005
Est. 1989 ***Stock size*** Large
Stock Silver, wood, brass, glass, Japanese woodblock prints
Open Tues noon–4.30pm Fri 10am–4.30pm Sat 10.30am–4.30pm

The Exchange
Contact John Caley
✉ **76 High Street, Totnes, Devon, TQ9 5SN**
☎ 01803 866836
Ⓔ bookworm1700@yahoo.com
Est. 1996 ***Stock size*** Large
No. of dealers 7
Stock Books, printed ephemera, tools, brass, African artefacts, china, stamps, toys, records, musical instruments and postcards
Open Mon–Sat 10am–5pm 5.30pm in summer
Services Valuations, restorations to instruments

Fine Pine
Contact Nick or Linda Gildersleve
✉ **Woodland Road, Harbertonford, Totnes, Devon, TQ9 7SU** Ⓟ
☎ 01803 732465
Ⓔ info@fine-pine-antiques.co.uk
Ⓦ www.fine-pine-antiques.co.uk
Est. 1973 ***Stock size*** Medium
Stock Pine and country antiques
Open Mon–Sat 9.30am–5pm Sun 11am–4pm
Services Valuations, restorations and stripping

Pandora's Box
Contact Sarah Mimpriss
5b High Street, Totnes, Devon, TQ9 5NN
01803 867799
07747 772527
Est. 1999 *Stock size* Small
Stock Georgian–Edwardian furniture, mirrors, china, collectables
Open Tues Thurs Fri Sat 10.30am–4pm

Past and Present James Sturges Antiques
Contact Mr J Sturges
94 High Street, The Narrows, Totnes, Devon, TQ9 5SN
01803 866086 01803 866086
Est. 1980 *Stock size* Small
Stock Georgian–early 20thC furniture and small items
Open Mon–Sat 10am–5pm closed Thurs

Pedlar's Pack Books (PBFA)
Contact Peter or Angela Elliott
4 The Plains, Totnes, Devon, TQ9 5DR
01803 866423
pedlar@aol.com
Est. 1983 *Stock size* Medium
Stock Antiquarian, second-hand, rare and modern books. Art and history books a speciality
Open Mon–Sat 9am–5pm summer Sun 10am–4pm
Fairs Local PBFA, also others (phone for details)
Services Valuations, book binding, book search

Rotherfold Antiques
Contact Miss Myra Van Heck
2 Rotherfold, Totnes, Devon, TQ9 5ST
01803 840303
rotherfoldantiques@yahoo.co.uk
Est. 1999 *Stock size* Large
Stock Interesting antiques, ceramics, pictures, rugs, furniture, lights, objets d'art, fabrics, etc
Open Mon–Sat 10am–5pm closed Thurs pm
Services Interior design

TYTHERLEIGH

The Trading Post Antique Centre
Contact Mr Remfry
Main Road, Tytherleigh, Axminster, Devon, EX13 7BE
01460 221330 01460 57005
07971 863192
Est. 1987 *Stock size* Large
No. of dealers 30
Stock General antiques, furniture, collectables, etc
Open Summer Mon–Sat 10am–5pm Sun 10am–4pm winter Mon–Sat 10am–4.30pm
Services Valuations, restorations, clock repairs, repair of cane chairs

YEALMPTON

Carnegie Paintings & Clocks
Contact Chris Carnegie
15 Fore Street, Yealmpton, Plymouth, Devon, PL8 2JN
01752 881170
www.paintingsandclocks.com
Est. 1996 *Stock size* Medium
Stock Pre-1940s paintings, clocks, barometers
Open Mon–Sat 10am–5.30pm
Fairs
Services Restorations

DORSET

BERE REGIS

Dorset Reclamation (SALVO)
Contact David Kirk or Steven Haycock
Cow Drove, Bere Regis, Wareham, Dorset, BH20 7JZ
01929 472200 01929 472292
info@dorsetrec.u-net.com
www.dorset-reclamation.co.uk
Est. 1992 *Stock size* Large
Stock Decorative architectural and garden antiques including flagstones, flooring, bathroom fittings, radiators, chimney pieces, traditional building materials
Open Mon–Fri 8am–5pm Sat 9am–4pm
Services Delivery

Legg of Dorchester
Contact Mrs H Legg
The Old Mill, West Street, Bere Regis, Wareham, Dorset, BH20 7HS
01305 264964
Est. 1930 *Stock size* Large
Stock General, mostly furniture
Open Mon–Sat 9.30am–5.30pm

BLANDFORD FORUM

Antiques for All
Contact Mr D G Corbin
Higher Shaftesbury Road, Blandford Forum, Dorset, DT11 7TA
01258 458011 01258 458022
Est. 1997 *Stock size* Large
No. of dealers 100
Stock Antique furniture, lighting, collectables
Open Mon–Sat 9.30am–5pm Sun 10.30am–5pm

Milton Antiques & Restoration
Contact Nigel Church
Bere's Yard, Market Place, Blandford Forum, Dorset, DT11 7HV
01258 450100
Est. 1989 *Stock size* Medium
Stock Period furniture
Open Mon–Sat 9am–5pm
Services Restorations

Robert A Warry Auctioneer (FNAVA)
Contact Mr R Warry
1a Alfred Street, Blandford Forum, Dorset, DT11 7JJ
01258 452454 01258 452454
auctioneers@rwarry.freeserve.co.uk
www.rwarry.freeserve.co.uk
Est. 1956
Open Mon–Fri 9am–5pm
Sales Antiques and collectables sale every 3 weeks, Fri 10am, viewing Wed 2–5pm Thurs 9.30am–7.30pm morning of sale
Frequency Every 3 weeks
Catalogues Yes

BOURNEMOUTH

Abbey Models
Contact Nick Powner
42 Littledown Drive, Littledown, Bournemouth, Dorset, BH7 7AQ
01202 395999 01202 395999
npowner@bournemouth.demon.co.uk
www.the-internet-agency.com/abbeymodels
Est. 1992 *Stock size* Large
Stock Old toys, Dinky, Corgi, Matchbox

Open By appointment
Fairs Sandown Park, NEC Toys
Services Valuations, mail-order catalogues available

Aladdins Antiques
Contact Paul
Flat 3, 54 Lansdowne Road, Bournemouth, Dorset, BH1 1RS
☎ 01202 298805 Ⓜ 07779 250940
Ⓔ paulboysen@cwcom.net
Ⓦ www.aladdinsantiques.cwc.net
Est. 1992 *Stock size* Small
Stock Furniture, ceramics
Open Mon–Sat 9am–6pm closed Wed

Altamira Deco
Contact Mr Ganley
14 Seamoor Road, Bournemouth, Dorset, BH4 9AR
☎ 01202 766444 Ⓜ 07885 778342
Ⓔ gallery@altamiradeco.com
Ⓦ www.altamiradeco.com
Est. 1992 *Stock size* Large
Stock Art Deco furniture, glass, ceramics, bronze
Open Tues–Sat 9.30am–5pm
Services Valuations

The Antiques Exchange
Contact Robert L Draycey
877 Christchurch Road, Boscombe, Bournemouth, Dorset, BH7 6AT
☎ 01202 430005 /433456
Ⓕ 01202 431318
Ⓔ info@AntiquesExchange.com
Ⓦ www.AntiquesExchange.com
Est. 1966 *Stock size* Large
Stock Furniture, glass, china, collectables, reproduction Tiffany lamps
Open Mon–Fri 10am–6pm Sat 10am–5pm
Services Exchange deal for trade

Books & Maps
Contact Mr R J Browne
1–3 Jewelbox Buildings, Cardigan Road, Winton, Bournemouth, Dorset, BH9 1BB
☎ 01202 521373 Ⓕ 01202 529403
Ⓔ sales@booksandmaps.freeserve.co.uk
Ⓦ www.booksandmaps.freeserve.co.uk
Est. 1984 *Stock size* Large
Stock Antiquarian, rare, second-hand books, maps. Books on Africa and dogs a speciality
Open Mon–Sat 9am–5.30pm
Fairs Russell Hotel
Services Valuations

Boscombe Militaria
Contact Mr E A Browne
86 Palmerston Road, Bournemouth, Dorset, BH1 4HU
☎ 01202 304250 Ⓕ 01202 733696
Est. 1982 *Stock size* Medium
Stock 20thC militaria, uniforms, medals, badges
Open Mon–Sat 10am–1pm 2–5pm closed Wed
Fairs Farnham, Aldershot

Boscombe Toy Collectors
Contact Mr Harvey
802b Somerset Road, Boscombe, Bournemouth, Dorset, BH7 6DD
☎ 01202 398884
Est. 2001 *Stock size* Medium
Stock Trains, Action Man, Star Wars, die-cast and Dragon figures
Open Mon–Sat 10am–5pm closed Wed

Chorley-Burdett Antiques
Contact Ray Burdett
828 Christchurch Road, Bournemouth, Dorset, BH7 6DF
☎ 01202 423363 Ⓕ 01202 423363
Est. 1992 *Stock size* Medium
Stock Victorian–Edwardian furniture, oak, mahogany, new and reclaimed pine
Open Mon–Sat 9am–5.30pm

Dalkeith Auctions Bournemouth
Contact Mr P Howard
Dalkeith Hall, Dalkeith Steps, rear of 81 Old Christchurch Road, Bournemouth, Dorset, BH1 1YL
☎ 01202 292905 Ⓕ 01202 292931
Ⓔ how@dalkeith-auctions.co.uk
Ⓦ www.dalkeith-auctions.co.uk
Est. 1992
Open Mon–Sat 9am–3pm
Sales Collectors' sales of ephemera and other collectors' items 1st Sat of month 11am, viewing week before 9am–3pm
Frequency Monthly
Catalogues Yes

The Emporium Antiques Centre
Contact Rebecca Hood
908 Christchurch Road, Boscombe, Bournemouth, Dorset, BH7 6DL
☎ 01202 422380 Ⓕ 01202 433348
Est. 1996 *Stock size* Large
No. of dealers 10
Stock General antiques, decorative arts
Open Mon–Sat 9.30am–5.30pm
Services Tea shop

Lionel Geneen Ltd (LAPADA)
Contact Mr Robert Geneen
811 Christchurch Road, Boscombe, Bournemouth, Dorset, BH7 6AP
☎ 01202 422961/520417
Ⓕ 01202 422961 Ⓜ 07770 596781
Est. 1902 *Stock size* Medium
Stock 19thC English, Continental, Oriental furniture, porcelain, bronzes, glass. Ornamental decorative pieces, dessert services, tea and dinner services
Open Mon–Fri 9am–1pm 2–5pm Sat 9am–noon or by appointment
Services Valuations

Hardy's Collectables
Contact Mr J Hardy
823 Christchurch Road, Boscombe, Bournemouth, Dorset, BH7 6AP
☎ 01202 473744
Ⓜ 07970 056858/613077
Est. 1987 *Stock size* Large
Stock 20thC collectables, mainly smalls, toys, metalware, ceramics
Open Mon–Sat 10am–5pm
Fairs Alexandra Palace, Kempton

Holloway's Antiques
Contact Mr M C Holloway
731 Christchurch Road, Bournemouth, Dorset, BH7 6AQ
☎ 01202 300330
Est. 1998 *Stock size* Large
Stock Victorian–Edwardian furniture, imports from the Far East
Open Mon–Sat 10am–5pm

Kebo Antiques Market
Contact Mr K Lawrence
823a Christchurch Road, Bournemouth, Dorset, BH7 6AP

☎ 01202 417052
Est. 1989 *Stock size* Small
No. of dealers 5
Stock General antiques
Open Mon–Sat 10am–5pm
Services Valuations

Manor Antiques
Contact D R or T W Vendy
✉ **739 Christchurch Road, Bournemouth, Dorset, BH7 6AN** P
☎ 01202 392779
Est. 1969 *Stock size* Large
Stock General antiques, furniture, silver, porcelain
Open Mon–Sat 10am–1pm 2–5pm

Norman D Landing Militaria
Contact Mr Kenneth Lewis
✉ **76 Alma Road, Winton, Bournemouth, Dorset, BH9 1AN** P
☎ 01202 521944 Ⓕ 01202 521944
Ⓜ 07711 790044
Ⓔ kenneth@44doughboy.fsnet.co.uk
Ⓦ norman-d-landing.com
Est. 1995 *Stock size* Large
Stock US uniforms and equipment 1900–45. US Army uniforms and equipment 1910–45
Open Thurs–Sat 10am–5pm, Mon–Wed by appointment
Fairs Stoneleigh, Warwicks (Jan), Beltring, Kent (July)
Services Valuations, mail order, hires to film and TV. Author of *Doughboy to GI*

Not Just Antiques
Contact Simon or Bryn Davies
✉ **Northbourne House, 1262 Wimborne Road, Bournemouth, Dorset, BH10 7AQ** P
☎ 01202 572315 Ⓜ 07970 376817
Est. 2000 *Stock size* Medium
Stock A varied selection of English and French furniture, collectables, garden and decorative items
Open Mon–Sat 9.30am–5.30pm Sun 10.30am–4pm
Services Upholstery

George A Payne & Son Ltd
Contact Mr Payne
✉ **742 Christchurch Road, Boscombe, Bournemouth, Dorset, BH7 6BZ** P
☎ 01202 394954
Est. 1900 *Stock size* Medium
Stock Jewellery and silver
Open Mon–Sat 9.15am–5.30pm
Services Valuations, restorations

Pokesdown Antique Centre
Contact Mr C Lane
✉ **848 Christchurch Road, Boscombe, Bournemouth, Dorset, BH7 6AP** P
☎ 01202 433263
Est. 1989 *Stock size* Large
No. of dealers 10
Stock Decorative antiques, wristwatches, lighting, pine, collectables (Georgian to Modern), paintings
Open Mon–Sat 9am–5.30pm
Services Valuations, delivery, wristwatch repairs

Portabellows
Contact Mrs V A McKnight
✉ **819 Christchurch Road, Boscombe, Bournemouth, Dorset, BH7 6AP** P
☎ 01202 432928
Stock General, mainly furniture
Open Mon–Sat 10am–4.30pm closed Wed

R E Porter
✉ **2–6 Post Office Road, Bournemouth, Dorset, BH1 1BA** P
☎ 01202 554289
Est. 1930 *Stock size* Large
Stock Silver, Baxter prints
Open Mon–Sat 9.30am–5pm
Services Valuations, restorations

Rawlinsons
Contact Mr M Rawlinson
✉ **884 Christchurch Road, Bournemouth, Dorset, BH7 6DJ** P
☎ 01202 433394
Est. 1983 *Stock size* Large
Stock General, smalls, furniture, glass, china, metalware, clocks, Art Deco
Open Mon–Sat 10am–5.30pm

Recollections
Contact Mrs B Francis
✉ **5 Royal Arcade, Boscombe, Bournemouth, Dorset, BH1 4BT** P
☎ 01202 304441
Ⓔ recollections@cwcom.net
Ⓦ www.recollections.mcmail.com
Est. 1994 *Stock size* Large
Stock Collectables, china, Poole pottery, commemoratives, Beatrix Potter figures, Art Deco
Open Mon Thurs–Sat last Sunday every month 9.30am–5pm

Riddetts of Bournemouth
Contact Keith Harris
✉ **177 Holdenhurst Road, Bournemouth, Dorset, BH8 8DQ** P
☎ 01202 555686 Ⓕ 01202 311004
Ⓔ auctions@riddetts.co.uk
Ⓦ www.riddetts.co.uk
Est. 1879
Open Mon–Fri 9am–5.30pm closed 1–2pm
Sales Sales usually Tues or Wed 10am and 2pm, viewing Mon 10am–7pm morning of sale 9–10am
Frequency Fortnightly
Catalogues Yes

H Rowan
Contact Mr H Rowan
✉ **459 Christchurch Road, Boscombe, Bournemouth, Dorset, BH1 4AD** P
☎ 01202 398820
Est. 1968 *Stock size* Large
Stock Antiquarian books, second-hand books, maps, prints. Local interest, art and antiques topics a speciality
Open Mon–Sat 9.30am–5.30pm
Services Valuations

The Sage Door
Contact Philip Richards
✉ **920 Christchurch Road, Bournemouth, Dorset, BH7 6DL** P
☎ 01202 434771
Est. 1975 *Stock size* Large
Stock Antique and decorative furniture, lighting, soft furnishings
Open Mon–Sat 10am–5pm
Services Interior design

Sainsburys of Bournemouth Ltd (LAPADA)
Contact Jonathan Sainsbury
✉ **23–25 Abbott Road, Bournemouth, Dorset, BH9 1EU** P

☎ 01202 529271 ⓕ 01202 510028
ⓔ sales@sainsburys-antiques.com
Est. 1918 *Stock size* Large
Stock Antique furniture and accessories, exceptional replica chairs
Open By appointment
Services Furniture made from antique timbers

Sandy's Antiques
Contact Michael Sandy
✉ **790–792 Christchurch Road, Boscombe, Bournemouth, Dorset, BH7 6DD** Ⓟ
☎ 01202 301190 ⓕ 01202 301190
ⓜ 07836 367384
Est. 1970 *Stock size* Large
Stock Edwardian, Victorian, shipping, furniture
Open Mon–Sat 10am–5.30pm

Smith & Sons
Contact Matthew Smith
✉ **903 Christchurch Road, Bournemouth, Dorset, BH7 6AX** Ⓟ
☎ 01202 429523/01425 476705
ⓔ enquiries@dsmithandsons.demon.co.uk
ⓦ www.dsmithandsons.demon.co.uk
Est. 1968 *Stock size* Medium
Stock Country furniture and china
Open Mon–Sat 10am–5pm
Services Restorations

Southbourne Antiques
Contact Mr Guyatt
✉ **23 Southbourne Grove, Southbourne, Bournemouth, Dorset, BH6 3QS** Ⓟ
☎ 01202 430313
Est. 2000 *Stock size* Medium
Stock Collectables, curios, lighting, records, jewellery
Open Mon–Sat 10am–5.30pm

Southern Stoves & Fireplaces
Contact Ms L Godfrey
✉ **797 Christchurch Road, Pokesdown, Bournemouth, Dorset, BH7 6AW** Ⓟ
☎ 01202 430050 ⓕ 01202 430050
ⓦ www.southernoriginalfireplaces.co.uk
Est. 1996 *Stock size* Small
Stock Architectural antiques, stoves, original cast-iron fireplaces
Open Mon–Sat 10am–6pm or by appointment
Services Valuations, restorations

Sterling Coins and Medals (OMRS)
Contact Mr V Henstridge
✉ **2 Somerset Road, Boscombe, Bournemouth, Dorset, BH7 6JH** Ⓟ
☎ 01202 423881 ⓕ 01202 423881
ⓔ agagia@aol.com
Est. 1985 *Stock size* Medium
Stock Coins and medals
Open Mon–Sat 9am–3.30pm Wed 9am–12.15pm
Services Valuations and medal mounting

Victorian Chairman
Contact Mrs M Leo
✉ **883 Christchurch Road, Bournemouth, Dorset, BH7 6AU** Ⓟ
☎ 01202 420996
Est. 1977 *Stock size* Medium
Stock Victorian tables and chairs, wrought iron, glass tables
Open Mon–Sat 10am–5pm
Services Upholstery restoration, French polishing

Vintage Clobber
Contact Richard Mason
✉ **874 Christchurch Road, Bournemouth, Dorset, BH7 6DJ** Ⓟ
☎ 01202 429794 ⓜ 07779 324109
ⓔ mail@vintageclobber.com
ⓦ www.vintageclobber.com
Est. 1997 *Stock size* Medium
Stock 1920–70 clothing
Open Mon–Sat 10am–5pm
Services Valuations

Volume One Books and Records
Contact Richard Cargill
✉ **1073 Christchurch Road, Boscombe East, Bournemouth, Dorset, BH7 6BE** Ⓟ
☎ 01202 417652 ⓕ 01202 483686
Est. 1989 *Stock size* Large
Stock Books, LP records, cassettes and CDs (classical, easy listening, jazz, stage and screen, country, rock and pop)
Open Mon Tues Fri 10am–5.30pm Wed 10am–1pm Sat 10am–1pm closed 3rd Sat in each month
Fairs Midhurst Monthly Market, Sussex; others – please phone
Services Record search and mail order

Wonderworld
Contact Mr David Hern
✉ **540 Christchurch Road, Boscombe, Bournemouth, Dorset, BH1 4BE** Ⓟ
☎ 01202 394918 ⓕ 01202 393613
ⓔ davejh4000@aol.com
ⓦ www.wonderworld.uk.com
Est. 1977 *Stock size* Large
Stock Modern collectables, Star Wars, comics, Beanie Babies
Open Mon–Sat 10am–6pm

Yesterdays Books (PBFA)
Contact David Weir
✉ **6 Cecil Avenue, Bournemouth, Dorset, BH8 9EH** Ⓟ
☎ 01202 522442
ⓜ 07946 548420
ⓔ david@yesterdaysbooks.demon.co.uk
Est. 1974 *Stock size* Medium
Stock Antiquarian books. African topics a speciality
Open By appointment
Fairs PBFA at London, Oxford and elsewhere, the London Travel Bookfair
Services Valuations, book search

BRIDPORT

The Auction House Bridport
Contact Michael Dark
✉ **38a St Michael's Trading Estate, Bridport, Dorset, DT6 3RR** Ⓟ
☎ 01308 459400 ⓕ 01308 459685
ⓜ 07905 481388
ⓔ sales@theauctionhouse.dabsol.co.uk
ⓦ www.theauctionhouse.dabsol.co.uk
Est. 1998
Open Mon–Fri 9.30am–5pm
Sales Antiques and modern sale last Fri each month 10am, viewing prior Wed Thurs 10am–5pm
Frequency Monthly
Catalogues Yes

Batten's Jewellers
Contact Gemma Batten
✉ **26 South Street, Bridport, Dorset, DT6 3NQ** Ⓟ
☎ 01308 456910
Est. 1978 *Stock size* Medium
Stock Jewellery, clocks, watches, silver
Open Mon–Fri 9am–5pm Thurs Sat 9am–1pm

DORSET • CHRISTCHURCH

P E L Bedford
Contact Patrick Bedford
81 East Street, Bridport, Dorset, DT6 3LB
01308 421370
Est. 1956 *Stock size* Large
Stock Oriental and general antiques, porcelain, paintings, jewellery
Open Variable, phone call advisable

Benchmark Antiques
Contact Meg Standage
West Allington, Bridport, Dorset, DT6 5BG
01308 420941 01308 420941
hohobird@netscape.net
Est. 1992 *Stock size* Medium
Stock 18thC furniture and related items
Open Mon–Sat 9am–5pm
Fairs NEC
Services Valuations

Bridport Antique Centre
Contact Mr John Higgins
5 West Allington, Bridport, Dorset, DT6 5BJ
01308 425885
Est. 1970 *Stock size* Large
No. of dealers 6
Stock Collectables, general antiques, pine furniture
Open Mon–Sat 9.30am–5pm

Bridport Old Books (PBFA)
Contact Ms C MacTaggart
11 South Street, Bridport, Dorset, DT6 3NR
01308 425689
Est. 1998 *Stock size* Medium
Stock Antiquarian, second-hand, children's illustrated, WWI, T E Lawrence, modern first edition books
Open Mon–Sat 10am–5pm
Services Valuations

Jack's
Contact Mrs Jini Emery
24 South Street, Bridport, Dorset, DT6 3NQ
01308 420700
Est. 1985 *Stock size* Medium
Stock Oriental rugs, pine furniture, antiques, collectables
Open Mon–Sat 9am–5pm
Services Restorations (rugs)

William Morey & Son
Contact Malcolm Wilson
The Sale Room, St Michael's Lane, Bridport, Dorset, DT6 3RB
01308 422078 01308 422078
07748 356376
Est. 1870
Open Mon–Fri 9am–5pm
Sales Antiques auction every 3 weeks Thurs 9.30am, viewing Wed 9am–4pm
Frequency Every 3 weeks
Catalogues Yes

Ann Quested Antiques
Contact Ann Quested
59 East Street, Bridport, Dorset, DT6 3LB
01308 422576/421551
Est. 1990 *Stock size* Medium
Stock Pine and country furniture, brass
Open Wed–Sat 10.30am–5pm
Services Valuations

CHRISTCHURCH

Ancient and Gothic (ADA)
Contact Mr C Belton
PO Box 356, Christchurch, Dorset, BH23 1XQ
01202 431721
Est. 1977
Stock Prehistoric, ancient and medieval antiquities, mail order only
Open Mon–Sat 11am–7pm
Services Bi-monthly sales list

Antique Pine Stores
Contact Russell Davey
91 Bargates, Christchurch, Dorset, BH23 1QQ
01202 475515
www.antiquepinestore.com
Est. 2001 *Stock size* Large
Stock Antique pine furniture from Eastern Europe
Open Mon–Sat 10am–4.30pm

Classic Pictures (PTA)
Contact Betty Underwood
12a Castle Street, Christchurch, Dorset, BH23 1DT
01202 470276
classicpictures@talk21.com
Est. 1989 *Stock size* Large
Stock Old postcards, Edwardian pictures, prints
Open Tues–Sat 9.30am–5pm
Fairs New Forest Show, Bournemouth International Centre
Services Valuations

H L B Antiques
Contact Mr H L Blechman
139 Barrack Road, Christchurch, Dorset, BH23 2AW
01202 482388
Est. 1967 *Stock size* Medium
Stock General collectables, gramophones, postcards, walking sticks, Art Deco, ivory
Open Sat 10am–4pm or by appointment on 01202 429252
Fairs New Caledonian Market in Bermondsey
Services Valuations

Gerald Hampton
Contact Gerald Hampton
12 Purewell, Christchurch, Dorset, BH23 1EP
01202 484000
Est. 1930 *Stock size* Medium
Stock General antiques
Trade only Yes
Open By appointment

M & R Lankshear Antiques
Contact Mike Lankshear
18 Plantation Drive, Walkford, Christchurch, Dorset, BH23 5SA
01425 277332 07811 018476
Est. 1977 *Stock size* Medium
Stock General antiques, military items
Open Mon–Sat 9.30am–5pm
Services Valuations

Past 'n' Present
Contact Pete Woodford
4 St Catherine's Parade, Fairmile Road, Christchurch, Dorset, BH23 2LQ
01202 478900
Est. 1997 *Stock size* Large
Stock Collectables
Open Mon–Sat 9.30am–5pm
Services Valuations, restorations

Tudor House Antiques (LAPADA)
Contact Mrs P Knight or Mrs D Burton
420 Lymington Road, Highcliffe, Christchurch, Dorset, BH23 5HE
01425 280440

Est. 1940 *Stock size* Medium
Stock General
Open Tues–Sat 10am–5pm
closed Wed

CRANBORNE

Tower Antiques
Contact Mr P White
The Square, Cranborne, Dorset, BH21 5PR
☎ 01725 517552
Est. 1973 *Stock size* Small
Stock Georgian, Victorian furniture
Open Mon–Sat 8.30am–5.30pm

DORCHESTER

The Antiques Emporium
Contact Bruce Clarke-Williams
9 High East Street, Dorchester, Dorset, DT1 1HS
☎ 01305 261546
Est. 1997 *Stock size* Medium
Open Mon–Sat 9.30am–5.30pm

Box of Porcelain
Contact Robert Lunn
51d Icen Way, Dorchester, Dorset, DT1 1EW
☎ 01305 250856 Ⓕ 01305 265517
Ⓜ 07721 351761
Ⓔ rlunn@btconnect.com
Ⓦ www.boxofporcelain.com
Est. 1987 *Stock size* Large
Stock Doulton, Beswick, Royal Worcester, Spode
Open Mon–Sat 10.30am–5pm
closed Thurs

Chattels
Colliton Antique Centre, 3 Colliton Street, Dorchester, Dorset, DT1 1XH
☎ 01305 263620
Est. 1993 *Stock size* Large
Stock General, Edwardian, Victorian furniture
Open Mon–Sat 9am–5pm

Colliton Antique Centre
Contact Tony Phillips
3a Colliton Street, Dorchester, Dorset, DT1 1XH
☎ 01305 269398/260115
Est. 1983 *Stock size* Large
No. of dealers 6
Stock General Victorian, Georgian, Edwardian furniture, jewellery, silver, old pine
Open Mon–Sat 9am–5pm
Sun by appointment
Services Restoration of metalwork, silver and jewellery valuations

De Danann Antiques Centre
Contact Mr J Burton
27 London Road, Dorchester, Dorset, DT1 1NF
☎ 01305 250066/264123
Ⓕ 01305 250113
Ⓦ www.dedanann.co.uk
Est. 1994 *Stock size* Medium
No. of dealers 20
Stock General antiques
Open Mon–Sat 9am–5pm

The Dorchester Bookshop
Contact Michael Edmonds
3 Nappers Court, Charles Street, Dorchester, Dorset, DT1 1EE
☎ 01305 269919
Est. 1993 *Stock size* Medium
Stock Second-hand, antiquarian books
Open Tues–Sat 10am–5pm
Fairs Local book fairs
Services Valuations, restorations and book search

Hy Duke & Son (SOFAA)
Contact Mr Guy Schwinge or Mr Gary Batt
The Dorchester Fine Art Salerooms, Weymouth Avenue, Dorchester, Dorset, DT1 1QS
☎ 01305 265080 Ⓕ 01305 260101
Ⓜ 07778 523962
Ⓔ enquiries@dukes-auctions.com
Ⓦ www.dukes-auctions.com
Est. 1823
Open Mon–Fri some Sats 9am–1pm 2–5.30pm
Sales Specialist sales of paintings, furniture, ceramics, silver, jewellery and furniture, viewing week prior Sat 9.30am–noon Mon 9.30am–5pm Tues 9.30am–7pm Wed 9.30am–5pm morning of sale
Frequency 9 per annum
Catalogues Yes

Fordington Antiques
Contact Brian Dodington
60 Kings Road, Dorchester, Dorset, DT1 1NH
☎ 01305 251502
Est. 1999 *Stock size* Large
Stock Country furniture, tools, garden items, kitchenware
Open Mon–Sat 8am–6.30pm

Legg of Dorchester
Contact Mrs H Legg
Regency House, 51 High East Street, Dorchester, Dorset, DT1 1HU
☎ 01305 264964
Est. 1930 *Stock size* Large
Stock General, mostly furniture
Open Mon–Sat 9.30am–5.30pm

Santiques
Contact Tony Phillips
Colliton Antique Centre, 3 Colliton Street, Dorchester, Dorset, DT1 1XH
☎ 01305 260115
Est. 1975 *Stock size* Medium
Stock Jewellery, silver, china, furniture
Open Mon–Sat 9am–5pm
Sun by appointment
Services Restorations of metal and woodwork, silver and jewellery valuations

John Walker Antiques (BADA, BACA Award Winner 2002)
Contact Mr J Walker
52 High West Street, Dorchester, Dorset, DT1 1UT
☎ 01305 260324 Ⓜ 07880 528436
Est. 1973 *Stock size* Medium
Stock Early oak, textiles, ceramics, metalwork
Open Tues–Sat 9.30am–5pm

GILLINGHAM

Talisman (LAPADA)
Contact Mr Ken Bolan
The Old Brewery, Wyke Road, Gillingham, Dorset, SP8 4NW
☎ 01747 824423 Ⓕ 01747 823544
Ⓔ arcadia@talisman-antiques.co.uk
Ⓦ www.talisman-antiques.co.uk
Est. 1979 *Stock size* Large
Stock Antiques and garden statuary
Open Mon–Fri 9am–5pm
Sat 10am–4pm
Fairs Summer Olympia

LYME REGIS

The Commemorative Man
Contact Mr Harris

✉ **Lyme Regis Antiques & Craft Centre, Marine Parade, Lyme Regis, Dorset, DT7 3JH** P
☎ 01297 32682
Est. 1994 *Stock size* Large
Stock Political and sporting commemoratives
Open April–Oct Mon–Sun 11am–6.30pm Nov–Mar Fri Sat Sun 11am–4.30pm
Services Mail order and search service

Patsy Lewis
Contact Mrs P Lewis
✉ **Lyme Regis Antiques & Craft Centre, Marine Parade, Lyme Regis, Dorset, DT7 3JH** P
☎ 01297 445053
Est. 1990 *Stock size* Medium
Stock Linen, tablecloths, sheets and pillowcases
Open Apr–Oct Mon–Sun 11am–6.30pm Nov–Mar Fri Sat Sun 11am–4.30pm

Lyme Regis Antique & Craft Centre
Contact Mr C Willis
✉ **Marine Parade, Lyme Regis, Dorset, DT7 3JH** P
☎ 01297 445053
Est. 1995 *Stock size* Large
No. of dealers 35
Stock Commemoratives, stamps, coins, toys, linen, brass taps, Art Deco, lamps, lighting
Open Apr–Oct Mon–Sun 11am–6.30pm Nov–Mar Fri Sat Sun 11am–4.30pm

Pennies
Contact Penny Ross
✉ **15 Broad Street, Lyme Regis, Dorset, DT7 3QE** P
☎ 01297 444933
Est. 1992 *Stock size* Small
Stock Victorian, Art Deco china, gold, silver
Open Mon–Sun 10.30am–5.30pm

LYTCHETT MINSTER

Button Shop Antiques
Contact Thelma Johns
✉ **Dorchester Road, Lytchett Minster, Dorset, BH16 6JF** P
☎ 01202 622169
ⓔ info@oldbuttonshop.fsnet.co.uk
Est. 1979 *Stock size* Small
Stock General and cottage antiques, Dorset buttons
Open Tues–Fri 2–5pm Sat 11am–1pm
Services Valuations, restorations

MAIDEN NEWTON

Dynasty Antiques
Contact Gareth Clarke-Williams
✉ **Newton Hall, Dorchester Road, Maiden Newton, Dorchester, Dorset, DT2 0BD** P
☎ 01300 321313 Ⓜ 07966 256648
Ⓦ www.dynastyantiques.co.uk
Est. 2000 *Stock size* Medium
Stock Chinese, Tibetan antique furniture
Open By appointment

MELBURY OSMOND

Hardy Country
Contact Mr S Groves
✉ **Meadow View, Drive End, Melbury Osmond, Dorchester, Dorset, DT2 0NA** P
☎ 01935 83440 Ⓜ 07778 658581
Est. 1972 *Stock size* Large
Stock Old pine
Open Mon–Sat 9am–6pm Sun by appointment
Services Valuations, restorations

POOLE

Branksome Antiques
Contact Brian Neal
✉ **370 Poole Road, Branksome, Poole, Dorset, BH12 1AW** P
☎ 01202 763324 Ⓕ 01202 763643
Est. 1972 *Stock size* Medium
Stock General antiques, scientific, medical, marine, silver, brass, copper
Open Mon Tues Thur Fri 10am–5pm
Fairs Scientific Fair, Portman Hotel

Castle Books
Contact Mr Clark
✉ **2 North Street, Poole, Dorset, BH15 1NX** P
☎ 01202 660295
Est. 1980 *Stock size* Medium
Stock Antiquarian, modern second-hand, collectable books
Open Mon–Sat 10am–5pm
Fairs London Book Fairs (June), HD promotions
Services Valuations

Davey & Davey (NAVA)
Contact Neil Davey
✉ **13 St Peters Road, Parkstone, Poole, Dorset, BH14 0NZ** P
☎ 01202 748567 Ⓕ 01202 716258
Est. 1946
Open Mon–Fri 9am–1pm 2–5.30pm
Sales General antiques and collectables every 2 months, Tues 10am, viewing Mon 10am–4pm
Frequency Every 2 months
Catalogues Yes

Down To The Woods Ltd
Contact Vanessa Harris
✉ **92 The Dolphin Centre, Poole, Dorset, BH15 1SR** P
☎ 01202 669448
ⓔ downttw@globalnet.co.uk
Est. 1998 *Stock size* Large
Stock Bears, soft toys, bean-bag collections, dolls' houses. Collectables rather than antiques
Open Mon–Sat 9.30am–5.30pm
Services Layaway, mail order

Fireplaces 'n' Things
Contact Mr D L Shackford
✉ **87–89 Alder Road, Parkstone, Poole, Dorset, BH12 2AB** P
☎ 01202 735301 Ⓕ 01202 735301
Est. 1980 *Stock size* Large
Stock Antique and reproduction fireplaces
Open Mon–Sat 10am–5pm half day Wed
Services Valuations, restorations

Great Expectations
Contact Mr Carter
✉ **115 Penn Hill Avenue, Lower Parkstone, Poole, Dorset, BH14 9LY** P
☎ 01202 740645
Est. 2000 *Stock size* Medium
Stock General antiques, paintings, prints, objets d'art
Open Wed–Sat 10.30am–5pm

W A Howe
Contact Mr W A Howe
✉ **5 Merrow Avenue, Branksome, Poole, Dorset, BH12 1PY** P
☎ 01202 743350
Est. 1999 *Stock size* Small
Stock Antiquarian and second-

hand books, modern first editions, cookery, golf
Open Mon–Sun 8am–8pm
Fairs Local book fairs
Services Valuations

Laburnum Antiques
Contact Mrs D Mills
Lonbourne House, 250 Bournemouth Road, Poole, Dorset, BH14 9HZ
01202 746222 01202 736777
enquiries@laburnumantiques.co.uk
www.laburnumantiques.co.uk
Est. 1997 *Stock size* Medium
Stock Georgian–Edwardian furniture, accessories, ottomans, stools and cushions
Open Tues–Sat 10am–5.30pm
Services Complete home furnishing service and fully qualified furniture restorations

Stocks and Chairs
Contact Mrs Carole Holding-Parsons
11 Bank Chambers, Penn Hill Avenue, Poole, Dorset, BH14 9NB
01202 718618
www.stockandchairsantiques.com
Est. 1979 *Stock size* Large
Stock 18th–19thC furniture, some smalls
Open Mon–Sat 11am–5pm closed Wed
Services Restoration of hand-dyed leather

Stocks and Chairs
Contact Mrs Carole Holding-Parsons
The Old Church Hall, Hardy Road, Poole, Dorset, BH14 9HN
01202 718418 01202 718918
www.stocksandchairsantiques.com
Est. 1979 *Stock size* Large
Stock Antique leather chairs and settees
Open Mon–Fri 8.30am–5.30pm and by appointment
Services Restoration of hand-dyed leather

Threeways Antique Pine
Contact Keith Norman
55 Commercial Road, Poole, Dorset, BH14 0JB
01202 730501 01202 730501
Est. 1998 *Stock size* Medium
Stock Antique English and Eastern European pine furniture
Open Mon–Sat 10am–5pm
Services Restorations

Christopher Williams (PBFA)
Contact Mr C Williams
19 Morrison Avenue, Poole, Dorset, BH12 4AD
01202 743157 01202 743157
cw4finebooks@lineone.net
www.abebooks.com/home/cw
Est. 1967 *Stock size* Small
Stock Antiquarian books and fine modern books. Lacemaking, needlework, cookery, art, antiques, collecting and local history topics a speciality
Open By appointment. Trades mostly through fairs/postal order
Fairs PBFA fairs
Services Valuations

PUDDLETOWN

Antique Map and Bookshop (PBFA, ABA)
Contact Mrs H M Proctor
32 High Street, Puddletown, Dorchester, Dorset, DT2 8RU
01305 848633 01305 848992
proctor@puddletown.demon.co.uk
Est. 1976 *Stock size* Medium
Stock Antique maps, antiquarian, second-hand books
Open Mon–Sat 9am–5pm
Fairs Oxford, Russell Hotel (June) – PBFA
Services Valuations, restorations, book catalogues (4–6 a year)

SEMLEY

Dairy House Antiques
Contact Andrew Stevenson
Station Road, Semley, Shaftesbury, Dorset, SP7 9AN
01747 853317
Est. 1998 *Stock size* Large
No. of dealers 9
Stock Antiques and collectables
Open Mon–Sat 9am–5pm

Semley Auctioneers
Contact Mr Simon Pearce
Station Road, Semley, Shaftesbury, Dorset, SP7 9AN
01747 855122 01747 855222
simon.pearce@semleyauctioneers.com
www.semleyauctioneers.com
Est. 1990
Open Mon–Fri 9am–5pm
Sales Sat 10am, viewing Friday prior 9am–9pm and morning of sale. Items of higher quality appear in these sales about every 6 weeks
Frequency Fortnightly
Catalogues Yes

SHAFTESBURY

Robert Morgan Antiques
Contact Robert Morgan
Mustons Yard, Mustons Lane, Shaftesbury, Dorset, SP7 8AD
01747 858770 07767 416106
robert@robertmorganantiques.co.uk
www.robertmorganantiques.co.uk
Est. 1985 *Stock size* Medium
Stock Small furniture, unusual items, medals, coins
Open By appointment
Fairs Kempton Park, Newark
Services Valuations

Mr Punch's Antique Market
Contact Mr C Jolliffe
33 Bell Street, Shaftesbury, Dorset, SP7 8AE
01747 855775 01747 855775
www.mrpunchs.biz
Est. 1994 *Stock size* Large
No. of dealers 20
Stock General, furniture, collectables, militaria
Open Mon–Sat 10am–6pm
Services Valuations, restorations, pine stripping, house clearance, Punch museum

Shaston Antiques
Contact Mr J D Hine
16a Bell Street, Shaftesbury, Dorset, SP7 8AE
01747 850405
Est. 1996 *Stock size* Medium
Stock Georgian–Victorian quality furniture
Open Mon Tues Thurs Sat 9am–5pm Wed 9am–1pm
Services Restorations

SHERBORNE

Abbas Antiques
Contact Trevor F J Jeans
Sherborne World of Antiques & Fine Art, Long Street, Sherborne, Dorset, DT9 3BS

☎ 01935 816451 ⓕ 01935 816240
Est. 1991 *Stock size* Medium
Stock 19thC furniture and smalls
Open Mon–Sat 9.30am–5pm
Services Valuations, restorations

Antiques of Sherborne (LAPADA, SAADA)
Contact Clive or Linda Greenslade
1 The Green, Sherborne, Dorset, DT9 3HZ
☎ 01935 816549 ⓕ 01935 816549
ⓜ 07971 019173
ⓔ clive@antiquesofsherborne.fsnet.co.uk
Est. 1988 *Stock size* Medium
Stock Town and country furniture, Georgian–Edwardian period, sofas, armchairs, linen, tantalus, chess and mah jong sets
Open Mon–Sat 10am–5pm
Fairs Shepton Mallet
Services Valuations, upholstery

Bonhams
Sherborne, Dorset, OX16 0TH
☎ 01935 815271 ⓕ 01935 816416
ⓔ bill.allan@bonhams.com
ⓦ www.bonhams.com
Open Mon–Fri 9am–5.30pm

Chapter House Books (PBFA)
Contact Mr or Mrs Hutchison
Trendle Street, Sherborne, Dorset, DT9 3NT
☎ 01935 816262
ⓔ chapterhousebooks@tiscali.co.uk
Est. 1988 *Stock size* Large
Stock Antiquarian books (mostly hardback), out-of-print, paperbacks, pictures
Open Mon–Sat 10am–5pm
Services Valuations, book repair, book search

Greystoke Antiques
Contact Mr F Butcher
4 Swan Yard, Cheap Street, Sherborne, Dorset, DT9 3AX
☎ 01935 812833
Est. 1974 *Stock size* Large
Stock Silver, Georgian and Victorian, English blue transfer-printed pottery 1790–1850
Open Mon–Sat 10am–4.30pm closed Wed
Services Valuations, restorations

Keeble Antiques
Contact Mr C Keeble
2 Tilton Court, Digby Road, Sherborne, Dorset, DT9 3NL
☎ 01935 816199 ⓕ 01935 816199
ⓔ clivekeeble@btconnect.com
ⓦ www.keebleantbks.co.uk
Est. 1969 *Stock size* Medium
Stock Eclectic pieces, pictures, mirrors, clocks, boxes, antique and fine art books
Open Mon–Sat 8am–6pm
Sun 9.30am–5.30pm
Services Book search

The Nook Antiques (SAADA)
Contact Mrs Jill Morley
South Street, Sherborne, Dorset, DT9 3LX
☎ 01935 813987
Est. 1969 *Stock size* Large
Stock Small, useful, refurbished furniture. China, glass, brass, copper and collectables
Open Tues–Sat 10am–5pm

Phoenix Antiques (SAADA)
Contact Neil or Sally Brent Jones
21 Cheap Street, Sherborne, Dorset, DT9 3PU
☎ 01935 812788
Est. 1982 *Stock size* Medium
Stock 18th–20thC English and Continental furniture. Mahogany, rosewood, painted country furniture, furnishings and lighting
Open Mon–Sat 9.30am–5.30pm or by appointment

Piers Pisani Antiques (SAADA)
Contact Mr Piers Pisani
The Court Yard, Newland, Sherborne, Dorset, DT9 3JG
☎ 01935 815209 ⓕ 01935 815209
ⓔ antiques@pierspisani.sagehost.co.uk
ⓦ www.pierspisani.com
Est. 1987 *Stock size* Large
Stock English and French furniture, upholstery
Open Mon–Sat 10am–5pm
Services Valuations, restorations, furniture copy

Renaissance
Contact Malcolm Heygate Browne
South Street, Sherborne, Dorset, DT9 3NG
☎ 01935 815487 ⓕ 01935 815487
Est. 1984 *Stock size* Large
Stock 18th–19thC English furniture, pottery, porcelain, Middle Eastern carpets
Open Mon–Sat 10am–5pm
Sun 11am–3pm
Services Valuations, restorations

Sherborne World of Antiques
Contact Mr T F J Jeans
Long Street, Sherborne, Dorset, DT9 3BS
☎ 01935 816451 ⓕ 01935 816240
ⓔ info@sherborneworldofantiques.co.uk
ⓦ www.sherborneworldofantiques.co.uk
Est. 2000 *Stock size* Large
No. of dealers 40
Stock General antiques, fine art, jewellery, clocks, porcelain
Open Mon–Sat 9.30am–5pm
Services Valuations, restorations, shipping, book search

Timecraft Clocks (BHI)
Contact Mr G Smith
Unit 2, 24 Cheap Street, Sherborne, Dorset, DT9 3PX
☎ 01935 817771
Est. 1994 *Stock size* Small
Stock Clocks, barometers, musical boxes
Open Tue–Fri 10.30am–5.30pm
Sat 10.30am–5pm
Services Restorations, repairs

Victor & Co (SAADA)
Contact Victor Barwick
The Stores, Trendle Street, Sherborne, Dorset, DT9 3NT
☎ 01935 817595
Est. 1995 *Stock size* Large
Stock Domestic antiques, textiles, glass, china
Open Mon–Sat 9.30am–5pm

Wessex Antiques (SAADA)
Contact Frances Bryant
6 Cheap Street, Sherborne, Dorset, DT9 3PX
☎ 01935 816816 ⓕ 01935 816816
ⓔ drucie.bryant@virgin.co.uk
Est. 1986 *Stock size* Small
Stock Furniture, Staffordshire figures, 19thC glass, Oriental rugs
Open Tues–Sat 10am–5pm

Henry Willis (Antique Silver)
Contact Henry Willis
38 Cheap Street, Sherborne, Dorset, DT9 3PX

WEST COUNTRY

☎ 01935 816828 Ⓜ 07971 171818
Est. 1975 *Stock size* Medium
Stock English silver medieval–1940
Open Mon–Sat 10am–5pm
Fairs Olympia (June)

STOURPAINE

Onslow Auctions Ltd
Contact Patrick Bogue
✉ **The Coach House, Manor Road, Stourpaine, Dorset, DT11 8TQ** Ⓟ
☎ 01258 488838 Ⓕ 01258 488838
Ⓔ onslow.auctions@btinternet.com
Ⓦ www.onslows.uk
Est. 1984
Open Mon–Fri 9.30am–5pm by appointment
Sales Collectors' sales, vintage travel, aeronautical, posters, railways, motoring, Titanic, ocean liners, advisable to phone for details
Frequency 4 per annum
Catalogues Yes

SWANAGE

New, Secondhand & Antiquarian Books
Contact Mrs J Blanchard
✉ **35 Station Road, Swanage, Dorset, BH19 1AD**
☎ 01929 424088
Est. 1987 *Stock size* Large
Stock New, second-hand, antiquarian books. First and pocket editions.
Open Summer Mon–Sun 9.30am–5.00pm winter closed Sun

WAREHAM

Cottees of Wareham
Contact Mr Bullock
✉ **The Market, East Street, Wareham, Dorset, BH20 4NR** Ⓟ
☎ 01929 552826 Ⓕ 01929 554916
Ⓔ auctions@cottees.fsnet.co.uk
Ⓦ www.auctionsatcottees.co.uk
Est. 1902
Open Mon–Fri 9am–5pm closed 1–2pm
Sales General antique sales fortnightly Tues 10am and 2pm, viewing Mon 10am–1pm 2–5pm 6–8pm. Regular quality antique and fine art sales. Poole pottery, Clarice Cliff, Moorcroft pottery, Art Deco and collectable toy sales
Frequency Fortnightly
Catalogues Yes

Heirlooms Antique Jewellers & Silversmiths
Contact Mr or Mrs Young
✉ **21 South Street, Wareham, Dorset, BH20 4LR** Ⓟ
☎ 01929 554207 Ⓕ 01929 554207
Est. 1985 *Stock size* Small
Stock Antique and period jewellery and silver
Open Mon–Sat 9.30am–5pm closed Wed Sun
Services Jewellery, silver, watch, clock repair

Yesterdays
Contact Mrs Joyce Hardie
✉ **32 South Street, Wareham, Dorset, BH20 4LU** Ⓟ
☎ 01929 550505
Est. 1994 *Stock size* Large
Stock 1920–1930s porcelain and china, Poole, Shelley, Carlton ware, Susie Cooper, modern collectables
Open Mon–Sat 10am–4.30pm closed Wed pm in winter
Fairs Shepton Mallet, Exeter livestock
Services Postal

WEYMOUTH

Books Afloat
Contact John Ritchie
✉ **66 Park Street, Weymouth, Dorset, DT4 7DE** Ⓟ
☎ 01305 779774
Est. 1983 *Stock size* Large
Stock Antiquarian, rare and second-hand books. Shipping, naval antiques and memorabilia, old postcards. ship models, paintings
Open Mon–Sat 9.30am–5.30pm

Books & Bygones
Contact Denise Nash
✉ **26 Great George Street, Weymouth, Dorset, DT4 7AS** Ⓟ
☎ 01305 777231
Est. 1985 *Stock size* Medium
Stock Antiques, collectables, out-of-print, rare and antiquarian books
Open Mon–Sat 10am–5pm
Services Valuations

The Crows Nest
Contact Julia Marko
✉ **3 Hope Square, Weymouth, Dorset, DT4 8TR** Ⓟ
☎ 01305 786930 Ⓕ 01305 786930
Est. 1992 *Stock size* Large
Stock China, glass, pictures, farming, ships' lamps, nautical, collectables
Open Mon–Sun 10am–5pm
Fairs Shepton Mallet, Exeter Livestock Market
Services Restorations

The Curiosity Shop on the Quay
Contact David Pinches
✉ **13 Trinity Road, Weymouth, Dorset, DT4 8TJ** Ⓟ
☎ 01305 769988 Ⓕ 01305 769988
Est. 1990 *Stock size* Large
Stock General collectors' shop, Victoriana, collectables, Moorcroft, Poole pottery and Pendelfin
Open Mon–Sun 10am–5pm
Fairs Shepton Mallet, Exeter West Point

Hy Duke & Son (SOFAA)
Contact Bob Bover
✉ **The Weymouth Auction Rooms, St Nicholas Street, Weymouth, Dorset, DT4 8AA** Ⓟ
☎ 01305 761499 Ⓜ 01305 260101
Est. 1823
Open Mon–Fri 9am–5.30pm closed 1–2pm
Sales Twice-monthly sales on Tues at 10.30am of general antiques and household effects. Viewing Mon prior 9.30am–5pm
Catalogues No

Nautical Antique Centre
Contact Mr D C Warwick
✉ **3a Cove Passage, off Hope Square, near Brewers Quay, Weymouth, Dorset, DT4 8TR** Ⓟ
☎ 01305 777838/783180
Ⓜ 07833 707247
Ⓔ nauticalantiques@tinyworld.co.uk
Ⓦ www.nauticalantiquesweymouth.co.uk
Est. 1988 *Stock size* Large
Stock Original maritime items, telescopes, sextants, clocks, barometers, ships' models, nautical collectables and memorabilia for collectors or commercial and domestic interior decor

Open Tues–Fri 10am–1pm 2–5pm (please ring in case shop is closed for fairs) evenings and weekends by appointment

⊞ Paddy Cliff's Clarice! (CCCC)
Contact Mrs Joan Ferguson
✉ **77 Coombe Valley Road, Preston, Weymouth, Dorset, DT3 6NL**
☎ 01305 834945 Ⓕ 01305 837369
Ⓜ 0793 0116265
Ⓔ bizarre@uk.packardbell.org
Ⓦ www.paddycliff.com
Est. 1999 *Stock size* Large
Stock Clarice Cliff pieces sold by mail order or via Internet
Open By appointment
Fairs NEC, Leeds Royal Armoury

⊞ The Shrubbery
Contact Mrs Sally Dench
✉ **15 Westham Road, Weymouth, Dorset, DT4 8NS** Ⓟ
☎ 01305 768240
Est. 1997 *Stock size* Large
Stock Collectable dolls, dolls' houses, toys
Open Mon–Sat 10am–54pm
Fairs Weymouth (Nov)

⊞ The Treasure Chest
Contact Mr P Barrett
✉ **29 East Street, Weymouth, Dorset, DT4 8BN** Ⓟ
☎ 01305 772757
Est. 1969 *Stock size* Medium
Stock Curios, coins, medals, local prints, brass, copper, china, army badges
Open Mon–Sat 10am–5pm closed 1–2.30pm Wed 10am–1pm
Services Medal mounting, full size or miniature medals

WIMBORNE

⊞ Minster Books
Contact Mr or Mrs Child
✉ **12 Cornmarket, Wimborne, Dorset, BH21 1JL**
☎ 01202 883355
Est. 1991 *Stock size* Large
Stock Antiquarian and second-hand books
Open Mon–Sat 10am–5pm
Services Valuations, restorations

⊞ Rectory Rocking Horses
Contact Geoff Boyd
✉ **The Barn, Pamphill Dairy, Pamphill, Wimborne, Dorset, BH21 4ED** Ⓟ
☎ 01202 881100 Ⓕ 01202 881100
Ⓦ www.antiquerockinghorses.co.uk
Est. 1997 *Stock size* Medium
Stock Antique rocking horses
Open Tues–Fri 10am–5pm Sat Sun 11am–3pm
Services Restorations

⊞ The Wimborne Emporium
Contact Trisha Gurney
✉ **9 West Borough, Wimborne, Dorset, BH21 1LT** Ⓟ
☎ 01202 883994
Est. 1999 *Stock size* Large
Stock Antiques and collectables
Open Mon–Sat 9am–5pm

SOMERSET

ABBOTS LEIGH

⊞ David & Sally March Antiques (LAPADA, CINOA)
Contact David March
✉ **Oak Wood Lodge, Stoke Leigh Woods, Abbots Leigh, Bristol, BS8 3QB** Ⓟ
☎ 01275 372422 Ⓕ 01275 372422
Ⓜ 07774 838376
Ⓔ david.march@lineone.net
Est. 1973 *Stock size* Medium
Stock 18thC English porcelain figures, Plymouth and Bristol a speciality
Open By appointment only
Fairs LAPADA, NEC
Services Valuations

AXBRIDGE

⊞ The Old Post House
Contact Ray or Mollie Seaman
✉ **Turnpike Road, Lower Weare, Axbridge, Somerset, BS26 2JF** Ⓟ
☎ 01934 732372 Ⓕ 01934 733377
Est. 1981 *Stock size* Medium
Stock General antiques, country pine furniture, paintings
Open Tues–Sat 10am–5pm
Services Free delivery (25 miles radius)

BATH

⊞ A J Antiques (BABAADA)
Contact Patrick Anketell-Jones
✉ **13 Broad Street, Bath, Somerset, BA1 5LJ**
☎ 01225 447765 Ⓕ 01225 447765
Est. 1977 *Stock size* Medium
Stock Georgian–1950s furniture
Open Mon–Sat 10am–5.30pm

⊞ Abbey Galleries (NAG, NPA)
Contact Richard Dickson
✉ **9 Abbey Church Yard, Bath, Somerset, BA1 1LY**
☎ 01225 460565 Ⓕ 01225 484192
Est. 1950 *Stock size* Large
Stock Jewellery, Oriental porcelain, silver
Open Mon–Sat 10.30am–5pm
Services Restorations

⊞ Alderson (BADA, CINOA)
Contact Mr C J Alderson
✉ **2 Princes Buildings, George Street, Bath, Somerset, BA1 2ED** Ⓟ
☎ 01225 421652 Ⓕ 01225 421652
Ⓔ kit.alderson@amserve.net
Est. 1976 *Stock size* Medium
Stock 18th–19thC furniture and works of art
Open Mon–Fri 9.30am–5.30pm closed 1–2pm Sat 9.30am–1pm or by appointment
Fairs BADA, Olympia

Aldridges of Bath
Contact Mr I Street
✉ **Newark House, 26–45 Cheltenham Street, Bath, Somerset, BA2 3EX** Ⓟ
☎ 01225 462830 Ⓕ 01225 311319
Ⓦ www.invaluable.com/aldridges
Est. 1740
Open Mon–Fri 9am–5pm Sat 9am–noon
Sales Tues 10am, Victorian and general sales fortnightly, specialist antiques sales 6–8 weeks, collectors' sales 6–8 weeks
Catalogues Yes

⊞ Antique Glass (BABAADA)
Contact Margaret Hopkins
✉ **33 Belvedere, Lansdown Road, Bath, Somerset, BA1 5HR** Ⓟ
☎ 01225 312367 Ⓕ 01225 312367
Ⓔ mh@antique-glass.co.uk
Ⓦ www.antique-glass.co.uk
Est. 1988 *Stock size* Medium
Stock Georgian glass, collectors' drinking glasses, rummers, ales,

friggers, decanters, other curiosities
Open Tues–Sat 10am–6pm
Services Search

Antique Linens & Lace (BABAADA)
Contact Rosalind Mellor
11 Pulteney Bridge, Bath, Somerset, BA2 4AY
01225 465782 01225 867551
rosalind.mellor@telinco.co.uk
Est. 1969 *Stock size* Large
Stock Tablecloths, bed linen, cushions, baby bonnets, wedding veils, shawls, christening gowns, textiles, quilts, bead bags
Open Mon–Sat 10am–5.30pm or by appointment

Antique Textiles and Lighting (BABAADA, BACA Award winner 2002)
Contact Joanna Proops
34 Belvedere, Lansdown Road, Bath, Somerset, BA1 5HR
01225 310795 01225 443884
www.antiquetextiles.co.uk
Est. 1970 *Stock size* Large
Stock Antique textiles, tapestries, samplers, Paisleys, fans, beadwork, linen, lace, wall and ceiling lighting, chandeliers
Open Tues–Fri 10am–5pm
Sat 9am–1pm
Fairs Bath Decorative Fair
Services Valuations

The Antiques Warehouse (BABAADA)
Contact Mr or Mrs R D Waterfall
57 Walcot Street, Bath, Somerset, BA1 5BN
01225 444201 07990 690240
Est. 1991 *Stock size* Medium
Stock Georgian, Victorian and early 20thC furniture and collectables
Open Mon–Sat 10.30am–5.30pm
Services Deliveries

Assembly Antiques Centre (BABAADA)
Contact Linda Brine
5–8 Saville Row, Bath, Somerset, BA1 5PF
01225 426288 01225 429661
www.assemblyantiques.co.uk
Est. 1969 *Stock size* Large
No. of dealers 5
Stock 18th–19thC furniture, lighting, chess sets, tea caddies, jewellery, scent bottles, porcelain
Open Mon–Sat 10am–5pm
Wed 8am–5pm
Services Valuations, restorations and gemologist

Bartlett Street Antiques Centre (BABAADA)
Contact Anne Linham
5–10 Bartlett Street, Bath, Somerset, BA1 2QZ
01225 469998 01225 444146
info@antiques-centre.co.uk
www.antiques-centre.co.uk
Est. 1983 *Stock size* Large
No. of dealers 50–60
Stock Antiques and collectables
Open Mon–Sat 9.30am–5pm
Wed 8am–5pm
Services Restaurant

Bath Antiquities Centre
Contact Antonia Kent
4 Bladud Buildings, Bath, Somerset, BA1 5LS
01225 316889
Est. 1998 *Stock size* Medium
No. of dealers 9
Stock Prehistoric, neolithic, medieval, Chinese, Greek, Egyptian antiques
Open Mon–Sat 9.30am–5pm

Bath Old Books (PBFA)
Contact Steven Ferdinando
9c Margaret's Buildings, Bath, Somerset, BA1 2LP
01225 422244
bathbooks@hotmail.com
Est. 1991 *Stock size* Medium
Stock Antiquarian and second-hand books
Open Mon–Sat 10am–5pm
Fairs PBFA
Services Valuations, book binding, book searches

George Bayntun (ABA)
Contact Mr Edward Bayntun-Coward
1 Manvers Street, Bath, Somerset, BA1 1JW
01225 466000 01225 482122
ebc@georgebayntun.com
www.georgebayntun.com
Est. 1894 *Stock size* Large
Stock Antiquarian and rare books, English literature first editions, fine bindings
Open Mon–Fri 9am–1pm
2–5.30pm Sat 9am–1pm
Services Valuations, restorations, binding service

Bedsteads (BABAADA)
Contact Nicola Ashton
2 Walcot Buildings, London Road, Bath, Somerset, BA1 6AD
01225 339182
www.bed-steads.co.uk
Est. 1990 *Stock size* Medium
Stock Antique bedsteads in iron, brass and exotic woods
Open Mon–Sat 10am–6pm
Sun by appointment
Services Restorations

Bonhams
1 Old King Street, Bath, Somerset, BA1 2JT
01225 788988 01225 446675
bath@bonhams.com
www.bonhams.com
Open Mon–Fri 9am–5.30pm
Sales Bath Saleroom

Bonstow and Crawshay Antiques
Contact Simon Crawshay
Bartlett Street Antique Centre, 5–10 Bartlett Street, Bath, Somerset, BA1 2QZ
01803 390850 01803 390850
07989 418592
bonstowandcrawshayantiques@talk21.com
Est. 1996 *Stock size* Medium
Stock Pre-1830 period English furniture, decorative items, marble, stonework, mirrors, sculpture
Open Mon–Sat 9am–5pm
Wed 8am–5pm
Fairs West Point
Services Valuations, restorations

Lawrence Brass
Apple Studio, Bath, Somerset, BA1 5YX
01225 852222
Est. 1973 *Stock size* Medium
Stock Furniture
Open Mon–Sat 9am–5pm
Services Valuations, restorations

Geoffrey Breeze (BABAADA)
Contact Mr Breeze
6 George Street, Bath, Somerset, BA1 2EH
01225 466499 01225 466499
geoffrey@geoffreybreeze.co.uk
Est. 1972 *Stock size* Medium
Stock 19thC furniture

Open Mon–Sat 10am–5pm
Fairs Bath Decorative and Antiques Fair

⊞ Lynda Brine Antiques
Contact Lynda Brine
✉ **Assembly Antiques, 5–8 Saville Row, Bath, Somerset, BA1 2QP** Ⓟ
☎ 01225 448488 Ⓕ 01225 429661
Ⓜ 07715 673716
Ⓔ lyndabrine@yahoo.com
Ⓦ www.scentbottlesandsmells.co.uk
Est. 1986 *Stock size* Large
Stock Perfume bottles, vinaigrettes, pomanders, objects of virtue, jewellery, silver
Open Tues–Sat 10am–5pm
Fairs NEC, USA
Services Valuations

⊞ Bryers Antiques
Contact Sheila Haines
✉ **Guildhall Market, High Street, Bath, Somerset, BA2 4AW**
☎ 01225 460535
Est. 1945 *Stock size* Medium
Stock Silver, silver plate, china, antique glass
Open Mon–Sat 10am–5.30pm

⊞ Camden Books (PBFA)
Contact Victor or Elizabeth Suchar
✉ **146 Walcot Street, Bath, Somerset, BA1 5BL** Ⓟ
☎ 01225 461606 Ⓕ 01225 461606
Ⓔ suchcam@msn.com
Ⓦ www.camdenbooks.com
Est. 1984 *Stock size* Large
Stock Antiquarian books, architecture, philosophy and science
Open Mon–Sat 10am–5pm
Fairs PBFA

⊞ Julia Craig (BABAADA)
Contact Julia Craig
✉ **Bartlett Street Antique Centre, 5–10 Bartlett Street, Bath, Somerset, BA1 2QZ** Ⓟ
☎ 01225 448202/310457
Ⓕ 01225 444432 Ⓜ 07771 786846
Ⓔ juliacraig@fsmail.net
Est. 1980 *Stock size* Large
Stock Antique lace and linen, costumes, costume accessories
Open Mon–Sat 10am–5pm
Fairs P & A Fairs, Hammersmith
Services Valuations

⊞ Brian and Caroline Craik Ltd
Contact Mrs C Craik
✉ **8 Margarets Buildings, Bath, Somerset, BA1 2LP** Ⓟ
☎ 01225 337161
Est. 1962 *Stock size* Medium
Stock General portable items, china and metalwork
Open Mon–Sat 10am–4pm

⊞ Mary Cruz Antiques (LAPADA, CINOA, BABAADA)
Contact Ms M Cruz
✉ **5 Broad Street, Bath, Somerset, BA1 5LJ** Ⓟ
☎ 01225 334174 Ⓕ 01225 423300
Est. 1974 *Stock size* Large
Stock 18th–19thC English and French furniture, 18th–20thC paintings, bronze and marble statues
Open Mon–Sat 10am–7pm
Services Valuations, restorations

⊞ D & B Dickinson (BADA, BABAADA)
Contact Mr Dickinson
✉ **22 New Bond Street, Bath, Somerset, BA1 1BA**
☎ 01225 466502
Est. 1917 *Stock size* Large
Stock Silver, jewellery, silver plate
Open Mon–Sat 9.30am–1pm 2–5pm

⊞ Frank Dux Antiques (BABAADA)
Contact Mr F Dux
✉ **33 Belvedere, Lansdown Road, Bath, Somerset, BA1 5HR** Ⓟ
☎ 01225 312367 Ⓕ 01225 312367
Ⓔ m.hopkins@antique-glass.co.uk
Ⓦ www.antique-glass.co.uk
Est. 1988 *Stock size* Medium
Stock 18th–19thC glass
Open Tues–Sat 10am–6pm
Services Search

⊞ Frogmore House Antiques
Contact Andrew Tinson
✉ **Bartlett Street Antique Centre, Bartlett Street, Bath, Somerset, BA1 2QZ** Ⓟ
☎ 01225 445054 Ⓕ 01225 445054
Ⓜ 07976 225988
Est. 1976 *Stock size* Large
Stock Novelties, objects of virtue, silver, good smalls
Open Mon–Sat 9.30am–5pm
Wed Trade Day 8am–5pm
Fairs NEC, Newark

⊞ Christina Grant
Contact Mr P Scott
✉ **Bartlett Street Antiques Centre, Bath, Somerset, BA1 2QZ** Ⓟ
☎ 01225 310457 Ⓕ 01225 319821
Ⓜ 07850 639770
Est. 1981 *Stock size* Medium
Stock Antique prints, decorative items
Open Mon–Sat 9.30am–5pm

⊞ George Gregory
Contact Mr Bayntun-Coward
✉ **Manvers Street, Bath, Somerset, BA1 1JW** Ⓟ
☎ 01225 466055 Ⓕ 01225 482122
Ⓔ ebc@georgebayntun.com
Ⓦ www.georgebayntun.com
Est. 1846 *Stock size* Large
Stock Antiquarian books, prints
Open Mon–Fri 9am–1pm 2–5.30pm Sat 9am–1pm

⊞ Indigo
Contact Marion Bender
✉ **59 Walcot Street, Bath, Somerset, BA1 5BN** Ⓟ
☎ 01225 311795
Ⓔ indigo_uk@compuserve.com
Ⓦ www.indigo-uk.com
Est. 1982 *Stock size* Medium
Stock Indian, Chinese and Japanese antique furniture, small handicraft and decorative items, furniture from Indonesia made from recycled teak
Open Mon–Sat 10am–6pm
Fairs House and Garden fair, DMG fairs
Services Restorations

⊞ Simon and Frauke Jackson
Contact Mr Simon Jackson
✉ **24 Mount Road, Southdown, Bath, Somerset, BA2 1LD**
☎ 01225 422221 Ⓕ 01225 422221
Ⓜ 07771 887771
Est. 1987 *Stock size* Medium
Stock Antique furniture
Open By appointment
Services Restorations

⊞ Jadis Antiques Ltd (BABAADA)
Contact Ms M Taylor

✉ **14 & 15 Walcot Buildings, London Road, Bath, Somerset, BA1 6AD** 🅿
☎ 01225 333130 Ⓕ 01225 333130
Ⓜ 07768 232133
Ⓔ jadpalad@aol.com
Ⓦ www.jadis-ltd.com
Est. 1970 ***Stock size*** Large
Stock French furniture and decorative items
Open Mon–Sat 9.30am–6pm or by appointment
Fairs Bath Decorative and Antiques Fair
Services Design service, mural painting

⊞ Kembery Antique Clocks Ltd (BABAADA)
Contact Mr Paul Kembery
✉ **Bartlett Street Antique Centre, 5–10 Bartlett Street, Bath, Somerset, BA1 2QZ** 🅿
☎ 0117 9565281 Ⓕ 0117 9565281
Ⓜ 07850 623237
Ⓔ kembery@kdclocks.co.uk
Ⓦ www.kdclocks.co.uk
Est. 1993 ***Stock size*** Medium
Stock Longcase, wall, mantel, bracket, carriage clocks and barometers
Open Mon–Sat 9.30am–5pm
Fairs NEC
Services Valuations, restorations, shipping

⊞ Ann King Antique Clothes
Contact Mrs Ann King
✉ **38 Belvedere, Lansdown Road, Bath, Somerset, BA1 5HR** 🅿
☎ 01225 336245
Est. 1980 ***Stock size*** Medium
Stock Antique clothes, quilts, lace
Open Mon–Sat 10am–5pm
Services Valuations

⊞ Lansdown Antiques (BABAADA)
Contact Chris or Ann Kemp
✉ **23 Belvedere, Lansdown Road, Bath, Somerset, BA1 5ED** 🅿
☎ 01225 313417
Ⓜ 07801 013663
Ⓔ lansdown-antiques@lineone.net
Est. 1983 ***Stock size*** Medium
Stock Painted pine and country furniture, metalware and decorative items
Open Mon–Sat 9.30am–5.30pm From 8am on Wed
Fairs Bath Decorative and Antiques Fair

⊞ Le Boudoir
Contact Sue Turner
✉ **Bartlett Street Antique Centre, 5–10 Bartlett Street, Bath, Somerset, BA1 2QZ** 🅿
☎ 01225 311061 Ⓕ 0117 9608 309
Ⓔ info@bathantiquesonline.com
Ⓦ www.bathantiquesonline.com
Est. 1988 ***Stock size*** Large
Stock Perfume bottles, dolls, decorative interior items, jewellery, Art Deco ceramics, Bakelite, petit point and beaded purses
Open Mon–Sat 9am–5pm Wed 8am–5pm
Services Valuations, restorations of ceramics

⊞ Looking Glass of Bath
Contact Anthony Reed
✉ **94 Walcot Street, Bath, Somerset, BA1 5BG** 🅿
☎ 01225 461969 Ⓕ 01225 316191
Ⓜ 07831 323878
Ⓔ info@lookingglassofbath.co.uk
Ⓦ www.lookingglassofbath.co.uk
Est. 1968 ***Stock size*** Medium
Stock Antique and replica period mirrors, picture frames
Open Mon–Sat 9am–6pm
Fairs House & Garden Olympia
Services Valuations, restorations, shipping

⊞ E P Mallory and Son Ltd (BADA)
Contact N Hall or P Mallory
✉ **1–4 Bridge Street, Bath, Somerset, BA2 4AP** 🅿
☎ 01225 788800 Ⓕ 01225 442210
Ⓔ mail@mallory-jewellers.com
Ⓦ www.mallory-jewellers.com
Est. 1898 ***Stock size*** Large
Stock Silver, jewellery
Open Mon–Sat 9.30am–5pm
Services Valuations

⊞ S Millard Antiques (BABAADA)
Contact Simon Millard
✉ **Bartlett Street Antiques Centre, 5–10 Bartlett Street, Bath, Somerset, BA1 2QZ** 🅿
☎ 01225 469785
Ⓔ tmillard@dircon.co.uk
Est. 1987 ***Stock size*** Medium
Stock Jewellery
Open Mon–Sun 10am–5pm Wed 8am–5pm
Fairs NEC
Services Valuations, restorations, insurance

⌂ Old Bank Antiques Centre (BABAADA)
Contact David Moore
✉ **16–17 Walcot Buildings, London Road, Bath, Somerset, BA1 6AD** 🅿
☎ 01225 469282/338813
Ⓔ alexatmontague@aol.com
Est. 2002 ***Stock size*** Large
No. of dealers 4
Stock 17th–early 20thC English and Continental furniture, glass, ceramics, textiles, metalwork
Open Mon–Sat 10am–6pm closed Thur Sun 11am–4pm
Services Valuations, shipping

⊞ Orient Expressions (BABAADA)
Contact Patricia Wilkinson
✉ **7 Lansdown Place, East Street, Bath, Somerset, BA1 5ET** 🅿
☎ 01225 313399 Ⓕ 01255 425446
Ⓔ amandaleader@aol.com
Ⓦ www.antiquesbulletin.com/orientexpressions
Est. 1999 ***Stock size*** Medium
Stock Mostly early 19thC provincial Chinese furniture, accessories
Open By appointment

⊞ Patterson Liddle (ABA, PBFA)
Contact John Patterson or Steve Liddle
✉ **10 Margaret's Buildings, Brock Street, Bath, Somerset, BA1 2LP** 🅿
☎ 01225 426722 Ⓕ 01225 426722
Ⓔ mail@pattersonliddle.com
Ⓦ www.pattersonliddle.com
Est. 1982 ***Stock size*** Medium
Stock Antiquarian and second-hand books
Open Mon–Sat 10am–5.30pm

⊞ Penny Philip
Contact Mrs P Philip
✉ **Abbey House, Abbey Green, Bath, Somerset, BA1 1NR** 🅿
☎ 01225 469564 Ⓕ 01225 469564
Est. 1979 ***Stock size*** Small
Stock Dyed antique linen sheets
Open By appointment

⊞ Piccadilly Antiques (BABAADA)
Contact John Davies
⊠ **280 High Street, Batheaston, Bath, Somerset, BA1 2QZ** 🅿
☎ 01225 851494 Ⓕ 01225 851120
Ⓔ piccadillyantiques@ukonline.co.uk
Est. 2001 *Stock size* Medium
Stock English and French furniture, decorative accessories aimed at the US market
Open Mon–Sat 9.30am–5.30pm Sun 10.30am–4.30 pm or by appointment

⊞ Quiet Street Antiques (BABAADA)
Contact Mr Kerry Hastings-Spital
⊠ **14–15 John Street, Bath, Somerset, BA1 2JG** 🅿
☎ 01225 483003
Ⓜ 07860 818212
Ⓔ kerry@quietstreetantiques.co.uk
Ⓦ www.quietstreetantiques.co.uk
Est. 1985 *Stock size* Large
Stock 18th–19thC furniture, clocks, tea caddies, boxes, mirrors, Royal Worcester, works of art
Open Mon–Sat 10am–6pm
Services Valuations, free delivery within 100 miles, export services

⊞ Quiet Street Antiques (BABAADA)
Contact Mr Kerry Hastings-Spital
⊠ **3 Quiet Street, Bath, Somerset, BA1 2JS** 🅿
☎ 01225 315727 Ⓕ 01225 448300
Ⓜ 07860 818212
Ⓔ kerry@quietstreetantiques.co.uk
Ⓦ www.quietstreetantiques.co.uk
Est. 1985 *Stock size* Large
Stock 18th–19thC furniture, clocks, tea caddies, boxes, mirrors, Royal Worcester, works of art
Open Mon–Sat 10am–6pm
Services Valuations, free delivery within 100 miles and export services

⊞ Roland Gallery (BABAADA)
Contact Mike Pettitt
⊠ **33 Monmouth Street, Bath, BA1 2AN** 🅿
☎ 01225 312330/319464
Ⓕ 01225 312330
Ⓜ 07889 723272
Ⓔ therolandgallery@aol.com
Est. 2000 *Stock size* Large
Stock Eclectic mix of 20thC design including silver, ivory, decorative items, paintings
Open Wed Sat 10am–5pm or by appointment

⊞ Michael Saffell Antiques (BABAADA)
Contact Mr M Saffell
⊠ **3 Walcot Buildings, London Road, Bath, Somerset, BA1 6AD** 🅿
☎ 01225 315857 Ⓕ 01225 315857
Ⓜ 07941 158049
Ⓔ michael.saffell@virgin.net
Est. 1975 *Stock size* Medium
Stock Advertising items, British tins (biscuit, tobacco, confectionery, mustard etc), decorative items
Open Mon–Fri 9am–5pm (best to phone in advance) or by appointment
Fairs Newark
Services Valuations

⊞ Peter Scott
Contact Mr P Scott
⊠ **Bartlett Street Antiques Centre, 5–10 Bartlett Street, Bath, Somerset, BA1 2QZ** 🅿
☎ 01225 310457 Ⓕ 01225 319821
Ⓜ 07850 639770
Est. 1984 *Stock size* Large
Stock White transfer ware, early English pottery including Mason's
Open Mon–Sat 9.30am–5pm
Fairs Newton, Shepton Mallet

⊞ Tim Snell Antiques (BABAADA)
Contact Tim Snell
⊠ **5–6 Cleveland Terrace, Bath, Somerset, BA1 5DF**
☎ 01225 423045 Ⓕ 01225 423045
Est. 1979 *Stock size* Large
Stock 19th–20thC oak furniture, Arts and Crafts
Open Mon–Sat 9am–5pm
Services Valuations, restorations, house clearances

⊞ Source (BABAADA)
Contact Mr R Donaldson
⊠ **93–95 Walcot Street, Bath, Somerset, BA1 3SD** 🅿
☎ 01225 469200
Ⓦ www.source-antiques.co.uk
Est. 1978 *Stock size* Medium
Stock Architectural antiques and lights including 1950s aluminium kitchens
Open Tues–Fri 10am–5pm Sat 9am–5pm
Fairs Bath Decorative and Antiques Fair
Services Valuations

⊞ Susannah (BABAADA, The Textiles Society)
Contact Mrs S Holley
⊠ **25 Broad Street, Bath, Somerset, BA1 5LW** 🅿
☎ 01225 445069 Ⓕ 01225 339004
Est. 1989 *Stock size* Medium
Stock General, decorative items, textiles
Open Mon–Sat 10am–5pm please phone in advance
Fairs Bath Decorative and Antiques Fair, Kensington Brocante, The Textiles Society Fair in Manchester

⊞ James Townshend Antiques (BABAADA)
Contact Mr Townshend
⊠ **1 Saville Row, Bath, Somerset, BA1 2QP** 🅿
☎ 01225 332290 Ⓕ 01225 332290
Ⓜ 01225 332290
Ⓔ sales@jtownshendantiques.co.uk
Ⓦ www.jtownshendantiques.co.uk
Stock size Large
Stock 19thC furniture, decorative items, mirrors
Open Mon–Sat 10am–5pm
Fairs Kempton
Services Valuations, restorations

⊞ Vintage to Vogue (BABAADA)
Contact Teresa Langton
⊠ **28 Milsom Street (entry in the passage off Broad Street car park), Bath, BA1 1DG** 🅿
☎ 01225 337323
Ⓦ www.vintagetovoguebath.com
Est. 1994 *Stock size* Large
Stock 1850s–1950s period clothing and accessories, costume lace, white linens, textiles
Open Tues–Sat 10.30am–5pm

⊞ Walcot Reclamation Ltd (BABAADA)
Contact Rick Knapp
⊠ **108 Walcot Street, Bath, Somerset, BA1 5BG** 🅿
☎ 01225 444404 Ⓕ 01225 448163
Ⓔ rick@walcot.com
Ⓦ www.walcot.com
Est. 1975 *Stock size* Large
Stock Architectural antiques

including bathrooms, radiators, fireplaces, garden furniture and reproductions of hard-to-find items
Open Mon–Fri 9am–5.30pm
Fairs The Country Living Fairs, Business Design Centre Islington (spring)
Services Restorations of marble, stone and old radiators

BITTON

Barrow Lodge Antiques
Contact Derek Wookey
Kings Square, Bitton, Bristol, BS30 6HR
☎ 0117 9324205 Ⓜ 07836 293993
Est. 1975 *Stock size* Large
Stock Furniture
Open By appointment
Fairs Newark, Ardingly
Services Restorations, stripping

BLACKFORD

L D Watts
Contact L D Watts
Blackford County Primary School, Sexey's Road, Blackford, Somerset, BS28 4NX
☎ 01934 712372
Est. 1970 *Stock size* Medium
Stock 18th–19thC furniture
Open By appointment
Services Valuations

BRIDGWATER

Memory Lane
Contact Belinda or Adam
6–8 York Buildings, Bridgwater, Somerset, TA6 3BS
☎ 01278 434373/434555
Ⓔ collectables@memorylane.fsbusiness.co.uk
Est. 2000 *Stock size* Medium
Stock Antiques and collectables
Open Mon–Sat 10am–4pm
Fairs Shepton Mallett, Newark

Tamlyn and Son
Contact Kathleen Macey
56 High Street, Bridgwater, Somerset, TA6 3BN
☎ 01278 445251/458241
Ⓕ 01278 458242 Ⓜ 07850 335928
Ⓔ saleroom@tamlynandson.co.uk
Ⓦ www.tamlynandson.co.uk
Est. 1893
Open Mon–Fri 9am–5.30pm
Sales Antiques and general sales monthly, 2 catalogue sales per annum May and Nov. Viewing day before sale
Frequency Monthly
Catalogues Yes

BRISTOL

A & C Antique Clocks (BWCG)
Contact Mr David Andrews
The Clock Shop, 86 Bryants Hill, Hanham, Bristol, BS5 8QT
☎ 01179 476141
Ⓔ info@antiquecorner.co.uk
Ⓦ www.antiquecorner.co.uk
Est. 1992 *Stock size* Large
Stock Clocks, furniture, ceramics, Winstanley cats, dolls
Open Tues–Sat 10am–4pm closed Wed
Services Clock repair service, valuations, restorations, shipping

The Antiques Warehouse Ltd (RADS)
Contact Chris Winsor
430 Gloucester Road, Horfield, Bristol, BS7 8TX
☎ 0117 9424500 Ⓕ 0117 9424140
Ⓔ chriswinsor@theantiqueswarehouseltd.co.uk
Ⓦ www.theantiqueswarehouseltd.co.uk
Est. 1994 *Stock size* Large
Stock Georgian–Edwardian and post-Edwardian furniture, carpets, mirrors
Open Mon–Sun 10am–6pm
Services Valuations, restorations and reupholstery

Arcadia Antiques
Contact Julia Irish
4 Boyces Avenue, Clifton, Bristol, BS8 4AA
☎ 0117 9144479 Ⓕ 0117 9239308
Ⓔ r.irish@phoenix-net.co.uk
Est. 1994 *Stock size* Small
Stock Furniture, collectables, upholstery, prints, paintings
Open Tues–Sat 10am–5.30pm

Aristocratz
Contact Mr Zaid
115 Coldharbour Road, Redlands, Bristol, BS6 7SD
☎ 0117 904 0091 Ⓜ 07770 393020
Ⓦ www.aristocratz.co.uk
Est. 1980 *Stock size* Medium
Stock General antiques
Open Mon–Sat 10am–5pm
Fairs Newark, Ardingly
Services Valuations, shipping

Gloria Barnes of Clifton Antiques Centre
Contact Gloria Barnes
The Clifton Antiques Centre, 18 The Mall, Clifton, Bristol, BS8 4DR
☎ 0117 9737843
Ⓔ jonathanbarnes@hotmail.com
Est. 1979 *Stock size* Medium
Stock Russell Flint prints, paintings, Indian art, stone jewellery
Open Tues–Sat 10am–6pm
Services Valuations

The Bed Workshop
Contact Dr Scott Jones
The Old Pickle Factory, Braunton Road, Bristol, BS3 3AA
☎ 0117 963 6659
Ⓔ thebedworkshop@aol.com
Est. 1981 *Stock size* Large
Stock French antique furniture
Open Mon–Sat 9.30am–6pm

Bedsteads (BABAADA)
Contact Nicola Ashton
15 Regent Street, Clifton, Bristol, BS8 4HW
☎ 0117 923 9181 Ⓕ 0117 923 9181
Ⓦ www.bed-steads.co.uk
Est. 1990 *Stock size* Medium
Stock Antique bedsteads in iron, brass and exotic woods
Open Mon 11.30am–5.30pm Tues–Sat 10am–6pm
Services Restorations

Bishopston Books
Contact Bill Singleton
259 Gloucester Road, Bishopston, Bristol, BS7 8NY
☎ 0117 9445303
Ⓔ bishopstonbook@btinternet.com
Est. 1993 *Stock size* Small
Stock Antiquarian and second-hand books
Open Thurs Fri 10am–5.30pm Sat 9.30am–4.30pm
Services Book search

Bristol Auction Rooms
Contact David Rees
St John's Place, Apsley Road, Clifton, Bristol, BS8 2ST
☎ 0117 9737201 Ⓕ 0117 9735671
Ⓔ info@bristolauctionrooms.com
Ⓦ www.bristolauctionrooms.com

Est. 1858
Open Mon–Fri 8.45am–6pm
Sales Antiques and decorative items. Sale Tues 10.30am, viewing Sat 9.30am–1pm Mon 9.30am–7pm day of sale from 9am
Frequency 5-weekly
Catalogues Yes

Bristol Auction Rooms
Contact David Rees
Saleroom 2, Baynton Road, Ashton, Bristol, BS3 2EB
0117 9531603 Ⓕ 0117 9531598
Est. 1858
Open Mon–Fri 8.45am–6pm
Sales Victorian and modern furniture and effects sale Thurs 10.30am, viewing Wed 11am–6pm day of sale from 9am
Frequency Fortnightly
Catalogues Yes

Bristol Brocante
Contact David or Elizabeth Durant
123 St Georges Road, College Green, Hotwells, Bristol, BS1 5UW
0117 9096688
Est. 1970 *Stock size* Large
Stock French antiques
Open Mon–Sat 11am–6pm
Fairs Newark, Kensington Brocante (Sept), Sandown Park Fair (Oct)

Bristol Trade Antiques
Contact Mr L Dyke
192 Cheltenham Road, Bristol, BS6 5RB
0117 9422790
Est. 1969 *Stock size* Medium
Stock Victorian–Edwardian furniture
Open Mon–Sat 9am–5.30pm
Services Valuations, exports to the USA

Caledonia Antiques
Contact Mrs M T Kerridge
6 The Mall, Clifton, Bristol, BS8 4DR
0117 974 3582 Ⓕ 0117 946 7997
Ⓜ 07710 434431
Est. 1981 *Stock size* Medium
Stock Jewellery and silver
Open Mon–Sat 10am–5.30pm

Circle Books
Contact Mr Mike Piddock
65 North Street, Bedminster, Bristol, BS3 1ES
0117 9662622
Est. 1999 *Stock size* Medium
Stock Antiquarian, second-hand, rare and out-of-print books
Open Mon–Sat 10am–5.30pm closed Tues
Services Valuations, café in shop

Clifton Antique Centre
Contact Mrs Barnes or Marlene Risdale
18 The Mall, Clifton, Bristol, BS8 4DR
0117 9737843
Est. 1965 *Stock size* Large
No. of dealers 6
Stock Silver, silver plate, paintings, clocks, ceramics, Moorcroft
Open Tues–Sat 10am–6pm
Services Valuations

Clifton Hill Textiles
Contact Mrs Hodder
4 Lower Clifton Hill, Clifton, Bristol, BS8 1BT
0117 9290644
Ⓔ cliftex@yahoo.com.co.uk
Est. 1984 *Stock size* Large
Stock Textiles, buttons, buckles
Open Mon–Sat 11am–5.30pm
Services Valuations

Cotham Antiques
Contact Susan Miller
39a Cotham Hill, Cotham, Bristol, BS6 6JZ
0117 9733 326
Est. 1983 *Stock size* Medium
Stock General
Open Tues–Sat 10.30am–5.30pm
Services Friendly advice

Cotham Galleries
Contact Mr D Jury
22 Cotham Hill, Bristol, BS6 6LF
0117 9736026
Ⓜ 07885 166811
Est. 1969 *Stock size* Medium
Stock General
Open Mon–Fri 9am–5.30pm Sat 10am–noon
Services Valuations, restorations

Cotham Hill Bookshop (PBFA)
Contact Roger Plant
39a Cotham Hill, Bristol, BS6 6JY
0117 9732344
Est. 1975 *Stock size* Medium
Stock Antiquarian and second-hand books and antiquarian prints
Open Mon–Sat 9.30am–5.30pm
Fairs PBFA
Services Valuations

Focus on the Past
Contact Mrs Alison Roylance
25 Waterloo Street, Clifton, Bristol, BS8 4BT
0117 9738080
Est. 1978 *Stock size* Large
Stock Furniture, pine, kitchenware, china, glass and books, jewellery, 20thC collectables
Open Mon–Sat 9.30am–5.30pm Sun 11am–5.30pm
Fairs Ardingly, Newark

Grey-Harris & Co
Contact Mr Grey-Harris
12 Princess Victoria Street, Clifton, Bristol, BS8 4BP
0117 9737365
Est. 1969 *Stock size* Large
Stock Antique jewellery, silver
Open Mon–Sat 9am–6pm
Services Valuations, restorations

Grimes Militaria
Contact Christopher or Hazel Grimes
13–14 Lower Park Row, Bristol, BS1 5BN
0117 929 8205
Est. 1967 *Stock size* Medium
Stock Scientific instruments, nautical memorabilia, militaria
Open Mon–Sat 11am–6pm
Fairs Exeter (Marsh Barton), Shepton Mallet
Services Valuations

Margaret R Jubb
Contact Mrs Jubb
6 The Clifton Arcade, Boyces Avenue, Clifton, Bristol, BS8 4AA
0117 9733105
Ⓜ 07974 095554
Ⓔ maggsy@kenmoor.demon.co.uk
Ⓦ www.kenmoor.demon.co.uk/antiques
Est. 1974 *Stock size* Medium
Stock General antiques
Open Mon–Fri 10am–6pm Sat 10.30am–6pm
Services Valuations

Marlenes
Contact Marlene Risdale
Clifton Antiques Centre, 18 The Mall, Clifton, Bristol, BS8 4DR
0117 9737645
Est. 1958 *Stock size* Medium
Stock Silver, jewellery
Open Tues–Sat 10am–6pm
Fairs Sandown, Stafford
Services Valuations

Robert Mills Architectural Antiques (SALVO)
Contact Bob Mills
Narroways Road, Eastville, Bristol, BS2 9XB
0117 9556542 F 0117 9558146
E sales@rmills.co.uk
W www.rmills.co.uk
Est. 1970 *Stock size* Large
Stock Architectural antiques including Gothic church fittings, stained glass, pub interiors
Open Mon–Fri 9.30am–5.30pm Sat 10am–5pm

Jan Morrison
Contact Jan Morrison
5 Clifton Arcade, Boyces Avenue, Clifton, Bristol, BS8 4AA
0117 970 6822 F 0117 970 6822
M 07789 094428
E jan@artibition.com
Est. 1979 *Stock size* Medium
Stock 18th–19thC glass and silver, modern jewellery
Open Tues–Sat 10am–5.30pm
Services Valuations

Oldwoods
Contact Sid Duck
4 Colston Yard, Bristol, BS1 5BD
0117 929 9023
Est. 1982 *Stock size* Small
Stock Victorian and pine furniture, decorative items
Open Mon–Fri 10am-5pm or by appointment
Services Restorations

Olliff's Architectural Antiques (SALVO)
Contact Marcus Olliff
19–21 Lower Redland Road, Redland, Bristol, BS6 6TB
0117 923 9232 F 0117 923 9880
M 07850 235793
E marcus@olliffs.com
W www.olliffs.com
Est. 1993 *Stock size* Large
Stock Georgian–Edwardian marble, stone and timber fireplaces, garden statuary, garden decorative items, doors, door furniture, stone doorways and windows, gates, lighting, mirrors, oak flooring
Open Fri–Sat 10am–5pm or by appointment
Services Valuations, restorations, shipping

Pastimes (OMRS)
Contact Mr A H Stevens
22 Lower Park Row, Bristol, BS1 5BN
0117 9299330
Est. 1974 *Stock size* Large
Stock Militaria
Open Mon–Sat 10.30am–1.45pm 2.45–5pm Wed 11am–5pm
Fairs Mark Carter Fairs
Services Medal mounting

Period Fireplaces
Contact John Ashton
The Old Station Building, Station Road, Montpelier, Bristol, BS6 5EE
0117 944 4449 F 0117 942 4091
E enquiries@periodfireplaces.co.uk
W www.periodfireplaces.co.uk
Est. 1984 *Stock size* Large
Stock Fireplaces
Open Mon–Fri 9am–5pm Sat 10am–4pm
Services Restorations

Piano Export
Contact Mr T W Smallridge
Bridge Road, Kingswood, Bristol, BS15 4FW
0117 956 8300
Est. 1982 *Stock size* Medium
Stock Grand pianos – Steinway, Bechstein and decorative pianos
Open Mon–Fri 8am–5pm or by appointment

Porchester Antiques
Contact Mrs Devonia Andrews
58 The Mall, Clifton, Bristol, BS8 4JG
0117 373 0256 F 01275 810629
M 07970 970449
E devonia.porchesterantiques@deepacres.freeserve.co.uk
Est. 1978 *Stock size* Medium
Stock Moorcroft, enamels and pottery, Okra glass, Sally Tuffin pottery, jewellery
Open Tues–Sat 10am–6pm
Services Valuations

Pride & Joy Antiques
Contact Martin Williams
25 North View, Westbury Park, Bristol, BS6 7SD
0117 973 5806
Est. 1994 *Stock size* Medium
Stock Victorian–Edwardian furniture
Open Mon–Sat 10.30am–1pm 2–5pm
Services Reupholstery

Raw Deluxe
Contact Mr J Stewart
148 Gloucester Road, Bishopston, Bristol, BS7 8NT
0117 9426998
Est. 1998 *Stock size* Medium
Stock General antiques, collectables
Open Mon–Sat 10am–5pm closed Wed
Services Restorations

Vincents of Clifton
Contact Vincent Risdale
Clifton Antique Centre, 18 The Mall, Clifton, Bristol, BS8 4DR
0117 9737645
Est. 1984 *Stock size* Medium
Stock Jewellery, silver and gold
Open Tues–Sat 10am–6pm
Fairs Cheltenham, Sandown and Stafford

Whiteladies Antiques & Collectables
Contact Sylvia Skerritt
49c Whiteladies Road, Clifton, Bristol, BS8 2LS
0117 973 5766
Est. 2001 *Stock size* Large
No. of dealers 25
Stock Antiques and collectables, small furniture
Open Mon–Sat 10.30am–5pm Sun noon–4pm

BROOMFIELD

Pines Antique & Gift Centre
Contact Sue Keohane
The Pines, Buncombe Hill, Broomfield, Taunton, Somerset, TA5 1AX
01823 451704 F 01278 671864

Est. 1999 *Stock size* Small
Stock Bric-a-brac
Open Wed–Sun 10.30am–5.30pm

BRUTON

The Antiques Shop Bruton
Contact David Gwilliam
5 High Street, Bruton, Somerset, BA10 0AB
01749 813264
Est. 1976 *Stock size* Medium
Stock Furniture, brass, copper, jewellery, silver, china and collectables
Open Thurs Fri Sat 10am–5.30pm
Services Jewellery repairs, re-stringing, watch, clock repairs

European Accent
Contact Steve Green
Station Road, Bruton, Somerset, BA10 0EH
01749 812460 F 01749 813932
M 0797 7496762
E enquiries@europeanaccent.co.uk
W www.europeanaccent.co.uk
Est. 1998 *Stock size* Medium
Stock Country decorative, painted, pine and fruitwood furniture, smalls
Open Mon–Fri 8.30am–5.30pm Sat 9am–1pm for trade
Fairs Newark, Shepton Mallet
Services Valuations

Michael Lewis Gallery
Contact Mrs J L Lewis
17 High Street, Bruton, Somerset, BA10 0AB
01749 813557
Est. 1980 *Stock size* Large
Stock Antiquarian maps and prints
Open Mon–Sat 9.30am–5.30pm closed Thurs 1pm

M G R Exports
Contact Mr M Read
Station Road, Bruton, Somerset, BA10 0EH
01749 812460 F 01749 812882
E enquiries@mgrexports.co.uk
W www.mgrexports.co.uk
Est. 1979 *Stock size* Large
Stock General
Open Mon–Fri 8.30am–5.30pm Sat 9am–1pm for trade
Services Packing, shipping and containers packed

Mr Gompy's Antiques & Curious
Contact Anne Sidford
6 High Street, Bruton, Somerset, BA10 0AA
01749 813238
Est. 1993 *Stock size* Large
Stock Country furniture, soft furnishings, miniatures, dolls and dolls' houses
Open Thurs–Fri 9.30am–1pm 2–5.30pm Sat 9.30am–1pm 2–4pm
Services Restorations, upholstery

BURNHAM-ON-SEA

Adam Antiques
Contact Mrs R Combes
30 Adam Street, Burnham-on-Sea, Somerset, TA8 1PQ
01278 783193 F 01278 793709
Est. 1977 *Stock size* Large
Stock General wide range of antiques and collectables
Open Mon–Sat 9am–5pm

Adams Auctions
Contact Mrs R Combes
28 Adam Street, Burnham-on-Sea, Somerset, TA8 1PQ
01278 793709 F 01278 793709
Est. 1993
Open Mon–Sat 10am–5pm
Sales Antique and general sales, monthly, Wed 6pm viewing Tues 2–6pm Wed 10am–6pm
Frequency Monthly
Catalogues Yes

The Burnham Model & Collectors Shop
Contact W Loudon
3 College Court, College Street, Burnham-on-Sea, Somerset, TA8 1AR
01278 780066 F 01278 780066
Est. 1994 *Stock size* Large
Stock Ephemera, postcards, banknotes, coins, medals, die-cast models, cigarette cards
Open Mon–Sat 9.30am–5pm
Services Valuations

Heape's
Contact Mrs M Heap
39 Victoria Street, Burnham-on-Sea, Somerset, TA8 1AN
01278 782131 F 01278 782131
Est. 1988 *Stock size* Large
Stock Porcelain, silverware, fine art, glass, collectables
Open Mon 10am–1pm Tue Thurs–Sat 10am–4.30pm Wed 10am–1pm
Services Bespoke framing, hand-made lampshades, specialist table lamps

CASTLE CARY

Antiquus
Contact Gerald Davison
West Country House, Woodcock Street, Castle Cary, Somerset, BA7 7BJ
01963 351246 M 07968 810092
W www.chinesemarks.com
Est. 2002 *Stock size* Medium
Stock English and Oriental antiques
Open Tues Wed Fri Sat 10am–5pm
Services Lectures on Chinese ceramics

Cary Antiques
Contact Mrs J A Oldham
2 High Street, Castle Cary, Somerset, BA7 7AW
01963 350437
Est. 1977 *Stock size* Large
Stock General antiques
Open Tues–Sat 10.30am–5pm closed Wed
Fairs Shepton Mallet
Services Picture framing

Chinns Antiques
Contact Clive or Carletta Chinn
Market Place, Castle Cary, Somerset, BA7 7AL
01963 351484
Est. 1982 *Stock size* Large
Stock Furniture, English, Continental and Oriental ceramics, jewellery, paintings
Open Mon–Sat 9am–5pm
Services Valuations

Pandora's Box
Contact Sally Comer
Fore Street, Castle Cary, Somerset, BA7 7BG
01963 350926
M 07798 692633
Est. 1988 *Stock size* Medium
Stock Furniture, quilts, textiles and decorative items
Open Mon–Sat 9.30am–5.30pm
Fairs Newark, Shepton Mallet

Alan and Kathy Stacey (LAPADA, BABAADA, BAFRA)
Contact Alan Stacey
Castle Cary, Somerset, BA9 9YY
01963 441333 F 01963 441330
E sales@antiqueboxes.uk.com
W www.antiqueboxes.uk.com
Est. 1990 *Stock size* Medium
Stock Tortoiseshell, ivory, shagreen and mother of pearl tea caddies and boxes
Open By appointment
Fairs Lapada, Penman Harrogate
Services Valuations, restorations

CHARD

Nick Chalon Antiques
Contact Nick Chalon
Field Bars House, Shepherds Lane, High Street, Chard, Somerset, TA20 1QX
01460 6239005
Est. 1972 *Stock size* Small
Stock Period English and French country furniture
Open By appointment

Chard Antiques Centre
Contact Julie Hills or Alistair Smith
23 High Street, Chard, Somerset, TA20 1QF
01460 63517
E julie@chardantiques.fsnet.co.uk
Est. 1997 *Stock size* Medium
No. of dealers 9
Stock General antiques, furniture, ceramics and decorative items
Open Mon–Sat 10am–5pm or by appointment

Chez Chalon Antiques
Contact Jake Chalon
The Old Telephone Exchange, East Street, Chard, Somerset, TA20 1EP
01460 68679 F 07813 117358
E antiques@chezchalon.freeserve.co.uk
Est. 1972 *Stock size* Large
Stock Period English and French country furniture
Open Mon–Sat 9am–5pm out of hours by appointment
Services Restorations

CHEDDAR

Matthew Bayly Antiques
Contact Matthew Bayly
Mark Hole Cottage, The Cliffs, Cheddar, Somerset, BS27 3QH
01934 743990
Est. 1972 *Stock size* Small
Stock General small antiques
Open By appointment
Services Valuations, restorations

Tinkers Antiques
Contact Mrs Sharpe
The Cottage Shop, Bath Street, Cheddar, Somerset, BS28 4EB
01934 713618
Est. 1993 *Stock size* Medium
Stock Country pine furniture, jewellery, general antiques
Open Mon–Sat 10am–5pm

CHILCOMPTON

Billiard Room Antiques (LAPADA, BABAADA, CINOA)
Contact Mrs J Mckeivor
The Old School, Church Lane, Chilcompton, Bath, Somerset, BA3 4HP
01761 232839 F 01761 232839
E info@billiardroom.co.uk
W www.billiardroom.co.uk
Est. 1990 *Stock size* Medium
Stock Billiard room furnishings
Open By appointment only
Fairs Olympia
Services Valuations, restoration and shipping

CHIPPING SODBURY

Sodbury Antiques
Contact Millicent Brown
70 Broad Street, Chipping Sodbury, Bristol, BS37 6AG
01454 273369 F 01454 273369
Est. 1989 *Stock size* Medium
Stock China, jewellery and bric-a-brac
Open Mon–Sat 9.30am–5.30pm closed Wed

CLEVEDON

Clevedon Books (PBFA)
Contact Mr or Mrs Douthwaite
The Gallery, 29 Copse Road, Clevedon, Somerset, BS21 7QN
01275 790579/872304
F 01275 342817
E clevedonbooks@globalnet.co.uk
Est. 1970 *Stock size* Medium
Stock Antiquarian books, maps and prints, second-hand books. History, science and technology a speciality
Open Thurs–Sat 11am–4.30pm
Fairs PBFA
Services Print and map colouring

Clevedon Salerooms
Contact Marc Burridge
Herbert Road, Clevedon, Somerset, BS21 7ND
01275 876699 F 01275 343765
E clevedon-salerooms@blueyonder.co.uk
W www.clevedon-salerooms.com
Est. 1880
Open Mon–Fri 9am–5.30pm
Sales Fine art and antiques sales, Thurs 10.30am, view Tues 2–5.30pm Wed 10am–6.30pm 9am morning of sale. Fortnightly sales of Victorian and later household furniture, effects, Thurs 10am, viewing Wed 10am–7.30pm morning of sale 9am
Frequency Quarterly
Catalogues Yes

The Collector
Contact Malcolm or Tina Simmonds
14 The Beach, Clevedon, Somerset, BS21 7QU
01275 875066
Est. 1992 *Stock size* Small
Stock Smalls and collectables including Beatrix Potter figures
Open Mon–Sat 10am–5pm Sun noon–5pm closed Thurs
Fairs Malvern Three Counties, Brunel Temple Meads, Bristol
Services Valuations

Nostalgia
Contact Wendy Moore
65a Hill Road, Clevedon, Somerset, BS21 7PD
01275 342587
Est. 1984 *Stock size* Medium
Stock General antiques including linen, furniture, china
Open Tues–Sat 10am–4.30pm
Services House calls to buy

COXLEY

Mrs Mitchell
Contact Mrs Mitchell
Clover Close House, Main Road, Coxley, Somerset, BA5 1QZ
01749 679533
Est. 1984 *Stock size* Medium
Stock General antiques
Open Mon–Sat 9am–5pm
Services Valuations, caning and upholstery

CREWKERNE

Antiques and Country Pine
Contact Mrs Wheeler
14 East Street, Crewkerne, Somerset, TA18 7AG
01460 75623
Est. 1979 *Stock size* Medium
Stock Antique and country pine furniture
Open Tues–Sat 10am–5pm

Books Galore
Contact Mrs Hall
The Old Warehouse, North Street, Crewkerne, Somerset, TA18 7AJ
01460 74465 F 01460 74465
M 07957 986053
E hallbook@aol.com
Est. 1969 *Stock size* Large
Stock Second-hand books. Countryside topics a speciality
Open Mon–Sat 10am–1pm 2.30–5pm
Services Book search

The Bookshop
Contact Mr Lemmey
15 Falkland Square, Crewkerne, Somerset, TA18 7JS
01460 76579
Est. 1990 *Stock size* Medium
Stock Antiquarian and second-hand books, early Penguins a speciality
Open Mon–Sat 10am–5pm

Crewkerne Antiques
Contact Eddie Blewden
16 Market Street, Crewkerne, Somerset, TA18 7LA
01460 77111 F 01460 77111
Est. 1991 *Stock size* Large
No. of dealers 20
Stock General antiques
Open Mon–Sat 9.30am–4.30pm
Services Valuations, restorations

East Street Interiors
Contact Mr C Hennessy
42 East Street, Crewkerne, Somerset, TA18 7AG
01460 78600 F 01460 78600
E info@veryold.co.uk
W www.veryold.co.uk
Est. 1974 *Stock size* Large
No. of dealers 2
Stock French and English country furniture, decorative items, architectural pieces, pine furniture
Open Mon–Sat 10am–5pm or by appointment

Gresham Books (PBFA, ABA)
Contact James Hine
31 Market Street, Crewkerne, Somerset, TA18 7JU
01460 77726 F 01460 52479
E jameshine@gresham-books.demon.co.uk
Est. 1972 *Stock size* Large
Stock Antiquarian and second-hand books including early cookery and architectural
Open Mon–Sat 10am–5pm
Fairs London Bookfair (monthly), most major book fairs (phone for details)
Services Valuations

Lawrence Fine Art Auctioneers Ltd (ARVA, SOFAA)
Contact Leah Ferguson
4 Linen Yard, South Street, Crewkerne, Somerset, TA18 8AB
01460 73041 F 01460 270799
E enquiries@lawrences.co.uk
W www.lawrences.co.uk
Est. 1900
Open Mon–Fri 9am–5pm
Sales 5 fine art sales a year. General household sale every Wed 9.30am, viewing Tues 9.30am–7pm
Frequency Bi-monthly – Fine Art Weekly – General
Catalogues Yes

Noah's
Contact Mrs Edmonds
41 Market Square, Crewkerne, Somerset, TA18 7LP
01460 77786
Est. 2001 *Stock size* Medium
Stock Fine art and antiques, silver, jewellery
Open Mon–Sat 10am–4.30pm
Services Valuations

CROWCOMBE

Newmans (BAFRA)
Contact Tony Newman
Tithe Barn, Crowcombe, Somerset, TA4 4AQ
M 07778 615945
E tony@cheddon.fsnet.co.uk
Est. 1991 *Stock size* Small
Stock 18th–19thC furniture
Open Sun–Mon 9am–5pm or by appointment
Services Valuations, restorations

DULVERTON

Acorn Antiques
Contact Peter Hounslow
39 High Street, Dulverton, Somerset, TA22 9DW
01398 323286
E Peter@exmoorantiques.co.uk
W www.acornantiquesexmoor.co.uk
Est. 1988 *Stock size* Medium
Stock 18th–19thC furniture, decorative items and general antiques
Trade only Yes
Open Mon–Sat 9.30am–5.30pm or Sun by appointment
Services Interior design

Guy Dennler
Contact Mr G Dennler
The White Hart, 23 High Street, Dulverton, Somerset, TA22 9HB
01398 324300 F 01398 324301
Est. 1979 *Stock size* Medium
Stock 18th–19thC English furniture, decorative items
Open Mon–Sat 10am–5pm
Fairs Battersea Decorative Fair
Services Restorations

Out Of The Blue
Contact Finny or Nigel Muers-Raby
4 Fore Street, Dulverton, Somerset, PA22 9EX
01398 324155
Est. 2001 *Stock size* Medium
Stock Decorative items for you and your home
Open Tues–Sat 10.30am–4pm

Anthony Sampson
Contact Mr A Sampson
Holland House, Bridge Street, Dulverton, Somerset, TA22 9HJ
01398 324247 F 01398 324027
M 07767 842409

Est. 1968 *Stock size* Medium
Stock Furniture, general antiques
Open Mon–Sat 9.30am–5.30pm
Sun by appointment
Services Valuations

DUNSTER

The Crooked Window

Contact Robert Ricketts
7 High Street, Dunster, Somerset, TA24 6SF
01643 821606 ⓜ 077641 75627
Est. 1987 *Stock size* Medium
Stock 17th–18thC English furniture, Chinese and European ceramics and works of art, including jade
Open Mon–Sat 10am–5.30pm
Fairs Wilton House
Services Valuations

The Linen Press

Contact Anne Fisher
22 Church Street, Dunster, Somerset, TA24 6SH
01643 821802
Est. 1986 *Stock size* Large
Stock Antique and new English and French linen and textiles
Open Mon–Sun 10.30am–5pm
Services Mail order

EAST PENNARD

Cottage Collectibles

Contact Mrs S Kettle
2 Pennard House, East Pennard, Somerset, BA4 6TP
01749 860266 ⓕ 01749 860732
ⓜ 07967 713512
ⓔ sheila@cottagecollectibles.co.uk
ⓦ www.cottagecollectibles.co.uk
Est. 1995 *Stock size* Medium
Stock English and Continental country antiques, kitchenware, pine furniture, garden and dairy tools
Open Mon–Sat 10am–5pm
Services Restorations

Pennard House Antiques (BABAADA, LAPADA)

Contact Martin Dearden
East Pennard, Shepton Mallet, Somerset, BA4 6TP
01749 860731 ⓕ 01749 860732
ⓜ 07802 243569
ⓔ pennardantiques@ukonline.co.uk
Est. 1979 *Stock size* Large
Stock French and English country furniture and decorative items
Open Mon–Sat 9.30am–5.30pm or by appointment
Fairs Bath Decorative and Antiques Fair Battersea Decorative and Textile Fair
Services Restorations, shipping and deliveries

FRESHFORD

Freshfords (LAPADA, CINOA, BABAADA)

Contact Mr Simon Powell
High Street, Freshford, Bath, Somerset, BA2 7WF
01225 722111 ⓕ 01225 722991
ⓜ 07970 517332 or 07720838877
ⓔ antiques@freshfords.com
ⓦ www.freshfords.com
Est. 1973 *Stock size* Large
Stock Regency period furniture
Open Mon–Fri 10am–5pm Sat by appointment 10am–1pm
Fairs Olympia, Chelsea
Services Valuations, restorations, shipping, book search

FROME

Antiques and Country Living

Contact Mrs D M Williams
43–44 Vallis Way, Frome, Somerset, BA11 3BA
01373 463015 ⓜ 07808 933076
Est. 1994 *Stock size* Large
No. of dealers 4
Stock 18th–19thC pottery and porcelain, Georgian–Edwardian furniture, books
Open Mon–Sun 9.30am–5.30pm

Steve Vee Bransgrove Collectables

Contact Steve
6 Catherine Hill, Frome, Somerset, BA11 1BY
01373 453225 ⓜ 0797 769 4537
Est. 1995 *Stock size* Medium
Stock Collectables, advertising, vintage magazines, ephemera and nostalgia
Open Mon–Sat 10am–5pm Thurs closed in winter 10am–2pm in summer
Services Valuations

Cooper and Tanner Chartered Surveyors

Contact Gillian Holland
The Agricultural Centre, Standerwick, Frome, Somerset, BA11 2QB
01373 831010 ⓕ 01373 831103
Est. 1900
Open Mon–Fri 9am–5pm
Sales Furniture, fine art and antiques sale Wed 10.30am, viewing Wed 7.30am prior to sale
Frequency Weekly
Catalogues No

Frome Reclamation (SALVO)

Contact Steve Horler
Station Approach, Frome, Somerset, BA11 1RE
01373 463919 ⓕ 01373 453122
ⓜ 07836 277507
Est. 1987 *Stock size* Large
Stock Architectural antiques, including roofing, flooring, period fireplaces, doors, bathrooms, etc
Open Mon–Fri 8am–5.30pm Sat 8am–4.30pm

GLASTONBURY

Bookbarn Ltd

Contact Mr Belton
17–18 Market Place, Glastonbury, Somerset, BA6 9HL
01458 835698
ⓔ bookbarn@netcomuk.co.uk
ⓦ www.bookbarn.co.uk
Est. 1997 *Stock size* Large
Stock Antiquarian and second-hand books
Open Mon–Sat 10am–6pm Sun noon–5pm

Courtyard Books

Contact Mr Mills
2–4 High Street, Glastonbury, Somerset, BA6 9DU
01458 831800
Est. 1995 *Stock size* Large
Stock Antiquarian, esoteric, New Age and magic books
Open Mon–Sun 9.30am–5.30pm

Metropolis Art Deco (SCC)

Contact Helen Smith
3 Monarch Mews, 15 High Street, Glastonbury, Somerset, BA6 9DP
01458 833240/253120
ⓦ www.metropolisartdeco.co.uk
Est. 1984 *Stock size* Large

Stock Art Deco including ceramics, light fittings, Moorcroft, Susie Cooper, Clarice Cliff, small furniture, Shelley
Open Thurs–Sat 10am–4.30pm closed Wed or by appointment
Fairs Battersea Art Deco
Services Valuations, selling on commission

HIGHBRIDGE

Colin Dyte Exports Ltd
Contact Mr C Dyte
The Old Bacon Factory, Huntspill Road, Highbridge, Somerset, TA9 3DE
☎ 01278 788590 F 01278 788604
M 07836 594610 or 07836 572323
Est. 1949 ***Stock size*** Large
Stock General antiques and shipping
Open Mon–Sat 7.30am–6pm or by appointment
Fairs Newark, Ardingly
Services Packing service

ILCHESTER

Gilbert and Dale
Contact Roy Gilbert or Joan Dale
The Old Chapel, Church Street, Ilchester, Yeovil, Somerset, BA22 8LN
☎ 01935 840464 F 01935 841599
Est. 1969 ***Stock size*** Medium
Stock English and French country furniture and accessories
Trade only Mainly trade
Open Mon–Fri 9am–5.30pm

LANGPORT

Myrtle Antiques
Contact David or Chris Knight
Staceys Court, Bow Street, Langport, Somerset, TA10 9PQ
☎ 01458 252666 F 01458 252666
M 07967 355490
W www.myrtleantiques.co.uk
Est. 1992 ***Stock size*** Medium
Stock English and European furniture, reproduction pine and elm
Open Mon–Fri 9am–5.30pm Sat 9.30am–3pm
Services Restoration and furniture makers

Oldnautibits
Contact Geoff Pringle
PO Box 67, Langport, Somerset, TA10 9WJ
☎ 01458 241816 M 07947 277833
E geoff.pringle@oldnautibits.com
W www.oldnautibits.com
Est. 2002 ***Stock size*** Medium
Stock Maritime, aeronautical antiques
Open Mon–Fri 9am–5pm
Fairs Bath and West, Carmarthen

LYDEARD ST LAWRENCE

The Coach House
Contact Clare Roberts
Handycross Farmhouse, Handycross, Lydeard St Lawrence, Taunton, Somerset, TA4 3PL
☎ 01984 667568
Est. 1996 ***Stock size*** Large
No. of dealers 11
Stock A wide range of furniture, collectables, silver, ceramics
Open Thurs–Sun Bank Holidays 11am–5pm

MARTOCK

Bowen & Co
Contact Jason Bowen
9B The Green, Martock, Somerset, TA12 6NE
☎ 01935 822100
Est. 2001 ***Stock size*** Medium
Stock Furniture, jewellery, china, crystals, coins
Open Wed–Sun 9.30am–5.30pm
Fairs Wembley
Services Restorations

Castle Reclamation (SALVO)
Contact Mr A Wills
Parrett Works, Martock, Somerset, TA12 6AE
☎ 01935 826483 F 01935 826791
E info@castlereclamation.com
W www.castlereclamation.com
Est. 1989 ***Stock size*** Medium
Stock Architectural antiques, stone masonary, hand-carved natural stone fireplaces, oak flooring
Open Mon–Fri 8.30am–5pm Sat 10am–1pm
Fairs Bath and West, Dyrham Park, Kingston Lacy

MIDSOMER NORTON

Somervale Antiques (BADA, LAPADA, CINOA, BABAADA)
Contact Wing Commander Ron Thomas
The Poplars, 6 Radstock Road, Midsomer Norton, Radstock, Somerset, BA3 2AJ
☎ 01761 412686 F 01761 412686
M 07885 088022
E ronthomas@somervaleantiquesglass.co.uk
W www.somervaleantiquesglass.co.uk
Est. 1972 ***Stock size*** Large
Stock English 18th–19thC drinking glasses, decanters, cut and coloured, Bristol and Nailsea glass, scent bottles
Open By appointment. Trains to Bath met by arrangement
Services Valuations

MINEHEAD

Chris's Crackers
Contact Peter Marshall
Townsend Garage, Main Road, Carhampton, Minehead, Somerset, BA24 6LH
☎ 01643 821873
W www.chriscrackers.net
Est. 1995 ***Stock size*** Large
Stock Reclamation, agricultural antiques, junkshop
Open Mon–Sun 11am–5.30pm

Memory Lane
Contact Mr M Ryan
53a The Avenue, Minehead, Somerset, TA24 5BB
☎ 01643 708991
Est. 1998 ***Stock size*** Large
Stock Furniture and collectables
Open Mon–Sat 10am–4pm Sat 10am–1pm closed Wed
Services Valuations

NORTH CHERITON

Paper Pleasures (PBFA)
Contact Lesley Tyson
Holt Farm, North Cheriton, Somerset, BA8 0AQ
☎ 01963 33718
E lesley@paperpleasures.bchip.com
Stock size Small
Stock Antiquarian and second-hand books
Open By appointment
Services Book search

NORTH NEWTON

Asian Art.co.uk Ltd
Contact The Manager
Big Bere Farm, Coxshill, North Newton, Somerset, TA7 0BT

☎ 01278 662535
Ⓔ james@asianart.co.uk
Ⓦ www.asianart.co.uk
Est. 1982 *Stock size* Large
Stock Oriental antiques, furniture, kilims, carpets
Open By appointment

NORTH PETHERTON

Jays Antiques and Collectables
Contact Mrs J Alba
✉ **121a Fore Street, North Petherton, Bridgwater, Somerset, TA6 6SA** Ⓟ
☎ 01278 662688
Est. 1994 *Stock size* Medium
Stock China, glass, clocks
Open Mon 10am–1pm Tues–Sat 10am–4.30pm closed Wed
Fairs Talisman Fairs, Bristol

PORLOCK

Magpie Antiques & Collectables
Contact Glenys Battams
✉ **High Street, Porlock, Somerset, TA24 8PT** Ⓟ
☎ 01643 862775 or 01271 850669
Ⓜ 07721 679020
Est. 1980 *Stock size* Medium
Stock Antique jewellery, silver, scent bottles, objects of virtue
Open Telephone call advisable
Fairs NEC, Westpoint
Services Valuations, restorations

Rare Books & Berry Ltd
Contact Michael Berry
✉ **Lowerbourne House, High Street, Porlock, Somerset, TA24 8PT** Ⓟ
☎ 01643 863255 Ⓕ 01643 863092
Ⓔ info@rarebooksandberry.co.uk
Ⓦ www.rarebooksandberry.co.uk
Est. 1982 *Stock size* Medium
Stock Antiquarian and second-handbooks
Open Mon–Sat 9.30am–5pm
Services Book search

QUEEN CAMEL

Steven Ferdinando (PBFA)
Contact Mr Steven Ferdinando
✉ **The Old Vicarage, Queen Camel, Yeovil, Somerset, BA22 7NG** Ⓟ
☎ 01935 850210
Est. 1978 *Stock size* Medium
Stock Antiquarian and second-hand books
Open Visitors welcome by appointment
Fairs PBFA
Services Valuations, book search

SHEPTON MALLET

Edward Marnier Antiques (BABAADA)
Contact Mr E Marnier
✉ **Old Bowlish House, Forum Lane, Bowlish, Shepton Mallet, Somerset, BA4 5JA** Ⓟ
☎ 01749 343340 Ⓜ 07785 110122
Ⓔ emarnier@ukonline.co.uk
Est. 1989 *Stock size* Medium
Stock 17th–20thC furniture, pictures, mirrors, interesting items, antique rugs, carpets
Open Mon–Sun 9am–6pm or by appointment
Fairs Olympia, Bath, Battersea
Services Valuations

MJM's
Contact Miranda Powell
✉ **F Block, Anglo Trading Estate, Commercial Road, Shepton Mallet, Somerset, BA4 5BY** Ⓟ
☎ 01749 344881
Ⓜ Antiques enquiries 07774 935079 Reclamation enquiries 07976 361948
Est. 1993 *Stock size* Large
No. of dealers 17
Stock General and architectural antiques, period bathrooms and collectables
Open Mon–Sat 10.30am–4.30pm

Parkways Antiques
Contact Pauline Brereton
✉ **31 High Street, Shepton Mallet, Somerset, BA4 5AQ** Ⓟ
☎ 01749 345065
Est. 1972 *Stock size* Small
Stock Period and Victorian furniture and reproduction pine
Open Mon–Fri 10am–4pm closed Wed
Services Reproduction pine made to order

SOMERTON

John Gardiner
Contact Mr John Gardiner
✉ **Monteclefe House, Kirkham Street, Somerton, Somerset, TA11 7NL** Ⓟ
☎ 01458 272238 Ⓕ 01458 274329
Ⓜ 07831 274427
Est. 1968 *Stock size* Medium
Stock General antiques, decorative items
Open Appointment advisable
Services Workshop facilities

Knole Barometers
Contact David Crawshaw
✉ **Bingham House, West Street, Somerton, Somerset, TA11 7PS** Ⓟ
☎ 01458 241015 Ⓕ 01458 241706
Ⓜ 07785 364567
Ⓔ dccops@btconnect.com
Est. 1997 *Stock size* Medium
Stock Barometers, scientific instruments
Open Mon–Fri 9am–5pm
Services Valuations, restorations

London Cigarette Card Company Ltd
Contact Mr Laker
✉ **West Street, Somerton, Somerset, TA11 6QP** Ⓟ
☎ 01458 273452 Ⓕ 01458 273515
Ⓔ cards@londoncigcard.co.uk
Ⓦ www.londoncigcard.co.uk
Est. 1927 *Stock size* Large
Stock Cigarette cards
Open Mon–Sat 9.30am–5pm closed Wed Sat pm
Services Direct sales, public/postal auctions. Publishes catalogues, card collectors magazines, trade cards

Simon's Books
Contact Mr B Ives
✉ **Broad Street, Somerton, Somerset, TA11 7NH** Ⓟ
☎ 01458 272313
Est. 1979 *Stock size* Medium
Stock General antiquarian and second-hand books
Open Mon–Sat 10am–4.30pm

Somerton Antique Centre
Contact Maurice Waite
✉ **Market Place, Somerton, Somerset, TA11 7NB** Ⓟ
☎ 01458 274423
Est. 1997 *Stock size* Large
No. of dealers 42

Stock General antiques including paintings, linen, militaria, pine and oak
Open Mon–Sat 10am–5pm
Services Restorations

⊞ Westville House Antiques
Contact Derek or Margaret Stacey
✉ **Westville House, Littleton, Somerton, Somerset, TA11 6NP** 🅿
☎ 01458 273376 Ⓕ 01458 273376
Ⓔ antique@westville.co.uk
Ⓦ www.westville.co.uk
Est. 1986 *Stock size* Large
Stock Antique country, pine, oak and mahogany furniture
Open Mon–Sat 9am–5.30pm or by appointment

SOUTH PETHERTON

⊞ Rostrum Antiques (BABAADA)
Contact Peter Skupien
✉ **The Old Flax Mill, Flaxdrayton, Yeabridge, South Petherton, Somerset, TA13 5LR** 🅿
☎ 01460 249249 Ⓜ 07831 444148
Ⓔ rostrum.uk@virgin.net
Est. 1988 *Stock size* Medium
Stock Fine 17th–19thC furniture, collectors' boxes, objets d'art and other interesting items
Open By appointment
Services Restoration, French polishing, giltwood restoration

STOKE SUB HAMDON

⊞ R G Watkins (PBFA)
Contact Mr R G Watkins
✉ **9 North Street Workshops, Stoke Sub Hamdon, Somerset, TA14 6QR** 🅿
☎ 01935 822891 Ⓕ 01935 822891
Ⓔ rgw@eurobell.co.uk
Ⓦ www.rgw.eurobell.co.uk
Est. 1985 *Stock size* Small
Stock Antiquarian books, prints, portraits. Books on art and antiques a speciality
Open Fri 10am–5pm or by appointment
Fairs PBFA
Services Valuations

STRATTON-ON-THE-FOSSE

⊞ Notts Pine
Contact Jeff Nott
✉ **Old Redhouse Farm, Stratton-on-the-Fosse, Radstock, Bath, Somerset, BA3 4QE** 🅿
☎ 01761 419911
Est. 1986 *Stock size* Medium
Stock Antique pine furniture
Open Mon–Fri 9am–6pm

TAUNTON

⊞ Aarons Antiques
✉ **27–29 Silver Street, Taunton, Somerset, TA1 3DH** 🅿
☎ 01823 698295
Est. 1982 *Stock size* Large
Stock Small antiques, collectables
Open Mon 9am–4pm

⊞ The Bookshop
Contact Sarah Allen
✉ **13a Paul Street, Taunton, Somerset, TA1 3PF** 🅿
☎ 01823 326963 Ⓕ 01458 241007
Ⓜ 07971 245301
Est. 1997 *Stock size* Medium
Stock Rare and second-hand books
Open Mon Tues Fri Sat 10am–4.30pm Thurs noon–4.30pm
Services Book search

Greenslade Taylor Hunt (SOFAA)
Contact Stuart Triggol
✉ **Magdalene House, Church Square, Taunton, Somerset, TA1 1SB** 🅿
☎ 01823 332525 Ⓕ 01823 353120
Ⓔ maghouse@dircom.co.uk
Ⓦ www.auction-net.co.uk
Est. 1843
Open Mon–Fri 9am–5pm
Sales Monthly fine art sales last Thurs 10am, viewing Tues 9.30am–4.30pm Wed 9.30am–7.30pm. Weekly household sale Wed 10am, viewing Tues 2.30–5pm. Also specialist clocks, silver, jewellery, books, collectors' sales. Phone for details
Frequency Monthly
Catalogues Yes

⊞ Hallidays (LAPADA)
Contact James Halliday
✉ **6 St James Street, Taunton, Somerset, TA1 1JH** 🅿
☎ 01823 324073 Ⓕ 01823 324073
Est. 1987 *Stock size* Medium
Stock 18th–19thC furniture, upholstery, ceramics
Open Mon–Sat 9.30am–5.30pm
Services Valuations, reupholstery, furniture renovation

Lawrences Taunton Ltd (ARVA)
Contact Angela Morley
✉ **The Corfield Hall, Magdalene Street, Taunton, Somerset, TA1 1SG** 🅿
☎ 01823 330567 Ⓕ 01823 330596
Ⓔ enquiries.taunton@lawrences.co.uk
Ⓦ www.lawrences.co.uk
Est. 1975
Open Mon–Fri 9am–5pm
Sales Fortnightly general sale first and third Tues 11am (no catalogue), viewing Mon 9am–7pm Tues 9am–11am prior to sale. 4 fine art sales a year Tues 11am, viewing Sat 9.30am–12.30pm Mon 9am–7pm. Bi-annual collectors' sale Feb and August Tues 9.30am, viewing as fine arts sale. Biannual sporting sale April and October Tues 11am, viewing as fine arts sale
Frequency Fortnightly
Catalogues Yes

⊞ O'Marley's Ghost
Contact C Harvey
✉ **8 Station Road, Taunton, Somerset, TA1 1NH** 🅿
☎ 01823 334080
Est. 2000 *Stock size* Medium
Stock Antique pine furniture, garden items
Open Mon–Sat 10.30am–4.30pm closed Wed
Services Stripping

⊞ Russell Books
Contact Mr Desmond Kerr
✉ **21 Bath Place, Taunton, Somerset, TA1 4ER**
☎ 01823 330887
Est. 1998 *Stock size* Medium
Stock Antiquarian and second-hand books
Open Mon–Sat 10am–5.30pm
Services Book search

⊞ Selwoods Antiques
Contact Mr J R Selwood
✉ **Queen Anne Cottage, Mary Street, Taunton, Somerset, TA1 3PE**
☎ 01823 272780

Est. 1927 *Stock size* Large
Stock Furniture
Open Mon–Sat 9.30am–5pm

Staple Grove Antiques Centre
Contact Norman Clarke
7–9 Staplegrove Road, Taunton, Somerset, TA1 1DE
01823 283050 Ⓕ 01823 283050
Est. 2000 *Stock size* Large
No. of dealers 18
Stock Period furniture, ceramics, jewellery, stamps, collectables
Open Mon–Sat 10am–5pm
Sun 11am–4pm
Services Valuations

Taunton Antiques Market
Contact Mike Spooner
25–29 Silver Street, Taunton, Somerset, TA1 3DH
020 7969 1500 Ⓕ 020 7969 1639
Est. 1978
No. of dealers 100
Stock General antiques and collectables including specialists in most fields
Open Mon 9am–4pm including Bank Holidays

TEMPLE CLOUD

Bookbarn Ltd
Contact Mr Belton
White Cross, Temple Cloud, Somerset, BS39 6EX
01761 451777
Ⓔ bookbarn@netcomuk.co.uk
Ⓦ www.bookbarn.co.uk
Est. 1997 *Stock size* Large
Stock Antiquarian and second-hand books
Open Mon–Sat 10am–6pm
Sun noon–5pm

THORNBURY

Thornbury Antiques
Contact Mrs H Hill
3a High Street, Thornbury, Bristol, BS35 2AE
01454 413722
Est. 1993 *Stock size* Medium
Stock Victorian pine furniture
Open Mon–Sat 10am–5pm

TIMSBURY

Ministry of Pine
Contact Tony Lawrence or Susan Dunn
Timsbury Village Workshop, Unit 2, Timsbury Industrial Estate, Hayeswood Road, Timsbury, Bath, Somerset, BA3 1HQ
01761 472297/434938
Ⓜ 07770 588536
Ⓔ ministryofpine.uk@virgin.net
Ⓦ www.ministryofpine.co.uk
Est. 1980 *Stock size* Large
Stock Antique pine furniture both painted and stripped
Open Mon–Fri 9am–6pm
Sat Sun 10am–4pm
Services Valuations, restorations and stripping

WATCHET

Clarence House Antiques
Contact Mr or Mrs Cotton
41 Swain Street, Watchet, Somerset, TA23 0AE
01984 631389
Est. 1972 *Stock size* Medium
Stock Antiques, curios, collectables
Open Mon–Sat 11am–5.30pm

WEDMORE

Slade Antiques
Contact Peter Kelley
King Alfred Mews, Church Street, Wedmore, Somerset, BS28 4AB
01934 710101
Ⓜ 07949 104617
Est. 2000 *Stock size* Medium
Stock Georgian, Victorian , Edwardian furniture, general antiques, rocking horses
Open Mon–Sat 10am–5pm closed Thurs
Services Restorations

WELLS

Alcove Antiques
Contact Nancy Alcock
1 Priest Row, Wells, Somerset, BA5 2PY
01749 672164 Ⓕ 01749 678925
Ⓜ 07885 508736
Est. 1979 *Stock size* Medium
Stock China, brass, copper, pine, Victorian and Edwardian mahogany
Open Tues Thurs–Sat 10.30am–5pm
Wed 10.30am–1pm
Services Restorations

Bookbarn Ltd
Contact Mr Belton
West Street, Wells, Somerset, BA5 2HJ
01749 689040
Ⓔ bookbarn@netcomuk.co.uk
Ⓦ www.bookbarn.co.uk
Est. 1997 *Stock size* Large
Stock Antiquarian and second-hand books
Open Mon–Sat 10am–6pm
Sun noon–5pm

Bookbarn Ltd
Contact Mr Belton
23 Broad Street, Wells, Somerset, BA5 2DJ
01749 670008
Ⓔ bookbarn@netcomuk.co.uk
Ⓦ www.bookbarn.co.uk
Est. 1997 *Stock size* Large
Stock Antiquarian and second-hand books
Open Mon–Sat 10am–6pm
Sun noon–5pm

Country Brocante (BABAADA)
Contact Tim Ovel
Fir Tree Farm, Lower Godney, Wells, Somerset, BA5 1RZ
01458 833052 Ⓕ 01458 835611
Ⓜ 07970 719708
Ⓔ ovel@compuserve.com
Est. 1993 *Stock size* Large
Stock French furniture, chandeliers, early mirrors
Open By appointment
Fairs Newark, Shepton Mallet

Kym Grant Bookseller
Contact Mr K Grant
82 Southover Wells, Wells, Somerset, BA5 1UH
01749 675618
Est. 1995 *Stock size* Small
Stock Antiquarian and second-hand books, children's annuals and books
Open By appointment
Fairs Bloomsbury (monthly)

Bernard G House Longcase Clocks
Contact Mr B G House
13 Market Place, Wells, Somerset, BA5 2RF
01749 672607 Ⓕ 01749 672607
Est. 1971 *Stock size* Medium
Stock Longcase clocks, barographs, barometers, clocks, telescopes, scientific instruments

Open Mon–Sat 10am–5.30pm or by appointment
Services Repairs and restorations to clocks and barometers

田 E A Nowell & Daughter (BADA)
Contact Edward or Mary-Ellen Nowell
✉ **Beryl, Hawkers Lane, Wells, Somerset, BA5 3JP** Ⓟ
☎ 01749 672415 Ⓕ 01749 670508
Ⓔ stay@beryl-wells.co.uk
Ⓦ www.beryl-wells.co.uk
Est. 1952 *Stock size* Medium
Stock 18th–19thC furniture, Sheffield plate, silver, jewellery
Open Mon–Sat 9.30am–5pm or by appointment
Services Restorations

Wells Auction Rooms
Contact Nick Ewing or Cynthia Peak
✉ **66–68 Southover, Wells, Somerset, BA5 1UH** Ⓟ
☎ 01749 678094 or 0117 973 7201
Est. 1845
Sales Sale monthly Wed 1.30pm, viewing Tues noon–5pm day of sale from 9am
Frequency Monthly
Catalogues Yes

田 Wells Reclamation Company
✉ **Coxley, Wells, Somerset, BA5 1RQ** Ⓟ
☎ 01749 677087 Ⓕ 01749 671098
Ⓔ enquiries@wellsreclamation.com
Ⓦ www.wellsreclaimation.com
Est. 1984 *Stock size* Large
Stock Architectural antiques, bricks, tiles, slates, fireplaces, doors, finials, pews, etc
Open Mon–Fri 8.30am–5.30pm Sat 9am–4pm
Services Oak studded doors made to order

WESTBURY-ON-TRYM

田 Kemps
Contact Michael Kemp
✉ **9 Carlton Court, Westbury-on-Trym, Somerset, BS9 3DF** Ⓟ
☎ 0117 950 5090 *Stock size* Medium
Stock Jewellery
Open Mon–Fri 9am–5.15pm Sat 9am–1pm

WESTON-SUPER-MARE

田 Clifton House Furniture
Contact Michael Barrett
✉ **67 Clifton Road, Weston-super-Mare, Somerset, BS23 1BW** Ⓟ
☎ 01934 625217
Est. 1987 *Stock size* Medium
Stock Furniture, mainly pine
Open Mon–Sat 10am–6pm
Services Restorations

田 David Hughes Antiques
Contact Mr Hughes
✉ **37 Baker Street, Weston-super-Mare, Somerset, BS23 3AD** Ⓟ
☎ 01934 628007 Ⓜ 07860 964100
Est. 1974 *Stock size* Medium
Stock General antiques, Arts and Crafts, Art Nouveau
Open Mon Sat 9am–1pm Tues Fri 9am–1pm 2–4pm
Fairs Newark, Ardingly
Services House clearances

田 Sterling Books (ABA, PBFA)
Contact Mr Nisbet
✉ **43a Locking Road, Weston-super-Mare, Somerset, BS23 3DG** Ⓟ
☎ 01934 625056
Ⓔ sterling.books@talk21.com
Est. 1966 *Stock size* Large
Stock Antiquarian and second-hand books on every subject
Open Tues–Sat 10am–5.30pm Thurs 10am–1pm
Services Valuations, book binding and picture framing

田 Terry's Antiques and Collectables
Contact Terry
✉ **The Inshops, Regent Street, Weston-super-Mare, Somerset, BS23 1SR** Ⓟ
☎ 01934 643374
Ⓜ 07980 408943
Est. 1986 *Stock size* Medium
Stock Victorian Furniture, ceramics and silver
Open Mon–Sat 9am–5.30pm Sun 11am–5pm
Services House clearance

田 Richard Twort
Contact Richard Twort
✉ **12 Sand Road, Sand Bay, Weston-super-Mare, Somerset, BS22 9UH** Ⓟ
☎ 01934 641900 Ⓕ 01934 641900
Ⓜ 07711 939789
Ⓔ walls@mirage-interiors.com
Est. 1962 *Stock size* Medium
Stock Barographs, thermographs, rain gauges, all types of meteorological instruments
Open By appointment

WILLITON

田 Courtyard Antiques
Contact Liz Cain
✉ **The Courtyard, St Audries, Williton, Somerset, TA4 4DP** Ⓟ
☎ 01984 633701
Ⓔ sales@courtyardantiques.net
Ⓦ www.courtyardantiques.net
Est. 1995 *Stock size* Medium
Stock Country furniture, pine, oak and elm, decorative items
Open Mon Tues Thurs Fri Sun 10am–4pm Sat 10am–1pm
Services Restorations

WINCANTON

田 Green Dragon Antiques and Crafts Centre
Contact Sally Denning
✉ **24 High Street, Wincanton, Somerset, BA9 9JF** Ⓟ
☎ 01963 34111
Ⓦ www.greendragonantiques.com
Est. 1991 *Stock size* Large
Stock General antiques, jewellery, crafts
Open Mon–Sun 9am–5pm
Services Valuations, free gift wrap, jewellery repairs

田 The Old School Rooms Antiques
Contact Philip Broomfield
✉ **16 Mill Street, Wincanton, Somerset, BA9 9AP** Ⓟ
☎ 01963 824259 Ⓜ 07768 726276
Ⓔ oldschoolantiques@aol.com
Est. 1987 *Stock size* Large
Stock Furniture
Open Tues Wed Fri Sat 10am–4pm
Services Restorations

田 Wincanton Antiques
Contact Tony or Clare
✉ **3 Church Street, Wincanton, Somerset, BA9 9AA** Ⓟ
☎ 01963 32223

Est. 1997 *Stock size* Large
Stock Georgian–Edwardian furniture, beds, French antiques
Open Mon–Sat 9.30am–5pm
Services Upholstery

WIVELISCOMBE

Yew Tree Antiques Warehouse
Contact N Nation
Old Brewery, Wiveliscombe, Taunton, Somerset, TA4 2NT
01984 623950/623914
Stock size Large
Stock Victorian, Edwardian and French furniture, Lloyd Loom
Open Tue–Fri 11am–4.30pm
Sat 10am–5pm

YEOVIL

Gilbert & Dale
Contact Roy Gilbert
Old Chapel, Church Street, Yeovil, Somerset, BA22 8LN
01935 840464 F 01935 841599
E roy@roygilbert.com
Est. 1972 *Stock size* Medium
Stock 18th–19thC French and English country furniture and accessories
Open Mon–Sat 9am–5.30pm

Phone Cards Centre (TCC)
Contact Mr Fowle
16 Boundary Road, Houndstone, Yeovil, Somerset, BA22 8SF
01935 431314 F 01935 427412
E jfowle8142@aol.com
Est. 1993 *Stock size* Medium
Stock Phone cards bought, sold and exchanged
Open By appointment
Fairs Wessex Fairs, Telephone Collectors Club Fair
Services Valuations

Yeovil Collectors Centre
Contact Barry Scott
16 Hendford, Yeovil, Somerset, BA20 1TE
01935 433739 F 01935 433739
Est. 1969 *Stock size* Small
Stock Militaria, postcards, general collectables, animals, blue-and-white pottery, Toby jugs
Open Mon Wed–Sat 9am–5pm

WILTSHIRE

AVEBURY

Avebury Antiques
Contact Brian Sumbler
High Street, Avebury, Wiltshire, SN8 1RF
01672 539436
Est. 1984 *Stock size* Small
Stock Antiques and collectables
Open Mon–Sun 10am–6pm

BRADFORD-ON-AVON

Audley House Antiques (BABAADA)
Contact Mr R B Brown
5 Wooley Street, Bradford-on-Avon, Wiltshire, BA15 1AD
01225 862476
Est. 1993 *Stock size* Large
Stock Victorian and Edwardian furniture, silver, pictures, porcelain
Open Mon–Sat 9am–6pm
Sun by appointment
Fairs Westonbirt, Arley, Snape
Services Valuations

Avon Antiques (BADA)
Contact Andrew Jenkins
25–27 Market Street, Bradford-on-Avon, Wiltshire, BA15 1LL
01225 862052 F 01225 868763
E avonantiques@aol.com
Est. 1963 *Stock size* Large
Stock 17th–mid-19thC furniture, clocks, barometers, metalwork, needlework, treen, English furniture, folk art pictures
Open Mon–Sat 9.30am–5.30pm
Fairs Grosvenor House Antiques Fair

Andrew Dando (BADA, LAPADA, BACA Award Winner 2002)
Contact Andrew Dando
34 Market Street, Bradford-on-Avon, Wiltshire, BA15 1LL
01225 865444
E andrew@andrewdando.co.uk
W www.andrewdando.co.uk
Est. 1915 *Stock size* Large
Stock Pottery and porcelain 1750–1870
Open Tues–Sat 10am–5pm
Fairs BADA

Granary Pine (BABAADA)
Contact Julia or Tony Chowles
The Granary, Pound Lane, Bradford-on-Avon, Wiltshire, BA15 1LF
01225 867781 F 01225 867781
E tony@granarypine.co.uk
W www.granarypine.co.uk
Est. 1987 *Stock size* Large
Stock Country pine furniture, collectables
Open Mon–Sun 10am–5pm

Mac Humble Antiques (BADA)
Contact Mr Humble
7–9 Woolley Street, Bradford-on-Avon, Wiltshire, BA15 1AD
01225 866329 F 01225 866329
M 07702 501888
E mac.humble@virgin.net
W www.machumbleantiques.co.uk
Est. 1979 *Stock size* Small
Stock 18th–19thC furniture, needlework, samplers, metalware and decorative items
Open Mon–Fri 9am–6pm
Sat 9am–1pm
Fairs Olympia (Nov) BADA Fair (March)
Services Valuations, restorations

Moxhams Antiques (LAPADA, BABAADA)
Contact Roger, Jill or Nick Bichard
17, 23 & 24 Silver Street, Bradford-on-Avon, Wiltshire, BA15 1JZ
01225 862789 F 01225 867844
M 07768 960295
E Jill@moxhams-antiques.demon.co.uk
Est. 1967 *Stock size* Large
Stock Good 17th–early 19thC mahogany and oak furniture, ceramics, tapestries and objects
Open Mon–Sat 9am–5.30pm
Fairs Olympia (June and Nov)

No. 32
Contact Katie Banks
32 Silver Street, Bradford-on-Avon, Wiltshire, BA15 1JX
01225 862981
Est. 1996 *Stock size* Medium
Stock Antique pine, collectables
Open Tues–Sun 10am–5pm

Revival
Contact Douglas Vallance
Unit 8, Tythebarn Workshops, Pound Lane, Bradford-on-Avon, Wiltshire, BA15 1LF
01225 864780
Est. 1967 *Stock size* Medium
Stock Georgian–Edwardian furniture
Open Tues–Sun 10am–5pm
Services Restorations

Roundabout Shop
Contact Clive or Pam Freeman
1–2 Silver Street, Bradford-on-Avon, Wiltshire, BA15 1JX
01225 863241
Est. 1960 *Stock size* Large
Stock Thousands of antiquarian and general books
Open Mon–Sun 9.30am–5.30pm half day Wed out of season
Services Cutting and mounting prints, framing

BRINKWORTH

North Wilts Exporters
Contact Caroline Thornbury
Farm Hill House, The Street, Brinkworth, Swindon, Wiltshire, SN5 5AJ
01666 510876
Est. 1974 *Stock size* Large
Stock Eastern European pine, oak, and mahogany furniture
Open Mon–Sat 9am–6pm or by appointment
Fairs Newark
Services Packers and shippers

BROAD HINTON

Bookmark (PBFA)
Contact Leonora Excell or Anne Excell
Fortnight, Wick Down, Broad Hinton, Swindon, Wiltshire, SN4 9NR
01793 731693 F 01793 731782
M 07788 841305
E leonora.excell@btinternet.com
Est. 1972 *Stock size* Medium
Stock Children's and illustrated antiquarian books. Mail order business with 3–4 catalogues a year
Open By appointment
Fairs PBFA
Services Book search

CALNE

Calne Antiques
Contact Malcolm Blackford
2a London Road, Calne, Wiltshire, SN11 0AB
01249 816311
Est. 1981 *Stock size* Large
Stock English and Continental pine furniture
Open Mon–Sun 9.30am–5pm

CHERHILL

P A Oxley Antique Clocks & Barometers (LAPADA)
Contact Mr M Oxley
The Old Rectory, Cherhill, Calne, Wiltshire, SN11 8UX
01249 816227 F 01249 821285
E info@paoxley.com
W www.british-antiqueclocks.com
Est. 1971 *Stock size* Large
Stock Antique clocks and barometers, longcase clocks a speciality
Open Mon–Sat 9.30am–5pm closed Wed Sun or by appointment
Services Delivery and shipping

CHIPPENHAM

Chippenham Auction Rooms
Contact Richard Edmonds
St Mary's Street, Chippenham, Wiltshire, SN15 3JM
01249 462222 F 01249 462222
M 07980 745441
E richard@chippenhamauctionrooms.co.uk
Est. 2001
Open Mon–Fri 9am–1pm 2–6pm
Sales General antiques monthly Sat 10am viewing Thurs 4–9pm, Fri 10am–5pm, Sat 8.30–10am. 5 fine art sales a year at Lackham College, Lackham on Tues 10am, viewing Sun noon–6pm Mon 10am–5pm. Also garden and farm machinery sales
Catalogues Yes

Collectors Corner
Contact Karen Groves
36 The Causeway, Chippenham, Wiltshire, SN15 3DB
01249 461617/01249 446044
Est. 1990 *Stock size* Large
Stock Antiques, collectables, musical instruments
Open Mon–Sat 9am–5pm

CHRISTIAN MALFORD

Harley Antiques
Contact Mr Harley
The Comedy, Main Road, Christian Malford, Chippenham, Wiltshire, SN15 4BS
01249 720112 F 01249 720553
Est. 1959 *Stock size* Large
Stock General antiques including decorative and unusual items, conservatory furniture and objects
Open Mon–Sun 9am–6pm

CORSHAM

Automattic Comics
Contact Matthew Booker
Unit 2, 17 Pickwick Road, Corsham, Wiltshire, SN13 9BQ
01249 701647
E matt@automatticcomics.com
W www.automatticcomics.com
Est. 1995 *Stock size* Large
Stock American import comics, old and new action figures, Star Wars figures
Open Mon Tues noon–5pm Thurs–Sat 10am–5pm
Fairs NEC Memorabilia (March, Nov)

Matthew Eden
Contact Mrs M Eden or Matthew Eden
Pickwick End, Corsham, Wiltshire, SN13 0JB
01249 713335 F 01249 713644
M 07899 926076
E mail@mattheweden.co.uk
W mattheweden.com
Est. 1952 *Stock size* Large
Stock General including garden furniture
Open Mon–Sat 9am–6pm
Fairs Chelsea Flower Show

Gardiner Houlgate
Contact Nicholas Houlgate
9 Leafield Way, Corsham, Wiltshire, SN13 9SW
01225 812912 F 01225 811777
E auctions@gardiner-houlgate.co.uk
W www.invaluable.com
Est. 1987
Open Mon–Fri 9am–5.30pm
Sales Quarterly antiques and works of art sales, 8 Victoriana

and later furnishings sales, Thurs 10.30am, view Tues Wed 9am–5.30pm and morning of sale. Also specialist sales of clocks, musical instruments, decorative art and silver
Catalogues Yes

CRUDWELL

Philip A Ruttleigh Antiques incorporating Crudwell Furniture
Contact Philip Ruttleigh
Odd Penny Farm, Crudwell, Wiltshire, SN16 9SJ
01285 770970 Ⓜ 07989 250077
www.crudwellfurniture.co.uk
Est. 1989 *Stock size* Small
Stock General antique furniture
Open Mon–Fri 9am–5pm or by appointment
Services Restorations

DEVIZES

Henry Aldridge & Son
Contact Alan Aldridge
Unit 1, Bath Road Business Centre, Devizes, Wiltshire, SN10 1XA
01380 720199
andrew.aldridge@virgin.net
www.henry-aldridge.co.uk
Est. 1989
Open Mon–Fri 10am–4pm
Sales Monthly antiques sales, bi-annual maritime and Titanic sale on Wed 6pm, viewing Mon noon–4pm Tues noon–6.30pm Wed noon–6.30pm.
Catalogues Yes

Devizes Auction Centre
Contact Alan Aldridge
New Park Street, Devizes, Wiltshire, SN10 1DX
01380 720900 Ⓕ 01380 721200
andrew.aldridge@virgin.net
www.henry-aldridge.co.uk
Est. 1989
Open Mon–Fri 10am–4pm
Sales Sale every Tues 10am, viewing Mon 4–7pm
Frequency Weekly
Catalogues Yes

Margaret Mead Antiques
Contact Mrs M Mead
19 Northgate Street, Devizes, Wiltshire, SN10 1JT
01380 721060 or 01793 533085
Ⓜ 07740 536560
Est. 1982 *Stock size* Medium
Stock General antiques, Georgian–Edwardian furniture, clocks, china
Open Tues–Sat 10am–5pm closed Wed
Services Restorations

St Mary's Chapel Antiques (BABAADA)
Contact Richard Sanke
St Mary's Chapel, Northgate Street, Devizes, Wiltshire, SN10 1DE
01380 721399 Ⓕ 01380 721399
richard@rsankey.freeserve.co.uk
Est. 1971 *Stock size* Large
Stock Original painted and country furniture, garden antiques and accessories
Open Mon–Sat 10am–6pm closed Wed
Fairs Bath Decorative and Antiques Fair
Services Selective restorations

Upstairs Downstairs
Contact Judy Coom
40 Market Place, Devizes, Wiltshire, SN10 1JG
01380 730266 Ⓕ 01380 739352
Ⓜ 07974 074220
devizesantiques@amserve.com
Est. 2002 *Stock size* Large
No. of dealers 32
Stock Antiques and collectables, furniture, post cards, pictures, toys, dolls, china
Open Mon–Sat 9.30am–4.30pm Sun 9.30am–3pm closed Wed
Services Doll repair

DRAYCOT CERNE

Crosshayes Antiques (LAPADA)
Contact David Brooks
Unit 6 Westbrook Farm, Draycot Cerne, Chippenham, Wiltshire, SN15 5LH
01249 720033 Ⓕ 01249 720033
david@crosshayes.co.uk
www.crosshayes.co.uk
Est. 1976 *Stock size* Large
Stock Furniture
Open Mon–Fri 9am–5pm or by appointment
Services Container packing service

DURRINGTON

Cannon Militaria
Contact Mr L Webb
21 Bulford Road, Durrington, Salisbury, Wiltshire, SP4 8DL
01980 655099
Est. 1995 *Stock size* Large
Stock Military collectables
Open Thurs Fri 9.30am–5pm Sat 9.00am–1pm
Services Valuations

LANGLEY BURRELL

Harriet Fairfax Fireplaces and General Antiques
Contact Harriet Fairfax
Langley Green, Langley Burrell, Wiltshire, SN15 4LL
01249 652030
Est. 1972 *Stock size* Small
Stock Furniture, fireplaces
Open By appointment

LYNEHAM

Pillars Antiques
Contact Mr K Clifford
10 The Banks, Lyneham, Chippenham, Wiltshire, SN15 4NS
01249 890632
Est. 1986 *Stock size* Large
Stock Old pine, 1940s and mahogany furniture, bric-a-brac
Open Mon–Sat 10am–5pm Sun 11am–5pm Wed by appointment closed Thurs

MALMESBURY

Athelstan's Attic
Contact Tim Harvey
The Cross Hayes, Malmesbury, Wiltshire, SN16 9AU
01666 825544/822678
tharvey@freeserve.co.uk
Est. 1997 *Stock size* Large
Stock General house clearance items
Open Mon Wed Fri Sat 9.30am–4.30pm
Services House clearance

Andrew Britten Antiques
Contact Mr T M Tyler
48 High Street, Malmesbury, Wiltshire, SN16 9AT
01666 823376 Ⓕ 01666 825563

maidolph@aol.com
Est. 1974 *Stock size* Small
Stock Small items of furniture, decorative accessories
Open Mon–Sat 9am–5.30pm
Services Valuations

Hilditch Auction (NAVA)
Contact Mr Hilditch
Gloucester Road Trading Estate, Malmesbury, Wiltshire, SN16 9JT
01666 822577 01666 825597
sales@hilditchauctions.co.uk
www.hilditchauctions.co.uk
Est. 1990
Open Mon–Fri 8.30am–5pm
Sales General household sale 4th Sat 10am every month, viewing Fri 10am–7pm, call for alternate dates
Frequency Monthly
Catalogues Yes

Rene Nicholls
Contact Mrs I Nicholls
56 High Street, Malmesbury, Wiltshire, SN16 9AT
01666 823089
Est. 1979 *Stock size* Medium
Stock English pottery and porcelain
Open Mon–Sat 9.30am–6pm or by appointment
Services Valuations, restorations

MANINGFORD BRUCE

Indigo
Contact Marion Bender or Richard Lightbown
Dairy Barn, Maningford Bruce, Wiltshire, SN9 6JW
01672 564722 01672 564733
07867 982233
indigo_uk@compuserve.com
www.indigo-uk.com
Est. 1982 *Stock size* Large
Stock Antique Indian, Chinese, Japanese and Indonesian furniture
Trade only Yes
Open By appointment
Fairs House and Garden fair
Services Restorations

MARLBOROUGH

Blanchard Ltd (LAPADA)
Contact Orlando Harris
Froxfield, Marlborough, Wiltshire, SN8 3LD
01488 680666 01488 680668
orlando@jwblanchard.com
Est. 1989 *Stock size* Large
Stock English and Continental furniture, decorative items, works of art
Open Mon–Fri 9.30am–5.30pm Sat 10am–5pm
Fairs June Olympia

Brocante Antiques Centre
Contact Peter Randall
6 London Road, Marlborough, Wiltshire, SN8 1PH
01672 516512 01672 516512
Est. 1995 *Stock size* Large
No. of dealers 20
Stock General antiques and collectables
Open Mon–Sat 10am–5pm
Services Restorations, valuations, pine stripping

The Cats Whiskers Antiques
Contact Sue Rumbold
3 Kingsbury Street, Marlborough, Wiltshire, SN8 1HU
01672 511577 or 01264 850801
07712 018543
Est. 2002 *Stock size* Medium
Stock Antiques, collectables, blue-and-white china, quilts, gardening items
Open Mon–Sat 10am–5.30pm telephone call advisable

Eureka Antiques
Contact Mr Newman
5 London Road, Marlborough, Wiltshire, SN8 1PH
01672 512072
Est. 1979 *Stock size* Medium
Stock Antique pots and furniture
Open Mon–Sun 9am–6pm

Graylings Antiques
Contact Gail Young
Brocante Antiques Centre, 6 London Road, Marlborough, Wiltshire, SN8 1PH
01264 710077 01264 710077
07732 293302
tremorfa@ntlworld.com
www.staffordshire-figures.com
Est. 1995 *Stock size* Medium
Stock Staffordshire pottery
Open By appointment
Fairs Newark
Services Valuations

Hamptons International Auctioneers and Valuers
Contact Sheldon Cameron
20 High Street, Marlborough, Wiltshire, SN8 1AA
01672 516161 01672 515882
camerons@hamptonsinternational.com
www.hamptons.co.uk
Open Mon–Fri 9am–5pm
Sales An eclectic mix of antique, collectables and household items on Wed 10.30am, viewing Mon Tues 9am–5pm and morning of sale.
Frequency Three weekly
Catalogues Yes

Katharine House Gallery (PBFA)
Contact Christopher Gange
Katharine House, The Parade, Marlborough, Wiltshire, SN8 1NE
01672 514040
Est. 1983 *Stock size* Medium
Stock Antiquarian and second-hand books, 20thC British pictures, general antiques and antiquities
Open Mon–Sat 10am–5.30pm
Fairs PBFA (Russell Hotel)

The Marlborough Parade Antique Centre
Contact Terry Page
The Parade, Marlborough, Wiltshire, SN8 1NE
01672 515331
Est. 1985 *Stock size* Large
No. of dealers 50
Stock Small items, general antiques, very good quality
Open Mon–Sun 10am–5pm closed Christmas, Boxing and New Year's Day

The Rope Works
Contact Richard Nadin or Patrick Macintosh
The House (1860–1925), Katharine House Yard, Kennet Place, Marlborough, Wiltshire, SN8 1NQ
01672 512111
Est. 2000 *Stock size* Large
Stock Furniture, mirrors and lighting 1600–1970
Open Mon–Sat 10am–4pm or by appointment
Services Valuations

Annmarie Turner Antiques
Contact Annmarie Turner
22 Salisbury Road, Marlborough, Wiltshire, SN8 4AD
01672 515396
Est. 1986 *Stock size* Small
Stock Country and rustic furniture, allied decorative items
Open Sat 9am–7pm

Nick Wheatley
Contact Nick Wheatley
The House (1860–1925), Katharine House Yard, Kennet Place, Marlborough, Wiltshire, SN8 1NQ
01672 512111
nick@thehouse1860–1925.com
www.thehouse1860–1925.com
Est. 1999 *Stock size* Large
Stock Furniture and accessories of the Arts and Crafts Movement
Open Mon–Sat 10am–4pm or by appointment
Services Valuations, restorations, interior design and furnishing

D P White
Contact Mr White
59 High Street, Ramsbury, Marlborough, Wiltshire, SN8 2QN
01672 520261
Est. 1969 *Stock size* Large
Stock Victorian oil lamps, oil lamp spares (old and new stocked), 50 oil lamps always in stock, brass, copper, furniture, clocks
Open Tues–Sat 10am–1pm 2–5pm closed Wed or by appointment
Services Longcase clock restoration

MELKSHAM

Peter Campbell Antiques (BABAADA)
Contact Mr P Campbell
59 Bath Road, Atworth, Melksham, Wiltshire, SN12 8JY
01225 709742
Est. 1976 *Stock size* Medium
Stock Country furniture and decorative items
Open Mon–Sat 10am–5pm Thurs and Sun by appointment

Dann Antiques Ltd (BABAADA)
Contact Gary Low
Unit S1, New Broughton Road, Melksham, Wiltshire, SN12 8BS
01225 707329 01225 790120
113665.1341@compuserve.com
Est. 1984 *Stock size* Large
Stock English mahogany furniture, furniture accessories
Open Mon–Fri 8.30am–5.30pm Sat 9am–1pm or by appointment
Services Restorations

Jaffray Antiques (BABAADA)
Contact Mrs J Carter
16 The Market Place, Melksham, Wiltshire, SN12 6EX
01225 702269 01225 790413
jaffray.antiques@talk21.com
Est. 1955 *Stock size* Large
Stock 18th–19thC furniture, tallboys, desks, linen presses, bamboo, dining tables, chests-of-drawers, Staffordshire, metalware
Open Mon–Fri 9am–5pm or by appointment

King Street Curios
Contact Lizzie Board
8–10 King Street, Melksham, Wiltshire, SN12 6HD
01225 790623
Est. 1987 *Stock size* Large
Stock General antiques, collectables
Open Mon–Sat 10am–5pm
Fairs Shepton Mallet, Royal Fairs, Walcot Street Antique Market

Polly's Parlour
Contact Pauline Hart
2–4 King Street, Melksham, Wiltshire, SN12 6HD
01225 706418
Est. 1999 *Stock size* Large
Stock General antiques, collectables, decorative items
Open Mon–Sat 10am–4.30pm or by appointment

MERE

Finan and Co
Contact Robert Finan
The Square, Mere, Wiltshire, BA12 6DJ
01747 861411 01747 861944
enquiries@finanandco.co.uk
www.finanandco.co.uk
Est. 1997
Open Tues Thurs Sat 10am–6pm or by appointment
Sales Two antiques sales April and October Sat, viewing Thurs Fri 10am–7pm Sat 9–11am prior to sale. Two collectables sales Jan and July
Frequency Bi-annual
Catalogues Yes

NETHERHAMPTON

Edward Hurst Antiques
Contact Edward Hurst
The Garden Room, Netherhampton, Wiltshire, SP2 8PU
01722 743042 07768 255557
Est. 1985 *Stock size* Medium
Stock 17th–18thC British furniture and associated works of art
Open By appointment

Victor Mahy (BADA)
Contact John H Parnaby
Netherhampton House, Netherhampton, Salisbury, Wiltshire, SP2 8PU
01722 743131 01722 743042
johnparnaby@netherhamptonhouse.co.uk
www.netherhamptonhouse.co.uk
Est. 1918 *Stock size* Large
Stock 17th–18thC furniture
Open Mon–Sat 9.30am–5.30pm

NORTH WRAXALL

Delomosne & Son Ltd (BADA, BABAADA)
Contact Mr T N M Osborne
Court Close, North Wraxall, Chippenham, Wiltshire, SN14 7AD
01225 891505 01225 891907
timosborne@delomosne.co.uk
www.delomosne.co.uk
Est. 1905 *Stock size* Large
Stock Glass, porcelain, pottery, enamels, needlework pictures, treen, bygones, period glass lighting
Open Mon–Fri 9.30am–5.30pm or by appointment
Fairs International Ceramics Fair, Winter Olympia
Services Valuations, restorations, commission buying

OAKSEY

Lyon Oliver Antiques (TADA)
Contact Lyon Oliver
Laynes House, Oaksey, Wiltshire, SN16 9SE
01666 577603
lyon@lyon-oliver.demon.co.uk
Est. 1995 *Stock size* Large
Stock English and Irish country house antiques and provincial Chinese
Open By appointment
Fairs Olympia, Decorative Fair

PEWSEY

Rupert Gentle Antiques (BADA)
Contact Mrs Belinda Gentle
The Manor House, Milton Lilbourne, Pewsey, Wiltshire, SN9 5LQ
01672 563344 01672 563563
Est. 1976 *Stock size* Small
Stock 17th–19thC English and Continental domestic metalwork, treen, needlework
Open Mon–Sat 9am–6pm or by appointment
Fairs Grosvenor House (June), Olympia, BADA (March, Chelsea)
Services Valuations

Time Restored
Contact J H Bowler-Reed
20 High Street, Pewsey, Wiltshire, SN9 5AQ
01672 563544
Est. 1978 *Stock size* Small
Stock Antique clocks, musical boxes and barometers
Open Mon–Fri 10am–6pm
Services Restorations

RAMSBURY

Heraldry Today (ABA)
Contact Mrs Henry
Parliament Piece, Ramsbury, Marlborough, Wiltshire, SN8 2QH
01672 520617 01672 520183
heraldry@heraldrytoday.co.uk
www.heraldrytoday.co.uk
Est. 1954 *Stock size* Large
Stock Antiquarian books on heraldry, geneaology and peerage
Open Mon–Fri 9.30am–4.30pm

Inglenook Antiques
Contact Dennis White
59 High Street, Ramsbury, Wiltshire, SN8 2QN
01672 520261
Est. 1969 *Stock size* Large
Stock Victorian oil lamps, longcase clocks
Open Tues Thur Fri Sat 10am–5pm or by appointment

SALISBURY

Antiquities Français Ltd
Contact Guy Davies Bateman
61 Milford Street, Salisbury, Wiltshire, SP1 2BP
01722 333375
guy@antiques-french.co.uk
www.antiques-french.co.uk
Est. 2002 *Stock size* Medium
Stock French antiques and collectables
Open Tues–Sat 9.30am–5pm
Services Valuations

The Barn Book Supply
Contact John Head
88 Crane Street, Salisbury, Wiltshire, SP1 2QD
01722 327767
Est. 1958 *Stock size* Large
Stock Antiquarian books, specializing in all field sports
Open By appointment
Services Book search

Robert Bradley Antiques
Contact Mr R Bradley
71 Brown Street, Salisbury, Wiltshire, SP1 2BA
01722 333677 01722 339922
Est. 1970 *Stock size* Medium
Stock 17th–18thC furniture
Open Mon–Fri 9.30am–5.30pm

Castle Galleries (OMRS)
Contact John Lodge
81 Castle Street, Salisbury, Wiltshire, SP1 3SP
01722 333734 01722 333734
07980 225059
john.lodge1@tesco.net
Est. 1971 *Stock size* Medium
Stock Coins, medals, small items and jewellery
Open Tues Thurs Fri 9am–4.30pm Sat 9am–1pm
Services Valuations

Fisherton Antiques Market
Contact Nigel Roberts
53 Fisherton Street, Salisbury, Wiltshire, SP2 7SU
01722 422147
Est. 1997 *Stock size* Small
Stock Victorian and Edwardian furniture, jewellery, modern and collectables
Open Mon–Sat 9.30am–5pm

Jonathan Green Antiques
Contact Jonathan Green
The Antiques Market, 37 Catherine Street, Salisbury, Wiltshire, SP1 2DH
01722 332635 01722 332635
Est. 1979 *Stock size* Medium
Stock Silver, silver plate and decorative items
Open Mon–Sat 10am–5pm

Myriad
Contact Karen Montlake
48–54 Milford Street, Salisbury, Wiltshire, SP1 2BP
01722 413595/718203
01722 416395
enquiries@myriad-antiques.co.uk
www.myriad-antiques.co.uk
Est. 1994 *Stock size* Large
Stock Georgian–Victorian furniture in pine, mahogany oak. Lamps, clocks, mirrors, rugs
Open Mon–Sat 9.30am–5pm Sun by appointment
Services Stripping, collection and delivery within 80 miles, antique search

Pennyfarthing Antiques
Contact Mr J M Scott
52–54 Winchester Street, Salisbury, Wiltshire, SP1 1HG
01722 505955 07778 300316
Est. 1993 *Stock size* Medium
Stock Country furniture
Open Mon–Sat 9am–5.30pm Sun 11am–4pm
Services Restorations

Salisbury Antiques Market
37 Catherine Street, Salisbury, Wiltshire, SP1 2DH
01722 326033
www.salisburyantiques.com
Est. 1977 *Stock size* Large
No. of dealers 40

WEST COUNTRY

Stock General antiques
Open Mon–Fri 10am–5pm
Sat 9.30am–5pm

Salisbury Antiques Warehouse Ltd
Contact Kevin Chase
94 Wilton Road, Salisbury, Wiltshire, SP2 7JJ
☎ 01722 410634 F 01722 410635
E kevin@salisbury-antiques.co.uk
Est. 1965 *Stock size* Large
No. of dealers 12
Stock 18th–19thC furniture, paintings, clocks, bronzes, barometers
Open Mon–Fri 9.15am–5.30pm
Sat 10am–4pm

Steven Shell
Contact Andrew Piggott
Old Sarum Airfield, Salisbury, Wiltshire, SP4 6BJ
☎ 01722 320120 F 01722 328828
Stock size Small
Stock Indonesian furniture, accessories
Trade only Yes
Open Mon–Fri 8am–5pm

Trevan's Old Books
Contact John Cocking
30 Catherine Street, Salisbury, Wiltshire, SP1 2DA
☎ 01722 325818 F 01722 341181
E john.cocking@virgin.net
W www.abebooks.com/home/trevan
Est. 1994 *Stock size* Large
Stock General bookseller with some antiquarian
Open Mon–Sat 9.30am–5.30pm
Services Full Internet book search

Chris Wadge Clocks
Contact Patrick Wadge
83 Fisherton Street, Salisbury, Wiltshire, SP2 7ST
☎ 01722 334467
Est. 1985 *Stock size* Small
Stock Carriage clocks, Vienna regulators, dial and mantel clocks, 1890–1900
Open Tues–Sat 9am–4pm
closed 1–2pm
Services Restorations

Woolley and Wallis Salisbury Salerooms Ltd (SOFAA, BACA Award Winner 2002)
Contact Sarah Bennie
51–61 Castle Street, Salisbury, Wiltshire, SP1 3SU
☎ 01722 424500 F 01722 424508
E enquiries@woolleyandwallis.co.uk
W www.woolleyandwallis.co.uk
Est. 1884
Open Mon–Fri 9am–5.30pm
Sat 9am–noon
Sales Household sales generally fortnightly on Fri at 10am, viewing Thurs 10am–7pm. 30 specialist sales a year including furniture, ceramics, rugs and textiles, silver and jewellery, wine, books and maps, paintings
Catalogues Yes

SWINDON

Antiques and All Pine
Contact Mr or Mrs Brown
11 Newport Street, Swindon, Wiltshire, SN1 3DX
☎ 01793 520259
Est. 1978 *Stock size* Large
Stock Antique and reproduction pine, reproduction brass and iron beds, old lace, linen and costume jewellery
Open Tues–Sat 10am–5.30pm
Mon 10am–4pm closed
Wed Sun

Penny Farthing Antiques
Contact Ann Farthing
Victoria Centre, 138–139 Victoria Road, Swindon, Wiltshire, SN1 3BU
☎ 01793 536668
Est. 1999 *Stock size* Large
No. of dealers 9
Stock Antiques and collectables
Open Mon–Sat 10am–5pm
Services Valuations

Sambourne House Antique Pine Ltd
Contact Tim or Kim Cove
Units 49–51, Brunel Shopping Centre, Swindon, Wiltshire, SN1 1LF
☎ 01793 610855
E tkcove34@globalnet.co.uk
W www.sambourne-antiques.co.uk
Est. 1986 *Stock size* Large
Stock Antique and reproduction pine furniture, smalls, decorative items
Open Mon–Sun 9am–5pm
Services Hand-built kitchens

Allan Smith
Contact Mr A Smith
Amity Cottage, 162 Beechcroft Road, Upper Stratton, Swindon, Wiltshire, SN2 7QE
☎ 01793 822977 F 01793 822977
M 07778 834342
E allansmithclocks@lineone.net
W www.allan-smith-antique-clocks.co.uk
Est. 1988 *Stock size* Large
Stock Decorative, unusual, good quality clocks including automata, Moonphase, painted dial, 30 hour, 8 day etc in mahogany, lacquer, walnut and marquetry. Mostly English longcase and bracket clocks. 50–60 fully restored longcases
Open By appointment any time
Services Valuations and clockfinder service

Swindon Auction Rooms
Contact Mrs H Burgin
The Planks, Old Town, Swindon, Wiltshire, SN3 1QP
☎ 01793 615915
Est. 1959
Open Mon–Fri 9am–5pm
Sales Periodic antique sales
Frequency Periodic

John Williams (PBFA)
Contact Mr Williams
93 Goddard Avenue, Swindon, Wiltshire, SN1 4HT
☎ 01793 533313
E john.williams24@virgin.net
W www.jwbooks.com
Est. 1994 *Stock size* Small
Stock Antiquarian and second-hand children's and illustrated books. Three catalogues a year
Open By appointment
Fairs PBFA

Dominic Winter Book Auctions
Contact Admin Office
The Old School, Maxwell Street, Swindon, Wiltshire, SN1 5DR
☎ 01793 611340 F 01793 491727
E info@dominicwinter.co.uk
W www.dominicwinter.co.uk
Est. 1988
Open Mon–Fri 9.30am–5.30pm
Sales General book sale Wed 11am, viewing day prior to sale 10am-7pm. Specialist single

category sale Thurs 11am, viewing day prior to sale 10am–7pm
Frequency 5 weeks
Catalogues Yes

WARMINSTER

Cassidy Antiques and Restorations (BABAADA)
Contact Matthew Cassidy
7 Silver Street, Warminster, Wiltshire, BA12 8PS
01985 213313 F 01985 213313
M 07050 206806
E matcas@supernet.com
W www.cassidyantiques.com
Est. 1994 *Stock size* Medium
Stock Georgian–Victorian furniture
Open Mon–Fri 9am–5pm
Sat 10am–5pm
Services Restorations

Choice Antiques
Contact Avril Bailey
4 Silver Street, Warminster, Wiltshire, BA12 8PS
01985 218924
Est. 1987 *Stock size* Medium
Stock Small, the unusual, furniture, decorative objects
Open Mon–Sat 10am–5.30pm
Services Valuations, shipping

Collectable Interiors
Contact David Swanton
33 Silver Street, Warminster, Wiltshire, BA12 8PT
01985 217177
Est. 1967 *Stock size* Medium
Stock Furniture and accessories
Open Mon–Sat 10am–5pm

European Accent (BABAADA)
Contact Claire Green
11 Silver Street, Warminster, Wiltshire, BA12 8PS
01985 219376 F 01749 813932
M 07941 116789
W www.europeanaccent.co.uk
Est. 2002 *Stock size* Small
Stock Decorative furniture and accessories, extensive range of items from country and primitive to formal and sophisticated
Open Mon–Fri 10am–5pm
Sat 10am–4pm
Fairs Newark

Annabelle Giltsoff (BABAADA)
Contact Anabelle Giltsoff
10 Silver Street, Warminster, Wiltshire, BA12 8PS
01985 218188
Est. 1984 *Stock size* Medium
Stock Paintings and frames
Open Mon–Sat 9.30am–1pm 2–5pm
Fairs Shepton Mallet, Newark, NEC (June)
Services Picture restoration and gilding

Isabella Antiques (BABAADA)
Contact Mr B W Semke
11 Silver Street, Warminster, Wiltshire, BA12 8PS
01985 218933
Est. 1990 *Stock size* Medium
Stock 18th–19thC mahogany furniture,
Open Mon–Sat 10am–5pm

Obelisk Antiques (LAPADA, BABAADA)
Contact Mr P Tanswell
2 Silver Street, Warminster, Wiltshire, BA12 8PS
01985 846646 F 01985 219901
M 07718 630673
E all@obelisk-antiques.freeserve.co.uk
Est. 1979 *Stock size* Large
Stock 18th–19thC French, English and Continental furniture
Open Mon–Sat 10am–1pm 2–5.30pm

Warminster Antique Centre (BABAADA)
Contact Mr P Walton
6 Silver Street, Warminster, Wiltshire, BA12 8PT
01985 847269 F 01985 211778
M 07860 584193
Est. 1993 *Stock size* Large
No. of dealers 15
Stock Wide range of antiques and collectable items, furniture, clocks, paintings, models, linens, fabrics, etc
Open Mon–Sat 10am–5pm
Services Valuations

WEST YATTON

Heirloom & Howard Ltd (BABAADA)
Contact David or Angela Howard
Manor Farm, West Yatton, Chippenham, Wiltshire, SN14 7EU
01249 783038 F 01249 783039
Est. 1973 *Stock size* Medium
Stock Chinese armorial and other porcelain, armorial paintings, coach panels, hall chairs, portrait engravings
Open Mon–Fri 10am–6pm
Sat 10am–6pm or by appointment
Services Bidding at auction

WESTBURY

Ray Coggins Antiques
Contact Mr R Coggins
1 Fore Street, Westbury, Wiltshire, BA13 3AU
01373 826574 F 01373 827996
Est. 1974 *Stock size* Large
Stock Antique, country and decorative furniture, architectural antiques
Open Mon–Fri 9am–5pm

WILTON

Bay Tree Antiques
Contact Mrs J D Waymouth
26 North Street, Wilton, Wiltshire, SP2 0HJ
01722 743392 F 01722 743392
Est. 1997 *Stock size* Medium
Stock Period furniture, decorative furniture and items
Open Mon–Sat 9am–5.30pm
Fairs Battersea Decorartive

Hingstons of Wilton
Contact Nick Hingston
36 North Street, Wilton, Wiltshire, SP2 0HJ
01722 742263
E nick@hingston-antiques.freeserve.co.uk
W hingston-antiques.freeserve.co.uk
Est. 1976 *Stock size* Large
Stock 18th–early 20thC furniture, clocks, pictures
Open Mon–Fri 9am–5pm
Sat 10am–4pm
Services Valuations

Carol Musselwhite Antiques
Contact Mrs C Musselwhite
6 West St, Wilton, Salisbury, Wiltshire, SP2 0DF
01722 742573
E carolmusselwhite@hotmail.com
Est. 1990 *Stock size* Large
Stock China, glass, linen, lace, out-of-production Derby
Open Tues–Sat 10am–5pm

EAST

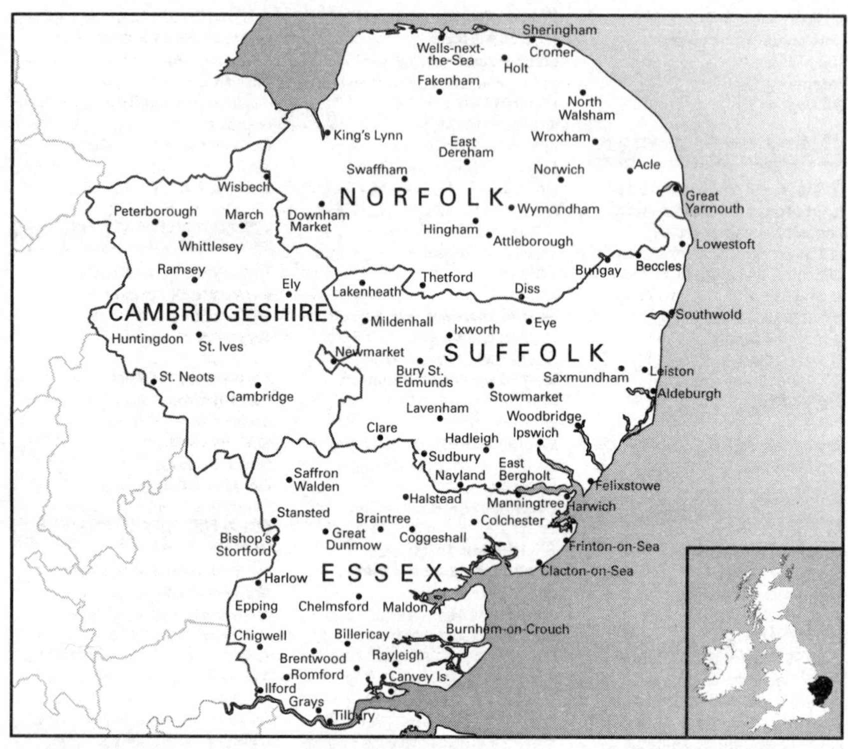

CAMBRIDGESHIRE

BALSHAM

⊞ Ward-Thomas Antiques
Contact Mr C R F Ward-Thomas
✉ **7 High Street, Balsham, Cambridge, Cambridgeshire, CB1 6DJ** P
☎ 01223 892431 Ⓕ 01223 892367
Ⓔ ward-thomas@freecom.uk.com
Est. 1997 ***Stock size*** Large
Stock Continental pine furniture, furniture accessories
Open Mon–Fri 9am–5pm
Sat 10am–5pm Sun 10am–4pm
Fairs Newark, Kempton Park
Services Restorations, mail order

BARTON

⊞ Bagatelle Antiques
Contact Mr Martyn Jeffrey
✉ **Burwash Manor Barns, New Road, Barton, Cambridge, Cambridgeshire, CB3 7AY** P
☎ 01223 264400 Ⓕ 01223 264445
Ⓜ 07714 104519
Ⓔ martyn@bagatelle-antiques.co.uk
Ⓦ www.bagatelle-antiques.co.uk
Est. 1998 ***Stock size*** Medium
Stock General antiques, decorative items, garden items
Open Mon–Fri 9am–5pm
Sat noon–5pm

BURWELL

⊞ Antiques Emporium
Contact Mr Stephen Hunt
✉ **59 High Street, Burwell, Cambridge, Cambridgeshire, CB5 0HD** P
☎ 01638 741155
Est. 1994 ***Stock size*** Medium
Stock General antiques
Open Mon–Sat 10.30am–5pm
Sun 11am–5pm closed Wed Thurs
Fairs Rowley Mile, Kempton
Services Restorations

⊞ Peter Norman Antiques
Contact Mr Tony Marpole
✉ **55 North Street, Burwell, Cambridge, Cambridgeshire, CB5 0BA** P
☎ 01638 616914
Est. 1979 ***Stock size*** Medium
Stock 18th–19thC furniture, Oriental rugs, clocks, pictures, prints
Open Mon–Sat 9am–5.30pm
Fairs Stafford, Newmarket
Services Restorations

CAMBRIDGE

⊞ Jess Applin (BADA)
Contact Mr J Applin
✉ **8 Lensfield Road, Cambridge, Cambridgeshire, CB2 1EG** P
☎ 01223 315168
Est. 1975 ***Stock size*** Medium
Stock 17th–19thC furniture, works of art
Open Mon–Sat 9.30am–5.30pm

⊞ John Beazor & Sons Ltd (BADA)
Contact Mr M Beazor

✉ **78–80 Regent Street, Cambridge, Cambridgeshire, CB2 1DP**
☎ 01223 355178 Ⓕ 01223 355183
Ⓜ 07774 123379
Ⓔ martin@johnbeazorantiques.co.uk
Ⓦ www.johnbeazorantiques.co.uk
Est. 1875 *Stock size* Large
Stock English furniture late 17th–early 19thC furniture, clocks, barometers, decorative items
Open Mon–Fri 9.15am–5pm Sat 10am–4pm
Services Valuations

Bonhams
✉ **17 Emmanuel Road, Cambridge, Cambridgeshire, CB1 1JW**
☎ 01223 366523 Ⓕ 012223 300208
Ⓔ cambridge@bonhams.com
Ⓦ www.bonhams.com
Open Mon–Fri 8.30am–5pm

The Book Shop
Contact Mr P Bright or Mr H Hardinge
✉ **24 Magdalene Street, Cambridge, Cambridgeshire, CB3 OAF**
☎ 01223 362457
Est. 1996 *Stock size* Medium
Stock Antiquarian, second-hand and out-of-print books
Open Mon–Sat 10am–5.30pm

Books & Collectables Ltd
Contact Mr A Doyle
✉ **Unit 7–8, Railway Arches, Coldhams Road, Cambridge, Cambridgeshire, CB1 3EW** Ⓟ
☎ 01223 412845 Ⓕ 01223 412845
Ⓜ 07703 795206
Ⓔ ask@booksandcollectables.com
Ⓦ www.booksandcollectables.com
Est. 1996 *Stock size* Large
Stock 16thC–modern books, comics, toys, postcards, cigarette cards, records, pop memorabilia, magazines, china, furniture
Open Mon–Sat 9.30am–5pm Sun 10am–4pm
Services Valuations, shipping

Buckies (NAG, LAPADA)
Contact Mrs L Buckie
✉ **31 Trinity Street, Cambridge, Cambridgeshire, CB2 1TB**
☎ 01223 357910 Ⓕ 01233 357920
Est. 1953 *Stock size* Medium
Stock Jewellery, silver
Open Tues–Fri 9.45am–5pm Sat 9.30am–5.30pm
Services Valuations

Cheffins
Contact J G Law, C B Ashton or R Haywood
✉ **2 Clifton Road, Cambridge, Cambridgeshire, CB1 4BW** Ⓟ
☎ 01223 213343 Ⓕ 01223 413396
Ⓔ fine.art@cheffins.co.uk
Ⓦ www.cheffins.co.uk
Est. 1824
Open Mon–Fri 9am–5pm
Sales 45 sales a year of antiques and later furnishings, specialist fine art and furniture sales. Catalogues and information available on website
Frequency Fortnightly
Catalogues Yes

Peter Crabbe Antiques
Contact Mr P Crabbe
✉ **3 Pembroke Street, Cambridge, Cambridgeshire, CB2 3QY**
☎ 01223 357117
Est. 1988 *Stock size* Large
Stock English furniture, Asian porcelain, works of art
Open Mon–Sat 9.30am–5pm
Services Valuations

G David (ABA, PBFA, BA)
Contact David Asplin, N T Adams or B L Collings
✉ **16 St Edward's Passage, Cambridge, Cambridgeshire, CB2 3PJ**
☎ 01223 354619 Ⓕ 01223 324663
Est. 1896 *Stock size* Large
Stock Antiquarian books, prints, publishers' remainders, fine antiquarian books a speciality
Open Mon–Sat 9.30am–5pm
Fairs PBFA Oxford, London (June), ABA (Nov)

Gabor Cossa Antiques
Contact David Theobald
✉ **34 Trumpington Street, Cambridge, Cambridgeshire, CB2 1QY** Ⓟ
☎ 01223 356049
Est. 1947 *Stock size* Large
Stock 18th–19thC ceramics, small items
Open Mon–Sat 10am–5.30pm

Granta Coins, Collectables and Antiquities
Contact Mr Alan Fordham
✉ **23 Magdalene Street, Cambridge, Cambridgeshire, CB3 0AF** Ⓟ
☎ 01223 361662 Ⓕ 01223 361662
Ⓜ 07713 513813
Ⓔ coingranta@aol.com
Est. 1978 *Stock size* Large
Stock Pre-Roman to modern coins
Open Mon–Sat 10am–5pm
Services Valuations, appraisals, probate

Gwydir Street Antiques
Contact Mrs P Gibb
✉ **Units 1 & 2, Dales Brewery, Gwydir Street, Cambridge, Cambridgeshire, CB1 2LJ** Ⓟ
☎ 01223 356391
Est. 1987 *Stock size* Medium
No. of dealers 10
Stock Furniture, bric-a-brac, collectables, decorative items
Open Mon–Sat 10am–5pm Sun 11am–5pm

The Haunted Bookshop (PBFA)
Contact Mrs Sarah Key
✉ **9 St Edward's Passage, Cambridge, Cambridgeshire, CB2 3PJ**
☎ 01223 312913 Ⓕ 08700 0569392
Ⓔ sarahkey@hauntedbooks.demon.co.uk
Est. 1987 *Stock size* Medium
Stock Antiquarian, second-hand, children's books, particularly girls' school stories
Open Mon–Sat 10am–5pm
Fairs PBFA
Services Mail order worldwide, book search for children's titles, catalogues, valuations

The Hive
Contact Mrs B Burch
✉ **Unit 3, Dales Brewery, Gwydir Street, Cambridge, Cambridgeshire, CB1 2LG** Ⓟ
☎ 01223 300269
Est. 1987
No. of dealers 10
Stock Antique pine, kitchenware, collectables, period lighting, pictures, Victorian–Edwardian furniture, bric-a-brac

Open Mon–Sat 9.30am–5.30pm Sun 11am–5pm
Services Commissions undertaken

La Belle Epoque
Contact Mrs C Keverne
55a Hills Road, Cambridge, Cambridgeshire, CB2 1NT
01223 506688
Est. 1986 *Stock size* Medium
Stock Period lighting, small items
Open Tues–Sat 11am–5pm

The Old Chemist Shop Antique Centre
Contact Mrs J Tucker
206 Mill Road, Cambridge, Cambridgeshire, CB1 3NF
01223 247324
Est. 1996 *Stock size* Large
Stock General antiques, collectables
Open Mon–Fri 10am–5pm Sat 10am–5.30pm
Services Clock repair, house clearance

Those Were The Days
Contact Julia or Richard Henderson
91 & 93 Mill Road, Cambridge, Cambridgeshire, CB1 2AW
Est. 1991 *Stock size* Large
No. of dealers 10
Stock Furniture, lighting, fireplaces
Open Mon–Sat 9.30am–5.30pm Sun 11am–5pm

Ken Trotman Ltd (PBFA)
Contact Mr or Mrs Brown
Unit 11, The Old Maltings, 135 Ditton Walk, Cambridge, Cambridgeshire, CB5 8PY
01223 211030 01223 212317
trotman@netcomuk.co.uk
www.kentrotman.ltd.uk
Est. 1950 *Stock size* Large
Stock Antiquarian and new books on military history. Catalogues available
Open By appointment

Valued History
Contact Mr Paul Murawski
13 Benet Street, Cambridge, Cambridgeshire, CB2 3PT
01223 319319 01223 319319
murawski@pmurawski.fsnet.co.uk
www.historyforsale.co.uk
Est. 1996 *Stock size* Medium
Stock Coins, antiquities
Open Tues–Sat 10am–5pm
Services Valuations

Willroy Antiques Centre
Contact Mr Roy Williams
Unit 5, Dales Brewery, Gwydir Street, Cambridge, Cambridgeshire, CB1 2LJ
01223 311687 01480 352853
07793 0193830
rwill61359@aol.com
Est. 1985 *Stock size* Large
No. of dealers 6
Stock General antiques
Open Mon–Sat 10am–5pm Sun noon–4pm
Services Restorations

CHATTERIS

James Fuller and Son
Contact Steven Fuller
51 Huntingdon Road, Chatteris, Cambridgeshire, PE16 6JE
01354 692740
Est. 1919 *Stock size* Large
Stock Telephone and letter boxes
Open Mon–Fri 8am–12.30pm 1.30pm–5pm

CHITTERING

Simon & Penny Rumble Antiques
Contact Mrs P Rumble
Causeway End Farmhouse, School Lane, Chittering, Cambridge, Cambridgeshire, CB5 9PW
01223 861831 07778 917300
penny@therumbles.freeserve.co.uk
Est. 1980 *Stock size* Small
Stock Early oak, country furniture, woodcarving
Open By appointment
Fairs NEC

COMBERTON

Comberton Antiques
Contact Mrs McEvoy
5A West Street, Comberton, Cambridgeshire, CB3 7DS
01223 262674
dewisem@free4all.co.uk
www.comberton_antiques.co.uk
Est. 1984 *Stock size* Large
Stock General furniture including Continental pine
Open Fri Sat Mon 10am–5pm Sun 2–5pm
Fairs Newark, Ardingly
Services Shipping

DUXFORD

Riro D Mooney
Contact Mr R Mooney
Mill Lane, Duxford, Cambridgeshire, CB2 4PS
01223 832252
Est. 1946 *Stock size* Large
Stock Victorian–Edwardian furniture
Open Mon–Sat 9am–6.30pm Sun 10am–noon 2.30–5pm
Services Restoration

ELY

Cloisters Antiques (PBFA)
Contact Barry Lonsdale
1a Lynn Road, Ely, Cambridgeshire, CB7 4EG
01353 668558 07767 881677
info@cloistersantiques.co.uk
www.cloistersantiques.co.uk
Est. 1997 *Stock size* Medium
Stock General clocks, china, second-hand and antiquarian books, mainly smalls
Open Mon–Sat 10.30am–4.30pm Sun 12.30–4.30pm closed Tues
Services Valuations

Mrs Mills' Antiques Etc.
Contact Mrs M Mills
1a St Mary's Street, Ely, Cambridgeshire, CB7 4ER
01353 664268
Est. 1968 *Stock size* Large
Stock Porcelain, silver, jewellery
Open Mon–Sat 10am–5pm closed Tues
Fairs Heritage Grosvenor Square

Rookery Farm Antiques
Contact Rachel Lemkow
Waterside Antiques, Ely, Cambridgeshire, CB7 4AU
01284 735141 01284 735161
rachel.lemkov@btinternet.com
07789 405635
www.antique-kitchenalia.co.uk
Est. 1989 *Stock size* Large
Stock Decorative furniture, bamboo, pine
Open Mon–Sat 9am–5.30pm Sun 11.30am–5.30pm
Fairs Newark

Rowley Fine Art
Contact Diane White
8 Downham Road, Ely, Cambridgeshire, CB6 1AH
01353 653020 01353 653022
mail@rowleyfineart.com
www.rowleyfineart.com
Est. 2001
Open Mon–Fri 9am–5pm
Sales General sales every 2nd Sat 10.30am, viewing Fri 9am–7pm
Frequency Bi-monthly
Catalogues Yes

Waterside Antiques
Contact Mr G Peters
The Wharf, Waterside, Ely, Cambridgeshire, CB7 4AU
01353 667066
Est. 1985
No. of dealers 68
Stock Furniture, collectables
Open Mon–Sat 9.30am–5.30pm Sun 11.30am–5.30pm
Services Valuations, clearances

FORDHAM

Phoenix Antiques
Contact Mr K Bycroft
Homelands, 1 Carter Street, Fordham, Ely, Cambridgeshire, CB7 5NG
01638 720363
Est. 1966 *Stock size* Medium
Stock Everything for a European interior prior to 1750
Open By appointment only
Services Valuations

GODMANCHESTER

The Bookshop Godmanchester (BA)
Contact J H or D L Lewis
11 Post Street, Godmanchester, Huntingdon, Cambridgeshire, PE18 8BA
01480 455020 01480 434619
Est. 1977 *Stock size* Large
Stock Antiquarian, second-hand and new books, children's books a speciality
Open Tues–Sat 9.30am–1pm 2–5.30pm
Services Book search

HADDENHAM

Hereward Books (PBFA)
Contact Mr R Pratt
17 High Street, Haddenham, Ely, Cambridgeshire, CB6 3XA
01353 740821 01353 741721
sales@herewardbooks.co.uk
www.herewardbooks.co.uk
Est. 1984 *Stock size* Medium
Stock Rare and collectable books, specializing in field sports and fishing
Open Mon Tues Thurs 10am–4pm Fri Sat 10am–1pm
Fairs PBFA Russell Hotel, CLA Game Fair

Ludovic Potts Antiques (BAFRA)
Contact Mr Ludovic Potts
Unit 1–1a, Station Road, Haddenham, Ely, Cambridgeshire, CB6 3XD
01353 741537 01353 741822
07889 341671
mail@restorers.co.uk
www.restorers.co.uk
Est. 2001 *Stock size* Small
Stock Polished wood furniture, upholstered chairs, sofas, soft furnishings, porcelain, gilt mirrors
Open By appointment
Services Restorations

HUNTINGDON

Huntingdon Trading Post
Contact Mr John De'Ath
1 St Mary's Street, Huntingdon, Cambridgeshire, PE29 3PE
01480 450998 01480 431142
j.death@ntlworld.com
www.huntingdontradingpost.co.uk
Est. 2001 *Stock size* Large
No. of dealers 35
Stock General antiques, including furniture, clocks, collectables, brassware, pictures
Open Mon–Sat 9am–5pm Sun 10am–2pm

Mark Seabrook Antiques
Contact Mr M Seabrook
PO Box 396, Huntingdon, Cambridgeshire, PE28 0ZA
01788 510772
07770 721931
enquiries@markseabrook.com
www.markseabrook.com
Est. 1996 *Stock size* Medium
Stock Early English oak and country furniture, metalware, treen, ceramics
Open By appointment 7 days
Fairs NEC, Kensington, Chelsea
Services Restorations

IMPINGTON

Woodcock House Antiques
Contact Mr A M Peat
83–85 Station Road, Impington, Cambridge, Cambridgeshire, CB4 9NP
01223 232858
Est. 1978 *Stock size* Large
Stock Late 19thC decorative furniture, Aesthetic items, smalls
Open Mon–Fri 10am–5pm or by appointment
Fairs Grosvenor House
Services Valuations

LANDBEACH

Cambridge Pianola Company and J V Pianos
Contact Tom Poole
The Limes, High Street, Landbeach, Cambridgeshire, CB4 8DR
01223 861348 01223 441276
ftpoole@talk21.com
www.cambridgepianolacompany.co.uk
Est. 1972 *Stock size* Medium
Stock Pianos, pianolas and player pianos
Open By appointment
Services Restorations

MARCH

Fagins
Contact Mrs P Humby
9 Station Road, March, Cambridgeshire, PE15 0JL
01354 656445
Est. 1998 *Stock size* Medium
Stock General antiques, furniture, collectables
Open Mon–Sat 10am–5pm closed Tues

PETERBOROUGH

Antiques & Curios Shop
Contact Mr M Mason
249 Lincoln Road, Millfield, Peterborough, Cambridgeshire, PE1 2PL
01733 314948 07974 548873

Est. 1989 *Stock size* Medium
Stock Mahogany, oak, pine, country furniture, fireplaces
Open Mon–Sat 10am–5pm
Fairs Newark, RAF Swinderby
Services Restorations

Cards 'N' Collectables
Contact Colin Dorman
25 Misterton, Orton Goldhay, Peterborough, Cambridgeshire, PE2 5SZ
01733 232272
www.cards-n-collectables.com
Est. 2000
Stock Trading cards, collectable card games, action figures, movie memorabilia
Open Mon 10am–4pm
Tues–Sat 10am–6pm
Sun noon–4pm

T V Coles
Contact Mr T V Coles
981 Lincoln Road, Peterborough, Cambridgeshire, PE4 6AH
01733 577268
Est. 1980 *Stock size* Medium
Stock Antiquarian, out-of-print and second-hand books, militaria, ephemera, postcards etc
Open Mon–Sat 9am–4.30pm

Fitzwilliam Antiques Centre
Contact Mr Paul Stafford
20–22 Fitzwilliam Street, Peterborough, Cambridgeshire, PE1 2RX
01733 566346 F 01733 565415
Est. 1990 *Stock size* Large
No. of dealers 20
Stock General antiques, collectables
Open Mon–Sat 10am–5pm
Services Valuations, restorations, repairs

Old Soke Books
Contact Peter or Linda Clay
68 Burghley Road, Peterborough, Cambridgeshire, PE1 2QE
01733 564147
Est. 1984 *Stock size* Small
Stock Antiquarian books, small antiques, pictures, prints, maps
Open By appointment only
Services Valuations

RAMSEY

Abbey Antiques
Contact Mr J Smith
63 Great Whyte, Ramsey, Cambridgeshire, PE26 1HL
01487 814753
Est. 1979 *Stock size* Medium
Stock General antiques, collectables
Open Tues–Sun 10am–5pm
Fairs Alexandra Palace
Services Valuations, Mabel Lucie Attwell Museum and Collectors' Club

Antique Barometers
Contact William Rae
Wingfield, 26 Biggin Lane, Ramsey, Cambridgeshire, PE26 1NB
01487 814060 F 01487 814060
antiquebarometers@talk21.com
Est. 1996 *Stock size* Medium
Stock Early stick and wheel barometers, barographs
Open By appointment
Fairs Hinchingbrook House, Putteridge Bury House
Services Valuations, restorations

SOHAM

Burwell Auctions
Contact Mr N Reed-Herbert
The Church Hall, High Street, Soham, Ely, Cambridgeshire, CB7 5HD
01353 727100 F 01353 727101
Est. 1984
Open By appointment
Sales General antique sales, viewing day prior to sale 9am–5pm and day of sale 9am–10.30am or by appointment
Frequency Variable
Catalogues Yes

ST IVES

Hyperion Auction Centre (ICOM)
Contact Mrs Pat Bernard or Mr Colin Gunter
Station Road, St Ives, Huntingdon, Cambridgeshire, PE27 5BH
01480 464140 F 01480 497552
M 07788 486590
enquiries@hyperion-auctions.co.uk
www.hyperion-auctions.co.uk
Est. 1995
Open Mon–Sat 9.30am–5pm
Sales General antiques sale 2nd Mon monthly 10.30am, viewing Sat prior 9.30am–5pm Mon 9.30–10.30am
Frequency Monthly
Catalogues Yes

Quay Court Antiques
Contact Mr M Knight
Bull Lane, Bridge Street, St Ives, Huntingdon, Cambridgeshire, PE17 4AZ
01480 468295
michaelknight@compuserve.com
Est. 1972 *Stock size* Medium
Stock Pottery, porcelain, pictures, jewellery
Open Mon 11am–2pm
Wed 10.30am–3pm
Fri 11am–2pm Sat 11am–4pm
Services Valuations, talks to antiques clubs

ST NEOTS

Brentside Programmes
Contact Mr Chris Ward
1 Dial Close, Little Paxton, St Neots, Huntingdon, Cambridgeshire, PE19 4QN
01480 474682 F 01480 370650
sales@brentside.co.uk
www.brentside.co.uk
Est. 1974 *Stock size* Medium
Stock Football memorabilia, mostly mail order
Open Mon–Fri 9am–5pm

Peggy's Pandora
Contact Mr B George
10 Crosskeys Mews, Market Square, St Neots, Huntingdon, Cambridgeshire, PE19 2AR
01480 403580
Est. 1991 *Stock size* Medium
Stock Postcards, medals, coins, toys, small items
Open Mon–Sat 9am–5pm

WHITTLESEY

Pinestrip
Contact Kent or Adele Griffin
Gildenburgh Waters, Eastrea Road, Whittlesey, Peterborough, Cambridgeshire, PE7 2AR
01733 351199 F 01733 840076
M 07960 279032
www.pinestrip-pine.co.uk
Est. 1992 *Stock size* Medium

Stock Antique Continental pine furniture
Open Mon–Fri 9am–5pm Sat 9am–3pm
Services Pine stripping

WISBECH

Steve Carpenter
Contact Mr S Carpenter
96 Norfolk Street, Wisbech, Cambridgeshire, PE13 2LF
01945 588411 F 01945 588411
M 07939 112569
Est. 1997 *Stock size* Medium
Stock 18th–19thC country furniture, longcase clocks, quality smalls
Open Mon–Sat 9am–5pm closed Wed

Peter A Crofts (BADA)
Contact Mr P A Crofts
117 High Road, Wisbech, Cambridgeshire, PE14 0DN
01945 584614 M 07803 740972
E crofts@bigwig.net
Est. 1949 *Stock size* Large
Stock General antiques, furniture, silver, china
Open Mon–Fri 8am–4.30pm or by appointment
Services Valuations

Granny's Cupboard Antiques
Contact Mr R J Robbs
34 Old Market, Wisbech, Cambridgeshire, PE13 1NF
01945 589606/870730
M 07721 616154
Est. 1985 *Stock size* Medium
Stock Victorian–Edwardian china, glass and furniture to 1950s
Open Tues Thurs 10.30am–4pm Sat 10.30am–3pm
Fairs The Maltings, Ely

Grounds & Co
Contact Mr R Barnwell
2 Nene Quay, Wisbech, Cambridgeshire, PE13 1AQ
01945 585041 F 01945 474255
M 07885 431520
Est. 1792
Open Mon–Fri 9am–5pm Sat 9am–4pm
Sales Antiques and collectors' sales 3 a year. Phone for details
Catalogues Yes

Maxey & Son
Contact John Maxey
Auction Hall, Cattle Market Chase, Wisbech, Cambridgeshire, PE13 1RD
01945 584609 F 01945 589440
E mail@maxeyandson.co.uk
W www.maxeyandson.co.uk
Est. 1856
Open Mon–Fri 9am–5pm Sat 9am–noon
Sales General sales with some antiques and collectables twice weekly on Wed and Sat 10am, viewing any day. Occasional special antiques sales
Catalogues No

ESSEX

BARKING

Collectors' Corner
Contact Mrs S Lee
401a Ripple Road, Barking, Essex, IG11 9RB
020 8591 4441
Est. 1999 *Stock size* Large
Stock General antiques, small items, china, glass, jewellery
Open Mon–Fri 9.30am–5.30pm
Services House clearance

BASILDON

Bear Essentials
Contact Kim Brown
64a Eastgate Shopping Centre, Basildon, Essex, SS14 1AF
01268 270154 F 01268 270154
E hugs@companyofbears.com
W www.companyofbears.com
Est. 2000 *Stock size* Large
Stock Collectable bears, Steiff, Dean's and Hermann Club store
Open Mon–Sat 10am–5.30pm

BATTLESBRIDGE

Battlesbridge Antiques Centre
Contact Mr Jim Gallie
Hawk Hill, Battlesbridge, Wickford, Essex, SS11 7RE
01268 575000 F 01268 575001
E jim.gallie@virgin.net
W www.battlesbridge.com
Est. 1969 *Stock size* Large
No. of dealers 80
Stock General antiques, collectables
Open Mon–Sun 10am–5.30pm
Services Valuations

The Bones Lane Antiques Centre
Contact Mr Pettitt
The Green, Chelmsford Road, Battlesbridge, Wickford, Essex, SS11 7RJ
01268 763500 F 01268 763500
Est. 1969 *Stock size* Medium
No. of dealers 12
Stock Gas, oil and early electric lighting, gramophones
Open Tues–Sun 10am–4.30pm closed Thurs
Services Restorations of lighting and gramophones

Bridgebarn Antiques (EADA)
Contact Mr Pettitt
The Bones Lane Antiques Centre, The Green, Chelmsford Road, Battlesbridge, Wickford, Essex, SS11 7RJ
01268 763500 F 01268 763500
Est. 1969 *Stock size* Medium
Stock Gas, oil and early electric lighting, gramophones
Open Tues–Sun 10am–4.30pm closed Thurs
Services Restorations of lighting and gramophones

Cottage Antiques
Contact Mr R Jarman
The Old Granary, Battlesbridge Antique Centre, Battlesbridge, Wickford, Essex, SS11 7RE
01268 764138 F 01268 764138
M 07958 618629
E bob@cottageantiquefurniture.com
W www.cottageantiquefurniture.com
Est. 1998 *Stock size* Large
Stock Georgian–Edwardian items, mainly furniture, collectables
Open Mon–Sun 10am–5.30pm
Services Furniture restoration, French polishing, furniture search

Phoenix Fireplaces
Contact John or Cris
Hawk Hill, Battlesbridge, Essex, SS11 7RE
01268 768844 F 01268 768844
M 07956 556442
W www.phoenix-fireplaces.co.uk
Est. 1991 *Stock size* Large
Stock Fireplaces
Open Mon–Sun 10am–5.30pm

Trails End Collectables Ltd
Contact Pat Stoneham
3rd Floor, The Old Granary, Battlesbridge Antique Centre, Battlesbridge, Wickford, Essex, SS11 7RE
01277 656750 F 01268 764138
M 07941 179031
E vintage@collectibles99.freeserve.co.uk
Est. 1991 *Stock size* Small
Stock 20thC US collectables
Open Mon–Sun 10am–5.30pm

BAYTHORN END

Swan Antiques
Contact Mr K Mercado
Baythorn End, Clare (between Clare and Haverhill), Essex, CO9 4AF
01440 785306 M 07850 426420
E swanantiques@aol.com
Est. 1993 *Stock size* Large
Stock Georgian–Edwardian furniture, fireplaces, firebacks, surrounds, pine furniture, glass, smalls
Open Mon–Sun 10am–5.30pm
Fairs Newark

BENFLEET

E J & C A Brooks (BNTA, IBNS)
Contact Mr E J Brooks
44 Kiln Road, Thundersley, Benfleet, Essex, SS7 1TB
01268 753835 M 07850 262629
Est. 1974 *Stock size* Large
Stock Coins, English and foreign bank notes
Open By appointment
Fairs York, Birmingham, Cumberland Hotel
Services Free valuations

BRENTWOOD

Le-Potier
Contact Mr S Hall
42 King's Road, Brentwood, Essex, CM14 4DW
01277 216310
Est. 1985 *Stock size* Small
Stock Collectables
Open Tues–Sun 10am–5pm closed Thurs
Services China restoration

BRIGHTLINGSEA

Shipwreck Centre
Contact Mr M K Kettle
22e Marshes Yard, Victoria Place, Brightlingsea, Colchester, Essex, CO7 0BX
01206 307307
W www.sos.uk.com
Est. 1995 *Stock size* Large
No. of dealers 15
Stock Collectables, furniture, books, arts, crafts
Open Mon–Sun 10am–5pm
Services House clearance

BROOMFIELD

The Cottage Collection
Contact Mr I Honeywood
93 Main Road, Broomfield, Chelmsford, Essex, CM1 7DQ
01245 442013 M 07741 448025
Est. 1994 *Stock size* Medium
Stock Antique pine furniture, ceramics, brass, pictures
Open Sun–Sat 11am–5pm
Services Free delivery

Hutchison Antiques and Interiors (EADA)
Contact Mr Gavin Hutchison
163 Main Road, Broomfield, Chelmsford, Essex, CM1 7DJ
01245 441184 F 01245 441184
Est. 1984 *Stock size* Large
Stock Period furniture, paintings, decorative items
Open Tues–Sat 11am–5pm
Fairs NEC
Services Restorations, interior design service

CHELMSFORD

Chelmsford Coin Centre
Contact Mr D Drury
219 Springfield Road, Chelmsford, Essex, CM2 6JS
01245 261278
Est. 1968 *Stock size* Medium
Stock Ancient and modern coins, medals
Open By appointment

Cooper Hirst Auctions
Contact Mr R L C Hirst FRICS
The Granary Saleroom, Victoria Road, Chelmsford, Essex, CM2 6LH
01245 260535 F 01245 345185
Est. 1950
Open Mon–Fri 9am–5pm
Sales Regular antiques sales and sales of household effects, furniture, electrical goods, machinery, tools. Phone for details
Catalogues Yes

S H Rowland
Contact Mr S H Rowland
42 Mildmay Road, Chelmsford, Essex, CM2 0DZ
01245 354251 F 01245 344466
Est. 1946
Open Mon–Fri 9am–5.30pm
Sales Lesser-quality goods alternate weeks, antiques 2–3 a year on Wed, viewing Tues 9am–4.30pm Wed 9–10am
Frequency 2 weeks
Catalogues Yes

CHIPPING ONGAR

Garners (EADA)
Contact Nick Garner
The Barn (Next to the Two Brewers), Greensted Road, Chipping Ongar, Essex, CM5 9HD
01245 261863
M 07970 206682
E nickgarner@btinternet.com
W www.ngarners.co.uk
Est. 1998 *Stock size* Large
Stock Studio and art pottery, Sally Tuffin, Dennis chinaworks, Lise Moorcroft, Dean Sherwin, Roger Cockram, Highland stoneware, Dartington pottery, Alexandra Copeland. Also general antiques
Open Sat Sun 10am–4pm
Services Valuations

COGGESHALL

Argentum Antiques
Contact Mrs Dianne Carr
1 Church Street, Coggeshall, Essex, CO6 1TU
01376 561365
Est. 1994 *Stock size* Medium
Stock Early oak furniture, silver, decorative items
Open Mon–Sat 10.30am–5pm closed Wed Sun

English Rose Antiques
Contact Mr M Barrett
7 Church Street, Coggeshall, Essex, CO6 1TU
01376 562683 F 01376 563450
M 07770 880790

englishroseantiques@hotmail.com
Est. 1983 *Stock size* Large
Stock Antiques and country pine furniture
Open Mon–Sun 10am–5.30pm
Fairs Ardingly, Newark
Services Stripping, finishing

Lion House Antiques Ltd (EADA)
Contact Mr P Young
10 East Street, Coggeshall, Colchester, Essex, CO6 1SH
01376 563282 07802 955829
lionpy@aol.com
Est. 1991 *Stock size* Large
Stock 17th–19thC English furniture, chairs, oak farmhouse tables
Open Mon–Sat 10am–5pm Sun by appointment
Fairs Newark, DMG fairs, Arthur Swallow fairs
Services Valuations, restorations, house clearance

Partners in Pine
Contact Mr W T Newton
63–65 West Street, Coggeshall, Colchester, Essex, CO6 1NS
01376 561972
Est. 1983 *Stock size* Medium
Stock Victorian pine furniture
Open Mon–Sun 10am–6pm closed Wed

COLCHESTER

Alphabets
Contact Mr Briggs
13 Trinity, Colchester, Essex, CO1 1JN
01206 572751
Est. 1974 *Stock size* Medium
Stock Antiquarian and second-hand books
Open Mon–Sat 10am–5pm closed Thurs

Elizabeth Cannon Antiques
Contact Mrs E Cannon
85 Crouch Street, Colchester, Essex, CO3 3EZ
01206 575817
Est. 1978 *Stock size* Large
Stock Antique glass, jewellery, silver, porcelain, furniture
Open Mon–Sat 9.30am–5.30pm

The Castle Book Shop (PBFA)
Contact Mr R Green
40 Osborne Street, Colchester, Essex, CO2 7DB
01206 577520 01206 577520
Est. 1947 *Stock size* Large
Stock Antiquarian and second-hand books, East Anglia, archaeology, modern first editions, maps, prints
Open Mon–Sat 9am–5pm
Fairs PBFA
Services Book search

Colton Antiques
Contact Mr G Colton
Station Road, Colchester, Essex, CO5 9NP
01376 571504
Est. 1992 *Stock size* Small
Stock 18th–19thC furniture, Georgian, decorative furniture
Open Mon–Sat 8am–5pm
Services Restorations

G K R Bonds Ltd (IBSS)
Contact Hazel Fisher
Unit 4, Park Farm, Inworth, Colchester, Essex, CO5 9SH
01376 571711 01376 570125
Est. 1979 *Stock size* Large
Stock Old bonds, share certificates
Open Mail order only
Services Valuations, annual and quarterly lists

Mill Antiques
Contact David Illingsworth
10 East Street, Colchester, Essex, CO1 2TX
01206 500996 *Stock size* Large
Stock Victorian, Edwardian mahogany furniture
Open Mon–Sat 10am–5pm

Reeman, Dansie, Howe & Son
Contact Mr J Grinter
12 Headgate, Colchester, Essex, CO3 3BT
01206 574271 01206 578213
auctions@reemans.com
Est. 1881
Open Mon–Fri 9am–5.30pm
Sales Antiques and general sales Wed 10am, viewing Tues 9am–7pm Wed 9am–10pm. Also weekly household goods sales
Frequency 6–8 weeks
Catalogues Yes

Revival
Contact Mrs B Addison
23b Drury Road, Colchester, Essex, CO2 7UY
01206 506162
Est. 1999 *Stock size* Large
Stock Architectural salvage, furniture, decorative curios
Open Tues–Sat 10am–4pm

Stanfords
Contact Mr David Lord
11 East Hill, Colchester, Essex, CO1 2QX
01206 868070 01206 869590
Est. 1995
Open Mon–Fri 9am–5.30pm
Sales General goods Tues 10am, antique furniture, collectables quarterly Tues 11am, viewing Sat 9am–1pm Mon noon–7pm Tues 9–10am
Frequency Weekly
Catalogues Yes

DANBURY

Danbury Antiques (EADA)
Contact Mrs Southgate
Eves Corner, Danbury, Chelmsford, Essex, CM3 4QF
01245 223035 01245 222740
07711 704652
Est. 1979 *Stock size* Large
Stock Jewellery, silver, ceramics, porcelain, furniture
Open Tues–Sat 10am–5pm Wed 10am–1pm Sun 10.30am–1pm
Fairs Furze Hill
Services Restorations

DEBDEN

Debden Antiques (EADA)
Contact Mr Edward Norman
Elder Street, Debden, Saffron Walden, Essex, CB11 3JY
01799 543007 01799 542482
info@debden-antiques.co.uk
www.debden-antiques.co.uk
Est. 1999 *Stock size* Large
No. of dealers 30
Stock 17th–19thC furniture, paintings, jewellery, silver, glass, rugs, garden ornaments, furniture
Open Mon–Sat 10am–5.30pm Sun 11am–4pm
Services Valuations, restorations, shipping

EPPING

Old Barn Antiques
Contact Mr T Quick
Hayleys Manor, Epping Upland, Epping, Essex, CM16 6PQ
01992 579007 F 01992 579008
Est. 1974 *Stock size* Large
Stock Furniture from 1850 onwards
Open Mon–Fri 9am–5pm or by appointment
Services Container packing

FINCHINGFIELD

Finchingfield Antiques Centre
Contact Mr Peter Curry
The Green, Finchingfield, Braintree, Essex, CM7 4JX
01371 810258
Est. 1996 *Stock size* Large
No. of dealers 45
Stock Furniture, silver, porcelain, antiquarian books, jewellery, collectables
Open Mon–Sun 10am–5.30pm

FRINTON-ON-SEA

Dickens Curios
Contact Miss M Wilsher
151 Connaught Avenue, Frinton-on-Sea, Essex, CO13 9AH
01255 674134
Est. 1970 *Stock size* Large
Stock Antiques, china, glass, pewter, copper, jewellery
Open Mon Fri 11am–1pm 2.15–5.30pm Tues Thurs 9.45am–1pm 2.15–5.30pm Sat 9.45am–5pm closed Wed pm
Services Buying from public

No 24 of Frinton
Contact Mr C Pereira
24 Connaught Avenue, Frinton-on-Sea, Essex, CO13 9PR
01255 670505
Est. 1993 *Stock size* Large
Stock Art Deco, general antiques, original prints
Open Mon–Sat 10am–5pm Sun 2–4pm closed Wed

Phoenix Trading
Contact Mr Tom Sheldon
130 Connaught Avenue, Frinton-on-Sea, Essex, CO13 9AD
01255 851094 F 01255 851094
Est. 1996 *Stock size* Large
Stock Antique pine
Open Tues–Sat 10am–4pm
Services Restorations, stripping, cabinet makers

GRAYS

Atticus Books
Contact Mr R Drake
8 London Road, Grays, Essex, RM17 5XY
01375 371200
M 07809 024845
Est. 1983 *Stock size* Large
Stock Antiquarian, out-of-print and second-hand books
Open Thurs–Sat 9am–4pm
Services Book search

GREAT BADDOW

The Antique Brass Bedstead Co Ltd
Contact Mr I Rabin
The Bringey, Church Street, Great Baddow, Chelmsford, Essex, CM2 7JW
01245 471137
Est. 1978 *Stock size* Large
Stock Victorian brass and iron bedsteads
Open Mon–Sat 10am–5pm Sun 11am–5pm
Services Restorations

Baddow Antique Centre (EADA)
The Bringey, Church Street, Great Baddow, Chelmsford, Essex, CM2 7JW
01245 476159
Est. 1974 *Stock size* Large
No. of dealers 20
Stock 18th–20thC furniture, silver, glass, porcelain, paintings, Victorian brass and iron bedsteads
Open Mon–Sat 10am–5pm Sun 11am–5pm
Services Valuations, restorations

GREAT CHESTERFORD

C & J Mortimer & Son
Contact Mr C Mortimer
School Street, Great Chesterford, Saffron Walden, Essex, CB10 1NN
01799 530261
Est. 1964 *Stock size* Medium
Stock Oak furniture
Open Thurs Sat 2.30–5pm or by appointment
Services Restorations

GREAT DUNMOW

Memories (EADA)
Contact Peter Berriman
11a Market Place, Great Dunmow, Essex, CM6 1AX
01371 872331 F 01371 872331
M 07774 937001
Est. 2000 *Stock size* Small
Stock General antiques, Victorian–Edwardian furniture, 18th–19thC clocks, 19th–20thC ceramics
Open Mon–Sat 9.30am–5pm
Fairs Brentwood
Services House clearance, reupholstery, repolishing

F B Neill
Contact Mr F B Neill
Ivydene, Chelmsford Road, White Roding, Great Dunmow, Essex, CM6 1RG
01279 876376
Est. 1975 *Stock size* Medium
Stock Antique furniture
Open By appointment

Clive Smith
Contact Mr C Smith
Brick House, North Street, Great Dunmow, Essex, CM6 1BA
01371 873171 F 01371 873171
E clivesmith@route56.co.uk
Est. 1975 *Stock size* Small
Stock Antiquarian books, British Isles, topography, military, natural history
Trade only Yes
Open Mail order or by appointment

Trembath Welch (NAVA)
Contact Clive Welch
The Old Town Hall, Great Dunmow, Essex, CM6 1AU
01371 873014 F 01371 878239
E trembathwelsh@ic24.net
W www.trembathwelchauctions.co.uk

Est. 1886
Open Mon–Fri 9am–5.30pm
Sales Chequers Lane, Great Dunmow, fine art and antiques sales quarterly, general sales every 2 weeks. Phone for details
Frequency Quarterly
Catalogues Yes

GREAT WALTHAM

The Stores,
Contact Scott Saunders
The Stores, Great Waltham, Chelmsford, Essex, CM3 1DE
01245 360277
Est. 1975 ***Stock size*** Large
Stock English antique pine and country furniture
Open Wed–Sat 10am–5pm
Sun 11am–4pm
Services Deliveries

HALSTEAD

The Antique Bed Shop
Contact Mrs V McGregor
Napier House, Head Street, Halstead, Essex, CO9 2BT
01787 477346 F 01787 478757
M 07801 626047
Est. 1976 ***Stock size*** Large
Stock Antique wooden beds
Open Thurs–Sat 9am–5pm or by appointment
Services Free delivery

Appleton's Allsorts
Contact Barry Appleton
9 Head Street, Halstead, Essex, CO9 2AT
01787 476273 M 07715 035934
Est. 1997 ***Stock size*** Large
Stock General antiques, second-hand and household items
Open Mon–Sat 9am–5pm
closed Wed
Services Stripping, house clearance

Townsford Mill Antiques Centre
Contact Rosemary Bennett
The Causeway, Halstead, Essex, CO9 1ET
01787 474451
Est. 1987 ***Stock size*** Large
No. of dealers 80
Stock Antiques, collectables, furniture, silver, porcelain, lace, copper, Beswick, Royal Doulton, kitchenware
Open Mon–Sat 10am–5pm
Sun Bank Holidays 11am–5pm

HARLOW

West Essex Antiques
Contact Mr C Dovaston
Stone Hall, Down Hall Road, Matching Green, Harlow, Essex, CM17 0RA
01279 730609 F 01279 730609
E chris@essexantiques.co.uk
W www.essexantiques.co.uk
Est. 1975 ***Stock size*** Large
Stock Furniture
Open Mon–Fri 9am–5pm
or by appointment

HARWICH

Harwich International Antique Centre
Contact Mr Hans Scholz
19 King's Quay Street, Harwich, Essex, CO12 3ER
01255 554719 F 01255 554719
E info@antiques-access-agency.com
W www.antiques-access-agency.com
Est. 1996 ***Stock size*** Large
No. of dealers 45
Stock A wide range of antiques, collectables and decorative items
Open Tues–Sat 10am–5pm
Sun 1–5pm

HIGH EASTER

Antique Workshop
Contact Mr Haldane
Haydens Farm, High Easter, Chelmsford, Essex, CM1 4QU
01245 231770 M 07867 533093
Est. 1989 ***Stock size*** Small
Stock Victorian–Edwardian furniture
Open By appointment
Services Trade restorations

HOLLAND-ON-SEA

Bookworm
Contact Mr A Durrant
100 Kings Avenue, Holland-on-Sea, Essex, CO15 5EP
01255 815984 F 01255 815984
E andy@adr-comms.demon.co.uk
W www.bookwormshop.com
Est. 1995 ***Stock size*** Medium
Stock Antiquarian and general second-hand books, fiction, modern first editions
Open Mon–Sat 9am–5pm
Bank Holidays 10am–4pm
Services Free book search

ILFORD

Goodwins
Contact Mr C E Goodwin
32 Cameron Road, Ilford, Essex, IG3 8LB
020 8590 4560
Est. 1964 ***Stock size*** Small
Stock General antiques
Open Mon–Sat 9am–6pm

INGATESTONE

Hutchison Antiques and Interiors (EADA)
Contact Mr Gavin Hutchison
60 High Street, Ingatestone, Essex, CM4 9DW
01277 353361 F 01277 353361
Est. 1984 ***Stock size*** Large
Stock Furniture, paintings, antique and contemporary lamps
Open Mon–Sat 10am–5pm
closed Wed
Fairs NEC
Services Valuations, interior design service

Megarry's Antiques (EADA, BACA Award Winner 2002)
Contact Judy Wood
Jericho Cottage, The Duckpond Green, Blackmore, Ingatestone, Essex, CM4 0RR
01277 821031
Est. 1994 ***Stock size*** Large
Stock General antiques, small furniture, collectables, ceramics, blue-and-white china, prints, mirrors, small silver plate
Open Wed–Sun 11am–5pm
Services Valuations, restoration advice

KELVEDON

G T Ratcliff Ltd
Contact Fiona Campbell
Brick House, Braxted Road, Kelvedon, Essex, CO5 9BS
01376 570234
Est. 1947 ***Stock size*** Medium
Stock English lacquer, decorative furniture
Open Mon–Fri 9am–5pm
Sat Sun by appointment

LEIGH-ON-SEA

Astoria Art Deco
Contact Mr or Mrs R Taylor
80 Rectory Grove, Leigh-on-Sea, Essex, SS9 2HJ
01702 471800 07711 332148
astoriaartdeco@aol.com
Est. 1987 *Stock size* Large
Stock Furniture, mirrors, lighting
Open Tues–Sat 10.30am–5pm closed Mon Wed
Fairs Battersea, Hove
Services Polishing, upholstery

Castle Antiques
Contact Mrs Barbara Gair
PO Box 1911, Leigh-on-Sea, Essex, SS9 1JG
01702 711390 01702 475732
07973 674355
castle@enterprise.net
www.castle-antiques.com
Est. 1979 *Stock size* Large
Stock 19thC Staffordshire figures, ironstone wares, tribal artefacts, good taxidermy
Trade only Yes
Open By appointment
Fairs NEC, Newark
Services Valuations

Chalkwell Auctions Ltd (EADA)
Contact Trevor or David
The Arlington Rooms, Leigh-on-Sea, Essex, SS0 8NU
01702 710383 01702 710383
Est. 1990
Sales Antiques and collectables sale monthly, normally 2nd Wed 6.30pm, viewing 4.30pm
Frequency Monthly
Catalogues Yes

Deja Vu Antiques
Contact Mr S Lewis
876 London Road, Leigh-on-Sea, Essex, SS9 3NQ
01702 470829
info@deja-vu-antiques.co.uk
www.deja-vu-antiques.co.uk
Est. 1994 *Stock size* Large
Stock 18th–19thC French furniture
Open Mon–Sat 9.30am–5.30pm Sun 10.30am–2pm
Services Restorations

Drizen Coins
Contact Mr Harry Drizen
1 Hawthorns, Leigh-on-Sea, Essex, SS9 4JT
01702 521094
Est. 1961 *Stock size* Medium
Stock Coins, tokens, medallions, medals
Open Mon–Sat 9am–9pm

Othellos
Contact Mr F Bush or Mrs M Layzell
1376 London Road, Leigh-on-Sea, Essex, SS9 2UH
01702 473334 07710 764175
othellos@hotmail.com
www.othellosbookshop.co.uk
Est. 1999 *Stock size* Large
Stock Out-of-print and second-hand books
Open Tues–Sat 9.30am–5pm

Pall Mall Antiques (EADA)
Contact Jo or Ray Webb
104c–d Elm Road, Leigh-on-Sea, Essex, SS9 1SQ
01702 477235 07970 494122
info@pallmallantiques.co.uk
www.pallmallantiques.co.uk
Est. 1974 *Stock size* Large
Stock Glass, silver, metalware, china, collectables
Open Mon–Sat 10am–5pm closed Wed
Fairs Newark
Services Restoration

Paris Antiques (EADA)
Contact N Rodgers
96 The Broadway, Leigh-on-Sea, Essex, SS9 1A3
01702 712832 01702 712832
enquiries@parisantiques.freeserve.co.uk
Est. 1983 *Stock size* Large
Stock 18th–early 20thC furniture, Art Nouveau
Open Mon–Fri 9.30am–5pm Sat 9.30am–6pm closed Wed
Services Valuations

John Stacey & Sons
Contact Mr P J Stacey
86–90 Pall Mall, Leigh-on-Sea, Essex, SS9 1RG
01702 477051 01702 470141
jstacey@easynet.co.uk
www.jstacey.com
Est. 1946 *Stock size* Medium
Stock Victorian–Edwardian furniture, clocks, ceramics
Open Mon–Fri 9am–5.30pm Sat 9am–1pm
Fairs Newark, Ardingly
Services Adult education courses, valuations, house clearance

John Stacey & Sons (Leigh Auction Rooms)
Contact Mr P J Stacey
86–90 Pall Mall, Leigh-on-Sea, Essex, SS9 1RG
01702 477051 01702 470141
jstacey@easynet.co.uk
Est. 1962
Open Mon–Fri 9am–5.30pm Sat 9am–1pm
Sales General antiques sales Tues 10.30am, viewing Sat Mon 10am–4pm Sun 10am–2pm. Occasional collectors' sale
Frequency 3 weeks
Catalogues Yes

J Streamer
Contact Mrs J Streamer
86 Broadway, Leigh-on-Sea, Essex, SS9 1AE
01702 472895
Est. 1963 *Stock size* Medium
Stock Jewellery, silver, small furniture, art items
Open Mon–Sat 9am–5pm closed Wed
Services Jewellery repair

J Streamer
Contact Mrs J Streamer
212 Leigh Road, Leigh-on-Sea, Essex, SS9 1BS
01702 472895
Est. 1963 *Stock size* Medium
Stock Objets d'art, small furniture
Open Mon–Sat 9am–5pm closed Wed

Tillys Antiques
Contact Mr S T Austen or R J Austen
1801 London Road, Leigh-on-Sea, Essex, SS9 2ST
01702 557170
07803 866318
Est. 1972 *Stock size* Large
Stock General antiques, furniture, antique dolls
Open Mon–Sat 9am–4.30pm closed Wed
Services Valuations, restorations

LITTLE WALTHAM

Collectors' Corner
Contact Mr P Workman or Alasdair MacInnes
100 The Street, Little Waltham, Chelmsford, Essex, CM3 3NT
01245 361166 01245 361166
Est. 1987 *Stock size* Large
Stock Paper-type collectables, postcards, cigarette cards, ephemera, books
Open Mon–Sun 9am–6pm
Services Picture framing

MALDON

All Books
Contact Mr K Peggs
2 Mill Road, Maldon, Essex, CM9 5HZ
01621 856214
www.collect-hobbies.co.uk
Est. 1975 *Stock size* Large
Stock Antiquarian and second-hand books, especially sailing and maritime history
Open Mon–Sat 10am–5pm Sun 1.30–5pm
Services Valuations

The Antique Rooms (RADS)
Contact Mrs Ellen Hedley
63d High Street, Maldon, Essex, CM9 5EB
01621 856985
Est. 1977 *Stock size* Large
Stock 19th–20thC general antiques
Open Mon–Sat 10am–4pm closed Wed
Services Scandinavian spoken

Clive Beardall (BAFRA, EADA)
Contact Mr Clive Beardall
104b High Street, Maldon, Essex, CM9 5ET
01621 857890 01621 850753
info@clivebeardall.co.uk
www.clivebeardall.co.uk
Est. 1982 *Stock size* Small
Stock 18th–20thC furniture
Open Mon–Fri 8am–5.30pm Sat 9am–4pm
Services Valuations, restorations

MANNINGTREE

Antiques (BAFRA)
Contact Mrs A Patterson
49 High Street, Manningtree, Essex, CO11 1AH
01206 396170
Est. 1977 *Stock size* Medium
Stock General antiques, furniture, glass, silver, porcelain, pictures, mirrors
Open Mon–Sat 10am–1pm 2–5pm
Services Restorations

NEWPORT

Brown House Antiques
Contact Brian Hodgkinson
The Brown House, High Street, Newport, Essex, CB11 3QY
01799 540238
Est. 1966 *Stock size* Medium
Stock Mainly 19thC pine and country furniture
Open Mon–Sat 10am–5.30pm

Omega Decorative Arts
Contact Mr Tony Phillips or Mrs Sybil Hooper
High Street, Newport, Saffron Walden, Essex, CB11 3PF
01799 540720
Est. 1985 *Stock size* Medium
Stock 1860–1960, Art Deco, Arts and Crafts
Open Mon–Sat 10am–6pm closed Thurs
Services Restorations

RAYLEIGH

F G Bruschweiler Antiques Ltd (LAPADA)
Contact Mr F Bruschweiler
41–67 Lower Lambricks, Rayleigh, Essex, SS6 8DA
01268 773761/773932
01268 773318
fred@fgbruschweiler.demon.co.uk or fbruschweiler@virgin.net
www.business.virgin.net/f.bruschweiler
Est. 1960 *Stock size* Large
Stock General antique furniture, public house bars
Open Mon–Fri 8.30am–5pm
Services Restorations

ROMFORD

Carey's Bookshop
Contact Mr Robert Carey
91 High Road, Chadwell Heath, Romford, Essex, RM6 6PB
020 8597 4165
Est. 1985 *Stock size* Medium
Stock Antiquarian and second-hand books, especially sci-fi and crime
Open Tues–Sat 10am–5pm

Off World
Contact Mr Mark Woollard
Romford Shopping Hall, Market Place, Romford, Essex, RM1 3AT
01708 765633
Est. 1995 *Stock size* Large
Stock Antique toys, collectables, *Star Wars* a speciality
Open Mon–Sat 9am–5.30pm
Fairs Luton

SAFFRON WALDEN

Bush Antiques (EADA)
Contact Mrs J M Hosford
26–28 Church Street, Saffron Walden, Essex, CB10 1JQ
01799 523277
Est. 1960 *Stock size* Medium
Stock Country furniture, copper, brass, treen, ceramics, glass
Open Mon–Sat 11am–4.30pm closed Thurs

Ickleton Antiques
Contact Mr B Arbury
4 Gold Street, Saffron Walden, Essex, CB10 1EJ
01799 513114
Est. 1995 *Stock size* Medium
Stock Militaria, postcards, collectables WWI, WWII
Open Mon–Fri 10am–4pm Sat 10am–5pm

Lankester Antiques & Books
Contact Mr P Lankester
The Old Sun Inn, Church Street, Saffron Walden, Essex, CB10 1JW
01799 522685
Est. 1967 *Stock size* Large
Stock General antiques, antiquarian and second-hand books
Open Mon–Sat 9.30am–5.30pm

⊞ Market Row Antiques & Collectables
Contact Mr P Bowyer or Mr D Miller
✉ **14 Market Row, Saffron Waldon, Essex, CB10 1HB**
☎ 01799 516131 Ⓜ 07759 493613
Est. 1994 ***Stock size*** Small
Stock General antiques, clocks, barometers
Open Mon–Wed Fri Sat 10am–5pm Thurs 2–5pm
Fairs London and Birmingham clock fairs
Services Clock and watch repairs

⊞ T. Reed & Son
Contact Meg Reed
✉ **22 Castle Street, Saffron Walden, Essex, CB10 1BJ** Ⓟ
☎ 01799 522363
Est. 1881 ***Stock size*** Small
Stock Country antiques
Open Tues Sat 10am–1pm 2–5pm

Saffron Walden Antiques Centre
Contact Mr P Rowell or Mrs J Rowell
✉ **1 Market Row, Saffron Walden, Essex, CB10 1HA** Ⓟ
☎ 01799 524534 Ⓕ 01799 524703
Ⓦ www.saffronwaldenantiquescentre.com
Est. 1997 ***Stock size*** Large
No. of dealers 40
Stock Huge range of antiques, collectables, bygones, furniture, silver, jewellery, porcelain, lighting, pictures, sporting memorabilia
Open Mon–Fri 10am–5.30pm Sat 9am–5.30pm Sun 11am–5pm

Saffron Walden Auctions
Contact Mr C Peeke-Voute
✉ **1 Market Street, Saffron Walden, Essex, CB10 1JB**
☎ 01799 513281 Ⓕ 01799 513334
Ⓔ info@saffronwaldenauctions.com
Ⓦ www.saffronwaldenauctions.com
Est. 1905
Open Fri 910am–4pm
Sales Antiques sales Sundays every 6 weeks, viewing Fri 10am–5pm Sat 10am–1pm
Frequency 6-weekly
Catalogues Yes

SIBLE HEDINGHAM

⊞ Hedingham Antiques (EADA)
Contact Mrs P Patterson
✉ **100 Swan Street, Sible Hedingham, Halstead, Essex, CO9 3HP** Ⓟ
☎ 01787 460360 Ⓕ 01787 469109
Ⓜ 07802 265702
Ⓔ patriciapatterson@totalise.co.uk
Ⓦ www.silberausengland.co.uk
Est. 1980 ***Stock size*** Medium
Stock Antique and early 20thC silver, silver plate, glass
Open By appointment
Services Silver and furniture restoration

⊞ Lennard Antiques (LAPADA)
Contact G Pinn
✉ **124 Swan Street, Sible Hedingham, Halstead, Essex, CO9 3HP** Ⓟ
☎ 01787 461127
Est. 1969 ***Stock size*** Medium
Stock Oak and country furniture, Delftware
Open Mon–Sat 9.30am–6pm
Fairs Olympia, Chelsea Spring and Autumn, Kensington

⊞ W A Pinn & Sons (LAPADA, BADA)
Contact Mr J Pinn or Mr K Pinn
✉ **124 Swan Street, Sible Hedingham, Halstead, Essex, CO9 3HP** Ⓟ
☎ 01787 461127
Est. 1969 ***Stock size*** Medium
Stock 17th–early 19thC furniture, accessories
Open Mon–Sat 9.30am–6pm
Fairs Olympia, Chelsea Spring and Autumn, Kensington

SOUTHEND-ON-SEA

⊞ CurioCity
Contact Carol or Matt
✉ **333–335 Chartwell Square, Victoria Plaza, Southend-on-Sea, Essex, SS2 5SP** Ⓟ
☎ 01702 611350
Est. 1998 ***Stock size*** Large
Stock Wide range of antiques, collectables
Open Mon–Fri 10am–5pm Sat 9am–5pm
Services Café

⊞ Dealers
Contact Gary Bell
✉ **659 London Road, Southend-on-Sea, Essex, SS0 9PD** Ⓟ
☎ 01702 300052 Ⓕ 01702 300050
Ⓦ www.les-and-gary.co.uk
Est. 1977 ***Stock size*** Large
Stock General antiques
Open Mon–Sun 9am–5pm

⊞ Lonsdale Antiques
Contact Mrs H Clark
✉ **86 Lonsdale Road, Southend-on-Sea, Essex, SS2 4LR** Ⓟ
☎ 01702 462643 Ⓜ 07899 771989
Est. 1980 ***Stock size*** Large
Stock General antiques, porcelain, small furniture, ceramics, gold and silver jewellery, costume jewellery, pictures
Open Mon–Sat 9.30am–5.30pm closed Wed
Fairs Essex, Enfield Middlesex

⊞ David Morton
Contact Mr D Morton
✉ **Rear of 61–69 Princes Street, Southend-on-Sea, Essex, SS1 1PT** Ⓟ
☎ 01702 354144
Est. 1967 ***Stock size*** Large
Stock 19thC furniture, general antiques
Trade only Yes
Open By appointment

⊞ R & J Coins
Contact Mr R Harvey
✉ **21b Alexandra Street, Market Place, Southend-on-Sea, Essex, SS1 1BX** Ⓟ
☎ 01702 345995
Est. 1967 ***Stock size*** Medium
Stock Coins, medals, bank notes, cap badges
Open Mon–Fri 10am–4pm Wed 10am–2pm Sat 10am–3pm

STANSTED MOUNTFITCHET

⊞ Harris Antiques Stansted (BAFRA, EADA)
Contact Brian Harris
✉ **40 Lower Street, Stansted Mountfitchet, Essex, CM24 8LR** Ⓟ
☎ 01279 812233
Est. 1956 ***Stock size*** Large
Stock 16th–20thC furniture, clocks, barometers, ceramics

Open Mon–Sat 9am–5pm
Fairs NEC
Services Valuations, restorations

Linden House Antiques
Contact Mr A W Sargeant
3 Silver Street, Stansted Mountfitchet, Essex, CM24 8HA
01279 812372
Est. 1962 *Stock size* Large
Stock 18th–19thC furniture, pictures
Open Mon–Sat 9.30am–5.30pm
Services Valuations

G E Sworder & Sons
Contact Mr Guy Schooling ARICS
14 Cambridge Road, Stansted Mountfitchet, Essex, CM24 8BZ
01279 817778 F 01279 817779
auctions@sworder.co.uk
www.sworder.co.uk
Est. 1782
Open Mon–Fri 9am–5pm
Sales Victoriana and lesser-quality antiques and collectables, Thurs, no catalogue, viewing Wed 2–5pm Thurs 9–11am. Antiques and fine art sale every 5 weeks Tues 10am, viewing Fri 10am–5pm Sat Sun 10am–1pm Mon 10am–5pm
Frequency Weekly
Catalogues Yes

Valmar Antiques (BADA, LAPADA, CINOA)
Contact J A or M R Orpin
Croft House Cottage, High Lane, Stansted Mountfitchet, Essex, CM24 8LQ
01279 813201 F 01279 816962
M 07831 093701
valmar-antiques@cwcom.net
Est. 1967 *Stock size* Large
Stock 18th–19thC furniture and accesssories, Arts and Crafts
Open By appointment only
Fairs Olympia BADA

STOCK

Sabine Antiques (EADA)
Contact Mrs S Sabine
38 High Street, Stock, Essex, CM4 9BW
01277 840553 F 01277 840553
Est. 1969 *Stock size* Small
Stock 18th–19thC furniture, silver, ceramics, clocks, general household
Open Phone for opening times
Services Valuations, restorations, French polishing

THORPE-LE-SOKEN

Jade Antiques
Contact Mrs J Ellis
Suffolk House, High Street, Thorpe-le-Soken, Clacton-on-Sea, Essex, CO16 0EA
01255 860040 M 07747 730852
Est. 1984 *Stock size* Small
Stock Fine porcelain, small furniture
Open Wed–Sat 10am–5pm

WESTCLIFF-ON-SEA

It's About Time (EADA)
Contact Mr Pane Williams
863 London Road, Westcliff-on-Sea, Essex, SS0 9SZ
01702 472574 F 01702 472574
iat@clocking-in.demon.co.uk
www.clocking-in.demon.co.uk
Est. 1979 *Stock size* Medium
Stock Clocks, furniture
Open Mon–Sat 9am–5.30pm
Services Restoration

Ridgeway Antiques (EADA)
Contact Trevor or Charles
66 The Ridgeway, Westcliff-on-Sea, Essex, SS0 8NU
01702 710383 F 01702 710383
www.ridgeweb.co.uk
Est. 1987 *Stock size* Medium
Stock 18thC–pre-war furniture, general antiques
Open Mon–Sat 10.30am–5pm
Fairs Hallmark, Ridgeway Fairs
Services Valuations

WOODFORD GREEN

Mill Lane Antiques
Contact Mr N McArtney
29 Mill Lane, Woodford Green, Essex, IG8 0UG
020 8502 9930
Est. 1987 *Stock size* Large
Stock Georgian–Victorian furniture, lighting, ironwork, collectables
Open Tues Thurs–Sat 10am–4.30pm
Fairs Kempton Park
Services House clearance

WRITTLE

Whichcraft Jewellery (EADA)
Contact Alan Turner
54–56 The Green, Writtle, Chelmsford, Essex, CM1 3DU
01245 420183
Est. 1978 *Stock size* Large
Stock Antique and modern jewellery, small silver items
Open Tues–Sat 9.30am–5.30pm
Services Jewellery repairs and restorations

NORFOLK

ACLE

Horners Auctioneers (ISVA)
Contact Mr N Horner-Glister FRICS
Acle Salerooms, Norwich Road, Acle, Norwich, Norfolk, NR13 3BY
01493 750225 F 01493 750506
auction@horners.co.uk
www.horners.co.uk
Est. 1900
Open Mon–Fri 9am–1pm 2–5pm
Sales General antiques sale Thurs 10am, viewing Wed 2–4pm, bi-monthly antiques and collectables sale Sat 10am
Frequency Weekly
Catalogues Yes

Ivy House Antiques
Contact Mr N L Pratt
Ivy House, The Street, Acle, Norwich, Norfolk, NR13 3BH
01493 750682
Est. 1985 *Stock size* Large
Stock General antiques, porcelain, furniture, pictures, metalware
Open Mon–Sat 9am–5pm
Services Valuations, restorations

ALDBOROUGH

Knight's Sporting Auctions
Contact Tim Knight
The Thatched Gallery, The Green, Aldborough, Norwich, Norfolk, NR11 7AA

☎ 01263 768488 Ⓕ 01263 768788
Ⓔ tim@knights.co.uk
Ⓦ www.knights.co.uk
Est. 1993
Open Mon–Fri 9am–5pm
Sales Sporting memorabilia, especially cricket and football, varied venues and dates, telephone for details, viewing day prior to sale
Frequency Quarterly
Catalogues Yes

AYLSHAM

Keys
Contact Mr D J Lines
✉ **Aylsham Salerooms, Off Palmers Lane, Aylsham, Norfolk, NR11 6JA** Ⓟ
☎ 01263 733195 Ⓕ 01263 732140
Ⓔ info@gakey.co.uk
Ⓦ www.aylshamsalerooms.co.uk
Est. 1953
Open Mon–Fri 9am–5pm closed 1–2pm Sat 9am–noon
Sales Weekly general sale, antique sale every 3 weeks Tues Wed. Every 2 months book sale Fri, collectors' sale Thurs, picture sales Fri. Phone for details
Frequency Every 3 weeks
Catalogues Yes

BAWDESWELL

The Norfolk Polyphon Centre
Contact Mr Norman Vince
✉ **Wood Farm, Reepham Road, Bawdeswell, Dereham, Norfolk, NR20 4RX** Ⓟ
☎ 01362 688230 Ⓕ 01362 688230
Est. 1966 *Stock size* Large
Stock Antique and new musical boxes
Open By appointment

BROOKE

Country House Antiques
Contact Mr G Searle
✉ **Green Acre, Seething, Nr Brooke, Norwich, Norfolk, NR15 1AL** Ⓟ
☎ 01508 558144 Ⓕ 01508 558144
Est. 1980 *Stock size* Medium
Stock 17th–19thC furniture
Trade only Yes
Open By appointment
Fairs Newark

BURNHAM MARKET

The Brazen Head Bookshop & Gallery
Contact David Kenyon
✉ **Greenside, Market Place, Burnham Market, King's Lynn, Norfolk, PE31 8HD** Ⓟ
☎ 01328 730700 Ⓕ 01328 730929
Ⓔ brazenheadbook@aol.com
Est. 1979 *Stock size* Large
Stock Antiquarian, second-hand and out-of-print books, specializing in children's books, also books concerning Nelson
Open Mon–Sat 9.30am–5pm
Services Valuations, book search

M & A Cringle
Contact Mr or Mrs Cringle
✉ **The Old Black Horse, Market Place, Burnham Market, Norfolk, PE31 8HD** Ⓟ
☎ 01328 738456
Est. 1965 *Stock size* Small
Stock Late 18thC furniture, prints, maps, china, pottery
Open Mon–Sat 9am–1pm 2–5pm closed Wed
Services Valuations

Market House Antiques (BADA)
Contact Mr or Mrs D Maufe
✉ **Market House, Burnham Market, Norfolk, PE31 8HF** Ⓟ
☎ 01328 738475 Ⓕ 01328 730750
Est. 1976 *Stock size* Medium
Stock 18th–early 19thC furniture and works of art, mirrors, bronzes
Open By appointment or by chance
Fairs BADA March, Summer and Winter Olympias

CAISTER-ON-SEA

Readers' Dream
Contact Miss T Kemp
✉ **17a Yarmouth Road, Caister-on-Sea, Great Yarmouth, Norfolk, NR30 5DL** Ⓟ
☎ 01493 720220
Est. 1998 *Stock size* Large
Stock Antiquarian books, first editions
Open Mon–Sat 10am–5.30pm Sun 10am–2pm
Services Book search

COLTISHALL

Roger Bradbury Antiques
Contact Roger Bradbury
✉ **Church Street, Coltishall, Norfolk, NR12 7DJ** Ⓟ
☎ 01603 737444 Ⓕ 01603 737018
Ⓜ 07860 372528
Est. 1967 *Stock size* Medium
Stock Chinese porcelain cargoes, 18th–19thC furniture, pictures, objets d'art

Coltishall Antique Centre
Contact Isabel Ford
✉ **7 High Street, Coltishall, Norwich, Norfolk, NR12 7AA** Ⓟ
☎ 01603 738306
Est. 1977 *Stock size* Medium
No. of dealers 8
Stock Glass, ceramics, militaria, jewellery, silver, fishing, golfing items, collectables
Open Mon–Sat 10am–4.30pm

Gwendoline Golder Antiques
Contact Mrs G Golder
✉ **Point House, 5 High Street, Coltishall, Norwich, Norfolk, NR12 7AA** Ⓟ
☎ 01603 738099
Est. 1979 *Stock size* Medium
Stock General antiques, furniture, silver, jewellery, porcelain
Open Mon–Sat 10am–1pm 2–5pm

CROMER

Bond Street Antiques (NAG, GAGTL)
Contact Mr M R T Jones
✉ **6 Bond Street, Cromer, Norfolk, NR27 9DA** Ⓟ
☎ 01263 513134
Est. 1970 *Stock size* Medium
Stock Silver, jewellery
Open Mon–Sat 9am–5pm
Services Valuations

Books Etc.
Contact Mr Kevin Reynor
✉ **15a Church Street, Cromer, Norfolk, NR27 9ES**
☎ 01263 515501
Ⓔ bookskcr@aol.com
Est. 1997 *Stock size* Large
Stock Antiquarian and second-hand books

Open Easter–Sept Sun–Mon 11am–4pm winter Wed–Sat 11am–4pm

Collectors' Cabin
Contact Diana Hazell Bennington
The Kiosk, North Lodge Park Promenade, Cromer, Norfolk, NR27 9HE
01263 512195 01263 515961
Est. 1997 *Stock size* Large
Stock Ceramics, glass, Crown Derby
Open Tues–Sun 10am–5pm
Services Restorations

Collectors' World
Contact Mrs Irene Nockels
6 New Parade, Church Street, Cromer, Norfolk, NR27 9EP
01263 515330/514174
nockels@25nr.fsnet.co.uk
Est. 1994 *Stock size* Large
Stock Furniture, general antiques, collectables
Open Tues–Sat 10am–5pm
Fairs Norwich, Newark
Services Valuations, house clearance

Little Gems Rock Shop
Contact Danny or Gail Hickling
2a Mount Street, Cromer, Norfolk, NR27 9DB
01263 519519
littlegems@breathemail.net
www.littlegemsrockshop.co.uk
Est. 1998 *Stock size* Large
Stock Fossils, gemstones, crystals from around the world
Open Mon–Sat 10am–5pm Sun noon–5pm

DEREHAM

Case & Dewing
Contact John Dewing
Church Street, Dereham, Norfolk, NR19 1DJ
01362 692004 01362 693103
info@case-dewing.co.uk
www.case-dewing.co.uk
Est. 1900
Open Mon–Fri 9am–5.30pm Sat 9am–3.30pm
Sales General antiques and effects Tues, viewing morning of sale
Frequency 2 weeks
Catalogues No

Tyrone R Roberts
Contact T R Roberts
Matlock Grange, 16 Greenfields Road, Dereham, Norfolk, NR20 3TE
01362 691267 01362 691267
07702 642362
tyroneroberts@yahoo.co.uk
www.tyroneroberts.com
Est. 1970
Open Mon–Sun 9am–5pm or by appointment
Sales General antiques
Frequency Monthly
Catalogues Yes

Village Books
Contact Mr Jack James
20a High Street, Dereham, Norfolk, NR19 1DR
01362 853066
villagebkdereham@aol.com
Est. 1996 *Stock size* Large
Stock General books, maps, ephemera
Open Mon Tues Thurs Fri 9.30am–4.30pm Wed 9.30am–1pm Sat 9.30am–5pm
Services Free book search, Readers' Club, postal sales

DISS

Antique and Collectors' Centre Diss
Contact Mr D Cockaday
The Works, 3 Cobbs Yard, St Nicholas Street, Diss, Norfolk, IP22 4LB
01379 644472
Est. 1999 *Stock size* Large
No. of dealers 28
Stock General antiques, 1850–1970, Art Deco china and glass, commemoratives
Open Mon–Thurs 10am–4.30pm Fri 9am–4pm Sat 10am–4.30pm
Services Valuations

Diss Antiques & Interiors (LAPADA)
Contact Mr Brian Wimshurst
2–3 Market Place, Diss, Norfolk, IP22 3JT
01379 642213 01379 642213
07770 477368
Est. 1971 *Stock size* Medium
Stock Tudor–Edwardian furniture, ceramics, silver
Open Mon–Sat 9am–5pm
Fairs Snape
Services Valuations, restorations

Thos Wm Gaze & Son (RICS)
Contact Alan M Smith FRICS
Diss Auction Rooms, Roydon Road, Diss, Norfolk, IP22 4LN
01379 650306 01379 644313
sales@dissauctionrooms.co.uk
www.twgaze.com
Est. 1857
Open Sat 9am–1pm Mon–Fri 9am–5pm
Sales Weekly Fri sales of antiques and collectables, Victorian pine and shipping furniture, modern furniture and effects. Periodic Fri sales of decorative arts, modern furniture and decor, 19th–20thC paintings, books, ephemera. Periodic Sat sales decorative arts, modern furniture, decor, toys, nostalgia, architectural salvage, statuary, rural and domestic bygones. Auction calendars available, viewing Thurs 2–8pm Fri Sat from 8.30am
Catalogues Yes

DOWNHAM MARKET

Antiques and Gifts
Contact Mrs Addrison
47 Bridge Street, Downham Market, Norfolk, PE38 9DW
01366 387700
Est. 1998 *Stock size* Medium
Stock Victorian–Edwardian furniture, second-hand books, china, glass, smalls, general antiques
Open Mon–Sat 9am–5pm

Downham Market Antique Centre
Contact Sue Cook
43 High Street, Downham Market, Norfolk, PE38 9HF
01366 384402
terry@misuzy.fsnet.co.uk
Est. 1990 *Stock size* Large
No. of dealers 40
Stock General antiques and collectables
Open Wed–Sun 10am–4pm

Barry L Hawkins
Contact Mr B Hawkins FRICS
15 Lynn Road, Downham Market, Norfolk, PE38 9NL
01366 387180 01366 386626

Ⓜ 07860 451721
Ⓔ Barry@barryhawkins.freewire.co.uk
Ⓦ www.barryhawkins.freewire.co.uk
Est. 1840
Open Mon–Fri 9am–5pm
Sales Monthly antiques and general sale of goods first Wed, viewing morning of sale 8–11am. Wine sales and Oriental carpet sales, catalogued
Frequency Monthly
Catalogues No

EAST WINCH

Holt's (GTA)
Contact Mr N Holt
✉ **The Old Vicarage, Church Lane, East Winch, King's Lynn, Norfolk, PE32 1NQ** Ⓟ
☎ 01553 777140 Ⓕ 01553 761657
Ⓔ enquires@holtandcompany.co.uk
Ⓦ www.holtandcompany.co.uk
Est. 1993
Open Mon–Fri 9am–5pm
Sales Fine modern and antique gun sales at the Duke of York's Barracks, Chelsea, London, Thurs 2pm, viewing Tues 10am–8pm Wed 9am–6pm morning of sale
Frequency 4 per annum
Catalogues Yes

FAKENHAM

James Beck Auctions
Contact Mr James Beck
✉ **The Cornhall, Cattle Market Street, Fakenham, Norfolk, NR21 9AW** Ⓟ
☎ 01328 851557 Ⓕ 01328 851044
Est. 1840
Open Tues 10am–1pm Thurs 10am–5pm Fri 10am–2pm
Sales General antiques sales on Thurs at 11am, specialist sales occasionally, viewing Wed 2–5pm Thurs 9–11am
Frequency Weekly
Catalogues No

Fakenham Antiques Centre
Contact Mandy Allen or Julie Hunt
✉ **The Old Congregational Church, 14 Norwich Road, Fakenham, Norfolk, NR21 8AZ** Ⓟ
☎ 01328 862941
Ⓔ mandyallen@cockthorpe.freeserve.co.uk
Est. 1984 *Stock size* Large
No. of dealers 20
Stock Period furniture, antiques, curios, collectables
Open Mon–Sat 10am–4.30pm
Services Restorations

Sue Rivett Antiques
Contact Sue Rivett
✉ **6 Norwich Road, Fakenham, Norfolk, NR21 8AX** Ⓟ
☎ 01328 862924
Est. 1969 *Stock size* Small
Stock General antiques, Victorian and pre-Victorian items
Open Mon–Sat 10am–1pm closed Wed

David Steward Antiques
Contact David Steward
✉ **8 Norwich Road, Fakenham, Norfolk, NR21 8AX** Ⓟ
☎ 01328 853535/853214
Ⓜ 07979 496193
Est. 1980 *Stock size* Medium
Stock Furniture, clocks, ceramics, glass
Open Mon–Sat 10am–3pm closed Wed

GREAT YARMOUTH

Barry's Antiques
Contact Mr Barry Nichols
✉ **35 King Street, Great Yarmouth, Norfolk, NR30 2PN** Ⓟ
☎ 01493 842713 Ⓕ 01493 745312
Ⓜ 07802 619579
Est. 1979 *Stock size* Large
Stock Jewellery, porcelain, silver
Open Mon–Sat 9.30am–4.30pm closed Thurs
Services Jewellery repair, insurance valuer and agent

Curiosity Too
Contact Mr or Mrs R Moore
✉ **163 Northgate Street, Great Yarmouth, Norfolk, NR30 1BY** Ⓟ
☎ 01493 859690
Est. 1983 *Stock size* Medium
Stock China, glass, pictures, general antiques, small furniture
Open Mon–Fri 10am–4.30pm Sat 10.30am–3.30pm closed Thurs
Services House clearance

Garry M Emms and Co Ltd
Contact Garry Emms
✉ **Great Yarmouth Salerooms, Beevor Road, Great Yarmouth, Norfolk, NR30 3PS** Ⓟ
☎ 01493 332668 Ⓕ 01493 728290
Ⓔ g_emms@gt-yarmouthauctions.com
Ⓦ www.gt-yarmouthauctions.com
Est. 1994
Open Thurs–Fri 10am–4pm to accept goods for sale
Sales Weekly sales of antiques Wed 10am, viewing Tues 2–8pm Wed 9–10am
Frequency Weekly
Catalogues No

David Ferrow (ABA, PBFA)
Contact David Ferrow
✉ **77 Howard Street South, Great Yarmouth, Norfolk, NR30 1LN** Ⓟ
☎ 01493 843800
Est. 1940 *Stock size* Large
Stock General antiquarian books, local topography
Open Mon–Wed Fri Sat 10am–5pm closed Bank Holidays
Services Valuations

King Street Bookshop (PBFA)
Contact Mr or Mrs C or J Read
✉ **129 King Street, Great Yarmouth, Norfolk, NR30 2PQ** Ⓟ
☎ 01493 857733
Est. 1993 *Stock size* Medium
Stock Antiquarian and out-of-print books, maritime, general history, country life, postcards, ephemera
Open Mon–Sat 10am–5pm closed Thurs
Fairs PBFA
Services Book search

HINDRINGHAM

Fullertons Booksearch
Contact Mr Humphrey Boon
✉ **The Duke's House, Moorgate Road, Hindringham, Fakenham, Norfolk, NR21 0PT** Ⓟ
☎ 01420 544088 Ⓕ 01420 542445
Ⓔ fullertonsbooks@aol.com
Est. 1991
Stock Books
Open Mon–Fri 9am–5pm
Services Out-of-print book searching facility. Mail order only. No obligation

HINGHAM

Hingham Antiques
Contact Mrs C Docwra
The Fairland, Hingham, Norwich, Norfolk, NR9 4HN
01953 850838 07789 114629
Est. 1996 *Stock size* Large
Stock General antiques
Open Tues–Sun 10am–4pm
Fairs Newark
Services Furniture restoration, reupholstery

Mongers Architectural Salvage (SALVO)
Contact Mrs Sam Coster
15 Market Place, Hingham, Norwich, Norfolk, NR9 4AF
01953 851868 01953 851870
sam@mongersofhingham.co.uk
www.mongersofhingham.co.uk
Est. 1997 *Stock size* Large
Stock Architectural salvage
Open Mon–Sat 9.30am–5.30pm Sun 11am–2pm
Fairs Newark
Services Stripping, fireplace restoration

Past & Present
Contact Christine George
16a Fairland, Hingham, Norwich, Norfolk, NR9 4HN
01953 851471
info@pastandpresentantiques.co.uk
www.pastandpresentantiques.co.uk
Est. 1999 *Stock size* Large
Stock Fine art and antiques
Open Tues–Sun 10am–5pm

HOLT

Baron Art
Contact Mr A Baron
9 Chapel Yard, Albert Street, Holt, Norfolk, NR25 6HJ
01263 713906 01263 711670
baronart@aol.com
Est. 1990 *Stock size* Large
Stock Art Deco, paintings
Open Mon–Sat 9am–5pm
Services Valuations

Baron Art
Contact Mr A Baron
17 Chapel Yard, Albert Street, Holt, Norfolk, NR25 6HG
01263 713430 01263 711670
baronart@aol.com
Est. 1990 *Stock size* Large
Stock Art Deco, paintings, antiquarian books
Open Mon–Sat 9am–5pm
Services Valuations, framing

Cobwebs
Contact Ann Buchanan
2 Fish Hill, Holt, Norfolk, NR25 6BD
01263 711955 01328 829592
07980 087889
Est. 1996 *Stock size* Large
Stock Bygones, collectables, woodworking and agricultural tools
Open Mon–Fri 10.30am–5pm Sat 10.30am–6pm

Cottage Collectables
Contact Philip or Linda Morris
Fish Hill, Holt, Norfolk, NR25 6BD
01263 711707
Est. 1984 *Stock size* Large
Stock General antiques, jewellery
Open Mon–Sun 10am–5pm
Fairs Newark, The International Antique and Collectables Fair, RAF Swinderby, Peterborough and Norwich showgrounds
Services Restorations, house clearance

Simon Gough Books Ltd
Contact Mr Tristram Hull
5 Fish Hill, Holt, Norfolk, NR25 6BD
01263 712650 01263 712276
tristram.hull@virgin.net
www.simongoughbooks.com
Est. 1974 *Stock size* Large
Stock General stock, antiquarian books
Open Mon–Sat 10am–5pm
Fairs The Hilton, Olympia

Heathfield Antiques
Contact Stephen Heathfield
Candlestick Lane, Thornage Road, Holt, Norfolk, NR25 6SU
01263 711609 01263 711609
info@antique-pine.net
www.antique-pine.net
Est. 1991 *Stock size* Large
Stock Antique pine, country items
Open Mon–Sat 8am–5pm
Services Restorations

Holt Antique Centre
Contact Mr D Attfield
Albert Street, Holt, Norfolk, NR25 6HX
01263 712097
Est. 1982 *Stock size* Large
No. of dealers 15
Stock Antiques, collectables
Open Mon–Sun 10am–5pm

Holt Antique Gallery
Contact Mrs J Holliday
2 Shire Hall Plain, Holt, Norfolk, NR25 6HT
01263 711991 01263 711991
Est. 1997 *Stock size* Large
Stock Antique furniture, china, brass
Open Mon–Sun 10am–5pm
Fairs Newark, The International Antique and Collectables Fair, RAF Swinderby

Mews Antique Emporium
Contact Mr Howard Heathfield
17 High Street, Holt, Norfolk, NR25 6BN
01263 713224
Est. 1998 *Stock size* Large
No. of dealers 14
Stock Furniture, pictures, pottery, china
Open Mon–Sat 10am–5pm Sun 11am–4pm
Services Valuations, restorations

Past Caring
Contact Mrs Lynda Mossman
6 Chapel Yard, Albert Street, Holt, Norfolk, NR25 6HG
01263 713771 01263 680078
pstcaring@aol.com
Est. 1987 *Stock size* Large
Stock Linen, lace, vintage clothing, accessories, costume jewellery 1800s–1950
Open Mon–Sat 11am–5pm closed Thurs
Fairs Alexandra Palace

Richard Scott Antiques
Contact Mr Richard Scott
30 High Street, Holt, Norfolk, NR25 6BH
01263 712479
Est. 1972 *Stock size* Large
Stock Ceramics, studio pottery, oil lamps
Open Mon–Fri 10am–5pm Sat 10am–5.30pm closed Thurs
Fairs Newark
Services Advice on valuation, restorations

Trinities
Contact Mrs Lois White
29a Bull Street, Holt, Norfolk, NR25 6HP
☎ 01263 711606 Ⓜ 07730 070290
Est. 1998 *Stock size* Large
Stock Antiques, Victorian beds fully restored, collectables, artefacts, memorabilia, antique bedsteads
Open Tues–Sat 10.30am–4pm
Fairs Newark

HOVETON

Bradley Hatch Jewellers
Contact Bradley Hatch
Tunstead Road, Hoveton, Norfolk, NR12 8QG P
☎ 01603 738723 Ⓕ 01603 784679
Ⓔ sales@bradleyhatch.com
Ⓦ www.bradleyhatch.com
Est. 1992 *Stock size* Large
Stock Antique and second-hand jewellery, silver, watches
Open Mon–Sat 9am–5pm Thurs 9.30am–5pm
Services Valuations, restorations

KING'S LYNN

The Old Curiosity Shop
Contact Mrs Wright
25 St James Street, King's Lynn, Norfolk, PE30 5DA P
☎ 01553 766591 Ⓜ 07802 348635
Est. 1984 *Stock size* Small
Stock General antiques, collectables, furniture
Open Mon–Sat 11am–5pm
Fairs Alexandra Palace, Lee Valley Park
Services Teddy bear restoration, clock, watch repairs, bead restringing

The Old Granary Antique Centre
Contact Mrs J L Waymouth
Kings Staithe Lane, King's Lynn, Norfolk, PE30 1LZ P
☎ 01553 775509
Est. 1979 *Stock size* Medium
Stock General antiques, collectables, coins, medals, stamps, books
Open Mon–Sat 10am–5pm (4.30pm in winter)
Services Valuations

Roderick Richardson
Contact Mr Roderick Richardson
The Old Granary Antique Centre, Kings Staithe Lane, King's Lynn, Norfolk, PE30 1LZ P
☎ 01553 670833 Ⓕ 01553 670833
Ⓦ www.coin.dealers-on-line.com/roderick
Est. 1995 *Stock size* Large
Stock English hammered and early milled gold and silver
Open Mon–Sat 10am–5pm
Fairs York Northern Fair, Midland Coin Fair, London Coin Fair

KIRSTEAD GREEN

Antique Chair Shop
Contact Simon Hunt
Kirstead Green, Norwich, Norfolk, NR15 1EB P
☎ 01508 550051
Ⓔ info@antiquechairshop.co.uk
Ⓦ www.antiquechairshop.co.uk
Est. 1985 *Stock size* Small
Stock Chairs
Open Mon-Sat 9am–5pm Thur 9am–12.30pm
Services Restorations

MARSHAM

Euro Antiques
Contact Mr Case Van Woerkom
1–6 Outbuildings, Grove Farm, Norwich Road, Marsham, Norwich, Norfolk, NR10 5SR P
☎ 01263 731377 Ⓕ 01263 731378
Ⓜ 07771 727420
Est. 1979 *Stock size* Medium
Stock Pine, general furniture
Open Mon–Fri 9am–5pm Sat 9am–1pm
Services Leathering

Brian Watson Antique Glass (LAPADA)
Contact Brian Watson
Foxwarren Cottage, High Street, Marsham, Norwich, Norfolk, NR10 5QA P
☎ 01263 732519 Ⓕ 01263 732519
Ⓜ 07718 860535
Ⓔ brian.h.watson@talk21.com
Est. 1991 *Stock size* Medium
Stock Georgian–Victorian drinking glasses, decanters and other glass of the period
Open By appointment
Fairs NEC, Penman fairs
Services Valuations

MELTON CONSTABLE

Steven Simpson Natural History Books
Contact Mr S J Simpson
23 Melton Street, Melton Constable, Norfolk, NR24 2DB
☎ 01263 862287 Ⓜ 07884 366387
Ⓔ sjs5555@fsmail,net
Est. 1986 *Stock size* Small
Stock Antiquarian books on natural history, fish topics a speciality
Open Mail order only
Services Valuations, brokerage, publisher distributor

MULBARTON

Junk and Disorderly
Contact Mr Tony Nash
The Dell, Birchfield Lane, Mulbarton, Norfolk, NR14 8AA P
☎ 01603 748801
Est. 1976 *Stock size* Large
Stock General antiques
Open Sat 8am–4pm
Services House clearance, removals

NORTH WALSHAM

The Angel Bookshop (PBFA)
Contact Mr E Green
4 Aylsham Road, North Walsham, Norfolk, NR28 0BH
☎ 01692 404054
Ⓔ angelbooks@onetel.net.uk
Est. 1989 *Stock size* Medium
Stock General antiquarian books, Norfolk and natural history topics a speciality
Open Mon–Fri 9.30am–5pm Sat 9.30am–3.30pm closed Wed
Fairs PBFA
Services Book search

Eric Bates & Sons
Contact Graham or Eric Bates
Melbourne House, Bacton Road, North Walsham, Norfolk, NR28 0RA P
☎ 01692 403221 Ⓕ 01692 404388
Ⓜ 07887 776149
Ⓔ furnitureebates.fsnet.co.uk
Ⓦ www.batesfurniture.co.uk
Est. 1982 *Stock size* Large
Stock General 19thC antiques, Victorian chairs
Open Mon–Fri 9am–5pm Sat 9am–4.30pm
Fairs Newark

Horners Auctioneers
Contact Mr N Horner-Glister FRICS
North Walsham Sales Rooms, Midland Road, North Walsham, Norfolk, NR28 9JR
01692 500603 01692 500480
auction@horners.co.uk
www.horners.co.uk
Est. 1993
Open Mon–Fri 9am–1pm 2–5pm
Sales Monthly antiques and collectables sale Sat 10am, viewing Fri 10am–8pm
Frequency Bi-monthly
Catalogues Yes

NORWICH

Antiques & Interiors
31–35 Elm Hill, Norwich, Norfolk, NR3 1HG
01603 622695 01603 632446
Est. 1996 ***Stock size*** Large
Stock Art Deco and other furniture, porcelain
Open Mon–Sat 10am–5pm

Black Horse Antiques Centre
Contact Mandy Allen
8–10 Wensum Street, Norwich, Norfolk, NR3 1HR
01603 623339 01603 623339
mandyallen@btconnect.com
Est. 2002 ***Stock size*** Large
No. of dealers 20
Stock Fine 17th–18thC furniture, period lighting, collectables, Art Deco, country pine
Open Mon–Sat 10am–5pm
Services Restorations, antique lighting fitting

Black Horse Gallery (LAPADA, BADA)
Contact Mr C Risebrook
10b Wensum Street, Norwich, Norfolk, NR3 1HR
01603 612428
Est. 1989 ***Stock size*** Medium
Stock Complete range of antiques, collectables
Open Mon–Sat 10am–5pm
Fairs Lomax Antiques Fairs
Services Valuations

Arthur Brett & Sons (BADA)
Contact Mrs T Lotis
42 St Giles Street, Norwich, Norfolk, NR2 1LW
01603 628171 01603 630245
Est. 1870 ***Stock size*** Large
Stock 17th–18thC furniture, fine art
Open Mon–Fri 9.30am–1pm 2–5pm
Fairs Olympia

The Collectors' Shop
Contact Mr L Downham
2 Angel Road, Norwich, Norfolk, NR3 3HP
01603 765672
Est. 1975 ***Stock size*** Large
Stock Stamps, postcards, coins, models, small items, collectables
Open Mon–Sat 9.30am–5.30pm closed Thurs
Fairs Bloomsbury

Deja Vu
Contact Mr V Engledew or Mr A Hawes
67–69 Magdalen Street, Norwich, Norfolk, NR3 1AA
01603 765489 01603 765489
Est. 1987 ***Stock size*** Large
Stock General antiques, furniture
Open Mon–Sun 10am–5pm
Fairs Newark, The International Antique and Collectables Fair, RAF Swinderby
Services Valuations, restorations

Clive Dennett (BNTA, IBNS)
Contact Mr C Dennett
66 St Benedict's Street, Norwich, Norfolk, NR2 4AR
01603 624315 01603 624315
Est. 1970 ***Stock size*** Large
Stock Coins, medals, banknotes, currency
Open Mon–Sat 9am–5pm closed Thurs
Fairs The Cumberland Coin Fairs

Nicholas Fowle Antiques (BADA)
Contact Mr N Fowle
Websdales Court, Bedford Street, Norwich, Norfolk, NR2 1AR
01603 219964 01692 630378
07831 218808
Est. 1995 ***Stock size*** Medium
Stock 18th–19thC furniture
Open Mon–Fri 9am–5.30pm Sat 9am–1pm
Fairs BADA, Olympia (Nov)
Services Valuations, restorations

Peter J Hadley (PBFA, ABA)
Contact Mr P J Hadley
29 Surrey Street, Norwich, Norfolk, NR1 3NX
01603 663411 01603 663411
books@hadley.co.uk
www.hadley.co.uk
Est. 1983 ***Stock size*** Medium
Stock Antiquarian books, English, architectural history, art reference, literature
Open Fri Sat 10am–6pm, telephone first during week
Fairs PBFA, ABA Chelsea
Services Valuation, catalogue every 8 weeks

The Inventory
Contact Jonty Young or Roy Benton
97 Upper St Giles Street, Norwich, Norfolk, NR2 1AB
01603 667640 01603 611833
Est. 2001 ***Stock size*** Large
Stock Architectural antiques, paintings, shop fittings, lighting, 20thC design
Open Mon–Sat 10am–5.30pm

Leona Levine Silver Specialist (BADA)
Contact Leona Levine
35 St Giles Street, Norwich, Norfolk, NR2 1JN
01603 628709 01603 628709
Est. 1865 ***Stock size*** Large
Stock Silver, old Sheffield plate
Open Mon–Sat 9am–5pm closed Thurs
Services Valuations, restorations

Maddermarket Antiques (NAG)
Contact Mr T Earl
18c Lower Goat Lane, Norwich, Norfolk, NR2 1EL
01603 620610 01603 620610
Est. 1984 ***Stock size*** Large
Stock Antique, second-hand, modern jewellery, silverware
Open Mon–Sat 9am–5pm

The Movie Shop
Contact Mr P Cossey
11 St Gregory's Alley, Norwich, Norfolk, NR2 1ER
01603 615239
petecossey@mcmail.com
www.the-movieshop.com
Est. 1985 ***Stock size*** Large
Stock General antiquarian

books, movie, TV, theatre and vinyl
Open Mon–Sat 10.30am–5pm
Services Valuations

Norwich Auction Rooms
Contact Mr J Sutton
The Auction Centre, Bessemer Road, Norwich, Norfolk, NR4 6DQ
01603 666502 01603 666502
Est. 1991
Open Mon–Fri 9am–5pm
Sales Monthly antiques and collectables Sun 10.30am, viewing day of sale 9am and Fri prior to sale 2–4pm. Special sales occasionally
Frequency Monthly
Catalogues Yes

St Michael at Plea Antiques and Collectors Centre
Contact Mr D Clarke
Redwell Street, Bank Plain, Norwich, Norfolk, NR2 4SN
01603 618989
Est. 1987 *Stock size* Large
Stock China, silver, toys, brass, prints, small items of furniture, books, coins, medals
Open Mon–Sat 9.30am–5pm
Services Valuations, restorations

Timgems Jewellers
Contact Tim Snelling
30 Elm Hill, Norwich, Norfolk, NR3 1HG
01603 623296 01603 666183
Est. 1969 *Stock size* Medium
Stock Antique jewellery, silverware
Open Tues–Sat 11am–4.30pm
Services Valuations, restorations

Tombland Antiques Centre
Contact Bob Gale
Augustine Stewart House, 14 Tombland, Norwich, Norfolk, NR3 1HF
01603 619129
Est. 1999 *Stock size* Large
No. of dealers 40
Stock A wide range of antiques and collectables
Open Mon–Sat 10am–5pm Sun 11am–3pm
Services Valuations

Tombland Bookshop
Contact Mr J Freeman
8 Tombland, Norwich, Norfolk, NR3 1HF
01603 490000 01603 760610
tombland.bookshop@virgin.net
Est. 1973 *Stock size* Large
Stock Antiquarian and second-hand books
Open Mon–Fri 9.30am–5pm Sat 9.30am–4.30pm

Malcolm Turner
Contact Mr M Turner
15 St Giles Street, Norwich, Norfolk, NR2 1JL
01603 627007 01603 627007
Est. 1971 *Stock size* Large
Stock Mixed porcelain, bronze figures, silver, jewellery
Open Tues–Sat 10am–5pm
Services Valuations

Tymewarp
Contact Mrs C Docwra
1 Magdalen Street, Tombland, Norwich, Norfolk, NR3 1LE
01603 616396
07789 114629
Est. 2000 *Stock size* Medium
Stock Art Deco, 20thC, Retro antiques
Open Tues–Sat 10am–4pm
Fairs Newark, Take Five, Woking

RAVENINGHAM

M D Cannell
Contact Mr M Cannell
Castell Farm, Beccles Road, Raveningham, Norfolk, NR14 6NU
01508 548406 01508 548406
07801 416355
mal@raveningham.demon.co.uk
Est. 1984 *Stock size* Large
Stock European decorative furniture, carpets, Oriental rugs
Open Fri–Mon 10am–6pm or by appointment
Fairs Newark, Bath Decorative

REEPHAM

Bonhams
The Market Place, Reepham, Norwich, Norfolk, NR10 4JJ
01603 871443 01603 872973
norfolk@bonhams.com
www.bonhams.com
Est. 1793
Open Mon–Fri 9am–1pm 2–5pm
Catalogues Yes

Echo Antiques
Contact Marion Stiesel
Church Hill, Reepham, Norwich, Norfolk, NR10 4JW
01603 873291
Est. 1997 *Stock size* Large
Stock General antiques, English and French furniture
Open Mon–Sat 10am–5pm closed Thurs
Services Valuations

SCRATBY

Keith Lawson Antique Clocks (BHI)
Contact Keith Lawson
Scratby Garden Centre, Beach Road, Scratby, Great Yarmouth, Norfolk, NR29 3AJ
01493 730950 01493 730658
Est. 1979
Stock Antique clocks
Open Mon–Sun 2–6pm
Services Valuations, restorations

SHERINGHAM

Kitty Blakes Shop
Contact Mrs J McMillan
57 Station Road, Sheringham, Norfolk, NR26 8RG
01263 825316
Est. 1998 *Stock size* Large
Stock General antiques, stamps, prints, old sheet music, postcards, china, collectables
Open Mon–Sat 9am–5pm
Fairs Norwich Sports Centre

Dorothy's Antiques
Contact Mrs D E Collier
23 Waterbank Road, Sheringham, Norfolk, NR26 8RB
01263 822319
Est. 1975 *Stock size* Medium
Stock Royal Worcestershire, Royal Doulton, small furniture, collectables
Open Mon–Sun 11.15am–3.30pm

SOUTH WALSHAM

Leo Pratt and Son (LAPADA)
Contact Mr Rodney Pratt
Curiosity Shop, South Walsham, Norwich, Norfolk, NR13 6EA
01603 270204 01603 270204
Est. 1890 *Stock size* Large

Stock General antiques, furniture, clocks, china
Open Mon–Sat 9.30am–5pm
Services Valuations

STALHAM

Stalham Antique Gallery (LAPADA)
Contact Mr Mike Hicks
29 High Street, Stalham, Norwich, Norfolk, NR12 9AH
01692 580636 Ⓕ 01692 580636
Ⓔ mbhickslink@talk21.com
Est. 1970 *Stock size* Large
Stock Period furniture, associated items
Open Mon–Fri 9am–5pm Sat 9am–1pm or by appointment
Services Valuations, restorations

SWAFFHAM

Cranglegate Antiques
Contact Mrs R D Buckie
59 Market Place, Swaffham, Norfolk, PE37 7LE
01760 721052
Ⓦ www.buckie-antiques.com
Est. 1973 *Stock size* Medium
Stock Furniture, decorative, small items
Open Tues Thurs Sat 10am–1pm 2–5.30pm
Fairs Newark

THETFORD

Thetford Antiques and Collectables
Contact Dennis Crawford
6 Market Place, Thetford, Norfolk, IP24 2AJ
01842 755511
Ⓜ 07961 302651
Est. 1998 *Stock size* Large
Stock Furniture, Doulton, Beswick, Wedgwood china, collectables including Toby jugs, silver
Open Mon–Sat 9.30am–5pm
Services Valuations

WATTON

J C Books (PBFA)
Contact Mr J A Ball
55 High Street, Watton, Thetford, Norfolk, IP25 6AB
01953 883488 Ⓕ 01953 883488
Ⓔ j.c.books@lineone.net
Est. 1990 *Stock size* Medium
Stock General antiquarian books, ephemera, Victorian and Edwardian theatre a speciality
Open Mon–Wed Fri Sat 10am–4.30pm Thurs 10am–1pm
Fairs PBFA
Services Book search

Watton Salerooms
Contact Mr S Roberts
Breckland House, Newgreen Business Park, Norwich Road, Watton, Thetford, Norfolk, IP25 6DU
01953 885676 Ⓕ 01953 885676
Ⓔ watton.salerooms@eidosnet.co.uk
Ⓦ www.thesalerooms.co.uk
Est. 1989
Open Mon 8am–8pm Tues 8am–6pm Wed–Fri 10am–3pm Sat 10am–1pm
Sales 7 or 8 antiques sales yearly on Bank Holidays and Sun, viewing day before the sale 3–6pm and day of sale from 9am. Also antiques and general household Tues, viewing Mon 4–8pm and day of sale
Frequency Weekly
Catalogues No

WELLS-NEXT-THE-SEA

Church Street Antiques
Contact Mrs P Ford or Mrs L Irons
2 Church Street, Wells-next-the-Sea, Norfolk, NR23 1JA
01328 711698
Est. 1989 *Stock size* Large
Stock Small collectables, costume jewellery, linen, lace, costume, hat pins
Open Summer Tues–Sun 10am–4pm winter Thurs–Sun 10am–4pm

Wells Antique Centre
Contact Mr Vallance
The Old Mill, Maryland, Wells-next-the-Sea, Norfolk, NR23 1LY
01328 711433
Est. 1989 *Stock size* Medium
No. of dealers 15
Stock General antiques, copper, brass, porcelain, glass, rugs, furniture, jewellery, linen, collectables
Open Mon–Sun 10am–4pm

WROXHAM

T C S Brooke (BADA)
Contact Mr S T Brooke
The Grange, Norwich Road, Wroxham, Norwich, Norfolk, NR12 8RX
01603 782644 Ⓕ 01603 782644
Est. 1936 *Stock size* Large
Stock General antiques, 18thC furniture, Georgian items, 18thC porcelain
Open Tues–Sat 9.15am–1pm 2.15–5.30pm
Services Valuations

Bradley Hatch Jewellers
Contact Mr Bradley Hatch
Tunstead Road, Wroxham, Norwich, Norfolk, NR12 8QG
01603 782233 Ⓕ 01603 784679
Ⓔ sales@bradleyhatch.com
Ⓦ www.bradleyhatch.com
Est. 1994 *Stock size* Medium
Stock Jewellery, watches, silver, clocks, gifts, pocket watches
Open Mon–Sat 9am–5pm
Services Valuations, restorations, shipping

WYMONDHAM

Margaret King
Contact Margaret King
16 Market Place, Wymondham, Norfolk, NR18 0AX
01953 604758
Est. 1975 *Stock size* Large
Stock General antiques, furniture, porcelain, glass, silver
Open Thurs–Sat 9am–1pm 2–4pm
Fairs Langley, Woolverstone, all Lomax Fairs

M and A C Thompson
Contact Mr A C Thompson
The Bookshop, 1 Town Green, Wymondham, Norfolk, NR18 0PN
01953 602244
Est. 1981 *Stock size* Medium
Stock Antiquarian, general second-hand books
Open Mon–Fri 10.30am–4.50pm closed Wed

Wymondham Antique Centre
Contact Kay Hipperson
3 Town Green, Wymondham, Norfolk, NR18 0PN
01953 604817 Ⓕ 01603 811112

Est. 1987 *Stock size* Large
Stock General antiques, china, furniture, books, pictures
Open Mon–Sun 10am–5pm
Services Valuations

SUFFOLK

ALDEBURGH

Bly Valley Antiques
Contact Mr Eric Ward
152 High Street, Aldeburgh, Suffolk, IP15 5AX
01728 454508 F 01502 675376
www.bly-valley-antiques.com
Est. 2000 *Stock size* Medium
Stock China, glass, pictures, furniture, antiquarian books
Open Thurs–Sat 10.30am–4.30pm

Mole Hall Antiques
Contact Mr P Weaver
102 High Street, Aldeburgh, Suffolk, IP15 5AB
01728 452361
Est. 1981 *Stock size* Large
Stock General antiques
Open Mon–Sat 10am–5pm
Fairs Snape

BECCLES

Besley's Books (PBFA, ABA)
Contact Piers or Gaby Besley
4 Blyburgate, Beccles, Suffolk, NR34 9TA
01502 715762 F 01502 675649
piers@besleysbooks.demon.co.uk
www.besleysbooks.demon.co.uk
Est. 1970 *Stock size* Medium
Stock Antiquarian books. Gardening, natural history, art, private press a speciality
Open Mon–Sat 9.30am–5pm closed Wed
Fairs PBFA, ABA
Services Valuations, restorations, booksearch, 2 catalogues a year

Blyburgate Antiques
Contact Mrs Kate Lee
27–29 Blyburgate, Beccles, Suffolk, NR34 9TB
01502 711174
katherine.lee@lineone.net
Est. 1997 *Stock size* Medium
Stock General antiques, furniture
Open Tues–Sat 10am–4.30pm closed Wed
Fairs Alexandra Palace
Services Valuations

Durrants Auction Rooms
Contact Mr Miles Lamdin
Gresham Road, Beccles, Suffolk, NR34 9QN
01502 713490 F 01502 711039
info@durrantsauctionrooms.com
www.durrantsauctionrooms.com
Est. 1853
Open Mon–Fri 9am–4pm Sat 9am–noon
Sales General antiques sales every Fri. Special sale once every 6 weeks, viewing every Thurs and sale day
Frequency Weekly
Catalogues No

Fauconberges
Contact Mr R D Howard or Mr R J Crozier
8 Smallgate, Beccles, Suffolk, NR34 9AD
01502 716147
Est. 1980 *Stock size* Medium
Stock 17th–19thC furniture, pictures, glass
Open Mon–Sat 10am–5pm
Fairs Lomax, Graham Turner (Long Melford)
Services Valuations for insurance and probate, sales on commission, decanter cleaning and renovation

M & A Ratcliffe
Contact Mrs A Ratcliffe
11 Saltgate, Beccles, Suffolk, NR34 9AN
01502 712776
Est. 1971 *Stock size* Medium
Stock General antiques, 18th–19thC furniture
Open Mon–Sat 10am–5pm early closing Wed

BUNGAY

Beaver Booksearch
Contact Mr N Watts
33 Hillside Road East, Bungay, Suffolk, NR35 1JU
01986 896698 F 01986 896698
nick@beaverbooksearch.co.uk
www.beaverbooksearch.co.uk
Est. 1996 *Stock size* Small
Stock Books, bridge a speciality
Open Mail order only
Services Book search

Black Dog Antiques
Contact Mr M Button
51 Earsham Street, Bungay, Suffolk, NR35 1AF
01986 895554
Est. 1985 *Stock size* Medium
Stock General, collectables, pine furniture
Open Mon–Sat 10am–5pm Sun 11am–4.30pm

Friend or Faux
Contact Jane Cudlipp or Kim Sisson
28 Earsham Street, Bungay, Suffolk, NR35 1AQ
01986 896170 F 01502 714246
Est. 1989 *Stock size* Medium
Stock Antiques, decorative objects, murals, paintings, hand-painted furniture
Open Fri–Sat 10am–5pm
Services Restorations, faux finishes

One Step Back
Contact Mrs Diane Wells
4a Earsham Street, Bungay, Suffolk, NR35 1AG
01986 896626
Est. 1998 *Stock size* Medium
Stock General antiques, furniture
Open Mon–Sat 10am–5pm closed Wed
Services Restorations

BURES

Major Iain Grahame (ABA)
Contact Major Iain Grahame
Daws Hall, Lamarsh, Bures, Suffolk, CO8 5EX
01787 269213 F 01787 269634
majorbooks@compuserve.com
www.iaingrahamerarebooks.com
Est. 1979 *Stock size* Medium
Stock Antiquarian books, especially sporting, natural history, Africana
Open By appointment
Fairs Olympia

BURROUGH GREEN

R E and G B Way (ABA, PBFA)
Contact Mr G Way
Brettons, Church Lane, Burrough Green, Newmarket, Suffolk, CB8 9NA

☎ 01638 507217 Ⓕ 01638 508058
Ⓔ waybks@msn.com
Est. 1950 *Stock size* Large
Stock Antiquarian, out-of-print, horse, hunting, racing, field-sport books
Open Mon–Sat 9am–5pm phone to check
Fairs Russell Book Fair

BURY ST EDMUNDS

Lacy Scott & Knight (SOFAA)
Contact Edward Crichton
10 Risbygate Street, Bury St Edmunds, Suffolk, IP33 3AA
☎ 01284 748600 Ⓕ 01284 748620
Ⓔ fineart@lsk.co.uk
Ⓦ www.lsk.co.uk
Est. 1869
Open Mon–Fri 9am–1pm 2–5.30pm
Sales Quarterly fine art sale and model and collectors' sales. Victoriana sales every 3–4 weeks, viewing Fri 3–7pm
Frequency Monthly
Catalogues Yes

Marshall Buck and Casson
Contact Mr B Moss
The Auction Rooms, Eastgate Street, Bury St Edmunds, Suffolk, IP33 1YQ
☎ 01284 756081 Ⓕ 01284 756081
Ⓜ 07768 324102
Est. 1999
Open Wed 8am–8pm
Sales Mixed antiques and general sales Sat, viewing Fri 2.30–8pm and Sat 8–9am. Periodic special antiques sales
Frequency Every 3 weeks
Catalogues Yes

Peppers Period Pieces
Contact Mr M Pepper
23 Churchgate Street, Bury St Edmunds, Suffolk, IP33 1RG
☎ 01284 768786 Ⓕ 01284 768786
Est. 1975 *Stock size* Small
Stock 16th–18thC English oak furniture, 15th–19thC metalware
Open Mon–Sat 10am–5pm
Services Restorations

CAMPSIE ASH

Abbotts Auction Rooms
Contact Mrs Linda Coates
Campsie Ash, Woodbridge, Suffolk, IP13 0PS
☎ 01728 746323 Ⓕ 01728 748173
Est. 1920
Open Mon–Sat 9am–5.30pm
Sales General auction every Mon 11am, viewing Sat 9–11am and 8.30–11am on day of sale. Special antiques auctions (9 per annum) Wed 10am, viewing Mon prior to sale 2–8pm Tues 10am–4pm and morning of sale from 8.30am
Frequency Weekly
Catalogues Yes

Ashe Antiques Warehouse
Contact Mr G Laffling
Station Road, Campsie Ash, Woodbridge, Suffolk, IP13 0PT
☎ 01728 747255 Ⓕ 01728 747255
Est. 1987 *Stock size* Large
Stock 18thC oak furniture, Victorian smalls, mirrors etc
Open Mon–Sun 10.30am–5pm
Fairs The International Antique and Collectables Fair, RAF Swinderby, Newark
Services French polishing, upholstery, ceramic restoration

CAVENDISH

Cavendish Rose Antiques
Contact Toby Patterson
1 Clarks Yard, High Street, Cavendish, Sudbury, Suffolk, CO10 8AT
☎ 01787 282133 Ⓕ 01787 280332
Ⓔ cavrose.antiques@easicom.co
Est. 1974 *Stock size* Large
Stock 18thC–Edwardian furniture, dining tables, chairs, desks, chests-of-drawers, bookcases
Open Mon–Sat 10.30am–5pm

CLARE

Clare Antique Warehouse
Contact Leonard Edwards
The Mill, Malting Lane, Clare, Suffolk, CO10 8NW
☎ 01787 278449 Ⓕ 01787 278449
Est. 1988 *Stock size* Large
No. of dealers 85
Stock General, pine, oak furniture
Open Mon–Sat 9.30am–5pm Sun 1–5pm
Services Restorations, shipping, valuations

Dyson & Son
Contact Mr N Dyson
The Auction Rooms, Church Street, Clare, Sudbury, Suffolk, CO10 8PD
☎ 01787 277993 Ⓕ 01787 277996
Ⓔ info@dyson-auctioneers.co.uk
Ⓦ www.dyson-auctioneers.co.uk
Est. 1977
Open Mon–Fri 9am–5pm closed 1–2pm Sat 9am–1pm
Sales General antiques sales every 3 weeks Sat, 600–700 lots, viewing Fri 9am–9pm and day of sale 9–11am. A yearly calendar is available on request
Frequency Every 3 weeks
Catalogues Yes

Christina Parker Antiques
Contact Christina Parker
Church Street, Clare, Suffolk, CO10 8PD
☎ 01787 278570 or 0207 628 4545
Ⓕ 0207 428 5942
Ⓔ chrisparker@hotmail.com
Ⓦ www.jewelpast.com
Est. 1999 *Stock size* Small
Stock Jewellery, ceramics, pictures, collectables, scent bottles, vintage clothing, textiles
Open Mon–Wed 11am–4pm Thurs–Sat 9.30am–5pm
Fairs Newmarket

F D Salter
Contact Mr F D Salter
1–2 Church Street, Clare, Sudbury, Suffolk, CO10 8PD
☎ 01787 277693
Est. 1960 *Stock size* Medium
Stock 18th–19thC furniture, porcelain, glass
Open Mon–Sat 9am–5pm closed Wed
Fairs West London, Harrogate
Services Furniture restorations

Sarah Smith Scent Bottles and Collectables
Contact Sarah Smith
2 Mortimer Place, Clare, Suffolk, CO10 8QP
☎ 01787 277609
Est. 2001 *Stock size* Small

Stock Scent bottles, handbags, compacts, jewellery
Open By appointment

⊞ Trinder's Fine Tools (PBFA)
Contact Mr P D Trinder
✉ **Malting Lane, Clare, Sudbury, Suffolk, CO10 8NW** 🅿
☎ 01787 277130 Ⓕ 01787 277677
Ⓔ peter@trindersfinetools.co.uk
Ⓦ www.trindersfinetools.co.uk
Est. 1974 *Stock size* Medium
Stock Woodworking tools including British infill planes by Norris, Spiers, Mathieson, Preston, second-hand, new books on furniture and woodworking, horology, architecture, art reference, collecting, metalworking, model engineering
Open Mon–Fri 10am–1pm 2–5pm Wed Sat 10am–1pm advisable to phone to check times

DEBENHAM

⊞ Debenham Antiques
Contact Simon Sodeaux or Chris Bigden
✉ **73 High Street, Debenham, Suffolk, IP14 6QS** 🅿
☎ 01728 860707 Ⓕ 01728 860333
Ⓜ 07836 260650
Ⓔ info@debenhamantiques.com
Est. 1974 *Stock size* Large
Stock 17th–19thC furniture, paintings
Open Mon–Sat 9.30am–5.30pm

DRINKSTONE

⊞ Denzil Grant (BADA, LAPADA)
Contact Mr D Grant
✉ **Drinkstone House, Gedding Rd, Drinkstone, Bury St Edmunds, Suffolk, IP30 9TG** 🅿
☎ 01449 736576 Ⓕ 01449 737679
Ⓜ 07836 223312
Ⓔ denzil@denzilgrant.com
Ⓦ www.denzilgrant.com
Est. 1979 *Stock size* Medium
Stock 17th–19thC country furniture
Open By appointment
Fairs LAPADA, Olympias

EASTON

⊞ Marilyn Garrow Fine Textile Art (LAPADA, BADA)
Contact Marilyn Garrow
✉ **2 Black and White Cottages, Easton, Suffolk, IP13 0EF** 🅿
☎ 01728 648671 Ⓕ 01728 648671
Ⓜ 07774 842074
Ⓔ marogarrow@aol.com
Est. 1977 *Stock size* Large
Stock Textiles
Open By appointment
Fairs Olympia, LAPADA
Services Valuations

EXNING

⊞ Exning Antiques & Interiors
Contact Mrs M Tabbron
✉ **5 Oxford Street, Exning, Newmarket, Suffolk, CB8 7EW** 🅿
☎ 01638 600073 Ⓕ 01638 600015
Est. 1993 *Stock size* Small
Stock Beds, canopies, covers, drapes, mirrors, original lighting
Open Tues–Sat 10am–5pm
Fairs Newark
Services Restoring and cleaning lighting

EYE

⊞ English and Continental Antiques
Contact Mr Steven Harmer
✉ **1 Broad Street, Eye, Suffolk, IP23 7AF** 🅿
☎ 01379 871199 Ⓕ 01379 871199
Ⓔ steveneca@aol.com
Est. 1975 *Stock size* Medium
Stock 17th–19thC furniture
Open Tues–Sat 10am–5pm
Services Restorations, upholstery

FELIXSTOWE

⊞ Ancient and Modern Collectables Centre
Contact Mr Brian Fahey
✉ **2 Bent Hill, Felixstowe, Suffolk, IP11 7DG** 🅿
☎ 01394 275709
Est. 1984 *Stock size* Large
Stock Antique ceramics, collectables
Open Mon–Sun 10am–4.30pm closed Wed
Services Ceramics bought on commission

Diamond Mills & Company (FSVA)
Contact Mr N J Papworth
✉ **117 Hamilton Road, Felixstowe, Suffolk, P11 7BL** 🅿
☎ 01394 282281 Ⓕ 01394 671791
Ⓔ diamondmills@easynet.co.uk
Ⓦ www.diamondmills.co.uk
Est. 1908
Open Mon–Fri 9am–6pm Sat 9am–4pm
Sales Antiques sales monthly, usually Wed, phone for details, 3 special sales annually
Frequency Monthly
Catalogues Yes

⊞ Poor Richard's Books
Contact Dick Moffat
✉ **17 Orwell Road, Felixstowe, Suffolk, IP11 7EP** 🅿
☎ 01394 283138
Ⓔ moffatsfx@aol.com
Est. 1997 *Stock size* Large
Stock General and antiquarian books, modern first editions
Open Mon–Sat 9am–5pm
Services Valuations, restorations, book search

⊞ Tea and Antiques
Contact David George
✉ **109 High Road, Old Felixstowe, Suffolk, IP11 9PS** 🅿
☎ 01394 277789
Est. 2000 *Stock size* Medium
Stock Antiques, collectables, furniture
Open Thurs–Sun Bank Holidays 10am–5pm
Services Tea shop

⊞ The Treasure Chest Books (PBFA)
Contact Mr Robert Green
✉ **61 Cobbold Road, Felixstowe, Suffolk, IP11 7BH** 🅿
☎ 01394 270717
Est. 1981 *Stock size* Large
Stock Antiquarian and second-hand books
Open Mon–Sat 9.30am–5.30pm

FINNINGHAM

⊞ Abington Books
Contact Mr J Haldane
✉ **Primrose Cottage, Westhorpe, Finningham, Stowmarket, Suffolk, IP14 4TW** 🅿
☎ 01449 780303 Ⓕ 01449 780202
Est. 1971 *Stock size* Medium

Stock Antiquarian books on Oriental and other carpets, classical tapestries
Open By appointment
Services Valuations, restorations, book search

FRAMLINGHAM

Richard Goodbrey Antiques
Contact Mrs M Goodbrey
29 Double Street, Framlingham, Woodbridge, Suffolk, IP13 9BN
01728 621191 F 01728 724626
M 07802 868622
E merlin@zetnet.co.uk
Est. 1965 *Stock size* Large
Stock 18th–19thC Continental antiques, some English furniture, sleigh beds, painted furniture, pottery, glass
Open Sat 9am–1pm 2–5.30pm or by appointment
Fairs Newark

The Green Room
Contact Mrs J Shand Kydd
2 Church Street, Framlingham, Woodbridge, Suffolk, IP13 9BE
01728 723009
Est. 1986 *Stock size* Medium
Stock Textiles, quilts, curtains, bed covers
Open Fri Sat 11am–4.45pm

The Theatre Antiques Centre
Contact Wig Darby
10 Church Street, Framlingham, Suffolk, IP13 9BH
01728 621069
E wig@darbyw.freeserve.co.uk
W www.darbyw.freeserve.co.uk
Est. 2002 *Stock size* Large
No. of dealers 9
Stock Country and fine furniture, smalls
Open Mon–Sat 9.30–5.30pm

HACHESTON

Pine and Country Furniture
Contact Mrs Joyce Hardy
Wisteria Cottage, The Street, Hacheston, Woodbridge, Suffolk, IP3 0DS
01728 746485
Est. 1962 *Stock size* Medium
Stock Antique pine furniture
Open Mon–Sat 9.30am–5.30pm Sun 10am–noon
Fairs Ardingly, Ipswich

HADLEIGH

Randolph Antiques (BADA)
Contact Mr Baden F Marston
97–99 High Street, Hadleigh, Ipswich, Suffolk, IP7 5EJ
01473 823789 F 01473 823867
Est. 1929 *Stock size* Medium
Stock English furniture up to 1830, accessories
Open By appointment only

IPSWICH

A Abbott Antiques
Contact Mr A Abbott
757 Woodbridge Road, Ipswich, Suffolk, IP4 4NE
01473 728900 F 01473 728900
M 07771 533413
E abbott_antiques@hotmail.com
Est. 1974
Stock General antiques, furniture, smalls, clocks
Open Mon–Sat 9.30am–5pm closed Wed
Fairs Newark, Ardingly

Antiques and Restoration
Contact Mr R Rush
Unit 5, Penny Corner, Farthing Road, Ipswich, Suffolk, IP1 5AP
01473 464609 F 01473 464609
M 07939 220041
E info@antiquesandrestoration.co.uk
W www.antiquesandrestoration.co.uk
Est. 1997 *Stock size* Medium
Stock 18th–19thC furniture
Open Mon–Fri 8am–6pm Sat 8am–1.30pm
Services Restorations

Bonhams
32 Boss Hall Road, Ipswich, Suffolk, IP1 5DJ
01473 740494 F 01473 741091
E ipswich@bonhams.com
W www.bonhams.com
Open Mon 9am–7pm Sat 9am–noon
Sales Ipswich Saleroom

Claude Cox Books (ABA, PBFA)
Contact Anthony Brian Cox
3–5 Silent Street, Ipswich, Suffolk, IP11 1TF
01473 254776 F 01473 254776
E books@claudecox.co.uk
W www.claudecox.co.uk
Est. 1974 *Stock size* Large
Stock Antiquarian and second-hand books, fine printing, private press, catalogues issued, Suffolk maps and prints a speciality
Open Wed–Sat 10am–5pm or by appointment

Andrew Drake Antiques
Contact Mr A Drake
211 Spring Road, Ipswich, Suffolk, IP4 5NF
01473 713608 F 01473 711164
Est. 1987 *Stock size* Large
Stock General
Open Mon–Sat 9am–4.30pm closed Wed
Fairs Swinderby

Hubbard's Antiques
Contact Mr Mark Hubbard
16 St Margaret's Green, Ipswich, Suffolk, IP4 2BS
01473 233034 F 01473 253639
E sales@hubbard-antiques.com
W www.hubbard-antiques.com
Est. 1965 *Stock size* Large
Stock 18th–19thC antique furniture, decorative items, works of art
Open Mon–Sat 9am–6pm or by appointment
Services Valuations by Internet

Lockdale Coins Ltd (BNTA)
Contact Dan Daley
37 Upper Orwell Street, Ipswich, Suffolk, IP4 1HP
01473 218588 F 01473 218588
E lockdales@shop1.freeserve.co.uk
W lockdales.co.uk
Est. 1994 *Stock size* Medium
Stock British and foreign coins, banknotes, metal detectors and accessories
Open Mon–Sat 9.30am–4.30pm
Fairs Cumberland Hotel Show, Olympia
Services Valuations, auctioneering

Lockdale Coins Ltd
Contact Dan Daley
37 Upper Orwell Street, Ipswich, Suffolk, IP4 1HP
01473 218588 F 01473 218588

ⓔ lockdales@shop1.freeserve.co.uk
ⓦ www.lockdales.com
Est. 1996
Open Mon–Sat 9.30am–5pm
Sales Phone for details of sales, held alternately between Ipswich and Norwich
Frequency Bi-monthly
Catalogues Yes

Maud's Attic
Contact Mrs W Childs
25 St Peter's Street, Ipswich, Suffolk, IP1 1XF
☎ 01473 221057 ⓕ 01473 221056
Est. 1996 *Stock size* Large
Stock Antiques, collectables
Open Tues–Sat 10am–5pm

Merchant House Antiques
Contact Mr G Childs
27–29 St Peter's Street, Ipswich, Suffolk, IP1 1XF
☎ 01473 221054 ⓕ 01473 221056
ⓜ 07768 068575
Est. 2000 *Stock size* Medium
Stock Antiques and reclamation
Open Tues–Sat 10am–5pm

The Suffolk Antique Bed Centre
Contact Mr A Sandham
273 Norwich Road, Ipswich, Suffolk, IP1 4BP
☎ 01473 252444
Est. 1985 *Stock size* Large
Stock Brass and iron bedsteads
Open Mon–Sat 9am–5.30pm
Services Hand-made mattresses

Suffolk Sci-fi Fantasy
Contact Mr M Milliard
17 Norwich Road, Ipswich, Suffolk, IP1 2ET
☎ 01473 400655 ⓕ 01473 400656
Est. 1992 *Stock size* Large
Stock Sci-fi collectables, ephemera, collectable card games, trade cards
Open Mon–Sat 9am–6pm

E F Wall Antiques
Contact Libby Wall
Cliff Quay, Ipswich, Suffolk, IP3 0BD
☎ 01473 225010 ⓕ 01473 254910
ⓜ 07885 374917
ⓔ libbyswall@ukonline.co.uk
Est. 1979 *Stock size* Large
Stock Reproduction French polished furniture
Trade only Yes
Open Mon–Fri 7am–6pm
Fairs NEC, USA
Services Restorations

IXWORTH

E W Cousins & Son (LAPADA)
Contact Mr Robert Cousins
Old School, Thetford Road, Ixworth, Bury St Edmunds, Suffolk, IP31 2HJ
☎ 01359 230254 ⓕ 01359 232370
ⓔ john@ewcousins.co.uk
ⓦ www.ewcousins.co.uk
Est. 1920 *Stock size* Large
Stock 18th–19thC furniture
Open Mon–Fri 8.30am–5pm Sat 8.30am–1pm
Services Restorations, containers packed

LAVENHAM

R G Archer Books
Contact Mr Richard Archer
7 Water Street, Lavenham, Sudbury, Suffolk, CO10 9RW
☎ 01787 247229
Est. 1970 *Stock size* Medium
Stock Second-hand and antiquarian books, especially of Suffolk and Norfolk interest
Open Mon–Sun 10am–5pm closed Wed
Services Book search

J & J Baker
Contact Mrs Joy Baker
12–14 Water Street, Lavenham, Sudbury, Suffolk, CO10 9RW
☎ 01787 247610
Est. 1970 *Stock size* Large
Stock General English antiques, furniture, porcelain
Open Mon–Sat 10am–5.30pm

One Bell
Contact Mr John Tinworth
46 High Street, Lavenham, Sudbury, Suffolk, CO10 9PY
☎ 01787 248206
Est. 1986 *Stock size* Medium
Stock Militaria, small collectables
Open Mon–Sun 11am–4.30pm closed Wed Thurs

Timbers Antiques & Collectables
Contact Mrs Ann Trodd or Brenda Preece
High Street, Lavenham, Sudbury, Suffolk, CO10 9PT
☎ 01787 247218
Est. 1996 *Stock size* Medium
Stock Antique furniture, silver, glass etc
Open Mon–Sun 10am–5pm closed Wed
Fairs Newark, Birmingham

LEISTON

Leiston Trading Post
Contact Mrs L Smith
13a High Street, Leiston, Suffolk, IP16 4EL
☎ 01728 830081
ⓜ 0771 259 6005
Est. 1967 *Stock size* Large
Stock Shipping goods, general antiques, china, bric-a-brac
Open Mon–Sat 9.30am–1pm 2–4.30pm half day Wed
Fairs Newark
Services Valuations

Warren Antiques
Contact Mr J Warren
31 High Street, Leiston, Suffolk, IP16 4EL
☎ 01728 831414 ⓕ 01728 831414
ⓜ 07989 865598
Est. 1970 *Stock size* Medium
Stock Late 18thC–1930s furniture
Open Mon–Tues 9am–1pm 2–5pm Thurs–Sat 9am–12.30pm
Fairs Newark, Ardingly (DMG)
Services Restorations

LONG MELFORD

Karen Bryan Antiques
Contact Karen Bryan
Little St Mary's, Long Melford, Sudbury, Suffolk, CO10 9LQ
☎ 01787 312613 ⓕ 01206 271727
Est. 1990 *Stock size* Medium
Stock Georgian, post-Georgian furniture, pictures, prints
Open Mon–Sat 10.30am–4.30pm closed Wed

Sandy Cooke Antiques
Contact Mr Sandy Cooke
Hall Street, Long Melford, Sudbury, Suffolk, CO10 9JQ
☎ 01787 378265 ⓕ 01284 830935
ⓔ sandycooke@englishfurniture.co.uk
ⓦ www.englishfurniture.co.uk
Est. 1974 *Stock size* Large
Stock 1700–1830 English furniture
Open Mon Fri Sat 10am–5pm

Alexander Lyall Antiques
Contact Mr A J Lyall
Belmont House, Hall Street, Long Melford, Sudbury, Suffolk, CO10 9JF
☎ 01787 375434 Ⓕ 01787 311115
Ⓔ alex@lyallantiques.com
Ⓦ www.lyallantiques.com
Est. 1977 *Stock size* Medium
Stock Georgian–Victorian furniture
Open Mon–Sat 10am–5.30pm closed Bank Holidays

Magpie Antiques
Contact Pat Coll
Hall Street, Long Melford, Sudbury, Suffolk, CO10 9JT
☎ 01787 310581 Ⓕ 01787 310581
Ⓔ terrycoll.magpie@ic24.net
Est. 1984 *Stock size* Large
Stock Stripped old pine, country collectables
Open Tues Thurs Fri 10.30am–1pm 2.15–4.30pm Sat 11am–5pm

Melford Antiques Warehouse
Contact Patrick
Hall Street, Long Melford, Sudbury, Suffolk, CO10 9JB
☎ 01787 379638
Ⓔ patrick@worldwideantiques.co.uk
Ⓦ www.antiques-access-agency.com
Est. 1979 *Stock size* Large
Stock 17th–20thC furniture, decorative items, large variety of dining tables, bookcases, chairs, clocks etc
Open Mon–Sat 9.30am–5pm Sun 1–5pm
Services Valuations, restorations, shipping

Noel Mercer Antiques
Contact Mr Noel Mercer
Aurora House, Hall Street, Long Melford, Suffolk, CO10 9JR
☎ 01787 311882
Est. 1991 *Stock size* Large
Stock Early English oak and walnut furniture
Open Mon–Sat 10am–5pm

Seabrook Antiques
Contact Mr John Tanner
Melford Gallery, Hall Street, Long Melford, Sudbury, Suffolk, CO10 9JF
☎ 01787 375787 Ⓕ 01787 375787
Est. 1978 *Stock size* Large
Stock 17th–19thC oak and decorative furniture
Open Mon–Sat 9.30am–5.30pm
Services Interior design

Stable Antiques
Contact Mrs P Gee
Hall Street, Long Melford, Sudbury, Suffolk, CO10 9JB
☎ 01787 310754
Est. 1980 *Stock size* Medium
Stock Victorian–1960s memorabilia
Open Mon–Sat 10am–5pm Sun 1–5pm closed Thurs

Suthburgh Antiques
Contact Mr R Alston
The Red House, Hall Street, Long Melford, Sudbury, Suffolk, CO10 9JQ
☎ 01787 374818 Ⓕ 01787 374818
Est. 1977 *Stock size* Large
Stock Early oak, walnut, Georgian, mahogany furniture, clocks, barometers, period portraits, early metalware, maps
Open Friday 10am–5pm Saturday noon–5pm or by appointment
Services Valuations, restorations

Trident Antiques (LAPADA)
Contact Mr Tom McGlynn
2 Foundry House, Hall Street, Long Melford, Sudbury, Suffolk, CO10 9JR
☎ 01787 883388 Ⓕ 01787 378850
Ⓜ 07860 221402
Ⓔ tridentoak@aol.com
Est. 1994 *Stock size* Large
Stock Early oak, English furniture, related objects, barometers
Open Mon–Sat 10am–5.30pm
Fairs LAPADA (Jan NEC)
Services Valuations, restorations, security implanting

Village Clocks
Contact Mr J Massey
Little St Mary's, Long Melford, Suffolk, CO10 0LQ
☎ 01787 375896
Est. 1989 *Stock size* Large
Stock Antique clocks
Open Mon–Sat 10am–4pm closed Wed
Services Restorations

LOWESTOFT

Lockdale Coins Ltd (BNTA)
Contact Dan Daley
168 London Road South, Lowestoft, Suffolk, NR33 0BB
☎ 01502 568468 Ⓕ 01502 568468
Ⓔ ddaley@lockdales.freeserve.co.uk
Ⓦ www.lockdales.co.uk
Est. 1998 *Stock size* Medium
Stock Gold, silver jewellery, British and world coins, banknotes, metal detectors, accessories
Open Mon–Sat 9.30am–4.30pm
Fairs Cumberland Hotel, Olympia
Services Valuations, jewellery, watch, clock repairs, auctioneering

Lockdale Coins Ltd
Contact Jean Daley
168 London Road South, Lowestoft, Suffolk, NR33 0BB
☎ 01502 568468 Ⓕ 01502 568468
Ⓔ ddaley@lockdales.freeserve.co.uk
Ⓦ www.lockdales.co.uk
Est. 1996
Open Mon–Sat 9.30am–4.30pm
Sales Phone for details of sales, held alternately between Ipswich and Norwich. Coins, jewellery, medals, militaria, ephemera, autographs
Frequency Bi-monthly
Catalogues Yes

Lowestoft Auction Rooms
Contact Mr J Peyto
Pinbush Road, South Lowestoft Industrial Estate, Lowestoft, Suffolk, NR33 7NL
☎ 01502 531532 Ⓕ 01502 531241
Ⓔ lowestoft@auctioneer.net
Est. 1985
Open Mon–Fri 8am–5.30pm
Sales Large house sales on site
Frequency Twice monthly
Catalogues Yes

Odds and Ends
Contact Mr B Smith
127 High Street, Lowestoft, Suffolk, NR32 1HP
☎ 01502 568569 Ⓕ 01502 568569
Stock All smalls, jewellery, collectables
Open Mon–Sat 10am–5pm
Services Valuations, restoration of jewellery and watches

M G Osborne
Contact Mr M G Osborne
140 High Street, Lowestoft, Suffolk, NR33 1HR
01502 508988
Est. 1988 *Stock size* Large
Stock General antiques
Open Mon–Sat 9.30am–4pm closed Thurs
Fairs The International Antique and Collectables Fair, RAF Swinderby

John Rolph
Contact Mr John Rolph
Manor House, Pakefield Street, Lowestoft, Suffolk, NR33 0JT
01502 572039
Est. 1948 *Stock size* Medium
Stock 17thC–1950, second-hand books
Open Tues–Sat 11am–1pm 2.30–5pm closed Thurs

MARLESFORD

The Antiques Warehouse
Contact John or Lesley Ball
The Old Mill, Main Road, Marlesford, Suffolk, IP13 0AG
01728 747438 01728 747627
omtc@antiqueswarehouse.fsnet.co.uk
Est. 1989 *Stock size* Large
Stock Country furniture, mirrors, lighting, general antiques
Open Mon–Fri 9am–4.30pm Sat 10am–4.30pm Sun 11am–4.30pm

MARTLESHAM

Martlesham Antiques
Contact Mr R Frost
Thatched Roadhouse, Main Road, Martlesham, Woodbridge, Suffolk, IP12 4RJ
01394 386732 01394 382959
bob@martleshamantiques.com
Est. 1983 *Stock size* Large
Stock 18th–20thC furniture
Open Mon–Fri 9am–5pm Sat 9am–12.30pm

NAYLAND

Town and Country Prints (EADA)
Contact Mr F E Jones
Longwood Cottage, Nayland, Colchester, Suffolk, CO6 4HT
01206 262483
jonesnayland@x-stream.co.uk
Est. 1976 *Stock size* Medium
Stock 18th–19thC maps, Essex and Suffolk a speciality, steel and copper engravings, woodblock illustrations, views and agricultural scenes
Open By appointment
Services Framing

NEEDHAM MARKET

Needham Market Antiques Centre
Contact Mrs Sheila Abbott
Old Town Hall, High Street, Needham Market, Suffolk, IP6 8AL
01449 720773
Est. 1979 *Stock size* Large
Stock Antiques, collectables
Open Mon–Sat 10am–5pm
Fairs Newark (DMG)
Services Restoration of jewellery

The Tool Shop (LAPADA)
Contact Mr Tony Murland
78 High Street, Needham Market, Ipswich, Suffolk, IP6 8AW
01449 722992 01449 722683
tony@antiquetools.co.uk
www.antiquetools.co.uk
Est. 1991 *Stock size* Large
Stock Antique woodworking tools, new quality French, Japanese, American
Open Mon–Sat 10am–5pm
Fairs All major national woodworking exhibitions

NEWMARKET

Jemima Godfrey Antiques
Contact Mrs A Lanham
5 Rous Road, Newmarket, Suffolk, CB8 8DH
01638 663584
Est. 1964 *Stock size* Small
Stock Small silver, linen, jewellery, Victorian china fairings, linen
Open Thurs Fri 10am–1pm 2pm–4.30pm

Rowley Fine Art
Contact Diane White
Tattersalls, Newmarket, Suffolk, CB8 9AU
01638 561313 01638 560251
mail@vosts.com
www.vosts.com
Est. 1994
Open Mon–Fri 9am–5pm
Sales Fine art and antique sales
Frequency 6 per annum
Catalogues Yes

ORFORD

Castle Antiques
Contact Ms S Simpkin
Market Hill, Orford, Woodbridge, Suffolk, IP12 2LH
01394 450100 01394 450536
stephanie@castle-estates.uk.com
Est. 1959 *Stock size* Small
Stock Furniture, lamps, pictures, glass, bric-a-brac
Open Mon–Sun 11am–4pm

PEASENHALL

Peasenhall Art & Antiques Gallery
Contact Mr M Wickens
The Street, Peasenhall, Saxmundham, Suffolk, IP17 2HJ
01728 660224
Est. 1972 *Stock size* Large
Stock 18th–early 20thC watercolours, oil paintings, country furniture in all woods
Open Mon–Sun 9am–6pm
Services Restorations

RISBY

Past and Present
Contact Joe Aldridge
The Risby Barn Complex, South Street, Risby, Bury St Edmunds, Suffolk, IP28 6QU
01284 811480
Est. 1996 *Stock size* Large
No. of dealers 30
Stock Furniture, antique to present day china, silver, jewellery, bric-a-brac, pictures, books, glass, pine, Victorian–Edwardian furniture, European furniture, collectable toys
Open Mon–Sat 10am–5pm Sun 10.30am–4.30pm
Services Restorations, coffee shop, garden centre

The Risby Barn Antique Centre
Contact Mr R Martin

Risby Barn, South Street, Risby, Bury St Edmunds, Suffolk, IP28 6QU P
☎ 01284 811126 Ⓕ 01284 810783
Ⓔ r.martin@lineone.net
Est. 1980 *Stock size* Large
No. of dealers 30
Stock Victorian furniture, china, silver, clocks, rural bygones
Open Mon–Sat 9am–5.30pm Sun Bank Holidays 10am–5pm
Services Coffee shop, restorations

SAXMUNDHAM

Keith A Savage
Contact Mr K A Savage
35 High Street, Saxmundham, Suffolk, IP17 IAJ P
☎ 01728 604538 or 01986 872231
Est. 1992 *Stock size* Medium
Stock Second-hand, collectors' books, second-hand ephemera, children's books a speciality
Open Mon Sat 10.30am–1pm Tues Wed Fri 10.30am–5pm

SOUTHWOLD

Architectural Artefacts
Contact Mr B Howard or Mrs J Twist
The Rope House, Station Road, Southwold, Suffolk, IP18 6AX P
☎ 01502 723075 Ⓕ 01502 724346
Ⓔ aa@ropehouse.easynet.co.uk
Est. 1996 *Stock size* Small
Stock Stained glass, architectural antiques, taps, sinks, chimney pots
Open Mon–Fri 9am–5pm
Services Stained glass design

Cannonbury Antiques Southwold
Contact Mr David Brinsmead
Bridgefoot Corner, Reydon, Southwold, Suffolk, IP18 6NF P
☎ 01502 722133
Est. 1998 *Stock size* Medium
Stock General, furniture, decorative antiques
Open Mon–Sat 10am–5pm Sun 11am–4pm
Services Valuations

Puritan Values at the Dome
Contact Anthony Geering
St Edmunds Business Park, St Edmunds Road, Southwold, Suffolk, IP18 6BZ P
☎ 01502 722211 Ⓕ 01502 722734
Ⓜ 07966 371676
Ⓔ sales@puritanvalues.com
Ⓦ www.puritanvalues.com
Est. 1985
Stock Arts & Crafts movement, Aesthetic movement, Gothic revival, important furniture
Open Mon–Sat 10am–6pm Sun 11am–5pm
Fairs NEC, SEC
Services Valuations, restorations

T Schotte Antiques
Contact Mrs Schotte
Old Bakehouse, Blackmill Road, Southwold, Suffolk, IP18 6AQ
☎ 01502 722083
Est. 1989 *Stock size* Small
Stock Antiques, decorative items
Open Mon–Sat 10am–4pm closed Wed

S J Webster-Speakman (BADA)
Contact Mrs S J Webster-Speakman
Southwold, Suffolk
☎ 01502 722252
Est. 1968 *Stock size* Medium
Stock 18th–19thC furniture, clocks, Staffordshire animals
Open By appointment
Fairs Louise Walker Harrogate Fair, Annual Chester Antiques and Fine Art Show, Guildford, Snape
Services Restoration of clocks

SPROUGHTON

Heritage Reclamations
Contact Mr Richard Howells
1a High Street, Sproughton, Ipswich, Suffolk, IP8 3AF P
☎ 01473 748519 Ⓕ 01473 748519
Ⓔ heritage@reclamations.fsnet.co.uk
Ⓦ www.heritage-reclamations.co.uk
Est. 1985 *Stock size* Large
Stock Interior fittings, stoves, ranges, fireplaces, garden ornaments
Open Mon–Fri 9am–5pm Sat 9.30am–5pm
Fairs Newark, Ardingly, Swinderby
Services Restorations

STOWMARKET

What-Not-Shop Antiques
Contact Mr F J Smith
28 Bury Street, Stowmarket, Suffolk, IP14 1HH P
☎ 01449 613126
Est. 1979 *Stock size* Medium
Stock Jewellery, china, glass
Open Mon–Sat 9am–4.30pm Tues 9am–1pm
Services Repairs

SUDBURY

Beckham Books (PBFA)
Contact Mrs Jenny Beckham
Chilton Mount, Newton Road, Sudbury, Suffolk, CO10 2RS P
☎ 01787 373683 Ⓕ 01787 375441
Ⓔ sales@beckhambooks.co.uk
Ⓦ www.beckhambooks.co.uk
Est. 1996 *Stock size* Small
Stock Antiquarian, theological books, bibles
Open By appointment
Fairs PBFA Fairs
Services Book search

Hobknobs Antiques and Gallery
Contact Mrs S Fletcher
16 Friars Street, Sudbury, Suffolk, CO10 2AA P
☎ 01787 881360
Ⓜ 07930 899737
Est. 1987 *Stock size* Medium
Stock General, small furniture, gallery
Open Mon–Sat 9.30am–12.45pm 1.45–5pm
Services Valuations, restorations

Napier House Antiques
Contact Mrs Veronica McGregor
3 Church Street, Sudbury, Suffolk, CO10 2BJ P
☎ 01787 375280 Ⓕ 01787 478757
Ⓜ 07768 703406
Est. 1976 *Stock size* Large
Stock 18th–19thC mahogany furniture
Open Mon–Sat 10am–4.30pm closed Wed
Services Free delivery UK mainland

Neate Militarian & Antiques (OMRS)
Contact Gary Neate
PO Box 3794, Preston St Mary, Sudbury, Suffolk, CO10 9PX P

☎ 01787 248168 ℻ 01787 248363
ⓔ gary@neatemedals.co.uk
ⓦ www.neatemedals.co.uk
Est. 1984 ***Stock size*** Medium
Stock Worldwide orders, decorations, medals, with an emphasis on British material
Open Mon–Fri 9am–6pm
Fairs Brittania Medal Fair, Aldershot Medal Fair
Services Valuations, restorations, mail order catalogue

Olivers (SOFAA)
Contact Mr J Fletcher
The Sale Room, Burkitts Lane, Sudbury, Suffolk, CO10 1HB Ⓟ
☎ 01787 880305 ℻ 01787 880305
Est. 1766
Open Mon–Fri 9am–5pm
Sales Regular sales of antiques and works of art. Victorian, later furniture, household effects fortnightly Thurs 1pm, viewing day of sale from 9am
Frequency Fortnightly
Catalogues Yes

Sasha
Contact Susan Bailey
79 Melford Road, Sudbury, Suffolk, CO10 1JT Ⓟ
☎ 01787 375582
Ⓜ 07781 453250
Est. 1986 ***Stock size*** Medium
Stock Small furniture, ceramics, collectables, books
Open Mon–Sat 10.30am–5pm
Services Book search

Sitting Pretty Antiques
Contact Mrs S Fletcher
16 Friars Street, Sudbury, Suffolk, CO10 2AA Ⓟ
☎ 01787 880908/881360
Ⓜ 07930 899737
Est. 1987 ***Stock size*** Large
Stock Re-upholstered period furniture, 18thC–1930s
Open Mon–Sat 9.30am–12.45pm 1.45–5pm
Services Upholstery, interior design consultations

Suffolk Rare Books
Contact Mr T Cawthorne
7 New Street, Sudbury, Suffolk, CO10 1JB Ⓟ
☎ 01787 372075
Est. 1975 ***Stock size*** Medium
Stock Antiquarian books, topography, military, history
Open Tues–Sat 10.30am–4.30pm closed Wed

WOODBRIDGE

Blake's Books (PBFA)
Contact Mr R Green
88 The Thoroughfare, Woodbridge, Suffolk, IP12 1AL
☎ 01394 380302
Stock Antiquarian and second-hand books, Suffolk and sailing books a speciality
Open Mon–Sat 9.30am–5pm
Fairs Woodbridge Book Fair

Church Street Centre
Contact Miss M Brown
6e Church Street, Woodbridge, Suffolk, IP12 1DH Ⓟ
☎ 01394 388887
Est. 1994 ***Stock size*** Large
No. of dealers 10
Stock Wide range of items including small furniture, jewellery, china, glass, silver, ephemera, textiles, pictures, bygones, clocks, collectables
Open Mon–Sat 10am–5pm closed Wed pm
Services Free local delivery

Collectors Books & CD Centre
Contact Mr P J Freeman
63A The Thoroughfare, Woodbridge, Suffolk, IP12 1AH Ⓟ
☎ 01394 383388
Est. 1997 ***Stock size*** Medium
Stock Includes some antiquarian books
Open Mon–Sat 10am–5pm

Dix-Sept Antiques
Contact Miss Sophie Goodbrey
17 Station Road, Woodbridge, Suffolk, IP13 9EA Ⓟ
☎ 01728 621505 ℻ 01728 724884
Est. 1985 ***Stock size*** Medium
Stock French antiques, furniture glass, pottery, textiles
Open Sat 10am–1pm 2–5.30pm or by appointment
Fairs Newark

David Gibbins (BADA)
Contact Mr David Gibbins
The White House, 14 Market Hill, Woodbridge, Suffolk, IP12 4LU Ⓟ
☎ 01394 383531 ℻ 01394 383531
Ⓜ 07702 306914
ⓔ david@gibbinsantiques.co.uk
Est. 1966 ***Stock size*** Medium
Stock 18thC furniture, Lowestoft porcelain
Open By appointment
Fairs The West London Antiques and Fine Art Fair, Louise Walker Harrogate Fair, BADA Fair
Services Valuations, restorations

Hamilton Antiques (LAPADA)
Contact Hamilton or Rosemary Ferguson
5 Church Street, Woodbridge, Suffolk, IP12 1DH
☎ 01394 387222 ℻ 01394 383832
Ⓜ 07747 033437
ⓔ hamiltonantiques@fsmail.net
Est. 1976 ***Stock size*** Large
Stock 18th–20thC furniture
Trade only Yes
Open Mon–Fri 8.30am–5pm Sat 10am–5pm
Services Restoration, polishing

Anthony Hurst (LAPADA)
Contact Mr Christopher Hurst
13 Church Street, Woodbridge, Suffolk, IP12 1DS Ⓟ
☎ 01394 382500 ℻ 01394 382500
Est. 1968 ***Stock size*** Large
Stock 18th–19thC furniture, mahogany, oak
Open Mon–Fri 9.30am–1pm 2–5.30pm Sat 10am–1pm closed Wed pm

Raymond Lambert
Contact Mr Raymond Lambert
24a Church Street, Woodbridge, Suffolk, IP12 1DH Ⓟ
☎ 01394 382380
Est. 1963 ***Stock size*** Medium
Stock 19thC furniture
Open Mon–Sat 9.30am–1pm 2–5pm closed Wed

Sarah Meysey-Thompson Antiques
Contact Sarah Meysey-Thompson
10 Church Street, Woodbridge, Suffolk, IP12 1DH Ⓟ
☎ 01394 382144
Est. 1961 ***Stock size*** Medium
Stock Georgian–Victorian furniture, curios, decorative pieces, textiles

Open Mon–Sat 10am–5pm
Fairs Battersea Park Decorative Antique and Textile Fair

Neal Sons & Fletcher
Contact Mr Edward Fletcher FRICS
26 Church Street, Woodbridge, Suffolk, IP12 1DP
01394 382263 01394 383030
enquiries@nsf.co.uk
www.nsf.co.uk
Est. 1951
Open Mon–Fri 9am–5.30pm Sat 9am–4pm
Sales General monthly antiques sales, viewing day prior to sale 2.15–4.30pm and 6.30–8pm and sale day 9.30–10.30am. Bi- or tri-annual specialist sales of period English and Continental furniture, pictures, books, carpets etc at The Theatre Street Sale Room, viewing Sat prior to sale 10am–1pm and day preceding sale 11am–4.30pm 6.30–8pm sale day 9.30–10.30am
Frequency Monthly
Catalogues Yes

Isobel Rhodes
Contact Mrs I Rhodes
10 & 12 Market Hill, Woodbridge, Suffolk, IP12 4LS
01394 382763
Est. 1964 *Stock size* Medium
Stock Oak, country furniture, pewter, pottery, brass
Open Mon–Sat 10am–1pm 2–5pm

Woodbridge Gallery
Contact Mr David Bethell
23 Market Hill, Woodbridge, Suffolk, IP12 4OX
01394 386500 01394 386500
Est. 1998 *Stock size* Large
No. of dealers 30–35
Stock General antiques, fine art gallery
Open Mon–Sat 10am–5.30pm Wed 10am–1pm

WOOLPIT

John Heather
Contact John Heather
Old Crown, The Street, Woolpit, Bury St Edmunds, Suffolk, IP30 9SA
01359 240297
07715 282600
john@johnheather.co.uk
Est. 1946 *Stock size* Medium
Stock Late 18thC furniture
Open Mon–Sun 9am–6pm
Services Restorations

WRENTHAM

Bly Valley Antiques
Contact Mr Eric Ward
Old Reading Rooms, 7 High Street, Wrentham, Beccles, Suffolk, NR34 7HD
01502 675376 or 01728 454508
01502 675376
www.bly-valley-antiques.com
Est. 1971 *Stock size* Large
Stock China, glass, pictures, furniture, antiquarian books
Open Tues–Sat 10.30am–4.30pm

Wren House Antiques
Contact Ms V Kemp
1 High Street, Wrentham, Beccles, Suffolk, NR34 7HD
01502 675276
07747 824229
Est. 1984 *Stock size* Medium
Stock Small antique furniture, collectables
Open Thurs–Sun 10.30am–5pm
Fairs Newark, Ardingly

Wrentham Antiques
Contact Mr B C Spearing
40–44 High Street, Wrentham, Beccles, Suffolk, NR34 7HB
01502 675583 01502 675707
wrentham.antiques@netcom.co.uk
www.business.netcom.co.uk/ransom
Est. 1974 *Stock size* Large
Stock Antique furniture, clocks
Open Mon–Fri 8.30am–5pm Sat 9am–4pm
Services Valuations, shipping

YOXFORD

The Garden House Bookshop
Contact Liza Adamczewski
High Street, Yoxford, Saxmundham, Suffolk, IP17 3ER
01728 668044
gardenhousebooks@hotmail.com
gardenhousebooks.co.uk
Est. 1969 *Stock size* Large
Stock Antiquarian, second-hand books, specializing in modernists, travel
Open Tues–Thurs Sat 10am–5pm winter by appointment
Services Valuations, book search

Suffolk House Antiques (BADA)
Contact Mr A Singleton
High Street, Yoxford, Saxmundham, Suffolk, IP17 3EP
01728 668122 01728 668122
07860 521583
andrew.singleton@suffolk-house-antiques.co.uk
www.suffolk-house-antiques.co.uk
Est. 1991 *Stock size* Large
Stock Early English furniture, ceramics, associated works of art
Open Mon–Sat 10am–1pm 2.15–5.15pm closed Wed
Fairs BADA, Snape

HEART OF ENGLAND

BEDFORDSHIRE

AMPTHILL

Ampthill Antiques
Contact Mrs A Olney
Market Square, Church Street, Ampthill, Bedfordshire, MK45 2EH
☎ 01525 403344 Ⓜ 07050 291011
Est. 1980 *Stock size* Large
Stock General antiques
Open Mon–Sat 11am–4pm Sun 2–5pm closed Wed

Ampthill Antiques Emporium
Contact Marc Legg
6 Bedford Street, Ampthill, Bedfordshire, MK45 2NB Ⓟ
☎ 01525 402131 Ⓕ 01582 737527
Ⓜ 07831 374919
Ⓔ info@ampthillantiquesemporium.co.uk
Ⓦ www.ampthillantiquesemporium.co.uk
Est. 1979 *Stock size* Large
No. of dealers 40
Stock Georgian–Edwardian furniture, smalls, shipping goods
Open Mon–Sun 10am–5pm closed Tues
Services Upholstery, valuations, shipping, furniture restoration, pine stripping, picture framing

Antiquarius
Contact Mr P Caldwell
107 Dunstable Street, Ampthill, Bedfordshire, MK45 2NG Ⓟ
☎ 01525 841799
Ⓔ peter.caldwell@tesco.net
Est. 1996 *Stock size* Medium
Stock Georgian–Edwardian sitting and dining room furniture
Open Mon–Sat 10.30am–5pm Sun 1–5pm
Services Restorations, reupholstery

House of Clocks (BHI)
Contact Mrs H Proud
102–104 Dunstable Street, Ampthill, Bedfordshire, MK45 2JP Ⓟ
☎ 01525 403136 Ⓕ 01525 402680
Ⓔ ian@houseofclocks.co.uk
Ⓦ www.houseofclocks.co.uk
Est. 1984 *Stock size* Large
Stock Fine-quality antiques, reproduction clocks
Open Mon–Sat 9am–5pm Sun 11am–5pm
Fairs Motorcycle Museum, NEC, Brunel University
Services Restorations

David Litt Antiques
Contact Mr D Litt
The Old Telephone Exchange, Claridges Lane, Ampthill, Bedfordshire, MK45 2HU Ⓟ
☎ 01525 404825 Ⓕ 01525 404563
Ⓜ 07802 449027
Ⓔ litt@ntlworld.com
Est. 1967 *Stock size* Large
Stock French provincial, 19thC furniture
Open Mon–Fri 7am–5pm
Fairs Battersea, Olympia
Services Restorations

Paris Antiques
Contact Mr Paul Northwood
97b Dunstable Street, Ampthill, Bedfordshire, MK45 2NG Ⓟ
☎ 01525 840488 Ⓕ 01525 840488
Ⓜ 07802 535059
Est. 1984 *Stock size* Medium
Stock 18th–early 20thC furniture and effects
Open Tues–Sun 9.30am–5.30pm
Services Valuations, restorations

Pilgrim Antiques
Contact Mr G Lester
111 Dunstable Street, Ampthill, Bedfordshire, MK45 2NG Ⓟ
☎ 01525 633023
Est. 1996 *Stock size* Large
Stock General antiques, Georgian–Edwardian furniture, glass, china, jewellery
Open Tues–Sun 10am–5pm closed Mon

The Pine Parlour
Contact Mrs J Barber
1 Chandos Road, Ampthill, Bedfordshire, MK45 2LF
01525 403030
Est. 1987 *Stock size* Medium
Stock Victorian–Edwardian original pine, wardrobes, dressers, chests, kitchenware, sleigh beds
Open Mon–Sun 10am–5pm

Transatlantic Antiques & Fine Art Ltd
Contact Mrs Deidre Higgins
101 Dunstable Street, Ampthill, Bedfordshire, MK45 2NG
01525 403346 01525 403346
Est. 1996 *Stock size* Large
Stock Very general 19th–early 20thC antiques including a good selection of English and European porcelain, glass, silver, decorative items, watercolours, lighting
Open Mon–Sat 10.30am–5pm Sun noon–5pm

BEDFORD

Architectural Antiques
Contact Mr Paul Hoare
70 Pembroke Street, Bedford, Bedfordshire, MK40 3RQ
01234 213131 01234 309858
07977 573767
Est. 1988 *Stock size* Large
Stock Architectural antiques, period fixtures and fittings, fireplaces, doors and general salvage
Open Mon–Fri noon–5pm Sat 9am–5pm
Services Installation, restorations

The Eagle Bookshop
Contact Mr Peter Budek
103 Castle Road, Bedford, Bedfordshire, MK40 3QP
01234 269295 01234 269295
customers@eaglebookshop.co.uk
www.eaglebookshop.co.uk
Est. 1991 *Stock size* Medium
Stock General second-hand speciality books on science and mathematics
Open Mon–Sat 10am–6pm closed Wed
Services Catalogues issued

Harpur Antiques
Contact Nigel Hill
58 Harpur Street, Bedford, Bedfordshire, MK40 2QT
01234 344831 01234 344831
info@harpurjewellery.com
www.harpurjewellery.com
Est. 1981 *Stock size* Medium
Stock Antique, contemporary and new jewellery, small collectables, watches, silver
Open Mon–Sat 10am–5pm closed Thurs

W & H Peacock
Contact Mark Baker or Simon Rowell
26 Newnham Street, Bedford, Bedfordshire, MK40 3JR
01234 266366 01234 269082
info@peacockauction.co.uk
www.peacockauction.co.uk
Est. 1901
Open Mon–Thurs 9am–5.30pm Fri 9am–8.30pm Sat 8.30am–5pm
Sales General and antiques sale Sat 9.30am, viewing Fri 9am–8pm Sat 8.30am prior to sale, also Thurs 11am, viewing Wed 9am–8pm Thurs 8.30am prior to sale. Monthly antiques and collectables sale first Fri 10.45am, viewing Fri 5–8pm in week before Thurs 9am–6pm in week of sale and Fri 8.30–10.45am prior to sale
Frequency Weekly
Catalogues Yes

Victoria House
Contact Helen Felts
70a Tavistock Street, Bedford, Bedfordshire, MK40 2RP
01234 320000
Est. 1998 *Stock size* Large
Stock Victorian–Edwardian furniture, antiques, reproduction and decorative pieces
Open Mon–Fri 11.30am–5pm Sat 11am–5pm Sun 12.30–4.30pm closed Wed
Services Interior design

BIGGLESWADE

Old Mother Hubbards
Contact Mrs D Dynes
38 Shortmead Street, Biggleswade, Bedfordshire, SG18 0AP
01767 600959 01767 151669
Est. 1994 *Stock size* Medium
Stock Collectables, old pine furniture, small items, china, glass
Open Mon Wed Fri Sat 10am–5pm
Services Made-to-measure pine furniture, waxing

Shortmead Antiques
Contact Mr S E Sinfield
46 Shortmead Street, Biggleswade, Bedfordshire, SG18 0AP
01767 601780
www.shortmead.co.uk
Est. 1989 *Stock size* Medium
Stock Victorian–Edwardian furniture, china, silver, glass, general antiques
Open Tues Wed Fri Sat 10am–4.30pm

Simply Oak
Contact Anna Kilgarriff or Dick Sturman
Oak Tree Farm, Potton Road, Biggleswade, Bedfordshire, SG18 0EP
01767 601559 01767 312855
antiques@simplyoak.freeserve.co.uk
Est. 1997 *Stock size* Large
Stock Late Victorian–1930s restored oak furniture
Open Mon–Sat 10am–5pm Sun 11am–4pm
Services Restorations

BROMHAM

Paperchase
Contact Brian Moakes
77 Wingfield Road, Bromham, Bedford, Bedfordshire, MK43 8JY
01234 825942
brianmoakes@aol.com
Est. 1991
Open Mon–Fri 9am–5pm
Sales Postal auction of transport-related paper memorabilia
Frequency 6 per annum
Catalogues Yes

EGGINGTON

Robert Kirkman Ltd (ABA, PBFA)
Contact Robert Kirkman
Kings Cottage, Eggington, Leighton Buzzard, Bedfordshire, LU7 9PG
01525 210647 01525 211184
robertkirkmanltd@btinternet.com
Est. 1988 *Stock size* Small

Stock Antiquarian books, specializing in English literature, Churchill, English Bibles, sets of standard authors
Open By appointment only
Fairs ABA, PBFA
Services Restorations, book binding, shipping

LEIGHTON BUZZARD

David Ball Antiques
Contact David Ball
59 North Street, Leighton Buzzard, Bedfordshire, LU7 1EQ
☎ 01525 382954 Ⓜ 07831 111661
Est. 1970 *Stock size* Medium
Stock Furniture, clocks, barometers, 18th–early 20thC porcelain
Open Mon–Sat 10am–5pm closed Thurs
Fairs Luton Antiques Fair, Mid Beds Antiques Fair
Services Restorations

LOWER STONDON

Dippers
Contact Mr Paul Monroe
52 Bedford Road, Lower Stondon, Henlow, Bedfordshire, SG16 6DZ
☎ 01462 811003 Ⓕ 01462 819197
Ⓔ monroe.dippers@virgin.net
Est. 1997 *Stock size* Large
Stock Architectural antiques, antique pine furniture
Open Mon–Fri 10am–6pm Sat 10am–5pm
Fairs Swinderby, Newark
Services Restorations, stripping

Memory Lane Antiques
Contact Mrs Liz Henry RAFA RJDip
14 Bedford Road, Lower Stondon, Henlow, Bedfordshire, SG16 6EA
☎ 01462 812716 Ⓜ 07702 715477
Est. 1998 *Stock size* Medium
Stock Furniture, silver, porcelain, crystal, collectables
Open Mon–Sun 10.30am–5pm closed Wed Thurs
Services Appraisals

LUTON

Bargain Box
Contact Dean Dickinson
4 & 6a Adelaide Street, Luton, Bedfordshire, LU1 5BB
☎ 01582 423809
Est. 1962 *Stock size* Medium
Stock Collectables
Open Mon–Sat 9.30am–5pm

Off World
Contact Mr J Woollard
141a–143a Market Hall, The Luton Arndale Centre, Luton, Bedfordshire, LU1 2TP
☎ 01582 736256
Est. 1995 *Stock size* Large
Stock Collectable toys, Star Wars, Transformers, comics, cards etc
Open Mon–Fri 9.30am–5.30pm Wed 9.30am–2pm

POTTON

Wesley J West & Son
Contact Mr A West
58 King Street, Potton, Sandy, Bedfordshire, SG19 2QZ
☎ 01767 260589
Est. 1931 *Stock size* Medium
Stock Georgian–Edwardian furniture
Open Mon–Fri 9am–5pm Sat 9am–noon
Services Restorations, upholstery

RAVENSDEN

Lisa Cordes Antiques
Contact Mr J E Harbridge
Struttle End, Oldways Road, Ravensden, Bedford, Bedfordshire, MK44 2RF
☎ 01234 771980 Ⓕ 01234 771980
Est. 1974 *Stock size* Medium
Stock Antique furniture up to 1900
Trade only Yes
Open Mon–Sat 9am–5pm
Services Restorations, cabinet-making

SHEFFORD

S and S Timms Antiques Ltd (LAPADA)
Contact Sue Timms
2–4 High Street, Shefford, Bedfordshire, SG17 5DG
☎ 01462 851051 Ⓕ 01462 817047
Ⓔ sstimms@highstshefford.freeserve.co.uk
Est. 1976 *Stock size* Large
Stock 18th–19thC town and country furniture
Open Mon–Fri 9.30am–5.30pm Sat Sun 11am–5pm or by appointment
Fairs Chelsea, LAPADA

SLAPTON

Nick & Janet's Antiques
Contact Janet Griffin
Bury Farm, Mill Road, Slapton, Leighton Buzzard, Bedfordshire, LU7 9BT
☎ 01525 220256 Ⓕ 01525 220757
Ⓔ nick@nickandjanets.co.uk
Ⓦ www.nickandjanets.co.uk
Est. 1991 *Stock size* Large
Stock Devon, Torquay, Brannam pottery, Martin Brothers, modern Moorcroft
Open By appointment
Fairs Shepton Mallet

TODDINGTON

Books for Collectors Ltd
Contact Nicky Holdsworth
Unit 1, 24–26 High Street, Toddington, Bedfordshire, LU5 6BY
☎ 01525 875100
Est. 1999 *Stock size* Large
Stock Antiquarian and second-hand books
Open Mon–Fri 10am–4pm
Fairs Detling, Edinburgh
Services Book search

WILSTEAD

Manor Antiques and Interiors
Contact Mrs S Bowen
The Manor House, Cotton End Road, Wilstead, Bedford, Bedfordshire, MK45 3BT
☎ 01234 740262 Ⓕ 01234 740262
Ⓜ 07831 419729
Est. 1979 *Stock size* Large
Stock 19thC and Edwardian furniture, antique and replica mirrors, lighting
Open Mon–Sat 10am–5pm
Fairs House & Gardens, Olympia

WOBURN

Bazaar Boxes (LAPADA)
Contact Andrew Grierson or Mark Brewster

✉ **Woburn Abbey Antiques Centre, Woburn, Bedfordshire, MK17 9WA** P
☎ 01992 504454 F 01992 504454
M 07970 909204/909206
E bazaarboxes@hotmail.com
Stock size Medium
Stock Tortoiseshell, ivory and mother-of-pearl tea caddies and boxes
Open 363 days a year 10am–5.30pm or by appointment
Fairs NEC, LAPADA

Collectors Carbooks
Contact Mr C Knapman
✉ **14 Bedford Street, Woburn, Bedfordshire, MK17 9QB** P
☎ 01525 290088 F 01525 290044
E sales@collectorscarbooks.com
W www.collectorscarbooks.com
Est. 1991 ***Stock size*** Large
Stock Rare, out-of-print, motoring and motor-racing books, magazines, posters, autographs, programmes, new car-related books
Open Mon–Sat 10am–5pm
Fairs All major historic race meetings, classic car shows
Services Free book search, international mail order

Geoffrey Hugall
Contact Mr G Hugall
✉ **Woburn Abbey Antique Centre, Woburn Abbey, Bedfordshire, MK17 9WA** P
☎ 020 7838 0457 or 01525 290350
M 07973 273485
Est. 1971 ***Stock size*** Medium
Stock General antiques, mirrors, period furniture
Open Mon–Sun 10am–5.30pm
Services Valuations

Christopher Sykes
Contact Mr C Sykes or Mrs Sally Lloyd
✉ **The Old Parsonage, Bedford Street, Woburn, Milton Keynes, Bedfordshire, MK17 9QL** P
☎ 01525 290259 F 01525 290061
E sykes.corkscrews@sykes-corkscrews.co.uk
W www.sykes-corkscrews.co.uk
Est. 1960 ***Stock size*** Large
Stock Items associated with wine, speciality corkscrews
Open Mon–Sat 9am–5pm

Town Hall Antiques
Contact Mr or Mrs Groves
✉ **Market Place, Woburn, Milton Keynes, Bedfordshire, MK17 9PZ** P
☎ 01525 290950 F 01525 290950
Est. 1993 ***Stock size*** Large
Stock Varied
Open Mon–Sat 10am–5.30pm Sun 11am–5.30pm
Services Valuations, picture framing

Woburn Abbey Antiques Centre
Contact Ian Osborn
✉ **Woburn, Bedfordshire, MK17 9WA** P
☎ 01525 290350 F 01525 292102
E antiques@woburnabbey.co.uk
Est. 1967 ***Stock size*** Large
No. of dealers 64
Stock Furniture (dateline 1910), porcelain, silver, paintings (dateline 1940)
Open 363 days a year 10am–5.30pm

Yew Tree
Contact Anna Maggs
✉ **Woburn Abbey Antiques Centre, Woburn, Bedfordshire, MK17 9WA** P
☎ 01582 872514 M 01582 873816
Est. 1983 ***Stock size*** Medium
Stock Farm and garden tools and related rural items, 18th–20thC decorative prints
Open 363 days a year 10am–5.30pm
Fairs NEC, Decorative Antiques & Textiles Fair, Battersea

WOBURN SANDS

Pine Love
Contact A Tracoshas
✉ **37 High Street, Woburn Sands, Bedfordshire, MK17 8RB** P
☎ 01908 585515 F 01908 585515
Est. 1995 ***Stock size*** Medium
Stock Antique pine furniture
Open Mon–Sat 10am–5.30pm closed Wed

BUCKINGHAMSHIRE

AMERSHAM

The Amersham Auction Rooms (RICS)
Contact Pippa Ellis
✉ **125 Station Road, Amersham, Buckinghamshire, HP7 0AH** P
☎ 01494 729292 F 01494 722337
E info@amershamauctionrooms.co.uk
W www.amershamauctionrooms.co.uk
Est. 1877
Open Mon–Fri 9am–5.30pm Sat 9–11.30am
Sales Antiques and collectors' sale first Thurs of month. Victorian and general furniture other Thurs weekly 10.30am, viewing Tues 2–5pm Wed 9.30am–7pm Thurs 9–10.15am
Frequency Weekly
Catalogues Yes

Old Amersham Auctions
Contact Mr M King
✉ **2 School Lane, Amersham, Buckinghamshire, HP7 0EL** P
☎ 01494 722758 F 01494 722758
Est. 1979
Open Mon–Sat 9am–5pm
Sales General and antiques sale Sat 11am, viewing Sat 9am prior to sale. Occasional house sales, phone for details
Frequency Fortnightly
Catalogues Yes

Pop Antiques
✉ **12 The Broadway, Amersham, Buckinghamshire, HP7 0HP** P
☎ 01494 434443 F 07970 043083
M 07768 366606
W www.popantiques.com
Est. 2001 ***Stock size*** Large
Stock Late 19thC French painted furniture, mirrors
Open Mon–Sat 10am–5pm
Services Shipping

Liz Quilter
Contact Liz or Jackie Quilter
✉ **38 High Street, Amersham, Buckinghamshire, HP7 0DJ** P
☎ 01494 433723 F 01494 433723
E jackie@quilters-antiques.fsnet.co.uk
Est. 1969 ***Stock size*** Large
Stock Old pine collectables, copper, brass, rustic furniture
Open Mon–Sat 10am–5pm

Sundial Antiques
Contact Mr A Macdonald
✉ **19 Whielden Street, Amersham, Buckinghamshire, HP7 0HU** P
☎ 01494 727955 M 07866 819314
Est. 1970 ***Stock size*** Medium
Stock 19thC copper and brass, small furniture, ceramics

Open Mon–Sat 9.30am–5.30pm closed Thurs
Services Antiques vouchers available

ASTON CLINTON

Dismantle & Deal Direct
Contact Mr T Pattison
108 London Road, Aston Clinton, Buckinghamshire, HP22 5HS
01296 632300 F 01296 631346
E info@dismandealdirect.com
W www.dismandealdirect.com
Est. 1992 *Stock size* Large
Stock Doors, entrance ways, chimney pieces, lighting, stained glass, mirrors, garden statuary, other architecturally unusual items
Open Mon–Sat 9.30am–5pm
Services Architectural salvage brokers

AYLESBURY

Gillian Neale Antiques (BADA)
Contact Gillian Neale
PO Box 247, Aylesbury, Buckinghamshire, HP20 1JZ
01296 423754 F 01296 334601
E gillianneale@aol.com
W www.gilliannealeantiques.co.uk
Est. 1980 *Stock size* Large
Stock English blue printed pottery 1780–1900
Open By appointment
Fairs Olympia, BADA
Services Valuations, restorations, export, search

BEACONSFIELD

Buck House Antique Centre
Contact Mrs B Whitby
47 Wycombe End, Beaconsfield, Buckinghamshire, HP9 1LZ
01494 670714 F 01494 670714
E bachantiques@supanet.com
Est. 1982 *Stock size* Medium
Stock Clocks, furniture, metalware, ceramics, general antiques
Open Mon–Sat 10am–5pm closed Wed

June Elsworth Beaconsfield Ltd
Contact June Elsworth
Clover House, 16 London End, Beaconsfield, Buckinghamshire, HP9 2JH
01494 675611 F 01494 671273
Est. 1986 *Stock size* Large
Stock 18th–19thC furniture, accessories
Open Tues–Sat 10am–5.30pm

Grosvenor House Interiors
Contact Mr T Marriott
51 Wycombe End, Beaconsfield, Buckinghamshire, HP9 1LX
01494 677498 F 01494 677498
M 07747 014098
Est. 1978 *Stock size* Large
Stock 18th–19thC furniture, pictures, mirrors, clocks, fireplaces
Open Mon–Sat 10am–1pm 2–5pm closed Wed

Period Furniture Showrooms (TVADA)
Contact Mr R E W Hearne
49 London End, Beaconsfield, Buckinghamshire, HP9 2HW
01494 674112 F 01494 681046
E sales@periodfurniture.net
W www.periodfurniture.net
Est. 1966 *Stock size* Large
Stock Victorian–Edwardian furniture
Open Mon–Sat 9am–5.30pm
Fairs TVADA Spring
Services Restoration of furniture

Spinning Wheel
Contact Mrs Meg Royle
86 London End, Beaconsfield, Buckinghamshire, 4P9 2JD
01494 673055
Est. 1969 *Stock size* Medium
Stock 18th–19thC furniture, china, glass
Open Tues–Sat 9.30am–4.30pm closed Wed

BOURNE END

Bourne End Antiques Centre
Contact Mr Simon Shepheard
67 The Parade, Bourne End, Buckinghamshire, SL8 5SB
01628 533298
M 07776 176876
Est. 1996 *Stock size* Large
No. of dealers 40
Stock General antiques, oak, pine, mahogany, silver, jewellery
Open Mon–Sat 10am–5.30pm Sun Bank Holidays noon–4pm

Bourne End Auction Rooms
Contact Mr S Brown
Station Approach, Bourne End, Buckinghamshire, SL8 5QH
01628 531500 F 01628 522158
Est. 1992
Open Mon–Fri 9am–5.30pm Sat 9am–noon
Sales Weekly general sale Wed 10.30am, 1st Wed monthly antiques sale 10.30am, viewing Tues 9.30am–7pm Wed 9–10.30am
Frequency Weekly
Catalogues Yes

La Maison
Contact Mr J Pratt
The Crossings, Cores End Road, Bourne End, Buckinghamshire, SL8 5AL
01628 525858 F 01494 670363
M 07885 209001
Est. 1994 *Stock size* Medium
Stock French mirrors, beds, tables, gifts, garden statuary
Open Mon 1–5.30pm Tues–Sat 10am–5.30pm Sun 11am–5pm
Services Upholstery

BUCKINGHAM

Buckingham Antiques Centre Ltd
Contact Mr P Walton
5 West Street, Buckingham, Buckinghamshire, MK18 1HL
01280 824464 M 07904 242877
E peterwalton@whsmithnet.co.uk
Est. 1992 *Stock size* Small
Stock General antiques, furniture, clocks, silver, china
Open Mon–Sat 9am–5pm closed Wed or by appointment
Services Valuations

Flappers Antiques
Contact Mr or Mrs N Goodwin
2 High Street, Buckingham, Buckinghamshire, MK18 1NT
01280 813115
Est. 1980 *Stock size* Large
Stock Country pine furniture, accessories
Open Mon–Sat 9.30am–5.30pm closed Thurs

CHALFONT ST GILES

Gallery 23 Antiques
Contact Mr F Vollaro
5 High Street, Chalfont St Giles, Buckinghamshire, HP8 4QH
01494 871512 01494 871512
Est. 1989 *Stock size* Large
Stock China, silver, furniture, glass, pictures, prints, clocks
Open Mon–Sat 10am–5pm
Services Valuations

St Giles Old Pine Company
Contact Toby Smith
The Furniture Village, London Road, Chalfont St Giles, Buckinghamshire, HP8 4RD
01494 873031 07860 265130
tobysmith@stgilesfurniture.com
Est. 1968 *Stock size* Large
Stock Antique, English and Continental oak and pine furniture
Open Mon–Sat 9am–5pm
Sun 11am–4pm

CHALFONT ST PETER

White House Antiques
Contact Mrs Betty St John-White
10 Market Place, Chalfont St Peter, Buckinghamshire, SL9 9EA
01753 885878
Est. 2000 *Stock size* Medium
Stock Early porcelain, glass, silver
Open Mon–Fri 10.15am–4.15pm
Sat 10.15am–2pm closed Thurs

CHESHAM

The Attic
Contact Karen Page
3 High Street, Chesham, Buckinghamshire, HP5 1BG
01494 794114
Est. 1998 *Stock size* Large
Stock Collectables, furniture, jewellery, paintings, pictures, china, pottery, clocks, brass, commemoratives
Open Mon–Sat 9.30am–5.30pm
Sun 11am–5pm

Chess Antiques (LAPADA)
Contact Mr Wilder
85 Broad Street, Chesham, Buckinghamshire, HP5 3EF
01494 783043 01494 791302
07831 212454
www.mike_wilder44@hotmail.com
Est. 1971 *Stock size* Medium
Stock Clocks
Open Mon–Fri 9am–5.30pm
Sat 10am–5pm
Services Valuations

A E Jackson
Contact Ann Jackson
Queen Anne House, 57 Church Street, Chesham, Buckinghamshire, HP5 1HY
01494 783811
Est. 1910 *Stock size* Medium
Stock Home antiques
Open Wed Fri Sat 10am–12.30pm
1.30–5pm

The Sovereign
Contact Mr Leadbeater
115 High Street, Chesham, Buckinghamshire, HP5 1DE
01494 783103 07961 865398
Est. 1999 *Stock size* Large
Stock Period furniture, militaria, glass, general objets d'art, textiles
Open Mon–Sat 9.30am–5.30pm
Sun 11am–4pm closed Wed
Services Valuations, restorations

Stuff & Nonsense
Contact Helen or Elaine Robb
70 Broad Street, Chesham, Buckinghamshire, HP5 3DX
01494 775988/782877
Est. 1998 *Stock size* Large
No. of dealers 20
Stock Collectables, books, antiques, furniture
Open Mon–Sat 9.30am–5.30pm
Sun 11am–5.30pm

HIGH WYCOMBE

Glade Antiques (BADA, LAPADA, CINOA)
Contact Sonia Vaughan
PO Box 873, High Wycombe, Buckinghamshire, HP14 3ZQ
01494 882818 07771 552328
sonia@gladeantiques.com
www.gladeantiques.com
Stock Oriental porcelain, bronzes, jades, antiquities
Open By appointment
Fairs BADA, Olympia, LAPADA
Services Valuations

IVER

Yester-Year
Contact Mr P J Frost
12 High Street, Iver, Buckinghamshire, SL0 9NG
01753 652072
Est. 1968 *Stock size* Medium
Stock General antiques, furniture, pictures, china, glass, metalwork
Open Mon–Sat 10am–6pm
Services Valuations, restorations, picture framing, clock repairs

LITTLE CHALFONT

Nightingale Antiques
Contact Mr L Andreou or Mr A Truss
17 Nightingale Corner, Little Chalfont, Amersham, Buckinghamshire, HP7 9PZ
01494 762163
Est. 1962 *Stock size* Large
Stock General antiques, silver, silver plate, fine china, porcelain
Open Tues–Sat 9.30am–5.30pm
Sun 10am–4pm
Services Restorations, valuations, silver-plating

MARLOW

Bosleys Military Auctioneers
Contact Mr S Bosley
The White House, Marlow, Buckinghamshire, SL7 1AH
01628 488188 01628 488111
www.bosleys.co.uk
Est. 1994
Open By appointment only
Sales Militaria sales Wed noon at Court Gardens, viewing Wed 8am–noon prior to sale
Frequency Quarterly
Catalogues Yes

Coldstream Military Antiques (LAPADA)
Contact Mr S Bosley
The White House, Marlow, Buckinghamshire, SL7 1AH
01628 488188 01628 488111
Est. 1978 *Stock size* Large
Stock Militaria including swords, medals, pictures, campaign furniture
Open By appointment only

Marlow Antiques Centre (TVADA)
Contact Marilyn Short
✉ **35 Station Road, Marlow, Buckinghamshire, SL7 1NW** P
☎ 01628 473223 F 01628 478989
M 07802 188345
Est. 1995 *Stock size* Large
No. of dealers 30
Stock 18th–20thC furniture, china, Staffordshire figures, chandeliers, silver, decorative glass, writing slopes, tea caddies, postcards, pens, cuff links, equestrian items
Open Mon–Sat 10.30am–5pm Sun 11am–4pm
Services Restorations, shipping

MEDMENHAM

Jack Harness Antiques
Contact Jack Harness
✉ **Unit 2, Westfield Farm, Medmenham, Marlow, Buckinghamshire, SL7 2HE** P
☎ 01491 410691 F 01491 419699
E jackharness@aol.com
Est. 1990 *Stock size* Large
Stock Antique country furniture for export only
Trade only Yes
Open By appointment

NAPHILL

A and E Foster (BADA, CINOA)
Contact Stephen Foster
✉ **Little Heysham, Naphill, Buckinghamshire, HP14 4SU** P
☎ 01494 562024 F 01494 562024
M 07802 895146
Est. 1970 *Stock size* Medium
Stock European works of art and sculpture
Open By appointment
Fairs Grosvenor House, Spring and Winter Olympia

NEWPORT PAGNELL

Ken's Paper Collectables (UACC, Ephemera Society)
Contact Ken Graham
✉ **29 High Street, Newport Pagnell, Buckinghamshire, MK16 8AR** P
☎ 01908 210683 or 610003
F 01908 610003
E ken@kens.co.uk
W www.kens.co.uk
Est. 1983 *Stock size* Large
Stock Autographs, vintage magazines, posters, historic newspapers, British comics, documents, printed, written ephemera, show business memorabilia
Open Mon–Wed Fri 9.30am–5pm Sat 9.30am–4pm
Fairs Alexandra Palace, ephemera fairs, film fairs

OLNEY

Archers
Contact Mr N Carter or Katherine Haslam
✉ **19 High Street, Olney, Buckinghamshire, MK46 4EB** P
☎ 01234 713050 F 01234 713050
E archersantiques@ukgateway.net
Est. 1999 *Stock size* Large
Stock Mahogany, pine, oak furniture
Open Mon–Sat 10am–5pm Sun 2–5pm closed Wed
Fairs Ardingly, Newark

Gilpin Antiques
Contact Mr J Swallow
✉ **100a High Street, Olney, Buckinghamshire, MK46 4BE** P
☎ 01234 711095 F 01234 711895
M 07808 200522
Est. 1979 *Stock size* Medium
Stock Furniture, porcelain, silver, jewellery, clocks
Open Mon–Sat 10am–1pm 2–5pm Sun 2–5pm closed Wed
Services Restorations

Robin Unsworth Antiques
Contact Robin Unsworth
✉ **1a Weston Road, Olney, Buckinghamshire, MK46 5BD** P
☎ 01234 711210 M 07860 809584
Est. 1972 *Stock size* Large
Stock 18th–19thC furniture, clocks
Open Mon–Sun 10am–4pm or by appointment

PENN

Penn Barn
Contact Paul Hunnings
✉ **By the Pond, Elm Road, Penn, Buckinghamshire, HP10 8LB** P
☎ 01494 815691
Est. 1968 *Stock size* Medium
Stock Antiquarian books, maps, prints, watercolours, oil paintings
Open Tues–Sat 10.30am–1pm 2–4pm

Penn Village Antique Centre
Contact John Merrifield
✉ **3 Hazlemere Road, Penn, High Wycombe, Buckinghamshire, HP10 8AA** P
☎ 01494 812244
Est. 1961 *Stock size* Large
No. of dealers 30
Stock Antiques and collectables
Open Mon–Sat 10am–5pm Sun noon–4.30pm

PRINCES RISBOROUGH

Well Cottage Antique Centre
Contact Mrs J Blaik
✉ **20–22 Bell Street, Princes Risborough, Buckinghamshire, HP27 0AD** P
☎ 01844 342002
Est. 1985 *Stock size* Medium
No. of dealers 9
Stock Furniture, early silver, general antiques
Open Mon Tues Thurs–Sat 10am–5pm Sun 1–5pm

STONY STRATFORD

Circa Antiques
Contact Victoria Holton
✉ **6 Church Street, Stony Stratford, Buckinghamshire, MK11 1BD** P
☎ 01908 567100
E info@circa-antiques.co.uk
W www.circa-antiques.co.uk
Est. 2000 *Stock size* Medium
Stock Victorian and Edwardian furniture, interesting pieces pre 1939
Open Tues–Sat 10am–5pm

Daeron's Books
Contact Mrs A Gardner
✉ **3 Timor Court, High Street, Stony Stratford, Milton Keynes, Buckinghamshire, MK11 1EJ** P
☎ 01908 568989 F 01908 266092
E books@daerons.co.uk
W www.daerons.co.uk
Est. 1993 *Stock size* Medium
Stock Fantasy, science fiction books, Tolkien and C S Lewis a speciality

Open Mon–Fri 9am–5pm Thurs Sun by appointment
Fairs Stony Stratford
Services Valuations, book search, book fair organizer

Periplus Books
Contact Mr J Phillips
2 Timor Court, High Street, Stony Stratford, Milton Keynes, Buckinghamshire, MK11 1EJ P
☎ 01908 263300
periplus@cix.co.uk
Est. 1997 ***Stock size*** Small
Stock General second-hand and antiquarian books
Open Tues–Sat 10.30am–5pm Thurs by appointment

WADDESDON

Junk and Disorderly
Contact Mrs R Mead
74 High Street, Waddesdon, Aylesbury, Buckinghamshire, HP18 0JD P
☎ 01296 658573 F 01296 651048
Est. 1993 ***Stock size*** Large
Stock General antiques
Open Mon–Sun 10am–5pm

WAVENDON

Jeanne Temple Antiques
Contact Mrs Temple
Stockwell House, 1 Stockwell Lane, Wavendon, Milton Keynes, Buckinghamshire, MK17 8LS P
☎ 01908 583597 F 01908 281149
Est. 1960 ***Stock size*** Medium
Stock Furniture, collectable items, lighting
Open Tues–Sat 10am–5pm Sun by appointment
Fairs Luton Fair

WENDOVER

Antiques at Wendover
Contact Mrs N Gregory
The Old Post Office, 25 High Street, Wendover, Buckinghamshire, HP22 6DU P
☎ 01296 625335 F 01296 620401
M 07712 032565
antiques@antiqueswendover.co.uk
www.antiqueswendover.co.uk
Est. 1987 ***Stock size*** Large
No. of dealers 30
Stock Town and country antiques, furniture, silver, glass, rugs, English garden tools and statuary, kitchenware, architectural antiques, barometers, antiquities, guns, pocket watches, Art Deco (dateline 1940)
Open Mon–Sat 10am–5.30pm Sun Bank Holidays 11am–5pm
Services Restoration of caning, ceramics, metals, jewellery, furniture

Bowood Antiques (LAPADA, TVADA)
Contact Miss P Peyton-Jones
Wendover Dean Farm, Bowood Lane, Wendover, Buckinghamshire, HP22 6PY P
☎ 01296 622113 F 01296 696598
Est. 1960 ***Stock size*** Medium
Stock General antiques, 17th–early 19thC furniture
Open Mon–Sat 10am–5pm phone call advisable

Sally Turner Antiques (LAPADA)
Contact Sally Turner
Hogarth House, High Street, Wendover, Buckinghamshire, HP22 6DU P
☎ 01296 624402 F 01296 624402
Est. 1979 ***Stock size*** Large
Stock 18th–19thC furniture, decorative items, jewellery, works of art
Open Mon–Sat 10am–5pm closed Wed
Fairs Olympia
Services Repairs

Wendover Antiques (LAPADA)
Contact Richard or Dorli Davies
1 South Street, Wendover, Buckinghamshire, HP22 6EF P
☎ 01296 622078
Est. 1979 ***Stock size*** Large
Stock 18th–19thC furniture, pictures, oils, watercolours, miniatures, silhouettes, silver
Open Mon–Sat 10am–5.30pm or by appointment

WHITCHURCH

Deerstalker Antiques
Contact Mrs. L. Eichler
28 High Street, Whitchurch, Buckinghamshire, HP22 4JT P
☎ 01296 641505
Est. 1978 ***Stock size*** Small
Stock General country antiques
Open Tues Wed Thurs Sat 10am–6pm or by appointment
Fairs Milton Keynes
Services Restorations of period furniture only

WINSLOW

Winslow Antique Centre
Contact Mr Taylor
15 Market Square, Winslow, Buckinghamshire, MK18 3AB P
☎ 01296 714540 F 01296 714556
Est. 1990 ***Stock size*** Large
No. of dealers 20
Stock Country-style antique centre, Staffordshire, pottery
Open Mon–Sat 10am–5pm Sun 1–5pm closed Wed

GLOUCESTERSHIRE

ANDOVERSFORD

Julian Tatham-Losh
Contact Mr Julian Tatham-Losh
Brereton House, Andoversford, Cheltenham, Gloucestershire, GL54 4JN P
☎ 01242 820646 F 01242 820563
jtlantiques@onetel.net.uk
Est. 1980 ***Stock size*** Large
Stock Majolica, Staffordshire, tea caddies, bamboo furniture, general decorative items
Trade only Yes
Open Mon–Fri 8am–6pm
Fairs NEC, Newark
Services Valuations

ASTON SUBEDGE

Cottage Farm Antiques
Contact Tony or Ann Willmore
Cottage Farm, Aston Subedge, Chipping Campden, Gloucestershire, GL55 6PZ P
☎ 01386 438263 F 01386 438263
info@cottagefarmantiques.co.uk
www.cottagefarmantiques.co.uk
Est. 1986 ***Stock size*** Large
Stock Original Victorian–Edwardian furniture, mostly pine, unfitted kitchens
Open Mon–Sun 9am–5pm
Services Restorations, shipping

BERKELEY

Berkeley Market
Contact Mr Keith Gardener
11 The Market Place, Berkeley, Gloucestershire, GL13 9BD
01453 511032 07802 304534
Est. 1988 ***Stock size*** Large
No. of dealers 5
Stock Bric-a-brac, period furniture, general antiques
Open Tues–Sat 9.30am–5pm or by appointment
Services Free tea or coffee

Proudfoot Antiques (FATG)
Contact Peter or Penny Proudfoot
16–18 High Street, Berkeley, Gloucestershire, GL13 9BJ
01453 811513 01453 511616
07802 911894
berkeleyframes@aol.com
www.berkeley-framing.co.uk
Est. 1956 ***Stock size*** Medium
Stock General antiques
Open Mon–Sun 9.30am–5.30pm
Services Valuations, picture framing

BIBURY

Mill Antiques Etc
Contact Mr B Goodall
Arlington Mill, Arlington, Bibury, Cirencester, Gloucestershire, GL7 5NL
01285 740199
07788 681998
Est. 1999 ***Stock size*** Large
Stock General antiques, gifts, souvenir collectables, exclusive tea towels
Open 7 days 9am–6pm

BISLEY

High Street Antiques
Contact Heather Ross
Bisley, Stroud, Gloucestershire, GL6 7BA
01452 770153 07703 755841
Est. 1975 ***Stock size*** Small
Stock Oriental rugs, small furniture, collectables
Open Mon–Sat 2–6pm
Fairs Malvern

BOURTON-ON-THE-WATER

Aquarius Books Ltd
Contact Mr S Dumbleton
Portland House, Victoria Street, Bourton-on-the-Water, Gloucestershire, GL54 2BX
01451 820352
Est. 1992 ***Stock size*** Large
Stock Antiquarian and second-hand books
Open Mon–Sun 9.30am–5.30pm
Services Book search

The Looking Glass
Contact Mrs A P Jones
Rear of Aquarius Bookshop, Victoria Street, Bourton-on-the-Water, Gloucestershire, GL54 2BX
01451 810818
Est. 2001 ***Stock size*** Small
Stock Glass, small furniture, collectables, silver, pottery, china, studio pottery
Open Mon–Sun 10am–5pm

Tayler & Fletcher
Contact Mr Martin Lambert
London House, High Street, Bourton-on-the-Water, Gloucestershire, GL54 2AP
01451 821666 01451 820818
07074 821666
lambert@tayler-and-fletcher.co.uk
www.taylerfletcher.com
Est. 1790
Open Mon–Fri 9am–5.30pm Sat 9am–12.30pm
Sales Monthly furniture sales Sat 10am, viewing Fri 1–6pm and morning of sale from 7.30am. Three fine art and antiques sales per annum Tues 10.30am, viewing Mon 1–7pm and morning of sale from 8am
Frequency Monthly
Catalogues Yes

CHALFORD

Minchinhampton Architectural Salvage Co (SALVO)
Contact Eve Guinan
Cirencester Road, Aston Down, Chalford, Stroud, Gloucestershire, GL6 8PE
01285 760886 01285 760838
masco@catbrain.com
www.catbrain.com
Est. 1983 ***Stock size*** Large
Stock Architectural antiques, garden ornaments, reclaimed materials, metalwork, gates, staddle stones, window frames, chimney pieces
Open Mon–Fri 9am–5pm Sat 9am–3pm
Services Valuations, garden design

CHARLTON KINGS

Latchford Antiques
Contact Mrs R Latchford
203 London Road, Charlton Kings, Cheltenham, Gloucestershire, GL52 6HX
01242 226263 01242 226263
Est. 1985 ***Stock size*** Medium
Stock Victorian pine and period furniture, jewellery, gifts
Open Mon–Sat 10am–5.30pm

CHELTENHAM

Art & Antiques (LAPADA)
Contact Mrs J Turner
16–17 Montpellier Walk, Cheltenham, Gloucestershire, GL50 1SD
01242 522939
Est. 1950 ***Stock size*** Large
Stock General antiques
Open Mon–Sat 9am–4pm closed Thurs
Fairs Westonbirt
Services Road shows

Cheltenham Antique Market
Contact Mr K Shave
54 Suffolk Road, Cheltenham, Gloucestershire, GL50 2AQ
01242 529812
Est. 1979 ***Stock size*** Large
Stock Victorian–20thC furniture, chandeliers
Open Mon–Sat 10am–5.30pm

Corner Cupboard Curios
Contact P. Larner
2 Church Street, Cheltenham, Gloucestershire, GL7 1LE
01285 655476
Est. 1975 ***Stock size*** Medium
Stock General antiques and collectables
Open By appointment
Fairs NEC

The Cotswold Auction Co Ltd
Contact Mrs Elizabeth Poole

✉ **Chapel Walk Sale Room, Chapel Walk, Cheltenham, Gloucestershire, GL50 3DS**
☎ 01242 256363 Ⓕ 01242 571734
Ⓔ info@cotswoldauction.co.uk
Ⓦ www.cotswoldauction.co.uk
Est. 1890
Open Mon–Fri 9am–5.30pm
Sales General and specialist sale Tues 11am, viewing day prior 10am–5pm day of sale 9–11am
Frequency Monthly
Catalogues Yes

⊞ Giltwood Gallery

Contact Mr Jeff Butt or Mrs Gill Butt
✉ **30 Suffolk Parade, Cheltenham, Gloucestershire, GL50 2AE**
☎ 01242 512482 Ⓕ 01242 512482
Est. 1994 ***Stock size*** Medium
Stock Georgian–Edwardian furniture, mirrors, chandeliers, pictures
Open Mon–Sat 9am–5.30pm
Services Restorations, upholstery

⊞ Greens of Cheltenham Ltd (GAGTL)

Contact Mr S Reynolds
✉ **15 Montpellier Walk, Cheltenham, Gloucestershire, GL50 1SD** Ⓟ
☎ 01242 512088 Ⓕ 01242 512088
Ⓔ steve@greensofcheltenham.co.uk
Est. 1947 ***Stock size*** Large
Stock Jewellery, Oriental works of art, silver
Open Mon–Sat 9am–1pm 2–5pm closed Wed
Fairs Olympia (June), Miami Beach (Jan)
Services Restorations

⊞ Catherine Hunt Oriental Antiques, (TADA)

Contact Catherine Hunt
✉ **PO Box 743, Cheltenham, Gloucestershire, GL52 5ZB** Ⓟ
☎ 01242 227794 Ⓕ 01242 227794
Ⓜ 07976 319344
Ⓔ cathyhunt@btinternet.com
Est. 1986 ***Stock size*** Large
Stock Chinese ceramics, Ming, Qing etc, furniture, textiles from Ming onwards
Open By appointment
Fairs Wilton House, Caroline Penman Fair Petersfield

⊞ H W Keil (Cheltenham) Ltd (BADA, LAPADA, CINOA)

Contact Miss Laura Stapleton
✉ **129–131 The Promenade, Cheltenham, Gloucestershire, GL50 1NW** Ⓟ
☎ 01242 522509 Ⓕ 01386 852069
Stock size Large
Stock Furniture, rugs
Open Mon–Sat 9.15am–12.45pm 2.15–5.30pm
Services Valuations, restorations

Mallams

Contact Robin Fisher
✉ **Grosvenor Galleries, 26 Grosvenor Street, Cheltenham, Gloucestershire, GL52 2SG** Ⓟ
☎ 01242 235712 Ⓕ 01242 241943
Ⓔ cheltenham@mallams.co.uk
Ⓦ www.mallams.co.uk/fineart
Est. 1788
Open Mon–Fri 9am–5.30pm Sat 9am–noon
Sales Antiques and general sale Thurs 11am, viewing Tues 9am–7pm Wed prior 9am–5pm. Ceramics sales, 2 per annum Thurs 11am, viewing Tues 9am–7pm Wed 9am–5pm
Frequency Monthly
Catalogues Yes

⊞ Montpellier Clocks (BADA, CINOA)

Contact Toby Birch
✉ **13 Rotunda Terrace, Cheltenham, Gloucestershire, GL50 1SW** Ⓟ
☎ 01242 242178 Ⓕ 01242 242178
Ⓔ montpellier.clocks@virgin.net
Ⓦ www.montpellierclocks.com
Est. 1959 ***Stock size*** Medium
Stock Longcase clocks, bracket clocks, chronometers, barometers, carriage clocks
Open Mon–Sat 9am–5pm
Services Restorations, conservation (BADA qualified)

⊞ Patrick Oliver Antiques

Contact Michael Oliver
✉ **4 Tivoli Street, Cheltenham, Gloucestershire, GL50 2UW** Ⓟ
☎ 01242 519538
Est. 1902 ***Stock size*** Medium
Stock General antiques
Open Mon–Fri 9am–1pm
Services Valuations

⊞ Promenade Antiques

Contact Mr B Mann
✉ **18 The Promenade, Cheltenham, Gloucestershire, GL50 1LR**
☎ 01242 524519
Est. 1980 ***Stock size*** Large
Stock Antique and second-hand jewellery, clocks, watches, silver, plated items
Open Mon–Sat 9am–5pm
Fairs Malvern Antiques Fair
Services Valuations, repairs

⊞ Q & C Militaria (OMRS)

Contact Mr John Wright
✉ **22 Suffolk Road, Cheltenham, Gloucestershire, GL50 2AQ** Ⓟ
☎ 01242 519815 Ⓕ 01242 519815
Ⓜ 07778 613977
Ⓔ john@qc-militaria.freeserve.co.uk
Est. 1994 ***Stock size*** Large
Stock Militaria
Open Tues–Sat 10am–5pm
Fairs Brittania Medal Fairs
Services Medal mounting

⊞ Michael Rayner Bookseller

Contact Michael Rayner
✉ **11 St Lukes Road, Cheltenham, Gloucestershire, GL53 7JQ** Ⓟ
☎ 01242 512806
Est. 1988 ***Stock size*** Medium
Stock Antiquarian and second-hand books
Open Wed Thurs Fri Sat 10am–6pm or by appointment
Services Valuations, restorations

⊞ Replay Period Clothing

Contact Ms Ruth Lane
✉ **7 Well Walk, Cheltenham, Gloucestershire, GL50 3JX** Ⓟ
☎ 01242 238864
Ⓔ replayperiodclothingruthlane@btinternet.com
Est. 1987 ***Stock size*** Large
Stock Period clothing 1800–1970, linen, lace, costume jewellery
Open Tues–Sat 10am–5pm closed 1–2pm
Fairs Chelsea Town Hall, Hammersmith Town Hall
Services Hat decoration, clothing hire considered

⊞ Sambourne House Antique Pine Ltd

Contact Tim or Kim Cove

✉ **Units 23, Regent Shopping Centre, Cheltenham, Gloucestershire, GL50 1JZ** 🅿
☎ 01242 210257
ⓔ tkcove34@globalnet.co.uk
ⓦ www.sambourne-antiques.co.uk
Est. 1986 ***Stock size*** Large
Stock Antique and reproduction pine furniture, smalls, decorative items
Open Mon–Sun 9am–5pm
Services Hand-built kitchens

Catherine Shinn Decorative Textiles
Contact Catherine Shinn
✉ **5–6 Well Walk, Cheltenham, Gloucestershire, GL50 3JX** 🅿
☎ 01242 574546 ⓕ 01242 578495
ⓦ www.catherineshinn.com
Est. 1988 ***Stock size*** Large
Stock Decorative textiles, antique cushions, furnishings, accessories
Open Mon–Sat 10am–5pm
Services Advice

Tapestry Antiques
Contact Mrs G Hall
✉ **33 Suffolk Parade, Cheltenham, Gloucestershire, GL50 2AE** 🅿
☎ 01242 512191
Est. 1984 ***Stock size*** Large
Stock Decorative antiques, pine, beds, garden furniture, mirrors
Open Mon–Sat 10am–5.30pm

Triton Gallery
Contact Mr L Bianco
✉ **27 Suffolk Parade, Cheltenham, Gloucestershire, GL50 2AE** 🅿
☎ 01242 510477
Est. 1984 ***Stock size*** Large
Stock Antique mirrors, chandeliers, paintings, Continental and English furniture
Open Mon–Sat 9am–5.30pm

Troubridge Antiques
Contact Mr I Lochhead
✉ **11 Great Norwood Street, Cheltenham, Gloucestershire, GL50 2AW** 🅿
☎ 01242 226919
Est. 1974 ***Stock size*** Large
Stock Mixture of general antiques
Open Tues–Sat 10am–5pm
Services Valuations

CHIPPING CAMDEN

Draycott Books
Contact Mr R H McClement
✉ **2 Sheep Street, Chipping Camden, Gloucestershire, GL55 6DX**
☎ 01386 841392
ⓔ draycottbooks@hotmail.com
Est. 1981 ***Stock size*** Medium
Stock Second-hand and antiquarian books
Open Mon–Fri 10am–1pm 2–5pm Sat 10am–5.30pm
Services Valuations, book search

Schoolhouse Antiques
Contact Mr Hammond
✉ **The Headmaster's House, The Old School, High Street, Chipping Camden, Gloucestershire, GL55 6HB** 🅿
☎ 01386 841474
ⓔ hamatschoolhouse@aol.com
ⓦ www.schoolhouseantiques.co.uk
Est. 1969 ***Stock size*** Large
Stock 17th–19thC furniture, pictures, clocks, Victorian oils, musical boxes
Open Mon–Sun 9am–5pm closed Thurs Oct–Mar
Services Valuations

CIRENCESTER

Cirencester Arcade
Contact Mr P Bird
✉ **25 Market Place, Cirencester, Gloucestershire, GL7 2NX** 🅿
☎ 01285 644214
Est. 1995 ***Stock size*** Large
No. of dealers 60
Stock Furniture, china, glass, jewellery, coins, stamps, postcards
Open Mon–Sun 9.30am–5pm
Services Shipping, book search, clock repair

Corinium Auctions (PTA)
Contact Mr K Lawson
✉ **25 Gloucester Street, Cirencester, Gloucestershire, GL7 2DJ** 🅿
☎ 01285 659057 ⓕ 01285 652047
Est. 1990
Open Mon–Fri 10am–1pm 3–7pm
Sales 3 sales in Jan June Oct selling printed ephemera, cigarette cards, books, postcards etc
Catalogues Yes

The Cotswold Auction Co Ltd (RICS)
Contact Elizabeth Poole
✉ **Swan Yard, West Market Place, Cirencester, Gloucestershire, GL7 2NH** 🅿
☎ 01285 642420 ⓕ 01285 642400
ⓔ info@cotswoldauction.co.uk
ⓦ www.cotswoldauction.co.uk
Est. 1890
Open Mon–Fri 9am–5.30pm
Sales Held at The Bingham Hall, King Street, Cirencester. General antiques and specialist sales Fri 10am, viewing Thurs prior 10am–8pm day of sale 9–10am
Frequency Monthly
Catalogues Yes

Forum Antiques
Contact Mr Weston Mitchell
✉ **Springfield Farm, Perrott's Brook, Cirencester, Gloucestershire, GL7 7DT** 🅿
☎ 01285 831821
ⓔ westie@forumants.freeserve.co.uk
Est. 1985 ***Stock size*** Small
Stock 18thC and earlier veneered walnut, early oak, Empire furniture
Open By appointment only

Hare's Antiques Ltd
Contact Allan Hare
✉ **4 Black Jack Street, Cirencester, Gloucestershire, GL7 2AA** 🅿
☎ 01285 640077 ⓕ 01285 653513
ⓜ 07860 350097/6
ⓔ hares@hares-antiques.com
ⓦ www.hares-antiques.com
Est. 1972 ***Stock size*** Large
Stock 18th–19thC English furniture, Howard upholstery
Open Mon–Sat 10am–5.30pm or by appointment
Fairs Olympia
Services Restorations, upholstery

Moore, Allen & Innocent (FNAVA)
Contact Mrs Marjorie Williams
✉ **Norcote, Cirencester, Gloucestershire, GL7 5RH** 🅿
☎ 01285 646050 ⓕ 01285 652862
ⓔ fineart@mooreallen.co.uk
ⓦ www.mooreallen.co.uk
Est. 1852
Open Mon–Fri 9am–5.30pm Sat 9am–noon
Sales Selective antiques sale quarterly Fri 10am. Sporting 6 monthly Fri 10am. Picture sale 6

monthly Fri 10am. General sale monthly Fri 9.30am, viewing, day prior 10.30am–8.00pm, sale day 9am–3pm
Frequency Twice monthly
Catalogues Yes

Original Architectural Antiques Co Ltd (SALVO)
Contact John Rawlinson
Ermin Farm, Cirencester, Gloucestershire, GL7 5PN
☎ 01285 869222 Ⓕ 01285 862221
Ⓜ 07774 979735
Ⓔ info@originaluk.com
Ⓦ www.originaluk.com
Est. 1980 *Stock size* Large
Stock Architectural antiques, fireplaces, columns, limestone troughs, oak doors
Open Mon–Sat 9am–5pm Sun 10am–4pm
Services Valuations, restorations

Parlour Farm Antiques
Contact Mr N Grunfeld
Unit 12B, Wilkinson Road, Love Lane Industrial Estate, Cirencester, Gloucestershire, GL7 1YT
☎ 01285 885336 Ⓕ 01285 885338
Ⓔ info@parlourfarm.com
Ⓦ www.parlourfarm.com
Est. 1994 *Stock size* Large
Stock Antique pine furniture, kitchens, garden furniture
Open Mon–Sun 10am–5pm

Rankine Taylor Antiques (LAPADA, CADA, CINOA)
Contact Mrs L Taylor
34 Dollar Street, Cirencester, Gloucestershire, GL7 2AN
☎ 01285 652529 Ⓕ 01285 652529
Ⓦ www.cirencestergalleries.com
Est. 1969 *Stock size* Large
Stock An eclectic collection of 16th–18thC furniture, silver, glass, pewter, copper, brass and rare associated objects
Open Mon–Sat 9am–5.30pm
Services Small repairs

Silver Street Antiques
Contact Mr S Tarrant
9 Silver Street, Cirencester, Gloucestershire, GL7 2BJ
☎ 01285 641600 Ⓕ 01285 641600
Est. 1994 *Stock size* Medium
Stock General antiques, kitchenware
Open Mon Tues Thurs–Sat 10am–5pm Wed Sun noon–5pm
Services House clearance

Specialised Postcard Auctions (PTA)
Contact Mr K Lawson
25 Gloucester Street, Cirencester, Gloucestershire, GL7 2DJ
☎ 01285 659057 Ⓕ 01285 652047
Est. 1976
Open As per viewing
Sales Every 5 weeks Mon 2pm, viewing Mon–Fri prior 10am–1pm 3–7pm day of sale 10am–2pm
Frequency Every 5 weeks
Catalogues Yes

William H Stokes (BADA, CADA)
Contact Mr Peter Bontoft
The Cloisters, 6–8 Dollar Street, Cirencester, Gloucestershire, GL7 2AJ
☎ 01285 653907 Ⓕ 01285 653907
Est. 1968 *Stock size* Medium
Stock Early oak furniture, associated items
Open Mon–Fri 9.30am–5.30pm Sat 9.30am–4.30pm

Patrick Waldron Antiques
Contact Patrick Waldron
18 Dollar Street, Cirencester, Gloucestershire, GL7 2AN
☎ 01285 652880
Est. 1994 *Stock size* Medium
Stock 18th–early 19thC English furniture
Open Mon–Sat 9.30am–6pm
Services Restorations

Bernard Weaver Antiques
Contact Bernard Weaver
28 Gloucester Street, Cirencester, Gloucestershire, GL7 2DH
☎ 01285 652055
Est. 1990 *Stock size* Medium
Stock General antiques
Open By appointment
Fairs Olympia

COLEFORD

Simon Lewis Transport Books
Contact Mr S Lewis
PO Box 9, Coleford, Gloucestershire, GL16 8YF
☎ 01594 839369 Ⓕ 01594 839369
Ⓔ simon@simonlewis.com
Ⓦ www.simonlewis.com
Est. 1985 *Stock size* Medium
Stock 1910–1990 transport-related books
Open By appointment

CUTSDEAN

Architectural Heritage (CADA)
Contact Alex Puddy
Taddington Manor, Taddington, Cutsdean, Gloucestershire, GL54 5RY
☎ 01386 584414 Ⓕ 01386 584236
Ⓔ puddy@architectural-heritage.co.uk
Ⓦ www.architectural-heritage.co.uk
Est. 1986 *Stock size* Large
Stock Garden ornaments, chimney pieces, wood wall panelling
Open Mon–Fri 9.30am–5.30pm Sat 10.30am–4.30pm
Fairs Chelsea
Services Valuations

EBRINGTON

Natural Craft Taxidermy (Guild of Taxidermy)
Contact John Burton
21 Main Street, Ebrington, Chipping Camden, Gloucestershire, GL57 6NL
☎ 01386 593231 Ⓜ 07850 356354
Est. 1973 *Stock size* Medium
Stock Victorian–Edwardian, modern natural history subjects
Open By appointment
Services Valuations, restorations, commissions

FAIRFORD

Blenheim Antiques (CADA)
Contact Mr Neil Hurdle
Acacia House, Market Place, Fairford, Gloucestershire, GL7 4AB
☎ 01285 712094
Est. 1973 *Stock size* Medium
Stock 18th–19thC town and country furniture, clocks, accessories
Open Mon–Sat 9am–6pm

Gloucester House Antiques (CADA)
Contact Mrs Chester-Master
Market Place, Fairford, Gloucestershire, GL7 4AB
01285 712790 01285 713324
Est. 1972 *Stock size* Large
Stock English and French country furniture, farmhouse tables, chairs, 18th–19thC French faïence and pottery
Open Mon–Sat 9am–5.30pm

Anthony Hazledine Oriental Carpets
Contact Anthony Hazeldine
High Street, Fairford, Gloucestershire, GL7 4AD
01285 713400 01285 713400
tonyhazrugs@aol.com
Est. 1982 *Stock size* Small
Stock Antique Oriental rugs and carpets
Open Mon–Sat 9.30am–5pm
Services Valuations, restorations, cleaning

FILKINS

Corner House Antiques
Contact Mr John Downes-Hall
Gardener's Cottage, Broughton Poggs, Filkins, Lechlade, Gloucestershire, GL7 3JH
01367 860078
jdhis007@btopenworld.com
www.cornerhouseantiques.co.uk
Est. 1995 *Stock size* Medium
Stock Antique silver, jewellery, country furniture, porcelain, objets d'art
Open By appointment
Services Designer and silversmith, restoration of old silver

GLOUCESTER

Agdar
Contact Mr Alan Giles
330 Barton Street, Gloucester, Gloucestershire, GL1 4JJ
01452 302272 01452 302272
07785 278878
Est. 1984 *Stock size* Medium
Stock General antiques, pine
Open Mon–Sat 9am–3pm
Services House clearance

The Cotswold Auction Co Ltd
Contact Robert Short FRICS
4–6 Clarence Street, Gloucester, Gloucestershire, GL1 1DX
01452 521177 01452 305883
info@cotswoldauction.co.uk
www.cotswoldauction.co.uk
Est. 1890
Open Mon–Fri 9am–5.30pm
Sales Antiques, collectables and general sale at St Barnabas Church Hall Tues 10am, viewing Mon 9am–9pm
Frequency Every 2 months
Catalogues Yes

The Cottage
Contact Mrs Helen Webb
55 Southgate Street, Gloucester, Gloucestershire, GL1 1TX
01452 526027
Est. 1998 *Stock size* Large
Stock Antiques, collectables, gifts of distinction
Open Mon–Sat 9.30am–4.30pm Wed 12.30–4.30pm
Services Repairs

Gloucester Antique Centre
Contact Mrs Wright
The Historic Docks, 1 Severn Road, Gloucester, Gloucestershire, GL1 2LE
01452 529716 01452 307161
www.antiques-center.com
Est. 1990 *Stock size* Large
No. of dealers 140
Stock General antiques, collectables
Open Mon–Sat 10am–5pm Sun 1–5pm
Services Valuations, shipping, book search

HQ 84
Contact J Williams
82–84 Southgate Street, Gloucester, Gloucestershire, GL12 DX
01452 556038
Est. 1962 *Stock size* Medium
Stock Militaria
Open Mon–Sun 9am–5pm

M & C Cards
Contact Mr M W Cant
Shop 30, The Antiques Centre, Severn Road, Gloucester, Gloucestershire, GL1 2LE
01452 506361 01452 307161
mick@mandccards.co.uk
www.mandccards.co.uk
Est. 1991 *Stock size* Medium
Stock Postcards, cigarette cards, advertising collectables
Open Thurs–Mon 10am–5pm Sun 1–5pm
Fairs Cheltenham Race Course Card Fair

M & C Stamps
Contact Mr M W Cant
Shop 30, The Antiques Centre, Severn Road, Gloucester, Gloucestershire, GL1 2LE
01452 506361 01452 307161
mick@mandcstamps.co.uk
www.mandcstamps.co.uk
Est. 1984 *Stock size* Medium
Stock Stamps, first day covers, accessories
Open Thurs–Mon 10am–5pm Sun 1–5pm
Fairs Stamp Fair Cheltenham Town Hall
Services Valuations, new issue service

W H Webber Antique Clocks
Contact W H Webber
First Floor, Gloucester Antique Centre, Historic Docks, Gloucester, Gloucestershire, GL1 2LE
029 2070 2313 029 2070 2313
07909 745155
whwebber@tesco.net
Est. 1994 *Stock size* Medium
Stock Antique clocks, especially longcase, wall clocks
Open Mon–Sat 10am–5pm Sun 1–5pm
Fairs Margam
Services Valuations, repairs, restorations

GREET

Stephen Cook Antiques (LAPADA)
Contact Stephen Cook
The Studio, Winchcombe Pottery, Becketts Lane, Greet, Cheltenham, Gloucestershire, GL54 5NU
01242 604770 01242 609098
07973 814656
stephen@scookantiques.com
www.scookantiques.com
Est. 1986 *Stock size* Medium

Stock Period oak, walnut and mahogany furniture
Open By appointment
Services Valuations, restorations

KEMPSFORD

Ximenes Rare Books Inc (ABA, PBFA)
Contact Mr Stephen Weissman
Kempsford House, Kempsford, Fairford, Gloucestershire, GL7 4ET
01285 810640 F 01285 810650
steve@ximenes.com
Est. 1965 *Stock size* Medium
Stock Rare books
Open By appointment only
Fairs Olympia (June)
Services Catalogues

LECHLADE

Jubilee Hall Antiques Centre
Contact Mr John Calgie
Oak Street, Lechlade, Gloucestershire, GL7 3AY
01367 253777
sales@jubileehall.co.uk
Est. 1997 *Stock size* Large
No. of dealers 25
Stock Furniture, objets d'art, metalware, pottery, porcelain,
Open Mon–Sat 10am–5pm Sun 11am–5pm
Services Shipping, delivery arranged

Lechlade Arcade
Contact Mr J Dickson
5–7 High Street, Lechlade, Gloucestershire, GL7 3AD
01367 252832
M 07949 130875
Est. 1990 *Stock size* Large
Stock 40 rooms of china, smalls, small furniture, cast-iron, farm tools and implements, antique pistols, guns, medals, Roman artefacts
Open Mon–Sun 9am–5pm
Services House clearance

The Old Ironmongers Antiques Centre
Contact Mark Serle or Geoff Allen
5 Burford Street, Lechlade, Gloucestershire, GL7 3AP
01367 252397
Est. 2000 *Stock size* Large
No. of dealers 40
Stock Tools, town and country furniture, gramophones, iron, copperware, architectural, books, gardening bygones, pot lids
Open Mon–Sun 10am–5pm
Services Restorations, shipping, book search

MINCHINHAMPTON

Mick & Fanny Wright
Contact Mr M Wright
The Trumpet, West End, Minchinhampton, Stroud, Gloucestershire, GL6 9JA
01453 883027
antiques@thetrumpet.free-online.co,uk
Est. 1979 *Stock size* Medium
Stock General antiques, more smalls than furniture, second-hand books, watches, clocks
Open Wed–Sat 10.30am–5.30pm
Fairs Kempton

MORETON-IN-MARSH

Benton Fine Art and Antiques (LAPADA)
Contact Melanie Benton
Regent House, High Street, Moreton-in-Marsh, Gloucestershire, GL56 0AX
01608 652153 F 01608 652153
bentonfineart@excite.co.uk
Est. 1972 *Stock size* Medium
Stock 19th–20thC oils and watercolours, 19th–20thC fine furniture
Open Mon–Sat 10am–5.30pm Sun 11am–5.30pm closed Tues
Fairs LAPADA London and Birmingham, NEC

Berry Antiques (LAPADA)
Contact Mr C Berry
3 High Street, Moreton-in-Marsh, Gloucestershire, GL56 0AH
01608 652929 F 01608 652929
chris@berryantiques.com
W www.berryantiques.com
Est. 1984 *Stock size* Medium
Stock 18th–19thC furniture, 19thC oil paintings
Open Mon–Sat 10am–5.30pm Sun 11am–5pm closed Tues

Chandlers Antiques
Contact Ian Kellam
Chandlers Cottage, High Street, Moreton-in-Marsh, Gloucestershire, GL56 0AD
01608 651347 F 01608 651347
Est. 1984 *Stock size* Large
Stock All small porcelain, glass, jewellery, silver
Open By appointment
Services Valuations

Cox's Architectural Salvage Yard Ltd (SALVO)
Contact Mr P Watson
10 Fosse Way Industrial Estate, Stratford Road, Moreton-in-Marsh, Gloucestershire, GL56 9NQ
01608 652505 F 01608 652881
coxs@fsbdial.co.uk
W www.salvo.co.uk/coxs
Est. 1991 *Stock size* Large
Stock Architectural antiques, doors, fireplaces, Gothic-style windows
Open Mon–Sat 9am–6pm
Services Valuations, shipping

Dale House
Contact Nicholas Allen
High Street, Moreton-in-Marsh, Gloucestershire, GL56 0AD
01608 652950 F 01608 652424
Est. 1973 *Stock size* Large
Stock 18th–early 20thC furniture, works of art
Open Mon–Sat 10am–5.30pm Sun 11am–5pm

Jeffrey Formby Antiques (LAPADA, BADA)
Contact Mr J Formby
Orchard Cottage, East Street, Moreton-in-Marsh, Gloucestershire, GL56 0LQ
01608 650558 M 07770 755546
jeff@formby-clocks.co.uk
W www.formby-clocks.co.uk
Est. 1994 *Stock size* Small
Stock English clocks, horological books, longcase, bracket, skeleton, lantern clocks
Open By appointment
Fairs Olympia, BADA

Jon Fox Antiques (CADA)
Contact Mr Jon Fox
High Street, Moreton-in-Marsh, Gloucestershire, GL56 0AD

☎ 01608 650714/650325
Est. 1983 *Stock size* Large
Stock Garden antiques, furniture, country bygones
Open Mon–Fri 9.30am–5.30pm closed Tues

Grimes House Antiques & Fine Art
Contact Stephen or Val Farnsworth
✉ **High Street, Moreton-in-Marsh, Gloucestershire, GL56 0AT** P
☎ 01608 651029
e grimes_house@cix.co.uk
w www.cranberryglass.co.uk
Est. 1977 *Stock size* Large
Stock Victorian and later coloured glass, Royal Worcester
Open Mon–Sat 9.30am–5.30pm closed 1–2pm
Services Valuations

London House Antique Centre
Contact Mr Dudley Thompson
✉ **London House, High Street, Moreton-in-Marsh, Gloucestershire, GL56 0AH** P
☎ 01608 651084
Est. 1979 *Stock size* Large
Stock General antiques, Chinese porcelain, furniture, silver, porcelain, pictures
Open Mon–Sun 10am–5pm

Oriental Gallery (LAPADA)
Contact Patricia Cater
✉ **Moreton-in-Marsh, Gloucestershire, GL56 0QW**
☎ 01451 830944 f 01451 870126
e patriciacaterorg@aol.com
w www.patriciacater-orientalart.com
Est. 1988 *Stock size* Medium
Stock Chinese ceramics, Asian works of art
Open By appointment only

Seaford House Antiques (LAPADA, CADA)
Contact Mr or Mrs D Young
✉ **Seaford House, High Street, Moreton-in-Marsh, Gloucestershire, GL56 0AD** P
☎ 01608 652423 f 01608 652423
m 07714 485632
Est. 1988 *Stock size* Medium
Stock 18th–early 20thC small furniture, porcelain, pictures, objets d'art
Open Wed–Sat 10am–5.30pm Sun 1am–4pm

Windsor House Antiques Centre
Contact Mr T Sutton
✉ **High Street, Moreton-in-Marsh, Gloucestershire, GL56 0AD** P
☎ 01608 650993 f 01858 565438
e windsorhouse@btinternet.com
w www.windsorhouse.co.uk
Est. 1992 *Stock size* Large
No. of dealers 48
Stock High-quality general antiques, porcelain, glass, silver, clocks, paintings, furniture
Open Mon–Sat 10am–5pm Tues Sun noon–5pm
Services Shipping, delivery

Gary Wright Antiques Ltd
Contact Gary or Gill Wright
✉ **2 Stratford Road, Moreton-in-Marsh, Gloucestershire, GL56 9NQ** P
☎ 01608 652007 f 01608 652007
m 07831 653843
e garywrightantiques@fsbdial.co.uk
w www.garywrightantiques.co.uk
Est. 1972 *Stock size* Large
Stock Georgian mahogany, walnut, marquetry, unusual, decorative objects, 17th–19thC good-quality furniture from £500 to £20,000
Open Mon–Sat 9.30am–5.30pm
Services Valuations, buys at auction

NEWENT

Jillings (LAPADA, CINOA, BADA)
Contact John or Doro Jillings
✉ **Croft House, 17 Church Street, Newent, Gloucestershire, GL18 1PU** P
☎ 01531 822100 f 01531 822666
m 07973 830110
e clocks@jillings.com
w www.jillings.com
Est. 1987 *Stock size* Medium
Stock 18th–early 19thC English and Continental clocks
Open Fri Sat 9.30am–5pm or by appointment
Fairs BADA, LAPADA, Olympia
Services Valuations, repair and restoration of all fine antique clocks

NEWNHAM ON SEVERN

Christopher Saunders (PBFA, ABA)
Contact Mr C Saunders
✉ **Kingston House, High Street, Newnham on Severn, Gloucestershire, GL14 1BB** P
☎ 01594 516030 f 01594 517273
e chrisbooks@aol.com
Est. 1980 *Stock size* Large
Stock Antiquarian cricket books, memorabilia
Open By appointment only
Fairs PBFA

NORTH LEACH

Keith Harding's World of Mechanical Music
Contact Keith Harding
✉ **The Oak House, High Street, North Leach, Gloucestershire, GL54 3ET** P
☎ 01451 860181 f 10451 861133
e keith@mechanicalmusic.co.uk
w www.mechanicalmusic.co.uk
Est. 1961 *Stock size* Medium
Stock Mechanical musical antiques, clocks
Open Mon–Sun 10am–6pm closed Christmas Day Boxing Day
Services Restorations, museum

NORTON

Ronson's Architectural Effects
Contact Ron Jones
✉ **North Barns, Wainlods Lane, Norton, Gloucestershire, GL2 9LN** P
☎ 01452 731326 f 01452 731888
e infor@ronsonsreclamation.co.uk
w www.ronsonsreclamation.com
Est. 1982 *Stock size* Large
Stock Architectural antiques
Open Mon–Sat 8am–5pm
Services Shipping

SOUTHAM

BK Art & Antiques (SOFAA)
Contact Mr Simon Chorley
✉ **The Tithe Barn Sale Room, Southam Lane, Southam, Cheltenham, Gloucestershire, GL52 3NY** P
☎ 01452 521267 f 01452 300184
e artantiques@bkonline.co.uk
w www.bkonline.co.uk
Est. 1862

Open Mon–Fri 8.30am–5.30pm
Sales Art and antiques sales, phone for details
Frequency Every 6 weeks
Catalogues Yes

STOW-ON-THE-WOLD

Ashton Gower Antiques (LAPADA)
Contact Chris Gower or Barry Ashton
9 Talbot Court, Market Square, Stow-on-the-Wold, Gloucestershire, GL54 1BQ P
☎ 01451 870699 F 01451 870699
E ashtongower@aol.com
Est. 1987 ***Stock size*** Large
Stock Gilded mirrors, French decorative furniture, 20thC Lucite
Open Mon–Sat 10am–5pm
Services Valuations

Baggott Church Street Ltd (BADA, CADA)
Contact Mrs C Baggott
Church Street, Stow-on-the-Wold, Gloucestershire, GL54 1BB
☎ 01451 830370 F 01451 832174
Est. 1976 ***Stock size*** Large
Stock English 17th–19thC furniture, paintings, objects
Open Mon–Sat 9.30am–5.30pm
Services Annual exhibition in October

Duncan J Baggott (LAPADA, CADA)
Contact Mrs C Baggott
Woolcomber House, Sheep Street, Stow-on-the-Wold, Gloucestershire, GL54 1AA
☎ 01451 830662 F 01451 832174
Est. 1967 ***Stock size*** Large
Stock English furniture, portraits, landscape paintings, domestic metalware, fireplace accoutrements, pottery, glass, garden statuary, ornaments
Open Mon–Sat 9.30am–5.30pm
Services Annual exhibition in October

Bears on the Wold
Contact Mrs Eileen Evers
Sheep Street, Stow-on-the-Wold, Gloucestershire, GL54 2EN P
☎ 01451 870133 F 01451 870133
E eileen@bearsonthewold.co.uk
W bearsonthewold.co.uk
Est. 1991 ***Stock size*** Large
Stock Old bears, Steiff, Hermann, Deans, Merrythought, Hermann Spielwaren, Leebert, Tickelpenny
Open Mon–Sat 10am–5pm Sun 11am–4pm closed Wed
Fairs Hugglets, Kensington, Teddy Bear Times, Hove

Bookbox (PBFA)
Contact Mrs C Fisher
Chantry House, Sheep Street, Stow-on-the-Wold, Gloucestershire, GL54 1AA P
☎ 01451 831214
Est. 1977 ***Stock size*** Medium
Stock Antiquarian, second-hand books, 19th–20thC good literature, art, topography
Open Mon–Sat 11am–1pm 2.30–5pm closed Wed winter open only Thurs–Sat

Bread & Roses
Contact Rose Smith
Durham House Antique Centre, Sheep Street, Stow-on-the-Wold, Gloucestershire, GL54 1AA P
☎ 01451 870404
Est. 1995 ***Stock size*** Large
Stock Kitchenware
Open Mon–Sat 10am–5pm Sun 11am–5pm
Fairs NEC, Newark

Church Street Antiques Centre
Contact Mrs Elizabeth Niner
3–4 Church Street, Stow-on-the-Wold, Gloucestershire, GL54 1BB P
☎ 01451 870186
Est. 1997 ***Stock size*** Large
No. of dealers 15
Stock General antiques, mid-17th–early 20thC, furniture, pictures, mirrors, pottery, porcelain, vintage leather goods, silver, Staffordshire animals, blue-and-white pottery, glass, lacquered furniture, copper, brass
Open Mon–Sat 9.45am–5pm

Christopher Clarke Antiques (LAPADA, CADA)
Contact Mr Simon Clarke
Fosseway, Stow-on-the-Wold, Gloucestershire, GL54 1JS P
☎ 01451 830476 F 01451 830300
M 07971 287733
E cclarkeantiques@aol.com
W www.antiques-in-england.com
Est. 1961 ***Stock size*** Large
Stock English furniture, works of art, animal antiques, campaign furniture, unusual decorative items
Open Mon–Sat 9.30am–5.30pm or by appointment
Fairs Olympia (June November), CADA (October)

Country Life Antiques
Contact Ann or David Rosa
Grey House, The Square, Stow-on-the-Wold, Gloucestershire, GL54 1AF P
☎ 01451 831564 F 01451 831564
Est. 1974 ***Stock size*** Large
Stock Scientific instruments, decorative accessories, metalware, furniture, paintings
Open Mon–Sat 10am–5pm

Durham House Antiques Centre
Contact Mr Alan Smith
Sheep Street, Stow-on-the-Wold, Gloucestershire, GL54 1AA P
☎ 01451 870404 F 01451 870404
E durhamhouse@compuserve.com
Est. 1994 ***Stock size*** Large
No. of dealers 36
Stock General antiques, silver, clocks, oak, mahogany, porcelain, Derby, Worcester, Staffordshire, Mason's, linens, prints, paintings
Open Mon–Sat 10am–5pm Sun 11am–5pm

Fosse Way Antiques (CADA)
Contact Mr M Beeston
Ross House, The Square, Stow-on-the-Wold, Gloucestershire, GL54 1AF P
☎ 01451 830776 F 01451 830776
E furnish@fossewayantiques.com
Est. 1969 ***Stock size*** Large
Stock 18th–early 19thC furniture, oil paintings, small period accessories
Open Mon–Sat 10am–5pm
Services Valuations, shipping

Fox Cottage Antiques
Contact Miss Sue London
Digbeth Street, Stow-on-the-Wold, Gloucestershire, GL54 1BN P
☎ 01451 870307
Est. 1995 ***Stock size*** Medium
No. of dealers 8

Stock Pottery, porcelain, glassware, silver, plated ware, small furniture, decorative items, country goods, mainly pre-1910
Open Mon–Sat 10am–5pm

⊞ Grandfather Clock Shop
Contact Mr W J Styles
✉ The Little House, Sheep Street, Stow-on-the-Wold, Gloucestershire, GL54 1JS 🅿
☎ 01451 830455 Ⓕ 01451 830455
Ⓔ info@stylesofstow.co.uk
Ⓦ www.stylesofstow.co.uk
Est. 1996 ***Stock size*** Large
Stock Clocks including longcase clocks, 18th–19thC furniture, 19th–20thC oil paintings and watercolours
Open Mon–Sat 10am–5pm or by appointment
Services Valuations, restorations

⊞ Keith Hockin Antiques (BADA, CADA)
Contact Mr K Hockin
✉ The Elms, The Square, Stow-on-the-Wold, Gloucestershire, GL54 1AF 🅿
☎ 01451 831058 Ⓕ 01451 831058
Ⓔ keith.hockin@talk21.com
Est. 1973 ***Stock size*** Medium
Stock 17th–early 18thC English oak furniture, pewter, early brass, 16th–17thC wood carvings
Open Thurs–Sat 10am–5pm closed 1–2pm or by appointment

⊞ Hungry Ghost
Contact Mrs V Kern
✉ 1 Brewery Yard, Sheep Street, Stow-on-the-Wold, Gloucestershire, GL54 1AA 🅿
☎ 01451 870101
Ⓦ www.hungry-ghost.co.uk
Est. 1998 ***Stock size*** Large
Stock Oriental antiques, gifts, china
Open Mon–Sat 9.30am–5.30pm Sun 10am–4.30pm
Fairs Battersea

⊞ Huntington Antiques Ltd (LAPADA, CADA, BACA Award Winner 2002)
✉ Church Street, Stow-on-the-Wold, Gloucestershire, GL54 1BE 🅿
☎ 01451 830842 Ⓕ 01451 832211
Ⓔ info@huntington-antiques.com
Ⓦ www.huntington-antiques.com
Est. 1975 ***Stock size*** Large
Stock Early furniture and works of art, tapestries, English and Continental metalwork
Open Mon–Sat 9.30am–5.30pm
Fairs LAPADA London and Birmingham
Services Valuations, restorations, interior decoration

⊞ La Chaise Antiques
Contact Roger Clark
✉ Beauport, Sheep Street, Stow-on-the-Wold, Gloucestershire, GL54 1AA 🅿
☎ 01451 830582
Stock size Medium
Stock Furniture
Open Mon–Sat 9am–6pm Sun 10am–4pm

⊞ Roger Lamb Antiques and Works of Art (LAPADA, CADA)
Contact Roger Lamb
✉ The Square, Stow-on-the-Wold, Gloucestershire, GL54 1AB 🅿
☎ 01451 831371 Ⓕ 01451 832485
Ⓜ 07860 391959
Est. 1993 ***Stock size*** Medium
Stock 18th–early 19thC period furniture, decorative oils, watercolours, antique lighting, accessories
Open Mon–Sat 10am–5pm
Fairs LAPADA
Services Valuations, restorations

⊞ Simon Nutter and Thomas King-Smith
Contact Mr T M King-Smith or Mr S W Nutter
✉ Wraggs Row, Fosseway, Stow-on-the-Wold, Gloucestershire, GL54 1JT
☎ 01451 830658 Ⓜ 07775 864394
Est. 1975 ***Stock size*** Medium
Stock 18th–19thC furniture, silver, porcelain
Open Mon–Sat 9.30am–5.30pm
Fairs Westonbirt
Services Valuations

⊞ Park House Antiques
Contact Mr George Sutton
✉ 8 Park Street, Stow-on-the-Wold, Gloucestershire, GL54 1AQ 🅿
☎ 01451 830159
Ⓔ teamsutton@btinternet.com
Est. 1987 ***Stock size*** Large
Stock Old toys, textiles, small furniture, porcelain, pottery
Open Feb–Apr June–Oct Wed Thurs Fri Sat 10am–1pm 2–4.30pm other times by appointment
Services Repairs, toy museum, teddy bear repair

⊞ Antony Preston Antiques (BADA)
Contact Antony Preston
✉ The Square, Stow-on-the-Wold, Gloucestershire, GL54 1AB 🅿
☎ 01451 831586
Est. 1977 ***Stock size*** Large
Stock Early 18th–19thC English furniture and objets d'art
Open Mon–Sat 9.30am–5.30pm
Fairs Grosvenor House, BADA

⊞ Priest's Antiques & Fine Arts
Contact Mr Andrew Priest
✉ The Malt House, Digbeth Street, Stow-on-the-Wold, Gloucestershire, GL54 1BN 🅿
☎ 01451 830592 Ⓕ 01451 830592
Est. 1986 ***Stock size*** Large
Stock 17th–early 20thC English furniture
Open Mon–Sat 10am–5pm

⊞ Michael Rowland Antiques
Contact Michael Rowland
✉ Little Elms, The Square, Stow-on-the-Wold, Gloucestershire, GL54 1AF 🅿
☎ 01451 870089 Ⓜ 07779 509753
Est. 1991 ***Stock size*** Medium
Stock 17th–18thC oak and fruitwood country furniture
Open Mon–Sat 10.30am–5pm

⊞ Ruskin Decorative Arts (CADA)
Contact Mr or Mrs T W Morris
✉ 5 Talbot Court, Stow-on-the-Wold, Gloucestershire, GL54 1DP 🅿
☎ 01451 832254 Ⓕ 01451 832167
Est. 1989 ***Stock size*** Small
Stock Decorative Arts 1860–1950, Arts and Crafts, Art Nouveau, Art Deco, the Cotswold Movement including the Guild of Handicraft, Gordon Russell, Gimson and the Barnsleys
Open Mon–Sat 10am–5.30pm
Fairs NEC, Antiques for Everyone
Services Valuations for insurance and probate

Samarkand Galleries (LAPADA, CADA, CINOA)
Contact Brian MacDonald
✉ **7–8 Brewery Yard, Sheep Street, Stow-on-the-Wold, Gloucestershire, GL54 1AA** P
☎ 01451 832322 F 01451 832322
E mac@samarkand.co.uk
W www.samarkand.co.uk
Est. 1979 *Stock size* Large
Stock Antique and contemporary rugs from Near East and central Asia, decorative carpets, nomadic weavings
Open Mon–Sat 10am–5.30pm
Fairs Hali Antique Textile Art Fair
Services Valuations, restorations, search

Arthur Seager Antiques
Contact Mr A Seager
✉ **50 Sheep Street, Stow-on-the-Wold, Gloucestershire, GL54 1AA** P
☎ 01451 831605
E stock@arthurseager.evesham.net
W www.arthurseager.com
Est. 1979 *Stock size* Medium
Stock 16th–17thC objects, oak furniture, carvings
Open Thurs–Sat 10am–4pm

Stow Antiques (CADA, LAPADA, CINOA)
Contact Mrs H Hutton-Clarke
✉ **The Square, Stow-on-the-Wold, Gloucestershire, GL54 1AF** P
☎ 01451 830377 F 01451 870018
E hazel@stowantiques.demon.co.uk
Est. 1969 *Stock size* Large
Stock 18th–19thC mahogany furniture, large tables, sets of chairs, sideboards, bookcases
Open Mon–Sat 10am–5.30pm or by appointment
Services Shipping

Tudor House
Contact Mr Peter Collingridge
✉ **Sheep Street, Stow-on-the-Wold, Gloucestershire, GL54 1AA** P
☎ 01451 830021 F 01451 830021
Est. 2001 *Stock size* Large
No. of dealers 12
Stock 18th–early 20thC furniture, clocks, watercolours, porcelain, metalware, fountain pens, garden furniture, lighting, Arts and Crafts
Open Mon–Sat 10am–5pm
Services Valuations

Vanbrugh House Antiques
Contact John or Monica Sands
✉ **Vanbrugh House, Park Street, Stow-on-the-Wold, Gloucestershire, GL54 1AQ** P
☎ 01451 830797
Est. 1978 *Stock size* Medium
Stock Early fine furniture, musical boxes, early maps
Open Mon–Sat 10am–5.30pm
Services Valuations

STROUD

Ian Hodgkins & Co Ltd (ABA)
Contact Mr Simon Weager
✉ **Upper Vatch Mill, The Vatch, Stroud, Gloucestershire, GL6 7JY** P
☎ 01453 764270 F 01453 755233
E i.hodgkins@dial.pipex.com
W www.ianhodgkins.com
Est. 1974 *Stock size* Medium
Stock Antiquarian, 19thC art, literature, children's books
Open By appointment
Fairs Chelsea (November)

Inprint
Contact Mr Mike Goodenough
✉ **31 High Street, Stroud, Gloucestershire, GL5 1AJ** P
☎ 01453 759731 F 01453 759731
E enquiries@inprint.co.uk
W www.inprint.co.uk
Est. 1979 *Stock size* Medium
Stock Antiquarian, second-hand and out-of-print books on fine, applied, performing arts
Open Mon–Sat 10am–5.30pm
Services Book search

TETBURY

Philip Adler Antiques (BADA)
Contact Mr P Adler
✉ **35 Long Street, Tetbury, Gloucestershire, GL8 8AA** P
☎ 01666 505759 F 01452 770525
M 07710 477891
E philipadlerantiques@hotmail.com
Est. 1979 *Stock size* Large
Stock Eclectic, general stock of decorative and period antiques
Open Mon–Sat 10am–6pm and by appointment
Fairs Bath Fair (December)
Services Valuations, restorations

The Antique & Interior Centre (TADA)
Contact Linda Townsend-Bateson
✉ **Unit 1, 51 Long Street, Tetbury, Gloucestershire, GL8 8AA** P
☎ 01666 505083
Est. 1995 *Stock size* Medium
No. of dealers 7
Stock Good quality furniture, porcelain, silver, pictures
Open Mon–Sat 10am–5pm Sun most Bank Holidays 1–5pm

The Antique Centre (TADA)
Contact Mrs Linda Townsend Bateman
✉ **51a Long Street, Tetbury, Gloucestershire, GL8 8AA** P
☎ 01666 505083
Est. 1995 *Stock size* Large
Stock French furniture, decorative pieces, 19thC Staffordshire textiles. Georgian–Edwardian furniture
Open Mon–Sat 10am–5pm Sun 1–5pm

The Antiques Emporium (TADA)
Contact Debbie Sayers
✉ **The Old Chapel, Long Street, Tetbury, Gloucestershire, GL8 8AA** P
☎ 01666 505281 F 01666 505661
Est. 1993 *Stock size* Large
No. of dealers 42
Stock Fine and country furniture, brass, copper, treen, kitchenware, paintings, miniatures, silver, jewellery, decorative items, pottery, porcelain, books, glass, luggage
Open Mon–Sat 10am–5pm Sun 1–5pm

Artique (TADA)
Contact George Bristow
✉ **Talboys House, 17 Church Street, Tetbury, Gloucestershire, GL8 8JG**
☎ 01666 503597 F 01666 503597
M 07836 337038
E george@artique.demon.co.uk
W www.artique.uk.com
Est. 1990 *Stock size* Large
Stock Central Asian artefacts, rugs, jewellery, furniture, textiles, architectural items
Open Mon Tues Wed 10am–6pm Thurs Fri 10am–8pm Sun noon–4pm

Ball & Claw Antiques (TADA)
Contact Mr Chris Kirkland
45 Long Street, Tetbury, Gloucestershire, GL8 8AA P
01666 502440
07957 870423
www.antiquesportfolio.com/ballclawantiques
Est. 1994 *Stock size* Medium
Stock 17th–19thC furniture, Arts and Crafts, engravings, pictures, linens, textiles, children's antique decorative toys, general antiques
Open Mon–Sat 10am–5pm
Services Valuations

Balmuir House Antiques (LAPADA)
Contact Mr P Whittam
14 Long Street, Tetbury, Gloucestershire, GL8 8AQ P
01666 503822 F 01666 505285
Est. 1989 *Stock size* Large
Stock 19thC furniture, paintings
Open Mon–Sat 9.30am–5.30pm
Services Restoration of furniture and paintings

The Black Sheep
Contact Mr Oliver Mcerlain
51 Long Street, Tetbury, Gloucestershire, GL8 8AA P
01666 505026
Est. 2000 *Stock size* Medium
Stock 18th–19thC decorative country furniture, 19thC pictures
Open Mon–Sat 10am–5pm or Sun noon–4pm

Bonhams
22a Long Street, Tetbury, Gloucestershire, GL8 8AQ
01666 502200 F 01666 505107
tetbury@bonhams.com
www.bonhams.com
Open Mon–Fri 9am–5.30pm

Bread & Roses
Contact Rose Smith
Antiques Emporium, The Old Chapel, Long Street, Tetbury, Gloucestershire, GL8 8AA P
01666 505281 F 01666 505661
Stock size Large
Stock Kitchenware
Open Mon–Sat 10am–5pm Sun 1–5pm

Breakspeare Antiques (LAPADA, CADA)
Contact Michael or Sylvia Breakspeare
36 & 57 Long Street, Tetbury, Gloucestershire, GL8 8AQ P
01666 503122
mark.breakspeare@hemscott.net
Est. 1962 *Stock size* Medium
Stock English period furniture, mahogany, 1750–1835, early veneered walnut, 1690–1740
Open Mon–Sat 10am–5pm

The Chest of Drawers (TADA)
Contact Mrs P Bristow
24 Long Street, Tetbury, Gloucestershire, GL8 8AQ P
01666 502105 M 07710 292064
Est. 1969 *Stock size* Medium
Stock English furniture, 17thC onwards
Open Mon–Fri 9.30am–5.30pm

Day Antiques (BADA, CADA)
Contact Mrs A or Roger Day
5 New Church Street, Tetbury, Gloucestershire, GL8 8DS P
01666 502413 F 01666 505894
07836 565763
dayantiques@lineone.net
www.dayantiques.com
Est. 1975 *Stock size* Medium
Stock Early oak, country furniture, related items
Open Mon–Sat 10am–5pm

The Decorator Source (TADA)
Contact Mr Colin Gee
39a Long Street, Tetbury, Gloucestershire, GL8 8AA P
01666 505358 F 01666 505358
Est. 1979 *Stock size* Large
Stock French provincial furniture, accessories, English country house furniture and objects
Open Mon–Sat 10am–5.30pm or by appointment
Services Shipping

Anne Fowler (TADA)
Contact Anne Fowler
35 Long Street, Tetbury, Gloucestershire, GL8 8AA P
01666 504043 M 07770 754043
Est. 1995 *Stock size* Medium
Stock Mirrors, lustres, oil paintings, prints, linen, early garden and painted furniture, faïence, pottery, French items a speciality
Open Mon–Sat 10am–5.30pm
Fairs Bath Fair (March)
Services Interior design

Jester Antiques (TADA)
Contact Mr Peter Bairsto
10 Church Street, Tetbury, Gloucestershire, GL8 8JG P
01666 505125 F 01666 505125
07974 232783
sales@jesterantiques.co.uk
www.jesterantiques.co.uk
Est. 1995 *Stock size* Medium
Stock Exciting, colourful stock of furniture, decorative items, lamps, mirrors, garden and architectural antiques
Open Mon–Sun 10am–5.30pm
Services Shipping

Merlin Antiques
Contact Mr Brian Smith
Shops 4 & 5, Chippingcourt Shopping Mall, Chipping Street, Tetbury, Gloucestershire, GL8 8ES P
01666 505008
Est. 1994 *Stock size* Large
Stock Mixed, china, pictures, Victorian–Edwardian furniture, costume jewellery, reproduction furniture, garden stoneware
Open Mon–Sat 9.30am–5pm Sun by appointment
Services Valuations, repairs, items purchased, single or house clearance

Bobbie Middleton (TADA, CADA)
Contact Bobbie Middleton
58 Long Street, Tetbury, Gloucestershire, GL8 8AQ P
01666 502761 F 01454 238619
07774 192660
bobbiemiddleton@lineone.net
Est. 1986 *Stock size* Medium
Stock Classic country house furniture including painted pieces, mirrors, decorative accessories, upholstered furniture
Open Mon–Sat 10am–5pm closed 1–2.30pm
Services Search for pieces

Morpheus Beds
Contact Mrs Betty Symes
Elgin House, 1 New Church Street, Tetbury, Gloucestershire, GL8 8DT P

☎ 01666 504068 Ⓕ 01666 503352
Ⓔ info@antique-beds.co.uk
Ⓦ www.antique-beds.co.uk
Est. 1984 *Stock size* Large
Stock Antique beds, bedroom furniture, accessories
Open Mon–Sat 9am–5.30pm
Sun by appointment

Peter Norden Antiques (LAPADA, TADA)
Contact Mr P Norden
✉ **61 Long Street, Tetbury, Gloucestershire, GL8 8AA** Ⓟ
☎ 01666 503854 Ⓕ 01666 505595
Ⓜ 07778 013108
Ⓔ petermorden_antiques@lineone.net
Ⓦ www.peter-norden-antiques.co.uk
Est. 1960 *Stock size* Medium
Stock Early oak and country furniture, early wood carvings, pewter, brass, treen
Open Mon–Sat 10am–5.30pm or by appointment
Services Valuations

Porch House Antiques (TADA)
Contact Mrs L A Woodburn
✉ **42 Long Street, Tetbury, Gloucestershire, GL8 8AQ** Ⓟ
☎ 01666 502687
Ⓜ 07715 32793
Est. 1976 *Stock size* Large
Stock 17th–20thC furniture, decorative items
Open Mon–Sat 10am–5pm
most Sundays

Sieff (TADA, LAPADA)
Contact Kirsty Sylvester
✉ **49 Long Street, Tetbury, Gloucestershire, GL8 8AA** Ⓟ
☎ 01666 504477 Ⓕ 01666 504478
Ⓔ sieff@sieff.co.uk
Ⓦ www.sieff.co.uk
Est. 1984 *Stock size* Large
Stock 18th–19thC French provincial fruitwood, 20thC furniture
Open Mon–Sat 10am–5.30pm
Fairs Decorative Antique & Textile Fair

Tetbury Old Books
Contact Mr P M Gibbons
✉ **4 The Chipping, Tetbury, Gloucestershire, GL8 8ET** Ⓟ
☎ 01666 504330 Ⓕ 01666 504458
Ⓔ oldbooks@tetbury.co.uk
Est. 1994 *Stock size* Medium
Stock Antiquarian and second-hand books, Black's colour books, prints
Open Mon–Sat 10am–6pm
Sun 11am–5pm

Westwood House Antiques (TADA)
Contact R Griffiths
✉ **29 Long Street, Tetbury, Gloucestershire, GL8 8AA** Ⓟ
☎ 01666 502328 Ⓕ 01666 502328
Est. 1993 *Stock size* Large
Stock 17th–19thC oak, elm and ash country furniture, some French fruitwood, decorative pottery, pewter, treen
Open Mon–Sat 10am–5.30pm

TEWKESBURY

Berkeley Antiques
Contact Peter or Susan Dennis
✉ **The Wheatsheaf, High Street, Tewkesbury, Gloucestershire, GL20 5JR** Ⓟ
☎ 01684 292034
Ⓜ 07836 243397
Est. 1973 *Stock size* Medium
Stock 17th–19thC antique furniture, accessories to match
Open Mon–Sat 10am–5.30pm
closed Thurs pm
Services Restorations

Cornell Books Ltd
Contact Mr G Cornell
✉ **93 Church Street, Tewkesbury, Gloucestershire, GL20 5RS** Ⓟ
☎ 01684 293337 Ⓕ 01684 273959
Ⓔ gtcornell@aol.com
Est. 1996 *Stock size* Medium
Stock Antiquarian and second-hand books
Open Mon–Sat 10.30am–5pm

Gainsborough House
Contact A or B Hillson
✉ **81 Church Street, Tewkesbury, Gloucestershire, GL20 5RX** Ⓟ
☎ 01684 293072
Est. 1962 *Stock size* Large
Stock Period furniture, porcelain, silver
Open Mon–Sat 10am–5pm
closed Thurs

Tewkesbury Antiques Centre
Contact Mrs Coral Pearce
✉ **Tolsey Hall, Tolsey Lane, Tewkesbury, Gloucestershire, GL20 5AE** Ⓟ
☎ 01684 294091/01531 822211
Ⓕ 01531 822211
Est. 1991 *Stock size* Medium
No. of dealers 13
Stock Antiques, bric-a-brac, collectables, books, records, jewellery, furniture, radios, old tools
Open Mon–Sat 10am–5pm
Sun 11am–5pm

Whatnots Antiques of Tewkesbury
Contact Mr D Lothian
✉ **24 St Mary's Lane, Tewkesbury, Gloucestershire, GL20 5SF** Ⓟ
☎ 01684 294154
Est. 1988 *Stock size* Large
Stock General small antiques, small furniture, pictures, curios
Open Mon–Sat 11am–5pm

THORNBURY

Castle Antiques
Contact Steven Davies
✉ **2 Castle Street, Thornbury, Gloucestershire, BS35 1HB** Ⓟ
☎ 01454 880006 Ⓕ 01454 880007
Est. 1995 *Stock size* Medium
Stock General antiques
Open Mon–Sat 10am–6pm

Thornbury Antiques
✉ **3a High Street, Thornbury, Gloucestershire, BS35 2AE** Ⓟ
☎ 01454 413722
Est. 1991 *Stock size* Medium
Stock Victorian and Edwardian furniture, ceramics
Open Mon–Sat 10am–4pm
Services Restorations

WICKWAR

Bell Passage Antiques (LAPADA)
Contact Mrs D Brand
✉ **36–38 High Street, Wickwar, Wotton-under-Edge, Gloucestershire, GL12 8NP** Ⓟ
☎ 01454 294251
Est. 1966 *Stock size* Medium
Stock General antiques, furniture, glass, porcelain
Open Mon–Sat 9am–5pm closed Thurs or by appointment
Services Restorations, upholstery, caning

WINCHCOMBE

Government House Quality Antique Lighting
Contact Mr M Bailey
✉ **St Georges House, High Street, Winchcombe, Cheltenham, Gloucestershire, GL54 5LJ** P
☎ 01242 604562 Ⓜ 07970 430684
Est. 1980 *Stock size* Large
Stock Antique pre-1939 lighting
Open By appointment
Services Restorations

In Period Antiques
Contact John Edgeler
✉ **Queen Anne House, High Street, Winchcombe, Gloucestershire, GL54 5LJ** P
☎ 01242 602319
Est. 1999 *Stock size* Medium
Stock 17th–19thC furniture, metalwork, glass, porcelain, decorative items
Open Thurs–Sat 9.30am–5pm or by appointment
Services Valuations

Newsum Antiques (CADA)
Contact Mark Newsum
✉ **2 High Street, Winchcombe, Gloucestershire, GL54 5HT**
☎ 01242 603446
Ⓜ 07968 196668
Ⓔ marknewsum@hotmail.com
Est. 1985 *Stock size* Medium
Stock Oak and country furniture, treen, Swedish metalware
Open Tues–Sat 10.30am–5pm
Fairs NEC, Caroline Penman Fairs Kensington, Chelsea, Petersfield

Prichard Antiques (CADA)
Contact Keith or Debbie Prichard
✉ **16 High Street, Winchcombe, Gloucestershire, GL54 5LJ** P
☎ 01242 603566
Est. 1979 *Stock size* Large
Stock 17th–19thC formal and country furniture, clocks, treen, boxes, metalware, decorative items, garden furniture
Open Mon–Sat 9am–5.30pm

WOTTON-UNDER-EDGE

Wotton Auction Rooms Ltd
Contact Mr Philip Taubenheim
✉ **Tabernacle Road, Wotton-under-Edge, Gloucestershire, GL12 7EB** P
☎ 01453 844733 Ⓕ 01453 845448
Ⓔ info@wottonauctionrooms.co.uk
Ⓦ www.wottonauctionrooms.co.uk
Est. 1991
Open Mon–Fri 9am–5pm
Sales Tues smalls, Wed furniture, viewing Mon 10am–7pm Tues 9–10.30am
Frequency Monthly
Catalogues Yes

HEREFORDSHIRE

HAY-ON-WYE

Addyman Annexe
Contact Mr Addyman
✉ **27 Castle Street, Hay-on-Wye, Herefordshire, HR3 5DF**
☎ 01497 821600
Ⓔ madness@addyman-books.demon.co.uk
Ⓦ www.addyman-books.co.uk
Est. 1987 *Stock size* Medium
Stock Antiquarian books on all subjects, modern first editions, occult, myths and legends, leather-bound sets
Open Mon–Sun 10.30am–5.30pm

Addyman Books
Contact Anne Brichto
✉ **39 Lion Street, Hay-on-Wye, Herefordshire, HR3 5AA**
☎ 01497 821136 Ⓕ 01497 821732
Ⓔ madness@addyman-books.demon.co.uk
Ⓦ www.addyman-books.co.uk
Est. 1987 *Stock size* Medium
Stock Antiquarian and second-hand books, specializing in English literature, modern first editions
Open Mon–Sat 10am–6pm Sun 10.30am–5.30pm

C Arden Bookseller (PBFA)
Contact Mrs C Arden
✉ **Radnor House, Church Street, Hay-on-Wye, Herefordshire, HR3 5DQ** P
☎ 01497 820471 Ⓕ 01497 820498
Ⓔ c.arden@virgin.net
Ⓦ www.ardenbooks.co.uk
Est. 1992 *Stock size* Large
Stock Antiquarian books on natural history, gardening, botany
Open Mon–Sat 10.30am–5.30pm Sun 11am–4pm please phone first
Fairs PBFA

The Book Shop
Contact Andy Cooke
✉ **Pavement House, The Pavement, Hay-on-Wye, Herefordshire, HR3 5BU**
☎ 01497 821341
Est. 1987 *Stock size* Large
Stock Antiquarian books, general stock
Open Mon–Sat 9am–8pm Sun 9am–5pm

Richard Booth's Bookshop Ltd
Contact Mr R G W Booth
✉ **44 Lion Street, Hay-on-Wye, Herefordshire, HR3 5AA** P
☎ 01497 820322 Ⓕ 01497 821150
Ⓔ postmaster@richardbooth.demon.co.uk
Ⓦ www.richardbooth.demon.co.uk
Est. 1969 *Stock size* Large
Stock Antiquarian and second-hand books
Open Mon–Sat summer 9am–8pm winter 9am–5.30pm Sun 11.30am–5.30pm
Services Mail order

Boz Books (ABA)
Contact Peter Harries
✉ **13a Castle Street, Hay-on-Wye, Herefordshire, HR3 5DF** P
☎ 01497 821277 Ⓕ 01497 821277
Ⓔ peter@bozbooks.demon.co.uk
Ⓦ www.bozbooks.co.uk
Est. 1989 *Stock size* Medium
Stock Antiquarian, rare and second-hand books, 19thC English literature
Open Mon–Sat 10am–5pm closed 1–2pm variable in winter
Services Book search

Bullring Antiques
Contact Mrs S Spencer or Marjorie Abel
✉ **Bear Street, Hay-on-Wye, Herefordshire, HR3 5AN**
☎ 01487 820467
Est. 1994 *Stock size* Medium
No. of dealers 6
Stock Wide general stock of good-quality antiques,

furniture, ceramics, pictures, glass, silver
Open Mon–Sat 10am–5pm
Sun 11am–5pm

The Children's Bookshop
Contact Judith Gardener
Toll Cottage, Pontvaen, Hay-on-Wye, Herefordshire, HR3 5EW
01497 821083 01497 821083
judith@childrensbookshop.com
www.childrensbookshop.com
Est. 1981 *Stock size* Medium
Stock 18th–20thC children's books
Open Mon–Sat 9.30am–5.30pm
Sun 10am–5pm
Services Book search catalogue on website

Hancock & Monks
Contact Jerry Monks
15 Broad Street, Hay-on-Wye, Herefordshire, HR3 5DB
01497 821784 01591 610778
jerry@hancockandmonks.co.uk
www.hancockandmonks.co.uk
Est. 1974 *Stock size* Medium
Stock Antiquarian books on music, antiquarian sheet music
Open Mon–Sat 11am–5pm
Services Book search

Hay Antique Market
Contact Jenny Price
6 Market Street, Hay-on-Wye, Herefordshire, HR3 5AF
01497 820175
Est. 1989 *Stock size* Large
No. of dealers 17
Stock China, glass, jewellery, linen, country furniture, period furniture, rural and rustic items, period clothing, lighting, pictures, brass
Open Mon–Sat 10am–5pm
Sun 11am–5pm

Hay Cinema Bookshop (PBFA)
Contact Mr Greg Coombes
The Old Cinema, Castle Street, Hay-on-Wye, Herefordshire, HR3 5DF
01497 820071 01497 821900
sales@haycinemabookshop.co.uk
www.haycinemabookshop.co.uk
Est. 1855 *Stock size* Large
Stock Antiquarian and second-hand books, leather-bound books, art, antiques topics a speciality
Open Mon–Sat 9am–7pm
Sun 11.30am–5.30pm
Fairs PBFA

Hay on Wye Booksellers
Contact Mrs J Jordan
14 High Town, Hay-on-Wye, Herefordshire, HR3 5AE
01497 820875 01497 847129
07977 141745
Est. 1969 *Stock size* Large
Stock Antiquarian, second-hand and cut-price new books, publishers' returns
Open Mon–Sat 9am–6pm
Sun 9.30am–6pm

G B & P E Hebbard
Contact Mrs P Hebbard
7–8 Market Street, Hay-on-Wye, Herefordshire, HR3 5AF
01497 820413
Est. 1964 *Stock size* Large
Stock 18th–19thC English pottery, porcelain
Open Mon–Sat 9am–4.30pm

Lion Fine Arts & Books
Contact Mr Charles Spencer
19 Lion Street, Hay-on-Wye, Herefordshire, HR3 5AD
01497 821726
www.hay-on-wye.co.uk/LionFine
Est. 1995 *Stock size* Medium
Stock Small antique furniture, porcelain, pottery, Georgian–early 19thC glass, old prints, treen, interesting collectables, antique books
Open Mon Thurs Sat 10am–5pm other days variable, open most afternoons, phone first

Lion Street Books
Contact Mr Mark Williams
1 St John's Place, Hay-on-Wye, Herefordshire, HR3 5BN
01497 820121 01497 820121
mark@boxingstuff.com
www.boxingstuff.com
Est. 1993 *Stock size* Large
Stock Boxing memorabilia, books, programmes, magazines, photos
Open Mon–Sat 10am–5pm
Services Mail order catalogue

Murder & Mayhem
Contact Mr Addyman
5 Lion Street, Hay-on-Wye, Herefordshire, HR3 5AA
01497 821613 01497 821732
madness@hay-on-wyebooks.com
www.hay-on-wyebooks.com
Est. 1997 *Stock size* Medium
Stock Antiquarian and second-hand books, specializing in detective fiction, crime, horror
Open Mon–Sat Sun in season 10.30am–5.30

Rose's Books
Contact Mrs M Goddard
14 Broad Street, Hay-on-Wye, Herefordshire, HR3 5DB
01497 820013 01497 820031
enquiry@rosesbooks.com
www.rosesbooks.com
Est. 1984 *Stock size* Medium
Stock Rare, out-of-print, children's, illustrated books
Open Mon–Sun 9.30am–5pm
Services Regular e-mail lists sent out for authors, illustrators on subjects of interest

Mark Westwood Books (ABA, PBFA)
Contact Evelyn Westwood
Grove House, High Town, Hay-on-Wye, Herefordshire, HR3 5AE
01497 820068 01497 821641
books@markwestwood.demon.co.uk
Est. 1976 *Stock size* Medium
Stock Antique, scholarly second-hand books on most subjects
Open Mon–Sun 10.30am–6pm
Fairs Oxford

HEREFORD

The Antique Tea Shop
Contact Miss J Cockin
5a St Peters Street, Hereford, Herefordshire, HR1 2LA
01432 342172
Est. 1990 *Stock size* Small
Stock Small items, pastry forks, afternoon tea knives, 1920s–1930s jewellery, French furniture, mirrors, ceramics
Open Mon–Sat 9.45am–5pm
Sun 10.15am–5pm
Services Tea shop

Bourneville Books
Contact Mr F Nutt
95 White Cross Road, Hereford, Herefordshire, HR4 0DQ
01432 261263
Est. 1990 *Stock size* Medium
Stock Second-hand, collectable, antiquarian and rare books, prints, watercolours, books for decoration
Open Mon–Sat 9.30am–5.30pm
Fairs Newark

I and J L Brown Ltd
Contact Mr Simon Hilton
Whitestone Park, Whitestone, Hereford, Herefordshire, HR1 3SE
01432 851991 01432 851994
enquiries@brownantiques.com
www.brownantiques.com
Est. 1978 *Stock size* Large
Stock English country, French provincial furniture, largest source in UK
Open Mon–Sat 9am–5.30pm or by appointment
Services Re-rushing, restoration, makes reproduction furniture especially Windsor chairs

Hereford Antique Centre
Contact Georgina Smith
128 Widemarsh Street, Hereford, Herefordshire, HR4 9HN
01432 266242
Est. 1989 *Stock size* Large
No. of dealers 35
Stock Furniture, pictures, fireplaces, china etc
Open Mon–Sat 10am–5pm Sun noon–5pm
Services Delivery

Hereford Map Centre (IMTA)
Contact Mr J Davey
24–25 Church Street, Hereford, Herefordshire, HR1 2LR
01432 266322 01432 341874
info@themapcentre.com
www.themapcentre.com
Est. 1984 *Stock size* Large
Stock Old maps of varying scales, 1:10,000, 1:2,500, 1:500, tythe maps, hand-painted, County Series maps
Open Mon–Sat 9am–5.30pm
Services Laminating, mounting

Sunderlands Sale Rooms
Contact Mr Graham Baker
Newmarket Street, Hereford, Herefordshire, HR4 9HX
01432 266894 01432 266901
www.sunderlandshereford.co.uk
Est. 1868
Open Mon–Fri 9am–5.30pm
Sales General furniture sale Mon 5pm. Antiques sale every 2 months Tues 11am, viewing Mon Tues prior to sale (phone Head Office on 01432 356161 for further details)
Frequency Fortnightly
Catalogues No

Waring's Antiques
Contact Mrs E Sullivan
45–47 St Owen Street, Hereford, Herefordshire, HR1 2JB
01432 276241
Est. 1959 *Stock size* Large
Stock General antiques, collectables, pine, both new and old
Open Mon–Sat 9am–5pm

KINGTON

Castle Hill Books
Contact Mr P Newman
12 Church Street, Kington, Herefordshire, HR5 3AZ
01544 231195 01544 231161
newmans@castlehill.books.co.uk
www.castlehillbooks.co.uk
Est. 1989 *Stock size* Medium
Stock New, antiquarian, out-of-print, second-hand books, general stock, most subjects covered, some specialist subjects including archaeology, British and Welsh topography
Open Mon–Fri 10.30am–1pm 2–6pm Sat 10.30am–1pm 2–5pm
Services Book search, valuations, restorations

LEDBURY

John Nash Antiques and Interiors (LAPADA, IDDA)
Contact John Nash
17c High Street, Ledbury, Herefordshire, HR8 1DS
01531 635714 01531 635050
07831 382970
www.johnnash.co.uk
Est. 1973 *Stock size* Medium
Stock 18th–19thC fine mahogany and walnut furniture
Open Mon–Sat 9am–5.30pm Sun by appointment
Services Valuations, restorations, interior design

H J Pugh and Co
Contact Mr Howard Pugh
Ledbury Sale Rooms, Market Street, Ledbury, Herefordshire, HR8 2AQ
01531 631122 01531 631818
auctions@hjpugh.com
www.hjpugh.com
Est. 1990
Open Mon–Fri 9am–5.30pm
Sales General antiques sale Tues 6pm, viewing Tues 10am–6pm prior to sale
Frequency Monthly
Catalogues Yes

Serendipity
Contact Mrs R Ford
The Tythings, Preston Court, Ledbury, Herefordshire, HR8 2LL
01531 660245 01531 660421
sales@serendipity-antiques.co.uk
www.serendipity-antiques.co.uk
Est. 1969 *Stock size* Large
Stock 18thC furniture, long dining tables, four-poster beds
Open Mon–Sat 9am–5.30pm
Fairs Olympia, Battersea
Services Restorations

Keith Smith Books (PBFA)
Contact Mr K Smith
78b The Homend, Ledbury, Herefordshire, HR8 1BX
01531 635336 0870 0529986
keith@ksbooks.demon.co.uk
Est. 1989 *Stock size* Medium
Stock Antiquarian, general, second-hand books, WWI poetry, needlecrafts
Open Mon–Sat 10am–5pm
Fairs Churchdown
Services Book search

LEOMINSTER

22 Broad Street
Contact Daphne Sturley
22 Broad Street, Leominster, Herefordshire, HR6 8BS
01568 620426
Est. 1999 *Stock size* Medium

Stock French furniture, textiles, decorative items, curtains
Open Mon–Sat 10.30am–5pm

🏪 The Barometer Shop
Contact Richard Cookson
✉ **25 New Street, Leominster, Herefordshire, HR6 8BT** 🅿
☎ 01568 610200
Ⓦ www.barometershop.co.uk
Stock size Medium
Stock Antiques, collectables, barometers, clocks, watches
Open Mon–Fri 9am–5pm Sat 10am–4pm
Services Restorations

Key to Symbols

🏪	=	Dealer
🏛	=	Antiques Centre
🔨	=	Auction House
✉	=	Address
🅿	=	Parking
☎	=	Telephone No.
Ⓜ	=	Mobile tel No.
Ⓕ	=	Fax No.
Ⓔ	=	E-mail address
Ⓦ	=	Website address

🔨 Brightwells
Contact Roger Williams
✉ **The Fine Art Sale Room, Ryelands Road, Leominster, Herefordshire, HR6 8NZ** 🅿
☎ 01568 611122 Ⓕ 01568 610519
Ⓔ fineart@brightwells.com
Ⓦ www.catalogs.icollector.com/brightwells
Est. 1846
Open Mon–Fri 9am–5pm
Sales Antiques sale Wed Thurs 10am, viewing Tues 9am–5pm. 5–6 ceramics sales per year Wed 11am, viewing Tues 9am–5pm
Frequency 3–4 sales per month
Catalogues Yes

🏪 Courts Miscellany
Contact Mr G Court
✉ **48a Bridge Street, Leominster, Herefordshire, HR6 8DZ** 🅿
☎ 01568 612995
Est. 1983 *Stock size* Medium
Stock Selection of collectables and antiques relating to social history, sporting, militaria, brewery, political
Open Mon–Sat 10.30am–5pm

🏪 Jeffery Hammond Antiques (LAPADA)
Contact Mr J Hammond
✉ **Shaftesbury House, 38 Broad Street, Leominster, Herefordshire, HR6 8BS** 🅿
☎ 01568 614876 Ⓕ 01568 614876
Ⓔ enquiries@jefferyhammondantiques.co.uk
Ⓦ www.jefferyhammondantiques.co.uk
Est. 1970 *Stock size* Medium
Stock Good quality 18th–early 19thC walnut, mahogany, rosewood furniture, some clocks, paintings, mirrors
Open Mon–Sat 9am–5.30pm or by appointment
Services Valuations for insurance, probate

🏛 Leominster Antique Centre
Contact Mr J Weston
✉ **34 Broad Street, Leominster, Herefordshire, HR6 8BS** 🅿
☎ 01568 615505
Est. 1998 *Stock size* Large
No. of dealers 35
Stock Period furniture, early porcelain, pottery, objets d'art, antiquarian books, garden furniture
Open Mon–Sat 10am–5pm Sun 11am–4pm
Services Tea rooms, gardens

🏛 Leominster Antique Market
Contact Mrs O G Dyke
✉ **14 Broad Street, Leominster, Herefordshire, HR6 8BS** 🅿
☎ 01568 612189
Est. 1975 *Stock size* Large
No. of dealers 16
Stock Glass, china, silver, pine, furniture
Open Mon–Sat 10am–5pm April–Sept Sun 11am–3pm

🏪 Leominster Clock Repairs
Contact Ashley Prosser
✉ **Unit 2, The Railway Station, Worcester Road, Leominster, Herefordshire, HR6 8AR** 🅿
☎ 01568 612298
Est. 2000 *Stock size* Small
Stock Georgian–Victorian longcase and dial clocks
Open Mon–Sat 9am–6pm
Services Repairs

🏛 Linden House Antiques
Contact Michael Clayton or Caroline Scott Mayfield
✉ **1 Drapers Lane, Leominster, Herefordshire, HR6 8ND** 🅿
☎ 01568 620350 Ⓜ 07790 671722
Ⓔ busca@lineone.net
Est. 1972 *Stock size* Large
No. of dealers 10
Stock Furniture, lighting, glass, silver, porcelain, paintings, early country pewter etc, collectables
Open Mon–Sat 10am–1pm 2–5pm Sun by appointment
Services Valuations (free if brought to shop on Sat)

🏛 Old Merchant's House Antiques Centre
Contact Elaine Griffin
✉ **10 Corn Square, Leominster, Herefordshire, HR6 8LR** 🅿
☎ 01568 616141 Ⓕ 01568 616141
Est. 1997 *Stock size* Large
No. of dealers 26
Stock General antiques, collectables, antiquarian and second-hand books
Open Mon–Sat 10am–5pm
Services Re-upholstery, cabinet making

🏪 The Old Shoe Box
Contact Stacey Williams or Eric Titchmarsh
✉ **2 Church Street, Leominster, Herefordshire, HR6 8NE** 🅿
☎ 01568 611414 Ⓜ 07980 286414
Ⓔ staceycharleswilliams@yahoo.com
Est. 1997 *Stock size* Small
Stock Collectables, furniture, soft furnishings, pictures, books
Open Tues–Sat 10am–5pm
Services Book search, picture valuation, restoration

🏪 Tea Gowns & Textiles
Contact Annie Townsend
✉ **28 Broad Street, Leominster, Herefordshire, HR6 8BS** 🅿
☎ 01568 612999 or 01982 560422
Ⓜ 07900 375410
Est. 2002 *Stock size* Medium
Stock Vintage clothing and accessories
Open Mon–Sat 10am–5pm

🏪 Utter Clutter
Contact Mrs L M Mackenzie
✉ **16 West Street, Leominster, Herefordshire, HR6 8ES** 🅿
☎ 01568 611277
Est. 1995 *Stock size* Medium

Stock General antiques, collectables, early toys
Open Mon–Sat 10am–4.30pm

Zany Lady
Contact Sue Humphreys
44 Broad Street, Leominster, Herefordshire, HR6 8BS
01568 612281 07980 286414
Est. 2001 ***Stock size*** Medium
Stock Decorative stock, country furniture, textiles, French garden furniture
Open Mon–Sat 10am–5pm

LONGTOWN

Abergavenny Reclamation
Contact Mr Simon Thomas
Lower Ponthendre, Longtown, Herefordshire, HR2 0NY
07970 318399
Est. 1993 ***Stock size*** Varies
Stock Architectural salvage, reclaimed building materials
Open By appointment

PONTRILAS

Nigel Ward & Co
Contact Mr Nigel Ward
The Border Property Centre, Pontrilas, Herefordshire, HR2 0EH
01981 240140 01981 240857
Est. 1988
Open Mon–Fri 9am–5.30pm
Sales Monthly sales of antique and country furniture, porcelain and collectables at Pontrilas Sale Room
Frequency monthly
Catalogues Yes

ROSS-ON-WYE

Fritz Fryer (LAPADA)
Contact Mr Fritz Fryer or Margaret Lewis
12 Brookend Street, Ross-on-Wye, Herefordshire, HR9 7EG
01989 567416 01989 566742
fritz@fritzfryer.co.uk
www.fritzfryer.co.uk
Est. 1982 ***Stock size*** Large
Stock Antique lighting 1820–1950, crystal chandeliers, gasoliers, wall lights, table lights, nickel and silver fittings, industrial and post-modern lights
Open Mon–Sat 10am–5.30pm
Fairs Olympia, NEC
Services Lighting design, restorations, conversion, shipping, removals and delivery

Andy Gibbs
29 Brookend Street, Ross-on-Wye, Herefordshire, HR9 7EE
01989 566833 07850 354480
Est. 1993 ***Stock size*** Large
Stock Furniture including dining tables, chairs, reformed Gothic and Gothic revival
Open Mon–Sat 10 am–1pm 2–5.30pm
Fairs Dublin Feb
Services Valuations, restorations

W John Griffiths Antiques
Contact Mr Griffiths
30a Brookend Street, Ross-on-Wye, Herefordshire, HR9 7EE
07768 606507
Est. 1997 ***Stock size*** Medium
Stock 18th–early 20thC primarily mahogany furniture, decorative objects, pictures, paintings, prints
Open Mon–Sat 10am–1pm 2–5.30pm

Robin Lloyd Antiques
Contact Mr R R Knightley
23–24 Brookend Street, Ross-on-Wye, Herefordshire, HR9 7EE
01989 562123 01989 562123
robin@robinlloydantiques.fsnet.co.uk
Est. 1972 ***Stock size*** Large
Stock Welsh country furniture, longcase clocks, farmhouse tables
Open Mon–Sat 10am–5.30pm
Services Valuations

The Merchant House
Contact Mr Neil Cockman
36 High Street, Ross-on-Wye, Herefordshire, HR9 5HD
01989 563010
Est. 1998 ***Stock size*** Large
Stock Antique lighting, country furniture, early oak, interior furnishings, small curio items, objets d'art
Open Mon–Sat 10am–5pm

Morris Bricknell
Contact Mr Nigel Morris
Stroud House, Gloucester Road, Ross-on-Wye, Herefordshire, HR9 5BU
01989 768320 01989 768345
Est. 1989
Open Mon–Fri 9am–5.30pm
Sales General antiques sale Sat 10.30am at V H Whitechurch and Goodrich, viewing Sat 8.30am prior to sale. Occasional special and marquee sales (phone for details)
Frequency Monthly
Catalogues No

Ross Old Books and Print Shop (PBFA)
Contact Mr P Thredder
51–52 High Street, Ross-on-Wye, Herefordshire, HR9 5HH
01989 567458 01989 567861
enquiries@rossoldbooks.co.uk
www.antiqueprints.com/abebooks.com
Est. 1987 ***Stock size*** Medium
Stock Antique, second-hand and rare books selling for £1–£1,000, also maps
Open Mon–Sat 10am–5pm closed mid-Jan to mid-Feb
Fairs PBFA
Services Post inland and overseas

Ross-on-Wye Antique Gallery
Contact Mr Michael Aslanian
Gloucester Road, Ross-on-Wye, Herefordshire, HR9 5BU
01989 762290 01989 762291
Est. 1996 ***Stock size*** Large
No. of dealers 50
Stock Gothic-style church, period furniture, oak, country furniture, works of art, antique books, silver, gold, jewellery, English and Continental porcelain, English and French glass, Oriental antiques, rugs, Art Deco, spoons, other cutlery, longcase clocks
Open Mon–Sat 10.30am–5pm Bank Holidays by appointment
Services Valuations

Waterfall Antiques
Contact Mr O McCarthy
2 High Street, Ross-on-Wye, Herefordshire, HR9 5HL
01989 563103

Est. 1991 ***Stock size*** Large
Stock Pine and country furniture
Open Mon–Sat 9.30am–4.30pm closed Wed Fri pm
Fairs Newark

Williams & Watkins Auctioneers Ltd
Contact Roger Garlick
Ross-on-Wye Auction Centre, Overcross, Ross-on-Wye, Herefordshire, HR9 7QF
01989 762225 F 01989 566082
Est. 1866
Open Mon–Fri 9am–5pm
Sales Wed 10am. General antiques sales, viewing Tues 1–7pm and day of sale 9–10am
Frequency monthly
Catalogues Yes

HERTFORDSHIRE

BALDOCK

Ralph & Bruce Moss
Contact Mr B Moss
26 Whitehorse Street, Baldock, Hertfordshire, SG7 6QQ
01462 892751 F 01462 892751
Est. 1973 ***Stock size*** Large
Stock 17th–early 19thC furniture, porcelain, clocks, maps, prints, silver, small items
Open Mon–Sat 9am–6pm

BARNET

Antiques Little Shop
Contact Mrs F O'Gorman
2 Bruce Road, Barnet, Hertfordshire, EN5 4LS
020 8449 9282
Est. 1996 ***Stock size*** Medium
Stock Furniture, collectables, Georgian–1950s
Open Wed–Sat 10am–5pm Fri 11am–5pm
Services House clearance

Barnet Bygones
Contact Mrs M Phillips
2 Bruce Road, Barnet, Hertfordshire, EN5 4LS
020 8440 7304
Est. 1994 ***Stock size*** Large
No. of dealers 5
Stock Furniture, smalls, collectables
Open Wed Fri Sat 9am–5pm

C Bellinger Antiques
Contact Mr C Bellinger
91 Wood Street, Barnet, Hertfordshire, EN5 4BX
020 8449 3467
Est. 1971 ***Stock size*** Small
Stock General antiques
Open Thurs–Sat 10am–3pm

BERKHAMSTED

Berkhamsted Auction Rooms
Contact Mr A Harris
Middle Road, Berkhamsted, Hertfordshire, HP4 3EQ
01442 865169
Est. 1920
Open Mon–Fri 9am–4.30pm
Sales Antiques, modern furniture and effects Wed 10am, viewing day prior 10am–4pm 6–8pm
Frequency Monthly
Catalogues Yes

BOREHAMWOOD

Barnet-Cattanach Antiques (BADA, LAPADA)
Contact Mr R J Gerry
The Old Marble Works, Glenhaven Avenue, Borehamwood, Hertfordshire, WD6 1BB
020 8207 6792 F 020 8381 5889
E acattana@uk.packardbell.org
Est. 1964 ***Stock size*** Large
Stock 18thC period furniture, accessories
Open By appointment only
Fairs Olympia (June, Sept)
Services Restorations, carriage

The Book Exchange
Contact Mr Brian Berman
120 Shenley Road, Borehamwood, Hertfordshire, WD6 1EF
020 8236 0966 F 020 8953 6673
E dee4bee@compuserve.com
Est. 1993 ***Stock size*** Large
Stock General antiquarian, second-hand, some new books
Open Mon–Sat 9.30am–5.30pm
Services Book search

BUSHEY

C and B Antiques
Contact Carol Epstein
22 Brooke Way, Bushey Heath, Watford, Hertfordshire, WD23 4LG
020 8950 1844 F 020 8950 1844
M 07831 647274
Est. 1979 ***Stock size*** Large
Stock 1790–1930 porcelain and small furniture
Open By appointment or at fairs
Fairs The Moat House, The Bell House, Shepton Mallet
Services Valuations

Circa Antiques
Contact Kay Wildman
43 High Street, Bushey, Watford, Hertfordshire, WD2 1BD
020 8950 9233
E kayesley@aol.com
Est. 1969 ***Stock size*** Large
Stock Victorian–Edwardian furniture, china, silver, clocks
Open Mon–Sat 9.30am–5pm
Fairs NEC
Services House clearance

Country Life Interiors
Contact Mr Peter Myers
33a High Street, Bushey, Watford, Hertfordshire, WD23 1BD
020 8950 8575 F 020 8950 6982
E info@countrylifeinteriors.com
W www.countrylifeinteriors.com
Est. 1982 ***Stock size*** Large
Stock Victorian pine, reproduction pine in old wood, oak furniture, limited-edition prints, watercolours, general smalls, giftware, fitted kitchens
Open Mon–Sat 10am–6pm Sun 11am–4pm
Services Worldwide shipping arranged

Marcel Cards (Cartophilic Society)
Contact Marcel Epstein
22 Brooke Way, Bushey Heath, Watford, Hertfordshire, WD23 4LG
020 8950 1844 F 020 8950 1844
M 07887 648255
Est. 1991 ***Stock size*** Large
Stock Cigarette cards 1890–1939, new collectors' cards, tea, bubblegum cards
Open By appointment and at Marcel Fairs
Fairs Peterborough, Ardingly, Dunstable
Services Odd cards to complete sets, card search, valuations

CHESHUNT

Cheshunt Antiques
Contact Mr Peter Howard
126–128 Turners Hill, Cheshunt, Waltham Cross, Hertfordshire, EN8 9BN
01992 637337
Est. 1991 *Stock size* Large
Stock Georgian–early 20thC furniture
Open Tues–Fri 10am–2pm Sat 10am–4pm
Fairs Newark
Services Restorations, French polishing

FROGMORE

Dobson's Antiques
Contact Mr Fred W Dobson
107 Radlett Road, Frogmore, St Albans, Hertfordshire, AL2 2QA
01727 873589
Est. 1969 *Stock size* Medium
Stock General antiques, shipping
Open Mon–Sun 10am–6pm
Services House clearance

HEMEL HEMPSTEAD

Architectural Salvage
Contact Mr L Leadbetter
Wood Lane, Paradise Industrial Estate, Hemel Hempstead, Hertfordshire, HP2 4TL
01442 219936
Est. 1998 *Stock size* Medium
Stock Victorian pews, roll-top baths, internal and external doors, stained glass, French burners, Victorian fireplaces, reclaimed bricks, tiles, floor boarding
Open Mon–Fri 8am–5pm Sat 9am–4.30pm
Services Supply and fit flooring

Bushwood Antiques (LAPADA)
Contact Mr A Bush
Stags End Equestrian Centre, Gaddesden Lane, Hemel Hempstead, Hertfordshire, HP2 6HN
01582 794700 01582 792299
antiques@bushwood.co.uk
www.bushwood.co.uk
Est. 1967 *Stock size* Large
Stock 18th–19thC English and Continental furniture, accessories, objets d'art
Open Mon–Fri 8.30am–4pm Sat 10am–4pm

Cherry Antiques
Contact Mr R S Cullen
101–103 High Street, Hemel Hempstead, Hertfordshire, HP1 3AH
01442 264358
Est. 1981 *Stock size* Medium
Stock General antiques
Open Mon–Sat 9.30am–4.30pm Wed 9.30am–1pm
Services Valuations

Libritz Stamps
Contact Mr R Hickman
70 London Road, Apsley, Hemel Hempstead, Hertfordshire, HP3 9SD
01442 242691 01442 242691
libritzstampshop@aol.com
Est. 1967 *Stock size* Large
Stock Banknotes, stamps, coins, cigarette cards, accessories, albums, catalogues
Open Mon–Sat 10am–5pm
Services Want lists serviced

Off The Wall Antique Mini Centre
Contact Deborah Tanswell
52 High Street, Hemel Hempstead, Hertfordshire, HP1 3AF
01442 218300
Est. 1998 *Stock size* Large
Stock Eccentric European antiques, collectables
Open Mon–Sat 10am–5.30pm Sun noon–4.30pm
Services Eco-friendly house clearance

HERTFORD

Beckwith and Son
Contact Mr G Gray
St Nicholas Hall, St Andrew Street, Hertford, Hertfordshire, SG14 1HZ
01992 582079
sales@beckwithandsonantiques.co.uk
www.beckwithandsonantiques.co.uk
Est. 1903 *Stock size* Large
Stock 17thC–1930s mahogany, pine, oak furniture, silver, glass, pictures, metalware, general antiques, clocks
Open Mon–Fri 9am–1pm 2–5.30pm Sat 9am–5.30pm
Services Restorations, valuations

Gillmark Map Gallery
Contact Mr Mark Pretlove
25 Parliament Square, Hertford, Hertfordshire, SG14 1EX
01992 534444 01992 554734
gillmark@btinternet.com
www.gillmark.com
Est. 1997 *Stock size* Large
Stock Antique maps, prints, second-hand books
Open Tues–Sat 10am–5pm Thurs closed pm
Services Restorations, conservation, framing, hand colouring

Hertford Antiques
Contact Mr S Garratt
51 St Andrew Street, Hertford, Hertfordshire, SG14 1HZ
01992 504504 01920 460648
Est. 1994 *Stock size* Large
No. of dealers 60
Stock Everything from period furniture to jewellery
Open Mon–Sun 10am–5.30pm

Tapestry Antiques
Contact Mrs P Stokes
27 St Andrew Street, Hertford, Hertfordshire, SG14 1HZ
01992 587438
pjstokes27@yahoo.com
Est. 1974 *Stock size* Large
Stock General 18th–19thC furniture, brass, copper, porcelain, Staffordshire figures
Open Mon–Sat 10am–5pm
Services Valuations, probate

HITCHIN

Antiques' Collectables & Furniture
Contact Mr Godfrey
92 Walsworth Road, Hitchin, Hertfordshire, SG4 9SX
01462 632288 07711 843032
Est. 1999 *Stock size* Medium
Stock Oil lamp spares, furniture, fixtures and fittings, collectors' reference books, polishes
Open Mon–Sat 10am–5pm Sun 11am–4pm
Fairs Welwyn, Potters Bar
Services Upholstery

The Book Bug
Contact Mrs S Jevon
1 The Arcade, Hitchin, Hertfordshire, SG5 1ED P
01462 431309
Est. 1984 *Stock size* Large
Stock General second-hand and antiquarian books
Open Mon Tues Thurs Sat 9am–5pm Wed 9am–2pm

Michael Gander
Contact Mr M Gander
10 & 11 Bridge Street, Hitchin, Hertfordshire, SG5 2DE P
01462 432678 M 07885 728976
Est. 1974 *Stock size* Medium
Stock Period furniture, small items
Open Wed Thurs Sat 9am–5pm or by appointment

Hanbury Antiques
Contact Mrs M D Hanbury
86 Tilehouse Street, Hitchin, Hertfordshire, SG5 2DU P
01462 420487
Est. 1989 *Stock size* Medium
Stock 18th–20thC furniture, small items
Open Mon–Sat 9am–5pm
Services Valuations

Eric T Moore
Contact Katie Maynard-Smith
24 Bridge Street, Hitchin, Hertfordshire, SG5 2DF P
01462 450497
E booksales@erictmoore.co.uk
W www.erictmoore.co.uk
Est. 1965 *Stock size* Large
Stock Antiquarian books, maps, loose prints
Open Mon–Fri 9.30am–5pm Sat 9.30am–5.30pm
Services Bookbinding, book search, coffee served to customers

Geoffrey Norman
Contact Mr G Norman
93 Walsworth Road, Hitchin, Hertfordshire, SG4 9SX
01462 421138
Est. 1995 *Stock size* Medium
Stock Collectables, furniture, books, coins, clocks, watches, general antiques
Open Mon–Sat 10am–6pm

Phillips of Hitchin Antiques Ltd (BADA)
Contact Mr J Phillips
The Manor House, 26 Bancroft, Hitchin, Hertfordshire, SG5 1JW P
01462 432067 F 01462 441368
Est. 1884 *Stock size* Medium
Stock English furniture, 1730–1830, unusual items such as campaign furniture, new and out-of-print reference books on antique furniture
Open Mon–Fri 9am–5.30pm

KING'S LANGLEY

Past & Present Antiques and Collectables
Contact Sue Smith
42 High Street, King's Langley, Hertfordshire, WD4 9HT P
01923 291181 M 07740 122903
Est. 1996 *Stock size* Medium
Stock Art Deco, jewellery, 1940s–1960s, Victorian furniture
Open Tues–Sat 10am–6pm Sun 11am–5pm Nov Dec Mon–Sat 10am–6pm Sun 11am–5pm
Services Valuations

LEAVESDEN

Peter Taylor and Son
Contact Mr P Taylor
1 Ganders Ash, Leavesden, Watford, Hertfordshire, WD25 7HE P
01923 663325
E taylorbooks@clara.co.uk
Est. 1973 *Stock size* Medium
Stock Tudor and medieval history antique books, documents
Open Catalogue order
Services Valuations

REDBOURNE

J N Antiques
Contact Mrs J Brunning
86 High Street, Redbourne, St Albans, Hertfordshire, AL3 7BD P
01582 793603
Est. 1974 *Stock size* Large
Stock General antiques
Open Mon–Sat 9am–6am
Services Valuations

Tim Wharton (LAPADA)
Contact Mr T Wharton
24 High Street, Redbourne, St Albans, Hertfordshire, AL3 7LL P
01582 794371 F 01727 751973
M 07850 622880
E tim@timwhartonantiques.co.uk
Est. 1973 *Stock size* Large
Stock 17th–19thC oak, country furniture, some period mahogany, metalware, treen, country pictures
Open Tues Wed Fri 10am–5pm Sat 10am–4pm Thurs by appointment
Fairs LAPADA (Birmingham), Olympia

RICKMANSWORTH

Galliard Antiques
Contact Mrs E Harriman
144 High Street, Rickmansworth, Hertfordshire, WD3 1AB P
01923 778087 F 01923 778087
M 07714 068989
E galliardi@aol.com
Est. 1996 *Stock size* Medium
Stock General antiques, furniture, pictures, china, militaria, unusual items, coins, Roman and medieval pottery
Open Mon–Thurs Sat 9.30am–5.30pm Fri 9.30am–7pm
Services Valuations

ROYSTON

Philip Dawes Antiques
37–39 Kneesworth Street, Royston, Hertfordshire, SG8 5AB P
01736 243039
Est. 1997 *Stock size* Medium
Stock General antiques, garden furniture
Open Tues–Sat 9.30am–5pm
Services Upholstery, chair caning

SAWBRIDGEWORTH

Arcane Antiques Centre (EADA)
Contact Mr Nigel Hoy or Miss Nicola Smith
The Maltings, Station Road, Sawbridgeworth, Hertfordshire, CM21 9JX P
01279 600562
M 07957 551899
E charnwoodantiques@tiscali.co.uk
Est. 1999 *Stock size* Large
No. of dealers 25
Stock Ceramics, glass, silver, oil paintings, watercolours, fine prints, clocks, jewellery, Georgian–Edwardian furniture

Open Tues–Fri 10am–5pm
Sat Sun 11am–5pm
Services Antique furniture restoration, cabinet-making, upholstery, cabinet-lining, French polishing, glass repair, picture framing

Herts & Essex Antiques Centre
Contact Robert Sklar
The Maltings, Station Road, Sawbridgeworth, Hertfordshire, CM21 9JX
☎ 01279 722044 Ⓕ 01279 725445
Ⓔ webmaster@antiques-of-britain.co.uk
Ⓦ www.antiques-of-britain.co.uk
Est. 1980 *Stock size* Large
No. of dealers 130
Stock All sorts of antiques, collectables
Open Mon–Sun 10am–5pm
Services Tea room

Riverside Antiques Centre
Contact Mr J Maynard
Unit 1, The Maltings, Station Road, Sawbridgeworth, Hertfordshire, CM21 9JX
☎ 01279 600985
Est. 1998 *Stock size* Large
No. of dealers 185
Stock Probably the largest antiques centre in Hertfordshire and Essex. Antiques, collectables, furniture, etc
Open Mon–Sun 10am–5pm
Services Restoration and repair of furniture, glass, ceramics

ST ALBANS

Magic Lanterns
Contact J A Marsden
By George, 23 George Street, St Albans, Hertfordshire, AL3 4ES
☎ 01727 865680
Est. 1987 *Stock size* Large
Stock 1800–1950 antique lighting, mirrors, jewellery
Open Mon–Fri 10am–5pm
Sat 10am–5.30pm Sun 1–5pm
Services Reproduction Victorian lampshades made to order, lighting consultancy for period houses

Paton Books
Contact Richard Child
34 Holywell Hill, St Albans, Hertfordshire, AL1 1DE
☎ 01727 853984 Ⓕ 01727 865764
Ⓔ patonbooks@aol.com
Ⓦ www.patonbooks.co.uk
Est. 1962 *Stock size* Large
Stock General secondhand and antiquarian books
Open Mon–Sat 9am–6pm
Sun 10am–6pm

STANDON

Grand Prix Top Gear
Contact Mr N Grint
Unit 3, Mill End, Standon, Ware, Hertfordshire, SG11 1LR
☎ 07000 553949 Ⓕ 01279 842072
Ⓔ f1@topgear.org
Ⓦ www.topgear.org
Est. 1989 *Stock size* Large
Stock Memorabilia. Formula One collectables including car body parts, original team clothing, signed photos, models, caps
Open Mon–Sat 9am–6pm phone first
Fairs Autosport Show NEC, Silverstone GP
Services Mail order and trade suppliers

STEVENAGE

Ayuka Ltd
Contact Mune Ota
25 Broom Walk, Stevenage, Hertfordshire, SG1 1UU
☎ 01438 362494 Ⓕ 01438 228494
Ⓔ sales@ayuka.com
Stock size Medium
Stock Pine furniture, small oak, mahogany, other wood furniture
Trade only Yes
Open Mon–Sun 9am–8pm

TRING

John Bly (BADA)
Contact Mr Parris
The Old Billiards Room, Church Yard, Tring, Hertfordshire, HP23 5AG
☎ 01442 890802
Est. 1891 *Stock size* Large
Stock Georgian furniture, porcelain, silver, glass, other quality antiques
Open Tues–Sat 10am–4pm
Fairs Grosvenor House, Florida
Services Valuations, restorations

Country Clocks
Contact Mr Terry Cartmell
3 Pendley Bridge Cottages, Tring Station, Tring, Hertfordshire, HP23 5QU
☎ 01442 825090
Est. 1976 *Stock size* Medium
Stock 18th–19thC wall, longcase, mantel clocks
Open Mon–Fri by appointment
Sat 9am–5pm Sun 2–5pm
Services Valuations, restorations, repairs

Farrelly Antiques
Contact Mr Paul Farrelly
Rear of 50 High Street, Tring, Hertfordshire, HP23 5AG
☎ 01442 891905
Est. 1979 *Stock size* Medium
Stock Antique furniture up to 1900
Open Mon–Sat 10am–5pm
Services Restorations

New England House Antiques
Contact Mr S Munjee
50 High Street, Tring, Hertfordshire, HP23 5AG
☎ 01442 827262 Ⓕ 01442 827262
Ⓜ 07711 224422
Ⓔ enquiries@newenglandhouseantiques.co.uk
Ⓦ www.newenglandhouseantiques.co.uk
Est. 1992 *Stock size* Large
Stock Georgian–Edwardian furniture, silver, glass, paintings, clocks
Open Tues–Sat 10.30am–5pm
Services Restorations, free search and find for furniture

WATFORD

Bygone Years
Contact Mrs H Alsop
250 St Albans Road, Watford, Hertfordshire, WD2 4AX
☎ 01923 210623 Ⓕ 01923 210623
Est. 1998 *Stock size* Medium
Stock Victorian and new furniture, pine, very varied stock of interesting items
Open Mon Tues 10am–2.30am
Wed 10am–1pm Thurs–Sat
9am–5.30pm or by appointment
Fairs Newark, Swinderby, Goodwood

⊞ Cards Inc
Contact Mr P Freedman
✉ **Unit 9, Woodshots Meadow, Croxley Business Park, Watford, Hertfordshire, WD1 8YU** Ⓟ
☎ 01923 200138 Ⓕ 01923 200134
Ⓔ paul@cardsinc.com
Ⓦ www.cardsinc.com
Est. 1987 *Stock size* Small
Stock Collectable trading cards
Open By appointment

⊞ Collectors Corner
Contact Mr L Dronkes
✉ **Charter Place, Watford Market, Watford, Hertfordshire, WD1 2RN** Ⓟ
☎ 01923 248855 or 020 8904 0552
Est. 1968 *Stock size* Small
Stock Coins, medals, bank notes, cigarette cards, small collectables
Open Tues Fri Sat 10am–5pm
Services Valuations, medal mounting

⊞ Pine Furniture Store
Contact Mrs Sheward
✉ **304a Lower High Street, Watford, Hertfordshire, WD1 2JE** Ⓟ
☎ 01923 441604
Est. 1979 *Stock size* Medium
Stock Reclaimed, new, old pine furniture, pine and iron beds, mirrors
Open Tues Fri Sat 10am–5pm Sun 10am–4pm
Services Stripping

⊞ Quicktest
Contact Raffi Katz
✉ **Park House, Greenhill Crescent, Watford Business Park, Watford, Hertfordshire, WD18 8QU** Ⓟ
☎ 01923 220206
Ⓜ 07976 831953
Ⓔ info@quicktest.co.uk
Ⓦ www.quicktest.co.uk
Est. 1986 *Stock size* Large
Stock Testers, magnifiers, weighing machines, jewellery boxes, hand tools
Open Mon–Thurs 8am–6pm Fri 8am–3pm
Fairs Newark, Alexandra Palace, Ardingly, Kempton, Shepton, Birmingham, Sandown

WHEATHAMPSTEAD

⊞ Collins Antiques
Contact Mr Michael Collins
✉ **Corner House, Church Street, Wheathampstead, Hertfordshire, AL4 8AP** Ⓟ
☎ 01582 833111
Est. 1907 *Stock size* Medium
Stock 17th–19thC furniture, including oak and mahogany tables, chairs, chests-of-drawers
Open Mon–Sat 9am–1pm 2–5pm
Services Valuations

⊞ The Old Bakery Antiques Ltd
Contact Mr Maurice Shifrin
✉ **3 Station Road, Wheathampstead, Hertfordshire, AL4 8BU** Ⓟ
☎ 01582 831999 Ⓕ 01582 831555
Est. 1997 *Stock size* Large
Stock Mainly Victorian–Edwardian furniture, Oriental carpets
Open Mon–Sun 10am–5pm closed Wed
Fairs Newark, Ardingly

⊞ Thomas Thorp (ABA, PBFA)
Contact Mr Jim Thorp
✉ **35–37 High Street, Wheathampstead, Hertfordshire, AL4 8BB** Ⓟ
☎ 01582 834757 Ⓕ 01582 834757
Ⓔ thorpbooks@compuserve.com
Est. 1883 *Stock size* Small
Stock General antiquarian books, specializing in early printed English history, literature, modern, private press editions
Open Mail order or by appointment
Fairs Olympia (Jun), Chelsea (Nov)

WILSTONE

⊞ W J Hazle
Contact Mr W J Hazle
✉ **36 Grange Road, Wilstone, Tring, Hertfordshire, HP23 4PG**
☎ 01442 890493 Ⓕ 01442 890493
Ⓜ 07850 474672
Ⓔ all-our-yesterdays@hotmail.com
Ⓦ www.allouryesterdays.co.uk
Est. 1995 *Stock size* Large
Stock Original, reproduction, modern collectors' cards
Open Mail order or by appointment

OXFORDSHIRE

ASCOTT-UNDER-WYCHWOOD

⊞ William Antiques
Contact Mr R Gripper
✉ **Manor Barn, Manor Farm, Ascott-under-Wychwood, Chipping Norton, Oxfordshire, OX7 6AL** Ⓟ
☎ 01993 831960 Ⓕ 01993 830395
Ⓔ robgripper@aol.com
Est. 1982 *Stock size* Medium
Stock Good-quality decorative antiques, Georgian–Victorian furniture
Open Mon–Fri 9am–5pm
Services Restorations

BANBURY

Bonhams
✉ **48 North Bar, Banbury, Oxfordshire, OX16 0TH**
☎ 01295 272723 Ⓕ 01295 272726
Ⓔ banbury@bonhams.com
Ⓦ www.bonhams.com
Open Mon–Fri 9am–5.30pm

⊞ Comic Connections
Contact Mr Glyn Smith
✉ **56–57 George Street, Banbury, Oxfordshire, OX16 8BH**
☎ 01295 268989 Ⓕ 01295 268989
Est. 1994 *Stock size* Large
Stock American comic books, graphic novels, action figures, science-fiction items
Open Mon–Wed 10.30am–5pm Thurs Fri 10am–5pm Sat 9.30am–5pm
Fairs D and J Fair, NEC
Services Standing order for comics, magazines, videos

Holloways (RICS)
Contact Mr Tim Holloway
✉ **49 Parsons Street, Banbury, Oxfordshire, OX16 5PF** Ⓟ
☎ 01295 817777 Ⓕ 01295 817701
Ⓔ enquiries@hollowaysauctioneers.co.uk
Ⓦ www.hollowaysauctioneers.co.uk
Open Mon–Fri 9am–5.30pm Sat 9am–noon
Sales Fortnightly general sales Mon 11am, viewing Fri 9am–5pm Sat 9am–12.30pm. Every 2 months specialist sales Wed 11am, viewing Sat 9am–12.30pm Mon 9am–7pm Tues 9am–5pm and day of sale
Catalogues No

BICESTER

R A Barnes Antiques (LAPADA)
Contact John Langin
PO Box 82, Bicester, Oxfordshire, OX25 1RA P
☎ 01844 237388
Est. 1970 *Stock size* Medium
Stock Continental glass, English and Continental porcelain, Art Nouveau, paintings, English metalware, 18th–19thC brass, Belleek, Wedgwood
Open By appointment
Fairs NEC, Little Chelsea
Services Valuations

Lisseters Antiques
Contact Mr M Lisseter
3 Kings End, Bicester, Oxfordshire, OX6 7DR P
☎ 01869 252[illegible]02
Ⓜ 07801 667[illegible]48
Est. 1959 *Stock size* Large
Stock Antiques, used furniture
Open Mon–Sat 9am–5pm

Mallams (SOFAA)
Contact C Turner
Pevensey House, 27 Sheep Street, Bicester, Oxfordshire, OX26 6JF P
☎ 01869 252901 Ⓕ 01869 320283
Ⓔ bicester@mallams.co.uk
Ⓦ www.mallams.co.uk/fineart
Est. 1788
Open Mon–Fri 9am–5pm
Sat 9am–1pm
Sales General antiques sale Mon 11am, viewing Fri 9am–5pm Sat 9am–1pm morning of sale 8–11am. Valuations service
Frequency 16 per year
Catalogues Yes

Serendipity
Contact Mr A J Slade
22 Wesley Lane, Bicester, Oxfordshire, OX6 7JW P
☎ 01869 322533
Est. 1993 *Stock size* Large
Stock New, old, collectable teddy bears, dolls
Open Mon Thurs–Sat 9am–5pm
Fairs NEC, Donnington Park
Services Bear, doll restorations

BIX

Easy Strip
Contact Mr R Cane
Old Manor Farm, Bix, Henley-on-Thames, Oxfordshire, RG9 6BX P
☎ 01491 577289 Ⓜ 07785 938580
Est. 1969 *Stock size* Large
Stock Victorian doors, architectural antiques
Open By appointment
Services Stripping doors

BLEWBURY

Blewbury Antiques
Contact E Richardson
London Road, Blewbury, Didcot, Oxfordshire, OX11 9NX P
☎ 01235 850366
Est. 1970 *Stock size* Medium
Stock General, furniture, garden ornaments, books, glass, china, clocks
Open Mon–Sun 10am–6pm closed Tues Wed

BLOXHAM

Antiques of Bloxham
Contact Mr S Robinson
Church Street, Bloxham, Banbury, Oxfordshire, OX15 4ET P
☎ 01295 721641
Est. 1996 *Stock size* Large
Stock General antiques
Open Mon–Sun 10am–4.30pm
Services Delivery, clock repairs

BURFORD

Antiques @ The George
Contact Coral Oswald
104 High Street, Burford, Oxfordshire, OX18 4QJ P
☎ 01993 823319
Est. 1992 *Stock size* Large
No. of dealers 20
Stock China, glass, furniture, treen, books, pictures, rugs, carpets
Open Mon–Sat 10am–5pm
Sun noon–5pm

Boxroom Antiques
Contact Mr Glyn Roberts
59 High Street, Burford, Oxfordshire, OX18 4QA P
☎ 01993 824268
Est. 1998 *Stock size* Large
Stock Jewellery, silver, linen, small furniture, porcelain, glass, collectables, cutlery
Open Mon–Sun 10am–6pm

Burford Antiques Centre
Contact Mr G Viventi
The Roundabout, Cheltenham Road, Burford, Oxfordshire, OX18 4JA P
☎ 01993 823227
Est. 1988 *Stock size* Large
Stock General antiques, 1930s–modern, period reproduction furniture
Open Mon–Sat 10am–6pm
Sun noon–5pm

Bygones
Contact Mrs Jenkins
29 Lower High Street, Burford, Oxfordshire, OX18 4RN P
☎ 01993 823588 Ⓕ 01993 704338
Est. 1986 *Stock size* Medium
Stock General collectables, curios
Open Mon–Sat 10am–1pm 2–5pm Sun noon–5pm

Jonathan Fyson Antiques (CADA)
Contact Mr J Fyson
50–52 High Street, Burford, Oxfordshire, OX18 4QF
☎ 01993 823204 Ⓕ 01993 823204
Ⓔ j@jonathanfysonantiques.com
Ⓦ www.jonathanfysonantiques.com
Est. 1971 *Stock size* Large
Stock English and Continental furniture, brass, lighting, fireplaces, accessories, club fenders, papier mâché, tôle, treen, porcelain, glass, prints, jewellery
Open Mon–Fri 9.30am–5.30pm closed 1–2pm Sat 10am–5.30pm closed 1–2pm
Services Valuations

Gateway Antiques (CADA)
Contact Mr Paul Brown or Mr Michael Ford
Cheltenham Road, Burford, Oxfordshire, OX18 4JA P
☎ 01993 823678 Ⓕ 01993 823857
Ⓦ www.gatewayantiques.co.uk
Est. 1985 *Stock size* Large
Stock 17th–19thC furniture, farmhouse furniture, Arts and Crafts, decorative objects, accessories,
Open Mon–Sat 10am–5.30pm
Sun 2–5pm
Services Shipping worldwide, multi-lingual courier service and driver, accomodation, storage

Horseshoe Antiques
Contact Mr B Evans
97 High Street, Burford, Oxfordshire, OX18 4QA
01993 823244 07711 525383
Est. 1979 *Stock size* Medium
Stock 17th–18thC furniture, oil paintings, copper, brass, horse brasses, clocks, longcase clocks
Open Mon–Sat 9.30am–5pm

David Pickup (BADA, CADA)
Contact Mr D Pickup
115 High Street, Burford, Oxfordshire, OX18 4RG
01993 822555
Est. 1980 *Stock size* Medium
Stock Fine English furniture, emphasis on the Cotswold Arts and Crafts movement early 20thC
Open Mon–Fri 9.30am–5.30pm Sat 10.30am–4.30pm
Fairs Olympia (Spring, Nov)

Saracen Antiques Ltd
Contact Mr C Mills
Upton Downs Farm, Burford, Oxfordshire, OX18 4LY
01993 822987 01993 823701
cmills6702@aol.com
Est. 1996 *Stock size* Large
Stock Predominantly 18th–19thC English furniture
Open Mon–Sat 9am–5.30pm
Services Restorations

Manfred Schotten Antiques (CADA, BACA Award Winner 2002)
109 High Street, Burford, Oxfordshire, OX18 4RG
01993 822302 01993 822055
antiques@schotten.com
www.schotten.com
Est. 1976 *Stock size* Large
Stock Sporting antiques, library furniture, leather furniture
Open Mon–Sat 9.30am–5.30pm
Fairs Olympia

Swan Gallery (CADA)
Contact Mr D Pratt
127 High Street, Burford, Oxfordshire, OX18 4RE
01993 822244 01993 822244
Est. 1977 *Stock size* Large
Stock Early oak and period furniture
Open Mon–Sat 10am–5.30pm

CHALGROVE

Hitchcox's Antiques
Contact Rupert Hitchcox
The Garth, Warpsgrove, Chalgrove, Oxford, Oxfordshire, OX44 7RW
01865 890241 01865 890241
Est. 1957 *Stock size* Large
Stock 18th–20thC English furniture
Open Mon–Sat 10am–5pm Sun 2–5pm
Services Valuations, buys at auction

CHARNEY BASSETT

Brian Davis Antiques
Contact Mr B Davis
Goosey Wick Farm, Goosey Wick, Charney Bassett, Wantage, Oxfordshire, OX12 0EY
01367 718933
Est. 1981 *Stock size* Large
Stock English and Continental period pine
Open Tues–Sat 9am–5.30pm

CHILTON

Country Markets Antiques & Collectables
Contact Mr G Vaughan
Wyevale Garden Centre, Newbury Road, Chilton, Didcot, Oxfordshire, OX11 0QN
01235 835125 01235 833068
country.markets.antiques@breathemail.net
www.countrymarkets.co.uk
Est. 1989 *Stock size* Large
No. of dealers 35
Stock Furniture, glass, jewellery, cased fish, porcelain, ceramics etc
Open Mon 10.30am–5.30pm Tues–Sat 10am–5.30pm Sun Bank Holidays 10.30am–4.30pm
Services Valuations, restorations

CHINNOR

Mr Booth Antiques
Contact Mr G Booth
6 Thame Road, Chinnor, Oxfordshire, OX9 4QS
01844 354344
Est. 1994 *Stock size* Small
Stock Wide range of collectables, period furniture, mirrors, pictures
Open Sat Mon 9.30am–5.30pm
Fairs Kempton Park

CHIPPING NORTON

Antique English Windsor Chairs (BADA, CINOA, CADA)
Contact Michael Harding-Hill
9 Horse Fair, Chipping Norton, Oxfordshire, OX7 5AL
01608 643322 01608 644322
07798 653134
michael@antique-english-windsor-chairs.com
www.antique-english-windsor-chairs.com
Est. 1971 *Stock size* Large
Stock Antique English Windsor chairs 18th–19thC, sets, singles for collectors and everyday use
Open 10am–5pm Mon–Sat or by appointment
Fairs Olympia (June, Nov)

Chipping Norton Antique Centre
Contact Michael Mence
Ivy House, Middle Row, Chipping Norton, Oxfordshire, OX7 5NH
01608 644212 01608 641369
Est. 1986 *Stock size* Large
No. of dealers 15
Stock General antiques, collectables, Georgian and Edwardian furniture, china, silver, kitchenware
Open 10am–5.30pm Mon–Sun
Services Tea room

Georgian House Antiques (LAPADA)
Contact Sheila Wissinger
21 West Street, Chipping Norton, Oxfordshire, OX7 5EU
01608 641369 01608 641369
Stock size Large
Stock Period oak, mahogany, walnut furniture, paintings, chairs, farmhouse furniture
Open Mon–Sun 10am–5pm or by appointment
Services Delivery, shipping arranged

Greensleeves Books (BA)
Contact Mrs C Seers

✉ **PO Box 156, Chipping Norton, Oxfordshire, OX7 3NJ**
☎ 01608 644707 Ⓕ 01608 644707
Ⓔ greensleeves@v21mail.co.uk
Ⓦ www.greensleevesbooks.co.uk
Est. 1981 ***Stock size*** Medium
Stock Rare and second-hand books, mind, body and spirit books a speciality
Open Mail order only
Services Book search, catalogues

Kellow Books
Contact Mr P Combellack
✉ **6 Market Place, Chipping Norton, Oxfordshire, OX7 5NA** Ⓟ
☎ 01608 644293
Est. 1998 ***Stock size*** Medium
Stock Antiquarian, rare, second-hand collectable books
Open Mon–Sat 10am–4.30pm
Services Book search

Key Antiques (BADA, CADA)
Contact Jane Riley
✉ **11 Horsefair, Chipping Norton, Oxfordshire, OX7 5AL** Ⓟ
☎ 01608 643777 Ⓜ 07860 650112
Est. 1972 ***Stock size*** Medium
Stock Period oak, country furniture, related objects of 17th–18thC
Open Wed–Sat 10am–5.30pm
Services Valuations of period oak, metalware

The Quiet Woman Antiques Centre
Contact Ann Marriott
✉ **Southcombe, Chipping Norton, Oxfordshire, OX7 5QH** Ⓟ
☎ 01608 646262 Ⓕ 01608 646262
Ⓜ 07860 889524
Est. 1998 ***Stock size*** Medium
No. of dealers 20
Stock Furniture, china, general antiques
Open Mon–Fri 10am–6pm
Sat 10am–5.30pm
Sun 10am–4pm
Services Coffee shop

Station Mill Antiques Centre
Contact Tracey Hewlett
✉ **Station Road, Chipping Norton, Oxfordshire, OX7 5HX** Ⓟ
☎ 01608 644563 Ⓕ 01327 860952
Ⓔ TL@stationmill.com
Ⓦ www.stationmill.com
Est. 1996 ***Stock size*** Large
No. of dealers 70
Stock Complete range of antiques, collectables
Open Mon–Sun 10am–5pm
Services Tea room

CHURCHILL

Clive Payne (LAPADA)
Contact Clive Payne
✉ **Unit 4, Mount Farm, Junction Road, Churchill, Chipping Norton, Oxfordshire, OX7 6NP** Ⓟ
☎ 01608 658856 Ⓕ 01608 658856
Ⓜ 07801 088363
Ⓔ clive.payne@virgin.net
Ⓦ www.clivepayne.com
Est. 1986 ***Stock size*** Medium
Stock 17thC–early Victorian furniture
Open Mon–Fri 9am–5pm
Services Antique furniture restoration

DEDDINGTON

Castle Antiques Ltd (LAPADA)
Contact John or Judy Vaughan
✉ **Manor Farm, Clifton, Deddington, Oxfordshire, OX15 0PA** Ⓟ
☎ 01869 338688
Est. 1972 ***Stock size*** Large
Stock General antiques, furniture, metalware, silver, reproduction garden furniture
Open Mon–Sat 10am–6pm
Sun 10am–4pm

Deddington Antique Centre (TVADA)
Contact Mrs Brenda Haller
✉ **Laurel House, Bullring, Deddington, Banbury, Oxfordshire, OX15 0TT** Ⓟ
☎ 01869 338968 Ⓕ 01869 338916
Est. 1977 ***Stock size*** Large
No. of dealers 20
Stock Period furniture, silver, porcelain, oil and watercolours, jewellery, clocks etc
Open Mon–Sat 10am–5pm
Sun 11am–5pm
Services Porcelain, silver and jewellery repairs

DORCHESTER

Dorchester Antiques (TVADA, LAPADA)
Contact Mrs S or Jonty Hearnden
✉ **The Barn, 3 High Street, Dorchester, Oxfordshire, OX10 7HH** Ⓟ
☎ 01865 341373 Ⓕ 01865 341373
Est. 1992
Stock Georgian furniture, interesting country pieces

Open Tues–Sat 10am–5pm
Fairs TVADA
Services Finding service

Hallidays (Fine Antiques) Ltd (LAPADA, CINOA, TVADA)
Contact Mr E M Reily Collins
High Street, Dorchester, Oxfordshire, OX10 7HL
01865 340028 Ⓕ 01865 341149
Ⓔ antiques@hallidays.com
Ⓦ www.hallidays.com
Est. 1942 *Stock size* Large
Stock 17th–19thC English furniture, decorative items, paintings
Open Mon–Fri 9am–5pm
Sat 10am–4pm
Fairs Olympia, LAPADA (Jan)
Services Shipping

EAST HAGBOURNE

Craig Barfoot Clocks
Contact Craig Barfoot
Tudor House, East Hagbourne, Oxfordshire, OX11 9LR
01235 818968 Ⓕ 01235 818968
Ⓜ 07710 858158
Ⓔ craig.barfoot@tiscali.co.uk
Est. 1991 *Stock size* Medium
Stock Longcase, organ and musical clocks
Open By appointment
Services Restorations, buys at auction

E M Lawson and Co (ABA, ILAB)
Contact Mr J Lawson
Kingsholm, Main Road, East Hagbourne, Didcot, Oxfordshire, OX11 9LN
01235 812033
Est. 1919 *Stock size* Small
Stock Rare and antiquarian books, early English literature, science, medicine, economics, travel
Open Mon–Fri 9am–6pm or by appointment

HENLEY-ON-THAMES

Bonhams
The Coach House, 66 Northfield End, Henley-on-Thames, Oxfordshire, RG9 2JN
01491 413636 Ⓕ 01494 413637
Ⓔ henley@bonhams.com
Ⓦ www.bonhams.com
Open Mon Fri 9am–5pm
1st Sat of month 10am–1pm

The Country Seat (TVADA, LAPADA)
Contact William Clegg
Huntercombe Manor Barn, Henley-on-Thames, Oxfordshire, RG9 5RY
01491 641349 Ⓕ 01491 641533
Ⓔ ferryandclegg@thecountryseat.com
Ⓦ www.thecountryseat.com
Est. 1971 *Stock size* Large
Stock Furniture designed by architects 17th–20thC, post-war furniture, art pottery, metalwork, Whitefriars glass
Open 9am–5pm
Fairs TVADA, 20thC Olympia

The Ferret (Friday Street Antiques Centre)
Contact Mrs D Etherington
4 Friday Street, Henley-on-Thames, Oxfordshire, RG9 1AH
01491 574104 Ⓕ 01491 641039
Est. 1984 *Stock size* Medium
No. of dealers 6
Stock Jewellery, silver, furniture, china, books, collectables
Open Mon–Sat 10am–5.30pm
Sun noon–5.30pm

Henley Antique Centre
Contact Mr D Shepherd
2–4 Reading Road, Henley-on-Thames, Oxfordshire, RG9 1AG
01491 411468
Est. 1999 *Stock size* Large
No. of dealers 48
Stock Furniture, glass, china, silver, coins, scientific instruments, tools
Open Mon–Sat 10am–5.30pm
Sun noon–5.30pm

Jackdaw Antique Centres Ltd
Contact Mrs J Mayle
5 Reading Road, Henley-on-Thames, Oxfordshire, RG9 0AS
01491 572289 Ⓕ 01491 682885
Ⓦ www.jackdawantiques.co.uk
Est. 1998 *Stock size* Medium
No. of dealers 24
Stock Furniture, ceramics, glass, collectables, general antiques
Open Mon–Sat 10am–5.30pm
Sun Bank Holidays noon–5pm
Services Furniture, ceramic restoration, upholstery

Jonkers (ABA, PBFA)
Contact Sam Jonkers
24 Hart Street, Henley-on-Thames, Oxfordshire, RG9 2AU
01491 576427 Ⓕ 01491 573805
Ⓔ info@jonkers.co.uk
Ⓦ www.jonkers.co.uk
Est. 1990 *Stock size* Medium
Stock Antiquarian literature, 19th–20thC first editions, illustrated and children's books
Open Mon–Sat 10am–5.30pm
Fairs Olympia

Simmons & Sons (RICS)
Contact Mr S Jones or Mrs E Latham
32 Bell Street, Henley-on-Thames, Oxfordshire, RG9 2BH
01491 571111 Ⓕ 01491 579833
Ⓔ auctions@simmonsandsons.com
Ⓦ www.simmonsandsons.com
Est. 1802
Open Mon–Fri 9am–5.30pm
Sat 9am–noon
Sales 8 sales of general antiques per annum, valuations
Catalogues Yes

Tudor House Antiques and Collectables
Contact Mr D Potter
49 Duke Street, Henley-on-Thames, Oxfordshire, RG9 1UR
01491 573680 Ⓜ 07709 987892
Est. 1996 *Stock size* Large
Stock General antiques, collectables
Open Mon–Sun 10am–5pm
Services Valuations, house clearance

Ways Bookshop (ABA)
Contact Diana Cook
54b Friday Street, Henley-on-Thames, Oxfordshire, RG9 1AH
01491 576663 Ⓕ 01491 576663
Est. 1977 *Stock size* Medium
Stock Rare and second-hand books bought and sold
Open Mon–Sat 10am–5.30pm
Services Book search, bookbinding, valuations

The Worm Hole Antique Centre
Contact Mr Doug Shephard
8 Greys Road, Henley-on-Thames, Oxfordshire, RG9 1RY
☎ 01491 413333
Est. 1998 *Stock size* Large
No. of dealers 13
Stock Furniture, collectors' items
Open Mon–Sat 10am–5pm
Sun noon–5pm

LONG HANBOROUGH

Hanborough Antiques
Contact Mrs S Holifield or Mrs L Pearce
125a–127 Main Road, Long Hanborough, Witney, Oxfordshire, OX29 8JX
☎ 01993 882767
Est. 1997 *Stock size* Medium
Stock Pine, smalls, olive pots, Islamic and Turkish rugs, new garden pots
Open Thurs–Sat 11am–5pm

MIDDLE ASTON

Cotswold Pine
Contact Mr Bob Prancks
The Poultry Unit, Middle Aston, Bicester, Oxfordshire, OX25 5QL
☎ 01869 340963 F 01869 340963
Est. 1972 *Stock size* Large
Stock General antique furniture including mahogany, oak, pine
Open Mon–Sat 9am–6pm
Sun 10am–4.30pm
Services Restorations, stripping

NETTLEBED

Nettlebed Antique Merchants (TVADA)
Contact Mr W Bicknell
1 High Street, Nettlebed, Henley-on-Thames, Oxfordshire, RG9 5DA
☎ 01491 642062 F 01491 628811
M 07770 554559
W www.nettlebedantiques.co.uk
Est. 1980 *Stock size* Large
Stock 1600–1970s from the fine to the funky, architectural, garden items
Open Mon–Sat 10am–5.30pm or by appointment
Fairs TVADA (Spring, Autumn)
Services Upholstery, restorations, finding service, copying and making furniture

NORTHMOOR

Soames Country Auctioneers
Contact Gary Martin Soame
Pinnocks Farm, Northmoor, Witney, Oxfordshire, OX29 5AY
☎ 01865 300626 F 01865 300432
E soame@msn.com
W www.soamesauctioneers.co.uk
Est. 1991
Open By appointment
Sales General antiques sales Sat 10.30am viewing Thurs noon–6pm Fri 10am–8pm
Frequency Monthly
Catalogues Yes

OXFORD

Antiques on High Ltd (TVADA)
Contact Mr P Lipson or Mrs S Young
85 High Street, Oxford, Oxfordshire, OX1 4BG
☎ 01865 251075
Est. 1997 *Stock size* Large
No. of dealers 38
Stock Smalls, collectables
Open Mon–Sat 10am–5pm
Sun Bank Holidays 11am–5pm
Services Repairs

Barclay Antiques
Contact Mr Colin Barclay
107 Windmill Road, Headington, Oxford, Oxfordshire, OX3 7BT
☎ 01865 769551
Est. 1980 *Stock size* Large
Stock China, glass, silver, bronzes, lighting
Open Mon–Sat 10am–5.30pm closed Wed
Services Repairs to lighting

Blackwell's Rare Books (ABA, PBFA)
Contact Mr P Brown
48–51 Broad Street, Oxford, Oxfordshire, OX1 3BQ
☎ 01865 333555 F 01865 794143
E rarebooks@blackwell.co.uk
W www.rarebooks.blackwell.co.uk
Est. 1879 *Stock size* Large
Stock Modern first editions, private press books, antiquarian English literature, juvenilia, general antiquarian books
Open Mon Wed–Sat 9am–6pm
Tues 9.30am–6pm
Fairs Olympia, Chelsea Book Fair, 1 American fair per year east or west coast
Services Shipping, book search

Bonhams
39 Park End Street, Oxford, Oxfordshire, OX1 1JD
☎ 01865 723524 F 01865 791064
E oxford@bonhams.com
W www.bonhams.com
Open Mon–Fri 9am–5.30pm
Sales Oxford Saleroom

Robert Clark (PBFA, ABA)
Contact Mr R Clark
6a King Street, Jericho, Oxford, Oxfordshire, OX2 6DF
☎ 01865 552154 F 01865 552154
E rclark@rarebooks.u-net.com
Est. 1984 *Stock size* Medium
Stock English 17thC books, English literature, history, theology
Open By appointment
Fairs PBFA, ABA
Services Valuations

Reginald Davis (Oxford) Ltd (BADA, NAG)
Contact David Marcus
34 High Street, Oxford, Oxfordshire, OX1 4AN
☎ 01865 248347 F 01865 200915
E davisr@mail.globalnet.co.uk
Est. 1966 *Stock size* Large
Stock Jewellery, silver, old Sheffield plate
Open Tues–Fri 9am–5pm
Sat 10am–6pm
Services Valuations, repairs, restorations

Jericho Books (PBFA)
Contact Mr F Stringer
48 Walton Street, Oxford, Oxfordshire, OX2 6AD
☎ 01865 511992
M 07870 1315166
E shop@jerichobooks.com
W www.jerichobooks.com
Est. 1996 *Stock size* Medium
Stock Rare and second-hand books
Open Mon–Sun 10am–6.30pm
Fairs Russell Square, London
Services Valuations, restorations, book search

Roger Little Antique Pottery (English Ceramic Circle)
Contact Roger Little
White Lodge, Osler Road, Headington, Oxford, Oxfordshire, OX3 9BJ
01865 762317 01865 741595
rogerlittle@hotmail.com
Est. 1985 *Stock size* Medium
Stock English and Continental pottery, tiles, 1650–1800
Open By appointment only
Fairs NEC
Services Valuations

Mallams
Contact Mr B Lloyd
Bocardo House, St Michael's Street, Oxford, Oxfordshire, OX1 2DR
01865 241358 01865 725483
oxford@mallams.co.uk
www.mallams.co.uk
Est. 1788
Open Mon–Fri 9am–5.30pm
Sales Monthly fine antiques sales Wed 11am, viewing Sat 9am–1pm Mon Tues 9am–5pm. Jewellery and silver sales Apr Jun Nov. Antique books and pictures Apr Oct Dec
Catalogues Yes

Oxford Furniture Warehouse
Contact F or P K Mitchell
272 Abingdon Road, Oxford, Oxfordshire, OX1 4TA
01865 202221 01865 202221
oxfurniture@aol.com
www.oxford-furniture.co.uk
Est. 1992 *Stock size* Large
Stock Old pine, oak and general furniture, some Continental furniture
Open Mon–Sat 10am–5.30pm Sun 11am–4.30pm

Payne and Son (Goldsmiths) Ltd (BADA, NAG)
Contact Judy Payne or David Thornton
131 High Street, Oxford, Oxfordshire, OX1 4DH
01865 243787 01865 793241
silver@payneandson.co.uk
www.payneandson.co.uk
Est. 1790 *Stock size* Large
Stock 17thC–present day silver including Arts and Crafts and contemporary designs
Open Mon–Sat 9am–5pm
Fairs BADA Chelsea, Olympia
Services Restorations

St Clements Antiques
Contact Mr G Power
93 St Clements Street, Oxford, Oxfordshire, OX4 1AR
01865 727010 01865 864690
s_c_antiques@hotmail.com
Est. 1999 *Stock size* Medium
Stock Town and country pieces from home and abroad
Open Mon–Sat 10.30am–5pm
Services Valuations

Unsworths Booksellers Ltd (ABA, PBFA, BA)
Contact Mr Charlie Unsworth
15 Turl Street, Oxford, Oxfordshire, OX1 3DQ
01865 727928 01865 727206
books@unsworths.com
www.unsworths.com
Est. 1986 *Stock size* Medium
Stock Antiquarian, second-hand and remaindered books on humanities
Open Mon–Sat 10am–6pm Sun noon–5pm
Fairs See website for details

ROTHERFIELD GREYS

The Old French Mirror Company
Contact Bridget de Breanski
Nightingales, Greys Green, Rotherfield Greys, Henley-on-Thames, Oxfordshire, RG9 4QQ
01491 629913 01491 629913
info@frenchmirrors.co.uk
www.oldfrenchmirrors.co.uk
Est. 1999 *Stock size* Large
Stock Decorative gilded and painted French mirrors, mainly 19thC
Open By appointment
Fairs Old French Mirror Fairs, House & Garden Fair Olympia
Services Shipping, restorations, re-gilding

STANDLAKE

Manor Farm Antiques
Contact Charles Gower
159 Abingdon Road, Standlake, Witney, Oxfordshire, OX8 7RL
01865 300303 01865 300153
Est. 1964 *Stock size* Large
Stock Brass, iron, wooden bedsteads
Open Mon–Sat 10am–5pm

STEVENTON

Bennett and Kerr Books (PBFA, ABA)
Contact Mr E Bennett
Millhill Warehouse, Church Lane, Steventon, Abingdon, Oxfordshire, OX13 6SW
01235 820604
bennettkerr@aol.com
Est. 1982 *Stock size* Medium
Stock Antique, scholarly books on Middle Ages, Renaissance, medieval studies
Open By appointment
Fairs PBFA, Oxford
Services Catalogues issued

TETSWORTH

Gillian Gould Antiques
Contact Gill Gould
The Swan at Tetsworth, High Street, Tetsworth, Oxfordshire, OX9 7AB
020 7419 0500 020 7419 0400
07831 150060
gillgould@dealwith.com
Est. 1989 *Stock size* Small
Stock Scientific, marine, general gifts
Open By appointment only
Services Valuations, restorations

The Swan at Tetsworth (TVADA)
Contact Rita Woodman
High Street, Tetsworth, Thame, Oxfordshire, OX9 7AB
01844 281777 01844 281770
antiques@theswan.co.uk
www.theswan.co.uk
Est. 1994 *Stock size* Large
No. of dealers 80
Stock 80 dealers in historic Elizabethan coaching inn
Open Mon–Sun 10am–6pm
Services Renowned restaurant, delivery arranged, events, shipping

THAME

Rosemary & Time
Contact Mr Tom Fletcher
42 Park Street, Thame, Oxfordshire, OX9 3HR
01844 216923

Est. 1983 **Stock size** Large
Stock Clocks
Open Tues–Sat 9am–5.30pm
Services Restorations, repairs

WALLINGFORD

Alicia Antiques
Contact Mrs A Collins
Lamb Arcade, High Street, Wallingford, Oxfordshire, OX10 0BS
01491 833737
Est. 1979 **Stock size** Medium
Stock Silver, plate, glass, small furniture
Open Mon–Sat 10am–5pm
Services Silver repairs

M & J De Albuquerque
Contact Mrs J De Albuquerque
12 High Street, Wallingford, Oxfordshire, OX10 0BP
01491 832322 F 01491 832322
E janedealb@tiscali.co.uk
Est. 1982 **Stock size** Medium
Stock 18th–19thC French and English furniture, objects of the period
Open Mon–Sat 9.30am–5.30pm
Fairs Olympia, NEC, Newark, Ardingly
Services Restorations, framing, gilding

Toby English Antiquarian & Secondhand Books (PBFA)
Contact Mr T English
10 St Mary's Street, Wallingford, Oxfordshire, OX10 0EL
01491 836389 F 01491 836389
E toby@tobyenglish.com
W www.tobyenglish.com
Est. 1984 **Stock size** Large
Stock Art, architectural, Renaissance literature, large general stock
Open Mon–Sat 9.30am–5pm
Fairs PBFA
Services Book search, valuations, catalogues issued

The Lamb Arcade (TVADA)
Contact Mrs P Hayward
83 High Street, Wallingford, Oxfordshire, OX10 0BX
01491 835166 F 01491 824247
E pdhayward@netscapeonline.co.uk
W www.thelambarcade.co.uk
Est. 1979 **Stock size** Large
No. of dealers 39
Stock Everything from period furniture to small items
Open Mon–Fri 10am–5pm Sat 10am–5.30pm

O'Donnell Antiques
Contact Lin O'Donnell
26 High Street, Wallingford, Oxfordshire, OX10 0BU
01491 839332
Est. 1974 **Stock size** Large
Stock General antiques, Georgian–early 20thC furniture, taxidermy, rugs, English pine, Oriental items, silver, Gaudy Welsh, Staffordshire
Open Mon–Sat 9.30am–5pm

Otter Antiques
Contact Mr P Otter
20 High Street, Wallingford, Oxfordshire, OX10 0BP
01491 825544 F 01865 407396
W www.otterantiques.co.uk
Est. 1994 **Stock size** Medium
Stock 18th–19thC boxes, period furniture
Open Mon–Sat 9.30am–5pm Sun 10.30am–5pm
Services Restoration of boxes

Summers Davis Antiques Ltd (TVADA, LAPADA)
Contact Mr J Driver-Jones
Calleva House, 6 High Street, Wallingford, Oxfordshire, OX10 0BP
01491 836284 F 01491 833443
E antiques@summersdavis.co.uk
W www.summersdavis.co.uk
Est. 1915 **Stock size** Large
Stock 11 showrooms. 17th–19thC English and Continental furniture
Open Mon–Fri 9am–5.30pm Sat 9am–5pm Sun 11am–5pm
Fairs TVADA

Tooley, Adams and Co (IMCOS, ABA)
Contact Steve Luck
PO Box 174, Wallingford, Oxfordshire, OX10 0YT
01491 838298 F 01491 834616
E steve@tooleys.co.uk
W www.tooleys.co.uk
Est. 1982 **Stock size** Large
Stock Antiquarian maps, atlases
Open By appointment
Fairs IMCoS, Bonnington Map Fair (monthly)
Services Valuations

WANTAGE

The Arbery Centre (TVADA)
Contact Sheila Briggs
Market Place, Wantage, Oxfordshire, OX12 8AB
01235 767331 F 01235 765242
W www.arberys.co.uk
Est. 2001 **Stock size** Large
No. of dealers 40
Stock Town and country furniture, lamps, glass, porcelain, silver, jewellery, paintings, costumes, textiles, gramophones, books, maps
Open Mon–Sat 9.30am–5pm Sun Bank Holidays 11.30am–5pm
Services Jewellery and violin restoration, tea room

WHEATLEY

Country Collections
Contact Mrs A Descenclos
47 High Street, Wheatley, Oxford, Oxfordshire, OX33 1XX
01865 875701
Est. 1992 **Stock size** Medium
Stock Small items, furniture, general antiques
Open Mon–Sat 10am–4.30pm closed Wed pm
Fairs Milton Keynes

WITNEY

Church Green Books (PBFA)
Contact Margaret or Roger Barnes
46 Market Square, Witney, Oxfordshire, OX8 6AL
01993 700822
E books@churchgreen.co.uk
W www.churchgreen.co.uk
Est. 1995 **Stock size** Medium
Stock General second-hand and antiquarian books, books on bellringing a speciality
Open Mon–Sat 10am–4pm
Services Book search

Colin Greenway Antiques (CADA)
Contact Jean Greenway
90 Corn Street, Witney, Oxfordshire, OX28 6BU

☎ 01993 705026 Ⓕ 01993 705026
Ⓜ 07831 585014
Est. 1974 *Stock size* Medium
Stock 17th–early 20thC furniture, general antiques, interesting, unusual items
Open Mon–Fri 9.30am–5.30pm Sat 10am–4pm
Services Valuations

W R Harvey & Co (Antiques) Ltd (BADA, CADA)
Contact Mr David Harvey
86 Corn Street, Witney, Oxfordshire, OX28 6BU
☎ 01993 706501 Ⓕ 01993 706601
Ⓔ antiques@wrharvey.co.uk
Ⓦ www.wrharvey.co.uk
Est. 1950 *Stock size* Large
Stock Important stock of English furniture, clocks, pictures, mirrors, works of art, 1680–1830
Open Mon–Sat 9.30am–5.30pm
Fairs Chelsea Spring & Autumn Fair, BADA, Olympia (June)
Services Valuations, restorations, conservation, buying at auction for clients

Teddy Bears of Witney
Contact Ian Pout
99 High Street, Witney, Oxfordshire, OX28 6HY
☎ 01993 702616 Ⓕ 01993 702344
Ⓦ www.teddybears.co.uk
Est. 1985 *Stock size* Large
Stock Steiff, Merrythought, Deans, Hermann, artists' bears
Open Mon–Fri 9.30am– 5.30pm Sat 9.30am–5pm Sun 10.30am–4.30pm
Services Valuations

Witney Antiques (BADA, LAPADA, CADA)
Contact Mrs C J Jarrett
96–100 Corn Street, Witney, Oxfordshire, OX28 6BU
☎ 01993 703902 Ⓕ 01993 779852
Ⓔ witneyantiques@community.co.uk
Ⓦ www.witneyantiques.com
Est. 1963 *Stock size* Large
Stock 17th–early 19thC furniture, clocks, works of art, needleworks, probably the largest selection of samplers in the UK
Open Tues Wed–Sat 10am–5pm other times by appointment
Fairs Grosvenor House, BADA
Services Restorations, catalogues

WOODSTOCK

Chris Baylis Country Chairs (TVADA)
Contact Mr C Baylis
16 Oxford Street, Woodstock, Oxfordshire, OX20 1TS
☎ 01993 813887 Ⓕ 01993 812379
Ⓔ rwood@mcmail.com
Ⓦ www.realwoodfurniture.co.uk
Est. 1979 *Stock size* Large
Stock English country chairs 1780–present day. Windsors, rush-seated ladder and spindleback chairs, kitchen chairs etc
Open Tues–Sat 10.30am–5.30pm Sun 11am–5pm

Bees Antiques (TVADA)
Contact Mr J Bateman
30 High Street, Woodstock, Oxfordshire, OX20 1TG
☎ 01993 811062
Est. 1989 *Stock size* Medium
Stock Fine 18th–19thC British and Continental ceramics, glass, jewellery, decorative furniture, metalware
Open Mon–Sat 10am–1pm 1.30–5pm Sun 11am–5pm closed Tues or by appointment
Services Valuations for ceramics, glass, jewellery

The Chair Set
Contact Allan James
18 Market Place, Woodstock, Oxfordshire, OX20 1TA
☎ 01428 707301 Ⓕ 01428 707457
Ⓔ allanjames@thechairset.com
Ⓦ www.thechairset.com
Est. 1985 *Stock size* Large
Stock 18th–19thC sets of chairs and dining room antiques
Open Mon–Sun 10.30am–5.30pm
Services Valuations, search

Span Antiques (TVADA)
Contact Mrs B Johnson or Miss R Mobey
6 Market Place, Woodstock, Oxfordshire, OX20 1TA
☎ 01993 811332
Est. 1978 *Stock size* Medium
No. of dealers 10
Stock An interesting variety of silver, decorative textiles,19th–20thC pictures, Art Deco, Art Nouveau, porcelain, books
Open Mon–Sat 10am–5pm Sun 1pm–5pm

The Woodstock Bookshop (PBFA)
Contact Mr Mark Wratten
3 Market Place, Woodstock, Oxfordshire, OX20 1SY
☎ 01993 811005 Ⓕ 01993 811005
Ⓔ markwrat@dircon.co.uk
Est. 1989 *Stock size* Small
Stock Antiquarian and second-hand books on literature, travel, topography, art, history of art, prints
Open Mon–Sun 10am–5pm closed 1–2pm
Fairs PBFA

YARNTON

Yarnton Antique Centre
Contact Mr M Dunseath
within Yarnton Nurseries, Sandy Lane, off A44, Yarnton, Kidlington, Oxfordshire, OX5 1PA
☎ 01865 379600
Est. 1998 *Stock size* Large
No. of dealers 45 (21 cabinets)
Stock Furniture, silver, china, brass, books, jewellery, lighting, decorative items
Open Mon–Sun 10am–4.30pm

MIDLANDS

DERBYSHIRE

ALFRETON

Alfreton Antique Centre
Contact Helen Dixon
✉ **11 King Street, Alfreton, Derbyshire, DE55 7AF** P
☎ 01773 520781 Ⓜ 07970 786968
Ⓔ alfretonantiques@supanet.com
Ⓦ www.alfretonantiques.supanet.com
Est. 1996 *Stock size* Large
No. of dealers 35
Stock General antiques, collectables, furniture, clocks, silver, militaria, books, postcards, lighting
Open Mon–Sat 10am–4.30pm Sun 11am–4.30pm
Services Derby replacement service

Curiosity Shop
Contact Kenneth Allsop
✉ **37 King Street, Alfreton, Derbyshire, DE55 7BY** P
☎ 01773 832429 Ⓜ 07932 7674663
Est. 1974 *Stock size* Medium
Stock General antiques
Open Mon–Sat 9.30am–5pm

ALPORT

Peter Bunting (LAPADA, BADA, CINOA)
Contact Mr P Bunting
✉ **Harthill Hall, Alport, Bakewell, Derbyshire, DE45 1LH** P
☎ 01629 636203 Ⓕ 01629 636101
Ⓜ 07860 540870
Ⓔ peter@peterbunting.com
Ⓦ www.peterbunting.com
Est. 1975 *Stock size* Medium
Stock English oak and country furniture, tapestries, portraits
Open By appointment
Fairs Olympia, NEC

ASHBOURNE

Ashbourne Antiques Ltd
Contact Robert Allsebrook
✉ **Blake House Farm, Shirely, Ashbourne, Derbyshire, DE6 3AS** P
☎ 01332 290280
Ⓜ 07970 094883
Est. 1975 *Stock size* Large
Stock 18th–20thC furniture
Open By appointment
Services Restorations, shipping

M G Bassett
Contact Mrs G Bassett or Mr M Bassett
✉ **38 Church Street, Ashbourne, Derbyshire, DE6 1AJ**
☎ 01335 300061/347750 (workshop) Ⓕ 01335 300061
Ⓔ mgbassett@aol.com
Est. 1979 *Stock size* Large
Stock General antiques
Open Mon–Sat 10am–5pm closed Wed

Daniel Charles Antiques
Contact Keith Phillips-Moul

33 Church Street, Ashbourne, Derbyshire, DE6 1AE
01335 300002 01335 348200
keith@danielcharlesantiques.com
www.danielcharlesantiques.com
Est. 2000 *Stock size* Medium
Stock 17th–20thC furniture, paintings, chandeliers, decorative items
Open Mon–Sat 10am–5pm
Services Restorations

Pamela Elsom Antiques (LAPADA)
Contact Mrs P Elsom
5 Church Street, Ashbourne, Derbyshire, DE6 1AE
01335 343468/344311
Est. 1965 *Stock size* Medium
Stock General antiques
Open Thurs–Sat 10am–5pm
Services Valuations

Hotspur & Nimrod
Contact Mrs Jarrett
14 Church Street, Ashbourne, Derbyshire, DE6 1AE
01335 342518 07718 634605
www.hotspurandnimrodantiques.co.uk
Est. 1997 *Stock size* Medium
Stock General antiques
Open Mon–Sat 10am–5pm Sun noon–4pm
Services Coffee shop

J H S Antiques Ltd (LAPADA, CINOA, Pewter Society, Metalware Society)
Contact Mr J H Snodin
41a Church Street, Ashbourne, Derbyshire, DE6 1AJ
01335 347733 07810 122248
www.antiques-atlas.com/jhs.htm
Est. 1970 *Stock size* Medium
Stock Period oak, metalware, carving, treen
Open Tues–Sat 10am–5pm closed Wed

Prestwood Antiques
Contact Mr Chris Ball
28b & 39 Church Street, Ashbourne, Derbyshire, DE6 1AJ
01335 342198 01335 342198
07976 767629
chris@spurrier-smith.co.uk
Est. 1989 *Stock size* Large
Stock General antiques
Open Mon–Sat 10am–5pm closed Wed
Services Restorations

Rose Antiques
Contact Mrs G Rose
37 Church Street, Ashbourne, Derbyshire, DE6 1AE
01335 343822 01335 343822
Est. 1984 *Stock size* Medium
Stock General antiques
Open Mon–Sat 10am–5pm closed Wed

Spurrier-Smith Antiques (LAPADA, CINOA)
Contact Mr I Spurrier-Smith
28b & 39 Church Street, Ashbourne, Derbyshire, DE6 1AE
01335 343669 01335 342198
07831 454603
ivanspurrier-smith@fsnet.com
www.spurrier-smith.co.uk
Est. 1974 *Stock size* Large
Stock General antiques, large pine warehouse, furniture, decorative items
Open Mon–Sat 10am–5pm closed Wed
Services Valuations

Top Drawer Antiques
Contact Justin Flint
30 Church Street, Ashbourne, Derbyshire, DE6 1AE
01335 342198 07966 133171
sarah@topdrawerantiques.freeserve.co.uk
Est. 1990 *Stock size* Large
Stock General antiques, pine, kitchenware, decorative items
Open Mon–Sat 10am–5pm closed Wed or by appointment
Services Restorations

Watson & Watson
Contact Mrs Lucie-Clare Watson
29 Church Street, Ashbourne, Derbyshire, DE6 1AE
01335 345796 01335 345628
info@watson-watson.co.uk
www.watson-watson.co.uk
Est. 1994 *Stock size* Medium
Stock 18th–19thC French country furniture
Open Mon–Sat 10am–5pm
Services Interior design

BAKEWELL

Chappells Antiques Centre, Bakewell (BADA)
Contact Mrs J Chappell
King Street, Bakewell, Derbyshire, DE45 1DZ
01629 812496 01629 814531
ask@chappellsantiquescentre.com
www.chappellsantiquescentre.com
Est. 1992 *Stock size* Large
No. of dealers 30
Stock 17th–20thC items
Open Mon–Sat 10am–5pm Sun 11am–5pm
Services Restoration, valuation for sale, wedding lists, finance

J Dickinson
Chappells Antiques Centre, King Street, Bakewell, Derbyshire, DE45 1DZ
01246 551370 07885 174890
Est. 1995
Stock Antique maps, 16th–19thC prints, Derbyshire books and related items
Open By appointment only
Fairs NEC and quality fairs throughout the UK
Services Valuations, restorations

G W Ford & Son Ltd (LAPADA)
Contact Mr I Thomson
Stand 1, Chappells Antique Centre, King Street, Bakewell, Derbyshire, DE45 1DZ
01246 410512 01246 419223
07740 025936
enquiries@gwfordantiques.co.uk
www.gwfordantiques.co.uk
Est. 1890 *Stock size* Small
Stock 18th–19thC mahogany, country furniture, 19thC–early 20thC sculpture, silver, Sheffield plate, treen, decorative items
Open Mon–Sat 10am–5pm Sun 11am–5pm
Services Restorations

Ganymede Antiques
Contact Keith Petts
Chappells Antiques Centre, King Street, Bakewell, Derbyshire, DE45 1DZ
0114 266 5015
ganymede@talk21.com
Est. 1992 *Stock size* Medium
Stock Scientific instruments, clocks, silver, metalwork
Open Mon–Sat 10am–5pm Sun 11am–5pm
Fairs International Antique Scientific & Medical Instrument Fair
Services Valuations, restorations

Martin and Dorothy Harper Antiques (LAPADA)
Contact Martin or Dorothy Harper
King Street, Bakewell, Derbyshire, DE45 1DZ
01629 814757 07885 347134
Est. 1971 *Stock size* Medium
Stock 18th–early 20thC furniture, metalware, decorative items
Open Tues Wed Fri Sat 10am–5pm or by appointment
Services Valuations

Michael Pembery Antiques
Contact Michael Pembery
Peppercorn House, Kings Street, Bakewell, Derbyshire, DE45 1FD
01629 814161
Est. 1967 *Stock size* Medium
Stock 17th–18thC oak and walnut furniture, Blue John, Ashford marble
Open Mon–Sat 10am–5pm closed Thurs
Services Restorations

BAMFORD

High Peak Antiques
Contact Pat Infanti
High Peak Garden Centre, Sickleholme, Bamford, Derbyshire, S33 0AH
01433 659595 07967 862093
Est. 1998 *Stock size* Large
Stock Sporting memorabilia, Flemish furniture, books, Victoriana, jewellery, Moorcroft, toys, garden items, kitchenware
Open Mon–Sun 10am–5pm

BARLOW

Hackney House Antiques
Contact Mrs J M Gorman
Hackney House, Hackney Lane, Barlow, Dronfield, Derbyshire, S18 7TF
0114 289 0248
Est. 1981 *Stock size* Medium
Stock Georgian–Edwardian furniture, silver, pictures, porcelain, glass, clocks
Open Tues–Sun 9am–6pm

BELPER

Derwentside Antiques
Contact Mr M J Adams
Derwent Street, Belper, Derbyshire, DE56 1WN
01773 828008 01773 828983
enquiries@derwentsidehomecentre.co.uk
www.derwentsidehomecentre.co.uk
Est. 1994 *Stock size* Large
Stock General antiques
Open Mon–Sun 8.30am–5.30pm
Fairs Newark, Swinderby
Services Architectural salvage

Sweetings Antiques Belper
Contact Mr or Mrs Sweeting
1 & 1a The Butts, Belper, Derbyshire, DE56 1HX
01773 825930 01773 822780
07973 658640
Est. 1972 *Stock size* Large
Stock General antiques, country pine furniture, home accessories
Open Mon–Sat 9.30am–5.30pm Sun 11am–4.30pm
Services Restorations and pine stripping

BRADWELL

Bradwell Antiques Centre
Contact Mr N Cottam
Newburgh Hall, Netherside, Bradwell, Derbyshire, S33 9JL
01433 621000 01433 621000
nick@bradwellantiques.com
www.bradwellantiques.com
Est. 2000 *Stock size* Large
No. of dealers 28
Stock Furniture, paintings, general antiques, collectables
Open Mon–Sat 10am–5pm Sun 11am–5pm
Services Licensed café, bar, booksearch, restoration

BUXTON

Antiques Warehouse
Contact Nigel Thompson
25 Lightwood Road, Buxton, Derbyshire, SK17 7BJ
01298 72967 01298 22603
07947 050552
Est. 1979 *Stock size* Large
Stock General antiques
Open Mon–Fri 10am–3pm Sat 10am–4pm Sun by appointment
Services Valuations, restorations

Back to Front
Contact Miss Simone Jordan-Lomas
9–11 Market Street, Buxton, Derbyshire, SK17 6JY
01298 23969
Est. 1974 *Stock size* Large
Stock Antique textiles
Open Mon–Sun 10am–8pm
Fairs Newark, The International Antique and Collectables Fair at RAF Swinderby
Services Seminars and valuations

A & A Needham
Contact Ann Needham
8 Cavendish Circus, Buxton, Derbyshire, SK17 6AT
01298 24546
07941 436931
Est. 1953 *Stock size* Small
Stock French, Dutch, English furniture, paintings, bronzes, works of art
Open Mon–Sat 9am–5pm
Fairs Buxton Fair, Chester

What Now Antiques
Contact Mrs L Carruthers
Unit 8, Cavendish Arcade, The Crescent, Buxton, Derbyshire, SK17 6BQ
01298 27178
Est. 1987 *Stock size* Medium
Stock General 19th–20thC antiques
Open Tues–Sat 10am–5pm Sun 1–4pm
Services Valuations, restorations

CASTLE DONNINGTON

The Gallery Book Shop
Contact Mrs J Ethelston
17 Borough Street, Castle Donnington, Derbyshire, DE74 2LA
01332 814391
Est. 2000 *Stock size* Medium
Stock Antiquarian and collectable books, prints
Open Mon–Fri 9am–4.30pm Sat 9am–1pm closed Wed
Services Picture framing

CASTLETOL

Hawkridge Books
Contact Irene or Joe Tierney
Crucu Barn, Cross Street, Castletol, Derbyshire, S33 8WH
01433 621999
www.hawkridge.co.uk
Est. 1995 *Stock size* Large

Stock Antiquarian, rare and second-hand books, ornithology
Open Mon–Fri 10am–5pm Sat 10am–5.30pm Sun noon–5.30pm

CHESTERFIELD

Ian Morris
Contact Mr I Morris
479 Chatsworth Road, Chesterfield, Derbyshire, S40 3AD
01246 235120
Est. 1974 *Stock size* Medium
Stock General antiques
Open Mon–Sat 9am–5pm

Marlene Rutherford Antiques
Contact Mrs M Rutherford
401 Sheffield Road, Whittington Moor, Chesterfield, Derbyshire, S41 8LS
01246 450209 07885 665440
Est. 1984 *Stock size* Large
Stock General antiques, upholstered furniture, oil lamps, clocks
Open Mon Tues Fri Sat 1–4pm Thurs 10am–4pm

CROMFORD

Antiques Loft
Contact Brendan Rogerson
Market Place, Cromford, Matlock, Derbyshire, DE4 3QH
01629 826565
Est. 1993 *Stock size* Large
Stock Victorian pine, shipping furniture
Open By appointment
Fairs Swinderby, Newark

DERBY

Antiques & Curios
Contact Mr McCann
8 Ashbourne Road, Derby, Derbyshire, DE22 3AA
01332 363330
Est. 2001 *Stock size* Small
Stock Furniture, ceramics
Open Mon–Sat 10am–5pm

Derventio Books
Contact Ian Briddon
43a Sadlergate, Derby, Derbyshire, DE1 3NQ
01332 343538
spikeydave@zoom.co.uk
www.derventio-books.co.uk
Est. 1996 *Stock size* Medium
Stock Antiquarian and second-hand books, antiquarian topographical prints, Derbyshire books a speciality
Open Mon–Sat 10.15am–5pm
Services On-line catalogue

Finishing Touches
Contact Lynne Robertson
224 Uttoxeter Old Road, Derby, Derbyshire, DE1 1NF
01332 721717
www.derbyantiques.co.uk
Est. 1994 *Stock size* Medium
Stock Georgian–Victorian fireplaces and fire surrounds, pine doors, locks, handles, window catches
Open Tues–Sat 10am–5.30pm

Friargate Antiques Company
Contact Glyn or Daryl Richards
120 Friargate, Derby, Derbyshire, DE1 1EX
01332 297966 01332 297966
07976 929456
daryl@friargateantiques.demon.co.uk
www.friargateantiques.co.uk
Est. 1978 *Stock size* Large
Stock General antiques, Royal Crown Derby
Open Mon–Fri 10am–4pm Sat 10am–5pm
Fairs Newark
Services Valuations, restorations

Friargate Pine Co Ltd
Contact John Marianszi
Old Pump House, Stafford Street, Derby, Derbyshire, DE1 1JL
01332 341215 01332 341215
enquiries@friargatepine.co.uk
www.friargatepine.co.uk
Est. 1984 *Stock size* Medium
Stock Antique, reproduction pine
Open Mon–Sat 9am–5pm
Services Made to measure

Brian Matsell
Contact Brian Matsell
1 Friargate Court, Friargate, Derby, Derbyshire, DE1 1HE
01332 365211 07747 702741
brian.matsell@btopenworld.com
Est. 1965 *Stock size* Medium
Stock Oriental ceramics, works of art, paintings, decorative objects
Open By appointment only
Services Buy at auction for clients

Neales Auctioneers (ARVA, SOFAA)
Contact Mr J Lewis
Becket Street, Derby, Derbyshire, DE1 1HU
01332 203601 01332 295543
derby@neales.co.uk
www.neales.co.uk
Est. 1840
Open Mon–Fri 9am–5.30pm
Sales Victorian and later sales fortnightly, quarterly antique furniture and effects sales
Frequency Fortnightly
Catalogues Yes

Rummages
Contact Mr P Lyttel
2 Monk Street, Derby, Derbyshire, DE22 3QB
01332 200590
Est. 1994 *Stock size* Small
Stock General antiques
Open Mon–Sat 9am–5pm

DUFFIELD

Wayside Antiques
Contact Brian Harding
62 Town Street, Duffield, Belper, Derbyshire, DE56 4GG
01332 840346
Est. 1976 *Stock size* Large
Stock 18th–19thC furniture
Open Mon–Sat 10am–6pm
Services Valuations

GLOSSOP

The Chair Shop
Contact Louise Jannetta
53 High Street East, Glossop, Derbyshire, SK13 8PN
01457 856389
Est. 1994 *Stock size* Medium
Stock Upholstered chairs, antique soft furnishings
Open Mon–Sat 9am–5pm
Services Restorations

Chapel Antiques
Contact Mr Norman Pogsom
126 Brookfield, Glossop, Derbyshire, SK13 6JE
01457 866711
Est. 1984 *Stock size* Medium
Stock Clocks, barometers, pottery, general antiques
Open Thurs–Sun 10am–5pm

MIDLANDS

DERBYSHIRE • HAYFIELD

Cottage Antiques
Contact Mrs J Shapter
Unit 13, Brookfield, Glossop, Derbyshire, SK13 6JF
01457 860092
Est. 1979 *Stock size* Large
Stock General antiques
Open Thurs–Sun Bank Holidays 10am–5pm
Services Valuations, restorations, house clearance

Derbyshire Clocks
Contact Terry or Judith Lees
104 High Street West, Glossop, Derbyshire, SK13 8BB
01457 862677
Est. 1971 *Stock size* Medium
Stock Clocks, barometers and other related items. Pre-1880 longcase and wall clocks
Open Thurs–Sat 9am–5pm Sun noon–4.30pm
Services Restorations

Glossop Antique Centre
Contact Mr G Conway
Brookfield, Glossop, Derbyshire, SK13 6JE
01457 863904
Stock size Medium
No. of dealers 12
Stock General antiques
Open Thurs–Sun 10am–5pm
Services Valuations, restorations, café

HAYFIELD

Paul Pickford Antiques
Contact Paul Pickford
Top of the Town, Hayfield, High Peak, Derbyshire, SK22 2JE
01663 747276/743356
07887 585891
paul@pickfordantiques.co.uk
www.pickfordantiques.co.uk
Est. 1974 *Stock size* Medium
Stock General antiques, furniture, stripped pine, light fittings
Open Tues Thurs Sat 11am–4pm Sun 1–5pm

HEANOR

Heanor Antiques Centre
Contact Jane Richards
Church Square, 1–2 Ilkeston Road, Heanor, Derbyshire, DE75 7AE
01773 531181
Est. 1997 *Stock size* Large
No. of dealers 150
Stock General antiques and small collectable items
Open Mon–Sun 10.30am–4.30pm

ILKESTON

Flourish Farm Antiques
Contact Joyce Mumford
Dale Abbey, Ilkeston, Derbyshire, DE7 4PQ
01332 667820
07970 055151
Est. 1995 *Stock size* Medium
Stock Original pine furniture, cast-iron fireplaces, doors and door fittings
Open Tues–Sat 10am–5pm Sun 11am–4pm closed Wed pm
Services Wood stripping

MATLOCK

Antique Centre
Contact Margaret O'Reilly or Keith Allsop
190 South Parade, Matlock Bath, Derbyshire, DE4 3NR
01629 582712
Est. 1970 *Stock size* Large
Stock Georgian–Edwardian furniture, upholstered furniture
Open Mon–Sun 10am–5pm or later

R F Barrett Rare Books
Contact Mr R Barrett
87 Dale Road, Matlock, Derbyshire, DE4 3LU
01629 57644
RFBarrett@gas.com
Est. 1979 *Stock size* Medium
Stock Antique, rare and second-hand books
Open Mon–Sun 10am–5pm

Country Cottage Antiques
Contact Barbara or Sally Powell
69 Matlock Green, Matlock, Derbyshire, DE43BT
01629 57109/582762
07974 954956
Est. 1983 *Stock size* Medium
Stock General antiques, upholstered chairs
Open Tues–Fri 1–5pm Wed 2–5pm Sat 11am–4.30pm or by appointment
Fairs Buxton
Services Upholstery and removals

Matlock Antiques & Collectables
Contact Miss Wendy Shirley
7 Dale Road, Matlock, Derbyshire, DE4 3LT
☎ 01629 760808 Ⓕ 01629 760808
Ⓦ www.matlock-antiques-collectables.cwc.net
Est. 1996 *Stock size* Large
No. of dealers 70
Stock General antiques, collectables
Open Mon–Sun 10am–5pm
Services Delivery, riverside café

Noel Wheatcroft & Son (FNAVA)
Contact Mrs J Kinnear
Matlock Auction Gallery, The Old Picture Palace, Dale Road, Matlock, Derbyshire, DE4 3LT
☎ 01629 57460 Ⓕ 01629 57956
Ⓔ mag@wheatcroft-noel.co.uk
Ⓦ www.wheatcroft-noel.co.uk
Est. 1923
Open Mon–Fri 10am–4pm closed Thurs
Sales Monthly sales (phone for details)
Catalogues Yes

NEW MILLS

Michael Allcroft Antiques
Contact Michael Allcroft
203 Buxton Road, Newtown, New Mills, Nr Stockport, SK12 2RA
☎ 01663 744014 Ⓕ 01663 744014
Ⓜ 07798 781642
Est. 1986 *Stock size* Large
Stock General antiques
Open Mon–Wed noon–5pm Thurs 11am–5.30pm Sat 9am–noon
Fairs Newark

Antiques & Pine Shop
Contact Mrs Pickering
2 High Street, New Mills, Derbyshire, SK22 4AL
☎ 01663 744710
Est. 1979 *Stock size* Medium
Stock Antique and pine furniture, bric-a-brac, giftware, pictures, glass
Open Thurs Fri Sat 11.30am–5.30pm or by appointment
Services House clearance

OCKBROOK

The Good Olde Days
Contact Mr S Potter
6 Flood Street, Ockbrook, Derby, Derbyshire, DE72 3RF
☎ 01332 544244
Est. 1995 *Stock size* Large
Stock General antiques
Open Tues–Sat 10am–5pm Wed noon–5pm
Fairs Newark, Cheltenham, Kettering
Services Valuations

RIDDINGS

South Street Trading Co
Contact Mr R Evison
31 South Street, Riddings, Alfreton, Derbyshire, DE55 4EJ
☎ 01773 541527 Ⓕ 01773 541527
Ⓜ 07713 514320
Ⓔ raevison@aol.com
Ⓦ www.steammodels.uk.com
Est. 1990 *Stock size* Large
Stock Old and new live steam models
Open Mon–Fri 9am–5pm

RIPLEY

A A Ambergate Antiques
Contact Mr C Lawrence
8 Derby Road, Ripley, Derbyshire, DE5 3HR
☎ 01773 745201
Ⓜ 07885 327753
Est. 1971 *Stock size* Large
Stock Edwardian bedroom furniture
Open Mon–Sat 9.30am–4.30pm
Services Valuations, restorations

Memory Lane Antiques
Contact Jim Cullen
Nottingham Road, Ripley, Derbyshire, DE5 3AS
☎ 01773 570184 Ⓜ 07703 115626
Ⓔ JamesGC1@aol.com
Est. 1993 *Stock size* Large
No. of dealers 40
Stock General antiques, collectables, shipping goods, kitchenware, Denby
Open Mon–Sun 10.30am–4pm only closed Christmas Day
Services Valuations, talks, house clearance. A permanent display of all 150+ Derby domestic ware patterns produced from 1940

Wartime Wardrobe
Contact Mr Barry Draycott
193 Church Street, Waingroves, Ripley, Derbyshire, DE5 9TF
☎ 01773 744427 Ⓕ 01773 744427
Ⓜ 07966 450726
Est. 1995 *Stock size* Medium
Stock Military and civilian1940s vintage clothing, general militaria
Open Any time by appointment
Fairs Most 1940s themed events throughout the UK, some military shows
Services Valuations, advice

SHARDLOW

Shardlow Antiques
Contact Nina or Nigel
24 The Wharf, Shardlow, Derbyshire, DE72 2GH
☎ 01332 792899
Est. 1977 *Stock size* Large
Stock Georgian furniture, general antiques
Open Mon–Thurs 10.30am–5pm Sat 10am–5pm Sun noon–5pm
Fairs Newark

WHALEY BRIDGE

Nimbus Antiques
Contact Mr H C Brobbin
14 Chapel Road, Whaley Bridge, High Peak, Derbyshire, SK23 7JZ
☎ 01663 734248 Ⓕ 01663 734248
Ⓔ nimbusantiques@hotmail.com
Ⓦ www.antiques-atlas.com/nimbus.htm
Est. 1979 *Stock size* Large
Stock General antiques, Georgian–Victorian furniture and clocks
Open Mon–Fri 9am–5.30pm Sat 10am–5.30pm Sun 2–5.30pm

LEICESTERSHIRE

ASHBY DE LA ZOUCH

Affordable Antiques
Contact Mrs J Sidwells
The Old Forge, North Street, Ashby de la Zouch, Leicestershire, LE65 1HS
☎ 01530 413744 Ⓜ 07966 424861
Est. 1994 *Stock size* Medium
Stock Pre-1950s furniture and effects

MIDLANDS

LEICESTERSHIRE • COALVILLE

Open Mon–Sat 10am–5pm
closed Wed
Fairs Newark, Swinderby
Services Pine, oak stripping

COALVILLE

Keystone Antiques (LAPADA)
Contact Miss H McPherson
9 Ashby Road, Coalville, Leicestershire, LE67 3LF
☎ 01530 835966 F 01530 817773
E heather@heathermcpherson.co.uk
Est. 1980 *Stock size* Medium
Stock General antiques, jewellery, silver, small collectables
Open Mon–Wed by appointment
Thurs–Sat 10am–5pm
Fairs NEC
Services Valuations

EARL SHILTON

The Glory Hole
Contact Mark Crowston
69 High Street, Earl Shilton, Leicestershire, LE9 7DH
☎ 01455 847922 M 07710 101364
W www.gloryholeantiques.co.uk
Est. 1994 *Stock size* Large
Stock Victorian–Edwardian furniture, general antiques
Open Mon–Sat 10am–5.30pm
Sun 10am–4pm
Fairs Newark, Ardingly
Services Restorations, door and furniture stripping

EAST LEAKE

Booklore (SOBB)
Contact Mr R Corbett
4 Brookside, East Leake, Loughborough, Leicestershire, LE12 6PB
☎ 01509 852044 F 01509 852044
Est. 1994 *Stock size* Medium
Stock Antiquarian and collectable books, maps
Open Mon–Sat 9.30am–5.30pm
Wed 9.30am–1.30pm
Fairs Buxton Book Fair, Bloomsbury
Services Restorations, binding

GREAT GLAN

Sitting Pretty
Contact Mrs J Jones-Fenleigh
45a Main Street, Great Glan, Leicestershire, LE8 9EH
☎ 01162 593711
Est. 1979 *Stock size* Medium
Stock Antique furniture
Open Thurs–Sat 10am–6pm
Services Upholstery restoration

GRIMSTON

Ancient and Oriental Ltd (ADA)
Contact Mr Alex Szolin
Park View, Grimston, Melton Mowbray, Leicestershire, LE14 3BZ
☎ 01664 812044
E alex@antiquities.co.uk
W www.antiquities.co.uk
Est. 1992
Stock Ancient art and items of archaeological interest from major world cultures, ancient–medieval
Open By appointment
Services Mail order, catalogues and website

HINCKLEY

House Things Antiques
Contact P Robertson
44 Mansion Street, Trinity Lane, Hinckley, Leicestershire, LE10 0AU
☎ 01455 618518
Est. 1976 *Stock size* Medium
Stock General antiques
Open Mon–Sat 10am–6pm
closed Tues
Services Valuations, restorations

Magpie Antiques & Collectables
Contact Michelle Johnston
126 Castle Street, Hinckley, Leicestershire, LE10 1DD
☎ 01455 891819 M 07713 099744
Est. 1983 *Stock size* Medium
Stock Antique furniture, collectables, pre-1950s ephemera and effects
Open Mon–Sat 9am–5pm

HOBY

Withers of Leicester
Contact Simon Frings
The Old Rutland, 6 Regent Road, Hoby, Leicestershire, LE14 3DU
☎ 01664 434803 M 07836 526595
Est. 1860 *Stock size* Medium
Stock 17th–early 20thC furniture
Open Mon–Sat phone first
Services Valuations, restorations

KIBWORTH

Kibworth Pine Co
Contact Mrs Burdett
16 Harcourt Estate, Kibworth, Leicestershire, LE8 0NE
☎ 0116 279 3475
W www.kibworthpinecompany.com
Est. 1981 *Stock size* Large
Stock Antique pine furniture
Open Tues–Sat 9.30am–5.30pm
Sun noon–4pm

LEICESTER

Betty's Antiques
Contact Mr A Smith
9 Knighton Fields Road West, Leicester, Leicestershire, LE2 6LH
☎ 0116 283 9048
Est. 1983 *Stock size* Small
Stock General antiques
Open Mon–Sat 10am–5pm

The Black Cat Bookshop
Contact Mr P Woolley
90 Charles Street, Leicester, Leicestershire, LE1 1GE
☎ 01162 512756 F 01162 813545
E blackcatuk@aol.com
W www.blackcatbookshop.com
Est. 1987 *Stock size* Large
Stock Antiquarian, rare and second-hand books, British comics, magazines, printed ephemera
Open Mon–Sat 9.30am–5pm
Fairs Memorabilia Fair (NEC)
Services Worldwide mail order, book search, catalogues

Churchgate Auctions Ltd
Contact Mr D Dearman
66 Churchgate, Leicester, Leicestershire, LE1 4AL
☎ 01162 621416 F 01162 517711
E info@churchgateauctions.co.uk
W www.churchgateauctions.co.uk
Est. 1966
Open Mon–Fri 8.30am–6pm
Sat 8.30am–noon
Sales General and antiques sales Fri 10am viewing Thurs 2–6pm
Frequency Weekly
Catalogues Yes

⊞ Clarendon Books (PBFA)
Contact Mr J Smith
✉ **144 Clarendon Park Road, Leicester, Leicestershire, LE2 3AE** P
☎ 01162 701856 F 01162 709020
M 07710 683996
E clarendonbooks@aol.com
Est. 1986 *Stock size* Medium
Stock Antiquarian, rare and second-hand books
Open Mon–Sat 10am–5pm
Fairs PBFA

⊞ Corry's Antiques (LAPADA)
Contact Mrs E I Corry
✉ **26 Francis Street, Stoneygate, Leicester, Leicestershire, LE2 2BD** P
☎ 01162 703794 F 01162 703794
W www.corrys-antiques.com
Est. 1964 *Stock size* Large
Stock General antiques, clocks, mirrors
Open Mon–Sat 10am–5pm
Fairs LAPADA
Services Restorations

Key to Symbols
- ⊞ Dealer
- Auction House
- Antiques Centre
- ✉ Address
- P Parking
- ☎ Telephone No.
- M Mobile No.
- F Fax No.
- E E-mail address
- W Web Address

⊞ John Hardy Antiques
Contact John Hardy
✉ **91 London Road, Oadby, Leicester, Leicestershire, LE2 5DP** P
☎ 01162 7128622
Est. 1969 *Stock size* Medium
Stock General antiques
Open Mon–Sat 10am–6pm

Heathcote Ball and Co Fine Art Auctioneers & Valuers
Contact Stuart West
✉ **Castle Auction Rooms, 78 St Nicholas Circle, Leicester, Leicestershire, LE1 5NW** P
☎ 01162 536789 F 01162 538517
E heathcote-ball@clara.co.uk
W www.heathcote-ball.clara.co.uk
Est. 1977
Open Mon–Fri 9am–1pm 2–5.30pm
Sales General antiques and fine art sales (phone for details)
Frequency 5 to 6 weeks
Catalogues Yes

Leicester Antiques Warehouse
✉ **Clarkes Road, Wigston, Leicester, Leicestershire, LE18 2BG** P
☎ 0116 288 1315 F 0116 281 1742
E webmaster@antiques-of-britain.co.uk
W www.antiques-of-britain.co.uk
Est. 2002 *Stock size* Large
No. of dealers 60
Stock General antiques, collectables
Open Tues–Sat 10am–5pm Sun noon–5pm

⊞ Letty's Antiques
Contact Mr Dubberley
✉ **6 Rutland Street, Leicester, Leicestershire, LE1 1RA**
☎ 01162 626435
M 07050 163532
Est. 1952 *Stock size* Small
Stock General antiques, jewellery and silver
Open Mon–Sat 9.30am–4.45pm closed Thurs except Nov Dec
Services Free verbal valuations

⊞ Oxford Street Antique Centre
Contact Mr P Giles
✉ **16–26 Oxford Street, Leicester, Leicestershire, LE1 5XU** P
☎ 0116 2553006 F 0116 2555863
Est. 1987 *Stock size* Large
Stock Victorian to present-day furniture
Open Mon–Fri 10am–5.30pm Sat 10am–5pm Sun 2–5pm
Services Export, container packing

⊞ Retrobuy
Contact Mr Mark Williamson
✉ **62 Silver Arcade, Leicester, Leicestershire, LE1 5FB**
☎ 0116 242 5949 F 0116 242 5949
E retrobuy@ntlworld.com
W www.retrobuy.co.uk
Est. 1997 *Stock size* Large
Stock Retro toys, clothes, arcade, home, music, records
Open Mon–Sat noon–5pm
Fairs NEC, Donnington
Services Valuations, Mail order

⊞ The Rug Gallery
Contact Mr R Short
✉ **50 Montague Road, Leicester, Leicestershire, LE2 1TH**
☎ 01162 700085 F 01162 700113

MIDLANDS

LEICESTERSHIRE • LOUGHBOROUGH

Est. 1987 *Stock size* Large
Stock Old and new Oriental rugs and Kilims, antique Oriental furniture
Open Fri Sat 10am–4pm or by appointment

⊞ Treasure Trove Books
Contact Linda Sharman
✉ **21 Mayfield Road, Leicester, Leicestershire, LE2 1SR** Ⓟ
☎ 0116 2755933
ⓔ info@horizon-books.co.uk
Est. 1993 *Stock size* Medium
Stock Second-hand books, records (pop and classical), CDs, tapes
Open Mon–Sat 9.30am–5.30pm
Fairs Leicestershire, Missing Book Fair

Warner Auctions Ltd
Contact Amanda Harding
✉ **52 Sanvey Gate, Leicester, Leicestershire, LE1 4BQ** Ⓟ
☎ 01162 512510 ⓕ 01162 510204
ⓔ enquiries@warnerauctions.co.uk
ⓦ www.warnerauctions.co.uk
Est. 1846
Open Mon–Fri 9am–5.30pm
Sales General sale Wed 10.30am, viewing Tues noon–6pm Wed 9–10.30am prior to sale. Antiques and fine art sale quarterly Wed 11am, viewing Tues 9am–5pm Wed 9–11am prior to sale, also occasional books and collectors' sales
Frequency Fortnightly
Catalogues Yes

⊞ West End Antiques
Contact Mrs C Vaughan
✉ **1 Lothair Road, Aylestone Road, Leicester, Leicestershire, LE2 7QE** Ⓟ
☎ 0116 2440086
Est. 1985 *Stock size* Medium
Stock General antiques
Open Tues–Sat 10am–4.30pm
Fairs Donnington

LOUGHBOROUGH

⊞ Malcolm Hornsby
Contact Mr Malcolm Hornsby
✉ **41 Church Gate, Loughborough, Leicestershire, LE11 1UE** Ⓟ
☎ 01509 269860 ⓕ 01509 269860
ⓔ hornsby@webleicester.co.uk
Est. 1969 *Stock size* Large
Stock Antique, rare and second-hand books, eastern Mediterranean travel books a speciality
Open Mon–Sat 9.30am–5.30pm

⊞ Loughborough Antiques Centre
Contact Richard or Carol Wesley
✉ **50 Market Street, Loughborough, Leicestershire, LE11 3ER**
☎ 01509 239931
Est. 1979 *Stock size* Medium
Stock General antiques, jewellery, clocks
Open Tues Thurs–Sat 10am–5pm
Fairs NEC, Newark
Services Valuations

⊞ Lowe of Loughborough
Contact Richard Lowe
✉ **37–40 Church Gate, Loughborough, Leicestershire, LE11 1UE** Ⓟ
☎ 01509 212554/217876
Est. 1846 *Stock size* Medium
Stock Furniture, clocks, maps
Open Mon–Fri 8am–5.30pm
Services Restorations

LUBENHAM

⊞ Oaktree Antiques
Contact Gillian Abraham
✉ **The Drapers House, Main Street, Lubenham, Market Harborough, Leicestershire, LE16 9TF** Ⓟ
☎ 01858 410041
ⓦ www.oaktreeantiques.co.uk
Stock size Large
Stock Town and country 17th–19thC furniture, longcase clocks, works of art
Open Wed–Sun 10am–6pm

MARKET BOSWORTH

⊞ Bosworth Antiques
Contact Mr J H Thorp
✉ **12 Main Street, Market Bosworth, Leicestershire, CV13 0JW** Ⓟ
☎ 01455 292134
Est. 1986 *Stock size* Medium
Stock General antiques and collectables
Open Mon–Sat 10am–5pm closed Tues
Services Valuations

⊞ Corner Cottage Antiques
Contact Jill or Bob Roberts
✉ **7 Market Place, Market Bosworth, Leicestershire, CV13 0LF** Ⓟ
☎ 01455 282583 ⓜ 07909 920903
ⓔ bobandjill@btinternet.com
Est. 1969 *Stock size* Large
Stock 18th–early 20thC furniture, silver, porcelain, copper, brass, glass, oil lamps
Open Tues–Sat 10am–5pm
Fairs Newark

MARKET HARBOROUGH

⊞ Aquarius Books
Contact Mr R Lack
✉ **17 St Marys Road, Market Harborough, Leicestershire, LE16 7DS**
☎ 01858 431060
ⓦ www.aquariusbooks.co.uk
Est. 1989 *Stock size* Medium
Stock Antiquarian, rare and second-hand books
Open Mon–Sat 10am–4pm

Bonhams
✉ **34 High Street, Market Harborough, Leicestershire, BN3 2JN** Ⓟ
☎ 01858 438900 ⓕ 01858 438909
ⓔ marketharborough@bonhams.com
ⓦ www.bonhams.com
Est. 1793
Open Mon–Fri 9am–1pm 2–5pm
Catalogues Yes

⊞ The Furniture Barn
Contact Richard Kimbell
✉ **Rockingham Road, Market Harborough, Leicestershire, LE16 7QE** Ⓟ
☎ 01858 433444 ⓕ 01858 461301
ⓦ www.thefurniturebarn.com
Est. 1969 *Stock size* Medium
Stock Antique, pine and country furniture, upholstery, end-of-line fabrics
Open Mon Tues Wed Fri 10am–6pm Thurs 10am–8pm Sat 9am–6pm Sun 10.30am–4.30pm

Gildings
Contact John Gilding
✉ **Roman Way, Market Harborough, Leicestershire, LE16 7PQ** Ⓟ
☎ 01858 410414 ⓕ 01858 432956
ⓔ sales@gildings.co.uk
ⓦ www.gildings.co.uk

Est. 1980
Open Mon–Fri 9am–5pm
Sales Regular fine art, antiques, specialist sales, weekly Victoriana and collectables sales
Frequency Monthly
Catalogues Yes

Mosstique
Contact Mrs Andre C Moss
6 Adam & Eve Street, Market Harborough, Leicestershire, LE16 7LT
01858 469448 F 01604 882399
M 07889 365423
E mossfairs@hotmail.com
Est. 1995 *Stock size* Medium
No. of dealers 6
Stock Collectables, furniture, books, ephemera, militaria, commemoratives, postcards, cigarette cards
Open Mon–Sun 10am–4pm

J Stamp & Sons
Contact Mark Stamp
The Chestnuts, 15 Kettering Road, Market Harborough, Leicestershire, LE16 8AN
01858 462524 F 01858 465643
Est. 1946 *Stock size* Medium
Stock Georgian–Edwardian furniture
Open Mon–Fri 8.30am–5.30pm Sat 9am–1pm or by appointment
Services Valuations, restorations

MELTON MOWBRAY

Flagstones Pine and Country Furniture
Contact Julie Adcock
24 Burton Street, Melton Mowbray, Leicestershire, LE13 1AF
01664 566438 M 07971 299206
Est. 1984 *Stock size* Medium
Stock Pine and country furniture, old and reproduction lighting, accessories
Open Mon–Sat 9.30am–5.15pm Sun 10.30am–3.30pm
Services Stripping service, custom-built furniture

NARBOROUGH

Ken Smith Antiques Ltd (LAPADA)
Contact Mr K Smith
215–217 Leicester Road, Narborough, Leicester, Leicestershire, LE9 5BE
0116 286 2341
E KSL@kensmithltd.co.uk
W www.kensmithltd.co.uk
Est. 1888 *Stock size* Medium
Stock General antiques, furniture and collectables
Open Mon–Sat 9.30am–5pm
Fairs Newark

OSGATHORPE

David E Burrows Antiques (LAPADA)
Contact Mr David Burrows
Manor House Farm, Osgathorpe, Loughborough, Leicestershire, LE12 9SY
01530 222218 F 01530 223139
E david.burrows2@virgin.net
Est. 1970 *Stock size* Large
Stock Pine, oak, mahogany and walnut furniture, clocks, pictures
Trade only Yes
Open By appointment
Services Valuations, shipping

David Stanley Auctions
Contact David Stanley
Stordon Grange, Osgathorpe, Loughborough, Leicestershire, LE12 9SR
01530 222320 F 01530 222523
E auctions@davidstanley.com
W www.davidstanley.com
Est. 1979
Open Mon–Sat 8am–5pm
Sales Antique woodwork tools (phone for details)
Frequency Bi-monthly
Catalogues Yes

QUENIBOROUGH

J Green & Son
Contact Mr R Green
1 Coppice Lane, Queniborough, Leicestershire, LE7 3DR
01162 606682 F 01162 606682
M 07860 513121
Est. 1949 *Stock size* Medium
Stock Georgian and period furniture
Open By appointment

QUORN

Quorn Pine
Contact Steven Yates or Steven Parker
The Mills, Leicester Road, Quorn, Leicestershire, LE12 8ES
01509 416031 F 01509 416051
W www.quorn-pine.co.uk
Est. 1983 *Stock size* Large
Stock Mainly antique pine and country furniture, clocks, doors, fireplaces
Open Mon–Fri 9am–6pm Sat 9.30am–5.30pm Sun 2–5pm
Services Restorations, door stripping

SEAGRAVE

Miller Services
Contact Robert Miller
43–45 Swan Street, Seagrave, Leicestershire, LE12 7NN
01509 812037 F 01509 812037
Est. 1986
Open Mon–Fri 9am–5pm Sat 10am–12.30pm
Sales Monthly antiques and jewellery sales, Seagrave Village Hall, Sun 12.30pm, viewing 10am
Frequency Monthly
Catalogues Yes

Miller Services
Contact Robert Miller
43–45 Swan Street, Seagrave, Leicestershire, LE12 7NN
01509 812037 F 01509 812037
Est. 1986
Stock Pottery, glass, silver
Open Mon–Fri 9am–5pm Sat 10am–12.30pm
Fairs Arthur Swallow, DMG
Services Auctions, valuations

SWINFORD

Old Timers (BHI)
Contact Mr M Harris
High Street, Swinford, Lutterworth, Leicestershire, LE17 6BL
01788 860311 F 01788 860311
M 07836 505111
W www.old-timers.co.uk
Est. 1993 *Stock size* Medium
Stock Antique clocks including longcase, furniture
Open Mon–Sat 9am–5pm Sun 10am–1.30pm advised to call first
Services Valuations, restorations

WHITWICK

⊞ Charles Antiques
Contact Mr Haydon
✉ **3 Market Place, Whitwick, Leicestershire, LE67 5AE** 🅿
☎ 01530 836982 Ⓜ 07831 204406
Ⓔ charles.antiques@btopenworld.com
Est. 1973 *Stock size* Large
Stock Clocks, furniture, ceramics
Open Fri Sat 10am–5pm or by appointment
Fairs Birmingham Motorcycle Museum

WOODHOUSE EAVES

⊞ Paddock Antiques
Contact Carole Bray
✉ **The Old Smithy, Brand Hill, Woodhouse Eaves, Loughborough, Leicestershire, LE1 5SS** 🅿
☎ 01509 890264 Ⓜ 07860 785325
Est. 1974 *Stock size* Large
Stock Porcelain, small furniture
Open Tues Fri Sat 9.30am–5.30pm
Fairs NEC, Shepton Mallet
Services Valuations, restorations

WYMESWOLD

⊞ N F Bryan-Peach Antiques
Contact Mr N Bryan-Peach
✉ **28 Far Street, Wymeswold, Loughborough, Leicestershire, LE12 6TZ** 🅿
☎ 01509 880425 Ⓕ 01509 880425
Ⓜ 07860 559590
Ⓔ norm@bryanpeach.demon.co.uk
Ⓦ www.country-focus.co.uk/antiques
Est. 1974 *Stock size* Medium
Stock 18th–19thC furniture, clocks, barometers
Open Mon–Sat 9.30am–5pm closed Thurs
Services Valuations, restorations

WYMONDHAM

⊞ The Old Bakery Antiques
Contact Mrs T Bryan
✉ **The Old Bakery, Main Street, Wymondham, Melton Mowbray, Leicestershire, LE14 2AG** 🅿
☎ 01572 787472
Est. 1990 *Stock size* Medium
Stock Antique kitchenware, pine, stained glass, door hardware, chimney pots, tiles, decorative items, garden items, architectural antiques
Open Mon–Sat 10am–5.30pm closed Thurs

NORTHAMPTONSHIRE

BRACKLEY

⌂ The Brackley Antique Cellar
Contact Debby Perry
✉ **Drayman's Walk, Brackley, Northamptonshire, NN13 6BE** 🅿
☎ 01280 841841 Ⓕ 01280 841851
Est. 2000 *Stock size* Large
No. of dealers 102
Stock General antiques, smalls, collectables, furniture, militaria
Open Mon–Sun 10am–5pm
Services Valuations, restorations, tea room

⊞ Brackley Antiques
Contact Mrs B H Nutting
✉ **69 High Street, Brackley, Northamptonshire, NN13 7BW** 🅿

☎ 01280 703362 Ⓕ 01280 703362
Ⓜ 07761 443726
Est. 1979 *Stock size* Medium
Stock General antiques
Open Mon–Sat 10am–6pm
Wed by appointment
Services Traditional upholstery

Juno Antiques
Contact Mrs van Bergen
4 Bridge Street, Brackley, Northamptonshire, NN13 7EP
☎ 01280 700639
Est. 1983 *Stock size* Medium
Stock General antiques
Open Tues–Sat 10am–1pm 2–5pm
closed Wed

The Old Hall Bookshop (ABA, PBFA, ILAB)
Contact Tom Dixon
32 Market Place, Brackley, Northamptonshire, NN13 7DP Ⓟ
☎ 01280 704146 Ⓕ 01280 705131
Ⓔ books@oldhallbooks.com
Ⓦ www.oldhallbooks.com
Est. 1977 *Stock size* Large
Stock A wide range of second-hand and antiquarian books
Open Mon–Fri 9.30am–5.30pm
Sat 9.30am–1pm 2–5.30pm
Fairs ABA, PBFA
Services Book search for out-of-print books

EVENLEY

Amors of Evenley
Contact Mr Amor
Evenley, Brackley, Northamptonshire, NN13 5SB Ⓟ
☎ 01869 811342
Ⓔ amorsofevenley@hotmail.com
Est. 1960 *Stock size* Large
No. of dealers 6
Stock 17th–19thC furniture, porcelain, ceramics, paintings
Open Mon–Sat 9am–5.30pm
Sun 10am–4pm
Services Valuations, house clearance

FINEDON

Antiques en France
Contact Mr K Day
3 Church Street, Finedon, Wellingborough, Northamptonshire, NN9 5NA Ⓟ
☎ 01933 682515 Ⓕ 01933 682951
Ⓔ kenday@btinternet.com
Est. 1994 *Stock size* Large
Stock General French and English decorative furniture
Open Mon–Sat 9.30am–5.30pm
Sun by appointment
Services Valuations, shipping

Aspidistra Antiques (RADS)
Contact Patricia Moss
51 High Street, Finedon, Wellingborough, Northamptonshire, NN9 9JN Ⓟ
☎ 01933 680196 Ⓕ 01933 680196
Ⓜ 07768 071948
Ⓔ aspidistra@patandgeoff.demon.co.uk
Ⓦ www.aspidistra.antiques.com
Est. 1994 *Stock size* Medium
No. of dealers 6
Stock Specialist in decorative arts, good selection of smalls and furniture, 1960s–1970s items
Open Mon–Sat 10am–5pm
Sun 11am–5pm
Services Valuations, commission sales, restoration

Simon Banks Antiques
Contact Mr S Banks
28 Church Street, Finedon, Wellingborough, Northamptonshire, NN9 5NA Ⓟ
☎ 01933 680371 Ⓜ 07976 787539
Est. 1984 *Stock size* Large
Stock General antiques, dining room furniture, clocks, silver, silver plate, pottery, porcelain
Open Mon–Fri 10am–5.30pm
Sat 10am–5.30pm
Sun 11am–4.30pm
Services Valuations

Robert Cheney Antiques
Contact Robert Cheney
11–13 High Street, Finedon, Wellingborough, Northamptonshire, NN9 5JN Ⓟ
☎ 01933 681048 Ⓜ 07939 373901
Est. 1992 *Stock size* Medium
Stock General antiques
Open Mon–Sat 9am–5pm
Sun 11am–4pm
Services Valuations and house clearances

E K Antiques
Contact E Kubacki
37 High Street, Finedon, Northamptonshire, NN9 5JN Ⓟ
☎ 01933 681882 Ⓜ 07711 245530
Est. 1991 *Stock size* Medium
Stock General antiques
Open Mon–Sat 9.30am–5pm
Sun 11am–4pm
Fairs Hinchingbrooke, Hunts
Services Valuations, restorations, house clearance

Finedon Antiques Ltd (LAPADA)
Contact Roy Kirkpatrick, Michael Chapman or Stephen Burnett
11–25 Bell Hill, Finedon, Wellingborough, Northamptonshire, NN9 5ND Ⓟ
☎ 01933 681260/682210
Ⓕ 01933 682210
Ⓔ sales@finedonantiques.com
Ⓦ www.finedonantiques.com
Est. 1972 *Stock size* Large
No. of dealers 35
Stock 18th–19thC English and French furniture, pottery, porcelain, decorative items
Open Mon–Sat 9am–5.30pm
Sun 11am–5pm
Services Valuations, restorations

Village Antiques
Contact John Kerti
59 High Street, Finedon, Northamptonshire, NN9 5JN Ⓟ
☎ 01933 681522 Ⓜ 07951 071896
Est. 2000 *Stock size* Small
Stock Furniture
Open Mon–Sun 9am–6pm

FLORE

Richard Sear
Contact Mr Richard Sear
The Huntershields, The Avenue, Flore, Northampton, Northamptonshire, NN7 4LZ Ⓟ
☎ 01327 340718 Ⓕ 01327 349263
Est. 1964 *Stock size* Medium
Stock General antiques, 17th–19thC metalwork, replicas, decorative items
Open Mon–Fri 10am–6pm
Sat Sun by appointment
Fairs Newark, Stoneleigh
Services Valuations

GUILSBOROUGH

Nick Goodwin Exports
Contact Mr N Goodwin
The Firs, Nortoft, Guilsborough, Northamptonshire, NN6 8QB Ⓟ
☎ 01604 740234 Ⓕ 01604 740827
Est. 1974 *Stock size* Medium

MIDLANDS

Stock General antiques
Open By appointment
Fairs Ardingly, Swinderby
Services Packing, shipping

HARPOLE

Inglenook Antiques
Contact Tony or Pamela Havard
23 High Street, Harpole, Northamptonshire, NN7 4DH
01604 830007
Est. 1971 *Stock size* Small
Stock Small country items, copper, brass, Victoriana, general antiques
Open Mon–Sat 9am–6.30pm
Services Longcase clock restoration

IRTHLINGBOROUGH

Hock & Dough Antiques
Contact Brian F Knight
82 High Street, Irthlingborough, Northamptonshire, NN7 4DH
01933 650109
Est. 1919 *Stock size* Small
Stock Silver, general antiques
Open By appointment
Services Valuations, restorations

KETTERING

Dragon Antiques
Contact Sandra Hunt
85 Rockingham Road, Kettering, Northamptonshire, NN16 8LA
01536 517017
Est. 1982 *Stock size* Small
Stock General antiques, paintings
Open Mon–Sat 10am–4pm closed Thurs
Services Picture framing, restoration

John Roe Antiques
Contact Mr John Roe
Furnace Site, Kettering Road, Kettering, Northamptonshire, NN14 3JW
01832 732937 F 01832 732937
Est. 1969 *Stock size* Large
Stock General antique furniture
Open Mon–Fri 9am–6pm Sat 10am–5pm Sun by appointment
Fairs Newark
Services Shipping, packing

NORTHAMPTON

Cave's
Contact Allan Cave
111 Kettering Road, Northampton, Northamptonshire, NN1 4BA
01604 638278 F 01604 230177
Est. 1879 *Stock size* Large
Stock Georgian furniture
Open Mon–Sat 9am–5.30pm closed Thurs

Laila Gray Antiques
Contact Ms L Gray
25 Welford Road, Northampton, Northamptonshire, NN2 8AQ
01604 715277 F 01604 715277
M 07941 263236
Est. 1984 *Stock size* Medium
Stock Antique pine furniture
Open By appointment
Fairs Newark, Swinderby
Services Restorations, stripping

Legends
Contact Paul Edwards
4 Victoria Road, Northampton, Northamptonshire, NN1 5ED
01604 473133 F 01604 473881
E legends@myth-and-magic.co.uk
W www.myth-and-magic.co.uk
Est. 1996 *Stock size* Large
Stock Tudor Mint, pewter, Myth and Magic crystal figures
Open Mon–Sat 10am–5pm
Services Valuations for insurance, mail order worldwide

Merry's Auctions
Contact Mrs Denise Cowling FGA
Northampton Auction & Sales Centre, Liliput Road, Brackmills, Northampton, Northamptonshire, NN4 7BY
01604 769990 F 01604 763155
M 0781 800 3786
E denise@northantsauctions,co.uk
W www.northantsauctions.com
Est. 1815
Open Mon–Fri 9am–5pm or by appointment
Sales Bi-monthly antique, fine art and collectables sale. Victorian, later and general antiques sale twice per month. Bar and cafeteria
Catalogues Yes

Giuseppe Miceli (OMRS)
Contact Mr Giuseppe Miceli
204 Bants Lane, Northampton, Northamptonshire, NN5 6AH
01604 581533
Est. 1969 *Stock size* Medium
Stock Coins, medals
Open Mon–Sat 9am–6pm
Services Valuations

The Old Brigade
Contact Mr S Wilson
10a Harborough Road, Kingsthorpe, Northampton, Northamptonshire, NN2 7AZ
01604 719389 F 01604 712489
E theoldbrigade@easynet.co.uk
W www.theoldbrigade.co.uk
Est. 1985 *Stock size* Medium
Stock 1850–1945 militaria, Third Reich
Open Mon–Sat 10.30am–5pm by appointment only
Services Valuations

OUNDLE

Goldsmiths Howard
Contact Mr Ian Goldsmith
15 Market Place, Oundle, Northamptonshire, PE8 4BA
01832 272349 F 01832 275000
E goldsmithshoward@goldsmithshoward.co.uk
W www.goldsmithshoward.co.uk
Est. 1964
Open Mon–Fri 9am–6.30pm Sat 9am–4pm Sun 11am–3pm
Sales Antiques sales Sat 10.30am, viewing Fri 2.30–6pm and sale day 9–10.30am. Sale room is at South Road, Oundle
Frequency Bi-monthly
Catalogues Yes

POTTERSPURY

Reindeer Antiques Ltd (LAPADA, BADA)
Contact John Butterworth or Nicholas Fuller
43 Watling Street, Potterspury, Northamptonshire, NN12 7QD
01908 542407/542200
F 01908 542121 M 07711 446221
E nicholas@reindeerantiques.co.uk
W www.reindeerantiques.co.uk
Est. 1969 *Stock size* Large
Stock Early 17th–mid-19thC fine English furniture, 17thC–contemporary works of art
Open Mon–Fri 9am–6pm

Sat Sun by appointment, phone call advisable
Fairs BADA, LAPADA
Services Valuations, restorations

Tillmans Antiques
Contact Nick Tillman
Wakefield Country Courtyard, Wakefield Farm, Potterspury, Northamptonshire, NN12 7QX P
☎ 01327 811882 Ⓜ 07711 570798
Ⓔ nick_tillman@lineone.net
Est. 1999 *Stock size* Medium
No. of dealers 17
Stock Porcelain, silver, glass, small range of furniture, pictures
Open Wed–Sat 10am–5pm
Sun Bank Holidays 10.30am–4.30pm

RUSHDEN

Magpies
Contact Mr J E Ward
1 East Grove, Rushden, Northamptonshire, NN10 0AP P
☎ 01933 411404
Est. 1994 *Stock size* Medium
Stock General antiques
Open Mon–Sat 10am–5pm
Sun noon–4pm

D W Sherwood Ltd
Contact Mrs S Sherwood
59 Little Street, Rushden, Northamptonshire, NN10 0LS P
☎ 01933 353265
Est. 1959 *Stock size* Large
Stock General antiques, paintings, clocks, furniture, prints, maps, glass, china, lace bobbins
Open Tues–Sat 11am–5pm closed Thurs
Services Valuations

THRAPSTON

Southam & Sons (RICS)
Contact Mr N Croskell
Corn Exchange, High Street, Thrapston, Kettering, Northamptonshire, NN14 4JJ P
☎ 01832 734486 Ⓕ 01832 732409
Est. 1900
Open Mon–Fri 9am–5pm
Sales Antiques, sporting memorabilia, guns, household
Frequency Monthly
Catalogues Yes

TOWCESTER

Ron Green
Contact M or N Green
227 & 239 Watling Street West, Towcester, Northamptonshire, NN12 6DD P
☎ 01327 350615 Ⓕ 01327 350387
Ⓜ 07740 774152
Ⓔ ron@green227.freeserve.co.uk
Ⓦ www.rongreenantiques.com
Est. 1954 *Stock size* Medium
Stock General antiques, furniture, paintings, decorative items
Open Mon–Sat 8.30am–5.30pm
Sun by appointment
Services Valuations for probate and insurance

R J K Nicholas
Contact Mr R Nicholas
161 Watling Street, Towcester, Northamptonshire, NN12 6BX P
☎ 01327 350639
Est. 1969 *Stock size* Medium
Stock Glass, prints, silver
Open Mon–Sat 9.30am–5pm
Fairs NEC

WEEDON

Helios and Co
Contact Mr B Walters
25–27 High Street, Weedon, Northamptonshire, NN7 4QD P
☎ 01327 340264 Ⓕ 01327 342235
Est. 1976 *Stock size* Large
Stock General antiques, reproduction 18thC-style oak furniture
Open Tues–Sat 9.30am–5.30pm
Sun 10.30am–4pm
Mon 1.30–4.30pm
Services Valuations, restorations

Rococo Antiques & Interiors
Contact Neville Griffiths
5 New Street, Lower Weedon, Northamptonshire, NN7 4QS P
☎ 01327 341258 Ⓜ 07939 212542
Ⓦ www.nevillegriffiths.co.uk
Est. 1983 *Stock size* Medium
Stock Antiques, architectural salvage
Open Mon–Sat 10am–5pm Sun by appointment
Services Restorations, metal polishing, conservation of period property

Rococo Antiques & Interiors
Contact Neville Griffiths
Bridge Street, Lower Weedon, Northamptonshire, NN7 4PN P
☎ 01327 341288 Ⓜ 07939 212542
Ⓦ www.nevillegriffiths.co.uk
Est. 1983 *Stock size* Medium
Stock Antiques and architectural salvage
Open Mon–Sat 10am–5pm
Sun by appointment
Services Restorations, metal polishing, conservation of period property

Rococo Antiques & Interiors
Contact Neville Griffiths
High Street, Lower Weedon, Northamptonshire, NN7 4PX P
☎ 01327 342606 Ⓜ 07939 212542
Ⓦ www.nevillegriffiths.co.uk
Est. 1983 *Stock size* Medium
Stock Antique furnishings
Open Mon–Sat 10am–5pm
Sun by appointment

Shabby Genteel
Contact Mrs N Hesketh
29A High Street, Weedon, Northamptonshire, NN7 4QD
☎ 01327 342139/340218
Est. 1994 *Stock size* Medium
Stock General antiques, collectables
Open Mon–Fri 11am–4pm
Sat Sun 11am–5pm
Services Free local delivery

Streeton Antiques Ltd
Contact Les Streeton
Watling Street, Weedon, Northamptonshire, NN7 4QG P
☎ 01327 340999 Ⓕ 01327 342234
Ⓦ www.streetons.com
Est. 1986 *Stock size* Large
Stock Pine furniture
Open Mon–Sat 9am–5pm

The Village Market Antiques
Contact Mrs M Howard
62 High Street, Weedon, Northamptonshire, NN7 4QD P
☎ 01327 342015
Est. 1981 *Stock size* Large
No. of dealers 40
Stock General antiques
Open Mon–Fri 9.30am–5.15pm
Sat 10am–5.15pm Sun Bank Holidays 10.30am–5.15pm

MIDLANDS

NORTHAMPTONSHIRE • WELLINGBOROUGH

Weedon Antiques
Contact Nick Tillman
23 High Street, Weedon, Northamptonshire, NN7 4QD P
01327 349777 M 07711 570798
nick_tillman@lineone.net
Est. 2000 *Stock size* Large
No. of dealers 21
Stock Porcelain, silver, glass, small range of furniture, pictures
Open Wed–Sat 10am–5pm
Sun 10.30am–4.30pm

WELLINGBOROUGH

Bryan Perkins Antiques,
Contact John Perkins
52–54 Cannon Street, Wellingborough, Northamptonshire, NN8 4DJ P
01933 228812 F 01933 228812
Est. 1967 *Stock size* Medium
Stock Georgian, Victorian and shipping furniture
Open Mon–Fri 9am–5.30pm

Wilfords
Contact Mr S Wilford
76 Midland Road, Wellingborough, Northamptonshire, NN8 1NB P
01933 222760 F 01933 271796
Est. 1934
Open Mon–Fri 8am–5pm
Sat 8am–11am
Sales General antiques, weekly on Thurs 9.30am
Frequency Weekly
Catalogues No

WEST HADDON

Barber Antiques
Contact Miss A Barber
8 High Street, West Haddon, Northampton, Northamptonshire, NN6 7AP P
01788 510315 F 01788 510315
ali@barberantiques.freeserve.co.uk
www.barberantiques.co.uk
Est. 1992 *Stock size* Large
Stock Staffordshire pottery, blue-and-white pottery, writing boxes, tea caddies, glass, samplers, majolica
Open Tues–Sat 10am–5pm
Services Valuations, restorations

Paul Hopwell Antiques (BADA, LAPADA)
Contact Mr or Mrs P Hopwell
30 High Street, West Haddon, Northampton, Northamptonshire, NN6 7AP P
01788 510636 F 01788 510044
paulhopwell@antiqueoak.co.uk
www.antiqueoak.co.uk
Est. 1969 *Stock size* Large
Stock 17th–18thC English oak furniture, metalware, treen, Delftware
Open Mon–Sat 10am–6pm
Sun by appointment
Fairs Olympia, Chelsea, NEC
Services Valuations, restorations

WESTON FAVELL

Discovery Antiques
Contact Mrs M Eales
1a Park Way, Weston Favell, Northampton, Northamptonshire, NN3 3BS P
01604 401116
M 07815 022184
Est. 1996 *Stock size* Medium
Stock Antique furniture, china, collectables
Open Mon–Sat 10am–5pm
Services Valuations, restorations

NOTTINGHAMSHIRE

BALDERTON

The Blacksmiths Forge
Contact Mr or Mrs K Sheppard
74 Main Street, Balderton, Newark, Nottinghamshire, NG24 3NP P
01636 700008
Est. 1984 *Stock size* Medium
Stock Antique fireplaces
Open By appointment
Fairs Swinderby
Services Restorations

BEESTON

Turner Violins
Contact Monique
1–5 Lily Grove, Beeston, Nottinghamshire, NG9 1QL P
0115 943 0333 F 0115 943 0444
info@turnerviolins.co.uk
www.turnerviolins.co.uk
Est. 1980
Stock Violins, double basses, violas, cellos, bows
Open Mon–Fri 9am–6pm, Sat 9am–5pm
Services Valuations, restorations, part exchange

BUDBY

Dukeries Antiques Centre
Contact John Coupe
Thoresby Park, Budby, Nottinghamshire, NG22 9EX P
01623 822252 F 01623 822209
M 07836 635312
dukeriesantiques@aol.com
Est. 2001 *Stock size* Large
No. of dealers 18

Stock Antique furniture, paintings, porcelain, glass, silver
Open Mon–Sun 10am–5pm
Services Valuations, restorations

DUNHAM ON TRENT

R G Antiques
Contact Mr R G Barnett
Main Street, Dunham on Trent, Newark, Nottinghamshire, NG22 0TY
☎ 01777 228312 Fax 01777 228312
Est. 1979 *Stock size* Medium
Stock General antiques
Open Mon–Sun 10am–6pm
Fairs Newark
Services Valuations

EASTWOOD

Millennium Collectables
Contact Mrs Carol Hadwick
PO Box 146, Eastwood, Nottingham, Nottinghamshire, NG16 3SP
☎ 01773 535333 Fax 01773 535374
mail@millenniumcollectables.co.uk
www.millenniumcollectables.co.uk
Est. 1997 *Stock size* Large
Stock Royal Doulton, special commissions, advertising-related memorabilia, limited edition Guinness enamel badges
Open Mail order only

FARNSFIELD

A B Period Pine
Contact Alan Baker
The Barn, 38 Main Street, Farnsfield, Newark, Nottinghamshire, NG22 8EA
☎ 01623 882288 Fax 01623 882288
alan@abperiodpine.fsnet.co.uk
www.periodpine.co.uk
Est. 1998 *Stock size* Large
Stock Pine
Open Mon–Fri 10am–3pm
Sat 10am–5pm closed Wed
Services Farmhouse and painted pine kitchens

GOTHAM

T Vennett-Smith Auctioneers and Valuers
Contact T or M A Vennett-Smith
11 Nottingham Road, Gotham, Nottingham, Nottinghamshire, NE11 0HE
☎ 0115 983 0541 Fax 0115 983 0114
info@vennett-smith.com
www.vennett-smith.com
Est. 1989
Open Mon–Fri 9am–5.30pm
Sales Autographs, postcards, cigarette cards, 5 sales per year, 2 postal auctions
Frequency 5 per annum
Catalogues Yes

GRINGLEY ON THE HILL

Peter Young Auctioneers
Contact Mr P Young
Hillside, Beacon Hill Road, Gringley on the Hill, Nottinghamshire, DN10 4RQ
☎ 01777 816609
Mobile 07801 079818
Est. 1961
Open Mon–Fri 9.30am–5.30pm
Sales Antiques and collectables Sat 10am, viewing Fri 4–9pm Sat 9–10am. Quarterly antiques and collectables sales. Held at Lord Barnby Memorial Hall, Blyth
Frequency Quarterly
Catalogues Yes

HOCKLEY

Retrospect
Contact Mr Duffy
17 Heathcote Street, Hockley, Nottinghamshire, NG1 3AQ
☎ 0115 956 1182
Est. 1993 *Stock size* Small
Stock Decorative arts, 1880–1980
Open Wed–Sun 9am–5pm

KIRKBY IN ASHFIELD

Kyrios Books
Contact Mr K Parr
11 Kingsway, Kirkby in Ashfield, Nottingham, Nottinghamshire, NG17 7BB
☎ 01623 452556
kyriosbooks@tiscali.co.uk
www.kyrios.webspace.fish.co.uk
Est. 1989 *Stock size* Large
Stock Rare and second-hand Christian and philosophy books
Open Mon Tues Thur Fri 10.30am–noon 1–2.30pm Sat 10am–1pm or by appointment
Services Mail order. Bi-monthly catalogue available from the web

LANGFORD

T Baker
Contact Mr T Baker
Langford House Farm, Langford, Newark, Nottinghamshire, NG23 7RR
☎ 01636 704026
Est. 1966 *Stock size* Medium
Stock Period and Victorian furniture
Open Mon–Fri 8am–5pm or by appointment
Fairs Newark

LONG EATON

Miss Elany
Contact Mr D Mottershead
2 Salisbury Street, Long Eaton, Nottinghamshire, NG10 1BA
☎ 0115 973 4835 Fax 0115 973 4835
www.misselany.com
Est. 1977 *Stock size* Large
Stock Antiques and pianos
Open Mon–Sat 9am–5pm
Fairs Newark, Swinderby
Services Valuations

MANSFIELD

Antiques & Clock Shop (BWCG)
Contact Mr Tom Matthews
34a Bancroft Lane, Mansfield, Nottinghamshire, NG18 5LQ
☎ 01623 476097 Mobile 07808 693559
tomclockrepairs@lineone.net
www.tomclockrepairs.co.uk
Est. 1974 *Stock size* Large
Stock General antiques
Open Mon–Fri 8.30am–5pm
Sat 8.30am–3pm
Fairs Birmingham Clock Fair
Services Valuations, restorations of clocks and jewellery

Fair Deal Antiques
Contact Mr Low
138 Chesterfield Road North, Mansfield, Nottinghamshire, NE19 7PE
☎ 01623 653768
Est. 1979 *Stock size* Large
Stock General antiques
Open Mon–Sun 8am–6pm or by appointment
Services Container packing

Mansfield Antique Centre
Contact Dave Buckinger

MIDLANDS

NOTTINGHAMSHIRE • NEWARK

⊠ 185 Yorke Street, Mansfield Woodhouse, Mansfield, Nottinghamshire, NG19 2NJ 🅿
☎ 01623 661122 ⓕ 01623 631738
Est. 1992 *Stock size* Medium
Stock General antiques
Open Thurs–Sun 10am–5.30pm

NEWARK

Castlegate Antique Centre
Contact John Dench
⊠ 55 Castle Gate, Newark, Nottinghamshire, NG24 1BE 🅿
☎ 01636 700076 ⓕ 01636 700144
Est. 1983 *Stock size* Large
No. of dealers 9
Stock General antiques
Open Mon–Sat 9.30am–5.30pm
Services Valuations, restorations

Galerie
Contact Gillian Jennison
⊠ 1 Bar Gate, Newark, Nottinghamshire, NG24 1ES 🅿
☎ 01636 705400 ⓜ 07951 691487
Est. 2000 *Stock size* Small
Stock French furniture, lights, mirrors
Open Wed–Sat 10am–5pm

Lawrence Books
Contact Mr A Lawrence
⊠ Newark Antique Centre, Lombard Street, Newark, Nottinghamshire, NG24 1XR 🅿
☎ 01636 605865/701619
ⓔ arthurlawrence@totalise.co.uk
Est. 1987 *Stock size* Small
Stock Antiquarian, rare and second-hand books
Open Mon–Sat 9.30am–5pm Sun 11am–4pm
Services Valuations

R R Limb Antiques
Contact Mr R Limb
⊠ 31/35 North Gate, Newark, Nottinghamshire, NG24 1HD 🅿
☎ 01636 674546
Est. 1955 *Stock size* Large
Stock General antiques, pianos
Open By appointment
Fairs Newark, Swinderby
Services Piano exporters

M B G Antiques (BGA)
Contact Margaret Begley-Gray DGA
⊠ 41b Castlegate, Newark, Nottinghamshire, NG24 1BE 🅿
☎ 01636 704442 ⓕ 01636 679586
ⓜ 07702 209808
ⓔ mbgantiques@mail.com
Est. 1982 *Stock size* Medium
Stock Period jewellery, quality pictures, diamond rings
Open Wed–Sat 11am–4pm closed Thurs
Services Valuations, picture search

Newark Antiques Centre
Contact Mr M Tinsley
⊠ Regent House, Lombard Street, Newark, Nottinghamshire, NG24 1XP 🅿
☎ 01636 605504 ⓕ 01636 605101
ⓜ 07931 109860
Est. 1988 *Stock size* Large
No. of dealers 101
Stock General antiques
Open Mon–Sat 9.30am–5pm Sun Bank Holidays 11am–4pm
Services Valuations, upholstery, clock repairs, specialist book service

Newark Antiques Warehouse Ltd
Contact Nick Mellors
⊠ Kelham Road, Newark, Nottinghamshire, NG24 1BX 🅿
☎ 01636 674869 ⓕ 01636 612933
ⓜ 07974 429185
ⓔ enquiries@newarkantiques.co.uk
ⓦ www.newarkantiques.co.uk
Est. 1984 *Stock size* Large
No. of dealers 80
Stock Good furniture, collectables, smalls
Open Mon–Fri 8.30am–5.30pm Sat 9.30am–4pm Sun at Newark Antiques Fair 9am–7pm
Services Valuations

No. 1 Castlegate Antiques
⊠ 1–3 Castlegate, Newark, Nottinghamshire, NG24 1AZ 🅿
☎ 01636 701877
Est. 1974 *Stock size* Large
No. of dealers 10
Stock 18th–19thC antique furniture, clocks, barometers, decorative items
Open Mon–Fri 9.30am–5pm Sat 9.30am–5.30pm
Services Valuations, restorations of clocks and barometers

Pearman Antiques & Interiors
Contact Jan Parnham
⊠ 9 Castle Gate, Newark, Nottinghamshire, NG24 1AZ 🅿
☎ 01636 679158/01949 837693
Est. 2001 *Stock size* Medium
Stock Oak and mahogany furniture
Open Wed–Sat 10am–4pm

Tudor Rose Antiques
Contact Mrs C Rose
⊠ Yew Tree Farm, Carlton-on-Trent, Newark, Nottinghamshire, NG23 6NL 🅿
☎ 01636 6821841 ⓜ 07970 972191
Est. 1979 *Stock size* Medium
Stock Small collectable antiques, antique furniture, silver, metalware, treen, country items
Open By appointment
Services Valuations

NOTTINGHAM

Acanthus Antiques & Collectables
Contact Trak or Sandra Smith
⊠ 140 Derby Road, Nottingham, Nottinghamshire, NG7 1LR 🅿
☎ 0115 924 3226
ⓔ trak.e.smith@btinternet.com
ⓦ www.acanthusantiques.co.uk
Est. 1979 *Stock size* Medium
Stock General antiques
Open Tues–Fri 10am–3pm Sat noon–4pm Sun by appointment
Fairs Newark, Swinderby
Services Valuations, lectures and teaching

Antiques Across the World (LAPADA)
Contact Mr Rimes
⊠ James Alexander Buildings, London Road, Manvers Street, Nottingham, Nottinghamshire, NG2 3AE 🅿
☎ 0115 979 9199 ⓕ 0115 958 8314
ⓜ 07785 777787
ⓔ tonyrimes@btinternet.com
Est. 1992 *Stock size* Large
Stock Georgian–Edwardian furniture
Open Mon–Fri 9am–5pm Sat 10am–2pm
Fairs Newark
Services Valuations, courier service, antique finder service

The Autograph Collectors' Gallery
Contact Mr or Mrs G Clipson

✉ 7 Jessops Lane, Gedling, Nottingham, Nottinghamshire, NG4 4BQ
☎ 0115 961 2956/987 6578
Ⓕ 0115 961 2956
Ⓔ graham.clipson@btinternet.com or postmaster@autograph-gallery.co.uk
Ⓦ www.autograph-gallery.co.uk
Est. 1990 *Stock size* Large
Stock Signed photographs, documents, letters
Open Telephone 9am–8pm
Services Mail order only

Bonhams
✉ **57 Mansfield Road, Nottingham, Nottinghamshire, NG1 3PL** Ⓟ
☎ 0115 947 4414 Ⓕ 0115 947 4885
Ⓔ nottingham@bonhams.com
Ⓦ www.bonhams.com
Open Mon–Fri 10am–5pm

Castle Antiques
Contact Mr L Adamson
✉ **78 Derby Road, Nottingham, Nottinghamshire, NG1 5FD** Ⓟ
☎ 0115 947 3913
Est. 1979 *Stock size* Medium
Stock General antiques, pictures, maps, prints, lighting
Open Mon–Sat 9.30am–5pm

Cathay Oriental Antiques
Contact Jenny Bu
✉ **74 Derby Road, Nottingham, Nottinghamshire, NG1 5FD** Ⓟ
☎ 0115 988 1216
Ⓔ paulshum@hotmail.com
Est. 2000 *Stock size* Medium
Stock Furniture, porcelain, ceramic, pottery, Chinese folk art
Open Mon–Sat 10am–5pm

Collectors World
Contact Mr M Ray
✉ **188 Wollaton Road, Wollaton, Nottingham, Nottinghamshire, NG8 1HJ** Ⓟ
☎ 0115 928 0347 Ⓕ 0115 928 0347
Est. 1991 *Stock size* Large
Stock Coins, banknotes, cigarette cards, postcards
Open Tues–Sat 10.30am–5pm
Fairs Newark, specialist
Services Valuations, currency exchange, framing

Dutton & Smith Medal Collectors
Contact Mr A Dutton
✉ **Room 143, 48 Derby Road, Nottingham, Nottinghamshire, NG1 5FQ** Ⓟ
☎ 0115 987 6949 Ⓕ 0115 982 2137
Ⓔ duttonf@019.mbe.uk.com
Ⓦ www.acanthusantiques.co.uk
Est. 1991 *Stock size* Medium
Stock Campaign medals
Open By appointment
Fairs Newark, Swinderby
Services Valuations

Fourways Antiques
Contact Mr Peter Key
✉ **38 Owen Avenue, Nottingham, Nottinghamshire, NG10 2FS** Ⓟ
☎ 0115 972 1830 Ⓜ 07850 973889
Est. 1974 *Stock size* Medium
Stock General antiques
Open By appointment
Fairs Newark, Swinderby

Gatehouse Workshops
Contact Mr S J Waine
✉ **163 Castle Boulevard, Nottingham, Nottinghamshire, NG7 1FS** Ⓟ
☎ 0115 948 3954 Ⓕ 0115 948 3954
Ⓦ www.gatehouseworkshops.co.uk
Est. 1979 *Stock size* Medium
Stock Architectural antiques, stained glass
Open Mon–Fri 9.30am–4pm Sat 9am–5pm
Services Pine stripping

Hallam Antique and Diamond Jewellery
Contact Stuart Thexton
✉ **Kings Walk Corner, 30 Upper Parliament Street, Nottingham, Nottinghamshire, NG1 2AG** Ⓟ
☎ 0115 941 1276
Est. 1998 *Stock size* Medium
Stock Range of dining room pieces, condiment sets, watches
Open Mon–Sat 9am–5.30pm
Services Valuations, watch repair

Harlequin Antiques
Contact Peter Hinchley
✉ **79/81 Mansfield Road, Nottingham, Nottinghamshire, NG5 6BH** Ⓟ
☎ 0115 967 4590
Ⓔ sales@antiquepine.net
Ⓦ www.antiquepine.net
Est. 1993 *Stock size* Large
Stock Antique pine furniture
Open Mon–Fri 9.30am–5pm Sat 9am–5pm or by appointment
Fairs Newark
Services Restorations of all period furniture

Andy Holmes (PBFA)
✉ **82 Highbury Avenue, Bulwell, Nottingham, Nottinghamshire, NG6 9DB** Ⓟ
☎ 0115 979 5603 Ⓕ 0115 979 5616
Ⓔ holmesbook@aol.com
Est. 1996 *Stock size* Large
Stock Antiquarian, rare and second-hand books, 19thC travel, gypsies, folklore and general topics
Open By appointment only
Fairs London Royal National, Buxton
Services Valuations, book search

D D & A Ingle (ORMS)
Contact Mr D Ingle
✉ **380 Carlton Hill, Carlton, Nottingham, Nottinghamshire, NG4 1JA** Ⓟ
☎ 0115 987 3325 Ⓕ 0115 987 3325
Ⓔ ddaingle@talk21.com
Est. 1968 *Stock size* Medium
Stock General antiques
Open Mon–Sat 9am–5pm
Services Valuations

Ivory Gate Antiques
Contact Mr B Orridge
✉ **106 Derby Road, Nottingham, Nottinghamshire, NG1 5FB** Ⓟ
☎ 0115 947 3054
Ⓔ ivorygateantiques@hotmail.com
Est. 1979 *Stock size* Large
Stock General antiques
Open Mon–Sat 9.45am–4.45pm closed Fri
Fairs Newark, Swinderby
Services Restoration of furniture

Jeremy & Westerman
Contact Geoff Blore
✉ **203 Mansfield Road, Nottingham, Nottinghamshire, NG1 3FF**
☎ 0115 947 4522
Est. 1981 *Stock size* Medium
Stock Antique and second-hand books
Open Mon–Sat 11am–5pm
Fairs H & D Book Fairs

Arthur Johnson & Sons
Contact Mr R Hannersley
✉ **Nottingham Auction Centre, Meadow Lane, Nottingham, Nottinghamshire, NG2 3GY** Ⓟ

MIDLANDS

NOTTINGHAMSHIRE • NOTTINGHAM

☎ 0115 986 9128 Ⓕ 0115 986 2139
Est. 1899
Open Mon–Fri 9am–5pm closed lunch
Sales Antique and export furniture Sat 10am, viewing Fri 2–6.45pm Sat from 9am
Frequency Weekly
Catalogues Yes

⊞ Lights, Camera, Action (UACC)
Contact Mr N Straw
✉ **36 Cyril Avenue, Nottingham, Nottinghamshire, NG8 5BA** Ⓟ
☎ 0115 913 1116 Ⓕ 0115 913 1116
Ⓜ 0797 034 2363
Est. 1998 *Stock size* Large
Stock Collectors' items, autographs, Titanic memorabilia
Open By appointment
Fairs NEC, Olympia, Newark
Services Valuations

⊞ Michael D Long Ltd (GTA), BACA Award Winner 2001
Contact Mr M D Long
✉ **96–98 Derby Road, Nottingham, Nottinghamshire, NG1 5FB** Ⓟ
☎ 0115 941 3307 Ⓕ 0115 941 4199
Ⓔ sales@michaeldlong.com
Ⓦ www.michaeldlong.com
Est. 1964 *Stock size* Large
Stock Fine antique arms and armour
Open Mon–Fri 9.30am–5.15pm Sat 10am–4pm
Fairs London Arms Fair, Birmingham, Nottingham
Services Valuations

⊞ Luna
Contact Paul Rose
✉ **23 George Street, Nottingham, Nottinghamshire, NG1 3BH** Ⓟ
☎ 0115 924 3267
Ⓔ info@luna-online.co.uk
Ⓦ www.luna-online.co.uk
Est. 1993 *Stock size* Medium
Stock 1950s–1970s objects for the home
Open Mon–Sat 10.30am–5.30pm
Fairs Newark
Services Sourcing items, hire

⚒ Mellors & Kirk (RICS)
Contact Nigel Kirk or Martha Parvin
✉ **The Auction House, Nottingham, Nottinghamshire, NG7 2NL** Ⓟ
☎ 0115 979 0000 Ⓕ 0115 978 1111
Ⓔ mellkirk@dircon.co.uk
Ⓦ www.mellors-kirk.com
Est. 1993
Open Mon–Fri 8.30am–5pm Sat 9am–noon
Sales Weekly general sale on Tues. Fine art sale every six weeks
Frequency Six weekly
Catalogues yes

⊞ N S E Medal Department (OMRS)
Contact Dennis Henson
✉ **97 Derby Road, Nottingham, Nottinghamshire, NG1 5BB** Ⓟ
☎ 0115 950 1882
Ⓔ nsemed@totalserve.com
Est. 1974 *Stock size* Large
Stock Antique coins and medals, cap badges
Open Mon–Sat 9am–3.30pm
Services Valuations

⚒ Neales Auctioneers (SOFAA, ARVA)
Contact Bruce Fearn
✉ **192 Mansfield Road, Nottingham, Nottinghamshire, NG1 3HU** Ⓟ
☎ 0115 962 4141 Ⓕ 0115 985 6890
Ⓔ fineart@neales.co.uk
Ⓦ www.neales.co.uk
Est. 1840
Open Mon–Fri 9am–5.30pm Sat 9am–12.30pm
Sales Specialist antique and fine art sales every 2–3 months plus general antiques and collectables sales
Frequency Weekly
Catalogues Yes

⊞ Nottingham Coin Centre
Contact Mr P Muir
✉ **28 Alfreton Road, Nottingham, Nottinghamshire, NG7 3NG**
☎ 0115 942 42777
Est. 1987 *Stock size* Medium
Stock Coins, medals, collectables
Open Mon–Sat 10am–2pm
Services Valuations

⊞ P & P Antiques
Contact Mr J Pollard
✉ **Nottingham Auction Centre, Gregory Street, Nottingham, Nottinghamshire, NG7 2NL** Ⓟ
☎ 0115 924 4447 Ⓕ 0115 978 3135
Ⓔ no1export@aol.com
Est. 1994 *Stock size* Large
Stock General antiques, shipping goods
Open Mon–Fri 9am–5pm
Services Courier, shipping containers

⊞ David & Carole Potter (LAPADA)
Contact Mr or Mrs D Potter
✉ **76 Derby Road, Nottingham, Nottinghamshire, NG1 5FD** Ⓟ
☎ 07940 123485 Ⓜ 07973 689962
Est. 1966 *Stock size* Medium
Stock General antiques, 18th–19thC furniture, quality decorative items
Open By appointment only
Fairs NEC, Olympia
Services Valuations

⊞ John Priestley
Contact Mr John Priestley
✉ **48–50 Avenue B, Sneinton Market, Nottingham, Nottinghamshire, NG1 1DU** Ⓟ
☎ 0115 910 3393
Est. 1989 *Stock size* Large
Stock Autographs, football programmes, postcards
Open Mon–Fri 10.30am–4.30pm
Fairs Glasgow, NEC
Services Valuations

⚒ John Pye & Sons Ltd (NAVA)
Contact Adam Pye FNAVA
✉ **James Shipstone House, Radford Road, Nottingham, Nottinghamshire, NG7 7EA**
☎ 0115 970 6060 Ⓕ 0115 942 0100
Ⓔ ap@johnpye.co.uk.
Ⓦ www.johnpye.co.uk
Est. 1969
Open Mon–Fri 8am–4.30pm
Sales General
Frequency Fortnightly
Catalogues No

⊞ Top Hat Antiques
Contact Mrs J Wallis
✉ **62 Derby Road, Nottingham, Nottinghamshire, NG1 5FD** Ⓟ
☎ 0115 941 9143
Ⓔ decodealers@ntlworld.com
Ⓦ www.tophat-antiques.co.uk
Est. 1979 *Stock size* Large
Stock General antiques
Open Mon–Sat 10am–5pm

RETFORD

Bonhams
20 Square, Retford, Nottinghamshire, DN22 6XE
01777 708 633 01777 706724
retford@bonhams.com
www.bonhams.com
Open Mon–Fri 9am–5pm

Lynn Guest Antiques
Contact Lynn Guest
15 Mill Lane, Rockley, Retford, Nottinghamshire, DN22 0QP
01777 838498
Est. 1979 *Stock size* Medium
Stock General antiques and collectables
Open Mon–Fri 9am–6pm or by appointment
Fairs Newark
Services Valuations, house clearance

SANDIACRE

The Glory Hole
Contact Mr or Mrs C Reid
14 Station Road, Sandiacre, Nottingham, Nottinghamshire, NG10 5BG
0115 939 4081 0115 939 4085
Est. 1984 *Stock size* Medium
Stock Antique furniture, fireplaces
Open Mon–Sat 9.30am–5.30pm
Services Restorations

SOUTHWELL

Strouds of Southwell Antiques
Contact Mr V Stroud
3/7 Church Street, Southwell, Nottinghamshire, NG25 0HQ
01636 815001 01636 815001
Est. 1969 *Stock size* Large
Stock Antique fine period furniture
Open Tues–Sat 9.30am–5pm or by appointment
Services Valuations, restorations

SUTTON-IN-ASHFIELD

Carol's Curiosity Shop
Contact Mrs C Wilcockson
33 High Street, Station Hill, Sutton-in-Ashfield, Nottinghamshire, NG17 3GG
01623 555903
Est. 1998 *Stock size* Medium
Stock General antiques
Open Mon 10am–4pm Tues 9am–5pm Wed 10am–1pm Thurs Fri 9am–5.30pm Sat 9am–4pm
Fairs Newark, Swinderby

C B Sheppard & Son
Contact Mr B Sheppard
The Auction Gallery, 87 Chatworth Street, Sutton-in-Ashfield, Nottinghamshire, NG17 4GG
01623 556310 07714 798244
Est. 1951
Open Fri (auction weeks Tues–Fri) 9am–4pm
Sales General antiques
Frequency Monthly
Catalogues Yes

Yesterday and Today
Contact Mr J Turner
82 Station Road, Sutton-in-Ashfield, Nottinghamshire, NG17 5HB
01623 442215 07957 552753
Est. 1984 *Stock size* Medium
Stock Collectables, 1920s and 1930s oak furniture
Open Mon–Sat 9am–5pm
Fairs Newark, Swinderby

WEST BRIDGFORD

Bridgford Antiques
Contact Joe Domeika
2a Rushworth Avenue, West Bridgford, Nottingham, Nottinghamshire, NG2 7LF
0115 982 1835
Est. 1974 *Stock size* Medium
Stock General antiques and collectables
Open Mon–Sat 10am–5pm
Fairs Newark, Swinderby

Joan Cotton
Contact Mrs Joan Cotton
5 Davies Road, West Bridgford, Nottingham, Nottinghamshire, NG2 5JE
0115 981 3043
Est. 1964 *Stock size* Medium
Stock General antiques except furniture
Open Mon–Sat 9am–4pm closed Wed Sun

Portland Antiques & Curios
Contact Brendan or Carole Sprakes
5 Portland Road, West Bridgford, Nottingham, Nottinghamshire, NG2 6DN
0115 914 2123
Est. 1999 *Stock size* Large
Stock General antiques
Open Wed–Sat 9.30am–5pm

RUTLAND

MANTON

David Smith Antiques
Contact Mr D Smith
20 St Mary's Road, Manton, Oakham, Rutland, LE15 8SY
01572 737244/737607
Est. 1952 *Stock size* Medium
Stock General antiques
Open Mon–Sat 9am–5pm or by appointment
Fairs Kettering
Services Valuations, restorations

OAKHAM

Swans Antiques and Interiors
Contact Mr Peter Jones
17 Mill Street, Oakham, Rutland, LE15 6EA
01572 724364 01572 755094
07860 304084
info@swansofoakham.co.uk
www.swansofoakham.co.uk
Est. 1986 *Stock size* Large
Stock Antique beds, English and French decorative furniture
Open Mon–Sat 9am–5.30pm Sun 2–5pm
Fairs Newark
Services Valuations, restorations

Treedale Antiques
Contact Mr G Warren
10b Mill Street, Oakham, Rutland, LE15 6EA
01572 757521 01572 757521
Est. 1968 *Stock size* Medium
Stock 17th–18thC furniture, specializing in walnut and oak
Open Mon–Sat 9am–5.30pm Sun 2–5pm
Services Restorations

UPPINGHAM

Clutter Antiques
Contact Maureen Sumner
14 Orange Street, Uppingham, Oakham, Rutland, LE15 9SQ
01572 823745/717243
01162 697729
cfi@sumnerlikeithot.fsnet.co.uk
Est. 1982 *Stock size* Medium
Stock Victorian kitchen and

parlour clutter, textiles, linens, treen, glass, china
Open Mon–Fri 10am–5pm
Sat 10am–6pm or by appointment

⊞ John Garner Antiques
Contact John Garner
✉ **51 and 53 High Street East, Uppingham, Oakham, Rutland, LE15 9PY** Ⓟ
☎ 01572 823607 Ⓕ 01572 821654
Ⓜ 07850 596556
Ⓦ www.johngarnerantiques.com
Est. 1966 *Stock size* Large
Stock General antiques, 18th–19thC furniture and paintings, garden statuary, clocks, bronzes, sporting prints
Open Mon–Sat 9am–5.30pm
Services Valuations, restorations

⊞ Goldmark Books
Contact Ian Broughton
✉ **14 Orange Street, Uppingham, Oakham, Rutland, LE15 9SQ** Ⓟ
☎ 01572 822694 Ⓕ 01572 821503
Ⓔ Mike@mgoldmark.freeserve.co.uk
Est. 1974 *Stock size* Large
Stock General stock including antiquarian and second-hand books, art and poetry a speciality
Open Mon–Sat 9.30am–5.30pm
Sun 2.30–5.30pm
Services Book search

⊞ Tattersalls
Contact Mrs J Tattersall
✉ **14b Orange Street, Uppingham, Oakham, Rutland, LE14 2AG** Ⓟ
☎ 01572 821171
Est. 1985 *Stock size* Medium
Stock Antique and old Persian rugs
Open Tues–Sat 9.30am–5pm
Services Restorations

⊞ Woodmans House Antiques
Contact Mr or Mrs J Collie
✉ **35 High Street East, Uppingham, Oakham, Rutland, LE15 9PY** Ⓟ
☎ 01572 821799
Ⓔ woodmanshouse@aol.com
Ⓦ www.woodmanshouse-antiques.co.uk
Est. 1992 *Stock size* Medium
Stock Georgian furniture, designer fabrics
Open Mon–Sat 9.30am–5pm or Sun by appointment
Fairs NEC, Olympia
Services Valuations, restorations, reference library, complete interior design service

SHROPSHIRE

ATCHAM

⊞ Mytton Antiques
Contact M A Nares
✉ **Norton Crossroads, Atcham, Shrewsbury, Shropshire, SY4 4UH** Ⓟ
☎ 01952 740229 Ⓕ 01952 461154
Ⓜ 07860 575639
Ⓔ nares@myttonantiques.freeserve.co.uk
Est. 1979 *Stock size* Medium
Stock 18th–19thC furniture and smalls, longcase clocks, country furniture, restoration materials
Open Mon–Sat 10am–5pm or by appointment
Services Valuations, restoration, shipping, courier service

BISHOPS CASTLE

⊞ Autolycus
Contact Mr David Wilkinson
✉ **Porch House, High Street, Bishops Castle, Shropshire, SY9 5BE** Ⓟ
☎ 01588 630078 Ⓕ 01588 638686
Ⓔ autolycusbc@aol.com
Ⓦ www.booksonline.uk.com
Est. 1996 *Stock size* Medium
Stock Antiquarian and quality second-hand books, specializing in modern first editions, illustrated, children's, travel, topography, fine sporting prints and pictures
Open Mon–Fri 11am–4.30pm
Sat 10.30am–5pm

⊞ Decorative Antiques
Contact Richard Moulson
✉ **47 Church Street, Bishops Castle, Shropshire, SY9 5AD** Ⓟ
☎ 01588 638851 Ⓕ 01588 638851
Ⓔ enquiries@decorative-antiques.co.uk
Ⓦ www.decorative-antiques.co.uk
Est. 1996 *Stock size* Medium
Stock Art Deco 1860–1960, Arts and Crafts, pottery, glass, jewellery, metalware, evening bags, early plastics
Open Most days 10am–6pm
Services Identification and informal valuations

BRIDGNORTH

⊞ The Book Passage
Contact Mr David Lamont
✉ **57a High Street, Bridgnorth, Shropshire, WV16 4DX** Ⓟ
☎ 01746 768767
Est. 1999 *Stock size* Large
Stock Antiquarian and second-hand books
Open Mon–Sat 9am–5.30pm

⊞ Bookstack
Contact Mrs E Anderson
✉ **The Harp Yard, St Leonards Close, Bridgnorth, Shropshire, WV16 4EJ** Ⓟ
☎ 01746 767089 Ⓕ 01746 768008
Est. 1992 *Stock size* Small
Stock Antiquarian and second-hand books
Open Mon–Fri 9am–5pm
Services Restorations, bookbinding

Bridgnorth Antiques Centre
Contact Mr Richard Lewis
✉ **Whitburn Street, Bridgnorth, Shropshire, WV16 4QP** Ⓟ
☎ 01746 768055
Ⓔ antiquesrl@fsb.com
Ⓦ www.as4uk.com
Est. 1994 *Stock size* Large
No. of dealers 19 (6 rooms)
Stock Late Victorian, Edwardian and 1930s furniture, collectables
Open Mon–Sat 10am–5.30pm
Sun 10.30am–4.30pm
Services Clock repairs

⊞ English Heritage
Contact Mrs M Wainwright
✉ **2 Whitburn Street, Bridgnorth, Shropshire, WV16 4QN** Ⓟ
☎ 01746 762097
Est. 1988 *Stock size* Medium
Stock General antiques, giftware, medals, coins and silverware
Open Mon–Sat 10am–5pm closed Thurs

⊞ Malthouse Antiques
Contact Mrs Susan Mantle
✉ **6 Underhill Street, Bridgnorth, Shropshire, WV16 4BB** Ⓟ
☎ 01746 763054 Ⓕ 01746 763054
Est. 1979 *Stock size* Large
Stock Victorian–Edwardian furniture, chandeliers

Open Mon–Sat 10am–6pm
Sun 2–5pm closed Wed
Services Restorations

Old Mill Antique Centre
Contact Mr Dennis Ridgeway
48 Mill Street, Bridgnorth, Shropshire, WV15 5AG
☎ 01746 768778 Ⓕ 01746 768944
Est. 1996 *Stock size* Large
No. of dealers 90
Stock Complete range of antiques and collectables
Open Mon–Sun 10am–5pm
Services Restaurant

Perry & Phillips
Contact Dennis Ridgeway
Old Mill Auction Rooms, Mill Street, Bridgnorth, Shropshire, WV15 5AG
☎ 01746 762248 Ⓕ 01746 768944
Ⓔ sales@perryandphillips.co.uk
Ⓦ www.perryandphillips.co.uk
Est. 1835
Open Mon–Fri 9am–5pm
Sales General antiques sales Tues 10.30am, viewing Sat–Mon 10am–5pm, occasional special sales
Frequency Monthly
Catalogues Yes

BURLTON

North Shropshire Reclamation and Antique Salvage (SALVO)
Contact Mrs J Powell
Wackley Lodge Farm, Wackley, Burlton, Shrewsbury, Shropshire, SY4 5TD
☎ 01939 270719 Ⓕ 01939 270895
Ⓜ 07802 315038
Est. 1997 *Stock size* Large
Stock Garden statuary, bricks, baths, hand basins, tiles, doors, architectural salvage of all types
Open Mon–Fri 9am–6pm
Sat Sun 9am–5.30pm
Services Paint stripping

CHURCH STRETTON

Church Stretton Books (PBFA)
Contact Mr Roger Toon
Victoria House, 48 High Street, Church Stretton, Shropshire, SY6 6BX
☎ 01694 724337 Ⓕ 01694 724337
Ⓔ csbooks@btinternet.com
Ⓦ www.abebooks.com
Est. 1994 *Stock size* Medium
Stock High-quality second-hand and antiquarian books, Malcolm Saville books a speciality
Open Mon–Sat 10am–5pm
Wed 10am–1pm
Fairs Bloomsbury

Old Post Office Antiques
Contact Mr A Walker
46 Sandford Avenue, Church Stretton, Shropshire, SY6 6BH
☎ 01694 724491 Ⓕ 01694 724491
Est. 1998 *Stock size* Large
Stock Jewellery, Halcyon Days, Steiff bears
Open Mon–Sat 10am–5pm

The Snooker Room
Contact Mr A Walker
46a Sandford Avenue, Church Stretton, Shropshire, SY6 6BH
☎ 01694 724491 Ⓕ 01694 724491
Ⓜ 07790 906570
Est. 1939 *Stock size* Large
Stock Snooker tables, lighting, accessories
Open Mon–Sat 10am–5pm
Fairs Olympia

Stretton Antiques Market
Contact Terry or Lisa Elvins
36 Sandford Avenue, Church Stretton, Shropshire, SY6 6BH
☎ 01694 723718 Ⓕ 01694 723718
Est. 1985 *Stock size* Large
No. of dealers 60
Stock Wide range of antiques and collectables
Open Mon–Sat 9.30am–5.30pm
Sun 10.30am–4.30pm

COSFORD

Martin Quick Antiques (LAPADA)
Contact Mr C Quick
Unit 2, Next to Cosford Auctions, Long Lane, Cosford, Shropshire, TF11 8PJ
☎ 01902 754703 Ⓜ 07774 124859
Ⓔ cqantiques@aol.com
Est. 1970 *Stock size* Large
Stock Georgian–Victorian and later furniture, French furniture
Trade only Yes
Open By appointment or chance
Fairs Newark
Services Valuations

Walker, Barnett & Hill
Contact Christopher Sidebottom
Cosford Auction Rooms, Long Lane, Cosford, Shropshire, TF11 8PJ
☎ 01902 375555 Ⓕ 01902 375566
Ⓔ wbhauctions@lineone.net
Ⓦ www.walker-barnett-hill.co.uk
Est. 1780
Open Mon–Fri 9.30am–5pm
Sales Fortnightly antique and contemporary furniture sales, fine art sales 6-weekly
Frequency Fortnightly
Catalogues Yes

CRAVEN ARMS

Marine
Contact Mark Jarrold
Lower House Farm, Middlehope, Craven Arms, Shropshire, SY7 9JT
☎ 01584 841210 Ⓕ 01584 841210
Ⓜ 07776 193193
Ⓔ mark.jarrold@btinternet.com
Est. 1989
Stock Binoculars, ships' models, navigational instruments, chronometers, clocks, optical equipment
Open By appointment
Fairs Birmingham International Arms Fair
Services Valuations, restorations

Portcullis Furniture
Contact Mr John Cox or Mrs Sally Allen
Ludlow Road, Craven Arms, Shropshire, SY7 9QL
☎ 01588 672263 Ⓕ 01588 673321
Ⓜ 07966 188364
Est. 1995 *Stock size* Large
Stock Antique, reproduction and new furniture, copper, brass, silver, china, clocks
Open Mon–Sat 10am–5.30pm
Sun 10.30am–4.30pm
Fairs Newark
Services Shipping

DITTON PRIORS

Priors Reclamation (SALVO)
Contact Miss V Bale

MIDLANDS

SHROPSHIRE • ELLESMERE

✉ **Unit 2a, Ditton Priors Industrial Estate, Ditton Priors, Bridgnorth, Shropshire, WV16 6SS** 🅿
☎ 01746 712450 Ⓕ 01746 712450
Ⓜ 07989 302488
Ⓔ vicki@priorsrec.co.uk
Ⓦ www.priorsrec.co.uk
Est. 1998 *Stock size* Large
Stock Reclaimed flooring, new oak flooring, reclaimed doors, doors made to order from reclaimed timber
Open By appointment at any time
Services Delivery

ELLESMERE

Bowen, Son & Watson
Contact Mr Eddie Bowen
✉ **Wharf Road, Ellesmere, Shropshire, SY12 0EJ** 🅿
☎ 01691 622534 Ⓕ 01691 623603
Ⓔ bsw.ellesmere@virgin.net
Ⓦ www.bowensonandwatson.co.uk
Est. 1869
Open Mon–Fri 9am–5pm Sat 9am–noon
Sales Antique and household goods monthly Tues 11am, viewing Mon 9am–5pm Tues 9–11am
Frequency Monthly
Catalogues No

IRONBRIDGE

Bears on the Square
Contact Margaret Phillips
✉ **2 The Square, Ironbridge, Telford, Shropshire, TF8 7AQ** 🅿
☎ 01952 433924 Ⓕ 01952 433926
Ⓔ bernie@bearsonthesquare.com
Ⓦ www.bearsonthesquare.com
Est. 1991 *Stock size* Large
Stock Steiff, Deans, Hermann, Spielwaren, Artist and second-hand bears, country life
Open Mon–Sun 10am–5pm
Services Worldwide mail order

Tudor House Antiques
Contact Mr Peter Whitelaw
✉ **11 Tontine Hill, Ironbridge, Telford, Shropshire, TF8 7AL** 🅿
☎ 01952 433783
Ⓔ tudoriron@aol.com
Ⓦ www.tudorhouse.co.uk
Est. 1964 *Stock size* Large
Stock Coalport, Caughley, general English ceramics
Open Mon–Sat 10am–5pm
Sun by appointment
Services Valuations

LONGNOR

Oriental & African Books (PBFA)
Contact Mr Paul Wilson
✉ **The Corbett Rooms, Longnor Hall, Longnor, Shropshire, SY25 7PZ** 🅿
☎ 01743 718367 Ⓕ 01743 719001
Ⓔ abumoya@dial.pipex.com
Ⓦ www.africana.co.uk
Est. 1982 *Stock size* Medium
Stock Rare, antiquarian and out-of-print books on Africa and the Middle East
Open By appointment

LUDLOW

Bayliss Antiques
Contact Mr A B Bayliss
✉ **22–24 Old Street, Ludlow, Shropshire, SY8 1NP** 🅿
☎ 01584 873634 Ⓕ 01584 873634
Ⓜ 07831 672211
Est. 1968 *Stock size* Medium
Stock Oak and mahogany furniture, paintings
Open Mon–Sat 9am–6pm or by appointment
Fairs Bailey Fairs, NEC
Services Valuations

R G Cave & Sons Ltd (LAPADA, BADA)
Contact Mr R G Cave or John Cave
✉ **17 Broad Street, Ludlow, Shropshire, SY8 1NG** 🅿
☎ 01584 873568 Ⓕ 01584 875050
Est. 1965 *Stock size* Medium
Stock Period furniture, metalwork, works of art
Open Mon–Sat 9.30am–5.30pm
Services Valuations for probate and insurance, shippers of Bordeaux wine

John M Clegg
Contact Mr J Clegg
✉ **12 Old Street, Ludlow, Shropshire, SY8 1NP** 🅿
☎ 01584 873176
Est. 1974 *Stock size* Large
Stock Period oak, mahogany furniture and associated items
Open Mon–Fri 8.30am–5pm
Sat 10.30am–5pm

Corve Street Antiques
Contact Mr Jones or Mr McAvoy
✉ **141a Corve Street, Ludlow, Shropshire, SY8 2PG** 🅿
☎ 01584 879100
Est. 2001 *Stock size* Medium
Stock Longcase clocks, oak country, mahogany furniture, copper, brass, pictures
Open Mon–Sat 10am–5pm
Services Valuations

Garrard Antiques
Contact Mrs C Garrard
✉ **139a Corve Street, Ludlow, Shropshire, SY8 2PG** 🅿
☎ 01584 876727 Ⓕ 01584 781277
Ⓜ 07971 588063
Est. 1985 *Stock size* Large
Stock Period pine, oak and country furniture, pottery, porcelain, glass, treen, books, collectables
Open Mon–Fri 10am–1pm 2–5pm
Sat 10am–5pm

Leon Jones
Contact Mr L Jones
✉ **Mitre House Antiques, Corve Bridge, Ludlow, Shropshire, SY8 1DY** 🅿
☎ 01584 872138 Ⓜ 07976 549013
Est. 1972 *Stock size* Large
Stock Country furniture, mahogany, clocks
Open Mon–Sat 9am–5pm
Fairs Newark, Ardingly

Little Paws
Contact Mr Martin Rees-Evans
✉ **4 Castle Street, Ludlow, Shropshire, SY8 1AT** 🅿
☎ 01584 875286
Est. 1992 *Stock size* Medium
Stock Traditional teddy bears, dolls
Open Mon–Sat 10am–5pm

Ludlow Antique Beds & Fireplaces
Contact Mr G Jones or Mrs S Small
✉ **142 Corve Street, Ludlow, Shropshire, SY8 2PG** 🅿
☎ 01584 875506 Ⓜ 07850 841609
Est. 1987 *Stock size* Medium
Stock Victorian and Edwardian original fireplaces, brass, iron and wooden beds of all sizes, country furniture, garden furniture

Open Mon and Fri 11am–4pm
Sat 11am–5pm

McCartneys
Contact Mr N Carter or Miss Mary-Jane Hughes
The Ox Pasture, Overton Road, Ludlow, Shropshire, SY8 4AA
01584 872251 01584 875727
fineart@mccartneys.co.uk
www.maccartneys.co.uk
Est. 1874
Open Mon–Fri 9am–5.30pm
Sales Fine art, antiques and household effects Fri 10.30am, viewing Thurs 2–8pm day of sale 9–10.30am. Occasional specialist sales
Frequency Monthly
Catalogues Yes

K W Swift
Contact Mr K W Swift
56 Mill Street, Ludlow, Shropshire, SY8 1BB
01584 878571 01746 714407
ken@kwswift.demon.co.uk
Est. 1989 *Stock size* Medium
No. of dealers 20
Stock Book market total circa 5,000 volumes (frequently changed)
Open Mon–Sat 10am–5pm
Services Mounting, framing

M & R Taylor Antiques
Contact Michael Taylor
1 Pepper Lane, Ludlow, Shropshire, SY8 1PX
01584 874169 01584 874169
Est. 1977 *Stock size* Small
Stock Furniture, copper, brass
Open Mon–Sat 10am–4pm closed Thurs

MARKET DRAYTON

Deppner Antiques
Contact Mr J Deppner
Towers Lawn, Cheshire Street, Market Drayton, Shropshire, TF9 3EB
01630 654111 07974 020642
Est. 1987 *Stock size* Medium
Stock Stripped pine furniture, French antiques
Open Mon Wed Fri Sat 9am–5.30pm
Fairs Newark, Ardingly
Services Courier service for Newark and Ardingly fairs and at all other times, pine stripping

Kev 'n' Di's Antiques
Contact Mr K Williams
Country Needs, Rosehill Road, Market Drayton, Shropshire, TF9 2JU
01630 638320 01630 638658
07976 547174
Kevanddi.williams@btinternet.com
Est. 1980 *Stock size* Large
Stock Edwardian and Victorian shipping furniture, memorabilia, kitchenware, pine, enamel, house clearance, antiques purchased
Open Flexi hours and by appointment
Fairs Swinderby, Newark
Services Valuations, courier service

MUCH WENLOCK

Cruck House Antiques
Contact Mrs B Roderick Smith
23 Barrow Street, Much Wenlock, Shropshire, TF13 6EN
01952 727165 01952 727165
Est. 1984 *Stock size* Medium
Stock Silver, pictures, small furniture, collectables
Open Mon–Sat 10am–5pm

John King (BADA)
Contact Mr J King
Raynalds Mansion, Much Wenlock, Shropshire, TF13 6AE
01952 727456 01952 727456
Est. 1967 *Stock size* Large
Stock Period furniture and associated items
Open By appointment only
Fairs Olympia (June)

NEWPORT

Davies, White & Perry
Contact Mr J P Davies
45–47 High Street, Newport, Shropshire, TF10 7AT
01952 811003 01952 811439
newport@davieswhiteperry.co.uk
www.davieswhiteperry.co.uk
Est. 1806
Open Mon–Fri 8.15am–5pm
Sat 9am–4pm closed noon–2pm
Sun 11am–4pm
Sales Occasional antiques sales on site
Catalogues Yes

NORBURY

Brook Farm Antiques
Contact Mr Tucker or Mr James
Brook Farm, Gauntons Bank, Norbury, Shropshire, SY13 4HY
01948 666043 07754 418777
Est. 1983 *Stock size* Medium
Stock Victorian–Edwardian dining tables
Open Mon–Sun 9am–5pm
Fairs Stafford Bingley Hall, DMG Shepton Mallet
Services Restorations

OSWESTRY

Arcadia
Contact Joyce or Rod Whitehead
6 Upper Brook Street, Oswestry, Shropshire, SY10 2TB
01691 655622
Est. 1997 *Stock size* Large
Stock Antique and contemporary works of art, ceramics, pictures, books, textiles, designer jewellery, small furniture
Open Mon–Sat 9.30am–5.30pm or by appointment
Services Home decoration

Bookworld
Contact Mr J Cranwell
32 Beatrice Street, Oswestry, Shropshire, SY11 1QG
01691 657112 01691 657112
bookworld@arrowweb.co.uk
www.tgal.co.uk/bookworld
Est. 1995 *Stock size* Medium
Stock Antiquarian and second-hand books
Open Mon–Sat 9am–5.30pm
Services Book search

Judith Charles Antiques & Collectables
Contact Judith Charles
67 Beatrice Street, Oswestry, Shropshire, SY11 1QT
01691 653524 01691 624416
07855 253617
Est. 2001 *Stock size* Large
Stock Royal Doulton, china, porcelain, small items, furniture, Beswick, Royal Albert, Sadler, jewellery
Open Mon–Fri 10am–3pm
Sat 10am–5pm
Fairs Ellesmere
Services Valuations

MIDLANDS
SHROPSHIRE • PREES HEATH

PREES HEATH

Whitchurch Antique Centre
Contact Mr John Simcox
Heath Road, Prees Heath, Whitchurch, Shropshire, SY13 2AD
01948 662626 F 01948 662604
www.whitchurchantiques.co.uk
Est. 1979 *Stock size* Large
Stock French and English furniture
Open Mon–Sun 9am–5pm
Services Packing, shipping

SHERIFFHALES

Corner Farm Antiques
Contact Mr Tim Dams
Weston Heath, Sheriffhales, Shropshire, TF11 8RY
01952 691543 F 01952 691543
M 07971 578585
www.1cfa.co.uk
Est. 1995 *Stock size* Large
Stock Georgian–Victorian and dining furniture, clocks, barometers, longcase clocks, collectables
Open Mon–Sun 10am–5pm
Services Restorations, clock repairs, valuations

SHIFNAL

Davies, White & Perry
Contact Mr J P Davies
18 Market Place, Shifnal, Shropshire, TF11 9AZ
01952 460523
Est. 1806
Open Mon–Fri 9am–5pm closed 1pm–2pm Sat 9am–noon
Sales Occasional antiques sales on site
Catalogues Yes

SHREWSBURY

Bear Steps Antiques
Contact John or Sally Wyatt
2 Bear Steps, Fish Street, Shrewsbury, Shropshire, SY1 1UR
01743 344298 M 07720 675813
www.bear-steps-antiques.co.uk
Est. 1990 *Stock size* Large
Stock 18th–early 19thC English porcelain
Open Mon–Sat 9am–5pm
Fairs NEC Antiques for Everyone

Candle Lane Books
Contact Mr J Thornhill
28 Princess Street, Shrewsbury, Shropshire, SY1 1LW
01743 365301 F 01952 771127
Est. 1965 *Stock size* Large
Stock Antiquarian and second-hand books
Open Mon–Sat 9.30am–1pm 2–4.45pm

Collectors Gallery (IBNS, IBSS, ANA, BNTA)
Contact Mr Veissid
24 The Parade, St Mary's Place, Shrewsbury, Shropshire, SY1 1DL
01743 272140 F 01743 366041
E m.veissid@btinternet.com
www.collectors-gallery.co.uk
Est. 1976 *Stock size* Medium
Stock Coins, medals, stamps, bank notes, postcards, bonds and shares
Open Mon–Sat 9am–5.30pm
Services Mail order

Collectors Place
Contact Mr Keith Jones or Mrs June Jones
29a Princess Street, Shrewsbury, Shropshire, SY1 1LW
01743 246150
Est. 1996 *Stock size* Large
Stock Antique bottles, pot lids, Wade, Beswick, Carlton ware, Art Deco, collectables
Open Mon–Fri 10am–4pm closed Thurs Sat 9.30am–5pm
Fairs The Antique Bottle Fair
Services Valuations on bottles

Deborah Paul
Contact Debbie or Paul
23 Belle Vue Road, Shrewsbury, Shropshire, SY3 7LN
01743 357696 M 07890 926530
E pgurden@aol.com
Est. 2000 *Stock size* Medium
Stock Decorative and period furniture
Open Mon–Sat 10am–5pm or by appointment
Services Clock restorer on site

Deja Vu Antiques
Contact Mr I Jones
48 High Street, Shrewsbury, Shropshire, SY13 1EU
01743 362251
M 07772 691939
E dejavuantiques@lineone.net
www.antiquephones.co.uk
Est. 1984 *Stock size* Medium
Stock Antique telephones, Art Deco, pine furniture
Open Mon–Sat 9.30am–5pm usually closed Thurs
Fairs Chester, Leeds and Loughborough Art Deco fairs
Services Valuations, restorations, repairs, mail order service

Expressions
Contact Mrs J Griffiths
17 Princess Street, Shrewsbury, Shropshire, SY1 1LP
01743 351731
Est. 1991 *Stock size* Medium
Stock Art Deco, furniture, pictures, glass, ceramics
Open Mon–Sat 10am–4pm

Halls Fine Art Auctions (ARVA)
Contact Mr Richard Allen or Jeremy Lamond
Welsh Bridge, Shrewsbury, Shropshire, SY3 8LA
01743 231212 F 01743 271014
E fineart@halls-auctioneers.ltd.uk
www.halls-auctioneers.ltd.uk
Est. 1865
Open 9am–5pm
Sales Antiques sales every 6 weeks, general and collectors sales every Fri 10.30am, viewing Thurs 9.30am–7pm
Frequency Every 6 weeks
Catalogues Yes

Hutton Antiques
Contact Mrs C Brookfield
18 Princess Street, Shrewsbury, Shropshire, SY1 1LP
01743 245810
Est. 1979 *Stock size* Medium
Stock Silver, porcelain and small furniture
Open Tues–Sat 9.30am–4pm

The Little Gem (NAG)
Contact Mrs M A Bowdler
18 St Marys Street, Shrewsbury, Shropshire, SY1 1ED
01743 352085 F 01743 352085
E mbowdler@littlegem.freeserve.co.uk
www.thelittlegem.co.uk
Est. 1960 *Stock size* Medium
Stock Antique and second-hand

jewellery, modern Waterford crystal, lighting, handmade jewellery
Open Mon–Sat 9am–5.30pm closed Thurs except Dec
Services Jewellery and watch repair

F C Manser & Son Ltd (LAPADA)
Contact Paul Manser
Coleham Head, Shrewsbury, Shropshire, SY3 7BJ
01743 351120 01743 271047
mansers@theantiquedealers.com
www.theantiquedealers.com
Est. 1944 ***Stock size*** Large
Stock Antiques, furniture, porcelain, glassware
Open Mon–Sat 9am–5pm
Fairs LAPADA – NEC
Services Valuations, restorations

Princess Antique Centre
Contact Mr John Langford
14a The Square, Shrewsbury, Shropshire, SY1 1LH
01743 343701
Est. 1984 ***Stock size*** Large
No. of dealers 100
Stock Complete range of antiques and collectables
Open Mon–Sat 9.30am–5.15pm

Quayside Antiques
Contact Mr Chris Winter
9 Frankwell, Shrewsbury, Shropshire, SY3 8JY
01743 360490 or 01948 830363
07715 748223
www.quaysideantiques.co.uk
Est. 1974 ***Stock size*** Large
Stock Victorian and Edwardian mahogany furniture, large tables, sets of chairs
Open Tues–Sat 10am–4pm closed Thurs
Fairs NEC
Services Restorations

Remains To Be Seen
Contact Mr Moseley or Ms Roberts
62 Wyle Cop, Shrewsbury, Shropshire, SY1 1UX
01743 361560
07715 597137
Est. 1991 ***Stock size*** Medium
Stock Arts & Crafts, Art Nouveau, Gothic revival
Open Mon–Fri 10am–5pm Sat 10am–6pm

Shrewsbury Antique Centre
Contact Mr John Langford
15 Princess House, The Square, Shrewsbury, Shropshire, SY1 1JZ
01743 247704
Est. 1984 ***Stock size*** Large
No. of dealers 70
Stock Wide range of stock
Open Mon–Sat 9.30am–5.15pm

Shrewsbury Antique Market
Contact Mr W Williams
Frankwell Quay Warehouse, Frankwell, Shrewsbury, Shropshire, SY3 8LG
01743 350916
Est. 1979 ***Stock size*** Medium
No. of dealers 45
Stock Antique and period collectables
Open Mon–Sat 9.30am–5pm

Shrewsbury Clock Shop (BHI)
Contact Mr A Donnelly
The Clock Shop, 7 The Parade, St Mary's Place, Shrewsbury, Shropshire, SY1 1DL
01743 361388 01743 361388
clockshopshrewsbury@hotmail.com
Est. 1987 ***Stock size*** Medium
Stock Clocks, especially longcase and barometers
Open By appointment
Fairs NEC Spring
Services Clock and barometer repairs and restorations

STANTON UPON HINE HEATH

Marcus Moore Antiques
Contact Mr M Moore
Booley House, Booley, Stanton upon Hine Heath, Shrewsbury, Shropshire, SY4 4LY
01939 200333 01939 200333
07976 228122
mmooreantiques@aol.com
www.marcusmoore-antiques.com
Est. 1980 ***Stock size*** Large
Stock Georgian–Victorian oak, country and mahogany furniture and associated items
Open By appointment any time
Services Restorations, upholstery, search, courier

WALL UNDER HEYWOOD

Mullock & Madeley (RICS, ISVA)
Contact John Mullock or Paul Madeley
The Old Shippon, Wall under Heywood, Church Stretton, Shropshire, SY6 7DS
01694 771771 01694 771772
info@mullockmadeley.co.uk
www.mullockmadeley.co.uk
Est. 1997
Open Mon–Fri 9am–5pm
Sales Sporting memorabilia, vintage fishing tackle. Sales held London, Ludlow Race Course, Kempton Park, Solihull
Frequency Every 3 months

WEM

The Deermoss Gallery
Contact Colin C Moodley
The Old School, Edstaton, Wem, Shrewsbury, Shropshire, SY4 5RJ
01948 880984 01948 880984
colin.moodley@pipemedia.co.uk
Est. 1989 ***Stock size*** Large
Stock Antiques and curios from pre-1920
Open Thurs Fri Sat 10am–5pm
Services Framing, shipping and packing

Heritage Antiques
Contact M Nelms
Unit 2, Trench Farm, Tilley Green, Wem, Shropshire, SY4 5PJ
01939 235416
www.heritageantiques.co.uk
Est. 1988 ***Stock size*** Medium
Stock Regency–Edwardian furniture and collectables
Open Mon–Fri 9am–5pm Sat by appointment
Services Restorations

WOORE

Woore House Interiors
Contact Ms G Hargreaves-Jones or Mr R F M Jackson
Unit 7–8, Nantwich Road, Woore, Shropshire, CW3 9SA
01630 647888 07803 497938
Est. 1994 ***Stock size*** Small
Stock Victorian, Edwardian and

later furniture, sofas, winged armchairs, chaise longues etc, fully restored and unrestored
Open By appointment
Services Upholstery, designer fabrics

STAFFORDSHIRE

ALREWAS

Poley Antiques
Contact Mr D Poley
5 Main Street, Alrewas, Burton-on-Trent, Staffordshire, DE13 7AA
☎ 01283 791151 Ⓕ 01283 791151
Ⓜ 07976 676228
Ⓔ dennis.poley@which.net
Est. 1977 *Stock size* Medium
Stock Ceramics, small furniture, silver, brass, copper items
Open Thurs–Sat 10am–5.30pm
Fairs Alexandra Palace, Newark, NEC
Services Valuations

BREWOOD

David & Paula Whitfield
Contact David or Paula Whitfield
Passiflora, 25 Stafford Street, Brewood, Staffordshire, ST19 9DX
☎ 01902 851557
Ⓔ paula.whitfield@ukonline.co.uk
Est. 1988 *Stock size* Large
Stock Antiques and collectables dating back to Victorian times, glass, china, pottery, copper, brass, cast-iron, curios, leather, ephemera, postcards, children's books, bric-a-brac, garden statuary, small furniture, decorative items including Mabel Lucie Attwell
Open By appointment
Fairs Stafford Bingley Hall, West Midlands Fairs
Services Valuations and house clearance

BURTON-ON-TRENT

Burton Antiques
Contact Mr M Rodgers
1/2 Horninglow Road, Burton-on-Trent, Staffordshire, DE14 2PR
☎ 01283 542331
Est. 1978 *Stock size* Medium
Stock Antique pine and other antique furniture, shipping
Open Mon–Sat 9am–5pm
Sun 11am–4pm
Services Valuations and pine stripping

Byrkley Books Ltd
Contact Mrs P Tebbett
159 Station Street, Burton-on-Trent, Staffordshire, DE14 1BE
☎ 01283 565900
Est. 1963 *Stock size* Medium
Stock Antiquarian, second-hand and remainder books, horse racing a speciality
Open Mon–Fri 9.30am–5pm
Sat 9am–5pm

Martin Gilbert Antiques
Contact Mr M Gilbert
Unit 3, Manor Trading Estate, Hawkins Lane, Burton-on-Trent, Staffordshire, DE14 1QX
☎ 01283 517717
Ⓔ mgilbertantiques@aol.com
Est. 1987 *Stock size* Medium
Stock Georgian and Victorian mahogany and oak furniture, fully restored
Open Mon–Fri 8.30am–5pm or by appointment
Fairs Newark

Roy C Harris (LAPADA)
Contact Roy Harris
Burton-on-Trent, Staffordshire
☎ 01283 520355
Ⓔ rchclocks@aol.com
Est. 1983 *Stock size* Medium
Stock Longcase clocks, bracket, mantel and wall clocks
Open By appointment
Fairs NEC
Services Valuations, restorations, shipping

One Off
Contact Mr P Walton
35 Outwoods Street, Burton-on-Trent, Staffordshire, DE14 2PL
☎ 01283 563565
Est. 1989 *Stock size* Small
Stock Hand-painted furniture of all types
Open Mon–Sat 9am–6pm

Richard Winterton Auctioneers and Valuers (NAVA)
Contact Mr A Rathbone or Mr R Winterton
School House Auction Rooms, Hawkins Lane, Burton-on-Trent, Staffordshire, DE14 1PT
☎ 01283 511224 Ⓕ 01283 568650
Ⓔ adrianrathbone@btconnect.com
Ⓦ www.icollector.com
Est. 1864
Open Mon–Fri 9am–5pm
Tues 9am–6.30pm
Sales Weekly auctions of ceramics, glass, silver, fine art, jewellery, furniture, toys, sporting memorabilia, collectors' items, antiquarian books, shipping furniture
Frequency Weekly
Catalogues Yes

CHEADLE

Country Pine Trading Co
Contact Mr S Beard
Unit D, The Green, Cheadle, Staffordshire, ST10 1PH
☎ 01538 756894 Ⓕ 01538 750244
Ⓜ 07959 585133
Ⓦ www.countrypinetrading.co.uk
Est. 1974 *Stock size* Large
Stock Country pine and antique pine furniture
Open Mon–Fri 8am–5pm Sat 8am–1pm or by appointment
Fairs Newark
Services Restorations and pine stripping

ECCLESHALL

Cottage Collectibles
Contact Mrs S Kettle
62 High Street, Eccleshall, Staffordshire, ST21 6BZ
☎ 01785 850210 Ⓕ 01785 850757
Ⓜ 07967 713512
Ⓔ sheila@cottagecollectibles.co.uk
Ⓦ www.cottagecollectibles.co.uk
Est. 1995 *Stock size* Medium
Stock English and Continental country antiques, kitchenware, pine furniture, garden and dairy tools
Open By appointment only
Services Restorations

Worldwide Arms Ltd (GTA)
Contact Mrs Marita Rawlins
PO Box 5, Eccleshall, Staffordshire, ST21 6SN
☎ 01785 851515 Ⓕ 01785 850035
Ⓔ sales@worldwidearms.com
Ⓦ www.worldwidearms.com

Est. 1974 *Stock size* Large
Stock From medieval armour to deactivated machine guns
Open Telephone sales 9am–5.30pm
Fairs Many in UK and Germany
Services Mail order only, 3 colour catalogues annually

HARRISEAHEAD

David J Cope
Contact Mr D Cope
Fox Earth, Harriseahead Lane, Harriseahead, Stoke-on-Trent, Staffordshire, ST7 4RF
01782 511926 01782 516931
07712 880695
Est. 1979 *Stock size* Medium
Stock Moorcroft, Royal Worcester, Royal Doulton and porcelain
Open Mon–Sun 10am–5pm
Fairs Newark
Services Valuations

LEEK

The Antique Store
Contact Mrs J Hopwood
1 Clerk Bank, Leek, Staffordshire, ST13 5HE
01538 386555 01782 570119
Est. 1999 *Stock size* Medium
Stock Painted furniture, decorative items, garden items, architectural antiques, French items, ecclesiastical items
Open Mon–Sat 10am–5pm

Antiques Within
Contact Mr R Hicks or Mrs K Hicks
Ground Floor, Compton Mill, Compton, Leek, Staffordshire, ST13 5NJ
01538 387848 01538 387848
antiques.within@virgin.net
www.antiques-within.com
Est. 1994 *Stock size* Large
Stock Pine, oak, mahogany and Continental furniture, brass, copper, mirrors, collectables
Open Mon–Sat 10am–5.30pm
Fairs Newark, Swinderby and Ardingly
Services Shipping

Anvil Antiques
Contact Mrs Lynn Davis
Cross Street Mill, Cross Street, Leek, Staffordshire, ST13 6BL
01538 371657 01538 385118
Est. 1975 *Stock size* Medium
Stock Reproduction and old pine furniture, old French dark-wood furniture
Open Mon–Fri 9am–5pm Sat 10am–5pm Sun by appointment
Services Restorations

Bury & Hilton
Contact John Hilton
6 Market Street, Leek, Staffordshire, ST13 6HZ
01538 383344 01538 371314
Est. 1887
Open Mon–Fri 9am–5.30pm
Sales Antiques sales, 1st Thurs monthly 10am, special antiques sales April and October.
Frequency Monthly
Catalogues Yes

Compton Mill Antique Emporium
Contact Mrs S K Butler
Compton Mill, Compton, Leek, Staffordshire, ST13 5NJ
01538 373396 01538 399092
kelly@comptonmill.fsnet.co.uk
www.comptonmill.com
Est. 1996 *Stock size* Large
No. of dealers 25
Stock Wide range of antiques
Open Mon–Sat 10am–5.30pm Sun 1–5pm
Services Pine furniture made from reclaimed timber

Cornerhouse Antiques
Contact Ms H Balmer
2 Brook Street, Leek, Staffordshire, ST13 5JE
01538 399901 01538 399901
07973 189468
Est. 1996 *Stock size* Medium
Stock Georgian, Victorian, pine and mahogany furniture, brass, copper, iron, steel, kitchenware, country items, 1920s antiques
Open Mon–Sat 10am–5pm
Fairs Stafford Bowmans, Swinderby, Newark
Services Metal polishing

K Grosvenor
Contact Mr K Grosvenor
71 St Edward Street, Leek, Staffordshire, ST13 5DH
01538 385669 01538 385669
keith.grosvenor@virgin.net
Est. 1970 *Stock size* Large
Stock Clocks, barometers, scientific instruments
Open Mon–Sat 9am–4pm or by appointment
Services Restorations, repairs of clocks

Roger Haynes Antique Finder
Contact Mr R Haynes
31 Compton, Leek, Staffordshire, ST13 5NJ
01538 385161 01538 385161
Est. 1959 *Stock size* Large
Stock Decorative English and French items, pine and country small items, collectables
Trade only Yes
Open By appointment only
Services Export trade

Stephen Hibbert's Antiques
Contact Mr S Hibbert
24St Edward Street, Leek, Staffordshire, ST13 5DL
01538 381274 07768 835032
Est. 1984 *Stock size* Large
Stock Lalique, Gallé, tapestries, carved furniture, chandeliers, carpets, beds, furniture, clocks
Open Mon–Sat 10am–5.30pm
Services Valuations

Johnsons
Contact Mr P Johnson
120 Mill Street, Leek, Staffordshire, ST13 8HA
01538 386745 01538 386745
07714 288765
Est. 1976 *Stock size* Medium
Stock English and French country furniture, decorative accessories, unique objects
Open Mon–Fri 8am–5pm Sat Sun by appointment
Services Suppliers to export market

Jonathan Charles Antiques
Contact Mr J Heath
6 Broad Street, Leek, Staffordshire, ST13 5NS
01538 381883/385922 (workshops)
Est. 1999 *Stock size* Medium
Stock Pine furniture, country furniture, iron and brass bedsteads, collectables
Open Mon–Sat 11am–5pm
Services One-off pieces made to measure

Leek Antiques Centre (Barclay House)
Contact Mr P Lumley

MIDLANDS

STAFFORDSHIRE • LICHFIELD

✉ 4–6 Brook Street, Leek, Staffordshire, ST13 5JE 🅿
☎ 01538 398475 Ⓜ 07721 413095
Est. 1969 *Stock size* Large
No. of dealers 78
Stock Wide range of antiques including dining tables, sets of chairs, bedroom furniture, chests-of-drawers, pottery, watercolours, oil paintings, pine
Open Mon–Sat 10am–5pm
Services Restoration, polishing and upholstery

Molland Antique Mirrors
Contact John Molland
✉ 2 Duke Street, Leek, Staffordshire, ST13 5NH 🅿
☎ 01538 372553 Ⓕ 01538 372553
Ⓜ 07774 226042
Ⓔ sales@mollandmirrors.co.uk
Ⓦ www.mollandmirrors.co.uk
Est. 1988 *Stock size* Large
Stock 19thC French and English mirrors
Open Mon–Sat 8am–5pm
Fairs NEC
Services Export packing

Odeon Designs Ltd (Lighting Association)
Contact Mr S Ford
✉ 76–78 St Edward Street, Leek, Staffordshire, ST13 5DL 🅿
☎ 01538 387188 Ⓕ 01538 387188
Ⓜ 07973 317961
Ⓔ odeonantiques@hotmail.com
Ⓦ www.odeonantiques.co.uk
Est. 1993 *Stock size* Large
Stock Antique and some reproduction country furniture, lighting, small decorative objects
Open Mon–Sat 11am–5pm
Services Valuations, restorations of lighting

Page Antiques
Contact Dennis Page
✉ Antiques Within Ltd, Ground Floor, Compton Mill, Leek, Staffordshire, ST13 5NJ 🅿
☎ 01663 732358 Ⓕ 01663 732358
Ⓜ 07966 154993
Est. 1979 *Stock size* Medium
Stock General antiques, Georgian–Edwardian furniture
Open Mon–Sat 10am–5pm
Fairs Swinderby, Buxton, Newark, Chester
Services Valuations, exports

Roberts & Mudd Antiques
Contact Mr C Mudd
✉ Compton Mill, Compton, Leek, Staffordshire, ST13 5NJ 🅿
☎ 01538 371284 Ⓕ 01538 371284
Ⓜ 07768 845942
Ⓔ robertsmudd@compuserve.com
Ⓦ www.robertsandmudd.com
Est. 1993 *Stock size* Large
Stock French, pine and country furniture, decorative items
Open Mon–Fri 8am–6pm
Sat 9am–noon
Services Restorations

Simpsons
Contact Mr M Simpson
✉ 39 St Edward Street, Leek, Staffordshire, ST13 5DH 🅿
☎ 01538 371515 Ⓕ 01538 371515
Est. 1989 *Stock size* Medium
Stock Original decorative, painted and pine furniture for home and garden
Open Mon–Sat 10am–5pm
Thurs 11am–4pm

LICHFIELD

Cathedral Gallery
Contact Mrs R Thompson-Yates
✉ 22 Dam Street, Lichfield, Staffordshire, WS13 6AA
☎ 01543 253115
Est. 1984 *Stock size* Large
Stock Antique maps, prints
Open Mon–Sat 9.30am–5pm closed Wed
Services Valuations, restorations, framing, colouring

Cordelia & Perdy's Antique Shop
Contact Mrs Cordelia Mellor-Whiting
✉ 53 Tamworth Street, Lichfield, Staffordshire, WS13 6JW 🅿
☎ 01543 263223
Est. 1974 *Stock size* Medium
Stock Wide range of antiques including furniture, porcelain and collectables
Open Tues–Fri 10am–4pm
Sat 10am–5pm

Curborough Hall Farm Antiques Centre (ADA)
Contact Mr J Finnemore
✉ Unit 10, Curborough Hall Farm, Watery Lane, Lichfield, Staffordshire, WS13 7SE 🅿
☎ 01543 417100 Ⓜ 07885 285053
Est. 1995 *Stock size* Large
No. of dealers 31
Stock Furniture, china, collectables, jewellery, books, linen, pictures
Open Tues–Sun Bank Holidays 10.30am–5pm
Services Restaurant

The Essence of Time (BHI)
Contact Malcolm Hinton
✉ Unit 2, Curborough Antiques and Lichfield Craft Centre, Curborough Hall Farm, Watery Lane, Lichfield, Staffordshire, WS13 8ES 🅿
☎ 01543 418239/01902 764900 (evenings)
Ⓜ 07944 245064 (any time)
Est. 1990 *Stock size* Large
Stock Longcase, Vienna, wall, mantel and novelty clocks
Open Wed–Sun 10.45am–5pm

James A Jordan (BHI)
Contact Mr J Jordan
✉ 7 The Corn Exchange, Conduit Street, Lichfield, Staffordshire, WS13 6JR 🅿
☎ 01543 416221
Est. 1988 *Stock size* Large
Stock Jewellery, watches, clocks, silver, small antique furnishings
Open Mon–Sat 9am–5pm closed Wed
Services Watch, clock and barometer repairs

Milestone Antiques (LAPADA)
Contact Humphrey and Elsa Crawshaw
✉ 5 Main Street, Whittington, Lichfield, Staffordshire, WS14 9JU 🅿
☎ 01543 432248
Est. 1988 *Stock size* Medium
Stock Georgian–early Victorian traditional English furniture, 19thC English porcelain, decorative items
Open Thurs–Sat 10am–6pm
Sun 11am–3pm or by appointment

Royden Smith
Contact Mr R Smith
Church View House, Farewell Lane, Burntwood, Lichfield, Staffordshire, WS7 9DP
01543 682217
Est. 1973 *Stock size* Large
Stock Antiquarian, second-hand books
Open Sat 10am–4.30pm Sun 11am–4.30pm or by appointment
Services Valuations

The Staffs Bookshop
Contact Mr P Stockham
4 & 6 Dam Street, Lichfield, Staffordshire, WS13 6AA
01543 264093
Est. 1930 *Stock size* Large
Stock Children's, antiquarian, second-hand and new books, Samuel Johnson, 18thC literature
Open Mon–Sat 9.30am–5pm
Services Valuations

Wintertons Ltd (SOFAA)
Contact Charles Hanson
Lichfield Auction Centre, Fradley Park, Lichfield, Staffordshire, WS13 8NF
01543 263256 F 01543 415348
E enquiries@wintertons.co.uk
W www.wintertons.co.uk
Est. 1864
Open Mon–Fri 9am–5.30pm
Sales Victorian and general sales, every 2 or 3 weeks Thurs 10.30am, viewing Wed 1–7pm. Bi-monthly 2-day fine art sale, Wed Thurs 10.30am, viewing Tues noon–8pm and day of sale
Frequency Bi-monthly
Catalogues Yes

NEWCASTLE-UNDER-LYME

Richard Midwinter Antiques
Contact Mr R Midwinter
31 Bridge Street, Newcastle-under-Lyme, Staffordshire, ST5 2RY
01782 712483 or 01630 672289
F 01630 672289 M 07830 617361
E antiques@midwinter.fslife.co.uk
Est. 1972 *Stock size* Medium
Stock 16th–19thC oak, mahogany and walnut furniture
Open By appointment
Fairs Olympia
Services Restorations

PENKRIDGE

Golden Oldies
Contact Mr Knowles
5 Crown Bridge, Penkridge, Staffordshire, ST19 5AA
01785 714722
Est. 1973 *Stock size* Large
Stock Antique and reproduction stock mainly furniture and general antiques
Open Mon–Sat 9.30am–5.30pm
Fairs Newark

RUGELEY

Rugeley Antique Centre
Contact Mrs M Edwards
161 Main Road, Brereton, Rugeley, Staffordshire, WS15 1DX
01889 577166
E info@rugeleyantiquecentre.co.uk
W www.rugeleyantiquecentre.co.uk
Est. 1980 *Stock size* Large
No. of dealers 35
Stock Antiques and collectables
Open Mon–Sat 9am–5pm Sun Bank Holidays noon–4.30pm
Services Small parcel shipping

STAFFORD

Windmill Antiques
Contact Mr I Kettlewell
9 Castle Hill, Broad Eye, Stafford, Staffordshire, ST16 2QB
01785 228505 F 01785 228505
Est. 1992 *Stock size* Large
Stock Antiques, jewellery, decorative items
Open Mon–Sat 10am–5pm
Services Valuations, barometer and ceramic restoration

STOKE-ON-TRENT

Abacus Gallery
Contact Mr D Mycock
56 & 58 Millrise Road, Milton, Stoke-on-Trent, Staffordshire, ST2 7BW
01782 543005
Est. 1980 *Stock size* Medium
Stock Antiquarian and second-hand books, prints, engravings
Open Mon–Fri 9am–5pm Sat 9am–4pm
Fairs Buxton Book Fair

Ann's Antiques
Contact Mrs A Byatte
26 Leek Road, Stockton Brook, Stoke-on-Trent, Staffordshire, ST9 9NN
01782 503991
Est. 1969 *Stock size* Large
Stock Victorian–Edwardian furniture, cranberry glass, Victorian oil lamps, jewellery, pottery, porcelain, rocking horses, dolls houses
Open Fri Sat 10am–5pm or by appointment

Antiquities of Hartshill
Contact Mrs J Brunetti
311 Hartshill Road, Hartshill, Stoke-on-Trent, Staffordshire, ST4 7NR
01782 620222
Est. 1996 *Stock size* Large
Stock Wide range of antiquities including furniture, china, dolls, porcelain
Open Mon–Sat 10am–4.30pm
Services Valuations, Hummel figures found

Ceramics International
Contact Christine Cope
Unit 1, Canal Lane, Tunstall, Stoke-on-Trent, Staffordshire, ST6 4NZ
01782 575545 F 01782 814447
E theoldchintzcompany@compuserve.com
Est. 1996 *Stock size* Large
Stock English, imported ceramics, Worcester, Wedgewood, Moorcroft, chintz, flow blue
Trade only Yes
Open Mon–Fri 9am–5.30pm

Checkley Interiors
Contact Mr S Clegg
493–495 Hartshill Road, Hartshill, Stoke-on-Trent, Staffordshire, ST4 6AA
01782 717522 F 01782 717522
Est. 1998 *Stock size* Medium
Stock Victorian and Edwardian upholstered and occasional furniture
Open Mon–Sat 9.30am–5pm closed Thurs
Services Restorations, upholstery, room interior service

MIDLANDS

STAFFORDSHIRE • STONE

H Chesters & Sons
Contact Mr H Chesters
✉ **196 Waterloo Road, Burslem, Stoke-on-Trent, Staffordshire, ST6 3HQ** P
☎ 01782 822344
Est. 1912
Open Mon–Fri 10am–5pm telephone service 7am–noon
Sales Fine antiques sales, 2 per annum, Feb and Sept, viewing advertised locally
Catalogues Yes

On the Hill Antiques
Contact Ms Sue Bird
✉ **450 Hartshill Road, Stoke-on-Trent, Staffordshire, ST4 7PL** P
☎ 01782 252249 F 01782 252249
M 07932 726035
Est. 1996 *Stock size* Large
Stock 1930s oak furniture, pottery, collectables
Open Mon–Sat 9am–5pm
Fairs Bingley, Staffordshire
Services Valuations

Potteries Antique Centre
Contact Ms K Ware
✉ **271 Waterloo Road, Cobridge, Stoke-on-Trent, Staffordshire, ST6 3HR** P
☎ 01782 201455 F 01782 201518
E www@potteriesantiquecentre.com
W www.potteriesantiquecentre.com
Est. 1990 *Stock size* Large
Stock Wedgwood, Doulton, Beswick, Moorcroft, Crown Devon, Coalport, Minton, Clarice Cliff, Crown Derby, Wade, Shelley, Carlton ware
Open Mon–Sat 9am–5.30pm Sun 10am–4pm
Fairs Newark, Ardingly
Services Valuations

Potteries Specialist Auctions
Contact Stella M Ashbrook
✉ **271 Waterloo Road, Cobridge, Stoke-on-Trent, Staffordshire, ST6 3HR** P
☎ 01782 286622 F 01782 213777
W www.potteriesauctions.com
Est. 1986
Open Mon–Fri 9am–5pm
Sales Mainly British 20thC pottery, last Sat of each month 11.30am, viewing Fri prior 9am–7pm day of sale from 9am
Frequency Monthly
Catalogues Yes

The Pottery Buying Centre
Contact Mr P Hume
✉ **535 Etruria Road, Basford, Stoke-on-Trent, Staffordshire, ST5 0PN** P
☎ 01782 635453 M 07971 711612
Est. 1997 *Stock size* Medium
Stock Fine ceramics, collectables, Doulton, Moorcroft, Beswick, small furniture
Open Mon–Sat 10am–4pm
Services Valuations, restoration of ceramics

Louis Taylor Fine Art Auctioneers
Contact Mr C Hillier ARICS
✉ **Britannia House, 10 Town Road, Hanley, Stoke-on-Trent, Staffordshire, ST1 2QG** P
☎ 01782 214111 F 01782 215283
Est. 1877
Open Mon–Fri 9am–5pm closed 1–2pm
Sales Quarterly 2-day fine art sales Mon Tues 10am, viewing Thurs 10am–7pm Fri 10am–4pm day of sale from 9am. Specialist Doulton and Beswick quarterly, viewing as for fine art. General and Victoriana every two weeks Mon 10am, viewing Fri 10am–4pm Sat 9am–noon
Frequency Fortnightly
Catalogues Yes

The Tinder Box
Contact Mrs P Yarwood
✉ **61 Lichfield Street, Hanley, Stoke-on-Trent, Staffordshire, ST1 3EA** P
☎ 01782 261368 F 01782 261368
M 07946 445659
Est. 1969 *Stock size* Large
Stock Jewellery, pottery, silver, lamps, spares for oil lamps
Open Mon–Sat 9.30am–6.30pm
Services Valuations, restorations

Top of the Hill Antiques
Contact Mr A Phillips
✉ **12/14–14a Mile Street, Burslem, Stoke-on-Trent, Staffordshire, ST6 2AF** P
☎ 01782 834506 F 01782 834506
E info@ceramic.search.co.uk
W www.ceramic-search.mcmail.com
Est. 1995 *Stock size* Large
Stock Staffordshire ceramics, general antiques, collectables, antique and reproduction beds
Open Mon–Sat 9.30am–5pm
Fairs Specialist Doulton and Beswick fairs
Services Valuations, restorations, ceramic search service

Wooden Heart
Contact Mrs Y Quirke
✉ **51 Stoke Road, Shelton, Stoke-on-Trent, Staffordshire, ST4 2QN** P
☎ 01782 411437
Est. 1995 *Stock size* Large
Stock Edwardian–Victorian mahogany furniture and decorative items
Open Mon–Fri 8.30am–5pm Sat 10.30am–3.30pm
Services Restorations

STONE

Hallahan
Contact Hilary Jeffries
✉ **13 Station Road, Stone, Staffordshire, ST15 8JP** P
☎ 01785 815187 F 01785 815187
Est. 1995 *Stock size* Large
Stock 1960s–70s collectables, antiques, upholstered furniture, antiquarian books, jewellery
Open Mon–Sat 9.30am–5pm closed Wed
Services Upholstery

TAMWORTH

Aldergate Antiques
Contact Mr Mike Foster
✉ **George Street, Tamworth, Staffordshire, B79 7LQ** P
☎ 01827 62164
E aldergate.antiques@virgin.net
Est. 1998 *Stock size* Medium
Stock Ceramics, silver, ivory, smalls
Open By appointment
Fairs Malvern Fair, Donnington, NEC

TUTBURY

The Clock Shop (MBHI)
Contact Ms A James
✉ **1 High Street, Tutbury, Burton-on-Trent, Staffordshire, DE13 9LP** P
☎ 01283 814596 F 01283 814594

Ⓜ 07710 161949
Ⓔ sales@antique-clocks-watches.co.uk
Ⓦ www.antique-clocks-watches.co.uk
Est. 1987 *Stock size* Large
Stock Antique clocks, longcase clocks, watches
Open Mon–Sat 10am–5pm
Services Valuations, restorations and repairs

The Old Chapel Antiques & Collectables Centre (OCS)
Contact Mr R Clarke
High Street, Tutbury, Burton-on-Trent, Staffordshire, DE13 9LP Ⓟ
☎ 01283 815255
Est. 1996 *Stock size* Large
No. of dealers 26
Stock Wide range of antiques and collectables
Open Mon–Sun 10am–5pm

Tutbury Mill Antique Centre
Contact Mrs L Carlin
Tutbury Mill Mews, Lower High Street, Tutbury, Burton-on-Trent, Staffordshire, DE13 9LU Ⓟ
☎ 01283 520074 Ⓜ 07973 153246
Ⓦ www.antiquesplus.co.uk
Est. 1995 *Stock size* Large
No. of dealers 25
Stock Wide range of antiques and collectables
Open Mon–Sat 10.00am–5.30pm, Sun noon–5pm

UTTOXETER

Lion Antiques Centre
Contact Mrs Vicky Jacques
8 Market Place, Uttoxeter, Staffordshire, ST14 8HP Ⓟ
☎ 01889 567717 Ⓕ 01889 567717
Est. 1999 *Stock size* Large
No. of dealers 28
Stock Wide range of antiques
Open Mon–Sat 10am–5pm Sun 1–5pm
Services Sourcing service, design

Mouse Mill Antique Centre
Contact Mrs De Ville
The Old Warehouse, Market Street, Uttoxeter, Staffordshire, ST14 8JA Ⓟ
☎ 01889 565032
Est. 1999 *Stock size* Large
No. of dealers 10
Stock General antiques, collectables, Arts and Crafts, Art Deco, Victoriana
Open Mon–Sat 10am–5pm

WOODSEAVES

A D Antiques
Contact Alison Davey
PO Box 1623, Woodseaves, Stafford, Staffordshire, ST20 0SF
Ⓜ 07939 508171
Ⓔ alison@adantiques.freeserve.co.uk
Ⓦ www.adantiques.com
Est. 1997 *Stock size* Medium
Stock Decorative arts, ceramics and metalware
Open By appointment
Fairs NEC, Bingley Hall, GMEX

YOXALL

H W Heron & Son Ltd (LAPADA)
Contact Mrs J Heron
The Antique Shop, King Street, Yoxall, Burton-on-Trent, Staffordshire, DE13 8NF Ⓟ
☎ 01543 472266 Ⓕ 01543 473800
Ⓔ shop@hwheronantiques.com
Ⓦ www.hwheronantiques.com
Est. 1949 *Stock size* Medium
Stock Period furniture, ceramics, objects, paintings
Open Mon–Fri 9am–6pm Sat 9am–5.30pm Sun 2–6pm
Fairs Newark
Services Valuations

WARWICKSHIRE

ALCESTER

Malthouse Antiques Centre
Contact Pat Alcock
4 Market Place, Alcester, Warwickshire, B49 5AE Ⓟ
☎ 01789 764032
Est. 1984 *Stock size* Large
No. of dealers 15–20
Stock 18th–early 20thC furniture, ceramics, silver, collectables etc
Open Mon–Sat 10am–5pm, Sun 1–4pm

Justin Neales Antiques & Interiors
Contact Mr Justin Neales
3 Evesham Street, Alcester, Warwickshire, B49 5DS Ⓟ
☎ 01789 766699
Ⓦ www.justinnealesantiques.co.uk
Est. 1987 *Stock size* Large
Stock Georgian, Victorian and Edwardian furniture, painted furniture, tapestry, cushions, mirrors, silver picture frames
Open Mon–Fri 9am–5pm Sat 10am–5pm
Services Restorations, reupholstery

BIDFORD-ON-AVON

Bidford Antique Centre
Contact Mr B Owen
Warwick House, 94–96 High Street, Bidford-on-Avon, Alcester, Warwickshire, B50 4AF Ⓟ
☎ 01789 773680
Est. 1974 *Stock size* Large
No. of dealers 6
Stock General antiques and collectables
Open Tues–Sat 10am–5pm

Steven B Bruce Auctioneers Ltd (NAVA)
Contact Mr S Bruce
Unit 5, Clayhall Farm, Honeybourne Road, Bidford-on-Avon, Warwickshire, B49 5PD
☎ 01789 490450
Ⓜ 07778 595952
Ⓔ stevenbruce@hotmail.com
Ⓦ www.antiquesvaluers.co.uk
Est. 1995
Open Mon–Sat9.30am–5.30pm
Sales Antiques sales held at local venues in Warwickshire, Worcestershire, Gloucestershire. Occasional specialist sales, on-site country house sales
Frequency Bi-Monthly
Catalogues Yes

BRINKLOW

Annie's Attic
Contact Ann Wilson
19a Broad Street, Brinklow, Warwickshire, CV23 0LS Ⓟ
☎ 01788 833094
Est. 1998 *Stock size* Medium
Stock Clocks, small furniture, metalwork, oil lamps, old and interesting objects
Open Fri Sat 11am–5pm Sun 11am–4pm also some Wed
Services Clock restoration

MIDLANDS
WARWICKSHIRE • DUNCHURCH

The Victorian Ironmonger
Contact Mr D Thompson
The Old Garage, 70 Broad Street, Brinklow, Rugby, Warwickshire, CV23 0LN
01788 832292
dave@thevictorianironmonger.co.uk
www.thevictorianironmonger.co.uk
Est. 1993 *Stock size* Large
Stock Original Victorian ironmongery, fireplaces, doors, house fittings
Open Fri–Sat 10am–5pm Sun 11am–3pm

DUNCHURCH

Dunchurch Antiques Centre
Contact Graham Sutherland
16a Daventry Road, Dunchurch, Rugby, Warwickshire, CV22 6NS
01788 522450
Est. 1999 *Stock size* Medium
No. of dealers 10
Stock General antiques, collectables, antiquarian books
Open Mon–Sun 10am–5pm

Now & Then
Contact Mike Best
6 The Green, Dunchurch, Rugby, Warwickshire, CV22 6NX
01788 811211
07711 248951
Est. 2001 *Stock size* Large
Stock General antiques
Open Mon–Sun 10am–5pm

HATTON

The Stables Antique Centre
Contact Mr John Colledge
Hatton Country World, Dark Lane, Hatton, Warwick, Warwickshire, CV35 8XA
01926 842405 01926 842023
Est. 1992 *Stock size* Large
No. of dealers 25
Stock Old clocks, furniture, curios, china etc
Open Mon–Sun 10am–5pm
Services Craft centre, café, bar, clock repairs

HENLEY-IN-ARDEN

Henley Antiques & Collectables Centre
Contact Mrs Rosie Montague
Rear of Henley Bakery, 92 High Street, Henley-in-Arden, Warwickshire, B95 5BY
01564 795979 07950 324376
Est. 2000 *Stock size* Large
No. of dealers 20
Stock Georgian–Edwardian furniture, wide range of antiques, ceramics, glass, silver, collectables
Open Mon–Sat 10.30am–5pm Sun Bank Holidays 11am–4pm

ILMINGTON

Peter Finer (BADA)
Contact Peter Finer or Nickki Eden
The Old Rectory, Ilmington, Shipston-on-Stour, Warwickshire, CV36 4JQ
01608 682267 01608 682575
pf@peterfiner.com
www.peterfiner.com
Stock size Large
Stock Arms, armour and related objects
Open Strictly by appointment
Fairs New York, Texas
Services Restorations

LEAMINGTON SPA

Kings Cottage Antiques (LAPADA)
Contact Mr A Jackson
4 Windsor Street, Leamington Spa, Warwickshire, CV32 5EB
01926 422927 01926 422927
Est. 1993
Stock Early oak and country furniture
Open Mon–Fri 9am–5pm Sat by appointment

BBG Locke & England
Contact Nicola Ellis
18 Guy Street, Leamington Spa, Warwickshire, CV32 4RT
01926 889100 01926 470608
info@leauction.co.uk
www.leauction.co.uk
Open 9am–1pm 2–5.30pm
Sales Household and Victoriana auctions weekly, antiques and fine art auctions monthly
Frequency Weekly
Catalogues Yes

The Old Pine House
Contact Keith Platt
16 Warwick Street, Leamington Spa, Warwickshire, CV32 5LL
01926 470477 01926 470477
Est. 1993 *Stock size* Large
Stock Victorian stripped pine
Open Tues–Fri 10am–5.30pm Sat 9am–5.30pm evenings by appointment

Portland Books
Contact Mr Martyn Davies
7 Campion Terrace, Leamington Spa, Warwickshire, CV32 4SU
01926 888776 01926 888775
portlandbooks@quicknetuk.com
www.portlandbooks.com
Est. 1974 *Stock size* Large
Stock Antiquarian and second-hand books, Warwickshire history a speciality
Open Thurs–Sat 9.30am–6pm or by appointment
Services Valuations, book search

Portland Books
Contact Mr Martyn Davies or Gareth Wyatt
93 Warwick Street, Leamington Spa, Warwickshire, CV32 4RJ
01926 888118 01926 885305
twiceportlandbooks@quicknetuk.com
www.portlandbooks.com
Est. 1974 *Stock size* Large
Stock Antiquarian, second-hand and new books, Warwickshire history a speciality, modern books at discounted prices
Open Mon–Sat 9.30am–5.30pm Sun 11am–4pm
Services Valuations, book search

Yesterdays
Contact Mrs Shona Caldwell
21 Portland Street, Leamington Spa, Warwickshire, CV32 5EZ
01926 450238
Est. 1985 *Stock size* Medium
Stock General antiques shop, period furniture, pictures, bric-a-brac
Open Tues Wed Fri Sat 10am–5pm

LONG MARSTON

Barn Antique Centre
Contact Bev and Graham Simpson
Station Road, Long Marston, Stratford-upon-Avon, Warwickshire, CV37 8RP
01789 721399 01789 721390
info@barnantique.co.uk
www.barnantique.co.uk
Est. 1978 *Stock size* Large
No. of dealers 40
Stock Huge barn full of antiques and collectables.13,000+ sq ft
Open Mon–Sat 10am–5pm Sun noon–6pm
Services Licensed French restaurant

MIDDLETON

Middleton Hall Antiques (BAFRA)
Contact Mr S Herberholz
Middleton Hall, Middleton, Tamworth, Warwickshire, B78 2AE
01827 282858 07973 151681
Est. 1997 *Stock size* Small
Stock 18th–19thC furniture, porcelain
Open Wed–Sun 11am–5pm

NUNEATON

The Granary Antiques
Contact Gordon Stockdale
Hoar Park, Craft Village, Ansley, Nuneaton, Warwickshire, CV10 0QU
024 7639 5551 024 7639 4433
jl@hpcv.freeserve.co.uk
www.hpcv.freeserve.co.uk
Est. 1996 *Stock size* Large
Stock General antiques, pine, kitchenware, Edwardian furniture, porcelain and Mason's ironstone in a 17thC converted building
Open Tues–Sun 10am–5pm
Services Restaurant

G Payne Antiques
Contact Mr G Payne
25 Watling Street, Nuneaton, Warwickshire, CV11 6JJ
024 7632 5178 07836 754489
Est. 1991 *Stock size* Medium
Stock Mahogany and oak furniture
Open Mon–Sat 8am–6pm

POLESWORTH

G & J Chesters (PBFA)
Contact Mr G Chesters
14 Market Street, Polesworth, Tamworth, Warwickshire, B78 1HW
01827 894743
gandjchesters@bun.com
Est. 1970 *Stock size* Large
Stock Antiquarian and second-hand books, maps, prints
Open Mon–Sat 9.30am–5.30pm Wed 9.30am–9pm
Fairs NEC Antiques for Everyone fairs

RUGBY

272 Antiques
Contact Sue Walters
272 Hillmorton Road, Rugby, Warwickshire, CV22 5BW
01788 541818 01788 541818
Est. 2001 *Stock size* Small
Stock French country and English pine furniture
Open Wed–Sat 10.30am–5pm
Services Restorations, pine stripping

Old Forge Antiques
Contact April Blackburn
Main Street, Rugby, Warwickshire, CV23 0PF
01788 832191
enquiries@oldforge-antiques.co.uk
www.oldforge-antiques.co.uk
Est. 1992
Stock Edwardian–Victorian furniture, ceramics, brass, copper, linen, mirrors, pictures, clocks
Open Fri–Sun 11am–4pm or by appointment
Services Upholstery

The Rugby Salerooms
Contact Mrs M or Miss L Seaman
16–18 Albert Street, Rugby, Warwickshire, CV21 2RS
01788 542367/543445
Est. 1979
Sales Weekly auction of antiques and general household goods. Held at 6 Payne's Lane, Rugby on Mondays at 7pm. Viewing Sun 11am–3pm Mon noon–7pm
Frequency Weekly
Catalogues Yes

M G Seaman
Contact Mrs M Seaman
16–18 Albert Street, Rugby, Warwickshire, CV21 2RS
01788 560998 01788 570425
Est. 1979 *Stock size* Large
Stock 1920s–1960s antiques, glass, china, clothing, accessories, jewellery
Open Mon–Sat 9am–5pm closed Wed

SHENTON

Whitemoors Antique Centre
Contact Mr Colin Wightman
Main Street, Shenton, Warwickshire, CV13 6BZ
01455 212250
Est. 1993 *Stock size* Large
No. of dealers 15
Stock Furniture, pottery, clocks, bric-a-brac, paperweights
Open Mon–Sun summer 11am–5pm winter 11am–4pm

SHIPSTON-ON-STOUR

Church Street Gallery
Contact Mr Robert Field
24 Church Street, Shipston-on-Stour, Warwickshire, CV36 4AP
01608 662431 01608 662431
www.churchstreetgallery.co.uk
Est. 1979 *Stock size* Large
Stock Antique maps and prints, late 19th–early 20thC watercolours, oils, furniture, bric-a-brac
Open Mon–Fri 9.30am–6pm Thurs 9.30am–1pm Sat 10am–5.30pm
Services Picture framing and restoration

Pine & Country Antiques
Contact Mr C Harvey
28 Church Street, Shipston-on-Stour, Warwickshire, CV36 4AP
01608 662168 01608 662168
Est. 1973 *Stock size* Large
Stock General range of antiques, decorative items, French oak and mahogany furniture
Open Mon–Sat 9am–5.30pm or by appointment

MIDLANDS
WARWICKSHIRE • SNITTERFIELD

Pine and Things
Contact Mr R Wood
Portobello Farm, Campden Road, Shipston-on-Stour, Warwickshire, CV36 4PY
01608 663849 01608 663849
mailus@pinethings.co.uk
www.pinethings.co.uk
Est. 1991 *Stock size* Large
Stock Victorian and earlier pine furniture
Open Mon–Sat 9am–5pm

SNITTERFIELD

Phillips Brothers (NAVA)
Contact Robin Phillips
The Sale Room, Bearley Road, Snitterfield, Stratford-upon-Avon, Warwickshire, CV37 0EZ
01789 731114 01789 731114
Est. 1980
Open Mon–Fri 9.30am–5pm
Sales General and antiques sales Sat 10am, viewing from 9am. Occasional antiques sales Sat, viewing 9am
Frequency Fortnightly
Catalogues Yes

STRATFORD-UPON-AVON

Arbour Antiques Ltd
Contact Mr Colwell
Poets Arbour, Sheep Street, Stratford-upon-Avon, Warwickshire, CV37 6EF
01789 293453
Est. 1954 *Stock size* Large
Stock 17th–18thC arms and armour
Open Mon–Fri 9am–5pm

Thomas Crapper & Co (SALVO)
Stable Yard, Alscot Park, Stratford-upon-Avon, Warwickshire, CV37 8BL
01789 450522 01789 450523
wc@thomas-crapper.co.uk
www.thomas-crapper.co.uk
Est. 1861 *Stock size* Medium
Stock Victorian–Edwardian and unusual bathroom fittings. Art Deco and coloured 1930s bathrooms
Open Mon–Fri 9am–5.30pm or by appointment
Services Restorations, catalogues (£5 refundable on purchase)

Goodbye To All That
Contact Mr Briggs
Ely Street, Stratford-upon-Avon, Warwickshire, CV37 6LN
01789 204180
Est. 1999 *Stock size* Small
Stock Firearms, scientific instruments
Open Mon–Sun 10am–5.30pm

Pickwick Gallery
Contact Mr H D Dankenbring
32 Henley Street, Stratford-upon-Avon, Warwickshire, CV37 6QW
01789 294861
meridienmaps@btinternet.com
Est. 1986 *Stock size* Medium
Stock Antique maps, sporting prints, 1600–1880
Open Mon–Sat 10am–5pm Sun Bank Holidays 11am–4.30pm

Riverside Antiques
Contact Mr Richard Monk
60 Ely Street, Stratford-upon-Avon, Warwickshire, CV37 6LN
01789 262090 07931 512325
Est. 1996 *Stock size* Medium
Stock Clarice Cliff, antique and designer jewellery
Open Mon–Sun Oct–Mar 10am–5pm Jun–Sept 10am–5.30pm
Services Rings designed and made

Stratford Antiques and Interiors
Contact Mr or Mrs Kerr
Dodwell Trading Estate, Evesham Road, Stratford-upon-Avon, Warwickshire, CV37 9SY
01789 297729 01789 297710
drewkerr@tiscali.co.uk
www.stratfordantiques.co.uk
Est. 1995 *Stock size* Large
No. of dealers 20
Stock A wide range of antiques and collectables, home furnishings and decorative items
Open Mon–Sun 10am–5pm

Stratford Antiques Centre
Contact Mr Mike Conway
59–60 Ely Street, Stratford-upon-Avon, Warwickshire, CV37 6LN
01789 204180
Est. 1981 *Stock size* Large
No. of dealers 50
Stock Wide range of antiques and collectables. One of the largest antiques markets in the Midlands
Open Mon–Sun summer 10am–5.30pm winter 10am–5pm
Services Restaurant

Robert Vaughan Antiquarian Booksellers (ABA, PBFA)
Contact Mrs Colleen Vaughan
20 Chapel Street, Stratford-upon-Avon, Warwickshire, CV37 6EP
01789 205312
Est. 1953 *Stock size* Large
Stock Fine and first editions of English literature, theatre, allied subjects, Shakespeare
Open Mon–Sat 9.30am–5.30pm
Services Valuations, search

TIDDINGTON

Bigwood Auctioneers Ltd (SOFAA)
Contact Mr C Ironmonger
The Old School, Tiddington, Stratford-upon-Avon, Warwickshire, CV37 7AW
01789 269415 01789 294168
sales@bigwoodauctioneers.co.uk
www.bigwoodauctioneers.co.uk
Est. 1849
Open Mon–Fri 9am–5.30pm closed 12.45–2pm Sat 9am–noon
Sales Quarterly fine furniture and works of art, monthly antiques and collectables, sporting memorabilia (Mar Sept) wine sales (March June Sept Dec) collectables, games, toys, (April Oct)
Frequency 45 per annum
Catalogues Yes

WARWICK

Apollo Antiques Ltd (LAPADA, CINOA)
Contact Roger Mynott
The Saltisford, Warwick, Warwickshire, CV34 4TD
01926 494746/494666
01926 401477
mynott@apolloantiques.com
www.apolloantiques.com
Est. 1968 *Stock size* Large
Stock English 18th–19thC furniture, sculpture, paintings,

decorative items, arts and crafts, Gothic revival
Open Mon–Fri 9am–6pm Sat 9.30am–12.30pm
Services Free delivery service to London

W J Casey Antiques (LAPADA, CINOA)
Contact Mr Bill Casey
9 High Street, Warwick, Warwickshire, CV34 4AP
☎ 01926 499199
Ⓜ 07771 920475 ***Stock size*** Large
Stock 18th–19thC furniture, especially dining room furniture
Open Mon–Sat 10am–5pm or by appointment

Castle Antiques
Contact Julia Reynolds
24 Swan Street, Warwick, Warwickshire, CV34 4BJ
☎ 01926 401511
Est. 1998 ***Stock size*** Large
Stock Edwardian–Victorian furniture, small items
Open Mon–Sat 10am–5pm
Services Restorations

Dorridge Antiques
Contact Mrs P Spencer
Warwick Antique Centre, 22–24 High Street, Warwick, Warwickshire, CV34 4AP
☎ 01926 499857
Est. 1981 ***Stock size*** Medium
Stock Silver, jewellery
Open Mon–Sat 10am–5pm

Emscote Antiques
Contact Mr Paul Hannan
152 Emscote Road, Warwick, Warwickshire, CV34 5QN
☎ 01926 407979
Est. 1994 ***Stock size*** Medium
Stock Original and reproduction painted pine furniture
Open Thurs–Sat 10am–5pm
Fairs Newark, Ardingly
Services Pine stripping

English Antiques
Contact Mrs Jean Fair
3 High Street, Warwick, Warwickshire, CV34 4AP
☎ 01926 408656 Ⓕ 01926 408656
Ⓜ 07802 419536
Est. 1957 ***Stock size*** Large
Stock 18th–19thC furniture and decorative items
Open Mon–Sat 10am–5.30pm or by appointment

Entente Cordiale
Contact Carol Robson
9 High Street, Warwick, Warwickshire, CV34 4AP
☎ 01926 403733 Ⓕ 01905 754129
Est. 2000 ***Stock size*** Small
Stock Mixture of English and French generally small furniture
Open Mon–Sat

John Goodwin & Sons
Contact Mr Neil Goodwin
22–24 High Street, Warwick, Warwickshire, CV34
☎ 01926 853332
Est. 1969 ***Stock size*** Large
Stock General antiques, furniture, pictures, collectables
Open Mon–Sat 8.30am–5.30pm

Keith Gormley Antiques
Contact Mr Keith Gormley
56 West Street, Warwick, Warwickshire, CV34 6AW
☎ 01926 419880 Ⓜ 07866 314504
Est. 1996 ***Stock size*** Large
Stock Period and decorative furniture, accessories
Open Mon–Fri 10am–5pm

Russell Lane Antiques
Contact Mr Lane
2–4 High Street, Warwick, Warwickshire, CV34 4AP
☎ 01926 494494 Ⓕ 01926 492972
Ⓔ russell.laneantiques@virgin.net
Est. 1974 ***Stock size*** Large
Stock Antique jewellery and silver. Official jewellers to the Royal Show
Open Mon–Sat 10am–5pm
Services Replacement insurance claims

Patrick & Gillian Morley (LAPADA)
Contact Mr P Morley
62 West Street, Warwick, Warwickshire, CV34 6AW
☎ 01926 494464
Ⓜ 07768 835040
Est. 1969 ***Stock size*** Large
Stock Period decorative and unusual furniture, works of art
Open Mon–Fri 10am–5.30pm or by appointment

Christopher Peters Antiques
Contact Mr C or Mrs J Peters
28 West Street, Warwick, Warwickshire, CV34 6AN
☎ 01926 494106/02476 303300
Ⓕ 02476 303300
Ⓔ enquiries@christopherpetersantiques.co.uk
Ⓦ www.christopherpetersantiques.co.uk
Est. 1985 ***Stock size*** Large
Stock 17th–19thC painted fruitwood and country furniture
Open Mon–Sat 10am–5.30pm or by appointment
Fairs NEC (Spring, Summer)

Quinneys of Warwick
Contact James Reeve
9 Church Street, Warwick, Warwickshire, CV34 4AB
☎ 01926 498113 Ⓕ 01926 498113
Est. 1865 ***Stock size*** Large
Stock 17th–19thC English furniture
Open Mon–Fri 9.30am–5.30pm Sat 9.30am–1pm
Services Restorations

Don Spencer Antiques
Contact Don Spencer
36a Market Place, Warwick, Warwickshire, CV34 4SH
☎ 01926 407989 Ⓕ 01564 775470
Ⓜ 07836 525755
Ⓔ antiques@btinternet.com
Ⓦ www.antique-desks.co.uk
Est. 1974 ***Stock size*** Large
Stock Old desks, oak, mahogany, walnut, Victorian, Edwardian, roll-top, writing tables, desk chairs
Open Mon–Sat 10am–5pm
Services Free delivery anywhere in the UK

Summersons
Contact Mr Peter Lightfoot
172 Emscote Road, Warwick, Warwickshire, CV34 5QN
☎ 01926 400630 Ⓕ 01926 400630
Ⓔ clocks@summersons.com
Ⓦ www.summersons.com
Est. 1979 ***Stock size*** Medium
Stock Clocks, barometers
Open Mon–Fri 9am–5pm Sat 10am–1pm
Services Restorations, repairs of clocks and barometers, sales of materials for restoration

Tango Art Deco & Antiques
Contact Jenny and Martin Wills
46 Brook Sreet, Warwick, Warwickshire, CV34 4BL

☎ 01926 496999 Ⓕ 0121 704 4969
Ⓜ 07889 046969
Ⓔ info@tango-artdeco.co.uk
Ⓦ www.tango-artdeco.co.uk
Est. 1987 *Stock size* Large
Stock Decorative arts 1880–1940, ceramics, furniture, accessories
Open Thurs–Sat 10am–5pm

The Tao Antiques
Contact Mr A Ross
✉ **59 Smith Street, Warwick, Warwickshire, CV34 4HU** Ⓟ
☎ 01926 411772
Est. 1964 *Stock size* Medium
Stock Victorian furniture, copper, brass, china, general antiques
Open Mon–Sat 2pm–6pm

Vintage Antiques Centre
Contact Mr Peter Sellors
✉ **36 Market Place, Warwick, Warwickshire, CV34 4SH** Ⓟ
☎ 01926 491527
Ⓔ vintage@globalnet.co.uk
Est. 1979 *Stock size* Large
No. of dealers 20
Stock Victorian glass, 19thC ceramics, 20thC collectables, 1950s, smalls
Open Mon–Sat 10am–5pm
Sun 11.30am–4.30pm

Warwick Antique Centre
Contact Mr P Viola
✉ **22–24 High Street, Warwick, Warwickshire, CV34 4AP** Ⓟ
☎ 01926 491382 Ⓜ 07770 897707
Est. 1971 *Stock size* Large
No. of dealers 30
Stock General antiques, collectables
Open Mon–Sat 10am–5pm
Services Valuations

John Williams Antique & Collectables
Contact Mr John Williams
✉ **Warwick Antiques Centre, 22–24 High Street, Warwick, Warwickshire, CV34 4AP** Ⓟ
☎ 01926 419966
Est. 1981 *Stock size* Medium
Stock Cameras, toys, tools, collectables, militaria, porcelain
Open Mon–Sat 10am–4.30pm
Fairs Alexandra Palace, Birmingham Rag Market, NEC, Motorcycle Museum – Birmingham
Services Valuations

WOOTTON WAWEN

Le Grenier
Contact Joyce Ellis
✉ **Yew Tree Farm, Stratford Road, Wootton Wawen, Stratford-upon-Avon, Warwickshire, B95 6BY** Ⓟ
☎ 01564 795401 Ⓕ 01564 795401
Ⓜ 07712 126048
Ⓔ info@legrenierantiques.com
Ⓦ www.legrenierantiques.com
Est. 1989 *Stock size* Large
Stock French country furniture, fine period furniture
Open Tues–Sun 9am–5.30pm
Services Restorations for painted furniture, pen work, general restoration

WEST MIDLANDS

BIRMINGHAM

Acme Toy Company
Contact Mr P Hall
✉ **17 Station Road, Erdington, Birmingham, West Midlands, B23 6UB** Ⓟ
☎ 0121 384 8835
Ⓦ www.solnet.co.uk/acme
Est. 1995 *Stock size* Medium
Stock Antique and collectable toys – TV, Sci-Fi, Action Man
Open Mon–Thurs 11am–3pm
Fri Sat 11am–5pm
Fairs D & G Fairs

Biddle & Webb Ltd
Contact Mr Thornton
✉ **Icknield Square, Ladywood, Middleway, Birmingham, West Midlands, B16 0PP** Ⓟ
☎ 0121 455 8042 Ⓕ 0121 454 9615
Ⓔ antiques@biddleandwebb.freeserve.co.uk
Ⓦ www.invaluable.com.biddleandwebb.
Est. 1955
Open Mon–Fri 9am–5pm
Sales Pictures and prints 11am 1st Fri of month, viewing Sat prior 9am–noon Wed Thur 10am–4pm. Antiques and later furnishings, porcelain, glass sale 2nd Fri, viewing as previously. Toys, juvenalia 3rd Fri alternate months. Jewellery 4th Fri
Catalogues Yes

The Birmingham Antique Centre
Contact Mr Baldock
✉ **1407 Pershore Road, Stirchley, Birmingham, West Midlands, B30 2JR** Ⓟ
☎ 0121 459 4587 Ⓕ 0121 689 6565
Est. 1994 *Stock size* Large
No. of dealers 65
Stock Antique furniture, partly used furniture, bric-a-brac
Open Mon–Sat 9am–5.30pm
Sun 10am–5pm
Services Valuations, house clearance

Birmingham Coins
Contact Mr D Harris
✉ **30 Shaftmoor Lane, Acocks Green, Birmingham, West Midlands, B27 7RS** Ⓟ
☎ 0121 707 2808 Ⓕ 0121 707 2808
Est. 1996 *Stock size* Large
Stock General, world and British coins and bank notes, collectors' models, medals
Open Tues Thurs Fri 10.30am–5pm

Cambridge House Antiques
Contact Mr T McIntosh
✉ **168 Gravelly Lane, Birmingham, West Midlands, B23 5SN** Ⓟ
☎ 0121 386 1346
Est. 1998 *Stock size* Large
Stock General antiques
Open Mon–Sat 10am–5.30pm
Fairs Newark, Birmingham Rag Market

Chesterfield Antiques
Contact Mrs Mara Cirjanic
✉ **181 Gravelly Lane, Birmingham, West Midlands, B23 5SG** Ⓟ
☎ 0121 373 3876
Est. 1974 *Stock size* Large
Stock Victorian, Edwardian and 1930s furniture and sets of chairs
Open Mon–Sat 9.30am–5.30pm

Cross's Curios
Contact Mrs Valerie Cross
✉ **928 Pershore Road, Selly Park, Birmingham, West Midlands, B29 7PU** Ⓟ
☎ 0121 415 4866 Ⓜ 07961 841492
Est. 1970 *Stock size* Medium

Stock General antiques and old toys
Open Tues–Sat 10.30am–5pm closed Wed or by appointment
Services Valuations

Fellows & Sons (BJA)
Contact Mr S Whittaker
Augusta House, 19 Augusta Street, Birmingham, West Midlands, B18 6JA
☎ 0121 212 2131 Ⓕ 0121 212 1249
Ⓔ info@fellows.co.uk
Ⓦ www.fellows.co.uk
Est. 1876
Open Mon–Thurs 9am–5pm Fri 9am–4pm
Sales 5 antique furniture, porcelain, pictures, clocks and collectables sales per annum. Also general furniture and household contents sales. Fortnightly sales of jewellery and watches from pawnbrokers nationwide. 8 antique and modern jewellery, watches and silver sales per annum
Catalogues Yes

Format Coins (IAPN, BNTA)
Contact Mr D Vice
18–19 Bennetts Hill, Birmingham, West Midlands, B2 5QJ
☎ 0121 643 2058 Ⓕ 0121 643 2210
Est. 1970 ***Stock size*** Medium
Stock Coins, medallions, bank notes.
Open Mon–Fri 9.30am–5pm
Fairs London Coinex

Lindsay Architectural Antiques
Contact Mr G Lindsay
25 Passfield Road, Stetchford, Birmingham, West Midlands, B33 8EU
☎ 0121 789 8295 Ⓜ 07966 221632
Ⓔ glindsay@zoom.co.uk
Ⓦ www.authenticfireplaces.co.uk
Est. 1996 ***Stock size*** Large
Stock Architectural salvage, fireplaces, quarry tiles, wrought-iron gates
Open Mon–Sat 10am–5pm Sun 10am–4pm
Fairs Newark, Swinderby
Services Restoration and fitting service

MDS Ltd
Contact Mr R Wootton
14–16 Stechford Trading Estate, Lyndon Road, Stechford, Birmingham, West Midlands, B33 8BU
☎ 0121 783 9274 Ⓕ 0121 783 9274
Ⓜ 07836 649064
Est. 1969 ***Stock size*** Medium
Stock Architectural antiques
Open Mon–Sun 8am–6pm

Midland Football Programme Shop
Contact Mr John Garrad
253a Oxhill Road, Birmingham, West Midlands, B21 8ED
☎ 0121 551 1683 Ⓕ 0121 551 1683
Est. 1976 ***Stock size*** Medium
Stock Football programmes, memorabilia
Open Tues–Sat 10am–4.15pm
Services Catalogue available

Moseley Emporium
Contact Miss G Dorney
116 Alcester Road, Moseley, Birmingham, West Midlands, B13 3EF
☎ 0121 449 3441 Ⓜ 07973 156902
Est. 1993 ***Stock size*** Large
Stock Victorian, Edwardian and period furniture, architectural antiques
Open Mon–Sat 9.30am–6pm
Services Restoration

Raven Reclaim & Architectural Salvage Ltd
Contact Mr M Coughlan
453 Stockfield Road, Yardley, Birmingham, West Midlands, B25 8JH
☎ 0121 765 4840
Est. 1979 ***Stock size*** Medium
Stock Architectural antiques
Open Mon–Sat 8am–5.30pm

Weller & Dufty Ltd (GTA)
Contact Mr W Farmer
141 Bromsgrove Street, Birmingham, West Midlands, B5 6RQ
☎ 0121 692 1414 Ⓕ 0121 622 5605
Ⓔ wellerdufty@freewire.co.uk
Ⓦ www.wellerandduffy.co.uk
Est. 1835
Open Mon–Fri 9am–4.30pm
Sales Fine art and antiques
Frequency 6–8 per annum
Catalogues Yes

Stephen Wycherley (PBFA)
Contact Mr S Wycherley
508 Bristol Road, Selly Oak, Birmingham, West Midlands, B29 6BD
☎ 0121 471 1006
Ⓔ s.wycherley@btopenworld.com
Est. 1971 ***Stock size*** Large
Stock Traditional general second-hand and antiquarian bookshop
Open Mon–Sat 10am–5pm closed Wed Jul Aug Thurs–Sat 10am–5pm
Fairs PBFA
Services Valuations

BRIERLEY HILL

Cast Offs
Contact Mr Terence Young
Moor Street Industrial Estate, Moor Street, Brierley Hill, West Midlands, DY5 3EH
☎ 01384 486456 Ⓜ 07711 661135
Est. 1996 ***Stock size*** Medium
Stock Quarry tiles, pavors, cast-iron fireplaces, troughs, baths, radiators, sinks, taps, doors, furniture, chimney pots, gates, fencing, bricks
Open Mon–Fri 9am–5pm Sat 9am–2pm

COVENTRY

Duncan M Allsop (ABA)
Contact Mr D Allsop
68 Smith Street, Coventry, West Midlands, CV6 5EL
☎ 01926 493266 Ⓕ 01926 493266
Ⓔ duncan@allsop-books.freeserve.co.uk
Ⓦ www.allsop-books.freeserve.co.uk
Est. 1966 ***Stock size*** Medium
Stock Varied stock of books including antiquarian, fine bindings and modern books
Open Mon–Sat 9.30am–5.30pm
Fairs Royal National

Antiques Adventure
Contact Lesley Lawrence
Rugby Road, Binley Woods, Coventry, West Midlands, CV3 2AW
☎ 024 7645 3878 Ⓕ 024 7644 5847
Ⓔ sales@antiquesadventure.com
Ⓦ www.antiquesadventure.com
Est. 2000 ***Stock size*** Large
No. of dealers 35
Stock Antiques, collectables

MIDLANDS

WEST MIDLANDS • CRADLEY HEATH

Open Mon–Fri 9.30am–5.30pm
Sat Sun 10am–5pm
Services Shipping, delivery

Armstrong's Books & Collectables
Contact Mr Colin Armstrong
178 Albany Road, Earlsdon, Coventry, West Midlands, CV5 6NG
024 7671 4344
Est. 1983 *Stock size* Medium
Stock General second-hand books, special sci-fi comics, annuals, magazines, posters, postcards
Open Mon–Sat 10am–5pm

The Bookshop
Contact Mr A R Price
173 Walsgrave Road, Coventry, West Midlands, CV2 4HH
024 7645 5669
Est. 1990 *Stock size* Medium
Stock Antiquarian and second-hand books on all subjects
Open Mon–Sat 9am–5pm
Services Valuations

Cobwebs
Contact Mr R Clutterbuck
58 Far Gosford Street, Coventry, West Midlands, CV1 5DZ
024 7622 2032
Est. 1988 *Stock size* Large
Stock Victorian furniture and antiques, modern wares
Open Mon–Sat 9.30am–5pm
Fairs Newark, Towcester

Earlsdon Antiques
Contact Mrs V Kemp
35 Hearsall Lane, Coventry, West Midlands, CV5 6HF
024 7667 5456
Est. 1984 *Stock size* Medium
Stock General antiques and collectables
Open Fri Sat noon–5pm

Nicholas Green Antiques
Contact Mr N Green
Binley Common Farm, Rugby Road, Binley, Coventry, West Midlands, CV3 2AW
024 7645 3878 Fax 024 7644 5847
Est. 1969 *Stock size* Large
No. of dealers 10
Stock Victorian, shipping furniture
Open Mon–Sat 9.30am–5.30pm
Sun 10am–4.30pm
Services Valuations, container storage

Luckmans Antiques
Contact Mr D Auker
40 Far Gosford Street, Coventry, West Midlands, CV1 5DW
024 7622 3842
Est. 1890 *Stock size* Small
Stock Bric-a-brac, books, medals, cigarette cards, postcards, records
Open Tues–Sat 8.30am–4.30pm

Warwick Auctions (NAVA)
Contact Mr R Beaumont
3 Queen Victoria Road, Coventry, West Midlands, CV1 3JS
024 7622 3377 Fax 024 7622 0044
www.warwickauctions.com
Est. 1947
Open Mon–Fri 9am–5pm
Sales General household goods Wed 10am, viewing Tues 9am–4.30pm Wed 9–10am. Antiques and collectables sales first Wed of each month, except Jan
Frequency Weekly
Catalogues Yes

CRADLEY HEATH

R & L Furnishings
Contact Mr R Randall
244 Halesowen Road, Old Hill, Cradley Heath, West Midlands, B64 6NH
01384 410077
Est. 1980 *Stock size* Medium
Stock Antique furniture, bric-a-brac
Open Mon–Sat 10.30am–5.30pm closed Wed
Services House clearance

Yesterdays Treasures
Contact Mrs Christine Tildesley
205 Halesowen Road, Old Hill, Cradley Heath, West Midlands, B64 6HE
01384 413768 Fax 01384 413768
Est. 1994 *Stock size* Large
Stock General antiques and collectables
Open Mon–Fri 9.30am–5pm
Sat 10am–5pm

HALESOWEN

Anvil Books
Contact Mr J K Maddison
52 Summer Hill, Halesowen, West Midlands, B63 3BU
0121 550 0600
jkm@anvilbookshalesowen.co.uk
www.anvilbookshalesowen.co.uk
Est. 1997 *Stock size* Small
Stock General second-hand and antiquarian books, local history, transport and maritime topics specialities
Open Tues–Sat 10am–5pm
Fairs Kinver Book Fair, Waverley Fairs
Services Book search

Tudor House Antiques
Contact Mr D J Taylor
68 Long Lane, Halesowen, West Midlands, B62 9LS
0121 561 5563
Est. 1991 *Stock size* Medium
Stock Architectural antiques, stripped pine furniture
Open Tues–Sat 9.30am–5pm
Services Restorations, stripping

OLDBURY

The Glory Hole
Contact Mr Colin Dickens
431 Moat Road, Oldbury, West Midlands, B68 8EJ
0121 544 1888
Est. 1989 *Stock size* Medium
Stock Quality second-hand furniture, antiques and collectables
Open Mon–Sat 9.30am–5.30pm
Fairs Malvern Three Counties, Peterborough, Norwich
Services House clearance

S R Furnishings
Contact Mr S Wilder
18 Stanley Road, Oldbury, West Midlands, B68 0DY
0121 422 9788 Fax 0121 585 5611
Est. 1975 *Stock size* Large
Stock General antiques, shipping furniture, silver, china
Open Mon–Sat 9.30am–5.30pm
Fairs Stafford

Warley Antique Centre
Contact Mrs Hamilton
146 Pottery Road, Warley Woods, Oldbury, West Midlands, B68 9HD
0121 434 3813

Est. 1989 *Stock size* Medium
No. of dealers 40
Stock 19th–20thC furniture and collectables
Open Mon–Sat 10am–5pm
Services Valuations, picture framing, jewellery repairs

SOLIHULL

Alscot Bathroom Company (SALVO)
Contact Mr Cockroft
1 Oak Farm, Hampton Lane, Catherine de Barnes, Solihull, West Midlands, B92 0JB
0121 709 1901 0121 709 1800
worldwide@b920jb.fsnet.co.uk
www.alscotbathrooms.co.uk
Est. 1960 *Stock size* Large
Stock Victorian–Edwardian and Art Deco sanitary ware, roll-top baths
Open By appointment
Services Restorations

Dorridge Antiques & Collectables Centre
Contact Colleen Swift
7 Forest Court, Dorridge, Solihull, West Midlands, B93 8HN
01564 779336 or 01564 779768
Est. 1996 *Stock size* Large
Stock Guns, swords, brass ware, furniture, ceramics, paintings, prints, jewellery, silver, bric-a-brac
Open Mon–Sat 11am–6pm
Services Valuation & restoration advice

Yoxall Antiques & Fine Arts
Contact Mr Paul Burrows
68 Yoxall Road, Solihull, West Midlands, B90 3RP
0121 744 1744 07860 168078
sales@yoxallantiques.co.uk
www.yoxallantiques.co.uk
Est. 1988 *Stock size* Large
Stock Period furniture, quality porcelain, glassware, clocks, barometers
Open Mon–Sat 9.30am–5pm closed Wed or by appointment
Fairs NEC
Services Restorations

STOURBRIDGE

Crown Furnishers
Contact Mr C Cartwright
Unit 97 Crown Centre, Crown Lane, Stourbridge, West Midlands, DY8 1YD
01384 441488
Est. 1995 *Stock size* Large
Stock Antique furniture and collectables
Fairs Malvern

Memory Lane Antiques
Contact Mr Paul Jones
129 Brettell Lane, Stourbridge, West Midlands, DY8 4BA
01384 370348 07801 139949
Est. 1989 *Stock size* Large
Stock Country furniture, architectural antiques
Open Mon–Sat 10am–6pm
Fairs Newark, Ardingly

Pickwicks Antiques
Contact Mrs J Smith
35 Audnam, Amblecote, Stourbridge, West Midlands, DY8 4AG
01384 443404/79335
Est. 1987 *Stock size* Medium
Stock Antiques, Victorian and Edwardian furniture, textiles etc
Open By appointment only
Fairs Stafford, Bowmans

Walton & Hipkiss
Contact Mr J Carter
111 Worcester Street, Hayley, Stourbridge, West Midlands, DY9 0NE
01562 886688 01562 886655
walton-hipkiss&stour@lineone.net
www.walton-hipkiss.co.uk
Est. 1929
Open Mon–Fri 9am–5.30pm Sat 9am–4pm
Sales General antiques occasionally Sat 10.30am, viewing Fri 6–8pm Sat 8.30–10.30am, phone for details
Catalogues Yes

SUTTON COLDFIELD

Acres Fine Art Auctioneers & Valuers
Contact Mr I Kettlewell
28 Beeches Walk, Sutton Coldfield, West Midlands, B73 6HN
0121 355 1133 0121 354 5251
www.acres.co.uk
Est. 1992
Open Mon–Sat 9am–5.30pm
Sales Antiques sales. Telephone for details
Frequency Quarterly
Catalogues Yes

Thomas Coulborn and Sons (BADA, CINOA)
Contact Jonathan Coulborn
Vesey Manor, 64 Birmingham Road, Sutton Coldfield, West Midlands, B72 1QP
0121 354 3974 0121 354 4614
07941 252299
jc@coulborn.com
www.coulborn.com
Est. 1940 *Stock size* Large
Stock 18thC furniture and works of art, 19th–20thC paintings and watercolours
Open Mon–Sat 9.15am–1pm 2–5.30pm
Services Valuations

H & R L Parry Ltd
Contact Mrs Rachel Parry
23 Maney Corner, Sutton Coldfield, West Midlands, B72 1QL
0121 354 1178
Est. 1942 *Stock size* Medium
Stock Silver, jewellery, porcelain
Open Mon–Sat 9.30am–5pm closed Wed
Services Valuations

S & J Antiques
Contact Mr Steve Dowling
431 Birmingham Road, Wylde Green, Sutton Coldfield, West Midlands, B72 1AX
0121 384 1595
Est. 1988 *Stock size* Large
Stock Silver, silver plate, oak, period and stripped pine furniture, coins
Open Mon–Sat 10am–5.30pm
Fairs Birmingham Rag Market, Newark
Services Restorations, re-plating

WALSALL

Collectors Centre
Contact Mr Tom Moran
66 Bridge Street, Walsall, West Midlands, WS1 1JG
01922 625518
Est. 1979 *Stock size* Large

Stock Coins, medals, militaria, postcards, cigarette cards, toys, antique jewellery
Open Mon–Sat 9am–5pm Thurs 9am–1pm
Services Valuations

WEDNESBURY

Abacus
Contact Mr Lambert
37 Lower High Street, Wednesbury, West Midlands, WS10 7AQ
☎ 0121 502 4622
Est. 1988 *Stock size* Medium
Stock General second-hand and antiquarian books
Open Mon–Sat 9am–2pm closed Wed
Services Book search

WOLVERHAMPTON

Antiquities
Contact Mrs M Konczyk
75–76 Dudley Road, Wolverhampton, West Midlands, WV2 3BY
☎ 01902 459800
Est. 1968 *Stock size* Large
Stock General antiques
Open Mon–Sat 10.30am–5pm

Bookstack
Contact Mrs E Anderton
53 Bath Road, Wolverhampton, West Midlands, WV1 4EL
☎ 01902 421055 F 01902 421055
E bookstack@ntl.com
Est. 1975 *Stock size* Large
Stock Antiquarian and second-hand books
Open Tues–Sat 10am–5pm
Services Book search

Doveridge House Antiques (BADA, LAPADA, CINOA)
Contact Commander Harry Bain
PO Box 1856, Wolverhampton, West Midlands, WV3 9XH
☎ 01902 312211
Est. 1976 *Stock size* Large
Stock Fine antique furniture, lamps, paintings, silver, decorative objects
Open By appointment
Fairs NEC (Spring Autumn pre-Christmas)
Services Customer advice

Lamb Antique Fine Arts & Craft Originals (LAPADA)
Contact Beris or Cheryl Lamb
77 Fancourt Avenue, Penn, Wolverhampton, West Midlands, WV4 4HZ
☎ 01902 338150 F 01902 830805
M 07850 406907
E berislamb.artscrafts@virgin.net
W www.antiques-originals.com
Est. 1985 *Stock size* Medium
Stock Arts and Crafts, pottery, pewter, prints, silver, glass, jewellery, copper, furniture
Open By appointment only
Fairs Bowman Fairs, NEC

Newhampton Road Antiques
Contact Mr R G Hill
184–184a Newhampton Road East, Wolverhampton, West Midlands, WV1 4PQ
☎ 01902 334363/712583
M 07930 894719
Est. 1985 *Stock size* Large
Stock Antiques and collectables
Open Mon–Sat 9.30am–3.30pm
Fairs Newark, Swinderby
Services House clearance

No. 9 Antiques
Contact Miss C Weaver
9 Upper Green, Tettenhall, Wolverhampton, West Midlands, WV6 8QQ
☎ 01902 755333
Est. 1995 *Stock size* Medium
Stock 19thC furniture, porcelain, silver, watercolours
Open Wed–Fri 10am–6pm Sat 9am–5.30pm

Martin Taylor Antiques (LAPADA)
Contact Mr Martin Taylor
140b Tettenhall Road, Wolverhampton, West Midlands, WV6 0BQ
☎ 01902 751166 F 01902 746502
M 07836 636524
E enquiries@mtaylor-antiques.co.uk
W www.mtaylor-antiques.co.uk
Est. 1976 *Stock size* Large
Stock Furniture c1800–1930, quality replica furniture
Open Mon–Fri 8.30am–5.30pm Sat 9.30am–4pm
Services Search, restoration and delivery

West Midlands Collectors Centre
Contact Mr S Moran
9 Heatin House, Salop Street, Wolverhampton, West Midlands, WV3 0SQ
☎ 01902 772570
Est. 1983 *Stock size* Small
Stock Stamps, coins, medals, bank notes, curios
Open Mon–Sat 9.30am–5pm

Wood 'n' Things
Contact Mrs K Carter
388 Penn Road, Wolverhampton, West Midlands, WV4 4DF
☎ 01902 333324 M 07808 444786
Est. 1983 *Stock size* Medium
Stock Antiques, collectables, Victorian, Edwardian and 1920s furniture
Open Mon–Sat 10am–5pm Wed 10am–1pm
Services Restorations

Woodward Antique Clocks Ltd (LAPADA)
Contact Patricia Woodward
14 High Street, Tettenhall, Wolverhampton, West Midlands, WV6 8QT
☎ 01902 745608 F 01902 743565
E woodwardclocks@bun.com
W www.antiqnet.co.uk/woodward
Est. 1993 *Stock size* Large
Stock Antique clocks, decorative French mantel clocks, longcase, bracket, carriage and wall clocks
Open Wed–Sat 11am–5.30pm
Fairs NEC
Services Valuations, restorations

WORCESTERSHIRE

BARNT GREEN

Barnt Green Antiques
Contact Neville Slater
93 Hewell Road, Barnt Green, Birmingham, B45 8NL
☎ 0121 445 4942 F 0121 445 4942
Est. 1977 *Stock size* Medium
Stock Furniture, clocks
Open Mon–Fri 9am–5.30pm Sat 9am–1pm
Services Valuations, restorations

BEWDLEY

Antiques Unlimited
Contact Mr M Mayall

✉ **44 Load Street, Bewdley, Worcestershire, DY12 2AP** 🅿
☎ 01299 401431 Ⓜ 07968 050439
Est. 1998 *Stock size* Medium
Stock 18th–19thC decorative furniture, decorative items
Open Tues–Sat 10.30am–5.30pm closed Wed
Services Restorations

Bewdley Antiques
Contact Mrs A Hamilton
✉ **62a Load Street, Bewdley, Worcestershire, DY12 2AP** 🅿
☎ 01299 405636 Ⓕ 01299 841568
Est. 1999 *Stock size* Medium
No. of dealers 30
Stock 19th–20thC furniture, collectables, small decorative pieces
Open Mon–Sat 10am–5.30pm Sun 11am–4.30pm
Services Valuations, picture framing, jewellery repairs

Gerard Guy Antiques
Contact Mr C Mason
✉ **The Old Post Office, 24 Kidderminster Road, Bewdley, Worcestershire, DY12 1AG** 🅿
☎ 01299 400032
Est. 1990 *Stock size* Large
Stock Pine and oak Victorian furniture, mirrors, prints, collectables etc
Open Mon–Sat 11am–4pm
Services Restorations

BROADWAY

Fenwick & Fenwick Antiques (CADA)
Contact Mr G Fenwick
✉ **88–90 High Street, Broadway, Worcestershire, WR12 7AJ** 🅿
☎ 01386 853227/841724
Ⓕ 01386 858504
Est. 1980 *Stock size* Large
Stock 17th–early 19thC oak, mahogany, walnut furniture and works of art, treen, boxes, pewter, lace bobbins, Chinese porcelain, corkscrews, early metalware
Open Mon–Sat 10am–6pm

Gallimaufry
Contact Chris Stone
✉ **51a High Street, Broadway, Worcestershire, WR12 7DP** 🅿
☎ 01386 852898
Est. 1992 *Stock size* Medium
Stock China, glass, furniture, pictures, collectables
Open Mon–Sat 10am–5pm Sun 11am–5pm

Howards of Broadway
Contact Robert Light
✉ **27a High Street, Broadway, Worcestershire, WR12 7DP** 🅿
☎ 01386 858924 Ⓜ 07850 066312
Ⓔ robert.light@talk21.com
Est. 1989 *Stock size* Medium
Stock Antique and modern silver and jewellery
Open Mon–Sat 10am–5.30pm
Services Valuations, restorations

H W Keil Ltd (BADA, CADA)
Contact Mr Keil
✉ **Tudor House, Broadway, Worcestershire, WR12 7DB** 🅿
☎ 01386 852408 Ⓕ 01386 852069
Ⓔ info@hwkeil.co.uk
Ⓦ www.hwkeil.co.uk
Est. 1932 *Stock size* Large
Stock Early 17th–early 19thC furniture, works of art
Open Mon–Sat 9.15am–1.15pm 2.15–5.30pm
Services Restorations

John Noott Galleries (BADA, LAPADA, CADA)
Contact Kathryn Plume
✉ **High Street, Broadway, Worcestershire, WR12 7DP** 🅿
☎ 01386 854868 Ⓕ 01386 854919
Ⓔ info@john-noott.com
Ⓦ www.john-noott.com
Est. 1972 *Stock size* Large
Stock 19th–early 20thC oils and watercolours
Open Mon–Sat 10am–1pm 2–5pm
Fairs NEC, Harrogate
Services Valuations, restorations, shipping

BROMSGROVE

Adrian Jennings Antiques
Contact Mr A Jennings
✉ **144 New Road, Astonfields, Nr Bromsgrove, B60 2LE** 🅿
☎ 01527 835300 Ⓕ 01527 835300
Ⓜ 07802 251423
Ⓔ adrian.j@talk21.com
Ⓦ www.adrianjenningsantiques.co.uk
Est. 1992 *Stock size* Medium
Stock 18th–20thC furniture, decorative items for home and garden, country oak furniture
Open Wed 8.30am–12.30pm Fri–Sat 10.30am–5.30pm or by appointment
Fairs Stafford
Services Valuations for insurance and probate

Worcester Medal Service Ltd (OMRS)
Contact Mrs K McDermott
✉ **56 Broad Street, Sidemoor, Bromsgrove, Worcestershire, B61 8LL** 🅿
☎ 01527 835375 Ⓕ 01527 576798
Ⓔ wms@worcmedals.com
Ⓦ www.worcmedals.com
Est. 1988 *Stock size* Large
Stock Medals and medal mountings
Open Mon–Fri 9am–5pm Thurs 9am–noon Sat 9–11.30am
Services Suppliers of specialist cases, medal mounting, valuations

CLEOBURY MORTIMER

M & M Baldwin
Contact Dr M Baldwin
✉ **24 High Street, Cleobury Mortimer, Kidderminster, Worcestershire, DY14 8BY** 🅿
☎ 01299 270110 Ⓕ 01299 270110
Ⓔ mb@mbaldwin.free-online.co.uk
Est. 1978 *Stock size* Medium
Stock Second-hand and antiquarian books, books on transport, industrial history and WWII intelligence and codebreaking a speciality
Open Wed 2–6pm Fri (Easter–October) 10am–1pm 2–6pm Sat 10am–1pm 2–6pm or by appointment
Services Book search, valuations

DROITWICH SPA

Robert Belcher Antiques
Contact Mr R Belcher
✉ **128 Worcester Road, Droitwich Spa, Worcestershire, WR9 8AN** 🅿

☎ 01905 772320
Est. 1984 *Stock size* Large
Stock Georgian–Edwardian furniture, ceramics, silver, glass, pictures etc
Open Tues–Sat 9.30am–5.30pm
Fairs NEC
Services Furniture restoration, picture framing

EVESHAM

Bookworms of Evesham (PBFA)

Contact Mr T Sims
81 Port Street, Evesham, Worcestershire, WR11 3LF
☎ 01386 45509
Est. 1971 *Stock size* Medium
Stock Second-hand and antiquarian books on most subjects, Gloucestershire and Worcestershire topics specialities
Open Tues–Sat 10am–5pm
Fairs Churchdown, Gloucestershire Book Fair (1st Sunday of each month)

FLADBURY

The Hayloft Antiques

Contact Mrs S Pryse-Jones
Craycombe Farm, Old Worcester Road, Fladbury, Evesham, Worcestershire, WR10 2QS
☎ 01386 861166
Est. 1994 *Stock size* Medium
No. of dealers 9
Stock Antique furniture, stripped pine, collectables, china, glass, paintings, prints, books, linen, textiles
Open Mon–Sun summer 10.30am–5pm winter 10.30am–4pm
Services Pine stripping, French polishing, furniture restoration

KIDDERMINSTER

The Antique Centre

Contact Mrs V Bentley
5–8 Lion Street, Kidderminster, Worcestershire, DY10 1PT
☎ 01562 740389 Ⓕ 01562 740389
Est. 1980 *Stock size* Large
No. of dealers 12
Stock Furniture, china, glass, silver, jewellery, architectural salvage, cast-iron fireplaces, surrounds, tiles, books
Open Mon–Sat 10am–5.30pm
Services Jewellery and clock repairs, furniture and door stripping, furniture restoration

BBM Jewellery, Coins & Antiques (BJA)

Contact Mr W V Crook
9 Lion Street, Kidderminster, Worcestershire, DY10 1PT
☎ 01562 744118 Ⓕ 01562 829444
Ⓔ williamvcrook@aol.com
Est. 1980 *Stock size* Large
Stock Antique and second-hand jewellery, coins, medals, porcelain, silver
Open Wed Thurs Fri Sat 10am–5pm
Services Restorations and repairs

Kidderminster Market Auctions

Contact Mr B Cooke
Wholesale Market, Comberton Hill, Kidderminster, Worcestershire, DY10 1QH
☎ 01562 741303 Ⓕ 01562 865495
Est. 1957
Open Mon–Fri 9am–5pm Sat 9am–1pm
Sales General antiques sale Thurs 10.30am furniture 2.30pm, viewing Wed 4–8pm Thurs from 7am
Frequency Weekly

Phipps & Pritchard

Contact Mr A Mayall
Bank Buildings, 31 Worcester Street, Kidderminster, Worcestershire, DY10 1EQ
☎ 01562 822244 Ⓕ 01562 825401
Ⓜ 07970 218140
Est. 1848
Open Mon–Fri 9am–5.15pm Sat 9am–3.30pm
Sales General antiques and collectables Sat 10.30am, viewing Fri 3–6.30pm Sat from 8.30am. Sale held at Hartlebury Village Hall
Frequency Every 7–8 weeks
Catalogues Yes

MALVERN

Carlton Antiques

Contact Mr D W Roberts
43 Worcester Road, Malvern, Worcestershire, WR14 4RB
☎ 01684 573092
Ⓔ dave@carlton-antiques.com
Ⓦ www.carlton-antiques.com
Est. 1991 *Stock size* Medium
Stock Furniture, ephemera, postcards, bottles, die-cast toys, second-hand books etc
Open Mon–Sun 10am–5pm

Foley Furniture

Contact Mr D W Roberts
Foley Bank, Malvern, Worcestershire, WR14
☎ 01684 891255
Ⓔ dave@carlton-antiques.com
Ⓦ www.carlton-antiques.com
Est. 1991 *Stock size* Medium
Stock Furniture of all periods, postcards, bottles, die-cast toys, books etc
Open Wed–Sun 10am–5pm

Great Malvern Antiques

Contact Mr R Rice or Mr L Sutton
Salisbury House, 6 Abbey Road, Malvern, Worcestershire, WR14 3HG
☎ 01684 575490
Ⓔ gmantiques@dial.pipex.com
Est. 1984 *Stock size* Medium
Stock Decorative furniture and furnishings, paintings
Trade only Yes
Open By appointment
Fairs Bath Decorative Antiques Fair, Decorative Antiques and Textiles Fair

Kimber & Son

Contact Mr E M Kimber
6 Lower Howsell Road, Malvern, Worcestershire, WR14 1EF
☎ 01684 574339
Est. 1950 *Stock size* Medium
Stock 18th–early 20thC furniture, English, European and American markets
Open Mon–Fri 9am–5.30pm Sat 9am–1pm
Fairs Newark

Philip Laney

Contact Mr P Laney
Malvern Auction Centre, Portland Road, off Victoria Road, Malvern, Worcestershire, WR14 2TA
☎ 01684 893933 Ⓕ 01684 577948
Ⓔ philiplaney@compuserve.com

Est. 1969
Open Mon–Fri 9am–1pm 2–4.30pm
Sales General antiques and collectables sales
Frequency Monthly
Catalogues Yes

Lechmere Antiquarian Books
Contact Mr R Lechmere
Primswell, Evandrine, Colwall, Malvern, Worcestershire, WR13 6DT
☎ 01684 540340
Est. 1945 ***Stock size*** Small
Stock Antiquarian, rare and second-hand books on Hereford, Worcester, Australia
Open Mail order only
Services Mail order

The Malvern Bookshop
Contact Howard Hudson
7 Abbey Road, Malvern, Worcestershire, WR14 3ES P
☎ 01684 575915 F 01684 575915
E browse@malvern-bookshop.co.uk
Est. 1954 ***Stock size*** Medium
Stock Antiquarian, rare and second-hand books, books on music and sheet music a speciality
Open Mon–Sat 10am–5pm
Services Book search

Malvern Link Antiques Centre
Contact Mr R Hales
154 Worcester Road, Malvern, Worcestershire, WR14 1AA P
☎ 01684 575750
Est. 1997 ***Stock size*** Large
No. of dealers 10
Stock China, glass, Victorian–Edwardian furniture, jewellery, mirrors, pictures etc
Open Mon–Sat 10am–5.30pm Sun 11am–5pm
Services National or international delivery

Malvern Studios (BAFRA, UKIC, LCGI, NCCR)
Contact Jeff Hall
56 Cowleigh Road, Malvern, Worcestershire, WR14 1QD P
☎ 01684 574913 F 01684 569475
Est. 1961
Stock 18th–20thC furniture
Open Mon Tues Thurs 9am–5.15pm Fri Sat 9am–4.45pm
Services Restorations

Miscellany Antiques
Contact R S or E A Hunaban
20 Cowleigh Road, Malvern, Worcestershire, WR14 1QD P
☎ 01684 566671 F 01684 560562
E liz.hunaban@virgin.net
W www.freespace.virgin.net/lizhunaban
Est. 1974 ***Stock size*** Medium
Stock Georgian–Edwardian furniture, some country oak, bronzes, ivories, silver, jewellery, decorative items
Open By appointment
Services Valuations, restorations

Priory Books
Contact Mr L P Kelly
Church Walk, Malvern, Worcestershire, WR14 2XH P
☎ 01684 560258
Est. 1985 ***Stock size*** Medium
Stock Wide range of antiquarian and second-hand books
Open Tues–Sat 10am–5pm closed 1–2pm
Services Valuations, book search

Promenade Antiques & Books
Contact Mr M Seldester
41 Worcester Road, Malvern, Worcestershire, WR14 4RB P
☎ 01684 566876 F 01684 566876
E promant@bigfoot.com
Est. 1990 ***Stock size*** Medium
Stock Victorian–Edwardian furniture, collectables, decorative items, reproduction lamps, books
Open Mon–Sat 10am–5pm Sun noon–5pm

St James Antiques
Contact Mr Hans Van Wyngaarden
De Lys, Wells Road, Malvern, Worcestershire, WR14 4JL P
☎ 01684 563404
Est. 1992 ***Stock size*** Large
Stock Pine furniture, lighting, decorative items
Open Mon–Sat 9am–5.30pm closed Wed

PERSHORE

Coach House Books
Contact Mr P Ellingworth
17a Bridge Street, Pershore, Worcestershire, WR10 1AJ
☎ 01386 552801/556100
F 01386 552801
E sue@chb.co.uk
Est. 1982 ***Stock size*** Large
Stock Antiquarian, rare, new and second-hand books, prints
Open Mon–Sat 9am–5pm
Services Book search, picture framing

Hansen Chard Antiques (BHI)
Contact Mr P Ridler
126 High Street, Pershore, Worcestershire, WR10 1EA P
☎ 01386 553423
Est. 1984 ***Stock size*** Large
Stock Clocks, barometers, old and antique model steam engines, scientific instruments
Open Tues–Sat 10am–4.30pm closed Thurs or by appointment
Fairs Brunel Clock Fair, Birmingham Clock Fair, Haydock, Balderton
Services Valuations, restorations

Lion Antiques
Contact Mrs R Mansfield
12 Bridge Street, Pershore, Worcestershire, WR10 1AT P
☎ 01386 555688/750214
F 01386 555688 M 07816 834481
E lionantiques@talk21.com
Est. 1982 ***Stock size*** Medium
Stock Lighting, mirrors, bed canopies, pine, oak and mahogany furniture, sculptures
Open Tues–Sat 9.30am–4.30pm Mon Thurs by appointment

Ian K Pugh Books
Contact Mr I Pugh
40 Bridge Street, Pershore, Worcestershire, WR10 1AT P
☎ 01386 552681
Est. 1974 ***Stock size*** Medium
Stock Antiquarian, rare and second-hand books on most subjects. Antiques, fine art, horticulture and military topics specialities
Open Wed–Fri 10.30am–5pm Sat 9.30am–5pm
Services Valuations, book search

S W Antiques
Contact Mr Adrian Whiteside
Abbey Showrooms, Newlands, Pershore, Worcestershire, WR10 1BP P
☎ 01386 555580 F 01386 556205
E sw-antiques@talk21.com
W www.sw-antiques.co.uk
Est. 1978 ***Stock size*** Large

MIDLANDS
WORCESTERSHIRE • REDDITCH

Stock 19th–early 20thC furniture, antique beds
Open Mon–Sat 9am–5pm
Services Valuations, restorations

REDDITCH

Angel Antiques
Contact Mrs C Manners
211 Mount Pleasant, Redditch, Worcestershire, B97 4JG
01527 545844
Est. 1989 *Stock size* Medium
Stock Georgian–Edwardian antique furniture, decorative items
Open Mon Tues Thurs Fri 10am–3.30pm Wed 10am–2pm Sat 10am–5pm
Services Restorations

Arrow Auctions (NAVA)
Contact Mr A Reeves
Bartleet Road, Washford, Redditch, Worcestershire, B98 0DG
01527 517707 01527 510924
enquiries@arrowauctions.co.uk
www.arrowauctions.co.uk
Est. 1982
Open Mon–Fri 8.30am–5pm
Sales General household sale every Tues 6pm, viewing from 9am. Specialist bi-annual fine art sales Tues 11am. Free valuations. Removal, collection and storage facilities available. On-site restaurant
Frequency Weekly
Catalogues Yes

TENBURY WELLS

Antiques & Anything
Contact Mr S Deakin
13 Teme Street, Tenbury Wells, Worcestershire, WR15 8BB
01584 810830
07971 869256 or 07977 579278
Est. 1999 *Stock size* Medium
Stock Furniture, porcelain, china, decorative items, collectables
Open Mon–Sat 9am–5pm Sun 11am–4pm

UPTON-UPON-SEVERN

Boar's Nest Trading
Contact Mr G Smith
37a–37b Old Street, Upton-upon-Severn, Worcester, Worcestershire, WR8 0HN
01684 592540 07881 797443
Est. 1992 *Stock size* Large
Stock Second-hand and antiquarian books, non-fiction a speciality
Open Mon–Sun 10.30am–6pm
Services Valuations

WHITBOURNE

Juro Farm and Garden Antiques
Contact Mr R Hughes
Whitbourne, Worcester, Worcestershire, WR6 5SF
01886 821261 01886 821261
roy@juro.co.uk
www.juro.co.uk
Est. 1991 *Stock size* Large
Stock Garden antiques, staddle stones, troughs, cider mills, statuary, farming and garden implements
Open Mon–Sat 9am–5pm
Fairs Newark, Hampton Court, Malvern Spring Garden Show
Services Valuations

WORCESTER

Antiques & Curios
Contact Mr B Inett
50 Upper Tything, Worcester, Worcestershire, WR1 1JZ
01905 25412 01905 25412
Est. 1980 *Stock size* Large
Stock Victorian–Edwardian furniture, mirrors, clocks, porcelain, glass, decorative items
Open Mon–Sat 9.30am–5.30pm
Services Valuations, restorations

The Antiques Warehouse
Contact Mr D Venn
74 Droitwich Road (rear), Worcester, Worcestershire, WR1 8BW
01905 27493
Est. 1979 *Stock size* Large
Stock Pine furniture, Victorian interior doors, antique and reproduction fireplaces
Open Mon–Fri 8am–6pm Sat 10am–5pm
Services Restorations

The Barbers Clock
Contact Graham Gopsill
37 Droitwich Road, Worcester, Worcestershire, WR3 7LG
01905 29022 07710 486598
Graham@barbersclock37@fsnet.co.uk
Est. 1993 *Stock size* Medium
Stock Clocks from 1840–1930, wind-up gramophones, Art Deco
Open Mon–Sat 9am–5pm
Services Valuations, gramophone and clock repairs

Box Bush Antiques
Contact Mrs P Difford
43 Upper Tything, Worcester, Worcestershire, WR1 1JZ
01905 28617 01905 28617
Est. 1995 *Stock size* Medium
Stock 18th–19thC pine, mahogany and walnut furniture, decorative items, silver
Open Mon–Sat 9am–5.30pm
Services Valuations, restorations, wood turning

B Browning & Son
Contact Mr A Browning
35a Wylds Lane, Worcester, Worcestershire, WR5 1DA
01905 355646
Est. 1904 *Stock size* Medium
Stock Modern and antique general household furniture
Open Mon–Sat 9am–5pm closed Thurs
Services House clearance

Bygones by the Cathedral (LAPADA, FGA)
Cathedral Square, Worcester, Worcestershire, WR1 2JD
01905 25388 01905 23132
Est. 1946 *Stock size* Medium
Stock Decorative antiques, silver, jewellery, porcelain, furniture, paintings, glass, metalwork
Open Mon–Fri 9.30am–5.30pm Sat 9.30am–1pm 2–5.30pm

Bygones of Worcester (LAPADA)
Contact Gabrielle Bullock
55 Sidbury, Worcester, Worcestershire, WR1 2HU
01905 23132 01905 23132
Est. 1946 *Stock size* Medium
Stock 17th–20thC furniture, paintings, bronzes, silver, porcelain
Open Mon–Sat 9.30am–1pm 2–5.30pm

Andrew Grant Fine Art Auctioneers
St Marks Close, Worcester, Worcestershire, WR5 3DJ
01905 357547 01905 763942
fine.arts@andrew-grant.co.uk
www.andrew-grant.co.uk

Est. 1980
Open Mon–Fri 9am–5.30pm
Sales Quarterly antiques and fine art sale Thurs, viewing day prior 10am–7pm. Monthly Victoriana and collectables sale Sat, viewing day prior 10am–5pm
Frequency Quarterly
Catalogues Yes

Grays Antiques
Contact Mr D Gray
29 The Tiding, Worcester, Worcestershire, WR1 1JL
☎ 01905 724456 Ⓕ 01905 723433
Ⓔ enquiries@grays-antiques.com
Ⓦ www.grays-antiques.com
Est. 1984 *Stock size* Large
Stock Early 19th–early 20thC furniture and furnishings and decorative items including chandeliers
Open Mon–Sat 8.30am–5.30pm
Services Valuations, restorations

Heirlooms
Contact Mrs L Rumford
46 Upper Tything, Worcester, Worcestershire, WR1 1JZ Ⓟ
☎ 01905 23332
Est. 1988 *Stock size* Large
Stock Antique and old reproduction furniture, china, glass, decorative items
Open Mon–Sat 9.30am–4.30pm

P J Hughes Antiques
Contact Mr P J Hughes
3 Barbourne Road, Worcester, Worcestershire, WR1 1RS Ⓟ
☎ 01905 610695 Ⓜ 07774 204127
Est. 1972 *Stock size* Large
Stock Jewellery, collectables, china, silver, small furniture
Open Tues–Sat 9.30am–5pm
Fairs St Martin's Market, Birmingham
Services Valuations

M Lees & Son (LAPADA)
Contact Mr M Lees
Tower House, 1 Castle Place, Severn Street, Worcester, Worcestershire, WR1 2NB Ⓟ
☎ 01905 26620 Ⓕ 01905 26620
Ⓜ 07860 826218
Est. 1974 *Stock size* Medium
Stock Period furniture, china, pictures, decorative items, mirrors
Open Mon–Fri 9.30am–4.45pm Thurs 9.30am–12.45pm Sat 10.30am–4pm
Services Valuations

The Old Toll House
Contact Mr D Askew
1 Droitwich Road, Worcester, Worcestershire, WR3 7LG Ⓟ
☎ 01905 20608
Ⓔ derek@theoldtollhouse.freeserve.co.uk
Est. 1980 *Stock size* Medium
Stock Pine furniture, reclaimed wooden doors, pottery, porcelain, glass
Open Mon–Sat 10am–6pm
Services Restorations, stripping

Round the Bend
Contact Gabrielle Bullock FGA
1 Deansway, Worcester, Worcestershire, WR1 2JD Ⓟ
☎ 01905 616516
Est. 1992 *Stock size* Medium
Stock Eccentricities
Open Mon–Sat 10am–5.30pm

Philip Serrell FSVA
Contact P Serrell FRICS
Sansome House, 6 Sansome Walk, Worcester, Worcestershire, WR1 1LH Ⓟ
☎ 01905 26200 Ⓕ 01905 21202
Ⓔ serrell.auctions@virgin.net
Ⓦ www.serrell.com
Open Mon–Fri 9am–5pm closed 1–2pm
Sales General and fine art sales at the Malvern Sale Room, Malvern
Frequency Fortnightly
Catalogues Yes

Tything Antiques Centre
Contact Mr or Mrs Shuckburgh
39 The Tything, Worcester, Worcestershire, WR1 1JL Ⓟ
☎ 01905 723322
Est. 1994 *Stock size* Large
No. of dealers 12
Stock General antiques
Open Mon–Sat 10am–5.30pm

Worcester Antiques Centre
Contact Mr S Zacaroli
Unit 15, Reindeer Court, Mealcheapen Street, Worcester, Worcestershire, WR1 4DS Ⓟ
☎ 01905 610680
Est. 1991 *Stock size* Large
No. of dealers 45
Stock Porcelain, early Worcester, furniture, silver, jewellery, Art Nouveau, Arts and Crafts

YORKS & LINCS

EAST RIDING OF YORKSHIRE

BEVERLEY

Hawley Antiques (LAPADA)
Contact John Hawley
5 North Bar Within, Beverley, East Riding of Yorkshire, HU17 8AP P
☎ 01482 868193 F 01482 874672
M 07850 225805
E antiques@hawleys.org.uk
W www.hawleys.org.uk
Est. 1966 *Stock size* Medium
Stock General antiques, mainly Georgian–Victorian
Open Mon–Fri 10am–4pm Sat 9.30am–5pm
Fairs Newark
Services Valuations, restorations

Time and Motion (BHI, BWCG)
Contact Mr Peter Lancaster
1 Beckside, Beverley, East Riding of Yorkshire, HU17 0PB P
☎ 01482 881574
Est. 1984 *Stock size* Large
Stock Antique clocks and barometers
Open Mon–Sat 10am–5pm closed Thurs
Services Valuations, restorations

BRIDLINGTON

Dixons Medals (OMRS)
Contact Mr C J Dixon
23 Prospect Street, Bridlington, East Riding of Yorkshire, YO15 2AE P
☎ 01262 603348 F 01262 606600
E chris@dixonsmedals.co.uk
W www.dixonsmedals.co.uk

Est. 1969 *Stock size* Large
Stock Medals from Peninsular war, Victorian campaigns to present day
Open Mon–Fri 9.30am–5pm
Fairs OMRS convention
Services Restorations to medals, catalogue, mail order worldwide, Dixons Gazette

The Emporium
Contact Mr Burdall
59 St John Street, Bridlington, East Riding of Yorkshire, YO16 7NN
01262 677560 07779 200335
Est. 1979 *Stock size* Large
Stock Sanitary ware, doors, radiators, pine furniture, cast-iron fires, French stoves, brass ware, reclaimed timber etc
Open Tues–Sat 10am–5.30pm or by appointment
Services Valuations, restorations, stripping

The Georgian Rooms
Contact David Rothwell
56 High Street, Bridlington, East Riding of Yorkshire, YO16 4QA
01262 608600
Est. 2000 *Stock size* Large
No. of dealers 15
Stock General antiques, silver, jewellery, furniture, paintings
Open Mon–Sat 10am–5pm

Michael James Antiques & Curios
Contact Mr M James
45 High Street, Bridlington, East Riding of Yorkshire, YO16 4PR
01262 401909 07977 327364
Est. 1992 *Stock size* Medium
Stock Pre-war shipping furniture, decorative items
Open Mon–Sat 9am–5pm

The Magpie's Nest
Contact Ms R Szpakowski
92 St John Street, Bridlington, East Riding of Yorkshire, YO16 7JS
01262 400533 07721 090414
Est. 1994 *Stock size* Medium
Stock Antiques, bric-a-brac, collectables
Open Fri–Sat 10am–5pm
Fairs Wetherby, Harrogate, Swinderby

BROUGH

Lincoln House Antiques (LAPADA)
Contact Mr J Daggett
51 Market Place, South Cave, Brough, East Riding of Yorkshire, HU15 2BS
01430 424623 07764 273695
Est. 1993 *Stock size* Medium
Stock Georgian–Edwardian furniture, porcelain, pictures, clocks
Open Mon–Sat 10am–5pm closed Wed or by appointment
Fairs Burleys, Harrogate
Services Valuations

Pennyfarthing Antiques
Contact Miss Caroline E Dennett
Albion House, 18 Westgate, North Cave, Brough, East Yorkshire, HU15 2NJ
01430 422958 07980 624583
Est. 1989 *Stock size* Medium
Stock Brass and iron beds, sofas, silver, decorative items, furniture, porcelain
Open Mon–Sat 9.30am–6pm
Fairs Newark
Services Valuations

DRIFFIELD

The Crested China Co
Contact Mr David Taylor
Station House, Railway Station, Driffield, East Riding of Yorkshire, YO25 6PX
01377 255002/257042
dt@thecrestedchinacompany.com
www.thecrestedchinacompany.com
Est. 1980 *Stock size* Large
Stock Goss and Crested china
Open Mon–Fri 9am–5pm or by appointment
Fairs Goss Collectors Club Fairs
Services Mail order, bi-monthly catalogue

Dee, Atkinson and Harrison
Contact Owen Nisbet or Helen Pickering
The Exchange, Driffield, East Riding of Yorkshire, YO25 6LD
01377 253151 01377 241041
driffield@dee.atkinson.harrison.co.uk
www.dee.atkinson.harrison.co.uk
Est. 1880
Open 9am–5.30pm
Sales 6 Antique and collectors' sales per annum, 2 collectors' sports and toy sales per annum, fortnightly 19thC and modern sales
Catalogues Yes

Smith & Smith Designs, Antique Pine and Country Furniture
Contact Mr D Smith
58a Middle Street North, Driffield, East Riding of Yorkshire, YO25 6SU
01377 256321 01377 256070
07941 034446
shop@pine-on-line.co.uk
www.pine-on-line.co.uk
Est. 1976 *Stock size* Medium
Stock Antique and reproduction pine furniture, other period furniture, decorative items, lighting, water features
Open Mon–Sat 9.30am–5.30pm
Services Restorations

GOOLE

Arcadia Antiques Centre
Contact Mr Martin Spavin
10–14 The Arcade, Goole, East Yorkshire, DN14 5QT
01405 720549 01405 750549
07775 557499
Est. 1991 *Stock size* Medium
No. of dealers 20
Stock Collectables, costume jewellery, pictures, furniture etc
Open Mon–Sat 10am–5pm Sun by appointment
Services Valuations, clock and watch repairs

Clegg & Son
Contact Mr C Clegg
68 Aire Street, Goole, East Riding of Yorkshire, DN14 5QE
01405 763140 01405 764235
gooleoffice@cleggandson.co.uk
www.cleggandson.co.uk
Est. 1895
Open Mon–Fri 9am–5pm
Sales Antiques and household sale Sat am, viewing day of sale 9am–sale. Held at St Mary's Church Hall, Goole
Catalogues Yes

HORNSEA

Second Time Around
Contact Mr T Brown
61–61a Southgate, Hornsea, East Riding of Yorkshire, HU18 1AL
01964 532037
Est. 1981 *Stock size* Large
Stock General antiques, furniture, pottery, collectables, china
Open Mon–Sat 10am–4.30pm closed Wed
Fairs Newark, Birmingham
Services Restorations, upholstery

HOWDEN

Kemp Booksellers (ABA, PBFA, BA)
Contact Mike Kemp
5–7 Vicar Lane, Howden, East Riding of Yorkshire, DN14 7BP
01430 432071 01430 431666
kemp.books@dial.pipex.com
www.kempbooksellers.co.uk
Est. 1979 *Stock size* Medium
Stock Mervyn Peake, modern first editions, Yorkshire and Lincolnshire topography
Open Mon–Sat 9am–5pm
Fairs ABA, PBFA, BA

HULL

Anderson Antiques (UK) Ltd
Contact Mr Anderson
Anderson Wharf, Wincomlee, Hull, East Riding of Yorkshire, HU2 8AH
01482 609691
www.andersonantiques.com
Est. 1972 *Stock size* Large
Stock Georgian, Edwardian, 1930s, shipping furniture, general antiques, collectables
Open Mon–Fri 9am–5pm Sat Sun 10am–4pm
Services Valuations, shipping

David Hakeney Antiques
Contact David Hakeney
PO Box 65, Hull, East Riding of Yorkshire, HU10 7XT
01482 651177 07860 507774
Est. 1970 *Stock size* Medium
Stock General antiques, quality items
Open By appointment
Services Restorations

Imperial Antiques
Contact M Langton
397 Hessle Road, Hull, East Riding of Yorkshire, HU3 4EH
01482 327439
Est. 1980 *Stock size* Medium
Stock Pine furniture
Open Mon–Sat 9am–5pm

Kilnsea Antiques
Contact Tony Smith
The Old Barn, Kilnsea Road, Hull, East Riding of Yorkshire, HU12 0UB
01964 650311
tony@smith-antiques.freeserve.co.uk
Est. 1981 *Stock size* Medium
Stock Furniture and collectables from the late 1800s
Open Tues–Sun 10am–5pm

Mill Antiques
Contact John Mills
388–390 Beverley Road, Hull, East Riding of Yorkshire, HU5 1LN
01482 342248
john@millantiques.co.uk
Est. 1971 *Stock size* Medium
Stock Antique pine, brass beds, cast-iron fireplaces, architectural
Open Mon–Sat 9am–5pm
Services Valuations, pine stripping

Pine-Apple Antiques
Contact Diane Todd
321–327 Beverley Road, Hull, East Riding of Yorkshire, HU5 1LD
01482 441384 01482 441073
07860 874480
diane@pine-apple.co.uk
www.pine-apple.co.uk
Est. 1981 *Stock size* Large
Stock Architectural antiques, pine, lighting, clocks, pottery, curios, fireplaces
Open Mon–Sat 9am–5.30pm Sun 11am–4pm

MARKET WEIGHTON

R Hornsey & Sons
Contact Mr M Swann
33 High Street, Market Weighton, East Riding of Yorkshire, YO43 3AQ
01430 872551 01430 871387
07711 200854
sales@hornseys.uk.com
www.hornseys.uk.com
Est. 1884
Open Mon–Fri 9am–5pm Sat 9am–noon
Sales General antiques
Frequency Periodic
Catalogues No

Mount Pleasant Antiques Centre
Contact Linda Sirrs
46 Cliffe Road, Market Weighton, East Riding of Yorkshire, YO43 3BP
01430 872872
Est. 1999 *Stock size* Large
No. of dealers 20
Stock Good-quality furniture, collectables
Open Mon–Sun 9.30am–5pm
Services Restorations, tea room

PATRINGTON

Clyde Antiques
Contact Ms S Nettleton
12a Market Place, Patrington, Hull, East Riding of Yorkshire, HU12 0RB
01964 630650
Est. 1980 *Stock size* Medium
Stock Wide range of antique stock from collectables to period furniture
Open Tues–Sat 10am–5pm closed Wed
Services Valuations

Frank Hill & Son
Contact Mr R E Ward
18 Market Place, Patrington, Hull, East Yorkshire, HU12 0RB
01964 630531 01964 631203
07860 123057
Est. 1926
Open Mon–Fri 9am–5pm Sat 9am–noon
Sales Antique and modern household furniture and effects quarterly, phone for details, viewing morning of sale. Held at Church Hall, Ottringham
Frequency Quarterly
Catalogues Yes

THORNTON

Abacus Fireplaces
Contact Mr J White
Common End Farm, Thornton, Melbourne, East Riding of Yorkshire, YO42 4RZ
01759 318575 01423 524999
07703 517544

Est. 1969 *Stock size* Large
Stock Architectural antiques, fireplaces, fireplace furnishings
Open Mon–Sat 9am–4.30pm
Services Restorations to all antiques, custom-made castings

WITHERNSEA

Mathy's Emporium
Contact Mr M Quinn
2 Pier Road, Withernsea, East Riding of Yorkshire, HU19 2JS
☎ 01964 615739
Est. 1994 *Stock size* Large
Stock Brass, furniture, pottery, Wade, collectables
Open Mon–Sun 10am–5pm closed Wed
Services Valuations

NORTH YORKSHIRE

ALLERTON MAULEVERER

Mauleverer Antiques
Contact Ms Caroline Louise Forster
Allerton Park Castle, Allerton Mauleverer, Knaresborough, North Yorkshire, HG5 0SE
☎ 01423 340170 F 01423 340170
M 07974 255087
Est. 1984 *Stock size* Medium
Stock 1650–1850 early English oak and provincial furniture
Open By appointment only
Fairs NEC, The Northern Antique Fair, Harrogate

ASKRIGG

J R Hopper & Co
Contact Mr D Lambert
Wood End Countersett, Askrigg, North Yorkshire, DL8 3DE
☎ 01969 650776 F 01969 624319
E brian.carlisle@easynet.co.uk
Est. 1886
Open Possible to contact at all times
Sales General antiques, household furnishings
Frequency Monthly
Catalogues Yes

AUSTWICK

Austwick Hall Books
Contact Michael Pearson
Townhead Lane, Austwick, Nr Settle, North Yorkshire, LA2 8BS
☎ 01524 251794
E austwickhall@btinternet.com
Est. 2000 *Stock size* Medium
Stock Antiquarian, rare and second-hand books, including natural history and science
Open By appointment only
Services Book search

BEDALE

Bedale Antiques
Contact Mr or Mrs R C Stubley
2a Sussex Street, Bedale, North Yorkshire, DL8 2AJ
☎ 01677 427765
Est. 1998 *Stock size* Medium
Stock Period furniture, pottery, lighting
Open Mon–Sat 10am–4.30pm closed Thurs

Bennetts Antiques & Collectables Ltd
Contact Paul Bennett
7 Market Place, Bedale, North Yorkshire, DL8 1ED
☎ 01677 427900 F 01677 426858
E info@bennetts.uk.com
W www.bennetts.uk.com
Est. 1997 *Stock size* Large
Stock Furniture, clocks, works of art, 19thC Yorkshire paintings, collectables
Open Mon–Sat 9am–5pm Sun by appointment
Services Restorations, clock repair

Bonhams
14 Market Place, Bedale, North Yorkshire, DL8 1EQ
☎ 01667 424 114 F 01677 424 115
E bedale@bonhams.com
W www.bonhams.com
Open Mon–Fri 9am–1pm 2–5pm

M W Darwin & Son
Contact Mr M W Darwin
The Dales Furniture Hall, Bridge Street, Bedale, North Yorkshire, DL8 2AD
☎ 01677 422846 F 01609 779072
E mwdarwin1@estategazette.net
Est. 1959
Open Mon–Fri 9am–4.30pm Thurs 9am–noon
Sales General antiques sales held on Fri
Frequency Every 3 weeks
Catalogues No

Dovetail Interiors of Bedale
Contact Brian Jutsum
Bridge Street, Bedale, North Yorkshire, DL8 2AD
☎ 01677 426464 F 01677 426464
W www.dovetailinteriors.com
Est. 1997 *Stock size* Medium
Stock Antiques, bespoke furniture, ethnic artefacts
Open Mon–Sun 10am–5pm

BILLINGHAM

Margaret Bedi Antiques and Fine Art (LAPADA)
Contact Mrs Margaret Bedi
5 Station Road, Billingham, Stockton-on-Tees, TS23 1AG
☎ 01642 782346 M 07860 577637
Est. 1976 *Stock size* Large
Stock Fine furniture 1660–1920, watercolours, oils
Open By appointment only
Fairs Northern Antiques Fair, Harrogate
Services Valuations, restorations

BOLTON ABBEY

Grove Country Bookshop
Contact Mr A Sharpe
The Old Post Office, Bolton Abbey, Skipton, North Yorkshire, BD23 6EX
☎ 01756 710717
Est. 1997 *Stock size* Medium
Stock Antique, rare and second-hand books, local topography a speciality
Open Tues–Sun 10.30am–4pm variable during winter
Services Restorations, book search

BOROUGHBRIDGE

Oswald Lister & Haigh incorporating James Johnston
Contact Mr Paul Johnston
5 St James Square, Boroughbridge, North Yorkshire, YO51 9AS
☎ 01423 322382 F 01423 324735
M 07885 497825
E boroughbridge@listerhaugh.co.uk
W www.listerhaugh.co.uk
Est. 1919
Open Mon–Fri 9am–5.30pm Sat 9–11.30am

Sales General antiques and periodic catalogue sales
Frequency Monthly
Catalogues Yes

St James House Antiques & Restoration (LAPADA)
Contact Mr John Wilson or Mr P Wilson
St James Square, Boroughbridge, North Yorkshire, YO5 9AR
☎ 01423 322508 Ⓕ 01423 326690
Est. 1989 *Stock size* Medium
Stock General antiques, 18th–19thC furniture
Open Mon–Sat 9am–5.30pm or by appointment
Services Valuations, restorations

R S Wilson & Son
Contact Mr R Wilson
PO Box 41, Boroughbridge, North Yorkshire, YO51 9WY
☎ 01423 322417 Ⓕ 01423 322417
Ⓜ 07711 794801
Est. 1917 *Stock size* Medium
Stock 17th–19thC furniture
Open By appointment

EASINGWOLD

Country House Furniture
Contact Judith O'Brien
108 Long Street, Easingwold, North Yorkshire, YO61 3HY
☎ 01347 822977
Est. 1978 *Stock size* Medium
Stock English and French period pine, country furniture, decorative items, upholstered chairs etc
Open Mon–Sat 10.30am–5pm
Fairs Galloway Fairs

Milestone Antiques
Contact Mr A Streetley
Farnley House, 101 Long Street, Easingwold, York, North Yorkshire, YO61 3HY
☎ 01347 821608
Est. 1982 *Stock size* Medium
Stock Furniture, clocks
Open Mon–Sat 9am–5.30pm Sun by appointment
Services Valuations

Vale Antiques (GADAR)
Contact J M Leach
Mooracres, North Moor, Easingwold, York, North Yorkshire, YO61 3NB
☎ 01347 821298 Ⓕ 01347 821298
Ⓔ chris.leach@ukonline.co.uk
Est. 1990 *Stock size* Medium
Stock Georgian, Victorian and later furniture, collectables
Open Mon–Sun 9am–5pm
Services Furniture restoration

FARNHAM

Mauleverer Antiques
Contact Ms Caroline Louise Forster
The Old Cottage, Shaw Lane, Farnham, Knaresborough, North Yorkshire, HG5 9JE
☎ 01423 340170 Ⓕ 01423 340170
Ⓜ 07974 255087
Est. 1984 *Stock size* Medium
Stock 1650–1850 early English oak and provincial furniture
Open By appointment only
Fairs NEC, The Northern Antique Fair, Harrogate

FLAXTON

Flaxton Antique Gardens (SALVO)
Contact Tim Richardson
Glebe Farm, Flaxton, North Yorkshire, YO60 7RU
☎ 01904 468468 Ⓕ 01904 468468
Ⓦ www.salvo.co.uk/dealers/flaxton
Est. 1990 *Stock size* Large
Stock Garden antiques, terracotta urns, seats, Victorian edging, bird baths, troughs, sun dials
Open Mon–Sun 10am–4pm closed Tues winter times telephone call advisable
Services Valuations

GARGRAVE

Dickinson Antiques
Contact H H or A E Mardall
Estate Yard, West Street, Gargrave, North Yorkshire, BD23 3PH
☎ 01756 748257
Est. 1959 *Stock size* Medium
Stock Antique early furniture
Open Mon–Fri 9am–5.30pm or by appointment

Gargrave Gallery
Contact Mr B Herington
48 High Street, Gargrave, Skipton, North Yorkshire, BD23 1JP
☎ 01756 749641
Est. 1974 *Stock size* Medium
Stock General antiques, Georgian–Victorian furniture
Open Mon–Sat 10am–4pm

R N Myers & Son (BADA)
Contact Simon Myers
Endsleigh House, High Street, Gargrave, Skipton, North Yorkshire, BD23 3LX
☎ 01756 749587 Ⓕ 01756 749322
Ⓜ 07801 310126
Ⓔ rnmyersson@aol.com
Est. 1890 *Stock size* Medium
Stock Georgian furniture, works of art
Open Mon–Sat 9am–5pm or by appointment
Services Valuations

GUISBOROUGH

Curiosity Corner
Contact Mr B Wilson
47 Church Street, Guisborough, Cleveland, North Yorkshire, TS14 6HG
☎ 01287 636660
Est. 1987 *Stock size* Medium
Stock General antiques, longcase clocks
Open Mon–Sat 9am–4.30pm
Fairs Newark, Swinderby

HARROGATE

Armstrong Antiques (BADA, LAPADA)
Contact M A Armstrong
10–11 Montpellier Parade, Harrogate, North Yorkshire, HG1 2TJ
☎ 01423 506843 Ⓕ 01423 506843
Ⓜ 07802 721815
Est. 1983 *Stock size* Medium
Stock Fine 18th–early 19thC English furniture
Open Mon–Sat 10am–5.30pm
Fairs Olympia
Services Valuations

Richard Axe Books
Contact Mr R Axe
12 Cheltenham Crescent, Harrogate, North Yorkshire, HG1 1DH
☎ 01423 561867 Ⓕ 01423 561837
Ⓔ rja@axebooks.com
Est. 1980 *Stock size* Large
Stock Antiquarian, rare and

second-hand books, Yorkshire topics a speciality
Open Mon–Sat 10am–5.30pm

Margaret Bedi's Antiques and Fine Art (LAPADA)
Contact Mrs Margaret Bedi
Corn Exchange Building, The Ginnel, Harrogate, North Yorkshire, HG1 2RB
01642 782346 Ⓜ 07860 577637
Est. 1976 *Stock size* Large
Stock Fine furniture 1660–1920, watercolours, oils
Open By appointment only
Fairs Northern Antiques Fair, Harrogate
Services Valuations, restorations

Carlton Hollis Ltd
Contact Paul Hollis
10 Montpellier Mews, Montpellier Street, Harrogate, North Yorkshire, HG1 2TQ
01423 500216 Ⓕ 01423 500283
Est. 2000 *Stock size* Medium
Stock Antique silver and jewellery
Open Mon–Sat 10am–5pm
Services Valuations, restorations

Crown Jewellers of Harrogate
Contact Steve Kramer
23 Commercial Street, Harrogate, North Yorkshire, HG1 1UB
01423 502000 Ⓕ 01423 502000
Ⓔ sask@crownjewellers.freeserve.co.uk
Ⓦ www.crownjewellersharrogate.co.uk
Est. 2000 *Stock size* Medium
Stock Jewellery, porcelain, glass, silver
Open Mon–Sat 10am–5pm closed Wed
Services Valuations, jewellery repairs

John Daffern Antiques
Contact John Daffern
38 Forest Lane Head, Harrogate, North Yorkshire, HG2 7TS
01423 889832
Est. 1968 *Stock size* Medium
Stock Fine 17th–18thC furniture, clocks
Open Mon Wed Fri Sat 10.30am–5.30pm

Derbyshire Antiques Ltd
Contact Mr R Derbyshire
27 Montpellier Parade, Harrogate, North Yorkshire, HG1 2TG
01423 503115 Ⓜ 07860 580836
Est. 1962 *Stock size* Medium
Stock Early oak pieces, associated items, Georgian furniture to 1820
Open Mon–Sat 10am–5.30pm

Dragon Antiques
Contact Mr Peter Broadbelt
10 Dragon Road, Harrogate, North Yorkshire, HG1 5DF
01423 562037
Est. 1964 *Stock size* Medium
Stock General antiques, ephemera, postcards
Open Mon–Sat 11am–6pm

G W Ford & Son Ltd (LAPADA)
Contact Mr I Thomson
The Ginnell Antiques Centre, The Ginnell, Harrogate, North Yorkshire, HG1 2RB
01423 508857 Ⓕ 01423 508857
Ⓜ 07740 025936
Ⓔ enquiries@gwfordantiques.co.uk
Ⓦ www.gwfordantiques.co.uk
Est. 1890 *Stock size* Small
Stock 18th–19thC mahogany, country furniture, 19thC–early 20thC sculpture, silver, Sheffield plate, treen, decorative items
Open Mon–Sat 10am–5pm Sun 11am–5pm
Services Restorations

Garth Antiques (LAPADA)
Contact Mr or Mrs J Chapman
16 Montpellier Parade, Harrogate, North Yorkshire, HG1 2TG
01423 530573
Est. 1989 *Stock size* Small
Stock General antiques
Open Mon–Sat 10am–5.30pm
Services Restorations

The Ginnel Antiques Centre
Contact Mrs P Stephenson
Corn Exchange Building, The Ginnel, Harrogate, North Yorkshire, HG1 2RB
01423 508857 Ⓕ 01423 508857
Ⓔ info@theginnel.com
Ⓦ www.theginnel.co.uk
Est. 1986 *Stock size* Large
No. of dealers 50
Stock Quality datelined antiques
Open Mon–Sat 9.30am–5.30pm
Services Courier service, café, licensed restaurant

Grandad's Attic
Contact Miss B F Dawson
2 Granville Road, Harrogate, North Yorkshire, HG1 1BY
01423 503003
Est. 1984 *Stock size* Medium
Stock Antique usable tools, garden tools, kitchenware
Open Thurs Fri Sat 10.30am–4.30pm or by appointment

Havelocks Pine and Antiques
Contact Philip Adam
13–17 Westmoreland Street, Harrogate, North Yorkshire, HG1 5AY
01423 506721 Ⓕ 01423 506721
Ⓜ 07802 914419
Est. 1986 *Stock size* Large
Stock General antiques
Open Mon–Sat 10am–5pm Sun 11am–4pm
Fairs Newark
Services Restorations, pine stripping, valuations

Charles Lumb & Sons Ltd (BADA)
Contact Mr A Lumb
2 Montpellier Gardens, Harrogate, North Yorkshire, HG1 2TF
01423 503776 Ⓕ 01423 530074
Ⓔ charles.lumb@virgin.net
Est. 1910 *Stock size* Medium
Stock 18th–19thC English furniture, works of art, metalware
Open Mon–Sat 9.30am–6pm closed 1–2pm

Christopher Matthews
Contact Christopher Matthews
23 Mount Street, Harrogate, North Yorkshire, HG2 8DQ
01423 871756 Ⓕ 01423 879700
Est. 1989
Open Mon–Fri 9am–5pm
Sales Quarterly antiques auctions, phone for details
Catalogues Yes

Montpellier Mews Antique Market
Contact Murray Burgess
✉ **Montpellier Street, Harrogate, North Yorkshire, HG1 2TQ** Ⓟ
☎ 01423 530484
Est. 1987 *Stock size* Medium
No. of dealers 10
Stock General antiques, collectables, golf antiques, silver, china
Open Mon–Sat 10am–5pm

Morphets of Harrogate (SOFAA)
Contact Elizabeth Pepper-Darling
✉ **6 Albert Street, Harrogate, North Yorkshire, HG1 1JL**
☎ 01423 530030 Ⓕ 01423 500717
Ⓦ www.morphets.co.uk
Est. 1895
Open Mon–Fri 9am–5.30pm Wed 9am–6pm Sat 9am–noon
Sales Fine art and antiques sale quarterly Thurs 10am, viewing Tues 2–7pm Wed 10am–5pm Thurs 8.30–10am. Victorian and later furniture and effects Thurs 10am, viewing Wed 10am–7pm Thurs 8.30–10am
Catalogues Yes

Paul M Peters (LAPADA)
Contact Mr Paul Peters
✉ **15a Bower Road, Harrogate, North Yorkshire, HG1 1BE** Ⓟ
☎ 01423 560118 Ⓕ 01423 560118
Ⓜ 07803 082378
Est. 1964 *Stock size* Large
Stock Chinese, Japanese, European ceramics, Oriental works of art
Open Mon–Fri 10am–5pm
Fairs Olympia

Elaine Phillips Antiques Ltd (BADA)
Contact Elaine, Colin or Louise Phillips
✉ **1–2 Royal Parade, Harrogate, North Yorkshire, HG1 2SZ** Ⓟ
☎ 01423 569745 Ⓜ 07710 793753
Ⓔ elainephillips@heliscott.co.uk
Est. 1965 *Stock size* Medium
Stock 17th–18thC oak furniture, metalware, treen, some mahogany
Open Mon–Sat 9.30am–5.30pm or by appointment
Fairs Harrogate (Apr Sept)
Services Interior design

Shieling Antiques
Contact Mrs Irene Meyler
✉ **5 Montpellier Mews, Montpellier Street, Harrogate, North Yorkshire, HG1 2TQ** Ⓟ
☎ 01423 521884
Est. 1994 *Stock size* Small
Stock Pine and country furniture, brass and copper, decorative items for the country kitchen
Open Mon–Sat 10am–5pm

St Julien
Contact Mr J White
✉ **4 Royal Parade, Harrogate, North Yorkshire, HG1 2SZ** Ⓟ
☎ 01423 526569 Ⓕ 01423 524999
Ⓜ 07703 517544
Ⓔ abacus03@globalnet.co.uk
Est. 1998 *Stock size* Large
Stock Antique and period lighting, door furniture, fireplaces
Open Mon–Sat 10am–5.30pm
Fairs Newark
Services Restorations, light fittings, custom-made brass castings

Tennants Auctioneers
Contact Mr N Smith
✉ **34 Montpellier Parade, Harrogate, North Yorkshire, HG1 2TG** Ⓟ
☎ 01423 531661 Ⓕ 01423 530990
Ⓦ www.tennants.co.uk
Est. 1899
Open Mon–Fri 9am–5pm Sat 9.30am–3.30pm
Sales 3 general antiques sales per month, quarterly fine art sales, 2 books and collectors' sales, 2 militaria sales per annum
Catalogues Yes

Thorntons of Harrogate (LAPADA)
Contact Mr Jason O'Hugh
✉ **1 Montpellier Gardens, Harrogate, North Yorkshire, HG1 2TF** Ⓟ
☎ 01423 504118 Ⓕ 01423 528400
Ⓔ tofh@harrogateantiques.com
Ⓦ www.harrogateantiques.com
Est. 1973 *Stock size* Medium
Stock 18th–19thC furniture, clocks, barometers, decorative items
Open Mon–Sat 9.30am–5.30pm or by appointment
Fairs Harrogate (Apr May)
Services Restorations, valuations

Walker Galleries (BADA, LAPADA, CINOA)
Contact Ian Walker
✉ **1 Crown Place, Harrogate, North Yorkshire, HG1 2RY** Ⓟ
☎ 01423 520599 Ⓕ 01423 536664
Ⓔ walkermodern@aol.com
Ⓦ www.walkerfineart.co.uk
Est. 1972 *Stock size* Large
Stock 20thC British paintings, French impressionist paintings
Open Tues–Sat 9.30am–5.30pm
Fairs Olympia, BADA, Harrogate Fine Art and Antique Fair
Services Valuations, restorations

Walker Galleries (BADA, LAPADA, CINOA)
Contact Ian Walker
✉ **6 Montpellier Gardens, Harrogate, North Yorkshire, HG1 2TF** Ⓟ
☎ 01423 567933 Ⓕ 01423 536664
Ⓔ wgltd@aol.com
Ⓦ www.walkerfineart.co.uk
Est. 1972 *Stock size* Large
Stock 18th–20thC British and continental watercolours and oil paintings, small furniture, bronzes
Open Mon–Sat 9.30am–5.30pm
Fairs Olympia, BADA, Harrogate Fine Art and Antique Fair
Services Valuations, restorations

Weatherell's Antiques (LAPADA)
Contact Mr J Weatherell
✉ **29–30 Montpellier Parade, Harrogate, North Yorkshire, HG1 2TG** Ⓟ
☎ 01423 507810 Ⓕ 01423 520005
Est. 1964 *Stock size* Large
Stock 18th–early 20thC English and Continental furniture, paintings, objets d'art
Open Mon–Sat 9am–5.30pm

Chris Wilde Antiques (LAPADA)
Contact Mr C Wilde
✉ **134 Kings Road, Harrogate, North Yorkshire, HG1 5HY** Ⓟ
☎ 01423 525855 Ⓕ 01423 552301
Ⓜ 07831 543268
Ⓔ chris@harrogate.com
Ⓦ www.antiques.harrogate.com
Est. 1995 *Stock size* Large
Stock Georgian–Victorian furniture, longcase clocks, pictures

Open Mon–Sat 10am–5pm
Fairs NEC Antiques for Everyone, Bailey Fair, Harrogate
Services Valuations, restorations

Year Dot Interiors
Contact Lyn Pickles or Terry Kindon
4A Regent Parade, Harrogate, North Yorkshire, HG1 5AN
01423 817007 01423 817007
sales@yeardotinteriors.com
www.yeardotinteriors.com
Est. 1970
Stock Painted, pine, oak and country furniture
Open Mon–Sat 9am–5pm

HAWES

Cellar Antiques
Contact Mr Ian Iveson
Bridge Street, Hawes, North Yorkshire, DL8 3QL
01969 667224
Est. 1987 *Stock size* Medium
Stock General antiques, country oak period furniture, clocks, longcase clocks
Open Mon–Sun 10am–5pm
Services Valuations, house clearance

Sturmans Antiques (LAPADA)
Contact Mr Peter Sturman
Main Street, Hawes, North Yorkshire, DL8 3QW
01969 667742
sturmansantiques@tinyonline.co.uk
Est. 1984 *Stock size* Medium
Stock 18th–19thC furniture, clocks, porcelain
Open Mon–Sat 10am–5.30pm Sun 11am–5pm
Services Valuations, restorations, nationwide delivery, overseas shipping arranged

HELMSLEY

Buckingham Antiques
Contact Mrs H Wilson
17 Bridge Street, Helmsley, York, North Yorkshire
01439 771642
Est. 1997 *Stock size* Large
Stock General antiques
Open Tues–Sat 10am–4pm

Church Street Antiques
Contact Mr D Hartshorne
15 Church Street, Helmsley, York, North Yorkshire, YO62 5AD
01439 770370 01439 770370
Est. 1999 *Stock size* Large
Stock General antiques
Open Mon–Sun 10.30am–5pm
Services Valuations

Helmsley Antiquarian & Secondhand Books
Contact Mr M Moorby
Old Fire Station, Borogate, Helmsley, North Yorkshire, YO62 5BN
01439 770014
Est. 1985 *Stock size* Medium
Stock Antique, rare and second-hand books, Yorkshire topography a speciality
Open Mon–Sat 10am–5pm Sun noon–5pm

Westway Pine
Contact Mr J Dzierzek
Carlton Lane, Helmsley, North Yorkshire, YO62 5HB
01439 771399 01439 770172
derzie@supanet.co.uk
Est. 1987 *Stock size* Large
Stock Pine
Open Mon–Fri 9am–5pm Sat 10am–5pm
Services Valuations, restorations

York Cottage Antiques (LAPADA)
Contact G or E M Thornley
7 Church Street, Helmsley, North Yorkshire, YO62 5AD
01439 770833
Est. 1965 *Stock size* Medium
Stock Early oak and country furniture, metalware, pewter, blue-and-white pottery, maps, prints
Open Fri Sat 10am–4pm or by appointment

KILLINGHALL

Thompson Auctioneers
Contact Mr B D Thompson
The Dales Salesroom, Levens Hall Park, Lund Lane, Killinghall, Harrogate, North Yorkshire, HG3 2BG
01423 709086 01423 709085
thompsonsauctions@excite.co.uk
thompsonsauctioneers.co.uk
Est. 1989
Open Mon–Fri 9am–5pm Sat 9.30am–noon closed Thurs pm
Sales General antiques Fri 1pm, quarterly antiques and collectables sale
Frequency Weekly
Catalogues No

KNARESBOROUGH

H & L Bowkett
Contact Mr E Starkie
9 Abbey Road, naresborough, North Yorkshire, HE5 8HY
01423 866112
barbara@rivermidd.freeserve.co.uk
Est. 1974 *Stock size* Medium
Stock General antiques
Open Mon–Sat 9am–6pm

Early Oak
Contact Mr André Gora, **Knaresborough, North Yorkshire**
01423 860878
info@earlyoak.co.uk
www.earlyoak.co.uk
Stock size Medium
Stock Oak and country furniture, samplers, rugs, Delft and other ceramics, pewter, metalware
Open By appointment
Fairs Newark

John Thompson Antiques (LAPADA)
Contact Mr John Thompson
Swadforth House, Gracious Street, Knaresborough, North Yorkshire, HG5 8DT
01423 864698 01423 864698
07831 899948
Est. 1967 *Stock size* Medium
Stock Fine 18th–19thC furniture, related decorative objects
Open Mon–Sat 9am–5.30pm or by appointment
Fairs Olympia

Thornton & Linley
Contact Mr I A Thornton
2–4 Jockey Lane, High Street, Knaresborough, North Yorkshire, HG5 0HG
01423 862271 01423 862271
Est. 1909
Open Tues–Fri 9am–5pm closed 1–2pm
Sales General antiques
Frequency Periodic
Catalogues Yes

LEALHOLM

Stepping Stones
Contact Mrs J Davies
Lealholm, Whitby, North Yorkshire, YO21 2AJ P
01947 897382
Est. 1974 *Stock size* Medium
Stock General antiques, books
Open Daily 10am–5pm
Services Bed and breakfast

LEYBURN

Tennants Auctioneers (BACA Award Winner: Auctioneer of the Year 2000, Best Regional Auction House 2001)
Contact Mr Rodney Tennant
The Auction Centre, Leyburn, North Yorkshire, DL8 5SG P
01969 623780 F 01969 624281
E enquiry@tennants-ltd.co.uk
W www.tennants.co.uk
Open Mon–Fri 9am–5pm
Sales General sales Sat 9.30am 3–4 per month, viewing day prior 9am–7pm. 3 fine art sales per annum, 2 book sales and collectors' sales per annum
Catalogues Yes

MALTON

Boulton & Cooper Fine Art (SOFAA)
Contact Mr A McMillan
Forsyth House, Market Place, Malton, North Yorkshire, YO17 7LR P
01653 696151 F 01653 600311
E antiques@boultoncooper.co.uk
Est. 1801
Open Mon–Fri 9am–5.30pm Sat by appointment
Sales General antiques
Frequency Alternate months
Catalogues Yes

Cundalls
Contact Mr F Dimmey
15 Market Place, Malton, North Yorkshire, YO17 7LP
01653 697820 F 01653 698305
W www.cundalls.co.uk
Est. 1860
Open Mon–Fri 9am–5.30pm
Sales General antiques sales, phone for details
Frequency 8–10 per annum
Catalogues Yes

Magpie Antiques
Contact Mrs Gwyneth Warren
9–13 The Shambles, Malton, North Yorkshire, YO17 7LZ P
01653 691880/658335
M 07801 854636
Est. 1987 *Stock size* Medium
Stock General antiques, kitchenware, small collectables
Open Mon–Sat 10am–4pm closed Thurs
Fairs Newark
Services Will buy to order bric-a-brac to decorate pubs, shops etc

Malton Antique Market
Contact Mrs Cleverly
2 Old Maltongate, Malton, North Yorkshire, YO17 7EG P
01653 692732
Est. 1970 *Stock size* Medium
Stock 18th–19thC furniture, glass, silver, brass, copper, china
Open Mon–Sat 10am–4pm closed Thurs

Matthew Maw
Contact Mr M Maw
18 Castlegate, Malton, North Yorkshire, YO17 7DT
01653 694638 F 01653 694638
Stock size Medium
Stock General antiques
Open Mon–Sat 9am–5pm

Old Talbot Gallery
Contact Mrs C Bull
Old Talbot Gallery, 9 Market Street, Malton, North Yorkshire, YO17 7LY P
01653 696142
Est. 1981 *Stock size* Medium
Stock Books, prints, pictures, maps
Open Please telephone
Services Valuations, restorations

MASHAM

Aura Antiques
Silver Street, Masham, North Yorkshire, HE4 4DX P
01765 689315
E robert@aura-antiques.co.uk
W www.aura-antiques.co.uk
Est. 1986 *Stock size* Medium
Stock Georgian, Regency, mahogany and oak furniture
Open Mon–Sat 10am–4.30pm
Services Delivery throughout UK

MIDDLEHAM

Castle Antiques
Contact Mr D Jarvill or Mrs J Jarvill
34 Market Place, Middleham, North Yorkshire, DL8 4QW P
01969 624655
Est. 1992 *Stock size* Large
No. of dealers 20
Stock Furniture, art pottery, porcelain, glassware, blue-and-white pottery, pictures, prints, clocks, scientific instruments, lamps, jewellery, books, general antiques, collectors' items
Open Wed–Mon 10am–5.30pm Tues by appointment

Middleham Antiques
Contact Mr Mike Pitman
The Corner Shop, Kirkgate, Middleham, North Yorkshire, DL8 4PF P
01969 622982 F 01969 622982
Est. 1986 *Stock size* Small
Stock Pre-1830 oak and country furniture, longcase clocks, curios etc
Open Most days 10am–5.30pm Wed by appointment call before visiting recommended

NORTHALLERTON

Northallerton Auctions Ltd
Contact Mr P Richardson
Applegarth Sales Rooms, Romanby Road, Northallerton, North Yorkshire, DL7 8LZ P
01609 772034 F 01609 778786
Open Mon–Sat 9am–5pm
Sales General antiques Fri 1pm fortnightly
Frequency Fortnightly
Catalogues Yes

NORTON

Northern Antiques Co
Contact Mrs Ashby-Arnold
2 Parliament Street, Scarborough Road, Norton, Malton, North Yorkshire, YO17 9HE P
01653 697520 F 01653 690056
Est. 1990 *Stock size* Medium
Stock Georgian–Victorian furniture, decorative accessories
Open Mon–Fri 9am–5pm closed 1–2pm Sat 9.30am–12.30pm

PATELEY BRIDGE

H S C Fine Arts & Antiques
Contact David Hinchliffe
45 High Street, Pateley Bridge, North Yorkshire, HG3 5LB
☎ 01423 712218
rhinch4426@aol.com
Est. 1997 *Stock size* Medium
Stock Small furniture, porcelain, Royal Worcester, pictures, 18thC wine glasses
Open By appointment

Brian Loomes (BACA Award Winner 2001)
Contact Brian Loomes
Calf Haugh Farm, Pateley Bridge, Harrogate, North Yorkshire, HG3 5HW
☎ 01423 711163
brianloomes@antiqueclocks.freeserve.co.uk
www.brianloomes.com
Est. 1966 *Stock size* Large
Stock British clocks
Open By appointment
Services Restoration, valuation, author of several books on British clocks

Needfull Things Ltd
Contact Rebecca Hinchliffe
off High Street, Pateley Bridge, North Yorkshire, HG3 5AW
☎ 01423 712851 F 01423 712851
rhinch4426@aol.com
Est. 1999 *Stock size* Medium
Stock Jewellery, glassware, ceramics
Open Fri–Sun 10am–4pm or by appointment

PICKERING

Country Collector
Contact Grahame Berney
11–12 Birdgate, Pickering, North Yorkshire, YO18 7AL
☎ 01751 477481
gaggie@btinternet.com
Est. 1992 *Stock size* Small
Stock Ceramics, blue-and-white china, glass, silver, metalware, collectables, antiquities
Open Mon–Sat 10am–5pm closed Wed
Services Valuations

Inch's Books (PBFA, ABA)
Contact Mr P Inch
6 Westgate, Pickering, North Yorkshire, YO18 8BA
☎ 01751 474928 F 01751 475939
inchs.books@dial.pipex.com
www.inchsbooks.co.uk
Est. 1982 *Stock size* Medium
Stock Antiquarian and second-hand books
Open By appointment
Fairs ABA Chelsea, PBFA June fair
Services Mail order, catalogues (8 per year)

Pickering Antique Centre
Contact Mrs C Vance
Southgate, Pickering, North Yorkshire, YO18 8BN
☎ 01751 477210 F 01751 477210
sales@pickantiques.freeserve.co.uk
Est. 1998 *Stock size* Large
No. of dealers 32
Stock General antiques, books, postcards, pictures
Open Mon–Sun 10am–5pm
Services Valuations, metal restoration service

C H & D M Reynolds
Contact Mr Colin Reynolds
The Curiosity Shop, 122 Eastgate, Pickering, North Yorkshire, YO18 7DW
☎ 01751 472785 M 07714 355676
Est. 1949 *Stock size* Large
Stock General antiques, furniture, curios
Open Mon–Sat 9.30am–5.30pm Sun by appointment
Services Valuations

Stable Antiques
Contact Mrs Yvonne Kitching-Walker
Pickering Antique Centre, Southgate, Pickering, North Yorkshire, YO18 8BN
☎ 01751 477210
Est. 1998 *Stock size* Medium
Stock General antiques
Open Mon–Sun 10am–5pm

RICHMOND

Recollections
Contact Mrs J M Farquhar
35 Market Road, Richmond, North Yorkshire, DL10 4QG
☎ 01748 823568
Est. 1998 *Stock size* Medium
Stock General antiques
Open Mon–Sat 9.30am–4.30pm Sun noon–4pm
Fairs Newark
Services Valuations

Vokes Books Ltd (PBFA)
43 Bargate, Richmond, North Yorkshire, DL10 4QY
☎ 01748 824946 F 01748 824946
M 07790 793823
vokes-vokesbooksltd@tinyworld.co.uk

Stock size Medium
Stock Antiquarian, rare and second-hand books, military, north of England topography, travel, gardening, horticulture, natural history
Open By appointment
Services Valuations, booksearch

York House (Antiques)
Contact Mrs Christine Swift
60 Market Place, Richmond, North Yorkshire, DL10 4JQ
01748 850338 01748 850338
07711 307045
Est. 1997 *Stock size* Medium
Stock Pine, general antiques
Open Mon–Sat 9.30am–5.30pm Sun noon–4pm
Fairs Newark, Swinderby
Services Restorations, pine stripping

RIPON

Crown Auctions
Contact Mr C. Hanby
The Old Sale Room, St Wilfrid's Road, Ripon, North Yorkshire, HG4 2AR
01765 600111 07779 224474
Est. 1994
Open Mon–Fri 9–10.30am Sat 10–11.30am

Hornsey's of Ripon
Contact Bruce, Susan or Daniel Hornsey
3 Kirkgate, Ripon, North Yorkshire, HG4 1PA
01765 602878 01765 601692
daniel@rarebooks.freeserve.co.uk
Est. 1974 *Stock size* Large
Stock Antiques, collectables, rare books, fine linen, lace
Open Mon–Sat 9am–5.30pm or by appointment
Services Valuations

Hug & Plum
Contact Mr B M Plummer or Miss S A Hugill
5 Kirkgate, Ripon, North Yorkshire, HG4 1PA
01765 690428
bpbazz1@aol.com
Est. 1996 *Stock size* Medium
Stock General antiques, collectables
Open Mon–Sat 10am–4.30pm
Fairs Swinderby, Harrogate
Services House clearance, valuations, restorations

Sigma Antiques
Contact Mr David Thomson
The Old Opera House, Water Skellgate, Ripon, North Yorkshire, HG4 1BH
01765 603163 01765 603163
Est. 1964 *Stock size* Large
Stock General antiques
Open Mon–Sat 9am–5.30pm

Skellgate Curios
Contact Mrs J Wayne
2 Low Skellgate, Ripon, North Yorkshire, HG4 1BE
01765 601290
Est. 1975 *Stock size* Medium
Stock General antiques
Open Mon–Sat 11am–5pm closed Wed

ROBIN HOOD'S BAY

John Gilbert Antiques
Contact John Gilbert
King Street, Robin Hood's Bay, Whitby, North Yorkshire, YO22 4SY
01947 880528
Est. 1990 *Stock size* Medium
Stock 18th–19thC oak, country furniture
Open Sat 10am–1pm Sun 10am–5pm or by appointment
Services Valuations, restorations

SALTBURN-BY-THE-SEA

Anderson Antiques
Contact Mrs K Anderson
20 Milton Street, Saltburn-by-the-Sea, Cleveland, North Yorkshire, TS12 1DG
01287 624810 01287 625349
07798 587622
andersak@fsbdial.co.uk
Est. 1996 *Stock size* Medium
Stock Furniture, pictures, porcelain, jewellery, clocks, linen
Open Mon–Sat 10am–5pm closed Wed
Fairs Newark, Swinderby, Harrogate, Edinburgh
Services Valuations

J C Simmons & Son
Contact Mr G Aked
Saltburn Salerooms, Diamond Street, Saltburn-by-the Sea, North Yorkshire, TS12 1EB
01287 622366
Est. 1949
Open Viewing Mon–Sat 10am–4pm
Sales General antiques
Frequency Periodic
Catalogues Yes

Jösef Thompson
Contact Jösef Thompson
Saltburn Bookshop, 3 Amber Street, Saltburn-by-the-Sea, Cleveland, North Yorkshire, TS12 1DT
01287 623335
josefthompson@freeuk.com
Est. 1977 *Stock size* Large
Stock Second-hand books
Open March–Oct Mon–Sat 11am–1pm 2–5pm Nov–Feb Mon–Sat 11am–1pm 2–4pm
Services Book search

SCARBOROUGH

Antique and Collector's Centre (PTA)
Contact Colin Spink
35 St Nicholas Cliff, Scarborough, North Yorkshire, YO11 2ES
01723 365221 07730 202405
spink@collectors.demon.co.uk
www.collectors.demon.co.uk
Est. 1965 *Stock size* Medium
Stock General antique jewellery, ephemera, cigarette cards, coins, postcards, antiques, commemorative ware, etc
Open Mon–Sat 10am–4.30pm
Services Valuations

Bar Bookstore (The Antiquary Ltd) (PBFA)
Contact Mr M Chaddock
4 Swan Hill Road, Scarborough, North Yorkshire, YO11 1BW
01723 500141
antiquary@btinternet.com
Est. 1976 *Stock size* Medium
Stock Antiquarian, rare and second-hand books
Open Tues–Sat 10.30am–5pm
Fairs York, Harrogate, Darlington
Services Valuations, book search

Bar Street Antiques
Contact Mr D Lowe
40 Bar Street, Scarborough, North Yorkshire, YO11 2HT
01723 376447

Est. 1998 *Stock size* Medium
Stock General antiques
Open Mon–Sat 10am–5pm

David Duggleby Fine Art
Contact Jane Duggleby
The Vine Street Salerooms, Scarborough, North Yorkshire, YO11 1XN
01723 507111 Ⓕ 01723 507222
Ⓔ auctions@davidduggleby.com
Ⓦ www.davidduggleby.com
Est. 1996
Open Mon–Fri 8.30am–5pm
Sales Fortnightly 500-lot house contents and Victoriana sales, 700 lots of fine art and antiques every 8 weeks
Catalogues Yes

Allen Reed
Contact Mr A Reed
109 Fallsgrave Road, Scarborough, North Yorkshire, YO12 5EG
01723 360251
Est. 1999 *Stock size* Large
Stock General antiques
Open Mon–Sat 11am–4pm

Allen Reed
Contact Mr A Reed
188–190 Victoria Road, Scarborough, North Yorkshire, YO12 5EG
01723 360251
Est. 1969 *Stock size* Large
Stock General antiques
Open Mon–Sat 11am–4pm

Charles Smith & Son
54 Ramshill Road, Scarborough, North Yorkshire, YO11 2QG
01723 500378
Ⓔ charlessmith@btinternet.com
Est. 1984 *Stock size* Large
Stock General antiques, 19thC watercolours
Open Mon–Sat 9am–5pm
Services Valuations, restorations

Ward Price Ltd (ASVA)
Contact Mr I Smith
Royal Auction Rooms, 14–15 Queen Street, Scarborough, North Yorkshire, YO11 1HA
01723 353581 Ⓕ 01723 369926
Ⓦ www.wardprice.co.uk
Est. 1901
Open Mon–Fri 9am–5pm
Sat 10am–2pm
Sales General antiques
Frequency Alternate months
Catalogues Yes

SESSAY

Potterton Books
Contact Mrs Clare Jameson
The Old Rectory, Sessay, Nr Thirsk, North Yorkshire, YO7 3LZ
01845 501218 Ⓕ 01845 501439
Ⓔ enquiries@pottertonbooks.sagehost.co.uk
Ⓦ www.pottertonbooks.co.uk
Est. 1982
Stock Fine and decorative arts books
Open Mon–Fri 9am–5pm
Fairs Fine Art Olympia, Decorex International
Services Book search

SETTLE

Nanette Midgley
Contact Mr or Mrs J Midgley
Roundabout, 41 Duke Street, Settle, North Yorkshire, BD24 9DJ
01729 823324
Ⓔ midglui@aol.com
Est. 1953 *Stock size* Small
Stock 18th–19thC pottery, porcelain
Open Tues Fri Sat 11am–12.30pm 2–5.30pm
Services Valuations

Mary Milnthorpe & Daughters
Contact Miss Judith Milnthorpe
Market Place, Settle, North Yorkshire, BD24 9DX
01729 822331 Ⓕ 01729 823062
Est. 1959 *Stock size* Medium
Stock Antique jewellery, silver
Open Mon–Sat 9.30am–5pm closed Wed
Services Valuations, repairs

Nanbooks
Contact Mr or Mrs J L Midgley
Roundabout, 41 Duke Street, Settle, North Yorkshire, BD24 9DJ
01729 823324
Ⓔ midglui@aol.com
Est. 1955 *Stock size* Medium
Stock English and Continental ceramics, some 18th–19thC glass
Open Tues Fri Sat 11am–5pm closed 12.30–2pm or by appointment

Anderson Slater
Contact K C Slater
Duke Street, Settle, North Yorkshire, BD24 9DW
01729 822051
Est. 1959 *Stock size* Large
Stock 18th–19thC oak, mahogany furniture
Open Mon–Sat 10am–5pm
Services Valuations, restorations, interior designs

Thistlethwaite Antiques
Contact Mr E C Thistlethwaite
Market Square, Settle, North Yorkshire, BD24 9EF
01729 822460
Est. 1978 *Stock size* Medium
Stock 18th–19thC country furniture, metalware
Open Mon–Sat 9am–5pm closed Wed

SHERBURN-IN-ELMET

The Glass-House
Contact Sara Qualter
Low Street Farm, Sherburn-in-Elmet, North Yorkshire, LS25 6BB
01977 689119 Ⓕ 01977 682673
Ⓜ 07890 134063
Ⓔ theglasshouse@ic24.net
Est. 2001 *Stock size* Medium
Stock Antiques and collectables, oak and country furniture, pine, 20thC design
Open Tues–Sun 9am–5pm
Fairs Swinderby, Newark
Services Shipping

SKIPTON

Cherub Antiques
Contact G or V Hutchinson
2 Albert Street, Skipton, North Yorkshire, BD23 1JD
01756 700899
Ⓜ 07899 996571
Ⓔ mail@cherubantiques.co.uk
Ⓦ www.cherubantiques.co.uk
Est. 1997 *Stock size* Medium
Stock General antiques, collectables, textiles, small furniture
Open Mon–Sat 10.30am–4.30pm closed Tues
Services China restorations

Corn Mill Antiques
Contact Mr or Mrs Hawkridge
High Corn Mill, Chapel Hill, Skipton, North Yorkshire, BD23 1NL
01756 792440
Est. 1983 *Stock size* Medium
Stock Georgian–Edwardian furniture, porcelain, pictures etc
Open Mon Thurs Fri Sat 10am–4pm

Skipton Antiques & Collectors Centre
Contact Ann Hall
The Old Foundry, Cavendish Street, Skipton, North Yorkshire, BD23 2AB
01756 797667
Est. 1995 *Stock size* Large
No. of dealers 30
Stock General antiques and collectables, Art Deco, clocks, books, ceramics, pine, etc
Open Mon–Sat 10.30am–4pm Sun 11am–4pm

SLINGSBY

Tony Popek Antiques
Contact Mr E Popek
West View, Railway St, Slingsby, York, North Yorkshire, YO62 24A
01653 628533
Est. 1989 *Stock size* Medium
Stock General antiques
Open Tues Fri Sat 10am–5pm or by appointment
Fairs Harrogate

SPOFFORTH

Nicholas Merchant
Contact Mr N Merchant
11 High Street, Spofforth, Harrogate, North Yorkshire, HG3 1BQ
01937 591022 F 01937 591033
E merchantn@btconnect.com
Est. 1989 *Stock size* Small
Stock Antique and collectors' books, decorative, fine arts, reference books a speciality
Open By appointment
Services Valuations, mail order, out-of-print search

STOCKTON-ON-TEES

Paraphernalia
Contact Mrs R Thomas
12 Harland Place, High Street, Norton, Stockton-on-Tees, North Yorkshire, TS20 1AL
01642 535940 F 01642 535940
Est. 1984 *Stock size* Large
Stock General antiques
Open Mon–Sat 9.30am–5pm
Services Restorations, repairs, Victorian tea rooms

STOKESLEY

Fiddlesticks
Contact Mr Bennett
1 Bridge Road, Stokesley, Middlesbrough, North Yorkshire, TS9 5AA
01642 713247 M 07947 108174
Est. 1991 *Stock size* Medium
Stock Victorian–Edwardian furniture, pine, smalls
Open Mon–Sat 10.30am–5pm
Services Restoration

Lithgow & Partners
Contact Richard Storry
The Auction Houses, Station Road, Stokesley, North Yorkshire, TS9 7AB
01642 710158 F 01642 712641
E info@lithgowsauctions.com
W www.lithgowsauctions.com
Est. 1868
Open Mon–Fri 9am–5pm
Sales Weekly sale Wed 10.30am viewing Tues noon–4pm
Frequency Weekly
Catalogues Yes

Mantle Antiques
Contact Mr Derek Bushby
23 College Square, Stokesley, North Yorkshire, TS9 5DN
01642 714313 M 07713 155772
Est. 1973 *Stock size* Medium
Stock Victorian furniture, architectural antiques
Open Tues Thurs Fri Sat 10am–4pm

TADCASTER

Scarthingwell Antiques
Contact Mr B Brier
Scarthingwell Centre, Scarthingwell Farm, Tadcaster, North Yorkshire, LS24 9PG
01937 557877 F 01937 558084
Est. 1989 *Stock size* Large
Stock General antiques
Open Mon–Sun 10am–5pm closed Sat

Scarthingwell Auction Centre
Contact John Griffiths or Christine Bridge
Scarthingwell, Tadcaster, North Yorkshire, LS24 9PG
01937 557955 F 01937 557955
M 07778 520463
E scarthingwell@lineone.net
W www.scarthingwellauctions.co.uk
Est. 1990
Open Mon–Fri 10am–5pm
Sales Antiques and general sales Tues 5pm every 2–3 weeks, viewing Sun prior to sale noon–5pm Tues 2pm or by appointment
Frequency Every 2–3 weeks
Catalogues Yes

THIRSK

The Book & Stamp Shop
Contact Mr R O'Brien
7 Westgate, Thirsk, North Yorkshire, YO7 1QR
01845 524615
Est. 1995 *Stock size* Medium
Stock Antiquarian, rare and second-hand books, prints, British and Commonwealth stamps
Open Mon–Sat 10.30am–4.30pm closed Wed
Services Valuations, bookbinding

Hambleton Books
Contact Mr T F Parr
43 Market Place, Thirsk, North Yorkshire, YO7 1HA
01845 522343
E hambooks@btinternet.com
Est. 1979 *Stock size* Medium
Stock Antique, rare and second-hand books, books on cricket a speciality
Open Mon–Sat 9am–5.30pm Sun 10am–4pm

Millgate Antiques
Contact Tim Parvin
Abel Grange, Newsham Road, Thirsk, North Yorkshire, YO7 4DB
01845 523878 F 01845 523878
M 07966 251609
E babs.jenkins@btinternet.com
Est. 1991 *Stock size* Large
Stock Pine furniture, panelled doors
Open Mon–Sat 8.30am–5pm
Fairs Newark, Swinderbury
Services Stripping, restoration

Millgate Pine & Antiques
Contact Tim Parvin
12 Millgate, Thirsk, North Yorkshire, YO7 1AA
01845 523878 01845 523878
07966 251609
babs.jenkins@btinternet.com
Est. 1991 *Stock size* Large
Stock Pine furniture, panelled doors
Open Mon–Sat 8.30am–5pm
Fairs Newark, Swinderbury
Services Stripping

THORNTON-LE-DALE

Cobweb Books
Contact Mr Robin Buckler
Ye Olde Corner Shoppe, 1 Pickering Road, Thornton-le-Dale, North Yorkshire, YO19 7LG
01751 476638
sales@cobwebbooks.co.uk
www.cobwebbooks.co.uk
Est. 1991 *Stock size* Medium
Stock Antiquarian, rare and second-hand books
Open Tues–Sun 10am–5pm
Fairs Royal National Hotel Book Fair, London
Services Book search

TOCKWITH

Tomlinson Antiques (LAPADA, CINOA)
Contact Mike Grant
Moorside, Tockwith, North Yorkshire, YO26 7QG
01423 358833 01423 358188
info@tomlinsonfurniture.com
antique-furniture.co.uk
Est. 1977 *Stock size* Large
Stock Quality Georgian–pre-war furniture, china, silver, silver plate, longcase clocks, rugs
Open Mon–Sat 9am–4.30pm Sun 10am–4pm
Services Restorations, shipping

UPPER POPPLETON

D Wombell & Son
Contact Mr W Rice
Northminster Business Park, Upper Poppleton, York, North Yorkshire, YO41 4AR
01904 790777 01904 798018
www.invaluable.com/wombell
Est. 1984
Open Mon–Fri 10am–5pm
Sales General antiques monthly
Frequency Monthly
Catalogues Yes

WHITBY

Abbey Antiques
Contact Mr A L Barsby
4 & 5 Grape Lane, Whitby, North Yorkshire, YO22 4DD
01947 821424
Est. 1996 *Stock size* Large
Stock General antiques, collectables
Open Flexible, please telephone

Clewlow Antiques (PBFA)
Contact Mr A Clewlow
Sandringham House, 6–8 Skinner Street, Whitby, North Yorkshire, YO21 3AJ
01947 821655
fiona.clewlow@virgin.net
www.members.ebay.com/abcutme/gonzostuff
Est. 1977 *Stock size* Large
Stock General antiques
Open Summer Mon–Sat 10am–5pm winter Sat only

Curio Corner
Contact Mr A L Barsby
7 Market Plate, Whitby, North Yorkshire, YO22 4DD
01947 821424
Est. 1969 *Stock size* Small
Stock General antiques, collectables
Open Mon–Sun 10am–5pm or by appointment

Endeavour Books
Contact Mrs L Allison
1 Grape Lane, Whitby, North Yorkshire, YO22 4BA
01947 821331
linda@enbooks.co.uk
www.enbooks.co.uk
Est. 1989 *Stock size* Medium
Stock Rare and second-hand books
Open Mon–Sun summer 10am–8pm winter 10.30am–5pm

Eskdale Antiques
Contact Mr P Smith
85 Church Street, Whitby, North Yorkshire, YO22 4BH
01947 600512 07813 589117
Est. 1982 *Stock size* Medium
Stock Antique china, collectables
Open Daily 10.30am–5pm

Eskdale Antiques
Contact Mr P Smith
164 Coach Road, Whitby, North Yorkshire, YO22 5EQ
01947 810297 07813 589117
Est. 1979 *Stock size* Medium
Stock Antique stripped pine, garden ornaments
Open Daily 9.30am–5pm

Picfair Antiques
Contact Mr J Robertson
67 Haggersgate, Whitby, North Yorkshire, YO21 3PP
01947 602483
picfair@amserve.net
www.picfair.com
Est. 1987 *Stock size* Medium
Stock General antiques including glass, costume jewellery, porcelain
Open Mon–Sun noon–6pm
Services Valuations, advice to collectors

Quarter Deck Antiques
Contact Mr M B Taylor
8 Silver Street, Whitby, North Yorkshire, YO21 3BU
01947 820220
Est. 1982 *Stock size* Large
Stock General antiques, furniture, bric-a-brac, antiquities
Open Mon–Sun 8.30am–4.30pm

Venus Trading
Contact Mr Tim Ruff
4 Sandgate, Whitby, North Yorkshire, YO22 4DB
01947 601221
Est. 1976 *Stock size* Large
Stock Victorian, Edwardian and pre-war furniture, fireplaces
Open Mon–Sun 9am–6pm

WHIXLEY

Garth Antiques (LAPADA)
Contact Mr or Mrs J Chapman
The Old School, Franks Lane, Whixley, North Yorkshire, YO26 8AP
01423 331055 01423 331733
Est. 1978 *Stock size* Medium
Stock General antiques
Open Tues–Sat 10am–5pm
Services Restorations

YARM

Arts & Memorabilia
Contact J E or M H Parker
111 High Street, Yarm, Cleveland, North Yorkshire, TS15 9BB
01642 787178
Est. 1987 *Stock size* Medium
Stock General antiques
Open Mon–Sat 10am–5.30pm

Farthing
Contact Shirley Smith or Sybil Watson
63 High Street, Yarm, Cleveland, North Yorkshire, TS15 9BH
01642 785881
Est. 1977 *Stock size* Medium
Stock General antiques, prints, gifts
Open Mon–Sat 9.30am–5.30pm
Services Picture framing

Ruby Snowden Antiques
Contact Ruby Snowden
Glenisle House, 10 High Street, Yarm, Cleveland, North Yorkshire, TS15 9AE
01642 801188/830246
Est. 1976 *Stock size* Medium
Stock Georgian–Edwardian furniture, porcelain, smalls, copper, brass, local prints, pictures
Open Mon–Sat 9.30am–5pm

YORK

Advena Antiques & Fairs
Contact Alan White
Stonegate Antique Centre, 41 Stonegate, York, North Yorkshire, YO1 8AW
01904 668785 07713 150510
advenantiques@ntlworld.com
Est. 1992 *Stock size* Medium
Stock Antique silver, jewellery
Open Mon–Sat 9am–6pm Sun 10am–4pm
Services Valuations, repairs

Ancient World (ADA)
Contact John Moor
16 High Petergate, York, North Yorkshire, YO1 7EH
01904 624062
Est. 1975 *Stock size* Medium
Stock Ancient coins, antiquities
Open Mon–Sun 10am–5pm
Fairs ADA
Services Valuations for probate etc

Margaret Bedi Antiques and Fine Art (LAPADA)
Contact Mrs Margaret Bedi
The Red House Antique Centre, Duncombe Place, York, North Yorkshire, YO1 2EF
01642 782346 07860 577637
Est. 1976 *Stock size* Large
Stock Fine furniture 1660–1920, watercolours, oils
Open By appointment only
Fairs Northern Antiques Fair, Harrogate
Services Valuations, restorations

Bishopgate Antiques
Contact Mr R Weatherill
23/24 Bishopgate, York, North Yorkshire, YO23 1JH
01904 623893 01904 626511
Est. 1965 *Stock size* Medium
Stock General antiques
Open Mon–Sat 9.15am–6pm Sun noon–5pm

Barbara Cattle (BADA)
Contact Mr Richard Pool
45 Stonegate, York, North Yorkshire, YO1 8AW
01904 623862
info@hl-brown.co.uk
Stock Jewellery, silver, old Sheffield plate
Open Mon–Sat 9am–5.30pm
Services Valuations, repairs, restorations

Cavendish Antiques & Collectors Centre
Contact A Gilberthorpe
44 Stonegate, York, North Yorkshire, YO1 8AS
01904 621666 01904 644400
www.yorkantiquescentre.co.uk
Est. 1999 *Stock size* Large
No. of dealers 60
Stock General antiques
Open Mon–Sun 9am–6pm

Cook's Cottage Antiques
Contact E Cook
The Red House Antique Centre, Duncombe Place, York, North Yorkshire, YO1 2EF
01904 637000 or 01642 701664
cooks4antiques@aol.com
Est. 1996 *Stock size* Medium
Stock Quality furniture, Victorian paintings, silver, ceramics
Open Mon–Wed 9.30am–5.30pm Thurs–Sat 9.30am–8pm Sun in summer 10am–5pm
Services Restorations

Jack Duncan
Contact Mr Jack Duncan
36 Fossgate, York, North Yorkshire, YO1 9TF
01904 641389 01904 672184
Est. 1984 *Stock size* Medium
Stock Antique, scholarly and second-hand books, English literature a speciality
Open Mon–Sat 10am–5.30pm

Mike Fineron Cigarette Cards & Postcards
Contact Mike Fineron
28 The Pastures, Dringhouses, York, North Yorkshire, YO24 2JE
01904 703911
Est. 1997 *Stock size* Medium
Stock Cigarette cards, postcards, Yorkshire postcards a speciality
Open By appointment
Fairs Pudsey, Chester Le Street, Sheffield
Services Valuations, postal service

French House Antiques
Contact Steve
74 Micklegate, York, North Yorkshire, YO1 6LF
01904 624465 01904 629965
info@thefrenchhouse.co.uk
www.thefrenchhouse.co.uk
Est. 1995 *Stock size* Large
Stock Antique French furniture
Open Mon–Sat 9.30am–5.30pm
Services Restorations

Harpers Jewellers Ltd
Contact Nicholas Wiseman
2/6 Minster Gates, York, Yorkshire, YO1 7HL
01904 632634 01904 673370
harpersyork@btopenworld.com
www.vintage-watches.co.uk
Est. 1990 *Stock size* Large
Stock Jewellery
Open Mon–Sat 9am–5.30pm
Services Valuations

Hudsons of York
Contact Mr I Hudson
8 The Stonebow, York, North Yorkshire, YO1 7NY
01904 643131 01904 643132

Ⓜ 07050 136828
Ⓔ enq@hudsonsofyork.com
Ⓦ www.hudsonsofyork.com
Est. 1997 *Stock size* Large
Stock General antiques, European and oak furniture
Open Mon–Sat 9.30am–5pm Sun 11am–4pm
Fairs Newark, Swinderby

Hunts Pine (GADAR)
Contact Mr W Dougherty
✉ **Unit 6a, Victoria Farm, Water Lane, York, North Yorkshire, YO30 6PQ** P
☎ 01904 690561 Ⓕ 01904 690561
Est. 1995 *Stock size* Medium
Stock Antique pine furniture
Open Mon–Fri 9am–5.30pm Sat 9am–2pm
Fairs Newark
Services Stripping

Laurel Bank Antiques
Contact Mr K Lamb
✉ **52 Clarence Street, York, North Yorkshire, YO31 7EW** P
☎ 01904 676030 Ⓕ 01904 438700
Ⓔ sales@laurelbankantiques.co.uk
Ⓦ www.laurelbankantiques.co.uk
Est. 1997 *Stock size* Medium
Stock General antiques, collectables, Georgian–Edwardian furniture, longcase, wall and mantel clocks
Open Mon–Sat 10am–5pm closed Tues Sun
Services Restorations, French polishing

Minstergate Bookshop (PBFA)
Contact Mr N Wallace
✉ **8 Minster Gates, York, North Yorkshire, YO1 7HL**
☎ 01904 621812 Ⓕ 01904 622960
Ⓔ rarebooks@minstergatebooks.co.uk
Ⓦ www.minstergatebooks.co.uk
Est. 1977 *Stock size* Medium
Stock Books, children's and illustrated a speciality
Open Mon–Sun 10am–5.30pm
Services Valuations, book search

The Mulberry Bush Antique Shop
Contact Mr P A Young
✉ **36 Goodramgate, York, North Yorkshire, YO1 7LF**
☎ 01904 638842 Ⓕ 01904 468665
Ⓔ mulberryan@aol.com
Ⓦ www.yorkantiques.co.uk
Est. 1994 *Stock size* Medium
Stock General antiques, watercolours, oils, clocks
Open Mon–Sat 9.30am–5pm
Services Clock and furniture restorations, valuations

Janette Ray Rare Books (PBFA, ABA)
Contact Miss J Ray
✉ **8 Bootham, York, North Yorkshire, YO30 7BL** P
☎ 01904 623088 Ⓕ 01904 625528
Ⓔ books@janetteray.co.uk
Ⓦ www.janetteray.co.uk
Est. 1995 *Stock size* Medium
Stock Architectural and decorative arts, rare and second-hand books, landscape design, gardens, specializing in 19thC Arts & Crafts, Art Deco, Modernism
Open Fri–Sat 10am–5.30pm other times by appointment
Fairs York PBFA, London PBFA
Services Book search, valuations

The Red House Antique Centre
Contact Mrs P Stephenson
✉ **Duncombe Place, York, North Yorkshire, YO1 2EF** P
☎ 01904 637000 Ⓕ 01904 637000
Ⓦ www.redhouseyork.co.uk
Est. 1999
No. of dealers 60
Stock Datelined stock
Open Mon–Wed 9.30am–5.30pm Thurs–Sat 9.30am–8pm Sun 10.30am–5.30pm
Services Antiques and arts lecture programmes, café and restaurant, antiques parties, courier service

John Simpson (ASVA)
Contact Mr John Simpson
✉ **4 Forest Grove, York, North Yorkshire, YO3 0BL** P
☎ 01904 424797
Est. 1984
Open By appointment
Sales General antiques
Frequency Quarterly
Catalogues Yes

J Smith (BNTA)
Contact Mr J Smith
✉ **47 Shambles, York, North Yorkshire, YO1 7LX**
☎ 01904 654769 Ⓕ 01904 677988
Est. 1963 *Stock size* Large
Stock Coins, stamps, medals
Open Mon–Sat 9am–4.30pm
Services Valuations

Ken Spelman (ABA, PBPA, ILAB)
Contact P Miller or A Fothergill
✉ **70 Micklegate, York, North Yorkshire, YO1 6LF** P
☎ 01904 624414 Ⓕ 01904 626276
Ⓔ rarebooks@kenspelman.com
Ⓦ www.kenspelman.com
Stock size Large
Stock Antique, rare, second-hand books
Open Mon–Sat 9am–5.30pm
Fairs Olympia
Services Valuations, restorations, catalogues

Stonegate Antiques Centre
Contact Mr Gilberthorpe
✉ **41 Stonegate, York, North Yorkshire, YO1 8AW**
☎ 01904 613888 Ⓕ 01904 644400
Ⓦ www.yorkantiquescentre.co.uk
Est. 1996 *Stock size* Large
No. of dealers 120
Stock General antiques
Open Mon–Sun 9am–6pm
Services Café

Taikoo Books Ltd
Contact Mr David Chilton
✉ **46 Bootham, York, North Yorkshire, YO30 7BZ** P
☎ 01904 641213
Est. 1978 *Stock size* Medium
Stock Books on Africa and the Orient
Open Mon–Fri 10am–5pm or by appointment

York Antiques Centre
Contact Mr S Revere
✉ **2a Lendal, York, North Yorkshire, YO1 8AA**
☎ 01904 641445
Est. 1984 *Stock size* Large
No. of dealers 15
Stock General antiques
Open Mon–Sat 10am–5pm

York Vale Antiques (GADAR)
Contact Mr W Dougherty
✉ **Unit 6a, Victoria Farm, Water Lane, York, North Yorkshire, YO30 6PQ** P
☎ 01904 690561 Ⓕ 01904 690561
Est. 1995 *Stock size* Medium
Stock General antique furniture

Open Mon–Fri 9am–5.30pm
Sat 9am–2pm
Fairs Newark
Services Restorations, repairs

SOUTH YORKSHIRE

BARLOW

Byethorpe Antiques
Contact John Gelsthorpe
Shippen Rural Business Centre, Church Farm, Barlow, South Yorkshire, S18 7TR P
☎ 0114 289 9111
www.byethorpe.com
Est. 1977 *Stock size* Medium
Stock Traditional oak and mahogany furniture
Open Mon–Sat 9am–5.30pm

BARNSLEY

BBR Auctions
Contact Mr Alan Blakeman
Elsecar Heritage Centre, Barnsley, South Yorkshire, S74 8HJ P
☎ 01226 745156 F 01226 361561
E sales@bbrauctions.co.uk
W www.bbrauctions.co.uk
Est. 1979
Open Mon–Fri 9am–4pm
Sales Antique bottles and pot lids, 3 per annum. Antique advertising every 6 months. Doulton, Beswick and 20thC pottery, 2 per annum. Kitchenware, 2 per annum. Breweriana and pub jugs, 2 per annum. All sales Sun 11am, viewing full week prior 9am–5pm
Catalogues Yes

BENTLEY

Phoenix Trading Company – South Yorkshire
Contact John A Hallam
127–129 Askern Road, Bentley, Doncaster, South Yorkshire, DN5 0JH P
☎ 01302 872547 F 01302 875735
M 07801 631072
E JHallamPTC@aol.com
Est. 1995 *Stock size* Large
Stock Georgian–Victorian furniture, shipping items, brass, copper, ceramics, silver, curios
Open Mon–Sat 9am–5pm
Fairs Newark, Harrogate
Services Restorations, repairs, valuations

BIRDWELL

Birdwell Lodge Craft & Antiques Centre
Contact Mrs C Vaines
Pilley Lane, Birdwell, Barnsley, South Yorkshire, S70 5UD P
☎ 01226 743489 M 07714 353481
Est. 1998 *Stock size* Large
Stock Dolls' houses, dolls' furniture, antique jewellery, pottery, furniture, paintings, stained glass, crafts
Open Mon 1pm–4pm
Tues–Sun 11am–4pm closed Fri
Services Painting classes, sugar craft, coffee shop

CAWTHORNE

Cawthorne Antiques Centre
Contact Mr P Gates
2 Church Street, Cawthorne Village, Barnsley, South Yorkshire, S75 4HP P
☎ 01226 792237
Est. 1997 *Stock size* Large
No. of dealers 50
Stock Wide range of antique stock, collectables
Open Mon–Sat 10am–4pm
Sun 10.30am–4.30pm closed Wed
Services Tea room

DONCASTER

Harrison Sales
Contact Mr F Harrison
3 Carr Hill, Balby, Doncaster, South Yorkshire, DN4 8BS P
☎ 01302 769400 F 01302 812958
Est. 1995
Open Mon–Sat 9am–6pm
Sales Antiques sale last Sat of the month 11am, vewing day prior noon–7pm Sat 9–11am. Weekly general sale Sat noon, viewing Fri 4–7pm Sat 9am–noon
Frequency Monthly
Catalogues Yes

ECCLESFIELD

Any Old Iron
Contact Miss Leigh Bell
10 Town End Road, Ecclesfield, Sheffield, South Yorkshire, S35 9YY P
☎ 0114 257 7117 M 07971 522448
Est. 1996 *Stock size* Large
Stock Victorian cast-iron fireplaces
Open Thurs–Sun 10am–5pm
Fairs Swinderby, Newark
Services Restorations

Courthouse Antiques Centre
Contact Mrs S M Grayson
2–6 Town End Road, Ecclesfield, Sheffield, South Yorkshire, S35 9YY P
☎ 0114 257 0641
Est. 1994 *Stock size* Large
No. of dealers 35
Stock Town and country furniture, jewellery, kitchenware, clocks, textiles, decorative items, French furniture, mirrors, lighting
Open Mon–Sat 10.30am–5pm
Sun 11.30am–5pm

GREAT HOUGHTON

Farmhouse Antiques
Contact Mrs A Calvert
7 High Street, Great Houghton, Barnsley, South Yorkshire, S72 0AA P
☎ 01226 754057
Est. 1992 *Stock size* Small
Stock 19th–20thC decorative furniture, associated objects, Art Deco, Susie Cooper
Open Mon Sat 10am–noon 1–5pm or by appointment
Fairs NEC
Services Free advice on values and laying out of rooms

KILLAMARSH

Havenplan Ltd
Contact Mrs M Buckle
The Old Station, Station Road, Killamarsh, Sheffield, South Yorkshire, S21 1EN P
☎ 0114 248 9972 F 0114 248 9972
M 07720 635889
Est. 1972 *Stock size* Large
Stock Mainly Victorian pine furniture, architectural items, panelling, doors, fireplaces, troughs, gates, lighting
Open Tues–Sat 10am–3pm
Services Prop hire

PARKGATE

John Shaw Antiques Ltd
Contact Ms D Ellis
The Old Methodist Chapel, Broad Street, Parkgate, Rotherham, South Yorkshire, S62 6DL
01709 522340 F 01709 528593
Est. 1969 *Stock size* Large
Stock Wide range of Victorian–Edwardian furniture, clocks, pictures, mirrors etc
Open Mon–Fri 9am–5pm Sat 9.30am–5pm
Services Valuations Sat 10am–noon

PENISTONE

Penistone Pine & Antiques
Contact Mr P W Lucas
Unit 2–3, Sheffield Road, Penistone, Sheffield, South Yorkshire, S36 6HG
01226 370018
Est. 1985 *Stock size* Large
Stock Antique, original Victorian pine furniture
Open Mon–Sat 9am–5pm
Services Restorations, stripping

ROTHERHAM

Roger Appleyard Ltd (LAPADA)
Contact Roger Appleyard
Fitzwilliam Road, Eastwood Trading Estate, Rotherham, South Yorkshire, S65 1SL
01709 367670 F 01709 829395
E apple.antiques@dial.pipex.com
Est. 1971 *Stock size* Large
Stock Turn-of-the-century and shipping furniture
Trade only Yes
Open Mon–Fri 8am–5pm
Services Shipping

SHEFFIELD

Abbeydale Antiques
Contact Mr D Barks
639 Abbeydale Road, Sheffield, South Yorkshire, S7 1TB
0114 255 5646 F 0114 255 2555
Est. 1974 *Stock size* Large
Stock 1950s furniture
Open By appointment

Acorn Antiques
Contact Mr B Priest
298 Abbeydale Road, Sheffield, South Yorkshire, S7 1FL
0114 255 5348 F 0114 225 5348
E info@acornantique.co.uk
Est. 1988 *Stock size* Large
Stock General antiques, small furniture, collectables
Open Mon–Sat 10am–6pm

Antics
Contact Bronwen Stone
224 Abbeydale Road, Sheffield, South Yorkshire, S7 1FL
0114 255 1664 F 0114 250 8480
M 07812 517331
E anticsantiques@hotmail.com
Est. 1997 *Stock size* Large
Stock Furniture, fireplaces, dressers, oil paintings, old French enamelled fires, soft furnishings, contemporary design
Open Mon–Sat 10am–5pm Sun by appointment
Fairs Newark
Services Advice on furniture renovation, reupholstery

Banners Collectors & Antiques Centre
Contact Miss S Bates
Banners Business Centre, Attercliffe Road, Sheffield, South Yorkshire, S9 3QS
0114 244 0742
Est. 1997 *Stock size* Large
No. of dealers 40
Stock Wide range of antiques, collectables, Wade, Beanies, McDonald's, clocks etc
Open Mon–Sat 10am–5pm Sun 11am–5pm
Services Lists of goods wanted, deliveries, all collectables bought

Barmouth Court Antique Centre (LAPADA)
Contact Annette or Norman Salt
Barmouth Court, Barmouth Road, Sheffield, South Yorkshire, S7 2DH
0114 255 2711 F 0114 258 2672
M 07801 101363
Est. 1999 *Stock size* Large
No. of dealers 60
Stock Complete range of antiques, Art Deco, collectables
Open Mon–Sat 10am–5pm Sun 11am–4pm
Services Valuations, restorations

Beech House
Contact Mr M Beech
361 Abbeydale Road, Sheffield, South Yorkshire, S7 1FS
0114 250 1004 F 0114 250 1004
E beech.house@lineone.net
Est. 1996 *Stock size* Medium
Stock Rustic country pine furniture, cupboards, tables, dressers, chairs, fine art
Open Mon–Sat 10am–5pm closed Thurs or by appointment
Fairs Newark, Swinderby

Calico by Carol Anne
Contact Mrs C Slack
35 Abbey Lane, Sheffield, South Yorkshire, S8 0BJ
0114 249 3131
W www.woodseats.com
Est. 1991 *Stock size* Large
Stock Antique and reproduction giftware, decorative items, Tiffany lamps
Open Mon–Sat 10am–4.30pm

Chapel Antiques Centre
Contact Mrs Kate Bonshall
99 Broadfield Road, Sheffield, South Yorkshire, S8 0XH
0114 258 8288 F 0114 258 8288
E info@antiquesinsheffield.com
W www.antiquesinsheffield.com
Est. 1997 *Stock size* Medium
No. of dealers 20
Stock English and French antique furniture, mirrors, chandeliers, gardenalia, discounted upholstery fabrics
Open Mon–Sat 10am–5pm Sun Bank Holidays 11am–5pm
Services Restorations, upholstery, French polishing, custom-made furniture from reclaimed wood, paint effecting, finding service

Cobwebs
Contact Mrs S Sleath
208 Whitham Road, Sheffield, South Yorkshire, S10 2SS
0114 268 1923 M 07836 765695
Est. 1979 *Stock size* Medium
Stock Wide range of French decorative items, small furniture etc
Open Mon Wed Fri Sat 10am–5pm
Fairs Sheffield City Fairs

A E Dowse & Son (NAVA)
Contact Michael Dowse ANAVA

✉ **Cornwall Galleries, Scotland Street, Sheffield, South Yorkshire, S3 7DE**
☎ 0114 272 5858 Ⓕ 0114 249 0550
Ⓦ www.aedowseandson.com
Est. 1915
Open Mon–Fri 9.30am–4pm
Sales Antiques and collectables monthly. Fine art and antiques quarterly Wed 11am. Die-cast, tinplate and collectors' toys quarterly Sat 11am, viewing for Wed sales Mon 4–7pm Tues 10am–7pm Wed 9–11am, viewing for Sat sales Fri 2.30–7.30pm Sat 9.30–11am
Frequency Monthly
Catalogues Yes

ELR Auctions Ltd
Contact Liz Dashper
✉ **The Nichols Building, Shalesmoor, Sheffield, South Yorkshire, S3 8UJ** Ⓟ
☎ 0114 281 6161 Ⓕ 0114 281 6162
Ⓔ liz.dashper@virgin.net
Ⓦ www.elrauctions.com
Est. 1840
Open Mon–Fri 9am–5pm
Sales Quarterly antiques Fri 10.30am, viewing Wed 2–7.30pm Thurs 9am–7.30pm Fri 8.30am–sale. Antiques and collectables Fri 11am, viewing Thurs 10am–6.30pm Fri 9–11am
Frequency Fortnightly
Catalogues Yes

Filibuster & Booth Ltd
Contact Mr A Booth
✉ **158 Devonshire Street, Sheffield, South Yorkshire, S3 7SG** Ⓟ
☎ 0114 275 2311
Stock Unusual, eclectic mixture of genuine things
Open Please telephone, times irregular
Services Valuations

Just Military Ltd
Contact Mr T Smith
✉ **701 Abbeydale Road, Sheffield, South Yorkshire, S7 2BE** Ⓟ
☎ 0114 255 0536
Est. 1994 *Stock size* Large
Stock Militaria, WWI–Falklands, 1940s clothing, memorabilia, uniforms etc
Open Mon–Fri 10am–4.30pm Sat 10am–5pm
Services Medal mounting, uniform hire

Nichols Antique Centre
Contact Mr T Vickers
✉ **Nichols Building, Shalesmoor, Sheffield, South Yorkshire, S3 8UJ** Ⓟ
☎ 0114 281 2811 Ⓕ 0114 281 2812
Est. 1994 *Stock size* Large
No. of dealers 65
Stock Wide range of antique stock, specializing in Victorian furniture
Open Mon–Sun 10.30am–5pm
Services In-house auctioneers, French polishing

Paraphernalia
Contact W K Keller
✉ **66–68 Abbeydale Road, Sheffield, South Yorkshire, S7 1FD** Ⓟ
☎ 0114 255 0203
Est. 1969 *Stock size* Large
Stock Large range of antique stock including porcelain, glass, light fittings, brass, iron beds, chimney pots, kitchenware
Open Mon–Sat 9.30am–5pm

Renishaw Antique & Pine Centre
Contact Mr B Findley
✉ **32 Main Road, Sheffield, South Yorkshire, S21 3UT** Ⓟ
☎ 01246 435521
Est. 1988 *Stock size* Medium
Stock Victorian–Edwardian and 1930s furniture, pine, architectural items
Open Mon–Fri 8am–1pm Sun 11am–2pm

N P and A Salt Antiques (LAPADA)
Contact Mrs Annette Salt
✉ **Barmouth Court Antiques Centre, Barmouth Road, Sheffield, South Yorkshire, S7 2DH** Ⓟ
☎ 0114 2552711 Ⓕ 0114 2582672
Ⓜ 07801 101363
Est. 2000 *Stock size* Large
Stock General antiques, collectables, furniture, jewellery, toys
Open Mon–Sat 10am–5pm Sun 11am–4pm
Services Restorations

Sheffield Antiques Emporium
Contact Susan Sleath
✉ **15–19 Clyde Road, off Broadfield Road, Sheffield, South Yorkshire, S8 0YD** Ⓟ
☎ 0114 258 4863 Ⓕ 0114 255 5609
Ⓔ info@sheffieldantiquesemporium.com
Ⓦ www.sheffieldantiquesemporium.com
Est. 1992 *Stock size* Large
No. of dealers 70
Stock General antiques, collectables, militaria, jewellery, pottery, Clarice Cliff
Open Mon–Sat 10am–5pm Sun Bank Holidays 11am–5pm
Services Coffee shop

Michael J Taylor Antiques
Contact Michael Taylor
✉ **Barmouth Court Antiques Centre, Barmouth Road, Sheffield, South Yorkshire, S7 2DH** Ⓟ
☎ 01226 340595 Ⓜ 07970 437248
Est. 1995 *Stock size* Large
Stock Georgian–Edwardian furniture, porcelain
Open Mon–Sat 10am–5pm Sun 11am–4pm
Services Valuations

Tilleys Vintage Magazine Shop
Contact Mr A Tilley
✉ **281 Shoreham Street, Sheffield, South Yorkshire, S1 4SS** Ⓟ
☎ 0114 275 2442 Ⓕ 0114 275 2442
Ⓜ 07939 066872
Ⓔ tilleys281@aol.com
Ⓦ www.tilleysmagazines.com
Est. 1978 *Stock size* Large
Stock Antique, rare, second-hand books, magazines
Open Mon 1.30–4.30pm Tues–Fri 10am–4.30pm Sat 10am–1.30pm 3.15–4.30pm

Vision Thing
Contact Miss Jin Brook
✉ **368 Abbeydale Road, Sheffield, South Yorkshire, S7 1FH** Ⓟ
☎ 0114 255 5896 Ⓕ 0114 255 5896
Ⓜ 07714 207797
Ⓔ webmaster@sheffieldscene.co.uk
Ⓦ www.sheffieldscene.co.uk.
Est. 1984 *Stock size* Large
Stock Period interiors 1840–1960,

chenilles, linen, quilts, cushions etc, decorative items, period clothing
Open Thurs Fri Sat 10am–5.30pm Wed 1–5pm or by appointment
Fairs Swinderby
Services Theatrical costumes made

Paul Ward Antiques
Contact Paul or Christine Ward
Owl House, 8 Burnell Road, Sheffield, South Yorkshire, S6 2AX
0114 233 5980 F 0114 233 5980
M 07702 309000
Est. 1977 *Stock size* Large
Stock Country chairs
Trade only Yes
Open By appointment only

Y S F Books Ltd
Contact Mr R Eldridge or Mrs J Eldridge
365 Sharrowvale Road, Sheffield, South Yorkshire, S11 8ZG
0114 268 0687
E ysf@globalnet.co.uk
W www.ysfbooks.com
Est. 1986 *Stock size* Large
Stock General range of antiquarian, rare and second-hand books
Open Mon–Sat 9am–5pm

THURCROFT

Wilkinson & Beighton
Contact Miss S Lally
Woodhouse Green, Thurcroft, Rotherham, South Yorkshire, S66 9AQ
01709 700005 F 01709 700244
E wb.auctioneers@virgin.net
W www.wb-auctioneers.co.uk
Est. 1987
Open Mon–Fri 9am–5pm
Sales Antiques and general Sun 11am, viewing Fri prior 2–5pm Sun 9–11am. Quarterly fine art sales Sun 11am, see press for details
Frequency Fortnightly
Catalogues Yes

WADWORTH

Whittontique Curios & Collectables
Contact M Leaney
1 Main Street, Wadworth, Doncaster, South Yorkshire, DH9 11AY
01302 850339 M 07808 755444
E m.leaney@talk21.co.uk
Est. 1994 *Stock size* Small
Stock Pottery, porcelain, clocks, curios, collectables
Open By appointment
Fairs Newark

WENTWORTH

Holly Farm Antiques
Contact Mrs Linda Hardwick
Holly Farm, Harley, Wentworth, Rotherham, South Yorkshire, S62 7UD
01226 744077
Est. 1989 *Stock size* Medium
Stock Porcelain, Coalport, Worcester, Rockingham, silver, silver plate, jewellery, mirrors, furniture, lamps
Open Sat Sun 10am–5pm weekdays by appointment
Services Valuations

WEST YORKSHIRE

ABERFORD

Aberford Country Furniture
Contact J W H Long
Hicklam House, Aberford, Leeds, West Yorkshire, LS25 3DP
0113 281 3209 F 0113 281 3121
M 07712 657867
E johnwhlong@aol.com
W www.aberfordpine.co.uk
Est. 1973 *Stock size* Medium
Stock Oak and pine country furniture
Open Tues–Sat 9am–5.30pm Sun 10am–5.30pm
Services Restorations

BAILDON

The Baildon Furniture Co
Contact Mr R Parker
Spring Mills, Otley Road, Baildon, Bradford, West Yorkshire, BD17 6AD
01274 414345 F 01274 414345
E baildonfurniture@aol.com
Est. 1974 *Stock size* Large
Stock General antique furniture
Open Mon–Sat 10.30am–4.30pm
Services Valuations, restorations

Browgate Antiques
Contact Mrs D Shaw
13 Browgate, Baildon, Shipley, West Yorkshire, BD17 6BP
01274 597494
Est. 1995 *Stock size* Medium
Stock Georgian–Victorian furniture, clocks, porcelain
Open Mon–Sun 10.30am–5pm closed Thurs
Services Valuations

BATLEY

Tansu
Contact Mr N Hall or Mr C Battye
Red Brick Mill, 218 Bradford Road, Batley Carr, Batley, West Yorkshire, WF17 6JF
01924 460044/459441
F 01924 462844
E tansu@tansu.co.uk
W www.tansu.co.uk
Est. 1992 *Stock size* Large
Stock Japanese antique furniture
Open Mon–Sat 9.30am–5.30pm Sun 11am–5pm
Fairs Ideal Homes
Services Storage, restorations, valuations, customer pickup service, airports and train stations

Village Antiques
Contact Mr K Tuckwell
Jessops Mill Complex, 10 Station Road, Bottom Soothill Lane, Batley, West Yorkshire, WF17 5SU
01924 478002 F 01924 472301
E enquiries@jessopsmill.co.uk
W jessopsmill.co.uk
Est. 1996 *Stock size* Large
No. of dealers 28
Stock General antiques, collectables, music memorabilia
Open Mon–Sun 10am–4pm

Dale Wood & Co
Contact Mr Dale Wood
20 Station Road, Batley, West Yorkshire, WF17 5SU
01924 479439 F 01924 472291
M 07711 645236
E dalewoodandco@hotmail.com
Est. 1989
Open Mon–Fri 9am–5pm
Sales General antiques and general furnishings
Frequency Fortnightly
Catalogues Yes

BINGLEY

⊞ Antique Interiors
Contact Mrs L Dickens
✉ **16 Mornington Road, Bingley, West Yorkshire, BD16 4NJ** Ⓟ
☎ 01274 568024 Ⓕ 01274 568024
Est. 1993 *Stock size* Medium
Stock Victorian–Edwardian furniture, china, glass
Open Mon–Sat 10am–6pm Sun noon–6pm
Services Restorations

BRADFORD

⊞ Cottingly Antiques
Contact Mr P Nobbs
✉ **286 Keighley Road, Bradford, West Yorkshire, BD9 4LH** Ⓟ
☎ 01274 545829
Est. 1979 *Stock size* Medium
Stock General antiques, pine furniture
Open Tues–Sat 9am–4.30pm
Services Restorations

de Rome
Contact Mr S Le Blancq
✉ **12 New John Street, Bradford, West Yorkshire, BD1 2QY**
☎ 01274 734116 Ⓕ 01274 729970
Ⓦ www.deromes.co.uk
Est. 1948
Open Mon–Fri 9am–5.15pm
Sales General antiques
Frequency Periodic
Catalogues Yes

Windle & Co
Contact Mr A Windle
✉ **535 Great Horton Road, Bradford, West Yorkshire, BD7 4EG** Ⓟ
☎ 01274 572998 Ⓕ 01274 572998
Est. 1971
Open Mon–Thurs 9.15am–5.30pm Fri 9.15am–noon
Sales General antiques Wed 6.30pm, viewing Wed from 10am
Frequency Weekly

BRAMHAM

⊞ Priory Furnishing
Contact Mr or Mrs J Furniss
✉ **The Biggin', Bramham Park, Bramham, West Yorkshire, LS2 3 6LR** Ⓟ
☎ 01937 843259 Ⓕ 01937 843259
Ⓔ jeanette@priory-oak-furniture.in2home.co.uk
Est. 1992 *Stock size* Large
Stock 17th–18thC oak, mahogany and walnut furniture
Open Tues–Sun 10am–5pm
Services Valuations

BURLEY IN WHARFEDALE

⊞ Beacon Antiques
Contact L Cousins
✉ **128 Main Street, Burley in Wharfedale, West Yorkshire, LS29 7JP** Ⓟ
☎ 01943 864095 Ⓜ 07887 812858
Ⓔ les@beacon-antiques.co.uk
Ⓦ beacon-antiques.co.uk
Est. 1994 *Stock size* Medium
Stock Porcelain, silver, small Georgian–Edwardian furniture
Open Tues Wed 12.30–4.30pm Thurs Fri 10.30am–4.30pm Sat 9.30am–1pm
Fairs Harrogate, Stafford

BURTON SALMON

⊞ Old Hall Antiques
Contact Mr J Fenteman
✉ **21 Main Street, Burton Salmon, Leeds, West Yorkshire, LS25 5JS** Ⓟ
☎ 01977 607778
Est. 1998 *Stock size* Large
Stock Antique oak and country furniture
Open Tues–Sun 10am–5pm

CROSS HILLS

⊞ Heathcote Antiques
Contact Mr Michael Webster
✉ **Skipton Road Junction Crossroads, Cross Hills, Keighley, West Yorkshire, BD20 7DS** Ⓟ
☎ 01535 635250/635703
Ⓕ 01535 637205 Ⓜ 07836 259640
Ⓔ heathcote1@btopenworld.com
Est. 1974 *Stock size* Large
Stock General antiques, original English unstripped pine, pottery, porcelain
Open Wed–Sat 10am–5.30pm Sun 12.30–4.30pm
Services Most

DENBY DALE

⊞ Worlds Apart
Contact Mrs Sharon Dawson
✉ **Unit 6A, Springfield Mill, Norman Road, Denby Dale, Huddersfield, West Yorkshire, HD8 8TH** Ⓟ
☎ 01484 866713 Ⓜ 07801 349960
Ⓔ shaz@chris216.fsnet.co.uk
Est. 1995 *Stock size* Large
Stock Antiques, collectables
Open Mon–Sat 10am–5pm Sun noon–5pm

DEWSBURY

⊞ Collectors Corner
Contact Mr Tranter
✉ **246 Lees Hall Road, Dewsbury, West Yorkshire, WF12 9HF** Ⓟ
☎ 01924 464111 Ⓕ 01924 464111
Est. 1995 *Stock size* Medium
Stock General collectables
Open Mon–Fri 9.30am–3.30pm Sat 9am–noon
Fairs Newark, Leeds
Services Valuations

FEATHERSTONE

⊞ A645 Trading Post
Contact Mr G Thomas
✉ **Chapel Works, Wakefield Road, Featherstone, Pontefract, West Yorkshire, WF7 5HL** Ⓟ
☎ 01977 695255
Est. 1982 *Stock size* Large
Stock Furniture, collectables, books, die-cast toys, ceramics
Open Mon–Sat 10am–5pm Sun 11am–5pm closed Wed

GREETLAND

⊞ West Vale Trading Post
Contact Mr T Gresty
✉ **61–63 Saddleworth Road, Greetland, West Vale, Halifax, West Yorkshire, HX4 8AG** Ⓟ
☎ 01422 311630 Ⓕ 01422 311630
Est. 1989 *Stock size* Large
Stock General antiques, second-hand items
Open Wed–Sat 9am–5pm
Fairs Newark

HALIFAX

⊞ Antiquary Antiques
Contact Mrs B Hardy
✉ **231 King Cross Road, King Cross, Halifax, West Yorkshire, HX1 3JL** Ⓟ
☎ 01422 341770
Est. 1990 *Stock size* Medium

Stock General antiques, Victorian furniture
Open Mon–Sat 10am–4.30pm closed Wed
Services Valuations

Art Deco Originals/Muir Hewitt
Contact Mr M Hewitt
Halifax Antiques Centre, Queens Road Mills, Gibbet Street, Halifax, West Yorkshire, HX1 4LR
01422 347377 01422 347377
muir.hewitt@virgin.net
www.muirhewitt.com
Est. 1982 *Stock size* Large
Stock Art Deco ceramics, decorative arts, furniture, lighting, mirrors, chrome
Open Tues–Fri 10.30am–4.30pm Sat 10.30am–5pm closed Bank Holidays please phone for seasonal time changes
Fairs Chester, Leeds Art Deco fairs
Services Valuations

Collectors Old Toy Shop
Contact Simon Haley
89 Northgate, Halifax, West Yorkshire, HX1 1XF
01422 822148/360434
collectorsoldtoy@aol.com
Est. 1983 *Stock size* Medium
Stock Dinky, Corgi, die-casts, tin-plate toys, railways, money boxes
Open Mon–Sat 10.30am–4.30pm closed Thurs
Fairs Sandown Park, Harrogate International
Services Insurance valuations

Halifax Antique Centre
Contact Mr M Carroll
Queens Road, Halifax, West Yorkshire, HX1 4LR
01422 366657 01422 369293
info@halifaxantiques.co.uk
www.halifaxantiques.co.uk
Est. 1981 *Stock size* Large
No. of dealers 30
Stock French and English furniture, Art Deco, costume, kitchenware, collectables, Italian chandeliers
Open Tues–Sat 10am–4.30pm
Services Valuations, restorations, café

Holmfirth Antiques
Contact Ken Priestley
Halifax Antiques Centre, Queens Road, Gibbet Street, Halifax, West Yorkshire, HX1 4LR
01484 686854 01484 686854
07973 533478
kenpriestley@fonograf.demon.co.uk
www.fonograf.demon.co.uk
Est. 1988 *Stock size* Medium
Stock Mechanical music, gramophones, phonographs
Open Tues–Sat 10am–5pm
Services Valuations, restorations, mail order

HAWORTH

Bingley Antiques
Contact J B or J Poole
Springfield Farm Estate, Flappit, Haworth, Keighley, West Yorkshire, BD21 5PT
01535 646666 01535 646666
john@bingley-antiques.co.uk
www.bingley-antiques.co.uk
Est. 1969 *Stock size* Large
Stock General antiques, see website
Open Thurs Fri Sat 9am–5pm
Services Valuations

Yorkshire Relics
Contact Colin Ruff
11 Main Street, Haworth, West Yorkshire, BD22 8DA
01535 642218 or 662093
01535 642218 07808 757851
Est. 1987 *Stock size* Large
Stock Antiquarian and collectable books, records, general collectables
Open Mon–Fri noon–5pm Sat Sun 11am–5pm

HEBDEN BRIDGE

Cornucopia
Contact Mrs C Nassor
13 West End, Hebden Bridge, West Yorkshire, HX7 8JP
01422 844497
Est. 1974 *Stock size* Medium
Stock General antiques
Open Thurs–Fri Sun noon–5pm Sat 11am–5pm
Fairs Newark, Nottinghamshire

Re-Collections
Contact Mr A Cooper
24 Market Street, Hebden Bridge, West Yorkshire, HX7 6AA
01422 845764 01422 845764
07979 404757
ae.cooper@talk21.com
Est. 1989 *Stock size* Medium
Stock Wide range of general antiques, furniture
Open Mon–Fri 10.30am–4pm Sat 11am–4.30pm Sun noon–5pm
Fairs Newark

G J Saville (BADA)
Contact Graham Saville
Foster Clough, Hebden Bridge, West Yorkshire, HX7 5QZ
01422 882808 01422 882808
07889 750711
g.j.saville@btinternet.com
Est. 1968 *Stock size* Large
Stock 1750–1830 caricatures, caricature reference books
Open By appointment
Fairs Olympia, BADA
Services Valuations

Weather House Antiques (BADA, LAPADA)
Contact Kym Walker
Foster Clough, Hebden Bridge, West Yorkshire, HX7 5QZ
01422 882808/886961 (workshop) 01422 882808
07889 750711
kymwalker@btinternet.com
Est. 1986
Stock Barometers, weather instruments
Open By appointment only
Fairs Olympia, BADA
Services Restorations

HOLMFIRTH

Old Friendship Antiques
Contact Mr C J Dobson
77 Dunford Road, Holmfirth, Huddersfield, West Yorkshire, HD7 1DT
01484 682129
Est. 1984 *Stock size* Large
Stock Antique furniture, old pine, clocks
Open Mon–Fri 9.30am–5.30pm Sat 9am–4pm Sun 2–4pm
Fairs Newark
Services Pine stripping

William Sykes & Son
Contact Mr R Dixon
Sude Hill Saleroom, New Mill, 38 Huddersfield Road, Holmfirth, Huddersfield, West Yorkshire, HD7 1JH P
☎ 01484 683543 F 01484 683543
Est. 1866
Open Mon–Fri 9am–5.15pm Sat 9am–2pm Sun 11am–2pm
Sales General antiques every 3rd Friday
Frequency Every 3 weeks

Upperbridge Antiques
Contact Mr I Ridings
9 Huddersfield Road, Holmfirth, Huddersfield, West Yorkshire, HD7 1JR
☎ 01484 687200
Est. 1987 *Stock size* Medium
Stock General antiques
Open Wed–Sat 1–5pm Sun 2–5pm
Fairs Newark, Swinderby

HORBURY

Horbury Antique Workshop
Contact Mr J R Smithson
17 High Street, Horbury, Wakefield, West Yorkshire, WF4 5AB P
☎ 01924 271911
Est. 1997 *Stock size* Medium
Stock General antiques, Victorian–Edwardian furniture
Open Mon–Sat 9am–5pm
Services Restorations

John Walsh & Co.
Contact Mr J Walsh
55 Jenkin Road, Horbury, Wakefield, West Yorkshire, WF4 6DP P
☎ 01924 264030 F 01924 267758
M 07976 241587
E auctions@john-walsh.co.uk
W www.john-walsh.co.uk
Est. 1989
Open Mon–Fri 9am–6pm
Sales General antiques
Frequency Alternate months
Catalogues Yes

HUDDERSFIELD

Christopher J L Dawes
Contact Mr C Dawes
26 Lidget Street, Lindley, Huddersfield, West Yorkshire, HD3 3JP P
☎ 01484 649515
Est. 1999 *Stock size* Small
Stock General antiques, porcelain, glass, silver
Open Tues–Sat 10am–5pm closed Wed
Fairs Mytholmroyd, West Yorkshire

Huddersfield Picture Framing Co.
Contact Miss P Ward
Cloth Hall Street, Huddersfield, West Yorkshire, HD1 2EG P
☎ 01484 546075
Est. 1979 *Stock size* Medium
Stock Paintings, prints, swept frames, ovals, circles, mouldings etc
Open Mon Tues Thurs Fri 9am–5pm Wed 9am–1pm Sat 9am–4pm
Services Restorations, framing

Pat's Antique and Reproduction Pine Furniture and Gift Shop
Contact Pat or Jonathan Marsden
29–37 Beast Market, Huddersfield, West Yorkshire, HD1 1QF P
☎ 01484 430830 F 01484 431231
W www.patsantiques@bh-cc.co.uk
Est. 1987 *Stock size* Large
Stock Antique and reproduction pine furniture
Open Mon–Fri 10am–6pm Sat 10am–5.30pm Sun 11am–5pm
Services Furniture custom made to size, gift shop

Serendipity Antiques
Contact Mr Franco
1 Bridge Street, Huddersfield, West Yorkshire, HD4 6EL P
☎ 01484 428223
M 07967 919292
E samfranco59@hotmail.com
Est. 1988 *Stock size* Medium
Stock Situated in a Georgian coach house, selling general antiques, pine, porcelain, Victorian–Edwardian furniture
Open Wed–Sat 10.30am–5pm
Services Valuations, restorations

ILKLEY

Coopers of Ilkley (LAPADA)
Contact Charles Cooper
46–50 Leeds Road, Ilkley, West Yorkshire, LS29 8EQ P
☎ 01943 608020 F 01943 604321
E enquiries@coopersantiquesilkley
W www.coopersantiquesilkley
Stock size Medium
Stock Period and Victorian furniture
Open Mon–Fri 9am–1pm 2pm–5.30pm Sat 9am–5.30pm
Services Restorations

The Grove Bookshop (PBFA)
Contact Mr A Sharpe
10 The Grove, Ilkley, West Yorkshire, LS29 9EG P
☎ 01943 609335 F 01943 817086
E antiquarian@grovebookshop.co.uk
W www.grovebookshop.co.uk
Est. 1976 *Stock size* Medium
Stock Antiquarian, rare, and collectable books, specializing in Yorkshire topography, angling, field sports, literature
Open Mon–Sat 9am–5.30pm

Andrew Hartley Fine Arts (ISVA, SOFAA)
Contact Mr A D Hartley
Victoria Hall, Little Lane, Ilkley, West Yorkshire, LS29 8EA P
☎ 01943 816363 F 01943 817610
E info@andrewhartleyfinearts.co.uk
W www.andrewhartleyfinearts.co,uk
Est. 1906
Open Mon–Fri 9am–5.30pm Sat 9am–12.30pm
Sales Victorian and later every Wed 10am, viewing Tues prior 9am–7pm. Antique and fine art sale every two months Wed Thurs 10am, viewing Sat prior 9.30am–12.30pm Mon Tues prior 9.30am–4.30pm day of sale 9–10am
Frequency Weekly
Catalogues Yes

KEIGHLEY

Revival
Contact Peter Pryimuk
104–106 South Street, Keighley, West Yorkshire, BD21 1EH P
☎ 01535 606837

Est. 1987 *Stock size* Medium
Stock General antiques, architectural items, pine, bric-a-brac
Open Mon–Sat 10am–5pm telephone call advisable

LEEDS

Abbey Auctions
Contact John Midgely
11 Morris Lane, Kirkstall, Leeds, West Yorkshire, LS5 3JT P
0113 275 8787
Open Mon–Fri 8am–5pm Sat 8am–noon
Sales General antiques sales Tues 10am
Frequency Weekly
Catalogues No

Aquarius Antiques
Contact Peter McGlade
Abbey Mills, Abbey Road, Leeds, West Yorkshire, LS5 3HP P
0113 278 9216
Est. 1979 *Stock size* Medium
Stock General antiques, Georgian–Victorian furniture
Open Mon–Sat 9am–5pm
Services Repairs, restorations

Bonhams
17a East Parade, Leeds, West Yorkshire, LS1 2BH
0113 244 8011 F 0113 242 9875
E leeds@bonhams.com
W www.bonhams.com
Open Mon–Fri 9am–5pm

Cottage Antiques
Contact Mr D Atkinson
78 Otley Road, Leeds, West Yorkshire, LS6 4BA P
0113 2955125
Est. 1993 *Stock size* Medium
Stock General antiques
Open Mon Thurs 11am–4pm Tues Wed Fri Sat 10am–5pm
Fairs Newark, Ardingly
Services Valuations, French polishing

Headrow Antiques
Contact Sally Hurrell
Level 3, The Headrow Shopping Centre, The Headrow, Leeds, West Yorkshire, LS1 6JE P
0113 245 5344
W www.headrowantiques.com
Est. 1992 *Stock size* Large
No. of dealers 26
Stock General antiques
Open Mon–Sat 10am–5pm Nov Dec Sun 11am–4pm

Swiss Cottage Furniture
Contact Mr J Howorth
85 Westfield Crescent, Burley, Leeds, West Yorkshire, LS3 1DJ P
0113 242 9994
W www.swisscottageantiques.com
Est. 1987 *Stock size* Large
Stock General antiques, salvage yard
Open Mon–Sat 10am–5pm Sun 1–5pm closed Tues
Fairs Newark

Woodstock Antiques
Contact Mr R J Link
134 Woodhouse Street, Leeds, West Yorkshire, LS6 2JN
0113 246 1296
Est. 1990 *Stock size* Medium
Stock General antiques
Open Mon–Sat 10am–5pm
Fairs Newark

Works of Iron
Contact Mr G Higgins
Beaver Works, 36 Whitehouse Street, Leeds, West Yorkshire, LS10 1AD P
0113 234 0555 F 0113 234 2555
Est. 1985 *Stock size* Large
Stock Antique beds
Open Daily 11am–5pm
Services Valuations, restorations

Year Dot
Contact Mr Adrian Glithro
16 Market Street Arcade, Leeds, West Yorkshire, LS1 6DH P
0113 246 0860
Est. 1977 *Stock size* Medium
Stock General antiques, jewellery
Open Mon–Sat 9.30am–5pm

LEPTON

K L M & Co
Contact Mr K L Millington
Wakefield Road, Lepton, West Yorkshire, HD8 0EL P
01484 607763 F 01484 607763
M 07860 671547
Est. 1981 *Stock size* Large
Stock Antiques, 1940s furniture
Open Mon–Sat 10.30am–5pm

LUDDENDENFOOT

Calder Valley Auctioneers (RICS)
Contact Mr I Peace
Fairlea Mill, Ellenholme Road, Luddendenfoot, Halifax, West Yorkshire, HX2 6EP P
01422 8886648
Est. 1995
Open By appointment
Sales General antiques Thurs, viewing day prior 2–7pm and morning of sale
Frequency Monthly
Catalogues Yes

MENSTON

J Hanlon Antiques
Contact Mrs J Hanlon
101 Bradford Road, Menston, Ilkley, West Yorkshire, LS29 6BU P
01943 877634
Est. 1974 *Stock size* Medium
Stock Small collectables, textiles, jewellery, silver
Open Mon Thurs–Sat 2.30–5pm
Fairs Newark

Park Antiques
Contact Mr or Mrs Roe
2 North View, Main Street, Menston, Ilkley, West Yorkshire, LS29 6JU P
01943 872392 F 01943 878004
M 07801 624530
E parkantiques@nr-ilkley.demon.co.uk
Est. 1975 *Stock size* Medium
Stock 19thC fine quality rosewood, walnut and mahogany furniture
Open Wed–Sat 10am–6pm Sun 10am–5pm
Services Upholstery

OTLEY

Frantique
Contact Mr I Hughes
26 Cross Green, Otley, West Yorkshire, LS21 1HD P
01943 463380 F 01943 463380
M 07802 740012
E ivor@frantique.fsnet.co.uk
W www.frantique.co.uk
Est. 1998 *Stock size* Large
Stock Continental decorative arts, including faïence, kitchen antiques, clocks, bronzes, stoves, metalware, architectural, enamelware

Open Mon–Sat 10am–6pm closed Sun Wed
Services Anglo-French antiques press relations and translation

PONTEFRACT

Wards Collectables
Contact Mrs S Ward
53 South Avenue, Pontefract, West Yorkshire, WF8 4EW
01977 703970
Est. 1989 *Stock size* Small
Stock General antiques, collectables
Open By appointment
Fairs Newark

PUDSEY

Geary Antiques
Contact Mr J A Geary
114 Richardshaw Lane, Pudsey, Leeds, West Yorkshire, LS28 6BN
0113 256 4122 07802 441245
jag@t-nlbi.demon.co.uk
Est. 1933 *Stock size* Large
Stock General antique English furniture
Open Mon–Sat 10am–5.30pm Sun noon–4pm
Services Restorations, interior design, furnishing fabrics, wallpapers

SALTAIRE

Mick Burt (Antique Pine)
Contact Andrew Draper
The Victoria Centre, 3–4 Victoria Road, Saltaire, Shipley, West Yorkshire, BD18 3LA
01274 530611 01274 533722
Est. 1994 *Stock size* Medium
Stock Restored antique pine furniture
Open Wed–Sun 10am–5pm
Services Restorations

Harwood Antiques
Contact Mr R Harwood
The Victoria Centre, 3–4 Victoria Road, Saltaire, Shipley, West Yorkshire, BD18 3LA
01274 874138
07885 137573
Est. 1974 *Stock size* Medium
Stock Antique furniture, clocks
Open Wed–Sun 10.30am–5.30pm
Services Valuations

John Lewis
The Victoria Centre, 3–4 Victoria Road, Saltaire, Shipley, West Yorkshire, BD18 3LA
01274 533722 01274 530611
Est. 1988 *Stock size* Large
Stock Burmantoft's art pottery
Open Tues–Sun 10.30am–5.30pm
Fairs NEC, Alexandra Palace

Swan Antiques
Contact Mrs B Harwood
The Victoria Centre, 3–4 Victoria Road, Saltaire, Shipley, West Yorkshire, BD18 3LA
01274 533722
Est. 1998 *Stock size* Small
Stock General antiques, country furniture
Open Wed–Sun 10.30am–5.30pm

The Victoria Centre
Contact Mr Andrew Draper
3–4 Victoria Road, Saltaire, Shipley, West Yorkshire, BD18 3LA
01274 533722 01274 533722
info@victoriacentre.co.uk
www.victoriacentre.co.uk
Est. 1994 *Stock size* Large
No. of dealers 50
Stock General antiques, furniture, fine art and collectables
Open Wed–Sun 10.30am–5.30pm
Services Valuations, restorations

SHERBURN-IN-ELMET

Malcolms No1 Auctioneers & Valuers
Contact Mr Malcolm Dowson
The Chestnuts, 16 Park Avenue, Sherburn-in-Elmet, Leeds, West Yorkshire, LS25 6EF
01977 684971 01977 681046
07774 130784
info@malcolmsno1auctions.co.uk
www.malcolmsno1auctions.co.uk
Est. 1980
Open Mon–Fri 9am–5pm
Sales Antiques and collectables, named ceramics (all periods), viewing Mon 10am–6.15pm Sun 1–6pm. Venue Trustees Hall, High Street, Boston Spa, Wetherby, North Yorkshire
Frequency Monthly
Catalogues Yes

SHIPLEY

Victoria Antiques
Contact Mr Andrew Draper
27–31 Atkinson Street, Shipley, West Yorkshire, BD18 3QS
01274 533722 01274 533722
info@victoriacentre.co.uk
www.victoriacentre.co.uk
Est. 1994 *Stock size* Large
Stock Furniture, including pine
Open Mon–Sun 10am–4.30pm
Services Valuations, restorations

SOWERBY BRIDGE

Old Cawsey Antiques
Contact Miss S Stirrup
22 Wharf Street, Sowerby Bridge, West Yorkshire, HX6 2AE
01422 832140 07711 519545
Est. 1989 *Stock size* Medium
Stock Early oak, country furniture, accessories
Open Tues–Sat 10am–4.30pm

Talking Points Antiques
Contact Mr Paul Austwick
66 West Street, Sowerby Bridge, West Yorkshire, HX6 3AP
01422 834126
tpagrams@aol.com
Est. 1985
Stock Gramophones, other mechanical antiques
Open Thurs Fri Sat 10.30am–5.30pm and by appointment
Fairs NEC Vintage Communications Fair, Blackpool Vintage Technology Fair

WAKEFIELD

The Old Vicarage Bookshop
Contact Mr J Longfellow
24 Zetland Street, Wakefield, West Yorkshire, WF1 1QT
01924 380432
vicarage.books@virgin.net
Est. 1987 *Stock size* Large
Stock Antique, rare and second-hand books

Open Daily 10.30am–5pm closed Wed Sun
Services Valuations

D Turner Antiques
Contact Miss D Turner
574 Leeds Road, Outwood, Wakefield, West Yorkshire, WF1 2DT
01924 835942
Est. 1987 *Stock size* Small
Stock General antiques
Open Mon–Sat 11am–5pm closed Thurs
Services Valuations, house clearance

LINCOLNSHIRE

ALLINGTON

Garth Vincent Antique Arms and Armour (LAPADA)
Contact Garth Vincent
The Old Manor House, Allington, Nr Grantham, Lincolnshire, NG32 2DH P
01400 281358 F 01400 282658
M 077285 352151
E garthvincent@compuserve.com
W www.guns.co.uk
Est. 1980 *Stock size* Large
Stock International guns, swords, helmets, reproduction arms and armour
Open By appointment only
Fairs Birmingham and London Arms Fairs
Services Valuations

AYLESBY

Robin Fowler Period Clocks (LAPADA)
Contact Mr R Fowler
Washingdales, Washingdales Lane, Aylesby, Grimsby, Lincolnshire, DN37 7LH P
01472 751335 F 01472 751335
M 07949 141891
E periodclocks@washingdales.fsnet.co.uk
Est. 1968 *Stock size* Large
Stock Antique clocks, barometers, scientific instruments
Open By appointment
Fairs LAPADA, Bailey, Galloway
Services Valuations, restorations

BARTON UPON HUMBER

Ken Mannion Fossils
Contact Mr K Mannion
59 Barrow Road, Barton upon Humber, Lincolnshire, DN18 6AE P
01652 634827 F 01652 660700
E kenmannion@btinternet.com
W www.kenmannion.btinternet.co.uk
Est. 1980 *Stock size* Medium
Stock Fossils, meteorites, artefacts
Open By appointment
Services Valuations, restorations

BELTON

Richard Ellory
Contact Richard Ellory
Unit 5, Sandtoft Industrial Estate, Sandtoft Road, Belton, Lincolnshire, DN9 1PN P
01427 874064 F 01427 873626
E richard@ellory.fsnet.co.uk
Est. 1981 *Stock size* Medium
Stock English pine
Open Mon–Sat 8am–4.30pm Sun 10am–4pm

BOSTON

Antique Workshop Ltd
Contact Mr Murphy
4a Pulverstoft Lane, Boston, Lincolnshire, PE21 8TA P
01205 368692
Est. 1967 *Stock size* Large
Stock General antique furniture
Open Mon–Sat 8am–5pm
Services Restorations

Tony Coda Antiques
Contact Mr T Coda
121 High Street, Boston, Lincolnshire, PE21 8TJ P
01205 352754
M 07979 943084
Est. 1966 *Stock size* Medium
Stock General antiques, clocks, silver, paintings
Open Mon–Sat 9.30am–5pm closed Wed
Fairs Newark, The International Antique and Collectables Fair at RAF Swinderby
Services Valuations

Junktion Antiques
Contact Mr Jack Rundle
The Old Railway Station, Main Road, New Bolingbroke, Boston, Lincolnshire, PE22 7LN P
01205 480068 F 01205 480132
M 07836 345491
Est. 1983 *Stock size* Large
Stock Early toys, advertising, bygones, architectural and mechanical antiques 1880–1960
Open Wed Thurs Sat 10am–5pm
Fairs Newark, Swinderby

Pennyfarthing Antiques
Contact Mr Hale
1 Red Lion Street, Boston, Lincolnshire, PE21 6NY P
01205 362988
Est. 2000 *Stock size* Medium
Stock General antiques
Open Tues Wed Fri Sat 10am–4.30pm

BOURNE

Antique and Second Hand Traders
Contact Mr C Thompson
39 West Street, Bourne, Lincolnshire, PE10 9N3 P
01778 394700 F 01778 394700
M 07958 941728
Est. 1969 *Stock size* Large
Stock General antiques
Open Mon–Sat 10am–5pm closed Wed Thurs
Fairs Newark, Ardingly
Services House clearance, removals

BRIGG

DDM Auction Rooms
Contact Mr R Horner
Old Courts Road, Brigg, North Lincolnshire, DN20 8JD P
01652 650172 F 01652 650085
M 07970 126311
E sales@ddmauctionrooms.co.uk
W www.ddmgroup.co.uk
Est. 1884
Open Mon–Fri 9am–5.30pm
Sales Fine art and collectables sale every 6 weeks Tues Wed 9.30am. Fortnightly sale of general, household and shipping Sat 9.30am, ring for details, viewing day prior 2–7pm day of sale from 8.30am
Frequency Every 6 weeks
Catalogues Yes

CLEETHORPES

Cleethorpes Collectables
Contact Mr A Dalton

34 Alexandra Road, Cleethorpes, Lincolnshire, DN35 8LF
☎ 01472 291952 Ⓕ 01472 291952
Est. 1999 *Stock size* Large
Stock General antiques, collectables, curios
Open Mon–Sun 10am–5pm
Services Valuations

Yesterdays Antiques
Contact Mr N Bishop
86 Grimsby Road, Cleethorpes, Lincolnshire, DN35 7DP
☎ 01472 343020
Ⓔ n.bishop2@ntlworld.com
Ⓦ yesterdaysantiques.org.uk
Est. 1987 *Stock size* Large
Stock General antiques, fireplaces a speciality
Open Mon–Sat 9am–5pm or by appointment
Services Valuations, restorations, polishing

EPWORTH

Ellory & Chaffer
Contact Mr R Ellory
25a Burnham Road, Epworth, Lincolnshire, DN9 1BX
☎ 01427 874064 Ⓕ 01427 874064
Est. 1985 *Stock size* Medium
Stock Antique English reproduction pine furniture
Open Mon–Fri 8am–4.30pm Sat 8am–noon
Services Restorations, stripping

GAINSBOROUGH

Drewery and Wheeldon
Contact Mr M G Tomson
124 Trinity Street, Gainsborough, Lincolnshire, DN21 1JD
☎ 01427 616118 Ⓕ 01427 811020
Ⓔ auctions@drewery-&-wheeldon.co.uk
Est. 1879
Open Mon–Fri 9am–5.30pm Sat 9am–12.30pm
Sales General antiques sales, phone for details
Frequency Periodic
Catalogues Yes

Pilgrims Antiques Centre
Contact Mr M Wallis
66a Church Street, Gainsborough, Lincolnshire, DN21 2JR
☎ 01427 810897 Ⓕ 01427 810897
Est. 1985 *Stock size* Large
No. of dealers 8
Stock General antiques
Open Tues–Sat 10am–4.30pm closed Wed

R M Antiques
Contact Mr R Maclennan
4a Tennyson Street, Gainsborough, Lincolnshire, DN21 2GJ
☎ 01427 810624 Ⓕ 01427 810624
Est. 1984 *Stock size* Large
Stock General antiques
Trade only Yes
Open Mon–Sat 9am–3pm
Services Export

GRANTHAM

Golding Young & Co (NAVA)
Contact Mr Colin Young
The Grantham Auction Rooms, Old Wharf Road, Grantham, Lincolnshire, NG31 7AA
☎ 01476 565118 Ⓕ 01476 561475
Ⓔ enquiries@goldingyoung.com
Ⓦ www.goldingyoung.com
Est. 1900
Open Mon–Fri 9am–5pm closed 1–2pm
Sales Fortnightly general antiques sale, bi-monthly antique and fine art sale
Frequency Fortnightly
Catalogues Yes

Grantham Clocks
Contact M R Conder
30 Lodge Way, Grantham, Lincolnshire, NG31 8DD
☎ 01476 561784
Est. 1987 *Stock size* Medium
Stock Clocks
Open By appointment
Services Valuations, restorations

Grantham Furniture Emporium
Contact K or J E Hamilton
4–6 Wharf Road, Grantham, Lincolnshire, NG31 6BA
☎ 01476 562967 Ⓜ 07710 483865
Est. 1976 *Stock size* Large
Stock Victorian–Edwardian and 1920s shipping furniture,
Open Tues–Sun 11am–4pm closed Wed

Harlequin Antiques
Contact Tony or Sandra Marshall
46 Swinegate, Grantham, Lincolnshire, NG31 6RL
☎ 01476 563346
Est. 1995 *Stock size* Medium
Stock General antiques
Open Mon–Sat 9am–5pm
Services Valuations

Notions Antiques Centre
Contact Mr or Mrs L Checkley
1–2A Market Place, Grantham, Lincolnshire, NG31 6LQ
☎ 01476 563603 Ⓜ 07974 683120
Ⓔ scheckley@fsbdial.co.uk
Est. 1984 *Stock size* Large
No. of dealers 70
Stock General antiques
Open Mon–Fri 10am–5pm Sat 9.30am–5pm Sun 11am–4pm

Marilyn Swain Auctions (SOFAA)
Contact John Munroe
The Old Barracks, Sandon Road, Grantham, Lincolnshire, NG31 9AS
☎ 01476 568861 Ⓕ 01476 576100
Ⓔ swain.auctions@virgin.net
Est. 1991
Open Mon–Fri 9am–5.30pm
Sales General antiques
Frequency Fortnightly
Catalogues Yes

Marcus Wilkinson Jewellers & Antiques (BHI, AHS, NAWCC)
Contact Mr Marcus Wilkinson
The Tyme House, 1 Blue Court, Guildhall Street, Grantham, Lincolnshire, NG31 6NJ
☎ 01476 560400 Ⓕ 01476 568791
Ⓜ 07966 154590
Ⓔ marcus@timeshop.freeserve.co.uk
Ⓦ www.englishclocks.com or www.englishclocks.net
Est. 1935 *Stock size* Small
Stock Clocks, watches, jewellery
Open Mon–Sat 10am–4.30pm
Fairs San Francisco Fall Antique Show, Los Angeles Spring Antique Show
Services Valuations, restorations, repairs

GRIMSBY

Bell Antiques
Contact Mr Victor Hawkey
68 Harold Road, Grimsby, Lincolnshire, DN32 7NQ
☎ 01472 695110

Est. 1964 *Stock size* Large
Stock Clocks, music boxes
Open By appointment
Services Valuations

Jackson Green & Preston
Contact Mr D Arliss
New Cartergate, Grimsby, Lincolnshire, DN31 1RB
01472 311115 F 01472 311114
auction@jacksongreenpreston.co.uk
www.jacksongreenpreston.co.uk
Est. 1920
Open By appointment
Sales General household and antiques
Frequency Weekly
Catalogues No

HEMSWELL

Advena Antiques & Fairs
Contact Alan White
Building II, Hemswell Antique Centre, Caenby Corner Estate, Hemswell Cliff, Gainsborough, Lincolnshire, DN21 5TJ
01427 668389 F 01427 668935
M 07713 150510
advenantiques@ntlworld.com
Est. 1992 *Stock size* Large
Stock Antique silver, jewellery, silver plate
Open Mon–Sun 10am–5pm
Services Valuations, repairs

Astra House Antique Centre
Contact Mr M J Frith
Old RAF Hemswell, Nr Caenby Corner, Gainsborough, Lincolnshire, DN21 5TL
01427 668312 F 01427 668312
astraantiqueshemswell@btinternet.com
Est. 1992 *Stock size* Large
No. of dealers 50
Stock General antiques and collectables including second-hand items
Open Mon–Sun 10am–5pm
Services Shipping

Barleycorn Antiques
Contact Shirley or John Wheat
Hemswell Antiques Centre, Caenby Corner Estate, Hemswell Cliff, Gainsborough, Lincolnshire, DN21 5TW
01427 668789 M 07850 673965
www.barleycorn-antiques.co.uk
Est. 1982
Stock Furniture, brass, lighting, ceramics, clocks,
Open Mon–Sun 10am–5pm

Guardroom Antiques
Contact Mr C Lambert
RAF Station Hemswell, Gainsborough, Lincolnshire, DN21 5TU
01427 667113
Est. 1993 *Stock size* Large
No. of dealers 50
Stock General antiques including Victorian and Georgian furniture
Open Mon–Sun 10am–5pm

Hemswell Antique Centres
Contact Robert Miller
Caenby Corner Estate, Hemswell Cliff, Gainsborough, Lincolnshire, DN21 5TJ
01427 668389 F 01427 668935
info@hemswell-antiques.com
www.hemswell-antiques.com
Est. 1989 *Stock size* Large
No. of dealers 270
Stock General antiques
Open Daily 10am–5pm
Services Furniture restoration

Trevor Moss Antiques
Contact Mr T Moss
Building 1, Room 2, Caenby Corner Estate, Gainsborough, Hemswell Cliff, Lincolnshire, DN21 5TW
01427 667767 F 01427 614506
info@tsmossantiques.co.uk
www.tsmossantiques.co.uk
Est. 1985 *Stock size* Large
Stock General antiques
Open Mon–Sun 10am–5pm
Fairs Newark, Swinderby
Services Restorations

Second Time Around
Contact Mr Geoff Powis
Hemswell Antique Centre, Caenby Corner Estate, Hemswell Cliff, Gainsborough, Lincolnshire, DN21 5TJ
01522 543167 or 01427 668389
M 07860 679495
Est. 1984 *Stock size* Large
Stock Period longcase and bracket clocks, other clocks 17th–19thC and up to 1940s
Open Mon–Sun 10am–5pm
Services Valuations, restorations

Smithson Antiques
Contact Skip or Janie Smithson
Hemswell Antique Centre, Caenby Corner Estate, Hemswell Cliff, Lincolnshire, DN21 5TJ
01754 810265 M 07831 399180
Est. 1984 *Stock size* Medium
Stock Victorian kitchen and dairy antiques
Open Daily 10am–5pm

HOLBEACH

P J Cassidy
Contact Mr P Cassidy
1 Boston Road, Holbeach, Spalding, Lincolnshire, PE12 7LR
01406 426322
bookscass@aol.com
Est. 1974 *Stock size* Large
Stock Antiquarian books, maps, prints, and Lincolnshire topography
Open Mon–Sat 10am–6pm
Services Framing

HOLTON LE CLAY

C A Johnson
Contact Mr C A Johnson
32 Pinfold Lane, Holton Le Clay, Grimsby, Lincolnshire, DN36 5DH
01472 822406 F 01472 822406
Est. 1979 *Stock size* Medium
Stock General antiques
Open By appointment
Fairs Newark
Services Valuations

HORNCASTLE

G Baker Antiques
Contact Geoffrey or Christine Baker
16 South Street, Horncastle, Lincolnshire, LN9 6DX
01507 526553 M 07767 216264
Est. 1973 *Stock size* Medium
Stock Period and general furniture
Open Mon–Sat 9am–5pm or by appointment
Fairs Newark, Swinderby
Services Restorations

Clare Boam
Contact Clare Boam
22–38 North Street, Horncastle, Lincolnshire, LN9 5DX

☎ 01507 522381 Ⓕ 01507 524202
Ⓔ clareboam@btconnect.com
Ⓦ www.greatexpectationshorncastle.co.uk
Est. 1976 *Stock size* Large
Stock General antiques and collectables
Open Mon–Sat 9am–5pm
Sun 2–4.30pm

Great Expectations
Contact Miss M C Boam
✉ **37–43 East Street, Horncastle, Lincolnshire, LN9 6AZ** Ⓟ
☎ 01507 524202 Ⓕ 01507 524202
Ⓔ clareboam@btconnect.com
Ⓦ www.greatexpectationshorncastle.co.uk
Est. 1996 *Stock size* Large
No. of dealers 60
Stock General antiques
Open Mon–Sat 9am–5pm Sun 1–4.30pm and Bank Holidays

Horncastle Antique Centre
Contact Mrs P Sims or Mr D Sims
✉ **26 Bridge Street, Horncastle, Lincolnshire, LN9 3H2** Ⓟ
☎ 01507 527777/525898
Ⓕ 01507 527777
Ⓦ www.freeshop.co.uk/antiques
Est. 1976 *Stock size* Large
Stock General antiques and collectables
Open Mon–Sat 9.30am–5pm
Sun 1–5pm
Services Valuations, restorations, shipping

Lindsay Court Architectural
Contact Mr Lindsay White
✉ **Lindsay Court, Horncastle, Lincolnshire, LN9 5DH** Ⓟ
☎ 01507 527794/578413
Ⓜ 07768 396117
Ⓔ horncastlestone@aol.com
Est. 1987 *Stock size* Large
Stock Architectural antiques, stoneware, garden statuary salvage, reclaims
Open Tues Thurs Fri Sat
9.30am–5pm or by appointment
Fairs Newark
Services Export, container packing

Alan Read
Contact Mr A Read
✉ **60 & 62 West Street, Horncastle, Lincolnshire, LN9 5AD** Ⓟ
☎ 01507 524324/525548
Ⓕ 01507 525548
Ⓜ 07778 873838 *Stock size* Large
Stock 17th–18thC English furniture and decorative items
Open Tues–Sat 10am–4.30pm closed Wed or by appointment 7 days a week
Services Valuations, bespoke replicas made

Seaview Antiques
Contact Mr M Chalk
✉ **Stanhope Road, Horncastle, Lincolnshire, LN9 5DG** Ⓟ
☎ 01507 524524
Ⓔ tracey@seaviewantiques.co.uk
Ⓦ www.seaviewantiques.co.uk
Est. 1972 *Stock size* Large
Stock General antiques
Open Mon–Sat 9am–5pm
Fairs Newark

KIRTON

Kirton Antiques (LAPADA)
Contact Alan Marshall
✉ **3 High Street, Kirton, Lincolnshire, PE20 1DR** Ⓟ
☎ 01205 722595 Ⓕ 01205 722895
Ⓜ 07860 531600
Ⓔ alan.marshall@modcomp.net
Est. 1973 *Stock size* Large
Stock General antiques including period furniture
Open Mon–Fri 8am–5pm
Sat 8.30am–noon or by appointment
Services Valuations, property hire

LINCOLN

Eric A Bird Jewellers (BHI)
Contact Mr S Thompson
✉ **1 St Mary's Street, Lincoln, Lincolnshire, LN5 7EQ**
☎ 01522 520977 Ⓕ 01522 560586
Ⓦ www.eric-a-bird.co.uk
Est. 1959 *Stock size* Medium
Stock Antique and modern clocks, pocket watches
Open Mon–Sat 9am–5pm
Services Valuations, restorations and repairs

C & K Dring
Contact Mr C Dring
✉ **111 High Street, Lincoln, Lincolnshire, LN5 7PY** Ⓟ
☎ 01522 540733
Est. 1977 *Stock size* Medium
Stock Victorian and Edwardian inlaid furniture, clocks, music boxes, tinplate toys
Open Mon–Sat 10am–5pm closed Wed
Fairs Newark, Swinderby
Services Valuations, restorations

David J Hansord and Son (BADA, BACA Award Winner 2001)
Contact John Hansord
✉ **6–7 Castle Hill, Lincoln, Lincolnshire, LN1 3AA** Ⓟ
☎ 01522 530044 Ⓕ 01522 530044
Ⓜ 07831 183511
Est. 1972 *Stock size* Large
Stock 18thC English furniture, works of art and objects
Open Mon–Sat 10am–5pm
Fairs Olympia
Services Valuations, restorations

Harlequin Gallery (PBFA)
Contact Mrs Anna Cockram
✉ **20–22 Steep Hill, Lincoln, Lincolnshire, LN2 1LT** Ⓟ
☎ 01522 522589
Ⓔ harlequin@acockram.fsbusiness.co.uk
Est. 1964 *Stock size* Large
Stock Antiquarian and second-hand books, maps, prints
Open Mon–Sat 10.30am–5.45pm
Wed 11am–4.30pm
Services Valuations, antique globe restoration

Dorrian Lamberts
Contact Mr R Lambert
✉ **64 & 65 Steep Hill, Lincoln, Lincolnshire, LN2 1LR** Ⓟ
☎ 01522 545916
Est. 1984 *Stock size* Medium
Stock General antiques
Open Mon–Sat 10am–5pm
Fairs Newark, Swinderby
Services Valuations

Thomas Mawer & Son Ltd
Contact Mr J C Slingsby
✉ **Dunston House, Portland Street, Lincoln, Lincolnshire, LN5 7NN** Ⓟ
☎ 01522 524984
Ⓔ auctions@thos-mawer.co.uk
Ⓦ www.thos-mawer.co.uk
Est. 1864
Open Mon–Thurs 9am–5.30pm
Fri 9am–4pm Sat 9am–noon

Sales Victorian and later first Sat of every month, quarterly antiques, regular specialist sales
Frequency Monthly
Catalogues Yes

Whatnots
Contact Mr D Fowler
Cobb Hall, St Pauls Lane, Bailgate, Lincoln, Lincolnshire, LN1 3AX P
01522 544723 Ⓜ 07931 988974
Est. 1996 *Stock size* Medium
Stock General antiques, collectables
Open Mon–Sun 10am–5pm

LONG SUTTON

Chapel Emporium
Contact Miss B Hill or Miss Jennifer Beck
London Road, Long Sutton, Spalding, Lincolnshire, PE12 9EA P
01406 364808
Est. 1983 *Stock size* Large
Stock General antiques
Open Mon–Sun 10am–5pm
Services Restorations

Long Sutton Antique and Craft Centre
Contact Ms G Shergold
72–74 London Road, Long Sutton, Spalding, Lincolnshire, PE12 9EB P
01406 362991
Est. 1998 *Stock size* Large
No. of dealers 64
Stock General antiques, collectables and craft centre
Open Mon–Sat 10.30am–5.30pm Sun 11am–5pm

LOUTH

The Old Maltings Antique Centre
Contact Mr Norman Coffey
Aswell Street, Louth, Lincolnshire, LN11 9HP P
01507 608257
Ⓔ margaret@eastcoast88.freeserve.co.uk
Est. 1979 *Stock size* Large
No. of dealers 20
Stock General antiques, collectables, Victorian–Edwardian furniture
Open Mon–Sat 10am–4.30pm
Services Valuations, restorations

John Taylor's
Contact Mrs A Laverack
The Wool Mart, Kidgate, Louth, Lincolnshire, LN11 9EZ
01507 611107 Ⓕ 01507 601280
Ⓔ johntaylors@btconnect.com
Ⓦ www.johntaylors.com
Est. 1869
Open Mon–Fri 9am–5.15pm Sat 9am–2pm
Sales General antiques
Frequency Monthly
Catalogues Yes

MARKET DEEPING

Market Deeping Antiques & Craft Centre
Contact John Strutt
50–56 High Street, Market Deeping, Lincolnshire, PE6 8EB P
01778 380238
Est. 1995 *Stock size* Large
No. of dealers 70
Stock General antiques, collectables, crafts
Open Mon–Sat 10am–5pm Sun 11am–5pm

Portland House Antiques
Contact Mr Cree
23 Church Street, Market Deeping, Lincolnshire, PE6 8AN P
01778 347129
Est. 1971 *Stock size* Large
Stock 18thC–early 19thC furniture, pictures and clocks
Open Sat 10am–4pm or by appointment
Services Valuations

NETTLEHAM

Autumn Leaves
Contact Mrs Susan Young
Unit 2 Co-op Building, 19 The Green, Nettleham, Lincoln, Lincolnshire, LN2 2NR P
01522 750779
Ⓔ leaves@onetel.net.uk
Ⓦ www.abebooks.com/home/autumn_leaves
Est. 1997 *Stock size* Medium
Stock Second-hand books on all subjects
Open Tues–Thurs 9.15am–4.30pm Fri 9.15am–5pm Sat 9.15am–12.30pm
Services Book search

Homme de Quimper
Contact Mr S Toogood
Hillstead, 11 Church Street, Nettleham, Lincoln, Lincolnshire, LN2 2PD P
01522 753753 Ⓜ 07831 773622
Ⓔ steve.toogood@ntlworld.com
Ⓦ www.hommedequimper.co.uk
Est. 1996 *Stock size* Medium
Stock Antique French pottery, Quimper
Open Mon–Sun 9am–6pm
Services Valuations, restorations

Juke Box World
Contact Mr S Toogood
Hillstead, 11 Church Street, Nettleham, Lincoln, Lincolnshire, LN2 2PD P
01522 753753
Ⓔ steve.toogood@tesco.net
Est. 1985 *Stock size* Medium
Stock 20thC juke boxes
Open Mon–Sun 9am–6pm
Fairs Ascot Racecourse, Copthorne
Services Valuations, restorations

SCUNTHORPE

Canter & Francis (NAEA)
Contact Mr S J Francis, NAEA
41 Oswald Road, Scunthorpe, Lincolnshire, DN15 7PN P
01724 858855 Ⓕ 01724 858855
Est. 1947
Open Mon–Fri 9am–5pm
Sales General antiques
Frequency Periodic
Catalogues No

SOUTH HYKEHAM

Naylors Auctions
Contact Mr R Phillips
The Hall, Meadow Lane, South Hykeham, Lincoln, Lincolnshire, LN6 9PF P
01522 696496 Ⓕ 01522 6980006
Ⓜ 07778 604401
Ⓔ ray@southhykeham.com
Ⓦ www.countrysales.co.uk
Est. 1979
Open By appointment
Sales General antiques
Frequency Monthly
Catalogues No

SPALDING

A P Sales
Contact Alan Porter
23a High Street, Spalding, Lincolnshire, PE11 1TX
☎ 01775 762795 Ⓕ 01775 712091
Ⓔ auctions@apsales.co.uk
Ⓦ www.apsales.co.uk
Est. 1983
Open Mon–Fri 9am–5pm or by appointment
Sales Monthly antiques and collectables sale 3rd Fri (phone for details), general antiques sales every Sat and Tues
Frequency Monthly
Catalogues Yes

R Longstaff & Co
Contact Mr J A Smith
5 New Road, Spalding, Lincolnshire, PE11 3YZ
☎ 01775 766766 Ⓕ 01775 762289
Ⓔ admin@longstaff.com
Ⓦ www.longstaff.com
Est. 1770
Open Mon–Fri 9am–6pm Sat 9am–3pm Sun 11am–3pm
Sales General antiques, house clearance
Frequency Bi-monthly
Catalogues No

Munton & Russell (ISVA)
Contact Mr James Smith
16 Sheep Market, Spalding, Lincolnshire, PE11 1BE
☎ 01775 722475 Ⓕ 01775 769958
Ⓦ www.muntonandrussell.co.uk
Est. 1964
Open Mon–Fri 9am–6pm
Sales General antiques
Frequency Periodic
Catalogues No

Penman Clockcare (BWCG)
Contact Mr M Strutt
Unit 4–5, Pied Calf Yard, Sheepmarket, Spalding, Lincolnshire, PE11 1BE
☎ 01775 714900 Ⓜ 07940 911167
Ⓔ strutt@clara.net
Ⓦ www.antique-clockrepairs.co.uk
Est. 1997 *Stock size* Medium
Stock Antique clocks, watches and jewellery
Open Mon–Sat 9am–5pm
Services Restorations, full repair service, home calls

Spalding Antiques
Contact Mr John Mumford
1 Abbey Path, Spalding, Lincolnshire, PE11 1AY
☎ 01775 713185
Est. 1987 *Stock size* Medium
Stock General antiques, clocks, watches
Open Mon–Sat 10am–5pm

STAMFORD

Robert Loomes Clock Restoration (BWCG MBHI)
Contact Mr R Loomes
3 St Leonards Street, Stamford, Lincolnshire, PE9 2HU
☎ 01780 481319
Ⓦ www.dialrestorer.co.uk
Est. 1987 *Stock size* Small
Stock Clocks
Open Mon–Fri 9am–5pm or by appointment
Services Restorations

Graham Pickett Antiques
Contact Mrs H Pickett
7 High Steet, St Martins, Stamford, Lincolnshire, PE9 2LF
☎ 01780 481064 Ⓜ 07710 936948
Ⓔ graham@pickettantiques.demon.co.uk
Ⓦ www.pickettantiques.demon.co.uk
Est. 1987 *Stock size* Medium
Stock English and French provincial furniture, beds
Open Mon–Sat 10am–5.30pm Sun 11.30am–4pm
Fairs Newark

St Georges Antiques
Contact Mr G Burns
1 St Georges Square, Stamford, Lincolnshire, PE9 2BN
☎ 01780 754117 Ⓜ 07779 528713
Est. 1974 *Stock size* Large
Stock General antiques, furniture
Trade only Yes
Open Mon–Fri 9am–1pm 2–4.30pm

St Martins Antique Centre
Contact Mr P Light
23a High Street, St Martins, Stamford, Lincolnshire, PE9 2LF
☎ 01780 481158 Ⓕ 01780 481158
Ⓔ peter@st-martins-antiques.co.uk
Ⓦ www.st-martins-antiques.co.uk
Est. 1992 *Stock size* Large
No. of dealers 58
Stock General antiques, collectables, objets d'art, 20thC items
Open Mon–Sat 10am–5pm Sun 10.30am–5pm
Services Restorations, shipping

St Mary's Books & Prints
Contact Mr Tyers
9 St Mary's Hill, Stamford, Lincolnshire, PE9 2DP
☎ 01780 763033 Ⓕ 01780 763033
Ⓔ info@stmarysbookscom
Ⓦ www.stmarysbooks.com
Est. 1971 *Stock size* Large
Stock Antiquarian, rare and second-hand books, Wisden's Cricket Almanac a speciality
Open Mon–Sun 8am–6.30pm
Services Valuations, restorations and book search

St Paul's Street Bookshop (PBFA)
Contact Mr J Blessett
7 St Paul's Street, Stamford, Lincolnshire, PE9 2BE
☎ 01780 482748/343175
Ⓕ 01778 38053
Ⓔ jimblessett@aol.com
Est. 1978 *Stock size* Medium
Stock Antiquarian, rare and second-hand books, specializing in motoring books
Open Mon–Sat 10am–5pm closed Wed
Services Valuations

Staniland Booksellers (PBFA)
Contact Mr B J Valentine-Ketchum
4–5 St Georges Street, Stamford, Lincolnshire, PE9 2BJ
☎ 01780 755800 Ⓕ 01780 755800
Ⓔ stanilandbooksellers@btinternet.com
Est. 1972 *Stock size* Large
Stock Antiquarian, library sets and bindings, rare and second-hand scholarly books, architecture, applied art, art, philosophy, music history, literature, natural history
Open Mon–Sat 10am–1pm 2–5pm

Fairs London Book Fairs
Services Valuations, probate and insurance valuations

Andrew Thomas
Contact Mr A Thomas
Old Granary, 10 North Street, Stamford, Lincolnshire, PE9 1EH P
☎ 01780 762236 F 01780 762236
Est. 1969 ***Stock size*** Large
Stock General antiques and antique painted furniture
Open Mon–Sat 9am–6pm

Key to Symbols

⊞	=	Dealer
⌂	=	Antiques Centre
⚒	=	Auction House
✉	=	Address
P	=	Parking
☎	=	Telephone No.
M	=	Mobile tel No.
F	=	Fax No.
E	=	E-mail address
W	=	Website address

Undercover Books
Contact Mr T Dobson
30 Scotgate, Stamford, Lincolnshire, PE9 2YQ P
☎ 01780 480989 F 01780 763963
E undercoverbooks@btinternet.com
W www.ukbookworld.com/members/undercover
Est. 1989 ***Stock size*** Large
Stock Antiquarian, rare and second-hand books, law enforcement a speciality
Open Tues–Sat 10am–5pm

Vaughan Antiques (LAPADA)
Contact Mr Barry Vaughan
45 Broad Street, Stamford, Lincolnshire, PE9 1PX P
☎ 01780 765888 F 01778 342053
M 07712 657414
E vaughanantiques@aol.com
Est. 1994 ***Stock size*** Large
Stock English furniture, clocks, decorative items, 17th–19thC furniture a speciality
Open Mon–Sat 10am–5pm
Fairs NEC, LAPADA

STICKNEY

B & B Antiques
Main Road, Stickney, Boston, Lincolnshire, PE22 8AD P
☎ 01205 480204
Stock General antiques
Open By appointment

SUTTON BRIDGE

Old Barn Antiques
Contact Mr Steve Jackson
48–50 Bridge Road, Sutton Bridge, Spalding, Lincolnshire, PE12 9UA P
☎ 01406 359123/350435 (warehouse) F 01406 359158
M 07956 677228
E oldbarnants@aol.com
Est. 1984 ***Stock size*** Large
Stock Victorian, Edwardian and 1920s furniture
Trade only Yes
Open Mon–Fri 9am–5pm Sat 10am–5pm Sun 11am–4pm
Fairs Newark
Services Containers packed

Old Barn Antiques
Contact Mr S Jackson
220 New Road, Sutton Bridge, Spalding, Lincolnshire, PE12 9QE P
☎ 01406 359123/350435 (warehouse) F 01406 359158
M 07956 677228
E oldbarnants@aol.com
Est. 1983 ***Stock size*** Large
Stock Victorian, Edwardian and 1920s furniture
Open Mon–Fri 8.30am–5.30pm and by appointment
Fairs Newark
Services Containers packed

SWINDERBY

Graham the Hat
Contact Graham Rodwell
Newark Road, Swinderby, Lincolnshire, LN6 9HN
☎ 01493 650217 F 01493 650217
M 07899 892337
E graham@grahamthehat.com
W www.grahamthehat.com
Est. 1997 ***Stock size*** Large
Stock Collectables
Open By appointment
Fairs Swinderby, Ardingly
Services Trade prices on request

TATTERSHALL

Wayside Antiques
Contact Mr G Ball
10 Market Place, Tattershall, Lincolnshire, LN4 4LQ P
☎ 01526 342436
Est. 1972 ***Stock size*** Medium
Stock General antiques
Open By appointment

WAINFLEET

Ann-Tiques
Contact Mrs M Bark
40 High Street, Wainfleet, Lincolnshire, PE24 43H P
☎ 01754 880770
Est. 1981 ***Stock size*** Medium
Stock General antiques
Open Tues–Sat 10am–12.30pm 1.30–4pm closed Thurs
Fairs Swinderby
Services Repair of clocks and jewellery

Naylor's Auctions (RICS, ISVA, NAEA,)
Contact Mr Ian Naylor
20 St Johns Street, Wainfleet, Skegness, Lincolnshire, PE24 4DJ P
☎ 01754 881210 F 01754 881210
M 07989 372671
E raymondphillips@oden.org.uk
Est. 1994
Open By appointment
Sales General antiques, weekly, monthly, periodic
Frequency Weekly
Catalogues No

WALESBY

Lincolnshire Antiques and Fine Art
Contact Mr N J Rhodes
1 White House, Walesby, Market Rasen, Lincolnshire, LN8 3UW P
☎ 01673 838278 M 07950 271898

Est. 1979
Stock Quality 17th–19thC oil paintings and furniture
Open By appointment only

WOODHALL SPA

M & J Antiques
Contact Mr J Goodyear
Tattershall Road, Woodhall Spa, Lincolnshire, LN10 6QJ
☎ 01526 352140
Stock General antiques
Open Flexible

Underwood Hall Antiques
Contact G Underwood
5 The Broadway, Woodhall Spa, Lincolnshire, LN10 6ST P
☎ 01526 353815
Est. 1974 *Stock size* Medium
Stock Small furniture, 19th–20thC pottery, porcelain, silver, jewellery, postcards
Open Mon–Sat 10.30am–4.30pm Sun 1–4pm or by appointment
Fairs Newark
Services Valuations

VOC Antiques (LAPADA)
Contact David Leyland
27 Witham Road, Woodhall Spa, Lincolnshire, LN10 6RW P
☎ 01526 352753 F 01526 352753
E djleyland@tinyworld.co.uk
Est. 1975 *Stock size* Medium
Stock Georgian–Victorian furniture, brass, copper, general antiques
Open Mon–Sat 9.30am–5.30pm Sun 2–5pm
Services Valuations, restorations

CO DURHAM

BARNARD CASTLE

Edward Barrington-Doulby
Contact Mike or Fiona
23 The Bank, Barnard Castle, Co Durham, DL12 8PH P
☎ 01833 630500 Ⓜ 07817 287204
Est. 1994 *Stock size* Medium
Stock Furniture, smalls, ironmongery, kitchenware
Open Tues–Sat 11am–5pm Sun 1–5pm

James Hardy Antiques Ltd
Contact Alan Hardy or Amanda Longstaff
12 The Bank, Barnard Castle, Co Durham, DL12 8PQ P
☎ 01833 695135 Ⓕ 01833 695135
Ⓜ 07710 162003
Ⓔ alan@jameshardyantiques.co.uk
Ⓦ www.jameshardyantiques.co.uk
Est. 1993
Stock 18th–19thC furniture, silver, porcelain, metalware
Open 10am–5pm closed Thurs Sun
Fairs Harrogate
Services Restorations of silver and furniture

Kingsley & Co
Contact David Harper
Springwood Cottage, Barnard Castle, Co Durham, DL12 9DD P
☎ 01833 650551 Ⓕ 01833 650551
Ⓜ 07711 639035
Ⓔ kingsleyandco@btopenworld.com
Ⓦ www.kingsleyantiques.co.uk
Est. 2000 *Stock size* Medium
Stock Furniture, smalls, Asian works of art
Open Mon–Sat 10.30am–5.30pm
Services Valuations, restorations, upholstery, renovation

Robson's Antiques
Contact Mr or Mrs Robson
36 The Bank, Barnard Castle, Co Durham, DL12 8PN P
☎ 01833 690157 Ⓕ 01833 638700
Ⓜ 07977 146584
Ⓔ dale.hunter.robson@virgin.net
Ⓦ www.robsonsantiques.co.uk
Est. 1975 *Stock size* Large
Stock Fireplaces, Durham quilts, glass, silver, cutlery
Open Mon–Fri 10am–5.30pm Sat 10am–6pm Sun 1.30–5pm
Fairs Birmingham Glass Fair, Newark, Manchester Textile Fair, NEC
Services Fireplace restoration and fitting

BISHOP AUCKLAND

Eden House Antiques
Contact Chris Metcalfe
10 Staindrop Road, West Auckland, Bishop Auckland, Co Durham, DL14 9JX P
☎ 01388 833013
Ⓔ chrismetcalfe@aol.com
Ⓦ www.antiques.co.uk
Est. 1977 *Stock size* Medium
Stock Furniture, clocks, china, pottery
Open Mon–Sun 10am–6pm
Services Valuations, restorations

G H Edkins and Son
Contact Denis Edkins
Auckland Auction Rooms, 58 Kingsway, Bishop Auckland, Co Durham, DL14 7JF P
☎ 01388 603095 Ⓕ 01388 661239
Ⓜ 07762 150932
Est. 1907
Open Mon–Thurs 9.30am–4.30pm Fri 9.30am–4pm
Sales General antiques household sale every Thurs, viewing Wed 9.30am–noon 2–5pm
Frequency Fortnightly
Catalogues No

Something Different
Contact Mr Peter Reeves or Mr Melvin Holmes
34a Maude Terrace, St Helen Auckland, Bishop Auckland, Co Durham, DL14 9BD P
☎ 01388 664366 Ⓜ 07718 391880
Ⓔ melh@bishopauck.freeserve.co.uk
Est. 1980 *Stock size* Large
Stock Memorabilia, militaria, furniture, clocks, collectables, silver, lights, decorative items, carpets, rugs, Continental antiques
Open Mon–Sat 9.30am–5.30pm Sun 10am–5pm
Services Valuations, clock restorations, delivery

CONSETT

Harry Raine
Contact Mr N C Raine
Kelvinside House, 91 Villa Real Road, Consett, Co Durham, DH8 6BL
☎ 01207 503935 Ⓜ 07758 838328
Est. 1965 *Stock size* Medium
Stock General antiques
Trade only Yes
Open By appointment only

Westend Antiques & Jewellery
Contact Peter Ray
63 Middle Street, Consett, Co Durham, DH8 5QG
☎ 01207 582228 Ⓕ 01207 582228
Ⓜ 07778 288096
Ⓔ peterray@westendantiques.freeserve.co.uk
Est. 1996 *Stock size* Large
Stock General antiques, jewellery, Roman, medieval artefacts, bric-a-brac
Open Mon–Sat 9am–5pm
Fairs Newark
Services Valuations, restorations, clock, watch and pottery repairs,

DARLINGTON

Collectables Antiques
Contact Mr Ken Bradley
154 Gladstone Street, Darlington, Co Durham, DL3 6LD
☎ 01325 351195 Ⓜ 07968 941588
Est. 1980 *Stock size* Small
Stock Furniture, paintings, architectural items, objets d'art
Open Mon–Sat 10am–5pm
Fairs Ardingly, Swinderby
Services Valuations

Alan Ramsey Antiques (LAPADA)
Contact Mr Alan Ramsey
Dudley Road, Darlington, Co Durham, DL1 4GG
☎ 01325 361679/01642 711311
Ⓕ 01325 469739 Ⓜ 07702 523246
Est. 1970 *Stock size* Large
Stock Georgian–Edwardian furniture, clocks
Open Mon–Fri 9.30am–4pm or by appointment

Tango Curios
3a Houndgate, Darlington, Co Durham, DL1 5RL
☎ 01325 465768
Ⓜ 07977 979770
Est. 1986 *Stock size* Large
Stock 20thC Decorative Arts, glass, ceramics, metalware, pictures
Open Mon 10am–1pm 2–5pm Fri 10am–1pm 2–5pm Sat 10am–5pm
Fairs Antiques for Everyone, Loughborough Art Deco Antiques Fair
Services Valuations

DURHAM

Finley's Finds
Contact Mr B Finley
23 Flambard Road, Durham, Co Durham, DH1 5HY
☎ 0191 384 1643
Est. 1995
Stock Furniture, china, jewellery
Open Mon–Fri 9am–5pm
Fairs Newark, Swinderby
Services Valuations, house clearance

Old & Gold
Contact Pam Tracey
88 Claypath, Durham, Co Durham, DH1 1LG
☎ 0191 386 0728 Ⓜ 07831 362252
Ⓔ pampaul@traceyppt.freeserve.co.uk
Est. 1989 *Stock size* Medium
Stock General antiques
Open Mon–Fri 10am–4.30pm Sat 10am–2pm closed Wed
Fairs Newark
Services Jewellery repairs

MIDDLETON IN TEESDALE

Brown's Antiques Collectables
Contact JR or V Brown
13 Chapel Row, Middleton in Teesdale, Co Durham, DL12 0SN
☎ 01833 640276
Ⓔ antiques@13chapelrow.freeserve.co.uk
Ⓦ www.browns-antiques.co.uk
Est. 1991 *Stock size* Medium
Stock Antique furniture, ceramics, metalware, kitchenware
Open Mon–Sat 10am–5pm

NORTHUMBERLAND

ALNWICK

Barter Books
Contact Stuart Manley
Alnwick Station, Alnwick, Northumberland, NE66 2NP
☎ 01665 604888 Ⓕ 01665 604444
Ⓔ bb@barterbooks.co.uk
Ⓦ www.barterbooks.co.uk
Est. 1991 *Stock size* Large
Stock Antiquarian and second-hand books, records, CDs, videos
Open Summer Mon–Sun 9am–7pm winter Mon–Sun 9am–5pm Thurs 9am–7pm
Services Book search, valuations

John Smith of Alnwick Ltd
Contact Mr P Smith
West Cawledge Park Gallery, Alnwick, Northumberland, NE66 2HJ
☎ 01665 604363
Est. 1972 *Stock size* Medium
Stock Country and general antiques, rugs, pictures, furniture
Open Mon–Sun 9am–5pm

Tamblyn Antiques
Contact Professor Hirst
12 Bondgate Without, Alnwick, Northumberland, NE66 1PP
☎ 01665 603024
Ⓔ profbehirst@tamblyn.freeserve.co.uk
Est. 1981 *Stock size* Medium
Stock Small period furniture, ceramics, Finnish, Swedish and Dutch glass
Open Mon–Sat 9.30am–4.30pm
Services Valuations

BERWICK-UPON-TWEED

Leslies Mount Road Auction Galleries
Contact Miss A Watson
Mount Road, Tweedmouth, Berwick-upon-Tweed, Northumberland, TD15 2BA
☎ 01289 304635 Ⓕ 01289 304635
Ⓔ auctionhouse@rocketmail.com
Est. 1995
Open Mon–Fri 10am–5pm
Sales General antiques auction monthly Mon 10.30am, viewing Sat 11.30am–6pm Sun 1–5pm Mon 9.30–10.30am
Frequency Monthly
Catalogues Yes

James E McDougall
Contact James E McDougall MRICS

✉ **St Duthus,**
6 Palace Street East,
Berwick-upon-Tweed,
Northumberland, TD15 1HT Ⓟ
☎ 01289 330791
ⓔ james.mcdougall@caucasian-rugs.co.uk
ⓦ www.caucasian-rugs.co.uk
Est. 1989 *Stock size* Small
Stock Antique carpets, rugs
Open By appointment
Services Valuations

CHATTON

Jim Railton
Contact Jim Railton
✉ **Nursery House,**
Chatton, Alnwick,
Northumberland, NE66 5PY Ⓟ
☎ 01668 215323 ⓕ 01668 215400
ⓜ 07774 241111
ⓔ jim@jimrailton.com
ⓦ www.jimrailton.com
Est. 1993
Open Mon–Sat 9am–5pm or by appointment
Sales General antiques sale, specializing in country house sales at historic properties
Frequency 4 per annum
Catalogues Yes

CORBRIDGE

Judith Michael
Contact Gillian Anderson or Judith Troldahl
✉ **20a Watling Street,**
Corbridge, Northumberland,
NE45 5AH Ⓟ
☎ 01434 633165 ⓕ 01434 633165
ⓔ jma@supanet.com
ⓦ www.judithmichael.co.uk
Est. 1989 *Stock size* Medium
Stock General antiques, decorative items, jewellery, small furniture, glass, china, gardening section
Open Tues–Sat 10am–5pm
Sun noon–4pm
Services Interior design

HEXHAM

Boadens Antiques
Contact Christopher Boaden
✉ **29/30 Market Place,**
Hexham, Northumberland,
NE46 3PB Ⓟ
☎ 01434 603187 ⓕ 01434 603474
ⓔ antiques@boadens.fsnet.co.uk
Est. 1948 *Stock size* Large
Stock General antiques, furniture, silver, china, jewellery
Open Mon–Sat 9am–5pm
Services Valuations

Hedley's of Hexham
Contact Mrs P Torday
✉ **3 St Mary's Chare, Hexham,**
Northumberland, NE46 1NQ Ⓟ
☎ 01434 602317
ⓔ hedley@torday.fsbusiness.co.uk
Est. 1819 *Stock size* Medium
Stock General antiques, furniture, collectables, china, clocks, Moorcroft
Open Mon 10am–4pm
Tues–Sat 9.30am–5pm
Services Restorations

Hencotes Books and Prints (PBFA)
Contact Mrs Penny Pearce
✉ **8 Hencotes, Hexham,**
Northumberland, NE46 2EJ Ⓟ
☎ 01434 605971
ⓔ hencotebooks@btinternet.com
Est. 1992 *Stock size* Medium
Stock Antiquarian and second-hand books, specializing in local history, literature, children's books, gardening, cookery
Open Mon–Sat 10.30am–5pm closed Thurs
Fairs Local PBFA, Durham, Newcastle
Services Booksearch

Hexham and Northern Mart
Contact Mr Brian Rogerson
✉ **Mart Office,**
Tyne Green, Hexham,
Northumberland, NE46 3SG Ⓟ
☎ 01434 605444/01669 620392 (Rothbury)
ⓔ furniture@hexhammart.co.uk
ⓦ www.hexhammart.co.uk
Est. 1850
Open Mon–Fri 9am–5pm
Sales House clearances, antiques sales (held at Rothbury), viewing 2 days prior to sale
Frequency Every 2 or 3 months
Catalogues No

Hexham Antiques
Contact John and Dorothy Latham
✉ **Unit 10,**
Acomb Industrial Estate,
Acomb, Hexham,
Northumberland, NE46 4SA
☎ 01434 603851
Est. 1978 *Stock size* Large
Stock General antiques, collectables, pictures, bric-a-brac
Open Mon Tues Sat 10.30am–4pm or by appointment
Fairs Hexham, Carlisle
Services Picture framing, valuations, house clearance

O'Neil's Old Warehouse Antiques
Contact Neil Perry
✉ **45 Hallstile Bank,**
Hexham, Northumberland,
NE46 3PQ Ⓟ
☎ 01434 600510
Est. 1988 *Stock size* Large
Stock Georgian, Victorian, pine and country furniture
Open Mon–Fri 10am–4pm
Sat 9am–5pm
Fairs Newark

Pine Workshop (ADA)
Contact John Askell
✉ **28 Priestpopple,**
Hexham, Northumberland,
NE46 1PQ Ⓟ
☎ 01434 601121
Est. 1987 *Stock size* Medium
Stock Antique pine and oak
Open Mon–Sat 9am–5pm

Priestpopple Books
Contact Mr J B Patterson
✉ **9B Priestpopple,**
Hexham,
Northumberland, NE46 1PF
☎ 01434 607773
ⓔ priestpopple.books@tinyworld.co.uk
Est. 1998 *Stock size* Large
Stock Antiquarian books, general antiques, militaria, music, entertainment, art
Open Mon–Sat 9am–5pm
Services Valuations, restorations

MORPETH

Grove Antiques
Contact Lorna Gates
✉ **Green Tiles,**
Main Street, Red Row, Morpeth,
Northumberland,
NE61 5AD
☎ 01670 760330 ⓜ 07710 342965
ⓔ northumbrian@btinternet.com
Est. 1986 *Stock size* Medium
Stock General antiques
Trade only Yes
Open By appointment
Fairs International Antique and Collectables Fair RAF Swinderby

Louis Johnson
Contact John Hayes
63 Bridge Street, Morpeth, Northumberland, NE61 1PQ
01670 513025 01670 503267
lj@lj-estates.fsbusiness.co.uk
Est. 1955
Open Mon–Fri 9am–5pm
Sales General antiques, cars and motorcycles on Sat, viewing 2 days prior to sale. Advisable to call for details
Frequency Monthly
Catalogues Yes

Pottery Bank Antiques
Contact Mr Everitt
43 Bullers Green, Morpeth, Northumberland, NE61 1DF
01670 516160
apope@morpethnet.co.uk
www.morpethnet.co.uk
Est. 1977 *Stock size* Medium
Stock General antiques, furniture, silver
Open Mon–Sat 11.30am–5.30pm or by appointment

ROTHBURY

Golfark International
Contact Michael Arkle
5 Tollgate Crescent, Rothbury, Northumberland, NE65 7RE
01669 620487 01669 620487
07710 693860
michael@golfark.freeserve.co.uk
www.vsne16742pwp.blueyonder.com
Est. 1997 *Stock size* Small
Stock Old golf clubs, bags and balls, sporting antiques, golfing memorabilia
Open By appointment

SCREMERSTON

Woodside Reclamation (SALVO)
Contact Keith Allan
Woodside, Scremerston, Berwick-upon-Tweed, Northumberland, TD15 2SY
01289 331211/302658
01289 330274
woodside@bridgestudios.freeserve.co.uk
www.redbaths.co.uk
Est. 1990 *Stock size* Medium
Stock Fireplaces, antique baths, bathroom ware, doors, timber, beams, flooring
Open Tues–Sat 9am–5pm
Services Furniture and door stripping, restoration

WOOLER

Hamish Dunn Antiques
Contact Mr Dunn
17 High Street, Wooler, Northumberland, NE71 6BU
01668 281341 01668 281341
07940 530123
hamishdunn@wooler20.freeserve.co.uk
Est. 1986 *Stock size* Medium
Stock General antiques, second-hand and antiquarian books
Open Mon–Sat 9am–4.30pm

James Miller (LAPADA)
Contact James Miller
1–5 Church Street, Wooler, Northumberland, NE71 6BZ
01668 281500 01668 282383
www.millersantiquesofwooler.com
Est. 1947 *Stock size* Large
Stock Georgian and Victorian furniture
Open Mon–Fri 9.30am–5pm

TYNE AND WEAR

EAST BOLDEN

Bolden Auction Galleries
Contact Mr Hodges
Front Street, East Bolden, Tyne and Wear, NE36 0SJ
0191 537 2630 0191 536 3875
Est. 1981
Sales General antiques sales Wed 10am, viewing Tues 2–6pm, 4 antiques sales annually, 2 collectors' toy and 20thC modern design sales annually
Frequency Weekly
Catalogues Yes

GATESHEAD

Mulroys Antiques
Contact Miss J Mulroy
24 The Boulevard, Metro Centre, Gateshead, Tyne and Wear, NE11 9YL
0191 461 1211 0191 461 1211
Est. 1959 *Stock size* Large
Stock General antiques and period jewellery
Open Mon–Fri 10am–8pm Thurs 10am–9pm Sat 9am–7pm Sun 11am–5pm
Fairs Newark, Swinderby
Services Valuations, restorations

GOSFORTH

Anna Harrison Antiques (LAPADA)
Contact Mr or Mrs Harrison
Harewood House, 49 Great North Road, Gosforth, Newcastle-upon-Tyne, Tyne and Wear, NE3 2DG
0191 284 3202 0191 284 3202
annaharrisonantiques@ukgateway.net
Est. 1976 *Stock size* Large
Stock Early porcelain, Georgian–Edwardian furniture, dining and lounge furniture
Open Mon–Fri 8am–5pm Sat 10am–5pm or by appointment
Fairs Galloways Fairs, Bailey Fairs
Services Restorations

NEWCASTLE-UPON-TYNE

Acquisitions Antique & Handmade Furniture
Contact Mr J Maughan
57b Sanderson Road, Newcastle-upon-Tyne, Tyne and Wear, NE2 2DZ
0191 281 6690 0191 281 6690
07930 558823
acqpine@aol.com
Est. 1979 *Stock size* Medium
Stock Antique furniture, handmade furniture to order
Open Mon–Fri 9.30am–4pm Sat 10am–2pm
Services Restorations

Aladdins Architectural Antiques (SALVO)
Contact Mr D Crowley
626 Welbeck Road, Walker, Newcastle-upon-Tyne, Tyne and Wear, NE6 1DJ
0191 262 7373 07762 527640
Est. 1976 *Stock size* Large
Stock General antiques
Open Mon–Sat 10am–6pm
Services Valuations, restorations

Anderson & Garland (SOFAA)
Contact Mr A McCoull
Marlborough House, Marlborough Crescent, Newcastle-upon-Tyne, Tyne and Wear, NE1 4EE
0191 232 6278 0191 261 8665
garland@compuserve.com
www.auction-net.co.uk
Est. 1840

Open Mon–Fri 9am–5.30pm
Sales Fine art sales every 3 months, general antiques sales fortnightly
Frequency Fortnightly
Catalogues Yes

Antique Centre
Contact Mr C Parkin
2nd Floor, 142 Northumberland Street, Newcastle-upon-Tyne, Tyne and Wear, NE1 7DG
0191 232 9832
timeantiques@zoom.co.uk
www.timeantiques.co.uk
Est. 1983 ***Stock size*** Large
No. of dealers 13
Stock General antiques
Open Mon–Sat 10am–5pm
Services Tea rooms, jewellery and clock repairs

Antiques at H & S Collectables
Contact Mrs Shorrick
Little Theatre Antiques Centre, Fern Avenue, Jesmond, Newcastle-upon-Tyne, Tyne and Wear, NE3 2RA
0191 284 6626
Est. 1987 ***Stock size*** Large
Stock General antiques, curios, Victoriana, silver, Tyneside Maling pottery 1817–1963
Open Mon–Sat 10am–5.30pm
Fairs Colin Caygill
Services Valuations, restorations

Bonhams
30–32 Grey Street, Newcastle-upon-Tyne, Tyne and Wear, NE1 6AE
0191 233 9930 0191 233 9933
www.bonhams.com
Open Mon–Fri 9am–5pm

B J Coltman Antiques
Contact B J Coltman
80 Meldon Terrace, Heaton, Newcastle-upon-Tyne, Tyne and Wear, NE6 5XP
0191 224 5209
inquiries@coltmanantiques.co.uk
www.coltmanantiques.co.uk
Est. 1993 ***Stock size*** Medium
Stock General antiques
Open Mon–Fri 9am–5pm
Fairs Newark
Services Restorations

Corbitt's (ASDA, APS, BNTA)
Contact Mr D McMonaghe
5 Mosley Street, Newcastle-upon-Tyne, Tyne and Wear, NE1 1YE
0191 2327268 0191 2614130
info@corbitts.com
www.corbitts.com
Est. 1964 ***Stock size*** Medium
Stock Antiques, coins, stamps, medals, ephemera
Open Mon–Fri 9am–5pm Sat 9.30am–4pm
Services Valuations

Corbitt's
Contact Mr D McMonaghe
5 Mosley Street, Newcastle-upon-Tyne, Tyne and Wear, NE1 1YE
0191 2327268 0191 2614130
info@corbitts.com
www.corbitts.com
Est. 1964
Open Mon–Fri 9am–5pm
Sales Antique coins, medals, 3 per year. Stamps, history 4 per year. Cigarette cards, ephemera 2 per year
Catalogues Yes

Cradlewell Antiques
Contact Mr S Bardy
4 Churchill Gardens, Jesmond, Newcastle-upon-Tyne, Tyne and Wear, NE2 1HB
0191 212 1500
www.cradlewell.co.uk
Est. 1979 ***Stock size*** Medium
Stock General antiques, 20thC design classics
Open Thurs–Sat 11am–5pm Sun noon–4pm
Fairs Newark

Dog Leap Antiques
Contact Mr N MacDonald
61 The Side, Newcastle-upon-Tyne, Tyne and Wear, NE1 3JE
0191 232 7269
Est. 1969 ***Stock size*** Medium
Stock Antiquarian prints and reproductions
Open Mon–Fri 9.15am–5pm Sat 9am–1pm

Owen Humble Antiques (LAPADA)
Contact Mr M Humble
11–12 Clayton Road, Jesmond, Newcastle-upon-Tyne, Tyne and Wear, NE2 4RP
0191 281 4602 0191 281 9076
07836 261107
antiques@owenhumble.com
Est. 1959 ***Stock size*** Large
Stock General antiques
Open Mon–Sat 9am–5pm or by appointment
Fairs LAPADA
Services Valuations, restorations, trade warehouse

Intercoin
Contact Mr Brian
103 Clayton Street, Newcastle-upon-Tyne, Tyne and Wear, NE1 5PZ
0191 232 2064
Est. 1964 ***Stock size*** Large
Stock Coins, medals, bank notes
Open Mon–Sat 9.30am–4.30pm
Services Valuations

Little Theatre Antiques Centre
Contact Mr J Bell
Fern Avenue, Jesmond, Newcastle-upon-Tyne, Tyne and Wear, NE2 2RA
0191 2094321
john@bennett-bell.demon.co.uk
www.bennett-bell.demon.co.uk
Est. 1993 ***Stock size*** Large
No. of dealers 13
Stock General antiques
Open Mon–Sat 10am–5.30pm

Thomas N Miller Auctioneers
Contact Mr A Scott
Algernon Road, Byker, Newcastle-upon-Tyne, Tyne and Wear, NE6 2UZ
0191 265 8080 0191 265 5050
millerlot1@aol.com
Est. 1902
Open Mon–Fri 8.30am–5pm
Sales General antiques, later furniture, viewing Sun 10am–noon Mon Tues 9.30am–4pm
Frequency Weekly
Catalogues Yes

Oxfam Books
Contact Mr A Chadwin
7 St Mary's Place, Newcastle-Upon-Tyne, Tyne and Wear, NE1 87PG
0191 232 2476
Est. 2000 ***Stock size*** Medium

Stock General and antiquarian books
Open Mon–Sat 9.30am–5.30pm
Services Book search

Phoenix Design & Antiques
Contact Mrs M Ryle
The Old Monastery, Blackfriars, Newcastle-upon-Tyne, Tyne and Wear, NE1 4XN
0191 230 3804
Est. 1984 *Stock size* Small
Stock General antiques
Open Mon–Fri 11.30am–4.30pm Sat 10.30am–5pm

Shiners Snobs Knobs (SALVO)
Contact Mr Barry Lawson
81 Fern Avenue, Jesmond, Newcastle-Upon-Tyne, Tyne and Wear, NE2 2RA
0191 281 6474 0191 281 9041
07966 155350
Est. 1983 *Stock size* Large
Stock Internal fittings, antique doors and door furniture, fireplaces
Open Mon–Sat 10am–5pm
Services Polishing

Graham Smith Antiques (LAPADA)
Contact Mr Graham Smith
83 Fern Avenue, Jesmond, Newcastle-upon-Tyne, Tyne and Wear, NE2 2RA
0191 281 5065 0191 281 5072
gsmithantiques@aol.com
Est. 1973 *Stock size* Medium
Stock Furniture, clocks, smalls
Open Mon–Sat 10am–5pm

Frank Smith Maritime Aviation Books (PBFA)
Contact Alan Parker
100 Heaton Road, Newcastle-upon-Tyne, Tyne and Wear, NE6 5HL
0191 265 6333 0191 224 2620
books@franksmith.freeserve.co.uk
Est. 1981 *Stock size* Medium
Stock Antiquarian, rare and out-of-print books, maritime and aviation
Open Mon–Fri 10am–4pm Sat 10am–1pm
Fairs PBFA
Services Free monthly catalogues on maritime and aviation

Robert D Steedman (ABA)
Contact Mr David Steedman
9 Grey Street, Newcastle-upon-Tyne, Tyne and Wear, NE1 6EE
0191 2326561
Est. 1907 *Stock size* Medium
Stock Second-hand and antiquarian books
Open Mon–Fri 9am–5pm Sat 9am–12.30pm
Fairs Olympia, Edinburgh

Turnburrys Ltd (SALVO)
257 Jesmond Road, Newcastle-upon-Tyne, Tyne and Wear, NE2 1LB
0191 281 1770 0191 240 2569
info@turnburrys.co.uk
www.turnburrys.co.uk
Est. 1996 *Stock size* Medium
Stock Hardwood flooring, fireplaces, doors, radiators, mirrors, bespoke doors, etched and stained glass
Open Mon–Sat 9am–6pm Sun 11am–3pm
Services Valuations

NORTH SHIELDS

Chimney Pieces
Contact Mr T Chester
98a Howard Street, North Shields, Tyne and Wear, NE30 1NA
0191 2572118
www.chimneypieces.com
Est. 1985 *Stock size* Medium
Stock Antique chimney pieces, architectural antiques, fireplaces in marble and wood
Open Mon–Sat 10am–5pm
Fairs Newark
Services Restorations

The Clock Shop
Contact Mr G Ball
1a John Street, Cullercoates, North Shields, Tyne and Wear, NE30 4PL
0191 290 1212 07808 231306
Est. 1997 *Stock size* Medium
Stock General antiques
Open Mon–Sat 10am–5pm
Fairs Swinderby, Newark
Services Valuations, restorations, clock repairs

Keel Row Books
Contact Bob and Brenda Cook
11 Fenwick Terrace, Preston Road, North Shields, Tyne and Wear, NE29 0LU
0191 296 0664/287 3914
Est. 1980 *Stock size* Large
Stock General antiquarian books. Children's, military, mountaineering, local history, cinema a speciality
Open Mon–Sat 10.30am–5pm closed Wed

Tynemouth Architectural Salvage (SALVO)
Contact Mr Robin Archer
28 Tynemouth Road, North Shields, Tyne and Wear, NE30 4AA
0191 296 6070 0191 296 6097
robin@tynemoutharchitecturalsalvage.com
www.tynemoutharchitecturalsalvage.com
Stock size Large
Stock Architectural antiques
Open Mon–Fri 10am–6pm Sat 10am–5pm
Fairs Newark
Services Door stripping, bath restorations

The Curiosity Shop
Contact Mr G Davies
16 Frederick Street, South Shields, Tyne and Wear, NE33 5EA
0191 456 5560 0191 427 7597
07860 219949
glenda47@hotmail.com
Est. 1969 *Stock size* Medium
Stock General antiques, Royal Doulton
Open Mon–Sat 9am–5pm closed Wed
Fairs Newark
Services Valuations

SOUTH SHIELDS

De-Ja-Vu
Contact Mr J Atkinson
2 Imeary Street, South Shields, Tyne and Wear, NE33 4EG
0191 425 0031
Est. 1998 *Stock size* Small
Stock General antiques
Open Mon–Sat 10am–5pm

SUNDERLAND

Peter Smith Antiques (LAPADA)
Contact Mrs Smith
12–14 Borough Road, Sunderland, Tyne and Wear, SR1 1EP
☎ 0191 567 3537/514 0008
F 0191 514 2286 M 07802 273372
E petersmithantiques@btinternet.com
W www.petersmithantiques.co.uk
Est. 1968 ***Stock size*** Large
Stock General antiques
Open Mon–Fri 9.30am–4.30pm Sat 10am–1pm or by appointment
Services Valuations

TYNEMOUTH

Coast Antiques
Contact Mrs Dorothy Wadge or Mr Alex Beacham
10 Front Street, Tynemouth, Tyne and Wear, NE30 4RG
☎ 0191 296 0700 F 0191 296 0700
M 07977 780248
Est. 1989 ***Stock size*** Medium
Stock Victorian, Edwardian furniture and associated items
Open Mon–Sat 10.30am–4.30pm Sun noon–4pm or by appointment
Services Interest-free credit, free local delivery

Curio Corner
Contact Mrs S Welton
Units 5 & 6, Land of Green Ginger, Front Street, Tynemouth, North Shields, Tyne and Wear, NE30 4BP
☎ 0191 296 3316 F 0191 296 3319
M 07831 339906
W www.curiocorner.com.uk
Est. 1988 ***Stock size*** Large
Stock General antique furniture
Open Mon–Sat 11am–4.30pm
Fairs Newark
Services Restorations

Ian Sharp Antiques (LAPADA, CINOA)
Contact Mr Ian Sharp
23 Front Street, Tynemouth, North Shields, Tyne and Wear, NE30 4DX
☎ 0191 296 0656 F 0191 296 0656
M 07850 023689
E iansharp@sharpantiques.demon.co.uk
W www.sharpantiques.demon.co.uk
Est. 1988 ***Stock size*** Medium
Stock Georgian–Edwardian furniture, pottery
Open Mon–Sat 10am–1pm 1.30–5.30pm or by appointment
Fairs Newark

WHITLEY BAY

Bay Books
Contact Mr J Cairns
10A Norham Road, Whitley Bay, Tyne and Wear, NE16 2SB
☎ 0191 251 4448
Est. 1989 ***Stock size*** Medium
Stock Quality second-hand books, records, cassettes, CDs
Open Mon–Thurs 11am–4pm Fri Sat 11am–5pm
Fairs Tynemouth Station
Services Book search

Olivers Bookshop
Contact Mr John Oliver
48a Whitley Road, Whitley Bay, Tyne and Wear, NE26 2NF
☎ 0191 251 3552
Est. 1986 ***Stock size*** Medium
Stock Antiquarian, rare and second-hand books
Open Mon Thurs Fri Sat 11am–5pm
Fairs Tynemouth Book Fair

Treasure Chest Antiques
Contact Mr J Rain
2a–4 Norham Road, Whitley Bay, Tyne and Wear, NE26 2SB
☎ 0191 251 2052 M 07808 966611
Est. 1969 ***Stock size*** Medium
Stock General antiques
Open Mon–Sat 10.30am–4pm closed 1–2pm

NORTH WEST

CHESHIRE

ALDERLEY EDGE

⊞ Anthony Baker (LAPADA)
Contact Ms A Price
✉ **14 London Road, Alderley Edge, Cheshire, SK9 7JS** Ⓟ
☎ 01625 582674
Est. 1976 *Stock size* Medium
Stock Wide range of antique stock including 18th–19thC furniture, barometers and collectors' items
Open Tues–Sat 10am–5.30pm closed Wed

ALSAGER

⊞ Trash 'n' Treasure
Contact George G Ogden
✉ **48 Sandbach Road South, Alsager, Cheshire, ST7 2LP** Ⓟ
☎ 01270 873246/872972
Est. 1962 *Stock size* Medium
Stock Furniture, ceramics, pictures
Open Tues–Sat 10am–4pm closed Wed
Services Valuations

ALTRINCHAM

⊞ Abacus Books
Contact Mr C Lawton
✉ **24 Regent Road, Altrincham, Cheshire, WA14 1RP** Ⓟ
☎ 0161 928 5108
Est. 1979 *Stock size* Medium
Stock Antiquarian and second-hand books. Arts, gardening and crafts books specialities
Open Mon–Sat 10am–5pm
Services Valuations

⊞ Antique Fireplace Company Ltd
✉ **120 Manchester Road, Altrincham, Cheshire, WA14 4PY** Ⓟ
☎ 0161 929 6669 Ⓕ 0161 428 2212
Ⓔ sally@oldfireplaces.co.uk
Ⓦ www.oldfireplaces.co.uk
Stock size Large
Stock Victorian and Edwardian cast-iron fireplaces, oak, mahogany, pine, stone, slate, marble surrounds
Open Sat 10am–4.30pm
Services Shipping

Patrick Cheyne Auctions (FSVA)
Contact Mr P Cheyne
✉ **38 Hale Road, Altrincham, Cheshire, WA14 2EX** Ⓟ
☎ 0161 941 4879 Ⓕ 0161 941 4879
Est. 1982
Open Mon–Fri 10am–5.30pm
Sales Every 2 months Fri 10.30am, viewing Thurs 2–4.30pm 6–8pm Fri 9–10.30am. Held at St Peters Assembly Rooms, Hale
Frequency Every 2 months
Catalogues Yes

⊞ Church Street Antiques Ltd (LAPADA)
Contact Mr A Smalley
✉ **4–4a Old Market Place, Altrincham, Cheshire, WA14 4NP** Ⓟ
☎ 0161 929 5196 Ⓕ 0161 929 5196
Ⓜ 07768 318661
Ⓔ sales@churchstreetantiques.com
Ⓦ www.churchstreetantiques.com
Est. 1992 *Stock size* Large

Stock Fine Georgian and Victorian furniture, art, objets d'art, carpets, decorative items
Open Mon–Sat 10am–5pm Sun noon–4pm closed Tues
Fairs Baileys, Coopers
Services Valuations, restorations

Squires Antiques
Contact Mrs V Phillips
25 Regent Road, Altrincham, Cheshire, WA14 1RX
01161 928 0749 Ⓜ 07831 682229
Est. 1977 ***Stock size*** Large
Stock Silver, jewellery, porcelain, brass, copper, lighting, small fine furniture
Open Tues–Sat 10am–5pm closed Wed
Services Valuations

Village Farm Antiques
Contact Mr C Thomason
Village Farm, Station Road, Dunham Massey, Altrincham, Cheshire, WA14 5SA
0161 929 4468 Ⓜ 07977 139708
Ⓦ villlagefarmantiques.co.uk
Est. 1987 ***Stock size*** Large
Stock Wide range of stock including pine furniture, architectural antiques, fireplaces, chaise longues etc
Open Mon–Sun 9am–5pm
Fairs Newark, Swinderby
Services Wood stripping, upholstery

BARTON

Derek & Tina Rayment Antiques (BADA, LAPADA, CINOA)
Contact Derek or Tina Rayment
Orchard House, Barton, Farndon, Cheshire, SY14 7HT
01829 270429 Ⓕ 01829 270893
Ⓔ raymentantiques@aol.com
Ⓦ www.antique-barometers.com
Est. 1960 ***Stock size*** Large
Stock Antique barometers
Open By appointment
Fairs Olympia, Chelsea, LAPADA, NEC (Jan)
Services Restorations, repairs

BEESTON

Beeston Reclamations
Contact Mr D Malam
The Old Coal Yard, Whitchurch Road, Beeston, Tarporley, Cheshire, CW6 9NW
01829 260299 Ⓜ 07721 424400
Est. 1998 ***Stock size*** Large
Stock Garden statuary, bricks, slates, oak beams, pine beams, floor boards, York stone, fireplaces, block flooring
Open Mon–Sat 8am–5pm
Services Valuations, restorations

Wright-Manley
Contact Mr W T Witter
Beeston Castle Salerooms, Beeston Castle, Tarporley, Cheshire, CW6 9NZ
01829 262150 Ⓕ 01829 261829
Ⓔ wendymiller@wrightmanley.co.uk
Ⓦ www.wrightmanley.co.uk
Est. 1861
Open Mon–Fri 8.30am–5pm
Sales Victoriana 1st and 3rd Thurs of month 10.30am, viewing Wed 10am–6pm. Quarterly fine art sale (phone for details)
Frequency Fortnightly
Catalogues Yes

BELGRAVE

Antique Garden
Contact Maria Hopwood
Grosvenor Garden Centre, Wrexham Road, Belgrave, Chester, Cheshire, CH4 9EB
01244 629191 Ⓜ 07976 539990
Est. 1991 ***Stock size*** Medium
Stock Garden items
Open Mon–Sun 10am–4.30pm
Services Valuations, shipping

BOWDON

English Garden Antiques
Contact Bill Seddon
The White Cottage, Church Brow, Bowdon, Altrincham, Cheshire, WA14 2SF
0161 929 8081 Ⓕ 0161 928 0854
Ⓔ bill@english-garden-antiques.co.uk
Ⓦ www.english-garden-antiques.co.uk
Est. 1996 ***Stock size*** Large
Stock English garden antiques including stone troughs, sundials, bird baths, cast-iron urns, staddle stones, gargoyles
Open 10am–5pm confirm by phone
Services Valuations, restorations, repair

Richmond Antiques
Contact Mr J Freeman
The Hollies, Richmond Road, Bowdon, Altrincham, Cheshire, WA14 2TT
0161 928 1229 Ⓕ 0161 233 0431
Ⓜ 07720 416055
Ⓔ info@richmondantiques.com
Ⓦ www.richmondantiques.com
Est. 1993 ***Stock size*** Large
Stock Decorative furniture, chandeliers, mirrors including 19thC French and English
Open Tues–Sat noon–6pm or by appointment
Services Valuations, restorations

CHESTER

Adams Antiques of Chester (LAPADA)
Contact Mr B Adams
65 Watergate Row, Chester, Cheshire, CH1 2LE
01244 319421
Est. 1975 ***Stock size*** Medium
Stock 18th–19thC furniture, clocks, glass, 19th–early 20thC small silver, mechanical devices, lighting
Open Mon–Sat 10am–5pm
Services Valuations, restorations, export service

Aldersey Hall Ltd
Contact Anthony Wilding
Aldersey Hall, 47 Northgate Street, Chester, Cheshire, CH1 2HQ
01244 324885
Est. 1990 ***Stock size*** Medium
Stock General antiques
Open Mon–Sat 8.30am–5.45pm
Fairs Deco Fair Chester

Antique Scientific Instruments
Contact Charles Tomlinson
11 Blackfriars, Chester, Cheshire, CH1 2NU
01244 318395 Ⓕ 01244 318395
Ⓔ charles.tomlinson@lineone.net
Ⓦ www.lineone.net/~charles.tomlinson
Est. 1980
Stock Slide rules, calculators, early scientific instruments and drawing equipment
Open By appointment
Services Valuations

The Antique Shop
Contact Peter Thornber
40 Watergate Street, Chester, Cheshire, CH1 2LA

☎ 01244 316286
Est. 1987 *Stock size* Medium
Stock Small items, mainly brass, copper, pewter
Open Mon–Sat Sun from Easter to Christmas 10am–5.30pm
Services Metal repair, restoration, polishing

Ask Simon
Contact Mr S Cleveland
✉ **25 Christleton Road, Chester, Cheshire, CH3 5UF** P
☎ 01244 320704
M 07815 559431 *Stock size* Large
Stock Decorative antiques, domestic paraphernalia, sporting and farming items, pictures, collectables, furniture
Open Mon–Sat 10am–5pm
Fairs Newark, Ardingly

Bonhams
✉ **New House, 150 Christleton Road, Chester, Cheshire, CH3 5TD**
☎ 01244 313936 F 01244 340028
E chester@bonhams.com
W www.bonhams.com
Sales Chester Saleroom

Borg's Antiques
Contact Mr R Borg
✉ **14 and 26 Christleton Road, Chester, Cheshire, CH3 5UG** P
☎ 01244 400023 M 07939 227165
Est. 1991 *Stock size* Medium
Stock Silver, furniture, porcelain, Royal Doulton, small decorative items etc
Open Mon–Sat 10am–5.30pm Sun 11am–4pm
Fairs Swinderby, Newark

Bowstead Antiques (LAPADA)
Contact Olwyn Bowstead
✉ **59–61 Watergate Row South, Chester, Cheshire, CH1 2LE** P
☎ 01244 342300
Est. 1981 *Stock size* Medium
Stock 18th–19thC town and country furniture, oil paintings, metalware
Open Mon–Sat 10am–6pm
Fairs NEC
Services Valuations

Cestrian Antiques
Contact Mr Malcolm Tice
✉ **28 Watergate Street, Chester, Cheshire, CH1 2LA** P
☎ 01244 400444
Est. 1993 *Stock size* Large
Stock Small items of furniture, oak coffers, boxes, silver, glass, ceramics, longcase clocks, mantel clocks, wall clocks, pictures, lighting
Open Mon–Sat 10am–5.30pm or by appointment Sun eves
Services Valuations

Chester Antique Furniture Cave
Contact Mrs L Jones or G A Hadley
✉ **Congregational Church, 97a Christleton Road, Boughton, Chester, Cheshire, CH3 5UQ** P
☎ 01244 314798 F 01829 782330
M 07710 622749
E www.netcentral.co.uk/chester/cave
Est. 1984 *Stock size* Large
Stock Furniture of all periods and types including large dining tables, desks, bureaux, chairs etc
Open Mon–Sat 10am–5pm

D K R Refurbishers
Contact Mr D Wisinger
✉ **26b High Street, Saltney, Chester, Cheshire, CH4 8SE** P
☎ 01244 680290
Est. 1984 *Stock size* Large
Stock Original pine and oak furniture
Open Mon–Sat 10am–4.30pm Sun 2–4pm
Services Valuations, restorations

Dollectable
Contact Mo Harding
✉ **53 Lower Bridge Street, Chester, Cheshire, CH1 1RS**
☎ 01244 344888/679195
F 01244 679469
Est. 1972 *Stock size* Large
Stock Antique dolls
Open Fri noon–5pm Sat 10am–5pm
Fairs Kensington, Chelsea, Newark
Services Valuations, restorations

Farmhouse Antiques
Contact Ms K Appleby
✉ **23 Christleton Road, Boughton, Chester, Cheshire, CH3 5UF** P
☎ 01244 322478 F 01244 322478
M 07768 645818
Est. 1973 *Stock size* Large
Stock Wide range of antiques, country furniture, collectables, longcase clocks and other clocks
Open Mon–Sat 9am–5pm

Halls Fine Art (Chester) Ltd (ARVA)
Contact Mr A Byrne
✉ **Booth Mansion, 30 Watergate Street, Chester, Cheshire, CH1 2LA** P
☎ 01244 312300 F 01244 312112
E fineart@halls-auctioneers.ltd.uk
W www.halls-auctioneers.ltd.uk
Est. 1999
Open Mon–Fri 9am–5.30pm
Sales General sales last of every month Wed 11am, viewing day prior noon–7pm. Quarterly antiques sales Fri 11am, viewing Mon Tues 10am–5pm. Bi-annual wine sales and collectors' models, toys, scientific instruments and juvenilia sales three times a year
Frequency Monthly
Catalogues Yes

Uri Jacobi Oriental Carpet Gallery (LAPADA)
Contact Uri Jacobi
✉ **55–57 Watergate Row, Chester, Cheshire, CH1 2LE** P
☎ 01244 311300 F 01244 311300
M 07973 760722
E urijacobi@aol.com
W www.urijacobi.co.uk
Est. 1994 *Stock size* Medium
Stock Contemporary and antique carpets, rugs and tapestries
Open Mon–Sat 9am–5pm
Fairs NEC, LAPADA
Services Valuations, restorations, cleaning

Jamandic Ltd
Contact Dominic McParland
✉ **22 Bridge Street Row, Chester, Cheshire, CH1 1NN** P
☎ 01244 312822
Est. 1975 *Stock size* Small
Stock General antiques
Open Mon–Fri 9.30am–5.30pm Sat 9.30am–1pm
Services Interior design

K D Antiques
Contact Mrs D Gillett
✉ **11 City Walls, Chester, Cheshire, CH1 1LD**
☎ 01244 314208
Est. 1997 *Stock size* Medium

Stock Boxes, Staffordshire figures, prints, collectables, glass
Open Mon–Sat 10am–5pm
Fairs Welsh circuit, Manchester G-Mex

Kayes (LAPADA, NAG)
Contact Mr Nick Kaye
9 St Michaels Row, Chester, Cheshire, CH1 1EF
01244 327149/343638
F 01244 318404
E kayesgem@globalnet.co.uk
W www.kayeschester.com
Est. 1949 ***Stock size*** Large
Stock Second-hand, antique and new jewellery and silver
Open Mon–Sat 9.30am–5pm
Services Valuations, restorations

Lowe and Sons (NAG, BACA Award Winner 2002)
Contact Kevin Parry
11 Bridge Street Row, Chester, Cheshire, CH1 1PD
01244 325850
E lowes.chester@virgin.net
Est. 1770 ***Stock size*** Large
Stock Antiques, silver, jewellery, decorative arts, Lalique
Open Mon–Sat 9am–5.30pm

Made of Honour
Contact Mr Eric Jones
11 City Walls, Chester, Cheshire, CH1 1LD
01244 314208
E eric.antiques@virginnet.co.uk
Est. 1969 ***Stock size*** Medium
Stock 18th–19thC British pottery and porcelain, decorative items, boxes, caddies, Staffordshire figures
Open Mon–Sat 10am–5pm
Fairs Welsh circuit, Anglesey
Services Talks, lectures

McLarens Antiques & Interiors
Contact Sara Ewing
Boughton House, 38 Christleton Road, Chester, Cheshire, CH3 5UE
01244 320774 F 01244 314774
Est. 1983 ***Stock size*** Large
Stock French and Italian furniture, European and reclaimed pine
Open Mon–Sat 10am–6pm Sun 11am–5pm

Melody's Antique Galleries (LAPADA)
Contact G Melody
32 City Road, Chester, Cheshire, CH1 3AE
01244 660204
E george.melody@btinternet.com
Est. 1977 ***Stock size*** Large
Stock 17th–20thC furniture, varied small items, paintings
Open Mon–Sat 10am–5.30pm or by appointment
Fairs Newark
Services Valuations, shipping, nationwide delivery

Moor Hall Antiques
Contact John Murphy
27 Watergate Row, Chester, Cheshire, CH1 2LE
01244 340095
Est. 1993 ***Stock size*** Medium
Stock 18th–19thC British furniture
Open Mon–Sat 10–5pm

O'Keeffe Antiques
Contact Mr D O'Keeffe
2 Christleton Road, Chester, Cheshire, CH3 5UG
01244 311279
Est. 1998 ***Stock size*** Large
Stock Antique lighting, architectural antiques
Open Tues–Sat 10am–5pm

Objets d'Art
Contact Martin or Sonja De Rooy
67–71 Watergate Row, Chester, Cheshire, CH1 2LE
01244 312211 F 01244 400880
Est. 1998 ***Stock size*** Large
Stock Clocks, furniture, quality decorative items
Open Mon–Sat 10am–5pm
Services Restorations

The Old Warehouse Antiques
Contact Mrs U O'Donnell
7–9 Delamere Street, Chester, Cheshire, CH1 4DS
01244 383942 M 07790 533850
Est. 1989 ***Stock size*** Large
Stock Victorian–Edwardian furniture, beds, soft furnishings
Open Mon–Sat 10am–5.30pm
Services Valuations

Richmond Galleries
Contact Mrs M Armitage
Watergate Buildings, New Crane Street, Chester, Cheshire, CH1 4JE
01244 317602 F 01244 317602
Est. 1974 ***Stock size*** Large
Stock New and old country pine furniture, decorative items
Open Mon–Sat 9.30am–5pm

Saltney Restoration Services
Contact Mr J Moore
50 St Marks Road, Chester, Cheshire, CH4 8DQ
01244 312529 F 01244 312529
M 07713 823383
Est. 1967 ***Stock size*** Small
Stock Lighting, sanitary ware, furniture, ironware
Open By appointment
Services Restorations

Second Time Around
Contact Graham Shacklady
6 Christleton Road, Boughton, Chester, Cheshire, CH3 5UG
01244 316394 F 01244 322042
Est. 1979 ***Stock size*** Large
Stock Georgian–Edwardian furniture
Open Mon–Sat 9am–5pm
Fairs Newark
Services Packing, courier, export

Second Time Around
Contact Graham Shacklady
Staff Yard, 34 Spital Walk, Boughton, Chester, Cheshire, CH3 5DB
01244 316439 F 01244 322042
Est. 1979 ***Stock size*** Large
Stock Georgian–Edwardian furniture
Services Packing, courier, export

Stothert Old Books (PBFA)
Contact Mr A Checkley
4 Nicholas Street, Chester, Cheshire, CH1 2NX
01244 340756 M 07778 137461
Est. 1998 ***Stock size*** Large
Stock Wide range of antiquarian and second-hand books including local history, topography, natural history, good illustrated books etc
Open Mon–Sat 10am–5pm
Fairs PBFA, North West Book Fairs
Services Valuations, book search

Watergate Antiques
Contact Mr A Shindler
56 Watergate Street, Chester, Cheshire, CH1 2LD
01244 344516 F 01244 320350
E watergate.antiques@themail.co.uk
Est. 1968 *Stock size* Large
Stock Silver, silver plate, ceramics
Open Mon–Sat 9.30am–5pm
Fairs Newark
Services Restorations, repairs

Wheatsheaf Antiques Centre
Contact Jeremy Marks
57 Christleton Road, Boughton, Chester, Cheshire, CH3 5UF
01244 403743 F 01244 351713
E info@antiquesonlineuk.com
W www.antiquesonlineuk.com
Stock size Large
No. of dealers 7
Stock General antiques 17thC–1930s, books, china, prints, clocks, silver plate, vintage clothing
Open Mon–Sat 11am–4pm Sun noon–4pm or by appointment
Services Shipping

CONGLETON

Whittaker & Biggs (RICS)
Contact Mr J W Robinson
The Auction Room, Macclesfield Road, Congleton, Cheshire, CW12 1NS
01260 279858 F 01260 271629
W www.whittakerandbiggs.co.uk
Est. 1931
Open Mon–Fri 9am–5pm
Sales General household furniture and effects 1st Sat of month and 2nd and 4th Fri 10am. Antiques, reproduction and collectables auction 3rd Fri 4pm, viewing evening prior 5–7pm
Frequency Weekly
Catalogues Yes

CREWE

Antique & Country Pine
Contact Mr S Blackhurst
102 Edleston Road, Crewe, Cheshire, CW2 7HD
01270 258617
Est. 1990 *Stock size* Small
Stock English and Continental original and stripped pine, hand-made reproductions
Open Mon–Sat 9.30am–5.30pm closed Wed
Services Restorations

Cheshire Cast Company
Contact Mr D Davis
17 Crewe Hall, Weston Road, Crewe, Cheshire, CW1 6UV
01270 873111 F 01270 873222
Est. 1994 *Stock size* Large
Stock Original cast-iron radiators
Open By appointment
Services Refurbishing and rebuilding original cast-iron radiators

Copnal Books
Contact Mr P Ollerhead
18 Meredith Street, Crewe, Cheshire, CW1 2PW
01270 580470
Est. 1982 *Stock size* Medium
Stock Wide variety of second-hand, antiquarian and religious books
Open Mon Fri Sat 9.30am–5pm or by appointment
Services Valuations

J D Luffman
Contact Mr J D Luffman
Bank House, 13 Bradeley Road, Haslington, Crewe, Cheshire, CW1 5PW
01270 500199 F 01270 500199
M 07836 592898
Est. 1970 *Stock size* Medium
Stock Clocks, country furniture, militaria, musical boxes
Open By appointment

CUDDINGTON

www.horsebrass.co.uk
Contact Diane Wilkinson
Cuddington Lane, Cuddington, Northwich, Cheshire, CW8 2SY
01606 882555 F 01606 882555
E brasses@horsebrass.co.uk
W www.horsebrass.co.uk
Stock size Large
Stock Horse brasses
Open By appointment only
Fairs DMG, Antiques for Everyone
Services Valuations

DAVENHAM

Davenham Antiques Centre & Tea Room
Contact Mr G Maxwell
461 London Road, Davenham, Northwich, Cheshire, CW9 8NA
01606 44350 F 01606 782317
E maxwells@connectfree.co.uk
W www.antiques-atlas.com/davenham.htm
Est. 1984 *Stock size* Large
No. of dealers 15
Stock Wide range of antiques, furniture, collectables, china, silver, books
Open Mon–Sat 10am–5pm Sun 11am–5pm closed Wed
Services Tea room

DISLEY

Crescent Antiques
Contact Mr J Cooper
7 Buxton Road, Disley, Stockport, Cheshire, SK12 2DZ
01663 765677
Est. 1972 *Stock size* Medium
Stock Wide range of furniture, silver, porcelain
Open Mon–Sun 10am–5.30pm
Services Valuations

Mill Farm Antiques
Contact Mr S Berry
50–54 Market Street, Disley, Stockport, Cheshire, SK12 2DT
01663 764045 F 01663 762690
Est. 1971 *Stock size* Medium
Stock Longcase and other clocks, general antiques, mechanical music
Open Mon–Sat 9am–6pm Sun noon–6pm
Services Valuations, clock restorations, mechanical music, barometers

HALE

Bonhams
The Stables, 213 Ashley Road, Hale, Cheshire, WA15 9TB
0161 927 3822 F 0161 927 3824
E manchester@bonhams.com
W www.bonhams.com
Open Mon–Fri 9am–5pm

French Country Style
Contact Margaret Ernstone

✉ **61 Stamford Park Road, Hale, Altrincham, Cheshire, WA15 9EZ** 🅿
☎ 0161 927 9041 Ⓕ 0161 980 8949
Est. 2000 *Stock size* medium
Stock French decorative items, furniture, lighting, mirrors
Open Tues–Sat 10am–5pm or by appointment
Services Restorations

Porcupine
Contact Ms V Martin
✉ **110 Ashley Road, Hale, Altrincham, Cheshire, WA14 2UN**
☎ 0161 928 4421
Est. 1982 *Stock size* Medium
Stock Antique pine, pottery
Open Mon–Sat 9.30am–5.30pm

HALEBARNS

Cottage Antiques
Contact Joy or John Gholam
✉ **Hasty Lane, Halebarns, Ringway, Altrincham, Cheshire, WA15 8UT** 🅿
☎ 0161 980 7961
Est. 1975 *Stock size* Medium
Stock General antiques, oak, mahogany furniture, brass, copper, paintings, ceramics
Open Mon–Sat 9am–5pm or by appointment
Services Valuations

HATTON

H & H Classic Auctions Ltd
Contact Simon Hope or Mark Hamilton
✉ **Whitegate Farm, Hatton Lane, Hatton, Cheshire, WA4 4BZ** 🅿
☎ 01925 730630 Ⓕ 01925 730830
Ⓔ info@classic-auctions.co.uk
Ⓦ www.classic-auctions.co.uk
Est. 1993
Open Mon–Fri 9am–5pm
Sales Vintage and classic car sales 6 per annum, Wed 1pm, viewing day prior 2–7pm. Vintage and classic motorbike sales 2 per annum, Tues noon, viewing day prior 2–7pm. Held at the Pavilion Gardens, Buxton
Catalogues Yes

HELSBY

Sweetbriar Gallery Ltd (Paperweight Collectors Association)
Contact Anne Metcalfe
✉ **Sweetbriar House, 106 Robin Hood Lane, Helsby, Cheshire, WA6 9NH** 🅿
☎ 01928 723851 Ⓕ 01928 723153
Ⓜ 07860 907532
Ⓔ sweetbr@globalnet.co.uk
Ⓦ www.sweetbriar.co.uk
Est. 1988 *Stock size* Large
Stock Paperweights
Open Mon–Fri 9am–5pm
Fairs The Glass Fairs, DMG Fairs
Services Valuations

HUNTINGTON

Huntington Antiques
Contact Mrs Gregson
✉ **53 Chester Road, Huntington, Cheshire, CH3 6BS** 🅿
☎ 01244 324162
Est. 1994 *Stock size* Small
Stock Furniture, clocks, paintings
Open Mon–Fri 9am–5.30pm
Services Restorations

KNUTSFORD

Forest Books of Cheshire
Contact Mrs I Mottershead
✉ **Past & Presents Antique Centre, 35 King Street, Knutsford, Cheshire, WA16 6DW** 🅿
☎ 01565 653599
Ⓔ info@forest-books.co.uk
Est. 1996 *Stock size* Small
Stock Antiquarian, rare, second-hand, new books, pictures, prints
Open Mon–Sat 11am–5pm Sun 1.30–4.30pm closed Wed
Fairs Buxton Book Fair

King Street Antiques
Contact Mrs E L MacDougal
✉ **1 King Street, Knutsford, Cheshire, WA16 6DW** 🅿
☎ 01565 750387
Est. 1993 *Stock size* Small
Stock Furniture, porcelain, silver
Open Tues–Fri 10.30am–5pm Sat 10am–5pm closed Wed
Services Valuations

The Lemon Tree
Contact Mr S Nelson
✉ **103 King Street, Knutsford, Cheshire, WA16 6EQ** 🅿
☎ 01565 751101 Ⓕ 01565 751101
Est. 1997 *Stock size* Medium
Stock English country furniture in satin walnut, stripped pine
Open Mon–Sat 10am–5.30pm Sun noon–5pm

Frank R Marshall & Co
Contact Mr A Partridge
✉ **Marshall House, Church Hill, Knutsford, Cheshire, WA16 6DH** 🅿
☎ 01565 653284 Ⓕ 01565 652341
Ⓜ 07808 483435
Ⓔ antiques@frankmarshall.co.uk
Ⓦ www.antiques@frankmarshall.co.uk
Est. 1969
Open Mon–Fri 9am–5.30pm closed noon–1pm
Sales General antiques and collectors' sales, 5 per annum, Tues 10am. Fortnightly household sales Tues 10am, viewing Mon 9am-6.30pm
Frequency Fortnightly
Catalogues Yes

Past & Presents
Contact Lindsey Bowman
✉ **35 King Street, Knutsford, Cheshire, WA16 6DW** 🅿
☎ 01565 653599 Ⓕ 01565 653599
Est. 1997 *Stock size* Large
Stock General antiques, model ships, extensive range of clocks, collectables, furniture
Open Mon–Sat 10.30am–5.30pm Sun 1.30–5.30pm or by appointment
Services Clock and furniture restoration

LYMM

Baron Antiques (LAPADA)
Contact Mrs Roberts
✉ **Port of Willow Pool, Burford Lane, Lymm, Cheshire, WA13 0SH** 🅿
☎ 01925 757827 Ⓕ 01925 758101
Est. 1964 *Stock size* Medium
Stock Architectural antiques, decorative arts, resalvaged and general antiques
Open Mon–Sun 9am–6pm
Fairs Newark, Ardingly
Services Tea shop

Reflections (AMU)
Contact Mr John Sprague
✉ **11 The Cross, Lymm, Cheshire, WA13 0HR** 🅿
☎ 01925 753555/757331
Est. 1995 *Stock size* Large
Stock Furniture, china, glass, bric-a-brac, 1850s–1950s

Open Tues–Sat 9.30am–5pm
Sun by appointment
Services Polishing, traditional upholstery

MACCLESFIELD

Churchills Auction Room
Contact Mr P Ginsberg
Union Street, Macclesfield, Cheshire, SK11 6QG
01625 420088
Est. 1997 *Stock size* Large
Stock Antique, new and reproduction furniture, pianos, clocks, collectables, china, glass
Open Mon–Sun 11am–5pm
Services Valuations, restorations, occasional auctions

Gatehouse Antiques
Contact Mr W Livesley
72 Chestergate, Macclesfield, Cheshire, SK11 6DY
01625 426476 01625 426476
Est. 1974 *Stock size* Large
Stock Wide range of antiques including 18th–20thC furniture, jewellery, silver, glass
Open Mon Tues Thurs Fri 9am–5pm Wed 9am–1pm
Sat 10am–5pm
Services Valuations, restorations, repairs

Derek Hill Antiques
Contact Mr D Hill
Unit 47, Market Hall, Grosvenor Centre, Macclesfield, Cheshire, SK11 6AR
01625 420777 07711 855937
hillsantiques@tinyworld.co.uk
www.hillsantiques.co.uk
Est. 1969 *Stock size* Large
Stock Collectables, brass, copper, militaria, jewellery, stamps, cigarette cards etc
Open Mon–Sat 9am–5.30pm
Services Valuations, jewellery repairs

Mereside Books
Contact Ms S Laithwaite
75 Chestergate, Macclesfield, Cheshire, SK11 6DG
01625 425352
Est. 1996 *Stock size* Small
Stock Antiquarian and second-hand, local history and illustrated books specialities
Open Wed–Sat 10am–5pm
Fairs Cheshire, Buxton
Services Book search

MOBBERLEY

Limited Editions
Contact Charles Fogg
The Barn, Oak Tree Farm, Knutsford Road, Mobberley, Cheshire, WA16 7PU
0161 480 1239
info@ltd-editions.co.uk
www.antique-co.com
Est. 1974 *Stock size* Large
Stock Mostly furniture, especially dining tables and chairs
Open Thurs–Sat 10am–5.30pm
Sun noon–4pm
Services Restorations, joinery, polishing, upholstery

NANTWICH

Adams Antiques (BADA, LAPADA)
Contact Mrs Sandy Summers
Churche's Mansion, 50 Hospital Street, Nantwich, Cheshire, CW5 5RY
01270 625643 01270 625643
07901 855200
sandy@0800260.com
Est. 1970 *Stock size* Large
Stock Early oak, walnut and country furniture, Welsh dressers, Mason's ironstone, longcase clocks
Open 10am–6pm
Fairs NEC, BADA
Services Valuations, restorations, vetting

Antiques Traders of Nantwich
Contact Jonathan Coupe
The Manor House, 7 Beam Street, Nantwich, Cheshire, CW5 5LR
01270 611125 07973 686378
antiquetraders@hotmail.com
www.antique-traders. co.uk
Est. 1990 *Stock size* Small
Stock Antique furniture
Open Mon–Fri 10am–5pm
Sat 9am–5pm
Services House clearance

Barn Antiques
Contact Mr Brian Lee
8 The Cocoa Yard, Pillory Street, Nantwich, Cheshire, CW5 5BL
01270 627770
j.lee@btinternet.com
Est. 1993 *Stock size* Medium
Stock Wide range of china, small furniture, copper, brass, collectables including Carlton ware, Beswick
Open Mon Tues 10am–4pm
Thurs Fri 9.30am–4.30pm
Sat 9.30am–5pm closed 12.30–1.30pm

Chapel Antiques
Contact Mrs D Atkin
47 Hospital Street, Nantwich, Cheshire, CW5 5RL
01270 629508
Est. 1983 *Stock size* Medium
Stock Georgian–Victorian furniture, decorative items, mirrors
Open Tues–Sat 9.30am–5.30pm
Services Furniture restoration

Clock Corner (BHI)
Contact Mr M Green
176 Audlem Road, Nantwich, Cheshire, CW5 7QJ
01270 624481
clocks.corner@virginnet
clockscorner.com
Est. 1975 *Stock size* Large
Stock Antique clocks of all types – bracket, Vienna, longcase, mantel etc
Open By appointment
Services Valuations

Dagfields Crafts & Antiques Centre
Contact Mr I Bennion
Dagfields Farm, Walgherton, Nantwich, Cheshire, CW5 7LG
01270 841336 01270 842604
ian@dagfields.co.uk
www.dagfields.co.uk
Est. 1989 *Stock size* Large
No. of dealers 150
Stock Collectables and furniture of all periods
Open Mon–Sun 10am–5pm
Services 2 restaurants

Roderick Gibson
Contact Mrs R Gibson
70–72 Hospital Street, Nantwich, Cheshire, CW5 5RP
01270 625301 01270 629603
antiques@sfc.co.uk
www.sfc.co.uk/antiques
Est. 1975 *Stock size* Medium
Stock Antique and reproduction furniture, small collectables
Open Mon–Sat 9am–5pm
Services Valuations, probate service

Love Lane Antiques
Contact Mary Simon
Love Lane, Nantwich, Cheshire, CW5 5BH
01270 626239
Est. 1979 *Stock size* Medium
Stock General antiques
Open Mon–Sat 10am–5pm closed Wed

Nantwich Antiques
Contact Tony Coupe
The Manor House, 7 Beam Street, Nantwich, Cheshire, CW5 5LR
01270 611125 Ⓕ 01270 610637
Ⓜ 07939 500733
Ⓔ tony@indianfurniture.co.uk
Ⓦ www.indianfurniture.co.uk
Est. 1979 *Stock size* Large
Stock Period and reproduction furniture, Oriental rugs, silver, prints, paintings, jewellery, Indian furniture
Open Mon–Sat 10am–5pm
Fairs Many nationwide
Services Valuations, restorations

Richardson Antiques Ltd
Contact Mr Richardson
90 Hospital Street, Nantwich, Cheshire, CW5 5RP
01270 625963
Est. 1984 *Stock size* Medium
Stock Furniture, china
Open By appointment
Fairs Newark, Ardingly, Swinderby
Services Restorations, French polishing

Peter Wilson (SOFAA)
Contact Mr D Morgan-Wynne
Victoria Gallery, Market Street, Nantwich, Cheshire, CW5 5DG
01270 623878 Ⓕ 01270 610508
Ⓔ auctions@peterwilson.co.uk
Ⓦ www.peterwilson.co.uk
Est. 1955
Open Mon–Fri 9am–5.30pm Sat 9.30am–noon
Sales 2-day sales, 5 per annum, Wed Thurs 10.30am, viewing Sun prior 2–4pm Mon Tues 10am–4pm. Uncatalogued fast weekly sale Thurs 11am, viewing Wed 10am–4pm
Frequency 40 per annum
Catalogues Yes

NORTHWICH

Northwich Antiques Centre
Contact Freddie Cockburn
132 Witton Street, Northwich, Cheshire, CW9 5NP
01606 47540 Ⓜ 07980 645738
Ⓔ ron2@cockburn2686.fsnet
Est. 1999
No. of dealers 6
Stock Period furniture, collectables, china
Open Mon–Sun 10am–5pm

POYNTON

Recollections
Contact Angela Smith
69 Park Lane, Poynton, Stockport, Cheshire, SK12 1RD
01625 859373 Ⓜ 07778 993307
Est. 1984 *Stock size* Medium
Stock Furniture, costume jewellery, decorative china, glass
Open Mon–Sat 10am–5pm
Services House clearance

SANDBACH

Andrew Hilditch & Son Ltd
Contact Mr T Spencer Andrew
Hanover House, 1a The Square, Sandbach, Cheshire, CW11 1AP
01270 767246 Ⓕ 01270 767246
Est. 1866
Open Mon–Fri 9am–5pm closed 12.30–2pm
Sales Quarterly general antiques Wed 10.30am, viewing Mon 10.30am–3pm Tues 10am–3.30pm 7–8.30pm. General sale weekly, Wed 10am, viewing Tues 10.30am–3.30pm
Catalogues Yes

Saxon Cross Antiques Emporium
Contact John Jones
Town Mill, High Street, Sandbach, Cheshire, CW11 1AH
01270 753005 Ⓕ 01270 753005
Ⓦ www.saxonantique.co.uk
Est. 1999 *Stock size* Large
No. of dealers 32
Stock Fine antiques from 17th–20thC, porcelain, silver, collectables
Open Tues–Sat 10am–5pm Sun 11am–4pm

STOCKTON HEATH

Bridge Antiques
Contact Mrs N White
123 Fairfield Road, Stockton Heath, Warrington, Cheshire, WA4 2BU
01925 486365
Est. 1999 *Stock size* Medium
Stock Old and new pine furniture and other furniture, decorative items
Open Mon–Sat 10am–5pm

STRETTON

Harlequin Antiques
Contact Bernard Snagg
Roadside Farm, London Road, Stretton, Cheshire, WA4 5PG
01925 730031/730781
Est. 1997 *Stock size* Large
Stock Victorian pine, oak and mahogany furniture
Open Tues–Sun 10am–6pm

TARPORLEY

Tarporley Antique Centre
Contact Peter Wright
76 High Street, Tarporley, Cheshire, CW6 0AT
01829 733919
Est. 1991 *Stock size* Large
No. of dealers 10
Stock Pictures, brass, copper, glass, books
Open Mon–Sat 10am–5pm Sun 11am–4pm

TATTENHALL

Great Northern Architectural Antiques Co Ltd
Contact Mrs J Devoy
New Russia Hall, Chester Road, Tattenhall, Chester, Cheshire, CH3 9AH
01829 770796 Ⓕ 01829 770971
Ⓔ gnaacoltd@enterprise.net
Est. 1990 *Stock size* Large
Stock Stone, church exteriors, fireplaces, doors, brass ware, sanitary ware, pews, statuary etc
Open Mon–Sun 9.30am–5pm or by appointment
Services Valuations, restorations

WARRINGTON

Rocking Chair Antiques
Contact Michael Barratt
Unit 3, St Peters Way, Warrington, Cheshire, WA2 7BL
01925 652409 01925 652409
Est. 1976 *Stock size* Large
Stock Victorian–Edwardian bedroom and dining room furniture
Open Mon–Fri 8am–5pm Sat 10am–4pm
Fairs Swinderby
Services Valuations

WAVERTON

Antique Exporters of Chester
Contact Mike Kilgannon
Guy Lane Farm, Guy Lane, Waverton, Chester, Cheshire, CH3 7RZ
01829 741001/01244 570069
Est. 1969 *Stock size* Large
Stock 18thC–1930s furniture
Open Mon–Sun 9am–7pm
Services Restorations, shipping

White House Antiques & Stripped Pine
Contact Mrs E Rideal
The White House, Whitchurch Road, Waverton, Chester, Cheshire, CH3 7PB
01244 335063 01244 335098
rideal@whitehousescientifics.com
Est. 1979 *Stock size* Large
Stock German and English stripped-pine furniture of all types
Open Mon–Sat 10am–5pm

WIDNES

Iain Campbell (PBFA)
Contact Iain Campbell
Unit A5, Moor Lane Business Centre, Moor Lane, Widnes, Cheshire, WA8 7AQ
0151 420 5545
Est. 1970 *Stock size* Medium
Stock Antiquarian and second-hand books (mainly 19thC), maps, prints, ephemera, drawings, watercolours
Open By appointment
Fairs PBFA, Newark, Ephemera Society

WILMSLOW

Wilmslow Antiques
Contact Mr M Dale
5 Church Street, Wilmslow, Cheshire, SK9 1AX
01625 540472
pmdale99@aol.com
Est. 1996 *Stock size* Large
No. of dealers 20
Stock Wide range of stock including furniture, silver, copper, brass, pottery, china, pictures
Open Mon–Sat 10am–5pm

WOODFORD

Maxwells of Wilmslow incorporating Dockrees
Contact Mr M Blackmore ARICS
133a Woodford Road, Woodford, Cheshire, SK7 1QD
0161 439 5182 0161 439 5182
Est. 1989
Open Mon–Fri 9am–5pm
Sales 2 general chattels' sales per month, quarterly antiques sales
Frequency 2 per month
Catalogues Yes

CUMBRIA

ALSTON

Alston Antiques
Contact Mrs J Bell
10 Front Street, Alston, Cumbria, CA9 3HU
01434 382129
07778 624021
Est. 1974 *Stock size* Large
Stock Wide range of antiques, furniture, clocks, barometers, china, textiles etc
Open Mon–Sat 10am–5pm Sun 1–5pm closed Tues
Fairs Newark

APPLEBY IN WESTMORLAND

Bridge End Antiques
Contact Mrs S Murton
3 Bridge End, The Sands, Appleby in Westmorland, Cumbria, CA16 6XL
017683 520502
Est. 1979 *Stock size* Large
Stock General antiques and decorative items, collectables, small items of furniture
Open Mon–Sat 9am–5pm

Barry McKay Rare Books (PBFA)
Contact Mr B McKay
Kingstone House, Battlebarrow, Appleby in Westmorland, Cumbria, CA16 6XT
017683 52282 017683 52946
barry.mckay@britishlibrary.net
Est. 1986 *Stock size* Medium
Stock Antiquarian, second-hand and new books, specializing in all aspects of book production and distribution, some books on Cumbria and the North
Open Mon–Sat 10am–4pm preferably by appointment
Services Book search, catalogue

BARROW-IN-FURNESS

P J Cassells
Contact Mr P J Cassells
138 Cavendish Street, Barrow-in-Furness, Cumbria, LA14 1DJ
01229 834747 07788 905324
Est. 1993 *Stock size* Large
Stock Edwardian and Victorian furniture, longcase clocks
Open Mon–Sat 10am–4pm
Fairs Newark, Swinderby
Services Valuations

BOWNESS-ON-WINDERMERE

The White Elephant
Contact Mrs J Moore
66 Quarry Rigg, Bowness-on-Windermere, Windermere, Cumbria, LA23 3DO
01539 446962 01539 446962
mooredsr@paveyarkfreeserve.co.uk
Est. 1989 *Stock size* Large
Stock General range of antiques, furniture, porcelain, pewter, mahogany furniture
Open Mon–Sun 10am–5pm

BRAMPTON

Cumbrian Antiques Centre
Contact Mr Sumerson-Wright
St Martins Hall, Front Street, Brampton, Cumbria, CA8 1NT
016977 42515 or 42741
www.cumbrianantiques.co.uk

Est. 2001 *Stock size* Large
No. of dealers 42
Stock General antiques and collectables
Open Mon–Sat 10am–5pm
Sun noon–5pm

⊞ Something Old, Something New
Contact Mrs J Potts
⊠ **46 Main Street, Brampton, Cumbria, CA8 1SB** Ⓟ
☎ 0169 7741740
Est. 1979 *Stock size* Large
Stock Victorian pine furniture, country items, French decorative furniture
Open Mon–Sat 10am–4.30pm

⊞ Watsons Antiques
Contact Mr M Watson
⊠ **40 Front Street, Brampton, Cumbria, CA8 1NG** Ⓟ
☎ 01697 741066
Ⓔ enquiries@watsonline-ltd.co.uk
Ⓦ www.watsonline-ltd.co.uk
Est. 1987 *Stock size* Large
Stock Linen, lace, badges, medals, china, glass etc
Open Internet only
Services House clearance

Key to Symbols

⊞	=	Dealer
⌂	=	Antiques Centre
⚒	=	Auction House
⊠	=	Address
Ⓟ	=	Parking
☎	=	Telephone No.
Ⓜ	=	Mobile tel No.
Ⓕ	=	Fax No.
Ⓔ	=	E-mail address
Ⓦ	=	Website address

CARLISLE

⚒ Bonhams
⊠ **48 Cecil Street, Carlisle, Cumbria, CA1 1NT**
☎ 01228 542422 Ⓕ 01228 590106
Ⓔ carlisle@bonhams.com
Ⓦ www.bonhams.com
Open Mon Tues Thurs Fri 8.30am–1pm 2–5pm

⊞ Bookcase
Contact Mr S Matthews
⊠ **17–19 Castle Street, Carlisle, Cumbria, CA3 8SY** Ⓟ
☎ 01228 544560 Ⓕ 01228 544775
Ⓔ bookcasecarlisle@aol.com
Ⓦ www.bookscumbria.com
Est. 1978 *Stock size* Large
Stock Antiquarian, rare and second-hand books, maps, prints, classical CDs and LPs, art gallery
Open Mon–Sat 10am–5pm
Services Book search, repairs, valuations

⌂ Carlisle Antique Centre
Contact Mrs W Mitton
⊠ **Cecil Hall, 40a Cecil Street, Carlisle, Cumbria, CA1 1NT** Ⓟ
☎ 01228 536910 Ⓕ 01228 536910
Ⓔ wendymitton@aol.com
Est. 1986 *Stock size* Large
No. of dealers 6
Stock Wide range of antiques, clocks, watches, jewellery, silver, porcelain
Open Mon–Sat 9am–5pm
Services Restaurant

⚒ Cumbria Auction Rooms (NAVA)
Contact Howard Naylor
⊠ **12 Lowther Street, Carlisle, Cumbria, CA3 8DA** Ⓟ
☎ 01228 525259 Ⓕ 01228 597183
Ⓦ www.invaluable.com/cumbria
Est. 1880
Open Mon–Fri 9am–5pm at 9am–noon
Sales Weekly sale of Victorian and later furniture and effects Mon. Quarterly antiques and works-of-art sales Mon 10am, viewing Fri 9am–5pm Sat 9am–noon
Frequency Weekly
Catalogues Yes

⊞ The Eddie Stobart Fan Club Shop
Contact Mrs G Collins
⊠ **27 Castle Street, Carlisle, Cumbria, CA3 8TP** Ⓟ
☎ 01228 515166 Ⓕ 01228 590955
Est. 1996 *Stock size* Medium
Stock Eddie Stobart collection, die-cast models, clothing, ceramics, pens, mugs, limited editions
Open Mon–Sat 9am–5.30pm

⊞ Eddie Stobart Promotions Ltd
Contact Ms Debbie Rodgers
⊠ **Kingstown Industrial Estate, Carlisle, Cumbria, CA3 0EH** Ⓟ
☎ 01228 514151 Ⓕ 01228 515158
Ⓔ promotions@eddiestobart.co.uk
Est. 1993 *Stock size* Large
Stock Eddie Stobart collection, die-cast models, clothing, ceramics, pens, limited editions
Open Mon–Fri 8.30am–5.30pm
Services Mail-order service with catalogue

⊞ Souvenir Antiques
Contact Mr J Higham
⊠ **Treasury Court, 4 Kinmont Arcade, Carlisle, Cumbria, CA3 8RF** Ⓟ
☎ 01228 401281 Ⓕ 01228 401281
Ⓔ cumbriamaps@fsnet.co.uk
Est. 1986 *Stock size* Large
Stock Wide range of antiques and collectables, Roman and medieval coins, local maps, prints
Open Mon–Sat 10am–5pm

⊞ St Nicholas Galleries Ltd
Contact Mr C Carruthers
⊠ **39 Bank Street, Carlisle, Cumbria, CA3 8HJ** Ⓟ
☎ 01228 544459 Ⓕ 01228 511015
Est. 1975 *Stock size* Medium
Stock Late Victorian–Edwardian furniture, watercolours, silver, silver plate, Doulton figures, Rolex and Omega watches, diamond and other jewellery
Open Tues–Sat 10am–5pm
Services Jewellery repairs

⚒ Thomson, Roddick & Medcalf Auctioneers
Contact John Thomson
⊠ **Coleridge House, Shaddongate, Carlisle, Cumbria, CA2 5TU** Ⓟ
☎ 01228 528939 Ⓕ 01228 592128
Ⓔ auctions@thomsonroddick.com
Est. 1880
Sales 10 Antiques and collectors' sales per annum plus specialist sales of pictures, books
Frequency 20 per annum
Catalogues Yes

COCKERMOUTH

⊞ CG's Curiosity Shop
Contact Corrine Ritchie or Colin Graham

✉ **Cocker Bridge,
43 Market Place, Cockermouth,
Cumbria, CA13 9LT** Ⓟ
☎ 01900 824418 or 016973 21108
Ⓜ 07712 206786
Ⓔ cgcuriosity@hotmail.com
Est. 1987 ***Stock size*** Large
Stock Unusual items, pictures, militaria, furniture, porcelain, glass, books, records
Open Mon–Sat 10am–12.45pm 1.45–5pm
Fairs Newark, Swinderby
Services Restorations, house clearance

⊞ Cockermouth Antiques
Contact Ms E Bell
✉ **5 Station Street, Cockermouth, Cumbria, CA13 9QW** Ⓟ
☎ 01900 826746
Ⓔ elainebell@aol.com
Est. 1984 ***Stock size*** Large
Stock Large range of antiques, ceramics, glass, metalware, silver, jewellery, books, pictures, fireplaces
Open Mon–Sat 10am–5pm closed 1–2pm

Cockermouth Antiques & Craft Market
Contact Mrs P Gilbert
✉ **The Old Courthouse, Main Street, Cockermouth, Cumbria, CA13 9LU** Ⓟ
☎ 01900 824346
Est. 1978 ***Stock size*** Large
No. of dealers 4
Stock Wide range of antiques including jewellery, china, glass, postcards, books, ephemera
Open Mon–Sat 10am–5pm
Services Pine stripping and French polishing

Mitchell's Auction Company (ISVA)
Contact Mr M Wise or Mr K Scott
✉ **The Furniture Hall, 47 Station Road, Cockermouth, Cumbria, CA13 9PZ** Ⓟ
☎ 01900 827800 Ⓕ 01900 828073
Ⓔ MFineart@aol.com
Ⓦ www.mitchellsauction.co.uk
Est. 1873
Open Mon–Fri 9am–5pm
Sales 6 Fine art and antique sales per annum Thurs Fri 10am, weekly general sale Thurs 9.30am
Frequency Weekly
Catalogues Yes

GRANGE-OVER-SANDS

⊞ Anthemion (BADA, LAPADA)
Contact Jonathan Wood
✉ **Cartmel, Grange-over-Sands, Cumbria, LA11 6QD** Ⓟ
☎ 015395 36295 Ⓕ 015395 38881
Ⓜ 07768 443757
Est. 1989 ***Stock size*** Large
Stock Georgian furniture, decorative items
Open Mon–Sun 10am–5pm
Fairs BADA, LAPADA, Olympia (June), Harrogate

Gedyes Auctioneers & Estate Agents (NAEA)
Contact Mr N Gedyes
✉ **The Auction Centre, Main Street, Grange-over-Sands, Cumbria, LA11 6AB** Ⓟ
☎ 015395 33366 Ⓕ 015395 33366
Ⓜ 07740 174537
Ⓔ gedyes@aol.com
Est. 1968
Open Mon–Fri 9am–noon
Sales General and antiques sales Fri 10am, viewing Thurs 1–6pm
Frequency Monthly
Catalogues No

⊞ Norman Kerr (PBFA)
Contact Mrs H Kerr
✉ **Priory Barn, Priest Lane, Cartmel, Grange-over-Sands, Cumbria, LA11 6PX** Ⓟ
☎ 015395 36247
Est. 1933 ***Stock size*** Medium
Stock Second-hand and antiquarian books concerning art, architecture, travel, natural history, sport
Open By appointment only
Services Valuations

⊞ Utopia Antiques Ltd
Contact Mrs J Wilkinson
✉ **Yew Tree Barn, High Newton, Grange-over-Sands, Cumbria, LA11 6JP** Ⓟ
☎ 015395 30065 Ⓕ 015242 71867
Ⓔ utopiaantique@utopiaantique.com
Ⓦ www.utopiaantique.com
Est. 1993 ***Stock size*** Large
Stock Pine and country furniture, Indian imports, handicrafts, furniture, fabrics, silver
Open Mon–Sat 10am–5pm Sun 11am–5pm
Fairs NEC Furniture Show (Jan)
Services Bespoke furniture, hand-built kitchens

GRASMERE

⊞ Lakes Craft & Antiques Gallery
Contact Joe or Sandra Arthy
✉ **3 Oakbank, Broadgate, Grasmere, Ambleside, Cumbria, LA22 9TA** Ⓟ
☎ 015394 35037 Ⓕ 015394 44271
Ⓔ allbooks@globalnet.co.uk
Est. 1991 ***Stock size*** Medium
Stock Antiques, craft and gift items, china, silver, jewellery, small furniture, antiquarian books, postcards, cameras etc
Open Mon–Sun March–Nov 9.30am–6pm winter 10am–4pm

GREAT SALKELD

⊞ G K Hadfield (BHI)
Contact G K Hadfield
✉ **Beck Bank, Great Salkeld, Penrith, Cumbria, CA11 9LN** Ⓟ
☎ 01768 870111 Ⓕ 01768 870111
Ⓜ 07968 775694
Ⓔ gkhadfield@dial.pipex.com
Est. 1966 ***Stock size*** Large
Stock Clocks, horological books, clock restoration materials
Open Mon–Sat 9am–5pm or by appointment
Fairs Specialist clock fairs
Services Gilding, dial restoration, silvering, book restoration, hand-cut hands, frets in wood or brass

GREYSTOKE

⊞ Roadside Antiques
Contact Mrs K Sealby
✉ **Watsons Farm, Greystoke Gill, Greystoke, Penrith, Cumbria, CA11 0UQ** Ⓟ
☎ 017684 83279
Est. 1988 ***Stock size*** Large
Stock Antique ceramics, glass, Staffordshire figures, longcase clocks, Victorian–Edwardian furniture, silver, jewellery, paintings
Open Mon–Sun 10am–6pm
Services Porcelain restoration

KENDAL

⊞ Dower House Antiques
Contact Mrs J H Blakemore
✉ **40 Kirkland, Kendal, Cumbria, LA9 5AD** Ⓟ
☎ 01539 722778

Est. 1959 *Stock size* Small
Stock 18th–19thC pottery, porcelain, furniture, pictures
Open By appointment
Services Valuations

Granary Collectables
Contact Mr B Cross
29 Allhallows Lane, Kendal, Cumbria, LA9 4JH
01539 740770
Est. 1998 *Stock size* Medium
Stock Kitchenware, advertising, stoneware, pottery, collectables, pictures
Open Tues–Sat 10am–4.30pm

Kendal Studio Pottery Antiques
Contact Mr R Aindow
2–3 Wildman Street, Kendal, Cumbria, LA9 6EN
01539 723291
Est. 1953 *Stock size* Medium
Stock Oak furniture, art pottery, maps, prints
Open 10.30am–4.30pm usually or by appointment

Lakeland Architectural Antiques
Contact Mr G Fairclough
146 Highgate, Kendal, Cumbria, LA9 4HW
01539 737147 01539 737147
gordonfairclough@cs.com
www.architecturalantiques.co.uk
Est. 1987 *Stock size* Medium
Stock Fireplaces, mirrors, lighting
Open Mon–Sat 10am–5pm
Services Valuations

The Lion's Den
Contact Mrs L Marwood
28c Finkle Street, Kendal, Cumbria, LA9 4AB
01539 720660
Est. 1998 *Stock size* Large
Stock Antique and reproduction jewellery, clocks, pottery etc
Open Mon–Sat 10am–5pm closed Wed
Services Hand-made gold jewellery

Shambles Antiques
Contact Mr John or Mrs Janet Smyth
17–19 New Shambles, Off Market Place, Kendal, Cumbria, LA9 4TS
01539 729947 07710 245059
j&jsmyth@shamblesantiques.demon.co.uk
Est. 1991 *Stock size* Medium
Stock Ceramics, glass, objects of virtue
Open Tues–Sat 10am–5pm
Services Valuations

John Smyth Antiques
Contact J Smyth
16 New Shambles, Off Market Place, Kendal, Cumbria, LA9 4TS
01539 729947
j&jsmyth@shamblesantiques.demon.co.uk
www.shamblesantiques.demon.co.uk
Est. 1992 *Stock size* Small
Stock Furniture, paintings, works of art
Open Tues–Sat 10am–5pm
Services Valuations

Thomond Antiques
Contact Mr D Masters
33 Allhallows Lane, Kendal, Cumbria, LA9 4JH
01539 736720
thomondantiques@aol.com
Est. 1998 *Stock size* Medium
Stock China, glass, silver plate, 18th–20thC ceramics
Open Mon–Sat 10am–4.30pm
Services Valuations

KESWICK

Keswick Bookshop (PBFA)
Contact Ms J Kinnaird
4 Station Street, Keswick, Cumbria, CA12 5HT
017687 75535
Est. 1994 *Stock size* Medium
Stock Antiquarian and second-hand books, maps, prints
Open Mon–Sat Easter–Oct 10.30am–5pm winter Sat 10.30am–5pm advisable to phone

Keswick Collectables
Contact Mr M Stainton or David Lomas
18 St Johns Street, Keswick, Cumbria, CA12 5AS
01768 774928
Est. 1997 *Stock size* Medium
Stock Collectables, stamps, books, records, Victoriana, Beatles memorabilia
Open Mon–Sat 10am–6pm Sun noon–6pm
Services Postal service

Lakes Antiques & Collectables
Contact Mrs B Wren
5 St Johns Street, Keswick, Cumbria, CA12 5AP
01768 775855
Est. 1992 *Stock size* Medium
Stock Collectables, china, glass, jewellery, hat pins etc
Open Mon–Sat 10am–5pm
Fairs Newark
Services Valuations

John Young & Son Antiques (LAPADA)
Contact Mr J Young
12–14 Main Street, Keswick, Cumbria, CA12 5JD
017687 73434 017687 73306
www.john-young-antiques.co.uk
Est. 1890 *Stock size* Large
Stock Fine selection of 17th–19thC oak and mahogany furniture, longcase clocks
Open Mon–Sat 9.30am–5pm advisable to ring Wed

KIRKBY STEPHEN

The Book House (PBFA)
Contact Mr C Irwin
Ravenstonedale, Kirkby Stephen, Cumbria, CA17 4NQ
015396 23634 015396 23434
mail@thebookhouse.co.uk
www.thebookhouse.co.uk
Est. 1984 *Stock size* Medium
Stock Wide range of general books, history of technology, gardening literature, children's and language
Open Mon–Sat 9am–5pm closed Tues
Fairs PBFA
Services Catalogues issued

Haughey Antiques (LAPADA)
Contact D M Haughey
28–30 Market Street, Kirkby Stephen, Cumbria, CA17 4QW
017683 71302 017683 72423
haugheyantiques@aol.com
Est. 1969 *Stock size* Large

Stock 17th–19thC furniture, decorative items
Open Mon–Fri 10am–5.30pm Sat 11am–6pm or by appointment
Fairs Olympia (June, Nov), LAPADA Birmingham (Jan)
Services Valuations, restorations

David Hill
Contact Mr D Hill
36 Market Square, Kirkby Stephen, Cumbria, CA17 4QT
01768 371598
Est. 1966 *Stock size* Medium
Stock Small antiques, kitchenware, collectables, metalware
Open Thurs–Sat 9.30am–4pm

LONG MARTON

Ben Eggleston Antiques Ltd
Contact Ben Eggleston
The Dovecote, Long Marton, Nr Appleby, Cumbria, CA16 6BJ
01768 361849 F 01768 361849
E ben@benegglestonantiques.co.uk
W www.benegglestonantiques.co.uk
Est. 1974 *Stock size* Large
Stock Restored and unrestored antique pine furniture
Open By appointment
Fairs Newark

LONGTOWN

T Potts
Contact Mr T Potts
Scaurbank House, Netherby Road, Longtown, Carlisle, Cumbria, CA6 5NX
01228 791513 M 07702 449770
Est. 1974 *Stock size* Large
Stock Period furniture
Open By appointment
Services Valuations

NEWBY BRIDGE

Townhead Antiques (LAPADA)
Contact Mr C P Townley
Townhead, Newby Bridge, Cumbria, LA12 8NP
01539 531321 F 01539 530019
E townhead@aol.com
W www.townhead.com
Est. 1960 *Stock size* Large
Stock Wide variety of antiques, including oak, mahogany, walnut, rosewood furniture, porcelain, glass, brass, silver etc
Open Mon–Sat 10am–5pm eves and Sun by appointment
Services Valuations

PENRITH

Antiques of Penrith
Contact Mrs S Tiffin
4 Corney Square, Penrith, Cumbria, CA11 7PX
01768 862801
Est. 1953 *Stock size* Large
Stock Varied stock of furniture, decorative items, collectables
Open Mon–Fri 10am–5pm closed noon–1.30pm Sat 10am–1pm closed Wed

Brunswick Antiques
Contact Mr Martin Hodgson
8 Brunswick Road, Penrith, Cumbria, CA11 7LU
01768 899338 M 07971 295991
Est. 1987 *Stock size* Medium
Stock 18th–19thC clocks, furniture, glass, ceramics, collectables
Open Mon–Sat 10am–4pm closed Wed
Services Clock repairs

Penrith Farmers' & Kidd's Plc
Contact Mr M Huddleston
Skirsgill Saleroom, Skirsgill, Penrith, Cumbria, CA11 0DN
01768 890781 F 01768 895058
E penrith.farmers@virgin.net
W www.i-collector.com
Est. 1876
Open Mon–Fri 9am–5pm Tues 9am–6pm
Sales General sales of Victoriana and later furnishings and effects fortnightly Wed 9.30am, viewing Tues noon–6pm
Frequency Weekly
Catalogues Yes

RAUGHTON HEAD

Cumbria Architectural Salvage (SALVO)
Contact Mr R Temple
Birkshill, Raughton Head, Carlisle, Cumbria, CA5 7DH
016974 76420 F 016974 76420
M 07703 881170
Est. 1986 *Stock size* Small
Stock Fireplaces, sanitary ware, oak beams, sandstone flags, doors, radiators, kitchen ranges
Open Mon–Fri 9am–5pm Sat 9am–noon
Services Fireplace restoration

SEDBERGH

R F G Hollett & Son (ABA)
Contact Mr C G Hollett
6 Finkle Street, Sedbergh, Cumbria, LA10 5BZ
01539 620298 F 01539 621396
E hollett@sedbergh.demon.co.uk
W www.holletts-rarebooks.co.uk
Est. 1960 *Stock size* Large
Stock Wide selection of antiquarian books including natural history, travel, northern topography
Open Wed–Sat 10am–noon 1.30–5pm
Services Valuations, catalogues

Stable Antiques
Contact Mrs S Thurlby
15–16 Back Lane, Sedbergh, Cumbria, LA10 5AQ
015396 20251
E antique.thurlby@amserve.net
W www.sedbergh-yes.net
Est. 1968 *Stock size* Medium
Stock Small antiques, tools, treen, silver, small items of furniture
Open Mon–Sat 9am–6pm and by appointment
Services Search, valuations

Avril Whittle, Bookseller
Contact Mrs A Whittle
7–9 Bembridge Road, Sedbergh, Cumbria, LA10 5AU
01539 620026 F 01539 621770
E whittray@aol.com
Est. 1980 *Stock size* Medium
Stock Scarce, out-of-print and antiquarian books on art, craft and design
Open By appointment
Fairs Northumberland Lacemakers, Embroiderers' Guild
Services Book search, catalogue, valuations

Avril Whittle, Bookseller
Contact Mrs A Whittle

✉ **Whittle's Warehouse, 7–9 (Rear) Bainbridge Road, Sedbergh, Cumbria, LA10 5AU** Ⓟ
☎ 01539 620026 Ⓕ 01539 621770
Ⓔ whittray@aol.com
Est. 1980 *Stock size* Medium
Stock Scarce, out-of-print and antiquarian books on art, craft and design
Open By appointment
Fairs Northumberland Lacemakers, Embroiderers' Guild
Services Book search, catalogue, valuations

SHAP

David A H Grayling (PBFA)
✉ **Verdun House, Shap, Penrith, Cumbria, CA10 3NG** Ⓟ
☎ 01931 716746 Ⓕ 01931 716746
Ⓔ graylingbook@fsbdial.co.uk
Ⓦ www.davidgraylingbooks.com
Est. 1972 *Stock size* Medium
Stock Rare, out-of-print and new books on big game, deer, shooting, angling, hunting and natural history
Open By appointment only
Fairs Game fairs
Services Book search, catalogue, mail order, valuations, fine binding

SKELTON

The Pen & Pencil Gallery
Contact Mrs J Marshall
✉ **Church House, Skelton, Penrith, Cumbria, CA11 9TE** Ⓟ
☎ 01768 484300 Ⓕ 01768 484300
Ⓜ 07787 613780
Ⓔ ppgallery@aol.com
Est. 1995 *Stock size* Large
Stock Vintage and modern fountain pens, writing equipment, pencils, dip pens, inkwells
Open By appointment
Fairs London, Northern, USA pen shows
Services Valuations, repairs

STAVELEY

Staveley Antiques
Contact Mr J Corry
✉ **27 Main Street, Staveley, Kendal, Cumbria, LA8 9LU** Ⓟ
☎ 01539 821393
Est. 1990 *Stock size* Large
Stock Brass and iron beds, French wooden beds, lighting, metalware
Open Mon–Sat 10am–5pm
Services Metalware restoration

THURSBY

Maurice Dodd Books (PBFA)
Contact Mr R McRoberts
✉ **Greenwood House, Thursby, Carlisle, Cumbria, CA5 6NU** Ⓟ
☎ 01228 710456 Ⓕ 01228 710456
Ⓔ doddrarebooks@btconnect.com
Est. 1946 *Stock size* Medium
Stock Antiquarian books including topography, poetry, the Lake District
Open By appointment only
Fairs Russell Hotel
Services Valuations

ULVERSTON

Brogden Books
Contact Mr I Chapman
✉ **11 Brogden Street, Ulverston, Cumbria, LA12 7AH** Ⓟ
☎ 01229 588222
Ⓦ brogdenbooks.co.uk
Est. 1998 *Stock size* Medium
Stock Antiquarian and second-hand books
Open Mon–Sat 10am–5pm closed Wed
Services Valuations

Elizabeth & Son
Contact Mr J Bevins
✉ **Market Hall, New Market Street, Ulverston, Cumbria, LA12 7LJ** Ⓟ
☎ 01229 582763
Est. 1961 *Stock size* Small
Stock Late 1800–1900s china, glass, jewellery, books
Open Mon–Sat 9am–5pm closed Wed
Services Valuations

WHITEHAVEN

Michael Moon (PBFA)
Contact Mr M Moon
✉ **19 Lowther Street, Whitehaven, Cumbria, CA28 7AL** Ⓟ
☎ 01946 599010 Ⓕ 01946 599010
Est. 1970 *Stock size* Large
Stock Rare, second-hand and antiquarian books on cinema, history, local history
Open Mon–Sat 9am–5pm closed Wed Jan–Easter
Services Valuations, book search, catalogues (2–3 a year)

WINDERMERE

Serpentine Antiques
Contact Mrs M Worsley
✉ **30 Main Road, Windermere, Cumbria, LA23 1DY** Ⓟ
☎ 01539 442189
Ⓔ mworsley@fsb.co.uk
Est. 1974 *Stock size* Medium
Stock Furniture, collectables, china, glass, pictures, jewellery
Open Mon–Sat 9.30am–5.30pm Sun by appointment

WORKINGTON

Castle Antiques
Contact Mr K Wallace
✉ **18 Pow Street, Workington, Cumbria, CA14 3AG** Ⓟ
☎ 01900 607499
Est. 1997 *Stock size* Medium
Stock Collectors' items, curios, furniture, pictures. Publisher of local history books
Open Mon–Sat 9am–5pm
Fairs Charnock Richard, Newark
Services Valuations

GREATER MANCHESTER

ASTLEY BRIDGE

Alpine Antiques
Contact Mr B Carney
✉ **15 Sharples Avenue, Astley Bridge, Bolton, Lancashire, BL1 7HB** Ⓟ
☎ 01204 303364 Ⓕ 01204 303364
Ⓔ maybern@alpineantiques.co.uk
Ⓦ www.alpineantiques.co.uk
Est. 1974 *Stock size* Medium
Stock Silver, glass, porcelain, collectables etc
Open Mon–Sat 9.30am–5pm
Fairs Chester
Services Valuations

Red Rose Cricket Books
Contact Mr M Tebay
✉ **196 Belmont Road, Astley Bridge, Bolton, Lancashire, BL1 7AR** Ⓟ
☎ 01204 596118 Ⓕ 01204 597070
Ⓔ redrosebooks@btinternet.com
Ⓦ www.cricketsupplies.com/books

Est. 1993 *Stock size* Small
Stock Antiquarian and second-hand books and prints on cricket
Open By appointment
Services Catalogues (5 per annum)

ATHERTON

The Emporium
Contact Mr G Wilson
486 Blackburn Road, Atherton, Bolton, Lancashire, BL1 8PE
01204 303090 01204 302299
Est. 1989 *Stock size* Large
Stock Wide variety of second-hand Edwardian–Victorian furniture, china, collectables, glass etc
Open Mon–Sat 9.30am–5pm Sun 11am–4pm
Services Valuations

BOLTON

Bolton Antique Centre
Contact Mr G Roberts
96 Great Moor Street, Bolton, Lancashire, BL3 6DS
01204 362694 0780 9012306
Est. 1992 *Stock size* Medium
No. of dealers 20
Stock Quality antique furniture, paintings, china, silver, Art Deco, collectables
Open Mon–Sat 10am–5pm
Services Valuations

Bolton Pianos & Antique Export
Contact Frank Sotgiu
Victoria Buildings, Hanover Street, Bolton, Lancashire, BL1 4TG
01204 362036 01204 380355
www.antica.co.uk
Est. 1983 *Stock size* Large
Stock Georgian–Edwardian furniture for export
Open Mon–Sat 9am–5pm
Services Shipping

B J Dawson (BNTA)
Contact Mr P Dawson
52 St Helens Road, Bolton, Lancashire, BL3 3NN
01204 63732 01204 63732
07801 537412
dawsoncoins@btconnect.com
historycoin.com
Est. 1966 *Stock size* Large
Stock Ancient coins – Greek, Roman, Byzantine, medallions, old English coins
Open Mon–Fri 9am–5pm Sat 9am–noon
Fairs London Coin Fair
Services Valuations, lists, medal mounting

Ironchurch Antique Centre
Contact Mr P Wilkinson
Iron Church, Blackburn Road, Bolton, Lancashire, BL1 8DR
01204 383616
Est. 1993 *Stock size* Large
No. of dealers 20
Stock Situated in an old church, offering antiques, furniture, pottery, porcelain, clocks, paintings
Open Mon–Sun 10am–5pm

G Oakes & Son
Contact Mr S Hughes
160–162 Blackburn Road, Bolton, Lancashire, BL1 8DR
01204 526587 07774 284609
ycs12@dial.pipex.com
www.Antique-DealerUK.com
Est. 1959 *Stock size* Large
Stock Antiques, Georgian–1920s furniture, shipping furniture
Open Tues–Sat noon–5pm or by appointment
Services Shipping

Olde Mill Antiques
Contact Paul Morris
Grecian Mill, Fletcher Street, Bolton, Lancashire, BL3 6NG
0800 542 5756 or 01204 528678
Est. 1980 *Stock size* Large
Stock Georgian–Victorian and shipping furniture
Open Mon–Fri 9am–5.30pm Sat Sun 9.30am–4pm

BREDBURY

The Old Curiosity Shop
Contact Mrs S Crook
123 Stockport Road West, Bredbury, Stockport, Greater Manchester, SK6 2AN
0161 494 9469
Est. 1983 *Stock size* Large
Stock 1920s furniture, barley twist a speciality, brass, clocks, pottery
Open Mon–Sat 10am–6pm Sun noon–5pm closed Wed
Services Hand stripping service

BROMLEY CROSS

Drop Dial Antiques
Contact Irene Roberts
Last Drop Village, Hospital Road, Bromley Cross, Bolton, Lancashire, BL7 9PZ
01204 307186 or 01257 480995
Est. 1974 *Stock size* Medium
Stock Clocks, barometers, boxes, small items of furniture
Open Tues–Sun 12.30–4.30pm closed Mon
Fairs Ripley Castle, Stoneyhurst (Galloway Fairs), Naworth Castle, Duncombe Park
Services Clock and barometer restoration

Ellis Books (PBFA)
Contact Siri Ellis
Last Drop Village, Hospital Road, Bromley Cross, Bolton, Lancashire, BL7 9PZ
01204 597511
mail@siriellisbooks.co.uk
www.siriellisbooks.co.uk
Est. 1998 *Stock size* Medium
Stock Antiquarian and second-hand illustrated and children's books
Open Mon–Fri noon–5pm Sat Sun 10am–5pm
Fairs Buxton, Pudsey, PBFA
Services Free book search

BURY

Newtons of Bury
Contact Mr Glen Wild
151 The Rock, Bury, Lancashire, BL9 0ND
0161 764 1863 0161 761 7129
Est. 1989 *Stock size* Medium
Stock Antiques, furniture, china etc
Open Mon–Sat 9am–5pm Sun noon–4pm
Services House clearance

CHEADLE HULME

John Arnold & Co
Contact Mr W Bradshaw
Central Salerooms, 15 Station Road, Cheadle Hulme, Cheshire, SK8 5AF
0161 485 2777 0161 485 3777
Est. 1865

Open Mon–Fri 10am–4pm
Sales Antiques and general sale Wed 11am, viewing day prior 11am–4pm day of sale 10–11am
Frequency Weekly
Catalogues No

Andrew Foott Antiques
Contact Andrew Foott
4 Claremont Road, Cheadle Hulme, Cheshire, SK8 6EG
0161 485 3559
Est. 1986 *Stock size* Small
Stock Georgian furniture, barometers
Open Mon–Fri 9am–5pm
Fairs NEC
Services Restorations

David Lloyd
Contact David Lloyd
10 Ravenoak Road, Cheadle Hulme, Cheshire, SK8 7DL
0161 486 6368 Ⓜ 07711 948403
dloyd@onetel.net.uk
Est. 1991 *Stock size* Medium
Stock 18th–20thC silver, silver plate, flatware
Open By appointment only
Fairs Newark, Staffordshire
Services Matching flatware for canteens

ECCLES

Stephen Shawcross & Son
Contact Mr J. McInnes
103 Church Street, Eccles, Manchester, Lancashire, M30 0EJ
0161 789 3537 Ⓕ 0161 787 8461
Est. 1870
Open Mon–Sat 9am–5pm closed Wed

FAILSWORTH

Failsworth Mill Antiques
Contact Mr I Macdonald
Failsworth Mill, Ashton Road West, Failsworth, Manchester, Lancashire, M35 0FD
0161 684 7440 Ⓕ 0161 681 7111
Est. 1993 *Stock size* Large
Stock Furniture, small collectables etc in one of the largest warehouses in North England
Open Mon–Fri 9am–5pm
Sun 10am–4pm closed Bank Holidays
Services Restorations, export

The New Cavern Antiques & Collectors' Centre
Contact Mr Peter Stanley
Failsworth Mill, Ashton Road West, Failsworth, Manchester, Lancashire, M35 0FD
0161 684 7802 Ⓕ 0161 628 5999
Est. 1997 *Stock size* Large
No. of dealers 40
Stock Antiques, collectables, furniture
Open Mon–Sun 10am–4.30pm closed Sat
Services Shipping, valuations

R J O'Brien & Son Antiques Ltd
Contact Mr R O'Brien
Failsworth Mill, Ashton Road West, Failsworth, Manchester, Lancashire, M35 0FD
0161 688 4414 Ⓕ 0161 688 4414
obantiques@btinternet.com
www.antique-exports.com
Est. 1972 *Stock size* Large
Stock Antique furniture
Open Mon–Fri 9am–5pm or by appointment
Services Container and courier service

T L H & Company
Contact Mr Thomas Higham
Unit 5, Victory Industrial Estate, Mill Street, Failsworth, Manchester, Lancashire, M35 0BJ
0161 688 9099 Ⓕ 0161 688 9050
tlh@auctions1.freeserve.co.uk
Est. 1994
Open Mon–Sat 9am–5.30pm
Sales Weekly sales Tues 10am, viewing Mon 2–5.30pm Tues 9–10am
Frequency Weekly
Catalogues Yes

HAZEL GROVE

A F Brock & Co Ltd
Contact Mr A F Brock or Mrs W Jensen
269 London Road, Hazel Grove, Stockport, Cheshire, SK7 4PL
0161 456 5050 Ⓕ 0161 456 5112
info@afbrock.co.uk
www.afbrock.co.uk
Est. 1969
Open Mon–Fri 9am–5pm Sat 9am–4pm closed Wed
Sales 8 coins, jewellery and antiques sales per year, phone for details of sale. Specialist coin and banknote sales periodically. Held at the Acton Court Hotel, Stockport
Frequency 8 per year
Catalogues Yes

HEYWOOD

Heywood Antiques
Contact Mr Norman Marsh
5 Manchester Road, Heywood, Lancashire, OL10 2DZ
01706 621281
Est. 1989 *Stock size* Medium
Stock Late Victorian, Edwardian furniture, clocks
Open Mon–Sat 9.30am–5pm closed Tues
Fairs Newark, Camelot
Services Clock repairs, restorations

HOLLINGWORTH

Annatique
Contact Mr G MacKay
3 Wooley Lane, Hollingworth, Hyde, Cheshire, SK14 8NW
01457 852960
Est. 1977 *Stock size* Large
Stock Small furniture, clocks, lighting, mirrors, collectables
Open Thurs–Sat noon–6pm
Services Clock repairs

LITTLEBOROUGH

George Kelsall (PBFA)
Contact Mr B Kelsall
22 Church Street, Littleborough, Lancashire, OL15 9AA
01706 370244
kelsall@bookshop22.fsnet.co.uk
Est. 1979 *Stock size* Large
Stock Mainly second-hand, modern and antiquarian books on art, history, reference, topography of Northern England, industrial history, transport, social history
Open Mon 11am–5pm Tues 1–5pm Wed–Sat 10am–5pm
Fairs PBFA (Lancashire, Yorkshire)

Nostalgia
Contact Mr Philip Sunderland
24 Church Street, Littleborough, Lancashire, OL15 9AA
01706 377325 07711 503 755
Est. 1994 *Stock size* Medium
Stock General antiques, furniture, lighting, Victorian fireplaces
Open Mon–Sat 10.30am–5.30pm closed Tues

MANCHESTER

Capes, Dunn & Co (ISVA)
Contact Alison Lakin
38 Charles Street, Manchester, M1 7DB
0161 273 1911 0161 273 3474
capesdunn@compuserve.com
www.ukauctioneers.com
Est. 1826
Open Mon–Fri 9am–5pm
Sales Victorian and later period furniture and effects Mon noon, viewing from 10am day of sale. Specialist sales most Tues noon, viewing Mon 10am–4pm Tues 10–noon
Frequency Twice fortnightly
Catalogues Yes

Carl Ross Fireplaces
Contact Carl Ross
1026–1028 Stockport Road, Manchester, M19 3WX
0161 224 2550
Est. 1991 *Stock size* Large
Stock Fireplaces and accessories
Open Mon– 9.30am–4pm

Didsbury Antiques
Contact Mr Alan Willis
85 School Lane, Manchester, M20 6WN
0161 434 7487
Est. 1979 *Stock size* Medium
Stock General antiques
Open Mon–Sat 10am–5pm
Fairs Newark
Services Valuations, house clearance

Dollies Bear-Gere Ltd
Contact Robin Cottrill
61 Festival Village, The Trafford Centre, Manchester, M17 8FS
0161 202 9800 0161 749 9955
Est. 1998 *Stock size* Large
Stock New and second-hand Steiff and collectable bears, dolls
Open Mon–Fri 10am–10pm Sat 9am–7pm Sun noon–6pm

Dollies Bear-Gere Ltd
Contact Susan Cottrill
113 Regents Crescent, The Trafford Centre, Manchester, M17 8AR
0161 749 9898 0161 749 9955
Est. 1998 *Stock size* Large
Stock New and second-hand Steiff and collectable bears, dolls
Open Mon–Fri 10am–10pm Sat 9am–7pm Sun noon–6pm

Empire Exchange
Contact Mr David Ireland
1 Newton Street, Manchester, M1 1HW
0161 236 4445 0161 273 5007
empire@globalnet.co.uk
www.empir-uk.com
Est. 1986 *Stock size* Large
Stock Collectors' items, old and new books, toys, football memorabilia, dolls, teddy bears, jewellery, military
Open Mon–Sun 9am–7.30pm
Services Publishing company, valuations

Ginnell Gallery
Contact Mr J K Mottershead
The Ginnell, 18–22 Lloyd Street, Manchester, M2 5WA
0161 833 9037 0161 833 9037
www.antiques-atlas.com/ginnell.htm
Est. 1980 *Stock size* Large
No. of dealers 30
Stock General antiques, decorative arts 1900–present day, antiquarian and second-hand books
Open Mon–Sat 9.30am–5.30pm
Services Café, bar

Levenshulme Antiques Village
Contact Mr Tony Warburton
965 Stockport Road, Manchester, M19 3NP
0161 256 4644
Est. 1979
No. of dealers 20
Stock Furniture dealers situated in Old Town Hall
Open Mon–Sat 10am–5.30pm Sun 11am–4pm
Services Restoration, wood stripping

Malik Antiques
Contact Miss C Malik
10–12 Slade Lane, Manchester, M13 0QE
0161 225 4431 0161 225 4431
Est. 1985 *Stock size* Large
Stock Antique furniture, porcelain, architectural items, garden furniture
Open Mon–Fri 10am–6pm Sat by appointment

Secondhand & Rare Books
Contact Mr E Hopkinson
1 Church Street, Manchester, M4 1PN
0161 834 5964 or 01625 861608
Est. 1972 *Stock size* Medium
Stock Antiquarian and second-hand books, some topography and special interest
Open Mon–Sat noon–4pm

Select
Contact Mr Abushal
276a Claremont Road, Manchester, M14 4TS
0161 226 1152 0161 226 1152
Est. 1994 *Stock size* Medium
Stock General antiques, mostly furniture
Open Mon–Sat 10am–5pm

MARPLE BRIDGE

Townhouse Antiques
Contact Mr Paul Buxcey
21 Town Street, Marple Bridge, Stockport, Cheshire, SK6 5AA
0161 427 2228
Est. 1985 *Stock size* Medium
Stock Stripped pine furniture, carved wood, brass, iron beds, decorative antiques
Open Mon–Sat 10am–6pm

Vogue Antiques
Contact Mrs J Husband
80a Lower Fold, Marple Bridge, Stockport, Cheshire, SK6 5DU
0161 427 1070
Est. 1995 *Stock size* Medium
Stock French country provincial furniture, lighting, mirrors, decorative items
Open Wed–Sat 10.30am–4.30pm
Services Restorations

OLDHAM

The Collectors Centre
Contact Mr I Thorogood
12a Waterloo Street, Oldham, Lancashire, OL1 1SQ
0161 624 1365
Est. 1991 *Stock size* Large
No. of dealers 4
Stock Broad range of collectables – records, pop memorabilia, brass, pressed and old English glass, china, pottery, silver, videos, toys, etc
Open Mon–Sat 10am–5pm closed Tues
Services Valuations

Bob Lees
Contact Mr Bob Lees
65 George Street, Oldham, Lancashire, OL1 1LX
0161 628 4693
Est. 1994 *Stock size* Large
Stock General bookshop, second-hand, some antiquarian, local history
Open Mon–Sat 10.30am–6pm
Fairs North West Book Fairs, Pudsey, Cresta Court

Marks Antiques, Jewellers/Pawnbrokers
Contact Mrs Marks
16 Waterloo Street, Oldham, Lancashire, OL1 1SQ
0161 624 5975 F 0161 624 5975
M 07979 508495
E bmarks46@hotmail.com
Est. 1970 *Stock size* Medium
Stock Jewellery, pottery, good-quality furniture
Open Mon–Sat 9.30am–5pm closed Tues
Fairs Newark
Services Pawnbroker, valuations

PRESTWICH

Family Antiques
Contact Jean Ditondo
405–407 Bury New Road, Prestwich, Manchester, M25 1AA
0161 798 0036 F 0161 798 0036
Est. 1984 *Stock size* Large
Stock Antique furniture
Open Mon–Sat 10am–5pm
Fairs Newark, Swinderby
Services Valuations

Prestwich Antiques
Contact Mr S Harris or Mr T Finn
371 Bury New Road, Prestwich, Manchester, M25 1AW
07946 417074 F 07946 417074
E victorianimports@btinternet.com
W www.welcome.to/victorianimports
Est. 1984 *Stock size* Large
Stock Antique four-poster beds, furniture
Open Mon–Sat 10am–5.30pm
Fairs Newark, Ardingly
Services Valuations, restorations

Village Antiques
Contact Ruth Weidenbaum
416 Bury New Road, Prestwich, Manchester, M25 1BD
0161 773 3612
Est. 1981 *Stock size* Medium
Stock Porcelain, pottery, glass, pewter, small furniture
Open Mon–Sun 10am–5pm closed Wed pm

RADCLIFFE

Partners Antiques
Contact Mr L Ditondo
Walker Street, Radcliffe, Manchester, M26 1FH
0161 796 7095 F 0161 796 7095
E luigi.ditondo@btinternet.com
W www.luigi.ditondo@btinternet.com
Est. 1991 *Stock size* Large
Stock Victorian and shipping furniture
Open Mon–Sun 9am–6pm
Fairs Newark, Ardingly
Services Container service

ROCHDALE

Antiques & Bygones
Contact Mr K Bonn
100 Drake Street, Rochdale, Lancashire, OL16 1PQ
01706 648114
E ken.bonn@btopenworld.com
Est. 1983 *Stock size* Medium
Stock Small antique items including pottery, silver, coins, medals, jewellery, militaria, collectables
Open Wed–Sat 10am–4pm

Central Auction Rooms
Contact Terry Pickering
4 Baron Street, Rochdale, Lancashire, OL16 1SJ
01706 646298 F 01706 646298
Est. 1919
Open Mon–Fri 9.30am–4.30pm
Sales General household sales Tues 2pm, viewing Mon 9.30am–4.30pm. Occasional antiques and small items Tues 2pm, viewing Mon 9.30am–4.30pm
Frequency Fortnightly
Catalogues Yes

Rochdale Book Company (PBFA)
Contact Mr John Worthy
399 Oldham Road, Rochdale, Lancashire, L165LN
01706 631136 F 01706 713294
Est. 1972 *Stock size* Medium
Stock General stock of antiquarian and second-hand books
Open Sat 10.30am–5.30pm weekdays by appointment
Fairs PBFA (London, Lancashire and Yorkshire)
Services Valuations

ROMILEY

Romiley Antiques & Jewellery
Contact Mr Peter Green
42 Stockport Road, Romiley, Stockport, Cheshire, SK6 3AA
0161 494 6920
Est. 1984 *Stock size* Medium
Stock Antique and second-hand jewellery, Georgian and Victorian furniture, pottery, general antiques, clocks, barometers
Open Thurs–Sat 9am–5pm
Services Valuations, house clearance

SALFORD

A S Antique Galleries
Contact Audrey Sternshine
26 Broad Street, Pendleton, Salford, Greater Manchester, M6 5BY
0161 737 5938 or 07000 ART DECO F 0161 737 6626
E as@sternshine.demon.co.uk
Est. 1973 *Stock size* Large
Stock Art Nouveau and Art Deco, bronze and bronze and ivory figures, lighting, cameo glass, pewter, ceramics, furniture,

jewellery, silver and general antiques
Open Thurs–Sat 10am–5.30pm or by appointment
Services Valuations, restorations, commissions to purchase

STALYBRIDGE

Highams Auctions (NAVA)
Contact Mr M McLaughlin
Waterloo House, Waterloo Road, Stalybridge, Cheshire, SK15 2AU
☎ 0161 338 8698 ℱ 0161 338 4183
ⓔ info@hyamauctions.com
ⓦ www.highamsauctions.com
Est. 1941
Open Mon–Fri 9am–5pm
Sales General antiques sales Sat 10am, viewing Fri 1–4.30pm Sat 9–10am
Frequency Fortnightly
Catalogues Yes

STANDISH

Corner Cupboard Antiques
Contact Mrs B Calderbank
49 Preston Road, Standish, Wigan, Lancashire, WN6 0JH
☎ 01257 426454
Est. 1980 ***Stock size*** Small
Stock General antiques, furniture, old dolls, china, pottery
Open Thurs Fri 10am–4pm

STOCKPORT

Antique Furniture Warehouse
Contact Mr M Shields
Unit 3–4, Royal Oak Buildings, Cooper Street, Stockport, Cheshire, SK1 3QJ
☎ 0161 429 8590 ℱ 0161 480 5375
Est. 1981 ***Stock size*** Large
Stock Wide range of antiques Georgian–1940s including porcelain, English inlay furniture, decorative items, architectural antiques, credenzas, walnut and mahogany bookcases
Open Mon–Sat 9am–5pm

E R Antiques Centre
Contact Mrs E Warlowton
122 Wellington Street, Stockport, Cheshire, SK1 1YH
☎ 0161 429 6646 ℱ 0161 480 5598
Est. 1980 ***Stock size*** Large
No. of dealers 6
Stock Glass, china, pottery, scent bottles, costume jewellery, silver plate
Open Mon–Sat noon–7pm

Flintlock Antiques
Contact Mr F Tomlinson
28–30 Bramhall Lane, Stockport, Cheshire, SK2 6HR
☎ 0161 480 9973
Est. 1968 ***Stock size*** Medium
Stock Scientific instruments, telescopes, military items, paintings, marine models, furniture
Open Mon–Fri 10am–6pm

Hole in the Wall Antiques
Contact Mr A Ledger
20 Buxton Road, Heaviley, Stockport, Cheshire, SK2 6NU
☎ 0161 476 4013 ℱ 0161 285 2860
ⓔ paul@antiquesimportexport.freeserve.co.uk.
Est. 1963 ***Stock size*** Large
Stock 1850–1920 American, Georgian–Edwardian furniture
Open Mon–Sat 9.30am–5.30pm or by appointment
Fairs Newark, Ardingly
Services Courier

Imperial Antiques (LAPADA)
Contact Alfred Todd
295 Buxton Road, Great Moor, Stockport, Cheshire, SK2 7NR
☎ 0161 483 3322 ℱ 0161 483 3376
ⓔ alfred@imperial antiques.com
ⓦ imperialantiques.com
Est. 1975 ***Stock size*** Medium
Stock Oriental antiques, ceramics, carpets, lighting, silver, silver plate
Open Mon–Fri 9am–5pm
Fairs NEC
Services Valuations

Manchester Antique Company
Contact Mr J Long
Mac House, St Thomas Place, Stockport, Cheshire, SK1 3TZ
☎ 0161 355 5566 ℱ 0161 355 5588
ⓔ sales@manchester-antique.co.uk
ⓦ www.manchester-antique.co.uk
Est. 1969 ***Stock size*** Large
Stock General antiques, second-hand and Continental European furniture
Trade only Mainly trade
Open Mon–Fri 8am–5pm Sat 10am–4pm

Nostalgia
Contact Mrs E Durrant
Holland's Mill, 61 Shaw Heath, Stockport, Cheshire, SK3 8BH
☎ 0161 477 7706 ℱ 0161 477 2267
ⓔ info@nostalgia-uk.com
ⓦ www.nostalgia-uk.com
Est. 1977 ***Stock size*** Large
Stock Antique fireplaces 1780–1900, sanitary ware
Open Tues–Fri 10am–6pm Sat 10am–5pm

STRETFORD

Insitu (SALVO)
Contact Mr F Newsham
149–151 Barton Road, Stretford, Manchester, Lancashire, M32 8DP
☎ 0161 865 2110
Est. 1984 ***Stock size*** Large
Stock Complete range of antiques, fixtures and fittings
Open Mon–Sat 9am–5.30pm Sun 11am–5pm

WIGAN

Avaroot
Contact Mr P Prescott
53a Mesnes Street (rear), Wigan, Lancashire, WN1 1QX
☎ 01942 241500
Est. 1994 ***Stock size*** Large
Stock Collectables including Doulton, Beswick, books, cigarette cards, records, coins, badges, railwayana, lamps
Open Mon–Sat 10am–5pm

John Robinson Antiques
Contact Mrs E Halliwell
172–176 Manchester Road, Higher Ince, Wigan, Lancashire, WN2 2EA
☎ 01942 247773 ℱ 01942 824964
Est. 1963 ***Stock size*** Large
Stock Wholesale exporters, mostly shipping furniture
Trade only Yes
Open By appointment only

Colin de Rouffignac (BNTA)
Contact Mr C de Rouffignac
57 Wigan Lane, Wigan, Lancashire, WN1 2LF
01942 237927
Est. 1970 *Stock size* Medium
Stock 18th–early 20thC furniture, early coins, medals, general antiques, paintings
Open Mon–Sat 10am–4.30pm closed Wed
Fairs Tatton
Services Valuations

Steve's World Famous Movie Store
Contact Mr S Ellison
45 Cadogan Drive, Winstanley, Wigan, Lancashire, WN3 6JH
01942 213541 F 01942 213541
E movie.store@virgin.net
W www.worldfamousmovie.com
Est. 1973 *Stock size* Large
Stock Stills, posters, vinyl and CD soundtracks, books and movie magazines from 1916 onwards, other memorabilia, autographs
Open By appointment
Services Free search, mail order, valuations

Wiend Books & Collectables (PBFA)
Contact Mr P G Morris
8–10 & 12 The Wiend, Wigan, Lancashire, WN1 1PF
01942 820500 F 01942 820500
M 07976 604203
E wiendbooks@lycos.co.uk
W www.wiendbooks.co.uk
Est. 1997 *Stock size* Large
Stock General stock of antiquarian and second-hand books, printed collectables, comics, stamps, programmes, badges, Wade
Open Mon–Sat 9.30am–5pm closed Tues
Fairs PBFA
Services Valuations

WORSLEY

Northern Clocks (LAPADA)
Contact Robert or Mary Anne
Boothsbank Farm, Worsley, Manchester, M28 1LL
0161 790 8414 M 07970 820258
E info@northernclocks.co.uk
W www.northernclocks.co.uk
Est. 1997 *Stock size* Medium
Stock Longcase, bracket clocks
Open Thurs–Sat 10am–5pm or by appointment
Fairs Harrogate, G-Mex, Antiques for Everyone
Services Valuations, restoration

G White
Contact Mr G White
273 Chorley Road, Worsley, Manchester, M27 6AZ
0161 794 3806
Est. 1964 *Stock size* Medium
Stock General antiques, period furniture, clocks, sporting equipment
Open By appointment
Services Valuations, restorations

LANCASHIRE

ACCRINGTON

Almonds House Clearances
Contact Mr E Phillips
79 Burnley Road, Accrington, Lancashire, BB5 1AG
01254 391661 M 07881 407982
Est. 1984 *Stock size* Medium
Stock Victorian–modern furniture, pottery etc
Open Mon–Sat 9am–5pm closed Wed
Services Valuations

Alpha Coins & Medals (OMRS)
Contact Mr P Darlington
10 Water Street, Accrington, Lancashire, BB5 6PX
01254 395540 F 01254 393323
Est. 1994 *Stock size* Medium
Stock Post-1800 British coins and medals
Open Mon–Sat 9.30am–5pm
Fairs Bradford Coin Show, Outwood Memorial Hall Medal Show, Wakefield
Services Medal mounting

Bohemia
Contact Mr R Oldman
11 Warner Street, Accrington, Lancashire, BB5 1HN
01254 231119
Est. 1993 *Stock size* Large
Stock 1940s–70s clothing and accessories
Open Tues–Sat 10.30am–5pm closed Mon Wed
Fairs Manchester Textile Fairs

Revival
Contact Mr Ian Smith
34 Warner Street, Accrington, Lancashire, BB5 1HN
01254 382316
Est. 1989 *Stock size* Large
Stock Costume, textiles, jewellery from 1900–70s
Open Mon–Sat 10.30am–5pm closed Wed or by appointment
Fairs Hammersmith Textiles
Services Costume hire

BARTON

Kopper Kettle Furniture
Contact Mr Steve Round
639 Garstang Road, Barton, Preston, Lancashire, PR3 5DQ
01772 861064
Est. 1998 *Stock size* Medium
Stock Edwardian–Victorian furniture, some reproduction
Open Mon–Sun 10.30am–5.30pm closed Fri
Services Valuations, metal polishing

BLACKBURN

Ancient and Modern (NAG, OMRS)
Contact Zac Coles
17 Newmarket Street, Blackburn, Lancashire, BB1 7DR
01254 668818 F 01254 677866
Est. 1943 *Stock size* Large
Stock Georgian–modern jewellery, watches, silver, coins, medals
Open Mon–Sat 9am–5.30pm
Fairs Miami, Bangkok
Services Valuations, restorations

Decades (Textile Association)
Contact Janet Conroy
20 Lord Street West, Blackburn, Lancashire, BB2 1JX
01254 693320
Est. 1989 *Stock size* Large
Stock Costumes, textiles, accessories, pottery, small furniture, pictures, glass, curios, collectables
Open Mon–Sat 10.30am–5pm or by appointment
Fairs Margaret Bulger Art Fairs, Hammersmith

Fieldings Antiques & Clocks
Contact Mr Andrew Fielding
149 Blackmoor Road, Blackburn, Lancashire, BB1 2LG
01254 263358 07973 698961
Est. 1964 *Stock size* Large
Stock Longcase and other clocks, period furniture, steam engines, vintage motorcycles
Open Mon–Fri 9am–5pm

Mitchells Lock Antiques
Contact Mr S Mitchell
76 Bolton Road, Blackburn, Lancashire, BB2 3PZ
01254 664663
Est. 1973 *Stock size* Large
Stock General antiques
Open Mon–Sat 9am–5pm
Fairs Newark, Swinderby

BLACKPOOL

Ascot Antiques
Contact Mr C Winwood
106 Holmefield Road, Blackpool, Lancashire, FY2 9RF
01253 356383
Est. 1987 *Stock size* Medium
Stock Georgian–Victorian furniture and oil paintings
Trade only Yes
Open By appointment
Services Valuations

Peter Christian
Contact Mrs Ann Christian
400–402 Waterloo Road, South Shore, Blackpool, Lancashire, FY4 4BL
01253 763268 01253 763268
Est. 1978 *Stock size* Medium
Stock 1860s–1920s decorative arts
Open Mon–Sat 10am–5.30pm closed Wed
Fairs Newark, Swinderby

Robinsons Timber Building Supplies Ltd
Contact Mr A Robinson
3–7 Boothley Road, Blackpool, Lancashire, FY1 3RS
01253 628826 01253 627812
Est. 1938 *Stock size* Large
Stock Architectural antiques, doors, floors etc, garden items
Open Mon–Fri 8am–5.30pm Sat 8am–2pm
Services Restorations of timber flooring

B Scott-Spencer
Contact Mr J Neiman
228 Church Street, Blackpool, Lancashire, FY1 3PX
01253 294489 01253 626977
Stock Wide range of general antiques, jewellery, stamps, collectables etc
Open Mon–Fri 10am–4pm phone for appointment
Services Valuations, repairs, buying large diamonds

BRETHERTON

The Old Corn Mill Antique Centre
Contact Mr M Fellows
64 South Road, Bretherton, Lancashire, PR5 7AG
01772 601371 01772 601932
Est. 1999 *Stock size* Large
No. of dealers 50
Stock Antiques and collectables
Open Mon–Sat 10.30am–5.30pm Sun 11am–5pm

BURNLEY

Brun-Lea Antiques & Furnishings
Contact Mr John Waite
Unit 1, Travis Street, Burnley, Lancashire, BB10 1DG
01282 413513 01282 832769
07860 511842
www.antiques-atlas.com/brunlea.htm
Est. 1973 *Stock size* Large
Stock Period furniture
Open Mon–Thurs 8.30am–5.30pm Fri Sat 8.30am–4pm Sun noon–4pm

Lonesome Pine Antiques
Contact Mr P Berry
19 Bank Parade, Burnley, Lancashire, BB11 1UH
01282 428415
Est. 1987 *Stock size* Medium
Stock Antique pine furniture, period furniture, reclaimed pine furniture
Open Mon–Sat 9am–5pm
Services Bespoke furniture

BURSCOUGH

West Lancashire Antiques Export (LAPADA)
Contact Brett Griffiths
Victoria Mill, Victoria Street, Burscough, Lancashire, LN40 0SN
01704 894634
Est. 1969 *Stock size* Large
Stock Antique furniture
Open Mon–Fri 9am–5.30pm Sat Sun 10am–5.30pm
Fairs Swinderby, Newark
Services Shipping

CHARNOCK RICHARD

Park Hall
Contact Mr David Fletcher
Exhibition Halls, Charnock Richard, Lancashire, PR7 5LP
0161 773 7001 0161 773 7001
Stock size Medium
No. of dealers 100
Stock General antiques fair held every Sunday. £2 entrance fee
Open 8am–3pm

CHATBURN

T & J Brindle Antiques (LAPADA)
Contact T Brindle
6–8 Sawley Road, Chatburn, Clitheroe, Lancashire, BB7 4AS
01200 440025 01200 440090
www.antiqueweb.co.uk/tbrindle
Est. 1961 *Stock size* Large
Stock Good quality antiques
Open Mon–Fri 9am–5pm or by appointment
Fairs Olympia

CLEVELEYS

Smythe's
Contact Mr P Smythe
174 Victoria Road West, Cleveleys, Lancashire, FY5 3NE
01253 852184 01253 854084
Est. 1929
Open Mon–Fri 9am–5.30pm Sat 9am–noon
Sales General sales every 2 weeks, antiques sales every 6 weeks
Catalogues Yes

CLITHEROE

Brittons Watches (NAG)
Contact Mr P Walden, Glen Britton
4 King Street, Clitheroe, Lancashire, BB7 2EP

☎ 01200 425555 Ⓕ 01200 424200
Ⓔ info@brittons-watches.co.uk
Ⓦ www.brittons-watches.co.uk
Est. 1969 *Stock size* Large
Stock Quality pre-owned wrist watches from 1920s to present day, antique and quality second-hand jewellery
Open Mon–Sat 10am–5pm closed Tues
Services Watch and jewellery repairs, valuations

Clitheroe Collectables
Contact Mrs J Spensley
✉ **13 Duck Street, Clitheroe, Lancashire, BB7 1LP** Ⓟ
☎ 01200 422222 Ⓕ 01200 422223
Ⓔ sales@clicollect.fsnet.co.uk
Ⓦ www.clitheroecollectables.co.uk
Est. 1989 *Stock size* Medium
Stock Pottery, Victorian pine furniture
Open Mon–Sat 9am–5pm
Fairs Harrogate
Services Restorations of antique pine

Past and Present Fireplaces
Contact Mr David Hollings
✉ **22 Whalley Road, Clitheroe, Lancashire, BB7 1AW** Ⓟ
☎ 01200 428678/445373
Est. 1987 *Stock size* Large
Stock Architectural antiques, general antiques, fireplaces a speciality
Open Mon–Sat 10.30am–5pm Sun by appointment closed Wed
Fairs Newark
Services Fitting service, fire accessories

Roundstone Books
Contact Mr J Harding
✉ **120 Lowergate, Clitheroe, Lancashire, BB7 1AG** Ⓟ
☎ 01200 444242
Ⓔ joharbooks@aol.com
Ⓦ www.roundstonebooks.co.uk
Est. 1995 *Stock size* Medium
Stock Antiquarian and second-hand books, general stock including alternative medicine, poetry, literature, children's books
Open Tues–Sat 10am–5pm closed Wed
Services Book search

COLNE

Ingleside Antiques
Contact Mr Jack Fry
✉ **13 Keighley Road, Colne, Lancashire, BB8 0LP** Ⓟ
☎ 01282 860046
Ⓜ 07775 515014
Est. 1990 *Stock size* Medium
Stock Longcase, bracket, wall, mantel clocks, furniture
Open Mon Wed Fri Sat 10am–5pm
Services Repairs

DARWEN

Belgrave Antiques Centre
Contact Mr M Cooney
✉ **Brittania Mill, 136 Bolton Road, Darwen, Lancashire, BB3 1BZ** Ⓟ
☎ 01254 777714
Ⓔ belgraveantiques@aol.com
Est. 1997 *Stock size* Large
No. of dealers 40
Stock Furniture, pottery, Victorian stripped pine, architectural antiques, collectables
Open Mon–Sat 9.30am–5pm Sun 10am–4.30pm
Services Stripping, shipping

Grove Antiques
Contact Mr K Cooney
✉ **Hampden Mill, Springdale, Grimshaw Street, Darwen, Lancashire, BB3** Ⓟ
☎ 01254 776644
Est. 1984 *Stock size* Small
Stock Mixed stock of Edwardian furniture, bric-a-brac
Open Mon–Sat 10am–4pm
Fairs Newark, Kempton

K C Antiques (LAPADA)
Contact Mr C Davies
✉ **538 Bolton Road, Darwen, Lancashire, BB3 2JR** Ⓟ
☎ 01254 772252 Ⓕ 01254 704267
Ⓔ mickdavies@breathe.mail.net.
Est. 1970 *Stock size* Medium
Stock 18th–19thC furniture and decorative items
Open Mon–Sat 9am–5.30pm Sun 10am–4pm and by appointment
Fairs NEC LAPADA

ECCLESTON

Bygone Times
Contact Ged Wood
✉ **Grove Mill, The Green, Eccleston, Chorley, Lancashire, PR7 5PD** Ⓟ
☎ 01257 451889 Ⓕ 01257 451090
Ⓔ ged.wood@virgin.net
Ⓦ www.bygonetimes.co.uk
Est. 1988 *Stock size* Large
No. of dealers 250
Stock Antiques, furniture, small items, collectables, memorabilia
Open Mon–Sun 10am–6pm Wed 10am–8pm

Bygone Times International Plc
Contact Mr Charles Frankland
✉ **Grove Mill, The Green, Eccleston, Chorley, Lancashire, PR7 5PD** Ⓟ
☎ 01257 453780 Ⓕ 01257 450197
Ⓔ enquire@ebygone-times.co.uk
Ⓦ www.bygone-times.com
Est. 1987 *Stock size* Large
Stock Wide range of architectural antiques
Open Mon–Sun 10am–5pm
Fairs Plaza, L.I.W.

The Cutlery Chest
Contact Mr R W Metcalf
✉ **Unit 6, The Carrington Centre, The Green, Eccleston, Chorley, Lancashire, PR7 5UP** Ⓟ
☎ 01257 451281
Ⓔ Robert.W.Metcalf@btinternet.com
Est. 1989 *Stock size* Medium
Stock Silver-plated cutlery, linen, china, glass
Open Wed–Sat 10.30am–5pm
Fairs Newark, Ardingly
Services Cutlery repair and silver-plating

FLEETWOOD

Pavilion
Contact Mr Edward McLaughlin
✉ **228 Dock Street, Fleetwood, Lancashire, FY7 6NU** Ⓟ
☎ 01253 778851 Ⓕ 01253 779192
Ⓔ pavilion@propitup.demon.co.uk
Est. 1984 *Stock size* Medium
Stock Decorative items for the home
Open Mon–Sat 10am–5.30pm
Fairs Newark

GARSTANG

Acanthus
Contact Mrs L Stocks
Unit 3, Thomas Court, Thomas Weind, Garstang, Preston, Lancashire, PR3 1LL P
☎ 01995 604780
Est. 1987 *Stock size* Medium
Stock Wide variety of stock including small furniture, china, copper, brass, pictures etc
Open Mon–Sat 10am–5pm closed Wed

GREAT HARWOOD

Benny Charlsworth's Snuff Box
Contact Naomi Walsh
51 Blackburn Road, Great Harwood, Blackburn, Lancashire, BB6 7DF P
☎ 01254 888550
Est. 1983 *Stock size* Large
Stock Antique furniture, paintings, pottery, costume jewellery, linen etc
Open Mon–Fri 10am–1pm 2–5pm Sat 9.30am–4pm closed Tues
Fairs Newark

Jeans Military Memories
Contact Mrs J South
32 Queen Street, Great Harwood, Blackburn, Lancashire, BB6 7QQ P
☎ 01254 877825 F 01254 877825
M 07710 636069
Est. 1996 *Stock size* Large
Stock Militaria, guns of all types, edge weaponry 1800–2002
Open Mon–Fri 9am–5pm Sat 9am–4pm or by appointment

HAPTON

Pipkins Antiques
Contact Maurice Bradley
5 The Stables, Hapton, Nr Burnley, Lancashire, BB12 7LL P
F 01282 770548 M 07778 265909
E maurice@pipkins.fsbusiness.co.uk
W www.olddoors.co.uk
Est. 1996 *Stock size* Large
Stock Doors, door furniture, Belfast sinks, general architectural salvage
Open By appointment

HARLE SYKE

Kings Mill Antique Centre
Contact Linda Heuer
Unit 6, Kings Mill, Queen Street, Harle Syke, Burnley, Lancashire, BB10 2HX P
☎ 01282 431953 F 01282 839470
M 07803 153752
E antiques@kingsmill.demon.co.uk
W www.kingsmill.demon.co.uk
Est. 1996 *Stock size* Large
No. of dealers 30
Stock Antique furniture, Continental European collectables
Open Mon–Sat 10am–5pm Thurs 10am–8pm Sun 11am–5pm
Services Container service, export

HASLINGDEN

P J Brown Antiques
Contact Mrs K Brown
8 Church Street, Haslingden, Rossendale, Lancashire, BB4 5QU P
☎ 01706 224888 F 01706 224888
Est. 1979 *Stock size* Medium
Stock Georgian–Edwardian furniture, small antiques, advertising items, shop fittings, old bottles, pot lids
Open Mon–Fri 10am–5.30pm Sat 10am–4pm or by appointment
Fairs Newark
Services Containers

Fieldings Antiques & Clocks
Contact Mr Andrew Fielding
176–180 Blackburn Road, Haslingden, Rossendale, Lancashire, BB4 5HW P
☎ 01706 214254 M 07973 698961
Est. 1964 *Stock size* Large
Stock Longcase and other clocks, period furniture, steam engines, vintage motorcycles
Open Mon–Fri 9am–5pm

Holden Wood Antiques Centre
Contact John Ainslough
St Stephens, Grane Road, Haslingden, Rossendale, Lancashire, BB4 4AT P
☎ 01706 830803
E john@holdenwood.co.uk
W www.holdenwood.co.uk
Est. 1996 *Stock size* Large
No. of dealers 30
Stock Ceramics, clocks, watches, paintings, period and country furniture
Open Mon–Sun 10am–5pm
Services Valuations, restorations, tea rooms

HESKIN GREEN

Heskin Hall Antiques
Contact Mr Dennis Harrison
Wood Lane, Heskin Green, Chorley, Lancashire, PR7 5PA P
☎ 01257 452044 F 01257 450690
E heskinhallantiques@attglobal.net
Est. 1995 *Stock size* Large
No. of dealers 65
Stock A complete range of antiques and collectables
Open Mon–Sun 10am–5.30pm
Services Restorations

HORWICH

Stag's Head Antiques
Contact Mr George Bush
165 Chorley New Road, Horwich, Bolton, Lancashire, BL6 5QE P
☎ 01204 690962
Est. 1969 *Stock size* Medium
Stock General antiques mainly small furniture and bric-a-brac
Open Mon–Sat 10.30am–5pm closed 12.30–1.30pm

The Toy Shop
Contact Mr D Brandwood
138a Wright Street, Horwich, Bolton, Lancashire, BL6 7HU P
☎ 01204 669782 F 01204 669782
Est. 1972 *Stock size* Large
Stock Collectable toys, Dinky, Corgi, Hornby, Triang, Matchbox etc
Open Mon Thurs Fri 9.30am–5pm Tues Sat 9.30am–2pm
Services Valuations

KIRKBY LONSDALE

Architus Antiques & Collectables
Contact Mrs J Pearson
14 Main Street, Kirkby Lonsdale, Carnforth, Lancashire, LA6 2AE P

☎ 01524 272409
Est. 1994 *Stock size* Medium
Stock Wide range of antiques and collectables
Open Mon–Sat 10am–5pm
Services Valuations

Beck Head Books & Gallery
Contact Mr Stuart French or Mrs Barbara French
10 Beck Head, Kirkby Lonsdale, Lancashire, LA6 2AY
☎ 015242 71314
Est. 1984 *Stock size* Medium
Stock Furniture and decorative arts, chairs, small antiques, pictures, prints, antiquarian, out-of-print and second-hand books, antique maps, prints, old postcards
Open Tues–Sat 10am–5pm closed Wed

LANCASTER

Anything Old & Military Collectables
Contact Mr G H Chambers
55 Scotforth Road, Lancaster, Lancashire, LA1 4SA
☎ 01524 69933
Est. 1984 *Stock size* Medium
Stock Militaria including medals, cap badges, edged weapons, uniforms, helmets, Third Reich militaria
Open Wed Sat 1.30–6pm other times by appointment
Services Valuations, medal mounting

Atticus Bookshop
Contact Miss Tracey Mansell
26 King Street, Lancaster, Lancashire, LA1 1JY
☎ 01524 381413
trace@atticusbooks.demon.co.uk
Est. 1974 *Stock size* Medium
Stock General second-hand stock of books
Open Mon–Sat 10am–5pm
Services Book search

G B Antiques Centre
Contact Mr Alan Blackburn
Lancaster Leisure Park, Wyresdale Road, Lancaster, Lancashire, LA1 3LA
☎ 01524 844734 Ⓕ 01524 844735
Est. 1990 *Stock size* Large
No. of dealers 140
Stock Wide range of antiques, collectables
Open Mon–Sun 10am–5pm
Services Café, factory shop

Lancastrian Antiques & Co
Contact Mr S Wilkinson
70–72 Penny Street, Lancaster, Lancashire, LA1 1XF
☎ 01524 847004
info@rectorylancs.co.uk
Est. 1981 *Stock size* Medium
Stock General, period furniture, porcelain, pottery, paintings
Open Mon–Sat 10am–4.30pm closed Wed
Services Valuations

LONGRIDGE

Henry Holden & Son
Contact Mrs S MacCarthy
Central Salerooms, Towneley Road, Longridge, Preston, Lancashire, PR3 3EA
☎ 01772 783274 Ⓕ 01772 783274
www.holdenandsons.co.uk
Est. 1890
Open Tues–Fri 9am–5.30pm
Sales Fortnightly on Sat, household 10am, antiques noon, viewing Fri 10am–8pm day of sale 9–10am
Frequency Fortnightly

LYTHAM ST ANNE'S

Antiques at 35
Contact Mr A Sumner
35 St Andrew's Road South, Lytham St Anne's, Lancashire, FY8 1PZ
Ⓜ 07980 403516
arnold.antiques@talk21.com
Est. 1979 *Stock size* Medium
Stock General antiques
Open Mon–Sat 10.30am–4pm closed Wed
Fairs Newark

Mike Mallinson
Contact Mr M Mallinson
Lot 3 Auction Hall, 3 Kingsway, Lytham St Anne's, Lancashire, FY8 1AB
☎ 01253 731600 Ⓕ 01253 731614
Est. 1993
Open Mon–Fri 9am–5pm
Sales Antiques, reproductions and collectables every 3rd Wed 9.30am–2.30pm, viewing Sat 10–12am Mon 10am–6pm Tues 10am–5pm
Frequency Every 3rd Wed

The Victorian Shop
Contact Mr G O Freeman
19 Alexandria Drive, Lytham St Anne's, Lancashire, FY8 1JF
☎ 01253 725700
Est. 1974 *Stock size* Medium
Stock General antiques
Open Sat 10am–5pm or by appointment
Fairs Newark, Swinderby

Windmill Bookshop
Contact Gail Welsh
62a Preston Road, Lytham St Anne's, Lancashire, FY8 5AE
☎ 01253 732485 Ⓕ 01253 732485
Ⓜ 07710 378707
Est. 1993 *Stock size* Medium
Stock General stock of antiquarian and second-hand books
Open Mon–Sun 9.30am–5.30pm
Fairs Buxton, Pudsey

MORECAMBE

Lui Gino Vescovi Antiques
Rear of 1 & 3 Avondale Road, Morecambe, Lancashire, LA3 1XW
☎ 01524 416732 Ⓜ 07860 784856
Est. 1970 *Stock size* Medium
Stock Georgian–Edwardian furniture
Open By appointment any time
Services Valuations

NELSON

Brooks Antiques
Contact David & Susan Brooks
Russell Street, Nelson, Lancashire, BB9 7NL
☎ 01282 698148
Est. 1987 *Stock size* Large
Stock General antiques and collectables
Open Mon–Sat 9am–5pm closed Tues

ORMSKIRK

Browzaround
Contact Mrs P Graham
16 Derby Street West, Ormskirk, Lancashire, L39 3NH

☎ 01695 576999
Est. 1975 *Stock size* Medium
Stock Pre-war furniture, collectables and antique agricultural tools
Open Tues–Sat 10am–4pm closed Wed

⊞ Collectors Corner
Contact Mr B Jermyn
✉ **117 Aughton Street, Ormskirk, Lancashire, L39 3BN** Ⓟ
☎ 01695 577455 Ⓜ 07710 741250
ⓔ Beaniebob@fbtinternet.com
Est. 1997 *Stock size* Large
Stock Cigarette cards, Beanie Babies, dolls' houses
Open Thur–Sat 10.30am–5pm Wed 10.30am–4pm
Services Valuations

⊞ Green Lane Antiques
Contact Mr J Swift
✉ **Unit B20, Malthouse Business Centre, 48 Southport Road, Ormskirk, Lancashire, L39 1QR** Ⓟ
☎ 01695 580731
Est. 1998 *Stock size* Large
Stock Architectural antiques, period furniture, clocks, pine etc
Open Mon–Sun 10am–4pm
Services Restorations

⊞ A Grice
Contact Mr A Grice
✉ **106 Aughton Street, Ormskirk, Lancashire, L39 3BS** Ⓟ
☎ 01695 572007
Est. 1946 *Stock size* Small
Stock Furniture
Open Mon–Sat 10am–5pm closed Wed
Services Valuations, antique furniture restoration

PADIHAM

⊞ Discretion Antiques Ltd
Contact Iris Owen
✉ **37 Burnley Road, Padiham, Burnley, Lancashire, BB12 8BY** Ⓟ
☎ 01282 775693
Est. 1992 *Stock size* Medium
Stock Small modest-cost antiques and collectables
Open Mon–Fri 10.30am–4.45pm Sat 10.30am–12.30pm closed Tues

PRESTON

⊞ European Fine Arts & Antiques
Contact Mr Brian Beck
✉ **10 Cannon Street, Preston, Lancashire, PR1 3NR** Ⓟ
☎ 01772 883886 ⓕ 01772 823888
Ⓜ 07967 427710
ⓔ info@european-fine-arts.co.uk
ⓦ www.european-fine-arts.co.uk
Est. 1969 *Stock size* Large
Stock Victorian gallery, furniture, Louis XIV-style furniture
Open Mon–Sat 9.30am–5.30pm or by appointment

⊞ Fine Art Antiques
Contact Mr Mark Pedler
✉ **109 New Hall Lane, Preston, Lancashire, PR1 5PB** Ⓟ
☎ 01772 794010 Ⓜ 07798 635477
Est. 1987 *Stock size* Medium
Stock Georgian oak furniture, bracket and longcase clocks, barometers, general antiques
Open Mon–Fri 10am–4pm
Fairs Newark
Services Restorations, chandelier re-wiring

⊞ K C Antiques & K D Interiors at Samlesbury Hall
Contact Julie Robinson
✉ **The Long Gallery, Samlesbury Hall, Preston New Road, Preston, Lancashire, PR5 0UP** Ⓟ
☎ 01254 813883
ⓦ www.antique-interiors.co.uk
Est. 1990 *Stock size* Medium
Stock 18th–19thC furniture and decorative items
Open Mon–Fri 11am–4.30pm Sun 10am–4pm

⊞ Nelson Antiques
Contact Mr W Nelson
✉ **113 New Hall Lane, Preston, Lancashire, PR1 5PB** Ⓟ
☎ 01772 794896
Est. 1969 *Stock size* Medium
Stock General antiques, small items, silver, jewellery, copper, miners' lamps, collectables
Open Mon–Sat 9.30am–5pm
Fairs Newark

⊞ The Odd Chair Company
Contact Sue Cook
✉ **The Studio, Eaves Cottage Farm, Eaves, Preston, Lancashire, PR4 0BH** Ⓟ
☎ 01772 691777 ⓕ 01772 691888
ⓔ info@theoddchaircompany.com
ⓦ www.theoddchaircompany.com
Est. 1969 *Stock size* Large
Stock 19thC antique chairs, sofas and decorative furniture
Open By appointment only
Fairs Newark, Ardingly
Services Interior design

⛫ Preston Antique Centre Ltd
Contact Mrs S Shalloe
✉ **The Mill, New Hall Lane, Preston, Lancashire, PR1 5UH** Ⓟ
☎ 01772 794498 ⓕ 01772 651694
ⓔ prestonantiques@talk21.com
ⓦ www.prestonantiquescentre.com
Est. 1979 *Stock size* Large
No. of dealers 43
Stock Comprehensive range of English, French, German and Italian furniture, longcase clocks, shipping goods, small items, porcelain
Open Mon–Fri 8.30am–5.30pm Sat 10am–4pm Sun 10am–5pm

⊞ Priory Collectables
Contact Mr David Howden
✉ **7 Priory Lane, Penwortham, Preston, Lancashire, PR1 0AR** Ⓟ
☎ 01772 752090
Est. 1989 *Stock size* Medium
Stock Cutlery, silver plate, glassware, china, Doulton, Wade, clocks
Open Tues Thurs–Sat 11am–4pm Sat 10.30am–5pm Sun and trade by appointment

⊞ Ribble Reclamation (SALVO)
Contact Mr Joe Hindle
✉ **Ducie Place, Off New Hall Lane, Preston, Lancashire, PR1 4UJ** Ⓟ
☎ 01772 794534 ⓕ 01772 794604
ⓔ joe@ribble-reclamation.com
ⓦ www.ribble-reclamation.com
Est. 1977 *Stock size* Large
Stock Garden statuary, arches, stone flags, lamp posts, fountains, architectural antiques, reclaimed building materials

Open Mon–Fri 8am–5pm
Sat 8am–1pm
Fairs Holker Hall Country Garden Festival, Harrogate Spring Flower Show
Services Auctions, last Sat of April and Sept

SABDEN

Walter Aspinall Antiques
Contact Mr W Aspinall
Pendle Antiques Centre, Union Mill, Watt Street, Sabden, Clitheroe, Lancashire, BB7 9ED
☎ 01282 778642 Ⓕ 01282 778643
Ⓔ walter.aspinall@btinternet.com
Est. 1986 *Stock size* Large
Stock General antiques Victorian–1940s, shipping furniture, collectables, leaded windows etc
Open Mon–Thurs 9am–6pm Fri 9am–5pm Sat 10am–5pm Sun 11am–5pm or by appointment
Services Restorations, café

Pendle Antiques Centre Ltd
Contact Mr Jason Billington
Union Mill, Watt Street, Sabden, Clitheroe, Lancashire, BB7 9ED
☎ 01282 776311 Ⓕ 01282 777642
Ⓔ sales@pendleantiquescentre.co.uk
Est. 1984 *Stock size* Large
No. of dealers 15
Stock Wide range of antiques including architectural and shipping wares
Open Mon–Sat 10am–5pm Sun 11am–5pm
Services Shipping

TODMORDEN

The Border Bookshop (PBFA, BA)
Contact Mr V H Collinge
61a Halifax Road, Todmorden, Lancashire, OL14 5BB
☎ 01706 814721
Ⓔ collinge@borderbookshop.fsnet.co.uk
Est. 1979 *Stock size* Large
Stock Second-hand books, comics, story papers 1880–1965
Open Mon–Fri 10am–1pm 2–5pm Sat 9am–4pm closed Wed
Fairs PBFA
Services Book tokens

Cottage Antiques
Contact Angelica Slater
788 Rochdale Road, Walsden, Todmorden, Lancashire, OL14 7UA
☎ 01706 813612 Ⓕ 01706 813612
Ⓜ 07773 798032
Ⓦ www.ukcottageantiques.co.uk
Est. 1984 *Stock size* Medium
Stock Country furniture (particularly with original paint finishes), European antiques, country collectables, kitchenware
Open Tues–Sun 9.30am–5.30pm
Services Stripping, polishing, paint finishes, renovations, custom-built furniture

Echoes
Contact Mrs P Oldman
650a Halifax Road, Eastwood, Todmorden, Lancashire, OL14 6DW
☎ 01706 817505
Est. 1986 *Stock size* Large
Stock Clothing, textiles, pre-Victorian to late 1950s
Open Wed–Sat 11am–6pm Sun noon–5pm
Fairs Manchester Textile Fairs
Services Valuations

Fagin & Co
Contact Mr John Ratcliff
54 Burnley Road, Todmorden, Lancashire, OL14 5EY
☎ 01706 819499/814773
Ⓜ 07899 774257
Ⓔ mrhillside@aol.com
Est. 1994 *Stock size* Medium
Stock General antiques, collectables, advertising
Open Mon–Sat 10.30am–5pm closed Tues Sun
Services Valuations

Todmorden Antique Centre
Contact Mr E Hoogeveen
Sutcliffe House, Halifax Road, Todmorden, Lancashire, OL14 5BG
☎ 01706 818040 Ⓕ 01706 814344
Ⓔ mr.ed@freenat.co.uk
Est. 1994 *Stock size* Large
No. of dealers 30
Stock Wide range of antiques, collectables and collectors' cars
Open Mon–Fri 10am–5pm Sat 10am–4pm Sun noon–4pm

WHALLEY

As Time Goes By
Contact Mrs J Bland
3 Accrington Road, Whalley, Clitheroe, Lancashire, BB7 9TD
☎ 01254 822199 Ⓕ 01254 822199
Ⓜ 07989 063395
Est. 1989 *Stock size* Medium
Stock Antique and new furniture, decorative items, lighting, textiles etc
Open Tues–Sat 12.30–4.30pm by appointment
Services Upholstery

Brindle Fine Arts Ltd (LAPADA)
Contact Julian Brindle
King Street, Whalley, Lancashire, BB7 9SP
☎ 01254 825200 Ⓕ 01200 440090
Ⓦ www.antiqueweb.co.uk/tbrindle
Est. 1961 *Stock size* Large
Stock Good quality antiques
Open Mon–Fri 9am–5pm or by appointment
Fairs Olympia

Edmund Davies & Son Antiques
Contact Philip Davies
32 King Street, Whalley, Clitheroe, Lancashire, BB7 9SL
☎ 01254 823764 Ⓕ 01254 823764
Ⓜ 07879 877306
Est. 1960 *Stock size* Medium
Stock Longcase clocks, country furniture
Open Mon–Sat 10am–5pm
Services Clock and furniture restoration

MERSEYSIDE

BIRKENHEAD

D & T Architectural Salvage
Contact Mr Dave Lyons
106 Church Road, Birkenhead, Merseyside, CH42 0LJ
☎ 0151 670 0058
Est. 1990 *Stock size* Large
Stock Original interior doors, fireplaces, all salvage material
Open By appointment

Mistermicawber.Co Ltd
Contact Mr Barrington
100 Woodchurch Lane, Birkenhead, Merseyside, CH42 9PD

☎ 0151 608 5445
Ⓔ mistermicawber.co@btinternet.com
Est. 1974 ***Stock size*** Medium
Stock Pre-1930s furniture
Open Mon–Sat 9am–5pm closed Thurs
Services Valuations

Paraphernalia Antiques
Contact John
✉ **1 Woodchurch Road, Birkenhead, Merseyside, CH41 2XN**
☎ 0151 653 7530
Est. 1999 ***Stock size*** Medium
Stock Variety of Art Deco, Victorian, Edwardian furniture
Open Thurs Fri Sat 10am–5pm

BLUNDELLSANDS

Boydell Galleries (BADA, LAPADA)
Contact Paul Breen
✉ **48 Dowhills Road, Blundellsands, Liverpool, Merseyside, L23 8SW** Ⓟ
☎ 0151 932 9220 Ⓕ 0151 924 0199
Ⓔ boydellgalleries@btinternet.com
Ⓦ www.boydellgalleries.co.uk
Est. 1851 ***Stock size*** Medium
Stock British drawings and watercolours, early maps and prints
Open By appointment
Fairs The Watercolour Fair, Jan LAPADA

BROMBOROUGH

Full of Beans
Contact Kris Richards
✉ **Unit 34, Croft Retail Park, Dinsdale Road, Bromborough, Wirral, Merseyside, CH62 3PY** Ⓟ
☎ 0151 334 6999 Ⓕ 0151 334 0197
Ⓜ 07961 364284
Ⓦ www.fullofbeanies.com
Est. 1999 ***Stock size*** Large
Stock Beanie Babies and accessories
Open Mon–Sat 10am–5pm Sun Bank Holidays 10.30am–4pm

HESWALL

The Antique Shop
Contact Mr C Rosenberg
✉ **120–122 Telegraph Road, Heswall, Wirral, Merseyside, CH60 0AQ** Ⓟ
☎ 0151 342 1053 Ⓕ 0151 342 1053
Est. 1961 ***Stock size*** Medium
Stock Victorian jewellery, silver, bric-a-brac
Open Tues–Sat 10am–5pm closed Mon Wed
Services Jewellery repairs, silver repairs, valuations

Peninsula Books (PBFA)
Contact Mr Paul Cartmill
✉ **5 The Mount, Heswall, Wirral, CH60 4RE** Ⓟ
☎ 0151 342 5418
Est. 1986 ***Stock size*** Medium
Stock Antiquarian and second-hand books
Open Tues–Sat 10.30am–5pm
Fairs York, Oxford
Services Valuations, book search

HOYLAKE

Kingsleys Auctions Ltd
Contact Mr I McKellar
✉ **3–4 The Quadrant, Hoylake, Wirral, Merseyside, CH47 2EE** Ⓟ
☎ 0151 632 5821 Ⓕ 0151 632 5823
Ⓔ kingsleyauctions@msn.com
Est. 1972
Open Mon–Fri 9am–5pm closed 1–2pm Wed–Fri
Sales General auction sale Tues 10am, viewing Sat 9am–12.30pm Mon 9am–5pm day of sale 9–10am
Frequency Weekly
Catalogues Yes

Mansell Antiques & Collectables
Contact Mr Gary Challinor
✉ **Mulberry House, 128–130 Market Street, Hoylake, Wirral, Merseyside, CH47 3BH** Ⓟ
☎ 0151 632 0892 Ⓕ 0151 632 6137
Ⓦ www.antiquesatlas.com
Est. 1998 ***Stock size*** Large
Stock 20thC collectables, Art Deco, Carlton ware, Shelley etc
Open Mon–Sat 9am–5pm closed Wed
Fairs Birmingham Rag Market, Chester Racecourse

LIVERPOOL

Abram & Mitchell
Contact Mr Crane
✉ **6 Stanhope Street, Liverpool, Merseyside, L8 5RF** Ⓟ
☎ 0151 708 5180 Ⓕ 0151 707 2454
Ⓔ johncrane@cato-crane.co.uk
Ⓦ www.cato-crane.co.uk
Est. 1880
Open Mon–Fri 9am–5pm Sat by appointment
Sales Antique, general and household furnishings sales every Thursday
Frequency Weekly
Catalogues No

Black Cat Antiques
Contact Mr Barry Corbitt
✉ **100a High Street, Wavertree, Liverpool, Merseyside, L15 8HQ** Ⓟ
☎ 0151 734 1149
Est. 1969 ***Stock size*** Small
Stock Smalls, jewellery, ivories, miniatures, antique teddy bears
Open By appointment
Services Teddy bear repair

Cato Crane & Co
Contact Mr J Crane AMATA
✉ **6 and 33–41 Stanhope Street, Liverpool, Merseyside, L8 5RF** Ⓟ
☎ 0151 709 5559 Ⓕ 0151 707 2454
Ⓔ johncrane@cato-crane.co.uk
Ⓦ www.cato-crane.co.uk
Est. 1986
Open Mon–Fri 9am–5pm or by appointment
Sales Auctions every Thursday including antique Victorian and 20thC furniture, collectables and decorative objects. Quality antiques and fine art auction every two months
Frequency Weekly
Catalogues Yes

Circa 1900
Contact Mr W Colquhoun
✉ **11–13 Holts Arcade, India Buildings, Water Street, Liverpool, Merseyside, L2 0RR** Ⓟ
☎ 0151 236 1282 Ⓕ 0151 236 1282
Ⓦ www.merseyworld.com/circa1900
Est. 1996 ***Stock size*** Large
Stock Art Nouveau, classic Art Deco, applied arts
Open 10am–6pm or by appointment

Cottage Antiques
Contact Mr V Blundell
✉ **64 Moss Lane, Orrell Park, Liverpool, Merseyside, L9 8AN** Ⓟ
☎ 0151 284 6771

Est. 1994 *Stock size* Medium
Stock Victorian–Edwardian furniture, collectables, bric-a-brac
Open Mon–Sat 10.30am–6pm
Fairs Newark, Ardingly

Hartley & Co
Contact Mr J Brown
12–14 Moss Street, Low Hill, Liverpool, Merseyside, L6 1HF P
☎ 0151 263 6472/1865
F 0151 260 3417 M 07803 98 4199
Est. 1849
Open Mon–Fri 9am–4.30pm
Sales General household, antique and reproduction sales Fri 10.15am, viewing Thurs 9am–4.30pm Fri 9–10.15am. Merseyside Police lost property
Frequency Fortnightly
Catalogues No

Liverpool Militaria
Contact Mr Bill Tagg
15 Cheapside, Liverpool, Merseyside, L2 2DY P
☎ 0151 236 4404 F 0800 590009
Est. 1977 *Stock size* Medium
Stock General military antiques
Open Mon–Sat 10.30am–5pm closed Wed
Fairs Northern Arms & Armour, International – Birmingham

Maggs Shipping Ltd
Contact Mr R Webster
66–68 St Anne Street, Liverpool, Merseyside, L3 3DY P
☎ 0151 207 2555 F 0151 207 2555
E maggsantiques@compuserve.com
Est. 1971 *Stock size* Large
Stock Restored Georgian-style, country and pine furniture
Trade only Yes
Open Mon–Fri 9am–5pm
Services Restorations, packing, shipping

Mersey Collectables
Contact Mr J Foy
81 Renshaw Street, Liverpool, Merseyside, L1 2SJ P
☎ 0151 708 9012
E jfoy71160@aol.com
Est. 1995 *Stock size* Large
Stock Collectable toys
Open Mon–Sat 10am–5pm Sun 11am–4pm

Nothing Fancy
Contact Mr Robert M Adams
184 Derby Lane, Liverpool, Merseyside, L13 6QQ P
☎ 0151 259 1661
Est. 1979 *Stock size* Large
Stock Collectables, general antiques, bric-a-brac, fireplaces, doors, wrought-iron gates
Open Mon–Sat 8am–3pm closed Thurs

Outhwaite & Litherland (SOFAA)
Contact Mr Kevin Whay
Kingsway Galleries, Fontenoy Street, Liverpool, Merseyside, L3 2BE P
☎ 0151 236 6561 F 0151 236 1070
E auction@lots.uk.com
W www.lots.uk.com
Est. 1907
Open Mon–Fri 9am–5pm
Sales Antiques sales 4–5 per annum Wed. Weekly general household sales Tues 10.30am, viewing Mon 9am–5pm Tues 9–10.30am. Monthly cavalcade collectors' sales 1st Tues of month or day prior to major fine art and antiques sale
Frequency Weekly
Catalogues Yes

Pilgrim's Progress
Contact Selwyn Hyams
1a–3a Bridgewater Street, Liverpool, Merseyside, L1 0AR P
☎ 0151 708 7515
W www.pilgrimsprogress.co.uk
Est. 1979 *Stock size* Large
Stock Five floors of mainly 19th and early 20thC furniture
Open Mon–Fri 9am–5pm Sat 1–4pm
Services Valuations, restorations

Seventeen Antiques
Contact Mr J Brake
306 Aigburth Road, Liverpool, Merseyside, L17 9PW P
☎ 0151 727 1717 M 07712 189604
W www.seventeenantiques.gbr.cc
Est. 1997 *Stock size* Large
Stock Antique pine furniture, cast-iron fireplaces
Open Mon–Sat 10am–5.30pm closed Wed
Services Restorations, stripping

Stefani Antiques
Contact Mrs T Stefani
497 Smithdown Road, Liverpool, Merseyside, L15 5AE P
☎ 0151 734 1933/733 4836
M 07946 646395
Est. 1987 *Stock size* Large
Stock General antiques
Open Mon–Sat 10am–5pm closed Wed
Services Valuations, restorations

Turner & Sons (1787) (NAVA)
Contact Mr Kevin Davies
Century Salerooms, 28–36 Roscoe Street, Liverpool, Merseyside, L1 9DW P
☎ 0151 709 4005 F 0151 709 4005
M 07831 445816
E turnersauctions@aol.com
Est. 1787
Open Mon–Fri 9.15am–4.45pm
Sales General household, antique and commercial sales Thurs 11am, viewing Wed 9am–4.45pm Thurs 9–11am
Frequency Weekly
Catalogues No

Yazuka
Contact Mr Bill Tagg
15 Cheapside, Liverpool, Merseyside, L2 2DY P
☎ 0151 236 4404
Est. 1985
Stock Japanese swords and fittings
Open By appointment only
Fairs International – Birmingham, Northern Arms
Services Sword polishing

SOUTHPORT

Birkdale Antiques
Contact John Napp
119a Upper Aughton Road, Southport, Merseyside, PR8 5NH P
☎ 01704 550117 M 07973 303105
E john@birkdaleantiques.com
W www.birkdaleantiques.gbr.cc
Est. 1990 *Stock size* Small
Stock French bedroom suites 1820–1900s
Open Tues–Wed 10.30am–5.30pm or by appointment
Fairs Bingley Hall, Stafford
Services Valuations, restorations

Bonhams
✉ **Churchtown, Southport, Merseyside, PR9 7NE**
☎ 01704 507875 Ⓕ 01704 507877
Ⓔ southport@bonhams.com
Ⓦ www.bonhams.com
Open Mon–Fri 9am–1pm 2–5pm

Broadhursts of Southport Ltd (ABA, PBFA)
Contact Laurens Hardman
✉ **5–7 Market Street, Southport, Merseyside, PR8 1HD** Ⓟ
☎ 01704 532064 Ⓕ 01704 542009
Ⓔ litereria@aol.com
Est. 1926
Stock Wide range of scarce and collectable books
Fairs Chelsea, Olympia
Services Valuations, restorations, booksearch

King Street Antiques
Contact Mr John Nolan
✉ **27–29 King Street, Southport, Merseyside, PR8 1LH** Ⓟ
☎ 01704 540808 Ⓜ 07714 088388
Est. 1969 *Stock size* Large
Stock Antique furniture, interior design service
Open Mon–Sat 10am–5pm or by appointment
Services Packing, courier

Molloy's Furnishers Ltd
Contact Mr S Molloy
✉ **6–8 St James Street, Southport, Merseyside, PR8 5AE** Ⓟ
☎ 01704 535204 Ⓕ 01704 548101
Ⓔ sales@molloysfurnishers.co.uk
Ⓦ www.molloysfurnishers.co.uk
Est. 1976 *Stock size* Medium
Stock Antique shipping, reproduction furniture
Open Mon–Sat 9am–5.30pm

Osiris
Contact Mr Paul Wood
✉ **104 Shakespeare Street, Southport, Merseyside, PR8 5AJ** Ⓟ
☎ 01704 500991/560418
Ⓜ 07802 818500
Est. 1979 *Stock size* Medium
Stock Vintage clothing and textiles, Art Nouveau, Art Deco ceramics, glass, metalware, lighting
Open Mon–Sat 11am–5pm
Fairs Newark
Services Lectures, talks, valuations, period clothing hire

K A Parkinson Books
Contact K A or J Parkinson
✉ **359–363 Lord Street, Southport, Merseyside, PR8 1NH** Ⓟ
☎ 01704 547016 Ⓕ 01704 386416
Ⓔ info@parki.com
Ⓦ www.parki.com
Est. 1972 *Stock size* Large
Stock Antiquarian and second-hand books, sheet music, maps, prints, prehistoric, ancient and medieval antiquities, natural history items, vinyl records, autographs, manuscripts
Open Mon–Sat 10am–5pm Sun noon–5pm
Services Book search

David M Regan
Contact Mr David Regan
✉ **25 Hoghton Street, Southport, Merseyside, PR9 0NS** Ⓟ
☎ 01704 531266
Est. 1983 *Stock size* Medium
Stock Coins, postcards
Open Mon Wed Fri Sat 10am–5pm
Services Valuations

Southport Furnishings
Contact Steven Ross
✉ **119a Portland Street, Southport, Merseyside, PR8 6RA** Ⓟ
☎ 01704 533122 Ⓜ 07790 551117
Est. 1997 *Stock size* Large
Stock Victorian–Edwardian furniture
Open Mon–Sat 9am–5pm
Services Restorations

Southport Furnishings
Contact Steven Ross
✉ **4 Wesley Street, Southport, Merseyside, PR8 1BN** Ⓟ
☎ 07790 551117
Est. 1997 *Stock size* Large
Stock Victorian–Edwardian furniture
Open Mon–Sat 9am–5pm
Services Restorations

The Spinning Wheel Antiques (IBNS, TPCS)
Contact Roy or Pat Bell
✉ **1 Liverpool Road, Birkdale, Southport, Merseyside, PR8 4AR** Ⓟ
☎ 01704 568245 Ⓕ 01704 567613
Ⓜ 07833 314932
Est. 1974 *Stock size* Medium
Stock General collectables, coins, medals, porcelain, small fine furniture, clocks, violins, barometers, dolls, golf memorabilia etc
Open Mon–Sat 10.30am–5pm closed Tues
Fairs Most major fairs

WALLASEY

Arbiter
Contact Mr P Ferrett
✉ **10 Atherton Street, New Brighton, Wallasey, Merseyside, CH45 2NY** Ⓟ
☎ 0151 639 1159
Est. 1983 *Stock size* Medium
Stock Small objects, 1850–1970 decorative arts, Asian, tribal, base metal, treen, 20thC prints, Oriental, Islamic
Open Wed–Sat 1–5pm or by appointment
Services Valuations

Decade Antiques & Interiors
Contact A Duffy
✉ **62 Grove Road, Wallasey, Merseyside, CH45 3HW** Ⓟ
☎ 0151 638 0433 or 0151 639 6905
Ⓕ 0151 638 9995
Est. 1974 *Stock size* Medium
Stock English and Continental furniture, decorative items, textiles, upholstered furniture, pictures, china
Open Mon Tues Thurs 10.30am–1pm 2.15–5pm Sat 10.30am–1.30pm or by appointment
Fairs Manchester Textile Fairs

Victoria Antiques
Contact Mr J Collier
✉ **155–157 Brighton Street, Wallasey, Merseyside, CH44 8DU** Ⓟ
☎ 0151 639 0080
Ⓦ www.victoriaantiques.com
Est. 1990 *Stock size* Large
Stock Victorian–Edwardian furniture, grandfather clocks
Open Mon–Sat 9.30am–5.30pm closed Wed
Services Restorations

CARMARTHENSHIRE

CARMARTHEN

⊞ Audrey Bull Antiques
Contact Jane Bull
✉ **2a Jacksons Lane, Carmarthen, Carmarthenshire, SA31 1WD**
☎ 01267 222655
Est. 1949 *Stock size* Medium
Stock General Antiques, Georgian–Edwardian furniture, antique jewellery
Open Mon–Sat 10am–5pm
Services Valuations, restorations, repairs

Bonhams
✉ **Napier House, Spilman Street, Carmarthen, Carmarthenshire, SA31 1JY**
☎ 01267 238231 Ⓕ 02920 727989
Ⓔ carmarthen@bonhams.com
Ⓦ www.bonhams.com
Open Mon–Fri 9am–5pm

⊞ Cwmgwili Mill Antiques
Contact Michael Sandell
✉ **Cwmgwili Mill, Bronwydd Arms, Carmarthen, Carmarthenshire, SA33 6HX** Ⓟ
☎ 01267 231500/237215
Est. 1979 *Stock size* Large
Stock General antiques
Open Mon–Fri 9am–6pm Sat 10am–6pm or by appointment
Services Repairs, restorations

⊞ Mark's Mart
Contact Mark Terry
✉ **Colonial Buildings, Little Water Street, Carmarthen, SA31 1ER** Ⓟ
☎ 01267 236613
Ⓔ mterry@marksmart.f9.co.uk
Est. 1970 *Stock size* Large

Stock General antiques, mainly furniture
Open Mon–Fri 9am–5pm closed Thurs pm Sat 9am–4pm

The Pot Board
Contact Nigel or Gill Batten
30 King Street, Carmarthen, Carmarthenshire, SA31 1BS P
☎ 01267 236623 F 01267 236623
M 07785 924007
E Gill@potboard.co.uk
W www.potboard.co.uk
Est. 1980 *Stock size* Large
Stock Antique pine and country furniture, Welsh pine
Open Mon–Sat 9.30am–5.30pm

Roderick Price & Co
Contact Mr Deri Price
19–20 Lammas Street, Carmarthen, Carmarthenshire, SA31 3AL P
☎ 01267 230571 F 01267 238422
E enquiries@roderickprice.co.uk
W www.roderickprice.co.uk
Open Mon–Fri 9am–5pm Sat 9am–4pm Sun 10am–noon
Sales General antiques
Frequency Occasional
Catalogues Yes

CROSS HANDS

C J C Antiques
Contact Caroline Carpenter
Llanllyan Foelgastell, Cross Hands, Carmarthenshire, SA14 7HA P
☎ 01269 831094 F 01269 831094
E sales@cjcantiques.co.uk
W www.cjcantiques.co.uk
Est. 1979 *Stock size* Large
Stock Various Victorian items, musical instruments
Trade only Yes
Open By appointment
Services Shipping, valuations

Welsh Country Auctions
Contact Andrew or Bethan Williams
2 Carmarthen Road, Cross Hands, Llanelli, Carmarthenshire, SA14 6JP P
☎ 01269 844428 F 01269 844428
W www.welshcountryauctions.com
Est. 1995
Open Mon–Fri 9am–5pm Sat 9am–12.30pm
Sales General antiques
Frequency Every 3 weeks
Catalogues Yes

KIDWELLY

Country Antiques (Wales) (BADA, CINOA)
Contact R Bebb
Castle Mill, Kidwelly, Carmarthenshire, SA17 4UU P
☎ 01554 890534 F 01554 891705
E info@welshantiques.com
W www.welshantiques.com
Est. 1969 *Stock size* Large
Stock Welsh oak furniture, pottery, folk art, metalware
Open Tues–Sat 10am–5pm or by appointment
Services Valuations

Kidwelly Antiques (BADA, CINOA)
Contact Mr R Bebb
31 Bridge Street, Kidwelly, Carmarthenshire, SA17 4UU P
☎ 01554 890328 F 01554 891705
E info@welshantiques.com
W www.welshantiques.com
Est. 1969 *Stock size* Large
Stock Georgian–Victorian furniture and accessories
Open Tues–Sat 10am–5pm telephone call advisable

LLANDEILO

James Ash Antiques
Contact James Ash
The Warehouse, Station Road, Llandeilo, Carmarthenshire, SA19 6NG P
☎ 01558 823726/822130
F 01558 822130
E James@ashantiques.freeserve.co.uk
Est. 1976 *Stock size* Large
Stock Victorian and Welsh country furniture
Open Mon–Fri 8.30am–6pm or by appointment
Fairs Newark
Services Valuations

Jones & Llewelyn (NAEA)
Contact Mrs Ann Rees or Mr Hefin Jones
Llandeilo Auction Rooms, 21 New Road, Llandeilo, Carmarthenshire, SA19 6DE P
☎ 01558 823430 F 01558 822004
E enquiries@jonesllewelyn.freeserve.co.uk
W www.jonesllewelyn.freeserve.co.uk
Est. 1948
Open Mon–Fri 9am–5.30pm
Sales Quarterly general antiques and collectables, also property for sale
Frequency Quarterly
Catalogues Yes

Bob Jones Prytherch & Co Ltd
Contact Jonathon Morgan
50 Rhosmaen Street, Llandeilo, Carmarthenshire, SA19 6HA P
☎ 01558 822468 F 01558 823712
E property@bjpandco.s9.co.uk
W www.bjpproperty.co.uk
Est. 1996
Open Mon–Fri 9am–5.30pm
Sales General antiques
Frequency Quarterly
Catalogues No

Roderick Price & Co
Contact Mr Dewi Price
85 Rhosmaen Street, Llandeilo, Carmarthenshire, SA19 2DS P
☎ 01558 822280 F 01558 822824
E enquiries@roderickprice.co.uk
W www.roderickprice.co.uk
Open Mon–Fri 9am–5pm Sat 9am–noon
Sales General antiques
Frequency Occasional
Catalogues Yes

The Works Antiques Centre
Contact Steve Watts or Jon Storey
Station Road, Llandeilo, Carmarthenshire, SA19 6NH P
☎ 01558 823964
Est. 2001 *Stock size* Large
No. of dealers 44
Stock General antiques and collectables
Open Tues–Sat 10am–6pm Sun 10am–4pm
Services Restorations

LLANDOVERY

Clee Tompkinson & Francis
Contact Nick Jones
Ty Ocsiwn Tywi Auction House, Llandovery, Carmarthenshire, SA18 2LY P
☎ 01269 591884/01550 720440
F 01269 595482
E ctfamman@aol.com
W www.ctf-uk.com
Est. 1996
Open Mon–Fri 9am–5.30pm Sat 9am–1pm

Sales General antiques
Frequency Monthly
Catalogues No

Phillips Antiques & French Polishing Service
Contact Phillip Wyvill-Bell
11 Market Square, Llandovery, Carmarthenshire, SA20 0AB
01550 721355
Est. 1969 *Stock size* Large
Stock General antiques, porcelain, furniture
Open Mon–Sat 9am–5pm
Services French polishing, valuations, restoration, repairs

LLANELLI

Llanelli Antiques
Contact W Knapp
12 Great Western Crescent, Llanelli, Carmarthenshire, SA15 2RL
01554 759448
diane.knapp@btclick.com
Est. 1962 *Stock size* Medium
Stock General antiques, Victorian–Edwardian furniture
Open Mon–Sat 10am–1pm
Fairs Newark, Ardingly
Services Valuations, restorations

Radnedge Architectural Antiques
Contact Julian Cooper
Dafen Inn Row, Llanelli, Carmarthenshire, SA14 8LX
01554 755790 01554 755790
rantiques@radnedge.fsworld.co.uk
www.radnedge-arch-antiques.co.uk
Est. 1980 *Stock size* Large
Stock Architectural antiques, fireplaces, timber, stone etc
Open Mon–Sat 9am–5pm

LLANWRDA

Mark Rowan Antiques
Contact Mark Rowan
Garreg Fawr, Porthyrhyd, Llanwrda, Carmarthenshire, SA19 8NY
01558 650478 01558 650712
sales@markrowan.co.uk
www.markrowan.co.uk
Est. 1975 *Stock size* Medium
Stock Country furniture and antiques
Open By appointment only

LLANYBYDDER

Jen Jones Antiques
Contact Jen Jones
Pontbrendu, Llanybydder, Carmarthenshire, SA40 9UJ
01570 480610 01570 480112
quilts@jen-jones.com
www.jen-jones.com
Est. 1971 *Stock size* Large
Stock Welsh quilts and blankets, small Welsh country antiques
Open Mon–Sat 10am–6pm
Sun by appointment
Fairs BABAADA

NEWCASTLE EMLYN

The Old Saddler's Antiques
Contact Mr or Mrs Coomber
Bridge Street, Newcastle Emlyn, Carmarthenshire, SA38 9DU
01239 711615 (shop hours only)
07971 625113
Dotcoomb@aol.com
Est. 1995 *Stock size* Large
Stock General antiques, country-style furniture, horse-orientated antiques
Open Mon–Sat 10am–5pm
closed Wed in winter
Fairs Carmarthen

Riverside Antiques
Contact M Barton
Pine Croft, Carmarthen Road, Newcastle Emlyn, Carmarthenshire, SA38 9DA
01239 710384 07971 751562
Est. 1971 *Stock size* Large
Stock General antiques
Open Mon–Sun 9am–6pm
Fairs Ardingly, Newark
Services Valuation, restoration, repairs

CEREDIGION

ABERYSTWYTH

The Furniture Cave
Contact P David
33 Cambrian Street, Aberystwyth, Ceredigion, SY23 1NZ
01970 611234 01970 611234
07816 408871
thecave@btconnect.com
www.the-furniture-cave.co.uk
Est. 1979 *Stock size* Medium
Stock General antiques and pine
Open Mon–Fri 9am–5pm
Sat 10am–5pm
Fairs NEC, Birmingham Antiques Fair
Services Valuations, restoration, repairs

Lloyd Herbert & Jones
Contact J A Griffiths FRICS
10 Chalybeate Street, Aberystwyth, Ceredigion, SY23 1HS
01970 624328/612559
01970 617934
sales@lhj-property.co.uk
www.lhj-property.co.uk
Est. 1904
Open Mon–Sat 9am–5.30pm
Sales General antiques
Wed 11am, viewing 9–11am
Frequency Every 2 months
Catalogues No

Jim Raw-Rees & Co (ISVA)
Contact Charles
1–3 Chalybeate Street, Aberystwyth, Ceredigion, SY23 1HJ
01970 617179 019706 627262
07970 605040
propertysales@raw-rees.co.uk
www.raw-rees.co.uk
Est. 1948
Open Mon–Fri 9am–5.30pm
Sat 9.30am–4pm
Sales General antiques
Frequency Periodically
Catalogues No

Julian Shelley Books
Contact Julian Shelley
16 Northgate Street, Aberystwyth, Ceredigion, SY23 2JS
01970 627926
julianshelley@hotmail.com
Est. 1996 *Stock size* Medium
Stock Rare and second-hand books, jewellery, collectables, items on Welsh topography
Open Mon–Sat 10am–5pm
Services Book search

Ystwyth Books (BA)
Contact Mrs H M Hinde
7 Princess Street, Aberystwyth, Ceredigion, SY23 1DX
01970 617511
Est. 1976 *Stock size* Medium
Stock Rare and second-hand

books, specializing in Welsh-interest books
Open Mon–Sat 9.30am–5.15pm

CARDIGAN

J J Morris
Contact Mr Mal Evans
5 High Street, Cardigan, Ceredigion, SA43 1HJ
01239 612343 · 01239 615237
Est. 1969
Open Mon–Fri 9am–5.30pm
Sat 9am–noon
Sales General antiques
Frequency Periodically
Catalogues No

LLANDYSUL

Fred Davies & Co (FNAVA)
Contact Fred Davies
The Square Synod Inn, Llandysul, Ceredigion, SA44 6JA
01545 580005 · 01545 580006
07831 852511
Est. 1992
Open Mon–Fri 9am–5pm
Sat 10am–2pm
Sales General antiques, modern furniture
Frequency Monthly
Catalogues No

CONWY

COLWYN BAY

Colwyn Books
Contact John Beagan
66 Abergele Road, Colwyn Bay, Conwy, LL29 7PP
01492 530683
Est. 1989 *Stock size* Medium
Stock General stock of antiquarian and second-hand books
Open Mon–Sat 9am–5.30pm closed Wed
Services Book search

Cryers Antiques
Contact Mr Chris Cryer
24 Abergele Road, Colwyn Bay, Conwy, LL29 7PA
01492 532457
Est. 1974 *Stock size* Large
Stock General antiques and collectables
Open Mon–Sat 11am–4.30pm
Fairs Newark, Ardingly, Swinderby
Services Valuations

North Wales Antiques
Contact Mr F Robinson
58 Abergele Road, Colwyn Bay, Conwy, LL29 7PP
01492 530521 or 01352 720253 (after 6pm)
Est. 1959 *Stock size* Large
Stock Antique and old furniture bought and sold
Open Mon–Sat 10am–4pm
Fairs Newark
Services House clearance, probate valuations, valuations

Rogers Jones & Co
Contact Mr David Rogers Jones
33 Abergele Road, Colwyn Bay, Conwy, LL29 7RU
01492 532176 · 01492 533308
www.rogersjones.co.uk
Est. 1991
Open Mon–Thurs 9am–5pm
Fri 9am–noon
Sales Furniture, ceramics, silver, paintings, collectables last Tues in month, general and collectables bi-monthly
Frequency 3 per month
Catalogues Yes

CONWY

The Bookshop
Contact Mr D Crewe
21 High Street, Conwy, LL32 8DE
01492 592137
bookshopconwy.co.uk
Est. 1985 *Stock size* Medium
Stock Rare and second-hand books
Open Mon–Sat 9.30am–5pm

Paul Gibbs Antiques & Decorative Arts
Contact Paul Gibbs
25 Castle Street, Conwy, LL32 8AY
01492 593429 · 01492 593429
paul@teapotworld.co.uk
Est. 1959 *Stock size* Medium
Stock Ceramics, glass, decorative arts, focus on teapot design with reference collection open to the public exhibiting 1200 rare and early teapots
Open Mon–Sat 10am–5pm
Fairs Newark
Services Valuations, restoration, repairs

Knights Gone By
Contact Mr B Tunstall
Castle Square, Conwy, LL32 8AY
01492 596119 · 01492 596119
knightsgoneby@netscapeonline.co.uk
www.knightsgoneby.com
Est. 1998 *Stock size* Medium
Stock Collectable weaponry
Open Mon–Sun 11am–5pm

DEGANWY

Castle Antiques
Contact John Nickson
Victoria Building, 71 Station Road, Deganwy, Conwy, LL31 9DF
01492 583021 · 01492 596664
Est. 1980 *Stock size* Large
Stock General antiques
Open Mon–Sat 10am–5pm
Services Valuations

LLANDUDNO

Bryan Davies & Associates
Contact Bryan Davies
4 Mostyn Street, Llandudno, Conwy, LL30 2PS
01492 875125 · 01492 877292
llandudno@bdahomesales.co.uk
www.bdahomesales.co.uk
Est. 1908
Open Mon–Fri 9am–5pm
Sat 8.30am–4pm Sun 1–3pm
Sales General antiques
Frequency Phone for details
Catalogues Yes

More Books
Contact Sue Morley
102 Mostyn Street, Llandudno, Conwy, LL30 2SW
01492 878684
sales@morebooks.co.uk
www.morebooks.co.uk
Est. 1995 *Stock size* Medium
Stock Rare and second-hand books, stock of local Welsh history
Open Mon–Sat 10am–5pm
Sun 9.30am–5.30pm summer

Walters Antiques & Collectables
Contact Mrs Gillian Walters

✉ **6 Dunraven Street, Llandudno, CF40 1QE** P
☎ 01443 421524 F 01443 421824
Est. 1999 *Stock size* Medium
Stock General antiques
Open Mon–Fri 10am–5pm
Services House clearance

LLANDUDNO JUNCTION

Collinge Antiques
Contact Nicky Collinge
✉ **Old Fyffes Warehouse, Conwy Road, Llandudno Junction, Conwy, LL31 9LU** P
☎ 01492 580022 F 01492 580022
E sales@collinge-antiques.co.uk
W ww.collinge-antiques.co.uk
Est. 1980 *Stock size* Large
Stock General antiques, Georgian–Edwardian furniture
Open Mon–Sat 9am–5.30pm Sun 10.30am–4.30pm
Fairs Tatton Park
Services Restorations, valuations, shipping, upholstery

LLANRWST

Carrington House Antiques
Contact Richard Newstead
✉ **Ancaster Square, Llanrwst, Conwy, LL26 0LD** P
☎ 01492 642500 F 01492 642500
E richard@carringtonhouse.co.uk
W www.carringtonhouse.co.uk
Est. 1975 *Stock size* Medium
Stock Antiques, pine, mahogany and oak furniture
Open Tues–Sat 10.30am–5pm
Services Valuations

Prospect Books
Contact Mike Dingle
✉ **Albert House, 18 Denbigh Street, Llanrwst, Conwy, LL26 0LL** P
☎ 01492 640111 F 01492 640111
E prospectbooks@aol.com
W www.gunbooks.co.uk
Est. 1977 *Stock size* Small
Stock Rare and second-hand books including some on weapons
Open Tues–Sat 9am–5pm
Fairs Arms Fairs
Services Catalogues

PENMAENMAWR

Gwynedd Trading
Contact C Motter
✉ **Stanley Buildings, Bangor Road, Penmaenmawr, Conwy, LL34 6LF** P
☎ 01492 622189 F 01243 355499
M 07802 968819
Est. 1973 *Stock size* Large
Stock General antiques, shipping furniture, specializing in 17th–18thC furniture
Open By appointment only
Fairs Newark, Stafford
Services Shipping worldwide

RHOS-ON-SEA

Rhos Point Books
Contact Gwyn Morris
✉ **85 The Promenade, Rhos-on-Sea, Conwy, LL28 4PR** P
☎ 01492 545236 F 01492 540862
E rhos.point@btinternet.com
W www.rhos.point.btinternet.com
Est. 1984 *Stock size* Medium
Stock 20,000 antiquarian and second-hand titles, North Wales topography a speciality
Open Mon–Sun 10am–5.30pm July Aug 10am–9pm
Fairs Ludlow
Services Book search

DENBIGHSHIRE

CHIRK

Brocante Antiques
Contact Caroline Williams or Tina
✉ **3a St Mary's Precinct, Church Street, Chirk, Wrexham, Denbighshire, LL14 5HX** P
☎ 01691 778844 F 01691 778844
E brocanteantiques@btconnect.com
W brocanteantiques.com
Est. 1978 *Stock size* Large
Stock Furniture, Continental porcelain, textiles, linen, lace etc
Open Mon–Sat 10am–5.30pm
Services Valuations

Seventh Heaven
✉ **Chirk Mill, Chirk, Wrexham, Denbighshire, LL14 5BU** P
☎ 01691 777622 F 01691 777313
E requests@seventh-heaven.co.uk
W www.seventh-heaven.co.uk
Est. 1971 *Stock size* Large
Stock Antique beds, mattresses, bases, bed linen
Open Mon–Sat 9am–5pm Sun 10am–4pm

ERBISTOCK

Simon Wingett Ltd (LAPADA)
Contact Mr Simon Wingett
✉ **The Garden House, Erbistock, Wrexham, Denbighshire, LL13 0DL** P
☎ 01978 781144 F 01978 781144
M 07774 410889
Est. 1972 *Stock size* Medium
Stock 18th–19thC English furniture, paintings, objets d'art, garden sculpture
Open By appointment
Fairs LAPADA, Chelsea
Services Valuations

FRONCYSYLLTE

Chapel Antiques
Contact Mrs Eve Humber
✉ **Methodist Chapel, Holyhead Road, Froncysyllte, Denbighshire, LL20 7RA** P
☎ 01691 777624 F 01691 777624
Est. 1985 *Stock size* Medium
No. of dealers 8
Stock Wide range of antiques and collectables
Open Tues–Sun 10am–4pm

LLANGOLLEN

J & R Langford
Contact Mr P C Silverston
✉ **12 Bridge Street, Llangollen, Denbighshire, LL20 8PF** P
☎ 01978 860182
Est. 1952 *Stock size* Medium
Stock 18th–19thC Welsh dressers, 18th–early 20thC furniture, china, pictures
Open Mon–Sat 9.30am–5.30pm Thurs 9.30am–12.30pm
Services Valuations

Passers Buy
Contact Marie Evans
✉ **Oak Street/Chapel Street, Llangollen, Denbighshire, LL20 8NN** P
☎ 01978 860861
Est. 1978 *Stock size* Medium
Stock Range of furniture, china, brass, ceramics

Open Tues Fri Sat 11.30am–5pm or by appointment
Fairs Anglesey, Gwyn Davis Fair

RHYL

The Aquarius
Contact Mrs Gaynor Williams
18 Water Street, Rhyl, Denbighshire, LL18 1SW
01745 332436
Est. 1980 *Stock size* Medium
Stock Period clothing, accessories, costume jewellery, lace, collectables
Open Mon–Sat 10.30am–5pm winter closed Tues am

RUTHIN

Grandpa's Collectables
Contact Yvonne Jones
2 Market Street, Ruthin, Denbighshire, LL15 1BE
01824 705601
Est. 1998 *Stock size* Large
Stock Antiques, collectables, some French furniture
Open Tues–Sat 10am–5pm

TREVOR

Romantiques Antique Centre
Contact Mr Knight
Bryn Seion Chapel, Station Road, Trevor, Llangollen, Denbighshire, LL20 7TP
01978 822879
07778 279614 (day)
satkin1057@aol.com
www.romantiques.co.uk
Est. 1993 *Stock size* Large
Stock Antiques, collectables
Open Mon–Fri 10am–5pm Sat Sun 11am–4pm
Services Restoration of upholstery, clocks, furniture, barometers

WREXHAM

Wingett's
Contact Mr J Lloyd
29 Holt Street, Wrexham, Denbighshire, LL13 8DH
01978 353553 01978 353264
auctions@wingetts.co.uk
www.wingetts.co.uk
Est. 1942
Open Mon–Fri 9am–5pm
Sales Weekly general sale, 6-weekly antiques and fine art sale
Catalogues Yes

FLINTSHIRE

CONNAH'S QUAY

Whitehead & Sons
Contact Mr T Whitehead
264 High Street, Connah's Quay, Deeside, Flintshire, CH5 4DJ
01244 818414 01244 82290
Est. 1995
Open Mon–Sat 9am–6pm
Sales General sales including antique china, furniture, household goods, pawnbrokers' jewellery and regular bailiff sales
Frequency Every Tuesday

EWLOE

On The Air Ltd (British Vintage Wireless Society)
Contact Steve Harris
The Vintage Technology Centre, The Highway, Ewloe, Deeside, Flintshire, CH5 3DN
01244 530300 01244 530300
07778 767734
info@vintageradio.co.uk
www.vintageradio.co.uk
Est. 1990 *Stock size* Large
Stock Vintage radios, gramophones
Open Variable
Fairs NVCF (NEC)
Services Valuations, restorations, shipping

HAWARDEN

Capricorn Antiques
Contact Mr K Roberts
Ashfield Farm, Gladstone Way, Hawarden, Deeside, Flintshire, CH5 3HE
01244 535344
Est. 1987 *Stock size* Large
Stock Early pine and Edwardian furniture, 1920s stripped oak
Open Mon–Sat 9am–5pm Sun 11am–4pm
Services Restorations, wood stripping

MOLD

J Bradburne-Price & Co
Contact Mr Roger Griffiths
16 Chester Street, Mold, Flintshire, CH7 1EG
01352 753873 01352 700071
Est. 1904
Open Mon–Fri 9am–5pm Sat 9am–noon
Sales Periodic sales of antiques and modern furniture in Mold Market
Catalogues No

GWYNEDD

BANGOR

David Windsor Gallery (IPC, FATG)
Contact Mrs E Kendrick
173 High Street, Bangor, Gwynedd, LL57 1NU
01248 364639 01248 364639
Est. 1970 *Stock size* Medium
Stock 1580–1850 old maps, prints, lithographs, oil paintings, watercolours
Open Mon–Sat 10am–5pm closed Wed
Services Valuations, restoration, framing

BARMOUTH

Chapel Antiques Centre
Contact Danny Jones
High Street, Barmouth, Gwynedd, LL42 lDS
01341 281377 01341 281377
jonestheantique@supanet.com
www.chapelantiqueswales.co.uk
Est. 1993 *Stock size* Medium
No. of dealers 24
Stock General antiques, Gaudy Welsh china, country furniture
Open Mon–Sun 10.30am–5pm closed Wed out of season
Services Delivery within UK, shipping can be arranged

Fron House Antiques Decorative Items
Contact Mrs B Howard
Fron House, Jubilee Road, Barmouth, Gwynedd, LL42 1EE
01341 280649 01341 280649
07881 471875
Est. 1969 *Stock size* Medium
Stock General antiques, collectables
Open Mon–Sun 10am–5pm closed Wed Oct–April
Fairs Swinderby, Newark
Services Credit and debit cards accepted

Walter Lloyd Jones
Contact V West
High Street, Barmouth, Gwynedd, LL42 1DW
01341 281527 F 01341 280577
E staff@w-lloydjones.com
W www.w-lloydjones.com
Est. 1905 *Stock size* Medium
Stock Furniture, china, Gaudy Welsh, cranberry, books. Sales on commission at all times
Open Mon–Fri 10am–5.30pm Sat 10am–4.30pm winter closed Tues Wed

Walter Lloyd Jones Saleroom
Contact V West
High Street, Barmouth, Gwynedd, LL42 1DW
01341 281 527 F 01341 280577
E staff@w-lloydjones.com
W www.w-lloydjones.com
Est. 1905
Open Mon–Fri 10am–5.30pm Sat 10am–4.30pm winter closed Tues Wed
Sales Irregular sales of antique furniture, smalls, job lots held 4 times a year. Sales on commission at all times

BETHESDA

A E Morris Books (WBA)
Contact A E Morris
40 High Street, Bethesda, Bangor, Gwynedd, LL57 3AN
01248 602533
Est. 1986 *Stock size* Medium
Stock Rare and second-hand books, antiquarian prints
Open Mon–Sat 10am–5pm

O Law I Law
Contact Carys Dafydd
38 High Street, Bethesda, Bangor, Gwynedd, LL57 3AN
01248 600350 F 01248 605542
E gwynfor@olawilaw.co.uk
W www.olawilaw.co.uk
Est. 1995 *Stock size* Small
Stock General antiques
Open Mon–Sat 10am–5pm closed Wed
Fairs Anglesey

CAERNARFON

Days Gone By
Contact Sue
6 Palace Street, Caernarfon, Gwynedd, LL55 1RR
01286 678010 F 01286 678554
E sue@daysgonebyantiques.co.uk
W www.daysgonebyantiques.co.uk
Est. 1994 *Stock size* Medium
Stock General antiques, period furniture, collectables, jewellery
Open Mon–Sat 9.30am–5.30pm

CRICCIETH

Capel Mawr Collectors' Centre
Contact Alun Turner
21 High Street, Criccieth, Gwynedd, LL52 OBS
01766 523600
E collectables@capelmawr.free-online.co.uk
Est. 1998 *Stock size* Large
Stock Rare and second-hand books, old postcards, cigarette cards, antiques etc
Trade only Yes
Open Mid-May–end Sept Mon–Sun winter Tues Thurs–Sat 10am–5pm
Services Mail order

Criccieth Gallery Antiques
Contact Anita Evens
London House, High Street, Criccieth, Gwynedd, LL52 ORN
01766 522836
Est. 1971 *Stock size* Medium
Stock General antiques
Open Mon–Sun 9am–5.30pm
Fairs Newark, Mona, Towy
Services Restoration of pottery and porcelain

DOLGELLAU

Cader Idris Bookshop (PBFA, WBA)
Contact Barbara or Neil Beeby
2 Maldwyn House, Finsbury Square, Dolgellau, Gwynedd, LL40 1RF
01341 421288 and 01341 423779
Est. 1987 *Stock size* Medium
Stock Antiquarian and second-hand books including Welsh topography
Open Mon–Sat 9.30am–5pm Wed 9.30am–1pm
Services Book search

PENYGROES

Maen Dylan
Contact Ken Owen
Victoria Road, Penygroes, Caernarfon, Gwynedd, LL54 6HD
01286 880770
Est. 1979 *Stock size* Medium
Stock General antiques, good-quality second-hand items and household effects
Open Mon–Sat 9am–6pm
Fairs Anglesey

PONTLYFNI

Sea View Antiques
Contact Mr D Ramsell
Sea View, Pontlyfni, Caernarfon, Gwynedd, LL54 5EF
01286 660436 M 07990 976562
Est. 1997 *Stock size* Medium
Stock General antiques, collectables
Open Mon–Sun noon–6pm

PWLLDEFAID

T Evans Antiques
Contact T Evans
Pwlldefaid, Aberdafon, Pwllheli, Gwynedd, LL53 8BT
01758 760215
Est. 1984 *Stock size* Medium
Stock General antiques especially Welsh country furniture
Open Mon–Sun 9am–5pm
Fairs Carmarthen, Cardiff
Services House clearance

PWLLHELI

Rodney Adams Antiques
Contact Rodney Adams
Hall Place, 10 Penlan Street, Pwllheli, Gwynedd, LL53 5DU
01758 613173 F 01758 613173
Stock size Large
Stock General antiques, longcase clocks, early oak furniture
Open Mon–Sat 9am–5pm Thurs 9am–1pm
Services Valuations, repairs, restorations

Penlan Pine
Contact Michael Adams
Hall Place, 7 Penlan Street, Pwllheli, Gwynedd, LL53 7DH
01758 613173 F 01758 613173

Ⓜ 07785 313553 *Stock size* Small
Stock Reproduction and antique pine furniture
Open Mon–Sat 9am–5pm
Thurs 9am–1pm
Services Valuations, restoration and repair

Period Pine
Contact Allan Stanley
Units 1–3, Bron-y-Berth, Penrhos, Pwllheli, Gwynedd, LL53 7UL
☎ 01758 614343 Ⓕ 01758 614100
Ⓜ 07768 875875
Ⓔ allan@periodpine.fsnet.co.uk
Est. 1987 *Stock size* Large
Stock General antiques. Reproduction hand-made kitchens
Open Mon–Sun 9am–5pm
Services Restoration of antiques

ISLE OF ANGLESEY

BEAUMARIS

The Museum of Childhood Memories
Contact Robert Brown
1 Castle Street, Beaumaris, Isle of Anglesey, LL58 8AP
☎ 01248 712498
Ⓦ www.aboutbritain.com/museumofchildhoodmemories.htm
Est. 1973 *Stock size* Medium
Stock Childhood memorabilia, tinplate, childhood money boxes, pottery and glass, gift items based on museum exhibits
Open Mon–Sat 10.30am–5pm
March–Oct Sun noon–5pm
Services Valuations

HOLYHEAD

Gwynfair Antiques
Contact Mrs A McCann
74 Market Street, Holyhead, Isle of Anglesey, LL65 1UW
☎ 01407 763740 Ⓜ 079709 68484
Est. 1986 *Stock size* Medium
Stock Furniture, jewellery, ornaments
Open 10.30am–4.30pm
closed Tues Thurs Sun
Services Valuations

LLANERCHYMEDD

Two Dragons Oriental Antiques
Contact Tony Andrew
8 High Streeet, Llanerchymedd, Isle of Anglesey, LL71 8EA
☎ 01248 470204/470100
Ⓕ 01248 470040 Ⓜ 07811 101290
Est. 1979 *Stock size* Large
Stock Antique Chinese country furniture, signed limited-edition prints by Charles Tunnicliffe
Open By appointment only
Fairs Newark

MENAI BRIDGE

Better Days
Contact Mr & Mrs Rutter
33 High Street, Menai Bridge, Gwynedd, LL59 5EF
☎ 01248 716657
Ⓔ rosy@betterdaysantiques.co.uk
Ⓦ www.betterdaysantiques.co.uk
Est. 1988 *Stock size* Medium
Stock General antiques
Open Mon–Sat 10.30am–4.30pm
Wed 11am–1pm
Fairs Anglesey
Services House clearance

VALLEY

Ann Evans (LAPADA)
Contact Mrs Ann Evans
Carna Shop, Station Road, Valley, Isle of Anglesey, LL65 3EB
☎ 01407 741733 Ⓕ 01407 740109
Ⓜ 07753 650376
Ⓦ www.annevansantiques.com
Est. 1989 *Stock size* Medium
Stock Welsh dressers, Staffordshire figures, Cranberry glass, silver, country items
Open Thurs Fri Sat 10am–4.30pm
Fairs Portmeirion, Gwyn Davies
Services Valuations

MID GLAMORGAN

ABERDARE

Market Antiques
Contact Mr Toms Glanville
15 Duke Street, Aberdare, Mid Glamorgan, CF44 7ED
☎ 01685 870242 Ⓕ 01685 872453
Ⓔ toms@toms.worldonline.co.uk
Est. 1979 *Stock size* Large
Stock Second-hand and antique furniture, collectables, china, glass, pictures etc
Open Mon–Sat 9.30am–5pm
Fairs Abergavenny
Services House clearances

BRIDGEND

Nolton Antiques & Fine Art
Contact Mr J Gittings
66 Nolton Street, Bridgend, Mid Glamorgan, CF31 3BP
☎ 01656 667774
Ⓦ www.welsh-antiques.com
Ⓔ julian.gittings@connectfree.co.uk
Est. 1999 *Stock size* Large
Stock Antique furniture, ceramics, paintings, clocks, ephemera, books, stamps, decorative reproductions
Open Mon–Sat 9.30am–5.30pm
closed Wed
Services Valuations, house clearance

Utility
Contact Mr N Sutton
20b Queen Street, Bridgend, Mid Glamorgan, CF31 1HX
☎ 01656 766995
Est. 1987 *Stock size* Medium
Stock Late Victorian–Edwardian furniture and decorative items, Victorian cast-iron fireplaces and surrounds
Open Mon–Sat 10am–5pm
Services Maker of pine furniture

CAERPHILLY

G J Gittins & Sons
Contact Mr John Gittins
10 Clive Street, Caerphilly, Mid Glamorgan, CF83 1GE
☎ 029 2086 8835 Ⓜ 07941 213771
Est. 1928 *Stock size* Medium
Stock General antiques
Open Mon–Sat 10am–4pm
closed Wed
Services House clearance

EWENNY

Harvard Antiques
Contact Mrs E Budd
4 Wick Road, Ewenny, Bridgend, Mid Glamorgan, CF35 5BL
☎ 01656 766113
Est. 1989 *Stock size* Large
Stock Good-quality furniture, porcelain, clocks, longcase clocks
Open Sat 10am–5.30pm Sun noon–5.30pm or by appointment
Services Valuations

KENFIG HILL

J & A Antiques
Contact Mrs J Lawson
1 Prince Road, Kenfig Hill, Bridgend, Mid Glamorgan, CF33 6ED
01656 746681
Est. 1991 *Stock size* Medium
Stock Victorian–Edwardian china, glass, furniture
Open Mon–Fri 10am–4.30pm closed Wed Sat 10am–1pm

MERTHYR TYDFIL

Halfway Trading
Contact Mr J McCarthy
38 Portmorlais, Merthyr Tydfil, Mid Glamorgan, CF47 8UN
01685 350967
Est. 1995 *Stock size* Medium
Stock General range of antiques and new stock
Open Mon–Sat 9am–5pm
Services House clearances

Paul Williams Antiques
Contact Mr P Williams
The Warehouse, Warlow Street, Merthyr Tydfil, Mid Glamorgan, CF47 0YW
01685 721481 07775 828151
Est. 1985 *Stock size* Large
Stock Wide range of antique Victorian–Edwardian and Art Deco furniture, china, glass, pictures, mirrors
Open Mon–Fri 10am–5pm Sat 10am–2pm
Services House clearance

MOUNTAIN ASH

Old Oak Antiques Abercynon
Contact Mr M James
28 Margaret Street, Mountain Ash, Mid Glamorgan, CF45 4RE
01443 742553
oldoak_uk@yahoo.co.uk
Est. 1997 *Stock size* Medium
Stock Victorian–Art Deco furniture, decorative items, toys, collectors' items etc
Open Mon–Sat 9am–4.30pm
Services Valuations

Trading Post
Contact Julie Thomas or Del Francis
3–4 Oxford Buildings, Oxford Street, Mountain Ash, Mid Glamorgan, CF45 3HE
01443 478855 07989 332514
Est. 1997 *Stock size* Large
Stock Wide range of stock including furniture, china, glass, silver, jewellery, textiles, books, Continental furniture
Open Mon–Sat 10am–5pm closed Thurs

PONTYPRIDD

Holland & Welsh
Contact Michael Nap
13 Riverside Estate, Treforest, Pontypridd, Mid Glamorgan, CF37 5TG
029 2056 1795 029 2021 3370
hollandwelsh@msn.com
Est. 1997 *Stock size* Medium
Stock Antique flooring
Open Mon–Fri 9am–4.30pm Sat Sun 9.30am–1.30pm
Services Restoration

Pontypridd Auctions Ltd
Contact Mr K Hobbs ARICS
Old Co-op Bakery, Cefn Lane, Glyncoch, Pontypridd, Mid Glamorgan, CF37 3BP
01443 403764 01443 403764
Est. 1919
Open Mon–Fri 9am–5pm
Sales Auction Wed 10am, viewing Tues 2–7pm
Frequency Fortnightly
Catalogues Yes

PORTHCAWL

Harlequin Antiques
Contact John or Ann Ball
Dock Street, Porthcawl, Mid Glamorgan, CF36 3BL
01656 785910 07980 837844
Est. 1974 *Stock size* Medium
Stock General antiques, antiquarian books, textiles
Open Mon–Sat 10am–4pm
Services Valuations

Nostalgia
Contact Mr Paul Rossini
5 South Road, Porthcawl, Mid Glamorgan, CF36 3DH
01656 782933 01656 786913
07967 006820
Est. 1999 *Stock size* Medium
Stock General antiques
Open Mon–Fri Sat 9.30am–5pm
Services Valuations, restorations, house clearance

TONYPANDY

Jeff's Antiques
Contact Mrs J Howells
88 Dunraven Street, Tonypandy, Mid Glamorgan, CF40 1AP
01443 434963
Est. 1976 *Stock size* Large
Stock Shipping furniture, glass, porcelain, collectables
Open Mon–Sat 9.30am–5pm closed Thurs

TREHARRIS

Treharris Antiques
Contact Mr C Barker or Mrs Janet Barker
18 Perrott Street, Treharris, Mid Glamorgan, CF46 5ER
01443 413081
Est. 1971 *Stock size* Large
Stock Militaria, china, mining memorabilia, collectable records, Welsh collectables etc
Open Always open, ring first on weekends
Services Valuations

TREORCHY

Steven Evans Antiques
Contact Mrs P Evans
Melvyn Wine Cellars, Regent Street, Treorchy, Mid Glamorgan, CF42 6TR
01443 776410 01443 776982
07785 308567/746748
evans.antiques@virgin.net
Est. 1980 *Stock size* Large
Stock Victorian–1920s, furniture, decorative items etc
Open Mon–Fri 9am–5pm Sat 10am–5pm
Services Packing, shipping, Far East

MONMOUTHSHIRE

ABERGAVENNY

J Straker Chadwick & Sons
Contact Mr L H Trumper
Market Street Chambers, Market Street, Abergavenny, Monmouthshire, NP7 5SD
01873 852624 01873 857311

Ⓔ enquiries@strakerchadwick.co.uk
Ⓦ www.strakerchadwick.co.uk
Est. 1872
Open Mon–Fri 9am–5pm
Sat 9.30am–12.30pm
Sales General antiques
Frequency Monthly
Catalogues Yes

ABERSYCHAN

Emlyn Antiques
Contact Emlyn Edmonds
Ffrwd Road, Abersychan, Pontypool, Monmouthshire, NP4 8PP Ⓟ
☎ 01495 774982
Est. 1985 *Stock size* Medium
Stock General antiques
Open Mon–Sat 9.30am–6pm
Services Valuations

CHEPSTOW

Foxglove Antiques
Contact Lesley Brain
20 St Mary Street, Chepstow, Monmouthshire, NP16 5EW Ⓟ
☎ 01291 622386 Ⓜ 07949 244611
Ⓔ foxglovesants@foxglovesants.free-online.co.uk
Est. 1995 *Stock size* Medium
Stock Antiques and collectables
Open Mon–Sat 10am–5.30pm closed Wed
Services Valuations, restorations

Plough House Interiors
Contact Peter Jones
Plough House, Upper Church Street, Chepstow, Monmouthshire, NP16 5HU
☎ 01291 625200
Ⓔ ploughhouse@amserve.net
Est. 1979 *Stock size* Medium
Stock General antiques, furniture including tables and chairs
Open Mon–Sat 10am–5pm
Services Valuations, upholstery and polishing

LLANBADOC

Brindley John Ayers Antique Fishing Tackle
Contact Mr B J Ayres
Rivermill House, 1 Woodside Court, Llanbadoc, Usk, Monmouthshire, NP15 1SY Ⓟ
☎ 01291 672710 Ⓕ 01291 673464
Ⓔ bjayers@vintagefishingtackle.com
Ⓦ vintagefishingtackle.com
Est. 1988 *Stock size* Large
Stock Antique fishing tackle
Open By appointment
Fairs Newark, Canterbury
Services Catalogues, B & B (for customers)

MONMOUTH

Blestium Antique Centre
Contact Brent Watkins
The Malthouse, 10–14 St Mary Street, Monmouth, Monmouthshire, NP25 3DB
☎ 01600 713999 Ⓕ 01600 713999
Ⓔ brent@blestium.co.uk
Ⓦ www.blestium.co.uk
Est. 1999 *Stock size* Large
Stock Furniture, china, collectables, clocks, silver and architectural
Open Mon–Sat 10am–6pm Sun 1–5pm

Frost Antiques & Pine
Contact Nick Frost
8 Priory Street, Monmouth, Monmouthshire, NP25 3BR Ⓟ
☎ 01600 716687
Ⓔ nickfrost@frostantiques.com
Ⓦ www.frostantiques.com
Est. 1956 *Stock size* Medium
Stock Pine furniture, Staffordshire figures
Open Mon–Sat 9am–5pm or by appointment
Services Valuations, restorations

NEWPORT

Beechwood Antiques
Contact William Samuel
418 Chepstow Road, Newport, Monmouthshire, NP19 8JU Ⓟ
☎ 01633 279192 Ⓕ 01633 279192
Ⓜ 07712 1447913
Est. 1979 *Stock size* Medium
Stock General antiques
Open Mon–Sat 10.30am–5.30pm
Fairs Newark, Chepstow
Services Restoration and china repairs

Callie's Curiosity Shop
Contact Mrs K A Strangward
2 Speke Street, Maindee, Newport, Monmouthshire, NP19 8EX Ⓟ
☎ 01633 222005 Ⓜ 07801 149805
Est. 1996 *Stock size* Medium
Stock General antiques and collectables
Open Mon–Thurs 9.30am–4.30pm Fri Sat 10am–2pm
Fairs Berkeley Castle, Thame
Services Valuations, furniture repair and restoration

Welsh Salvage Co (SALVO)
Contact Mr S Lewis
Isca Yard, Milman Street, Newport, Monmouthshire, NP20 2JL Ⓟ
☎ 01633 212945 Ⓕ 01633 213458
Ⓦ www.welshsalvage.co.uk
Est. 1986 *Stock size* Large
Stock Fireplaces, flooring
Open Mon–Fri 8.30am–5.30pm Sat 8.30am–4pm Sun 11am–2pm
Services Restoration, repairs

TINTERN

Stella Books (PBFA)
Contact Mrs Chris Tomaszewski
Monmouth Road, Tintern, Monmouthshire, NP16 6SE Ⓟ
☎ 01291 689755 Ⓕ 01291 689998
Ⓔ enquiry@stellabooks.com
Ⓦ www.stellabooks.com
Est. 1990 *Stock size* Large
Stock Rare and out-of-print books, specializing in children's books and UK topography
Open Mon–Sun 9.30am–5.30pm
Services Book search

Tintern Antiques
Contact Dawn Floyd
The Old Bakehouse, Tintern, Chepstow, Monmouthshire, NP16 6SE Ⓟ
☎ 01291 689705 Ⓕ 01291 689705
Est. 1979 *Stock size* Medium
Stock General antiques including china, furniture, jewellery
Open Mon–Sun 10am–5pm

TREGARE

The Georgian Barn
Contact Sylvia Knee
Pen-y-Walk, Tregare, Usk, Monmouthshire, NP15 2LH Ⓟ
☎ 01291 690802
Est. 1986 *Stock size* Medium
Stock General antiques
Open Mon–Sun 10am–4pm
Services House clearance

PEMBROKESHIRE

FISHGUARD

J J Morris
Contact Mr D A Thomas
21 West Street, Fishguard, Pembrokeshire, SA65 9AL
01348 873836 01348 874166
mail@jjmestateagents.co.uk
www.jjmestateagents.co.uk
Est. 1949
Open Mon–Fri 9am–5.30pm
Sat 9am–noon
Sales General antiques
Frequency 6–8 weeks
Catalogues No

HAVERFORDWEST

Dyfed Antiques
Contact Giles Chaplin
The Wesleyan Chapel, Perrotts Road, Haverfordwest, Pembrokeshire, SA61 2JD
01437 760496 01437 760496
Est. 1969 *Stock size* Large
Stock General antiques, architectural salvage, bespoke furniture
Open Mon–Sat 10am–5pm
Services Advisory and refurbishment service

Gerald Oliver Antiques
Contact Gerald Oliver
14 Albany Terrace, Haverfordwest, Pembrokeshire, SA61 1RH
01437 762794
gerald.oliver@zoom.uk
Est. 1955 *Stock size* Medium
Stock General antiques, specializing in locally sourced items, furniture and bygones
Open Mon–Sat 9am–4.30pm
Thurs 9am–1pm
Services Valuations

Kent House Antiques
Contact Mr Graham Fanstone
Kent House, 15 Market Street, Haverfordwest, Pembrokeshire, SA61 1NF
01437 768175
Est. 1988 *Stock size* Medium
Stock General antiques
Open Tues–Sat 10am–5pm
Services Restorations

NARBERTH

Ichthus Antiques
Contact Cheryl Evans
2 Market Square, Narberth, Pembrokeshire, SA67 7AU
01834 860416
Est. 1998 *Stock size* Medium
Stock General antiques, linen, Welsh blankets
Open Mon–Sat 10.30am–5.30pm

The Malthouse
Contact P Griffiths or J Williams
Back Lane, High Street, Narberth, Pembrokeshire, SA67 7AR
01834 860303
Est. 1998 *Stock size* Medium
Stock General antiques, furniture, bric-a-brac
Open Mon–Sat 10am–5.30pm
Sun 11am–4pm
Services Pine stripping

NEWPORT

Carningli Centre
Contact Mrs Ann Gent
East Street, Newport, Pembrokeshire, SA42 0SY
01239 820724
info@carningli.co.uk
www.carningli.co.uk
Est. 1997 *Stock size* Medium
Stock General antiques, second-hand books, art gallery
Open Mon–Sat 10am–5.30pm
Services Furniture restoration and polishing

PEMBROKE

Pembroke Antiques Centre
Contact Michael Blake
Wesley Chapel, Main Street, Pembroke, Pembrokeshire, SA71 4DE
01646 687017
Est. 1979 *Stock size* Large
Stock General antiques, Victorian–Edwardian furniture, china, paintings, ephemera, postcards etc
Open Mon–Sat 10am–5pm
Services Repairs, restoration and valuations

Picton Collectables
Contact Mr A L Cuft
59 Main Street, Pembroke, Pembrokeshire, SA71 4DA
01646 621734
Est. 1992 *Stock size* Medium
Stock Collectables
Open Mon–Sat 10am–4pm
Fairs Towy
Services Valuations

PEMBROKE DOCK

Treen Box Antiques
Contact Mr M D Morris
61 Bush Street, Pembroke Dock, Pembrokeshire, SA72 6AN
01646 621800 01646 621800
07971 636148
Est. 1990 *Stock size* Large
Stock General antiques, small upholstered chairs
Open Mon–Sat 9am–5pm or by appointment
Fairs Ardingly, Stoneleigh
Services Restoration and repair, upholstery

Victoria Antiques
Contact Mr D Peter
49 Bush Street, Pembroke Dock, Pembrokeshire, SA72 6AN
01646 682652
Est. 1990 *Stock size* Medium
Stock General antiques, maritime artefacts
Open Tues Fri 10am–5pm
Wed 10am–1pm Sat 10am–3pm

TEMPLETON

Barn Court Antiques
Contact David Evans
Barn Court, Templeton, Narberth, Pembrokeshire, SA67 8SL
01834 861224
info@barncourtantiques.com
www.barncourtantiques.com
Est. 1976 *Stock size* Medium
Stock 18th–19thC fine quality furniture, china, glass
Open Mon–Sun 10am–5pm
winter closed Mon
Services Valuations, restorations

TENBY

Cofion Books & Postcards (PTA)
Contact A Smosarski
Bridge Street, Tenby, Pembrokeshire, SA70 7BU
01834 845741 01834 843864
albiesmosarski@hotmail.com

Est. 1987 *Stock size* Large
Stock Second-hand books, Edwardian postcards, varied collectables, specializing in Augustus and Gwen John publications
Open Mon–Sun 10.30am–5.30pm
Fairs Cardiff International Arena, Nottingham and London postcard fairs
Services Valuations, book search, postal approval on postcards

POWYS

BRECON

Antiques Etc
Contact Mrs S Thomas
Lion Street, Brecon, Powys, LD3 7AU
01874 622366 Ⓜ 07971 016356
sue@antiques-etc.co.uk
Est. 1995 *Stock size* Large
Stock General antiques
Open Mon–Sat 10am–5pm

Books, Maps & Prints
Contact Andrew Wakley
7 The Struet, Brecon, Powys, LD3 7LL
01874 622714 Ⓕ 01874 622714
Est. 1973 *Stock size* Medium
Stock Books, maps and prints
Open Mon–Sat 9am–5pm
Wed 9am–1pm
Services Framing

Montague Harris & Co
Contact John Lewis
16 Ship Street, Brecon, Powys, LD3 9AD
01874 623200 Ⓕ 01874 623131
jal@montague-harris.co.uk
www.montague-harris.co.uk
Est. 1900
Open Mon–Fri 9am–5pm
Sat 9am–1pm
Sales General antiques
Frequency Periodically
Catalogues Yes

F H Sunderland & Co (RICS, ISVA)
Contact David Pritchard
Coliseum House, 7 Wheat Street, Brecon, Powys, LD3 7DG
01874 622261 Ⓕ 01874 624705
Est. 1959
Open Mon–Sat 9am–5pm
Sales Antiques and general effects
Frequency Monthly
Catalogues Yes

BUILTH WELLS

McCartneys
Contact Mrs Diana Samuel
46 High Street, Builth Wells, Powys, LD2 3AB
01982 552259 Ⓕ 01982 552193
builth@mccartneys.co.uk
www.mccartneys.co.uk
Est. 1949
Open Mon–Fri 9am–5pm
Sat 9.30am–12.30pm
Sales General antiques, furniture and effects
Frequency Periodically
Catalogues No

Smithfield Antiques
Contact Suzanne Price
Smithfield Road, Builth Wells, Powys, LD2 3AN
01982 553022 Ⓕ 01982 553022
Ⓜ 07879 025577
suzanne@smithfieldjoinery.fsnet.co.uk
www.smithfield-joinery.com
Est. 2000 *Stock size* Medium
Stock General antiques, fireplaces, oak Welsh dressers
Open Mon–Sat 10am–5pm closed Wed

CILMERY

V Nejus
Contact Mr V Nejus
Comyn Cottage, Cilmery, Builth Wells, Powys, LD2 3LH
01982 553792
Est. 1972 *Stock size* Medium
Stock General antiques
Open By appointment only

FOUR CROSSES

Malthouse Antiques
Contact Neville Foulkes
The Old Malthouse, Pool Road, Four Crosses, Llanymynech, Powys, SY22 6PS
01691 830015 Ⓕ 01691 839099
Est. 1983 *Stock size* Medium
Stock Pine and country furniture
Open Mon–Sat 9am–6pm or by appointment
Services Valuations, restoration and repairs

KNIGHTON

Offa's Dyke Antique Centre
Contact Mr I Watkins or Mrs H Hood
4 High Street, Knighton, Powys, LD7 1AT
01547 528635
Est. 1987 *Stock size* Medium
No. of dealers 12
Stock General antiques, ceramics
Open Mon–Sat 10am–1pm and 2–5pm
Services House clearance

Islwyn Watkins Antiques
Contact Mr I Watkins
4 High Street, Knighton, Powys, LD7 1AT
01547 520145
Est. 1977 *Stock size* Large
Stock Ceramics and small country antiques
Open Mon–Sat 10am–1pm 2–5pm
Services Valuations

LLANFAIR CAEREINION

Heritage Restorations
Contact Jonathan Gluck
Llanfair Caereinion, Welshpool, Powys, SY21 0HD
01938 810384 Ⓕ 01938 810900
info@heritagerestorations.co.uk
www.heritagerestorations.co.uk
Est. 1970 *Stock size* Large
Stock 18th–19thC pine furniture
Open Mon–Sat 9am–5pm
Services Restorations

LLANFYLLIN

Galata Coins
Contact Paul Withers
Old White Lion, Market Street, Llanfyllin, Powys, SY22 5BX
01691 648765 Ⓕ 01691 648765
Paul@galata.co.uk
www.galata.co.uk
Est. 1974 *Stock size* Small
Stock Coin and medal dealers
Open By appointment
Services Valuations

Galata Print Ltd
Contact Paul Withers
Old White Lion, Market Street, Llanfyllin, Powys, SY22 5BX
01691 648765 Ⓕ 01691 648765
Paul@galata.co.uk

www.galata.co.uk
Est. 1974 *Stock size* Large
Stock Numismatic items, coins, tokens, commemorative medals
Open By appointment
Services Valuations

LLANIDLOES

The Great Oak Bookshop
Contact Ross Boswell or Karin Reiter
35 Great Oak Street, Llanidloes, Powys, SY18 6BW
01686 412959 01686 412959
greatoak@europe.com
www.midwales.com/gob
Est. 1992 *Stock size* Large
Stock New and second-hand books
Open Mon–Fri 9.30am–5.30pm Sat 9.30am–4.30pm
Services Book search

LLANSANTFFRAID

Tudor Antiques
Contact Menna Corbett
Central House, Llansantffraid, Powys, SY22 6AR
01691 829104
Est. 1996 *Stock size* Medium
Stock General antiques, Victorian china and small furniture
Open Wed–Sat 11am–5pm
Fairs Carmarthen, Anglesey

MACHYNLLETH

Dyfi Valley Bookshop (PBFA, WBA)
Contact Mr N. Beeby
6 Heol y Doll, Machynlleth, Powys, SY20 8BQ
01654 703849
beeb@dvbookshop.fsnet.co.uk
www.abebooks.com/home/dvbookshop
Est. 1988 *Stock size* Medium
Stock Rare and second-hand books specializing in archery, the Old West, firearms
Open Mon–Sat 9.30am–5pm
Services Book search, catalogues

NEWBRIDGE ON WYE

Newbridge Antiques
Contact P Allan
The Old Village Hall, Newbridge on Wye, Llandrindod Wells, Powys, LD1 6LA
01597 860654 01597 860655
Est. 1986 *Stock size* Large
Stock General antiques, furniture, architectural
Open Mon–Sat 10am–5pm Sun noon–5pm
Services Valuations, stripping and restoration

NEWTOWN

Morris Marshall & Poole
Contact Alun Davies
10 Broad Street, Newtown, Powys, SY16 2LZ
01686 625900 01686 623783
mmp@newtown.ereal.net
www.morrismarshall.co.uk
Est. 1862
Open Mon–Fri 9am–5pm Sat 9.30am–noon
Sales General antiques
Frequency Quarterly
Catalogues Yes

RHAYADER

Etcetera
Contact Mrs R A Hawthorn
Highbury Shop, North Street, Rhayader, Powys, LD6 5BT
01597 810676 or 811423
Est. 1992 *Stock size* Medium
Stock Period furniture
Open Mon–Sun 10am–5.30pm, Jan–Mar limited – phone first

TRECASTLE

The Fire & Stove Shop
Contact Andy Annear or Jim Portsmouth
Vicarage Row (on A40), Trecastle, Brecon, Powys, LD3 8UW
01874 636888 02920 614615
07973 916774
jim@solidfuelstoves.com
www.solidfuelstoves.com
Est. 1998
Stock Multi-fuel stoves, fires, fireplaces, tiles, inserts, surrounds, hearths, dog grates, radiators
Open Mon–Sun 10am–6pm

Trecastle Antique Centre
Contact Ro Williams
Trecastle, Brecon, Powys, LD3 8UN
01874 638007 07811 032248
Est. 1996 *Stock size* Large
No. of dealers 10
Stock General antiques
Open Mon–Sun 10am–5pm

WELSHPOOL

F E Anderson & Son (LAPADA)
Contact Ian Anderson
5 High Street, Welshpool, Powys, SY21 7JF
01938 553340 01938 590545
07889 896832
Est. 1842 *Stock size* Large
Stock General antiques, 17th–19thC furniture
Open Mon–Fri 9am–5pm Sat 9am–2pm
Fairs Olympia, Harrogate, Birmingham NEC, Kingston
Services Valuations

Norman Lloyd & Co
Contact John Harding
5 Broad Street, Welshpool, Powys, SY21 7RZ
01938 552371 01938 556314
normanlloyd@aol.com
www.normanlloyd.com
Est. 1900
Open Mon–Fri 9am–5.30pm
Sales General antiques
Frequency Periodically
Catalogues Yes

SOUTH GLAMORGAN

BARRY

Ray Hawkins Antiques
Contact Ray Hawkins
1A Arcade Workships, Atlantic Trading Estate, Barry, South Glamorgan, CF63 3RF
01446 744750 01222 711778
07971 575044
ray@hawkins.wholesalers.co.uk
Est. 1975 *Stock size* Medium
Stock Antique shipping furniture and statues
Open Mon–Fri 9am–5pm Sat 9am–1pm
Fairs Ardingly, Newark
Services Exports furniture to USA, packing facilities

Hawkins Brothers Antiques
Contact Mrs C Robertson
21–23 Romilly Buildings, Woodham Road, Barry Docks, Barry, South Glamorgan, CF63 4JE
01446 746561 F 01446 744750
E hawkinsbrosantiques@compuserve.com
Stock size Large
Stock General antiques
Open Mon–Sat 9am–5pm

CARDIFF

Anchor Antiques (Wales) Ltd
Contact B A Brownhill
The Pumping Station, Penarth Road, Cardiff, South Glamorgan, CF11 8TT
029 2023 1308 F 029 2023 2588
M 07967 264325
Est. 1989 *Stock size* Large
Stock General antiques, clocks and ceramics
Open Mon–Sun 9.30am–5.30pm
Fairs Carmarthen, Malvern and Newark

Bonhams
7–8 Park Place, Cardiff, South Glamorgan, CF10 3DP
02920 727980 F 02920 727989
E cardiff@bonhams.com
W www.bonhams.com
Open Mon–Fri 9am–5.30pm

Capital Bookshop
Contact Andrew Mitchell
27 Morgan Arcade, Cardiff, South Glamorgan, CF10 1AF
029 2038 8423
Stock size Medium
Stock Rare and second-hand books including Welsh interest
Open Mon–Sat 10am–5.30pm
Fairs Book fairs, Oxford

Cardiff Antique Centre
Contact Susan Wilding
10–12 Royal Arcade, Cardiff, South Glamorgan, CF10 1AE
029 2039 8891
Est. 1975 *Stock size* Large
Stock General antiques and collectables including Welsh china, jewellery
Open Mon–Sat 10am–5.30pm
Services Valuations

Cardiff Reclamation
Contact Jeff Evans
Unit 7, Tremorfa Industrial Estate, Martin Road, Tremorfa, Cardiff, South Glamorgan, CF24 5SD
029 2045 8995
Est. 1987 *Stock size* Medium
Stock Architectural antiques, specializing in fireplaces and bathrooms
Open Mon–Fri 9am–5pm Sat 9am–1pm Sun 10am–1pm
Services Bath refinishing, pine stripping, sandblasting

Charlotte's Antiques
Contact Peter Cason
129 Woodville Road, Cathays, Cardiff, South Glamorgan, CF24 4DZ
029 2075 9809 M 07831 619071
Est. 1975 *Stock size* Large
Stock General and period antiques
Open Mon–Fri 10am–5pm Sat 10am–1pm

Crwys Antiques
Contact Mr Elfed Caradog
51 Crwys Road, Cardiff, South Glamorgan, CF24 4ND
029 2022 5318
Est. 1985 *Stock size* Small
Stock General antiques
Open Mon–Sat 10am–6pm

Decorative Heating
Contact Jim Portsmouth
Unit 2, Victoria Arcade, The Pumping Station, Cardiff, South Glamorgan, CF11 8TT
029 2052 2000 M 07973 916774
E jim@solidfuelstoves.com
W www.solidfuelstoves.com
Est. 1998 *Stock size* Medium
Stock Multi-fuel stoves, fires, fireplaces, tiles, inserts, surrounds, hearths, dog grates, radiators
Open Mon–Sun 9am–5.30pm

W H Douglas
Contact Mr W H Douglas
161 Cowbridge Road East, Cardiff, South Glamorgan, CF11 9AH
029 2022 4861
Est. 1952 *Stock size* Medium
Stock General antiques
Open Mon–Fri 9am–5pm

Hera Antiques
Contact Neil Richards
140 Whitchurch Road, Cardiff, South Glamorgan, CF14 3LZ
029 2061 9472
Est. 1987 *Stock size* Large
Stock High-quality furniture, porcelain and pictures
Open Mon–Sat 10am–5pm closed Wed
Fairs The Orangery, Margam Abbey, Port Talbot
Services Restorations, valuations

Jacobs Antique Centre
Contact Mr Cooling
West Canal Wharf, Cardiff, South Glamorgan, CF10 5DB
029 2039 0939 F 029 2037 3587
Est. 1982 *Stock size* Medium
No. of dealers 40
Stock General antiques
Open Thurs–Sat 9.30am–5pm

Keepence Antiques
Contact Mr Clive Keepence
34 Clare Road, Cardiff, South Glamorgan, CF11 6RS
029 2025 5348
Est. 1969 *Stock size* Medium
Stock Victorian, Edwardian furniture, shipping goods
Open Mon–Fri 10am–4pm Sat 10am–2pm

Llanishen Antiques
Contact Mrs J Boalch
26 Crwys Road, Cardiff, South Glamorgan, CF24 4NL
029 2039 7244
Est. 1974 *Stock size* Medium
Stock General antiques including 19th–20thC furniture
Open Mon–Sat 10am–4pm
Fairs Carmarthen, Shepton Mallet
Services Restorations

Now & Then
Contact Mr A Williams
54 Crwys Road, Cardiff, South Glamorgan, CF24 4NN
029 2038 3268 F 029 2038 4945
E frongaled50@hotmail.com
Est. 1989 *Stock size* Medium
Stock General antiques
Open Mon–Sat 9am–5pm

The Pumping Station
Contact Mr A J Boyce
Penarth Road, Cardiff, South Glamorgan, CF11 8TT
029 2022 1085 F 029 2023 2588

Ⓜ 07774 449443
Est. 1989 *Stock size* Large
No. of dealers 35
Stock General antiques, militaria, model cars, railways
Open Mon–Sun 9.30am–5.30pm
Services Valuations

Roberts Emporium
Contact Ian Roberts
✉ **58–60 Salisbury Road, Cardiff, South Glamorgan, CF24 4AD** Ⓟ
☎ 029 2023 5630 Ⓕ 029 2039 5935
Est. 1997 *Stock size* Large
Stock General antiques, collectables, props for TV and theatre
Open Mon–Sat 11am–5.30pm
Fairs Newark, Cardiff
Services Valuations

Sambourne House Antique Pine Ltd
Contact Tim or Kim Cove
✉ **145 Colchester Avenue, Cardiff, South Glamorgan, CF23 9AN** Ⓟ
☎ 02920 487823
Ⓔ tkcove34@globalnet.co.uk
Ⓦ www.sambourne-antiques.co.uk
Est. 1986 *Stock size* Large
Stock Antique and reproduction pine furniture, smalls, decorative items
Open Mon–Sun 9am–5pm
Services Hand-built kitchens

Ty-Llwyd Antiques
Contact Mr Graham Rousell
✉ **Ty-Llwyd, Lisvane Road, Lisvane, Cardiff, South Glamorgan, CF14 0SF** Ⓟ
☎ 029 2075 4109
Est. 1988 *Stock size* Large
Stock General antiques, clocks
Open By appointment
Services House clearance

Whitchurch Books Ltd (WBA)
Contact Gale Canvin
✉ **67 Merthyr Road, Whitchurch, Cardiff, South Glamorgan, CF14 1DD** Ⓟ
☎ 029 2052 1956 Ⓕ 029 2062 3599
Ⓦ www.whitchurchbooks@barclays.net
Est. 1994 *Stock size* Medium
Stock Rare and second-hand books, specializing in archaeology and history
Open Tues–Sat 10am–5.30pm
Fairs Cardiff
Services Mail order catalogues on archaeology and history

COWBRIDGE

The Antique Centre
Contact Mike Haxley
✉ **Ebenezer Chapel, 48 Eastgate, Cowbridge, South Glamorgan, CF71 7AB** Ⓟ
☎ 01446 771190
Est. 1966 *Stock size* Large
No. of dealers 30
Stock General antiques
Open Mon–Sat 10am–5pm
Services Valuations, picture restorations, repairs

Castle Antique Clocks
Contact Mr William Webber
✉ **The Antique Centre, Ebenezer Chapel, 48 Eastgate, Cowbridge, South Glamorgan, CF71 7AB** Ⓟ
☎ 029 2070 2313 Ⓕ 029 2071 2141
Ⓔ whwebber@talk21.com
Est. 1995 *Stock size* Medium
Stock Longcase clocks
Open Mon–Sat 10am–5pm
Services Valuations, restorations

Collectors Corner
Contact M Haxley
✉ **The Antique Centre, Ebenezer Chapel, 48 Eastgate, Cowbridge, South Glamorgan, CF71 7AB** Ⓟ
☎ 01446 771190 Ⓜ 07977 091665
Ⓔ collectorscorner1@hotmail.com
Est. 1996 *Stock size* Medium
Stock Furniture, china, porcelain, collectables, jewellery, autographs
Open Mon–Sat 10am–5pm

Cowbridge Antiques Centre
Contact Mr T C Monaghan
✉ **75 Eastgate, Cowbridge, South Glamorgan, CF71 7AA** Ⓟ
☎ 01446 775841 Ⓜ 07773 486390
Ⓔ terryval@cowbridgeantiques.freeserve.co.uk
Est. 1995 *Stock size* Medium
No. of dealers 9
Stock Georgian–Edwardian furniture, small collectables
Open Mon–Sat 10am–5pm
Services Valuations, restorations

Eastgate Antiques
Contact Liz Herbert
✉ **6 High Street, Cowbridge, South Glamorgan, CF71 7AG** Ⓟ
☎ 01446 775111
Est. 1984 *Stock size* Medium
Stock General antiques
Open Mon–Sat 10am–1pm 2–5.30pm

WEST GLAMORGAN

CLYDACH

Celtic Antique Fireplaces
Contact Mr R Walker
✉ **Unit 13, John Player Industrial Estate, Clydach, Swansea, West Glamorgan, SA6 5BQ** Ⓟ
☎ 01792 476047 Ⓕ 01792 476047
Ⓜ 07973 253655
Ⓔ robin-walker@celticfireplaces.co.uk
Ⓦ www.celticfireplaces.co.uk
Est. 1992 *Stock size* Large
Stock Antique fireplaces
Open Wed Sat 10am–2pm or by appointment
Services Renovation

Clydach Antiques
Contact Mr R T Pulman
✉ **83 High Street, Clydach, Swansea, West Glamorgan, SA6 5LJ** Ⓟ
☎ 01792 843209
Est. 1981 *Stock size* Small
Stock General antiques
Open Mon–Fri 10am–5pm
Fairs Swansea
Services Clock repair

GURNOS

Gurnos Sales
Contact Mr Nigel Faulkner
✉ **10 Bethel Road, Gurnos, Lower Cwmtwrch, Swansea, West Glamorgan, SA9 2PS** Ⓟ
☎ 01639 849801 Ⓕ 01639 849801
Ⓔ nigel@gurnosales.fsnet.co.uk
Est. 1988 *Stock size* Medium
Stock General antiques and collectables
Open Mon–Fri 10am–5pm Sat 9am–1pm
Services House clearances

MUMBLES

Gower House Antiques
Contact Mrs E S Dodds
28–30 Dunns Lane, Mumbles, Swansea, West Glamorgan, SA3 4AA
01792 369844
Est. 1999 *Stock size* Medium
Stock General antiques, mirrors, lighting, chandeliers
Open Tues–Sat 10am–5.30pm
Services Valuations

NEATH

Neath Antiques
Contact Mrs S Thomas
6 Alfred Street, Neath, West Glamorgan, SA11 1EF
01639 645740
neathantiques.co.uk
Est. 1979 *Stock size* Medium
Stock General antiques, barometers and clocks
Open Mon–Sat 10am–4.30pm closed Thurs

Neath Market Curios (OMRS)
Contact Mr P D Owen
General Market, Green Street, Neath, West Glamorgan, SA11 1DP
01639 641775
Est. 1989 *Stock size* Medium
Stock General collectables
Open Mon–Sat 9am–5pm
Fairs Carmarthen, Cardiff

PONTARDULAIS

Collectors
Contact Mr J D Hyorns
48 Bryngwili Road, Hendy, Pontardulais, Swansea, West Glamorgan, SA4 1XA
01792 885141 01792 885141
pjexports@pj-collectors.fsnet.co.uk
Est. 1996 *Stock size* Medium
Stock General antiques
Open Mon–Sat 10am–5.30pm
Fairs Ardingly
Services Refurbishment

The Emporium
Contact Ms Laura Jeremy
112 St Teilo Street, Pontardulais, Swansea, West Glamorgan, SA4 1SR
01792 885185 07811 758896
laura@the-emporium.freeserve.co.uk
Est. 1990 *Stock size* Medium
Stock Small furniture, collectables, metalware
Open Mon–Fri 10am–5.30pm Sat 10am–1pm

SKETTY

Forget-Me-Nots
Contact Mr Anthony Thomas
43 Eversley Road, Sketty, Swansea, West Glamorgan, SA2 9DE
01792 201944 01792 201944
Est. 1999 *Stock size* Medium
Stock Small furniture, china, Poole, Mason's, Doulton, books
Open Mon–Fri 9.30am–5pm Sat 9.30am–4pm

Sketty Antiques
Contact Mrs P M Richards
87 Eversley Road, Sketty, Swansea, West Glamorgan, SA2 9DE
01792 201616
Est. 1995 *Stock size* Medium
Stock General antiques
Open Mon–Fri 11am–5pm Sat 10am–1pm
Fairs Towy Fairs

SWANSEA

Aladdin's Cave
Contact Pat Callen
2 Plymouth Street, Swansea, West Glamorgan, SA1 3QQ
01792 459576
Est. 1974 *Stock size* Large
Stock General antiques and collectables, Doulton Toby jugs, brass, copper, Winstanley cats
Open Mon–Fri 9.30am–5pm
Fairs Cowbridge, Chepstow

Bygone Antiques
Contact Mr C A Oliver
122 St Helens Road, Swansea, West Glamorgan, SA1 4AW
01792 468248
Est. 1970 *Stock size* Medium
Stock General antiques
Open Mon–Sat 10am–4.30pm

Collectors' Corner
Contact Mr J Tithecott
10–11 High Street, Swansea, West Glamorgan, SA1 1LE
01792 655506
Est. 1998 *Stock size* Medium
Stock Enamel badges, postcards, stamps, cigarette cards, old and new die-cast models
Open Mon–Fri 10am–4pm Sat 10am–1pm
Services Valuations

Stripped Pine Workshop
Contact Mr John Wood
Rear of 28 Catherine Street, Swansea, West Glamorgan, SA1 4JS
01792 461236
Est. 1970 *Stock size* Medium
Stock Furniture, doors, stripped pine
Open Mon–Sat 11.30am–6pm
Services Pine stripping

Swansea Antique Centre
Contact Mr W Wright
1 King Edward Road, Swansea, West Glamorgan, SA1 4LH
01792 475194
Est. 1999 *Stock size* Large
No. of dealers 2
Stock General antiques, good furniture
Open Mon–Sat 10am–5.30pm
Services Valuations, restorations, house clearance

Upstairs Antiques
Contact M Stanley
48 St Helens Road, Swansea, West Glamorgan, SA1 4AY
01792 466522
mariastanley@ntlworld.com
Est. 1994 *Stock size* Medium
Stock General antiques and restoration
Open Mon–Sat 10am–4pm phone call advisable
Services Re-caning and rush work

YSTRADGYNLAIS

Penybont Farm Antiques
Contact Mrs S Yankovic
Penybont Farm, Penycae, Ystradgynlais, Swansea, West Glamorgan, SA9 1SH
01639 730620
Est. 1990 *Stock size* Large
Stock General antiques, pine, china
Open Sat Sun 10am–5pm or by appointment
Services Restoration and hand stripping

SCOTLAND

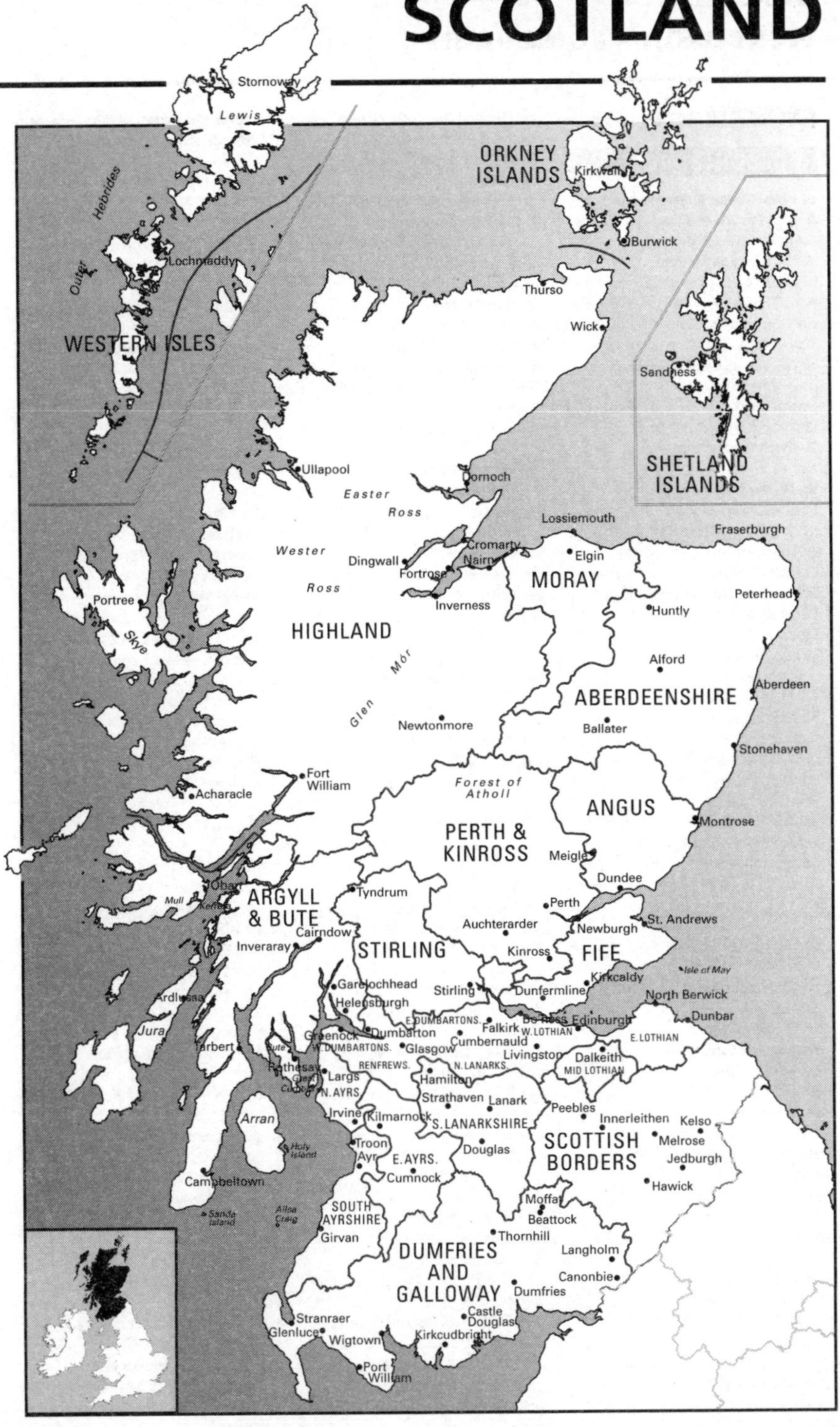

Stornoway
Lewis
Outer Hebrides
Lochmaddy
WESTERN ISLES
ORKNEY ISLANDS
Kirkwall
Burwick
Thurso
Wick
Sandness
SHETLAND ISLANDS
Ullapool
Dornoch
Easter Ross
Wester Ross
Lossiemouth
Fraserburgh
Cromarty
Elgin
Dingwall
Nairn
Fortrose
MORAY
Peterhead
Portree
Inverness
Huntly
Skye
HIGHLAND
Glen Mór
Alford
Aberdeen
ABERDEENSHIRE
Newtonmore
Ballater
Stonehaven
Fort William
Forest of Atholl
Acharacle
ANGUS
Montrose
PERTH & KINROSS
Meigle
Dundee
Oban
Mull
Kerrera
ARGYLL & BUTE
Tyndrum
Perth
Auchterarder
Newburgh
St. Andrews
Cairndow
Inveraray
STIRLING
Kinross
FIFE
Isle of May
Garelochhead
Stirling
Dunfermline
Kirkcaldy
North Berwick
Helensburgh
Ardlussa
E.DUMBARTONS.
Bo'ness
Edinburgh
Dunbar
Jura
Greenock
Dumbarton
Falkirk
W. LOTHIAN
E. LOTHIAN
W. DUMBARTONS.
Glasgow
Cumbernauld
Livingston
Tarbert
Bute
Rothesay
RENFREWS.
N. LANARKS.
Dalkeith
MID LOTHIAN
Great Cumbrae
Largs
Hamilton
N. AYRS.
Strathaven
Lanark
Peebles
Arran
Irvine
Kilmarnock
Innerleithen
Kelso
S. LANARKSHIRE
Melrose
Holy Island
Troon
Ayr
E. AYRS.
Douglas
SCOTTISH BORDERS
Jedburgh
Cumnock
Hawick
Campbeltown
Sanda Island
Ailsa Craig
SOUTH AYRSHIRE
Moffat
Beattock
Girvan
Thornhill
DUMFRIES AND GALLOWAY
Langholm
Canonbie
Dumfries
Stranraer
Castle Douglas
Glenluce
Wigtown
Kirkcudbright
Port William

SCOTLAND

EDINBURGH

EDINBURGH

Adam Antiques & Restoration
Contact Charles Bergius
23c Dundas Street, Edinburgh, EH3 6QQ
0131 556 7555 F 0131 556 7555
Est. 1983 *Stock size* Medium
Stock 18th–19thC mahogany furniture and associated furnishings
Open Tues–Sat 10.30am–6pm Mon by appointment
Services Restorations

Armchair Books
Contact Mr D Govan
72/74 West Port, Edinburgh, EH1 2LE
0131 229 5927
E armchairbooks@hotmail.com
Stock size Medium
Stock Books, especially Victorian illustrated books
Open Mon–Sun noon–5pm

Auckinleck
Contact William Stewart
86 Grassmarket, Edinburgh, EH1 9JR
0131 220 0505
Est. 1979 *Stock size* Medium
Stock General antiques, Georgian–Victorian
Open Tues–Sat 10.15am–5.15pm

Bébés et Jouets
Contact Dee Urquhart
c/o Post Office, 165 Restalrig Road, Edinburgh, EH7 6HW
0131 332 5650
M 07714 374995
E bebesetjouets@u.genie.co.uk
W www.you.genie.co.uk/bebesetjouets
Est. 1987 *Stock size* Medium
Stock Antique French bébés and German dolls, teddy bears, juvenilia and related items. Lay-away of items possible
Open By appointment only
Services Repair and restoration of antique dolls, teddies, antique costumes for dolls. Digital photographs and video of stock items. Postal service available. Author of articles on antique dolls

Belford Antiques
Contact John Belford
124 Buccleuch Street, Edinburgh, EH8 9NQ
0131 445 4368 M 07947 671963
Est. 1993 *Stock size* Small
Stock Furniture, collectables
Open Tues–Sat 2–6pm

Bonhams
65 George Street, Edinburgh, EH2 2JL
0131 225 2266 F 0131 220 2547
E edinburgh@bonhams.com
W www.bonhams.com
Sales Edinburgh saleroom

The Bookworm
Contact Peter Ritchie
210 Dalkeith Road, Edinburgh, EH16 5DT
0131 662 4357
E peter.book@talk21.com
Est. 1987 *Stock size* Medium
Stock Second-hand and antique books
Open Mon–Sat 9.30am–5.30pm
Services Valuations, book search

Bow-Well Antiques
Contact Murdo McLeod
103 West Row, Edinburgh, EH1 2JP
0131 225 3335 F 0131 226 1259
M 07710 600431
E murdoch.mcleod@virgin.net
Est. 1979 *Stock size* Large
Stock General and Scottish antiquities
Open Mon–Sat 10am–5pm
Services Shipping

Broughton Books
Contact Peter Galinsky
2a Broughton Place, Edinburgh, EH1 3RX
0131 557 8010
Est. 1971 *Stock size* Medium
Stock Rare and second-hand books
Open Tues–Fri noon–6pm Sat 10.30am–5.30pm

Cabaret Antiques
Contact Terry Cavers
37 Grassmarket, Edinburgh, EH1 2HS
0131 225 8618
Est. 1990 *Stock size* Large
Stock Art Deco, Scottish paperweights, compacts, glass, costume jewellery, ceramics
Open Mon–Sun 10.30am–5.30pm
Fairs Mammoth Fairs

Calton Gallery (BADA)
Contact Andrew Whitfield
10 Royal Terrace, Edinburgh, EH7 5AB
0131 556 1010 F 0131 558 1150
M 07887 793781
E calton.gall@virgin.net
Est. 1980 *Stock size* Large
Stock Fine art, Scottish, marine 19th–early 20thC paintings and watercolours
Open Mon–Fri 10am–6pm Sat 10am–1pm (during exhibitions)
Services Valuations, restorations

The Carson Clark Gallery – Scotland's Map Heritage Centre (IMTA)
Contact Paul Clark
181–183 Canongate, Edinburgh, EH18 8BN
0131 556 4710 F 0131 556 4710
E scotmap@aol.com
W www.carson-clark-gallery.co.uk
Est. 1972 *Stock size* Large
Stock Maps and charts, engravings, lithographs
Open Mon–Sat 10.30am–6pm
Services Valuations, appraisal, restoration, repair, framing, shipping

Castle Books
Contact Mrs K Choucha
20 Rankeillor Street, Edinburgh, EH8 9HY
0131 667 5174
E cathy@booksnet.freeserve.co.uk
Est. 1983 *Stock size* Small
Stock Rare and second-hand books
Open Mon–Fri 9am–5pm

D L Cavanagh Antiques
Contact Simon Cavanagh
49 Cockburn Street, Edinburgh, EH1 1BS
0131 226 3391
Est. 1972 *Stock size* Large
Stock Coins, medals, silver, jewellery, collectors' items
Open Mon–Sat 11am–5.30pm
Services Valuations

Chit Chat Antiques
Contact Victoria Reid
134 St Stephen Street, Edinburgh, EH3 5AA
0131 225 9660

Est. 1984 *Stock size* Small
Stock Flatware, silver plate, silver, ceramics
Open Tues–Sat 11am–5.30pm

Bobby Clyde Antiques
Contact Bobby Clyde
5a Grange Road, Edinburgh, EH9 1UH
0131 667 6718 07808 319496
Est. 1976 *Stock size* Medium
Stock General antiques
Open Mon Thurs Fri Sat 10.30am–5.30pm Sun noon–4pm
Services Stripping, delivery

Craiglea Clocks (BWCG)
Contact Mr Rafter
88 Corniston Road, Edinburgh, EH10 5QJ
0131 452 8568
craigclocks@btclick.com
www.craigleaclocks.com
Est. 1977 *Stock size* Medium
Stock Clocks and barometers
Open Mon–Fri 10am–4pm Sat 10am–1pm
Services Restorations

Da Capo Antiques
Contact Nick Carter
68 Henderson Row, Edinburgh, EH3 5BJ
0131 557 1918
Est. 1977 *Stock size* Medium
Stock 18th–early 20thC furniture, brass bedsteads, light fittings
Open Tues–Sat 10.30am–5.30pm
Services Valuations, restorations

Alan Day Antiques (LAPADA)
Contact Mr A Day
25A Moray Place, Edinburgh, EH3 6DA
0131 225 2590 07860 533922
doodah.day@virgin.net
Est. 1973 *Stock size* Medium
Stock General antiques
Trade only Yes
Open By appointment

Duncan & Reid
Contact Mrs Reid
5 Tanfield, Canon Mills, Edinburgh, EH3 5DA
0131 556 4591
msduncan@ecosse.net
Est. 1979 *Stock size* Medium
Stock 18th–19thC English, Chinese, Continental ceramics, glass, decorative objects, second-hand and antiquarian books
Open Tues–Sat noon–5.30pm

EASY Edinburgh & Glasgow Architectural Salvage Yard (SALVO)
Contact E Barrass
31 West Bowling Green Street, Edinburgh, EH6 5NX
0131 554 7077 0131 554 3070
enquiries@easy-arch-salv.co.uk
www.easy-arch-salv.co.uk
Est. 1987 *Stock size* Medium
Stock Architectural antiques, fireplaces, doors, ranges, pews, etc
Open Mon–Fri 9am–5pm Sat noon–5pm

ECS (LANA)
Contact Mr T D Brown
11 West Cross Causeway, Edinburgh, EH8 9JW
0131 667 9095/668 2928
0131 668 2926
Est. 1977 *Stock size* Large
Stock Antique coins and medals, stamps, ephemera, cigarette cards, medals
Open Mon–Sat 9am–5pm
Fairs Edinburgh, Castle Donnington
Services Valuations, auctions of coins and banknotes

Donald Ellis Antiques
Contact Donald Ellis
7 Bruntsfield Place, Edinburgh, EH10 4HN
0131 229 4720
Est. 1969 *Stock size* Medium
Stock General antiques
Open Mon–Fri 10am–5pm closed Wed pm
Fairs Buxton
Services Clock restorations

Georgian Antiques (LAPADA)
Contact P or J Dixon
10 Pattison Street, Leith, Edinburgh, EH6 7HF
0131 553 7286 0131 553 6299
info@georgianantiques.net
www.georgianantiques.net
Est. 1978 *Stock size* Large
Stock Very large collection of quality antiques
Open Mon–Fri 8.30am–5.30pm Sat 10am–2pm
Services Valuations, shipping

Gladrags
Contact Kate Cameron
17 Henderson Row, Edinburgh, EH3 5DH
0131 557 1916
Est. 1974 *Stock size* Large
Stock Unique selection of exquisite vintage clothes, accessories, costume jewellery, linen
Open Tues–Sat 10.30am–6pm

Goodwin's Antiques Ltd
Contact Mr B Goodwin
15–16 Queensferry Street, Edinburgh, EH2 4QW
0131 225 4717 0131 220 1412
bengoodwin@compuserve.com
Est. 1959 *Stock size* Large
Stock General antiques
Open Mon–Fri 9am–5.30pm Sat 9am–5pm
Services Valuations, repairs

Grant & Shaw Ltd (ABA)
Contact Alan Grant
62 West Port, Edinburgh, EH1 2LD
0131 229 8399 0131 229 8393
07967 001776
AGrant4227@aol.com
Est. 1989 *Stock size* Medium
Stock Antiquarian and travel literature
Open By appointment
Fairs Chelsea
Services Valuations

Harlequin Antiques
Contact Charles Harkness
30 Bruntsfield Place, Edinburgh, EH10 4HJ
0131 228 9446
Est. 1996 *Stock size* Medium
Stock General antiques
Open Mon–Sat 10am–5pm
Fairs Scone Place, Fife
Services Clock restoration

Holyrood Architectural Salvage
Contact Mr K Fowler
Holyrood Business Park, 146 Duddingston Road West, Edinburgh, EH16 4AP
0131 661 9305 0131 656 9404
Ken@has.abel.co.uk
www.holyroodarchitecturalsalvage.com
Est. 1993 *Stock size* Large
Stock Period fireplaces, baths, radiators, panelled doors, brassware, stained glass

Open Mon–Sat 9am–5pm
Sun noon–4pm
Services Restoration of baths

Gordon Inglis Antiques
Contact Gordon Inglis
8 Barclay Terrace, Edinburgh, EH10 4HP P
☎ 0131 221 1192 F 0131 221 1192
M 07966 505219
E gordon@inglisantiques.com
W www.inglisantiques.com
Est. 1990 *Stock size* Medium
Stock Wide range of inexpensive collectables, ephemera, vintage clothing, china, glass, etc
Open By appointment

Allan K L Jackson
67 Causewayside, Edinburgh, EH9 1QF P
☎ 0131 668 4532 M 07989 236443
Est. 1974 *Stock size* Medium
Stock General antiques
Open Mon–Sat 10am–5pm
Services House clearance

Kaimes Smithy Antiques
Contact Mr J Lynch
79 Howdenhall Road, Edinburgh, EH16 6PW P
☎ 0131 441 2076 M 07973 377198
E john@jlynch.freeserve.co.uk
Est. 1970 *Stock size* Medium
Stock 18th–19thC furniture, clocks, paintings (oils and watercolours), Chinese ceramics
Open Tues Wed Fri Sat 1.30–5pm

Alan Lawson & Son
Contact Mr A Lawson
181 Causewayside, Edinburgh, EH9 1PH P
☎ 0131 662 1991
Est. 1974 *Stock size* Medium
Stock General antiques and reproduction items
Open Mon–Sat 11.30am–5.30pm
Services Valuations, house clearance

London Road Antiques
Contact Mr R S Forrest
15 Earlston Place, Edinburgh, EH7 5SU P
☎ 0131 652 2790
E info@19thC.com
W www.19thC.com
Est. 1979 *Stock size* Large
Stock 19thC furniture, Victorian and Georgian wares, stripped pine
Open Mon–Sat 10am–5pm
Sun 1–5pm

J D Loue
Contact Mr J D Loue
15–17 Jane Street, Edinburgh, EH6 5HE P
☎ 0131 554 7609 F 0131 554 7609
M 07774 678423
Est. 1967 *Stock size* Medium
Stock General antiques
Open Mon–Sat 8.30am–4.30pm
Services Valuations, reproduction furniture

J Martinez Antiques
Contact Mr J Martinez
17 Brandon Terrace, Edinburgh, EH3 5DZ P
☎ 0131 558 8720 F 0131 558 8720
M 07836 608090
Est. 1979 *Stock size* Medium
Stock General antiques, jewellery, clocks
Open Mon–Sat 11am–5pm
Fairs NEC, Ingliston
Services Valuations

McNaughtan's Bookshop (ABA)
Contact Elizabeth Strong
3a & 4a Haddington Place, Edinburgh, EH7 4AE P
☎ 0131 556 5897 F 0131 556 8220
E mcnbooks@btconnect.com
Est. 1957
Stock Antiquarian and second-hand books, architecture, children's and Scottish topics
Open Tues–Sat 9.30am–5.30pm
Fairs ABA
Services Valuations

Meadow Lamps Gallery
Contact Mr Robertson
48 Warrender Park Road, Edinburgh, EH9 1HH P
☎ 0131 221 1212
Est. 1900 *Stock size* Medium
Stock Antique lighting
Open Tues Thurs Sat 10am–6pm
Fairs NEC Birmingham, Glasgow
Services Restorations

Millers Antiques
Contact Miss S Knott
187–191 Causewayside, Edinburgh, EH9 1PH P
☎ 0131 662 1429 F 0131 662 4187
Est. 1995 *Stock size* Large
Stock General antiques, Georgian–Edwardian furniture, mahogany, oak and pine, unusual collectables
Open Mon–Sat 10am–5.30pm
Fairs Newark, Swinderby
Services Pine – stripped, sanded and waxed, oak – hand stripped, French polishing

Montresor
Contact Gareth Jones
35 St Stephen Street, Edinburgh, EH3 5AH
☎ 0131 220 6877
Est. 1970 *Stock size* Large
Stock Vintage and designer costume jewellery, lighting, Art Nouveau, Art Deco
Open Mon–Sat 10.30am–1pm
2–6pm
Services Costume jewellery for hire

T & J W Neilson Ltd (National Fireplace Association)
Contact Mr or Mrs Neilson
76 Coburg Street, Edinburgh, EH6 6HJ P
☎ 0131 554 4704 F 0131 555 2071
E info@chimneypiece.co.uk
W www.chimneypiece.co.uk
Est. 1932 *Stock size* Large
Stock Antique chimney pieces, dog grates, register grates, fenders and fireplace accessories
Open Mon–Fri 9.30am–5pm
Sat 9.30am–4pm
Services Shipping

Now & Then
Contact Mr D Gordon
7 & 9 West Cross Causeway, Edinburgh, EH8 9JW P
☎ 0131 668 2927 F 0131 668 2926
M 07976 360283
E nowandthenuk@aol.com
W oldtoysandantiques.co.uk
Est. 1976 *Stock size* Medium
Stock Old toys, antiques, telephones, old clocks, cameras, bicycles, automobilia, railwayana, pre-WW1 office and domestic equipment, small items of furniture
Open Tues–Sat 1–5.30pm
Fairs Edinburgh, London
Services Valuations

The Old Children's Bookshelf (PBFA)
Contact Shirley Neilson

✉ **175 Canongate, Royal Mile, Edinburgh, EH8 8BN** 🅿
☎ 0131 558 3411
Ⓦ shirleyocb@aol.com
Est. 1998 ***Stock size*** Medium
Stock Children's novels, annuals, prints, comics
Open Mon–Fri 10.30am–5pm Sat 10am–5pm
Fairs PBFA, ESoc

The Old Town Bookshop (PBFA)
Contact Ron Wilson
✉ **8 Victoria Street, Edinburgh, EH1 2HG** 🅿
☎ 0131 225 9237 Ⓕ 0131 229 1503
Ⓜ 07740 625172
Ⓔ sales@oldtownbookshop.co.uk
Ⓦ www.oldtownbookshop.co.uk
Est. 1978 ***Stock size*** Medium
Stock Antiquarian and second-hand books, maps, prints, specializing in antiquarian art books
Open Mon–Sat 10.30am–6pm
Fairs Dublin, London, Edinburgh
Services Valuations, catalogues

Past & Present (PBFA)
Contact Gary Watt
✉ **54a Clerk Street, Edinburgh, EH8 9JR**
☎ 0131 667 2004 Ⓕ 0131 667 2004
Est. 1994 ***Stock size*** Medium
Stock General antiques, antiquarian children's books, Art Deco
Open Mon–Fri 10am–5pm Sat 10am–6pm Sun 2–6pm
Fairs Ingliston
Services Valuations, china repair

Reid & Reid
Contact Willie Reid
✉ **134 St Stephen Street, Edinburgh, EH3 5AA** 🅿
☎ 0131 225 9660
Est. 1981 ***Stock size*** Small
Stock Antiquuarian books and prints
Open Tues–Sat 11am–5.30pm

Royal Mile Curios
Contact Mr Martin
✉ **363 High Street, Edinburgh, EH1 1PW** 🅿
☎ 0131 226 4050
Est. 1875 ***Stock size*** Large
Stock Antique and Scottish jewellery
Open Mon–Sun 10.30am–5.30pm

Royal Mile Gallery
Contact J A Smith
✉ **272 Canongate, Edinburgh, EH8 8AA** 🅿
☎ 0131 558 1702
Ⓔ james@royalmilegallery.co.uk
Ⓦ www.royalmilegallery.co.uk
Est. 1994 ***Stock size*** Large
Stock Antiquarian maps, prints
Open Mon–Sat 11.30am–5pm
Services Valuations, framing service

Samarkand Galleries (LAPADA, CADA, CINOA)
Contact Brian MacDonald
✉ **16 Howe Street, Edinburgh, EH3 6TD** 🅿
☎ 0131 225 2010 Ⓕ 0131 225 2010
Ⓔ howe@samarkand.co.uk
Ⓦ www.samarkand.co.uk
Est. 1979 ***Stock size*** Large
Stock Antique and contemporary rugs from Near East and Central Asia, decorative carpets, nomadic weavings
Open Mon–Sat 10am–5.30pm
Fairs Hali Antique Textile Art Fair
Services Search

James Scott
Contact James Scott
✉ **43 Dundas Street, Edinburgh, EH3 6JN**
☎ 0131 556 8260
Est. 1964 ***Stock size*** Medium
Stock General antiques
Open Mon–Sat 11.30am–5.30pm closed 1–2pm closed Thurs
Services Valuations

Second Edition
Contact W A Smith
✉ **9 Howard Street, Edinburgh, EH3 5JP** 🅿
☎ 0131 556 9403
Est. 1979 ***Stock size*** Large
Stock Quality books, militaria, arts, Scottish books
Open Mon–Fri noon–5.30pm Sat 9.30am–5.30pm
Services Valuations, binding

Shapes Antiques & Fine Art Auctions
Contact Richard Longwill BA, MRICS
✉ **Bankhead Avenue, Sighthill, Edinburgh, EH11 4BY** 🅿
☎ 0131 453 3222 Ⓕ 0131 453 6444
Ⓔ auctionsadmin@shapesauctioneers.co.uk
Ⓦ www.shapesauctioneers.co.uk
Est. 1992
Open Mon–Fri 9am–5pm
Sales Fine art and antiques sale 1st Sat of every month 10am, viewing Thur 10am–7pm Fri 10am–4pm
Frequency Monthly
Catalogues Yes

Still Life
Contact Ewan Lamont
✉ **54 Candlemaker Row, Edinburgh, EH1 2QE**
☎ 0131 225 8524
Ⓔ ewanlamont@mac.com
Ⓦ http://homepage.mac.com/ewanlamont/PhotoAlbum.html
Est. 1984 ***Stock size*** Large
Stock General antiques, china, glass, pictures
Open Mon–Sat noon–5pm

The Talish Gallery
Contact John Martin
✉ **168 Canongate, Edinburgh, EH8 8DF** 🅿
☎ 0131 557 8435
Est. 1969 ***Stock size*** Large
Stock Small general antiques, Oriental wares, silver
Open Mon–Sat 10am–4pm
Fairs Newark

Thomson, Roddick & Medcalf
Contact Sybelle Medcalf
✉ **The Edinburgh and Lothian Sale Room, 44/3 Hardengreen Business Park, Eskbank, Edinburgh, EH22 3NX** 🅿
☎ 0131 454 9090 Ⓕ 0131 454 9191
Ⓔ t.rm@virgin.net
Est. 1999
Open Mon–Fri 9am–5pm
Sales Antiques, fine art, general furnishings, special quarterly sales
Frequency Weekly
Catalogues Yes

Till's Bookshop
Contact Mr R Till
✉ **1 Hope Park Crescent, Edinburgh, EH8 9NA** 🅿
☎ 0131 667 0895
Est. 1985 ***Stock size*** Medium
Stock Literature, fantasy, mystery, humanities, poetry, drama, cinema, general, first editions
Open Mon–Fri noon–7.30pm Sat 11am–6pm Sun noon–5.30pm
Services Valuations

Trinity Curios
Contact Alan Ferguson
4–6 Stanley Road, Edinburgh, EH6 4SG
0131 552 8481 07715 500719
adfer@btinternet.com
Est. 1987 *Stock size* Large
Stock Quality furniture, porcelain, silver, linen, collectables
Open Tues–Fri 10am–5pm Wed Sat noon–6pm Sun 2–5pm

Unicorn Antiques
Contact N Duncan
65 Dundas Street, Edinburgh, EH3 6RS
0131 556 7176
unicorn@ecosse.net
www.transcotland.com/unicorn
Est. 1969 *Stock size* Small
Stock General antiques, bric-a-brac
Open Mon–Sat 10.30am–6.30pm

West Port Books
Contact Mr H N Barrott
147 West Port, Edinburgh, EH3 9DD
0131 229 4431
west@portbooks.freeserve.co.uk
www.westport.freeserve.co.uk
Est. 1979 *Stock size* Large
Stock Second-hand and antiquarian books, especially fine art books and Indian imports
Open Mon–Sat 10.30am–5.30pm

Whytock & Reid
Contact Mr Reid
Sunbury House, Belford Mews, Edinburgh, EH4 3DN
0131 226 4911 0131 226 4595
whytockandreid.com
www.whytockandreid.com
Est. 1807 *Stock size* Large
Stock Whytock & Reid 19thC furniture, 18thC furniture, rugs, carpets
Open Mon–Fri 9am–5.30pm Sat 10am–2pm
Services Cabinet makers, French polishing

Wild Rose Antiques
Contact E or Kate Cameron
15 Henderson Row, Edinburgh, EH3 5DH
0131 557 1916
Est. 1974 *Stock size* Large
Stock Select decorative table silver, ladies' and gentlemen's jewellery, porcelain, pottery, glass, metalware
Open Tues–Sat 10.30am–6pm

Richard Wood Antiques
Contact Richard Wood
66 West Port, Edinburgh, EH1 2LD
0131 229 6344
Est. 1971 *Stock size* Large
Stock Small silver and Oriental items, collectables
Open Mon–Sat 10am–5pm
Fairs Ingliston Mammoth Fair

GLASGOW

GLASGOW

All Our Yesterdays
Contact Susie Robinson
6 Park Road, Kelvinbridge, Glasgow, G4 9JG
0141 334 7788 0141 339 8994
antiques@allouryesterdays.fsnet.co.uk
Est. 1989 *Stock size* Large
Stock General antiques, mineral and crystal specimens
Open Flexible Mon–Fri 11am–6pm Sat noon–5.30pm or by appointment
Services Valuations, search service

E A Alvarino
Contact E A Alvarino
13 Radnor Street, Kelvingrove, Glasgow, G3 7UA
0141 334 1213
EAAlvarino@aol.com
Est. 1976 *Stock size* Large
Stock General antiques
Open Mon–Fri 1–5pm
Services Valuations

Antichita
Contact Catherine Luporini
5 Abbot Street, Glasgow, G41 3XE
0141 632 5665
antichitauk@aol.co.uk
Est. 1989 *Stock size* Large
Stock General antiques
Open Mon–Sat 10am–5pm Sun noon–4pm
Services Valuations, restorations

The Antiques Warehouse
Contact Philip Mangan
Unit 3b, Yorkhill Quay Estate, Glasgow, G3 8QE
0141 334 4924 0141 400 4925
Est. 1979 *Stock size* Large
Stock General antiques
Open Mon–Fri 9am–5pm Sat 10am–5pm Sun noon–5pm
Services Valuations, restorations and repairs

Bonhams
176 St Vincent Street, Glasgow, G2 5SG
0141 223 8860 0141 223 8868
glasgow@bonhams.com
www.bonhams.com
Open Mon–Fri 8.30am–5pm

Browns Clocks
Contact Jim Cairns
13 Radnor Street, Glasgow, G3 7UA
0141 334 6308 0141 334 6308
james@jcairns.greatxscape.net
Est. 1933 *Stock size* Medium
Stock Longcase clocks
Open Mon–Fri 10am–5pm Sat 10am–1pm
Services Restoration of all antique clocks

Butler's Furniture Galleries
Contact Laurence Butler
39 Camelon Street, Carntyne Industrial Estate, Glasgow, G32 6JS
0141 7785720 07950 312355
butlersantiques@lineone.net
www.butlersfurnituregalleries.co.uk
Est. 1981 *Stock size* Large
Stock Georgian–Edwardian furniture
Open Mon–Fri 10am–5pm Sun by appointment
Services Valuations, restorations

Canning Antiques
Contact Kate
24–26 Millbrae Road, Langside, Glasgow, G42 9UT
0141 632 9853 0141 632 9853
kate@canning-antiques.com
www.canning-antiques.com
Est. 1997 *Stock size* Medium
Stock Georgian–Edwardian furniture, small mirrors
Open Mon–Fri 9am–5pm Sat 10am–5pm Sun noon–5pm
Fairs Antiques for Everyone
Services Restorations

Carpet Auctioneers Ltd (SAA)
Contact Mr T Severn

✉ **32 Washington Street, Glasgow, G3 8ZA** 🅿
☎ 0141 2219329
Est. 1959
Open Mon–Fri 10am–4.30pm Sat 9.30am–1.30pm
Sales Phone for details

⊞ Circa
Contact Sheila Murdoch
✉ **37 Ruthven Lane, Glasgow, G12 9BG**
☎ 0141 581 3307
Est. 2000 *Stock size* Large
Stock Vintage clothing, handbags, accessories, jewellery
Open Mon–Sat 11.30am–5.30pm Sun 1–5.30pm

Arthur E Collins & Son (SAA)
Contact Leonard Kerr
✉ **141 West Regent Street, Glasgow, G2 2ST**
☎ 0141 229 1326 Ⓕ 0141 248 1591
Est. 1899
Open Mon–Fri 9am–5pm
Sales Pawnbroker sales
Frequency 2 per week
Catalogues Yes

⊞ Cooper Hay Rare Books (ABA)
Contact Mr C Hay
✉ **182 Bath Street, Glasgow, G2 4HG** 🅿
☎ 0141 333 1992 Ⓕ 0141 333 1992
Ⓔ chayrbooks@aol.com
Ⓦ www.abebooks.com/home/haybooks
Est. 1984 *Stock size* Medium
Stock Books, prints, specializing in Scottish art and juvenile books
Open Mon–Fri 10am–5.30pm Sat 10am–1pm
Fairs Chelsea, Bath, Edinburgh
Services Valuations, book search

⊞ Finnie Antiques
Contact Bruce Finnie
✉ **103 Niddrie Road, Glasgow, G42 8PR** 🅿
☎ 0141 423 8515 Ⓕ 0141 423 8515
Ⓜ 07973 315460
Ⓔ finnie.antiques@net.ntl.com
Ⓦ www.finnieantiques.co.uk
Est. 1971 *Stock size* Large
Stock General antiques, furniture, Arts and Crafts, lighting
Open Mon–Fri 10.30am–4.30pm Sat Sun noon–4.30pm
Fairs Antiques for Everyone, Glasgow

⊞ Flying Dutchman Antiques
Contact Hannie Van Riel
✉ **Unit 3b, The Centre, Yorkhill Quay, Glasgow, G3 8QE** 🅿
☎ 0141 338 6834 Ⓕ 0141 338 6834
Ⓔ sales@flyingdutchman.freeserve.co.uk
Est. 1994 *Stock size* Large
Stock General antiques including continental European furniture
Open Mon–Fri 9am–5pm Sat 10am–5pm Sun noon–5pm

⊞ Gillmorehill Books
Contact Gerard McGonigle
✉ **43 Bank Street, Glasgow, G12 8NE**
☎ 0141 339 7504
Stock Rare and second-hand books
Open Mon–Sat 10am–6pm

Great Western Auctions
Contact Mr J H Duncan
✉ **29–37 Otago Street, Glasgow, G12 8JJ** 🅿
☎ 0141 339 3290
Ⓔ info@greatwesternauctions.com
Ⓦ www.greatwesternauctions.com
Est. 1988
Open Mon–Fri 9am–5pm
Sales General antiques
Frequency fortnightly
Catalogues Yes

⊞ A D Hamilton & Co
Contact Jeffrey Fineman
✉ **7 St Vincent Place, Glasgow, G1 2DW** 🅿
☎ 0141 221 5423
Ⓔ jefffineman@hotmail.com
Ⓦ www.antiquesglasgow.co.uk
Est. 1897 *Stock size* Medium
Stock Antique jewellery, silver, objets d'art coins, medals
Open Mon–Sat 10am–5pm
Services Valuations, repairs

Kerr & McAllister (SAA)
Contact Mr Thomas McAllister
✉ **140 Niddrie Road, Glasgow, G20 7XL** 🅿
☎ 0141 423 4271 Ⓕ 0141 423 7265
Est. 1969
Open Mon–Fri 9am–5pm
Sales Household goods
Frequency Every Thurs evening
Catalogues Yes

⊞ Kittoch Antiques
Contact Una Lambie or Laura McAlonan
✉ **336 Crow Road, Broomhill, Glasgow, GL11 7HT** 🅿
☎ 0141 339 7318
Est. 1995 *Stock size* Medium
Stock Small furniture, collectables, textiles, silver plate
Open Tues–Sat noon–5pm
Fairs Antiques for Everyone, Glasgow

⊞ Lovejoy Antiques
Contact Julie Gallagher
✉ **Unit 3b, Yorkhill Quay, Glasgow, G3 8QE** 🅿
☎ 0141 357 3559 Ⓕ 0141 357 3559
Ⓜ 07710 461484
Ⓔ julielovejoy@yahoo.co.uk
Est. 1995 *Stock size* Medium
Stock General antiques
Open Mon–Fri 9am–5pm Sat 10am–5pm Sun noon–5pm
Services Polishing, shipping

Robert McTear & Co (IAA)
Contact Miss Janet Stewart
✉ **Sky Park, 8 Elliot Place, Glasgow, G3 8EP** 🅿
☎ 0141 221 4456 Ⓕ 0141 204 5035
Ⓔ enquiries@mctears.co.uk
Ⓦ www.mctears.co.uk
Est. 1842
Open Mon–Fri 9am–5pm
Sales General antiques
Frequency Weekly
Catalogues Yes

⊞ Stuart Mylers
Contact Stuart Myler
✉ **93 West Regent Street, Glasgow, G2 2BA** 🅿
☎ 01236 843736
Ⓔ stuart@mylerantiques.demon.co.uk
Est. 1987 *Stock size* Medium
Stock General antiques
Open Mon–Sat 10am–5pm

⊞ Pastimes Vintage Toys
Contact Anne or Gordon Brown
✉ **126 Maryhill Road, St George's Cross, Glasgow, G27 7QS** 🅿
☎ 0141 331 1008 Ⓕ 0141 331 1496
Ⓔ anne@dinkydoll.com
Ⓦ www.dinkydoll.com
Est. 1976 *Stock size* Medium
Stock Vintage toys, Dinky, Hornby, dolls' houses, medals, militaria, small collectables
Open Mon–Sat 9.30am–5.30pm
Services Mail order, valuations

Patersons Auctioneers & Valuers
Contact Robert Paterson
8 Orchard Street, Paisley, Glasgow, PA1 1UZ
0141 889 2435 0141 887 5535
Est. 1848
Open Mon–Fri 9am–5pm
Sales General antiques
Frequency Fortnightly
Catalogues Yes

Relics
Contact Steven Currie
Dowanside Lane, Glasgow, G12 9BZ
0141 341 0007
Est. 1989 *Stock size* Medium
Stock General antiques, collectables including 1960s items
Open Mon–Sat 10.30am–6pm Sun 12.30–6pm
Services Valuations

The Renaissance Furniture Store
Contact Bruce Finnie
103 Niddrie Road, Glasgow, G42 8PR
0141 423 0022 0141 423 8515
07973 315460
finnie.antiques@net.nh.com
Est. 1992 *Stock size* Medium
Stock Furniture, silver, Arts and Crafts, fireplaces
Open Mon–Fri 10.30am–5pm Sat Sun noon–5pm
Services Valuations

Restore-It
Contact Jean Eddy Devion
22 Otago Lane, Glasgow, G12 8PB
0141 339 7776 0141 647 3182
07770 825555
www.restore-it.co.uk or www.maisonrouge.co.uk
Est. 1992 *Stock size* Medium
Stock General antiques, architectural salvage
Open Every day 10am–5pm
Services Restoration

Rusty Grates
Contact Tom Pearson
103 Niddrie Road, Queens Park, Glasgow, G42 8PR
0141 423 0022
Est. 1994 *Stock size* Medium
Stock Georgian, Victorian and Art Nouveau fireplaces
Open Mon–Fri 10am–5pm Sat Sun noon–5pm

R Rutherford
Contact Mrs R Rutherford
The Victorian Village, 93 West Regent Street, Glasgow, G2 2BA
0141 332 9808 0141 332 9808
Est. 1979 *Stock size* Medium
Stock General antiques, Scottish agates
Open Mon–Sat 10am–5pm
Services Valuations

Saratoga Trunk Yesteryear Costume & Textiles
Contact Cathie McLay
Fourth Floor, 61 Hyde Park Street, Glasgow, G3 8BW
0141 221 4433 0141 221 4433
07984 491066
Est. 1976 *Stock size* Large
Stock Vintage clothing, Victorian–1990s, linens, lace, costume jewellery, etc
Open Mon–Fri 10.30am–5pm
Fairs Manchester, Birmingham, Glasgow
Services Valuations, hire to film, television, theatre productions

Jeremy Sniders Antiques
Contact Jeremy Sniders
158 Bath Street, Glasgow, G2 4TB
0141 332 0043 0141 332 5505
jeremysniders@aol.com
www.jeremysnidersantiques.com
Est. 1981 *Stock size* Medium
Stock General antiques, Scandinavian antiques, silverware, jewellery, Georg Jensen specialist
Open Mon–Sat 9am–5pm
Services Valuations

Strachan Antiques
Contact Alex Strachan
40 Darnley Street, Pollokshields, Glasgow, G41 2SE
0141 429 4411 07950 262346
alex@strachan-antiques.freeserve.co.uk
www.strachan-antiques.freeserve.co.uk
Est. 1990 *Stock size* Large
Stock Arts and Crafts, Art Nouveau furniture, small decorative items
Open 10am–5pm Sun noon–5pm
Fairs SECC Glasgow

The Studio
Contact Liz McKelvie
DeCourcy's Arcade, 5–21 Cresswell Lane, Glasgow, G12 8AA
0141 334 8211 07909 742862
www.decourcys.co.uk
Est. 1998 *Stock size* Small
Stock Books, small furniture, ceramics, pictures, glass, textiles, Glasgow-style Arts and Crafts and Art Nouveau, Talwin Morris book bindings
Open Tues–Sat 10am–5.30pm Sun noon–5pm
Services Shipping, booksearch

The Treasure Bunker Militaria Shop
Contact Mr K J Andrew
21 King Street, Glasgow, G1 5Q2
0141 552 8164 0141 552 4651
info@treasurebunker.com
www.treasurebunker.com
Est. 1985 *Stock size* Large
Stock Military antiques, Battle of Waterloo–WWII
Open Tues–Sat 11am–5pm
Services Worldwide mail order catalogue

Victoria Antiques Ltd
Contact Geoff Lovatt
338–350 Pollockshaws Road, Glasgow, G41 1QS
0141 423 7216 0141 423 6497
antiquesgl@aol.com
Est. 1964 *Stock size* Large
Stock General antiques
Open Mon–Fri 9.30am–5pm Sat 10.30am–5pm
Services Valuations

Voltaire & Rousseau
Contact Mr J McGonagle
18 Otago Lane, Glasgow, G12 8PD
0141 339 1811
Est. 1972 *Stock size* Large
Stock Rare and second-hand books, specializing in Scotland and foreign languages
Open Mon–Sat 10am–6pm
Services Valuations

Tim Wright Antiques (LAPADA)
Contact Judy or Tim Wright

147 Bath Street, Glasgow, G2 4SQ P
☎ 0141 221 0364 F 0141 221 0364
E tim@timwright-antiques.com
W www.timwright-antiques.com
Est. 1972 *Stock size* Large
Stock Quality antiques, furniture, porcelain, glass, bronze, silver
Open Mon–Fri 10am–5pm Sat 10.30am–2.30pm
Services Valuations

Yesteryear
Contact Ian Taylor
Newlands, Glasgow
☎ 0141 423 0099 M 07887 592634
E jantaylo55@hotmail.com
Est. 1973 *Stock size* Medium
Stock General antiques
Open By appointment
Services Valuations

ABERDEENSHIRE

ABERDEEN

The Antiquary
Contact Mr Andy Murphy
13 Marischal Street, Aberdeen, Aberdeenshire, AB11 5AD P
☎ 01224 464959 M 07759 617530
Est. 2000 *Stock size* Large
Stock General antiques 1795–1975
Open Mon–Sat 10am–4pm closed Wed
Services Valuations

Bon-Accord Books (PBFA)
Contact Andrew Milne
69–75 Spital, Aberdeen, Aberdeenshire, AB24 3HX P
☎ 01224 643209
E bonaccordbooks@btinternet.com
W www.bon-accordbooks.co.uk
Est. 1998 *Stock size* Medium
Stock General and antiquarian books, Scottish, children's and modern topics, first editions
Open Mon–Fri 10.30am–5.30pm Sat 11am–4.30pm closed Wed
Fairs Aberdeen, Glasgow, York, London
Services Postcards, prints, pictures

Candle Close Gallery
Contact Mrs B Brown
123 Gallowgate, Aberdeen, Aberdeenshire, AB25 1BU P
☎ 01224 624940 F 01224 620548
Est. 1994 *Stock size* Medium
Stock Antique pine, collectors' items, curios
Open Mon–Fri 10am–5.30pm Thurs 10am–7pm Sat 9am–5pm Sun noon–4pm
Fairs Newark

Kings Quair
Contact M or R Murdoch
197 King Street, Aberdeen, Aberdeenshire, AB24 5AH
☎ 01224 637495
Est. 1994 *Stock size* Medium
Stock Rare and second-hand books
Open Mon–Sat 10am–5pm
Fairs Treetops – Aberdeen

John Milne Auctioneers (SAA)
Contact Robert Milne
9 North Silver Street, Aberdeen, Aberdeenshire, AB10 1RJ P
☎ 01224 639336 F 01224 645857
E info@john-milne.demon.co.uk
Est. 1867
Open Mon–Thur 8.30am–5pm Fri 8.30am–4pm
Sales Weekly general sales
Frequency Weekly
Catalogues Yes

The Odd Lot
Contact Mr G Mudie
24 Adelphi, Union Street, Aberdeen, Aberdeenshire, AB11 5BL P
☎ 01224 592551 F 01224 574404
M 07771 926736
E George@theoddlot.com
W www.theoddlot.com
Est. 1997 *Stock size* Medium
Stock General antiques, furniture, jewellery, Scottish antiques, books
Open Tues–Sat 11am–5pm
Fairs The Academy – Aberdeen
Services House clearance

The Old Aberdeen Bookshop
Contact Mr C Scott-Paul
140 Spital, Aberdeen, Aberdeenshire, AB24 3JU
☎ 01224 658355
Est. 1998 *Stock size* Small
Stock Rare and second-hand books
Open Mon–Sat 11am–5.30pm
Services Valuations

Rendezvous Gallery Ltd
Contact Mr C D Mead or Mr Andrew Allan
100 Forest Avenue, Aberdeen, Aberdeenshire, AB15 4TL P
☎ 01224 323247 F 01224 323247
E info@rendezvousgallery.freeserve.uk
W www.rendezvouz-gallery.co.uk
Est. 1975 *Stock size* Medium
Stock Art Nouveau, Art Deco, Scottish paintings
Open Mon–Sat 10am–6pm

Thistle Antiques (LAPADA)
Contact Mr P Bursill
28 Esslemont Avenue, Aberdeen, Aberdeenshire, AB25 1SN P
☎ 01224 634692 M 07759 429685
Est. 1969 *Stock size* Medium
Stock General antiques, Georgian–Victorian furniture, lighting
Open Mon–Fri 10am–5pm Sat 10am–1pm closed Wed

J R Webb Antiques
Contact J R Webb
23 Bon-Accord Terrace, Aberdeen, Aberdeenshire, AB11 6DP P
☎ 01224 586709 F 01224 586709
M 07801 192119
Est. 1908 *Stock size* Large
Stock General antiques, jewellery, arms and armour, especially Scottish artefacts and art
Open Mon–Fri 10am–6pm Sat 10am–1pm closed Wed
Services Valuations and probate service, restorations

Winram's Bookshop
Contact Mrs Margaret Davidson
32–36 Rosemount Place, Aberdeen, Aberdeenshire, AB25 2XB P
☎ 01224 630673 F 01224 630673
Est. 1975 *Stock size* Medium
Stock Rare and second-hand books, especially Scottish topics, postcards, local photographs
Open Mon–Sat 10am–5.30pm Wed 10am–1pm
Fairs Aberdeen
Services Valuations

Colin Wood Antiques Ltd
Contact Mr C Wood

✉ **25 Rose Street, Aberdeen, Aberdeenshire, AB10 1TX** 🅿
☎ 01224 643019/644786
Ⓕ 01224 644786
Est. 1969 ***Stock size*** Medium
Stock General and antique Scottish maps, prints
Open Mon–Sat 10am–5pm

ALFORD

David C Rogers Antiques & Interiors
Contact David Rogers
✉ **29 Main Street, Alford, Aberdeenshire, AB33 8PX** 🅿
☎ 01975 562799 Ⓕ 01464 831500
Ⓜ 07836 558797
Est. 1987 ***Stock size*** Medium
Stock General antiques, specializing in fishing items
Open Fri Sat 10am–4pm or by appointment
Fairs Newark
Services Valuations, restorations, repairs

BALLATER

Deeside Books
Contact Mr B Wayte
✉ **The Albert Memorial Hall, Station Square, Ballater, Aberdeenshire, AB35 5QB** 🅿
☎ 013397 54080 Ⓕ 013397 54080
Ⓔ deesidebk@aol.com
Est. 1998 ***Stock size*** Medium
Stock Out-of-print and antiquarian books, specializing in Scottish, military, topography and fishing topics
Open Tues–Sat 10am–5pm Sun noon–5pm
Services Valuations, book search

Rowan Antiques & Collectables
Contact Nikki Henderson
✉ **Tulchan House, 5–7 Victoria Road, Ballater, Aberdeenshire, AB35 5QQ** 🅿
☎ 013397 56035 Ⓕ 013397 56035
Ⓔ nikki.rowan@lineone.net
Est. 1986 ***Stock size*** Medium
Stock Victorian–1930s furniture, fine and country, jewellery, porcelain, prints
Open Mon–Sat 10am–5.30pm
Fairs Aberdeen Tree Tops
Services Valuations, shipping

CLOLA

Clola Antiques Centre
Contact David Blackburn
✉ **Shannas School, Clola, Aberdeenshire, Peterhead, AB42 5AB** 🅿
☎ 01771 624584 Ⓜ 07836 537188
Est. 1989 ***Stock size*** Large
No. of dealers 6
Stock Furniture, jewellery, china, glass
Open Mon–Sat 10am–5pm Sun 11am–5pm
Services Restorations, upholstery

DUNECHT

Magic Lantern
Contact Mrs J White
✉ **Nether Corskie, Dunecht, Aberdeenshire, AB32 7EL** 🅿
☎ 01330 860678
Est. 1978 ***Stock size*** Medium
Stock General antiques
Services Restorations to china

FYVIE

Grampian Books (PBFA)
Contact David Fleming
✉ **South Monkshill, Fyvie, Turriff, Aberdeenshire, AB53 8RQ** 🅿
☎ 01651 891524 Ⓕ 01651 891124
Ⓜ 07831 467495
Ⓔ dfleming@grampianbooks.sol.co.uk
Est. 1990 ***Stock size*** Large
Stock Out-of-print, antiquarian and second-hand books, specializing in Scottish topics
Open By appointment only
Fairs London, York, Glasgow, Edinburgh, Aberdeen
Services Valuations, purchasing libraries and book collections throughout the UK

HUNTLY

Huntly Antiques
Contact Jean Barker
✉ **43 Duke Street, Huntly, Aberdeenshire, AB54 8DT** 🅿
☎ 01466 793307
Est. 1984 ***Stock size*** Medium
Stock General antiques
Open Mon–Sat 10am–4pm or by appointment

G G & H R Lumsden
Contact G G Lumsden
✉ **Affleck, Huntly, Aberdeenshire, AB54 6XW** 🅿
☎ 01466 792686
Est. 1948
Open By appointment only
Sales General antiques
Frequency Monthly
Catalogues No

INVERURIE

Thainstone Specialist Auctions
Contact Mark Barrack or L Howie
✉ **Thainstone Centre, Inverurie, Aberdeen, Aberdeenshire, AB51 5XZ** 🅿
☎ 01467 623770 Ⓕ 01467 623771
Ⓔ tsa@goanm.co.uk
Ⓦ www.goanm.co.uk
Est. 1942
Open Mon–Fri 9am–5pm
Sales General antiques Tues 6pm
Frequency Weekly
Catalogues Yes

KINCARDINE O'NEIL

Dunmore Antiques
Contact Pauline Baird
✉ **27 North Deeside Road, Kincardine O'Neil, Aboyne, Aberdeenshire, AB34 5AA** 🅿
☎ 013398 84449 Ⓕ 013398 82640
Ⓜ 07711 886945
Ⓔ dunmore_antiques@talk21.com
Ⓦ www.dunmoreantiques.com
Est. 1988 ***Stock size*** Large
Stock General antiques, china, glass, amber jewellery
Open Thurs–Sat 10am–5pm
Fairs Newark, Treetops, Ardoe House Hotel, Aberdeen
Services Valuations

LAURENCEKIRK

James S T Liddle
Contact Mr B Liddle
✉ **Malvern, 65 Johnstone Street, Laurencekirk, Aberdeenshire, AB30 1AN** 🅿
☎ 01561 377420 Ⓕ 01561 377420
Est. 1989
Open Mon–Sat 8am–5pm
Sales General furniture
Frequency Monthly
Catalogues No

LONGHAVEN

Grannie Used To Have One
Contact Jacqui Harvey

✉ **Sanderling, Longhaven, Nr Peterhead, Aberdeenshire, AB42 0NX** 🅿
☎ 01779 813223 ⓕ 01779 813223
Ⓜ 07850 912364
ⓔ jacqui@grannieusedto.co.uk
ⓦ www.grannieusedto.co.uk
Est. 1991 ***Stock size*** Large
Stock Pottery, including Scottish pottery, porcelain, furniture, glass, metalware
Open Thurs Fri 1–5pm
Sat Sun 11am–5pm or by appointment
Fairs Treetops – Aberdeen
Services Valuations

TARLAND

The Tower Workshops
Contact George Pirie
✉ **Aberdeen Road, Tarland, Aboyne, Aberdeenshire, AB34 4TB** 🅿
☎ 013398 811544
Est. 1989 ***Stock size*** Large
Stock Edwardian mahogany and Georgian furniture, soft furnishings, small items, decorative objects
Open Mon–Fri 9am–5pm
Sat 11am–5pm
Services Valuations, restorations, complete house commissions

ANGUS

DUNDEE

Angus Antiques
Contact John Czerek or Stanley Paget
✉ **4 St Andrew Street, Dundee, Angus, DD1 2EX** 🅿
☎ 01382 322128
Est. 1972 ***Stock size*** Medium
Stock General antiques, militaria, jewellery
Open Mon–Fri 10am–4pm
Services Valuations

The Dundee Auction Rooms (Robert Curr & Dewar)
Contact D Dewar
✉ **Ward Road, Dundee, Angus, DD1 1LX** 🅿
☎ 01382 224185 ⓕ 01382 533350
Ⓜ 07889 734245
ⓔ derek@curranddewar-auction.totalserve.co.uk
Est. 1862
Open Mon–Fri 8.30am–5pm
Sat 8.30am–noon
Sales General furniture, antiques, jewellery, police lost property
Frequency Weekly
Catalogues No

Dundee Philatelic Auctions (SPTA, PTS, PTA)
Contact Frank Tonelli
✉ **15 King Street, Dundee, Angus, DD1 2JD** 🅿
☎ 01382 224946 ⓕ 01382 224946
Est. 1975
Open Mon–Fri 10am–1pm 2–5pm
Sat by appointment closed Wed
Sales Stamps, cigarette cards, postcards, banknotes. Public auctions held at Renfield Centre, 260 Bath St, Glasgow
Frequency 4 per annum
Catalogues Yes

B L Fenton & Son (SAA)
Contact Ben Fenton
✉ **84 Victoria Road, Dundee, Angus, DD1 2NY** 🅿
☎ 01382 226227
Est. 1919
Open Mon–Fri 9am–4.45pm
Sales Antique furniture, general auctioneers
Frequency Every Thurs
Catalogues No

Alastair Jamieson Antiques
Contact Alastair Jamieson
✉ **212 Perth Road, Dundee, Angus, DD1 4JY** 🅿
☎ 01382 322017
Est. 1997 ***Stock size*** Medium
Stock Wide range of antiques late Victorian–1970s
Open Mon–Sat 10am–5.30pm

Neil Livingstone (LAPADA)
Contact Neil Livingstone
✉ **3 Old Hawkhill, Dundee, Angus, DD1 5EU** 🅿
☎ 01382 907788 ⓕ 01382 566332
Ⓜ 07775 877715
ⓔ npl@hemscott.net
Est. 1971 ***Stock size*** Small
Stock Continental works of art and antiques
Open By appointment only

Taymouth Architectural Antiques
Contact Graham Ellis
✉ **49–51 Magdalen Yard Road, Dundee, Angus, DD1 4NF** 🅿
☎ 01382 666833 ⓕ 01382 666833
Est. 1991 ***Stock size*** Medium
Stock Antique fireplaces, Victorian fixtures and fittings, garden ornaments, antique bathrooms, doors, leaded glass
Open Tues–Sat 9.30am–5.30pm
Fairs Newark, Ardingly
Services Restorations of pine furniture, fireplaces etc

FORFAR

Forfar Auction Co Ltd
Contact Mr Rizza
✉ **Carseview Road, Forfar, Angus, DD8 3BT** 🅿
☎ 01307 462197 ⓕ 01307 464960
Est. 1990
Open Mon–Thurs 9.30am–5pm
Fri 9.30am to end of sale
Sales All household effects
Frequency Weekly
Catalogues Yes

Gow Antiques and Restoration (BAFRA)
Contact Jeremy Gow
✉ **Pitscandly Farm, Forfar, Angus, DD8 3NZ** 🅿
☎ 01307 465347 ⓕ 01307 468973
Ⓜ 07711 416786
ⓔ jeremy@gowantiques.co.uk
ⓦ www.gowantiques.co.uk
Est. 1991 ***Stock size*** Medium
Stock Furniture
Open Mon–Fri 9am–5pm or by appointment
Fairs SECC Glasgow
Services Restorations, organizes 3-day antique courses

FRIOCKHEIM BY ARBROATH

M J & D Barclay
Contact M J & D Barclay
✉ **29 Gardyne Street, Friockheim by Arbroath, Angus, DD11 4SQ** 🅿
☎ 01241 828265
Est. 1968 ***Stock size*** Medium
Stock General antiques, clocks, jewellery, porcelain
Open Mon–Sat 2pm–5pm closed Thurs
Fairs Treetops – Aberdeen

LETHAM

Idvies Antiques
Contact Mr T Slingsby

✉ **Idvies House, Letham, Forfar, Angus, DD8 2QJ** Ⓟ
☎ 01307 818402 Ⓕ 01307 818933
Ⓦ www.scotlandstreasures.co.uk
Est. 1989 *Stock size* Medium
Stock Furniture
Open By appointment
Services Valuations, restorations, cabinet-making

MONTROSE

Angus Architectural Antiques
Contact Les Morden
✉ **Balmain House, Lower Balmain Street, Montrose, Angus, DD10 8BQ** Ⓟ
☎ 01674 674291 Ⓕ 01241 830271
Ⓜ 07831 386998
Ⓔ courthill@lunan46.freeserve
Est. 1974 *Stock size* Medium
Stock Pine furniture, architectural and sanitary antiques, fireplaces
Open Mon–Sat 9am–5pm
Services Pine stripping

Harper–James (LAPADA)
Contact D James
✉ **25–27 Baltic Street, Montrose, Angus, DD10 8EX** Ⓟ
☎ 01674 671307 Ⓕ 01674 671307
Ⓜ 07970 173051
Ⓔ antiques@telco4u.net
Ⓦ www.harperjamesantiques.com
Est. 1989 *Stock size* Large
Stock 18th–19thC quality furniture, porcelain, silver
Open Mon–Fri 10am–5pm Sat 10am–4pm or by appointment
Fairs NEC, Aberdeen
Services Restorations, French polishing, modern polishing, upholstery

Sticks & Stones
Contact Mrs H McEwan
✉ **36–40 Baltic Street, Montrose, Angus, DD10 8EX** Ⓟ
☎ 01674 676764 Ⓜ 077647 69191
Est. 1995 *Stock size* Medium
Stock Victorian–Edwardian oak country furniture, Art Deco, Art Nouveau, stoves, fireplaces, baths
Open Mon–Sat 10am–5pm

ARGYLL & BUTE

COVE

Cove Curios
Contact Mrs Katherine Young
✉ **Shore Road, Clifton Place, Cove, Argyll & Bute, G84 8LR** Ⓟ
☎ 01436 842222 Ⓕ 01436 850261
Est. 1971 *Stock size* Medium
Stock General antiques including second-hand jewellery
Open Seasonal
Services Valuations, repairs

HELENSBURGH

McLaren Books (ABA, PBFA)
Contact George Newlands
✉ **91 West Clyde Street, Helensburgh, Argyll & Bute, G84 8BB** Ⓟ
☎ 01436 676453 Ⓕ 01436 673747
Ⓔ mclarenbooks@breathe.co.uk
Ⓦ www.mclarenbooks.co.uk
Est. 1976 *Stock size* Medium
Stock Rare and second-hand books, especially maritime topics
Open Mon–Sat 9.30am–5pm closed 1–2pm closed Wed
Services Valuations, books purchased, book search for maritime titles

Willow Antiques
Contact D J or Mrs C Weatherstone
✉ **93 West Clyde Street, Helensburgh, Argyll & Bute, G84 8BB** Ⓟ
☎ 01436 671174
Est. 1974 *Stock size* Medium
Stock General antiques
Open Tues Thurs Fri Sat 10.30am–5.30pm

OBAN

Oban Antiques
Contact Mrs P M Baker
✉ **35 Stevenson Street, Oban, Argyll & Bute, PA34 5NA** Ⓟ
☎ 01631 566203
Ⓔ enquiries@obantiques.com
Ⓦ www.obantiques.com
Est. 1969 *Stock size* Medium
Stock General antiques, second-hand books, prints
Open Tues–Sat 10am–4.30pm some seasonal variation

DUMFRIES & GALLOWAY

CANONBIE

John Mann Fine Antique Clocks
Contact John Mann
✉ **The Clock Showrooms, Canonbie, Dumfries and Galloway, DG14 0SY** Ⓟ
☎ 01387 371337 Ⓕ 01387 371337
Ⓜ 07850 606147
Ⓔ jmannclock@aol.com
Ⓦ www.johnmannantiqueclocks.co.uk
Est. 1987 *Stock size* Large
Stock Longcase, wall, bracket, mantel clocks, barometers, small antiques, collectables
Open Mon–Sun noon–5pm
Services Restoration

CASTLE DOUGLAS

Hazel's
Contact Mrs H Hall
✉ **St Andrew Street, Castle Douglas, Dumfries & Galloway, DG7 1EL** Ⓟ
☎ 01556 504573 Ⓕ 01556 504573
Ⓦ www.castledouglas.net
Est. 1989 *Stock size* Large
Stock General antiques
Open Mon–Sat 9.30am–5pm
Services Valuations

DUMFRIES

Cargenbank Antiques & Tearooms
Contact Laurence Hird
✉ **Cargen Bank, Dumfries, Dumfries & Galloway, DG2 8PZ** Ⓟ
☎ 01387 730303
Est. 1999 *Stock size* Medium
Stock 19thC furniture
Open Mon–Sun winter Thurs–Sun 1–5pm closed Wed

Quarrelwood Art & Antiques
Contact Miranda van Nieuwenhuizen (Fellow of Gemmological Association)
✉ **Quarrelwood, Kirkmahoe, (Kirton), Dumfries, Dumfries & Galloway, DG1 1TE** Ⓟ
☎ 01387 740654 Ⓕ 01387 740000

Ⓜ 07713 643434
Ⓔ miranda@quarrelwoodantiques.com
Ⓦ www.quarrelwoodantiques.com
Est. 1999 ***Stock size*** Medium
Stock Georgian–Victorian furniture, period jewellery, ceramics, glass, objets d'art
Open Wed–Sat 10am–5pm Sun 1–5pm
Services Valuations, restorations, shipping, advisory service, wedding lists

Thomson, Roddick & Medcalf
Contact Sybelle Medcalf
✉ **60 Whitesands, Dumfries, Dumfries & Galloway, DG1 2RS** Ⓟ
☎ 01387 279879 Ⓕ 01387 266236
Ⓔ office.trm@virgin.net
Est. 1899
Open Mon–Fri 9am–5pm
Sales Antiques, fine art, general furnishings
Frequency Weekly
Catalogues Yes

LOCHFOOT

Classic Pen Engineering (Writing Equipment Society)
Contact Mr D Purser
✉ **Auchenfranco Farm, Lochfoot, Dumfries, Dumfries & Galloway, DG2 8NZ** Ⓟ
☎ 01387 730208 Ⓕ 01387 730208
Ⓜ 0770 3690843
Ⓔ cpe@auchenfranco.freeserve.co.uk
Ⓦ www.auchenfranco.freeserve.co.uk
Est. 1994
Stock Fountain pens, dip pens, pencils
Open By appointment
Fairs Glasgow Antiques for Everyone, Edinburgh
Services Valuations, restorations

LOCKERBIE

Cobwebs of Lockerbie Ltd
Contact Irene Beck
✉ **30 Townhead Street, Lockerbie, Dumfries & Galloway, DG11 2AE** Ⓟ
☎ 01576 202554 Ⓕ 01576 203737
Ⓦ www.cobwebs-antiques.co.uk
Est. 1993 ***Stock size*** Large
Stock General antiques and collectables, porcelain, china, mostly Victorian–Edwardian
Open Mon–Sat 9am–5pm

MOFFAT

Ram Antiques
Contact Jean Gale
✉ **19 High Street, Moffat, Dumfries & Galloway, DG10 9SG** Ⓟ
☎ 01683 300451 Ⓜ 07887 641631
Ⓔ jeangale@ic24.net
Est. 1969 ***Stock size*** Small
Stock General antiques
Open By appointment
Services Valuations, house clearance

STRANRAER

Lochyran Furniture Stores
Contact A Patterson
✉ **1 Cairnryan Road, Stranraer, Dumfries & Galloway, DG9 8QJ** Ⓟ
☎ 01776 704442
Ⓦ www.lochyran.co.uk
Est. 1994 ***Stock size*** Large
No. of dealers 2
Stock Antiques, second-hand furniture
Open Mon Tues Thurs Sat 10am–4pm
Services Valuations, restorations

THORNHILL

The Hen Hoose
Contact Jo McGregor
✉ **Tynron, Thornhill, Dumfries & Galloway, DG3 4LA** Ⓟ
☎ 01848 200418
Ⓔ info@henhoose.co.uk
Ⓦ www.henhoose.co.uk
Est. 1994 ***Stock size*** Large
Stock Collectable items from 50p to £5,000, furniture, books, bric-a-brac
Open Tues–Sun 11am–5pm
Services Valuations, restorations, tea room

WHITHORN

Priory Antiques
Contact Mary Arnott
✉ **29 George Street, Whithorn, Dumfries & Galloway, DG8 8NS** Ⓟ
☎ 01988 500517 Ⓜ 07887 388714
Est. 1988 ***Stock size*** Medium
Stock General antiques
Open Usually Mon–Sun 10.30am–5pm phone call advisable
Services Valuations

WIGTOWN

The Bookcellar
Contact Robin or Marion Richmond
✉ **Beechwood, Acre Place, Wigtown, Dumfries & Galloway, DG8 9DU** Ⓟ
☎ 01988 402653 Ⓕ 01988 403472
Ⓔ bookcellar@aol.com
Est. 1999 ***Stock size*** Medium
Stock Collectables, antiquarian books, specializing in natural history and Scottish topics
Open Mon–Sun 11am–5pm
Services Book search and shipping worldwide

The Bookshop
Contact Shaun Bythel
✉ **17 North Main Street, Wigtown, Dumfries & Galloway, DG8 9HL** Ⓟ
☎ 01988 402499 Ⓕ 01988 402499
Ⓔ mail@the-bookshop.com
Ⓦ www.the-bookshop.com
Est. 1987 ***Stock size*** Large
Stock Antiquarian to modern books, specializing in Scottish topics and history
Open Mon–Sat 9am–5pm
Services Publishing

Ming Books
Contact Robin Richmond
✉ **Beechwood, Acre Place, Wigtown, Dumfries & Galloway, DG8 9DU** Ⓟ
☎ 01988 402653
Ⓦ www.mingbooks.com
Est. 1982 ***Stock size*** Large
Stock Antiquarian and rare books, modern first editions, crime fiction
Open Mon–Sun 10am–6pm
Services Book search

The Old Bank Bookshop (PBFA)
Contact John Carter
✉ **8 South Main Street, Wigtown, Newton Stewart, Dumfries & Galloway, DG8 9DU** Ⓟ
☎ 01988 402688
Est. 1987 ***Stock size*** Large
Stock Rare and second-hand books, specializing in archaeology and art topics
Open Mon–Sat 9am–5pm Sun 1–5pm
Services Framing

EAST AYRSHIRE

KILMARNOCK

D & D Programmes
Contact Mr D Stevenson
49 Titchfield Street, Kilmarnock, Ayrshire, KA1 1QS
☎ 01563 573316
ⓔ d-d-programmes@ukf.net
ⓦ www.d-d-programmes.ukf.net
Est. 1998 *Stock size* Medium
Stock Football memorabilia
Open Tues–Sat 10am–5pm Fri 10am–8pm
Fairs Glasgow, Alloway
Services Mail-order catalogue available

Q S Antiques and Cabinetmakers
Contact John Cunningham
Moorfield Industrial Estate, Kilmarnock, Ayrshire, KA2 0DP
☎ 01563 571071 ⓕ 01563 571055
ⓔ qsascotland@aol.com
Est. 1982 *Stock size* Large
Stock Victorian–Edwardian furniture
Open Mon–Fri 9am–5.30pm Sat 9am–5pm
Services Pine stripping, paint and varnish removal, Victorian-style solid wood kitchens

EAST LOTHIAN

GULLANE

Gullane Antiques
Contact Elizabeth Lindsey
5 Rosebery Place, Gullane, East Lothian, EH31 2AN
☎ 01620 842994
Est. 1980 *Stock size* Large
Stock General antiques, mixed porcelain, glass
Open Mon Tues Fri Sat 10.30am–1pm 2.30–5pm

HADDINGTON

Yester-Days
Contact Betty Logan
79 High Street, Haddington, East Lothian, EH41 3ET
☎ 01620 824543
Est. 1992 *Stock size* Small
Stock Antiques, collectables
Open Tues Wed Fri Sat 11am–4.30pm

NORTH BERWICK

Lindsey Antiques
Contact Stephen Lindsey
49a Kirk Ports, North Berwick, East Lothian, EH39 4HL
☎ 01620 894114
Est. 1995 *Stock size* Medium
Stock Furniture, ceramics, glass, pictures, etc
Open Mon–Sat 10.30am–5pm closed Thurs

The Penny Farthing
Contact Stuart Tait
23 Quality Street, North Berwick, East Lothian, EH39 4HR
☎ 01620 894400 ⓕ 01620 894400
Est. 1989 *Stock size* Medium
Stock Rare, antiquarian and second-hand books, specializing in travel and children's books
Open Mon–Sat 9am–5.30pm Sun 2–5.30pm
Fairs Meadowbank, Edinburgh

Soltire Antiques Ltd
Contact Andrew Young
Fenton Barns, Drem, North Berwick, East Lothian, EH39 5BW
☎ 01620 850677 ⓜ 07951 371861
Est. 2001 *Stock size* Large
Stock Antiques, collectables, pine, Victorian–Edwardian furniture, fireplaces, clocks, pews
Open Mon–Sun 10.30am–5pm

FIFE

ABERDOUR

Antiques & Gifts
Contact Mrs Jennifer Graham
26 High Street, Aberdour, Fife, KY3 0SW
☎ 01383 860523
Est. 1969 *Stock size* Small
Stock General antiques
Open Tues 2–5pm Wed 10am–12.30pm Thurs–Sat 10am–5pm closed 12.30–2pm

CERES

Ceres Antiques
Contact Evelyn Norrie
1 The Butts, Ceres, Cupar, Fife, KY15 5NF
☎ 01334 828384
Est. 1969 *Stock size* Medium
Stock General antiques, specializing in linen and lace
Open Mon–Sun 10am–6pm or by appointment
Fairs Newark, Birmingham and Harrogate

CUPAR

Oliver & Son
Contact Dorothy Wang
11 East Road, Cupar, Fife, KY15 4HQ
☎ 01334 657002 ⓕ 01334 653807
ⓜ 07850 013191
Est. 1998
Open Mon–Fri 9am–5pm Sat Sun 10am–4pm
Sales Quarterly antiques and collectors' sales, fortnightly general antiques and household furniture sales
Frequency Fortnightly
Catalogues Yes

DUNFERMLINE

Dunfermline Auction Company Ltd
Contact Mr G Mitchell
Castleblair Lane, Dunfermline, Fife, KY12 7DP
☎ 01383 727434 ⓕ 01383 729899
ⓦ www.dunfermlineauction.co.uk
Open Mon–Fri 9am–5.15pm Sat 9am–12.30pm
Sales Antiques, collectables
Frequency 3 per month
Catalogues Yes

DYSART

Second Notions Antiques
Contact Jim Sinclair
2 Normand Road, Dysart, Kirkcaldy, Fife, KY1 2XJ
☎ 01592 650505 ⓕ 01592 573341
ⓜ 07977 119787
ⓔ james@sinclair1155.freeserve.co.uk
ⓦ www.secondnotionsantiques.co.uk
Est. 1994 *Stock size* Medium
Stock General antiques
Open Mon–Fri noon–5pm Sat 10am–5pm
Fairs Swinderby, Newark
Services Exporting of containers

FALKLAND

Falkland Antiques
Contact Mrs Aileen Davies

✉ **High Street,**
Falkland, Fife, KY15 7BZ Ⓟ
☎ 01337 857966 Ⓕ 01337 857966
Ⓔ falklandantiques@hotmail.com
Est. 1989 *Stock size* Medium
Stock General antiques, Scottish and English ceramics, antique and second-hand jewellery, small pieces of furniture
Open Mon–Sun 10am–5.30pm
Services Professional china and ceramics restoration

INVERKEITHING

Bargain Centre
Contact Hilda Fleming
✉ **3 Boreland Road,**
Inverkeithing, Fife,
KY11 1NK Ⓟ
☎ 01383 416727 Ⓕ 01383 418054
Ⓦ www.bargaincentre.com
Est. 1982 *Stock size* Large
Stock General antiques, bric-a-brac, office furniture
Open Mon–Sat 9am–5pm

KIRKCALDY

A K Campbell & Son
Contact Mr A K Campbell
✉ **262 High Street,**
Kirkcaldy, Fife,
KY1 1LA Ⓟ
☎ 01592 597022
Est. 1977 *Stock size* Medium
Stock General antiques, militaria, furniture, bric-a-brac, postcards, banknotes
Open Mon–Sat 10am–5pm
Services Valuations, house and estate clearance

A K Campbell & Son
Contact Mr A K Campbell
✉ **277 High Street,**
Kirkcaldy, Fife, KY1 1JH Ⓟ
☎ 01592 264305/597161
Est. 1977 *Stock size* Medium
Stock Family jewellery including antique jewellery, silver
Open Mon–Sat 10am–5pm
Services Valuations, repairs, goods purchased

The Golden Past
Contact Fiona Campbell
✉ **90 Rosslyn Street,**
Kirkcaldy, Fife,
KY1 3AD Ⓟ
☎ 01592 653185
Est. 1983 *Stock size* Small
Stock General antiques, pine furniture
Open Tues–Sun 10am–5pm
Services Pine stripping

M D's Auction Co
Contact Mark Harnden
✉ **Unit 15–17,**
Smeaton Industrial Estate,
Hayfield Road, Kirkcaldy, Fife,
KY1 2HE Ⓟ
☎ 01592 599969 Ⓕ 01592 640969
Ⓜ 07970 737401
Ⓔ navatmds@aol.com
Ⓦ www.mdsauction.co.uk
Est. 1989
Open Mon–Fri 9am–5pm
Sat 10am–1pm
Sales 500 lots, Thurs 6.30pm
Frequency Weekly
Catalogues Yes

LEVEN

Johnson's Auctions
Contact Maureen Johnson
✉ **Station Road, Leven, Fife,**
KY8 4QU
☎ 01333 423438
Est. 1910
Open Mon–Fri 10am–5pm
Sales General antiques
Frequency Fortnightly
Catalogues No

MARKINCH

Squirrel Antiques
Contact Sheila Green
✉ **13 Commercial Street,**
Markinch, Fife, KY7 6DE Ⓟ
☎ 01592 754386 Ⓕ 01592 754386
Ⓜ 07850 912801
Est. 1984 *Stock size* Medium
Stock General antiques, restored pine, Scottish pottery
Open Mon–Sat 9am–5pm closed Wed or by appointment
Fairs Ingliston
Services Valuations

NEWBURGH

Henderson-Dark Antiques Ltd
Contact Dawn Dark
✉ **237–241 High Street,**
Newburgh, Fife, KY14 6DY Ⓟ
☎ 01337 842000
Est. 1990 *Stock size* Medium
Stock Good quality 18th–19thC small items, furniture
Open Every day 10am–5.30pm
Fairs NEC
Services Valuations, restorations and shipping

Newburgh Antiques
Contact Miss D J Fraser
✉ **222 High Street, Newburgh,**
Cupar, Fife, KY14 9HH Ⓟ
☎ 01337 841026
Est. 1989 *Stock size* Small
Stock General antiques
Open Tues–Sat 10am–5pm

NEWPORT-ON-TAY

Mair Wilkes Books (PBFA)
Contact James Mair
✉ **3 St Marys Lane,**
Newport-on-Tay, Fife,
DD6 8AH Ⓟ
☎ 01382 542260 Ⓕ 01382 542260
Est. 1969 *Stock size* Large
Stock Large selection of rare, second-hand, antiquarian and out-of-print books, specializing in Scottish topics and psychology
Open Tues–Fri 10am–5pm closed 12.30–2pm Sat 10am–5.30pm
Services Valuations, book search

PITTENWEEM

High Street Antiques
Contact R Clark
✉ **27 High Street, Pittenweem,**
Fife, KY10 2LA Ⓟ
☎ 01333 312870 Ⓜ 07711 300136
Est. 1984 *Stock size* Medium
Stock General antiques, Wemyss ware
Open Mon–Sun 10.30am–5pm
Services Valuations, goods purchased

ST ANDREWS

Bouquiniste
Contact Mrs E A Anderson
✉ **31 Market Street,**
St Andrews, Fife,
KY16 9NS
☎ 01334 476724
Est. 1981 *Stock size* Medium
Stock Rare and second-hand books
Open Mon–Sat 10am–5pm

A K Campbell & Son
Contact Mr A K Campbell
✉ **84c Market Street,**
St Andrews, Fife,
KY16 9PA Ⓟ

☎ 01334 474214
Est. 1977 *Stock size* Medium
Stock Jewellery
Open Mon–Sat 10am–5pm
Services Valuations, repairs

Macgregor Auctions
Contact Mrs Graham
56 Largo Road, St Andrews, Fife, KY16 8RP
☎ 01334 472431 Ⓕ 01334 479606
Est. 1857
Open Viewing and sale days only
Sales Sale Thurs Fri 10.30am, viewing day prior 9am–7pm
Frequency Fortnightly
Catalogues Yes

Old St Andrews Gallery
Contact David Brown
9 Albany Place, St Andrews, Fife, KY16 9HH
☎ 01334 477840
Est. 1969 *Stock size* Medium
Stock General antiques, Scottish jewellery, silver, golf memorabilia
Open Mon–Sat 10am–5pm
Services Valuations, restorations

UPPER LARGO

Waverley Antiques
Contact Dudley Stclair
13 Main Street, Upper Largo, Fife, KY8 6EL
☎ 01333 360437
Est. 1968 *Stock size* Small
Stock General antiques, furniture, china, etc
Open Mon–Sun 11am–5.30pm

HIGHLAND

AULDEARN

Auldearn Antiques
Contact Roger Milton
Dalmore Manse, Cethen Road, Auldearn, Nairn, Inverness-shire, IV12 5HZ
☎ 01667 453087 Ⓜ 07803 318801
Est. 1984 *Stock size* Large
Stock General antiques
Open Mon–Sun 9.30am–5.30pm
Services Valuations, restorations and repairs

BEAULY

Iain Marr (HADA)
Contact Iain Marr
3 Mid Street, Beauly, Inverness-shire, IV4 7DP
☎ 01463 782372 Ⓕ 01463 783263
Ⓜ 07860 914191
Ⓔ info@iain-marr-antiques.com
Ⓦ www.iain-marr-antiques.com
Est. 1974 *Stock size* Medium
Stock General antiques, authorized seller on Sothebys.com
Open Mon–Sat 10.30am–5.30pm closed 1–2pm closed Thurs
Services Valuations

CROMARTY

The Emporium (HOST)
Contact Vivienne Griffiths
11–13 High Street, Cromarty, Ross-shire, IV11 8UZ
☎ 01381 600551
Ⓔ emporium@tiscali.co.uk
Est. 1990 *Stock size* Small
Stock General antiques, small items, second-hand books, collectables
Open Mon–Sun 10.30am–5pm winter closed Mon
Services Valuations, tea and coffee shop

DINGWALL

Dingwall R U A Partnership (IAA)
Contact Kenneth MacKay
15 Tulloch Street, Dingwall, Ross-shire, IV15 9TT
☎ 01349 863252 Ⓕ 01349 865062
Ⓔ dingwallmart@cqm.co.uk
Open Mon–Fri 8am–5pm
Sales General antiques
Frequency weekly
Catalogues No

DORNOCH

Castle Close Antiques
Contact George or Joyce McLean
Castle Street, Dornoch, Highland, IV25 3SN
☎ 01862 810405 Ⓕ 01862 810405
Ⓔ enquiries@castle-close-antiques.com
Ⓦ www.castle-close-antiques.com
Est. 1983 *Stock size* Medium
Stock General antiques, jewellery, china
Open Mon–Sat 10am–1pm 2–5pm closed Thurs pm

Little Treasures
Contact Mrs A Taylor
Shore Road, Dornoch, Highland, IV25 3LS
☎ 01862 811175
Ⓔ alliandtrev@aol.com
Est. 1993 *Stock size* Medium
Stock General antiques, small items, curios, costume jewellery
Open Mon–Sat 10am–5pm
Services Valuations

FORTROSE

Cathedral Antiques
Contact Mrs Patricia MacColl
45 High Street, Fortrose, Ross-shire, IV10 8SU
☎ 01381 620161
Ⓔ cathant@hotmail.com
Est. 1996 *Stock size* Medium
Stock General antiques, 1780–1920 furniture, ceramics, silver, glass, decorative objects
Open Mar–Oct Thurs–Sat winter Fri–Sat 10am–5pm or by appointment
Fairs Highlands, Inverness, Hopetoun House, Edinburgh
Services Valuations

INVERNESS

County Furniture Antiques
Contact Mr F Rizza
8a Harbour Road, Inverness, Inverness-shire, IV1 1SY
☎ 01463 715688 Ⓜ 07769 906966
Est. 1984 *Stock size* Medium
Stock General antiques
Trade only Mainly trade
Open Mon–Wed 10am–5pm or by appointment
Services Valuations

Frasers Auctioneers
Contact Mrs A Henderson
8a Harbour Road, Inverness, Inverness-shire, IV1 1SY
☎ 01463 232395 Ⓕ 01463 233634
Est. 1900
Open Tues 9am–5pm Wed 9am–6pm
Sales General antiques
Frequency Weekly
Catalogues Yes

Gallery Persia
Contact Gordon MacDonald
Upper Myrtlesfield, Nairnside, Inverness, IV2 5BX
☎ 01463 798500 Ⓕ 01463 798500

mac@gallerypersia.co.uk
www.gallerypersia.co.uk
Est. 1989 *Stock size* Medium
Stock Old and antique rugs from Persia, Caucasus, Afghanistan, exemplary modern rugs
Open Mon–Sun by appointment Sat 11am–4pm
Fairs Scottish Game Fair
Services Restoration, repair, search service. Exhibition held in Spring and Autumn

NAIRN

Moray Antiques
Contact Melanie Muir
78 High Street, Nairn, Inverness-shire, IV12 4AU
01667 455570 01667 455570
Est. 1997 *Stock size* Medium
Stock General antiques, silver, porcelain
Open Mon–Sat 10.30am–5pm
Services Valuations, restorations

Sun-City Indoor Market
Contact S Morris
126 Harbour Street, Nairn, Inverness-shire, IV12 4AI
01667 456300
Est. 1989 *Stock size* Large
Stock General antiques
Open Mon 9am–5pm Sun noon–5pm
Services Valuations and house clearance

NEWTONMORE

The Antique Shop
Contact John Harrison
Main Street, Newtonmore, Inverness-shire, PH20 1DD
01540 673272 07713 093801
Est. 1990 *Stock size* Medium
Stock General antiques, scientific instruments, second-hand books
Open Mon–Sat 10am–5pm

MIDLOTHIAN

MUSSELBURGH

Early Technology
Contact Michael Bennett-Levy
Monkton House, Old Craighall, Musselburgh, Midlothian, EH21 8SF
0131 665 5753
levy@virgin.net
www.earlytech.com
Est. 1971 *Stock size* Large
Stock Early electrical and mechanical antiques
Open By appointment
Fairs Ingliston
Services Valuations, restorations

MORAY

ELGIN

West End Antiques (HADA)
Contact Mr F Stewart
35 High Street, Elgin, Moray, IV30 1EE
01343 547531 07977 821440
Est. 1971 *Stock size* Large
Stock General antiques, silver, furniture
Open Mon–Sat 9.30am–5pm closed 12.30–1.30pm closed Wed pm
Services Valuations

FORRES

Forres Saleroom
Contact Alexander Morris
Tytler Street, Forres, Moray, IV36 1EL
01309 672422 01309 673339
Est. 1895
Open Mon–Fri 9am–5pm Sat 9am–noon
Sales General antiques
Frequency Weekly
Catalogues Yes

GRANTOWN ON SPEY

Strathspey Gallery (LAPADA, HADA)
Contact James or Stephanie Franses
40 High Street, Grantown on Spey, Moray, PH26 3EH
01479 873290
07831 287762
antiques@strathspey.prestelc.o.uk
Est. 1969
Stock General antiques
Open Tues Wed Fri Sat 10am–5pm
Services Valuations

LOSSIEMOUTH

Harbour Treasures
Contact Janice Raynes
1 Pitgaveny Quay, Lossiemouth, Moray, IV31 6TW
01343 815880
Est. 1997 *Stock size* Large
Stock General antiques and collectables
Open Mon–Sun 10am–5pm
Fairs Newark, Swinderby and Ardingly
Services Tea rooms, free delivery within 200 miles

PORTGORDON

Hannah's Heirlooms
Contact Linda Sherman
9 Gordon Street, Portgordon, Moray, AB56 5QR
01542 832153
Est. 1997 *Stock size* Large
Stock General antiques, Victorian furniture and china
Open Mon–Sun 9.30am–5.30pm
Services Valuations, restorations and repairs

NORTH AYRSHIRE

FAIRLIE

E A Alvarino Fairlie Antiques
Contact E A Alvarino
86 Main Road, Fairlie, Largs, North Ayrshire, KA29 0AD
01475 568613
oldfairlie@aol.com
Est. 1976 *Stock size* Small
Stock General antiques
Services Valuations

ISLE OF ARRAN

The Stable Antiques
Contact Alistair Linton
Balmichael Visitors Centre, Shiskine Brodick, Isle of Arran, North Ayrshire, KA27 8DT
01770 860468
www.stableantiques-arran.co.uk
Est. 1984 *Stock size* Medium
Stock General antiques
Open Summer Mon–Sat 10am–5pm Sun noon–5pm winter Wed–Sat 10am–5pm Sun noon–5pm
Services Furniture restoration

LARGS

Narducci Antiques
Contact Mr G Narducci
11 Waterside Street, Largs, North Ayrshire, KA30 9LW

☎ 01475 672612 or 01294 461687
Ⓕ 01294 470002
Ⓜ 07771 577777 or 07831 100152
Est. 1969 *Stock size* Large
Stock General antiques, shipping goods
Open By appointment
Services Packing, shipping, European haulage

⊞ Nicolson Maps
Contact Malcolm Nicolson
✉ **3 Frazer Street, Largs, North Ayrshire, KA30 9HP** Ⓟ
☎ 01475 689242 Ⓕ 01475 689242
Ⓔ enquiries@nicolsonmaps.com
Ⓦ www.nicolsonmaps.com
Est. 1979 *Stock size* Medium
Stock General maps and charts
Open Mon–Fri 9am–5pm
Fairs International Map Association
Services Free postal service

PERTH & KINROSS

ABERNYTE

⊞ Newton Antiques
Contact Lindsay Newton
✉ **Scottish Antiques & Art Centre, Abernyte, Perthshire, PH14 9SJ** Ⓟ
☎ 018228 686401
Est. 1981 *Stock size* Medium
Stock General antiques, textiles, cushions, decorative items
Open Mon–Sun 10am–5pm

⊞ The Old Church Antiques
Contact George Whitla
✉ **The Old Church Scottish Antique and Art Centre, Abernyte, Perth, Perthshire, PH14 9SJ** Ⓟ
☎ 01828 686642 or 01250 886381
Ⓔ enquiries@oldchurchantiques.com
Ⓦ www.oldchurchantiques.com
Est. 1999 *Stock size* Medium
Stock Clocks, general antiques, books
Open Mon–Sun 11am–5pm
Services Valuations, clock repairs

⌂ Scottish Antique and Art Centre
Contact Tracy Walsh
✉ **Abernyte, Perthshire, PH14 9SJ** Ⓟ
☎ 01828 686401 Ⓕ 01828 686199
Ⓔ e.templeman@bopenworld.com
Ⓦ www.scottish-antiques.com
Est. 1999 *Stock size* Large
No. of dealers 130
Stock Georgian, Victorian, general antiques and collectables
Open Mon–Sun 10am–5pm
Services Valuations, restorations and repairs, shipping, coffee shop, food hall

AUCHTERARDER

⊞ Ian Burton Antique Clocks (NAWCC, AHS)
Contact Ian Burton
✉ **The Antiques Gallery, 125 High Street, Auchterarder, Perthshire, PH3 1AA** Ⓟ
☎ 01334 479979 Ⓜ 07785 114800
Ⓔ ian@ianburton.com
Ⓦ www.ianburton.com
Est. 1974 *Stock size* Large
Stock Antique clocks
Open Mon–Sat 9am–5pm

⊞ K Stanley & Son
Contact Chris Stanley
✉ **20b Townhead, Auchterarder, Perthshire, PH3 1AH** Ⓟ
☎ 01764 662252 Ⓕ 01764 662252
Ⓜ 07778 311653
Ⓔ ksantique@aol.com
Est. 1956 *Stock size* Medium
Stock General antiques
Open Mon–Sat 10am–5pm
Sun noon–5pm

⊞ Times Past Antiques
Contact Andrew or Neil Brown
✉ **Broadfold Farm, Auchterarder, Perthshire, PH3 1DR** Ⓟ
☎ 01764 663166 Ⓕ 01764 663166
Est. 1974 *Stock size* Large
Stock Stripped antique pine
Open Mon–Fri 8am–4.30pm
Sat Sun 10am–3.30pm
Services Restorations, stripping, exporting

⊞ John Whitelaw & Sons (LAPADA)
Contact Alan Whitelaw
✉ **125 High Street, Auchterarder, Perthshire, PH3 1AA** Ⓟ
☎ 01764 662482 Ⓕ 01764 663577
Ⓜ 07836 725558
Ⓔ jwsantique@aol.com
Ⓦ www.whitelawantiques.com
Est. 1959 *Stock size* Large
Stock General antiques, Georgian furniture
Open Mon–Sat 9am–5pm
Fairs NEC, LAPADA
Services Repairs, restorations

BLAIRGOWRIE

⊞ Roy Sim Antiques
Contact Roy Sim
✉ **The Granary Warehouse, Lower Mill Street, Blairgowrie, Perthshire, PH10 6AQ** Ⓟ
☎ 01250 873860 Ⓕ 01250 873860
Ⓔ roy.sim@lineone.net
Est. 1977 *Stock size* Large
Stock Antique furniture, decorative and collectable items, longcase clocks, wall and mantel clocks, copper, brassware
Open Mon–Sat 9am–5.30pm
Sun 12.30–5pm

BRIDGE OF EARN

⊞ Imrie Antiques & Interiors (LAPADA)
Contact Ian Imrie
✉ **Imrie House, Back Street, Bridge of Earn, Perth, Perthshire, PH2 9AE** Ⓟ
☎ 01738 812784
Est. 1966 *Stock size* Large
Stock General antiques
Open Mon–Sat 9am–5pm
Services Valuations, restorations and repairs

CRIEFF

⊞ Antiques & Fine Arts
Contact Mrs S Drysdale
✉ **11 Comrie Street, Crieff, Perthshire, PH7 4AX** Ⓟ
☎ 01764 654496
Est. 1984 *Stock size* Medium
Stock General antiques
Open Mon–Sat 10am–6pm
closed 1–2.20pm

DUNKELD

⊞ Dunkeld Antiques (LAPADA)
Contact David Dytch
✉ **Tay Terrace, Dunkeld, Perthshire, PH8 0AQ** Ⓟ
☎ 01350 728832 Ⓕ 01350 727008
Ⓜ 07713 074932
Ⓔ sales@dunkeldantiques.com
Ⓦ www.dunkeldantiques.com
Est. 1986 *Stock size* Large
Stock General antiques, specializing in 18thC–19thC furniture
Open Mon–Sat 10am–5pm
Sun noon–5pm

GLENDOICK

Becca Gauldie Antiques & Scribe Books
Contact Becca Gauldie
The Old School, Glendoick, Perth, Perthshire, PH2 7NR
01738 860870
Est. 1995 *Stock size* Large
Stock Scottish country antiques, large selection of Mauchlineware, antiquarian and second-hand books
Open Mon–Sat 10am–5pm

INCHTURE

Inchmartine Fine Art
Contact Paul Stephens
Inchmartine House, Inchture, Perth, Perthshire, PH14 9QQ
01828 686412 F 01828 686748
M 07702 190128
E fineart@inchmartine.freeserve.co.uk
Est. 1997 *Stock size* Medium
Stock 19th–early 20thC Scottish paintings
Open Mon–Sat 9am–5.30pm
Fairs Buxton, Chester, Glasgow
Services Valuations, cleaning and framing

Inchmartine Restorations
Contact Andrew Stephens
Inchmartine House, Inchture, Perth, Perthshire, PH14 9QQ
01828 686412 F 01828 686748
E ir@toolbazaar.freeserve.co.uk
W www.toolbazaar.co.uk
Est. 1989 *Stock size* Medium
Stock 18th–19thC furniture
Open Mon–Sat 9am–5.30pm
Fairs Buxton, Gleneagles
Services Valuations and cabinet-making

Inchmartine Tool Bazaar
Contact Andrew Stephens
Inchmartine House, Inchture, Perth, Perthshire, PH14 9QQ
01828 686096 F 01828 686748
E andrew@toolbazaar.freeserve.co.uk
W www.toolbazaar.co.uk
Est. 1991 *Stock size* Large
Stock Old cabinet-making and woodworking tools
Open Mon–Sat 9am–5.30pm
Fairs Buxton, Scone Palace, SECC Glasgow

C S Moreton Antiques
Contact Paul Stephens
Inchmartine House, Inchture, Perthshire, PH14 9QQ
01828 686412 F 01828 686748
M 07702 190128
E moreton@inchmartine.freeserve.co.uk
Est. 1854 *Stock size* Medium
Stock Period furniture, Oriental rugs, paintings, objets d'art, old hand tools
Open Mon–Sat 9am–5.30pm
Fairs Buxton, Chester, Glasgow
Services Valuations, restorations and shipping

KILLIN

Maureen H Gauld
Contact Maureen Gauld
Craiglee Main Street, Killin, Perthshire, FK21 8UN
01567 820475 F 01567 820605
E KillinGallery@FSBDial.co.uk
W www.killingallery,com
Est. 1973 *Stock size* Medium
Stock Silver, china, glass antiques
Open Mon–Sat 10am–5pm or by appointment

Killin Gallery
Contact J Gauld
Craiglea Main Street, Killin, Perthshire, FK21 8UN
01567 820475 F 01567 820605
E killingallery@FSBDial.co.uk
W www.killingallery.com
Est. 1994 *Stock size* Medium
Stock Furniture, paintings, etchings
Open Mon–Sat 10am–5pm or by appointment

KINROSS

Miles Antiques (LAPADA)
Contact Ken and Sue Miles
Mill Street, Kinross, Perth & Kinross, KY13 8DR
01577 864858 F 01577 863881
M 07836 315589
Est. 1978 *Stock size* Large
Stock Georgian–Victorian furniture, clocks, porcelain, decorative objects
Open Mon–Fri noon–5pm or by appointment

Tudor House Antiques
Contact John Neville
11 South Street, Milnathort, Kinross, Perth & Kinross, KY13 9XA
01577 863185 F 01577 863185
Est. 1978 *Stock size* Small
Stock General antiques
Open Tues Wed 1–5pm
Fri Sat 10am–5pm
Services Valuations, restorations and repairs

MEIGLE

Airlie Antiques
Contact J W McGill
Alyth Road, Meigle, Blairgowrie, Perthshire, PH12 8RS
01828 640617 F 01828 640617
M 07713 889205
E shop@airlieantiques.co.uk
W www.airlieantiques.co.uk
Est. 1981 *Stock size* Medium
Stock Antique glassware, Perthshire glass, Georgian–Victorian furniture
Open Mon–Sun noon–5pm or by appointment
Fairs Newark, Edinburgh
Services Valuations

Airlie Antiques (Textiles)
Contact Mrs J McGill
Alyth Road, Meigle, Blairgowrie, Perthshire, PH12 8RS
01828 640617 F 01828 640617
E jmcgill@tesco.net
Est. 1982 *Stock size* Medium
Stock Antique textiles, country antiques
Open Mon–Fri 2–5pm
Sat 10am–5pm closed Wed

Herrald of Edinburgh
Contact Bruce Herrald
Kings of Kinloch, Meigle, Blairgowrie, Perthshire, PH12 8QX
01828 640273 F 01828 640273
M 07711 285132
E herrald@sol.co.uk
W www.sol.co.uk/a/antiquesherrald
Est. 1882 *Stock size* Large
Stock General antiques
Open Mon–Sat 9.30am–5pm
Sun 2–5pm
Services Valuations, restorations and repairs

MUTHILL

Upstairs-Downstairs
Contact Elizabeth Richardson
18 Drummond Street, Muthill, Crieff, Perthshire, PH5 2AN P
☎ 01764 681737 Ⓜ 07803 461465
Est. 1996 *Stock size* Small
Stock General antiques, Victorian, Edwardian, Arts and Crafts, Art Nouveau, small furniture items, Continental glass, golf paraphernalia
Open Mon–Sun 2–5.30pm or by appointment

PERTH

Ainslie's Antiques
Contact Robert Ainslie
Unit 3, Gray Street, Perth, Perthshire, PH2 0JH P
☎ 01738 636825
Est. 1959 *Stock size* Large
Stock General antiques including Victorian and Edwardian furniture
Open Mon–Fri 9am–5pm or by appointment
Fairs Newark

Lindsay Burns & Co (SAA)
Contact Mr L Burns
6 King Street, Perth, Perthshire, PH2 8JA P
☎ 01738 633888 Ⓕ 01738 441322
Ⓔ lindsayburns@btconnect.com
Ⓦ www.lburnscoauctions.co.uk
Est. 1982
Open Mon–Fri 9am–5pm Sat 9am–noon
Sales General antiques, household effects bi-weekly Thurs 10.30am, viewing day prior to sale
Frequency Bi-weekly
Catalogues Yes

Design Interiors
Contact Margaret Blane
55 South Street, Perth, Perthshire, PH2 8PD P
☎ 01738 635360
Ⓔ robert.blane@btinternet.com
Est. 1989 *Stock size* Medium
Stock General antiques and collectables
Open Mon–Sat 10am–5.30pm
Services China restoration, picture cleaning, framing

Alexander S Deuchar & Son
Contact A S Deuchar
12 South Street, Perth, Perthshire, PH2 8PG P
☎ 01738 626297
Est. 1911 *Stock size* Medium
Stock General antiques
Open Mon–Fri 10am–5pm

Loves Auction Rooms (SAA, SOFAA)
Contact Mrs E Reid
52–54 Canal Street, Perth, Perthshire, PH2 8LF P
☎ 01738 633337 Ⓕ 01738 629830
Est. 1869
Open Mon–Fri 9am–5.30pm Sat 9am–noon
Sales Antiques quarterly, household effects weekly
Frequency Weekly & quarterly
Catalogues Yes (quarterly sales only)

Perth Antiques
Contact Robert Blane
50 South Street, Perth, Perthshire, PH2 8PD P
☎ 01738 440888 Ⓜ 07939 196750
Ⓔ robert.blane@btinternet.com
Est. 1998 *Stock size* Large
Stock General antiques, porcelain, Clarice Cliff, Belleek, Morecroft, Art Deco pottery, Monart glass, chintz
Open Mon–Sat 10am–5pm

Whisper of the Past
Contact Laura Wilson
15 George Street, Perth, Perthshire, PH1 5JY P
☎ 01738 635472
Est. 1981 *Stock size* Medium
Stock Country antiques
Open Mon–Sat 9.30am–5pm Jan–Mar closed Wed

Yesterdays Today
Contact W MacGregor
267 Old High Street, Perth, Perthshire, PH1 5QN P
☎ 01738 443534 Ⓜ 07713 897793
Ⓔ yesterdaystoday@talk21.com
Est. 1995 *Stock size* Medium
Stock Scottish pottery and glass, jewellery, silver, Royal Doulton, Beswick
Open Mon–Sat 9am–5pm
Services Valuations

PITLOCHRY

Blair Antiques
Contact Duncan Huie
Falls of Bruar, by Pitlochry, Perthshire, PH18 5TW P
☎ 01796 483264
Ⓔ adhuie@aol.com
Est. 1976 *Stock size* Medium
Stock General antiques, art
Open Mon–Fri 9am–5pm closed 12.30–2pm
Services Valuations

RAIT

Edward Bowry
Contact Edward Bowry
Rait Village Antique Centre, Rait, Perth, Perthshire, PH2 7RT P
☎ 01821 670318
Est. 1990 *Stock size* Medium
Stock Furniture, old woodworking tools, sporting items
Open Mon–Sat 10.30am–5pm
Services Valuations, restorations and repairs

Fair Finds Antiques
Contact Lynda Templeman
Rait Village Antiques Centre, Rait, Perth, Perthshire, PH2 7RT P
☎ 01821 670379 Ⓕ 01821 670379
Ⓜ 07720 394750
Ⓔ chris.comben@kanthal.com
Est. 1969 *Stock size* Large
Stock Furniture, Wemyss ware, general antiques
Open Mon–Sat 10am–5pm Sun 12.30–4.30pm

Gordon Loraine Antiques
Contact Liane or Gordon Loraine
The Sawmill, Rait Village Antiques Centre, Rait, Perth, Perthshire, PH2 7RT P
☎ 01821 670760 Ⓕ 01821 670760
Ⓜ 07798 550017
Est. 1991 *Stock size* Medium
Stock Good-quality Georgian–Edwardian furniture, decorative items and collectables
Open Mon–Sat 10am–5pm Sept–Mar noon–4pm

Rait Village Antiques Centre
Contact Lynda Templeman

✉ Rait, Perth, Perthshire, PH2 7RT 🅿
☎ 01821 670379 🅕 01821 670379
Ⓜ 07720 394750
Ⓔ chris.comben@kanthal.co,
Est. 1985 *Stock size* Large
No. of dealers 8
Stock Furniture, silver, pottery, porcelain, woodworking tools, Wemyss ware, rugs, paintings
Open Mon–Sat 10am–5pm Sun 12.30–4.30pm
Services Valuations, restorations, coffee shop

SCONE

Ian M Smith Auctioneers & Valuers
Contact Iain Smith
✉ Unit 18, Perth Airport Business Park, Scone, Perth, Perthshire, PH2 6NP 🅿
☎ 01738 551110 🅕 01738 551110
Ⓜ 07836 770664
Ⓔ imsauctions@beeb.net
Est. 1994
Open Mon–Fri 9am–5pm Sat 10am–1pm
Sales General antiques
Frequency Weekly
Catalogues No

STANLEY

Coach House Antiques Ltd (PADA)
Contact John Walker
✉ Charleston, Stanley, Perthshire, PN1 4PN 🅿
☎ 01738 828627 Ⓜ 07710 122244
Ⓦ www.goodtradecall.com
Est. 1970 *Stock size* Medium
Stock Period furniture, decorative items, garden items
Open By appointment
Services Valuations, restorations, shipping

RENFREWSHIRE

GREENOCK

McTear's (SAA, IAA)
Contact Brian Clements
✉ 22 Forsyth Street, Greenock, Renfrewshire, PA16 8DX 🅿
☎ 01475 730343 🅕 01475 726436
Ⓜ 07767 376642
Ⓔ enquiries@mctears.co.uk
Ⓦ www.mctears.co.uk
Est. 1842
Open Mon–Fri 8.30am–5pm
Sales General antiques
Frequency Weekly
Catalogues Yes

D B Warne Ltd (SAA)
Contact L Haynes
✉ 2 Houston Street, Greenock, Renfrewshire, PA16 8ND 🅿
☎ 01475 723150 🅕 01475 723150
Ⓔ corains@easynet.co.uk
Est. 1921
Open Mon–Fri 9.30am–4pm
Sales General antiques
Frequency Weekly
Catalogues Yes

KILBARCHAN

Gardners 'The Antique Shop' (LAPADA)
Contact George, Robert or David Gardner
✉ Wardend House, Kibbleston Road, Kilbarchan, Johnstone, Renfrewshire, PA10 2PN 🅿
☎ 01505 702292 🅕 01505 702292
Ⓔ gardantiques@colloquium.co.uk
Est. 1950 *Stock size* Large
Stock General antiques, Georgian–1930s
Open Mon–Fri 9am–6pm Sat 10am–5pm

McQuade Antiques
✉ 7 Shuttle Street, Kilbarchan, Johnstone, Renfrewshire, PA10 2JN 🅿
☎ 01505 704249 Ⓜ 07860 729598
Est. 1967 *Stock size* Medium
Stock General antiques
Open Mon–Fri 10am–5.30pm Sun 2–5.30pm
Fairs Newark

KILMALCOLM

Kilmalcolm Antiques
Contact Hilary McLean
✉ Stewart Place, Bridge of Weir Road, Kilmalcolm, Renfrewshire, PA13 4AF 🅿
☎ 01505 873149 🅕 01505 873149
Ⓜ 07850 126150
Est. 1974 *Stock size* Large
Stock General antiques, Scottish paintings, pottery, Georgian–Victorian furniture
Open Mon–Sat 10am–1pm 2.30–5.30pm
Fairs Hopeton House, Margam

PAISLEY

Corrigan Antiques
Contact Mr John Corrigan
✉ 23 High Calside, Paisley, Renfrewshire, PA2 6BY 🅿
☎ 0141 889 6653 🅕 0141 848 9700
Ⓜ 07802 631110
Ⓔ john.@corriganantiques3.freeserve.co.uk
Est. 1939 *Stock size* Small
Stock Decorative antiques
Open By appointment only

SCOTTISH BORDERS

COLDSTREAM

Fraser Antiques
Contact R Fleming
✉ 65 High Street, Coldstream, Scottish Borders, TD12 4DL 🅿
☎ 01890 882450 🅕 01890 882451
Ⓔ robertfleming698@msn.com
Est. 1968 *Stock size* Medium
Stock General antiques
Open Tues–Sat 10am–1pm 2–5pm
Services Valuations, restorations

GALASHIELS

Hall's Auctioneers
Contact Michael Hall
✉ Ladhope Vale House, Ladhope Vale, Galashiels, Scottish Borders, TD1 1BT 🅿
☎ 01896 754477 🅕 01896 754477
Est. 1995
Open Mon–Fri 9am–5pm Sat 9am–noon or by appointment
Sales General antiques and collectables
Frequency Monthly
Catalogues Yes

INNERLEITHEN

The Glory Hole
Contact Paul MacNaughton
✉ 29 High Street, Innerleithen, Scottish Borders, EH44 6HA 🅿
☎ 01896 831306 Ⓜ 07710 771055
Est. 1996 *Stock size* Medium
Stock General antiques, specializing in old printing items, coins
Open Mon–Fri 11am–5pm closed Tues
Fairs Border fairs

Keepsakes
Contact Mrs M Maxwell
96 High Street, Innerleithen, Scottish Borders, EH44 6HF
01896 831369 ⓜ 07773 477291
rmaxwells@keepsakes.freeserve.co.uk
www.website.lineone.net/~rmaxwell
Est. 1979 *Stock size* Medium
Stock General antiques, dolls, toys, Art Deco
Open Mon Thurs–Sat 11am–4.30pm
Fairs Ingliston

The Last Century Antiques
Contact Keith or Gill Miller
34 High Street, Innerleithen, Scottish Borders, EH44 6HF
01896 831759
last.century@btinternet.com
Est. 1989 *Stock size* Medium
Stock General antiques including glass, cutlery, curtains
Open Mon–Sat 11am–4.30pm
Fairs Inglestone
Services Valuations

JEDBURGH

R & M Turner (Antiques & Fine Art) Ltd (LAPADA)
Contact Mr R J Turner
34–36 High Street, Jedburgh, Roxburghshire, TD8 6AG
01835 863445 Ⓕ 01835 863349
Est. 1966 *Stock size* Large
Stock Fine art, clocks, furniture, jewellery, bric-a-brac, porcelain, reproductions
Open Mon–Fri 9.30am–5.30pm Sat 10am–5pm
Services Valuations, restorations, shipping

MELROSE

Birch House Antiques at Michael Vee Design
Contact Michael Vee
Birch House, High Street, Melrose, Scottish Borders, TD6 9PA
01896 822116 Ⓕ 01896 682320
ⓜ 07761 913349
michael.vee@btinternet.com
www.michaelveedesign.com
Est. 1990 *Stock size* Medium
Stock French decorative antiques
Open Mon–Sat 9am–5pm

Border Country Furniture
Contact Denni or Christine Reid
2 Palma Place, Melrose, Scottish Borders, TD6 9PR
01896 823700 Ⓕ 01896 823700
Est. 1974 *Stock size* Large
Stock General antiques, hand-made furniture
Open Mon–Sat 10am–5pm Thurs 10–1pm Sun 2–4pm
Services Made-to-measure tables and fireplaces

John Swan & Sons Plc
Contact Frank Forrest
Newtown St Boswells, Melrose, Scottish Borders, TD6 0PD
01835 822214 Ⓕ 01835 823860
stboswells@johnswan.demon.co.uk
Est. 1899
Open Mon–Fri 9am–5pm
Sales General antiques and house clearance
Catalogues Yes

PEEBLES

Veteran Antiques and Collectables
Contact Paul Kelly
61 High Street, Peebles, Scottish Borders, EH45 8AN
01721 724228
Est. 1996 *Stock size* Medium
Stock General antiques
Open Mon–Sat 10.30am–5pm or by appointment
Fairs NEC, Newark
Services Valuations

SOUTH AYRSHIRE

AYR

Lochyran Furniture Stores
Contact A Patterson
12 Kirkport, Ayr, South Ayrshire, KA7 1QB
01292 282821
www.lochyran.co.uk
Est. 1994 *Stock size* Large
No. of dealers 2
Stock General antiques
Open Mon–Sat 10am–5pm

GIRVAN

Ainslie Books
Contact Mr G Clark
28 Hamilton Street, Girvan, South Ayrshire, KA26 9EY
01465 715453 Ⓕ 01465 715453
Est. 1996 *Stock size* Medium
Stock Rare and second-hand books, specializing in Scottish and Ayrshire topics
Open Mon–Sat 10am–5pm
Services Book search

Clamjamfrey
Contact Ingrid Powell
26 Hamilton Street, Girvan, South Ayrshire, KA26 9EY
01465 715621
clamjam@tiscali.co.uk
Est. 1997 *Stock size* Medium
Stock General antiques, Denby and Poole pottery, 20thC ceramics
Open Mon–Sat 10am–5pm
Fairs Ingliston, Edinburgh, Swinderby
Services Valuations

PRESTWICK

Crossroads Antiques
Contact Mr T O'Keeffe
7 The Cross, Prestwick, South Ayrshire, KA9 1AJ
01292 474004
Est. 1989 *Stock size* Medium
Stock General antiques, furniture, china
Open Mon–Sat 10.30am–5pm

TROON

IDS Valuation Consultants (BWCG)
Contact Iain Sutherland
79 Templehill, Troon, South Ayrshire, KA10 6BQ
01292 315999 Ⓕ 01292 316611
Est. 1995 *Stock size* Medium
Stock General antiques
Open Mon–Sat 9.30am–5.30pm or by appointment
Fairs Ayr
Services Valuations, full consultation service

Tantalus Antiques (BWCG)
Contact Iain Sutherland
79 Templehill, Troon, South Ayrshire, KA10 6BQ

☎ 01292 315999 Ⓕ 01292 316611
Ⓔ idsantique@aol.com
Est. 1997 *Stock size* Medium
Stock General antiques, furniture, jewellery, clocks, watches
Open Mon–Sat 10am–5pm or by appointment
Fairs Ayr
Services Full consultation and restoration service

SOUTH LANARKSHIRE

HAMILTON

L S Smellie & Sons Ltd (SAA)
Contact Mr A Smellie
Lower Auchingramont Road, Hamilton, South Lanarkshire, ML3 6HW Ⓟ
☎ 01698 282007 Ⓕ 01698 207473
Ⓔ andrew@LSSmellie.co.uk
Ⓦ www.LSSmellie.co.uk
Est. 1874
Open Mon–Fri 8am–5pm
Sales General antiques
Frequency Weekly & quarterly
Catalogues Yes

STRATHAVEN

Suedan Antiques
Contact Mrs M Hardie
5 Main Street, Strathaven, South Lanarkshire, ML10 6AJ Ⓟ
☎ 01357 529854 Ⓜ 07801 367768
Est. 1997 *Stock size* Large
Stock General antiques
Open Mon–Sat 10.30am–4.30pm closed Wed
Services Valuations, repairs

WISTON

Sunnyside Antiques
Contact Mark Attwood
Castledykes, Wiston, Biggar, South Lanarkshire, ML12 6HT Ⓟ
☎ 01899 850552 Ⓕ 01899 850551
Ⓜ 07798 640629
Ⓔ info@periodantiques.net
Ⓦ www.periodantiques.net
Est. 1995 *Stock size* Medium
Stock 17th–19thC period furniture, longcase clocks
Open By appointment only
Fairs Newark
Services Restorations, shipping

STIRLING

BRIDGE OF ALLAN

Bridge of Allan Books (PBFA)
2 Henderson Street, Bridge of Allan, Stirling, FK9 4HT Ⓟ
☎ 01786 834483 Ⓕ 01786 834483
Ⓔ books@bridgeofallen.fsnet.co.uk
Est. 1985 *Stock size* Medium
Stock Antiquarian, rare and second-hand books, prints, specializing in Scottish and field sports
Open Mon–Sat 10am–5.30pm
Services Free book search

DOUNE

Bluebell Collectables
Contact Charlie Claydon
4 Main Street, Doune, Stirling, FK16 6BJ Ⓟ
☎ 01786 842828 Ⓕ 0141 571 5694
Ⓔ militaria@stirling.co.uk
Ⓦ www.militaria.stirling.co.uk
Est. 1994 *Stock size* Medium
Stock Collectables, regimental badges
Open Tues–Sat 10.30am–4.30pm closed Wed
Fairs Ingliston, Lancaster, Liverpool
Services Medal research

Scottish Antique and Arts Centre
Contact Victoria Templeman
Doune, Stirling, FK16 6HG Ⓟ
☎ 01786 841203 Ⓕ 01786 842561
Ⓔ victempleman@aol.com
Ⓦ www.scottish-antiques.com
Est. 1974 *Stock size* Large
No. of dealers 100
Stock Georgian–Victorian, general antiques and collectables
Open Mon–Sun 10am–5pm
Services Valuations, shipping, coffee shop

FALKIRK

Auction Rooms (NAVA)
Contact Robert Penman
Central Auction Hall, Bankside, Falkirk, Stirling, FK2 7XR Ⓟ
☎ 01324 623000 Ⓕ 01324 630343
Ⓔ robert@auctionroomsfalkirk.co.uk
Ⓦ www.auctionroomsfalkirk.co.uk
Est. 1999
Open Mon Thurs Fri 9am–5pm Tues 8am–8pm Wed 8am–6pm Sat 9am–noon
Sales General antiques sales every Wed evening
Frequency Weekly
Catalogues Yes

Fairweathers
Contact Jane Wheeler
54 Vicars Street, Falkirk, Stirling, FK1 1JB
☎ 01324 633569
Est. 1984 *Stock size* Small
Stock Collectors items, curios
Open Mon–Sat 9.30am–5.30pm

GARGUNNOCK

Country Home Antiques
Contact P Christie
Mains Farm, Gargunnock, Stirling, FK8 3AY Ⓟ
☎ 01786 860509 Ⓕ 01786 860509
Ⓔ gargunnock@aol.com or antiquestrader@aol.com
Ⓦ www.scotlandroom.com
Est. 1979 *Stock size* Large
Stock General antiques
Open Mon–Fri 9am–5pm Sat 10am–5pm Sun 12.30–5pm
Services Stripping, waxing, upholstery, French polishing, full restoration, shipping

STIRLING

Abbey Antiques
Contact Stuart Campbell
35 Friars Street, Stirling, FK8 1HA Ⓟ
☎ 01786 447840 Ⓜ 07801 692126
Est. 1979 *Stock size* Small
Stock Jewellery, silver, militaria, paintings, furniture, bric-a-brac
Open Mon–Sat 9am–5pm
Services Valuations

Stewart Sales Rooms
Contact Mrs Watson-Fargie
14 Dumbarton Road, Stirling, FK8 2LG Ⓟ
☎ 01786 473414
Est. 1969 *Stock size* Large
Stock General antiques
Open Mon–Sat 10am–4pm closed Wed
Services Valuations

STRATHBLANE

What Nots Antiques
Contact Frank Bruce
16 Milngavie Road, Strathblane, Stirling, G63 9EH
01360 770310
Est. 1969 *Stock size* Medium
Stock General antiques, clocks, selection of horse-drawn vehicles
Open Mon–Sun 9.30am–5pm

WEST LOTHIAN

BO'NESS

D J Manning Auctioneers, Valuers & Appraisers (NAVA)
Contact D J Manning
Bridgeness Road, Carriden, Bo'Ness, West Lothian, EH51 9SF
01506 827693 01506 826495
info@djmanning.co.uk
www.djmanning.co.uk
Est. 1969
Open Mon–Fri 9am–5pm
Sales Books, general antiques, collectables
Frequency Quarterly
Catalogues Yes

LINLITHGOW

County Antiques
Contact Mrs Flynn
30 High Street, Linlithgow, West Lothian, EH49 7AE
01506 671201
Est. 1992 *Stock size* Medium
Stock General antiques, jewellery
Open Mon–Sat 10am–5pm
Fairs Edinburgh
Services Valuations and jewellery repairs

Heritage Antiques
Contact Ann Davidson
222 High Street, Linlithgow, West Lothian, EH49 7ES
01506 847460
anantiques@aol.com
www.members.aol.com/antiques
Est. 1992 *Stock size* Medium
Stock General antiques
Open Mon–Sat 10.30am–5pm closed Wed
Fairs Ingliston
Services Valuations

CHANNEL ISLANDS

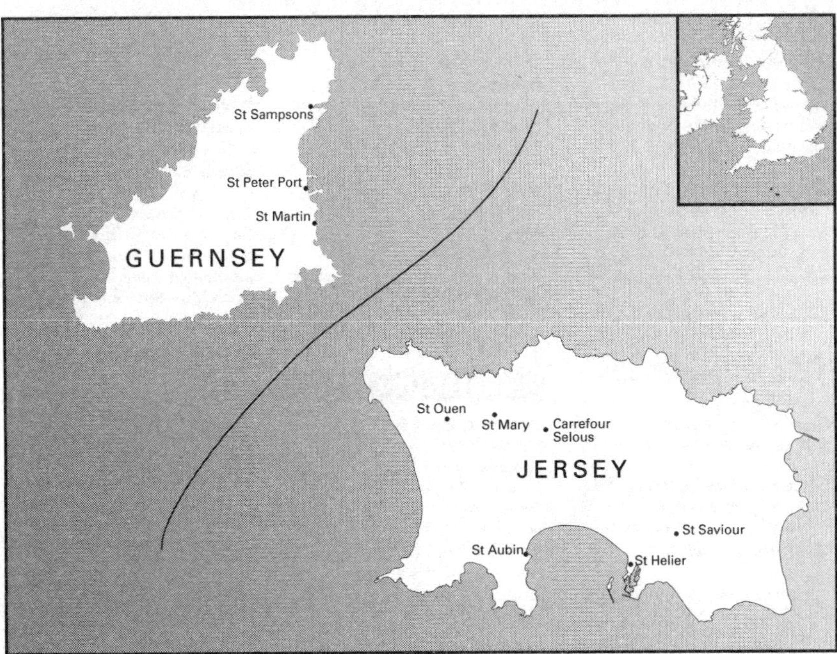

GUERNSEY

ST PETER PORT

Stephen Andrews Gallery
Contact Stephen Andrews
5 College Terrace, The Grange, St Peter Port, Guernsey, GY1 2PX P
☎ 01481 710380
Est. 1984 *Stock size* Large
Stock Pottery, porcelain, furniture, silver
Open Mon–Sat 9.30am–5pm
Fairs Guernsey Antiques Fair

Channel Islands Galleries Ltd
Contact Geoffrey Gavey
Trinity Square Centre, Trinity Square, St Peter Port, Guernsey, GY1 ILX P
☎ 01481 723247 Ⓕ 01481 714669
Ⓔ geoff.gavey@cigalleries.f9.co.uk
Ⓦ www.cigalleries.f9.co.uk
Est. 1970 *Stock size* Medium
Stock Channel Island antique maps, prints, watercolours, oil paintings, out-of-print books, bank notes, coins
Open Mon–Fri 10am–5pm
Sat 10am–1pm
Services Valuations, restorations, conservation, picture framing

The Collectors Centre
Contact Andrew Rundle
1 Sausmarez Street, St Peter Port, Guernsey, GY1 2PT P
☎ 01481 725209
Est. 1985 *Stock size* Medium
Stock Antique prints, engravings, old postcards, coins, bank notes, memorabilia, stamps
Open Mon–Sat 10.30am–6pm
Services Valuations for collectables, mail order, postal auctions, free catalogue

W De La Rue Antiques
Contact William de La Rue
29 Mill Street, St Peter Port, Guernsey, GY1 1HG
☎ 01481 723177
Est. 1975 *Stock size* Medium
Stock General antiques, collectors' items
Open Mon–Sat 10am–12.30pm
2–4pm closed Thurs pm
Services Valuations, buying

Ann Drury Antiques
Contact Ann Drury
1 Mansell Street, St Peter Port, Guernsey, GY1 1HP
☎ 01481 716193 Ⓜ 07781 104304
Est. 1969 *Stock size* Large
Stock 18th–20thC furniture and decorative antiques
Open Mon–Sat 10am–noon
2–4pm closed Thurs
Fairs Guernsey Antiques Fair
Services Valuations

Mahogany
Contact Angela Edwards
7 Mansell Street, St Peter Port, Guernsey, GY1 1HP
☎ 01481 727574 Ⓕ 01481 727574
Est. 1980 *Stock size* Large
Stock General antiques, collectables
Open Mon–Sat 10am–12.30pm
2–4pm Thurs closed pm
Fairs Guernsey Antiques Fair

N St J Paint and Sons Ltd (NAG)
Contact Michael or Paul Paint
26 Le Pollet, St Peter Port, Guernsey, GY1 1WQ
☎ 01481 722229 Ⓕ 01481 710241
Ⓔ paint@guernsey.net

CHANNEL ISLANDS

GUERNSEY • ST SAMPSONS

Est. 1947 *Stock size* Large
Stock General antiques, jewellery, silver, objets d'art
Open Mon–Sat 9am–5.30pm
Services Valuations, restorations and repairs (goldsmiths and silversmiths)

Parasol Antiques
Contact Marianne Barwick
23 Mansell Street, St Peter Port, Guernsey, GY1 1HP
01481 710780 01481 710780
07781 118715
Est. 1993 *Stock size* Medium
Stock Jewellery, silver, furniture, copper, brass, pictures
Open Mon–Sat 10am–5pm Thurs 10am–1pm
Fairs Guernsey Antiques Fair
Services Valuations, restorations

St James's Gallery Ltd
Contact Mrs C Whittam
Smith Street, St Peter Port, Guernsey, GY1 2JQ
01481 720070 01481 721132
stjamesantiques@gtonline.net
Est. 1979 *Stock size* Large
Stock Post-1830s furniture, paintings, silver, porcelain
Open Mon–Fri 9.30am–1pm 2–5pm Sat 9.30am–1pm
Fairs Olympia (under the name of Havilland Antiques Ltd)
Services Valuations

ST SAMPSONS

The Old Curiosity Shop
Contact Mrs Stevens-Cox
Commercial Road, St Sampsons, Guernsey, GY2 4QP
01481 245324
Est. 1978 *Stock size* Medium
Stock General small antiques, collectables, second-hand books
Open Tues Wed Fri Sat 10.30am–4.30pm
Fairs Guernsey Antiques Fair
Services Framing

Pretty Things
Contact Myrtle Domiall
Petites Capelles, St Sampsons, Guernsey, GY2 4GX
01481 47391 01481 42215
Est. 1984 *Stock size* Large
Stock General antiques and collectables (no furniture)
Open Mon–Sat 9.30am–12.30pm 2.30–5pm closed Thurs

Ray & Scott Ltd (NAG)
Contact M Search
The Bridge, St Sampsons, Guernsey, GY2 4QN
01481 244610 01481 244610
Est. 1962 *Stock size* Large
Stock Fine jewellery, clocks, silver, second-hand watches
Open Mon–Sat 9am–5pm
Fairs Guernsey Antiques Fair, Beau Sejours Fair
Services Valuations, restoration of jewellery, antique clocks, gold and silversmiths

JERSEY

CARREFOUR SELOUS

David Hick Antiques
Contact David Hick
Alexandra House, Carrefour Selous, St Lawrence, Jersey, JE3 1GL
01534 865965 01534 865448
hickantiques@localdial.com
Est. 1974 *Stock size* Large
Stock Furniture, silver, porcelain
Open Wed Fri Sat 9.30am–5pm

ST HELIER

Antiques Warehouse
Contact Tim Morley
Robin Place, St Helier, Jersey, JE2 4LT
01534 873932 01534 506833
07797 720234
Est. 1988 *Stock size* Large
Stock General antiques
Open Mon–Sat 8am–5.30pm
Fairs Mainly French fairs
Services Restorations, shipping

Bonhams & Langlois
39 Don Street, St Helier, Jersey, JE2 4TR
01534 722441 01534 759354
jersey@bonhams.com
www.bonhams.com
Est. 1940
Open Mon–Fri 9am–5pm

Brown's Times Past Antiques
Contact Mick Brown
28 Burrard Street, St Helier, Jersey, JE2 4WS
01534 737090/735264
Est. 1984 *Stock size* Medium
Stock Georgian–Edwardian furniture, ceramics, 19thC pottery and glass
Open Mon–Sat 9am–5pm or by appointment
Services Valuations

John Cooper Antiques
Contact John Cooper
16 Central Market, St Helier, Jersey, JE2 4WL
01534 723600
Est. 1982 *Stock size* Medium
Stock General, mostly small items including jewellery
Open Mon–Sat 9am–5.30pm Thurs half day

David Hick Antiques
Contact David Hick
45 Halkett Place, St Helier, Jersey, JE2 4WQ
01534 721162 01534 721162
hickantiques@localdial.com
Est. 1974 *Stock size* Large
Stock Furniture, silver, porcelain
Open Mon–Sat 10am–5pm

Jersey Coin Company
Contact V or S Dougan
26 Halkett Street, St Helier, Jersey, JE2 4WJ
01534 725743 01534 509094
Est. 1965 *Stock size* Medium
Stock Antique coins, bank notes, medals, WWII weapons
Open Mon–Sat 9am–5pm
Services Valuations, jewellery repairs

Peter Le Vesconte Collectables
Contact Peter Le Vesconte
62 Stopford Road, St Helier, Jersey, JE2 4LZ
01534 732481 01534 732481
p-l-v-collectables@psilink.co.je
Est. 1981 *Stock size* Large
Stock Dinky and Corgi toys, mint and boxed toys, militaria (especially WWII), new collectors' toys
Open Mon–Sat 10am–3pm closed Thurs
Fairs Jersey Toy and Phone Card Collectors Fair
Services Toy valuations

Park Antiques
Contact P Cowan
16 Burrard Street, St Helier, Jersey, JE2 4WF

☎ 01534 280784 Ⓕ 01534 618129
Ⓔ park@igl.net
Est. 1969 *Stock size* Large
Stock English and Continental furniture
Open By appointment

A & R Ritchie
Contact A and R Ritchie
✉ **7 Duhamel Place, St Helier, Jersey, JE2 4TP** Ⓟ
☎ 01534 873805
Est. 1973 *Stock size* Medium
Stock Collectables, brass, china, glass, toys, silver, jewellery, scent bottles, militaria
Open Mon–Sat 10am–5pm
Services Restorations – militaria and ivory

Robert's Antiques
Contact Robert Michieli
✉ **14 York Street, St Helier, Jersey, JE2 3RQ**
☎ 01534 509071 Ⓜ 07798 876553
Est. 1979 *Stock size* Medium
Stock English silver, porcelain, jewellery, glass
Open Mon–Sat 9am–5.30pm or by appointment
Services Valuations

Thomson's Antiques
Contact Ray or Chris Thomson
✉ **44 Don Street, St Helier, Jersey, JE2 4TR** Ⓟ
☎ 01534 618673 Ⓜ 07797 766806
Est. 1967 *Stock size* Large
Stock Collectors' items, furniture, clocks, silver, barometers
Open Mon–Sat 10am–5pm

Thomson's Antiques
Contact Ray or Chris Thomson
✉ **60 Kensington Place, St Helier, Jersey, JE2 3PA**
☎ 01534 723673 Ⓕ 01534 724673
Ⓜ 07797 766806
Est. 1967 *Stock size* Large
Stock General antiques, furniture
Open Mon–Sat 10am–5pm

ST MARY

Country House and Cottage Antiques
Contact Sarah Johnson
✉ **Rue Esboeufs, St Mary, Jersey, JE3 3EQ** Ⓟ
☎ 01534 862547
Est. 1984 *Stock size* Large
Stock Georgian–Edwardian, oak, pine and mahogany furniture, china, glass, ceramics, silver
Open Mon–Fri 10am–4pm
Sat 9am–1pm
Fairs St Mary's Fair
Services Valuations

ST OUEN

Stephen Cohu Antiques
Contact Stephen Cohu
✉ **The Village Gallery, La Ville de L'Eglise, St Ouen, Jersey, JE3 2LR** Ⓟ
☎ 01534 485177 Ⓜ 07797 723895
Est. 1993 *Stock size* Large
Stock General antiques
Open In season Sat 10am–5pm other times by appointment
Fairs Newark, NEC
Services Valuations, restorations

ST SAVIOUR

Pine for Pine Antiques
Contact Mrs Brenda Clyde Smith
✉ **Chateau Clairval, St Saviour, Jersey, JE2 7HN** Ⓟ
☎ 01534 737173/724748
Ⓕ 01534 618384
Est. 1974 *Stock size* Medium
Stock Georgian–Edwardian pine furniture
Open Mon–Fri 10am–4pm
Sat 10am–2pm

NORTHERN IRELAND

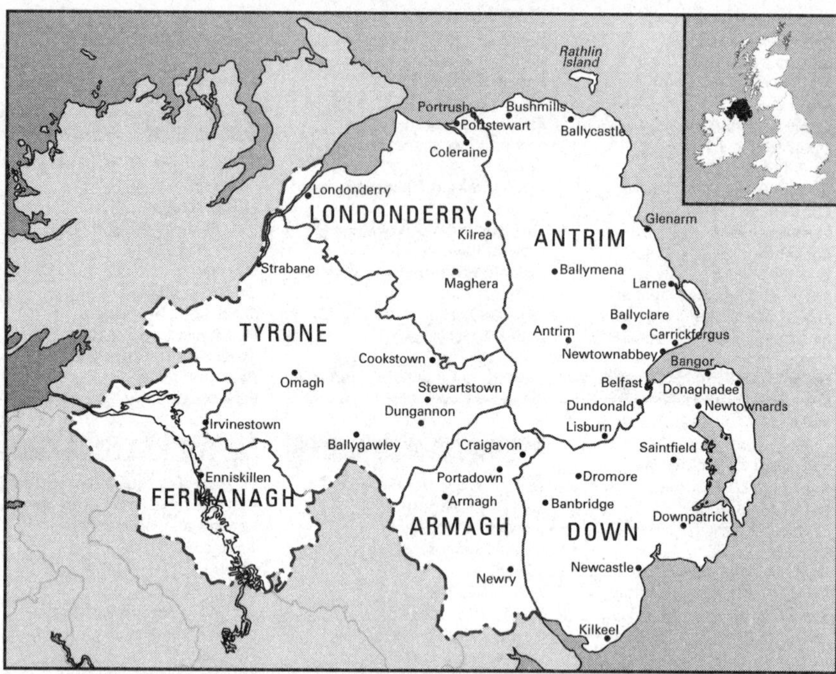

CO ANTRIM

AHOGHILL

⊞ Once Upon a Time Antiques
Contact Sean or Ronan McLaughlin
✉ The Old Mill, 2 Parkfield Road, Ahoghill, Co Antrim, BT42 2QF 🅿
☎ 028 2587 1244 Ⓕ 028 2565 6666
Est. 1973 *Stock size* Large
Stock Jewellery, furniture, general antiques
Open Mon–Sat 10am–6pm
Services Valuations, restorations, coffee shop, craft centre

ANTRIM

⊞ Country Antiques (LAPADA)
Contact David Wolfenden
✉ 219 Lisnevenagh Road, Antrim, BT41 2JT 🅿
☎ 028 9442 9498 Ⓕ 028 9442 9498
Ⓜ 07768 128800
Ⓔ antiquewolfirl@aol.com
Ⓦ www.country-antiques-wolfenden.co.uk
Est. 1984 *Stock size* Large
Stock Furniture, jewellery, general antiques
Open Mon–Sat 10am–6pm
Services Valuations, restorations

⊞ Past & Present Antiques
✉ Colin Paul, 21 Hillhead Road, Toomebridge, Antrim, BT41 3SF 🅿
☎ 028 7965 9603
Est. 1998 *Stock size* Large
Stock General antiques
Open Tues–Sat 10.30am–5pm
Services Valuations, restorations

⊞ Village Antiques
Contact Mr W J Baird
✉ 99 Main Street, Randalstown, Antrim, BT41 3BB 🅿
☎ 028 9447 8686 Ⓜ 07703 594522
Est. 1998 *Stock size* Medium
Stock General antiques, furniture
Open Mon–Sat 10am–6pm
Services Restorations and clock repairs

BALLINDERRY

⊞ Ballinderry Antiques
Contact Mr W Mills
✉ 2 Ballinderry Road, Ballinderry, Upper Lisburn, Co Antrim, BT28 2EP 🅿
☎ 028 9265 1046 Ⓕ 028 9265 1580
Est. 1959 *Stock size* Large
Stock Antique furniture, silver
Open Mon–Sat 10am–5.30pm Thurs 10am–9pm
Fairs Newark
Services Valuations

BALLYCASTLE

⚒ P J Mcilroy & Son
Contact Mr Sean Mcilroy FNAEA
✉ 11 Ann Street, Ballycastle, Co Antrim, BT54 6AA 🅿
☎ 028 2076 2353 Ⓕ 028 2076 2126
Ⓔ leo@pjmcilroy.freeserve.co.uk
Est. 1967
Open Mon–Fri 9am–5.30pm Sat 10am–12.30pm
Sales General antiques, paintings
Frequency Quarterly
Catalogues Yes

BALLYMENA

⊞ Angela's Antiques
Contact Angela McClelland

✉ **75 Wellington Street, Ballymena, Co Antrim, BT43 6AD**
☎ 028 2564 1999
Est. 1993 *Stock size* Large
Stock Porcelain, jewellery, furniture, general antiques
Open Mon–Sat 9.30am–5pm

Lorraine's Antiques
Contact Ms Lorraine Wylie
✉ **84 Galgorm Road, Ballymena, Co Antrim, BT42 1AA** P
☎ 028 2564 5359
Stock Porcelain, jewellery
Fairs Ulster Antique and Fine Art Fair, Temple Patrick (Mar)

BALLYMONEY

McAfee Auctions (NIAVI)
Contact Mr Gerry McAfee
✉ **51 Main Street, Ballymoney, Co Antrim, BT53 6AN** P
☎ 028 2766 7676 Ⓕ 028 2766 7666
Est. 1992
Open Mon–Fri 9am–5.30pm Sat 9.30am–12.30pm
Sales Monthly sales of general antiques. Quarterly specialist Irish art sales
Catalogues Yes

BELFAST

Anderson's Auction Rooms
Contact Mr Flanaghan
✉ **Unit 7 Prince Regent Business Park, Prince Regent Road, Castlereagh, Belfast, Co Antrim, BT5 6QR**
☎ 028 9040 1888 Ⓕ 028 9040 1177
Est. 1979
Open Mon–Thur 9am–5pm Fri 9am–4pm late viewing Tues until 8pm
Sales Antiques and general every Wednesday, specialized Art and antiques sales 3 times per annum
Catalogues No

Antiquarian
Contact Mr Eric Lauro
✉ **67 Royal Avenue, Belfast, Co Antrim, BT1 1FE** P
☎ 028 9032 7301
Stock Guns, swords, wartime memorabilia, watches, clocks, stamps, coins
Open Mon–Sat 9am–5.30pm Thurs 10am–9pm
Services Valuations, repairs

Archives Antique Centre
Contact Mr Laurence Johnston
✉ **88 Donegal Pass, Belfast, Co Antrim, BT7 1BX** P
☎ 028 9023 2383 Ⓜ 07889 104719
Est. 1989 *Stock size* Large
Stock General antiques and collectables, pub memorabilia, light fittings
Open Mon–Sat 10am–5.30pm or by appointment
Fairs Culloden
Services Valuations

B B Collectables
Contact Mr Robert Holden
✉ **17 Sunnyside Park, Belfast, Co Antrim, BT7 3DT**
☎ 028 9087 8133
Ⓔ bbcollectables@yahoo.com
Ⓦ www.holden.free-online.co.uk
Est. 1993 *Stock size* Medium
Stock General antique furniture, collectables, curios
Open Trades only at fairs
Fairs Mary Magdalen Hall, Newman House

The Bell Gallery
Contact Nelson Bell
✉ **13 Adelaide Park, Belfast, Co Antrim, BT9 6FX** P
☎ 028 9066 2998 Ⓕ 028 9038 1524
Ⓔ bellgallery@btinternet.com
Ⓦ www.bellgallery.com
Est. 1964 *Stock size* Small
Stock Irish art and contemporary Irish artists, prints, silver, bog oak, jewellery, Irish books
Services Valuations

Bloomfield Auctions
Contact Mr George Gribben
✉ **288 Deersbridge Road, Belfast, Co Antrim, BT5 1DX** P
☎ 028 9045 6404 Ⓕ 028 9045 6404
Est. 1991
Open Mon–Fri 10am–5pm
Sales Antiques, fine art
Frequency Every Tues at 6.30pm
Catalogues No

Bookfinders
Contact Miss Mary Denver
✉ **47 University Road, Belfast, Co Antrim, BT7 1ND**
☎ 028 9032 8269
Est. 1985 *Stock size* Large
Stock Antiquarian, rare and second-hand books
Open Mon–Sat 10am–5.30pm
Services Book search

Cellar Antiques
Contact Jonathan Megaw
✉ **Belfast Castle, Antrim Road, Belfast, Co Antrim, BT15 5GR** P
☎ 028 9077 6925 ext 31
Est. 1984 *Stock size* Medium
Stock Jewellery, general antiques, collectables
Open Mon–Sat 12.30–10pm Sun 12.30–5pm
Services Valuations, restorations and repairs

The Collector
Contact William Seawright
✉ **42 Rosscoole Park, Belfast, Co Antrim, BT14 8JX**
☎ 028 9071 0115
Est. 1964 *Stock size* Large
Stock Antique coins, medals, cigarette cards, postcards
Open Trades through fairs only
Fairs All major fairs in Dublin and Belfast

Harry Hall's Bookshop
Contact Mr Bernard Hope
✉ **39 Gresham Street, Belfast, Co Antrim, BT1 1JL**
☎ 028 9024 1923
Est. 1970 *Stock size* Large
Stock Antiquarian and second-hand books
Open Mon–Sat 10am–5pm
Fairs Belfast Book Fair

Kennedy Wolfenden
Contact Mr John Irwin
✉ **218 Lisburn Road, Belfast, Co Antrim, BT9 6GD** P
☎ 028 9038 1775 Ⓕ 028 9038 1147
Ⓜ 07831 453038
Ⓔ eleanorwolfenden@hotmail.com
Ⓦ www.antiquesni.co.uk or www.kwauctionsni.co.uk
Est. 1974 *Stock size* Large
Stock Antique furniture, porcelain, jewellery, silver, paintings
Open Mon–Sat 9am–5.30pm
Services Valuations

Morgan's Auctions
Contact Mr Haliday or Mr Morgan
✉ **6 Duncrue Crescent, Duncrue Road, Belfast, Co Antrim, BT3 9BW** P
☎ 028 9077 1552 Ⓕ 028 9077 4503
Est. 1985
Open Mon 9am–6pm Tues–Fri 9am–5pm

Sales General and antiques
Frequency Every Tues 11am
Catalogues No

⊞ Oakland Antiques
Contact Donald McCluskey
✉ **135 Donegal Pass, Belfast, Co Antrim, BT7 1DS** Ⓟ
☎ 028 9023 0176 Ⓕ 028 9024 8144
Ⓜ 07831 176438
Ⓔ sales@oaklandni.com
Ⓦ www.oaklandni.com
Est. 1975 *Stock size* Large
Stock Georgian–Edwardian furniture, silver, clocks, glass, bronze, spelter, marble, English and Oriental porcelain, oil paintings, watercolours, longcase clocks
Open Mon–Sat 10am–5.30pm
Fairs Ulster Antique and Fine Art Fair
Services Deliveries to anywhere in Northern Ireland

⊞ Past & Present
Contact Trevor or Frances McNally
✉ **58–60 Donegal Pass, Belfast, Co Antrim, BT7 1BU** Ⓟ
☎ 028 9033 3137 Ⓕ 028 9033 3137
Est. 1985 *Stock size* Medium
Stock Edwardian–Victorian furniture, collectables
Open Tues–Sat 10.30am–5pm

⊞ Petite Antiques
Contact Charlie Tosh
✉ **123–137 York Street, Belfast, Co Antrim, BT15 1AB** Ⓟ
☎ 028 9064 4632 Ⓕ 028 9043 9068
Ⓜ 07850 280777
Ⓔ enquiries@petiteantiques.com
Ⓦ www.petiteantiques.com
Stock size Small
Stock Clocks, porcelain, jewellery
Open Mon–Fri 9am–5pm
Sat 9.30am–12.30pm
Services Valuations

⊞ Phoenix Gallery
Contact Vivienne Jackson
✉ **82 Donegal Pass, Belfast, Co Antrim, BT7 1BX** Ⓟ
☎ 028 9023 8246
Est. 2000 *Stock size* Large
Stock General antiques, art
Open Mon–Sat 10am–5pm

John Ross & Company (NIAVI)
Contact Mr Daniel Clarke
✉ **37 Montgomery Street, Belfast, Co Antrim, BT1 4NX** Ⓟ
☎ 028 9032 5448 Ⓕ 028 9033 3642
Ⓔ info@rossbelfast.com
Ⓦ www.rossbelfast.com
Est. 1919
Open Mon–Fri 9am–5pm late viewing Wed
Sales Quarterly sales of Irish paintings, monthly sales of antiques, weekly general sales
Frequency Weekly
Catalogues Yes

⊞ P & B Rowan (IADA)
Contact Peter or Briad Rowan
✉ **Carleton House, 92 Malone Road, Belfast, Co Antrim, BT9 5HP** Ⓟ
☎ 028 9066 6448 Ⓕ 028 9066 3725
Ⓔ peter@pbrowan.thegap.com
Est. 1973 *Stock size* Large
Stock Antiquarian books
Open By appointment
Fairs Irish Antiques Dealers Fair, PBFA (May/June)
Services Valuations

⊞ Stormont Antiques
Contact Mrs Ann McMurray
✉ **2a Sandown Road, Upper Newtownards Road, Belfast, Co Antrim, BT5 6GY** Ⓟ
☎ 028 9047 2586
Est. 1979 *Stock size* Large
Stock Jewellery, silver
Open Mon–Fri 11.30am–5pm
Sat 11.30am–4pm
Services Valuations, restorations

⊞ Terrace Antiques
Contact Peter or Anne Houston
✉ **441a Lisburn Road, Belfast, Co Antrim, BT9 7EY** Ⓟ
☎ 028 9066 3943
Ⓔ peter.houston@btclick.com
Est. 1985 *Stock size* Medium
Stock Jewellery, small furniture, linens, general antiques
Open Tues–Sat 10.30am–5pm
Fairs Ulster Antique and Fine Art Fair
Services Jewellery repairs, valuations, house clearances

⊞ The Wake Table
Contact Mr P Rosenberg
✉ **40 Donegal Pass, Belfast, Co Antrim, BT7 1BS** Ⓟ
☎ 028 9032 2147
Est. 1996 *Stock size* Medium
Stock General antiques
Open Mon–Sat 9am–5pm
Fairs Ulster Antique and Fine Art Fair

BUSHMILLS

⊞ Brian R Bolt Antiques (IADA)
Contact Brian or Helen Bolt
✉ **88 Ballaghmore Road, Portballintrae, Bushmills, Co Antrim, BT57 8RL** Ⓟ
☎ 028 2073 1129 Ⓕ 028 2073 1129
Ⓜ 07712 579802
Ⓔ brianbolt@antiques88.freeserve.co.uk
Est. 1979 *Stock size* Medium
Stock Antique and 20thC silver and objects of virtue, decorative arts, antique and 20thC glass, treen, general small items
Open Tues–Sat 11am–5.30pm or by appointment
Services Valuations, search, worldwide postal service

⊞ Causeway Books
Contact Mr D Speers
✉ **110 Main Street, Bushmills, Co Antrim, BT57 8QD**
☎ 028 2073 2596
Est. 1989 *Stock size* Medium
Stock General antiquarian books
Open Mon–Sat 10am–5.30pm

⊞ Dunluce Antiques and Crafts
Contact Ms Clare Ross
✉ **33 Ballytober Road, Bushmills, Co Antrim, BT57 8UU** Ⓟ
☎ 028 207 31140
Est. 1978 *Stock size* Small
Stock General antiques
Open Mon–Thurs 10am–6pm
Sat 2–6pm
Services Valuations and porcelain restoration

CARRICKFERGUS

⊞ Robert Christie Antiques (IADA)
Contact Robert Christie
✉ **The Courtyard, 38 Scotch Quarter, Carrickfergus, Co Antrim, BT38 7DP** Ⓟ
☎ 028 9336 1333 Ⓕ 028 9334 1149
Ⓜ 07802 968846
Est. 1976 *Stock size* Medium
Stock 18th–19thC furniture, clocks, silver and plate, pottery, porcelain
Open Tue–Sat 11am–5pm or by appointment

Fairs Northern Ireland Antiques Fair, Ulster Antique and Fine Art Fair
Services Valuations

Lennox Auctions and Valuers
Contact Mr A Lennox
The Basement, 41b Ellis Street, Carrickfergus, Co Antrim, BT38 8AY
028 9335 1522 or 028 9337 8527 (pm) F 028 9335 1522
Est. 1987
Open Mon–Fri 9.30am–5pm Sat 9.30am–1pm
Sales Weekly sales Thurs 7pm, viewing all day Thurs. Telephone for details. Also total house clearance sales
Frequency Weekly
Catalogues No

CARRYDUFF

Carryduff Group Ltd
Contact Mr Robert Jenkins
10 Comber Road, Carryduff, Co Antrim, BT8 8AM
028 9081 3775 F 028 9081 4518
Est. 1996
Open Mon–Fri 9am–6pm
Sales General antiques
Frequency Monthly
Catalogues Yes

GLARRYFORD

Antique Builders Suppliers
Contact Mr Hastings White
94 Duneoin Road, Drumminning, Glarryford, Co Antrim, BT44 9HH
028 2568 5444 M 07860 675908
E sales@whites-architecturalsalvage.com
W www.whites-architecturalsalvage.com
Est. 1983 ***Stock size*** Large
Stock Architectural salvage, Bangor blue slates, beams, tiles, stained glass windows, chimney pots, weathervanes, hardwood flooring, baths, etc
Open Mon–Sat 7am–11pm
Services Delivery

GLENGORMLEY

Acorns
Contact Mr P McComb
4 Portland Avenue, Glengormley, Co Antrim, BT36 5EY
028 9080 4100
Est. 1999 ***Stock size*** Medium
Stock Furniture, general antiques
Open Mon–Sat 9.30am–5.30pm
Services Local delivery

KELLS

Cottage Antiques
Contact Rachael Hiles
25 Greenfield Road, Kells, Co Antrim, BT42 3JL
028 2589 2169 M 07808 161052
Est. 1969 ***Stock size*** Large
Stock General antiques
Open Fri–Sat 1–5.30pm

LARNE

Bric-A-Brac
Contact Mr J McIlwaine
4 Riverdale, Larne, Co Antrim, BT40 1LB
028 2827 5657
Est. 1974 ***Stock size*** Large
Stock General antiques including clocks, furniture, oil lamps, jewellery, paintings
Open Mon–Sat 9am–5.30pm Tues 9am–2pm

Cobwebs
Contact Mrs D Knox
94c Agnew Street, Larne, Co Antrim, BT40 1RE
028 2826 7127
Stock General antiques, clocks, antique fireplaces, antique pine
Open Wed–Sat 11am–4.30pm

Colin Wilkinson and Co (IRRV)
Contact Mr Colin Wilkinson
The Auction Mart, 7 Point Street, Larne, Co Antrim, BT40 1HY
028 2826 0037 F 028 2826 0497
Est. 1900
Open Mon–Fri 9.30am–5pm
Sales General antiques, paintings, silver, porcelain
Frequency Monthly
Catalogues No

LISBURN

Trevor Falconer Antiques
Contact Trevor Falconer
51 Bridge Street, Lisburn, Co Antrim, BT28 1BZ
028 9260 5879
Est. 1984 ***Stock size*** Medium
Stock Antique country furniture, militaria, clocks, Irish pine
Open Mon–Sat 10am–5pm
Services Restorations and pine stripping

Jiri Books
Contact Jim and Rita Swindall
11 Mill Road, Lisburn, Co Antrim, BT27 5TT
028 9082 6443 F 028 9082 6443
E jiri.books@dnet.co.uk
Est. 1978 ***Stock size*** Medium
Stock Largely Irish interest, second-hand and antiquarian books
Open By appointment only
Fairs Second-hand and Antiquarian Bookfair (part of the Belfast Festival)
Services Book searches

Parvis (IADA)
Contact Parvis or Meriel Sigaroudinia
Mountain View House, 40 Sandy Lane, Ballyskeagh, Lisburn, Co Antrim, BT27 5TL
028 9062 1824 F 028 9062 3311
M 07801 347358
E parvissig@aol.com
W www.parvis.co.uk
Est. 1973 ***Stock size*** Large
Stock General antiques and fine art
Open By appointment at any time
Fairs IADA Exhibition, Northern Ireland Antiques Fair
Services Valuations, restorations, consultancy, own exhibitions

Temple Auctions Ltd
Contact Mr Robin Graham
133 Carryduff Road, Temple, Lisburn, Co Antrim, BT27 6YL
028 9263 8777 F 028 9263 8640
Est. 1981
Open Mon–Fri 9am–5.30 pm or by appointment
Sales General antiques, jewellery, paintings
Frequency Every 3 weeks
Catalogues No

Van-Lyn Antiques
Contact V or W Hastings
300 Comber Road, Lisburn, Co Antrim, BT27 6TA
028 9263 8358 07899 935990
Est. 1979 *Stock size* Medium
Stock General, antique furniture, porcelain, brass, glass, books
Open Mon–Sat 9am–9pm

NEWTOWNABBEY

MacHenry Antiques (IADA)
Contact Rupert or Anne MacHenry
1–7 Glen Road, Jordanstown, Newtownabbey, Co Antrim, BT37 0RY
028 9086 2036 028 9085 3281
07831 135226
rupertmachenry@ntlworld.com
Est. 1964 *Stock size* Medium
Stock 18th–19thC furniture, paintings
Open Mon–Sat 2–7pm or by appointment
Fairs Ulster Antique and Fine Art Fair
Services Valuation for insurance, probate and family division, restoration

Wilson's Auctions (NAVA, IAVI)
Contact Mr Richard Bell
22 Mallusk Road, Newtownabbey, Co Antrim, BT36 8PP
028 9034 2626 028 9034 2528
richardbell@wilsonsauctions.com
www.wilsonsauctions.com
Est. 1964
Open Mon–Fri 9am–6pm, viewing Sun noon–5pm
Sales Monthly sales on the last Mon of month at 7pm, also quarterly sales of Irish art. Other specialist sales throughout the year
Frequency Monthly
Catalogues Yes

PORTRUSH

Alexander Antiques
Contact Mr David Alexander
108 Dunluce Road, Portrush, Co Antrim, BT56 8NB
028 7082 2783 028 7082 2364
alexanderantique@aol.com
Est. 1973 *Stock size* Large
Stock Georgian–Edwardian furniture
Open Mon–Sat 10am–6pm
Services Valuations, restorations

Atlantic Antiques
Contact Mr Samuel Dickie
22 Portstewart Road, Portrush, Co Antrim, BT56 8EQ
028 7082 5988
Est. 1997 *Stock size* Medium
Stock General antiques
Open Mon Sat 11am–6pm Sun 2–6pm

Kennedy Wolfenden
Contact Miss Eleanor Wolfenden
86 Main Street, Portrush, Co Antrim, BT56 8BN
028 7082 2995 028 7082 5587
07831 453038
eleanorwolfenden@hotmail.com
www.kwauctionsni.co.uk
Est. 1974 *Stock size* Large
Stock Antique furniture, porcelain, jewellery, silver and paintings
Open Mon–Sat 11am–5.30pm Jul–Aug later
Services Valuations

CO ARMAGH

ARMAGH

Craobh Rua Rare Book (PBFA)
Contact Mr James Vallely
12 Woodford Gardens, Armagh, BT60 2AZ
028 3752 6938
Craobh@btinternet.com
Est. 1990 *Stock size* Medium
Stock Books, prints, selection of newspaper prints relating to 19thC Ireland
Open By appointment only
Fairs National Book Fair, Dublin
Services Catalogue, mail order

LOUGHALL

Heritage Antiques
Contact Ms Heather Teggart
Dispensary House, 88 Main Street, Loughall, Co Armagh, BT61 8HZ
028 3889 1314 07710 38557
Est. 1981 *Stock size* Small
Stock Clocks
Open Tues–Fri 2–5pm Sat 11am–5.30pm
Services Clock and barometer repairs

MOIRA

Four Winds Antiques
Contact Mr John Cairns
66a Main Street, Moira, Co Armagh, BT67 0LQ
028 9261 2226
07768 292369 (John) or 07713 081748 (Tina)
Est. 1994 *Stock size* Large
Stock Georgian–Edwardian furniture, porcelain, longcase and bracket clocks
Open Mon–Sat 10am–5.30pm or by appointment

Moyrah Antiques
Contact Mrs Dorothy Smith
98 Main Street, Moira, Craigavon, Co Armagh, BT67 0LH
028 9261 1272 07710 611037
Est. 1987 *Stock size* Medium
Stock General antiques, porcelain, jewellery
Open Mon–Sat 10.30am–5.30pm

PORTADOWN

Wilson's Auctions Ltd (Portadown) (NAVA, IAVI)
Contact Michael Tomalin
65 Seagoe Industrial Estate, Portadown, Craigavon, Co Armagh, T63 5QE
028 3833 6433 028 3833 6618
mtomalin@virgin.net
www.wilsons-auctions.com
Est. 1964
Open Mon–Fri 9am–6pm and on auction nights
Sales Antiques, fine art and disposal auctions Wed 7pm. Advisable to phone ahead for sale details
Frequency Phone for details
Catalogues Yes

CO DOWN

BALLYNAHINCH

Davidson Books
Contact Mr Arthur Davidson
34 Broomhill Road, Spa, Ballynahinch, Co Down, BT24 8QD
028 9756 2502 028 9756 2502
Est. 1959 *Stock size* Large

Stock Antiquarian books, especially Irish
Open By appointment only
Fairs Annual Belfast Second-hand and Antiquarian Bookfair
Services Valuations

The French Warehouse
Contact Heather Cowdy
72 Dunmore Road, Spa, Ballynahinch, Co Down, BT24 8PR
02897 561774
frenchwarehouse@nireland.com
www.french-warehouse.com
Est. 1988 ***Stock size*** Large
Stock Antique French beds, 19thC French furniture
Open By appointment
Services Shipping

BANGOR

Annville Antiques
Contact A Chambers
28 Grays Hill, Bangor, Co Down, BT20 3BB
028 9145 2522
Est. 1984 ***Stock size*** Small
Stock General antiques
Open Mon–Sat 10.30am–4.30pm

Balloo Moon Antiques
Contact Marie Erwin
Unit 30, Balloo Drive, Bangor, Co Down, BT19 7QY
028 9145 6886 028 9145 3183
Est. 1979 ***Stock size*** Large
Stock General antiques
Open Mon–Sat 10am–5.30pm

Pages Bookshop
Contact Mr Harry Hichens
12 High Street, Bangor, Co Down, BT20 5AY
028 9145 3061
Est. 1979 ***Stock size*** Large
Stock Rare antiquarian books
Open Mon–Sat 10am–5.30pm
Services Book-finding service

Todd Antiques
Contact Mrs E Heyes
30 Gray's Hill, Bangor, Co Down, BT20 3BB
028 9145 5850
Est. 1988 ***Stock size*** Medium
Stock Silver jewellery, clocks, small furniture items
Open Tues–Sat 9.30am–4.30pm closed Thurs
Services Clock and jewellery repairs

COMBER

Bobby Douglas
Contact Mr Bobby Douglas
31 Ballykeigle Road, Comber, Co Down, BT23 5SD
028 9752 8351
Est. 1964 ***Stock size*** Medium
Stock Irish Georgian furniture (pre-1837)
Open Any time by appointment
Services Valuations

Reflections
Contact Mr Nick Williams
9 Killinchy Street, Comber, Co Down, BT23 5AP
028 9187 0809 07748 948325
Est. 1994 ***Stock size*** Small
Stock 19thC country furniture, decorative items, clocks
Open Mon–Sat 10am–5pm
Services Restoration and French polishing

DONAGHADEE

Antiquarian Booksellers
Contact M C McAlister
Prospect House, 4 Millisle Road, Donaghadee, Co Down, BT21 0HY
028 9188 2990 028 9188 2990
rarebooks@phb.dnet.co.uk
www.booksulster.com
Est. 1981 ***Stock size*** Medium
Stock Antiquarian and out-of-print books, Ireland, travel, fine buildings and natural history specialities
Open Strictly by appointment only
Fairs Wellington Park (Nov)

Ferran's Antiques
Contact Justin or Vivien Ferran
2 Meetinghouse Street, Donaghadee, Co Down, BT21 0HJ
028 9188 2642 07711 085563
clanferran@hotmail.com
Est. 1988 ***Stock size*** Medium
Stock 18th–19thC furniture
Open By appointment only

DUNDONALD

Stacks Bookshop
Contact Mr Jim Tollerton
67 Comber Road, Dundonald, Co Down, BT16 0AE
028 9048 6880
Est. 1992 ***Stock size*** Medium
Stock Antiquarian Irish, religious, military and poetry books
Open Mon–Sat 10am–6pm
Fairs Annual Belfast Second-hand and Antiquarian Bookfair

GREY ABBEY

Archway Antiques
Contact Mrs Boo Hughes
Hoops Courtyard, Main Street, Grey Abbey, Newtownards, Co Down, BT22 2NE
028 4278 8889 07703 330900
Est. 1989 ***Stock size*** Large
Stock 18th–19thC porcelain, 19thC glass, jewellery, furniture, silver, kitchenware, linen, pictures
Open Wed Fri Sat 11am–5pm or by appointment
Fairs Ulster Antique and Fine Art Fair, Culloden
Services Valuations, house clearances

Phyllis Arnold Antiques
Contact Ms Phyllis Arnold
Hoops Courtyard, Grey Abbey, Newtownards, Co Down, BT22 2NE
028 4278 8199 028 9185 3322
Est. 1973 ***Stock size*** Medium
Stock Maps, prints, furniture, silver, general
Open Wed Fri Sat 11am–5pm
Services Framing, conservation

Old Forge Collectables
Contact David or Christine Eynon
5 Main Street, Grey Abbey, Co Down, BT22 2NE
028 9181 0422 028 9181 0422
07808 605644
info@oldforge.downtownfm.com
www.oldforgecollectables.co.uk
Est. 1989 ***Stock size*** Medium
Stock Very comprehensive selection of discontinued porcelain and china
Open Tues–Fri 1–5pm
Sat 11am–5pm
Mon by appointment only

Ann Shaw Antiques
Contact Ann Shaw
Hoops Courtyard, 79 Main Street, Grey Abbey, Newtownards, Co Down, BT22 2NE
028 9066 0975
Est. 1972 ***Stock size*** Medium

Stock Jewellery, silver, furniture, general
Open Wed Fri Sat 11am–5pm
Fairs Olympia, Grosvenor House
Services Upholstery

HILLSBOROUGH

Bowers' Auctioneers
Contact Mr Bowers
1 Dromore Road, Hillsborough, Co Down, BT26 6HS
028 9268 3840 Ⓕ 028 9268 9528
Ⓔ billy@bowersantiques.co.uk
Est. 1987
Open Mon–Fri 9am–5pm
Sales Antique furniture, fine art, house sales
Frequency Quarterly
Catalogues Yes

HOLYWOOD

Jacquart Antiques
Contact Mr Dan Uprichard
10–12 Hibernia Street, Holywood, Co Down, BT18 9JE
028 9042 6642 Ⓕ 028 9752 1109
Ⓜ 07831 548803
Ⓔ jacquart@nireland.com
Ⓦ www.jacquart.co.uk
Est. 1992 *Stock size* Large
Stock Imported French antiques, mainly 19th century furniture (walnut, oak), mirrors, rare items
Open Mon–Sat 10am–5.30pm or by appointment
Fairs Ulster Antique and Fine Art Fair
Services Interior-design item search

KILLYLEAGH

Tout Le Monde
Contact Mr Tony Forsyth
12–14 Shore Street, Killyleagh, Co Down, BT30 9QJ
028 4482 8509 Ⓕ 028 4482 8509
Ⓔ aforsyth@mac.com
Ⓦ wwwtoutlemonde.co.uk
Est. 1998 *Stock size* Medium
Stock Old country furniture, French, Chinese, Irish antiques
Open Mon–Sat 9am–5pm or by appointment

NEWTOWNARDS

Ballyalton House Architectural Antiques (SALVO)
Contact Leonard Cave
Ballyalton House, 39 Ballyrainey Road, Newtownards, Co Down, BT23 5AD
028 9181 3235 Ⓕ 028 9181 3235
Ⓔ andrew@ballyalton.freeserve.co.uk
Ⓦ www.ballyalton.freeserve.co.uk
Est. 1993 *Stock size* Large
Stock General architectural antiques, largest stock of bathrooms in Ireland. Newly quarried stone, granite
Open Mon–Sat 8am–6pm

Bangor Auctions
Contact Mr G Holden-Downes
11 Greenway Industrial Estate, Conlig, Newtownards, Co Down, BT23 7SU
028 9145 0494 Ⓕ 028 9127 5993
Ⓔ info@bangorauctions.co.uk
Ⓦ www.bangorauctions.co.uk
Est. 1991
Open Mon Tues Fri 9am–5pm
Sales General antiques sales every Thurs 6pm
Frequency Weekly
Catalogues Yes

Castle Antiques
Contact Peter Moore
6 Regency Manor, Newtownards, Co Down, BT23 8ZD
028 9181 5710 Ⓜ 07113 451440
Ⓔ info@castleantiques.co.uk
Ⓦ www.castleantiques.co.uk
Est. 1989 *Stock size* Medium
Stock Collectables, clocks
Open By appointment only

PORTAFERRY

Time & Tide Antiques (IADA, MAPH)
Contact Mr David Dunlop
Rock Angus House, 2 Ferry Street, Portaferry, Co Down, BT22 1PB
028 4272 8935 Ⓕ 028 4272 9825
Est. 1990 *Stock size* Large
Stock Clocks, barometers, nautical items, marine instruments, fine small furniture
Open Wed Fri Sat noon–5.30pm or by appointment
Fairs Ulster Antique and Fine Art Fair
Services Restorations

SAINTFIELD

Agar Antiques
Contact Rosie Agar
92 Main Street, Saintfield, Co Down, BT24 7AB
028 9751 1214
Est. 1991 *Stock size* Medium
Stock Victorian furniture, ceramics, jewellery, Oriental antiques, Delftware, lighting
Open Mon–Sat 11am–5pm
Services Valuations

Antiques at the Stile
Contact Mr Graham Hancock
52 Main Street, Saintfield, Co Down, BT24 7AB
028 9751 0844
Ⓜ 07831 587078
Est. 1989 *Stock size* Large
Stock Georgian–Edwardian furniture, clocks, porcelain
Open Tues–Sat 10am–5.30pm or by appointment
Services Valuations

Ashley Pine
Contact Ms Trudy Martin
88 Main Street, Saintfield, Co Down, BT24 7AB
028 9751 1855 Ⓕ 028 9751 1855
Ⓔ trudy@ashleypine.totalserve.co.uk
Ⓦ www.ceenet.co.uk/ashleypine
Est. 1995 *Stock size* Medium
Stock General antiques, furniture, kitchens built using salvaged materials
Open Mon 12.30–5pm Tues–Fri 10.30am–5pm Sat 10am–5.30pm
Fairs International Antique and Collectables Fair at RAF Swinderby

Attic Antiques
Contact Mr Reuben Doyle
90 Main Street, Saintfield, Co Down, BT24 7AB
028 9751 1057 Ⓜ 07803 169799
Est. 1980 *Stock size* Large
Stock General antiques, jewellery, bric-a-brac, large selection of stripped pine
Open Mon–Fri 10am–5pm Sat 10am–5.30pm
Fairs Swinderby
Services Export worldwide, house clearance

Attic Pine
Contact Mr Reuben Doyle
88 Main Street, Saintfield, Co Down, BT24 7AB

☎ 028 9751 1057
Est. 1996 *Stock size* Large
Stock Irish and continental pine, reclaimed furniture
Open Mon–Sat 10am–5pm
Services Stripping

Peter Francis Antiques
Contact Mr Peter Francis
92 Main Street, Saintfield, Co Down, BT24 7AD
☎ 028 9751 1214
Est. 1997 *Stock size* Small
Stock Irish glass, pottery and oriental antiques
Open Mon–Sat 11am–5pm
Services Valuations

Saintfield Antiques & Fine Books
Contact Mr Joseph Leckey
68 Main Street, Saintfield, Co Down, BT24 7AB
☎ 028 9752 8428 Ⓕ 028 9752 8428
Ⓔ home@antiquesireland.com
Ⓦ www.antiquesireland.com
Est. 1982 *Stock size* Medium
Stock Porcelain 1750–1850, silver (especially Georgian), British and European glass, antiquarian books
Open Thurs–Sat 11.30am–5pm or by appointment
Fairs All fairs organized by L&M Fairs Ltd
Services Book search

SEAPATRICK

Mill Court Antiques
Contact Ms Gillian Close
99 Lurgan Road, Seapatrick, Banbridge, Co Down, BT32 4NE
☎ 028 4066 2909
Est. 1979 *Stock size* Medium
Stock Furniture, ceramics, collectables, jewellery
Open Mon–Sat 11.30am–5.30pm closed Thurs
Services Valuations, restorations

CO FERMANAGH

BALLINAMALLARD

Ballindullagh Barn
Contact Mr Roy Armstrong
Ballindullagh, Ballinamallard, Co Fermanagh, BT94 2NY
☎ 028 6862 1802
Est. 1988 *Stock size* Large
Stock Pine country furniture
Open Mon–Sat 8am–6pm
Services Valuations, restorations

ENNISKILLEN

Cloughcor House Antiques
Contact Mr Ian Black
22 Shore Road, Enniskillen, Co Fermanagh, BT74 7EF
☎ 028 6632 4805 Ⓕ 028 6632 8828
Ⓜ 07774 758827
Est. 1964 *Stock size* Large
Stock Victorian–Edwardian furniture, Continental European pine, small silver wares
Open Mon–Sat 9.30am–5.30pm
Services Valuations, restorations and delivery

TEMPO

Marion Langham
Contact Marion Langham
Claranagh, Tempo, Co Fermanagh, BT94 3FJ
☎ 028 8954 1247
Ⓔ LL@ladymarion.co.uk
Ⓦ www.ladymarion.co.uk
Est. 1982 *Stock size* Large
Stock Belleek, paperweights
Open By appointment
Fairs NEC
Services Valuations, advice

CO LONDONDERRY

AGHADOWEY

Sarah Rose Antiques
Contact Mr Jim McCaughey
51 Ardreagh Road, Aghadowey, Coleraine, Co Londonderry, BT51 4DN
☎ 028 7086 8722
Ⓦ www.srantiques.co.uk
Est. 1989 *Stock size* Medium
Stock General antiques, pine
Open Mon–Sat 10am–5.30pm

COLERAINE

The Forge Antiques
Contact Margaret or Graham Walker
24–26 Long Commons, Coleraine, Co Londonderry, BT52 1LH
☎ 028 7035 1339
Est. 1966 *Stock size* Large
Stock Jewellery, silver, porcelain, furniture, clocks.
Open Mon–Sat 10am–5.30pm closed Thurs

Fountain Antique Studios & Workshop
Contact Ms Anne Morton
Fountain Villas, 31 Millburn Road, Coleraine, Co Londonderry, BT52 1QT
☎ 028 703 52260 Ⓕ 028 703 54268
Ⓜ 07771 525650
Est. 1989 *Stock size* Medium
Stock Kitchenware, furniture, stripped pine, porcelain
Open Mon–Sat 2–5.30pm or by appointment

KILREA

Beeswax Antiques
Contact Pat McNeill
6 Church Street, Kilrea, Co Londonderry, BT51 5QU
☎ 028 2564 1104
Est. 1987 *Stock size* Large
Stock Mahogany and pine furniture, general smalls
Open Mon–Sat 10.30am–5.30pm
Fairs Newark fair every other month
Services Valuations, restorations

LONDONDERRY

Foyle Antiques
Contact Mr John Helfery
The Old Farmhouse, 16 Whitehouse Road, Londonderry, BT48 0NE
☎ 028 7126 7626 Ⓕ 028 7126 7626
Ⓔ john@foyleantiques.com
Ⓦ foyleantiques.com
Est. 1984 *Stock size* Large
Stock Antiques and reproduction furniture. Showhouse with 16 furnished period rooms
Open Mon–Sat 10am–6pm Sun 2–6pm
Services Restorations, upholstery

Foyle Books
Contact Ken Thatcher or A Byrne
12 Magazine Street, Londonderry, BT48 6HH
☎ 028 7137 2530
Ⓔ ken@thatcher30.freeserve.uk
Est. 1989 *Stock size* Medium
Stock Antiquarian books, general, books on Derry and Donegal a speciality

Open Mon–Fri 11am–5pm
Sat 10am–5pm
Services Valuations

Marcus Griffin Specialists in Silver Jewellery
Contact Ms Marcus Griffin
2 London Street, Londonderry, BT48 6RQ
028 7130 9495
Est. 1974 *Stock size* Large
Stock General antiques, furniture, silver, fossils, objets d'art
Open Mon–Sat 10am–5pm
Fairs International Antique and Collectables Fair at RAF Swinderby

The Whatnot
Contact Ms Margot O'Dowd
22 Bishop Street, Londonderry, BT48 6TP
028 7128 8333
Est. 1984 *Stock size* Medium
Stock General antiques
Open Mon–Sat 11am–5pm

PORTSTEWART

Irish Art Group (PTA)
Contact Michael Hughes
49 The Promenade, Portstewart, Co Londonderry, BT55 7AE
028 7083 4600 F 028 7083 4600
E michael@irishartgroup.com
W www.irishartgroup.com
Est. 1982 *Stock size* Large
Stock Irish art, prints, collectables, maps, postcards, cigarette cards, fountain pens
Open Mon–Sat 11am–1pm 2–5pm
Fairs NEC Spring & Autumn
Services Catalogue (6 times a year)

CO TYRONE

AUGHNACLOY

Lucy Forsythe Antiques
Contact Albert or Lucy Forsythe
The Old Rectory, 24 Carnteel Road, Aughnacloy, Co Tyrone, BT69 6DU
028 855 57522 F 028 855 57522
E jforsythe@mac.com
Est. 1962 *Stock size* Large
Stock French provincial farmhouse tables, Irish pine country furniture, Chinese rural antiques
Open Mon–Sat 9am–5pm or by appointment

BALLYCOLMAN

Melmount Auctions
Contact Mr Michael McNamee
Unit C, Ballycolman Industrial Estate, Ballycolman, Co Tyrone, BT82 9PH
028 7138 2223
Est. 1992
Open Mon–Fri 9.30am–5.30pm
Thurs 9.30am–1pm
Sales General antiques
Frequency Weekly
Catalogues Yes

BALLYGAWLEY

Keepers Cottage Antique Irish Pine
Contact Ann Ross
101 Kiloleeshill Road, Ballygawley, Co Tyrone, BT70 2HX
028 8556 8765
Est. 1987 *Stock size* Medium
Stock Antique Irish pine and country furniture
Open Mon–Sat 9am–5pm
Services Valuations

Old Mill Antiques
Contact Michael and Rose Lippett
The Old Mill, Tulnavern Road, Ballygawley, Co Tyrone, BT70 2HH
028 855 67470 F 028 855 67466
M 07831 866235
W www.oldmillantiques.ulsterguide.com
Est. 1970 *Stock size* Large
Stock General antiques
Open Mon–Sat 10am–5.30pm
Thurs 10am–9pm
Fairs Royal Dublin Society Show, King's Hall, Balmoral
Services Valuations

COOKSTOWN

Cookstown Antiques (RICS)
Contact Mrs Glynis Jebb
16 Oldtown Street, Cookstown, Co Tyrone, BT80 8EF
028 8676 5279 F 028 8676 2946
M 07808 0788417
Est. 1980 *Stock size* Small
Stock Jewellery, china, small antiques, militaria including WWI medals, coins
Open Thurs Fri 2–5.30pm
Sat 10.30am–5.30pm
Services Valuations

MOY

Moy Antique Pine
Contact Mr Barry MacNeice
15 Charlemont Street, Moy, Dungannon, Co Tyrone, BT71 7SG
028 8778 9909 F 028 8778 4895
M 07909 538784
E macneice@fsnet.co.uk
Est. 1974 *Stock size* Large
Stock General antiques
Open Mon–Sat 9am–6pm
Services Freestanding kitchens made with antique wood

Moy Antiques
Contact Mr Lawrence MacNeice
12 The Square, Moy, Dungannon, Co Tyrone, BT71 7SG
028 8778 4895/4755
F 028 8778 4895
E sales@moyantiques.freeserve.co.uk
Est. 1979 *Stock size* Large
Stock General antique furniture, garden statues, original marble fireplaces
Open Mon–Sat 9.30am–6pm
Fairs Newark, Ardingly
Services Valuations

OMAGH

Dromore Road Auction Rooms
Contact Mr Oliver Gormley
Unit 3, Dromore Road Industrial Estate, Omagh, Co Tyrone, BT78 1QZ
028 8224 7738 F 028 8225 2797
E info@gormleys.ie
W www.gormleys.ie
Est. 1989
Open Mon–Sat 9am–6pm
Sales General sales every Thurs, regular sales of antiques and paintings
Frequency Weekly
Catalogues Yes

Gormley Antique Gallery
Contact Mr Oliver Gormley
Unit 4, Dromore Road, Omagh, Co Tyrone, BT79 IQ2

☎ 028 8225 2797 Ⓕ 028 8225 2797
Est. 1989 *Stock size* Large
Stock General antiques and paintings
Open Mon–Sat 9am–6pm
Tues Fri 9am–8.30pm
Fairs Newark
Services Valuations, restorations

Kelly Antiques
Contact Mr Louis Kelly
✉ **Mullaghmore House, Old Mountfield Road, Omagh, Co Tyrone, BT79 7EX** Ⓟ
☎ 028 8224 2314 Ⓕ 028 8225 0262
Ⓔ sales@kellyantiques.com
Ⓦ www.kellyantiques.com
Est. 1936 *Stock size* Large
Stock Period fireplaces, hardwood furniture, bedroom suites, tables, chairs, lighting
Open Mon–Fri 10am–7pm
Sat 10am–5pm
Services Restorations, private auctions, due to open an international college teaching restoration techniques

Viewback Auctions
Contact Mr G Simpson
✉ **8–10 Castle Place, Omagh, Co Tyrone, BT78 5ER** Ⓟ
☎ 028 8224 6271 Ⓕ 028 8224 6271
Ⓜ 0776 0275247
Ⓔ viewback@talk21.com
Est. 1979 *Stock size* Large
Stock General antiques
Open Mon–Sat 10am–6pm
Fairs Newark
Services Auctioneering

STEWARTSTOWN

Silversaddle Antiques
Contact Vivian Smith
✉ **West Street, Stewartstown, Co Tyrone, BT71 5HT** Ⓟ
☎ 028 8773 8088
Est. 1900 *Stock size* Large
Stock Georgian–Edwardian furniture, clocks, Victorian chandeliers
Open Mon–Sat 10.30am–6pm
Thurs until 9pm
Services Valuations, restorations

P J Smith (Fair Trades)
Contact Patrick Smith
✉ **1 North Street, Stewartstown, Co Tyrone, BT71 5JE** Ⓟ
☎ 028 8773 8071
Ⓦ ww.pjsmith-antique-fireplace.co.uk
Est. 1979 *Stock size* Large
Stock Antique fireplaces (largest stock in Ireland), stained glass, beds
Open Mon–Fri 10.30am–1pm
1.40–6pm Thurs until 9pm
Sat 10.30am–6pm
Services Restorations

REPUBLIC OF IRELAND

CO CARLOW

BORRIS

Joe Dunne Auctioneers & Valuers (IAVI)
Contact Joe Dunne
Borris, Co Carlow, Ireland
050 373191 F 050 373536
E movehome@dunnesofborris.com
W www.dunnesofborris.com
Est. 1984
Open Tues–Sat 9.30am–5pm
Sales Antiques and general household, antiques sales twice yearly
Frequency Every 6 weeks
Catalogues Yes

CO CAVAN

BALLINEA

F J McAvenues & Son
Contact Dennis McAvenues
7 Lower Bridge Street, Ballinea, Co Cavan, Ireland
04995 22204
Est. 1964 *Stock size* Large
Stock General antiques, furniture, jewellery, silver, clocks
Open Mon–Fri 2–6pm Sat Sun 11am–5pm
Services Valuations

CO CLARE

CLARECASTLE

The Antique Loft
Contact Paul Walsh or Paul Deloughrey
Barrack Street, Clarecastle, Co Clare, Ireland
065 6841969 F 065 6841969
Est. 1991 *Stock size* Large
Stock Victorian furniture, collectables, Persian rugs
Open Mon–Sat 9am–6.30pm Sun by appointment only

ENNIS

Tony Honan
Contact Mr Tony Honan
14 Abbey Street, Ennis, Co Clare, Ireland
065 682 8137
Est. 1974 *Stock size* Large
Stock Clocks, oil lamps
Open Mon–Sat 10am–6pm

CO CORK

BALLYDEHOB

Schull Books
Contact Barbara or Jack O'Connell
Ballydehob, Co Cork, Ireland
028 37317 F 028 37317
E schullbooks@eircom.net
W www.schullbooks.com
Est. 1981 *Stock size* Medium
Stock Antiquarian and second-hand books, military history a speciality
Open June–Sept Mon–Sat 11am–6pm other times by appointment
Fairs All major Irish book fairs
Services Valuations

BANDON

Galvins Antiques
Contact Maisie Galvin
Clonakilty Road, Bandon, Co Cork, Ireland
023 20983 F 023 20555
Est. 1991 *Stock size* Medium
Stock Antiques and collectables
Open Mon–Sat 10am–5pm closed 1–2pm

BANTRY

The Bantry Bookstore (IAB)
Contact Michael Carroll
New Street, Bantry, Co Cork, Ireland
027 50064 F 027 52042
E bantrybk@iol.ie
W www.irelandbooks.com www.bantrybk.com
Est. 1992 *Stock size* Large
Stock Antiquarian books, including rare Irish books, Irish history books, collectors' items, second-hand books
Open Mon–Sun 9.30am–5.30pm closed Sun 15 Oct–15 Jun
Services Restorations

CHARLEVILLE

Fortlands Antiques (IADA)
Contact Mary or Carol O'Connor
Fortlands, Charleville, Co Cork, Ireland
063 81295 F 063 81295
Est. 1974 *Stock size* Large
Stock Georgian–Victorian furniture, silver, brass, china, objets d'art
Open Mon–Sat 11am–5pm Sun 2–5pm
Fairs Irish Antique Dealers' Fair
Services Valuations, restorations

CLONAKILTY

Boyle's Antiques
Contact Joyce Boyle
35 Ashe Street, Clonakilty, Co Cork, Ireland
02334 222
Est. 1993 *Stock size* Small
Stock Gilt mirrors, overmantels, jewellery
Open Mon–Sat 10am–6pm closed Wed pm Jan–Mar Thurs–Sat only
Services Valuations

CORK

Antiques & Curios Centre
Contact Liam Hurley
No 3 Adelaide Street, Cork, Ireland
021 439 5320
Est. 1987 *Stock size* Large
Stock Country furniture, general antiques
Open Mon–Sat 9.30am–5.30pm

Devonshire Antiques
Contact John O'Brien
9 Carroll's Quay, Cork, Ireland
021 450 9300
M 0863 081943
Est. 1995 *Stock size* Large
Stock Furniture, fireplaces
Open Mon–Sat 10am–5.30pm

Georgian Antiques (LAPADA, CINOA, IADA)
Contact Patrick Jones
21 Lavitts Quay, Cork, Ireland
021 427 8153 F 021 427 9365
M 0872 563721
E info@georgianantiquesltd.com
W www.georgianantiquesltd.com
Est. 1998 *Stock size* Large
Stock 18th–19thC Irish, English and Continental European furniture, decorations
Open Mon–Fri 2–5pm Sat 10am–5pm
Fairs Irish Antique Dealers' Fair, The Annual Cork Antiques Fair

⊞ Goodwood Pine Furniture
Contact Tedge or Cathy Mullane
✉ **Rosebank, Old Blackrock Road, Cork, Ireland** 🅿
☎ 021 431 8418 ⓕ 021 431 8418
Est. 1990 *Stock size* Large
Stock General antiques
Open Mon–Fri 9am–6pm
Sat 10am–2pm

⊞ Goodwoods
Contact Mr T O'Mullane
✉ **Rosebank, Old Blackrock Road, Cork, Ireland** 🅿
☎ 021 431 8418 ⓕ 021 431 8418
Est. 1992 *Stock size* Medium
Stock Architectural salvage, doors, baths, fireplaces, sinks, etc
Open Mon–Fri 9am–6pm
Sat 10am–2pm

⊞ Helga's Antiques
Contact Helga McCarthy Cleary or John McCarthy
✉ **7 Cross Street, Cork, Ireland** 🅿
☎ 021 427 0034 ⓕ 021 427 4222
ⓜ 0868 727075
Est. 1994 *Stock size* Large
Stock General antiques
Open Mon–Sat 9.30am–5pm or by appointment
Services Valuations, restorations, French polishing

⊞ Ann McCarthy
Contact Ann McCarthy
✉ **2 Paul's Lane, Huguenot Quarter, Cork, Ireland** 🅿
☎ 021 427 3755
Est. 1985 *Stock size* Large
Stock Silver, linen, china, glass, lace
Open Mon–Sat 10am–6pm
Services Valuations

⊞ Mills Antiques
Contact David Coon or Orla Clarke
✉ **3 Paul's Lane, Huguenot Centre, Cork, Ireland** 🅿
☎ 021 427 3528
ⓔ david-coon@eircom.net
Est. 1981 *Stock size* Large
Stock General small items, small furniture, paintings, prints, objets d'art
Open Mon–Sat 10am–6pm
Services Painting and frame restoration

⊞ Diana O'Mahony Antiques & Jewellery (IADA, BGA)
Contact Diana or Niamh O'Mahony
✉ **8 Winthrop Street, Cork, Ireland** 🅿
☎ 021 427 6599
Est. 1970 *Stock size* Large
Stock Victorian jewellery, diamond pieces, Georgian–Victorian silver, Cork and Dublin silver, small furniture
Open Mon–Sat 9.30am–5.30pm
Services Valuations, pearl restringing, remounting

⊞ Royal Carberry Books
Contact Gerald Feehan
✉ **36 Beechwood Park, Ballinlough, Cork, Ireland** 🅿
☎ 021 429 4191 ⓕ 021 429 4191
ⓔ mgfeehan@teircom.net
Est. 1976 *Stock size* Medium
Stock Antiquarian and out-of-print books, books of Irish interest, postcards
Open By appointment only
Fairs All major Irish book fairs
Services Valuations and book search facility

⊞ Stokes Clocks and Watches Ltd
Contact Philip Stokes
✉ **48 MacCurtain Street, Cork, Ireland** 🅿
☎ 021 455 1195 ⓕ 021 450 9125
ⓔ stokesclocks@eircom.net
Est. 1969 *Stock size* Large
Stock Clocks, watches, barometers
Open Mon–Fri 9.15am–6pm
Sat 10am–5pm
Services Valuations, restorations, repairs

⊞ Victoria's Antiques
Contact Ms Frances Lynch
✉ **2 Oliver Plunkett Street, Cork, Ireland** 🅿
☎ 021 427 2752 ⓕ 021 427 8814
Est. 1987 *Stock size* Large
Stock Jewellery, silver gifts, small items of furniture
Open Mon–Sat 10.30am–6pm
Services Valuations, restorations

Joseph Woodward & Sons Ltd (IAVI)
Contact Tom Woodward
✉ **26 Cook Street, Cork, Ireland** 🅿
☎ 021 427 3327 ⓕ 021 427 2891
ⓔ auctions@woodward.ie
ⓦ www.woodward.ie
Est. 1883
Open Mon–Fri 9am–5.30pm
Sales Antiques, paintings, silver, porcelain. Twice-yearly specialist Irish silver auctions. Internet catalogues available
Frequency Monthly
Catalogues Yes

FERMOY

⊞ Country Furniture
Contact Seamus Kirby
✉ **Johnstown, Fermoy, Co Cork, Ireland** 🅿
☎ 025 38244 ⓕ 025 38244
ⓜ 0868 126883
Est. 1990 *Stock size* Large
Stock Antique fireplaces, pine, salvage
Open Mon–Sat 9am–6pm
Sun 2–6pm other times by appointment only
Services Pine stripping

KINSALE

⊞ Linda's Antiques
Contact Linda or Laura Walsh
✉ **Main Street, Kinsale, Co Cork, Ireland**
☎ 021 477 4754 ⓕ 021 477 7582
ⓜ 0872 502467
ⓔ lindasjewellery@eircom.net
Est. 1992
Stock Jewellery, prints, silver, books, prints, oil paintings, watercolours, porcelain, objets d'art
Open Mon–Sat 10.30am–5.30pm
Sun 2–5.30pm Jan Feb Mar close 4.30pm
Fairs Cork Antiques Fair

LEAP

⊞ Ovne Antique Stoves
Contact Tom Keane or Claire Graham
✉ **Main Street, Leap, Co Cork, Ireland** 🅿
☎ 028 34917 ⓜ 0868 555635
ⓔ info@ovnestoves.com
ⓦ www.ovnestoves.com
Est. 1990 *Stock size* Medium
Stock Antique stoves from all around the world 1840–1950
Open Mon–Sat 10am–6pm

MALLOW

Linda's Antiques (IADA)
Contact Linda or Brendan Walsh
1st Floor, 151 West End, Mallow, Co Cork, Ireland
021 477 4754 F 021 477 7582
M 0872 502467
E lindasjewellery@eircom.net
Est. 1974 *Stock size* Large
Stock Antique jewellery, silver, porcelain, paintings, prints, books
Open Thurs–Sat 10.30am–5.30pm
Fairs Annual Cork Antiques Fair
Services Valuations, proprietor is a gemologist

McMahon's Antiques
Contact Mr McMahon
Dromagh, Mallow, Co Cork, Ireland
029 78119
Est. 1977 *Stock size* Large
Stock Pre-War, general antiques
Open Mon–Sat 10am–9pm Sun noon–9pm

SCHULL

Fuschia Books
Contact Ms Mary Mackey
Main Street, Schull, Co Cork, Ireland
028 28016 F 028 28016
E fuschiabooks@eircom.net
W www.fuschiabooks.com
Est. 1984 *Stock size* Small
Stock Antiquarian stock, especially Irish books, prints
Open Mon–Sat summer 10am–6pm winter 11am–4pm
Services Valuations and book searches

SKIBEREEN

Moylurg Antiques
Contact Timothy MacDermot-Roe
The Mall, Castletownshend, Skibbereen, Co Cork, Ireland
028 36396 F 028 36396
E moylurgantiques@eircom.net
Est. 1993 *Stock size* Small
Stock General, furniture, pictures, porcelain, Indian furniture and artefacts
Open May–Sept Tues–Sun 10.30am–7pm Mon by appointment only
Services Valuations

CO DONEGAL

BUNDORAN

Vincent McGowan Antiques
Contact Mr Vincent McGowan
2–3 Main Street, Bundoran, Co Donegal, Ireland
072 41536
Est. 1981 *Stock size* Medium
Stock Georgian–Edwardian furniture, small items, clocks, jewellery, Belleek
Open By appointment
Services Valuations, restorations

CARNDONAGH

The Bookshop
Contact Mr Michael Herron
Court Place, Pound Street, Carndonagh, Co Donegal, Ireland
077 74389 F 077 74313
Est. 1987 *Stock size* Large
Stock Irish interest, science, 19thC antiquarian section, general books
Open Mon–Fri 2–6pm Sat 11am–6pm Sun 2–6pm
Fairs Annual Belfast Second-hand and Antiquarian Bookfair
Services Catalogues 4 or 5 a year

DONEGAL

Millcourt Antiques
Contact Tom Dooley
Millcourt Mews, Donegal, Ireland
073 23222 F 073 23274
Est. 1995 *Stock size* Medium
Stock Georgian–Victorian furniture
Open Mon–Sat 9.30am–5.30pm
Services Valuations

Sean Thomas Antiques (IADA)
Contact Sean or Noreen Thomas
Killymard House, Donegal, Ireland
073 35024
Est. 1961 *Stock size* Small
Stock General
Open Mon–Sat 10am–6pm
Services Valuations

DUNFANAGHY

The Gallery
Contact Alan and Moira Harley
Dunfanaghy, Co Donegal, Ireland
074 36224
Est. 1968 *Stock size* Medium
Stock Silver, brass, Asian antiques, pottery, porcelain, jewellery, clocks, old prints, maps
Open Mon–Sat 10am–7pm
Services Picture framing

CO DUBLIN

BLACKROCK

Adams Blackrock (IAVI)
Contact Ms Martina Noonan
38 Main Street, Blackrock, Co Dublin, Ireland
01 288 5146 F 01 288 7820
E info@adamsblackrock.com
Est. 1947
Open Mon–Fri 9.30am–5.30pm
Sales 20 furniture fine art auctions per annum, 4 Irish and Continental European paintings auctions per annum, 4 jewellery and silver sales per annum, regular house contents sales
Catalogues Yes

De Burca Rare Books (IADA, ABA, PBFA)
Contact Mr Eamon de Burca
Cloonagashel, 27 Priory Drive, Blackrock, Co Dublin, Ireland
01 288 2159 F 01 283 4080
E deburca@indigo.ie
Stock Irish antiquarian fine books, maps, prints, manuscripts
Open Mon–Fri 9am–6pm Sat 10am–1pm
Fairs London and New York Book Fairs
Services Mail-order service, book search, valuations, book binding

HOK Fine Art (IAVI)
Contact Ms Sarah Kenny
4 Main Street, Blackrock, Co Dublin, Ireland
01 288 1000 F 01 288 0838
E fineart@hok.ie
W www.hok.ie
Est. 1944
Open 8.45am–5.45pm
Sales Biannual fine art and furniture sales held at Royal Dublin Society. Blackrock fine art and furniture sales Wed every 6 weeks. House contents sales countrywide. Phone for details
Frequency 6 weeks
Catalogues Yes

Peter Linden Oriental Rugs and Carpets (IADA)
Contact Mr Peter Linden
15 George's Avenue, Blackrock, Co Dublin, Ireland
01 288 5875 F 01 283 5616
lindorient@hotmail.com
www.peterlinden.com
Est. 1980 *Stock size* Large
Stock Oriental rugs, carpets, Kilims, tapestries
Open Tues–Sat 10am–5.30pm
Fairs Irish Antique Dealers' Fair
Services Valuations, restorations

Treasure Chest Antiques
Contact Mr Norman Ludgate
49 Main Street, Blackrock, Co Dublin, Ireland
01 288 9961 M 0872 831027
treasurechest@iol.ie
Est. 1992
Stock Lighting, small furniture, silver, jewellery, general antiques
Open Mon–Fri 11am–6pm Sat 11.30am–6pm closed Thurs

DUBLIN

James Adam
26 St Stephen's Green, Dublin 2, Ireland
01 676 0261 F 01 662 4725
info@jamesadam.ie
www.jamesadam.ie
Est. 1887
Sales Specialist sales throughout the year of Irish art, vintage wine, militaria, toys and ceramics, phone for details
Catalogues Yes

Anthony Antiques Ltd (IADA, CINOA)
Contact Jeffrey or Roger Dell
7 Molesworth Street, Dublin 2, Ireland
01 677 7222 F 01 677 7222
anthonyantiques@oceanfree.net
www.irelandantiques.com/anthony
Est. 1963 *Stock size* Large
Stock Decorative antique furniture, mirrors, brass, chandeliers
Open Mon–Sat 9am–6pm
Fairs Irish Antique Dealers' Fair

Antique Prints (IADA)
Contact Hugh or Anne Iremonger
16 South Anne Street, Dublin 2, Ireland
01 671 9523 or 01 269 8373
antiqueprints_irl@yahoo.ie
Est. 1969
Stock 17th–20thC prints, maps, books, incunabulae
Open Mon–Sat 11am–5.30pm

Architectural Antiques and Salvage
Contact Mr S Bird or Mr S Flanagan
31 South Richmond Street, Dublin, Ireland
01 478 4245 F 01 478 4245
www.arcantiques.ie
Est. 1996 *Stock size* Medium
Stock Architectural salvage, fonts, statues, fireplaces, ecclesiastical robes
Open Mon–Sat 10am–6pm

Architectural Classics
Contact Mr Niall McDonagh
South Gloucester Street, Dublin 2, Ireland
086 8207700 F 01 6773318
info@architecturalclassics.com
www.architecturalclassics.com
Est. 1986 *Stock size* Large
Stock Antique lighting, door furniture, period fireplaces, garden statuary
Open Mon–Fri 9am–5.30pm Sat 9am–2pm
Fairs IADA Fairs, Dublin
Services Valuations, restorations

Benezet Antiques
Contact Ms Sarah Halpin
101a Rathgar Road, Dublin 6, Ireland
01 490 8361 F 01 490 8361
Est. 1979 *Stock size* Medium
Stock Gilt furnishings, furniture, paintings
Open Mon–Sat 10am–5pm or by appointment
Services Valuations

Christy Bird
Contact Christy Bird
32 South Richmond Street, Dublin, Ireland
01 475 4049 F 01 475 8708
christybird@ireland.com
christybird.com
Est. 1945 *Stock size* Large
Stock Antique furniture
Open Mon–Sat 10am–6pm
Services Restorations

Lorcan Brereton (IADA)
Contact Mr Diarmuid Brereton
29 South Anne Street, Dublin 2, Ireland
01 677 1462 F 01 677 1125
Est. 1912
Stock Antique and modern jewellery, silver
Open Mon–Sat 9.15am–5.30pm
Fairs IADA
Services Valuations, restorations

Edward Butler (IADA)
Contact Peter or Elizabeth Bateman
14 Bachelor's Walk, Dublin 1, Ireland
01 873 0296 F 01 873 0296
M 0872 486916
bateman@iol.ie
www.edwardbutlerantiques.com
Est. 1850 *Stock size* Large
Stock Nautical and scientific instruments, 18th–19thC furniture, paintings, clocks
Open Mon–Fri 10.30am–4.45pm
Fairs Irish Antique Dealers' Fair

Cathach Books
Contact Mr Enda Cunningham
10 Duke Street, Dublin 2, Ireland
01 671 8676 F 01 671 5120
cathach@rarebooks.ie
www.rarebooks.ie
Est. 1964 *Stock size* Medium
Stock Irish 20thC literature, rare signed editions, Irish history, antiquarian maps
Open Mon–Sat 9.30am–5.45pm
Services Valuations

Caxton Prints (IADA CINOA)
Contact Ronan Teevan or Liam Fitzpatrick
63 Patrick Street, Dublin 8, Ireland
01 453 0060 F 01 453 0060
M 0872 429799
caxton@e-merge.ie
Est. 1989 *Stock size* Small
Stock Old Masters, 17th–18thC decorative prints
Open Mon–Sat 10.30am–5.30pm
Fairs Irish Antique Dealers' Fair
Services Valuations

Chapters Book and Music Store (BA)
Contact Mr William Kinsella
108–109 Middle Abbey Street, Dublin 1, Ireland

☎ 01 872 3297 (books) 01 873 0484 (music) Ⓕ 01 872 3044
Ⓔ chapterbooksandmusicstore@eircom.net
Est. 1983 *Stock size* Large
Stock Antiquarian books, collectable vinyls, CDs, Irish music
Open Mon–Sat 9.30am–6.30pm Thurs 9.30am–8pm Sun noon–6.30pm

Conlan Antiques
Contact Mr Michael Conlan
✉ **22 Lower Clanbrassil Street, Dublin 8, Ireland** Ⓟ
☎ 01 453 7323
Est. 1970 *Stock size* Large
Stock General antiques, prints, watercolours, paintings, clocks, fireplaces
Open Mon–Sat 10am–6pm

Courtville Antiques (IADA, CINOA)
Contact Ms Grainne Pierse
✉ **Powerscourt Townhouse Centre, South William Street, Dublin 2, Ireland** Ⓟ
☎ 01 679 4042 Ⓕ 01 679 4042
Est. 1964 *Stock size* Large
Stock Victorian and Art Deco jewellery, silver, paintings, decorative items
Open Mon–Sat 10am–6pm
Fairs Irish Antique Dealers' Fair
Services Commission purchasing

Delphi Antiques
Contact Mr Declan Corrigan
✉ **Powerscourt Townhouse Centre, South William Street, Dublin 2, Ireland** Ⓟ
☎ 01 679 0331
Ⓔ declancorrigan@netscape.net declancorrigan@sothebys.com
Est. 1987 *Stock size* Large
Stock Georgian–Edwardian jewellery, Continental and European ceramics, Irish Belleek
Open Mon–Sat 10.30am–5.30pm
Services Restorations

Michael Duffy Antiques
Contact Mr Michael Duffy
✉ **9–10 Parnell Street, Dublin 1, Ireland** Ⓟ
☎ 01 872 6928 Ⓕ 01 872 6928
Ⓜ 0872 562326
Est. 1949 *Stock size* Medium
Stock General Victorian antiques
Open Mon–Sat 10am–5pm

Samuel Elliot
Contact Mr Samuel Elliot
✉ **12 Fade Street, Dublin 2, Ireland** Ⓟ
☎ 01 671 1174
Est. 1961 *Stock size* Small
Stock Pocket watches, wrist watches, Rolex
Open Mon–Fri 9.30am–6pm Sat by appointment
Services Valuations, restorations

John Farrington Antiques (IADA)
Contact Mr John Farrington
✉ **32 Drury Street, Dublin 2, Ireland** Ⓟ
☎ 01 679 1899
Ⓔ johnfarringtonantiques@dircon.net
Est. 1979 *Stock size* Large
Stock Fine-quality jewellery, silver, gilt mirrors
Open Tues–Sat 10.30am–5pm
Fairs Dublin Horse Show, Irish Antique Dealers' Fair

Flanagans Ltd
Contact Brian or Peter Flanagan
✉ **Deerpark Road, Mount Merrion, Dublin, Ireland** Ⓟ
☎ 01 288 0218 Ⓕ 01 288 1336
Ⓔ flan@iol.ie
Ⓦ www.theflanagan.com
Est. 1974 *Stock size* Large
Stock Antique pianos, 19thC furniture
Open Mon–Sat 10am–6pm Thurs 10am–9pm
Services Restorations

Fleury Antiques (IADA)
Contact C or D Fleury
✉ **57 Francis Street, Dublin 8, Ireland**
☎ 01 473 0878 Ⓕ 01 473 0371
Ⓔ fleuryantiques@eircom.ie
Ⓦ www.fleuryantiques.com
Est. 1979 *Stock size* Large
Stock 18th–19thC furniture, sculptures, paintings, decorative objects, porcelain, silver
Open Mon–Sat 9am–6pm

Herman & Wilkinson (IAVI)
Contact Mr David Herman or Mr Ray Wilkinson
✉ **161 Lower Rathmines Road, Dublin 6, Ireland** Ⓟ
☎ 01 497 2245 Ⓕ 01 496 2245
Ⓔ hwauct@indigo.ie
Est. 1970
Open Mon–Fri 9.30am–5.30pm
Sales Monthly antiques and fine art sales, Thurs 10am, viewing Wed 10am–9pm
Frequency Monthly
Catalogues Yes

Patrick Howard Antiques (IADA)
Contact Patrick Howard
✉ **60 Francis Street, Dublin 8, Ireland** Ⓟ
☎ 01 473 1126 Ⓕ 01 473 1126
Ⓜ 0872 331870
Ⓔ phowardantiques@hotmail.com
Stock size Large
Stock Decorative arts, furniture, paintings, prints and lighting
Open Mon–Sat 9.30am–6pm
Fairs Irish Antique Dealers' Fair

The Jewel Casket (IADA)
Contact Mr Keith Cusack
✉ **17 South Anne Street, Dublin 2, Ireland**
☎ 01 671 1262
Est. 1989 *Stock size* Large
Stock Antique jewellery, silver, curios
Open Tues–Sat 9.30am–6pm
Services Jewellery repairs

Kevin Jones Antiques (IADA)
Contact Mr Kevin Jones
✉ **65–66 Francis Street, Dublin 8, Ireland** Ⓟ
☎ 01 454 6626 Ⓜ 0876 29790
Ⓔ jonesantiques@aircom.net
Est. 1989 *Stock size* Large
Stock 18th–19thC furniture, paintings, objets d'art
Open Mon–Sat 10am–5.30pm

Gerald Kenyon Antiques (IADA, CINOA)
Contact Mr Gerald A Kenyon
✉ **6 Great Strand Street, Dublin 1, Ireland** Ⓟ
☎ 01 873 0625 Ⓕ 01 873 0882
Ⓔ mark@kenyon-antiques.com
Ⓦ www.kenyon-antiques.com
Est. 1740 *Stock size* Large
Stock Fine Georgian furniture, works of art, collectors' items
Open Mon–Fri 9am–6pm
Fairs Irish Antique Dealers' Fair, Dublin Antiques Fair
Services Interior decoration

McGovern's Corner
Contact Pat McGovern
87–88 Cork Street, Dublin 8, Ireland
01 453 5979
Est. 1960 *Stock size* Large
Stock Architectural salvage
Open Mon–Fri 9am–5pm
Sat 9am–1pm

Mitofsky Antiques (IADA)
Contact Anne Citron
8 Rathfarnham Road, Terenure, Dublin 6, Ireland
01 492 0033 F 01 492 0188
E info@mintofskyartdeco.com
W www.mintofskyartdeco.com
Est. 1994 *Stock size* Large
Stock Art Deco, Art Nouveau, Arts and Crafts
Open Mon–Sat 10am–5.30pm
Fairs The Kings Hall (Belfast), IADA

Roxane Moorhead Antiques (IADA)
Contact Ms Roxane Moorhead
65–66 Francis Street, Dublin 8, Ireland
01 453 3962 M 0868 147451
Est. 1979 *Stock size* Medium
Stock 18th–19thC furniture, porcelain, mirrors, chandeliers
Open Mon–Sat 10am–5.30pm
Fairs Irish Antique Dealers' Fair
Services Valuations

Neptune Gallery (IADA, FATG)
Contact Mr Andrew Bonar Law
41 South William Street, Dublin 2, Ireland
01 671 5021 F 01 671 5021
E abl@neptune-gallery.ie
Est. 1963 *Stock size* Medium
Stock Irish maps, prints, watercolours, books
Open Mon–Fri 10am–6pm
Sat 10am–1pm
Fairs Irish Antique Dealers' Fair
Services Valuations, framing, restoration

Gordon Nichol Antiques (IADA, CINOA)
Contact Mr Gordon Nichol
67–68 Francis Street, Dublin 8, Ireland
01 454 3322 F 01 473 5020
Est. 1985 *Stock size* Large
Stock 18th–19thC Irish, English and Continental furniture, chimney pieces, decorative objects
Open Mon–Sat 10.30am–4pm

O'Reillys (IAVI)
Contact Mr Michael Jordan
126 Francis Street, Dublin 8, Ireland
01 453 0311 F 01 453 0226
Est. 1952
Open Mon–Fri 9.30am–5pm
Sales Fine jewellery and silverware monthly sale Wed 1pm, viewing Sun noon–4pm Mon Tues 11am–6pm Wed 10am–12.30pm prior to sale
Frequency Monthly
Catalogues Yes

O'Sullivan Antiques (IADA)
Contact Ms Chantal O'Sullivan
43–44 Francis Street, Dublin 8, Ireland
01 454 1143 F 01 454 1156
M 0862 543399
E info@osullivanantiques.com
W www.osullivanantiques.com
Est. 1991 *Stock size* Large
Stock 18th–19thC furniture, paintings, mirrors, chandeliers, mantelpieces, garden furniture
Open Mon–Fri 9am–6pm
Sat 10am–6pm
Fairs Irish Antique Dealers' Fair
Services Valuations, restoration and upholstery

Oman Antique Galleries (IADA)
Contact Rosemary Whelan
20–21 South William Street, Dublin 2, Ireland
01 872 4477 F 01 872 4520
E info@omanantiques.com
W www.omanantiques.com
Est. 1974 *Stock size* Large
Stock Georgian–Edwardian furniture, works of art
Open Mon–Sat 9am–5.30pm
Fairs Irish Antique Dealers' Fair, Kerrygold Horseshow Fair
Services Packing and shipping

Rathmines Bookshop (BABI)
Contact Mr James Kinsella
201 Lower Rathmines Road, Dublin 6, Ireland
01 496 1064 F 01 496 1064
Est. 1986 *Stock size* Large
Stock Irish books, first editions
Open Mon–Sat 10am–7pm

Rufus the Cat
Contact Aidan & Gail Kinsella
50 Drury Street, Dublin 2, Ireland
01 677 0406
Est. 1964 *Stock size* Large
Stock Gentlemen's clothing and collectable accessories – smoking jackets, hats, watches, cuff links, ash trays etc
Open Mon–Sat 10.30am–6pm

Esther Sexton Antiques (IADA)
Contact Ms Esther Sexton
51 Francis Street, Dublin 8, Ireland
01 473 0909 *Stock size* Large
Stock Victorian and Edwardian furniture, decorative items
Open Mon–Fri 10.30am–5.50pm
Fairs Irish Antique Dealers' Fair

The Silver Shop (IADA)
Contact Mr Ian Haslam
Powerscourt Townhouse Centre, South William Street, Dublin 2, Ireland
01 679 4147 F 01 679 4147
E ianhaslam@eircom.net
Est. 1979 *Stock size* Large
Stock 18th–19thC silver, porcelain, portrait miniatures
Open Mon–Sat 11am–6pm
Thurs 11am–8pm
Fairs Irish Antique Dealers' Fair
Services Valuations

Stokes Books
Contact Mr Stephen Stokes
19 Market Arcade, South Great George's Street, Dublin 2, Ireland
01 671 3584 F 01 671 3181
E stokesbooks@oceanfree.net
Est. 1982 *Stock size* Small
Stock General antiquarian. Catalogues available. Books on Irish history and literature a speciality
Open Mon–Sat 10.30am–5.30pm
Services Valuations for probate and insurance

Timepiece Antique Clocks (IADA)
Contact Kevin Chellar
57–58 Patrick Street, Dublin 8, Ireland

☎ 01 454 0774 Ⓕ 01 454 0744
Ⓜ 0872 260212
Ⓔ timepieceireland@eircom.net
Est. 1983 *Stock size* Large
Stock 18th–19thC clocks
Open Tues–Sat 10am–5pm
Fairs Irish Antique Dealers' Fair, Burlington Antiques Fair
Services Valuations, restorations

Town & Country Auctioneers (IAVI)
Contact Ms Helen Thornton
✉ **4 Lower Ormond Quay, Dublin 1, Ireland**
☎ 01 872 8300/7401 Ⓕ 01 872 8002
Est. 1992
Open Mon–Fri 9am–5pm
Sales Large house contents sales Sun, Victorian and Georgian furniture
Frequency Fortnightly

Upper Court Manor Antiques (IADA)
Contact Patrick Fitzgerald
✉ **54 Francis Street, Dublin 8, Ireland** Ⓟ
☎ 01 473 0037 Ⓕ 01 473 0037
Ⓔ uppercourtmanorantiques@iol.ie
Est. 1994 *Stock size* Large
Stock English and Irish 18th–19thC furniture
Open Mon–Sat 10am–6pm
Fairs IADA Exhibition

Jenny Vander
Contact Aidan or Gail Kinsella
✉ **50 Drury Road, Dublin 2, Ireland** Ⓟ
☎ 01 677 0406
Est. 1964 *Stock size* Large
Stock Clothing (including evening dress), lace, 1930s–1950s, jewellery, Victorian–1960s
Open Mon–Sat 10am–4pm

The Victorian Salvage and Joinery Co Ltd (SALVO)
Contact Mark McDonagh
✉ **46–47 Townsend Street, Dublin 2, Ireland** Ⓟ
☎ 01 672 7000 Ⓕ 01 672 7435
Ⓜ 0872 551299
Ⓔ vicsalv@indigo.ie
Ⓦ www.victorian-salvage.com
Est. 1999 *Stock size* Large
Stock Reclaimed building materials
Open Mon–Fri 8.30am–5.30 Sat 9am–2pm
Services Valuations, restorations, shipping

Weir and Sons
Contact Allan Kilpatrick
✉ **96–99 Grafton Street, Dublin 2, Ireland** Ⓟ
☎ 01 677 9678 Ⓕ 01 677 7739
Ⓔ weirs@indigo.ie
Ⓦ www.weirandsons.com
Est. 1869 *Stock size* Large
Stock Silverware (especially Irish), jewellery, pocket and wrist watches
Open Mon–Sat 9am–5.30pm Thurs 9am–8pm
Services Valuations, restorations

J W Weldon (IADA)
Contact James or Martin Weldon
✉ **55 Clarendon Street, Dublin 2, Ireland** Ⓟ
☎ 01 677 1638 Ⓕ 01 670 7958
Ⓔ antiques@weldonsofdublin.com
Ⓦ www.weldonsofdublin.com
Est. 1900 *Stock size* Large
Stock Irish and diamond jewellery, antique and provincial Irish silver
Open Mon–Sat 10am–5.30pm
Fairs IADA

Whyte's
Contact Ian Whyte
✉ **30 Marlborough Street, Dublin 1, Ireland** Ⓟ
☎ 01 676 2888 Ⓕ 01 676 2880
Ⓔ info@whytes.ie
Ⓦ www.whytes.ie
Est. 1783
Open Mon–Fri 10am–1pm 2–6pm
Sales 8–10 sales annually of Irish art and collectables
Catalogues Yes

The Winding Stair Bookshop
Contact Mr Kevin Connolly
✉ **40 Lower Ormond Quay, Dublin 1, Ireland**
☎ 01 873 3292 Ⓕ 01 873 3292
Ⓔ windingstairbooks@tinet.ie
Ⓦ www.windingstair.ie
Est. 1982 *Stock size* Large
Stock New, second-hand and antiquarian books, Irish-interest books a speciality
Open Mon–Sat 9.30am–6pm Sun 1–6pm

Yesteryear Antiques
Contact Cyril Wall
✉ **12 North Frederick Street, Dublin 1, Ireland** Ⓟ
☎ 01878 3567
Est. 1981 *Stock size* Small
Stock Collectables
Open Tues–Fri 10am–5.30pm Sat 10am–4pm

DUN LAOGHAIRE

James Fenning, Old and Rare Books (ABA)
Contact Mr James Fenning
✉ **12 Glenview, Rochestown Avenue, Dun Laoghaire, Co Dublin, Ireland** Ⓟ
☎ 01 285 7855 Ⓕ 01 285 7919
Ⓔ fenning@indigo.ie
Est. 1969 *Stock size* Small
Stock Antiquarian books
Open By appointment
Services Valuations

Naughton's Booksellers
Contact Ms Susan Naughton
✉ **8 Marine Terrace, Dun Laoghaire, Co Dublin, Ireland** Ⓟ
☎ 01 280 4392
Ⓔ sales@naughtonsbooks.com
Ⓦ www.naughtonsbooks.com
Est. 1978 *Stock size* Medium
Stock Second-hand and antiquarian books
Open By appointment

The Old Shop
Contact Ms Siobhan Nugent
✉ **St Michael's Mall, Dun Laoghaire Shopping Centre, Co Dublin, Ireland** Ⓟ
☎ 01 280 9915
Est. 1976 *Stock size* Large
Stock Jewellery, silver, porcelain
Open Mon–Sat 9.30am–6pm

Through the Looking Glass
Contact Ms Anna Connolly
✉ **2 Salthill Place, Dun Laoghaire, Co Dublin, Ireland** Ⓟ
☎ 01 280 6577
Est. 1989 *Stock size* Large
Stock Mirrors, general
Open Tues–Sat 10.30am–5.30pm
Services Restoration of mirrors

MALAHIDE

Drums Malahide
Contact Dennis Drum
Malahide, Co Dublin, Ireland
☎ 01 845 2819 Ⓕ 01 845 3356
Est. 1974
Open Mon–Fri 9am–5pm closed 1–2pm
Sales Fine art sales monthly on Thurs at 7pm, regular fortnightly mixed household sales Thurs
Catalogues Yes

Malahide Antique Shop
Contact Mr Frank Donellan
✉ **14 New Street, Malahide, Co Dublin, Ireland**
☎ 01 845 2900
Est. 1974 *Stock size* Large
Stock Jewellery, silver, Georgian furniture, pictures, porcelain
Open Mon–Sat 10am–5.30pm closed 1–2pm
Services Valuations, restorations

SANDYCOVE

Sandycove Fine Arts (IADA)
Contact Ms Fiona O'Reilly
✉ **55 Glasthule Road, Sandycove, Co Dublin, Ireland**
☎ 01 280 5956
Est. 1993 *Stock size* Medium
Stock Antique furniture, paintings, china, glass, silver, silver plate
Open Mon–Sat 10.30am–1pm 2–6pm

STILLORGAN

Beaufield Mews Antiques (IADA)
Contact Ms Jill Cox
✉ **Woodlands Avenue, Stillorgan, Co Dublin, Ireland**
☎ 01 288 0375 Ⓕ 01 288 6945
Ⓜ 0872 427360
Ⓔ beaumews@iol.ie
Ⓦ www.antiquesireland.ie
Est. 1948 *Stock size* Large
Stock Early Irish glass and porcelain, 18th–19thC small items of furniture, pictures
Open Tues–Sat 3–9pm Sun 1–5pm
Fairs Irish Antique Dealers' Fair
Services Valuations, award-winning restaurant on site

CO GALWAY

ATHLONE

Arcadia Antiques & Fine Art (IADA)
Contact Ms Imelda O'Flynn
✉ **Church Street, Athlone, Co Galway, Ireland**
☎ 0902 74671
Est. 1971 *Stock size* Large
Stock Fine Victorian jewellery, silver, objets d'art, prints, dolls
Open Mon–Sat 9.30am–6pm
Services Jewellery restoration

CLARENBRIDGE

Clarenbridge Antiques
Contact Mr Martin Griffin
✉ **Limerick Road (N18), Clarenbridge, Co Galway, Ireland**
☎ 091 796522 Ⓕ 091 796522
Ⓔ clarenbridgeantiques@tinet.ie
Ⓦ www.homepage.tinet.ie/~clarenbridgeantiques
Est. 1981 *Stock size* Large
Stock Irish pine furniture, country antiques, mahogany and collectables
Open Summer Mon–Sun winter Mon–Sat 9am–6pm
Services Pine stripping

GALWAY

Cobwebs (IADA)
Contact Mrs Phyllis MacNamara
✉ **7 Quay Lane, Galway, Ireland**
☎ 091 564388 Ⓕ 091 564235
Ⓜ 0872 375745
Ⓔ cobwebs@tinet.ie
Ⓦ www.cobwebsgalway.com
Est. 1972 *Stock size* Large
Stock Sporting antiques, jewellery, collectables
Open Mon–Sat 9.30am–5.30pm
Fairs Irish Antique Dealers Fair

Corrib Antiques
Contact Ms Gretta Boland
✉ **The Bridge Mills, Galway, Ireland**
☎ 091 564938
Est. 1987 *Stock size* Medium
Stock Mahogany and pine furniture, general, jewellery
Open Mon–Sat 10am–5.30pm
Fairs Galway Antique Fair – Galway Bay Hotel

Maguire Antiques of Galway Ltd
Contact Phillip or Martin Maguire
✉ **Tuam Rd Centre, Tuam Rd, Galway, Ireland**
☎ 091 770799 Ⓕ 091 771433
Est. 1949 *Stock size* Large
Stock General antiques, fine art, paintings, porcelain
Open Mon–Sat 9.30am–6pm
Services Valuations

Tempo Antiques
Contact Frank or Phil Greeley
✉ **9 Cross Street, Galway, Ireland**
☎ 091 562282
Ⓔ info@tempoantiques.com
Ⓦ www.tempoantiques.com
Est. 1995 *Stock size* Large
Stock Victorian–Edwardian, Art Deco antique jewellery, silver, porcelain, collectables
Open Mon–Sat 9.30am–6.30pm open later in summer
Fairs Galway Bay Hotel

Twice As Nice
Contact Ms Deirdre Grandee
✉ **5 Quay Street, Galway, Ireland**
☎ 091 566332
Ⓔ grandideirdre@hotmail.com
Est. 1987 *Stock size* Medium
Stock Period clothes, lace, linen, jewellery
Open Mon–Sat 10am–6pm

The Winding Stair
Contact Mr Val Tyrell
✉ **4 Mainguard Street, Galway, Ireland**
☎ 091 561682
Ⓔ tyrell@eircom.net
Est. 1991 *Stock size* Medium
Stock Prints, lighting, furniture, bathroom fittings, jewellery, collectables, general antiques
Open Mon–Sat 10am–6pm
Services Shipping – small items only

GORT

Honan's Antiques
Contact Brian or Margaret Honan
✉ **Crowe Street, Gort, Co Galway, Ireland**
☎ 091 631407 Ⓕ 091 631816
Ⓔ honansantique@eircom.net
Ⓦ www.honansantiques.com

Est. 1976 *Stock size* Large
Stock Antique pine, clocks, lamps, Victorian fireplaces, advertising signs, mirrors, pub fittings etc
Open Mon–Sat 10am–6pm
Services Pine stripping

KINVARA

Penny Farthing Antiques
Contact Olive or Neil Bradley
Main Street, Kinvara, Co Galway, Ireland
091 637720
www.pennyfarthing.ie
Est. 1997 *Stock size* Medium
Stock Furniture, china, pictures, collectables
Open Mon–Sun noon–5pm closed Tues

MOYCULLEN

Moycullen Village Antiques (IADA)
Contact Ms Maura Duffy
Main Street, Moycullen, Co Galway, Ireland
091 555303 F 091 555303
M 0868 235976
Est. 1989 *Stock size* Large
Stock Fine Regency–Edwardian furniture, paintings, prints, fine china, silver
Open Mon–Sat 9.45am–5.30pm Sun 2–5.30pm
Fairs Dublin Horse Show, IADA (Mar, Dec)
Services Valuations, restorations

CO KERRY

ABBEYDORNEY

Abbey Antiques
Contact Jerry O'Donovan
Main Street, Abbeydorney, Co Kerry, Ireland
066 7135460
Est. 1989 *Stock size* Large
Stock Victorian fireplaces, Georgian–Edwardian furniture
Open Sun or by appointment

CAHIRSIVEEN

Biggs Antique Shop (IADA)
Contact Denyce Biggs
Old Road, Cahirsiveen, Co Kerry, Ireland
066 947 2580
Est. 1975 *Stock size* Large
Stock 1830–1950s small portable antiques including cutlery
Open Tues–Sat 10.30am–6pm Sun call first
Services Valuations

TRALEE

O'Keeffe's Antiques and Interiors
Contact Maurice or Jane O'Keeffe
15 Princes Street, Tralee, Co Kerry, Ireland
066 718 0613/712 5635
F 066 712 5635
okeeffeantiques2@eircom.net
Est. 1860 *Stock size* Large
Stock 8 rooms in a Georgian town house, fully decorated in period furnishings, all items for sale
Open Tues–Sat 9.30am–6pm
Services Valuations, restorations

CO KILDARE

MAYMOOTH

Hugh Cash Antiques
Contact Hugh Cash
Main Street, Maynooth, Co Kildare, Ireland
01 628 5946 M 0872 434510
Est. 1969 *Stock size* Large
Stock Georgian–Edwardian furniture
Open By appointment only
Services Valuations

CO KILKENNY

CASTLECOMER

Mealy's Ltd (IAVI)
Contact Fonsie or George Mealy
Chatsworth Street, Castlecomer, Co Kilkenny, Ireland
056 41229/41413 F 056 41627
info@mealys.com
www.mealys.com
Est. 1934
Open Mon–Fri 9am–1pm 2–6pm
Sales 2 antiquarian book auctions per year, viewing days prior to auction. Also fine art sales
Frequency 8 per year
Catalogues Yes

FRESHFORD

Cass Freshford Antiques
Contact Michael Cass
Bohercrussia Street, Freshford, Co Kilkenny, Ireland
056 32240
cassantiques@dol.ie
Est. 1966 *Stock size* Medium
Stock Antique furniture
Open Mon–Sat 9am–5pm
Services Restorations

Upper Court Manor Antiques (IADA)
Contact Patrick Fitzgerald
Upper Court Manor, Freshford, Co Kilkenny, Ireland
056 32174 F 056 32325
antiques@indigo.ie
Est. 1989 *Stock size* Large
Stock English and Irish 19thC furniture
Open Mon–Fri 10am–5.30pm
Fairs Irish Antique Dealers' Fair, Burlington Antiques Fair
Services Restorations, shipping, packing

CO LAOIS

BALLACOLLA

Glebe Hall Collectables
Contact Carmel Corrigan-Griffin
Old Killernogh Rectory, Rathmakelly Glebe, Ballacolla, Co Laois, Ireland
050 234105 F 050 234154
Est. 1980 *Stock size* Large
Stock Pine country furniture, porcelain, linen, paintings, kitchenware, silver plate, books, jewellery
Open By appointment
Services Restorations, tuition

DURROW

C Sheppard and Sons (IAVI)
Contact Michael Sheppard
The Square, Durrow, Co Laois, Ireland
050 236123 F 050 236546
info@sheppards.ie
Est. 1949
Open Mon–Sat 10am–1pm 2–6pm

Sales General antiques, porcelain, furniture, fine arts
Frequency Every 2–3 months
Catalogues Yes

PORTARLINGTON

McDonnell's Antique Furniture
Contact Ray McDonnell
Cloneyhurke, Portarlington, Co Laois, Ireland P
☎ 050 243304
Est. 1981 *Stock size* Large
Stock Religious furniture, pulpits, pews, statuary, pine and farmhouse furniture
Open Mon–Sat 8am–8pm

CO LEITRIM

CARRICK ON SHANNON

Trinity Rare Books
Contact Nick or Joanna Kaszuk
Bridge Street, Carrick on Shannon, Co Leitrim, Ireland
☎ 078 22144
E nickk@indigo.ie
W www.indigo.ie/~nickk
Est. 1999 *Stock size* Medium
Stock Antiquarian fine bindings, books, modern first editions
Open Mon–Sat 9.30am–6pm
Services Book search

CO LIMERICK

ADARE

Carol's Antiques (IADA, CINOA)
Contact Ms Carol O'Connor
Main Street, Adare, Co Limerick, Ireland P
☎ 061 396977 F 061 396991
M 0862 478827
E coconnor@indigo.ie
W www.carolsantiquesadare.com
Est. 1979 *Stock size* Large
Stock Georgian–Victorian furniture, silver, brass, porcelain, objets d'art, jewellery
Open Mon–Sat 9.30am–5.30pm Sun 12.30–5pm
Fairs Irish Antique Dealers' Fair, Annual Cork Antiques Fair
Services Interior decoration

Manor Antiques
Contact Mr Simon Quilligan
Main Street, Adare, Co Limerick, Ireland P
☎ 061 396515 or 069 64869
M 0868 365196
Est. 1914 *Stock size* Large
Stock Georgian–Victorian furniture, general antiques
Open Sat 10am–5.30pm or by appointment
Services Shipping

George Stacpoole (IADA)
Contact Mr George Stacpoole
Main Street, Adare, Co Limerick, Ireland P
☎ 061 396409 F 061 396733
E stacpool@iol.ie
W www.georgestacpooleantiques.com
Est. 1962 *Stock size* Medium
Stock Furniture, silver, books, pictures, china, prints
Open Mon–Sat 10am–5.30pm
Fairs IADA
Services Valuations and interior decoration

LIMERICK

Ann's Antiques
Contact Ann O'Doherty
32 Mallow Street, Limerick, Ireland P
☎ 061 302492 F 061 413035
Est. 1984 *Stock size* Medium
Stock Mid–late Victorian furniture
Open Tues–Fri 11am–5pm or by appointment
Services Valuations, search

Bygones Antiques
Contact Mr John Costello
16 Nicholas Street, Limerick, Ireland P
☎ 061 417339
Est. 1979 *Stock size* Medium
Stock Antique pine furniture and beds
Open Mon–Fri 9am–5.30pm half day Sat
Services Pine stripping

John Gunning Antiques
Contact Mr John Gunning
2 Castle Street, Limerick, Ireland P
☎ 061 410535
Est. 1970 *Stock size* Large
Stock General antiques
Open Mon–Sat 10am–5pm

Noonan Antiques
Contact Jim Noonan
16–17 Ellen Street, Limerick, Ireland P
☎ 061 413861 F 061 413861
M 0872 539165
E jandanoonan@eircom.net
Est. 1985 *Stock size* Medium
Stock Antique jewellery, furniture
Open Mon–Sat 10am–5pm

O'Toole Antiques & Decorative Galleries (IADA)
Contact Noel O'Toole
Upper William Street, Limerick, Ireland P
☎ 061 414490 F 061 411378
M 0872 550985
E noel.o.toole.antiques@oceanfree.net
Est. 1979 *Stock size* Large
Stock 18th–19thC furniture, pictures, fireplaces, mirrors and porcelain
Open Mon–Sat 9.30am–6pm
Fairs IADA
Services Valuations, restorations

Tess Antiques
Contact Ms Tess Costello
5 Roches Street, Limerick, Ireland P
☎ 061 416643 M 0872 960624
E tessantiques@eircom.net
Est. 1980 *Stock size* Small
Stock Jewellery, silver, porcelain
Open Tues–Sat 10am–5pm

CO LOUTH

DROGHEDA

Greene's Antiques Galleries (IADA)
Contact Austin Greene
The Mall, Drogheda, Co Louth, Ireland P
☎ 041 983 8286/36212
F 041 983 8286
Est. 1886 *Stock size* Large
Stock Furniture, Irish silver, paintings
Open Mon–Sat 10am–12.30pm 2–5pm

DUNDALK

Hall's Curio Shop
Contact Margaret or Rory Hall
9/10 Jocelyn Street, Dundalk, Co Louth, Ireland
☎ 042 933 4902

Est. 1971 *Stock size* Large
Stock Jewellery, paintings, silver, general
Open Mon–Sat 10am–1pm 2–6pm closed Thurs or by appointment
Services Valuations

CO MAYO

ACHILL SOUND

Roger Grimes (IADA)
Contact Roger Grimes
Old Rectory, Achill Sound, Co Mayo, Ireland
098 27823 F 098 27823
E roger.grimes@eirecom.net
Est. 1977
Stock 17th–19thC provincial furniture, metalware, china, pictures, prints, eccentricities
Open Daily in the summer or by appointment
Fairs IADA
Services Valuations

Vanessa Parker Rare Books (IADA)
Contact Vanessa Parker
Old Rectory, Achill Sound, Co Mayo, Ireland
098 27823 F 098 27823
E vanessa.parker@eirecom.net
Est. 1977
Stock Antiquarian books, folklore, literature, Irish, 19th–20thC children's books.
Open Daily in the summer or by appointment
Fairs IADA
Services Valuations

WESTPORT

Jonathan Beech Antique Clocks (IADA, CINOA)
Contact Mr Jonathan Beech
Killeenacoff House, Cloona, Westport, Co Mayo, Ireland
098 28688 F 098 28688
M 0872 226247
E jbeech@anu.ie
W www.antiques-ireland.com
Est. 1984 *Stock size* Medium
Stock Clocks
Open Mon–Sat 9.30am–5.30pm or by appointment
Fairs Irish Antique Dealers' Fair, Dublin, Galway, Limerick
Services Valuations, restorations

Bygones of Ireland Ltd
Contact John or Lia Van Wensveen
Lodge Road, Westport, Co Mayo, Ireland
098 26132 F 098 26862
E bygones@anu.ie
W www.bygones-of-ireland.com
Est. 1983 *Stock size* Large
Stock Irish and European antique pine and country furniture
Open Mon–Sat 9am–5.30pm

Satch Kiely (IADA, LAPADA)
Contact Mrs Satch Kiely
Westport Quay, Westport, Co Mayo, Ireland
098 25775 F 098 25957
Est. 1985 *Stock size* Large
Stock 18th–19thC furniture, Irish and English silver, colonial lamps, fossil bog oak and Biedermeier
Open Mon–Sat 2–6pm or by appointment
Fairs Irish Antique Dealers' Fair, Annual Cork Antiques Fair, Galway and Hunt Museum, Limerick
Services Valuations

Westport House Antique Shop (IADA)
Contact Earl of Altamont
Westport, Co Mayo, Ireland
098 25430/25404 F 098 25206
E info@westporthouse.ie
W www.westporthouse.ie
Est. 1969 *Stock size* Medium
Stock General antiques, prints, postcards, silver, silver plate, jewellery
Open Daily April–June 2–5pm Jul Aug 11.30am–5.30pm or by appointment

CO MEATH

GORMANSTOWN

Delvin Farm Antiques
Contact J or B McCrane
Gormanstown, Co Meath, Ireland
01 841 2285 F 01 841 3730
E info@delvinfarmpine.com
W www.delvinfarmpine.com
Est. 1974 *Stock size* Large
Stock Antique country furniture
Open Mon–Sat 9am–5pm

KELLS

Oliver Usher (IAVI)
Contact Mr Oliver Usher
John Street, Kells, Co Meath, Ireland
046 41097 F 046 41097
E oliverusher@ireland.com
Est. 1978
Open Mon–Fri 9.30am–5.30pm
Sales Antique and high-class furniture sale Tues 5pm mid month at Kells, viewing Sun 2–6pm Mon 11am–7pm Tues 11am–5pm. Monthly general household sale in CYWS Hall, Navan first Fri of month 6.30pm (no catalogue), viewing Fri 11am–6.30pm. Spring and Autumn sale at The Conyngham Arms Hotel, Slane
Frequency Monthly
Catalogues Yes

George Williams Antiques (IADA)
Contact George Williams
The Annexe, Newcastle House, Kilmainhamwood, Kells, Co Meath, Ireland
046 52740 M 0872 529959
E gwilliams@eircom.net
W www.georgian-antiques.com
Est. 1987 *Stock size* Medium
Stock 18th–19thC furniture, paintings
Open By appointment only
Fairs IADA Exhibition, Dublin (Sept)
Services Purchasing on commission, valuations

OLDCASTLE

Mullen Bros Auctions
Contact Michael Mullen
Oldcastle, Co Meath, Ireland
049 854 1107 F 049 854 1107
Est. 1962
Open Tues–Fri 10am–6pm closed Sun Mon
Sales General antiques and household goods 1st Tues of every month 6.30pm, viewing 3 days prior
Catalogues No

CO OFFALY

BIRR

Ivy Hall Antiques (IADA, CINOA)
Contact Mrs Ena Hoctor
Carrig, Birr, Co Offaly, Ireland
0509 20148
Est. 1967 *Stock size* Large
Stock 18th–19thC silver, porcelain, furniture, pictures
Open By appointment

EDENDERRY

Edenderry Architectural Salvage Ltd
Contact Brian Murphy
Monasteroris Industrial Estate, Edenderry, Co Offaly, Ireland
040 533156 F 040 533156
M 0862 595367
E bpmurphy@iol.ie
Est. 1995 *Stock size* Large
Stock Reclaimed flooring, bricks, radiators, doors, baths, sinks, beams, railway sleepers, cobblestones, fireplaces
Open Mon–Fri 9am–5pm
Services Cutting and planing of reclaimed timber beams and flooring

CO SLIGO

SLIGO

Louis J Doherty and Sons
Contact Mr John McSharry
Tealing Street, Sligo, Ireland
071 69494 F 071 69494
E ljdoherty@tinet.ie
Est. 1976 *Stock size* Large
Stock Large furniture, bedroom suites, settees, display cabinets, overmantels, pianos, general antiques
Open Mon–Sat 9.30am–1pm 2–6pm
Services Valuations

Georgian Village Antiques
Contact Louis and John Doherty
Johnstons Court, Sligo, Ireland
071 62421 F 071 69494
E ljdoherty@tinet.ie
Est. 1976 *Stock size* Medium
Stock Small furniture items, jewellery, porcelain, glass
Open Mon–Sat 10am–6pm
Services Valuations

CO TIPPERARY

BALLINDERRY

Kilgarvan Antique Centre
Contact Denise Shaw
Kilgarvan Quay, Ballinderry, Nenagh, Co Tipperary, Ireland
067 22047
E deniseshaw27@hotmail.com
Est. 1947 *Stock size* Medium
Stock Georgian antiques, mirrors, general china
Open Mon–Sat 10am–7pm Sun after 3pm Apr–Oct by appointment
Services Restoration of giltwood mirrors and antique furniture, restoration and polishing of wooden and carved furniture

BIRDHILL

Delany Antiques
Contact Patrick Delaney
Cragg House, Cragg, Birdhill, Co Tipperary, Ireland
061 378180 F 061 378180
E pdelanyantiques@eircom.net
Est. 1979 *Stock size* Large
Stock Architectural salvage, bath fittings, accessories, decorative furniture, fine art, soft furnishings
Open By appointment
Services Valuations, upholstery

CAHIR

Abbey Antiques (IADA)
Contact Mr Michael Kennedy
Abbey Street, Cahir, Co Tipperary, Ireland
052 41187 F 052 41187
M 0872 728844
E celine@antiquesireland.ie
W www.antiquesireland.ie
Est. 1992 *Stock size* Large
Stock Georgian–Edwardian furniture, lighting, objets d'art
Open Mon–Sat 10.30am–5.30pm
Services Shipping

Fleury Antiques (IADA)
Contact C or D Fleury or P Reidy
The Square, Cahir, Co Tipperary, Ireland
052 41226 F 052 41819
E fleuryantiques@eircom.ie
W www.fleuryantiques.com
Est. 1978 *Stock size* Medium
Stock 18th–19thC furniture, sculptures, paintings, decorative objects, jewellery, porcelain, silver
Open Mon–Sat 9am–6pm
Fairs No

CO WATERFORD

WATERFORD

R J Keighery (IPAV)
Contact Rody or Ann Keighery
Georges Quay, Waterford, Ireland
051 873692 F 051 873692
Est. 1948
Open Mon–Sun 9am–5.30pm
Sales Six weekly antiques and general furniture sale Mon 2pm, viewing Fri Sat Sun noon–6pm
Frequency Six weekly
Catalogues Yes

R J Keighery
Contact Rody or Ann Keighery
27 William Street, Waterford, Ireland
051 873692
Est. 1948 *Stock size* Large
Stock Antiques, furniture, china, silver, collectables
Open Mon–Sat 9am–5.30pm
Services Valuations

The Salvage Shop
Contact Sean Corcoran
Airport Road, Waterford City, Ireland
051 873260 F 051 858323
M 0872 524657
E salvage@iol.ie
W www.bang2000.com
Est. 1991 *Stock size* Large
Stock Architectural salvage and reclaimed wood furniture
Open Mon–Fri 8am–5.30pm Sat 10am–3pm
Fairs Beyond the Hall Door
Services Restorations, interior design, catalogues

Times Past
Contact James O'Hanlon
28 Spring Garden Alley, Waterford, Ireland
051 853036 F 051 853036
M 0872 503557

Est. 1989 *Stock size* Large
Stock General antiques, fireplaces and furniture, smalls
Open Mon–Sat 10am–5pm
Services Pine stripping

CO WEXFORD

WEXFORD

Forum Antiques
Contact Nora Liddy
Selskar, Wexford, Ireland P
☎ 053 21055 F 053 23630
E info@selskarantiques.com
W www.selskarantiques.com
Est. 1996 *Stock size* Medium
Stock Antiquarian books, maps, prints, china, collectables
Open Tues–Sat 11am–5.30pm
Fairs National Book Fairs
Services Book valuations

Selskar Abbey Antiques
Contact Irene Walker
Selskar Court, Wexford, Ireland P
☎ 053 23630 F 053 23630
M 0876 791095
E selskarantiques@eircom.
Est. 1984 *Stock size* Medium
Stock Antique jewellery, pictures, fine china, small furniture items, glass, collectables
Open Mon–Sat 10am–6pm
Fairs O'Donnell Fairs, Wexford Opera Festival
Services Valuations

CO WICKLOW

BRAY

Clancy Chandeliers (IADA)
Contact Ger, Derek or Tommy Clancy
Villanova, Ballywaltrim, Bray, Co Wicklow, Ireland P
☎ 0128 63460 F 0128 63460
E info@clancychandeliers.com
W www.clancychandeliers.com
Est. 1989 *Stock size* Large
Stock Period and reproduction chandeliers, wall lights, hall lanterns
Open Strictly by appointment
Fairs IADA Exhibition, Dublin (Sept), Dublin Antiques Fair (Mar Nov)
Services Professional cleaning, restoration, hanging service

GREYSTONES

Beth-Nell Antiques
Contact Beth O'Riordan
Church Road, Greystones, Co Wicklow, Ireland P
☎ 01 287 5651
Est. 1990 *Stock size* Medium
Stock Furniture, porcelain, pottery, ceramics, silver, jewellery, linens, glass
Open Mon–Sat 10.30am–5.30pm

RADHDRUM

Cathair Books
Contact Mr Eugene Mallon
Pound Brook Lane, Radhdrum, Co Wicklow, Ireland P
☎ 040 446939 F 040 446939
E cathairbks@eircom.net
W www.abebooks.com/home/cathair_books
Est. 1974 *Stock size* Medium
Stock Irish-interest books, prints, maps, postcards
Open Mail order or by appointment
Fairs Dublin Book Fair and provincial fairs in Limerick and Belfast
Services Valuations

Associated Services

ARCHITECTURAL

Zygmunt Chelminski (UKIC)
Contact Mr Z Chelminski
✉ **Studio GE1, 2 Michael Road, London, SW6 2AD** P
☎ 020 7610 9731 Ⓕ 020 7610 9731
Ⓜ 07770 585130
Est. 1995
Services Marble, stone, terracotta, alabaster and coldstone repair and restoration. English Heritage approved contractor
Open Mon–Fri 10am–5pm appointment advisable

Heritage Architectural Restoration
Contact Richard Powell
✉ **Tyne Court, Haddington, East Lothian, EH41 4BL** P
☎ 01620 825499
Est. 1995
Services Refurbishing and restoration of all architectural woodwork, internal woodwork and furniture
Open By appointment

Iron Wright
Contact Mr F Sporik
✉ **Arch 13b, Parkfield Industrial Estate, Culvert Place, London, SW11 5BA** P
☎ 020 7622 7495 Ⓕ 020 7652 4089
Est. 1994
Services Repair and restoration of cast-iron fireplaces
Open Mon–Fri 8am–6pm
Sat by appointment

Melluish & Davis
Contact Mr J Davis
✉ **11 Hampton Lane, Hanworth, Middlesex, TW13 6NN** P
☎ 020 7622 5731 Ⓕ 020 8893 4178
Est. 1972
Services Restoration of marble chimney pieces, sculpture and garden ornaments
Open By appointment only

Saltney Restoration Services
Contact Mr J Moore
✉ **50 St Mark's Road, Chester, Cheshire, CH4 8DQ** P
☎ 01244 312529 Ⓕ 01244 312529
Ⓜ 07713 823383
Est. 1967
Services Brick, metal, steel, glass, furniture, stone, lighting and sanitary ware restoration
Open By appointment only

Salvo
Contact Hazel Maltravers
✉ **PO Box 333, Cornhill on Tweed, Northumberland, TD12 4YJ**
☎ 01890 820333 Ⓕ 01890 820499
Ⓔ admin@salvoweb.com
Ⓦ www.salvoweb.com
Est. 1992
Services Salvo networks information on architectural salvage, garden antiques, reclaimed building materials and reproductions. Salvo publish SalvoEMAILS several times a week, printed SalvoNEWS every 3 weeks, SALVO magazine intermittently and The Salvo Guide 2000.

BAROMETERS

The Restoration Shop (BHI)
Contact Mr R Cookson
✉ **25 New Street, Leominster, Herefordshire, HR6 8DP** P
☎ 01568 613652 Ⓜ 07771 548037
Est. 1969
Services Supply and restoration of antique mercurial, aneroid barometers, clocks and watches, furniture, ceramics, French polishing, wood finishing, dial painting
Open Mon–Fri 9am–5pm
Sat 10am–4pm

BOOKS

Antiquarian Bookcrafts
Contact Des Breen
✉ **Craft Centre, Marlay Park, Dublin 16, Ireland** P
☎ 01 494 2384 Ⓕ 01 494 2811
Ⓔ desbreen@eirecom.net
Est. 1962
Services Book-binding, restoration
Open Mon–Fri 7.45am–4.30pm

C & A J Barmby
Contact C Barmby
✉ **140 Lavender Hill, Tonbridge, Kent, TN9 2AY**
☎ 01732 771590 Ⓕ 01732 771590
Ⓔ bookpilot@aol.com
Est. 1970
Services Reference books on antiques, display stands, accessories, packaging material
Trade only Yes
Open By appointment

The Book Depot
Contact Conrad Wiberg
✉ **111 Woodcote Avenue, London, NW7 2PD**
☎ 020 8906 3708 Ⓕ 020 8906 3708
Est. 1980
Services Free book search for any book
Open Mon–Sun 9am–5pm postal business

Brignell Bookbinders
Contact Barry Brignell
✉ **25 Gwydir Street, Cambridge, Cambridgeshire, CB1 2LG** P
☎ 01223 321280 Ⓕ 01223 321280
Est. 1982
Services Book binding, repairs, presentation volumes
Open Mon–Thurs 8.30am–4.45pm Fri 8.30am–4pm

H P Book Finders
Contact Mr Martin Earl
✉ **Mosslaird, Brig O'Turk, Callander, Scotland, FK17 8HT** P
☎ 01877 376377 Ⓕ 01877 376377
Ⓔ martin@hp-bookfinders.co.uk
Ⓦ www.hp-bookfinders.co.uk
Est. 1984
Services Book search
Open 8am–6pm

F Hutton (Bookbinder) (SOBB, Designer Binders)
Contact Felicity Hutton
✉ **Langore House, Langore, Launceston, Cornwall, PL15 8LD** P
☎ 01566 773831
Est. 1985
Services Book binding and restoration
Open Telephone first

Meadowcroft Books
Contact Mr A Parry
✉ **21 Upper Bognor Road, Bognor Regis, West Sussex, PO21 1JA** P
☎ 01243 868614 Ⓕ 01243 868714
Ⓔ enquiries@meadowcroftbooks.demon.co.uk
Ⓦ www.meadowcroftbooks.demon.co.uk
Est. 1996

Services Book search
Open By appointment

BOXES

William Heffer Antiques
Contact Mr W Heffer
✉ **37 Victoria Park, Cambridge, Cambridgeshire, CB4 3EJ** P
☎ 01223 362825
ⓔ hefferw.vicpark@dial.pipex.com
Est. 1972
Services Small restoration work, caddies, jewellery boxes
Open By appointment

Alan and Kathy Stacy (LAPADA, BABAADA, BAFRA)
Contact Alan Stacey
✉ **Castle Cary, Somerset, BA9 9YY** P
☎ 01963 441333 ⓕ 01963 441330
ⓔ info@antiqueboxes.uk.com
ⓦ www.antiqueboxes.uk.com
Est. 1990
Services Restoration of tortoiseshell, ivory, shagreen, mother-of-pearl and bone
Open By appointment

CANING

The Cane & Rush Chair Repair Service
Contact R D Nolan
✉ **156 Horton Hill, Epsom, Surrey, KT19 8ST** P
☎ 01372 727063 ⓜ 07961 313933
Est. 1984
Services Cane and rush repairs
Open Mon–Fri 7.30am–5pm Sat 8am–noon

Cane and Rush Works (Basket Makers Association)
Contact Miss J Swan
✉ **6c Sylvan Road, London, E11 1QH** P
☎ 020 8530 7052
Est. 1981
Services Caning and rushing, country chairs, chair seats, bergère suites and sofas
Open By appointment

Cane Chairs Repaired
Contact Paul Bolton
✉ **Dunmayling, High Street, Burwash, East Sussex, TN19 7EP** P
☎ 0800 027 2201 ⓕ 01435 882299
ⓜ 07850 943091
ⓔ chairs@btconnect.com
ⓦ www.canechairs.co.uk
Est. 1995
Services Repair of all cane and Lloyd Loom chairs
Open Mon–Fri 8am–6pm

Cane Corner (Basket Makers Association, Devon Rural Skills Trust)
Contact Bridgette Stone
✉ **Behind East Budleigh Garage, Lower Budleigh, East Budleigh, Devon, EX9 7DL** P
☎ 01395 446166
Est. 1985
Services Antique and modern chairs professionally reseated with split cane and rush
Open Mon–Fri 9am–5.30pm

The Cane Workshop (Basket Makers Association)
Contact Mr K Mason
✉ **Squires Garden Centre, Sixth Cross Road, Twickenham, Middlesex, TW2 5PA** P
☎ 020 8943 4869 ⓕ 020 8943 4869
Est. 1976
Services Caning, rushing, cords and willows
Open Tues–Sat 9am–5pm

Caners & Upholders
Contact Steve Warrington
✉ **12 Soberton Road, Bournemouth, Dorset, BH8 9BG** P
☎ 01202 399339
ⓔ steven.warrington@virgin.net.
Est. 1989
Services Cane and rush repair and restoration
Open Mon–Fri 9am–5pm or by appointment

Peter Maitland
Contact Mr P J Maitland
✉ **27 Berkeley Road, Bishopstone, Bristol, BS7 8HF** P
☎ 0117 942 6870
Est. 1990
Services Chair restoration, rush seating and caning
Open Mon–Fri 9am–5pm or by appointment

CARPETS & RUGS

Barin Carpets Restoration
Contact H Barin
✉ **57a New Kings Road, London, SW6 4SE** P
☎ 020 7731 0546
Est. 1976
Services Cleaning and restoration of Oriental carpets and rugs, European tapestries, Aubussons. Listed by the conservation unit of The Museums and Galleries Commission
Open Mon–Sat 9am–6pm

Lannowe Oriental Textiles
Contact Joanna Titchell
✉ **Near Bath, Wiltshire**
☎ 01225 891487 ⓕ 01225 891182
ⓜ 0771 470 3535
ⓔ joanna@lannowe.co.uk
Est. 1976
Services Washing, restoration and conservation of Oriental carpets, rugs and tapestries
Open By appointment

M & M Restoration
Contact Marina Jezierzanska
✉ **Mantel House, Broomhill Road, London, SW18 4JQ** P
☎ 020 8871 5098 ⓕ 020 8877 1940
ⓜ 07949 107611
Est. 1985
Services Restoration and cleaning of antique tapestries, carpets, textiles
Open Mon–Fri 9am–6pm

CERAMICS

SOUTH EAST

Carol Basing
Contact Carol Basing
✉ **41 Prospect Road, Sevenoaks, Kent, TN13 3UA**
☎ 01732 456695
Est. 1984
Services Ceramic repair and restoration
Open Mon–Sun 9am–5pm

Grenville Godfrey
Contact Mr G Godfrey
✉ **60 Watts Lane, Eastbourne, East Sussex, BN21 2LL** P
☎ 01323 735595
Est. 1997

Services Repair and restoration of ceramics
Open By appointment

Helen Warren China Restoration
Contact Helen Warren
✉ **Unit 9, Slaney Place Farm, Headcorn Road, Staplehurst, Kent, TN12 0DT** 🅿
☎ 01622 891700
Ⓔ conservation@ifwarren.demon.co.uk
Ⓦ www.ifwarren.demon.co.uk
Est. 1990
Services Ceramic repair and restoration
Open By appointment

Laurie Wheeler Restorations
Contact Laurie Wheeler
✉ **Great Knell Farm Cottage, Molland Lane, Ash, Canterbury, Kent, CT3 2ED** 🅿
☎ 01304 813550 Ⓕ 01304 813550
Est. 1979
Services Restoration of antique porcelain, pottery, Parianware, gilding and enamelling
Open By appointment

LONDON

China Repairers
Contact Virginia Baron
✉ **The Coach House, King Street Mews, King Street, London, N2 8DY** 🅿
☎ 020 8444 3030
Ⓦ www.chinarepairers.co.uk
Est. 1953
Services Ceramic and glass repairs. Tuition available
Open Mon–Thurs 10am–4pm

G W Conservation (OCS)
Contact Ms Gillian Quartly-Watson
✉ **5S Hewlett House, Havelock Avenue, London, SW8 4AS** 🅿
☎ 020 7498 5938 Ⓕ 020 7498 5938
Ⓜ 07710 355743
Ⓔ stylish.moves@virgin.net
Est. 1991
Services Conservation of ceramics and related objects
Open Mon–Fri 10am–6pm or by appointment

The Conservation Studio (ICOM, IIC, UKIC)
Contact Mrs F Hayward
✉ **77 Troutbeck, Albany Street, London, NW1 4EJ** 🅿
☎ 020 7387 4994 Ⓕ 020 7387 4994
Ⓔ flu_flo@yahoo.co.uk
Est. 1993
Services Restoration and conservation of ceramics, glass, metalwork, ivory and soapstone, specializing in gilding, painting on glass and ceramics
Open Mon–Fri 8.30am–4.30pm Sat by appointment

Rosemary Hamilton China Repairs (IDDA)
Contact Mrs R Hamilton
✉ **44 Moreton Street, London, SW1V 2PB** 🅿
☎ 020 7828 5018 Ⓕ 020 7828 1325
Ⓔ rosemary@rosemaryhamilton.co.uk
Est. 1993
Services China repairs and restorations
Open Mon–Fri 9.30am–5.30pm

SOUTH

Brook Studio
Contact Mrs Joanna Holland
✉ **The Granary, 2 Church Road, Pangbourne, Berkshire, RG8 7AA** 🅿
☎ 0118 984 2014/971 3249
Ⓔ joanna@holland.demon.co.uk
Est. 1978
Services Good-quality china and porcelain restoration
Open By appointment

Norman Flynn Restorations
Contact Mr N Flynn
✉ **2 Lind Road, Sutton, Surrey, SM1 4QY** 🅿
☎ 020 8661 9505
Est. 1972
Services Porcelain, pottery, enamel restoration
Open Tues–Fri 8.30am–3.30pm

Sarah Peek
Contact Miss S Peek
✉ **The Battery House, Petworth House, Petworth, West Sussex, GU28 0DP** 🅿
☎ 01798 342763 Ⓕ 01798 342763
Ⓔ conservation@sarahpeek.co.uk
Ⓦ www.sarahpeek.co.uk
Est. 1995
Services Restoration of ceramics, glass, enamels
Open By appointment

Regency Antiques
Contact R De Santini
✉ **Bognor Regis, West Sussex**
☎ 01243 861643 Ⓕ 01243 861643
Ⓜ 07947 597311
Est. 1978
Services Porcelain and furniture restoration
Open Mon–Fri 9.30am–5.30pm by appointment only

Ryde Antiques
Contact Patricia Rowan
✉ **15 Royal Street, Sandown, Isle of Wight, PO36 8LP** 🅿
☎ 01983 402434
Est. 1975
Services Ceramic repair, matt finish a speciality
Open By appointment

Sheila Southwell Studio (BCPAA, IPAA)
Contact Mrs S Southwell
✉ **7 West Street, Burgess Hill, West Sussex, RH15 8NN** 🅿
☎ 01444 244307
Est. 1969
Services Restoration of ceramics, china, porcelain, earthenware. Commissions accepted for hand-painted, commemorative porcelain for any occasion
Open By appointment

WEST COUNTRY

Addington Studio Ceramic Repairs
Contact Pam Warner
✉ **1 Addington Cottages, Upottery, Honiton, Devon, EX14 9PN** 🅿
☎ 01404 861519 Ⓕ 01404 861308
Ⓔ addington.studio@virgin.net
Est. 1991
Services Restoration and conservation of ceramics and glass. Tuition given. Regular delivery and collection point now available
Open By appointment

Antique China and Porcelain Restoration
Contact Mr Carl Garratt

✉ **6 Enfield Drive, Evercreech, Shepton Mallet, Somerset, BA4 6LL** 🅿
☎ 01749 831116
Est. 1978
Services Restoration of antique china, oil paintings and objets d'art
Open By appointment

Ceramic Restoration
Contact Martina Gray or Emma Organ
✉ **Unit 1, 24 Cheap Street, Sherborne, Dorset, DT9 3PX** 🅿
☎ 01935 813128
Est. 1989
Services Restoration and conservation of ceramics
Open Mon–Fri 10am–12.30pm Sat 1.30pm–4pm by appointment

China and Glass Restoration
Contact Mrs Susan Birch
✉ **The Shoe, Old Hollow, Mere, Warminster, Wiltshire, BA12 6EG** 🅿
☎ 01747 861703
Est. 1993
Services China and glass restoration
Open By appointment

Peter Martin Ceramic Restoration
Contact Mr P Martin
✉ **11 Eastbourne Terrace, Westward Ho, Bideford, Devon, EX39 1HG** 🅿
☎ 01237 421446
ⓔ pmcr@madasafish.com
Est. 1996
Services Modern and antique ceramic restoration, specializing in decorative pottery and porcelain antiques
Open Strictly by appointment

Reference Works Ltd
Contact Joy or Barry Lamb
✉ **9 Commercial Road, Swanage, Dorset, BH19 1DF** 🅿
☎ 01929 424423 ⓕ 01929 422597
ⓔ sales@referenceworks.co.uk
ⓦ www.referenceworks.co.uk
Est. 1984
Services Mail order reference books on pottery and porcelain. Consultants and advisers on British ceramics. Monthly illustrated newsletters and book lists, extensive website. Small range of 18th–20thC pottery, porcelain
Open Mon–Fri 10.30am–4pm Sat 10.30am–1pm or by appointment

EAST

Emma Bradshaw Ceramic Restorations (UKIC)
Contact Emma Bradshaw
✉ **Blake House Craft Centre, 7 Blake End, Rayne, Nr Braintree, Essex, CM7 8SH** 🅿
☎ 01376 529180
Est. 1991
Services Conservation and restoration of bone china, earthenware, porcelain, stoneware, terracotta, early English pottery
Open By appointment

Ceramic Restorations
Contact Miss Syms
✉ **10 Valley Lane, Holt, Norfolk, NR25 6SF** 🅿
ⓜ 07748 901093
ⓔ victoriasyms@hotmail.com
Est. 1989
Services Ceramics, pottery and porcelain restorations, specializing in English blue-and-white transfer ware
Open By appointment

HEART OF ENGLAND

The China Repairers
Contact Mrs A Chalmers
✉ **1 Street Farm Workshops, Doughton, Tetbury, Gloucestershire, G18 8TH** 🅿
☎ 01666 503551
Est. 1989
Services China, mirror and picture frame restoration. By Appointment to HRH The Prince of Wales
Open Mon–Fri 9am–5pm

Gray Arts
Contact Mr A Gray
✉ **Unit 21b, The Maltings, School Lane, Amersham, Buckinghamshire, HP7 0ET** 🅿
☎ 01494 726502 ⓕ 01494 726502
ⓜ 07714 274410
Est. 1979
Services Porcelain restoration, clock and watch dial restoration
Trade only Yes
Open By appointment

George Perkins
Contact Mr George Perkins
✉ **2 Dell Spring, Buntingford, Hertfordshire, SG9 9BF** 🅿
☎ 01763 273139 ⓕ 01763 273139
Est. 1997
Services Porcelain restoration
Open By appointment

The Traditional Studio
Contact Miss V Green
✉ **Welwyn Equestrian Centre, Potters Heath Road, Welwyn, Hertfordshire, AL6 9SZ** 🅿
☎ 01438 814808 ⓕ 01438 814808
ⓜ 07899 745316
Est. 1997
Services Ceramics, porcelain, pottery, furniture, plaster, stonework repair, restoration, gilding, frame restoration.
Free estimates and advice
Open Mon–Fri 9am–5pm

MIDLANDS

Ashdale China Restoration
Contact Mr R Gregory
✉ **19 Boothby Avenue, Ashbourne, Derbyshire, DE6 1EL** 🅿
☎ 01335 345965
ⓜ 07961 957530
Est. 1984
Services Repairs and restorations
Open By appointment

Roger Hawkins Restoration
Contact R Hawkins
✉ **Unit 4, The Old Dairy, Winkburn, Newark, Nottinghamshire, NG22 8PQ**
☎ 01636 636666
Est. 1980
Services Restoration of all types of pottery, porcelain. Tuition given
Open By appointment

Ravensdale Studios
Contact Mr S Nicholls
✉ **77a Roundwell Street, Tunstall, Stoke-on-Trent, Staffordshire, ST6 5AW** 🅿
☎ 01782 836810 ⓕ 01782 836810
ⓔ restore@ravensdale69.fsnet.co.uk
ⓦ www.ravensdalestudios.co.uk

Est. 1988
Services Ceramic restoration
Open Mon–Fri 9am–5pm

Warwick-Wright Restoration
Contact Mr S MacGarvey
✉ **19b Wem Business Park, New Street, Wem, Shrewsbury, Shropshire, SY4 5JX** Ⓟ
☎ 01939 234879
Ⓦ www.porcelain-restoring.co.uk
Est. 1992
Services Porcelain restoration
Open Mon–Fri 8.30am–4.30pm

YORK & LINCS

A M Hurrell
Contact Miss A M Hurrell
✉ **49 Bolton Road, Silsden, Keighley, West Yorkshire, BD20 0JY** Ⓟ
☎ 01535 652969
Est. 1989
Services China restoration
Open By appointment

Kaleidescope Porcelain and Pottery Restorers
Contact Mr F Roberts
✉ **Rose Marie, Main Road, Potterhanworth, Lincoln, Lincolnshire, LN4 2DT** Ⓟ
☎ 01522 793869 Ⓕ 01522 793869
Est. 1985
Services Antique repairs and restorations, restoration of modern pieces on request
Open Mon–Fri 9am–7pm Sat 9am–noon

The Pottery & Porcelain Restoration Co
Contact Mr Tom Cosens
✉ **30 Wharf Street, Sowerby Bridge, West Yorkshire, HX6 2AE** Ⓟ
☎ 01422 834828 Ⓜ 07817 296381
Ⓔ octusnorth@aol.com
Est. 1990
Services Repairs, restoration to all ceramics and spelter
Open By appointment only

NORTH EAST

Artisans
Contact Mr C Hobs
✉ **Unit 68, Enterprise Centre, 70 Brunswick Street, Stockton-on-Tees, Cleveland, TS18 1DW** Ⓟ
☎ 01642 801020 Ⓕ 01642 391351
Ⓜ 07813 002820
Est. 1991
Services Restoration, repairs to antique china and glassware
Open Mon–Fri 9am–5pm Sat 9am–2pm

NORTH WEST

Domino Restorations
Contact Mrs J Hargreaves
✉ **c/o G B Antiques Centre, Lancaster Leisure Park, Wyresdale Road, Lancaster, Lancashire, LA1 3LA** Ⓟ
Ⓜ 07710 223170
Ⓔ r.j.hargreaves@ic24.net
Ⓦ www.domino-restoration.co.uk
Est. 1979
Services Porcelain and china restoration, jewellery repairs. Repair and restoration of glassware, metalware, tortoiseshell and ivory, spelter, bronze
Open By appointment

Monogram Studios
Contact Mr David R Adams
✉ **25 Kinsey Street, Congleton, Cheshire, CW12 1ES** Ⓟ
☎ 01260 273957
Est. 1962
Services Pottery and porcelain repair and restoration
Open Mon–Fri 8.30am–5pm

Porcelain Repairs
Contact Mr I Norman
✉ **240 Stockport Road, Cheadle Heath, Stockport, Cheshire, SK3 0LX** Ⓟ
☎ 0161 428 9599 Ⓕ 0161 286 6702
Ⓔ porcelain@repairs999.fsnet.co.uk
Est. 1976
Services Repair and restoration of all ceramics. Collection and delivery service to central London
Open By appointment only, during office hours

WALES

Ceramic Restoration (GADAR)
Contact Lynette Pierce
✉ **Woodlands Studio, Glanhafren, Abermule, Montgomery, Powys, SY15 6NA** Ⓟ
☎ 01686 630219 Ⓜ 07748 954609
Est. 1995
Services China and pottery repairs and restoration, figurines a speciality
Trade only Yes
Open By appointment

SCOTLAND

Ellen L Breheny (UKIC)
Contact Ellen L Breheny
✉ **10 Glenisla Gardens, Edinburgh, EH9 2HR** Ⓟ
☎ 0131 667 2620
Ⓔ ellen@breheny.com
Est. 1988
Services Conservation and restoration of ceramics, glass and related materials
Open Mon–Fri 10am–6pm

Renaissance China Restoration
Contact Miss S Harvey
✉ **30 West Annadale Street, Edinburgh, EH7 4JY** Ⓟ
☎ 0131 557 2762
Est. 1984
Services Invisible ceramic restoration
Open Mon–Fri 10am–1pm 2.30–5pm

REPUBLIC OF IRELAND

Lorna Barnes Conservation (IPCRA, ICOM)
Contact Lorna Barnes
✉ **158 Rialto Cottages, Rialto, Dublin 8, Ireland** Ⓟ
☎ 01 473 6205
Ⓔ barneslorna@hotmail.com
Est. 2000
Services Conservation of glass, ceramic and stone objects, condition surveys, advice on packaging and storage
Open Mon–Fri 9am–6pm

CLOCKS

Anthony Allen Conservation, Restoration, Furniture and Artefacts (BAFRA, UKIC)
Contact Anthony Allen
✉ **The Old Wharf Workshop, Redmoor Lane, Newtown, High Peak, Derbyshire, SK22 3JL** Ⓟ

☎ 01663 745274 Ⓕ 01663 745274
Est. 1970
Services Restoration of clock cases and movements, gilding, marquetry, Boulle, upholstery, metalwork, 17th–19thC furniture
Open Mon–Fri 8am–5pm

David Ansell (BAFRA, BHI)
Contact David Ansell
✉ **48 Dellside, Harefield, Middlesex, UB9 6AX** Ⓟ
☎ 01895 824648 Ⓜ 07976 222610
Ⓔ dansell@globalnet.co.uk
Est. 1990
Services Repairs and restoration of clocks
Open Mon–Sun 8.30am–5.30pm or by appointment

Antique Renovations
Contact Stephen or Alan Gartland
✉ **Unit 1, Lavenham Craft Units, Brent Eleigh Road, Lavenham, Sudbury, Suffolk, CO10 9PE** Ⓟ
☎ 01787 248511
Est. 1960
Services Repair, cabinet work and French polishing. Recommended by ERCOL. Specializing in clock case repair
Open Mon–Fri 8.30am–5pm Sat 9am–1pm

David Bates
Contact Mr David Bates
✉ **Church Cottage, Church Lane, Cawston, Norwich, Norfolk, NR10 4AJ** Ⓟ
☎ 01603 871687
Est. 1995
Services Restoration of painted and brass clock dials
Open Mon–Fri 9am–5pm

Neill Robinson Blaxill
Contact Neill Blaxill
✉ **21 St Johns Hill, Sevenoaks, Kent, TN13 3NX** Ⓟ
☎ 01732 454179
Ⓦ www.antique-clocks.co.uk
Est. 1980
Services Clock and barometer restoration
Open Mon–Sat 9am–6pm or by appointment

Symon E Boyd Clock Restorer (BHI)
Contact Mr S Boyd
✉ **54 Buxton Road, Disley, Stockport, Cheshire, SK12 2EY** Ⓟ
☎ 01663 763999
Est. 1984
Services Repair and restoration of clocks, barometers, musical boxes and automata
Open By appointment

J W Carpenter Antique Clock Restorer (BHI)
Contact John Carpenter
✉ **Whitehaven, Sandown Road, Sandwich, Kent, CT13 9NY** Ⓟ
☎ 01304 619787
Ⓔ john@ticking.freeserve.co.uk
Est. 1970
Services Antique clock repair and restoration
Open By appointment

Clockcraft
Contact Mr D Peveley
✉ **13 High Street, Bridlington, East Yorkshire, YO16 4PR** Ⓟ
☎ 01262 602802
Est. 1984
Services Clock repairs and restoration, all periods and all types
Open Mon–Sat 9am–5pm

Goodacre Engraving (BHI)
Contact John Skeavington
✉ **The Dial House, 120 Main Street, Sutton Bonington, Leicestershire, LE12 5PF** Ⓟ
☎ 01509 673082 Ⓕ 01509 673082
Est. 1948
Services Dial engraving, restoration and clock parts for English longcase and bracket clocks
Open Mon–Sat 9am–5pm phone for appointment

Gray Arts
Contact Mr A Gray
✉ **Unit 21b, The Maltings, School Lane, Amersham, Buckinghamshire, HP7 0ET** Ⓟ
☎ 01494 726502 Ⓕ 01494 726502
Ⓜ 07714 274410
Est. 1979
Services Porcelain restoration, clock and watch dial restoration
Trade only Yes
Open By appointment

Nick Hansford
Contact Nick Hansford
✉ **Nyth-fallanwrane, Hereford, Herefordshire, HR2 8JE** Ⓟ
☎ 01981 540460
Est. 1968
Services Clock and watch repairs
Open By appointment

Richard Higgins Conservation (BAFRA, UKIC)
Contact Richard Higgins
✉ **The Old School, Longnor, Nr Shrewsbury, Shropshire, SY5 7PP** Ⓟ
☎ 01743 718162 Ⓕ 01743 718022
Ⓔ richardhigginsco@aol.com
Est. 1988
Services Restoration of all fine furniture, clocks, movements, dials and cases, casting, plating, Boulle, gilding, lacquerwork, carving, period upholstery
Open Mon–Fri 8am–6pm

E Hollander (BWCG, BHI)
Contact Mr D J Pay
✉ **1 Bennets Castle, 89 The Street, Capel, Dorking, Surrey, RH5 5JX** Ⓟ
☎ 01306 713377 Ⓕ 01306 712013
Est. 1860
Services Repair and restoration of clocks, barometers, watches
Open Mon–Fri 8am–4.30pm or by appointment

Horological Workshops (BHI, BADA)
Contact Mr M D Tooke
✉ **204 Worplesdon Road, Guildford, Surrey, GU2 9UY** Ⓟ
☎ 01483 576496 Ⓕ 01483 452212
Ⓔ enquiries@horologicalworkshops.com
Est. 1968
Services Full restoration of antique clocks
Open Tues–Fri 8.30am–5.30pm Sat 9am–12.30pm

Gavin Hussey Antique Restoration (BAFRA)
Contact G Hussey
✉ **4 Brook Farm, Clayhill Road, Leigh, Reigate, Surrey, RH2 8PA** Ⓟ
☎ 01306 611634 Ⓕ 01306 611634
Ⓦ www.restoreantiques.com
Est. 1994
Services Full restoration of furniture and clocks
Open Mon–Fri 8.30am–5.30pm or by appointment

Leominster Clock Repairs (BHI)
Contact Ashley Prosser
✉ **Unit 2, The Railway Station, Worcester Road, Leominster, Herefordshire, HR6 8AR** P
☎ 01568 612298
Est. 2000
Services Clock repairs
Open Mon–Sat 9am–6pm

Llewellyn Clocks
Contact Mr C Llewellyn
✉ **12 Gibson Crescent, Sandbach, Cheshire, CW11 3HW** P
☎ 01270 768525
Est. 1976
Services Complete antique clock repair and restoration
Open By appointment only

Robert Loomes Clock Restoration (BWCG, MBHI)
Contact Mr R Loomes
✉ **3 St Leonards Street, Stamford, Lincolnshire, PE9 2HU** P
☎ 01780 481319
Ⓦ www.dialrestorer.co.uk
Est. 1987
Services Antique repair and restoration
Open Mon–Fri 9am–5pm or by appointment

William Mansell (BHI, NAG, BWCG)
Contact Bill Salisbury
✉ **24 Connaught Street, London, W2 2AF** P
☎ 020 7723 4154 Ⓕ 020 7724 2273
Ⓔ mail@williammansell.co.uk
Ⓦ www.williammansell.co.uk
Est. 1864
Services Repair, restoration and sale of clocks, watches, barometers, barographs
Open Mon–Fri 9am–6pm Sat 10am–1pm

Merim Restoration
Contact Ian Potts
✉ **Bow Street, Langport, Somerset, TA10 9PL** P
☎ 01458 252157 Ⓕ 01458 250747
Ⓔ merimianpots@hotmail.com
Ⓦ www.grandfather-clocks.org.uk
Est. 1979
Services Clock restoration, specializing in English longcase
Open Mon–Fri 8am–5pm Sat 8.30am–noon

C Moss
Contact Mr C Moss
✉ **59 Walcot Street, Bath, Somerset, BA1 5BN** P
☎ 01225 445892 Ⓕ 01225 445892
Ⓜ 07779 161731
Est. 1985
Services Clock case restoration, marquetry, parquetry, walnut furniture
Open By appointment

Oxford Longcase Clocks
Contact Mr Paul Carroll
✉ **76 Courtland Road, Rose Hill, Oxford, Oxfordshire, OX4 4JB** P
☎ 01865 779660
Est. 1978
Services Clock and barometer repair
Open Mon–Fri 8am–5pm Sat 8am–noon

Reeves Restoration at the Coach House Antiques
Contact Mrs L Reeves
✉ **The Coach House, 60 Station Approach, Gomshall, Surrey, GU5 9NP** P
☎ 01483 203838 Ⓕ 01483 202999
Ⓔ coach_house.antiques@virgin.net
Ⓦ www.coachhouseantiques.com
Est. 1984
Services Antique clock, furniture restoration
Open Mon–Sun 10am–5pm closed Thurs

J K Speed Antique Furniture Restoration
Contact Mr J Speed
✉ **The Workshop, Thornton Road, New York, Lincoln, Lincolnshire, LN4 4YL** P
☎ 01205 280313 Ⓜ 07761 242219
Est. 1964
Services Antique repair and restoration, light upholstery, specializing in case repair of longcase clocks
Open Mon–Fri 9am–5.30pm

Sundial Antique Clock Service
Contact Mr Peter Mole
✉ **64 The Parade, Brighton Road, Hooley, Coulsdon, Surrey, CR5 3EE** P
☎ 01737 551991 Ⓕ 01737 551991
Ⓜ 07733 408535
Ⓔ sundialclocks@hooley68.fsnet.co.uk
Est. 1965
Services Barometer and clock restoration, specializing in longcase clock repair
Open By appointment

Robert P Tandy (BAFRA)
Contact Robert P Tandy
✉ **Unit 5, Manor Workshops, West End, Nailsea, Bristol, BS48 4DD** P
☎ 01275 856378
Est. 1987
Services Antique furniture and longcase clock casework restoration
Open Mon–Fri 10am–6pm

Time Restored
Contact J H Bowler-Reed
✉ **20 High Street, Pewsey, Wiltshire, SN9 5AQ** P
☎ 01672 563544
Est. 1978
Services Restoration of antique clocks, musical boxes and barometers
Open Mon–Fri 10am–6pm

Timecraft Clocks (BHI)
Contact Mr G Smith
✉ **Unit 2, 24 Cheap Street, Sherborne, Dorset, DT9 3PX** P
☎ 01935 817771 Ⓕ 01935 817771
Est. 1994
Services Clock restoration and repair
Open Tue–Fri 10.30am–5.30pm Sat 10.30am–5pm

Chris Wadge Clocks
Contact Patrick Wadge
✉ **83 Fisherton Street, Salisbury, Wiltshire, SP2 7ST** P
☎ 01722 334467
Est. 1985
Services Repair, restoration of antique and modern clocks, 400-day Anniversary clocks a speciality
Open Tues–Sat 9am–4pm closed 1–2pm

Warwick Antique Restorations (UKIC)
Contact Mr R Lawman
✉ **32 Beddington Lane, Croydon, Surrey, CR0 4TB** P
☎ 020 8688 4511

Ⓔ boris@sutton74.freeserve.co.uk
Est. 1976
Services Antique clock restoration, leathering, rushing, upholstery, caning, brass
Open Tues–Sat 9.30am–5pm

Wheelers (BHI, BWCG)
Contact Mr T P Wheeler
✉ **14–16 Bath Place, Worthing, West Sussex, BN11 3AA**
☎ 01903 207656
Est. 1991
Services Antique clock repair, restoration, sales
Open Mon–Sat 9am–5pm

CONSERVATION

Archaeological Conservator (ICHAWI, IIC, IPCRA)
Contact Susannah Kelly
✉ **14 Greenmount Lawns, Terenure, Dublin 6, Ireland**
☎ 01 492 7695/01 716 8503
Ⓜ 08728 48752
Ⓔ csmchale@gofree.indigo.ie
Est. 1993
Services Conservation of archaeological and historical objects
Open Mon–Fri 9am–6pm

Heritage Care (ICHAWI, IPCRA, IMA)
Contact Adrian Kennedy
✉ **Dublin, Ireland**
☎ 01 459 9745
Ⓔ adrian@iegateway.net
Est. 1998
Services Conservation and restoration of museum, folk-life and religious type objects dating from the archaeological period to 20thC
Open Mon–Fri 7.30am–5.30pm

Plowden and Smith Ltd (MGR)
Contact James Fielden
✉ **190 St Ann's Hill, London, SW18 2RT** Ⓟ
☎ 020 8874 4005 Ⓕ 020 8874 7248
Ⓔ info@plowden-smith.com
Ⓦ www.plowden-smith.com
Est. 1966
Services Repair and restoration of paintings, furniture, stone, metalwork, decorative arts, object mounting, exhibitions
Open Mon–Fri 9am–5pm

Gordon Richardson
Contact Gordon Richardson
✉ **36 Silverknowes Road, Edinburgh, EH4 5LG** Ⓟ
☎ 0131 312 7959
Services Conservation and restoration of paintings, pictures, prints, drawings, globes, scientific instruments, silverware, metalware, military artefacts, ships' models, decorative objects
Open By appointment

Textile Conservation (UKIC)
Contact Fiona Hutton
✉ **Ivy House Farm, Wolvershill Road, Banwell, Somerset, BS29 6LB** Ⓟ
☎ 01934 822449
Ⓔ fiona@textileconservation.co.uk
Est. 1989
Services Textile conservation
Open Mon–Fri 9am–5pm

Textile Conservation Services
Contact Miss L Bond
✉ **3–4 West Workshops, Welbeck, Worksop, Nottinghamshire, S80 3LW** Ⓟ
☎ 01909 481655 Ⓕ 01909 481655
Ⓔ textile.conservation@tesco.net
Est. 1984
Services The conservation of costume, lace and small textiles. Talks and courses on costume and textiles
Open By appointment

Voitek Conservation of Works of Art (IPC)
Contact Mrs E Sobczynski
✉ **9 Whitehorse Mews, Westminster Bridge Road, London, SE1 7QD** Ⓟ
☎ 020 7928 6094 Ⓕ 020 7928 6094
Ⓔ voitekcwa@btinternet.com
Est. 1972
Services Conservation of prints, drawings, watercolours, maps, conservation mounting and project planning. Conservation of sculpture, marble, terracotta, wood
Open By appointment

CONSULTANCY

Tim Corfield Professional Antiques Consultant
Contact Tim Corfield
✉ **Beechcroft, Buckholt Road, Broughton, Stockbridge, Hampshire, SO20 8DA** Ⓟ
☎ 01794 301141 Ⓕ 01794 301141
Ⓜ 07798 881383
Ⓔ antique@tcp.co.uk
Ⓦ www.antiques-hunter.com
Est. 1992
Services Advising clients on purchases at auction or in the trade
Open By appointment

Robert Kleiner and Co Ltd (BADA, CINOA)
Contact Robert Kleiner or Jane de Hurtig
✉ **30 Old Bond Street, London, W1S 4AE** Ⓟ
☎ 020 7629 1814 Ⓕ 020 7629 1239
Ⓔ robert.kleiner@virgin.net
Ⓦ www.cloudband.com/gallery/kleiner/playthings
Est. 1989
Services Advice on purchase and sale of Chinese works of art, jades, porcelain, snuff bottles, valuations of collections. Specialist in Chinese snuff bottles
Open Mon–Fri 9.30am–5.30pm

DISPLAY EQUIPMENT

Arcade Arts Ltd
Contact Mr K Hewitt or Monika Wengraf-Hewitt
✉ **25 West Hill Road, London, SW18 1LL** Ⓟ
☎ 020 8265 2564 Ⓕ 020 8874 2982
Est. 1997
Services Repair and renovation of art objects and makers of display stands
Open By appointment

Timbercraft
Contact Mr A J Fishwick
✉ **Bottomley Yard, Bottomley Street, Nelson, Lancashire, BB9 9SW** Ⓟ
☎ 01282 611277 Ⓕ 01282 615651
Ⓦ www.subnet.co.uk/timbercraft.nw
Est. 1997
Services Makers of display units for antique thimbles, spoons, cabinets for medals etc
Open By appointment

DOCUMENTATION & PROVENANCE

DIVA (Digital Inventory and Visual Archive) (GADAR)
Contact Mr R Haycraft
✉ **The Lamb Arcade, High Street, Wallingford, Oxfordshire, OX10 0BS** P
☎ 01491 839622
e rohaycraft@fsbdial.co.uk
w www.juststolen.com
Est. 1980
Services Archive documentation, provision of logbook and provenance history, plus, if property is stolen, world-wide publicity on website
Open Mon–Fri 9am–5.30pm

ENAMEL

Mark Newland Enamel Restorer
Contact Mr M Newland
✉ **1 Whitehouse Way, Southgate, London, N14 7LX** P
☎ 020 8361 0429
Est. 1982
Services Restoration of enamelled jewellery and objets d'art
Open By appointment

ETHNOGRAPHICS

George Monger
Contact Mr G Monger
✉ **Unit 6, The Barn, Glebe Farm Industrial Units, Onehouse, Stowmarket, Suffolk, IP14 3HL** P
☎ 01449 677900 f 01449 674803
m 07703 441265
e geoMcons@tinyworld.co.uk
Est. 1995
Services Conservation and restoration, including social and industrial history and ethnography of pieces
Open By appointment

FLOORS

Holland & Welsh
Contact Michael Nap
✉ **Unit 13, Riverside Park, Treforest Industrial Estate, Pontypridd, Mid Glamorgan, CF37 5TG** P
☎ 01443 660255 f 01443 660651
Est. 1997
Services Supply and installation of antique flooring
Open Mon–Fri 9am–5pm
Sat Sun 9.30am–1.30pm

FRAMING

Baron Art
Contact Mr A Baron
✉ **9 Chapel Yard, Albert Street, Holt, Norfolk, NR25 6HJ** P
☎ 01263 713430 f 01263 711670
e baronart@aol.com
Est. 2001
Services Framing
Open Mon–Sat 9am–5pm

Douglas McLeod Period Frames
Contact Suzie McLeod
✉ **44 Trinity Street, Salisbury, Wiltshire, SP1 2BD** P
☎ 01722 337565 f 01722 337565
Est. 1982
Services Restoration of old frames, picture restoration, carving, gilding, lacewing framing
Open Mon–Fri 9am–5pm
Sat 10am–4pm

FURNITURE

SOUTH EAST

T M Akers Antique Restoration (BAFRA)
Contact Mr T M Akers
✉ **39 Chancery Lane, Beckenham, Kent, BR3 2NR** P
☎ 020 8650 9179 m 07768 948421
w www.akersofantiques.com
Est. 1979
Services Period antique furniture restoration
Open Mon–Fri 9am–5pm

Antique Restorations (BAFRA)
Contact Raymond Konyn
✉ **The Old Wheelwrights', Brasted Forge, Brasted, Kent, TN16 1JL** P
☎ 01959 563863 f 01959 561262
e antique@antique-restorations.org.uk
w www.antique-restorations.org.uk
Est. 1979
Services Full antique furniture restoration, pre-1900 furniture sourcing and acquisition, replica brass foundry castings
Open Mon–Fri 9am–5pm

Ashdown Antiques Restoration
Contact Robert Hale
✉ **Old Forge Farm, Old Forge Lane, Horney Common, Uckfield, East Sussex, TB22 3EL** P
☎ 01825 713003
Est. 1975
Services Furniture restorer
Open By appointment

Bespoke Furniture
Contact Mr M McEwan
✉ **Ladwood Farm, Acrise, Folkestone, Kent, CT18 8LL** P
☎ 01303 893635
Est. 1994
Services Restoration of antique furniture. Traditional or contemporary individual pieces of furniture made to order
Open Mon–Fri 8.30am–5pm
Sat 9am–2pm Sun by appointment

Bigwood Restoration
Contact Mr S Bigwood
✉ **Bigwood Antiques, High Street, Brasted, Kent, TN16 1JA** P
☎ 01959 564458
e sales@bigwoodantiques.com
w www.antiquesrestoration.co.uk
Est. 1984
Services Complete restoration of all antique furniture
Open Mon–Sat 10am–5pm
Sun noon–4pm

Maxwell Black
Contact Mr M Black
✉ **Brook House Studio, Novington Lane, East Chiltington, Lewes, East Sussex, BN7 3AX** P
☎ 01273 890175
Est. 1979
Services All types of antique furniture restoration
Open Mon–Fri 8am–6pm

Brightling Restoration
Contact D White
✉ **Little Worge Farm, Brightling, Robertsbridge, East Sussex, TN32 5HN** P
☎ 01424 838424 f 01424 838681
e brightlingrest@cs.com
Est. 2000
Services Restoration of English and Continental furniture
Open Mon–Fri 8am–4.30pm

Benedict Clegg (BAFRA)
Contact Mr Benedict Clegg
✉ **Rear of 20 Camden Road, Tunbridge Wells, Kent, TN1 2PY**
☎ 01892 548095
Est. 1987
Services Antique furniture repair and restoration
Open Mon–Fri 9am–5pm

D & C Antique Restorations
Contact Mr C Voles
✉ **1–4 Upper Gardner Street, Brighton, East Sussex, BN1 4AN** P
☎ 01273 670344
Est. 1993
Services Complete antique furniture restoration
Open Mon–Fri 8am–5.30pm

W H Earles
Contact Mr W H Earles
✉ **60 Castle Road, Tankerton, Whitstable, Kent, CT5 2EA** P
☎ 01227 264346
Est. 1978
Services English, Continental and most period furniture restoration and papier mâché
Open Mon–Fri 8.30am–6pm

Luke Evans Antiques
Contact Mr Luke Evans
✉ **19 Pycombe Street, Pycombe, East Sussex, BN45 7EE** P
☎ 01273 504359
Est. 1998
Services Furniture restoration, upholstery, re-caning, re-leathering, pine stripping, furniture finding service
Open Mon–Sat 9am–6pm

Farm Cottage Antiques
Contact Mrs Lynn Winder
✉ **Basement, 6a Claremont Road, Seaford, East Sussex, BN25 2AY** P
☎ 01323 896766 F 01323 894982
Est. 1995
Services Furniture restoration
Open By appointment

Glassenbury Country Furniture Ltd
Contact Clive Cowell
✉ **Iden Green, Goudhurst, Cranbrook, Kent, TN17 2PA** P
☎ 01580 212022 F 01580 212944
Est. 1985
Services Repair and restoration, make on commission
Open Mon–Fri 8.30am–5.30pm Sat by appointment

Heritage Restoration
Contact Mr D R Johnson
✉ **782 Lower Rainham Road, Rainham, Gillingham, Kent, ME8 7UD** P
☎ 01634 374609
Est. 1989
Services Antique furniture restoration
Open Mon–Fri 9am–5pm

T C Hinton
Contact T C Hinton
✉ **The Board Stores, Spencer Mews, Rear of 20 Camden Rd, Tunbridge Wells, Kent, TN1 2PY** P
☎ 01892 547515 F 01892 547515
E hintonbusiness@talk21.com
Est. 1979
Services Restoration and conservation of antique furniture, French polishing, gilding, painted furniture, antique paint effects
Open Mon–Fri 9am–1pm 2–5.30pm

R G Jones
Contact R G Jones
✉ **1 Brickfield Cottage, Bilting, Ashford, Kent, TN25 4ER** P
☎ 01233 812849
Est. 1985
Services Antique restoration, gilding
Open Mon–Fri 9am–4pm

R Lindsell
Contact R Lindsell
✉ **2b Southwood Road, Ramsgate, Kent, CT11 0AA** P
☎ 01843 588845
Est. 1973
Services Furniture repair and restoration, French polishing
Open Mon–Fri 9am–6pm

Timothy Long Restoration (BAFRA, CR)
Contact Timothy Long
✉ **St John's Church, London Road, Dunton Green, Sevenoaks, Kent, TN13 2TE** P
☎ 01732 743368
Est. 1978
Services Antique furniture restoration, marquetry, Boulle, clock cases, upholstery, cabinet work and polishing
Open Mon–Fri 8am–5pm

The Old Forge
Contact Mr Burgess
✉ **South Street, Rotherfield, Crowborough, East Sussex, TN6 3LR** P
☎ 01892 852060
Est. 1979
Services Furniture restoration
Open Mon–Fri 8am–6pm Sat 8am–2pm

Park View Antiques
Contact Patrick Leith-Ross
✉ **High Street, Durgates, Wadhurst, East Sussex, TN5 6DE** P
☎ 01892 740264 F 01892 740264
M 07970 202036
E leithross@btconnect.com
Est. 1985
Services Furniture restoration
Open By appointment

Phillburys
Contact Mr G C Rattenbury
✉ **Unit 2, Udimore Workshop, School Lane, Udimore, Rye, East Sussex, TN31 6AS** P
☎ 01797 222361
Est. 1982
Services Restoration of antique furniture
Open Mon–Sat 8am–6pm

Marco Pitt (BADA)
Contact Mr Marco Pitt
✉ **New England House, New England Street, Brighton, East Sussex, BN1 4GH** P
☎ 01273 685009 M 07721 022480
Est. 1978
Services Complete furniture restoration, specializing in Russian, French, European pieces
Open Mon–Fri 9am–6pm Sat 9am–1pm

Paul M Read Antique Furniture Restoration
Contact Paul Read
✉ **Brasted Forge, The Green, High Street, Brasted, Westerham, Kent, TN16 1JL** P
☎ 01959 565733 F 01959 565733
Est. 1986

ASSOCIATED SERVICES

FURNITURE

Services Furniture restoration, cabinet-making, marquetry, inlaying, carving, turning, gilding, leather work, clock restoration, upholstery, cane and rush seating, traditional French polishing, on-site polishing and specialist wood finishes
Open By appointment

T Straw Restoration
Contact Mr T Straw
✉ **Unit 4, The Oast Hurst Farm, Mountain Street, Chilham, Canterbury, Kent, CT4 8DH** Ⓟ
☎ 01227 732485 Ⓜ 07961 944014
Est. 1989
Services Antique furniture restoration
Open Mon–Fri 8am–6pm or by appointment

V Stringer
Contact Mr V Stringer
✉ **Unit 5, Acorn House, The Broyle, Ringmer, Lewes, East Sussex, BN8 5NN** Ⓟ
☎ 01273 814434 Ⓕ 01273 814434
Est. 1989
Services Antique restoration, reproduction polishers, furniture makers
Open Mon–Fri 8am–6pm
Sat 8am–noon

Temple Jones Restoration
Contact E or Miss B Temple Jones
✉ **The Workshop, Burwash Common Post Office, Heathfield Road, Burwash Common, East Sussex, TN19 7LT** Ⓟ
☎ 01435 883130 Ⓕ 01435 883130
Ⓜ 07802 415138
Ⓔ temple-jones@talk21.com
Est. 1996
Services Restoration and conservation work to period antique furniture
Open Mon–Sat 8am–6pm

LONDON

J Abrahart
Contact Mr J Abrahart
✉ **62a Valetta Road, London, W3 7TN** Ⓟ
☎ 020 8746 7260
Est. 1955
Services Antique furniture repair and restoration, French polishing
Open By appointment

Adams Restorations
Contact Mr A Klappholz
✉ **273 Green Lanes, Brownswood Road, London, N4 2EX** Ⓟ
☎ 020 7281 9604 Ⓕ 020 7281 9604
Ⓜ 07778 802877
Ⓔ aklappholz@ukgateway.net
Est. 1987
Services Furniture repair and restoration
Open Mon–Sat 8am–5pm

G Albanese
Contact Mr G Albanese
✉ **Unit 3a, 100 Rosebery Avenue, London, E12 6PS** Ⓟ
☎ 020 8471 5417
Est. 1978
Services Antiques restoration and cabinet-making
Trade only Yes
Open Mon–Fri 7am–5pm

Antique Restorations (BAFRA)
Contact Mr A Smith
✉ **45 Windmill Road, Brentford, Middlesex, TW8 0QQ** Ⓟ
☎ 020 8568 5249 Ⓕ 020 8568 5249
Est. 1987
Services Restorers of painted and decorated furniture. Specialists in Oriental lacquering, Japanning, gilding
Open Mon–Fri 9am–5.30pm or by appointment

B S H Antique Restorers Ltd
Contact Mr B S Howells
✉ **7a Tynemouth Terrace, Tynemouth Road, London, N15 4AP** Ⓟ
☎ 020 8808 7965 Ⓕ 020 8801 5313
Est. 1978
Services 18th–19thC antique furniture restoration, leatherwork, gilding, marquetry and copy brasswork
Open Mon–Fri 6.30am–3.30pm

Ballantyne Booth Ltd (UKIC)
Contact Miss H Mark or Mr Scott Bowram
✉ **Wendover House, 2a Wendover Road, London, NW10 4RT** Ⓟ
☎ 020 8965 2777 Ⓕ 020 8965 2777
Est. 1983
Services Cabinet work, veneering, glazing, carving, polishing, upholstery, aerial conservation and restoration
Open Mon–Fri 9am–5.30pm

Bell House Restoration
Contact Mr R Humphrey
✉ **20–22 Beardell Street, London, SE19 1TP** Ⓟ
☎ 020 8761 9002 Ⓕ 020 8761 9012
Ⓜ 07771 801269
Ⓔ bellhouserestore@aol.com
Est. 1984
Services Antique furniture restoration, gilding, polishing, colouring, turning, veneering, restorations abroad, simulation
Open Mon–Fri 8am–5pm

Church Lane Restorations (LAPADA)
Contact Mr Evans or Mr Vincent
✉ **1 Church Lane, Teddington, Middlesex, TW11 8PA** Ⓟ
☎ 020 8977 2526 Ⓕ 020 8977 2526
Est. 1969
Services Complete repair and restoration service, cabinet-making, polishing, carving
Open Mon–Thurs 7.30am–5pm
Fri 7.30am–4pm

The Collector's Workshop
Contact Mr B Brannan
✉ **Heathrow House, Factory Lane, London, N17 9BY** Ⓟ
☎ 020 8808 1920 Ⓕ 020 8808 1920
Ⓜ 07778 754754
Est. 1968
Services Antique furniture repair and restoration, upholstery, carving, gilding
Open By appointment

W J Cook (BAFRA)
Contact Mr B Cook
✉ **167 Battersea High Street, London, SW11 3JS** Ⓟ
☎ 020 7736 5329
Est. 1963
Services Furniture polishing, restoration, upholstery, gilding
Open By appointment

George Cooke
Contact Mr G Cooke
✉ **Unit GE 3, Cooper House, 2 Michael Road, London, SW6 2AD** Ⓟ

☎ 020 7610 9066 Ⓜ 07932 007412
Ⓔ george@gcrestoration.fsnet.co.uk
Est. 1993
Services Antique restoration and conservation, including French polishing, veneering, turning, cabinet-making
Open Mon–Fri 8am–6pm
Sat by appointment

The Craftsman's Joint
Contact Mrs Jo Hollis
✉ **175 Kingston Road, London, SW19 1LH** 🅿
☎ 020 8545 0655 Ⓕ 020 8395 4566
Ⓔ craftsmans_joint@yahoo.co.uk
Ⓦ www.craftsmansjoint.co.uk
Est. 1991
Services Furniture restoration, cabinet-making, French polishing, upholstery, caning, leatherwork
Open Mon–Fri 9.30am–5.30pm
Sat 10am–2pm closed Wed or by appointment

Crawford Antiques
✉ **87 Cricklewood Lane, London, NW2 1HR** 🅿
☎ 020 8450 3660
Est. 1969
Services Antiques repairs and French polishing
Open Mon–Sat 9am–6pm

Robert H Crawley (BAFRA)
Contact Mr R Crawley
✉ **75 St Mary's Road, London, W5 5RH** 🅿
☎ 020 8566 5074 Ⓕ 020 8810 0878
Ⓔ antique.restorer@virgin.net
Est. 1979
Services Antique furniture restoration
Open Mon–Fri 8.30am–4.30pm

G and D Davis Antique Restorers
Contact Mr G Davis
✉ **135 Bowes Road, London, N13 4SE** 🅿
☎ 020 8889 4951
Est. 1982
Services Antique furniture restoration, caning, upholstery
Open Mon–Sat 9am–6pm

Dyson Furniture
Contact Nick Dyson
✉ **Eel Pie Boatyard, Eel Pie Island, Twickenham, Middlesex, TW1 3DY**
☎ 020 8891 5309
Est. 1992
Services Complete furniture repair and restoration, turning, marquetry, inlay work, cabinet-making
Open Mon–Fri 10am–6pm

Elizabeth Street Antiques and Restoration Services
Contact Mr Naik
✉ **35 Elizabeth Street, London, SW1 9RP** 🅿
☎ 020 7730 6777
Est. 1993
Services Antique restoration, marquetry, French polishing, upholstery. Antiques sales
Open Mon–Sat 8am–7pm

Fens Restoration and Sales
Contact Mrs M Saville
✉ **46 Lots Road, London, SW10 0QF** 🅿
☎ 020 7352 9883
Est. 1979
Services Repair and restoration of furniture, stripping
Open Mon–Fri 9am–5pm
Sat by appointment

Ivo Geikie-Cobb
Contact Mr I Geikie-Cobb
✉ **Unit 32, Charterhouse Works, Eltringham Street, London, SW18 1TD** 🅿
☎ 020 8874 3767 Ⓕ 020 8874 3767
Ⓜ 07761 561569
Ⓔ restore@ivogc.com
Ⓦ www.ivogc.com
Est. 1991
Services Antique furniture conservation and restoration, gilding, upholstery, re-leathering, French polishing, veneering, architectural restoration
Open Mon–Fri 9.30am–5.30pm

Greenwich Conservation Workshops
Contact Richard Moy
✉ **22 Nelson Road, London, SE10 9JB** 🅿
☎ 020 8293 1067
Ⓦ www.spreadeagle.org
Est. 1957
Services Restoration of period furniture, oil, watercolours, picture frames, porcelain, pottery
Open Mon–Sat 10.30am–5.30pm

H J Hatfield and Son
✉ **42 St Michael's Street, London, W2 1QP** 🅿
☎ 020 7723 8265 Ⓕ 020 7706 4562
Ⓔ hjhatfield@msn.com
Est. 1834
Services Restoration of furniture, porcelain, paintings, Boulle, upholstery, lacquerwork, metalwork, chandeliers, marble
Open Mon–Fri 9am–1pm 2–5pm

Hatter Antiques & Restoration
Contact Mr P Harris
✉ **291 Sydenham Road, London, SE26 5EW** 🅿
☎ 020 8659 0333
Est. 1987
Services Antique furniture repair and restoration, upholstery, French polishing, woodwork repair
Open Mon–Sat 8.30am–7.30pm

Hens Teeth Antiques
Contact Mr M Murray
✉ **20 Park Hall Road, London, N2 9PU** 🅿
☎ 020 8883 0755 Ⓜ 07970 625359
Ⓔ hens.teeth@virgin.net
Est. 1997
Services Furniture repair and restoration, polishing, gilding, upholstery
Open By appointment

Hope and Piaget (BAFRA)
Contact Mr B Duffy or Mrs K Keate
✉ **Unit 12–13, Burmarsh Workshops, Marsden Street, London, NW5 3JA** 🅿
☎ 020 7267 6040 Ⓕ 020 7267 6040
Ⓔ mail@hope-piaget.co.uk
Est. 1982
Services Conservation and restoration of 18th–19thC furniture, Japanning, laquerwork, gilding, carving, tortoiseshelling
Open Mon–Fri 9.30am–6pm

Hornsby Furniture Restoration Ltd
Contact Mr M Gough
✉ **35 Thurloe Place, London, SW7 2HJ** 🅿
☎ 020 7225 2888 Ⓕ 020 7838 0235
Ⓔ sales@antiqueous.com
Ⓦ www.hornsbyleather.com
Est. 1890

Services Antique furniture restoration including gilding, cabinet-making, upholstery, bespoke furniture, French polishing, caning
Open Mon–Fri 8am–5.30pm Sat 9am–12.30pm

Magical Restorations
Contact Mr F Hussain
✉ **3 Wilson Walk, Chiswick, London, W4 1TP** Ⓟ
☎ 020 8741 3799
Est. 1997
Services Furniture repair and restoration, carving, gilding, French polishing
Open Mon–Fri 9am–5pm

M Merritt
Contact Mr M Merritt
✉ **8 Brightfield Road, London, SE12 8QF** Ⓟ
☎ 020 8852 7577 Ⓕ 020 8852 7577
Est. 1983
Services Antique furniture restoration, cabinet-making, veneering
Open Mon–Fri 9am–5pm

Richard G Phillips Ltd
Contact Mr R G Phillips
✉ **95–99 Shernhall Street, London, E17 9HS** Ⓟ
☎ 020 8509 9075 Ⓕ 020 8509 9077
Est. 1984
Services Antique furniture restoration. Also manufacturer of classical English furniture and decorative four-poster beds
Open By appointment

Piers Furniture Repair Workshop
Contact Mr P Tarrant-Willis
✉ **The Old Air Raid Shelter, Athlone Street, London, NW5 4LN** Ⓟ
☎ 020 7209 5824
Est. 1998
Services Antique furniture repair and restoration including French polishing
Open By appointment

Quality Restorations Limited
Contact Mr A Dwyer
✉ **Ionna House, Humber Road, London, NW2 6EN** Ⓟ
☎ 020 8830 5888 Ⓕ 020 8450 9296
Ⓔ info@qfw.co.uk
Ⓦ www.qfw.co.uk
Est. 1994
Services Full repair and restoration of all types of furniture, French polishing, waxing, high-density gloss and satin finish, oiling
Open By appointment

R M W Restorations
Contact Mr R Mark-Wardlaw
✉ **Unit B08, Acton Business Centre, School Road, London, NW10 6TD** Ⓟ
☎ 020 8965 2938 Ⓕ 020 8965 2938
Est. 1986
Services Antique furniture repair and restoration, traditional and modern finishes, insurance work, cabinet work, polishing
Open Mon–Fri 10am–6pm

Regency Restoration
Contact Mrs E Ball
✉ **Studio 21, Thames House, 140 Battersea Park Road, London, SW11 4NB** Ⓟ
☎ 020 7622 5275 Ⓕ 020 7498 1803
Est. 1987
Services Restoration of 18th–19thC mirrors, picture frames, English and Continental painted and gilded furniture, architectural gilding, church interiors, polychrome sculpture, lacquerwork, oil paintings, carving
Open Mon–Fri 9.30am–5.30pm

Remstone Contracts
Contact Mr D Louden
✉ **69a Southgate Road, London, N1 3JS** Ⓟ
☎ 020 7359 3536 Ⓕ 020 7359 3536
Est. 1968
Services Furniture restoration and repair, polishing, leather colouring
Open Mon–Fri 8am–5.30pm

Sears
Contact Mr D Foster
✉ **17–17A Nunhead Green, Peckham, London, SE15 3QQ** Ⓟ
☎ 020 7732 1968 Ⓕ 020 7732 1968
Est. 1975
Services Furniture restoration
Open Mon–Fri 8am–4pm

Michael Slade
Contact M Slade
✉ **42 Quernmore Road, London, N4 4QP** Ⓟ
☎ 020 8341 3194
Ⓔ mikeslade@ntl.com
Est. 1984
Services Antique repairs and restoration, furniture maker, upholstery, French polishing. Furniture sales
Open By appointment

H A Smith & Son
Contact Mr A Smith
✉ **36a Nelson Road, Harrow on the Hill, Harrow, Middlesex, HA1 3ET** Ⓟ
☎ 020 8864 2335
Est. 1920
Services Antique and modern furniture restoration, repair and upholstery
Open Mon–Fri 9am–6pm Sat 10am–2pm

Solomon
Contact Solomon
✉ **49 Park Road, London N8 8SY**
☎ 020 8341 1817 Ⓕ 020 8341 1817
Ⓔ solomon@solomonantiques.fsnet.co.uk
Est. 1981
Services Restoration, upholstery, polishing
Open Mon–Sat 9am–6pm

Tony's Antique Restoration
Contact Tony Brown
✉ **Unit 13 Downham Enterprise Centre, London, SE6 1TE** Ⓟ
☎ 020 8461 5757 Ⓕ 020 8461 5757
Est. 1997
Services Antiques restoration including stripping, polishing, marquetry and inlaying
Open Mon–Fri 9.30am–4.30pm

Angela Vernon Bates
Contact Mrs A Vernon Bates
✉ **Candid Studio, 3 Torrens Street, London, EC1V 1NQ** Ⓟ
☎ 020 7833 2133 Ⓕ 020 7833 2133
Est. 1991
Services Antiques repair and restoration of small items, painted surfaces, re-lining of boxes, frames, tôle gilding, papier mâché, painted textiles and furniture
Open By apppointment

P Walters Ltd
Contact David Walters
✉ **3 Harold Road, Harringey, London, N15 4PL**
☎ 020 8808 5889 Ⓕ 020 8808 0227
Est. 1937
Services Repair and restoration of antiques, cabinet-maker
Trade only Yes
Open Mon–Fri 8am–5.30pm

Woodbourne Antiques and Furniture Makers
Contact Mr G Evans
✉ **Unit 35 Cromwell Industrial Estate, Staffa Road, London, E10 7QZ** Ⓟ
☎ 020 8539 5575 Ⓕ 020 8539 5575
Est. 1984
Services Furniture makers, chair copying, repair and restoration of antique furniture
Open Mon–Fri 8am–6pm
Sat 8am–1pm

SOUTH

Allen Avery Interiors
Contact Paul Avery
✉ **No 1 High Street, Haselmere, Surrey, GU27 2AG** Ⓟ
☎ 01428 643883 Ⓕ 01428 656815
Est. 1970
Services Restoration
Open Mon Tues Thurs Fri
9am–1pm 2.15–5pm
Wed Sat 9am–1pm

Antique Restorers
Contact Mr W Barker
✉ **2 Station Approach, Stoneleigh, Epsom, Surrey, KT19 0QZ** Ⓟ
☎ 020 8393 9111
Est. 1980
Services Upholstery, French polishing, furniture repairs, cane and rush seating. Antique and second-hand tools for sale
Open Mon–Fri 9.30am–4.30pm

B H Woodfinishes
Contact Mr C Hopkins
✉ **Unit 22, Church Lane Industrial Estate, Church Lane, Horsham, West Sussex, RH13 6LU** Ⓟ
☎ 01403 891551 Ⓕ 01403 891551
Ⓜ 07850 051607
Ⓔ sales@bhwoodfinishes.co.uk
Ⓦ www.bhwoodfinishes.co.uk
Est. 1988
Services Strip and repolish, wood repairs, French polishing, leathering, gilding. On-site work (bannisters, staircases etc)
Open Mon–Fri 9am–5pm

Colin Bell, Ben Norris and Co (BAFRA)
Contact Colin Bell
✉ **Knowl Hill Farm, Knowl Hill, Kingsclere, Newbury, Berkshire, RG15 8NJ** Ⓟ
☎ 01635 297950 Ⓕ 01635 299851
Est. 1980
Services Restoration of antique furniture and gilding, reproduction cabinet-making, furniture made to order
Open Mon–Fri 8.30am–5pm

A E Booth and Son (BAFRA)
Contact David or Ann Booth
✉ **9 High Street, Ewell, Surrey, KT17 1SG** Ⓟ
☎ 020 8393 5245 Ⓕ 020 8393 5245
Est. 1934
Services Restoration of antique and reproduction furniture including polishing and upholstery
Open Mon–Sat 9am–4.45pm

C T Bristow
Contact Mr Bristow
✉ **Lydgate, Seale Lane, Seale, Farnham, Surrey, GU10 1LF** Ⓟ
☎ 01252 782775
Est. 1971
Services French polishing, fine antique furniture restoration
Open By appointment

The Cabinet Repair Shop
Contact Mrs M H Embling
✉ **Woodlands Farm, Blacknest Road, Blacknest, Alton, Hampshire, GU34 4BQ** Ⓟ
☎ 01252 793084 Ⓕ 01252 794260
Ⓦ www.dsembling.co.uk
Est. 1984
Services Restoration of antique and modern furniture, insurance claim work
Open Mon–Fri 8am–5pm
Sat by appointment

Peter Casebow (BAFRA)
Contact Mr P Casebow
✉ **Pilgrims Mill Lane, Worthing, West Sussex, BN13 3DE** Ⓟ
☎ 01903 264045 Ⓜ 07790 339602
Ⓔ pcasebow@hotmail.com
Est. 1987
Services Restoration of period furniture including square-piano restoration
Open By appointment

B Castle (Exhibitor of the Royal Academy & Mall Gallery)
Contact Mr B Castle
✉ **2 Charmandean Road, Worthing, West Sussex, BN14 9LB** Ⓟ
☎ 01903 239702
Est. 1982
Services Antique repair and restoration of small furniture, decorative items, woodcarver
Open Mon–Sat by appointment

Ralph Clee
Contact Mr R Clee
✉ **Quell Farm, Greatham, Pulborough, West Sussex, RH20 2ES** Ⓟ
☎ 01798 874228
Est. 1995
Services Furniture restoration, polishing
Open Mon–Fri 8.30am–6pm
Sat by appointment

Alan Cooper Antique Restorations
Contact Alan Cooper
✉ **Unit 7, Park Farm, Hundred Acre Lane, Wivelsfield Green, Haywards Heath, West Sussex, RH17 7RU** Ⓟ
☎ 01273 890017
Est. 1973
Services Antiques repair, French polishing, restoration
Open Mon–Fri 8am–3pm

Copperwheat Restoration (RICS)
Contact Carole Copperwheat
✉ **Rear of Pascall Atkey, 29–30 High Street, Cowes, Isle of Wight, PO31 7RX** Ⓟ
☎ 01983 281011 Ⓜ 07720 399670
Est. 1985
Services Antique furniture repair, restoration, commissions
Open Any time by prior phone call

Corwell
Contact Mr S Corbin
✉ **Unit 6, Amners Farm, Burghfield, Reading, Berkshire, RG30 3UE** P
☎ 0118 983 3404 ⓕ 0118 983 3404
ⓔ info@corwell.co.uk
ⓦ www.corwell.co.uk
Est. 1989
Services Antique restoration, cabinet-making
Open Mon–Fri 9am–5pm
Sat 9am–2pm

Davenports Antiques
Contact Mr C Height
✉ **Unit 5, Woodgate Centre, Oak Tree Lane, Woodgate, Chichester, West Sussex, PO20 6GU** P
☎ 01243 544242 ⓜ 07932 690210
Est. 1980
Services Antique furniture restoration
Open Mon–Fri 8.30am–6pm

Sonia Demetriou
Contact Sonia Demetriou
✉ **2 Elbridge Farm Buildings, Chichester Road, Bognor Regis, West Sussex, PO21 5EG** P
☎ 01243 842235 ⓕ 01243 842235
ⓔ sondem@intelynx.net
Est. 1977
Services Restoration of antique painted furniture and objets d'art
Open Mon–Fri 9.30am–6pm
Sat by appointment

R G Dewdney
Contact Mr R G Dewdney
✉ **Norfolk Road, South Holmwood, Dorking, Surrey, RH5 4LA** P
☎ 01306 888174 ⓕ 01306 742636
Est. 1968
Services General antiques repairs and restoration, leatherwork
Open Mon–Fri 9am–6pm

Downland Furniture Restoration
Contact Mr S Macintyre
✉ **Wepham Farmyard, Wepham, Arundel, West Sussex, BN18 9RQ** P
☎ 01903 883387
Est. 1984
Services Furniture restoration and conservation
Open Mon–Fri 9am–5pm

Dunn and Wright
Contact Mr A Dunn
✉ **Rear of 128 Sheen Road, Richmond, Surrey, TW9 1UR** P
☎ 020 8948 7032
Est. 1974
Services Furniture repair and restoration
Open Mon–Fri 8am–5.30pm

Richard Elderton
Contact R C Elderton
✉ **Home Farm, Mill Lane, Hawkley, Liss, Hampshire, GU33 6NU** P
☎ 01420 538374
ⓔ woodman@cix.co.uk
ⓦ www.cix.co.uk/~woodman/
Est. 1976
Services Antique furniture restorations, new bespoke solid wood furniture, metalworking repairs, woodturning
Open Mon–Fri 9am–5pm or by appointment

F and R Restorations
Contact Mr G R Fisher
✉ **39b Walton Street, Tadworth, Surrey, KT20 7RR** P
☎ 01737 819918 ⓕ 01737 819518
ⓔ fandr.restoration@virgin.net
ⓦ www.fandrrestorations.co.uk
Est. 1999
Services Antique furniture restorations, sales of antique and contemporary design furniture
Open Mon–Sat 8.30am–6pm

G and R Fraser-Sinclair (BAFRA)
Contact Mr G Fraser-Sinclair
✉ **Haysbridge Farm, Brickhouse Lane, South Godstone, Godstone, Surrey, RH9 8JW** P
☎ 01342 844112 ⓕ 01342 844112
Est. 1978
Services General restoration of 18thC furniture
Open Mon–Fri 8am–5.30pm

A D Gardner
Contact Mr Gardner
✉ **2a East Road, Reigate, Surrey, RH2 9EX** P
☎ 01737 222430
Est. 1969
Services Antique repair and restoration, fine French polishing, caning, leathering, upholstery
Open Mon–Fri 8.30am–5.30pm

Tony Gardner
Contact Mr T Gardner
✉ **The Boiler House, Morden Hall Park, Morden, Surrey, SM4 5JD** P
☎ 020 8687 1991 ⓜ 07979 642895
Est. 1980
Services Furniture restoration, French polishing, caning and rushing. Situated in a National Trust property
Open Thurs–Mon 10am–4pm

Goodwood Furniture Restoration (BAFRA)
Contact Bruce Neville
✉ **21 Richmond Road, Westerton, Chichester, West Sussex, PO18 0PQ** P
☎ 01243 778614 ⓜ 07719 778079
ⓔ bruce@goodwoodrestoration.co.uk
ⓦ www.goodwoodrestoration.co.uk
Est. 1991
Services Antique furniture restoration, cabinet-making
Open Mon–Sat 8.30am–5.30pm

G J Hall, Antique Furniture Restoration
Contact Mr G J Hall
✉ **Unit 1, Rear of Longreach, Branshill Road, Eversley, Hampshire, RG27 0PS** P
☎ 01189 737001 ⓜ 07711 846712
ⓔ garyh29@hotmail.com
Est. 1984
Services Restoration and conservation of fine antique furniture, copy chair making, French polishing, insurance work, design commissions
Open Mon–Fri 9.30am–5.30pm

Hedgecoe and Freeland (LAPADA, BAFRA)
Contact Justin Freeland
✉ **Rowan House, 21 Burrow Hill Green, Chobham, Woking, Surrey, GU24 8QP** P
☎ 01276 858206 ⓕ 01276 857352
ⓜ 07771 953870
Est. 1969
Services Cabinet-making, polishing, upholstery, metalwork, gilding, lacquerwork and paintwork
Open Mon–Fri 8am–5.30pm

Stuart Hobbs Antique Furniture Restoration (BAFRA)
Contact Mr S Hobbs

✉ Meath Paddock, Meath Green Lane, Horley, Surrey, RH6 8HZ 🅿
☎ 01293 782349 Ⓕ 01293 773467
Est. 1981
Services Furniture, longcase, bracket clock and barometer restoration
Open By appointment

Jeff Howlett Restoration (BAFRA)
Contact Jeff Howlett
✉ Unit 4, Charnham Lane, Hungerford, Berkshire, RG17 0EY 🅿
☎ 01488 684674 Ⓕ 01488 686178
Ⓔ jeffhowlett@antiquefurniturerestorers.com
Ⓦ www.antiquefurniturerestorers.com
Est. 1989
Services Full restoration and conservation of all antiques
Open Mon–Fri 8am–6pm Sat by appointment

Howard Hunt Antiques
Contact Mr H Hunt
✉ The White Hut, Thackhams Farm, Bottle Lane, Mattingley, Hook, Hampshire, RG27 8LJ 🅿
☎ 01256 881111 Ⓕ 01256 881111
Est. 1989
Services Repair and restoration of furniture, mirrors, porcelain, upholstery, leathering, gilding
Open Mon–Fri 9am–6pm Sat 9am–4pm

David C E Lewry (BAFRA, Woodwork Fellowship)
Contact Mr D Lewry
✉ Wychelms, 66 Gorran Avenue, Peel Common, Gosport, Hampshire, PO13 0NF 🅿
☎ 01329 286901 Ⓕ 01329 289964
Ⓜ 07785 766844
Ⓔ davidjoanlewry@talk21.com
Est. 1979
Services Complete repair and restoration service
Open By appointment

John Lloyd (BAFRA)
✉ Bankside Farm, Jacobs Post, Ditchling Common, West Sussex, RH15 0SJ 🅿
☎ 01444 480388 Ⓕ 01444 480388
Ⓜ 07941 124772
Ⓔ lloydjohn@aol.com
Ⓦ www.johnlloydfurniture.co.uk
Est. 1989
Services Complete repair and restoration of period, reproduction and modern furniture, short courses on care and repair of antiques and gilding
Open Mon–Fri 8.30am–5.30pm

C Lopez
Contact Mr C Lopez
✉ 151 London Road, Burgess Hill, West Sussex, RH15 8LH 🅿
☎ 01444 243176 Ⓕ 01444 254208
Est. 1977
Services Antique furniture restoration and hand-made chair copying
Open Mon–Fri 9am–1pm 2–6pm Sat 9am–1pm

Lush Restoration
Contact Mr M Lush
✉ 64d Old Milton Road, New Milton, Hampshire, BN25 6DX 🅿
☎ 01425 629680
Est. 1992
Services Repair and restoration
Open Mon–Fri 8am–1pm 2–5pm

Lymington Restoration
Contact Mr M Cooper
✉ Fairlea House, 110–112 Marsh Lane, Lymington, Hampshire, SO41 9EE 🅿
☎ 01590 677558 Ⓕ 01590 677558
Est. 1996
Services Restoration of antique furniture, gilding, upholstery
Open Mon–Fri 9am–5pm

Maybury Antique Restoration
Contact Mr B Everitt
✉ Maybury Rough Cottage, Lytton Road, Woking, Surrey, GU22 7EH 🅿
☎ 01483 762812
Est. 1989
Services All furniture repairs, gilding, leathering, upholstering, French polishing
Open Mon–Fri 8am–6pm Sat 8am–1pm

A F Mrozinski
Contact Mr Mrozinski
✉ 44 Elizabeth Road, Farncombe, Godalming, Surrey, GU7 3PZ 🅿
☎ 01483 415028
Est. 1979
Services Antique furniture repair, French polishing
Open Mon–Fri 7.30am–5pm

Timothy Naylor Associates (BAFRA)
Contact T Naylor
✉ 24 Bridge Road, Chertsey, Surrey, KT16 8JN 🅿
☎ 01932 567129 Ⓕ 01932 564948
Ⓔ timothy.naylor@talk21.com
Est. 1988
Services Georgian and Regency furniture restoration
Open Mon–Fri 8.30am–5pm

Simon Paterson (BAFRA)
✉ Whitelands, West Dean, Chichester, West Sussex, PO18 0RL 🅿
☎ 01243 811900
Ⓔ hotglue@lineone.net
Est. 1992
Services Repair and restoration of antique furniture and clocks, Boulle work, marquetry
Open By appointment

K S Pawlowski
Contact K S Pawlowski
✉ Unit 3, Turner Dumbrell Workshops, North End, Ditchling, Hassocks, West Sussex, BN6 8TG 🅿
☎ 01273 846003
Est. 1983
Services Conservation and restoration of antique furniture
Open Mon–Fri 9am–5.30pm Sat 9am–1pm

Eva-Louise Pepperall (BAFRA)
Contact E Pepperall
✉ Dairy Lane Cottage, Walberton, Arundel, West Sussex, BN18 0PT 🅿
☎ 01243 551282
Est. 1977
Services Restoration of antique furniture, gilding, lacquer work
Open By appointment

Mr Pickett's
Contact Mr M Pickett
✉ Top Barn, Old Park Lane, Bosham, Nr Chichester, West Sussex, PO18 8EX 🅿
☎ 01243 574573 Ⓕ 01243 572255

Ⓜ 07779 997012
Ⓔ info@mrpicketts.com
Ⓦ www.mrpicketts.com
Est. 1991
Services Paint stripping, sanding, waxing, full restoration, bespoke items made to order from reclaimed pine
Open Mon–Fri 8am–5pm
Sat 8am–4pm Sun by appointment

Albert Plumb Furniture Co (BAFRA)
Contact Mrs S Plumb
✉ **Itchenor Green, Chichester, West Sussex, PO20 7DA** Ⓟ
☎ 01243 513701 Ⓕ 01243 513700
Est. 1977
Services Antique furniture restorers and upholsterers. Bespoke cabinet-makers
Open Mon–Fri 8.30am–6.30pm or by appointment

D Potashnick
Contact Mr D Potashnick
✉ **7 The Parade, 73 Stoats Nest Road, Coulsdon, Surrey, CR5 2JJ** Ⓟ
☎ 020 8660 8403
Est. 1969
Services Restoration of furniture
Open Mon–Fri 9am–5pm or by appointment

Renaissance
Contact Mr Peter Cross
✉ **11 Enterprise Close, Croydon, Surrey, CR0 3RZ** Ⓟ
☎ 020 8664 9686 Ⓕ 020 8664 9737
Est. 1996
Services Furniture and frame repair and restoration
Open Mon–Fri 10am–6.30pm

The Restoration Co
Contact Mr J Howard
✉ **The Coach House, Dorney Court, Dorney, Windsor, Berkshire, SL4 6QL** Ⓟ
☎ 01628 660708
Est. 1991
Services Restoration of 18th–19thC furniture, carving, gilding, upholstery, metalwork
Open Mon–Fri 8am–5.30pm

Robinson Restorations
Contact Mr Nick Robinson
✉ **Unit 8, Seven House, 34–38 Town End, Caterham, Surrey, CR3 5UG** Ⓟ
☎ 01883 330111 Ⓜ 07970 255053
Ⓔ ted@gegriffin.freeserve.co.uk
Est. 1896
Services Antiques restoration, French polishing
Open Mon–Fri 8am–6pm
Sat 10am–4pm

David A Sayer Antique Furniture Restorer (BAFRA, Furniture History Society, Regional Furniture Society)
Contact David Sayer
✉ **Courtlands, Park Road, Banstead, Surrey, SM7 3EF** Ⓟ
☎ 01737 352429 Ⓕ 01737 373255
Ⓜ 07775 636009
Ⓔ dsayer@courtlands98.freeserve.co.uk
Ⓦ www.antiquerestorationssurrey.com
Est. 1985
Services Comprehensive repair, restoration and conservation service of English and Continental furniture
Open Mon–Fri 8am–6pm

Michael Schryver Antiques
Contact Mr M Schryver
✉ **The Granary, 10 North Street, Dorking, Surrey, RH4 1DN** Ⓟ
☎ 01306 881110 Ⓕ 01306 876168
Est. 1971
Services 18thC furniture restoration
Open Mon–Fri 8.30am–5.30pm
Sat 8am–noon or by appointment

Seagers Restorations
Contact Mr M L Cheater
✉ **Seagers Farm, Stuckton, Fordingbridge, Hampshire, SP6 2HG** Ⓟ
☎ 01425 652245
Est. 1962
Services Restoration of furniture of all ages
Open Mon–Fri 9am–5.30pm or by appointment

Andrew Sharp Antique Restoration Ltd
Contact Mr A Sharp
✉ **Unit 1, Forest Villa Courtyard, Lyndhurst Road, Brockenhurst, Hampshire, SO42 7RL** Ⓟ
☎ 01590 622577
Est. 1996
Services Sale and restoration of Georgian–Victorian furniture
Open Mon–Sat 9am–5.30pm

Surrey Restoration Ltd
Contact Emily McGhee
✉ **Highway Farm, Horsley Road, Downside, Cobham, Surrey, KT11 3JZ** Ⓟ
☎ 01932 868883 Ⓕ 01483 268285
Ⓔ emcghee@surreyrestoration.freeserve.co.uk
Est. 1994
Services Antique furniture restoration, interior wooden panelling of period houses
Open Mon–Sat 8.30am–6.30pm

Sussex Woodcraft
Contact Mr Waters
✉ **15 Drayton Cottages, Drayton Lane, Drayton, Chichester, West Sussex, PO20 6BN** Ⓟ
☎ 01243 788830
Est. 1937
Services Cabinet-making and restoration
Open Mon–Fri 8am–5pm

T S Restorations
Contact T Street
✉ **13 Blatchford Close, Horsham, West Sussex, RH13 5RG** Ⓟ
☎ 01403 273766
Est. 1989
Services Antiques repair and restoration
Open Mon–Fri 8am–5pm

Roy Temple Polishing
Contact Mr R Temple
✉ **Unit 14, Sheeplands Farm, Twyford Road, Wargrave, Reading, Berkshire, RG10 8DL** Ⓟ
☎ 01189 402211/01628 660106
Ⓕ 01189 402211
Est. 1996
Services Furniture repair and restoration, polishing, leathering
Open Mon–Sat 9am–5pm

Thread Bare Upholstery (AMU)
Contact Mr Martin Colwill
✉ **186a Bitterne Road, Bitterne, Southampton, Hampshire, SO18 1BE** Ⓟ
☎ 023 8021 1721 Ⓕ 023 8021 1721
Ⓜ 0789 9695479
Ⓦ www.threadbareupholstery.co.uk
Est. 1985
Services Furniture restoration, French polishing, reupholstery
Open Tue–Fri 10am–5pm
Sat 10am–4pm

T R J Troke
Contact T Troke
✉ **22 Fairview Road, Hungerford, Berkshire, RG17 0BT** Ⓟ
☎ 01488 683310
Est. 1975
Services Antique furniture repair and restoration
Open By appointment

Martin Tucker Antique Restoration
Contact M Tucker
✉ **Springbok Estate, Alfold, Cranleigh, Surrey, GU6 8HR** Ⓟ
☎ 01403 753090
Est. 1984
Services Furniture restoration, French polishing
Open Mon–Fri 9am–5pm

D G Weston
Contact Mr I L Weston
✉ **33 Rowan Drive, Newbury, Berkshire, RG14 1LY** Ⓟ
☎ 01635 43022 Ⓜ 07803 752420
Est. 1958
Services Antiques repair and restoration, French polishing, leather lining, upholstery
Open Mon–Fri 9am–5.30pm

G Williams
Contact Graham Williams
✉ **The Builders Yard, Church Street, Betchworth, Surrey, RH3 7DN** Ⓟ
☎ 01737 843266
Est. 1975
Services General restoration, desk-top leathering, gold tooling, French polishing
Open Mon–Fri 9am–6pm
Sat 10am–2pm

Wotruba and Son
Contact F F Wotruba
✉ **Manor Farm, Chilworth Old Village, Southampton, Hampshire, SO16 7JP** Ⓟ
☎ 023 8076 6411 Ⓜ 07887 712401
Est. 1995
Services Antiques restoration, upholstery
Open Mon–Fri 1–5pm or by appointment

WEST COUNTRY

4b Antiques and Interiors
Contact Jonathan Plant
✉ **4b Northgate Street, Devizes, Wiltshire, SN10 1JL** Ⓟ
☎ 01380 729275
Est. 1972
Services Furniture restoration
Open Mon–Fri 8am–5pm or by appointment

Antique Restoration (Furniture History Society, NACF)
Contact George Judd
✉ **East Farm, Winterbourne Gunner, Salisbury, Wiltshire, SP4 6EW** Ⓟ
☎ 01980 610576/611828
Est. 1975
Services Antique furniture, porcelain and painting restoration, cabinet-making, upholstery
Open Mon–Fri 9am–7pm

David Battle Antique Furniture Restoration and Conservation (BAFRA)
Contact David Battle
✉ **Brightley Pound, Umberleigh, Devon, EX37 9AL** Ⓟ
☎ 01769 540483
Ⓔ david@brightley.clara.net
Ⓦ brightley.clara.net
Est. 1984
Services Comprehensive service for English and Continental period furniture
Open By appointment

Peter Binnington (BAFRA, Society of Gilders)
Contact Mr Peter Binnington
✉ **Barn Studio, Botany Farm, East Lulworth, Wareham, Dorset, BH20 5QH** Ⓟ
☎ 01929 400224 Ⓕ 01929 400744
Est. 1979
Services General furniture restoration and gilding, specialist in verre églomisé
Open By appointment

Boughey Antique Restoration
Contact Dave Boughey
✉ **Manor Farm Workshop, Millbrook, Torpoint, Cornwall, PL10 1AN** Ⓟ
☎ 01752 829008 Ⓕ 01752 829008
Ⓜ 07970 540644
Est. 1960
Services Furniture restoration, cabinet-making, porcelain and pottery restoration
Open Mon–Fri 8am–5.30pm or by appointment

Jason Bowen
Contact Mr J Bowen
✉ **Unit 2, Alexandra Court, Yeovil, Somerset, BA21 5AL** Ⓟ
☎ 01935 474446
Est. 1984
Services Furniture restoration, French polishing, gilding, carving, cabinet-making
Open Mon–Sat 8.30am–5pm

M and S Bradbury (BAFRA)
Contact Mr S Bradbury
✉ **The Barn, Hanham Lane, Paulton, Bristol, BS39 7PF** Ⓟ
☎ 01761 418910
Est. 1988
Services Furniture restoration including clock cases
Open Mon–Fri 8am–5pm

Sarah & Gary Brumfitt
Contact Sarah or Gary Brumfitt
✉ **Watershed Studio, East Street, Salisbury, Wiltshire, SP2 7SF**
☎ 01722 335532/334877
Est. 1992
Services Antiques repair and restoration, gilding, painted effects
Open By appointment

J E Cadman
Contact Mr Cadman
✉ **15 Norwich Road, Bournemouth, Dorset, BH2 5QZ** Ⓟ
☎ 01202 290973
Est. 1901
Services Antiques restoration, mostly furniture
Open Mon–Fri 9am–5pm

Castle House (BAFRA)
Contact Mr Michael Durkee
✉ **Castle House, Units 1 and 3, Bennetts Field Estate, Wincanton, Somerset, BA9 9DT** Ⓟ
☎ 01963 33885 Ⓕ 01963 31278
Est. 1975
Services Antique furniture restoration and conservation
Open Mon–Fri 8.30am–5pm

Christopher Cole
Contact Mr C Cole
✉ **The Workshop, 36 Claude Avenue, Oldfield Park, Bath, Somerset, BA2 1AG** P
☎ 01225 310298 F 01225 310298
Est. 1994
Services Antique furniture restoration, carving, turning, French polishing
Open Mon–Fri 8.30am–7pm

David Collyer Antique Restorations
Contact David Collyer
✉ **Tunley Farm, Tunley, Bath, Somerset, BA2 0DL** P
☎ 01761 472727 F 01761 472727
M 07889 725508
E davidcollyer@fsbdial.co.uk
Est. 1985
Services Furniture restoration and repair
Open Mon–Fri 9am–5.30pm or by appointment

W J Cook (BAFRA)
Contact Mr B Cook
✉ **High Trees, Savernake Forest, Near Marlborough, Wiltshire, SN8 4NE** P
☎ 01672 513017 F 01672 514455
Est. 1963
Services Furniture polishing, restoration, upholstery, gilding
Open By appointment

Mark Coray Fine Antique Furniture Restoration (BAFRA)
Contact Mark Coray
✉ **The Coach House Workshops, Ford Street, Wellington, Somerset, TA21 9PG** P
☎ 01823 663766/667284
M 07979 245524
Est. 1999
Services All antique furniture restoration, gilding, furniture made to order
Open Mon–Fri 9am–5pm

N G and C Coryndon (BAFRA)
Contact N G Coryndon or Simon Butler
✉ **Rainscombe Farm, Oare, Marlborough, Wiltshire, SN8 4HZ** P
☎ 01672 562581 F 01672 563995
E simonbutler@coryndon.fsbusiness.co.uk
Est. 1964
Services General restoration of furniture, gilding, paint finishes. Collection and delivery if required
Open Mon–Fri 8.30am–4.30pm

D M Antique Restoration
Contact Mr D Pike
✉ **Purn Farm, Bridgewater, Bleadon, Weston-super-Mare, Somerset, BS24 0AN** P
☎ 01934 811120
Est. 1983
Services Restoration of furniture and chests-of-drawers
Open Mon–Fri 8am–5pm

M L Davis
Contact Mr M L Davis
✉ **Rear of 1079 Christchurch Road, Bournemouth, Dorset, BH7 6BQ** P
☎ 01202 434684
Est. 1987
Services Full restoration of furniture, brass cleaning
Open Mon–Fri 8.30am–5.30pm or by appointment

Simon Dodson
Contact Mr Dodson
✉ **The Workshop, Odd Penny Farm, Crudwell, Malmesbury, Wiltshire, SN16 9SJ** P
☎ 01285 770810
Est. 1992
Services Antique furniture restoration
Open Mon–Sat 9am–6pm

Christopher John Douglas
Contact Mr C J Douglas
✉ **Befferlands Farm Workshop, Berne Lane, Charmouth, Bridport, Dorset, DT6 6RD** P
☎ 01297 561120 M 07989 161019
Est. 1975
Services Restoration of antique furniture, old pine, Art Deco
Open Mon–Fri 9am–5.30pm

Dudley and Spencer
Contact John Spencer or Ray Dudley
✉ **Unit 21, Signal Way, Central Trading Estate, Swindon, Wiltshire, SN3 1PD** P
☎ 01793 535394
Est. 1969
Services Furniture restoration, upholstery
Open Mon–Fri 7am–6pm

A A Eddy and Son
Contact Mr K Eddy or Mr M Eddy
✉ **1a Elphinstone Road, Peverell, Plymouth, Devon, PL2 3QQ** P
☎ 01752 787138 F 01752 789013
Est. 1889
Services Full repairs and restoration, French polishing. Free estimates in the Plymouth area
Open Mon–Fri 7.30am–5pm

Esox Antique Restoration
Contact Mr B Elston
✉ **Unit 8, Dobles Lane Industrial Estate, Holsworthy, Devon, EX22 6HL** P
☎ 01409 259090 M 07967 283602
Est. 1987
Services Full furniture restoration, French polishing
Open Mon–Fri 9am–5pm or by appointment

Gilboy's
Contact Mr S Gilboys
✉ **Hall Farm, Riverford, Staverton, Totnes, Devon, TQ9 6AH** P
☎ 01803 762763
Est. 1992
Services Restoration, French polishing, modern furniture finishes (dining room table heatproofing). Maker of replacement doors
Open Mon–Fri 9am–5pm

John Hamblin
Contact John or Mark
✉ **Unit 6, 15 Oxford Road, Penmill Trading Estate, Yeovil, Somerset, BA21 5HR** P
☎ 01935 471154 F 01935 471154
M 07889 281659
Est. 1981
Services Antique furniture restoration, French polishing, cabinet-making
Open Mon–Sat 9am–5pm

Philip Hawkins Furniture (BAFRA)
Contact Mr P Hawkins
✉ **Glebe Workshop, Semley, Shaftesbury, Dorset, SP7 9AP** P
☎ 01747 830830 F 01747 830830
E hawkinssemley@hotmail.com

Est. 1987
Services Restoration and replication of antique furniture
Open Mon–Fri 9am–5pm or by appointment

Bruce Isaac
Contact Mr Bruce Isaac
✉ **Crown Works, 114a Rodden Road, Frome, Somerset, BA11 2AW** P
☎ 01373 453277 F 01373 830849
M 07711 399165
Est. 1990
Services Furniture restoration
Open Mon–Fri 8am–5pm

Mike Keeley
Contact Mike Keeley
✉ **205 Old Church Road, Clevedon, Somerset, BS21 7UD** P
☎ 01275 873418
E mikeandsheila@blueyonder.co.uk
Est. 1980
Services General repairs to antique furniture, specializing in dining furniture
Open By appointment Mon–Fri 9am–5pm

M & J Lazenby Antique Restoration
Contact Mark Lazenby
✉ **The Old Bakery, Terrace View, Horsecastles, Sherborne, Dorset, DT9 3HE**
☎ 01935 816716
Est. 1987
Services Full furniture restoration service
Open Mon–Fri 8am–5pm

Market Place Antiques Restorations
Contact Martin Bryan Turner
✉ **Nuttaberry Works, Nuttaberry Industrial Estate, Bideford East, Bideford, Devon, EX39 4DU** P
☎ 01237 476628
Est. 1984
Services Antique furniture restoration
Open By appointment

Alf McKay
Contact Mr A McKay
✉ **Manor Barn, Hewish, Crewkerne, Somerset, TA18 8QT** P
☎ 01460 78916 F 01460 78916
M 07720 810750
E info@cabinet-maker.biz
W www.cabinet-maker.biz
Est. 1972
Services Restorations, cabinet-maker, traditional furniture, architectural salvage
Open By appointment

Rod Naylor
Contact Angela Naylor
✉ **208 Devizes Road, Hilperton, Trowbridge, Wiltshire, BA14 7QP** P
☎ 01225 754497 F 01225 754497
E rod.naylor@virgin.net
W www.rodnaylor.com
Est. 1970
Services Restoration of antique wood carvings, supplier replicas of hard-to-find items and materials for caddies, boxes, desks etc, cabinet-making, supplier of power carving machinery and tools
Open By appointment only

Newmans (BAFRA)
Contact Tony Newman
✉ **Tithe Barn, Crowcombe, Somerset, TA4 4AQ** P
M 07778 615945
E tony@cheddon.fsnet.co.uk
Est. 1991
Services All types of restoration
Open Sun–Mon 9am–5pm or by appointment

Oakfield Cabinet Makers
Contact Mr X Haines
✉ **Unit 8, Mount Pleasant, Offwell, Honiton, Devon, EX14 9RN** P
☎ 01404 46858
Est. 1989
Services Cabinet-making and restoration
Open Mon–Fri 7.30am–6pm

Ottery Antique Restorers (BAFRA)
Contact Mr C James
✉ **Wincanton Business Park, Wessex Way, Wincanton, Somerset, BA9 9RR** P
☎ 01963 34572 F 01963 34572
M 07770 923955
E charles@otteryantiques.co.uk
W www.otteryantiques.co.uk
Est. 1986
Services Furniture restoration
Open Mon–Fri 7.30am–5.30pm

Park Lane Restoration
Contact Matthew Channell
✉ **Unit 2, Marston Park Lane, St Clement, Truro, Cornwall, TR1 1SX** P
☎ 01872 223944 M 07774 798198
Est. 1984
Services 18th–19thC furniture restoration, cabinet veneering, stripping and French polishing. Fire, flood, shipping damage insurance work
Open Mon–Fri 8am–6pm

Alexander Paul Restorations
Contact Dave Steele
✉ **Fenny Bridges, Honiton, Devon, EX14 1PJ** P
☎ 01404 850881 F 01404 850881
E alexanderpaulre@aol.com
Est. 2000
Services Full restoration including French polishing, turning, veneering
Open Mon–Fri 9am–5.30pm Sat 10am–4pm

R L Peploe
Contact Mr Peploe
✉ **18 Hughenden Road, Clifton, Bristol, BS8 2TT** P
☎ 0117 923 9349
Est. 1986
Services Cabinet work, gilding, carving, general finishing
Open Mon–Fri 9am–5pm

J Perrin
Contact Mr Perrin
✉ **Hope Chapel, Pitney, Langport, Somerset, TA10 9AE** P
☎ 01458 251150 F 01458 251150
Est. 1971
Services Furniture restoration
Open Mon–Sat 8am–6pm

Piers Pisani Antiques
Contact Mr Piers Pisani
✉ **The Old Chapel, Marston Road, Sherborne, Dorset, DT9 4BL** P
☎ 01935 814789 F 01935 815209
M 07973 373753
E antiques@pierspisani.com
W www.pierspisani.com
Est. 1987
Services Full furniture restoration, cabinet-making
Open Mon–Sat 10am–5pm

Revival
Contact Mr B Gould
✉ **South Road, Timsbury, Bath, Somerset, BA3 1LD** 🅿
☎ 01761 472255
Est. 1979
Services Antiques restoration, upholstery, French polishing
Open Mon–Fri 7am–4.30pm

Rostrum Antiques (BABAADA)
Contact Peter Skupien
✉ **The Old Flax Mill, Yeabridge, South Petherton, Somerset, TA13 5LR** 🅿
☎ 01460 249249 Ⓜ 07831 444148
Ⓔ rostrum.uk@virgin.net
Est. 1988
Services Furniture restoration, French polishing, wood turning, carving, veneering, water and oil gilding, giltwood restoration, restoration of painted surfaces, tortoiseshell and ivory
Open By appointment

Philip A Ruttleigh Antiques incorporating Crudwell Furniture
Contact Philip Ruttleigh
✉ **Odd Penny Farm, Crudwell, Wiltshire, SN16 9SJ** 🅿
☎ 01285 770970 Ⓜ 07989 250077
Ⓦ www.crudwellfurniture.co.uk
Est. 1989
Services Furniture restoration
Open Mon–Fri 9am–5pm or by appointment

F B Sadowski
Contact Mr Sadowski
✉ **Unit 2, Plot 1a, Rospeath Estate, Crowlas, Penzance, Cornwall, TR20 8DU** 🅿
☎ 01736 741083
Est. 1910
Services Furniture restoration. Repairs including Boulle work, marquetry
Open Mon–Fri 9.30am–5pm

Graham Sparks Restoration
Contact Mr Graham Sparks
✉ **Unit 63, Tone Mill, Tonedale, Wellington, Somerset, TA21 0AB** 🅿
☎ 01823 663636 Ⓕ 01823 667393
Est. 1979
Services Furniture restoration, upholstery, cabinet-making. Selection of desks, cabinets etc always in stock
Open Mon–Fri 8am–6pm Sat 8am–1pm

St Thomas Antiques
Contact Ken Holdsworth
✉ **74 St Thomas Street, Wells, Somerset, BA5 2UZ** 🅿
☎ 01749 672520
Est. 1969
Services Repairs, repolishing
Open Mon–Fri 10am–4pm closed Wed

Robert P Tandy (BAFRA)
Contact Robert P Tandy
✉ **Unit 5, Manor Workshops, West End, Nailsea, Bristol, North Somerset, BS48 4DD** 🅿
☎ 01275 856378
Est. 1987
Services Antique furniture and longcase clock casework restoration
Open Mon–Fri 10am–6pm

John Thorpe Fine Furniture
Contact Mr John Thorpe-Dixon
✉ **Units 1–2, Old Station Yard, Egloskerry, Launceston, Cornwall, PL15 8ST** 🅿
☎ 01566 785544 Ⓕ 01566 785544
Est. 1990
Services Antique furniture restoration, cabinetry, refinishing. London and all areas West
Open Mon–Fri 9am–5pm

N S L Tomson
Contact Nick Tompson
✉ **Unit 1, Centurion Works, Union Road, Kingsbridge, Devon, TQ7 1EF** 🅿
☎ 01548 854380
Est. 1981
Services French polishing and furniture restoration
Open Mon–Sat 8am–6pm and by appointment

Brian Walker
Contact Mr Walker
✉ **Westwood, Dinton Road, Forant, Salisbury, Wiltshire, SP3 5JW** 🅿
☎ 01722 714370 Ⓕ 01722 714853
Est. 1972
Services Furniture restoration and maker
Open Mon–Fri 8am–6pm or by appointment

Westmoor Furniture
Contact Gary Male
✉ **Unit 3, Alfords Yard, Westmoor Lane, Hambridge, Langport, Somerset, TA10 0AS** 🅿
☎ 01460 281535
Est. 1994
Services Antiques restoration and repairs, custom-made furniture
Open Mon–Fri 9am–6pm

N D Whibley Restorations
Contact Mr Whibley
✉ **1166 Ringwood Road, Bear Cross, Bournemouth, Dorset, BH11 9LG** 🅿
☎ 01202 575167
Est. 1975
Services Polishing and restoration of furniture, Georgian and Victorian clock cases, medical cases, scientific instrument cases
Open By appointment

Wood 'n' Things
Contact Mr William Page
✉ **Cross Lanes Farm, Cross Lanes, Pill, Bristol, BS20 0JJ** 🅿
☎ 01275 371660
Est. 1983
Services Furniture restoration, cabinet-making
Open Mon–Fri 9am–6pm advisable to call first

EAST

Abbey Antique Restorers
Contact Mr David Carter
✉ **Coxford Abbey Farmhouse, Coxford, King's Lynn, Norfolk, PE31 6TB** 🅿
☎ 01485 528043
Ⓦ www.abbey-restorations.co.uk
Est. 1969
Services Conservation and restoration of antique furniture
Open Mon–Sun 9am–6pm

Acorn Antique Restoration Services
Contact Mr V Lawson
✉ **9 Taverham Chase, Taverham, Norwich, Norfolk, NR8 6NZ** 🅿
☎ 01603 260446 Ⓜ 0771 322 5674
Est. 1998
Services French polishing,

furniture restoration, general small repairs, wood turning service
Open Mon–Sat 9am–6pm

Antiques and Restoration
Contact Mr R Rush
✉ **Unit 5, Penny Corner, Farthing Road, Ipswich, Suffolk, IP1 5AP** P
☎ 01473 464609 F 01473 464609
M 07939 220041
E info@antiquesandrestoration.co.uk
W www.antiquesandrestoration.co.uk
Est. 1997
Services Restorations
Open Mon–Fri 8am–6pm
Sat 8am–1.30pm

M Barrett Restoration
Contact Mr M Barrett
✉ **Unit 7, Warbraham Farm, Heath Road, Burwell, Cambridge, Cambridgeshire, CB5 0AP** P
☎ 01638 741700 F 01638 741700
Est. 1987
Services Pre-1940s furniture restoration
Open Mon–Fri 8.30am–5pm

Clive Beardall (BAFRA)
Contact Mr Clive Beardall
✉ **104b High Street, Maldon, Essex, CM9 7ET** P
☎ 01621 857890 F 01621 850753
E info@clivebeardall.co.uk
W www.clivebeardall.co.uk
Est. 1982
Services Specializing in period furniture restoration, traditional hand French polishing, wax polishing, reupholstery, marquetry, carving, gilding, leather desk-lining, rush and cane seating, decorative finishes, bespoke cabinet-making, valuations
Open Mon–Fri 8am–5.30pm
Sat 9am–4pm

Beechams Furniture (EADA)
Contact George or Stan Beecham
✉ **Asheton Farm, Tysea Hill, Stapleford Abbotts, Essex, RM4 1JU** P
☎ 01708 343431 F 01708 343431
M 07870 688925
E info@beechamsfurniture.co.uk
W www.beechamsfurniture.co.uk
Est. 1969
Services Chair, table, cabinet manufacture, restoration, polishing, upholstery, gilding, chair caning, interior decoration, refurbishment
Open Mon–Fri 8.30am–5pm

K W Box
Contact Mr K W Box
✉ **The Workshop, Upper Street, Stratford St Mary, Colchester, Essex, CO7 6JN** P
☎ 01206 322673
Est. 1985
Services 17th–18th and early 19thC furniture restoration and one-off cabinet-making to order. 22 years experience
Open Mon–Fri 8am–6pm
Sat 8am–1pm

Bradshaw Fine Wood Furniture Ltd
Contact Mr Chris Shaw-Williams
✉ **Unit 12, Clovelly Works, Chelmsford Road, Rawreth, Wickford, Essex, SS11 8SY** P
☎ 01268 571414 F 01268 571314
Est. 1988
Services French polishing, furniture restoration and repair work
Open Mon–Fri 8am–6pm

The Cabinet Maker
Contact Gary Fitzjohn
✉ **Unit 23, Boleness Road, Wisbech, Cambridgeshire, PE13 2RB** P
☎ 01945 475635 F 01945 475635
M 07813 391481
Est. 1997
Services Bespoke furniture manufacturers
Open Mon–Fri 8.30am–5pm

Clare Hall Co
Contact Mr M Moore
✉ **The Barns, Clare Hall, Clare, Sudbury, Suffolk, CO10 8PJ** P
☎ 01787 278445 F 01787 278803
Est. 1960
Services Restoration of all antiques including polishing and upholstery. Replicas of antique globes and four-poster beds, etc
Open By appointment

P Dawson Furniture Restorers
Contact Mr Paul Dawson
✉ **Unit 0, Dodnash Priory Farm, Hazel Shrub, Bentley, Ipswich, Suffolk, IP9 2DF** P
☎ 01473 311947 F 01473 462397
M 07718 958415
E paul@dawson21.freeserve.co.uk
Est. 1996
Services Restoration and sales of 17th–20thC furniture £50–£3,000 and reproductions
Open Mon–Sat 8am–6pm

Michael Dolling (BAFRA)
Contact Mr Michael Dolling
✉ **Church Farm, Barns, Glandford, Holt, Norfolk, NR25 7JR** P
☎ 01263 741115
Est. 1986
Services General furniture restoration and repair
Open Mon–Fri 9am–5pm

Essex Reupholstery Services
Contact Mr S T Richardson
✉ **49 Chestnut Grove, Southend on Sea, Essex, SS2 5HG**
☎ 01702 464775 F 01702 305684
Est. 1987
Services Restoration of antique furniture, paddings, re-upholstery
Open Mon–Fri 8am–5pm

Forge Studio Workshops
Contact Mr D Darton
✉ **Stour Street, Manningtree, Essex, CO11 1BE** P
☎ 01206 396222 F 01206 396222
Est. 1979
Services Antique furniture restoration
Open Mon–Fri 8.30am–5.30pm
Sat 8.30am–1pm

Furse Restoration
Contact Mr Fred Furse
✉ **Beechcroft, Damases Lane, Boreham, Chelmsford, Essex, CM3 3AL** P
☎ 01245 466744 F 01245 466744
E andrew@furserestoration.co.uk
W www.furserestoration.co.uk
Est. 1993
Services Antique restoration, bespoke cabinet-making, French polishing, veneer design and pressing
Open Mon–Fri 8am–6pm
Sat 9am–4pm

ASSOCIATED SERVICES
FURNITURE

Michael Goater Restoration
Contact Michael Goater
✉ **15 Red Barn Yards, Thornham Magna, Eye, Suffolk, IP23 8HH** 🅿
☎ 01379 788722
ⓔ goater@primex.co.uk
ⓦ www.michaelgoater.co.uk
Est. 1987
Services Full restoration and conservation of 18th–19thC furniture, particular interest in country furniture
Open Mon–Sun 9am–6pm

P Godden
Contact Mr P Godden
✉ **32 Darcy Road, Old Heath, Colchester, Essex, CO2 8BB** 🅿
☎ 01206 790349
Est. 1942
Services Antique furniture restoration
Open Mon–Sat 9am–5pm

Haig and Hosford
Contact Mr J Hosford
✉ **The Workshop, Trews Chase, High Street, Kelvedon, Colchester, Essex, CO5 9AQ** 🅿
☎ 01376 571502
Est. 1981
Services French polishing, antique restoration
Open Mon–Fri 8.30am–5pm Sat 8.30am–1pm

Brian Harris Furniture Restorations (BAFRA, EADA)
Contact Brian Harris
✉ **40 Lower Street, Stansted Mountfitchet, Essex, CM24 8LR** 🅿
☎ 01279 812233
Est. 1956
Services Antique furniture restoration including carving, gilding, French polishing, inlay work. Also restoration of clocks, barometers and ceramics
Open Mon–Sat 9am–5pm

Jeff Ingall
Contact Mr J Ingall
✉ **33 Hillside Road, Southminster, Essex, CM0 7AL** 🅿
☎ 01621 772686
Est. 1989
Services Antique furniture restorer, furniture maker
Open Mon–Sun 9am–6pm

S Layt
Contact Mr S Layt
✉ **Units 27 & 28, Barns Stables, Timworth Green, Bury St Edmunds, Suffolk, IP31 1HS** 🅿
☎ 01284 729072
Est. 1999
Services Antique furniture restoration, French polishing
Open Mon–Fri 8am–5.30pm

Lomas Pigeon & Co Ltd (BAFRA, AMU)
Contact Mr W A J Pigeon
✉ **37 Beehive Lane, Chelmsford, Essex, CM2 9TQ** 🅿
☎ 01245 353708 ⓕ 01245 355211
ⓔ wpigeon@compuserve.com
ⓦ www.lomas-pigeon.co.uk
Est. 1938
Services Upholstery, antique restoration, French polishing, cabinet-making
Open Mon–Fri 10am–4pm Sat 9am–noon closed Wed

Maisey Restoration
Contact Mr Steve Maisey
✉ **Clark's Yard, High Street, Cavendish, Sudbury, Suffolk, CO10 8AT** 🅿
☎ 01787 281331
Est. 1991
Services Repair, restoration and French polishing
Open Mon–Fri 8am–5pm

Andrew A Matthews Restoration (Graduate member BAFRA)
Contact Mr A A Matthews
✉ **Top Field Farm, 16 Cambridge Road, Barton, Cambridge, Cambridgeshire, CB3 7AR** 🅿
☎ 01223 264963 ⓜ 07808 590370
Est. 1998
Services Antiques restoration and conservation, cabinet work, veneering, turning, key-making, lock repair, polishing, upholstery, rushing and caning
Open By appointment

R J McPhee
Contact Mr R J McPhee
✉ **20 Muspole Street, Norwich, Norfolk, NR3 1DJ** 🅿
☎ 01603 667701 ⓕ 01603 667701
ⓔ richardj.mcphee@tesco.net
ⓦ www.yell.co.uk/sites/rjmcphee
Est. 1980
Services 17th–18thC fine antique furniture restoration
Open Mon–Fri 8am–1pm 2–5pm or Sat by appointment

Norfolk Galleries
Contact Mr G Cumbley or Mr B Houchen
✉ **1 Stanley Street, King's Lynn, Norfolk, PE30 1PF**
☎ 01553 765060
Est. 1971
Services Full restoration service
Open Mon–Fri 8.30am–5.30pm

Peter Norman Antiques
Contact Mr Tony Marpole
✉ **55 North Street, Burwell, Cambridge, Cambridgeshire, CB5 0BA** 🅿
☎ 01638 616914
Est. 1977
Services General antiques restoration, woodwork, caning, re-upholstery, relining and restoring oils
Open Mon–Sat 9am–5.30pm prior warning best

Mark Peters Antiques
Contact Mr M Peters
✉ **Green Farm Cottage, Oak Road, Thurston, Bury St Edmunds, Suffolk, IP31 3SN** 🅿
☎ 01359 230888 ⓕ 01359 233384
Est. 1977
Services Antique furniture restoration
Open Mon–Fri 8am–5pm Sat 9am–noon

Phoenix Restoration (EADA)
Contact Mr D Comben
✉ **Highlands Farm, Southend Road, Rettenden Common, Chelmsford, Essex, CM3 8EB** 🅿
☎ 01245 327111 ⓕ 01245 327111
Est. 1998
Services General antique furniture restoration
Open By appointment

Ludovic Potts Restorations (BAFRA)
Contact Mr Ludovic Potts
✉ **Unit 1/1a, Station Road, Haddenham, Ely, Cambridgeshire, CB6 3XD** 🅿

☎ 01353 741537 Ⓕ 01353 741822
Ⓜ 07889 341671
Ⓔ mail@restorers.co.uk
Ⓦ www.restorers.co.uk
Est. 2001
Services Modern and antique furniture restoration
Open By appointment

Repair Convert Furniture
Contact Mr John McKenna
✉ **The Barn, 86 Norsey Road, Billericay, Essex, CM11 1AT** Ⓟ
☎ 01277 653088
Est. 1969
Services Antique furniture restoration and cabinet-maker
Open Mon–Fri 8.30am–4.30pm

Richard's Polishing
Contact Mr R Bufton
✉ **Bentley Road, Weeley Heath, Clacton on Sea, Essex, CO16 9DP** Ⓟ
☎ 01255 831539 Ⓜ 07712 873864
Ⓔ sos@sos.uk.com
Ⓦ www.sos.uk.com
Est. 1979
Services Antique restoration, all polish finishes
Open Mon–Fri 7.30am–5pm

Robert's Antiques
Contact Mr Robert King
✉ **The Barn, South Street, Risby, Bury St Edmunds, Suffolk, IP28 6QU** Ⓟ
☎ 01284 811440 Ⓕ 01284 811440
Ⓔ roberts-antiques@ic24.com
Est. 1978
Services Upholstery, French polishing
Open Mon–Fri 8.30am–5pm

D J Short
Contact Mr D Short
✉ **The Stables, High Street, Horseheath, Cambridge, Cambridgeshire, CB1 6QN** Ⓟ
☎ 01223 891983
Est. 1969
Services Antique furniture restoration, upholstery
Open Mon–Fri 9am–5pm
Sat 9am–1pm

R J Smith Restoration
Contact Mr R J Smith
✉ **Unit 6A, Rear of Keimar House, Tut Hill, Fornham All Saints, Bury St Edmonds, Suffolk, IP28 6LE** Ⓟ
☎ 01284 704894 Ⓜ 07771 535863
Est. 1991
Services Repair and restoration of Georgian–Edwardian furniture, French polishing
Open Mon–Sat 8.30am–5.30pm

R A Surridge
Contact Mr R Surridge
✉ **The Barn, Thistledown, Latchingdon Road, Cold Norton, Chelmsford, Essex, CM3 6HR** Ⓟ
☎ 01621 828036 Ⓕ 01621 828036
Est. 1978
Services Antique restoration and cabinet-maker
Open Mon–Fri 8am–5pm

Teywood Ltd
Contact Mr K Cottee
✉ **East Gores Farm, Salmons Lane, Coggeshall, Essex, CO6 1RZ** Ⓟ
☎ 01376 563025 Ⓕ 01376 563025
Est. 1984
Services Antique furniture restoration and cabinet-maker
Open Mon–Fri 9am–5pm

Whitfield Restoration
Contact Mr J Palmor
✉ **London Road, Cockford, Colchester, Essex, CO6 1LG** Ⓟ
☎ 01206 213212
Est. 1990
Services Antique restoration of furniture, cabinet-making, French polishing
Open Mon–Sat 8.30am–5pm

Robert Williams (BAFRA)
Contact Mr Robert Williams
✉ **32 Church Street, Willingham, Cambridge, Cambridgeshire, CB4 5HT** Ⓟ
☎ 01954 260972
Est. 1980
Services Restoration of carving, ivory, mother of pearl, bonework, papier mâché, tortoiseshell, weapons. Also cabinet-maker and locksmith
Open Mon–Fri 9am–5pm

Justin Wood Restoration
Contact Justin Wood
✉ **Manor Farm Dairy, Manor Road, Hasketon, Woodbridge, Suffolk, IP13 6HZ** Ⓟ
☎ 01394 387791 Ⓜ 07712 131820
Ⓔ justin.wood@antique-restoration.net
Ⓦ www.antique-restoration.net
Est. 1997
Services Quality restoration, French polishing, woodcarving, cabinet-making
Open Mon–Fri 9am–5pm
Sat 9am–noon

Woodside Restoration Services (GADAR)
Contact Mr Tony Payne
✉ **Mulberry Farm, Ashfield Road, Elmswell, Bury St Edmunds, Suffolk, IP30 9HG** Ⓟ
☎ 01359 244244 Ⓕ 01359 244244
Ⓔ mulberry@hotmail.com
Est. 1969
Services Full restoration service of furniture, brass, steel and upholstery
Open By appointment

HEART OF ENGLAND

A C Restorations
Contact Mr Adrian Clark
✉ **Unit 9d, Quickbury Farm, Hatfield Heath Road, Sawbridgeworth, Hertfordshire, CM21 9HY** Ⓟ
☎ 01279 721583 Ⓜ 07905 156976
Ⓔ adrian.clark1@virgin.net
Est. 1993
Services Furniture restoration, polishing, leather lining, carving, general services
Open Mon–Fri 9am–5.30pm

Antique and Modern Restoration by Richard Parsons
Contact Mr R Parsons
✉ **85 Pondcroft Road, Knebworth, Hertfordshire, SG3 6DE** Ⓟ
☎ 01438 812200
Est. 1980
Services Antique and modern furniture restoration, French polishing
Open Mon–Fri 8.30am–6pm or by appointment

ASSOCIATED SERVICES
FURNITURE

Antique Restoration & Polishing
Contact Mr M P Wallis
✉ **1 The Row, Hawridge, Chesham, Buckinghamshire, HP5 2UH** 🅿
☎ 01494 758172 Ⓕ 01494 758701
Ⓔ mikewallis@hawridge.freeserve.co.uk
Est. 1968
Services General antique furniture restoration and polishing
Open By appointment

Keith Bawden (BAFRA)
Contact Keith Bawden
✉ **Mews Workshops, Montpelier Retreat, Cheltenham, Gloucestershire, GL50 2XG** 🅿
☎ 01242 230320
Est. 1975
Services Full antique restoration service of furniture, clocks, watercolours, jewellery, ceramics and Oriental carpets
Open Mon–Fri 7am–4.30pm

R Beesly
Contact Mr R Beesly
✉ **41 High Street, Broom, Biggleswade, Bedfordshire, SG18 9NA** 🅿
☎ 01767 314918
Est. 1974
Services Cabinet-maker, French polishing, clock repairs
Open Mon–Sat 8am–6pm or by appointment

Richard Bolton Furniture Restorer (BAFRA)
Contact Richard Bolton
✉ **Painswick House, Old Dairy Workshop, Gloucester Road, Painswick, Gloucestershire, GL6 6TH** 🅿
☎ 01452 814881
Est. 1981
Services Restoration of fine antique furniture
Open Mon–Fri 9am–5pm

Andy Briggs
Contact Andy Briggs
✉ **2 Folly View, Bampton Road, Black Bourton, Oxfordshire, OX18 2PD** 🅿
☎ 01865 301705 Ⓜ 07977 936882
Est. 1991
Services Restoration and conservation of town and country furniture, cabinet-making, items bought and sold, copies of stolen items made
Open By appointment

Peter Campion Restorations (BAFRA)
Contact Peter Campion
✉ **The Old Dairy, Rushley Lane, Winchcombe, Nr Cheltenham, Gloucestershire, GL54 5JE** 🅿
☎ 01242 604403 Ⓕ 01242 604403
Ⓔ petercampion@ukonline.co.uk
Ⓦ www.petercampion.co.uk
Est. 1959
Services Restoration and conservation of furniture, barometers, clock cases. Also cabinet work, inlays, brass, veneering, polishing, furniture designed and made to order
Open Mon–Fri 9am–5.30pm

Charnwood Antiques (EADA)
Contact Mr Nigel Hoy
✉ **Unit 2e, The Maltings, Station Road, Sawbridgeworth, Hertfordshire, CM21 9JX** 🅿
☎ 01279 600562 Ⓕ 01279 600562
Ⓜ 07957 551899
Est. 1988
Services Cabinet-maker, antique furniture restoration, upholstery, cabinet lining, French polishing
Open Tues–Fri 10am–5pm Sat Sun 11am–5pm

Chess Antique Restorations
Contact Mr T Chapman
✉ **85 Broad Street, Chesham, Buckinghamshire, HP5 3EF** 🅿
☎ 01494 783043 Ⓕ 01494 791302
Ⓔ chessres@aol.com
Est. 1969
Services All cabinet work, hand finishing, upholstery, ceramics, metalwork, picture restoration, traditional polishing
Open Mon–Fri 9am–5pm

N A Copp
Contact Nigel Copp
✉ **Red Lane, Tewkesbury, Gloucestershire, GL20 5BQ** 🅿
☎ 01684 293935
Est. 1984
Services Restoration of antique furniture, maker of kitchens
Open Mon–Fri 8.30am–5.30pm

Martin Coulborn Restorations
Contact Mr M Coulborn
✉ **Canterbury House, Bridge Road, Frampton on Severn, Gloucestershire, GL2 7HE** 🅿
☎ 01452 740334
Est. 1978
Services Antique furniture restoration, maker of replica 18thC-style furniture
Open Mon–Fri 9am–1pm 2–5pm

D H R Ltd (BAFRA, UKIC)
Contact Mr David Hordern
✉ **8–10 Lea Lane, Thame Road, Long Crendon, Aylesbury, Buckinghamshire, HP18 9RN** 🅿
☎ 01844 202213 Ⓕ 01844 202214
Est. 1985
Services All antique furniture restoration services
Open Mon–Fri 9am–5.30pm

D M E Restorations Ltd (BAFRA)
Contact Duncan Everitt
✉ **11 Church Street, Ampthill, Bedfordshire, MK45 2PL** 🅿
☎ 01525 405819 Ⓕ 01525 756177
Ⓜ 07778 015121
Ⓔ duncan@dmerestorations.com
Ⓦ www.dmerestorations.com
Est. 1986
Services Restoration and conservation of antique furniture
Open Mon–Fri 8am–5pm or by appointment

Deerstalker Antiques
Contact Mr or Mrs Eichler
✉ **28 High Street, Whitchurch, Buckinghamshire, HP22 4JT** 🅿
☎ 01296 641505
Est. 1978
Services Restoration of furniture pre-1850
Open By appointment

Dovetail Restoration
Contact Mr Robert Askham
✉ **Home Farm, Ardington, Wantage, Oxfordshire, OX12 8PD** 🅿
☎ 01235 833614 Ⓕ 01235 833110
Est. 1973
Services Antique and modern furniture restoration
Open Mon–Fri 8.30am–5.30pm or Sat by appointment

P M Dupuy
Contact Mr P Dupuy
✉ **132 Bletchley Road, Newton Longville, Milton Keynes, Buckinghamshire, MK17 0AA** P
☎ 01908 367168
Est. 1978
Services Restoration of antique furniture, all woodwork repairs, French and wax polishing, hand-stripping
Open Mon–Sat 9am–6pm

J W Eaton
Contact Mr J Eaton
✉ **The Barn, Tupsley Court Farm, Hampton Dene Road, Hereford, Herefordshire, HR1 1UX** P
☎ 01432 354344
Est. 1990
Services General antique restoration
Open Mon–Fri 9am–5pm

C G Elmer-Menage
Contact Mr C Elmer
✉ **Unit 12, Elmsfield Industrial Estate, Worcester Road, Chipping Norton, Oxfordshire, OX7 5XL** P
☎ 01608 644024
Est. 1978
Services Restoration of 18th–19thC furniture, marquetry, bespoke furniture maker
Open By appointment

Gloucestershire Furniture Hospital
Contact Mr M Deane
✉ **Commonfields Farm, Lower Boulsdon, Newent, Gloucestershire, GL18 1JH** P
☎ 01531 822881
Est. 1999
Services Antique and modern furniture repair including upholstery, caning and French polishing. Collection service
Open Mon–Sat 8am–6pm

Robert Gripper Restoration
Contact Mr R Gripper
✉ **Manor Barn, Manor Farm, Ascott-under-Wychwood, Chipping Norton, Oxfordshire, OX7 6AL** P
☎ 01993 831960 Ⓕ 01993 830395
Ⓔ robgripper@aol.com
Est. 1982
Services Antique furniture restoration, modern insurance work
Open Mon–Fri 9am–5pm

Hart Antiques
Contact Mr M Hart
✉ **Widmere Cottage, Parmoor, Frieth, Henley on Thames, Oxfordshire, RG9 6NH** P
☎ 01491 571669 Ⓕ 01491 571917
Ⓜ 07816 122730
Est. 1985
Services Antique furniture restoration including upholstery, gilding and lacquerwork
Open Mon–Sat 9am–6pm

Roland Haycraft (GADAR)
Contact Mr R Haycraft
✉ **The Lamb Arcade, High Street, Wallingford, Oxfordshire, OX10 0BS** P
☎ 01491 839622
Ⓔ rohaycraft@fsbdial.co.uk
Ⓦ www.juststolen.com
Est. 1980
Services Antique furniture restorations and cabinet-making
Open Mon–Fri 9am–5.30pm

Alan Hessel (BAFRA)
Contact Mr A Hessel
✉ **The Old Town Workshop, St George's Close, Moreton-in-Marsh, Gloucestershire, GL56 0LP** P
☎ 01608 650026 Ⓕ 01608 650026
Ⓜ 07860 225608
Est. 1975
Services Restoration of fine 17th–19thC furniture
Open Mon–Fri 8.30am–5pm or by appointment

Stephen Hill (BAFRA)
Contact Stephen Hill
✉ **11 Cirencester Workshops, Brewery Court, Cirencester, Gloucestershire, GL7 1JH** P
☎ 01285 658817 Ⓜ 07976 722028
Est. 1979
Services Restoration of 17th–19thC furniture
Open Mon–Fri 9am–5pm

John Hulme
Contact Mr J Hulme
✉ **11a High Street, Chipping Norton, Oxfordshire, OX7 5AD** P
☎ 01608 641692 Ⓕ 01608 641692
Est. 1980
Services Antique furniture restoration and conservation
Open Mon–Fri 7.30am–6pm

Icknield Restorations
Contact Simon Pallister
✉ **Icknield Farm, Tring Road, Dunstable, Bedfordshire, LU6 2JX** P
☎ 01525 222883
Est. 1994
Services Antique furniture restoration
Open Mon–Fri 9.30am–6pm

Ipsden Woodcraft
Contact Mr M Small
✉ **The Post Office, The Street, Ipsden, Wallingford, Oxfordshire, OX10 6AG** P
☎ 01491 680262
Est. 1981
Services Antique furniture restoration
Open Mon–Fri 8am–6pm

J R Jury & Son
Contact Mr Ken Jury
✉ **Springfields, Cobhall Common, Allensmore, Hereford, Herefordshire, HR2 9BJ** P
☎ 01432 279108
Est. 1974
Services Antique furniture restorers, French polishing
Open Mon–Fri 8am–5pm

Robert Lawrence-Jones
Contact Robert Lawrence-Jones
✉ **Frogmarsh Mill, Stroud, Gloucestershire, GL5 5ET** P
☎ 01453 872817
Est. 1980
Services Cabinet-maker, furniture restorer
Open Mon–Fri 9am–5pm

E C Legg and Son
Contact Mr C Legg
✉ **3 College Farm Buildings, Tetbury Road, Cirencester, Gloucestershire, GL7 6PY** P
☎ 01285 650695
Est. 1903
Services Furniture restoration, carving, rushing, leather laying
Open Mon–Fri 9am–5pm
Sat 9am–noon

FURNITURE

Andrew Lelliott
Contact Mr A Lelliott
✉ **6 Tetbury Hill, Avening, Tetbury, Gloucestershire, GL8 4LT**
☎ 01453 835783
ⓔ family@lelliotglass.freeserve.co.uk
Est. 1985
Services Furniture and clock case restoration, matching mouldings
Open By appointment

Clive Loader Restorations
Contact Mr C Loader
✉ **Stables Workshop, Lodge Cottage, High Street, Shipton under Wychwood, Oxfordshire, OX7 6DG** Ⓟ
☎ 01993 832727
Est. 1984
Services Antique furniture restoration
Open Mon–Fri 8am–5pm

M K Restorations
Contact Mr M Knight
✉ **Unit 8e4, Quickbury Farm, Hatfield Heath Road, Sawbridgeworth, Hertfordshire, CM21 9HY** Ⓟ
☎ 01279 726664 Ⓜ 07939 438587
Est. 1992
Services Antique furniture restoration
Open Mon–Sat 9am–6.30pm

Peter Makin (BAFRA)
Contact Mr P Makin
✉ **Dray House, The Maltings, School Lane, Amersham, Buckinghamshire, HP7 0ES** Ⓟ
☎ 01494 434688
ⓔ hotleybott@aol.com
Est. 1992
Services Repair and restoration of 18th–19thC furniture, clock cases etc, including French polishing, marquetry, veneer work, making historically accurate replicas
Open Mon–Fri 9am–5.30pm
Sat 9am–noon

Miracle Finishing
Contact Mr C Howes or Mr A Howes
✉ **The Cottage, Woodhall Farm, Hatfield, Hertfordshire, AL9 5NU** Ⓟ
☎ 01707 270587 Ⓕ 01707 270587
Ⓜ 07790 696631
Est. 1992
Services Furniture restoration, French polishing, re-upholstery, pine stripping
Open Mon–Fri 8.30am–5pm

J Moore Restorations
Contact Mr J Moore
✉ **College Farm House Workshops, Chawston Lane, Chawston, Bedford, Bedfordshire, MK44 3BH** Ⓟ
☎ 01480 214165
Est. 1975
Services All aspects of furniture restoration, particularly period furniture
Open Mon–Fri 9am–5pm

Clive Payne (BAFRA, LAPADA)
Contact Clive Payne
✉ **Unit 4, Mount Farm, Junction Road, Churchill, Chipping Norton, Oxfordshire, OX7 6NP** Ⓟ
☎ 01608 658856 Ⓕ 01608 658856
Ⓜ 07801 088363
ⓔ clive.payne@virgin.net
Ⓦ www.clivepayne.com
Est. 1986
Services Antique furniture restoration, specializing in country furniture and Georgian mahogany
Open Mon–Fri 9am–5pm

Charles Perry Restorations Ltd (BAFRA)
Contact John Carr
✉ **Praewood Farm, Hemel Hempstead Road, St Albans, Hertfordshire, AL3 6AA** Ⓟ
☎ 01727 853487 Ⓕ 01727 846668
ⓔ cperry@praewood.freeserve.co.uk
Est. 1986
Services Anything associated with antique furniture restoration including carving, gilding, caning and upholstery
Open Mon–Fri 8.30am–5.30pm

Nathan Polley Antique Restoration
Contact Mr N Polley
✉ **The Barn, Upton Grove, Tetbury Upton, Tetbury, Gloucestershire, GL8 8LR** Ⓟ
☎ 01666 504997
Ⓜ 07977 263236
ⓔ npolleyrestorations@yahoo.co.uk
Est. 1995
Services Repair and restoration
Open Mon–Fri 8am–6.30pm
Sat 8am–4pm

Alan J Ponsford Antique Restorations
Contact Alan Ponsford
✉ **Decora, Northbrook Road, Gloucester, Gloucestershire, GL4 3DP** Ⓟ
☎ 01452 307700
Est. 1962
Services Restoration
Open Mon–Fri 8am–5pm

R J Poynter
Contact Mr R Poynter
✉ **Lyndhurst, Westland Green, Little Hadham, Ware, Hertfordshire, SG11 2AF** Ⓟ
☎ 01279 842395
Est. 1984
Services Antique furniture restoration
Open Mon–Fri 10am–5pm
Sat by appointment only

Saracen Restoration
Contact Mr C Mills
✉ **Upton Downs Farm, Burford, Oxfordshire, OX18 4LY** Ⓟ
☎ 01993 822987 Ⓕ 01993 823701
Ⓜ 07958 907255
ⓔ cmills6702@aol.com
Est. 1992
Services Full restoration service including marquetry, French polishing, gilding
Open Mon–Sat 9am–5.30pm

J Smith
Contact Mr J Smith
✉ **Calleva House, 6 High Street, Wallingford, Oxfordshire, OX10 0BP** Ⓟ
☎ 01491 835185
Est. 1994
Services Antique furniture restoration, conservation of original finishes
Open Mon–Fri 9am–5.30pm

Starkadder
Contact Mr C Rosser
✉ **Unit 4–13, Ditchford Farm, Stretton on Fosse, Moreton-in-Marsh, Gloucestershire, GL56 9RD** Ⓟ
☎ 01608 664885
Est. 1998
Services Antique furniture restoration
Open By appointment

Sunningend Joiners and Cabinet Makers Ltd
Contact Mr R J Duester
✉ **Industrial Estate, Station Road, Bourton-on-the-Water, Cheltenham, Gloucestershire, GL54 2EP** Ⓟ
☎ 01451 820761 Ⓕ 01451 820761
Est. 1972
Services Joinery, cabinet-making, antique furniture restoration
Open By appointment

Timber Restorations
Contact Mr S Shannon
✉ **Hyde Hall Barn, Sandon, Buntingford, Hertfordshire, SG9 0RU** Ⓟ
☎ 01763 274849 Ⓕ 01763 274849
Ⓜ 07973 748644
Est. 1997
Services Spray lacquering, French polishing, furniture repairs, caustic and non-caustic stripping, wax polishing, furniture sales, leather top inlay
Open Mon–Sat 9am–5pm

Christopher Tombs
Contact Mr C G Tombs
✉ **Unit 45, Northwick Business Centre, Blockley, Moreton-in-Marsh, Gloucestershire, GL56 9RF** Ⓟ
☎ 01386 700085
Est. 1994
Services English furniture restoration
Open Mon–Fri 8am–5pm

Clifford J Tracy (BAFRA)
Contact Clifford Tracy
✉ **3 Shaftesbury Industrial Centre, Icknield Way, Letchworth, Hertfordshire, SG6 1HE** Ⓟ
☎ 01462 684855 Ⓕ 01462 684833
Ⓜ 07831 326488
Est. 1961
Services Antique furniture restoration, marquetry, brasswork, tortoiseshell, ivory work, wax polishing, re-upholstery, leather top lining, period panelling restoration, deinfestation. Specialist cabinet-makers
Open Mon–Thurs 7am–4pm
Fri 7am–3pm

Truman and Bates
Contact Mr P Truman
✉ **Classic Works, Station Road, Banbury, Oxfordshire, OX15 5LS** Ⓟ
☎ 01608 730433
Est. 1961
Services Restoration of antique furniture, French polishing
Open Mon–Fri 8am–5pm

P M Welch
Contact Mr P Welch
✉ **The Sitch, Longborough, Moreton-in-Marsh, Gloucestershire, GL56 0QJ** Ⓟ
☎ 01451 832046 Ⓕ 01451 870552
Ⓔ restoration.antiques@virgin.net
Ⓦ www.antiques-restorers.com
Est. 1969
Services Restoration of English and Continental furniture
Open Mon–Fri 7.45am–5.30pm
Sat 7.45am–noon

Richard J Young Antiques Restorer
Contact Richard Young
✉ **5 Macaroni Wood, Eastleach, Cirencester, Gloucestershire, GL7 3NF** Ⓟ
☎ 01367 850587
Ⓔ rjyrestor@aol.com
Est. 1980
Services Restoration of furniture and architectural antiques
Open By appointment

MIDLANDS

Anthony Allen Conservation, Restoration, Furniture and Artefacts (BAFRA, UKIC)
Contact Anthony Allen
✉ **The Old Wharf Workshop, Redmoor Lane, Newtown, High Peak, Derbyshire, SK22 3JL** Ⓟ
☎ 01663 745274 Ⓕ 01663 745274
Est. 1970
Services Restoration of 17th–19thC furniture, gilding, marquetry, Boulle, upholstery, metalwork, clock cases and movements
Open Mon–Fri 8am–5pm

The Antiques Workshop
Contact Mr Paul Burrows
✉ **68 Yoxall Road, Solihull, West Midlands, B90 3RP** Ⓟ
☎ 0121 744 1744 Ⓜ 07860 168078
Est. 1988
Services Furniture restoration
Open Mon–Sat 9am–5pm

M G Bassett
Contact Mrs G Bassett or Mr M Bassett
✉ **38 Church Street, Ashbourne, Derbyshire, DE6 1AJ** Ⓟ
☎ 01335 347750 (workshop)/ 300061 (shop) Ⓕ 01335 300061
Ⓔ mgbassett@aol.com
Est. 1979
Services Restoration of English and French country furniture and decorative items
Trade only Yes
Open Mon–Fri 9am–5pm
closed Wed

Belle Vue Restoration
Contact Mr Peter Grady
✉ **19 Belle Vue Road, Shrewsbury, Shropshire, SY3 7LN** Ⓟ
☎ 01743 272210
Est. 1984
Services Antique furniture restoration
Open Mon–Fri 8am–5.30pm

S C Brown
Contact Mr S C Brown
✉ **53 Melton Road, Birmingham, West Midlands, B14 7ET** Ⓟ
☎ 0121 441 1479
Est. 1981
Services Antique furniture restoration, furniture designed and made
Open Mon–Sat 8am–5.30pm

Jacob Butler – Period Joinery Specialist
Contact Jacob Butler
✉ **2 The Hall, Middleton, Matlock, Derbyshire, DE4 4LX** Ⓟ
☎ 01629 822170/825640
Ⓔ jacob@jpbutler.demon.co.uk
Ⓦ www.jpbutlerdemon.co.uk
Est. 1987
Services Repair and restoration of period joinery and furniture
Open By appointment

Century Tables
Contact Mr R Matthews
✉ **80 Hemming Street, Kidderminster, Worcestershire, DY11 6NB** Ⓟ

☎ 01562 747172
Est. 1974
Services Complete furniture restoration and repair, French polishing, marquetry, marble work etc
Open By appointment only

Ian Dewar
Contact Mr Ian Dewar
✉ **55 Whateleys Drive, Kenilworth, Warwickshire, CV8 2GY** 🅿
☎ 01926 856767
Ⓔ DewarRestoration@aol.com
Est. 1989
Services Antique furniture restoration, French polishing
Open Mon–Fri 8.30am–5.30pm

Joyce Ellis
Contact Joyce Ellis
✉ **Yew Tree Farm, Stratford Road, Wootton Wawen, Solihull, West Midlands, B95 6BY** 🅿
☎ 01564 795401 Ⓜ 07712 126048
Ⓔ info@legrenantiques.com
Ⓦ www.legrenantiques.com
Est. 1989
Services General restoration, specializing in French beds and farmhouse tables
Open Tues–Sun 9am–5.30pm

G M H Restoration
Contact Mr G Hale
✉ **56c Market Street, Kingswinford, West Midlands, DY6 9LE** 🅿
☎ 01384 279670
Est. 1993
Services Antique furniture restoration
Open Mon–Fri 8.30am–6pm

T J Gittins
Contact Mr T J Gittins
✉ **The Old Barn, Nagington Grange, Childs Ercall, Market Drayton, Shropshire, TF9 2TW**
☎ 01952 840409
Services Antique furniture restoration
Open By appointment

Guy Goodwin Restoration
Contact Mr Guy Goodwin
✉ **1a St John's, Warwick, Warwickshire, CV34 4NE** 🅿
☎ 01926 407409 Ⓕ 01926 407409
Est. 1979
Services Antique furniture restoration
Open Mon–Fri 9am–5.30pm

Grantham Workshops Cabinet Makers
Contact Peter Grantham
✉ **51a–57 Union Street, Kettering, Northamptonshire, NN16 9DA** 🅿
☎ 01536 411461 Ⓕ 01536 392239
Ⓔ info@grantham-workshops
Ⓦ www.grantham-workshops.co.uk
Est. 1979
Services Conservation and restoration of antique furniture. Veneer and inlay replacement, French polishing and colouring
Open Mon–Fri 9am–5.30pm

Richard Higgins Conservation (BAFRA, UKIC)
Contact Richard Higgins
✉ **The Old School, Longnor, Nr Shrewsbury, Shropshire, SY5 7PP** 🅿
☎ 01743 718162 Ⓕ 01743 718022
Ⓔ richardhigginsco@aol.com
Est. 1988
Services Restoration of all fine furniture, clocks, movements, dials and cases, casting, plating, Boulle, gilding, lacquerwork, carving, period upholstery
Open Mon–Fri 8am–6pm

Hope Antiques
Contact Mr D White
✉ **The Coach House, Spring Croft, Hartwell Lane, Rough Close, Stoke-on-Trent, Staffordshire, ST3 7NG** 🅿
☎ 01782 399022 Ⓕ 01782 399022
Ⓜ 07796 456773 or 07762 392712
Ⓔ hopeantiques@btintenet.com
Est. 1986
Services Repair and restoration of furniture, French polishing, pine stripping, inlay work. Country oak furniture made to order (from wood no less than 150 years old)
Open Mon–Sat 8am–6pm

John Hubbard Antiques Restoration & Conservation (LAPADA, CINOA)
Contact John Hubbard
✉ **Castle Ash, Birmingham Road, Blakedown, Worcestershire, DY10 3JE** 🅿
☎ 01562 701020 Ⓕ 01562 700001
Ⓜ 07775 872221
Ⓔ jphubbard@aol.com
Est. 1968
Services Furniture restoration, French polishing, desktop leathers, upholstery
Open By appointment Mon–Fri 9am–5.30pm

Kings of Loughborough
Contact Mr A King
✉ **9b Hanford Way, Loughborough, Leicestershire, LE11 1SL** 🅿
☎ 01509 236335
Est. 1971
Services Repairs, restorations and cabinet-making
Open Mon–Fri 8am–5pm

Lincoln Restorations
Contact Andrew Lincoln
✉ **54 Mill Road, High Heath, Pelsall, Walsall, West Midlands, WS4 1BS** 🅿
☎ 01922 693999
Est. 1986
Services Full antique furniture restoration
Open Mon–Fri 8.30am–6pm

Mackenzie & Smith (BAFRA, UKIC)
Contact Mr Tim Smith
✉ **4 The Bullring, Ludlow, Shropshire, SY8 1AD** 🅿
☎ 01584 877133
Est. 1998
Services Antique furniture 17th–19thC restoration, clock case restoration
Open Mon–Fri 9am–5pm

Malvern Studios (BAFRA, UKIC, NCCR)
Contact Jeff Hall
✉ **56 Cowleigh Road, Malvern, Worcestershire, WR14 1QD** 🅿
☎ 01684 574913 Ⓕ 01684 569475
Est. 1961
Services Restoration of any form of furniture and panelling, including Boulle, gilding, tortoiseshell, black lacquer, chinoiserie, satinwood, hand-painted cameos
Open Mon Tues Thurs 9am–5.15pm Fri Sat 9am–4.45pm

Nigel Mayall
Contact Mr N Mayall
44 Load Street, Bewdley, Worcestershire, DY12 2AP
01299 401431
Est. 1989
Services High-class French polishing, repairs, minor restorations, re-leathering, veneer repairs
Open Mon–Fri 10am–6pm

Melbourne Hall Furniture
Contact Mr N Collumbell
Old Saw Mill Craft Centre, Melbourne Hall, Melbourne, Derby, Derbyshire, DE73 1EA
01332 864131
Est. 1982
Services Repairs and restorations, French polishing
Open By appointment

Middleton Antiques (BAFRA)
Contact Mr S Herberholz
Middleton Hall, Middleton, Tamworth, Staffordshire, B78 2AE
01827 282858 07973 151681
Est. 1997
Services Complete repair and restoration of antique furniture including metalwork, turning, upholstery, carving, caning, gilding, porcelain restoration
Open Wed–Sun 11am–5pm

Paul Mitchell
Contact Mr P J Mitchell
The Restoration Workshop, Grove Place, Raunds, Wellingborough, Northamptonshire, NN9 6DU
01933 622336
mtchllmtch@aol.com
Est. 1974
Services Repairs, restorations, decorative paint finishes, gilding
Open By appointment

K Needham Restoration
Contact Kevin Needham
Unit 2, Old Hall Workshops, School Road, Beely, Derbyshire, DE4 2NU
01629 735455
Est. 1993
Services Repair and restoration
Open Mon–Sat 9am–5pm

Painswick Antiques
6 Churchgate, Retford, Nottinghamshire, DN22 6PQ
01777 706278
Est. 1977
Services Repair and restoration
Open Mon–Sat 9am–6pm

Perkins Stockwell and Co Ltd
Contact Mr J Stockwell
12 Abbey Gate, Leicester, Leicestershire, LE4 0AB
01162 516501 01162 510697
perkinsstockwell@aol.com
Est. 1760
Services Repair and restoration of furniture
Open Mon–Fri 7am–4pm

Regency Furniture Restoration
Contact Mr M Houghton
29 St Kenelm's Avenue, Halesowen, West Midlands, B63 1DW
0121 550 8356 0121 550 8356
07966 434947
Est. 1997
Services Antique furniture restoration and cabinet-making
Open Mon–Fri 8am–5pm or by appointment

Reindeer Restorations
Contact Mr K Stimpson
43 Watling Street, Pottersbury, Towcester, Northamptonshire, NN12 7QD
01908 542633
Est. 1984
Services Reproductions, restoration
Open Mon–Fri 8am–4.30pm or by appointment

Renaissance Antiques
Contact Mr S Macrow
18 Marshall Lake Road, Shirley, Solihull, West Midlands, B90 4PL
0121 745 5140
Est. 1979
Services Antique furniture restoration
Open Mon–Sat 9am–5pm

Restoration Rooms (AMU)
Contact Miss Jo MacDonald or Miss Susan Robinson
Machins Business Centre, Wood Street, Ashby de la Zouche, Leicestershire, LE65 1EL
01530 417510 01530 417510
Est. 1997
Services Repairs, restorations and re-upholstery
Open Mon–Fri 9am–5pm

Tim Ross-Bain
Contact Mr T Ross-Bain
Halford Bridge, Fosse Way, Halford, Shipston-on-Stour, Warwickshire, CV36 5BN
01789 740778 01789 740778
info@rossbain.com
www.rossbain.com
Est. 1979
Services Antique furniture restoration, interior decoration and repair, cabinet-making
Open 24 hours by appointment

Sealcraft
Contact Mr P M Sealey
107 New Road, Bromsgrove, Worcestershire, B60 2LJ
01527 872677
Est. 1995
Services Antiques restoration and repair, French polishing
Open By appointment

Simmons & Miles
Contact Mr S Simmons
The Workshop, Main Road, Wensley, Matlock, Derbyshire, DE4 2LH
01629 734826 01629 734826
info@simmondsandmiles.co.uk
www.simmonsandmiles.co.uk
Est. 1988
Services Antique furniture restoration. Specialist courses available, mail order of specialist restoration supplies
Open By appointment

Phillip Slater (BAFRA)
Contact Phillip Slater
93 Hewell Road, Barnt Green, Birmingham, West Midlands, B45 8NL
0121 445 4942 0121 445 4942
Est. 1977
Services Furniture and longcase clock restoration. All aspects of polishings and finishings including wax and French polishing, marquetry, inlay
Open Mon–Fri 9am–5.30pm Sat 9am–1pm

Anthony Smith
Contact Mr A Smith
✉ **Perton Court Farm, Jenny Walkers Lane, Wolverhampton, West Midlands, WV6 7HB** P
☎ 01902 380303 Ⓕ 01902 380303
Est. 1969
Services Antique and quality furniture restoration
Open Mon–Fri 8.30am–5pm

J A Snelson
Contact Mr J A Snelson
✉ **Jennett Tree Farm, Jennett Tree Lane, Callow End, Worcestershire, WR2 4UA** P
☎ 01905 831887 Ⓜ 07803 469122
Est. 1984
Services Fine antique restoration, French polishing, cabinet work
Open Mon–Fri 9am–5pm
Sat 9am–noon

J W Stevens and Son
Contact Mr M J Stevens
✉ **61 Main Street, Lubenham, Market Harborough, Leicestershire, LE16 9TF** P
☎ 01858 463521
Est. 1947
Services Antique furniture restorations
Open By appointment only

Sympathetic Restorations
Contact Mr N Welsh
✉ **21–22 Monkmoor Farm, Monkmoor Road, Shrewsbury, Shropshire, SY2 5TL** P
☎ 01743 340542 Ⓕ 01743 340542
Ⓜ 07813 835990
Ⓔ nicholas_welsh@hotmail.com
Est. 1994
Services Restoration of antique furniture, architectural features, insurance work, modern and traditional polishing, furniture made to order
Open Mon–Fri 8am–5pm
weekends by appointment

Treedale Antiques
Contact Mr G Warren
✉ **Pickwell Lane, Little Dalby, Melton Mowbray, Leicestershire, LE14 2XB** P
☎ 01664 454535 Ⓕ 01572 757521
Est. 1968
Services 16th–18thC furniture restoration
Open Mon–Sun 8am–6pm

Richard Walker – Antique Restoration
Contact Mr R Walker
✉ **302 Via Gellia Mills, Via Gellia Road, Bonsall, Matlock, Derbyshire, DE4 2AJ** P
☎ 01629 636012/825640
Est. 1992
Services Furniture repair and restoration
Open By appointment

Simon Waterhouse Designs
Contact Mr S Capewell
✉ **The Jinney Ring Craft Centre, Hanbury, Bromsgrove, Worcestershire, B60 4BU** P
☎ 01527 874787 or 821182
Services Complete restoration and repair service, French polishing, veneering, leathering, inlay work, upholstery, Japanning. Furniture copying service
Open Tues–Sun 10.30am–5.30pm

Wayside Antiques
Contact Brian Harding
✉ **62 Town Street, Duffield, Belper, Derbyshire, DE56 4GG** P
☎ 01332 840346
Est. 1976
Services Repairs and restorations
Open Mon–Sat 10am–6pm

Weedon Bec Antiques
Contact Mr N N Astbury
✉ **Rear of the Plough, Everdon, Daventry, Northamptonshire, NN11 3BL** P
☎ 01327 361614 Ⓕ 01327 361614
Est. 1989
Services Antique repair and restoration
Open By appointment

E White Antique Restoration
Contact Mr E White
✉ **Abbey House, 115 Woods Lane, Derby, Derbyshire, DE22 3UE** P
☎ 01332 331426
Ⓔ shirley.white1@btinternet.com
Est. 1969
Services Antique furniture repair and restoration
Open By appointment

Wizzards Furniture Transformers
Contact D Hayes
✉ **The Old Stables, Meadow Lane, Nottingham, Nottinghamshire, NG2 3HQ** P
☎ 0115 986 7484 Ⓕ 0115 986 7484
Est. 1994
Services Furniture repairs and restorations
Open Mon–Fri 8.30am–5pm

Wood Restorations
Contact Mr Peter Wood
✉ **Eastfields Farm, Crick Road, Rugby, Warwickshire, CV23 0AB** P
☎ 01788 822253 Ⓕ 01788 822253
Est. 1969
Services Antique furniture restoration
Open By appointment

YORKS & LINCS

David Bailes of Knaresborough
Contact Mr P Oliver
✉ **Finkle Street, Knaresborough, North Yorkshire, HG5 8AA** P
☎ 01423 868438
Est. 1961
Services Antiques repair, restoration
Open Mon–Sat 8am–5.30pm

Anthony James Beech (BAFRA, UKIC)
Contact Mr Anthony Beech
✉ **The Stable Courtyard, Burghley House, Stamford, Lincolnshire, PE9 3JY** P
☎ 01780 481199
Est. 1998
Services Period furniture conservation and restoration
Open By appointment only

Adrian J Black
Contact Mr A J Black
✉ **36a Freeman Street, Grimsby, Lincolnshire, DN32 7AG**
☎ 01472 355668
Est. 1968
Services Antique furniture repair and restoration
Open By apppointment

Byethorpe Furniture
Contact Mr B Yates
✉ **Shippen Rural Business Centre, Church Farm, Barlow, Yorkshire, S18 7TR** P
☎ 0114 289 9111 Ⓕ 0114 289 9111

Ⓦ www.byethorpe.com
Est. 1995
Services Antique restoration, maker of bespoke furniture
Open Mon–Sat 9.30am–5.30pm

Kenneth F Clifford
Contact Mr K Clifford
✉ **29 St Aubyn's Place, York, North Yorkshire, YO24 1EQ** P
☎ 01904 635780
Est. 1982
Services Antiques repair and restoration
Open By appointment

D A Copley
Contact Mr D A Copley
✉ **54a New Lane, Siddal, Halifax, West Yorkshire, HX3 9AL** P
☎ 01422 351854
Est. 1949
Services Antiques repairs and restorations, French polishing
Open Mon–Fri 8am–5pm Sat 8am–noon

Edmund Czajkowski & Son (BAFRA)
Contact Michael Czajkowski
✉ **96 Tor O Moor Road, Woodhall Spa, Lincolnshire, LN10 6SB** P
☎ 01526 352895 Ⓕ 01526 352895
Ⓔ michael.czajkowski@ntlworld.com
Ⓦ www.czajkowskiandson.com
Est. 1951
Services Restoration of antique furniture, clocks, barometers
Open Mon–Sat 8.30am–5pm

R D Dunning
Contact Mr R Dunning
✉ **Scaife Cottage, Gate Helmsley, York, North Yorkshire YO26 8AY**
☎ 01759 371961
Est. 1972
Services Antique furniture repair and restoration
Open Mon–Fri 9am–6pm

French House Antiques
Contact Steve
✉ **74 Micklegate, York, YO1 6LF** P
☎ 01904 624465 Ⓕ 01904 629965
Ⓔ info@thefrenchhouse.co.uk
Ⓦ www.thefrenchhouse.co.uk
Est. 1995
Services Restoration of antique French furniture
Open Mon–Sat 9.30am–5.30pm

Rodney S Kemble Fine Furniture (BAFRA)
Contact Rodney Kemble
✉ **16 Cragvale Terrace, Glusburn, Nr Keighley, West Yorkshire, BD20 8QU** P
☎ 01535 636954
Est. 1984
Services Restoration of 18th–19thC English furniture, especially mahogany and walnut including veneer work and gilding. Also restoration of clock cases, writing slopes, decorative boxes, barometers

Ogee Restorations
Contact Mr L Jackson
✉ **32a Cambridge Street, Cleethorpes, Lincolnshire, DN35 8HD** P
☎ 01472 601701 Ⓕ 01472 601701
Ⓜ 07977 860823
Est. 1973
Services Repair, restoration, veneering, inlaying
Open Mon–Sat 8am–5pm

Paraphernalia
Contact Mrs R Thomas
✉ **12 Harland Place, High Street, Norton, Stockton-on-Tees, North Yorkshire, TS20 1AL** P
☎ 01642 535940
Est. 1984
Services Repairs and restorations, tea room
Open Mon–Sat 9.30am–5pm

Period Furniture Ltd (LAPADA)
Contact Mr S Bowyer
✉ **Moorside, Tockwith, York, North Yorkshire, YO26 7QG** P
☎ 01423 358399 Ⓕ 01423 359050
Ⓔ pf@period-furniture.co.uk
Ⓦ www.antique-furniture.co.uk
Est. 1985
Services Antiques repair and restoration, sales of Georgian–Edwardian furniture
Trade only Sat
Open Mon–Fri 8am–4.30pm Sat 9am–4.30pm Sun 10am–4pm

T L Phelps Fine Furniture Restoration (BAFRA)
Contact Mr T Phelps
✉ **8 Mornington Terrace, Harrogate, North Yorkshire, HG1 5DH** P
☎ 01423 524604
Est. 1984
Services Repair, restoration and conservation of high-quality period furniture with old waxed and polished surfaces
Open By appointment

A G Podmore & Son
Contact Andrew Podmore
✉ **Unit 1D, North Minster Business Park, Northfield Lane, Poppleton, York, North Yorkshire, YO26 6QU** P
☎ 01904 799800
Est. 1968
Services Antique furniture restoration
Open Mon–Fri 9am–5pm

John W Saggers
Contact Mr J Saggers
✉ **Chapel Hill, Woolsthorpe by Belvoir, Grantham, Lincolnshire, NG32 1NG** P
☎ 01476 870756 Ⓕ 01476 870756
Est. 1966
Services Antiques repair and restoration
Open By appointment

K J Sarginson Fine Furniture (UKIC)
Contact Mr K Sarginson
✉ **The Joinery, Escrick Grange, Stillingfleet Road, Escrick, York, North Yorkshire, YO19 6EB** P
☎ 01904 728202 Ⓕ 01904 728202
Est. 1991
Services Antique restorations and repairs of fine furniture. Dining tables a speciality
Open Mon–Fri 8.15am–5.30pm or by appointment

Gerald Shaw
Contact Mr M G Shaw
✉ **Jansville, Quarry Lane, Harrogate, North Yorkshire, HG1 3HR** P
☎ 01423 503590 Ⓕ 01423 503590
Est. 1956
Services Repair, restoration of antique furniture
Open By appointment

Tony Smart Restorations
Contact Tony Smart
✉ **Fold House, Glebe Farm, Lund, Beverley, East Yorkshire, YO25 9TT** P
☎ 01377 217438

Est. 1971
Services General fine furniture restoration
Open Mon–Fri 9am–5pm

J K Speed Antique Furniture Restoration
Contact Mr J Speed
✉ **The Workshop, Thornton Road, New York, Lincoln, Lincolnshire, LN4 4YL** 🅿
☎ 01205 280313 Ⓜ 07761 242219
Est. 1964
Services Antique repair and restoration, light upholstery, specializing in case repair of longcase clocks
Open Mon–Fri 9am–5.30pm

Spires Restoration
Contact Mr G Bexon
✉ **32 Upgate, Louth, Lincolnshire, LN11 9ET** 🅿
☎ 01507 600707 Ⓕ 01507 602588
Ⓜ 07866 230725
Est. 1994
Services Repair and restoration of furniture
Open Mon–Fri 8am–5pm or by appointment

Tomlinson Antiques (LAPADA)
Contact Mike Grant
✉ **Moorside, Tockwith, North Yorkshire, YO26 7QG** 🅿
☎ 01423 358833 Ⓕ 01423 358188
Ⓔ info@tomlinsonfurniture.com
Ⓦ antique-furniture.co.uk
Est. 1977
Services Repair and restoration of furniture
Open Mon–Sat 9am–4.30pm
Sun 10am–4pm

Neil Trinder (BAFRA)
Contact Mr N Trinder
✉ **Burrowlee House, Broughton Road, Sheffield, South Yorkshire, S6 2AS** 🅿
☎ 0114 285 2428
Est. 1985
Services Furniture restoration including gilding, upholstery, marquetry etc
Open By appointment

Clive Underwood Antiques
Contact Mr Clive Underwood
✉ **Rose Cottage, 46 High Street, Colsterworth, Grantham, Lincolnshire, NG33 5NF** 🅿
☎ 01476 860689
Est. 1964
Services Restoration of 17th–18thC furniture, rushing and caning. Dining chairs made to match existing
Open Mon–Fri 8am–5.30pm

Westway Pine
Contact Mr J Dzierzek
✉ **Carlton Lane, Helmsley, York, YO62 5HB** 🅿
☎ 01439 771399 Ⓕ 01439 770172
Ⓜ 07798 651155
Ⓔ derzie@supanet.co.uk
Est. 1986
Services Antique reproductions and restoration
Open Mon–Fri 9am–5pm
Sat 10am–5pm
Sun by appointment

B D Whitham
Contact Mr B D Whitham
✉ **1 South View Cottage, Draughton, Skipton, North Yorkshire, BD23 6EF** 🅿
☎ 01756 710422
Est. 1984
Services Repair and restoration, upholstery
Open Mon–Fri 9am–6pm and by appointment

Nigel Wright
Contact Mr N Wright
✉ **Burrowlee House, Broughton Road, Sheffield, South Yorkshire, S6 2AS** 🅿
☎ 0114 234 1403
Est. 1983
Services Complete repair and restoration of antique furniture, veneering, inlays, French polishing, colouring etc
Open By appointment

NORTH EAST

G M Athey
Contact Mr Athey
✉ **Corner Shop, Narrowgate, Alnwick, Northumberland, NE66 1JQ** 🅿
☎ 01665 604229 Ⓜ 07836 718350
Ⓦ www.atheysantiques.com
Est. 1982
Services Full restoration, French polishing, upholstery. Sale of Georgian and Victorian furniture and china
Open Mon–Sat 8am–4.30pm

Richard Pattison
Contact Richard Pattison
✉ **Unit 4, New Kennels, Blagdon Estate, Seaton Burn, Newcastle-upon-Tyne, Tyne and Wear, NE13 6DB** 🅿
☎ 01670 789888
Est. 1977
Services Traditional antique furniture restoration
Open Mon–Sat 9am–5pm

Rainbow Bridge
Contact Mr N Lambert
✉ **57A Oxbridge Lane, Stockton-on-Tees, Cleveland, TS18 4AP** 🅿
☎ 01642 643033
Est. 1989
Services Antique repairs and restorations
Open Mon–Sat 10am–5pm

Richard Zabrocki & Son
Contact Mr I Zabrocki
✉ **Hoults Estate, Walker Road, Newcastle-upon-Tyne, Tyne & Wear, NE6 1AB** 🅿
☎ 0191 265 5989
Est. 1949
Services Repair and restoration of antique furniture
Open By appointment

NORTH WEST

Antique Furniture Restoration & Conservation (BAFRA)
Contact Eric Smith
✉ **The Old Church, Park Road, Darwen, Lancashire, BB3 2LD** 🅿
☎ 01254 776222 Ⓜ 07977 811067
Ⓔ ericsmith@restorations.ndo.co.uk
Est. 1965
Services Furniture restoration
Open Mon–Sun 9am–7pm

Arrowsmith Antiques & Restoration
Contact Mr P Arrowsmith
✉ **Unit 7–8, Waterside Mill, Waterside, Macclesfield, Cheshire, SK11 7HG** 🅿
☎ 01625 611880
Est. 1977
Services Complete repair and restoration service of high-quality antique furniture
Open Mon–Fri 8.30am–5.30pm
Sat 10am–2pm

K Bennett
Contact Mr Keith Bennett
✉ **Oak House Farm, Wycollar, Colne, Lancashire, BB8 8SY** 🅿
☎ 01282 866853
Est. 1973
Services Antique furniture restoration
Open By appointment

Steve Blackwell French Polishers
Contact Mr S Blackwell
✉ **Bute Mill, Essex Street, Preston, Lancashire, PR1 1QE** 🅿
☎ 01772 821004 Ⓕ 01772 432270
Ⓜ 07929 170114
Est. 1989
Services Full antique furniture restoration service and modern finishes
Open Mon–Thurs 8am–5pm
Fri 8am–4.30pm

M Bradley
Contact Mr M Bradley
✉ **588 Hawthorne Road, Bootle, Merseyside, L20 6JZ** 🅿
☎ 0151 922 5901
Est. 1969
Services Antique furniture restoration, French polishing, repairs, upholstery repairs
Open Mon–Fri 9am–5pm
Sat 9am–noon

Michael Clayton French Polisher
Contact Mr M Clayton
✉ **The Workshop, Lestrange Street, Cleethorpes, Lancashire, BU35 7HS** 🅿
☎ 01472 602795
Est. 1979
Services French polishing
Open By appointment

Cottage Antiques
Contact Angelica Slater
✉ **788 Rochdale Road, Walsden, Todmorden, Lancashire, OL14 7UA** 🅿
☎ 01706 813612 Ⓕ 01706 813612
Ⓜ 07773 798032
Ⓦ www.ukcottageantiques.co.uk
Services Stripping, polishing, renovations, paint finishes, custom-built furniture
Open Tues–Sun 9.30am–5.30pm

Rory Fraser
Contact Mr R Fraser
✉ **Goyt Mill, Upper Hibbert Lane, Marple, Stockport, Cheshire, SK6 7HX** 🅿
☎ 0161 427 2122
Est. 1993
Services Good-quality antique furniture restoration, French polishing, leathers fitted, woodturning, carving
Open Mon–Fri 9am–5pm

A Grice
Contact Mr A Grice
✉ **106 Aughton Street, Ormskirk, Lancashire, L39 3BS** 🅿
☎ 01695 572007
Est. 1984
Services Furniture restoration
Open Wed Sat 1.30–6pm or by appointment

Hamilton Antique Restoration
Contact Mr C Sayle
✉ **1a Orry Place, Douglas, Isle of Man**
☎ 01624 662483
Est. 1989
Services Complete furniture repair and restoration service, upholstery
Open By appointment

Michael Holroyd Restorations
Contact Mr M Holroyd
✉ **Pendle Antique Centre, Union Mill, Watt Street, Sabden, Clitheroe, Lancashire, BB7 9ED** 🅿
☎ 01282 771112 Ⓜ 07711 011465
Est. 1996
Services Complete repair and restoration service including spray finish, wax finish, French polishing, cabinet-making and veneering
Open Mon–Sat 8am–5pm

Hopkins Antique Restoration
Contact Mr Mark Hopkins
✉ **Unit 1, Excelsior Works, Charles Street, Heywood, Lancashire, OL10 2HW** 🅿
☎ 01706 620549
Est. 1987
Services Antique furniture restoration, French polishing
Open Mon–Sat 9am–5pm

J Kershaw Fine Furniture Restoration
Contact Mr J Kershaw
✉ **Normans Hall Farm, Shrigley Road, Pott Shrigley, Macclesfield, Cheshire, SK10 5SE** 🅿
☎ 01625 560808
Est. 1985
Services Full repair and restoration service including French polishing, inlay work, marquetry, lacquerwork
Open By appointment

Peter Lawrenson
Contact Margaret Lawrenson
✉ **Brook Cottage, Scronkey Pilling, Preston, Lancashire, PR3 6SQ** 🅿
☎ 01253 790671
Est. 1984
Services Furniture restoration
Open By appointment

M & M Restoration Work Ltd
Contact Mrs M Bean
✉ **Rock Cottage, Castletown, Isle of Man, IM9 4PJ** 🅿
☎ 01624 823620 Ⓕ 01624 822463
Est. 1993
Services Repair and restoration of furniture, upholstery, caning, rushing etc
Open By appointment

Macdonalds Restoration
Contact Mr A Macdonald
✉ **Unit 4, Gladstone Park, Ramsey, Isle of Man, IM8 2LE** 🅿
☎ 01624 812791
Est. 1980
Services Traditional antique and modern furniture repair and restoration, upholstery, cabinet-making etc
Open Mon–Sun 8am–6pm

Mansion House Antiques
Contact Mr Andrew Smith
✉ **11 Hand Lane, Leigh, Lancashire, WN7 3LP** 🅿
☎ 01942 605634
Est. 1995
Services Antique furniture restoration
Open By appointment

R S M Antique Restoration
Contact Mr Robin Stone

The Stables, Back Eaves Street, Blackpool, Lancashire, FY1 2HW P
☎ 01253 623839 F 01253 623839
Est. 1972
Services Antique furniture, clocks, barometer, restoration, marquetry cutting
Open Mon–Fri 9am–6pm

T N Richards
Contact Mr D Richards
Hamilton Place, Chester, Cheshire, CH1 2BH P
☎ 01244 320241
Est. 1975
Services Complete repair and restoration service
Open By appointment

R J H Rimmel
Contact Mr R J H Rimmel
3 Newton Bank Cottages, Newton Hall Road, Mobberley, Cheshire, WA16 7LB P
☎ 01565 873847
Est. 1974
Services Full furniture restoration service, special commissions and church work undertaken
Open By appointment

Seventeen Antiques
Contact Mr J Brake
306 Aigburth Road, Liverpool, Merseyside, L17 9PW P
☎ 0151 727 1717 M 07712 189604
W www.seventeenantiques.gbr.cc
Est. 1997
Services Furniture restoration, stripping
Open Mon–Sat 10am–5.30pm closed Wed

J D Worrall
Contact Mr J Worrall
Goyt Mill, The Old Brickworks, Pott, Shingley, Stockport, Cheshire, SK6 7HX P
☎ 01663 733817
Est. 1997
Services Complete antiques repair and restoration including upholstery, carving, gilding, veneer, inlay, cabinet work and French polishing
Open By appointment

WALES

Iain Ashcroft Furniture
Contact Mr Ian Ashcroft
Ty Canol Farm, Sunbank, Llangollen, Denbighshire, LL20 7UL P
☎ 01978 860392 F 01978 860392
Est. 1987
Services Antique furniture, restoration, carving, inlaying
Open Mon–Fri 9am–5pm

Craftsman Antiques
Contact Mark Haines
Unit 1, Maindy Lane, Maindy Road, Cathay, Cardiff, West Glamorgan, CF24 4XN P
☎ 01291 625145 F 01291 625145
M 07836 634712
E mark@oakden.co.uk
W www.oakden.co.uk
Est. 1968
Services Furniture, antiques repair and restoration, kitchenware
Open Mon–Sun 9am–5pm

D J Gravell
Contact D J Gravell
Unit 5, Aber Court, Ferryboat Close Enterprise Park, Morrison, Swansea, West Glamorgan, SA6 8QN P
☎ 01792 310202 F 01792 795471
E jgravell@universalwoodfinishers.co.uk
W www.universalwoodfinishers.co.uk
Est. 1989
Services Antique furniture repair and restoration
Open Mon–Fri 8.30am–5.30pm Sat 9–11am

Hera Restorations
Contact Neil Richards
Cardiff, South Glamorgan
☎ 029 2075 5379 F 01222 761660
Est. 1995
Services Full French polishing, veneering, carving
Open By appointment only

Heritage Workshop
Contact Mr G Lloyd
14B, rear of 1 Iestyn Street, Cardiff, South Glamorgan, CF11 9HT P
☎ 029 2039 0097 M 07931 681743
Est. 1981
Services Restoration of furniture. Oak and pine furniture made to order. Period architectural restoration, specializing in fireplaces
Open Mon–Sat 9am–5pm

B G Jones
Contact B G Jones
Cwmburry Honey Farm, Ferryside, Carmarthenshire, SA17 5TW P
☎ 01267 267318
E brian_jones@cwmburryfarm.freeserve.co.uk
Est. 1986
Services Antiques repair and restoration of furniture
Open Mon–Fri 9am–5pm

G A Parkinson
Contact Mr G A Parkinson
Glanrapon, Secontmill Road, Caernarfon, Gwynedd, LL55 2YL P
☎ 01286 672865
Est. 1949
Services French polishing, repairs, restoration
Open Mon–Sat 9am–5pm

Pastiche
Contact Mr S Pesticcio
15 Duxford Close, Llandaff, Cardiff, South Glamorgan, CF5 2DZ P
☎ 02920 309559 M 07811 594257
Est. 1975
Services Period and traditional restoration and redecoration of Victorian furniture and property
Open By appointment

Phoenix Conservation.com (BAFRA, UKIC)
Contact Hugh Haley
Selwyn Forge, Tenby Road, St Clears, Carmarthenshire, SA33 4JP P
☎ 01994 232109
E phoenixconservation@hotmail.com
W www.phoenixconservation.com
Est. 1992
Services Welsh oak and antique furniture restoration and repair
Open By appointment

T N Richards
Contact Mr D Richards
Caergynog, Llanbedr, Gwynedd, LL45 2PL P
☎ 01341 241485
Est. 1974
Services Complete repair and restoration service
Open By appointment

Snowdonia Antiques
Contact Jeffery Collins
✉ **Bank Building, Station Road, Llanrwst, Gwynedd, LL26 0EP** Ⓟ
☎ 01492 640789 Ⓕ 01492 641800
Ⓜ 07802 503552
Est. 1965
Services Antiques repair and restoration
Open Mon–Sat 9am–5pm
Sun by appointment

St Helens Restoration
Contact Jo McCarthy
✉ **87–88 St Helens Avenue, Swansea, West Glamorgan, SA1 4NN** Ⓟ
☎ 01792 465240 Ⓕ 01792 467788
Ⓔ jo@artsnetwork.co.uk
Est. 1979
Services Antiques repair and restoration, upholstery, French polishing
Open Mon–Fri 9am–5pm
Sat 9.30am–1pm

SCOTLAND

Adam Antiques & Restoration
Contact Charles Bergius
✉ **23c Dundas Street, Edinburgh, EH3 6QQ** Ⓟ
☎ 0131 556 7555 Ⓕ 0131 556 7555
Est. 1983
Services Quality repairs to 18th–19thC furniture. Sales of 18th–19thC mainly mahogany furniture and associated furnishings
Open Tues–Sat 10.30am–6pm
Mon by appointment

Antique Furniture Restoration
Contact David Carson
✉ **108b Causewayside, Edinburgh, EH9 1PU** Ⓟ
☎ 0131 667 1067 Ⓜ 07779 824543
Ⓔ carsonantrest@btinternet
Est. 1994
Services Repair and restoration of all old and antique furniture
Open Mon–Fri 10am–6pm
Sat 10am–2pm

Castle Restoration
Contact Peter Nicholson
✉ **Auchtertool House, Auchtertool, Kirkcaldy, Fife, KY2 5XW** Ⓟ
☎ 01592 780371 Ⓕ 01592 780371
Est. 1964
Services Repair and restoration of all antiques, French polishing
Open By appointment

The Chairman of Bearsden (Scottish Furniture Preservation Society)
Contact David Snutterton
✉ **At 16 Highborough Road, The Mews, Caledon Lane, Hillhead, Glasgow, G12 9YE** Ⓟ
☎ 0141 334 2727 Ⓕ 0141 334 4747
Ⓔ sales@thechairmanofbearsden.co.uk
Ⓦ www.thechairmanofbearsden.co.uk
Est. 1990
Services Furniture restoration and upholstery, French polishing, cabinet-making, bergère suites, cane and rush seating
Open Mon–Sat 9am–5pm

Chisholme Antiques
Contact Kim Roberts
✉ **5 Orrock Place, Hawick, Scottish Borders, TD9 0HQ** Ⓟ
☎ 01450 376928
Est. 1979
Services Antiques repair and restoration of furniture, cabinet-making
Open Mon–Fri 9am–5pm

Chylds Hall Fine Furniture Restoration
Contact Stephen Pickering
✉ **Old Dairy Cottage, Upper Stepford, Dunscore, Dumfries & Galloway, DG2 0JP** Ⓟ
☎ 01387 820558 Ⓕ 01387 280558
Est. 1991
Services Fine furniture restoration, period paint finish restoration, French polishing
Open By appointment only

Douglas & Kay
Contact Mr P Kay
✉ **Next to 200 Eglington Street, Glasgow, G5 9QJ** Ⓟ
☎ 0141 429 6908 Ⓜ 0797 4494618
Est. 1948
Services Repair and restoration of furniture, French polishing
Open By appointment

Roland Gomm
Contact Roland Gomm
✉ **65 Constitution Street, Edinburgh, EH6 7AF** Ⓟ
☎ 0131 467 5525 Ⓜ 07947 179774
Est. 1986
Services French polishing, restoration of fine antique furniture, upholstery
Open Mon–Sat 10am–6pm

Alastair Gunn
✉ **46e Bavelaw Road, Balerno, Midlothian, EH14 7AE** Ⓟ
☎ 0131 449 4032
Est. 1989
Services Antique reproduction and restoration
Open Mon–Sat 9am–6pm

The Hen Hoose
Contact Jo McGregor
✉ **Tynron, Thornhill, Dumfriesshire, DG3 4LA** Ⓟ
☎ 01848 200418
Ⓦ www.henhoose.co.uk
Est. 1994
Services French polishing, caning, rushing, upholstery, general antique repair
Open Tues–Sun 11am–5pm

Inchmartine Restorations (BAFRA)
Contact Andrew Stephens
✉ **Inchmartine House, Inchture, Perth, Perthshire, PH14 9QQ** Ⓟ
☎ 01828 686412 Ⓕ 01828 686748
Ⓔ ir@toolbazaar.freeserve.co.uk
Ⓦ www.toolbazaar.co.uk
Est. 1990
Services Restoration of antique furniture pre-1840
Open Mon–Sat 9am–5.30pm

The Tower Workshops
Contact George Pirie
✉ **Aberdeen Road, Tarland, Aboyne, Aberdeenshire, AB34 4TB** Ⓟ
☎ 013398 811544
Est. 1989
Services Antiques restorers and dealers
Open Mon–Fri 9am–5pm
Sat 11am–5pm

William Trist (BAFRA)
Contact Willliam Trist
✉ **135 St Leonard's Street, Edinburgh, EH8 9RB** Ⓟ
☎ 0131 667 7775 Ⓕ 0131 667 4333
Est. 1980
Services Restoration and conservation of antique furniture and panelling,

cabinet and chair-makers, cane and rush chair seating, upholstery
Open Mon–Fri 8am–6pm but appointment advisable

Graham Watson
✉ **The Workshop, Mill Lynd, Greenlaw, Scottish Borders, TD10 6UA** Ⓟ
☎ 01361 810770/810593
Est. 1996
Services Furniture restoration, French polishing
Open Mon–Sat 8am–5pm

NORTHERN IRELAND

Antique Services
Contact David Hosgood
✉ **288 Beersbridge Road, Belfast, Co Antrim, BT5 5DY** Ⓟ
☎ 028 9020 3933
Est. 1984
Services Restoration, re-polishing
Open Mon–Fri 8am–5pm
Sat 8am–1pm

Courtyard Restoration
Contact Cosi Shaker or Shaun Butler
✉ **The Old Mill, 2 Parkfield Road, Ahogill, Ballymena, Co Antrim, BT42 2QS** Ⓟ
☎ 028 2587 8875 Ⓜ 07967 144784
Est. 1996
Services Restoration of furniture, gilt frames, frame repairs, recarving, etc
Open Mon–Sat 10am–5pm

Crozier Antique Furniture Restoration
Contact Mr Peter Crozier
✉ **39 Tassagh Road, Keady, Co Armagh, BT60 3TU** Ⓟ
☎ 028 3753 8242
Est. 1986
Services Restoration
Open Mon–Fri 9am–6pm or by appointment

Kelly Antiques
Contact Mr Louis Kelly
✉ **Mullaghmore House, Old Mountfield Road, Omagh, Co Tyrone, BT79 7EX** Ⓟ
☎ 028 8224 2314 Ⓕ 028 8225 0262
Ⓔ sales@kellyantiques.com
Ⓦ www.kellyantiques.com
Est. 1936
Services Restorations, private bi-annual auctions, opening an International Centre of Excellence for conservation, heritage and restoration, with a full-time course in antique furniture restoration. College teaching restoration techniques
Open Mon–Fri 10am–7pm
Sat 10am–5pm

REPUBLIC OF IRELAND

Conservation Restoration Centre for Furniture and Wooden Artefacts (UKIC, ICHAWI)
Contact Colin Piper
✉ **Letterfrack, Co Galway, Ireland** Ⓟ
☎ 095 41036 Ⓕ 095 41112
Services Conservation and restoration of all historic furniture and related objects. Museum conservation, cabinet-making, French polishing, veneer work, turning and woodcarving, marquetry, Boulle work, metal work repairs, pietre dure and marble repair
Open Mon–Fri 9am–5.30pm or by appointment

E Fitzpatrick
Contact E Fitzpatrick
✉ **17 Sidney Park, Wellington Road, Cork, Ireland** Ⓟ
☎ 021 450 3084
Est. 1989
Services Repair and restoration of antique furniture
Open By appointment

Glebe Hall Restoration Studios
Contact Carmel Corrigan-Griffin
✉ **Old Killernogh Rectory, Rathnakelly Glebe, Ballacolla, Co Laois, Ireland** Ⓟ
☎ 0502 34105 Ⓕ 0502 34154
Est. 1980
Services Restoration, furniture, gilding, porcelain, ivory, jade
Open By appointment,
Sat 11am–4pm

Val Hughes (IPCRA)
Contact Mr Val Hughes
✉ **132 Arden Vale, Tullamore, Co Offaly, Ireland** Ⓟ
☎ 0506 22600
Ⓔ valhughestull@eircom.net
Est. 1990
Services Conservation and restoration of antique and fine furniture
Open Mon–Sat 8.30am–6pm

Stephen McDonnell (BAFRA)
Contact Mr McDonnell
✉ **2 Anglesea Lane, Dun Laoghaire, Co Dublin, Ireland** Ⓟ
☎ 01 280 7077 Ⓕ 01 284 2268
Ⓜ 0863 363537
Est. 1994
Services Furniture restoration, traditional finishing, French polishing, cabinet repairs
Open Tues–Sat 9am–5.30pm

GILDING

Alison Cosserat
Contact Miss Alison Cosserat
✉ **13f Tonedale Mills, Tonedale, Wellington, Somerset, TA21 0AW** Ⓟ
☎ 01823 665279 Ⓜ 07989 465427
Est. 1997
Services Gold leaf specialist
Open Mon–Fri 10am–6pm

Michael Ferris
Contact Mr M Ferris
✉ **Rose Cottage, Chapel Lane, South Cockerington, Louth, Lincolnshire, LN11 7EB** Ⓟ
☎ 01507 327463 Ⓕ 01507 327463
Est. 1979
Services Antiques repairs, restorations, gilding
Open By appointment

Mark Finamore
Contact Mark Finamore
✉ **63 Orford Road, Walthamstow, London, E17 9NJ** Ⓟ
☎ 020 8521 9407
Est. 1981
Services General antiques service, gilding, furniture restoration and conservation
Open Mon–Fri 10.30am–6pm or Sat by appointment

R G Jones
Contact R G Jones
✉ **1 Brickfield Cottage, Bilting, Ashford, Kent, TN25 4ER** Ⓟ
☎ 01233 812849
Est. 1985
Services Antique restoration, gilding
Open Mon–Fri 9am–4pm

Vigi Sawdon
Contact Vigi Sawdon
✉ **79–81 Ledbury Road, London, W11 2AG** P
☎ 020 7229 9321/2033 F 020 7229 2033
E vigisawdon@virgin.net
Est. 1994
Services Gilding and restoration of old wooden, gesso and composite mirrors, architectural pieces, frames. Also provides special paint effects
Open By appointment

GLASS

F W Aldridge Ltd
Contact Miss Angela Garwood
✉ **28 Mead Industrial Park Riverway, Harlow, Essex, CM20 2SE** P
☎ 01279 442876 F 01279 445764
E angela@fwaldridge.abk.co.uk
W www.fwaldridgeglass.com
Est. 1926
Services Repair and restoration of glass, supplier of Bristol glass for antique and modern table silverware, all glass and silver restoration
Open Mon–Fri 9am–5.30pm

Lorna Barnes Conservation (IPCRA, ICOM)
Contact Lorna Barnes
✉ **158 Rialto Cottages, Rialto, Dublin 8, Ireland** P
☎ 01 473 6205
E barneslorna@hotmail.com
Est. 2000
Services Conservation of glass, ceramic and stone objects, condition surveys, advice on packaging and storage
Open Mon–Fri 9am–6pm

Facets Glass Restoration
Contact Mrs K Moore
✉ **107 Boundary Road, London, E17 8NQ** P
☎ 020 8520 3392 F 020 8520 3392
M 07778 758304
E repairs@facetsglass.co.uk
W www.facetsglass.co.uk
Est. 1996
Services Antique glass restoration including supply of blue glass liners for table silverware, re-bristling hair brushes, cutlery restoration, flute and trumpet stopper suppliers
Open Tues 10am–5pm

Fran Hall Glass Restoration
Contact Mrs Fran Hall
✉ **49 Grove Road, Beccles, Suffolk, NR34 9RE** P
☎ 01502 717246
Services Glass restoration including decanter cleaning
Open By appointment

Looking Glass of Bath
Contact Anthony Reed
✉ **94 Walcot Street, Bath, Somerset, BA1 5BG** P
☎ 01225 461969 F 01225 316191
E info@lookingglassofbath.co.uk
W www.lookingglassofbath.co.uk
Est. 1968
Services Restoration of mirrors, picture frames, regilding, carving, manufacturers and supplier of antique mirror glass, paper and oil restoration
Open Mon–Sat 9am–6pm

Martyn Pearson Glass
Contact Martyn Pearson
✉ **The Stables Craft Centre, Halfpenny Green Vineyard, Tom Lane, Bobbington, Staffordshire, DY7 5EP** P
☎ 01384 221399 M 07951 305617
Est. 1995
Services Glass cutting, engraving and repairs
Open Mon–Sun 11am–5pm

Red House Glasscrafts
Contact Mrs J Oakley or B Taylor
✉ **Ruskin Glass Centre, Wollaston Road, Amblecote, Stourbridge, West Midlands, DY8 4HF** P
☎ 01384 399460 F 01384 399460
M 07751 392473
Est. 1987
Services Repair and restoration of antique crystal
Open Mon–Fri 9am–5pm
Sat 10am–4pm

Romanov Restoration
Contact Ludmila Romanova
✉ **51 Sutherland Avenue, London, SW9 2HF** P
☎ 020 7286 1430
Est. 1982
Services Painting and icon restoration using traditional Russian methods, glass and bronze restoration
Open By appointment

GRAMOPHONES & RADIOS

Philip Knighton (The Gramophone Man) (RETRA)
Contact Philip Knighton
✉ **Bush House, 17b South Street, Wellington, Somerset, TA21 8NR** P
☎ 01823 661618 F 01823 661618
E gramman@msn.com
Est. 1981
Services Supply and restoration of gramophones, early wirelesses, 78rpm records sold
Open Tues–Sat 10am–5pm closed Mon

Talking Points Antiques
Contact Mr Paul Austwick
✉ **66 West Street, Sowerby Bridge, West Yorkshire, HX6 3AP** P
☎ 01422 834126
E tpagrams@aol.com
Est. 1985
Services Repair, refurbishment and restoration of wind-up gramophones
Open Thurs Fri Sat 10.30am–5.30pm and by appointment

The Wireless Works
Contact Rob Rusbridge
✉ **40 Fore Street, Bugle, St Austell, Cornwall, PL26 8PE** P
☎ 01726 852284 F 01726 852284
E rob@wirelessworks.co.uk
W www.wirelessworks.co.uk
Est. 1995
Services Radio, gramophone and antique electronics repairs, restorations, rebuilding and trading
Open Mon–Sat 9am–5pm

INLAY WORK

Paul Waldmann Woodwork (Conservation Unit)
Contact Mr P Waldmann
✉ **41 Norfolk Street, Cambridge, Cambridgeshire, CB1 2LD** P
☎ 01223 314001 M 07740 167055
E paul.mann@cwcom.net

Est. 1982
Services Antique furniture restoration, cabinet-making
Open By appointment

JEWELLERY

Berkshire Antiques Co Ltd
Contact Mr Sutton
✉ **42 Thames Street, Windsor, Berkshire, SL4 1YY** P
☎ 01753 830100 F 01753 832278
E sales@jewels2go.co.uk
Est. 1981
Services Jewellery repair
Open Mon–Sat 10.30am–5.30pm Sun by appointment

LEATHER

Antique Leathers (LAPADA, AMU)
Contact Jackie Crisp
✉ **Unit 2, Bennetts Field Trading Estate, Wincanton, Somerset, BA9 9DT** P
☎ 01963 33163 F 01963 33164
E info@antique-leathers.co.uk
W www.antique-leathers.co.uk
Est. 1965
Services Hand-dyed leatherwork on desk tops, gold tooling, traditional upholstery, leather chair repairs and restorations, bookshelf edging
Open Mon–Fri 9.30am–5pm

J Crisp (AMU)
Contact Mr J Crisp
✉ **48 Roderick Road, London, NW3 2NL** P
☎ 020 7485 8566 F 020 7485 8566
Est. 1979
Services Loose leather services, traditional upholstery, French and leather polishing, table liners, leather gilding
Open Mon–Fri 10am–6pm visitors by appointment only

Director Furniture Leathergilders
Contact Mrs M Taylor
✉ **39 Severn Stoke, Worcester, Worcestershire, WR8 9JA** P
☎ 01905 371339
Est. 1984
Services Replacement leather tops for the antiques trade, gilded or ungilded. Full grainhide or skiver
Open By appointment

Leather Conservation Centre (UKIC, SSCR)
Contact Roy Thomson
✉ **University College Campus, Boughton Green Road, Moulton Park, Northampton, Northamptonshire, NN2 7AN** P
☎ 01604 719766 F 01604 719649
E lcc@northampton.ac.uk
Est. 1978
Services Conservation and restoration of leather objects, research, training and information for leather and leather conservation
Open Mon–Fri 9am–5pm

The Manor Bindery Ltd
Contact Philip Bradburn
✉ **Calshot Road, Fawley, Southampton, Hampshire, SO45 1BB** P
☎ 02380 894488 F 02380 899418
E manorbindery@btconnect.com
W www.falsebooks.co.uk
Est. 1976
Services Desk and table top leathering, edging. Supplier of leather-bound books and false books for display
Open Mon–Fri 8am–5pm

Stanstead Abbotts Leathers
Contact Mrs L Ray
✉ **Hedges, Commonside Road, Harlow, Essex, CM18 7EY** P
☎ 01279 453914 F 01279 432295
Est. 1981
Services Table liners
Open Mon–Fri 9am–5.30pm

Stocks and Chairs Antique Restoration
Contact Kevin Beale
✉ **The Old Church Hall, Hardy Road, Parkstone, Poole, Dorset, BH14 9HN** P
☎ 01202 718418 F 01202 718918
E email@stocksandchairsantiques.com
W www.stocksandchairsantiques.com
Est. 1979
Services Full restoration service, specializing in hand-dyed leather
Open Mon–Fri 9am–5pm weekends by appointment

Woolnough (AC) Ltd
Contact Mr A Cullen
✉ **Unit 7, Parmiter Industrial Estate, Parmiter Street, Bethnal Green, London, E2 9HZ** P
☎ 020 8980 9813 F 020 8980 9814
Est. 1885
Services Desk top leathering, leather upholstery, bookshelf edging, chairback embossing and distressed hand-stained leather upholstery
Open Mon–Fri 7am–3.30pm

LIGHTING

Dernier and Hamlyn Ltd
✉ **Unit 5, Croydon Business Centre, 214 Purley Way, Croydon, CR0 4XG** P
☎ 020 8760 0900 F 020 8760 0955
W www.dernier-hamlyn.com
Est. 1888
Services Traditional and contemporary bespoke lighting specialists, manufacturing and restoration. Holders of royal warrant for manufacture and restoration to HM Queen
Open Mon–Fri 9am–6pm

Karim Restorations
Contact Mr A Karim
✉ **Studio 6, The Bull Theatre Gallery, Barnet, Hertfordshire, EN5 5SJ** P
☎ 020 8449 928647
E aminsemail@e.mail.com
Est. 1984
Services Restoration of Art Nouveau, Arts and Crafts, pewter, castings and lighting
Open Mon–Fri 10am–5pm

David Malik & Son Ltd
Contact Sara Malik
✉ **5 Metro Centre, Britannia Way, Park Royal, London, NW10 7A** P
☎ 020 8965 4232 F 020 8965 2401
Est. 1950
Services Chandelier, wall bracket, candelabra restoration, re-wiring, re-gilding
Open Mon–Fri 9am–5pm

Sargeant Restorations
Contact David and Ann Sargeant
✉ **21 The Green, Westerham, Kent, TN16 1AX** P
☎ 01959 562130 F 01959 561989
M 07771 553624

Est. 1989
Services Restoration of all light fittings, lustres, candelabra
Open Mon–Sat 9am–5.30pm

Turn On Lighting
Contact Janet Holdstock
116–118 Islington High Street, Camden Passage, Islington, London, N1 8EG P
☎ 020 7359 7616 F 020 7359 7616
Est. 1976
Services Display lighting
Open Tues–Fri 10am–6pm
Sat 9.30am–4.30pm

David Turner
Contact Mr D Turner
✉ **24 Tottenham Road, London, N1 4BZ** P
☎ 020 7241 5400 F 020 7241 5416
E david.turner@teleregion.co.uk
Est. 1987
Services Repair and restoration of metalwork, lighting, decorative antiques
Open Mon–Fri 9.30am–6pm

MARBLE

Rimmer Restoration
Contact Mr J S Rimmer
✉ **14 Hastings Place, Lytham, Lancashire, FY8 5LZ** P
☎ 01253 794521 F 01253 794521
Est. 1987
Services Marble restorer
Open By appointment

MARQUETRY

A Dunn and Son
Contact Mr R Dunn
✉ **8 Wharf Road, Chelmsford, Essex, CM2 6LU** P
☎ 01245 354452 F 01245 494991
Est. 1896
Services Makers of marquetry and Boulle
Open Mon–Fri 8am–6pm
Sat by appointment

Gow Antiques and Restoration (BAFRA)
Contact Jeremy Gow
✉ **Pitscandly Farm, Forfar, Angus, DD8 3NZ** P
☎ 01307 465342 F 01307 468973
M 07711 416786
E jeremy@gowantiques.co.uk
W www.gowantiques.co.uk
Est. 1991
Services Specialists in restoration of European furniture, 17th–18thC marquetry
Open Mon–Fri 9am–5pm or by appointment

METAL

Antique Restorations
Contact Mr C Christofi
✉ **Unit 23a Rosebery Industrial Park, Rosebery Avenue, London, N17 9SR** P
☎ 020 8880 9697 F 020 8880 9697
Est. 1968
Services Repair, restoration and refinishing to all metalwork, re-gilding, repairing and casting
Open Mon–Fri 8am–6pm

John Armistead Restorations
Contact Mr John Armistead
✉ **Malham Cottage, Bellingdon, Chesham, Buckinghamshire, HP5 2UR** P
☎ 01494 758209 F 01494 758209
E j.armistead@ntlworld.com
Est. 1979
Services Repair and restoration of all antique metalwork including casting, replacement of missing parts, lighting
Open Mon–Fri 9am–5pm

B W Restorations
Contact Mr B W Harris
✉ **44 Hayling Rise, Worthing, West Sussex, BN13 3AG** P
☎ 01903 871562 F 01903 603846
M 07966 539854
Est. 1984
Services Restoration of bronze sculptures
Open Mon–Sun 8am–6pm

Bold as Brass Polishers
Contact Mark Mapley
✉ **Unit 13, Visicks Works, Perranarworthal, Truro, Cornwall, TR3 7NR** P
☎ 01872 864207
Est. 1994
Services Brass and copper polishing
Open Mon–Fri 9.15am–4.30pm

Bristol Restoration Workshop
Contact Mr Hall
✉ **8 Devon Road, Bristol, BS5 9AD** P
☎ 0117 954 2114 F 0117 954 2114
Est. 1979
Services Metalware restoration and repair
Open Mon–Fri 8am–5pm

Michael Brook Antique Metal Restoration (BAFRA)
Contact Mr M Brook
✉ **80 Newquay Road, London, SE6 2NP** P
☎ 020 7708 0467 F 020 7708 0467
W www.antiquemetalrestoration.co.uk
Est. 1988
Services Antique metal restoration, repair and patination of bronzes, specializing in ormolu cleaning and repair
Open By appointment

E Hansen
Contact Mr E Hansen
✉ **6 Shalbourne Close, Hungerford, Berkshire, RG17 0QH** P
☎ 01488 684772
M 07885 511986
E epgerdes-hans@amserve.net
Est. 1985
Services Metal restoration
Open Mon–Fri 9am–6pm

Rupert Harris Conservation (IIC, UKIC, NACF, SPAB, ICOM)
Contact Ms Roberts
✉ **Unit 5C, 1 Fawe Street, London, E14 6PD** P
☎ 020 7987 6231/7515 2020
F 020 7987 7994
E enquiries@rupertharris.com
W www.rupertharris.com
Est. 1982
Services Conservation and restoration of fine metalwork and sculpture
Trade only Yes
Open By appointment

Karim Restorations
Contact Mr A Karim
✉ **Studio 6, The Bull Theatre Gallery, Barnet, Hertfordshire, EN5 5SJ** P
☎ 020 8449 928647
E aminsemail@e.mail.com
Est. 1984
Services Restoration of Art

Nouveau, Arts and Crafts, pewter, castings and lighting
Open Mon–Fri 10am–5pm

Metalwork Restoration Services
Contact Ms G Salmon
✉ **59 Trafalgar Street, Sheffield, South Yorkshire, S1 4GN** Ⓟ
☎ 0114 249 3308
Est. 1993
Services Metalwork restoration, bronze, silver, brass etc
Open By appointment

Renaissance Ironwork
Contact Robert Helyer
✉ **Woodsend House, Old London Road, Copdock, Ipswich, Suffolk, IP8 3JP** Ⓟ
☎ 01473 730017 Ⓕ 01473 730017
Est. 1969
Services Makers of antique metal furniture fittings and decorative ironwork. Antique metal restorations
Trade only Yes
Open By appointment

Shawlan Antiques (LAPADA)
Contact Mr Shawn Parmakis
✉ **415a Whitehorse Road, Thornton Heath, Surrey, CR7 8SD** Ⓟ
☎ 020 8684 5082 Ⓕ 020 8684 5082
Ⓜ 07889 510253
Est. 1974
Services Metal restorations, foundry work, patination, gilding, chasing
Open Mon–Fri 8am–6pm
Sat 8am–5pm

David Turner
Contact Mr D Turner
✉ **24 Tottenham Road, London, N1 4BZ** Ⓟ
☎ 020 7241 5400 Ⓕ 020 7241 5416
Ⓔ david.turner@teleregion.co.uk
Est. 1987
Services Repair and restoration of metalwork, lighting, decorative antiques
Open Mon–Fri 9.30am–6pm

MILITARIA

Bailiff Forge Manufacturing
Contact Mr John Denbigh or Mr Tom Kay
✉ **Unit 53, Colne Valley Workshops, Linthwaite, Huddersfield, West Yorkshire, HD7 5QG** Ⓟ
☎ 01484 846973 Ⓕ 01484 846973
Ⓔ bailifforge@jedenbigh.freeserve.uk
Ⓦ www.baliff-forge.co.uk
Est. 1984
Services Restorations to swords and armour
Open Mon–Fri 10am–6pm
Sat 2–6pm

The Queen's Shilling
Contact Mrs A Wolf
✉ **87 Commercial Road, Parkstone, Poole, Dorset, BH14 0JD** Ⓟ
☎ 01202 723335
Est. 1986
Services Medal mounting, blazer badges for uniforms, sells memorabilia
Open Mon–Sat 9am–5pm half day Wed

Chris Rollason Home Counties Medal Services
Contact Mr C Rollason
✉ **53 Bodiam Crescent, Hampden Park, Eastbourne, East Sussex, BN22 9HQ** Ⓟ
☎ 01323 506012
Est. 1979
Services Full-size medals restored and mounted to wear or in frame or case. Miniature dress medals supplied and mounted. Regimental ties, blazer badges, buttons, medal accessories also supplied
Open Mon–Fri 9am–5pm

MUSICAL INSTRUMENTS

Cambridge Pianola Company and J V Pianos
Contact Tom Poole
✉ **The Limes, High Street, Landbeach, Cambridgeshire, CB4 8DR** Ⓟ
☎ 01223 861348 Ⓕ 01223 441276
Ⓔ ftpoole@talk21.com
Ⓦ www.cambridgepianolacompany.co.uk
Est. 1972
Services Restoration, transport and tuning of pianos
Open By appointment

A Frayling-Cork (BAFRA)
Contact Mr A Frayling-Cork
✉ **2 Mill Lane, Wallingford, Oxfordshire, OX10 0DH** Ⓟ
☎ 01491 826221
Est. 1979
Services Antique furniture repair, restoration, French polishing, metal fittings, specializing in musical instruments
Open By appointment 24hr answerphone

Peter Goodfellow
Contact Peter Goodfellow
✉ **Ivybank Croft, Lochietots Road, Miltonduff, Elgin, Moray, IV30 8WL** Ⓟ
☎ 01343 545045
Ⓔ peter@goodfellowviolins.com
Ⓦ www.goodfellowviolins.com
Est. 1996
Services Restoration of classic and modern violins, violas, cellos. Provides appraisal, valuation, makes new instruments
Open By appointment

Michael Parfett
Contact Mr M Parfett
✉ **Unit 058, 31 Clerkenwell Close, London, EC1R 0AT** Ⓟ
☎ 020 7490 8768 Ⓕ 020 7253 5535
Ⓜ 07939 334645
Ⓦ www.michaelparfett.co.uk
Est. 1990
Services Keyboard musical instrument restoration, also harps and stringed instruments, lacquerwork, gilding
Open By appointment

Guinevere Sommers-Hill Violins,
Contact Guinevere Sommers-Hill
✉ **The Arbery Centre, Market Place, Wantage, Oxfordshire, OX12 8AB** Ⓟ
☎ 01235 770094 Ⓕ 01235 770094
Ⓔ sommershill@yahoo.com
Est. 2001
Services Violin restoration and repair, bow work, makes new violins
Open Mon–Sat 9.30am–5pm
Sun Bank holidays 11.30am–5pm

ORIENTAL

E & C Royall
Contact Mr C Royall
✉ **10 Waterfall Way, Medbourne, Market Harborough, Leicestershire, LE16 8EE** Ⓟ
☎ 01858 565744

Est. 1981
Services Repairs, restorations
Open Mon–Sat 9am–5pm or by appointment

PACKERS AND SHIPPERS

Michael Allcroft Antiques
Contact Michael Allcroft
✉ **203 Buxton Road, Newtown, New Mills, Cheshire, SK12 2RA** P
☎ 01663 744014 F 01663 744014
M 07798 781642
Est. 1986
Services Packing and export to foreign countries, English oak ideal for the Japanese market
Open Mon–Fri noon–6pm Sat 10am–1pm or by appointment

Anglo Pacific (Fine Art) Ltd (LAPADA)
Contact Malcolm Disson
✉ **Unit 2, Bush Industrial Estate, Standard Road, London, NW10 6DF** P
☎ 020 8838 8008 F 020 8453 0225
E antiques@anglopacific.co.uk
W www.anglopacific.co.uk
Est. 1977
Services Packing, shipping and international removals. Also valuations and restorations
Open Mon–Fri 8.30am–5.30pm

Robert Boys Shipping
Contact Robert Boys
✉ **Unit D, Tunnel Avenue Trading Estate, Tunnel Avenue, Greenwich, London, SE10 0QH** P
☎ 020 8858 3355 F 020 8858 3344
E boysship@ftech.co.uk
Est. 1989
Services Shipping, packing, forwarding
Open Mon–Fri 8am–6pm

Derbyshire Removals
Contact Michael Powell
✉ **Butterley Cottage, Butterley Lane, Ashover, Derbyshire, S45 0JU** P
☎ 01629 582762/01246 202289
M 07774 422561
Est. 1987
Services Removal service of antique and fine furniture and packing
Open Ring anytime

Alan Franklin Transport
Contact Alan Franklin
✉ **26 Blackmoor Road, Verwood, Dorset, BH31 6BB**
☎ 01202 826539 F 01202 827337
E aft@afteurope.co.uk
W www.alanfranklintransport.co.uk
Est. 1975
Services Specialist carriers of antiques and fine art world-wide
Open Mon–Fri 8.30am–5.30pm

Gander and White Shipping Ltd (BADA, LAPADA)
Contact O Howell
✉ **21 Lillie Road, London, SW6 1UE** P
☎ 020 7381 0571 F 020 7381 5428
E info@ganderandwhite.com
W www.ganderandwhite.com
Est. 1933
Services Packing and shipping
Open Mon–Fri 9am–5.30pm

Hedleys Humpers (LAPADA, BADA, BIFA, BAR, IATA)
✉ **3 St Leonards Road, London, NW10 6SX** P
☎ 020 8965 8733 F 020 8965 0249
E mg@hedleyshumpers.com
W www.hedleyshumpers.com
Est. 1973
Services Door-to-door delivery by road, sea and air of single items to full container loads. Arrange collection, export, packing, insurance and all export and customs paperwork on customer's behalf
Open Mon–Fri 8am–6pm

International Furniture Exporters Ltd
Contact Iris Mitchell
✉ **Old Cement Works, South Heighton, Newhaven, East Sussex, BN9 0HS** P
☎ 01273 611251 F 01273 611574
W www.asweb.co.uk/ife
Est. 1990
Services Furniture exporters
Open By appointment

Kuwahara Ltd (LAPADA, HHGFAA)
Contact Yukio Kuwahara
✉ **6 McNicol Drive, London, NW10 7AW** P
☎ 020 8963 1100 F 020 8963 0100
E yukio@kuwahara.co.uk
W www.kuwahara.co.uk
Est. 1983
Services Fine art packing and shipping, door-to-door transport around the world by land, air or sea
Trade only Yes
Open Mon–Fri 9am–5.30pm

C and N Lawrence
Contact Mr N Lawrence
✉ **7 Church Walk, Brighton Road, Horley, Surrey, RH6 7EE**
☎ 01293 783243
Est. 1983
Services Removals, shipping, packing for antiques trade
Trade only Yes
Open Mon–Fri 9am–5pm

John Morgan and Sons (FIDI, OMNI, BAR, BAR Overseas Group, HHGFAA)
Contact Mr William Morgan
✉ **Removal House, 30 Island Street, Belfast, Co Antrim, BT4 1DH** P
☎ 028 9073 2333 F 028 9045 7402
E info@morganremovals.com
W www.morganremovals.com
Est. 1915
Services Specialist antique removals and local, worldwide household removals
Open Mon–Fri 9am–5.30pm

PDQ Air Freight/Art Move (LAPADA, CINOA, GTA, BIFA)
✉ **Unit 4, Court 1, Challenge Road, Ashford, Middlesex, TW15 1AX**
☎ 01784 243695 F 01784 242237
E artmove@pdq.uk.com
W www.pdq.uk.com
Est. 1983
Services Packing and shipping, fair logistics, hand-carry couriers, bonded warehouse
Open Mon–Fri 9am–5.30pm

Seabourne Mailpack Worldwide (LAPADA)
Contact Jonathan Cohen
✉ **Unit 13, Saxon Way, Moor Lane, Harmondsworth, Middlesex, UB7 0LW** P
☎ 020 8897 3888 M 07770 612134

Ⓦ www.seabourne-mailpack.co.uk
Est. 1962
Services Export packing and world wide delivery of fine art, antiques, furniture, etc
Open Mon–Fri 9am–5pm

The Shipping Company
Contact Matt Walton
✉ **Bourton Industrial Park, Bourton-on-the-Water, Cheltenham, Gloucestershire, GL54 2HQ** Ⓟ
☎ 01451 822451 Ⓕ 01451 810985
Ⓜ 07971 425978
Ⓔ enquiries@theshippingcompanyltd.com
Est. 1998
Services Packing and shipping of antiques worldwide
Open Mon–Fri 9am–6pm phone mobile at other times

A J Williams Shipping (LAPADA)
Contact Jennifer Williams
✉ **607 Sixth Avenue, Central Business Park, Petherton Road, Hengrove, Bristol, BS14 9BZ** Ⓟ
☎ 01275 892166 Ⓕ 01275 891333
Ⓔ aj.williams@btclick.com
Est. 1977
Services Packing and shipping of antiques and fine art worldwide
Open Mon–Fri 9am–5.30pm or by appointment

PAINTED FURNITURE

M Tocci
Contact Mr M Tocci
✉ **81 Southern Row, London, W10 5AL** Ⓟ
☎ 020 8960 4826
Est. 1978
Services Gilding, painted furniture restoration, lacquer on furniture and decorations
Open Mon–Fri 8am–4.30pm

PAPER

Cameron Preservation (IPCRA, IPC, SAPCON)
Contact Mr Elgin Cameron
✉ **Flush Business Centre, Flush Place, Lurgan, Co Armagh, BT66 7DT** Ⓟ
☎ 028 3834 3099 Ⓕ 028 3834 3099
Est. 1993
Services Restoration of art on paper, archives, manuscripts, books etc, also vellum, parchment, globes
Open Mon–Fri 8.30am–5.15 Sat 8.30am–noon

Voitek Conservation of Works of Art (IPC)
Contact Mrs E Sobczynski
✉ **9 Whitehorse Mews, Westminster Bridge Road, London, SE1 7QD** Ⓟ
☎ 020 7928 6094 Ⓕ 020 7928 6094
Ⓔ voitekcwa@btinternet.com
Est. 1972
Services Conservation of prints, drawings, watercolours, maps, conservation mounting and project planning
Open By appointment

PICTURE RESTORATION

Roger Allan
Contact Mr R Allan
✉ **The Old Red Lion, Bedlingfield, Eye, Suffolk, IP23 7LQ** Ⓟ
☎ 01728 628491
Est. 1973
Services Picture restorer, furniture restorer
Trade only Yes
Open By appointment

Alyson Lawrence
Contact Alyson Lawrence
✉ **Lev Antiques Ltd, 97a Kensington Church Street, London, W8 7LN** Ⓟ
☎ 020 7727 9248 Ⓕ 020 7727 9248
Ⓜ 07768 470473
Ⓔ alyson@richardlawrence.co.uk
Est. 1984
Services Restoration of 17th–20thC oil paintings
Open Tues–Sat 10.30am–5.45pm or by appointment

Romanov Restoration
Contact Ludmila Romanova
✉ **51 Sutherland Avenue, London, SW9 2HF** Ⓟ
☎ 020 7286 1430
Est. 1982
Services Painting and icon restoration using traditional Russian methods, glass and bronze restoration
Open By appointment

PINE

Heritage Restorations
Contact Jonathan Gluck
✉ **Llanfair Caereinion, Welshpool, Powys, SY21 0HD** Ⓟ
☎ 01938 810384 Ⓕ 01938 810900
Ⓔ info@heritagerestorations.co.uk
Ⓦ www.heritagerestorations.co.uk
Est. 1970
Services Antique furniture, repair and restoration, specializing in 18th–19thC pine
Open Mon–Sat 9am–5pm

Oldwoods Pine Furniture
Contact Sid Duck
✉ **Unit 4, Colston Yard, Colston Street, Bristol, BS1 5BD** Ⓟ
☎ 0117 9299023
Est. 1980
Services Furniture repairs, restorations, buying and selling
Open By appointment

The Pine Mine
Contact Mr David Crewe-Read
✉ **100 Wandsworth Bridge Road, London, SW6 2TF** Ⓟ
☎ 020 7736 1092 Ⓕ 020 7736 5283
Ⓔ pinemine@hotmail.com
Est. 1972
Services Country furniture and antique pine repair and restoration, bespoke furniture maker
Open Mon–Sat 9.30am–5.30pm Sun 11am–4pm

Ed Thomas Old Country Pine
Contact Mr E Thomas
✉ **Unit 9, Yates Brothers Estate, Lime Lane, Pelsall, Walsall, West Midlands, WS3 5AS** Ⓟ
☎ 01543 360097 Ⓕ 01543 360097
Ⓜ 07966 243477
Ⓔ edthomasoldcountrypine@altavista.com
Est. 1981
Services Made-to-measure pine furniture using only old original pine.
Open Mon–Sat 9am–5.30pm

Wood Be Good
Contact Mr Dennis Langford
✉ **1 Jarrow Road, London, SE16 3JR** Ⓟ

☎ 020 7232 2639 Ⓕ 020 8657 6610
Est. 1984
Services Pine furniture repair and restoration, pine stripping
Open Mon–Sat 7am–5pm

PLASTERWORK

Seamas O'Heocha Teoranta (IPCRA, Irish Georgian Society, An Taisce)

Contact Seamas O'Heocha
✉ **Corbally, Barna, Galway, Ireland** Ⓟ
☎ 091 590256 Ⓕ 091 590256
Ⓜ 0872 581150
Ⓔ soheocha@indigo.ie
Est. 1987
Services Ornate plasterwork restoration and conservation, contractors and consultants
Open Mon–Fri 9am–6pm

SCIENTIFIC

Osborne Antiques

Contact Mrs L Osborne
✉ **91 Chester Road, New Oscot, Sutton Coldfield, West Midlands, B73 5BA** Ⓟ
☎ 0121 355 6667 Ⓕ 0121 354 7166
Ⓔ chris@barometerparts.co.uk
Ⓦ www.barometerparts.co.uk
Est. 1975
Services Barometer parts suppliers, scientific glass blowers
Open Tues–Thurs 9am–5pm Fri 9am–5.30pm Sat 9.15am–1pm closed 1–2pm

SCULPTURE

Graciela Ainsworth (SSCR, UKIC)

Contact Graciela
✉ **Unit 10 Bonnington Mill, 72 Newhaven Road, Edinburgh, EH6 5QG** Ⓟ
☎ 0131 555 1294 Ⓕ 0131 467 7080
Ⓔ graciela@graciela-ainsworth.com
Est. 1990
Services Conservation of statues, monuments, stone sculptures. Carving commissions
Open Mon–Fri 9am–6pm

Taylor Pearce Restoration Services Ltd

Contact Mr K Taylor
✉ **Fishers Court, Besson Street, London, SE14 5AF** Ⓟ
☎ 020 7252 9800 Ⓕ 020 7277 8169
Ⓔ admin@taylorpearce.com
Est. 1985
Services Sculpture, conservation and restoration of stone, bronze, plaster and terracotta. By appointment to HM Queen
Open By appointment

Voitek Conservation of Works of Art (IPC)

Contact Mrs E Sobczynski
✉ **9 Whitehorse Mews, Westminster Bridge Road, London, SE1 7QD** Ⓟ
☎ 020 7928 6094 Ⓕ 020 7928 6094
Ⓔ voitekcwa@btinternet.com
Est. 1972
Services Conservation of sculpture, marble, terracotta, wood
Open By appointment

SILVER

Wellington Gallery (LAPADA)

Contact Mrs M Barclay
✉ **1 St John's Wood High Street, London, NW8 7NG** Ⓟ
☎ 020 7586 2620 Ⓕ 020 7483 0716
Est. 1979
Services Restoration of silver and silver plate, gilding, engraving, jewellery, glass, upholstery, paintings, porcelain, furniture, framing, valuations
Open Mon–Fri 10.30am–6pm Sat 10am–6pm

STONEWORK

Voitek Conservation of Works of Art

Contact Mr W Sobczynski
✉ **9 Whitehorse Mews, Westminster Bridge Road, London, SE1 7QD** Ⓟ
☎ 020 7928 6094 Ⓕ 020 7928 6094
Ⓔ voitekcwa@btinternet.com
Est. 1972
Services Conservation and restoration of marble, stone, terracotta, wood
Open By appointment

STRIPPING

Acorn Antique Interiors

Contact Brian or Margaret
✉ **Eddystone Road, Wadebridge, Cornwall, PL27 7AL** Ⓟ
☎ 01208 812815
Est. 1982
Services Paint stripping
Open Mon–Sat 9am–5pm

Back to the Wood

Contact Mr J Davis
✉ **Riverside Works, Riverside Road, Watford, Hertfordshire, WD1 4HY** Ⓟ
☎ 01923 222943 Ⓜ 07976 297008
Est. 1981
Services Pine stripping, Victorian–Edwardian fireplaces a speciality
Open Mon–Sat 9am–5pm

Cameo Antiques

Contact Mrs S Hinton
✉ **3 Liverpool Road East, Church Lawton, Stoke-on-Trent, Staffordshire, ST7 3AQ** Ⓟ
☎ 01782 772555
Est. 1985
Services Complete repair and restoration of furniture, stripping
Open Mon–Fri 9am–6pm Sat 9am–4pm

E Carty

Contact Mr E Carty
✉ **51 Trinity Street, Gainsborough, Lincolnshire, DN21 1JF** Ⓟ
☎ 01427 614452
Ⓜ 07733 474895
Est. 1976
Services Stripping and restoration
Open By appointment

Chiltern Strip & Polish

Contact Mr B Black
✉ **Kitchener Works, Kitchener Road, High Wycombe, Buckinghamshire, HP11 2SJ** Ⓟ
☎ 01494 438052
Est. 1986
Services Repairs and repolishing. Sale of antique furniture
Open Mon–Fri 9am–5pm Sat 9am–12.30pm

Dip 'n' Strip

Contact P Coates
✉ **88 Barkly Road, Beeston, Leeds, West Yorkshire, LS11 7ES** Ⓟ
☎ 0113 272 0064
Est. 1982

Services Antiques repairs and restorations
Open Mon–Fri 9am–6pm

Dip 'n' Strip
Contact Brendan Peoples
✉ **Singer Station, Singers Building, Kilbourne Road, Clydebank, Dunbartonshire, G81 2JQ** Ⓟ
☎ 0141 9529111460
Est. 1980
Services Furniture restoration
Open Mon–Fri 9am–5pm

The Door Stripping Company Ltd
Contact Mr B Findley
✉ **32 Main Road, Renishaw, Sheffield, South Yorkshire, S21 3UT** Ⓟ
☎ 01246 435521
Est. 1984
Services Pine stripping, non-caustic restoration of furniture
Open Mon–Fri 9am–5pm
Sat–Sun 11am–2pm

Hunts Pine Stripping Services
Contact Mr W Dougherty
✉ **Unit 6a, Victoria Farm, Water Lane, York, North Yorkshire, YO30 6PQ** Ⓟ
☎ 01904 690561
Est. 1984
Services Antiques repair and restoration
Open Mon–Fri 9am–5.30pm
Sat 9am–2.30pm

Miracle Stripping
Contact Mr C Howes or Mr A Howes
✉ **The Cottage, Woodhall Farm, Hatfield, Hertfordshire, AL9 5NU** Ⓟ
☎ 01707 270587 Ⓕ 01707 270587
Ⓜ 07790 696631
Est. 1992
Services Stripping of doors, cast-iron fireplaces etc
Open Mon–Fri 8.30am–5pm

Mr Dip
Contact Mr G Broadbridge
✉ **3 Knutsford Road, Alderley Edge, Cheshire, SK9 7SD** Ⓟ
☎ 01625 584896
Est. 1983
Services Wood stripping, hardwood, softwood and antique items, furniture and fireplaces
Open Mon–Fri 10am–4pm
Sat 10am–2pm closed Wed

Salisbury Stripping Co
Contact Karen Montlake
✉ **48–54 Milford Street, Salisbury, Wiltshire, SP1 2BP**
☎ 01722 413595/718203
Ⓕ 01722 416395
Ⓔ enquiries@myriad-antiques.co.uk
Ⓦ www.myriad-antiques.co.uk
Est. 1994
Services Paint and varnish stripping of furniture and doors, caustic and non-caustic processes, full restoration
Open Mon–Sat 9.30am–5pm
Sun by appointment

Strip It Ltd
Contact Mr Panton
✉ **109–111 Pope Street, Birmingham, West Midlands, B1 3AG** Ⓟ
☎ 0121 243 4001
Est. 1983
Services Stripping furniture
Open Mon–Sat 8am–5.30pm

Strippadoor Ltd
Contact Danny Russell
✉ **Victoria House, Higher Bury Street, Stockport, Cheshire, SK4 1BJ** Ⓟ
☎ 0161 477 8980 Ⓕ 0161 477 6302
Est. 1979
Services Stripping of doors, fireplaces, fire surrounds and furniture
Open Mon–Fri 8.30am–5.30pm
Sat 10.30am–2.30pm

Stripped Pine Workshop
Contact Mr John Wood
✉ **Rear of 28 Catherine Street, Swansea, West Glamorgan, SA1 4JS** Ⓟ
☎ 01792 461236
Est. 1970
Services Pine stripping
Open Mon–Sat 11.30am–6pm

The Stripper
Contact Mr K Pinder
✉ **Sneaton Lane, Ruswarp, Whitby, North Yorkshire, YO22 5HL** Ⓟ
☎ 01947 820035/880966
Est. 1995
Services Antiques repair and restoration
Open Mon–Fri 8am–6pm
Sat 8am–noon

The Stripping Store
Contact Jeff Low
✉ **57 Newhall Street, Glasgow, G40 1LA** Ⓟ
☎ 0141 550 8195 Ⓜ 07796 501633
Est. 1997
Services Hand stripping of period and traditional furniture
Open Mon–Sat 10am–6pm

Windsor Antiques
Contact Mr G Henderson
✉ **Rosemary Farm, Rosemary Lane, Castle Hedingham, Halstead, Essex, CO9 3AJ** Ⓟ
☎ 01787 461653
Est. 1981
Services Furniture and paint stripping
Open By appointment

SUPPLIERS

Richard Barry Southern Marketing Ltd
Contact Mr Richard Fill
✉ **Unit 1–2, Chapel Place, North Street, Portslade, Brighton, East Sussex, BN41 1DR** Ⓟ
☎ 01273 419471 Ⓕ 01273 421925
Est. 1978
Services Suppliers to the antiques trade of all wood-finishing materials
Open Mon–Fri 8am–5pm

Chemicals Ltd
Contact Sales department
✉ **Unit 2, Ringtail Place, Burscough Industrial Estate, Burscough, Lancashire, L40 7SD** Ⓟ
☎ 01704 897700 Ⓕ 01704 897237
Ⓔ sales@paramose.com
Est. 1982
Services Original and water washable strippers, Paramose stripping machines, restoration materials
Open Mon–Fri 9am–5pm

Classic Finishes
Contact Mark Baker
✉ **St Julien's Wharf, 131–133 King Street, Norwich, Norfolk, NR1 1QE** Ⓟ

☎ 01603 760374 Ⓕ 01603 660477
Ⓔ enq@classicfinishes.co.uk
Ⓦ www.classicfinishes.co.uk
Est. 1985
Services Restoration materials, advice, specialist paints, French and wax polishes
Open Mon–Fri 8.30am–5.30pm Sat 9am–1pm

Pendelfin Studio Ltd
Contact Mrs Morley
✉ **Cameron Mill, Housin Street, Burnley, Lancashire, BB10 1PP** Ⓟ
☎ 01282 432301 Ⓕ 01282 459464
Ⓔ boswell@pendelfin.co.uk
Ⓦ www.pendelfin.co.uk
Est. 1953
Services Suppliers to retail outlets of collectable stonecraft rabbits and village pieces
Open Mon–Fri 9am–5pm

John Penny Antique Services
Contact Mr J Penny
✉ **Unit 10, City Industrial Park, Southern Road, Southampton, Hampshire, SO15 0HA** Ⓟ
☎ 023 8023 2066 Ⓕ 023 8021 2129
Est. 1981
Services Suppliers of furniture restoration materials
Open Mon–Fri 9am–5pm Sat 9am–12.30pm

Restoration Supplies
Contact Mrs M O'Connell
✉ **The Corn Mill, Claremont, Wyke, Bradford, West Yorkshire, BD12 9JJ**
☎ 01274 691461
Est. 1989
Services Restoration supplies
Open Mon–Sat 10.30am–6pm closed Wed

Suffolk Brass Ltd
Contact Mr M Peters
✉ **Thurston, Bury St Edmunds, Suffolk, IP31 3SN**
☎ 01359 233383 Ⓕ 01359 233384
Ⓔ suffolkbrass@aol.com
Est. 1987
Services Supplies replica cast brass handles from catalogue
Trade only Yes
Open Mail order only

TEXTILES

Lannowe Oriental Textiles
Contact Joanna Titchell
✉ **Near Bath, Wiltshire**
☎ 01225 891487 Ⓕ 01225 891182
Ⓜ 0771 470 3535
Ⓔ joanna@lannowe.co.uk
Est. 1976
Services Washing, restoration and conservation of Oriental carpets, rugs and tapestries
Open By appointment

M & M Restoration
Contact Mrs M Druet
✉ **Mantel House, Broomhill Road, London, SW18 4JQ** Ⓟ
☎ 020 8871 5098 Ⓕ 020 8877 1940
Ⓜ 07850 310104
Est. 1985
Services Restoration and cleaning of antique tapestries, carpets and textiles
Open Mon–Fri 9am–6pm

The Restoration Studio
Contact Ela
✉ **63 Jeddo Road, London, W12 9EE** Ⓟ
☎ 020 8740 4977 Ⓜ 07711 157644
Ⓦ www.restorationstudio.co.uk
Est. 1987
Services Restoration of tapestries, needlework, embroidery, Aubussons
Open Mon–Fri 10am–5pm

The Textile Conservancy Co Ltd (UKIC)
Contact Alexandra Seth-Smith ACR
✉ **Pickhill Business Centre, Smallhythe Road, Tenterden, Kent, TN30 7LZ** Ⓟ
☎ 01580 761600 Ⓕ 01580 761600
Ⓔ alex@textile-conservation.co.uk
Ⓦ www.textile-conservation.co.uk
Est. 1997
Services Cleaning, repair, condition reports of historic textiles, costumes, tapestries, rugs. Advice on preventative conservation, storage, display, mounting
Open Mon–Fri 9am–6pm by appointment

Textile Conservation (UKIC)
Contact Fiona Hutton
✉ **Ivy House Farm, Wolvershill Road, Banwell, Somerset, BS29 6LB** Ⓟ
☎ 01934 822449
Ⓔ fiona@textileconservation.co.uk
Est. 1989
Services Textile conservation
Open Mon–Fri 9am–5pm

Textile Conservation Consultancy (UKIC)
Contact Sheila Landi
✉ **The Stable Yard, Burghley House, Stamford, Lincolnshire, PE9 3JY** Ⓟ
☎ 01780 480188 Ⓕ 01780 480188
Ⓔ landi@despina2.demon.co.uk
Est. 1989
Services Textile conservation
Open Mon–Fri 9.30am–5.30pm by appointment

Textile Conservation Services
Contact Miss Lyndall Bond
✉ **3–4 West Workshop, Welbeck, Worksop, Nottinghamshire, S80 3LW** Ⓟ
☎ 01909 481655 Ⓕ 01909 481655
Ⓔ textile.conservation@tesco.net
Est. 1984
Services The conservation of costume, lace and small textiles. Talks and courses on costume and textiles
Open By appointment

TOYS

Haddon Rocking Horses
Contact Paul Stollery
✉ **5 Telford Road, Clacton-on-Sea, Essex, CO15 4LP** Ⓟ
☎ 01255 424745 Ⓕ 01255 475505
Ⓔ millers@haddonrockinghorses.co.uk
Ⓦ www.haddonrockinghorses.co.uk
Est. 1971
Services Restorers and manufacturers of rocking horses
Open Mon–Thurs 8am–5pm Fri 8am–1pm

Recollect The Dolls Hospital
Contact Paul Jago
✉ **17 Junction Road, Burgess Hill, West Sussex, RH15 0HR** Ⓟ
Ⓔ dollshopuk@aol.com

Est. 1973
Services Complete restoration service for all dolls
Open Tues–Fri 10am–4pm
Sat 10am–1pm or
by appointment

Stevenson Brothers (British Toymakers Guild)
Contact Mark Stevenson or Sue Russell
✉ **The Workshop, Ashford Road, Bethersden, Ashford, Kent, TN26 3AP** 🅿
☎ 01233 820363 Ⓕ 01233 820580
Ⓔ sale@stevensonbros.com
Ⓦ www.stevensonbros.com
Est. 1982
Services Restoration of rocking horses and children's pedal cars
Open Mon–Fri 9am–6pm
Sat 10am–1pm

TUITION

Richard Bolton Furniture Restorer (BAFRA)
Contact Richard Bolton
✉ **Painswick House, Old Dairy Workshop, Gloucester Road, Painswick, Gloucestershire, GL6 6TH** 🅿
☎ 01452 814881
Est. 1981
Services Tuition on the restoration of fine antique furniture
Open Mon–Fri 9am–5pm

The Chippendale International School of Furniture (SSCR)
Contact Mr Anselm Fraser
✉ **Myreside, Gifford, Haddington, East Lothian, EH41 4JA** 🅿
☎ 01620 810680 Ⓕ 01620 810701
Ⓔ info@chippendale.co.uk
Ⓦ www.chippendale.co.uk
Est. 1982
Services International school of furniture, professional training of people to design, make and restore furniture
Open Mon–Fri 7.30am–5pm

Glebe Hall Restoration Studios
Contact Carmel Corrigan-Griffin
✉ **Old Killernogh Rectory, Rathnakelly Glebe, Ballacolla, Co Laois, Ireland** 🅿
☎ 0502 34105 Ⓕ 0502 34154
Est. 1980
Services Courses held on care and conservation of antiques, Saturday morning clinics by appointment
Open By appointment
Sat 11am–4pm

Gow Antiques and Restoration (BAFRA)
Contact Jeremy Gow
✉ **Pitscandly Farm, Forfar, Angus, DD8 3NZ** 🅿
☎ 01307 465342 Ⓕ 01307 468973
Ⓜ 07711 416786
Ⓔ jeremy@gowantiques.co.uk
Ⓦ www.knowyourantiques.com
Est. 1991
Services Three day Antique Furniture Recognition Courses. For dates and further information please telephone
Open Mon–Fri 9am–5pm or
by appointment

Leather Conservation Centre (UKIC, SSCR)
Contact Roy Thomson
✉ **University College Campus, Boughton Green Road, Moulton Park, Northampton, Northamptonshire, NN2 7AN** 🅿
☎ 01604 719766 Ⓕ 01604 719649
Ⓔ lcc@northampton.ac.uk
Est. 1978
Services Conservation and restoration of leather objects, research, training and information for leather and leather conservation
Open Mon–Fri 9am–5pm

The Wiston Project School
Contact Mr N Wears
✉ **The Old School, Wiston, Haverfordwest, Pembrokeshire, SA62 4PS** 🅿
☎ 01437 731579
Est. 1988
Services School of furniture making
Open By appointment

Peter Young Auctioneers
Contact Mr P Young
✉ **Barnby Memorial Hall, Blyth, Worksop, Nottinghamshire, DN10 4RQ** 🅿
☎ 01302 711770 Ⓕ 01302 711770
Ⓜ 07801 079818
Ⓔ pete@peteryoung.uk.com
Ⓦ www.peteryoung.com
Est. 1961
Services Regular timetable of antiques lectures for local further education groups, plus antiques visits, excursions and holidays
Open Mon–Fri 9.30am–5.30pm

UPHOLSTERY

SOUTH EAST

The Chair Repair Workshop
Contact Keith Woodcock or Cecilia Hall
✉ **The Corner Shop, 1–3 North Street, New Romney, Kent, TN28 8DR** 🅿
☎ 01797 364374 Ⓕ 01797 364374
Est. 2002
Services Upholstery
Open Mon–Fri 8.30am–5pm
Sat 9am–1pm

Deal Upholstery Services
Contact Mr P E Cavanagh
✉ **116 Downs Road, Walmer, Deal, Kent, G14 7TF** 🅿
☎ 01304 372297
Est. 1988
Services Antique and modern upholstery, loose covers
Open Mon–Fri 9am–5pm

Norris of Blackheath
Contact Paul Norris
✉ **Dimpleshaven, Pett Road, Pett, East Sussex, TN35 4HE** 🅿
☎ 01424 812129
Services Upholstery, free estimates, pick-up and delivery
Open Mon–Fri 8am–6pm

T J Upholstery
Contact Mr Tim Jenner
✉ **Unit One, Hill House Farm, High Street, Wadhurst, East Sussex, TN5 6AA** 🅿
☎ 01892 784417 Ⓜ 07867 672707
Est. 1979
Services Traditional upholstery
Open By appointment

The Upholsterers Workshop (Guild of Traditional Upholsterers, Association of Master Upholsterers)
Contact Mr Rodney Henham
✉ **Church Farm Studio, Penhurst, Battle, East Sussex, TN33 9QP** 🅿

☎ 01424 893277 Ⓕ 01424 893277
Est. 1996
Services Traditional upholsterers
Open Mon–Fri 8am–4.30pm
Sat 8am–1pm or by appointment

LONDON

Kantuta
Contact Mrs N Wright
✉ **1d Gleneagle Road, London, SW16 6AX** Ⓟ
☎ 020 8677 6701
Est. 1986
Services Upholstery and furniture and restoration
Open Mon–Sat 10am–6pm

SOUTH

Dee Cee Upholstery (AMU)
Contact Mr D A Caplen
✉ **502 Portswood Road, Portswood, Southampton, Hampshire, SO17 3SP** Ⓟ
☎ 023 8055 5888 Ⓕ 023 8067 6761
Ⓔ enquiries@deeceeupholstery.co.uk
Ⓦ www.deeceeupholstery.co.uk
Est. 1978
Services Traditional upholstery specialist, all upholstery and DIY supplies
Open Mon–Thurs 8am–5.30pm
Fri 8am–5pm Sat 9am–1pm or by appointment

Hartley Upholstery and Antique Restorations
Contact Paul Bligh
✉ **Unit 2, Priors Farm, Reading Road, Mattingley, Hook, Hampshire, RG27 8JU** Ⓟ
☎ 0118 932 6567 Ⓕ 0118 932 6567
Est. 1984
Services Upholstery, French polishing and cabinet work. Commissions undertaken
Open Mon–Sat 9am–5pm or by appointment

Hythe Furnishings
Contact Mr G Batchelor
✉ **16 Marsh Parade, Hythe, Southampton, Hampshire, SO45 6AN** Ⓟ
☎ 02380845727
Est. 1997
Services Re-upholstery and reconditioning of furniture
Open Mon–Fri 9am–5.30pm
Sat 9am–4pm closed Wed

A H Smith & Son
Contact Mr M Smith
✉ **3, 6–7 The Parade, Old Lodge Lane, Purley, Surrey, CR8 4DG** Ⓟ
☎ 020 8660 1211 Ⓕ 020 8660 1211
Est. 1949
Services Upholstery, French polishing, antiques repairs
Open Mon–Fri 9am–5pm
Sat 9am–1pm

Suite Dreams Upholstery
Contact Len Double
✉ **Larkwhistle Cottage, Christmas Hill, Sutton Scotney, Winchester, Hampshire, SO21 3ET** Ⓟ
☎ 01962 885630 Ⓕ 01962 885630
Ⓜ 07860 843691
Est. 1991
Services Traditional, modern upholstery, loose covers a speciality
Open Mon–Sat 9am–6pm

WEST COUNTRY

Rocco d'Ambrosio
Contact Mrs R Crees
✉ **94 Benedict Street, Glastonbury, Somerset, BA6 9EZ** Ⓟ
☎ 01458 831541
Est. 1969
Services Upholstery restoration, French polishing, dealer, furniture restoration
Open Mon–Fri 9am–6pm or by appointment

Daniel Fox Upholstery
Contact Mr D Fox
✉ **Goulds Farm, Nethercott, Braunton, Devon, EX33 1HT** Ⓟ
☎ 01271 815998
Est. 1994
Services Re-upholstery
Open Mon–Fri 9am–5pm

Russell Hudson Upholsterer
Contact Mr R Hudson
✉ **Unit 2e, Riverside Business Park, Riverside Road, Bath, Somerset, BA2 3DW** Ⓟ
☎ 01225 400003
Ⓔ russellhudson@lineone.net
Est. 1985
Services Antique re-upholstery
Open Mon–Fri 8.30am–5.30pm

M J R Upholstery
Contact Mr M J Rowbrey
✉ **Unit 7, Cornishway South, Galmington Trading Estate, Taunton, Somerset, TA1 5NQ** Ⓟ
☎ 01823 338793
Est. 1988
Services Re-upholstery
Open Mon–Fri 9am–5pm

Cyril C Wills
Contact Mr Wills
✉ **Oak Tree Yard, Upper Manor Road, Paignton, Devon, TQ3 2TP** Ⓟ
☎ 01803 558039 Ⓕ 01803 558039
Est. 1929
Services Upholstery, chair frame and furniture repair
Open Mon–Fri 9am–5pm

Wincanton Antiques
Contact Tony or Clare
✉ **3 Church Street, Wincanton, Somerset, BA9 9AA** Ⓟ
☎ 01963 32223
Est. 1997
Services Upholstery
Open Mon–Sat 9.30am–5pm

EAST

Decorcraft Upholsterers (AU)
Contact Mr A Wise
✉ **Sand Acre, Elmham Drive, Nacton, Ipswich, Suffolk, IP10 0DG** Ⓟ
☎ 01473 659396 Ⓕ 01473 659396
Est. 1975
Services Upholstery
Open Mon–Sat 9am–6pm

HEART OF ENGLAND

Churchill Upholstery
Contact David Matthews
✉ **Unit 1, Mount Farm, Junction Road, Churchill, Chipping Norton, Oxfordshire, OX7 6NP** Ⓟ
☎ 01608 658139 Ⓕ 01608 658139
Ⓜ 07957 355114
Est. 1986
Services Antique re-upholstery and soft furnishings
Open Mon–Fri 8am–5.30pm
Sat 8am–noon

Andrew & Philip Leach
Contact Andrew or Philip Leach
✉ **The Railway Station, Worcester Road, Leominster, Herefordshire, HR6 8AR** Ⓟ
☎ 01568 616404
Est. 1982
Services Upholstery, loose covers
Open Mon–Fri 8.30am–5.30pm

MIDLANDS

K Davenport
Contact Mr M Davenport
✉ **The Queens Yard, Madac Place, Beatrice Street, Oswestry, Shropshire, SY11 1QJ** Ⓟ
☎ 01691 652293 Ⓕ 01691 652293
Ⓜ 07885 817026
Ⓔ kdavenportinteriors@theinternetpages.co.uk
Ⓦ www.kdavenportinteriors.co.uk
Est. 1965
Services Re-upholstery and restoration of antique furniture
Open Mon–Fri 8.30am–5pm

Heath Upholstery
Contact Mr A Heath
✉ **Marychurch Road, Bucknall, Stoke-on-Trent, Staffordshire, ST2 9BJ** Ⓟ
☎ 01782 268802 Ⓕ 01782 268802
Ⓜ 07974 929221
Ⓔ a.heath@fsbdial.co.uk
Est. 1973
Services Antique upholstery and contract work
Open Mon–Fri 8.30am–6pm or by appointment

Imperial Upholstery
Contact Mr N Scattergood
✉ **Ferry Street, Stapenhill, Burton-on-Trent, Staffordshire, DE15 9EU** Ⓟ
☎ 01283 512327 Ⓕ 01283 512327
Est. 1993
Services Upholstery, antique restoration, French polishing
Open Mon–Sat 9am–6pm

John Reed and Son Upholsterers (AMU)
Contact Mr J Reed
✉ **141 Regent Street, Kettering, Northamptonshire, NN16 8QH** Ⓟ
☎ 01536 510584 Ⓕ 01536 510584
Ⓔ johnreed.andson@lineone.net
Ⓦ www.johnreedandsons.com
Est. 1973
Services Repairs, restorations, upholstery, French and spray polishing
Open Mon–Fri 8am–5.30pm

Sitting Pretty
Contact Mrs J Deaville
✉ **2 Groundslow Cottages, Tittensor, Stoke-on-Trent, Staffordshire, ST12 9HJ** Ⓟ
☎ 01782 373766 Ⓕ 01782 373766
Est. 1989
Services Upholstery, repair and restoration of furniture
Open By appointment only

P Woodcock & Co
Contact Mr Paul Day
✉ **56a Salop Road, Oswestry, Shropshire, SY11 2RQ** Ⓟ
☎ 01691 653317 or 0800 524 0008
Ⓕ 01691 679724
Est. 1954
Services Upholstery and restoration of antique furniture
Open Mon–Fri 7.15am–5pm Sat 9am–4pm

YORKS & LINCS

Paul Rawciffe Upholstery Services
Contact Mr P Rawciffe
✉ **Unit 10, New Enterprise Centre, Humber Bank South, South Quay, Grimsby, Lincolnshire, DN31 3SD** Ⓟ
☎ 01472 251732 Ⓜ 07714 436710
Est. 1989
Services Repair, restoration
Open Mon–Fri 8am–5pm

NORTH WEST

E Callister
Contact Mr E Callister
✉ **127 Lark Lane, Liverpool, Merseyside, L17 8UR** Ⓟ
☎ 0151 727 5679
Est. 1964
Services Re-upholstery, French polishing
Open Mon–Fri 9am–5pm Sat 9am–noon

J E Hatcher & Son
Contact Mr C Hatcher
✉ **121a Victoria Road West, Cleveleys, Thornton Cleveleys, Lancashire, FY5 3LA** Ⓟ
☎ 01253 853162
Est. 1946
Services Traditional upholstery
Open Mon–Fri 8.30am–5.30pm Sat 8.30am–11am

WALES

Cliff Amey & Son (AMU)
Contact Cliff Amey
✉ **12 Clive Road, Canton, Cardiff, South Glamorgan, CF5 1HJ** Ⓟ
☎ 02920 233462 Ⓕ 02920 233462
Ⓔ dennis.amey@talk21.com
Est. 1951
Services Upholstery
Open Mon–Fri 8am–5pm

S M Upholstery Ltd
Contact P Morgan
✉ **212a Whitchurch Road, Cardiff, South Glamorgan, CF14 3NB** Ⓟ
☎ 029 2061 7579 Ⓕ 029 2061 7579
Est. 1974
Services Traditional upholstery
Open Mon–Fri 9.30am–1pm 2–5pm Sat 9.30am–1pm

SCOTLAND

Just Chairs
Contact Mr R Kerr
✉ **Sunnyside, Baster Road, Edinburgh, EH7 5RA** Ⓟ
☎ 0131 652 0320
Est. 1984
Services Traditional upholstery, antique chairs (restored) bought and sold
Open Mon–Fri 8am–5pm

Sherman Upholstery
Contact Jim Sherman
✉ **Blairdaff Street, Buckie, Morayshire, AB56 1PT** Ⓟ
☎ 01542 834680 Ⓕ 01542 834680
Ⓜ 07703 881903
Ⓔ linda@sherman73.freeserve.co.uk
Est. 1956
Services Antiques repair, restoration, upholstery
Open Mon–Fri 8.30am–4.30pm Sat 8.30am–noon

W M Stark
Contact William Stark
✉ **88 Peddie Street, Dundee, Tayside, DD1 5LT** Ⓟ
☎ 01382 660040
Est. 1977
Services Upholstery, re-covering
Open Mon–Fri 8am–4.30pm

VALUERS

Lennox Auctions and Valuers

Contact Mr A Lennox
✉ **The Basement, 41b Ellis Street, Carrickfergus, Co Antrim, BT38 8AY** Ⓟ
☎ 028 9335 1522 or 028 9337 8527 (pm) Ⓕ 028 9335 1522
Est. 1987
Services Valuations on porcelain and glass
Open Mon–Fri 9.30am–5pm Sat 9.30am–1pm

Nicholas Somers Chartered Arts and Antiques Surveyor

Contact Nicholas Somers, FRICS, FRSA, FIAVI
✉ **45B Lurline Gardens, Battersea, London, SW11 4DD** Ⓟ
☎ 020 7627 1248
Ⓕ 020 7622 9587
Ⓜ 07836 698889
Est. 1990
Services Insurance valuations and sales advice for antiques, fine art and chattels. Expert witness work. Offices in Bath
Open By appointment

Sotheby's (International Auctioneers)

Contact William Montgomery
✉ **The Estate Office, Grey Abbey, Newtownards, Co Down, BT22 2QA** Ⓟ
☎ 028 4278 8668 Ⓕ 028 4278 8652
Ⓔ william.montgomery@sothebys.com
Ⓦ www.sothebys.com
Est. 1979
Services Sotheby's Northern Ireland office provides free valuations of antiques for sale by auction. Insurance valuations can be arranged, and advice given on buying, selling and restoration. Free transport of goods for auction is provided to Sotheby's in England
Open By appointment only

Weller King

Contact Alastair Dixon
✉ **36 High Street, Steyning, West Sussex, BN44 3YE** Ⓟ
☎ 01903 816633 Ⓕ 01903 816644
Ⓜ 07796 174381
Ⓔ enquiries@wellerking.com
Ⓦ www.wellerking.com
Est. 1993
Services Insurance, probate and market valuations, expert witness work
Open Mon–Fri 9am–5.30pm

Weller King

Contact Alastair Dixon
✉ **62 Pall Mall, London, SW1Y 5HZ** Ⓟ
☎ 020 7839 4702 Ⓕ 020 7839 0444
Ⓜ 07796 174381
Ⓔ enquiries@wellerking.com
Ⓦ www.wellerking.com
Est. 1993
Services Insurance, probate and market valuations, expert witness work
Open Mon–Fri 9am–5.30pm

WRITING

Classic Pen Engineering (Writing Equipment Society)

Contact Mr D Purser
✉ **Auchenfranco Farm, Lochfoot, Dumfries, Dumfries & Galloway, DG2 8NZ** Ⓟ
☎ 01387 730208 Ⓕ 01387 730208
Ⓜ 07703 690843
Ⓔ cpe@auchenfranco.freeserve.co.uk
Ⓦ www.auchenfranco.freeserve.co.uk
Est. 1994
Services Complete refurbishment of writing instruments. Sales and valuations of fountain pens, dip pens and pencils
Open By appointment

Fairs

Every effort has been made to ensure that this information is correct at the time of going to press. However it is highly recommended that you telephone to confirm the details are still as stated. You may also discover that the event organizer has several additional events, which could not be included at the time of going to press. If you would like your fair(s) to be included in next year's directory, please inform us by October 1st 2003. (FWC = Free with Card).

JANUARY

15–19

LAPADA Fine Art & Antiques Fair
☎ 0121 767 4789 Ⓕ 0121 767 3535
Ⓔ antiques@necgroup.co.uk
Ⓦ www.lapadafair.co.uk
Location NEC, Birmingham Ⓟ
Est. 1993
Open Weekdays 11am–7pm Sat Sun 11am–6pm
Entrance fee £10 single £16 double
Details 100 dealers

16–19

Penmans West London Antiques & Fine Art Fair
Contact Caroline Penman
☎ 01444 482514 Ⓕ 01444 482412
Ⓜ 07774 850044
Ⓔ info@penman-fairs.co.uk
Ⓦ www.penman-fairs.co.uk
Location Kensington Town Hall, Hornton Street, London W8 Ⓟ
Est. 1975
Open Thurs noon–8pm Fri Sat 10.30am–6pm Sun 10.30am–5pm
Entrance fee £4
Details A traditional mix of antiques and art

17–19

Shepton Mallet Antiques & Collectors Fair
Contact Caroline Cleary
☎ 01636 702326 Ⓕ 01636 707923
Ⓦ www.dmgantiquefairs.com
Location Royal Bath and West Showground, Shepton Mallet, Somerset Ⓟ
Est. 1997
Open Fri 1–6pm Sat 8.30am–5pm Sun 10am–4pm
Entrance fee Fri £10 Sat 8.30am £7.50 9.30am £5 Sun £5
Details Up to 600 exhibitors

18

Antiques Fair
Contact Barry Phillips
☎ 01945 870160 Ⓕ 01945 870660
Ⓜ 07860 517048
Location Castle Hall, The Wash, Hertford, Hertfordshire Ⓟ
Est. 1976
Open 10am–4.30pm
Entrance fee £1 Senior citizens 80p Trade FWC from 9am
Details Refreshments, ground floor, level access

Commonwealth Institute Coin Fair
Contact Mrs Monk
☎ 020 8656 4583 Ⓕ 020 8656 4583
Location The Commonwealth Institute, Kensington High Street, London W8 Ⓟ
Est. 1988
Open 9.30am–2.30pm
Entrance fee £1
Details English, foreign and ancient coins, antiquities, medallions, tokens and some bank notes

19

Biggleswade Antiques Fairs
☎ 01234 871449 Ⓕ 01234 871449
Ⓜ 07778 789917
Location The Weatherley Centre, Eagle Farm Road, Biggleswade, Bedfordshire
Open 9.30am–4.30pm

Hatfield Antiques & Collectors Fair
Contact Richard Millar
☎ 01279 871110 Ⓕ 01279 871917
Location Red Lion, Great North Road, Hatfield, Hertfordshire Ⓟ
Open Trade with card 9.30am Public 10.30am–4.30pm
Entrance fee Adults 90p Concessions 70p Children 16 and under free Trade FWC
Details Up to 54 stalls

Mark Carter Militaria & Medal Fairs
☎ 01753 534777
Location The Princes Hall, Princes Way, Aldershot, Hampshire Ⓟ
Open Preview 9.30am Public 10.30am–3.30pm
Entrance fee £1.50 Preview £3 Accompanied children free
Details Between 110 and 125 tables of quality militaria, books and medals

Monmouthshire County Antiques & Collectors Fair
Contact Mr G B Harris
☎ 01873 735811 Ⓕ 01873 735829
Ⓔ ghrr5@aol.com
Location The Market Hall (next to the Town Hall), Abergavenny, Monmouthshire Ⓟ
Est. 1996
Open 6am–5pm
Entrance fee Free
Details 60 dealers, refreshments

The London Textiles, Vintage Fashion and Accessories Fair
Contact Paola Francia-Gardiner
☎ 020 8543 5075 Ⓕ 020 8404 6262
Location Hammersmith Town Hall, King Street, London W6 Ⓟ
Open 8am–5pm
Entrance fee 8am £10 10am £4 1.30pm £3
Details 100 stands

22

The Big Brum
Contact Carol Baskin
☎ 01782 595805 Ⓕ 01782 596133
Ⓔ info@antiqueforumgroup.com
Ⓦ www.antiqueforumgroup.com
Location St Martins Market (The Rag), Edgbaston Street, Birmingham Ⓟ
Open From 7.30am
Entrance fee Free
Details 700 stands plus 500 unreserved stalls

25

Antique & Collectors Fair
Contact R M Torrens
☎ 01764 654555 Ⓕ 01764 654430
Location The Citadel Leisure Centre, Ayr Baths, South Beach Road, Ayr
Open 10am–4.30pm
Entrance fee £1
Details 100 stands

Chingford Antiques & Collectors Fair
Contact Richard Millar
☎ 01279 871110 Ⓕ 01279 871917
Location Assembly Hall, The Green, Station Road, Chingford, London E4 Ⓟ
Open Trade with card 9.30am Public 10.30am–4pm
Entrance fee Adults £1 Concessions 70p Children 16 and under free Trade FWC
Details 80 stalls

Pamela Robertson Antique & Collectors Fair
Contact Pamela Robertson

☎ 01244 678106
Ⓔ gprobertson@robertson58.fsnet.co.uk
Location Northgate Arena, Victoria Road, Chester 🅿
Open 10am–4.30pm
Entrance fee £1.50 Seniors £1
Details Capacity 150 stalls selling all small antiques and collectables

25–26

Bob Evans Fairs
☎ 01664 812627 Ⓕ 01664 813727
Location Sport Village, Drayton High Road, Hellesdon, Norwich 🅿
Est. 1977
Open Trade 8am Public 9.30am–4.30pm
Details 300 stalls

Buxton Antique & collectors Fair
Contact Mr David Fletcher
☎ 0161 773 7001
Location Pavilion Gardens, Buxton, Derbyshire 🅿
Est. 1976
Open 9am–5pm
Details 100 stalls

Detling International Antiques & Collectors Fair
Contact Caroline Cleary
☎ 01636 702326 Ⓕ 01636 707923
Ⓦ www.dmgantiquefairs.com
Location Kent County Showground, Detling, Nr Maidstone, Kent 🅿
Est. 1998
Open Sat 8.30am–5pm Sun 10am–4pm
Entrance fee Sat 8.30am £6 Sat 10am £4.50 Sun £4.50
Details Up to 500 exhibitors

The Original Long Melford Fair
Contact Tom Burt
☎ 01787 280306
Location The Old School, Long Melford, Suffolk 🅿
Est. 1976
Open Trade 7.30am Public 9.30am–4.30pm
Entrance fee Trade FWC Adults £1
Details 50 stalls each day

26

Antiques & Collectables Fair
Contact Joan Murray
☎ 00 353 1 6708260 Ⓕ 00 353 1 6708295
Ⓜ 00 353 87 2670607
Ⓔ AntiquesFairsIreland@esatclear.ie
Ⓦ www.antiquesfairsireland.com
Location Royal Marine Hotel, Dun Laoghaire, Co Dublin
Open 11am–6pm
Entrance fee €4 (£2.35)
Details 50 dealers

Antiques & Collectors Fair
Contact Barry Phillips
☎ 01945 870160 Ⓕ 01945 870660
Ⓜ 07860 517048
Ⓔ janba@supanet.com
Location Knights Hill Hotel, South Wooton, King's Lynn 🅿
Open 10am–4.30pm
Entrance fee £1 Senior citizens 80p Trade FWC from 9am
Details Refreshments, ground floor, level access

Art Deco Fair with 20thC Decorative Arts
Contact Ann Zierold
☎ 01824 750500 Ⓕ 01824 750490
Location Chester Racecourse 🅿
Est. 1996
Open 9.30am–4pm
Details 80 stands, no copies or reproductions

Biggleswade Antiques Fairs
☎ 01234 871449 Ⓕ 01234 871449
Ⓜ 07778 789917
Location The Addison Centre, Kempston, Bedford
Open 10am–4.30pm

Burford Antiques Fair
Contact Andy Briggs
☎ 01865 301705
Ⓜ 07977 936882
Ⓔ andy@fatcatfairs.co.uk
Ⓦ www.fatcatfairs.co.uk
Location Burford School, Burford, Oxfordshire 🅿
Est. 1990
Open 9am–4pm
Entrance fee Trade FWC
Details 40 stands, refreshments available

Dualco Promotions
Contact Mr Greenburg
☎ 0161 7662012 Ⓕ 0161 7662012
Location Reebok Stadium, Bolton, Jct 6 M61 🅿
Open 10am–5pm
Details 250 Stalls

M & S Antiques & Collectors Fair
Contact Jim Mansfield
☎ 01223 233059 Ⓕ 01223 500283
Ⓜ 07960 102889 or 07748 205647
Location Meldreth Village Hall, 2 miles north of Royston, Hertfordshire, off the A10 🅿
Open 9.30am–4pm

Entrance fee 70p
Details Antiques and collectables

Midland Clock & Watch Fair
☎ 01895 834694/834357
Ⓕ 01895 832329/832904
Location National Motorcycle Museum, M42 Exit 6, West Midlands Ⓟ
Open 9am–2.30pm
Entrance fee 9am £5
11am–2.30pm £2.50 Under 18s free
Details 153 stands, each fair displaying about £3 million worth of antique clocks, watches, parts and books, refreshments available, free valuations

V and A Fairs
Contact Julie Timmins
☎ 01938 580438 Ⓕ 01938 580438
Ⓔ vandafairs@talk21.com
Location The Community Hall, Low Town (on A442), Bridgnorth, Shropshire Ⓟ
Open Trade 8.30am Public 10am–4.30pm
Details 25 stands

28

Bushey Hall School
Contact David Maggs
☎ 01582 872514 Ⓕ 01582 873816
Location London Road, Bushey, Hertfordshire Ⓟ
Open Trade 8am Public 10am–4pm
Entrance fee £1
Details 80+ stalls, refreshments

30

Antique & Collectors Fair
Contact Stancie Kutler
☎ 01270 624288
Location Nantwich Civic Hall, Market Street, Nantwich, Cheshire, Jct 16 M6 Ⓟ
Est. 1974
Open Trade 8am Public 10am–5pm
Details Refreshments, up to 75 stalls

30–2 FEB

The 33rd Harrogate Winter Antiques and Fine Art Fair
☎ 01277 214677 Ⓕ 01277 214550
Ⓔ admin@baileyfairs.co.uk
Ⓦ www.baileyfairs.co.uk
Location Pavilions of Harrogate, Great Yorkshire Showground Ⓟ
Open Thurs 2–6pm Fri Sat 11am–6pm Sun 11am–5pm
Entrance fee £5
Details 82 dealers, vetted and datelined

31–2 FEB

The International Antiques & Collectors Fair at RAF Swinderby
Contact Mr J Ball
☎ 01298 27493/73188
Ⓜ 07860 797200
Location RAF Swinderby, A46 between Newark and Lincoln Ⓟ
Open Fri 7am–5pm Sat Sun 8am–5pm
Entrance fee Fri trade day £10 Sat Sun £3
Details Over 2000 stands

FEBRUARY

1

Antique & Collectors Fair
Contact R M Torrens
☎ 01764 654555 Ⓕ 01764 654430
Location Alberts Hall, Dumbarton Road, Stirling
Open 10am–4.30pm
Entrance fee £1
Details 135 stands

Buckingham Antique & Collectors Fair
Contact David Smith
☎ 01933 225674
Ⓔ david.smith34@ntlworld.com
Location Buckingham Community Centre, Cornwalls Meadow Shopping Precinct, Buckingham Ⓟ
Open 10am–4.30pm
Entrance fee £1

Marcel Fairs
Contact Marcel Epstein
☎ 020 8950 1844 Ⓕ 020 8950 1844
Ⓜ 07887 648255
Location St Paul's Church Hall, Mill Hill, Ridgeway, London NW7 Ⓟ
Open Trade 8am Public 9am–4pm
Entrance fee 50p
Details 1950's dateline, 30–35 dealers, small furniture

Victoriana's Fairs
Contact Mrs Kyzor
☎ 01543 425380
Location Walsall Town Hall, Walsall, West Midlands
Est. 1979
Open 10am–4pm
Details 35–40 stalls of antiques and collectables

2

Antique & Collectors Fair
Contact Graham Davey
☎ 01603 758252
Ⓔ graham@v21.me.uk
Location Leisure Centre, Exning Road, Newmarket Ⓟ
Open 10am–4pm
Entrance fee £1
Details 70 Stalls

Antique & Collectors Fair
Contact R M Torrens
☎ 01764 654555 Ⓕ 01764 654430
Location Meadowbank Stadium, London Road, Edinburgh
Open 10am–4.30pm
Entrance fee £1
Details 135 stands

Arun Fairs
Contact Stephanie Clark
☎ 01903 734112
Ⓔ cstephiemoo@aol.com
Location Woodland Centre, Woodlands Avenue, Rustington, West Sussex, off the A259 Ⓟ
Est. 1995
Open Trade 9am Public 10am–4pm
Details 40 stalls

Best of Fairs
Contact Tom Burt
☎ 01787 280306
Location The Village Hall, Copdock, 3 miles west of Ipswich Ⓟ
Est. 1990
Open Trade 7.30am Public 9am–4pm
Entrance fee Trade FWC
Details 50 stalls

Clock & Watch Dealers Fair
Contact Mr Lionel Parker
☎ 01691 831162
Ⓔ fairs@oswatch.fsnet.co.uk
Location The Grove Leisure Centre, London Road, Balderton, Nr Newark Ⓟ

Est. 2000
Open 8.30am–3pm
Entrance fee £5 before 10am £2 after
Details 65 stalls offering clocks, watches, barometers, books

Cross Country Fairs Ltd
Contact Mr Harding
☎ 07860 863300
Location Copthorne Hotel, Effingham Park, West Sussex P
Open 9am–4.30pm
Entrance fee £2 Children free Trade FWC until 10am
Details 145 stands

Decorative Antiques and Textiles for Interior
Contact Paola Francia-Gardiner
☎ 020 8543 5075 F 020 8404 6262
Location Chelsea Village Hotel, Stamford Bridge, Fulham Road, London SW6 P
Open 10am–5pm

Dualco Promotions
Contact Mr Greenburg
☎ 0161 766 2012 F 0161 766 2012
Location Huddersfield Sports Centre, Jct 23 & 24 M62 P
Open 10am–5pm
Details 200 stalls

Ipswich Antiques & Collectables Fair
Contact Vicky Roberts-Barber
☎ 01473 688201
Location Ipswich County Hotel (formerly Ipswich Moat House) Copdock, Ipswich, Suffolk P
Open Trade 8.30am Public 9am–5pm
Entrance fee £1.25 OAPs £1
Details Approximately 100 stalls covering all collectable items, refreshments available, licensed bar

Lechlade Antiques Fair
Contact Andy Briggs
☎ 01865 301705
M 07977 936882
E andy@fatcatfairs.co.uk
W www.fatcatfairs.co.uk
Location The New Memorial Hall, Burford Road, Lechlade, Gloucestershire P
Est. 1993
Open 9am–4pm
Entrance fee 50p Trade FWC
Details 35 stands, refreshments available

Malvern Antiques & Collectors Fair
Contact Caroline Cleary
☎ 01636 702326 F 01636 707923
W www.dmgantiquefairs.com
Location Three Counties Showground, Malvern, Worcestershire P
Est. 1997
Open 8.30am–5pm
Entrance fee 8.30am £4 10am £2.50
Details Up to 250 exhibitors

Mark Carter Militaria & Medal Fairs
☎ 01753 534777
Location Yate Leisure Centre, Kennedy Way, Yate, Bristol P
Open Preview 9.30am Public 10.30am–3.30pm
Entrance fee £1.50 Preview £3 Accompanied children free
Details Between 90 and 100 tables of quality militaria, books and medals

St Crispins Fair
Contact Mrs P Wyatt
☎ 0118 983 3020
Location St Crispins Sports Centre, A329, Wokingham, Berkshire P
Est. 1981
Open Trade 8.30am Public 10am–4pm
Entrance fee 50p
Details Variety of antique and collectors items, no furniture, refreshments and bar. 85 dealers

Twickenham Rugby Ground Art Deco Fair
Contact Jean May
☎ 0121 430 3767 F 0121 436 7912
Location Twickenham Rugby Ground P
Est. 2000
Open Trade 8.30am Public 9.30am–4.30pm
Entrance fee £2
Details 85 stalls, furniture

V and A Fairs
Contact Julie Timmins
☎ 01938 580438 F 01938 580438
E vandafairs@talk21.com
Location The Village Hotel & Leisure Club, Cheadle Road, Cheadle, Cheshire P
Open Trade 8.30am Public 10am–4.30pm
Entrance fee Trade FWC
Details 32 stands

Wessex Fairs
Contact Mrs Jo Wanford
☎ 01278 789568
Location Holiday Inn, Taunton, at Junction 25, M5 P
Est. 1986
Open 10am–4.30pm
Entrance fee £1 Trade FWC
Details Stall capacity 20, refreshments available

3–4

Newark International Antiques & Collectors Fair
Contact Caroline Cleary
☎ 01636 702326 F 01636 707923
W www.dmgantiquefairs.com
Location Newark & Notts Showground, Newark P
Est. 1997
Open Mon 5.30am–6pm Tues 8am–4pm
Entrance fee Mon £20 (includes Tuesday entry) Tues £5
Details Up to 4000 exhibitors

6

Paraphernalia Fairs
Contact Jill Robinson
☎ 01305 860012
Location Lyndhurst Community Centre, Lyndhurst, New Forest, Hampshire P
Est. 1995
Open Trade 9am Public 9.30am–4pm
Entrance fee 50p Trade FWC
Details 40 stands, antique and collectors flea market

6–9

Penmans Petersfield Antiques Fair
Contact Caroline Penman
☎ 01444 482514 F 01444 482412
M 07774 850044
E info@penman-fairs.co.uk
W www.penman-fairs.co.uk
Location Festival Hall, Heath Road, Petersfield, Hants P
Est. 1973
Open Fri Sat 10.30am–6pm Sun 10.30am–5pm
Entrance fee £3
Details 43 stands of vetted traditional and decorative antiques

7–9

Galloway Antiques Fairs
☎ 01423 522122 F 01423 522122
M 07966 528725
E susan@gallowayfairs.co.uk
W www.gallowayfairs.co.uk
Location Hengrave Hall, Bury St Edmunds, Suffolk P
Open 10.30am–5pm
Entrance fee £3.50–£4.50

Stafford Bingley Hall
Contact Helen Bowman or Ben Wray
☎ 07071 284333 F 07071 284334
E info@antiquesfairs.com
W www.antiquesfairs.com
Location The Bingley Hall County Showground, Stafford P
Est. 1974
Open Fri Trade 8.30am Public 10am–5pm Sat 9.30am–5pm
Entrance fee Sat £5 children under 14 free
Details Over 400 exhibitors including furniture

8

Chelsea Brocante
Contact Matthew Adams
☎ 020 7254 4054
W www.adams-antiques-fairs.co.uk
Location Chelsea Town Hall, King's Road, Chelsea, London SW3 P
Est. 1994
Open 10am–5pm
Entrance fee £2.50 accompanied children free
Details 70+ exhibitors

Devon County Antiques Fairs
☎ 01363 82571 F 01363 82312
E dcaf@antiques-fairs.com
W www.antiques-fairs.com
Location Matford Centre, Matford Park Road, Exeter P
Open 9am–4.30pm
Entrance fee 9–10am £3.50 10am–4.30pm £2.50 Children free
Details 230 stands inside, 350 outside, restaurant, bar, good disabled and wheelchair access

London Coin Fair
Contact Mr H Simmons
☎ 020 7831 2080 F 020 7831 2090
E lcf@simmonsgallery.co.uk
W www.simmonsgallery.co.uk
Location Holiday Inn, London Bloomsbury, Coram Street, London WC1 P
Est. 1970
Open 9.30am–5pm
Entrance fee £3 Concessions for families and OAPs
Details 70–85 dealers

8–9

Suffolk Book Markets
☎ 01787 210810
Location Long Melford Memorial Hall, Suffolk P
Open 10am–5pm
Details 30 dealers selling old books, prints, postcards, stamps, Victorian and later printed collectables, ephemera

9

Antique & Collectors Fair
Contact John Slade
☎ 020 8894 0218
W www.antiquefairs.co.uk
Location Woking Leisure Centre, Kingfield Road, Woking, Surrey P
Open 8.30am–4.30pm
Entrance fee £1.50
Details 175 stalls

Antiques & Collectables Fair
Contact Joan Murray
☎ 00 353 1 6708260
F 00 353 1 6708295
M 00 353 87 2670607
E AntiquesFairsIreland@esatclear.ie
W www.antiquesfairsireland.com
Location The Mansion House, Dawson Street, Dublin 2
Open 11am–6pm
Entrance fee €4 (£2.35)
Details 60 dealers from all parts of Ireland

Antiques & Collectors Fairs
☎ 01753 685098
Location Runnymeade Hotel & Spa, Windsor Road, Egham, Surrey P
Est. 1974
Open 11am–5pm
Details Approximately 70 stalls, refreshments available

Biggleswade Antiques Fairs
☎ 01234 871449 F 01234 871449
M 07778 789917
Location The Marriott Hotel, Huntingdon, Cambridgeshire, off A14
Open 10am–4.30pm

Bob Evans Fairs
☎ 01664 812627
F 01664 813727
Location Sports Connexion, Ryton on Dunsmore, Coventry P
Est. 1983
Open Trade 8am Public 9.30am–4.30pm
Details 300 stalls

Crispin Fairs
Contact Mrs P Wyatt
☎ 0118 983 3020
Location Victoria Hall, Hartley Wintney, Hampshire P
Est. 1985
Open Trade 8.30am Public 10am–4.30pm
Entrance fee 50p
Details 45 stalls

Dualco Promotions
Contact Mr Greenburg
☎ 0161 7662012 F 0161 7662012
Location Castle Armoury, Bury, Lancashire P
Open 10am–5pm
Details 100 stalls

Dualco Promotions
Contact Mr Greenburg
☎ 0161 766 2012 F 0161 766 2012
Location The Metrodome, Barnsley, Jct 37 M1 P
Open 10am–5pm
Details 200 stalls

J and K Fairs
☎ 01472 813281
Location Lincolnshire Showground, Lincoln, on A15 North of Lincoln P
Est. 1981
Open Trade 7am Public 10am–5pm
Entrance fee £1 Children under 14 free
Details 200 dealers

London Map Fairs
Contact Lee Jackson
☎ 020 7625 2157
F 020 7625 2157
E leejackson@btinternet.com
W www.londonmapfairs.com
Location The Bonnington Hotel,

Southampton Row, midway between Holborn and Russell Square tube stations, London WC1
Est. 1982
Open 10.30am–5pm
Entrance fee Free
Details 15 dealers

Lostwithiel Antiques Fair
Contact Richard Bonehill
☎ 01872 225200 or 01736 793213
Ⓜ 07811 919083
Ⓔ richard@bonehill3.freeserve.co.uk
Ⓦ www.bonehill3.freeserve.co.uk
Location Community Centre, Lostwithiel, Cornwall P
Est. 1989
Open Trade 9.30am Public 10am–4.30pm
Entrance fee 25p
Details 40 stands exhibit a wide range of antiques and collectables

M & S Collectors Fair
Contact Jim Mansfield
☎ 01223 233059
Ⓕ 01223 500283
Ⓜ 07960 102889 or 07748 205647
Location Cottenham Village College, 5 miles north of Cambridge, B1049 P
Open 10am–4pm
Entrance fee 70p
Details Collectables

Midas Antique Fair
Contact Joy Alder
☎ 01494 674170
Location The Bellhouse Hotel, Oxford Road (A40), Beaconsfield, Bucks P
Open 10.30am–5pm
Entrance fee Adults £1.50
Details 60 datelined stands of general antiques and collectables, refreshments, licenced bar

Pennyfarthing Fayres
Contact Maureen Carson
☎ 0208 4413425
Location Potters Bar P
Est. 1991
Open Trade 9am Public 10am–4.30pm
Entrance fee Trade FWC Public £1 OAPs 50p
Details 70 stands of antiques and collectables including furniture, no reproductions

13

Antique & Collectors Fair
Location Nantwich, Cheshire
Details See Antique & Collectors Fair 30 January

13–16

Penmans Chester Antiques & Fine Art Show
Contact Caroline Penman
☎ 01444 482514 Ⓕ 01444 482412
Ⓜ 07774 850044
Ⓔ info@penman-fairs.co.uk
Ⓦ www.penman-fairs.co.uk
Location County Grandstand, Chester Racecourse, Cheshire P
Est. 1990
Open Thurs noon–8pm Fri Sat 10.30am–6pm Sun 10.30am–5pm
Entrance fee £4
Details 60 stands on 3 floors, fine antiques and art

14–16

Galloway Antiques Fairs
☎ 01423 522122 Ⓕ 01423 522122
Ⓜ 07966 528725
Ⓔ susan@gallowayfairs.co.uk
Ⓦ www.gallowayfairs.co.uk
Location The Bowes Museum, Barnard Castle, Co Durham P
Open 10.30am–5pm
Entrance fee £3.50–£4.50

15

Blackpool Winter Gardens Collectors Market
Contact Mr Shaun Hoyle
☎ 01253 782828 Ⓕ 01253 714715
Ⓔ info@hoylespromotions.co.uk
Ⓦ www.hoylespromotions.co.uk
Location The Olympia at Blackpool Winter Gardens, Church Street, Blackpool, Lancashire P
Est. 1982
Open Trade 7.30am Public 9am–4pm
Entrance fee Trade FWC Public £1 accompanied children under 12 free
Details 200 stalls

Commonwealth Institute Coin Fair
Location London W8
Details See Commonwealth Institute Coin Fair 18 January

15–16

Albany Fairs
Contact Robert Davison
☎ 0191 584 2934
Ⓜ 07976 619009
Ⓔ enquiries@albanyfairs.com
Ⓦ www.albanyfairs.com
Location Pooley Bridge Village Hall, Cumbria P
Open 10am–4.30pm

Beckett Antique Fairs
Contact Alan
☎ 0114 2890656
Location Doncaster Race Exhibition Centre, Doncaster P
Open Trade 8.30am Public 10am–4.30pm
Entrance fee £2 OAPs Children £1
Details 240 stands, refreshments available

16

Antique & Collectors Fair
Contact R M Torrens
☎ 01764 654555 Ⓕ 01764 654430
Location Moir Hall, Mitchell Library, Granville Street, Glasgow
Open 10am–4.30pm
Entrance fee £1
Details 65 stands

Antiques & Collectors Fair
Location King's Lynn
Details See Antiques & Collectors Fair 26 January

Battersea Town Hall Art Deco Fair
Contact Jean May
☎ 0121 430 3767 Ⓕ 0121 436 7912
Location Battersea Town Hall P
Est. 1991
Open Trade 8.30am Public 9.30am–4.30pm
Entrance fee £2
Details 120 stalls, furniture

Bob Evans Fairs
☎ 01664 812627 Ⓕ 01664 813727
Location Leisure Village, Thurston Drive, Kettering P
Est. 1992
Open Trade 8am Public 9.30am–4.30pm
Details 300 stalls

Brunel Clock & Watch Fair
☎ 01895 834694/834357
Ⓕ 01895 832329/832904

Location Brunel University, Kingston Lane, Uxbridge, Middlesex P
Open 9am–2.30pm
Entrance fee 9am £5 11am–2.30pm £2.50 Accompanied children free
Details 153 stands, each fair displaying about £3 million worth of antique clocks, watches, parts and books, refreshments available, free valuations

Buxton Book Fair
Contact Mrs S Laithwaite
☎ 01625 425352
Location Pavilion Garden, Buxton, Derbyshire P
Est. 1982
Open 10am–5pm
Entrance fee 80p
Details 80 dealers

Devon County Antiques Fairs
☎ 01363 82571 F 01363 82312
E dcaf@antiques-fairs.com
W www.antiques-fairs.com
Location Westland Sports and Social Club, Westbourne Close, Yeovil, Somerset P
Open 9am–4.30pm
Entrance fee 9–10am £2 10am–4.30pm £1.50
Details 200 stands, restaurant, bar

Dualco Promotions
Contact Mr Greenburg
☎ 0161 766 2012 F 0161 766 2012
Location North Bridge Leisure Centre, Halifax, Jct 42 M62 P
Open 10am–5pm
Details 200 stalls

Dublin Toy and Train Fair
Contact Terry McNally or Brian Kelly
☎ 01 2849199 or 01 2803008
Location The Royal Marine Hotel, Marine Road, Dun Laoghaire, Co Dublin P
Open 11am–5pm
Entrance fee €4.50 (£2.87)

Hatfield Antiques & Collectors Fair
Location Hatfield, Hertfordshire
Details See Hatfield Antiques & Collectors Fair 19 January

Monmouthshire County Antiques & Collectors Fair
Location Abergavenny, Monmouthshire
Details See Monmouthshire County Antiques & Collectors Fair 19 January

V and A Fairs
Contact Julie Timmins
☎ 01938 580438 F 01938 580438
E vandafairs@talk21.com
Location The Civic Centre, High Street, Whitchurch, Shropshire P
Open Trade 8.30am Public 10am–4.30pm
Entrance fee Trade FWC
Details 60 stands

18

Biggleswade Antiques Fairs
Location Biggleswade, Bedfordshire
Details See Biggleswade Antiques Fairs 19 January

Crispin Fairs
Contact Mrs P Wyatt
☎ 0118 983 3020
Location Victoria Hall, Hartley Wintney, Hampshire P
Est. 1985
Open 8.30am–2.30pm
Entrance fee Free
Details 45 stalls

Sandown Park Antique & Collectors Fair
Contact Alan or Ludi Kipping
☎ 0207 249 4050 F 0207 249 5060
E alan&ludi@ww-antique-fairs.demon.co.uk
W www.ww-antique-fairs.demon.co.uk
Location Sandown Park Racecourse, Esher, Surrey P
Open Preview noon–2pm General admission 2–6pm
Entrance fee Noon £12 2pm £4
Details 550 stands under cover in 2 large exhibition halls

20

Antiques & Collectables Fair
☎ 01327 876540 M 0411 248951
Location Whilton Mill Racetrack, Daventry, M1 Junctions 16 and 18 P
Est. 1998
Open 7am–2pm
Entrance fee £2.50
Details 200 stands

22

Antique & Collectors Fair
Location Ayr
Details See Antique & Collectors Fair 25 January

Antiques & Collectors Fair
Contact Dennis Jewellery
☎ 01202 669061
M 07736 424231
Location Holy Angels Church Hall, Lilliput Road, Lilliput, Poole, Dorset
Est. 1976
Open 10am–4pm
Entrance fee 50p
Details 17 stands, jewellery, china, porcelain, books, postcards, linen, etc

Pamela Robertson Antique & Collectors Fair
Location Chester
Details See Pamela Robertson Antique & Collectors Fair 25 January

Southport Antiques & Collectors Fair
☎ 01253 782828 F 01253 714715
Location Southport Floral Hall, the Promenade, Southport, Merseyside P
Open Trade 8.30am Public 9.30am–4pm
Entrance fee Trade FWC Public £1.50 accompanied children under 12 free
Details 200 stalls

22–23

Antiques & Collectables Fair
Contact Sue Rumbold
☎ 01264 850801
M 07712 018543
Location Stockbridge Town Hall, near Winchester, Hampshire P
Est. 1997
Open 10am–5pm
Entrance fee 50p
Details 25 stands

Antiques & Collectors Fair
Contact Barry Phillips
☎ 01945 870160 F 01945 870660
M 07860 517048
E janba@supanet.com

Location Burgess Hall, St Ivo Leisure Centre, St Ives, Cambridgeshire P
Open 10am–4.30pm
Entrance fee £1 Senior citizens 80p Trade FWC from 9am
Details Café bar, ground floor, level access

The Original Long Melford Fair
Location Long Melford, Suffolk
Details See The Original Long Melford Fair 25–26 January

West Midlands Antique Fairs
Contact Jenny Wakeham
☎ 01743 271444 F 01743 352353
Location Prestwood Complex, Stafford County Showground P
Est. 1973
Open Trade 8.30am Public 10am–5pm
Entrance fee 8.30am £3 10am £2 Trade FWC
Details More than 280 stalls in 3 halls offering furniture, porcelain, paintings, clocks, Arts and Crafts, jewellery and collectables

23

Albany Fairs
Contact Robert Davison
☎ 0191 584 2934
M 07976 619009
E enquiries@albanyfairs.com
W www.albanyfairs.com
Location Lanchester Community Centre, Co Durham P
Open 10am–4.30pm

Antiques & Collectables Fair
Contact Joan Murray
☎ 00 353 1 670 8295
F 00 353 1 670 8295
M 00 353 872 670607
E antiquesfairsireland@esatclear.ie
W www.antiquesfairsireland.com
Location Clontarf Castle, Castle Avenue, Dublin P
Open 11am–6pm
Entrance fee €4 (£2.35)
Details 60 dealers, wide range of antiques and collectors items. Bar and restaurant

Art Deco Fair
Contact Nick Cox
☎ 01773 770422
E abbeyfairs@yahoo.co.uk
Location Warwick Hilton, Warwick
Open 9am–4pm
Entrance fee £2.50
Details 80 stands

Biggleswade Antiques Fairs
☎ 01234 871449 F 01234 871449
M 07778 789917
Location Kimbolton Castle, Huntingdon, Cambridgeshire
Open 10am–4.30pm
Details Dateline 1940s

Bloomsbury Postcard & Collectors Fair
☎ 020 8202 9080/8203 1500
F 020 8203 7031
E bloomsbury@memoriespostcards.co.uk
W www.memoriespostcards.co.uk
Location Galleon Suite, Royal National Hotel, Bedford Way, London WC1 P
Est. 1976
Open Early entry 8am Public 10am–4.30pm
Entrance fee £1 early entry £5
Details 120 stands of postcards, printed ephemera, autographs, programmes, photos, cigarette cards, postal history etc

Bob Evans Fairs
☎ 01664 812627 F 01664 813727
Location The Cresset, Bretton Centre, Peterborough P
Open Trade 8am Public 9.30am–4.30pm
Details 200 stalls

Burford Antiques Fair
Location Burford, Oxfordshire
Details See Burford Antiques Fair 26 January

Bushey Hall School
Location Bushey, Hertfordshire
Details See Bushey Hall 28 January

Chipping Norton Toy Fairs
Contact Don Davidson
☎ 01608 641870
Location Chipping Norton School, Burford Road, Chipping Norton, Oxfordshire P
Est. 1992
Open 10.30am–3pm
Entrance fee 70p
Details 20 dealers

Dualco Promotions
Contact Mr Greenburg
☎ 0161 766 2012 F 0161 766 2012
Location Clayton Arms Sports Centre, Oldham, Jct 20 M62 P
Open 10am–5pm
Details 150 stalls

Dualco Promotions
Contact Mr Greenburg
☎ 0161 7662012 F 0161 7662012
Location Pudsey Civic Hall, Leeds, Jct 26 & 27 M62 P
Open 10am–5pm
Details 100 stalls

M & S Antiques & Collectors Fair
Location Royston, Hertfordshire
Details See M & S Antiques & Collectors Fair 26 January

New Glass Fair
Contact Dr Graham Cooley
☎ 01223 810606
E graham.cooley@antenova.com
Location The Guildhall, Cambridge
Est. 2002
Open 11am–4pm
Entrance fee £2.50
Details Quality glass with specialist dealers offering a wide range of items from 18thC drinking glasses to contemporary decorative studio pieces

Newmarket Antiques & Collectors Fair
Contact Caroline Cleary
☎ 01636 702326 F 01636 707923
W www.dmgantiquefairs.com
Location Millennium Grandstand, Rowley Mile Racecourse, Newmarket, Suffolk P
Est. 1993
Open 8am–4pm
Entrance fee 8am £6 10am £3.50
Details Up to 250 exhibitors

Royal Horticultural Hall
Contact Matthew Adams
☎ 020 72544054
W www.adams-antiques-fairs.co.uk
Location Royal Horticultural Hall, Lawrence Hall, Greycoat Street, London SW1 P
Est. 1972
Open 9.30am–4.30pm
Entrance fee £2.50
Details 240+ antiques dealers

Wessex Fairs
Contact Mrs Jo Wanford
☎ 01278 789568
Location Winter Gardens, Weston-super-Mare P
Est. 1986
Open 10am–4.30pm
Entrance fee Trade FWC
Details Stall capacity 60+, refreshments available

25

Antiques Fair
Location Hertford, Hertfordshire
Details See Antiques Fair 18 January

25–2 MAR

The Olympia Spring Fine Art and Antiques Fair
☎ 020 7370 8186/8212
F 020 7370 8221
E olympia-antiques@eco.co.uk
W www.olympia-antiques.com
Location Olympia, London P
Est. 1994
Open 25th 5pm–10pm 26th 11am–9pm 27th–2nd 11am–8pm 2nd 11am–7pm 3rd 11am–5pm
Entrance fee £10 single £16 double reduced to £8 £14 if booked in advance
Details 180 exhibitors, offering wide range of antiques and works of art, all items examined by experts

27–2 MAR

The Milton Keynes Antiques Fair
Contact David Smith
☎ 01933 224674
Location Middleton Hall, Milton Keynes Shopping Centre P
Est. 1993
Entrance fee Free
Details Stand-fitted and tabletop sections, 1939 dateline, 86 dealers

28–2 MAR

Galloway Antiques Fairs
☎ 01423 522122 F 01423 522122
M 07966 528725
E susan@gallowayfairs.co.uk
W www.gallowayfairs.co.uk
Location Stonyhurst College, Nr Clitheroe, Lancashire P
Open 10.30am–5pm
Entrance fee £3.50–£4.50

MARCH

1

Antiques & Collectables Fair
Contact Sue Rumbold
☎ 01264 850801
M 07712 018543
Location Marlborough Town Hall, Wiltshire P
Est. 1997
Open 10am–5pm
Entrance fee 50p
Details 25 stands

Chingford Antiques & Collectors Fair
Location Chingford, London E4
Details See Chingford Antiques & Collectors Fair 25 January

Marcel Fairs
Location London NW7
Details See Marcel Fairs 1 February

Victoriana's Fairs
Location Walsall, West Midlands
Details See Victoriana's Fairs 1 February

1–2

Buxton Antique & Collectors Fair
Location Buxton, Derbyshire
Details See Buxton Antique & Collectors Fair 25–26 January

Devon County Antiques Fairs
☎ 01363 82571 F 01363 82312
E dcaf@antiques-fairs.com
W www.antiques-fairs.com
Location Westpoint Exhibition Centre, Clyst St Mary, Exeter P
Open 8am–5pm
Entrance fee Sat 8–10am £6.50 Sat Sun 10am–5pm £4.50
Details 500 stands, datelined section

1–3

Detling International Antiques & Collectors Fair
Location Detling, Nr Maidstone, Kent
Details See Detling International Antiques & Collectors Fair 25–26 January

2

Antique & Collectors Fair
Location Newmarket
Details See Antique & Collectors Fair 2 February

Antique & Collectors Fair
Location Edinburgh
Details See Antique & Collectors Fair 2 February

Arun Fairs
Location Rustington, West Sussex
Details See Arun Fairs 2 February

Best of Fairs
Location Copdock, Ipswich
Details See Best of Fairs 2 February

Bob Evans Fairs
☎ 01664 812627 F 01664 813727
Location Hinckley Leisure Centre, Coventry Road, Hinckley, Leicestershire P
Open Trade 8am Public 9.30am–4.30pm
Details 120 stalls

Chiswick Town Hall Art Deco Fair
Contact Jean May
☎ 0121 430 3767 F 0121 436 7912
Location Chiswick Town Hall P
Est. 1988
Open 9.30am–4pm
Entrance fee £1.50
Details 65 stalls, furniture

Cross Country Fairs Ltd
Location Effingham Park, West Sussex
Details See Cross Country Fairs Ltd 2 February

Dualco Promotions
Contact Mr Greenburg
☎ 0161 7662012 F 0161 7662012
Location Leeds United Exhibition Hall, Elland Road, Leeds P
Open 10am–5pm
Details 200 Stalls

Harlequin Fairs
Contact Colin Edwards
☎ 01462 671688 F 01462 641914
Location Centre for Epilepsy, Chalfont Common, Chalfont St Peter, Buckinghamshire
Open Trade 9.30am Public 10am–4.30pm
Details 50+ stalls, 1940 dateline

Ipswich Antiques & Collectables Fair
Location Copdock, Ipswich
Details See Ipswich Antiques & Collectables Fair 2 February

J and K Fairs
Location Lincoln
Details See J and K Fairs 9 February

Lechlade Antiques Fair
Location Lechlade, Gloucestershire
Details See Lechlade Antiques Fair 2 February

Malvern Antiques & Collectors Fair
Location Malvern, Worcestershire
Details See Malvern Antiques & Collectors Fair 2 February

St Crispins Fair
Location Wokingham, Berkshire
Details See St Crispins Fair 2 February

The London Textiles, Vintage Fashion and Accessories Fair
Location London W6
Details See The London Textiles, Vintage Fashion and Accessories Fair 19 January

Wessex Fairs
Location Taunton
Details See Wessex Fairs 2 February

4–5

Ardingly International Antiques & Collectors Fair
Contact Caroline Cleary
☎ 01636 702326 Ⓕ 01636 707923
Ⓦ www.dmgantiquefairs.com
Location South of England Centre, Ardingly, West Sussex Ⓟ
Est. 1997
Open Tues 10am–6pm Wed 8am–4pm
Entrance fee Tues £20 (includes Wed entry) Wed £5
Details Up to 1700 exhibitors

5–8

Bath Annual Decorative & Antiques Fair
Contact Robin Coleman
☎ 01225 851466 Ⓕ 01225 851120
Ⓔ bathdecorativefair@ukonline.co.uk
Ⓦ www.babaada.com
Location The Pavilion, North Parade Road, Bath Ⓟ
Est. 1983
Open Wed Trade only 1–8pm Thurs 1–7pm Fri 11am–7pm Sat 11am–5pm
Entrance fee £2.50 Trade FWC
Details 45 dealers, BABAADA members and invited guests

6

Paraphernalia Fairs
Location Lyndhurst, Hampshire
Details See Paraphernalia Fairs 6 February

6–8

Albany Fairs
Contact Robert Davison
☎ 0191 584 2934
Ⓜ 07976 619009
Ⓔ enquiries@albanyfairs.com
Ⓦ www.albanyfairs.com
Location Town Hall, Moffat, Dumfries & Galloway Ⓟ
Open 10am–4.30pm

6–9

The 34th Cheshire Spring Antiques Fair
☎ 01277 214677 Ⓕ 01277 214550
Ⓔ admin@baileyfairs.co.uk
Ⓦ www.baileyfairs.co.uk
Location Tatton Park, Knutsford Ⓟ
Open Thurs 2–6pm Fri Sat 11am–6pm Sun 11am–5pm
Entrance fee £5
Details 58 dealers, vetted and datelined

7–9

Galloway Antiques Fairs
☎ 01423 522122 Ⓕ 01423 522122
Ⓜ 07966 528725
Ⓔ susan@gallowayfairs.co.uk
Ⓦ www.gallowayfairs.co.uk
Location The Rose Bowl, Southampton, Hampshire Ⓟ
Open 10.30am–5pm
Entrance fee £3.50–£4.50

8

Antique & Collectors Fair
Location Stirling
Details See Antique & Collectors Fair 1 February

8–9

Carmarthen Antiques & Collectors Fair
Contact Carol Pugh
☎ 01267 236569 Ⓕ 01267 220444
Ⓜ 07885 333845
Ⓔ antiques@towy-fairs.co.uk
Ⓦ www.towy-fairs.co.uk
Location United Counties Showground, Carmarthen Ⓟ
Est. 1993
Open 10am–5pm
Entrance fee £3 Accompanied children free
Details 180 dealers

Suffolk Book Markets
Location Long Melford, Suffolk
Details See Suffolk Book Markets 8–9 February

9

Alexandra Palace
Contact Lindy Berkman
☎ 020 88837061 Ⓕ 020 82458361
Ⓦ www.pigandwhistlepromotions.com
Location Wood Green, London N22 Ⓟ
Open Trade 10am Public 11.30am–5pm
Entrance fee Trade £6 Public £4 Children free
Details London's largest antiques fair, over 700 stands plus furniture from 18th–20thC

Antique & Collectors Fair
Location Woking, Surrey
Details See Antique & Collectors Fair 9 February

Antiques & Collectables Fair
Location Dublin
Details See Antiques & Collectables Fair 9 February

Antiques & Collectors Fairs
☎ 01753 685098
Location Oakley Court, Windsor Road, Water Oakley (A308), Windsor, Berkshire Ⓟ
Est. 1974
Open 11am–5pm
Details Approximately 50 stalls, refreshments available

Crispin Fairs
Location Hartley Wintney, Hampshire
Details See Crispin Fairs 9 February

Dualco Promotions
Location Huddersfield
Details See Dualco Promotions 2 February

International Antique Textile Fair Manchester
Contact Walter Bowyer
☎ 020 8523 2399
Location Armitage Centre, Moseley Road, Fallowfield, Manchester P
Open Trade 8am Public 10am–5pm
Entrance fee Public £5 Trade £10
Details 70 stands

London Map Fairs
Location London WC1
Details See London Map Fairs 9 February

Lostwithiel Antiques Fair
Location Lostwithiel, Cornwall
Details See Lostwithiel Antiques Fair 9 February

M & S Collectors Fair
Location Cottenham, Cambridge
Details See M & S Collectors Fair 9 February

Mark Carter Militaria & Medal Fairs
☎ 01753 534777
Location Stratford Leisure & Visitor Centre, Stratford upon Avon, Warwickshire P
Open Preview 9.30am Public 10.30am–3.30pm
Entrance fee £1.50 Preview £3 Accompanied children free
Details 90 tables of quality militaria, books and medals

Midas Antique Fair
Location Beaconsfield, Bucks
Details See Midas Antique Fair 9 February

Midland Clock & Watch Fair
Location National Motorcycle Museum, West Midlands
Details See Midland Clock & Watch Fair 26 January

Pennyfarthing Fayres
Location Potters Bar
Details See Pennyfarthing Fayres 9 February

13

Antiques & Collectables Fair
Location Daventry
Details See Antiques & Collectables Fair 20 February

14–16

Albany Fairs
Location Pooley Bridge, Cumbria
Details See Albany Fairs 15–16 February

Cheshire County Antiques Fair
Contact Anne Harwood
☎ 01249 661111 F 01249 661111
W www.cooperantiquesfairs.co.uk
Location Arley Hall, Nr Knutsford, Cheshire
Open Fri noon–5pm Sat Sun 11am–5pm
Entrance fee £4 Children under 16 free

Stafford Bingley Hall
Location Stafford
Details See Stafford Bingley Hall 7–9 February

14–23

Penmans Chelsea Antiques Fair
Contact Caroline Penman
☎ 01444 482514 F 01444 482412
M 07774 850044
E info@penman-fairs.co.uk
W www.penman-fairs.co.uk
Location Chelsea Old Town Hall, King's Road, London SW3 P
Est. 1950
Open Weekdays 11am–8pm Sat 11am–7pm Sun 11am–5pm
Entrance fee £5
Details Fine traditional antiques from 40 top British exhibitors

15

Blackpool Winter Gardens Collectors Market
Location Blackpool, Lancashire
Details See Blackpool Winter Gardens Collectors Market 15 February

Commonwealth Institute Coin Fair
Location London W8
Details See Commonwealth Institute Coin Fair 18 January

Devon County Antiques Fairs
Location Exeter
Details See Devon County Antiques Fairs 8 February

15–16

2nd Whipsnade Antiques Fair
Contact David Smith
☎ 01933 225674
E david.smith34@ntlworld.com
Location The Cloisters Function Suite, Whipsnade Wild Animal Park, near Dunstable P
Entrance fee £2.50
Details 50 dealers in stand fitted and table top sections

Beckett Antique Fairs
Location Doncaster
Details See Beckett Antique Fairs 15–16 February

16

Antiques & Collectors Fair
Contact Sandra Mather
☎ 01744 750606 F 01744 750606
E sandracca@aol.com
W www.crafts@supanet.com
Location Wilmslow Leisure Centre, Wilmslow, Cheshire P
Open 10am–5pm
Entrance fee £1
Details 75 stalls, refreshments

Bob Evans Fairs
Location Coventry
Details See Bob Evans Fairs 9 February

Dualco Promotions
Location Bolton
Details See Dualco Promotions 26 January

Grand Glass Fair
Contact John Slade
☎ 020 8894 0218
W www.antiquefairs.co.uk
Location Woking Leisure Centre, Kingfield Road, Woking, Surrey P
Open 9.30am–4pm
Entrance fee £2.50
Details 145 stalls

Hatfield Antiques & Collectors Fair
Location Hatfield, Hertfordshire
Details See Hatfield Antiques & Collectors Fair 19 January

Monmouthshire County Antiques & Collectors Fair
Location Abergavenny, Monmouthshire
Details See Monmouthshire County Antiques & Collectors Fair 19 January

V and A Fairs
Location Cheadle, Cheshire
Details See V and A Fairs 2 February

17

13th Annual Antique and Fine Art Fair
☎ 028 9181 5710 Ⓕ 028 9182 0637
Ⓔ info@castleantiques.co.uk
Ⓦ www.castleantiques.co.uk
Location Templeton Hotel, Templepatrick Ⓟ
Open noon–9pm
Entrance fee £2.50 accompanied children free
Details 30 Plus dealers

18

Biggleswade Antiques Fairs
Location Biggleswade, Bedfordshire
Details See Biggleswade Antiques Fairs 19 January

Crispin Fairs
Location Hartley Wintney, Hampshire
Details See Crispin Fairs 18 February

19–25

The BADA Antiques and Fine Art Fair
☎ 020 7589 6108
Ⓦ www.bada-antiques-fair.co.uk
Location The Duke of York's Headquarters, King's Road, London SW3
Est. 1993
Open 13th 11am–9pm 14th 11am–5.30pm 15th 11am–8pm 16th–17th 11am–6pm 18th 11am–8pm 19th 11am-6pm
Entrance fee Single entry £10 Double entry £15. All tickets include a BADA Annual Handbook and one re-entry pass per person
Details Approximately 100 dealers, members of the British Antique Dealers Association, selling art and antiques

21–23

5th International Irish Antiques and Fine Art Fair
Contact Louis O'Sullivan
☎ 00 353 1 285 9294
Location Royal Dublin Society, Ballsbridge, Dublin 4, Ireland Ⓟ
Open 11am–7pm
Entrance fee €7 (£4.46)
Details Fair Datelines: pre-1900: prints, photos; pre-1925: furniture, metalwork, architectural fittings; pre-1930: glass, china, clocks; pre-1940: works of art, silver, etchings, lighting, clocks; pre-1950: jewellery, paintings, drawings

21–23

Shepton Mallet Antiques & Collectors Fair
Location Shepton Mallett Somerset
Details See Shepton Mallet Antiques & Collectors Fair 17–19 January

21–25

Galloway Antiques Fairs
☎ 01423 522122 Ⓕ 01423 522122
Ⓜ 07966 528725
Ⓔ susan@gallowayfairs.co.uk
Ⓦ www.gallowayfairs.co.uk
Location Naworth Castle, Brampton, Cumbria Ⓟ
Open 10.30am–5pm
Entrance fee £3.50–£4.50

22

Pamela Robertson Antique & Collectors Fair
Location Chester
Details See Pamela Robertson Antique & Collectors Fair 25 January

23

Antique & Collectors Fair
Details See Antique & Collectors Fair 16 February

Art Deco Fair with 20thC Decorative Arts
Contact Ann Zierold
☎ 01824 750500 Ⓕ 01824 750490
Location Leeds Royal Armouries Ⓟ
Est. 1997
Open 9.30am–4pm
Entrance fee £2.50
Details 90 stands, no copies or reproductions

Biggleswade Antiques Fairs
Location Kempston, Bedford
Details See Biggleswade Antiques Fairs 26 January

Bloomsbury Postcard & Collectors Fair
Location London WC1
Details See Bloomsbury Postcard and Collectors Fair 23 February

Burford Antiques Fair
Location Burford, Oxfordshire
Details See Burford Antiques Fair 26 January

Bushey Hall School
Location Bushey, Hertfordshire
Details See Bushey Hall 28 January

Buxton Book Fair
Contact Mrs S Laithwaite
☎ 01625 425352
Location Pavilion Garden, Buxton, Derbyshire Ⓟ
Est. 1982
Open 10am–5pm
Entrance fee 80p
Details 45 dealers

Dualco Promotions
Location Halifax
Details See Dualco Promotions 16 February

M & S Antiques & Collectors Fair
Location Royston, Hertfordshire
Details See M & S Antiques & Collectors Fair 26 January

Royal Horticultural Hall
Location London SW1
Details See Royal Horticultural Hall 23 February

Wessex Fairs
Location Weston-super-Mare
Details See Wessex Fairs 23 February

26

The Big Brum
Location Birmingham
Details See The Big Brum 22 January

27

Antique & Collectors Fair
Location Nantwich, Cheshire
Details See Antique & Collectors Fair 30 January

28–30

Wiltshire County Antiques Fair
Contact Anne Harwood
☎ 01249 661111 Ⓕ 01249 661111
Ⓔ enquiries@cooperantiquesfairs.co.uk
Ⓦ www.cooperantiquesfairs.co.uk
Location Marlborough College, Wiltshire
Open Sat Sun 11am–5pm
Entrance fee £4 Children under 16 free

29

Antique & Collectors Fair
Location Ayr
Details See Antique & Collectors Fair 25 January

Antiques & Collectors Fair
Location Poole, Dorset
Details See Antiques & Collectors Fair 22 February

Antiques Fair
Location Hertford, Hertfordshire
Details See Antiques Fair 18 January

Leeds Dolls & Teddy Fair
Contact Liz or David Bonmer
☎ 0191 424 0400 Ⓕ 0191 424 0400
Ⓔ fairs@dollydomain.com
Ⓦ www.dollydomain.com
Location Pudsey Civic Hall, Leeds Ⓟ
Est. 1981
Open 10.30am–4.30pm
Entrance fee £3 children 50p
Details 92 stalls of antique dolls and teddies

Southport Antiques & Collectors Fair
Location Southport, Merseyside
Details See Southport Antiques & Collectors Fair 22 February

29–30

Bob Evans Fairs
Location Norwich
Details See Bob Evans Fairs 25–26 January

The Original Long Melford Fair
Location Long Melford, Suffolk
Details See The Original Long Melford Fair 25–26 January

30

Antique & Collectors Fair
Contact Jocelyn Gibbons
☎ 01280 703454
Location Berkhampsted Sports Centre, Langley Meadow, Douglas Gardens, Berkhampsted, Hertfordshire
Open 10am–4.30pm
Details 130 stalls

Antiques & Collectors Fair
Location King's Lynn
Details See Antiques & Collectors Fair 26 January

Art Nouveau and Art Deco Fair
Contact John Slade
☎ 020 8894 0218
Ⓦ www.antiquefairs.co.uk
Location Woking Leisure Centre, Kingfield Road, Woking, Surrey Ⓟ
Open Trade 8am Public 9am–4pm
Entrance fee £2
Details 200 stalls

Clock & Watch Dealers Fair
Contact Mr Lionel Parker
☎ 01691 831162
Ⓔ fairs@oswatch.fsnet.co.uk
Location Haydock Park racecourse, Jct 23 M6 Ⓟ
Open 9am–3pm
Entrance fee £5 before 10am £2 after
Details 85 stalls offering clocks, watches and jewellery

Dualco Promotions
Location Pudsey
Details See Dualco Promotions 23 February

V and A Fairs
Location Bridgnorth, Shropshire
Details See V and A Fairs 26 January

Wessex Fairs
Contact Mrs Jo Wanford
☎ 01278 789568
Location Combe Lodge, A368, Blagdon, Nr Church Hill, North Somerset Ⓟ
Est. 2001
Open 10am–4.30pm
Entrance fee £1 Trade FWC
Details Stall capacity 40, refreshments available

APRIL

1

Sandown Park Antique & Collectors Fair
Location Sandown Park Racecourse, Esher, Surrey
Details See Sandown Park Antique & Collectors Fair 18 February

2–6

The 9th Claridge's Antiques and Fine Art Fair
☎ 01277 214677 Ⓕ 01277 214550
Ⓔ admin@baileyfairs.co.uk
Ⓦ www.baileyfairs.co.uk
Location Claridge's Hotel, London W1 Ⓟ
Entrance fee £5
Details 50 dealers, vetted and datelined

6

Antique & Collectors Fair
Location Edinburgh
Details See Antique & Collectors Fair 2 February

3

Paraphernalia Fairs
Location Lyndhurst, Hampshire
Details See Paraphernalia Fairs 6 February

3–6

Antiques for Everyone
Contact Philipa Alsop
☎ 0121 767 2596 Ⓕ 0121 767 3535
Ⓔ antiques@necgroup.co.uk
Ⓦ www.antiquesforeveryone.co.uk
Location NEC, Birmingham Ⓟ
Est. 1993

Open Thurs 11am–8pm Fri–Sun 11am–6pm
Entrance fee Thurs £8 Fri–Sun 11am–6pm
Details 650 stands

4–6

The International Antiques & Collectors Fair at RAF Swinderby
Location RAF Swinderby
Details See The International Antiques & Collectors Fair at RAF Swinderby 31 January–2 February

TVADA Spring Fair
Contact Elizabeth Fell
☎ 0208 693 3993
Location The Blue Coat School, Sonning-on-Thames, Berkshire P
Est. 1989
Open Fri Sat 11am–6pm Sun 11am–5pm
Entrance fee £5
Details 40+ stands, fully licensed restaurant

5

Buckingham Antique & Collectors Fair
Location Buckingham
Details See Buckingham Antique & Collectors Fair 1 February

Commonwealth Institute Coin Fair
Location London W8
Details See Commonwealth Institute Coin Fair 18 January

Marcel Fairs
Location London NW7
Details See Marcel Fairs 1 February

5–6

Buxton Antique & Collectors Fair
Location Buxton, Derbyshire
Details See Buxton Antique & Collectors Fair 25–26 January

6

Antique & Collectors Fair
Location Newmarket
Details See Antique & Collectors Fair 2 February

Arun Fairs
Location Rustington, West Sussex
Details See Arun Fairs 2 February

Battersea Town Hall Art Deco Fair
Location Battersea Town Hall
Details See Battersea Town Hall Art Deco Fair 16 February

Best of Fairs
Location Copdock, Ipswich
Details See Best of Fairs 2 February

Cross Country Fairs Ltd
Location Effingham Park, West Sussex
Details See Cross Country Fairs Ltd 2 February

Dualco Promotions
Location Oldham
Details See Dualco Promotions 23 February

Dualco Promotions
Contact Mr Greenburg
☎ 0161 766 2012 F 0161 766 2012
Location Morley Leisure Centre, Leeds, Jct 27 M62, Jct 41 M1 P
Open 10am–5pm
Details 120 stalls

Harlequin Fairs
Location Chalfont St Peter, Buckinghamshire
Details See Harlequin Fairs 2 March

Ipswich Antiques & Collectables Fair
Location Copdock, Ipswich, Suffolk
Details See Ipswich Antiques & Collectables Fair 2 February

Lechlade Antiques Fair
Location Lechlade, Gloucestershire
Details See Lechlade Antiques Fair 2 February

Malvern Antiques & Collectors Fair
Location Malvern, Worcestershire
Details See Malvern Antiques & Collectors Fair 2 February

Mark Carter Militaria & Medal Fairs
Location Aldershot, Hampshire
Details See Mark Carter Militaria & Medal Fairs 19 January

Royal Horticultural Hall
Location London SW1
Details See Royal Horticultural Hall 23 February

St Crispins Fair
Location Wokingham, Berkshire
Details See St Crispins Fair 2 February

V and A Fairs
Location Cheadle, Cheshire
Details See V and A Fairs 2 February

Wessex Fairs
Location Taunton
Details See Wessex Fairs 2 February

7–9

Newark International Antiques & Collectors Fair
Location Newark
Details See Newark International Antiques & Collectors Fair 3–4 February

8–13

The Decorative Antiques and Textiles Fair
Contact Patricia Harvey
☎ 020 76245173 F 020 76258326
E fairs@decorativefair.com
W www.decorativefair.com
Location The Marquee, Battersea Park P
Est. 1985
Open 8th noon–8pm 9th–10th11am–8pm 12th 11am–7pm 13th 11am–7pm
Entrance fee £6 including catalogue
Details 100 dealers exhibiting antiques and textiles in the context of room sets

11–13

Albany Fairs
Location Howtown, Cumbria
Details See Albany Fairs 15–16 February

Galloway Antiques Fairs
☎ 01423 522122 F 01423 522122
M 07966 528725
E susan@gallowayfairs.co.uk

Ⓦ www.gallowayfairs.co.uk
Location Ripley Castle, Ripley, Nr Harrogate, North Yorkshire Ⓟ
Open 10.30am–5pm
Entrance fee £3.50–£4.50

The 7th Harrogate Spring Antiques and Fine Art Fair
☎ 01277 214677 Ⓕ 01277 214550
Ⓔ admin@baileyfairs.co.uk
Ⓦ www.baileyfairs.co.uk
Location Pavilions of Harrogate, Great Yorkshire Showground Ⓟ
Open Thurs 2–6pm Fri Sat 11am–6pm Sun 11am–5pm
Entrance fee £5
Details 80 dealers, vetted and datelined

12

Antique & Collectors Fair
Location Stirling
Details See Antique & Collectors Fair 1 February

Chingford Antiques & Collectors Fair
Location Chingford, London E4
Details See Chingford Antiques & Collectors Fair 25 January

Devon County Antiques Fairs
☎ 01363 82571 Ⓕ 01363 82312
Ⓔ dcaf@antiques-fairs.com
Ⓦ www.antiques-fairs.com
Location Salisbury Leisure Centre, The Butts, Hulse Road, Salisbury Ⓟ
Open 9am–4.30pm
Entrance fee 9–10am £2 10am–4.30pm £1.50
Details 140 stands, snack bar, good disabled access

Victoriana's Fairs
Location Walsall, West Midlands
Details See Victoriana's Fairs 1 February

12–13

Suffolk Book Markets
Location Long Melford, Suffolk
Details See Suffolk Book Markets 8–9 February

West Midlands Antique Fairs
Location Stafford
Details See West Midlands Antique Fairs 22–23 February

13

Antique & Collectors Fair
Location Woking, Surrey
Details See Antique & Collectors Fair 9 February

Art Deco Fair with 20thC Decorative Arts
Location Chester Racecourse
Details See Art Deco Fair with 20thC Decorative Arts 26 January

Arun Fairs
Contact Stephanie Clark
☎ 01903 734112
Ⓔ cstephiemoo@aol.com
Location Arun Leisure Centre, Felpham Way, Bognor, West Sussex, on the A259 Ⓟ
Open Trade 9am Public 10am–4pm
Entrance fee £1
Details 100 stalls

Biggleswade Antiques Fairs
Location Huntingdon, Cambridgeshire, off A14
Details See Biggleswade Antiques Fairs 9 February

Bob Evans Fairs
☎ 01664 812627 Ⓕ 01664 813727
Location Hereford Leisure Centre, Holmer Road Ⓟ
Est. 1998
Open Trade 8am Public 9.30am–4.30pm
Details 200 stalls

Brunel Clock & Watch Fair
Location Uxbridge, Middlesex
Details See Brunel Clock & Watch Fair 16 February

Crispin Fairs
Location Hartley Wintney, Hampshire
Details See Crispin Fairs 9 February

Dualco Promotions
Location Barnsley
Details See Dualco Promotions 9 February

J and K Fairs
Location Lincoln
Details See J and K Fairs 9 February

London Map Fairs
Location London WC1
Details See London Map Fairs 9 February

Lostwithiel Antiques Fair
Location Lostwithiel, Cornwall
Details See Lostwithiel Antiques Fair 9 February

M & S Collectors Fair
Location Cottenham, Cambridge
Details See M & S Collectors Fair 9 February

Midas Antique Fair
Location Beaconsfield, Bucks
Details See Midas Antique Fair 9 February

Pennyfarthing Fayres
Location Potters Bar
Details See Pennyfarthing Fayres 9 February

The London Textiles, Vintage Fashion and Accessories Fair
Location London W6
Details See The London Textiles, Vintage Fashion and Accessories Fair 19 January

14–15

Little Chelsea Antiques Fair
Contact Carol Pugh
☎ 01267 236569 Ⓕ 01267 220444
Ⓜ 07885 333845
Ⓔ antiques@towy-fairs.co.uk
Ⓦ www.towy-fairs.co.uk
Location Chelsea Old Town Hall, King's Road, London SW3 Ⓟ
Open 10am–5pm
Entrance fee £3 Accompanied children free Trade FWC
Details Vetted and datelined quality fair

15

Crispin Fairs
Location Hartley Wintney, Hampshire
Details See Crispin Fairs 18 February

17

Antiques & Collectables Fair
Location Daventry

Details See Antiques & Collectables Fair 20 February

18

Antique & Collectors Fair

Location Woking, Surrey
Details See Antique & Collectors Fair 9 February

18–20

South Cotswolds Antiques Fair

Contact Anne Harwood
☎ 01249 661111 Ⓕ 01249 661111
Ⓔ enquiries@cooperantiquesfairs.co.uk
Ⓦ www.cooperantiquesfairs.co.uk
Location Westonbirt School, Nr Tetbury, Gloucestershire
Open Fri noon–5pm Sat Sun 11am–5pm
Entrance fee £4 Children under 16 free

18–21

Galloway Antiques Fairs

☎ 01423 522122 Ⓕ 01423 522122
Ⓜ 07966 528725
Ⓔ susan@gallowayfairs.co.uk
Ⓦ www.gallowayfairs.co.uk
Location Cranleigh School, Cranleigh, Surrey Ⓟ
Open 10.30am–5pm
Entrance fee £3.50–£4.50

19

Blackpool Winter Gardens Collectors Market

Location Blackpool, Lancashire
Details See Blackpool Winter Gardens Collectors Market 15 February

19–20

Devon County Antiques Fairs

Location Clyst St Mary, Exeter
Details See Devon County Antiques Fair 1–2 March

19–21

Beckett Antique Fairs

Location Doncaster
Details See Beckett Antique Fairs 15–16 February

The 3rd North Norfolk Fine Art and Antiques Fair

Contact Liz Allport
☎ 01603 737631 Ⓕ 01603 737631
Ⓜ 07747 843074
Ⓔ liz.allport@lineone.net
Ⓦ www.lomaxantiquesfairs.co.uk
Location Sussex Barn, Nr Burnham Market, Norfolk Ⓟ
Open 19th 11am–6pm 20th 10.30am–6pm 21st 10.30am–5pm

The Original Long Melford Fair

Location Long Melford, Suffolk
Details See The Original Long Melford Fair 25–26 January

20

Biggleswade Antiques Fairs

Location Biggleswade, Bedfordshire
Details See Biggleswade Antiques Fairs 19 January

Monmouthshire County Antiques & Collectors Fair

Location Abergavenny, Monmouthshire
Details See Monmouthshire County Antiques & Collectors Fair 19 January

Twickenham Rugby Ground Art Deco Fair

Location Twickenham Rugby Ground
Details See Twickenham Rugby Ground Art Deco Fair 2 February

20–21

Albany Fairs

Location Moffat, Dumfries & Galloway
Details See Albany Fairs 6–8 March

Antiques & Collectables Fair

Location Stockbridge, Hampshire
Details See Antiques & Collectables Fair 22–23 February

Antiques & Collectors Fair

Location St Ives, Cambridgeshire
Details See Antiques & Collectors Fair 22–23 February

Wessex Fairs

Location Weston-super-Mare
Details See Wessex Fairs 23 February

21

14th Annual Easter Antique and Fine Art Fair

☎ 028 9181 5710 Ⓕ 028 9182 0637
Ⓔ info@castleantiques.co.uk
Ⓦ www.castleantiques.co.uk
Location The Bohill Hotel & Country Club, Coleraine Ⓟ
Open 11am–7pm
Entrance fee £2.50 accompanied children free
Details 40 Plus dealers

Antique Collectors Jamboree

Contact Stancie Kutler
☎ 01270 624288
Location Nantwich Civic Hall, Market Street, Nantwich, Cheshire, Jct 16 M6 Ⓟ
Est. 1974
Open Trade 8am Public 10am–5pm
Details Refreshments, up to 75 stalls

Antiques & Collectables Fair

Location Dun Laoghaire, Co Dublin
Details See Antiques & Collectables Fair 26 January

Antiques & Collectors Fair

Location Wilmslow, Cheshire
Details See Antiques & Collectors Fair 16 March

Bob Evans Fairs

Location Kettering
Details See Bob Evans Fairs 16 February

Brunel Antiques & Collectors Fair

Contact Caroline Cleary
☎ 01636 702326 Ⓕ 01636 707923
Ⓦ www.dmgantiquefairs.com
Location Brunel University, Uxbridge, Middlesex Ⓟ
Est. 1997
Open 8am–4pm
Entrance fee 8am £5 10am £3.50
Details Up to 200 exhibitors

Buckhurst Hill Antiques & Collectors Fair
Contact Richard Millar
☎ 01279 871110 Ⓕ 01279 871917
Location St John's Centenary Hall, High Road, Buckhurst Hill, Essex Ⓟ
Open Trade with card 9.30am Public 10.30am–4.30pm
Entrance fee Adults 90p Concessions 70p Children 16 and under free Trade FWC
Details Up to 40 stalls

Dualco Promotions
Location Halifax
Details See Dualco Promotions 16 February

Pamela Robertson Antique & Collectors Fair
Location Chester
Details See Pamela Robertson Antique & Collectors Fair 25 January

23

Evening Antiques/Collectors Fairs
Contact Carol Baskin
☎ 01782 595805 Ⓕ 01782 596133
Ⓔ info@antiqueforumgroup.com
Ⓦ www.antiqueforumgroup.com
Location St Martins Market (The Rag), Edgbaston Street, Birmingham Ⓟ
Open 4–8pm
Entrance fee Free
Details 300 stalls only inside

24

Antique & Collectors Fair
Location Nantwich, Cheshire
Details See Antique & Collectors Fair 30 January

26

Antique & Collectors Fair
Location Ayr
Details See Antique & Collectors Fair 25 January

Antiques & Collectors Fair
Location Poole, Dorset
Details See Antiques & Collectors Fair 22 February

Antiques Fair
Location Hertford, Hertfordshire
Details See Antiques Fair 18 January

Southport Antiques & Collectors Fair
Location Southport, Merseyside
Details See Southport Antiques & Collectors Fair 22 February

26–27

Antiques & Collectables Fair
☎ 01327 876540
Ⓜ 07711 248951
Location Warwick Racecourse, Warwick Ⓟ
Est. 1998
Open 7am–2pm
Entrance fee £2
Details 200 stands

Cardiff Antiques & Collectors' Fair
Contact Carol Pugh
☎ 01267 236569 Ⓕ 01267 220444
Ⓜ 07885 333845
Ⓔ antiques@towy-fairs.co.uk
Ⓦ www.towy-fairs.co.uk
Location Cardiff Bowls Club, Sophia Gardens Ⓟ
Est. 2001
Open 10am–5pm
Entrance fee £3 Accompanied children free
Details 120 stands

Detling International Antiques & Collectors Fair
Location Detling, Nr Maidstone, Kent
Details See Detling International Antiques & Collectors Fair 25–26 January

The 70th London Arms Fair
Contact Adam Slough
☎ 01981 550145
Ⓦ www.antiquearmsfairsltd.co.uk
Location The Thistle London Heathrow, Bath Road, Longford, West Drayton Ⓟ
Est. 1968
Open Sat 9am Connoisseurs morning for pre-booked collectors and trade. Public noon–6pm Sun 9am–4pm
Entrance fee £15 Sat Sun pre-booked £7 per day
Details Antique arms, armour and militaria, 120 tables

27

Antiques & Collectors Fair
Location King's Lynn
Details See Antiques & Collectors Fair 26 January

Bloomsbury Postcard & Collectors Fair
Location London WC1
Details See Bloomsbury Postcard and Collectors Fair 23 February

Burford Antiques Fair
Location Burford, Oxfordshire
Details See Burford Antiques Fair 26 January

Bushey Hall School
Location Bushey, Hertfordshire
Details See Bushey Hall 28 January

Buxton Book Fair
Location Buxton, Derbyshire
Details See Buxton Book Fair 16 Feb

Chipping Norton Toy Fairs
Location Chipping Norton, Oxfordshire
Details See Chipping Norton Toy Fairs 23 February

Dualco Promotions
Location Bolton
Details See Dualco Promotions 16 February

Galway Antique Fair
Contact Ms Gretta Boland
☎ 091 564938
Location Galway Bay Hotel, Salthill, Co Galway Ⓟ
Est. 1993
Open Trade 10am Public 11am–7pm
Entrance fee €3 (£1.90) trade FWC
Details 45 stands, no reproductions, refreshments from bar and restaurant

M & S Antiques & Collectors Fair
Location Royston, Hertfordshire
Details See M & S Antiques & Collectors Fair 26 January

Mark Carter Militaria & Medal Fairs
Location Yate, Bristol
Details See Mark Carter Militaria & Medal Fairs 2 February

V and A Fairs
Location Whitchurch, Shropshire
Details See V and A Fairs 16 February

28–30

Albany Fairs
Location Pooley Bridge, Cumbria
Details See Albany Fairs 15–16 February

29–30

Ardingly International Antiques & Collectors Fair
Location Ardingly, West Sussex
Details See Ardingly International Antiques & Collectors Fair 4–5 March

MAY

1–5

The Harrogate Antique & Fine Art Fair
Contact Louise Walker
☎ 01823 323363 Ⓕ 01823 271072
Ⓦ www.harrogateantiquefair.com
Location Hall A and B, Harrogate International Centre, Ripon Road, Harrogate, North Yorkshire Ⓟ
Open Thurs Fri 11am–8pm Sat Sun 11am–6pm
Entrance fee £6 including catalogue
Details High quality antiques and fine art

2–5

Galloway Antiques Fairs
☎ 01423 522122 Ⓕ 01423 522122
Ⓜ 07966 528725
Ⓔ susan@gallowayfairs.co.uk
Ⓦ www.gallowayfairs.co.uk
Location The East Grinstead Country Club, East Grinstead, West Sussex Ⓟ
Open 10.30am–5pm
Entrance fee £3.50–£4.50

3

Antique & Collectors Fair
Location Stirling
Details See Antique & Collectors Fair 1 February

Buckingham Antique & Collectors Fair
Location Buckingham
Details See Buckingham Antique & Collectors Fair 1 February

Devon County Antiques Fairs
Location Exeter
Details See Devon County Antiques Fairs 8 February

Marcel Fairs
Location London NW7
Details See Marcel Fairs 1 February

Victoriana's Fairs
Location Walsall, West Midlands
Details See Victoriana's Fairs 1 February

The Original Long Melford Fair
Location Long Melford, Suffolk
Details See The Original Long Melford Fair 25–26 January

West Midlands Antique Fairs
Location Stafford
Details See West Midlands Antique Fairs 22–23 February

4

Antique & Collectors Fair
Location Newmarket
Details See Antique & Collectors Fair 2 February

Antique & Collectors Fair
Location Edinburgh
Details See Antique & Collectors Fair 2 February

Arun Fairs
Location Rustington, West Sussex
Details See Arun Fairs 2 February

Best of Fairs
Location Copdock, Ipswich
Details See Best of Fairs 2 February

Clock & Watch Dealers Fair
Location Haydock Park Racecourse
Details See Clock & Watch Dealers Fair 30 March

Cross Country Fairs Ltd
Location Effingham Park, West Sussex
Details See Cross Country Fairs Ltd 2 February

Harlequin Fairs
Location Chalfont St Peter, Buckinghamshire
Details See Harlequin Fairs 2 March

Ipswich Antiques & Collectables Fair
Location Copdock, Ipswich
Details See Ipswich Antiques & Collectables Fair 2 February

Lechlade Antiques Fair
Location Lechlade, Gloucestershire
Details See Lechlade Antiques Fair 2 February

Malvern Antiques & Collectors Fair
Location Malvern, Worcestershire
Details See Malvern Antiques & Collectors Fair 2 February

St Crispins Fair
Location Wokingham, Berkshire
Details See St Crispins Fair 2 February

The National Art Deco Fair
Contact Sylvia Weedon
☎ 0115 941 9143 Ⓕ 0115 877 4185
Location Town Hall, Market Place, Loughborough, Leicestershire Ⓟ
Open Trade 8am Public 10am–4pm
Entrance fee £2.50

V and A Fairs
Location Cheadle, Cheshire
Details See V and A Fairs 2 February

Wessex Fairs
Location Taunton
Details See Wessex Fairs 2 February

4–5

Albany Fairs
Location Moffat, Dumfries & Galloway
Details See Albany Fairs 6–8 March

5

9th Annual Charity Antique and Fine Art Fair
☎ 028 9181 5710 Ⓕ 028 9182 0637
Ⓔ info@castleantiques.co.uk
Ⓦ www.castleantiques.co.uk
Location Queen's Hall, Newtownards Ⓟ
Open 11am–5pm
Entrance fee £2 accompanied children free
Details 30 plus dealers

Antique Collectors Jamboree
Location Nantwich, Cheshire
Details See Antique Collectors Jamboree 21 April

Antiques & Collectables Fair
Location Dublin
Details See Antiques Fairs Ireland 23 February

Bob Evans Fairs
Location Peterborough
Details See Bob Evans Fairs 23 February

Buckhurst Hill Antiques & Collectors Fair
Location Buckhurst Hill, Essex
Details See Antiques & Collectors Fair 21 April

Dualco Promotions
Location Oldham
Details See Dualco Promotions 23 February

J and K Fairs
Location Lincoln
Details See J and K Fairs 9 February

Pamela Robertson Antique & Collectors Fair
Location Chester
Details See Pamela Robertson Antique & Collectors Fair 25 January

7

The Big Brum
Location Birmingham
Details See The Big Brum 22 January

8

Paraphernalia Fairs
Location Lyndhurst, Hampshire
Details See Paraphernalia Fairs 6 February

9–11

Albany Fairs
Location Howtown, Cumbria
Details See Albany Fairs 15–16 February

Shepton Mallet Antiques & Collectors Fair
Location Shepton Mallet, Somerset
Details See Shepton Mallet Antiques & Collectors Fair 17–19 January

The Period Living & Traditional Homes Show
Contact Kate Legg
☎ 020 7970 6543
Ⓔ kate.legg@centaur.co.uk
Location Business Design Centre, Upper Street, Islington, London N1 0QH
Open Fri Sat 10am–5pm Sun 10am–3.30pm
Details 130 diverse companies specializing in period and classic interiors and exteriors

10

Blackpool Winter Gardens Collectors Market
Location Blackpool, Lancashire
Details See Blackpool Winter Gardens Collectors Market 15 February

Chingford Antiques & Collectors Fair
Location Chingford, London E4
Details See Chingford Antiques & Collectors Fair 25 January

10–11

Suffolk Book Markets
Location Long Melford, Suffolk
Details See Suffolk Book Markets 8–9 February

11

Alexandra Palace
Location Wood Green, London
Details See Alexandra Palace 9 March

Antique & Collectors Fair
Location Woking, Surrey
Details See Antique & Collectors Fair 9 February

Antiques & Collectables Fair
Location Dublin
Details See Antiques & Collectables Fair 9 February

Antiques & Collectors Fairs
Location Egham, Surrey
Details See Antiques & Collectors Fair 9 February

Crispin Fairs
Location Hartley Wintney, Hampshire
Details See Crispin Fairs 9 February

Dualco Promotions
Location Barnsley
Details See Dualco Promotions 9 February

Dublin Toy and Train Fair
Location Dun Laoghaire, Co Dublin

Details See Dublin Toy and Train Fair 16 February

London Map Fairs
Location London WC1
Details See London Map Fairs 9 February

Lostwithiel Antiques Fair
Location Lostwithiel, Cornwall
Details See Lostwithiel Antiques Fair 9 February

M & S Collectors Fair
Location Cottenham, Cambridge
Details See M & S Collectors Fair 9 February

Midas Antique Fair
Location Beaconsfield, Bucks
Details See Midas Antique Fair 9 February

Pennyfarthing Fayres
Location Potters Bar
Details See Pennyfarthing Fayres 9 February

The Original National Glass Collectors Fair
Contact Patricia Hier
☎ 01260 271975 Ⓕ 01260 271975
Ⓔ dil.hier@talk21.com
Location National Motorcycle Museum, Junction 6 M42, Midlands P
Est. 1991
Open 9.30am–3.30pm
Details Over 100 dealers offering glass throughout the ages, including Ancient, 18thC drinking glasses, Victorian, pressed, Art Nouveau, Art Deco, paperweights, 1950s,1960s, 1970s, modern, studio

14–18

39th Buxton Antiques Fair
Contact Trudy Williams
☎ 01822 614671
Ⓦ www.buxtonantiquesfair.co.uk
Location Pavilion Gardens, Buxton, Derbyshire P
Est. 1965
Open Wed Thurs 11am–9pm Fri Sat 11am–7pm Sun 11am–5pm
Details Annual vetted and datelined fair

15

Antiques & Collectables Fair
Location Daventry
Details See Antiques & Collectables Fair 20 February

16–18

Albany Fairs
Location Pooley Bridge, Cumbria
Details See Albany Fairs 15–16 February

Galloway Antiques Fairs
☎ 01423 522122 Ⓕ 01423 522122
Ⓜ 07966 528725
Ⓔ susan@gallowayfairs.co.uk
Ⓦ www.gallowayfairs.co.uk
Location Brandling House, Gosforth Park, Newcastle P
Open 10.30am–5pm
Entrance fee £3.50–£4.50

17–18

Carmarthen Antiques & Collectors Fair
Location Carmarthen
Details See Carmarthen Antiques & Collectors Fair 8–9 March

18

Antique & Collectors Fair
Location Glasgow
Details See Antique & Collectors Fair 16 February

Antiques & Collectors Fair
Location King's Lynn
Details See Antiques & Collectors Fair 26 January

Biggleswade Antiques Fairs
Location Biggleswade, Bedfordshire
Details See Biggleswade Antiques Fairs 19 January

Dualco Promotions
Location Halifax
Details See Dualco Promotions 16 February

Hatfield Antiques & Collectors Fair
Location Hatfield, Hertfordshire
Details See Hatfield Antiques & Collectors Fair 19 January

Midland Clock & Watch Fair
Location National Motorcycle Museum, West Midlands
Details See Midland Clock & Watch Fair 26 January

Monmouthshire County Antiques & Collectors Fair
Location Abergavenny, Monmouthshire
Details See Monmouthshire County Antiques & Collectors Fair 19 January

Newmarket Antiques & Collectors Fair
Location Newmarket, Suffolk
Details See Newmarket Antiques & Collectors Fair 23 February

Royal Horticultural Hall
Location London SW1
Details See Royal Horticultural Hall 23 February

Wessex Fairs
Location Blagdon, North Somerset
Details See Wessex Fairs 30 March

20

Crispin Fairs
Location Hartley Wintney, Hampshire
Details See Crispin Fairs 18 February

24

Chelsea Brocante
☎ 020 7254 4054
Location Chelsea, London SW3
Details See Chelsea Brocante 8 February

Commonwealth Institute Coin Fair
Location London W8
Details See Commonwealth Institute Coin Fair 18 January

Southport Antiques & Collectors Fair
Location Southport, Merseyside
Details See Southport Antiques & Collectors Fair 22 February

FAIRS

MAY

24–26

The 11th Langley Park Spring Antiques Fair
Contact Liz Allport
☎ 01603 737631 Ⓕ 01603 737631
Ⓜ 07747 843074
Ⓔ liz.allport@lineone.net
Ⓦ www.lomaxantiquesfairs.co.uk
Location Langley Park School, Loddon, Norfolk Ⓟ
Open 24th 2–7pm
25th 10.30am–6pm
26th 10.30am–5pm

The Original Long Melford Fair
Location Long Melford, Suffolk
Details See The Original Long Melford Fair 25–26 January

25

Art Deco Fair
Location Warwick
Details See Art Deco Fair 23 February

Bloomsbury Postcard & Collectors Fair
Location London WC1
Details See Bloomsbury Postcard and Collectors Fair 23 February

Burford Antiques Fair
Location Burford, Oxfordshire
Details See Burford Antiques Fair 26 January

Bushey Hall School
Location Bushey, Hertfordshire
Details See Bushey Hall 28 January

Dualco Promotions
Location Pudsey
Details See Dualco Promotions 23 February

M & S Antiques & Collectors Fair
Location Royston, Hertfordshire
Details See M & S Antiques & Collectors Fair 26 January

Mark Carter Militaria & Medal Fairs
Location Stratford upon Avon, Warwickshire
Details See Mark Carter Militaria & Medal Fairs 9 March

The National Vintage Tackle Fair
Contact Bob Turner
☎ 01934 416492
Location Abbey Sports Stadium, Birmingham Road, Redditch, Worcestershire Ⓟ
Est. 1999
Open 10am–4pm
Entrance fee £1
Details 50 stalls

25–26

Albany Fairs
Location Moffat, Dumfries & Galloway
Details See Albany Fairs 6–8 March

Antiques & Collectables Fair
Location Stockbridge, Hampshire
Details See Antiques & Collectables Fair 22–23 February

Antiques & Collectors Fair
Location St Ives, Cambridgeshire
Details See Antiques & Collectors Fair 22–23 February

Beckett Antique Fairs
Location Doncaster
Details See Beckett Antique Fairs 15–16 February

Buxton Book Fair
Location Buxton, Derbyshire
Details See Buxton Book Fair 23 Mar

Wessex Fairs
Location Weston-super-Mare
Details See Wessex Fairs 23 February

26

Antique Collectors Jamboree
Location Nantwich, Cheshire
Details See Antique Collectors Jamboree 21 April

Antiques & Collectors Fair
Location Wilmslow, Cheshire
Details See Antiques & Collectors Fair 16 March

Bob Evans Fairs
Location Coventry
Details See Bob Evans Fairs 9 February

Brunel Antiques & Collectors Fair
Location Uxbridge, Middlesex
Details See Brunel Antiques & Collectors Fair 21 April

Buckhurst Hill Antiques & Collectors Fair
Location Buckhurst Hill, Essex
Details See Antiques & Collectors Fair 21 April

J and K Fairs
Location Lincoln
Details See J and K Fairs 9 February

29

Antique & Collectors Fair
Location Nantwich, Cheshire
Details See Antique & Collectors Fair 30 January

30–1 JUNE

The International Antiques & Collectors Fair at RAF Swinderby
Location RAF Swinderby
Details See The International Antiques & Collectors Fair at RAF Swinderby 31 January–2 February

31

Antique & Collectors Fair
Location Ayr
Details See Antique & Collectors Fair 25 January

Antiques & Collectors Fair
Location Poole, Dorset
Details See Antiques & Collectors Fair 22 February

Antiques Fair
Location Hertford, Hertfordshire
Details See Antiques Fair 18 January

V and A Fairs
Location Bridgnorth, Shropshire
Details See V and A Fairs 26 January

31–1 JUNE

Gawsworth Antiques Fair
Contact Sandra Mather
☎ 01744 750606 Ⓕ 01744 750606
Ⓜ 07966 499748

Ⓔ sandracca@aol.com
Ⓦ www.crafts@supanet.com
Location Gawsworth Hall, Macclesfield, off A536, Cheshire Ⓟ
Open 10am–5pm
Entrance fee £1.50
Details 75–85 stalls, refreshments

JUNE

1

Antique & Collectors Fair
Location Newmarket
Details See Antique & Collectors Fair 2 February

Antique & Collectors Fair
Location Edinburgh
Details See Antique & Collectors Fair 2 February

Arun Fairs
Location Rustington, West Sussex
Details See Arun Fairs 2 February

Best of Fairs
Location Copdock, Ipswich
Details See Best of Fairs 2 February

Clock & Watch Dealers Fair
Location Balderton, Nr Newark
Details See Clock & Watch Dealers Fair 2 February

Cross Country Fairs Ltd
Location Effingham Park, West Sussex
Details See Cross Country Fairs Ltd 2 February

Dualco Promotions
Location Huddersfield
Details See Dualco Promotions 2 February

Harlequin Fairs
Location Chalfont St Peter, Buckinghamshire
Details See Harlequin Fairs 2 March

Ipswich Antiques & Collectables Fair
Location Copdock, Ipswich
Details See Ipswich Antiques & Collectables Fair 2 February

Lechlade Antiques Fair
Location Lechlade, Gloucestershire
Details See Lechlade Antiques Fair 2 February

Malvern Antiques & Collectors Fair
Location Malvern, Worcestershire
Details See Malvern Antiques & Collectors Fair 2 February

St Crispins Fair
Location Wokingham, Berkshire
Details See St Crispins Fair 2 February

The London Textiles, Vintage Fashion and Accessories Fair
Location London W6
Details See The London Textiles, Vintage Fashion and Accessories Fair 19 January

V and A Fairs
Location Cheadle, Cheshire
Details See V and A Fairs 2 February

2

Antiques & Collectables Fair
Location Dun Laoghaire, Co Dublin
Details See Antiques & Collectables Fair 26 January

2–3

Newark International Antiques & Collectors Fair
Location Newark
Details See Newark International Antiques & Collectors Fair 3–4 February

5

Paraphernalia Fairs
Location Lyndhurst, Hampshire
Details See Paraphernalia Fairs 6 February

5–15

The Olympia Fine Art and Antiques Fair
☎ 020 7370 8186/8212 Ⓕ 020 7370 8221
Ⓔ olympia-antiques@eco.co.uk
Ⓦ www.olympia-antiques.com
Location Olympia, London Ⓟ
Est. 1971
Open 5th 11am–6pm 6th 11am–8pm 7th–8th 11am–7pm 9th closed 10th–14th 11am–8pm 14th 11am–7pm 15th 11am–5pm
Entrance fee £10 single £16 double reduced to £8 £14 if booked in advance
Details 400 exhibitors, offering wide range of antiques and works of art, all items examined by experts

5–7

Albany Fairs
Location Moffat, Dumfries & Galloway
Details See Albany Fairs 6–8 March

7

Antique & Collectors Fair
Location Stirling
Details See Antique & Collectors Fair 1 February

Antiques & Collectables Fair
Location Marlborough, Wiltshire
Details See Antiques & Collectables Fair 1 March

Buckingham Antique & Collectors Fair
Location Buckingham
Details See Buckingham Antique & Collectors Fair 1 February

Devon County Antiques Fairs
Location Exeter
Details See Devon County Antiques Fairs 8 February

London Coin Fair
Location London WC1
Details See London Coin Fair 8 February

London Map Fairs
Location London WC1
Open 9.30am–5pm
Details See London Map Fairs 9 February

Victoriana's Fairs
Location Walsall, West Midlands
Details See Victoriana's Fairs 1 February

7–8

Antiques & Collectables Fair
Location Warwick
Details See Antiques & Collectables Fair 26–27 April

8

Antique & Collectors Fair
Location Woking, Surrey
Details See Antique & Collectors Fair 9 February

Crispin Fairs
Location Hartley Wintney, Hampshire
Details See Crispin Fairs 9 February

Dualco Promotions
Location Oldham
Details See Dualco Promotions 23 February

Lostwithiel Antiques Fair
Location Lostwithiel, Cornwall
Details See Lostwithiel Antiques Fair 9 February

M & S Collectors Fair
Location Cottenham, Cambridge
Details See M & S Collectors Fair 9 February

Midas Antique Fair
Location Beaconsfield, Bucks
Details See Midas Antique Fair 9 February

Pennyfarthing Fayres
Location Potters Bar
Details See Pennyfarthing Fayres 9 February

Royal Horticultural Hall
Location London SW1
Details See Royal Horticultural Hall 23 February

11

The Big Brum
Location Birmingham
Details See The Big Brum 22 January

11–17

The Grosvenor House Art & Antiques Fair
Contact Nicola Winwood
☎ 020 7495 8743
Ⓕ 020 7495 8747
Ⓔ info@grosvenor-antiquesfair.co.uk
Ⓦ www.grosvenor-antiquesfair.co.uk
Location Le Méridien Grosvenor House, Park Lane, London W1K 7TN Ⓟ
Est. 1934
Open 11th 13th 11am–8pm 12th 14th–17th 11am–6pm
Entrance fee Single £16 Double £27
Details 90 of the world's leading art and antique dealers

13

The National Art Deco Fair
Location Loughborough, Leicestershire
Details See National Art Deco Fair 4 May

13–15

Galloway Antiques Fairs
☎ 01423 522122
Ⓕ 01423 522122
Ⓜ 07966 528725
Ⓔ susan@gallowayfairs.co.uk
Ⓦ www.gallowayfairs.co.uk
Location Duncombe Park, Helmsley, North Yorkshire Ⓟ
Open 10.30am–5pm
Entrance fee £3.50–£4.50

Stafford Bingley Hall
Location Stafford
Details See Stafford Bingley Hall 7–9 February

13–16

International Ceramics Fair & Seminar
Contact Tara Heffler
☎ 020 7734 5491
Ⓕ 020 7494 4604
Ⓔ d.stratton@haughton.com
Ⓦ www.haughton.com
Location Park Lane Hotel Ballroom, Piccadilly, London W1 Ⓟ
Est. 1982
Open 11am–7pm
Entrance fee £10
Details 40 exhibitors offering a broad range of European and Asian antique ceramics and glass, as well as 20thC studio ceramics and glass

14–15

Buxton Antique & Collectors Fair
Location Buxton, Derbyshire
Details See Buxton Antique & Collectors Fair 25–26 January

Suffolk Book Markets
Location Long Melford, Suffolk
Details See Suffolk Book Markets 8–9 February

15

Antique & Collectors Fair
Location Glasgow
Details See Antique & Collectors Fair 16 February

Antiques & Collectables Fair
Location Dublin 2
Details See Antiques & Collectables Fair 9 February

Battersea Town Hall Art Deco Fair
Location Battersea Town Hall
Details See Battersea Town Hall Art Deco Fair 16 February

Biggleswade Antiques Fairs
Location Biggleswade, Bedfordshire
Details See Biggleswade Antiques Fairs 19 January

Dualco Promotions
Location Morley
Details See Dualco Promotions 6 April

Monmouthshire County Antiques & Collectors Fair
Location Abergavenny, Monmouthshire
Details See Monmouthshire County Antiques & Collectors Fair 19 January

Newmarket Antiques & Collectors Fair
Location Newmarket, Suffolk
Details See Newmarket Antiques & Collectors Fair 23 February

17

Crispin Fairs
Location Hartley Wintney, Hampshire

Details See Crispin Fairs 18 February

Marcel Fairs
Location London NW7
Details See Marcel Fairs 1 February

19

Antiques & Collectables Fair
Location Daventry
Details See Antiques & Collectables Fair 20 February

19–20

Buxton Antique & Collectors Fair
Location Buxton, Derbyshire
Details See Buxton Antique & Collectors Fair 25–26 January

20–22

Albany Fairs
Location Pooley Bridge, Cumbria
Details See Albany Fairs 15–16 February

Cheshire County Antiques Fair
Location Knutsford, Cheshire
Details See Cheshire County Antiques Fair 14–16 March

Shepton Mallet Antiques & Collectors Fair
Location Shepton Mallet, Somerset
Details See Shepton Mallet Antiques & Collectors Fair 17–19 January

21

Antique & Collectors Fair
Location Ayr
Details See Antique & Collectors Fair 25 January

Antiques Fair
Location Hertford, Hertfordshire
Details See Antiques Fair 18 January

Commonwealth Institute Coin Fair
Location London W8
Details See Commonwealth Institute Coin Fair 18 January

21–22

Antiques & Collectables Fair
Location Stockbridge, Hampshire
Details See Antiques & Collectables Fair 22–23 February

22

Biggleswade Antiques Fairs
Location Kempston, Bedford
Details See Biggleswade Antiques Fairs 26 January

Bloomsbury Postcard & Collectors Fair
Location London WC1
Details See Bloomsbury Postcard and Collectors Fair 23 February

Brunel Clock & Watch Fair
Location Uxbridge, Middlesex
Details See Brunel Clock & Watch Fair 16 February

Burford Antiques Fair
Location Burford, Oxfordshire
Details See Burford Antiques Fair 26 January

Bushey Hall School
Location Bushey, Hertfordshire
Details See Bushey Hall 28 January

Mark Carter Militaria & Medal Fairs
Location Aldershot, Hampshire
Details See Mark Carter Militaria & Medal Fairs 19 January

V and A Fairs
Location Whitchurch, Shropshire
Details See V and A Fairs 16 February

Wessex Fairs
Location Blagdon, North Somerset
Details See Wessex Fairs 30 March

26

Antique & Collectors Fair
Location Nantwich, Cheshire
Details See Antique & Collectors Fair 30 January

27–28

Albany Fairs
Location Moffat, Dumfries & Galloway
Details See Albany Fairs 6–8 March

27–29

Galloway Antiques Fairs
☎ 01423 522122 Ⓕ 01423 522122
Ⓜ 07966 528725
Ⓔ susan@gallowayfairs.co.uk
Ⓦ www.gallowayfairs.co.uk
Location Blair Castle, Blair Atholl, Pitlochry, Perthshire P
Open 10.30am–5pm
Entrance fee £3.50–£4.50

28

Antiques & Collectors Fair
Location Poole, Dorset
Details See Antiques & Collectors Fair 22 February

Blackpool Winter Gardens Collectors Market
Location Blackpool, Lancashire
Details See Blackpool Winter Gardens Collectors Market 15 February

Pamela Robertson Antique & Collectors Fair
Location Chester
Details See Pamela Robertson Antique & Collectors Fair 25 January

28–29

The Original Long Melford Fair
Location Long Melford, Suffolk
Details See The Original Long Melford Fair 25–26 January

West Midlands Antique Fairs
Location Stafford
Details See West Midlands Antique Fairs 22–23 February

29

Antique & Collectors Fair
Location Berkhampsted, Hertfordshire
Details See Antique & Collectors Fair 30 March

Ardingly Antiques & Collectors Fair
Contact Caroline Cleary
☎ 01636 702326 ⓕ 01636 707923
ⓦ www.dmgantiquefairs.com
Location South of England Centre, Ardingly, West Sussex 🅿
Est. 1997
Open 8am–4pm
Entrance fee 8am £5 10am £3.50
Details Up to 200 exhibitors

Art Nouveau and Art Deco Fair
Location Woking, Surrey
Details See Art Nouveau and Art Deco Fair 30 March

Dualco Promotions
Location Pudsey
Details See Dualco Promotions 23 February

Wessex Fairs
Location Weston-super-Mare
Details See Wessex Fairs 24 February

JULY

1

V and A Fairs
Location Cheadle, Cheshire
Details See V and A Fairs 2 February

3

Paraphernalia Fairs
Location Lyndhurst, Hampshire
Details See Paraphernalia Fairs 6 February

4–6

Albany Fairs
Location Pooley Bridge, Cumbria
Details See Albany Fairs 15–16 February

North Cotswolds Antiques Fair
Contact Anne Harwood
☎ 01249 661111 ⓕ 01249 661111
ⓔ enquiries@cooperantiquesfairs.co.uk
ⓦ www.cooperantiquesfairs.co.uk
Location Stanway House, Winchcombe, Gloucestershire
Open Fri noon–5pm Sat Sun 11am–5pm
Entrance fee £4 Children under 16 free

5

Antiques & Collectables Fair
Location Marlborough, Wiltshire
Details See Antiques & Collectables Fair 1 March

Buckingham Antique & Collectors Fair
Location Buckingham
Details See Buckingham Antique & Collectors Fair 1 February

Marcel Fairs
Location London NW7
Details See Marcel Fairs 1 February

Victoriana's Fairs
Location Walsall, West Midlands
Details See Victoriana's Fairs 1 February

5–6

Devon County Antiques Fairs
Location Clyst St Mary, Exeter
Details See Devon County Antiques Fair 1–2 March

6

Antique & Collectors Fair
Location Newmarket
Details See Antique & Collectors Fair 2 February

Antique & Collectors Fair
Location Edinburgh
Details See Antique & Collectors Fair 2 February

Arun Fairs
Location Rustington, West Sussex
Details See Arun Fairs 2 February

Best of Fairs
Location Copdock, Ipswich
Details See Best of Fairs 2 February

Cross Country Fairs Ltd
Location Effingham Park, West Sussex
Details See Cross Country Fairs Ltd 2 February

Harlequin Fairs
Location Chalfont St Peter, Buckinghamshire
Details See Harlequin Fairs 2 March

Ipswich Antiques & Collectables Fair
Location Copdock, Ipswich
Details See Ipswich Antiques & Collectables Fair 2 February

J and K Fairs
Location Lincoln
Details See J and K Fairs 9 February

Lechlade Antiques Fair
Location Lechlade, Gloucestershire
Details See Lechlade Antiques Fair 2 February

St Crispins Fair
Location Wokingham, Berkshire
Details See St Crispins Fair 2 February

11–13

The 1st Southwold Summer Antiques Fair
Contact Liz Allport
☎ 01603 737631 ⓕ 01603 737631
ⓜ 07747 843074
ⓔ liz.allport@lineone.net
ⓦ www.lomaxantiquesfairs.co.uk
Location Saint Felix School. Southwold, Suffolk 🅿
Open 11th 2–7pm
12th 10.30am–6.pm
13th 10.30am–5pm

The 34th Cheshire Summer Antiques and Fine Art Fair
☎ 01277 214677 ⓕ 01277 214550
ⓔ admin@baileyfairs.co.uk
ⓦ www.baileyfairs.co.uk
Location Tatton Park, Knutsford 🅿
Open Fri 1–6pm Sat 11am–6pm Sun 11am–5pm
Entrance fee £5
Details 40 dealers, vetted and datelined

12

Antique & Collectors Fair
Location Alberts Hall, Dumbarton Road, Stirling
Details See Antique & Collectors Fair 1 February

12–13

Antiques & Collectables Fair
Location Stockbridge, Hampshire
Details See Antiques & Collectables Fair 22–23 February

Buxton Book Fair
Location Buxton, Derbyshire
Entrance fee £1
Details See Buxton Book Fair 16 February

13

Antique & Collectors Fair
Location Woking, Surrey
Details See Antique & Collectors Fair 9 February

Antiques & Collectables Fair
Location Dublin
Details See Antiques & Collectables Fair 9 February

London Map Fairs
Location London WC1
Details See London Map Fairs 9 February

Lostwithiel Antiques Fair
Location Lostwithiel, Cornwall
Details See Lostwithiel Antiques Fair 9 February

M & S Collectors and Dolls Fair
Contact Jim Mansfield
☎ 01223 233059 Ⓕ 01223 500283
Ⓜ 07960 102889 or 07748 205647
Location Cottenham Village College, 5 miles north of Cambridge, B1049 Ⓟ
Open 10am–4pm
Entrance fee 70p
Details Collectables and dolls

Malvern Antiques & Collectors Fair
Location Malvern, Worcestershire
Details See Malvern Antiques & Collectors Fair 2 February

Midas Antique Fair
Location Beaconsfield, Bucks
Details See Midas Antique Fair 9 February

Royal Horticultural Hall
Location London SW1
Details See Royal Horticultural Hall 23 February

The London Textiles, Vintage Fashion and Accessories Fair
Location London W6
Details See The London Textiles, Vintage Fashion and Accessories Fair 19 January

15

Crispin Fairs
Location Hartley Wintney, Hampshire
Details See Crispin Fairs 18 February

16

The Big Brum
Location Birmingham
Details See The Big Brum 22 January

17–20

36th Annual Snape Antiques Fair
Contact Anne Harwood
☎ 01249 661111 Ⓕ 01249 661111
Ⓔ enquiries@cooperantiquesfairs.co.uk
Ⓦ www.cooperantiquesfairs.co.uk
Location Snape, Suffolk
Open Daily 11am–5pm
Entrance fee £4 Children under 16 free

18–20

Albany Fairs
Location Pooley Bridge, Cumbria
Details See Albany Fairs 15–16 February

Galloway Antiques Fairs
☎ 01423 522122 Ⓕ 01423 522122
Ⓜ 07966 528725
Ⓔ susan@gallowayfairs.co.uk
Ⓦ www.gallowayfairs.co.uk
Location Ripley Castle, Harrogate, North Yorkshire Ⓟ
Open 10.30am–5pm
Entrance fee £3.50–£4.50

19

Commonwealth Institute Coin Fair
Location London W8
Details See Commonwealth Institute Coin Fair 18 January

Devon County Antiques Fairs
Location Exeter
Details See Devon County Antiques Fairs 8 February

19–20

Carmarthen Antiques & Collectors Fair
Location Carmarthen
Details See Carmarthen Antiques & Collectors Fair 8–9 March

Detling International Antiques & Collectors Fair
Location Detling, Nr Maidstone, Kent
Details See Detling International Antiques & Collectors Fair 25–26 January

Suffolk Book Markets
Location Long Melford, Suffolk
Details See Suffolk Book Markets 8–9 February

20

Antique & Collectors Fair
Location Glasgow
Details See Antique & Collectors Fair 16 February

Biggleswade Antiques Fairs
Location Biggleswade, Bedfordshire
Details See Biggleswade Antiques Fairs 19 January

Clock & Watch Dealers Fair
Location Haydock Park racecourse
Details See Clock & Watch Dealers Fair 30 March

Galway Antique Fair
Contact Ms Gretta Boland
☎ 091 564938
Location Galway Bay Hotel, Salthill, Co Galway Ⓟ
Est. 1993
Open Trade 10am Public 11am–7pm
Entrance fee €3 (£1.90) trade FWC
Details 45 stands, no reproductions, refreshments from bar and restaurant

Monmouthshire County Antiques & Collectors Fair
Location Abergavenny, Monmouthshire
Details See Monmouthshire County Antiques & Collectors Fair 19 January

Wessex Fairs
Location Weston-super-Mare
Details See Wessex Fairs 23 February

23–26

Kensington Fine Art & Antiques Fair
Contact Caroline Penman
☎ 01444 482514 Ⓕ 01444 482412
Ⓜ 07774 850044
Ⓔ info@penman-fairs.co.uk
Ⓦ www.penman-fairs.co.uk
Location Kensington Town Hall, Hornton Street, London W8 🅿
Est. 1975
Open Thurs 2–8pm Fri Sat 11am–6pm Sun 11am–5pm
Entrance fee £4
Details 50% art 50% antiques

24–26

Albany Fairs
Location Moffat, Dumfries & Galloway
Details See Albany Fairs 6–8 March

25–27

Galloway Antiques Fairs
Location Cranleigh, Surrey
Details See Galloway Antiques Fairs 18–21 April

Stafford Bingley Hall
Location Stafford
Details See Stafford Bingley Hall 7–9 February

26

Antique & Collectors Fair
Location Ayr
Details See Antique & Collectors Fair 25 January

Antiques & Collectors Fair
Location Poole, Dorset
Details See Antiques & Collectors Fair 22 February

Antiques Fair
Location Hertford, Hertfordshire
Details See Antiques Fair 18 January

Pamela Robertson Antique & Collectors Fair
Location Chester
Details See Pamela Robertson Antique & Collectors Fair 25 January

26–27

Antiques & Collectables Fair
Location Stockbridge, Hampshire
Details See Antiques & Collectables Fair 22–23 February

The Original Long Melford Fair
Location Long Melford, Suffolk
Details See The Original Long Melford Fair 25–26 January

27

Bloomsbury Postcard & Collectors Fair
Location London WC1
Details See Bloomsbury Postcard and Collectors Fair 23 February

Burford Antiques Fair
Location Burford, Oxfordshire
Details See Burford Antiques Fair 26 January

Bushey Hall School
Location Bushey, Hertfordshire
Details See Bushey Hall 28 January

Dualco Promotions
Location Pudsey
Details See Dualco Promotions 23 February

V and A Fairs
Location Bridgnorth, Shropshire
Details See V and A Fairs 26 January

31

Antique & Collectors Fair
Location Nantwich, Cheshire
Details See Antique & Collectors Fair 30 January

Antiques & Collectables Fair
Location Daventry
Details See Antiques & Collectables Fair 20 February

AUGUST

1–3

Albany Fairs
Location Pooley Bridge, Cumbria
Details See Albany Fairs 15–16 February

2

Antique & Collectors Fair
Location Stirling
Details See Antique & Collectors Fair 1 February

Buckingham Antique & Collectors Fair
Location Buckingham
Details See Buckingham Antique & Collectors Fair 1 February

Marcel Fairs
Location London NW7
Details See Marcel Fairs 1 February

3

Antique & Collectors Fair
Location Newmarket
Details See Antique & Collectors Fair 2 February

Antique & Collectors Fair
Location Edinburgh
Details See Antique & Collectors Fair 2 February

Arun Fairs
Location Rustington, West Sussex
Details See Arun Fairs 2 February

Best of Fairs
Location Copdock, Ipswich
Details See Best of Fairs 2 February

Cross Country Fairs Ltd
Location Effingham Park, West Sussex
Details See Cross Country Fairs Ltd 2 February

Dualco Promotions
Location Oldham
Details See Dualco Promotions 23 February

Harlequin Fairs
Location Chalfont St Peter, Buckinghamshire
Details See Harlequin Fairs 2 March

Lechlade Antiques Fair
Location Lechlade, Gloucestershire
Details See Lechlade Antiques Fair 2 February

Malvern Antiques & Collectors Fair
Location Malvern, Worcestershire
Details See Malvern Antiques & Collectors Fair 2 February

Mark Carter Militaria & Medal Fairs
Location Aldershot, Hampshire
Details See Mark Carter Militaria & Medal Fairs 19 January

St Crispins Fair
Location Wokingham, Berkshire
Details See St Crispins Fair 2 February

V and A Fairs
Location Cheadle, Cheshire
Details See V and A Fairs 2 February

4

Antiques & Collectables Fair
Location Dun Laoghaire, Co Dublin
Details See Antiques & Collectables Fair 26 January

7

Paraphernalia Fairs
Location Lyndhurst, Hampshire
Details See Paraphernalia Fairs 6 February

7–10

Antiques for Everyone
Location NEC, Birmingham
Details See Antiques for Everyone 3–6 April

9–10

Antiques & Collectables Fair
Location Warwick
Details See Antiques & Collectables Fair 26–27 April

10

Antique & Collectors Fair
Location Woking, Surrey
Details See Antique & Collectors Fair 9 February

Antique & Collectors Fair
Location Glasgow
Details See Antique & Collectors Fair 16 February

Bushey Hall School
Location Bushey, Hertfordshire
Details See Bushey Hall 28 January

Devon County Antiques Fairs
Location Yeovil, Somerset
Details See Devon County Antiques Fairs 16 February

Dualco Promotions
Location Huddersfield
Details See Dualco Promotions 2 February

London Map Fairs
Location London WC1
Details See London Map Fairs 9 February

Lostwithiel Antiques Fair
Location Lostwithiel, Cornwall
Details See Lostwithiel Antiques Fair 9 February

M & S Collectors Fair
Location Cottenham, Cambridge
Details See M & S Collectors Fair 9 February

Mark Carter Militaria & Medal Fairs
Location Yate, Bristol
Details See Mark Carter Militaria & Medal Fairs 2 February

Midas Antique Fair
Location Beaconsfield, Bucks
Details See Midas Antique Fair 9 February

Newmarket Antiques & Collectors Fair
Location Newmarket, Suffolk
Details See Newmarket Antiques & Collectors Fair 23 February

15–17

The International Antiques & Collectors Fair at RAF Swinderby
Location RAF Swinderby
Details See The International Antiques & Collectors Fair at RAF Swinderby 31 January–2 February

16

Commonwealth Institute Coin Fair
Location London W8
Details See Commonwealth Institute Coin Fair 18 January

16–17

Aberystwyth Antiques & Collectors Fair
Contact Carol Pugh
☎ 01267 236569 Ⓕ 01267 220444
Ⓜ 07885 333845
Ⓔ antiques@towy-fairs.co.uk
Ⓦ www.towy-fairs.co.uk
Location Penweddin School, Llanbadarn, Aberystwyth Ⓟ
Est. 2003
Open 10am–5pm
Entrance fee £3 Accompanied children free
Details 180 dealers

Suffolk Book Markets
Location Long Melford, Suffolk
Details See Suffolk Book Markets 8–9 February

17

Antiques & Collectables Fair
Location Dublin
Details See Antiques & Collectables Fair 9 February

Dualco Promotions
Location Morley
Details See Dualco Promotions 6 April

Midland Clock & Watch Fair
Location National Motorcycle

Museum, West Midlands
Details See Midland Clock & Watch Fair 26 January

Monmouthshire County Antiques & Collectors Fair
Location Abergavenny, Monmouthshire
Details See Monmouthshire County Antiques & Collectors Fair 19 January

18

Antique & Collectors Fair
Location Nantwich, Cheshire
Details See Antique & Collectors Fair 30 January

18–19

Newark International Antiques & Collectors Fair
Location Newark
Details See Newark International Antiques & Collectors Fair 3–4 February

19

Crispin Fairs
Location Hartley Wintney, Hampshire
Details See Crispin Fairs 18 February

22–25

Galloway Antiques Fairs
☎ 01423 522122 Ⓕ 01423 522122
Ⓜ 07966 528725
Ⓔ susan@gallowayfairs.co.uk
Ⓦ www.gallowayfairs.co.uk
Location Rookesbury Park School, Wickham, Nr Fareham, Hampshire Ⓟ
Open 10.30am–5pm
Entrance fee £3.50–£4.50

23

Antique & Collectors Fair
Location Ayr
Details See Antique & Collectors Fair 25 January

Devon County Antiques Fairs
Location Exeter
Details See Devon County Antiques Fairs 8 February

23–25

Albany Fairs
Location Moffat, Dumfries & Galloway
Details See Albany Fairs 6–8 March

Beckett Antique Fairs
Location Doncaster
Details See Beckett Antique Fairs 15–16 February

Buxton Antique & Collectors Fair
Location Buxton, Derbyshire
Details See Buxton Antique & Collectors Fair 25–26 January

The Original Long Melford Fair
Location Long Melford, Suffolk
Details See The Original Long Melford Fair 25–26 January

24

Bloomsbury Postcard & Collectors Fair
Location London WC1
Details See Bloomsbury Postcard and Collectors Fair 23 February

Dualco Promotions
Location Oldham
Details See Dualco Promotions 23 February

V and A Fairs
Location Whitchurch, Shropshire
Details See V and A Fairs 16 February

24–25

Antiques & Collectables Fair
Location Stockbridge, Hampshire
Details See Antiques & Collectables Fair 22–23 February

Antiques & Collectors Fair
Location St Ives, Cambridgeshire
Details See Antiques & Collectors Fair 22–23 February

Wessex Fairs
Location Weston-super-Mare
Details See Wessex Fairs 23 February

25

14th Annual August Antique and Fine Art Fair
☎ 028 9181 5710 Ⓕ 028 9182 0637
Ⓔ info@castleantiques.co.uk
Ⓦ www.castleantiques.co.uk
Location The Bohill Hotel & Country Club, Coleraine Ⓟ
Open 11am–7pm
Entrance fee £2.50 accompanied children free
Details 40 Plus dealers

Antiques & Collectors Fair
Location Wilmslow, Cheshire
Details See Antiques & Collectors Fair 16 March

Bob Evans Fairs
Location Hinckley, Leicestershire
Details See Bob Evans Fairs 2 March

Brunel Antiques & Collectors Fair
Location Uxbridge, Middlesex
Details See Brunel Antiques & Collectors Fair 21 April

Buckhurst Hill Antiques & Collectors Fair
Location Buckhurst Hill, Essex
Details See Antiques & Collectors Fair 21 April

Buxton Book Fair
Location Buxton, Derbyshire
Details See Buxton Book Fair 23 March

Dualco Promotions
Location Halifax
Details See Dualco Promotions 16 February

Pamela Robertson Antique & Collectors Fair
Location Chester
Details See Pamela Robertson Antique & Collectors Fair 25 January

28

Antiques & Collectables Fair
Location Daventry
Details See Antiques & Collectables Fair 20 February

28–29

Newbury Showground
Contact Matthew Adams
☎ 020 7254 4054
Location Newbury Showground, Chieveley, Berkshire 🅿
Open 10am–5pm
Entrance fee £4.50
Details 100 Indoor stands, 150 outdoor stands

29–31

Galloway Antiques Fairs
Location Brampton, Cumbria
Details See Galloway Antiques Fairs 21–25 March

South Cotswolds Antiques Fair
Location Tetbury, Gloucestershire
Details See South Cotswolds Antiques Fair 18–20 April

30

Antiques & Collectors Fair
Location Poole, Dorset
Details See Antiques & Collectors Fair 22 February

Antiques Fair
Location Hertford, Hertfordshire
Details See Antiques Fair 18 January

30–31

Gawsworth Antiques Fair
Location Gawsworth Hall, Cheshire
Details See Gawsworth Antiques Fair May 31–1 June

31

Antiques & Collectors Fair
Location King's Lynn
Details See Antiques & Collectors Fair 26 January

Bob Evans Fairs
Location Coventry
Details See Bob Evans Fairs 9 February

Chipping Norton Toy Fairs
Location Chipping Norton, Oxfordshire
Details See Chipping Norton Toy Fairs 23 February

J and K Fairs
Location Lincoln
Details See J and K Fairs 9 February

Wessex Fairs
Location Blagdon, North Somerset
Details See Wessex Fairs 30 March

SEPTEMBER

4

Paraphernalia Fairs
Location Lyndhurst, Hampshire
Details See Paraphernalia Fairs 6 February

4–7

The 34th Cheshire Autumn Antiques and Fine Art Fair
☎ 01277 214677 Ⓕ 01277 214550
Ⓔ admin@baileyfairs.co.uk
Ⓦ www.baileyfairs.co.uk
Location Tatton Park, Knutsford 🅿
Open Thurs 2–6pm Fri Sat 11am–6pm Sun 11am–5pm
Entrance fee £5
Details 50 dealers, vetted and datelined

5–7

Albany Fairs
Location Howtown, Cumbria
Details See Albany Fairs 15–16 February

Penmans Petersfield Antiques Fair
Location Petersfield, Hants
Details See Petersfield Antiques Fair 6–9 February

6

Buckingham Antique & Collectors Fair
Location Buckingham
Details See Buckingham Antique & Collectors Fair 1 February

Marcel Fairs
Location London NW7
Details See Marcel Fairs 1 February

6–7

Detling International Antiques & Collectors Fair
Location Detling, Nr Maidstone, Kent
Details See Detling International Antiques & Collectors Fair 25–26 January

Devon County Antiques Fairs
Location Clyst St Mary, Exeter
Details See Devon County Antiques Fair 1–2 March

7

Antique & Collectors Fair
Location Newmarket
Details See Antique & Collectors Fair 2 February

Antique & Collectors Fair
Location Edinburgh
Details See Antique & Collectors Fair 2 February

Antiques & Collectables Fair
Location Dublin
Details See Antiques & Collectables Fair 9 February

Arun Fairs
Location Rustington, West Sussex
Details See Arun Fairs 2 February

Battersea Town Hall Art Deco Fair
Location Battersea Town Hall
Details See Battersea Town Hall Art Deco Fair 16 February

Best of Fairs
Location Copdock, Ipswich
Details See Best of Fairs 2 February

Bob Evans Fairs
Location Peterborough
Details See Bob Evans Fairs 23 February

Brunel Clock & Watch Fair
Location Uxbridge, Middlesex
Details See Brunel Clock & Watch Fair 16 February

Cross Country Fairs Ltd
Location Effingham Park, West Sussex
Details See Cross Country Fairs Ltd 2 February

Dualco Promotions
Location Bolton
Details See Dualco Promotions 16 February

Harlequin Fairs
Location Chalfont St Peter, Buckinghamshire
Details See Harlequin Fairs 2 March

Ipswich Antiques & Collectables Fair
Location Copdock, Ipswich
Details See Ipswich Antiques & Collectables Fair 2 February

Lechlade Antiques Fair
Location Lechlade, Gloucestershire
Details See Lechlade Antiques Fair 2 February

Malvern Antiques & Collectors Fair
Location Malvern, Worcestershire
Details See Malvern Antiques & Collectors Fair 2 February

Royal Horticultural Hall
Location London SW1
Details See Royal Horticultural Hall 23 February

St Crispins Fair
Location Wokingham, Berkshire
Details See St Crispins Fair 2 February

V and A Fairs
Location Cheadle, Cheshire
Details See V and A Fairs 2 February

Wessex Fairs
Location Taunton
Details See Wessex Fairs 2 February

12–14

Albany Fairs
Location Pooley Bridge, Cumbria
Details See Albany Fairs 15–16 February

Galloway Antiques Fairs
☎ 01423 522122
Ⓜ 07966 528725
Ⓔ susan@gallowayfairs.co.uk
Ⓦ www.gallowayfairs.co.uk
Location Firle Place, Firle, Lewes, East Sussex 🅿
Open 10.30am–5pm
Entrance fee £3.50–£4.50

13

Antique & Collectors Fair
Location Stirling
Details See Antique & Collectors Fair 1 February

Chelsea Brocante
☎ 020 7254 4054
Location Chelsea, London SW3
Details See Chelsea Brocante 8 February

Southport Antiques & Collectors Fair
Location Southport, Merseyside
Details See Southport Antiques & Collectors Fair 22 February

13–14

Carmarthen Antiques & Collectors' Fair
Location Carmarthen
Details See Carmarthen Antiques & Collectors Fair 8–9 March

West Midlands Antique Fairs
Location Stafford
Details See West Midlands Antique Fairs 22–23 February

14

Antique & Collectors Fair
Location Woking, Surrey
Details See Antique & Collectors Fair 9 February

Antique & Collectors Fair
Location Glasgow
Details See Antique & Collectors Fair 16 February

Art Deco Fair
Location Warwick
Details See Art Deco Fair 23 February

Arun Fairs
Location Bognor, West Sussex
Details See Arun Fairs 13 April

Biggleswade Antiques Fairs
Location Huntingdon, Cambridgeshire
Details See Biggleswade Antiques Fairs 9 February

Bob Evans Fairs
Location Kettering
Details See Bob Evans Fairs 16 February

Crispin Fairs
Location Hartley Wintney, Hampshire
Details See Crispin Fairs 9 February

Dualco Promotions
Location Barnsley
Details See Dualco Promotions 9 February

London Map Fairs
Location London WC1
Details See London Map Fairs 9 February

Lostwithiel Antiques Fair
Location Lostwithiel, Cornwall
Details See Lostwithiel Antiques Fair 9 February

M & S Collectors Fair
Location Cottenham, Cambridge
Details See M & S Collectors Fair 9 February

Midas Antique Fair
Location Beaconsfield, Bucks
Details See Midas Antique Fair 9 February

Pennyfarthing Fayres
Location Potters Bar
Details See Pennyfarthing Fayres 9 February

The London Textiles, Vintage Fashion and Accessories Fair
Location London W6
Details See The London Textiles, Vintage Fashion and Accessories Fair 19 January

16

Crispin Fairs
Location Hartley Wintney, Hampshire
Details See Crispin Fairs 18 February

17

The Big Brum
Location Birmingham
Details See The Big Brum 22 January

17–21

Penmans Chelsea Antiques Fair
Location London SW3
Details See Penmans Chelsea Antiques Fair 14–23 March

The 53rd Northern Antiques Fair
☎ 01277 214677 Ⓕ 01277 214550
Ⓔ admin@baileyfairs.co.uk
Ⓦ www.baileyfairs.co.uk
Location Pavilions of Harrogate, Great Yorkshire Showground Ⓟ
Entrance fee £10
Details 70 dealers, vetted and datelined

18

Antiques & Collectables Fair
Location Daventry
Details See Antiques & Collectables Fair 20 February

18–20

Albany Fairs
Location Moffat, Dumfries & Galloway
Details See Albany Fairs 6–8 March

19

Wessex Fairs
Location Blagdon, North Somerset
Details See Wessex Fairs 30 March

19–21

Galloway Antiques Fairs
☎ 01423 522122
Ⓜ 07966 528725
Ⓔ susan@gallowayfairs.co.uk
Ⓦ www.gallowayfairs.co.uk
Location The Old Swan Hotel, Harrogate, North Yorkshire Ⓟ
Open 10.30am–5pm
Entrance fee £3.50–£4.50

Shepton Mallet Antiques & Collectors Fair
Location Shepton Mallet, Somerset
Details See Shepton Mallet Antiques & Collectors Fair 17–19 January

20

9th Annual Charity Antique and Fine Art Fair
Location Queen's Hall, Newtownards
Open 11am–5pm
Entrance fee £2 accompanied children free
Details 30 plus dealers

Blackpool Winter Gardens Collectors Market
Location Blackpool, Lancashire
Details See Blackpool Winter Gardens Collectors Market 15 February

Chingford Antiques & Collectors Fair
Location Chingford, London E4
Details See Chingford Antiques & Collectors Fair 25 January

Commonwealth Institute Coin Fair
Location London W8
Details See Commonwealth Institute Coin Fair 18 January

20–21

Bob Evans Fairs
Location Norwich
Details See Bob Evans Fairs 25–26 January

Suffolk Book Markets
Location Long Melford, Suffolk
Details See Suffolk Book Markets 8–9 February

21

Alexandra Palace
Location Wood Green, London
Details See Alexandra Palace 9 March

Art Deco Fair with 20thC Decorative Arts
Location Leeds Royal Armouries
Details See Art Deco Fair with 20thC Decorative Arts 23 March

Biggleswade Antiques Fairs
Location Biggleswade, Bedfordshire
Details See Biggleswade Antiques Fairs 19 January

Buxton Book Fair
Location Buxton, Derbyshire
Details See Buxton Book Fair 23 March

Clock & Watch Dealers Fair
Location Haydock Park Racecourse
Details See Clock & Watch Dealers Fair 30 March

Dublin Toy and Train Fair
Location Dun Laoghaire, Co Dublin
Details See Dublin Toy and Train Fair 16 February

Hatfield Antiques & Collectors Fair
Location Hatfield, Hertfordshire
Details See Hatfield Antiques & Collectors Fair 19 January

Monmouthshire County Antiques & Collectors Fair
Location Abergavenny, Monmouthshire
Details See Monmouthshire County Antiques & Collectors Fair 19 January

The National Art Deco Fair
Location Loughborough, Leicestershire
Details See National Art Deco Fair 4 May

23–28

The Decorative Antiques and Textiles Fair
Location Battersea Park
Details See The Decorative Antiques and Textiles Fair 8–13 April

24–28

Irish Antique Dealers Fair
Contact Louis O'Sullivan
☎ 00 353 1 2859294
Location Royal Dublin Society, Ballsbridge, Dublin 4, Ireland Ⓟ
Open 11am–7pm
Entrance fee €7 (£4.46)

Details Fair Datelines: pre-1900: prints, photos; pre-1925: furniture, metalwork, architectural fittings; pre-1930: glass, china, clocks; pre-1940: works of art, silver, etchings, lighting, clocks; pre-1950: jewellery, paintings, drawings

25

Antique & Collectors Fair
Location Nantwich, Cheshire
Details See Antique & Collectors Fair 30 January

26–28

Albany Fairs
Location Pooley Bridge, Cumbria
Details See Albany Fairs 15–16 February

26–30

The Harrogate Antiques Fair
Contact Louise Walker
☎ 01823 323363 Ⓕ 01823 271072
Ⓦ www.harrogateantiquefair.com
Location Hall A, Harrogate International Centre, Ripon Road, Harrogate, North Yorkshire Ⓟ
Entrance fee £7.50 including catalogue
Details High quality antiques and fine art, call for further information

27

Antique & Collectors Fair
Location Ayr
Details See Antique & Collectors Fair 25 January

Antiques & Collectors Fair
Location Poole, Dorset
Details See Antiques & Collectors Fair 22 February

Antiques Fair
Location Hertford, Hertfordshire
Details See Antiques Fair 18 January

Devon County Antiques Fairs
Location Salisbury
Details See Devon County Antiques Fairs 12 April

Pamela Robertson Antique & Collectors Fair
Location Chester
Details See Pamela Robertson Antique & Collectors Fair 25 January

27–28

Antiques & Collectables Fair
Location Stockbridge, Hampshire
Details See Antiques & Collectables Fair 22–23 February

Antiques & Collectables Fair
Location Warwick
Details See Antiques & Collectables Fair 26–27 April

Beckett Antique Fairs
Location Doncaster
Details See Beckett Antique Fairs 15–16 February

The 71st London Arms Fair
Location West Drayton, Middlesex
Details See The 70th London Arms Fair 26–27 April

The Original Long Melford Fair
Location Long Melford, Suffolk
Details See The Original Long Melford Fair 25–26 January

28

Antiques & Collectors Fair
Location King's Lynn
Details See Antiques & Collectors Fair 26 January

Ardingly Antiques & Collectors Fair
Location Ardingly, West Sussex
Details See Ardingly Antiques & Collectors Fair 29 June

Biggleswade Antiques Fairs
Location Kempston, Bedford
Details See Biggleswade Antiques Fairs 26 January

Bloomsbury Postcard & Collectors Fair
Location London WC1
Details See Bloomsbury Postcard and Collectors Fair 23 February

Bob Evans Fairs
Location Hereford
Details See Bob Evans Fairs 13 April

Burford Antiques Fair
Location Burford, Oxfordshire
Details See Burford Antiques Fair 26 January

Bushey Hall School
Location Bushey, Hertfordshire
Details See Bushey Hall 28 January

Royal Horticultural Hall
Location London SW1
Details See Royal Horticultural Hall 23 February

V and A Fairs
Location Bridgnorth, Shropshire
Details See V and A Fairs 26 January

Wessex Fairs
Location Weston-super-Mare
Details See Wessex Fairs 23 February

OCTOBER

2

Paraphernalia Fairs
Location Lyndhurst, Hampshire
Details See Paraphernalia Fairs 6 February

2–5

36th Surrey Antiques Fair
Contact Sue Ware
☎ 01822 614671
Ⓦ www.surreyantiquesfair.co.uk
Location Guildford Civic Centre, Guildford, Surrey Ⓟ
Est. 1968
Open Thurs–Sat 11am–7pm Sun 11am–6pm
Details Annual event with more than 40 dealers of antiques and fine art from around the country

The Milton Keynes Antiques Fair
Location Milton Keynes
Details See The Milton Keynes Antiques Fair 27–2 March

3–5

Albany Fairs
Location Howtown, Cumbria
Details See Albany Fairs 15–16 February

Stafford Bingley Hall
Location Stafford
Details See Stafford Bingley Hall 7–9 February

4

Marcel Fairs
Location London NW7
Details See Marcel Fairs 1 February

Victoriana's Fairs
Location Walsall, West Midlands
Details See Victoriana's Fairs 1 February

4–5

Buxton Antique & Collectors Fair
Location Buxton, Derbyshire
Details See Buxton Antique & Collectors Fair 25–26 January

5

Antique & Collectors Fair
Location Newmarket
Details See Antique & Collectors Fair 2 February

Antique & Collectors Fair
Location Edinburgh
Details See Antique & Collectors Fair 2 February

Antiques & Collectables Fair
Location Dublin
Details See Antiques Fairs Ireland 23 February

Arun Fairs
Location Rustington, West Sussex
Details See Arun Fairs 2 February

Best of Fairs
Location Copdock, Ipswich
Details See Best of Fairs 2 February

Chiswick Town Hall Art Deco Fair
Location Chiswick Town Hall
Details See Chiswick Town Hall Art Deco Fair 2 March

Cross Country Fairs Ltd
Location Effingham Park, West Sussex
Details See Cross Country Fairs Ltd 2 February

Devon County Antiques Fairs
Location Yeovil, Somerset
Details See Devon County Antiques Fairs 16 February

Dualco Promotions
Location Huddersfield
Details See Dualco Promotions 2 February

Grand Glass Fair
Location Woking, Surrey
Details See Grand Glass Fair 16 March

Harlequin Fairs
Location Chalfont St Peter, Buckinghamshire
Details See Harlequin Fairs 2 March

Ipswich Antiques & Collectables Fair
Location Copdock, Ipswich, Suffolk
Details See Ipswich Antiques & Collectables Fair 2 February

Lechlade Antiques Fair
Location Lechlade, Gloucestershire
Details See Lechlade Antiques Fair 2 February

Mark Carter Militaria & Medal Fairs
Location Yate, Bristol
Details See Mark Carter Militaria & Medal Fairs 2 February

St Crispins Fair
Location Wokingham, Berkshire
Details See St Crispins Fair 2 February

V and A Fairs
Location Cheadle, Cheshire
Details See V and A Fairs 2 February

Wessex Fairs
Location Taunton
Details See Wessex Fairs 2 February

6–7

Little Chelsea Antiques Fair
Location London SW3
Details See Little Chelsea Antiques Fair 14–15 April

7

Sandown Park Antique & Collectors Fair
Location Sandown Park Racecourse, Esher, Surrey
Details See Sandown Park Antique & Collectors Fair 18 February

8–12

LAPADA Fine Art & Antiques Fair
Ⓔ antiques@necgroup.co.uk
Ⓦ www.lapadafair.co.uk
Location Commonwealth Institute Galleries, Kensington High Street, London W8 Ⓟ
Est. 1993
Open Wed Thurs 11am–8pm Fri–Sun 11am–6pm
Entrance fee £10 single £16 double
Details 100 dealers

10–12

Albany Fairs
Location Pooley Bridge, Cumbria
Details See Albany Fairs 15–16 February

Cheshire County Antiques Fair
Location Knutsford, Cheshire
Details See Cheshire County Antiques Fair 14–16 March

11

Antique & Collectors Fair
Location Stirling
Details See Antique & Collectors Fair 1 February

Devon County Antiques Fairs
Location Exeter

Details See Devon County Antiques Fairs 8 February

12

Antique & Collectors Fair
Location Woking, Surrey
Details See Antique & Collectors Fair 9 February

Antiques & Collectables Fair
Location Dublin
Details See Antiques & Collectables Fair 9 February

Antiques & Collectors Fair
Location St Ives, Cambridgeshire
Details See Antiques & Collectors Fair 22–23 February

Antiques & Collectors Fairs
Location Egham, Surrey
Details See Antiques & Collectors Fair 9 February

Bob Evans Fairs
Location Hinckley, Leicestershire
Details See Bob Evans Fairs 2 March

Crispin Fairs
Location Hartley Wintney, Hampshire
Details See Crispin Fairs 9 February

Dualco Promotions
Location Halifax
Details See Dualco Promotions 16 February

London Map Fairs
Location London WC1
Details See London Map Fairs 9 February

Lostwithiel Antiques Fair
Location Lostwithiel, Cornwall
Details See Lostwithiel Antiques Fair 9 February

M & S Collectors Fair
Location Cottenham, Cambridge
Details See M & S Collectors Fair 9 February

Malvern Antiques & Collectors Fair
Location Malvern, Worcestershire
Details See Malvern Antiques & Collectors Fair 2 February

Pennyfarthing Fayres
Location Potters Bar
Details See Pennyfarthing Fayres 9 February

14

Midas Antique Fair
Location Beaconsfield, Bucks
Details See Midas Antique Fair 9 February

17–19

The 11th Buxton Autumn Fine Art and Antiques Fair
☎ 01277 214677 Ⓕ 01277 214550
Ⓔ admin@baileyfairs.co.uk
Ⓦ www.baileyfairs.co.uk
Location Pavilion Gardens, Buxton, Derbyshire Ⓟ
Open Fri 1–6pm Sat 11am–6pm Sun 11am–5pm
Entrance fee £5
Details 40 stands

The International Antiques & Collectors Fair at RAF Swinderby
Location RAF Swinderby
Details See The International Antiques & Collectors Fair at RAF Swinderby 31 January–2 February

18

Chingford Antiques & Collectors Fair
Location Chingford, London E4
Details See Chingford Antiques & Collectors Fair 25 January

Evening Antiques/Collectors Fairs
Location Birmingham
Details See Evening Antiques/Collectors Fairs 23 April

Leeds Dolls & Teddy Fair
Location Pudsey
Details See Leeds Dolls & Teddy Fair 29 March

19

Art Deco Fair with 20thC Decorative Arts
Location Chester Racecourse
Details See Art Deco Fair with 20thC Decorative Arts 27 January

Biggleswade Antiques Fairs
Location Biggleswade, Bedfordshire
Details See Biggleswade Antiques Fairs 19 January

Clock & Watch Dealers Fair
Location Balderton, Nr Newark
Details See Clock & Watch Dealers Fair 2 February

Dualco Promotions
Location Bolton
Details See Dualco Promotions 16 February

Hatfield Antiques & Collectors Fair
Location Hatfield, Hertfordshire
Details See Hatfield Antiques & Collectors Fair 19 January

Monmouthshire County Antiques & Collectors Fair
Location Abergavenny, Monmouthshire
Details See Monmouthshire County Antiques & Collectors Fair 19 January

Royal Horticultural Hall
Location London SW1
Details See Royal Horticultural Hall 23 February

V and A Fairs
Location Whitchurch, Shropshire
Details See V and A Fairs 16 February

20–21

Newark International Antiques & Collectors Fair
Location Newark
Details See Newark International Antiques & Collectors Fair 3–4 February

,21

Crispin Fairs
Location Hartley Wintney, Hampshire
Details See Crispin Fairs 18 February

23–25

Albany Fairs
Location Moffat, Dumfries & Galloway
Details See Albany Fairs 6–8 March

23–26

Penmans Chester Antiques & Fine Art Show
Location Chester Racecourse, Cheshire
Details See Penmans Chester Antiques & Fine Art Show 13–16 February

24–26

Albany Fairs
Location Pooley Bridge, Cumbria
Details See Albany Fairs 15–16 February

Galloway Antiques Fairs
Location Clitheroe, Lancashire
Details See Galloway Antiques Fairs 28 Feb–2 Mar

The 12th East Anglian Antique Dealers Fair
Contact Liz Allport
☎ 01603 737631 Ⓕ 01603 737631
Ⓜ 07747 843074
Ⓔ liz.allport@lineone.net
Ⓦ www.lomaxantiquesfairs.co.uk
Location Langley Park School, Loddon, Norfolk Ⓟ
Open 24th 2–7pm
25th 10.30am–6pm
26th 10.30am–5pm

25

Antique & Collectors Fair
Location Ayr
Details See Antique & Collectors Fair 25 January

Antiques & Collectors Fair
Location Poole, Dorset
Details See Antiques & Collectors Fair 22 February

Antiques Fair
Location Hertford, Hertfordshire
Details See Antiques Fair 18 January

Blackpool Winter Gardens Collectors Market
Location Blackpool, Lancashire
Details See Blackpool Winter Gardens Collectors Market 15 February

Commonwealth Institute Coin Fair
Location London W8
Details See Commonwealth Institute Coin Fair 18 January

Pamela Robertson Antique & Collectors Fair
Location Chester
Details See Pamela Robertson Antique & Collectors Fair 25 January

25–26

3rd Whipsnade Antiques Fair
Location Whipsnade Wild Animal Park, near Dunstable Ⓟ
Entrance fee £2.50
Details See 2nd Whipsnade Antiques Fair 15 March

Aberystwyth Antiques & Collectors'Fair
Location Aberystwyth
Details See Aberystwyth Antique & Collectors Fair 16–17 August

Antiques & Collectables Fair
Location Stockbridge, Hampshire
Details See Antiques & Collectables Fair 22–23 February

Suffolk Book Markets
Location Long Melford, Suffolk
Details See Suffolk Book Markets 8–9 February

The Original Long Melford Fair
Location Long Melford, Suffolk
Details See The Original Long Melford Fair 25–26 January

26

Antiques & Collectors Fair
Location King's Lynn
Details See Antiques & Collectors Fair 26 January

Art Nouveau and Art Deco Fair
Location Woking, Surrey
Details See Art Nouveau and Art Deco Fair 30 March

Battersea Town Hall Art Deco Fair
Location Battersea Town Hall
Details See Battersea Town Hall Art Deco Fair 16 February

Biggleswade Antiques Fairs
Location Huntingdon, Cambridgeshire
Details See Biggleswade Antiques Fairs 23 February

Bloomsbury Postcard & Collectors Fair
Location London WC1
Details See Bloomsbury Postcard and Collectors Fair 23 February

Bob Evans Fairs
Location Coventry
Details See Bob Evans Fairs 9 February

Burford Antiques Fair
Location Burford, Oxfordshire
Details See Burford Antiques Fair 26 January

Bushey Hall School
Location Bushey, Hertfordshire
Details See Bushey Hall 28 January

Buxton Book Fair
Location Buxton, Derbyshire
Details See Buxton Book Fair 16 February

Wessex Fairs
Location Weston-super-Mare
Details See Wessex Fairs 23 February

26–27

Antiques & Collectables Fair
Location Dun Laoghaire, Co Dublin
Details See Antiques & Collectables Fair 26 January

30

Antique & Collectors Fair
Location Nantwich, Cheshire
Details See Antique & Collectors Fair 30 January

Antiques & Collectables Fair
Location Daventry

Details See Antiques & Collectables Fair 20 February

31–2 NOV

Galloway Antiques Fairs
☎ 01423 522122 Ⓕ 01423 522122
Ⓜ 07966 528725
Ⓔ susan@gallowayfairs.co.uk
Ⓦ www.gallowayfairs.co.uk
Location Seaford College, Petworth, West Sussex Ⓟ
Open 10.30am–5pm
Entrance fee £3.50–£4.50

The 21st Hertfordshire Antiques and Fine Art Fair
☎ 01277 214677 Ⓕ 01277 214550
Ⓔ admin@baileyfairs.co.uk
Ⓦ www.baileyfairs.co.uk
Location Hatfield House, Hatfield, Hertfordshire Ⓟ
Open 11am–5pm
Entrance fee £4
Details 40 dealers, vetted and datelined

Wiltshire County Antiques Fair
Location Marlborough College, Wiltshire
Details See Wiltshire County Antiques Fair 28–30 Mar

NOVEMBER

1

Antique & Collectors Fair
Location Stirling
Details See Antique & Collectors Fair 1 February

Antiques & Collectables Fair
Location Marlborough, Wiltshire
Details See Antiques & Collectables Fair 1 March

Buckingham Antique & Collectors Fair
Location Buckingham
Details See Buckingham Antique & Collectors Fair 1 February

Chelsea Brocante
☎ 020 7254 4054
Location London SW3
Details See Chelsea Brocante 8 February

Marcel Fairs
Location London NW7
Details See Marcel Fairs 1 February

1–2

Beckett Antique Fairs
Location Doncaster
Details See Beckett Antique Fairs 15–16 February

Buxton Antique & Collectors Fair
Location Buxton, Derbyshire
Details See Buxton Antique & Collectors Fair 25–26 January

Devon County Antiques Fairs
Location Clyst St Mary, Exeter
Details See Devon County Antiques Fair 1–2 March

2

Antique & Collectors Fair
Location Newmarket
Details See Antique & Collectors Fair 2 February

Antique & Collectors Fair
Location Edinburgh
Details See Antique & Collectors Fair 2 February

Arun Fairs
Location Rustington, West Sussex
Details See Arun Fairs 2 February

Best of Fairs
Location Copdock, Ipswich
Details See Best of Fairs 2 February

Bob Evans Fairs
Location Peterborough
Details See Bob Evans Fairs 23 February

Chipping Norton Toy Fairs
Location Chipping Norton, Oxfordshire
Details See Chipping Norton Toy Fairs 23 February

Cross Country Fairs Ltd
Location Effingham Park, West Sussex
Details See Cross Country Fairs Ltd 2 February

Dualco Promotions
Location Oldham
Details See Dualco Promotions 23 February

Dualco Promotions
Location Morley
Details See Dualco Promotions 6 April

Harlequin Fairs
Location Chalfont St Peter, Buckinghamshire
Details See Harlequin Fairs 2 March

Ipswich Antiques & Collectables Fair
Location Copdock, Ipswich
Details See Ipswich Antiques & Collectables Fair 2 February

Lechlade Antiques Fair
Location Lechlade, Gloucestershire
Details See Lechlade Antiques Fair 2 February

Malvern Antiques & Collectors Fair
Location Malvern, Worcestershire
Details See Malvern Antiques & Collectors Fair 2 February

Mark Carter Militaria & Medal Fairs
Location Aldershot, Hampshire
Details See Mark Carter Militaria & Medal Fairs 19 January

St Crispins Fair
Location Wokingham, Berkshire
Details See St Crispins Fair 2 February

The London Textiles, Vintage Fashion and Accessories Fair
Location London W6
Details See The London Textiles, Vintage Fashion and Accessories Fair 19 January

The National Art Deco Fair
Location Loughborough, Leicestershire
Details See National Art Deco Fair 4 May

V and A Fairs
Location Cheadle, Cheshire
Details See V and A Fairs 2 February

Wessex Fairs
Location Taunton
Details See Wessex Fairs 2 February

4–5

Ardingly International Antiques & Collectors Fair
Location Ardingly, West Sussex
Details See Ardingly International Antiques & Collectors Fair 4–5 March

6

Paraphernalia Fairs
Location Lyndhurst, Hampshire
Details See Paraphernalia Fairs 6 February

7–9

Albany Fairs
Location Pooley Bridge, Cumbria
Details See Albany Fairs 15–16 February

Galloway Antiques Fairs
Location Helmsley, North Yorkshire
Details See Galloway Antiques Fairs 13–15 June

The 4th Tattersalls Antiques & Fine Art Fair
☎ 01277 214677 Ⓕ 01277 214550
Ⓔ admin@baileyfairs.co.uk
Ⓦ www.baileyfairs.co.uk
Location Park Paddocks, The Avenue, Newmarket Ⓟ
Open 11am–5pm
Details 30 dealers, vetted and datelined

8

21st Annual Belfast Book Fair
Contact Jim or Rita Swindall
☎ 028 90826443 Ⓕ 028 90826443
Ⓔ jiribooks@dnet.co.uk
Location Wellington Park Hotel, Malone Road, Belfast BT9 Ⓟ
Est. 1982
Open 10am–5.30pm
Entrance fee £2 Concessions £1
Details 35 dealers exhibiting from NI, ROI and GB, much Irish interest stock, refreshments

London Coin Fair
Location London WC1
Details See London Coin Fair 8 February

Southport Antiques & Collectors Fair
Location Southport, Merseyside
Details See Southport Antiques & Collectors Fair 22 February

8–9

Bob Evans Fairs
Location Norwich
Est. 1995
Details See Bob Evans Fairs 25–26 January

Detling International Antiques & Collectors Fair
Location Detling, Nr Maidstone, Kent
Details See Detling International Antiques & Collectors Fair 25–26 January

West Midlands Antique Fairs
Location Stafford
Details See West Midlands Antique Fairs 22–23 February

9

Antique & Collectors Fair
Contact John Slade
☎ 020 8894 0218
Ⓦ www.antiquefairs.co.uk
Location Canons Leisure Centre, Madeira Road, Mitcham, Surrey Ⓟ
Open 8.30am–4.30pm
Entrance fee £1.50
Details 145 stalls

Antique & Collectors Fair
Location Woking, Surrey
Details See Antique & Collectors Fair 9 February

Antiques & Collectables Fair
Location Dublin
Details See Antiques & Collectables Fair 9 February

Antiques & Collectors Fairs
Location Egham, Surrey
Details See Antiques & Collectors Fair 9 February

Art Deco Fair with 20thC Decorative Arts
Location Leeds Royal Armouries
Details See Art Deco Fair with 20thC Decorative Arts 23 March

Chiswick Town Hall Art Deco Fair
Location Chiswick Town Hall
Details See Chiswick Town Hall Art Deco Fair 2 March

Crispin Fairs
Location Hartley Wintney, Hampshire
Details See Crispin Fairs 9 February

Dualco Promotions
Location Halifax
Details See Dualco Promotions 16 February

London Map Fairs
Location London WC1
Details See London Map Fairs 9 February

Lostwithiel Antiques Fair
Location Lostwithiel, Cornwall
Details See Lostwithiel Antiques Fair 9 February

M & S Collectors Fair
Location Cottenham, Cambridge
Details See M & S Collectors Fair 9 February

Midas Antique Fair
Location Beaconsfield, Bucks
Details See Midas Antique Fair 9 February

Pennyfarthing Fayres
Location Potters Bar
Details See Pennyfarthing Fayres 9 February

The Original National Glass Collectors Fair
Location National Motorcycle Museum, West Midlands
Details See The Original National Glass Collectors Fair 11 May

FAIRS

NOVEMBER

10–16

The Olympia Winter Fine Art and Antiques Fair
Contact Roisin Fogarty
☎ 020 7370 8211 Ⓕ 020 7370 8221
Ⓔ roisin.fogarty@eco.co.uk
Ⓦ www.olympia-antiques.com
Location Olympia, London Ⓟ
Est. 1994
Open 25th 5–10pm 26th 11am–9pm 27th–2nd 11am–8pm 2nd 11am–7pm 3rd 11am–5pm
Entrance fee £10 single £16 double reduced to £8 £14 if booked in advance
Details 180 exhibitors, offering wide range of antiques and works of art, all items examined by experts

12

The Big Brum
Location Birmingham
Details See The Big Brum 22 January

14–16

Galloway Antiques Fairs
☎ 01423 522122 Ⓕ 01423 522122
Ⓜ 07966 528725
Ⓔ susan@gallowayfairs.co.uk
Ⓦ www.gallowayfairs.co.uk
Location Scone Palace, Perth Ⓟ
Open 10.30am–5pm
Entrance fee £3.50–£4.50

The 4th Wirral Antiques & Fine Art Fair
☎ 01277 214677 Ⓕ 01277 214550
Ⓔ admin@baileyfairs.co.uk
Ⓦ www.baileyfairs.co.uk
Location Hulme Hall, Port Sunlight, Wirral Ⓟ
Open 11am–5pm
Details 30 dealers, vetted and datelined

15

Antiques Fair
Location Hertford, Hertfordshire
Details See Antiques Fair 18 January

Commonwealth Institute Coin Fair
Location London W8
Details See Commonwealth Institute Coin Fair 18 January

16

Alexandra Palace
Location Wood Green, London
Details See Alexandra Palace 9 March

Biggleswade Antiques Fairs
Location Biggleswade, Bedfordshire
Details See Biggleswade Antiques Fairs 19 January

Bob Evans Fairs
Location Kettering
Details See Bob Evans Fairs 16 February

Dualco Promotions
Location Barnsley
Details See Dualco Promotions 9 February

Hatfield Antiques & Collectors Fair
Location Hatfield, Hertfordshire
Details See Hatfield Antiques & Collectors Fair 19 January

Midland Clock & Watch Fair
Location National Motorcycle Museum, West Midlands
Details See Midland Clock & Watch Fair 26 January

Monmouthshire County Antiques & Collectors Fair
Location Abergavenny, Monmouthshire
Details See Monmouthshire County Antiques & Collectors Fair 19 January

Royal Horticultural Hall
Location London SW1
Details See Royal Horticultural Hall 23 February

The National Vintage Tackle Fair
Location Abbey Sports Stadium, Birmingham Road, Redditch, Worcestershire
Details See The National Vintage Tackle Fair 25 May

18

Crispin Fairs
Location Hartley Wintney, Hampshire
Details See Crispin Fairs 18 February

Sandown Park Antique & Collectors Fair
Location Sandown Park Racecourse
Details See Sandown Park Antique Fair 18 February

20

Antiques & Collectables Fair
Location Daventry
Details See Antiques & Collectables Fair 20 February

21–23

Galloway Antiques Fairs
☎ 01423 522122 Ⓕ 01423 522122
Ⓜ 07966 528725
Ⓔ susan@gallowayfairs.co.uk
Ⓦ www.gallowayfairs.co.uk
Location Stansted House, Rowlands Castle, Hampshire Ⓟ
Open 10.30am–5pm
Entrance fee £3.50–£4.50

The 25th Lancashire Christmas Antiques & Fine Art Fair
☎ 01277 214677 Ⓕ 01277 214550
Ⓔ admin@baileyfairs.co.uk
Ⓦ www.baileyfairs.co.uk
Location Swallow Trafalgar Hotel, Preston, Lancashire Ⓟ
Open 11am–5pm
Details 25 dealers, vetted and datelined

22

Blackpool Winter Gardens Collectors Market
Location Blackpool, Lancashire
Details See Blackpool Winter Gardens Collectors Market 15 February

Devon County Antiques Fairs
Location Exeter
Details See Devon County Antiques Fairs 8 February

Pamela Robertson Antique & Collectors Fair
Location Chester
Details See Pamela Robertson Antique & Collectors Fair 25 January

22–23

Antiques & Collectables Fair
Location Stockbridge, Hampshire
Details See Antiques & Collectables Fair 22–23 February

Antiques & Collectors Fair
Location St Ives, Cambridgeshire
Details See Antiques & Collectors Fair 22–23 February

23

Battersea Town Hall Art Deco Fair
Location Battersea Town Hall
Details See Battersea Town Hall Art Deco Fair February 16

Biggleswade Antiques Fairs
Location Kempston, Bedford
Details See Biggleswade Antiques Fairs 26 January

Bloomsbury Postcard & Collectors Fair
Location London WC1
Details See Bloomsbury Postcard and Collectors Fair 23 February

Burford Antiques Fair
Location Burford, Oxfordshire
Details See Burford Antiques Fair 26 January

Bushey Hall School
Location Bushey, Hertfordshire
Details See Bushey Hall 28 January

Buxton Book Fair
Location Buxton, Derbyshire
Details See Buxton Book Fair 23 March

Dualco Promotions
Location Huddersfield
Details See Dualco Promotions 2 February

Dublin Toy and Train Fair
Location Dun Laoghaire, Co Dublin
Details See Dublin Toy and Train Fair 16 February

J and K Fairs
Location Lincoln
Details See J and K Fairs 9 February

M & S Antiques & Collectors Fair
Location Royston, Hertfordshire
Details See M & S Antiques & Collectors Fair 26 January

Newmarket Antiques & Collectors Fair
Location Newmarket, Suffolk
Details See Newmarket Antiques & Collectors Fair 23 February

Wessex Fairs
Location Blagdon, North Somerset
Details See Wessex Fairs 30 March

27

Antique & Collectors Fair
Location Nantwich, Cheshire
Details See Antique & Collectors Fair 30 January

27–30

Antiques for Everyone
Location NEC, Birmingham
Details See Antiques for Everyone 3–6 April

28–30

The Autumn Antiques Fair
Contact Louis O'Sullivan
☎ 00 3531 2859294
Location Royal Dublin Society, Ballsbridge, Dublin 4, Ireland P
Open 11am–7pm
Entrance fee €7 (£4.46)
Details Over 30 dealers

The International Antiques & Collectors Fair at RAF Swinderby
Location RAF Swinderby
Details See The International Antiques & Collectors Fair at RAF Swinderby 31 January–2 February

29

Antique & Collectors Fair
Location Ayr
Details See Antique & Collectors Fair 25 January

Antiques & Collectors Fair
Location Poole, Dorset
Details See Antiques & Collectors Fair 22 February

29–30

Buxton Antique & Collectors Fair
Location Buxton, Derbyshire
Details See Buxton Antique & Collectors Fair 25–26 January

Suffolk Book Markets
Location Long Melford, Suffolk
Details See Suffolk Book Markets 8–9 February

The Original Long Melford Fair
Location Long Melford, Suffolk
Details See The Original Long Melford Fair 25–26 January

30

Antique & Collectors Fair
Location Berkhampsted, Hertfordshire
Details See Antique & Collectors Fair 30 March

Antiques & Collectors Fair
Location King's Lynn
Details See Antiques & Collectors Fair 26 January

Biggleswade Antiques Fairs
Location Huntingdon, Cambridgeshire
Details See Biggleswade Antiques Fairs 9 February

Bob Evans Fairs
Location Hereford
Details See Bob Evans Fairs 13 April

Clock & Watch Dealers Fair
Location Haydock Park Racecourse
Est. 1998
Details See Clock & Watch Dealers Fair 30 March

Dualco Promotions
Location Bolton
Details See Dualco Promotions 16 February

V and A Fairs
Location Bridgnorth, Shropshire
Details See V and A Fairs 26 January

Wessex Fairs
Location Weston-super-Mare
Details See Wessex Fairs 23 February

DECEMBER

1

Harlequin Fairs
Location Chalfont St Peter, Buckinghamshire
Details See Harlequin Fairs 2 March

1–2

Newark International Antiques & Collectors Fair
Location Newark
Details See Newark International Antiques & Collectors Fair 3–4 February

4

Paraphernalia Fairs
Location Lyndhurst, Hampshire
Details See Paraphernalia Fairs 6 February

5–7

Galloway Antiques Fairs
Location Gosforth Park, Newcastle
Details See Galloway Antiques Fairs 16–18 May

6

Antique & Collectors Fair
Location Stirling
Details See Antique & Collectors Fair 1 February

Buckingham Antique & Collectors Fair
Location Buckingham
Details See Buckingham Antique & Collectors Fair 1 February

Devon County Antiques Fairs
Location Salisbury
Details See Devon County Antiques Fairs 12 April

Marcel Fairs
Location London NW7
Details See Marcel Fairs 1 February

7

Antique & Collectors Fair
Location Newmarket
Details See Antique & Collectors Fair 2 February

Antique & Collectors Fair
Location Edinburgh
Details See Antique & Collectors Fair 2 February

Art Deco Fair
Location Warwick
Details See Art Deco Fair 23 February

Arun Fairs
Location Rustington, West Sussex
Details See Arun Fairs 2 February

Best of Fairs
Location Copdock, Ipswich
Details See Best of Fairs 2 February

Cross Country Fairs Ltd
Location Effingham Park, West Sussex
Details See Cross Country Fairs Ltd 2 February

Dualco Promotions
Location Halifax
Details See Dualco Promotions 16 February

Ipswich Antiques & Collectables Fair
Location Copdock, Ipswich
Details See Ipswich Antiques & Collectables Fair 2 February

J and K Fairs
Location Lincoln
Details See J and K Fairs 9 February

Lechlade Antiques Fair
Location Lechlade, Gloucestershire
Details See Lechlade Antiques Fair 2 February

Malvern Antiques & Collectors Fair
Location Malvern, Worcestershire
Details See Malvern Antiques & Collectors Fair 2 February

Mark Carter Militaria & Medal Fairs
Location Yate, Bristol
Details See Mark Carter Militaria & Medal Fairs 2 February

Pennyfarthing Fayres
Location Potters Bar
Details See Pennyfarthing Fayres 9 February

Royal Horticultural Hall
Location London SW1
Details See Royal Horticultural Hall 10 February

St Crispins Fair
Location Wokingham, Berkshire
Details See St Crispins Fair 2 February

The London Textiles, Vintage Fashion and Accessories Fair
Location London W6
Details See The London Textiles, Vintage Fashion and Accessories Fair 19 January

V and A Fairs
Location Whitchurch, Shropshire
Details See V and A Fairs 16 February

V and A Fairs
Location Cheadle, Cheshire
Details See V and A Fairs 2 February

Wessex Fairs
Location Taunton
Details See Wessex Fairs 2 February

10

The Big Brum
Location Birmingham
Details See The Big Brum 22 January

11

Antique & Collectors Fair
Location Nantwich, Cheshire
Details See Antique & Collectors Fair 30 January

12–14

Stafford Bingley Hall
Location Stafford

Details See Stafford Bingley Hall 7–9 February

13

Pamela Robertson Antique & Collectors Fair
Location Chester
Details See Pamela Robertson Antique & Collectors Fair 25 January

13–14

Carmarthen Antiques & Collectors Fair
Location Carmarthen
Open 10am–4pm
Details See Carmarthen Antiques & Collectors Fair 8–9 March

The Original Long Melford Fair
Location Long Melford, Suffolk
Details See The Original Long Melford Fair 25–26 January

14

Antiques & Collectors Fairs
Location Egham, Surrey
Details See Antiques & Collectors Fair 9 February

Brunel Clock & Watch Fair
Location Uxbridge, Middlesex
Details See Brunel Clock & Watch Fair 16 February

Bushey Hall School
Location Bushey, Hertfordshire
Details See Bushey Hall 28 January

Crispin Fairs
Location Hartley Wintney, Hampshire
Details See Crispin Fairs 9 February

Devon County Antiques Fairs
Location Yeovil, Somerset
Details See Devon County Antiques Fairs 16 February

Dualco Promotions
Location Barnsley
Details See Dualco Promotions 9 February

London Map Fairs
Location London WC1
Details See London Map Fairs 9 February

Lostwithiel Antiques Fair
Location Lostwithiel, Cornwall
Details See Lostwithiel Antiques Fair 9 February

M & S Collectors Fair
Location Cottenham, Cambridge
Details See M & S Collectors Fair 9 February

Midas Antique Fair
Location Beaconsfield, Bucks
Details See Midas Antique Fair 9 February

16

Crispin Fairs
Location Hartley Wintney, Hampshire
Details See Crispin Fairs 18 February

18

Antiques & Collectables Fair
Location Daventry
Details See Antiques & Collectables Fair 20 February

20

Antique & Collectors Fair
Location Ayr
Details See Antique & Collectors Fair 25 January

Antiques Fair
Location Hertford, Hertfordshire
Details See Antiques Fair 18 January

Chingford Antiques & Collectors Fair
Location Chingford, London E4
Details See Chingford Antiques & Collectors Fair 25 January

Commonwealth Institute Coin Fair
Location London W8
Details See Commonwealth Institute Coin Fair 18 January

20–21

South Cotswolds Xmas Antiques Fair
Contact Anne Harwood
☎ 01249 661111 Ⓕ 01249 661111
Ⓔ enquiries@cooperantiquesfairs.co.uk
Ⓦ www.cooperantiquesfairs.co.uk
Location Tetbury, Gloucestershire
Open Sat Sun 11am–5pm
Entrance fee £3.50 Children under 16 free

21

Antiques & Collectors Fair
Location King's Lynn
Details See Antiques & Collectors Fair 26 January

Biggleswade Antiques Fairs
Location Biggleswade, Bedfordshire
Details See Biggleswade Antiques Fairs 19 January

Bloomsbury Postcard & Collectors Fair
Location London WC1
Details See Bloomsbury Postcard and Collectors Fair 23 February

Buxton Book Fair
Location Buxton, Derbyshire
Details See Buxton Book Fair 23 March

Hatfield Antiques & Collectors Fair
Location Hatfield, Hertfordshire
Details See Hatfield Antiques & Collectors Fair 19 January

Monmouthshire County Antiques & Collectors Fair
Location Abergavenny, Monmouthshire
Details See Monmouthshire County Antiques & Collectors Fair 19 January

26

Boxing Day Antique & Collectors Fair
☎ 01253 782828
Ⓕ 01253 714715

Location Empress Ballroom, Blackpool Winter Gardens, Blackpool, Lancashire P
Est. 1975
Open Trade 7.30am Public 9.30am–5pm
Entrance fee 7.30am–9pm £5 plus card 9.30am–5pm £3 accompanied children under 12 free
Details 200 stalls

27

Antiques & Collectors Fair
Location Poole, Dorset
Details See Antiques & Collectors Fair 22 February

Bob Evans Fairs
Location Kettering
Est. 1992
Details See Bob Evans Fairs 16 February

Brunel Antiques & Collectors Fair
Location Uxbridge, Middlesex
Details See Brunel Antiques & Collectors Fair 21 April

27–28

Beckett Antique Fairs
Location Doncaster
Details See Beckett Antique Fairs 15–16 February

Buxton Antique & Collectors Fair
Location Buxton, Derbyshire
Details See Buxton Antique & Collectors Fair 25–26 January

The Original Long Melford Fair
Location Long Melford, Suffolk
Details See The Original Long Melford Fair 25–26 January

27–29

West Midlands Antique Fairs
Location Stafford
Details See West Midlands Antique Fairs 22–23 February

28

Biggleswade Antiques Fairs
Location Kempston, Bedford
Details See Biggleswade Antiques Fairs 26 January

Bob Evans Fairs
Location Coventry
Details See Bob Evans Fairs 9 February

J and K Fairs
Location Lincoln
Details See J and K Fairs 9 February

Wessex Fairs
Location Weston-super-Mare
Details See Wessex Fairs 23 February

29

Art Nouveau and Art Deco Fair
Location Woking, Surrey
Details See Art Nouveau and Art Deco Fair 30 March

Indexes

In the Index of Specialists and the General Index, shops and businesses beginning with a forename are listed alphabetically by surname: thus R G Archer Books is listed under A and Michael Saffell Antiques appears under S.

The county in which a city, town or village has been placed in the Directory is also given In the Index of Place Names. Note that this is not always the county given in the address that forms part of the entry.

KEY TO MEMBER ORGANIZATIONS

In order to make the information in this book more concise we have used the following abbreviations where applicable.

AAFAA Alresford Antique & Fine Arts Association
ABA Antiquarian Booksellers' Association
ACC Antique Collectors' Club
ADA Antique Dealers' Association
ADDA Art Deco Dealers' Association
ADS Antique Dealers' Society
AFAA Association of Fine Art Auctioneers
AHA American Horological Association
AHS Antiquarian Horological Society
AMU Association Master Upholsterers
AMUSF Association of Master Upholsterers & Soft Furnishers
ANA American Numismatic Association
APS American Philatelic Society
ARVA Association of Regional Valuers & Auctioneers
ASDA American Stamp Dealers' Association
ASVA Association of Society of Valuers & Auctioneers
AU Association of Upholsterers
BA Booksellers' Association
BABAADA Bath & Bradford on Avon Antique Dealers' Association
BABI Booksellers' Association of Britain & Ireland
BACA British Antiques and Collectables Awards
BADA British Antique Dealers' Association
BAFRA British Antique Furniture Restorers' Association
BAR British Association of Removers
BCPAA British China & Porcelain Artists' Association
BGA British Gemologists' Association
BHI British Horological Institute
BIFA British International Freight Association
BJA British Jewellers' Association
BNTA British Numismatic Trade Association
BTCM British Traditional Cabinet Makers
BWCG British Watch & Clockmakers' Guild
CADA Cotswold Antique Dealers' Association
CC Clockmakers' Company
CCCC Clarice Cliff Collectors' Club
CINOA Confédération Internationale des Négociants en Oeuvres d'Art
CLPGS City of London Phonograph & Gramophone Society
CGCG Ceramics & Glass Conservation Group
CISS Channel Islands Specialists Society
CPADA Camden Passage Antique Dealers' Association
CPTA Camden Passage Traders' Association
CR Conservation Register
CSFAC Chartered Surveyors of Fine Art & Chattels
DADA Dorking Antique Dealers' Association
EADA Essex Antique Dealers' Association
ESoc Ephemera Society
FATG Fine Art Trade Guild
FIDI Fédération Internationale des Déménageurs Internationaux
FNAVA Federation of National Auctioneers & Valuers
FSVA Fellow of the Society of Valuers & Auctioneers
GADAR Guild of Antique Dealers & Restorers
GAGTL Gemmological Association and Gem Testing Laboratory of Great Britain
GAI Guild of Architectural Ironmongers
GCS Golf Collectors' Society (GB, USA)
GTA Gun Traders' Association
HADA Hudson Antique Dealers' Association
HHGFAA Household Goods Forwarders of America
IAA Institute of Antiques Auctioneers
IAB Irish Antiquarian Bookdealers
IADA Irish Antique Dealers' Association
IADAA International Association of Dealers in Ancient Art
IAPN International Society of Professional Numismatists
IATA International Air Transport Association
IAVI Irish Auctioneers & Valuers Institute
IBNS International Bank Note Society
IBSS International Bond and Share Society
ICA Institute of Contemporary Arts
ICHAWI Institute for the Conservation of Historic & Artistic Works in Ireland
ICOM International Council of Museums (Committee for Conservation)
IDDA Interior Decorators' & Designers' Association
IIC International Institute for Conservation of Historic & Artistic Work
ILAB International League of Antiquarian Booksellers
IMA Irish Museums Association
IMCOS International Map Collectors' Society
IMTA International Map Trade Association
IPAA International Porcelain Artists' Association
IPAV Institute of Professional Auctioneers & Valuers
IPC Institute of Paper Conservation
IPCRA Irish Professional Conservators' & Restorers' Association
ISVA Incorporated Society of Valuers & Auctioneers
IRRV Institute of Revenues, Ratings & Valuation
ITA Islington Trading Association

KEY TO MEMBER ORGANIZATIONS

KCSADA	Kensington Church Street Antique Dealers' Association
LAB	London Antique Books
LAPADA	London & Provincial Antique Dealers' Association
LJAJDA	London & Japan Antique Jewellery Dealers' Association
LSVA	London Silver Vaults Association
LPC	League of Professional Craftsmen
MAPH	Member of the Association of Professional Horologists
MBHI	Member of British Horological Society
MBWCG	Member of British Watch & Clockmakers' Guild
MGR	Museums and Galleries Register
NACF	National Art Collections Fund
NAEA	National Art Education Association
NAG	National Association of Goldsmiths
NAVA	National Association of Auctioneers & Valuers
NAWCC	National Association of Watch & Clock Collectors
NCCR	National Council for Conservation and Restoration
NIAVI	Northern Ireland Auctioneers & Valuers Institute
NPA	National Pawnbrokers Association
OCS	Oriental Ceramic Society
OMNI	Overseas Moving Network International
OMRS	Order Medals Research Society
OMSA	Orders and Medals Society of America
PAADA	Petworth Art & Antique Dealers' Association
PADA	Portobello Antique Dealers' Association
PBFA	Provincial Book Fair Association
PBSA	Provincial Book Sellers' Association
PLA	Private Libraries Association
PNG	Professional Numismatists' Guild
PO	Pewter Organisation
PTA	Postcard Traders' Association
PTS	Philatelic Traders' Society
RADS	Registered Antique Dealers' Association
RETRA	Radio, Electrical and Television Retailers' Association
RICS	Royal Institute of Chartered Surveyors
RWHA	Royal Warrant Holders' Association
SAA	Scottish Association of Auctioneers
SAADA	Sherborne Art & Antique Dealers' Association
SAPCON	South African Paper Conservation Group
SCC	Susie Cooper Club
SDA	Stamp Dealers' Association
SDADA	Saintfield & District Antique Dealers' Association
SLAD	Society of London Art Dealers
SIS	Scientific Instrument Society
SOBB	Society of Book Binders
SOFAA	Society of Fine Art Auctioneers
SPAB	Society for the Protection of Ancient Buildings
SPTA	Scottish Philatelic Traders' Association
SSA	Sussex Saleroom Association
SSCR	Scottish Society for Conservation & Restoration
TADA	Tetbury Antique Dealers' Association
TCC	Telephone Collectors' Club
TCS	Tennis Collectors' Society
TPCS	Torquay Pottery Collectors' Club
TRADA	Timber Research and Development Association
TVADA	Thames Valley Antique Dealers' Association
UACC	Universal Autograph Collectors' Club
UKIC	United Kingdom Institute for Conservation
UKPCC	UK Perfume Collectors' Club
WBA	Welsh Booksellers' Association
WCC	Worshipful Company of Clockmakers
WSADA	West Street Antique Dealers' Association
WKADA	West Kent Antique Dealers' Association

INDEX OF ADVERTISERS

INDEX OF SPECIALISTS

ADVERTISING

ARMS & ARMOUR

ARMOUR

ASIAN AND ISLAMIC

JAPANESE SWORDS

ART DECO

ART NOUVEAU

JEWELLERY

ARTS & CRAFTS

ASIAN WORKS OF ART

CENTRAL ASIA

CERAMICS

CHINESE ART

CHINESE SNUFF BOTTLES

EAST ASIAN ART AND ARCHAEOLOGY

FURNITURE

JAPANESE

JAPANESE IMARI

JAPANESE WOODCUT PRINTS

JEWELLERY

NORITAKE

OBJETS D'ART

AUTOMATA

BAROMETERS

BLACK FOREST

BOOKS

INDEX OF SPECIALISTS
BOOKS

INDEX OF SPECIALISTS
COLLECTABLES

FURNITURE

17THC ENGLISH

17TH–18THC

17TH–18THC ITALIAN

17TH–18THC OAK

17TH–19THC

18THC

INDEX OF SPECIALISTS

FURNITURE

INDEX OF PLACE NAMES

A

C

INDEX OF PLACE NAMES

D

D

E

F

INDEX OF PLACE NAMES

I

T

A

GENERAL INDEX

A

B

GENERAL INDEX

B

GENERAL INDEX

B

GENERAL INDEX

C

D

E

GENERAL INDEX

F

G

GENERAL INDEX

G

GENERAL INDEX
H

I

J

M

N

O

GENERAL INDEX

P

P

Q

R

GENERAL INDEX

R

S

GENERAL INDEX

S

T

GENERAL INDEX

T

U

V

X

Y

Z

MILLER'S

Antiques Shops, Fairs & Auctions in the UK & Eire 2004

ENTRY FORM

Please return a signed copy of this form to: Miller's Publications (Directory 2004), The Cellars, High Street, Tenterden, Kent TN30 6BN or fax to 01580 766100.

Name of Business: ....

Type of Entry *(Dealer/Auction House/Market or Centre/Associated Service)*: ....

Contact Name: ....

Street: ....

Town: .... County: .... Postcode: ....

Address for mailing *(if different from above)*: ....

....

Telephone: .... Fax: .... Mobile: ....

Email: .... Web address: ....

Trade only *(Yes/No)*: .... Parking nearby *(Yes/No)*: ....

Member of: .... Established: ....

Opening/Office hours: ....

Dealers only

Principal Stock: ....

If a Specialist Dealer, please give speciality *(one only)*: ....

Services offered *(Valuation/Restoration/Shipping/Book Search)*: ....

....

Exhibitor at which fairs? *(two only)*: ....

Quantity of stock held *(Small/Medium/Large)*: ....

Auction Houses only

Sale details: ....

Catalogues *(Yes/No)*: ....Frequency of main sale: ....

Markets/Centres only

Number of stalls/shops/dealers: ....

Associated Service only

Specialist area: ....

Services offered: ....

I agree that the above data may be included in the 2004 and future editions of Miller's Antiques Shops, Fairs & Auctions in the UK & Eire. I further acknowledge that it is my responsibility to keep this information up to date and agree to inform Octopus Publishing Group Ltd (OPG) of any changes to it.

Signature: ______________________ Name: ______________________ Date: ____________

Paragraph A: We Octopus Publishing Group Ltd (OPG) wish to share the information you have provided with our business partners for promotional and product development purposes, via a range of media including web sites and digital television. If you do not wish us to use your information in this way, then please tick here: ❑

If you no longer want to be included in the above publication or if you have any queries concerning the personal information held about you, please contact: Valerie Lewis, Miller's Publications, The Cellars, High Street, Tenterden, Kent TN30 6BN.